# Toward Liberal Education

❧ ❧ ❧ *Readings for Liberal Education*

# Toward Liberal Education

❧ ❧ ❧ *Third Edition*

Edited by

Louis G. Locke
*Madison College*

William M. Gibson
*New York University*

George Arms
*The University of New Mexico*

*Rinehart & Company Inc., New York*

". . . Some will then be chosen for higher privilege. The studies which they pursued without order in their early years will now be brought together, and the students will see the relationship of these studies to one another and to truth."

"Yes," he said. "That is the only kind of knowledge which takes lasting root."

PLATO, The Republic

❦ ❦ ❦

# Preface

THE IDEA for the book of which this volume is a part began several years ago when we were thinking and reading and arguing with our colleagues about liberal education in America. Our constant purpose has been to make an anthology that would help first-year college students understand what liberal education can mean to them.

As it seemed to us, the reading provided in most freshman courses went a good way toward realizing this purpose. But the effort was often partial and sometimes fitful. The principal differences between *Toward Liberal Education* and earlier collections of readings are those of development rather than of radical change. First, it points steadily in the direction indicated by its title. Without deviating into models at one time or mere entertainment at another, it seeks systematically to explore the skills and disciplines of our humanistic culture. Second, it makes this exploration by the use of writing chosen for its intrinsic worth. It does not talk down to its readers.

In this volume of *Readings for Liberal Education*, the first three parts are concerned with the skills of a liberal education: learning, reading and writing, and thinking. The four parts that follow these represent the great areas of liberal learning: the arts, science, society, and philosophy and religion. The second volume, *Introduction to Literature*, turns to that discipline which is particularly cherished by teachers of English: literature of the imagination.

The development of all these parts aims at presenting the material to the student with force and meaning. In arranging the parts in their final order, we thus feel that we have provided a sound framework for a course which uses the anthology. Yet we recognize that each school and each teacher may properly wish to rearrange the order for special needs.

For material we have chosen writing that bears the stamp of permanent value. This standard has not meant that we have stayed in the past. But it has meant the exclusion of superficial journalizing and disregard for the timeliness of yesterday's newspaper. Freshmen, we believe, not only are capable of hard, solid reading, but are happier when they are expected to do it. Such reading is not dull, as we hope this book demonstrates; for certainly not wisdom alone, but the sweetness and joy of wisdom, determines a classic.

The third edition keeps the same approach and the same quality of readings that have characterized the original and revised editions. From our own experience, as well as from the advice of many others who have taught the two earlier editions, we have learned where certain improvements could be made; we have, accordingly, made a limited number of changes in selections, which we believe will enhance the value of the book.

In revising we have given special attention to the sections on "Reading and Writing" and on "The Arts," since these portions of the book are always of highest importance in any course taught by members of departments of English. We hope that our changes in these sections have given them an even greater significance that will enlarge students' understanding and contribute to teachers' sense of accomplishment.

Though the most extensive revision appears in these sections, readers will find that new essays have been introduced in every part and that some older essays no longer appear. Although regretting the omission of some of these, we believe we have replaced them with better essays. And we have, consequently, been delighted to introduce new work of high merit, not only in the interest of freshness, but also to work toward a better multivoiced statement of the meaning of liberal education, even while we know that we cannot ever hope to find— and indeed would not want to find—a finality that lacks the essential of further growth. As in the earlier editions, we have provided teachers with a wide range of material with the expectation that few will want to assign every essay, but with confidence that such abundance of readings provides a latitude of choice which gives individuality and richness to the course.

In this edition we have provided for the first time an alternate table of contents arranged by rhetorical types.

We have removed the questions from this edition since we have felt that most teachers preferred phrasing their own to using those prepared by the editors. Likewise, we have believed that not facing the student with printed questions will help him develop the sense of maturity and independence that this book constantly attempts to foster. In cooperation with this policy, the publishers have agreed to make available to those who want it a pamphlet containing questions prepared by the editors, together with editorial observations and teaching suggestions.

L.G.L.
W.M.G.
*January, 1957*                                                                    G.A.

❦ ❦ ❦

# Acknowledgments

MANY teachers who used the original and revised editions in their classes have generously made their experience and wisdom available to us, and we wish to make full acknowledgment to them. For help in earlier editions we again thank Professors Morris Bein, Wallace C. Brown, Alan S. Downer, Richard Eastman, J. Stuart Goodman, Hyatt H. Waggoner, Howard A. Wilson, and James L. Wortham. We also appreciate the assistance of Professors Frank Adams, W. P. Albrecht, E. W. Baughman, Samuel N. Bogorad, George C. Booth, Frederick Bracher, C. A. Brown, Edith Buchanan, Irving L. Churchill, Fletcher Collins, Jr., J. Hal Connor, W. Raymond Cooper, Ethel C. Cox, Norton B. Crowell, Herbert N. Dillard, Grace Donaldson, Ethel A. Fleming, Signi Falk, Morris Freedman, Eleanor J. Gibson, James J. Gibson, L. P. Goggin, Milton A. Goldberg, Robert M. Gorrell, Françoise C. Gourier, Willis D. Jacobs, William R. Keast, Julia Keleher, John Pendy Kirby, Jane Kluckhohn, Arthur Kreisman, David G. Kroft, Daniel Kroll, Joseph M. Kuntz, Juanita Kytle, Vernon Lichtenstein, Richard C. R. Louder, Edward G. Lueders, Raymond R. MacCurdy, Catherine Mims, Mary E. Osborn, Herbert B. Nelson, T. M. Pearce, Paul Roberts, Macha L. Rosenthal, Ernest Samuels, Katherine Simons, Dane F. Smith, Hugh L. Smith, Jr., F. Smoyer, E. W. Tedlock, Jr., Margaret Trotter, Herbert S. Turner, R. G. Webster, Alfred Westfall, C. V. Wicker, and Horace Williston.

Particularly for help with this edition we wish to thank Professor Harold Martin and the staff of General Education A at Harvard and Professor Francis Christensen and the Committee on English Communication at the University of Southern California, as well as Professors Geraldine Hammond of the University of Wichita, Janice D. Warnke of New York University, Irwin Griggs of Temple University, John Weimer of the University of Michigan, and Charles T. Davis of Princeton. We are further aware of indebtedness extending back over many years to teachers, students, and acquaintances of the past.

# Contents

## III. Thinking

## IV. The Arts

### The Fine Arts

### The Popular Arts

### Literature and Criticism

## V. *Science*

### The Nature of Science

### The Sciences

### Technology

### Challenges to Science and Technology

## VI. *Society*

### Social Attitudes

## Problems of the Social Sciences

## VII. *Philosophy and Religion*

### The Good Life

### Religion

# The Nature of Reality

# Can Philosophy Save Civilization?

❦ ❦ ❦

# Contents

*Arranged by Rhetorical Types*

## Cause and Effect

## Comparison and Contrast

## Analogy

## Classification

## Definition

## Analysis

## Historical Writing

## Biography and Autobiography

## Persuasion:  Sermon

## Persuasion:  Ceremonial  Essay

# Toward Liberal Education

# ❦ ❦ ❦ I. Learning

# The Campus

James Thurber

## University Days[1]

I PASSED all the other courses that I took at my University, but I could never pass botany. This was because all botany students had to spend several hours a week in a laboratory looking through a microscope at plant cells, and I could never see through a microscope. I never once saw a cell through a microscope. This used to enrage my instructor. He would wander around the laboratory pleased with the progress all the students were making in drawing the involved and, so I am told, interesting structure of flower cells, until he came to me. I would just be standing there. "I can't see anything," I would say. He would begin patiently enough, explaining how anybody can see through a microscope, but he would always end up in a fury, claiming that I could *too* see through a microscope but just pretended that I couldn't. "It takes away from the beauty of flowers anyway," I used to tell him. "We are not concerned with beauty in this course," he would say. "We are concerned solely with what I may call the *mechanics* of flars." "Well," I'd say, "I can't see anything." "Try it just once again," he'd say, and I would put my eye to the microscope and see nothing at all, except now and again, a nebulous milky substance—a phenomenon of maladjustment. You were supposed to see a vivid, restless clockwork of sharply defined plant cells. "I see what looks like a lot of milk," I would tell him. This, he claimed, was the result of my not having adjusted the microscope properly; so he would readjust it for me, or rather, for himself. And I would look again and see milk.

I finally took a deferred pass, as they called it, and waited a year and tried again. (You had to pass one of the biological sciences or you couldn't graduate.) The professor had come back from vacation brown as a berry, bright-eyed, and eager to explain cell-structure again to his classes. "Well," he said to me, cheerily, when we met in the first laboratory hour of the semester, "we're going to see cells this time, aren't we?" "Yes, sir," I said. Students to right of me and to left of me and in front of me were seeing cells; what's more, they were quietly drawing pictures of them in their notebooks. Of course, I didn't see anything.

"We'll try it," the professor said to me, grimly, "with every adjustment of the microscope known to man. As God is my witness, I'll arrange this glass so that you see cells through it or I'll give up teaching. In twenty-two years of botany, I—" He cut off abruptly for he was beginning to quiver all over, like Lionel Barrymore, and he genuinely wished to hold onto his temper: his scenes with me had taken a great deal out of him.

So we tried it with every adjustment of the microscope known to man. With only one of them did I see anything but blackness or the familiar lacteal opacity, and that time I saw, to my pleasure and amazement, a variegated constellation of flecks, specks, and dots. These I hastily drew. The instructor, noting my activity, came back from an adjoining desk, a smile on his lips and his eyebrows high in hope. He looked at my cell drawing. "What's that?" he demanded, with a hint of a squeal in his voice. "That's what I saw," I said. "You didn't, you didn't, you *didn't!*" he screamed, losing control of his temper instantly, and he bent over and squinted into the microscope. His head snapped up. "That's your eye!" he shouted. "You've fixed the lens so that it reflects! You've drawn your eye!"

Another course that I didn't like, but somehow managed to pass, was economics. I went to that class straight from the botany class, which didn't help me any in understanding either subject. I used to get them mixed up. But not as mixed up as another student in my economics class who came there direct from a physics laboratory. He was a tackle on the football team, named Bolenciecwcz. At that time Ohio State University had one of the best football teams in the country, and Bolenciecwcz was one of its outstanding stars. In order to be eligible to play it was necessary for him to keep up in his studies, a very difficult matter, for while he was not dumber than an ox he was not any smarter. Most of his professors were lenient and helped him along. None gave him more hints, in answering questions, or asked him simpler ones than the economics professor, a thin, timid man named Bassum. One day when we were on the subject of transportation and distribution, it came Bolenciecwcz's turn to answer a question. "Name one means of transportation," the professor said to him. No light came into the big tackle's eyes. "Just any means of transportation," said the professor. Bolenciecwcz sat staring at him. "That is," pursued the professor, "any medium, agency, or method of going from one place to another." Bolenciecwcz had the look of a man who is being led into a trap. "You may choose among steam, horse-drawn, or electrically propelled vehicles," said the instructor. "I might suggest the one which we commonly take in making long journeys across land." There was a profound silence in which everybody stirred uneasily, including Bolenciecwcz and Mr. Bassum. Mr. Bassum abruptly broke this silence in an amazing manner. "Choo-choo-choo," he said, in a low voice, and turned instantly scarlet. He glanced appealingly around the room. All of us, of course, shared Mr. Bassum's desire that Bolenciecwcz should stay abreast of the class in economics, for the Illinois game, one of the hardest and most important of the season, was only a week off. "Toot, toot, too-toooooooot!" some student with a deep voice moaned; and we all looked encouragingly at Bolenciecwcz. Somebody else gave a fine imitation of a locomotive letting off steam. Mr. Bassum himself rounded off the little show. "Ding, dong, ding, dong," he said, hopefully. Bolenciecwcz was staring at the floor now, trying to think, his great brow furrowed, his huge hands rubbing together, his face red.

"How did you come to college this year, Mr. Bolenciecwcz?" asked the professor. "*Chuffa* chuffa, *chuffa* chuffa."

"M'father sent me," said the football player.

"What on?" asked Bassum.

"I git an 'lowance," said the tackle, in a low, husky voice, obviously embarrassed.

"No, no," said Bassum. "Name a means of transportation. What did you *ride* here on?"

"Train," said Bolenciecwcz.

"Quite right," said the professor. "Now, Mr. Nugent, will you tell us——"

If I went through anguish in botany and economics—for different reasons—gymnasium work was even worse. I don't even like to think about it. They wouldn't let you play games or join in the exercises with your glasses on and I couldn't see with mine off. I bumped into professors, horizontal bars, agricultural students, and swinging iron rings. Not being able to see, I could take it but I couldn't dish it out. Also, in order to pass gymnasium (and you had to pass it to graduate) you had to learn to swim if you didn't know how. I didn't like the swimming pool, I didn't like swimming, and I didn't like the swimming instructor, and after all these years I still don't. I never swam but I passed my gym work anyway, by having another student give my gymnasium number (978) and swim across the pool in my place. He was a quiet, amiable blonde youth, number 473, and he would have seen through a microscope for me if we could have got away with it, but we couldn't get away with it. Another thing I didn't like about gymnasium work was that they made you strip the day you registered. It is impossible for me to be happy when I am stripped and being asked a lot of questions. Still, I did better than a lanky agricultural student who was cross-examined just before I was. They asked each student what college he was in—that is, whether Arts, Engineering, Commerce, or Agriculture. "What college are you in?" the instructor snapped at the youth in front of me. "Ohio State University," he said promptly.

It wasn't that agricultural student but it was another a whole lot like him who decided to take up journalism, possibly on the ground that when farming went to hell he could fall back on newspaper work. He didn't realize, of course, that that would be very much like falling back full-length on a kit of carpenter's tools. Haskins didn't seem cut out for journalism, being too embarrassed to talk to anybody and unable to use a typewriter, but the editor of the college paper assigned him to the cow barns, the sheep house, the horse pavilion, and the animal husbandry department generally. This was a genuinely big "beat," for it took up five times as much ground and got ten times as great a legislative appropriation as the College of Liberal Arts. The agricultural student knew animals, but nevertheless his stories were dull and colorlessly written. He took all afternoon on each of them, because he had to hunt for each letter on the typewriter. Once in a while he had to ask somebody to help him hunt. "C" and "L," in particular, were hard letters for him to find. His editor finally got pretty much annoyed at the farmer-journalist because his pieces were so uninteresting. "See here, Haskins," he snapped at him one day, "why is it we never have anything hot from you on the horse pavilion? Here we have two hundred head of horses on this campus—more than any other university in the Western Conference except Purdue—and yet you never get any real low-down on them. Now shoot over to the horse barns and dig up something lively." Haskins shambled out and came back in about an hour; he said he had something. "Well, start it off snappily," said the editor. "Something people will read." Haskins set to work and in a couple of hours brought a sheet of typewritten paper to the desk; it was a two-hundred word story about some disease that had broken out among the horses. Its opening sentence was simple but arresting. It read: "Who has noticed the sores on the tops of the horses in the animal husbandry building?"

Ohio State was a land grant university and therefore two years of military drill was compulsory. We drilled with old Springfield rifles and studied the tactics of the Civil War even though the World War was going on at the time. At 11 o'clock each morning thousands of freshmen and sophomores used to deploy over the campus, moodily creeping up on the old chemistry building. It was good training for the kind of warfare that was waged at Shiloh but it had no connection with what was going on in Europe. Some people used to think there was German money behind it, but they didn't dare say so or they would have been thrown in jail as German spies. It was a period of muddy thought and marked, I believe, the decline of higher education in the Middle West.

As a soldier I was never any good at all. Most of the cadets were glumly indifferent soldiers, but I was no good at all. Once General Littlefield, who was commandant of the cadet corps, popped up in front of me during regimental drill and snapped, "You are the main trouble with this university!" I think he meant that my type was the main trouble with the university but he may have meant me individually. I was mediocre at drill, certainly—that is, until my senior year. By that time I had drilled longer than anybody else in the Western Conference, having failed at military at the end of each preceding year so that I had to do it all over again. I was the only senior still in uniform. The uniform which, when new, had made me look like an interurban railway conductor, now that it had become faded and too tight made me look like Bert Williams in his bell-boy act. This had a definitely bad effect on my morale. Even so, I had become by sheer practise little short of wonderful at squad manoeuvres.

One day General Littlefield picked our company out of the whole regiment and tried to get it mixed up by putting it through one movement after another as fast as we could execute them: squads right, squads left, squads on right into line, squads right about, squads left front into line, etc. In about three minutes one hundred and nine men were marching in one direction and I was marching away from them at an angle of forty degrees, all alone. "Company, halt!" shouted General Littlefield, "That man is the only man who has it right!" I was made a corporal for my achievement.

The next day General Littlefield summoned me to his office. He was swatting flies when I went in. I was silent and he was silent too, for a long time. I don't think he remembered me or why he had sent for me, but he didn't want to admit it. He swatted some more flies, keeping his eyes on them narrowly before he let go with the swatter. "Button up your coat!" he snapped. Looking back on it now I can see that he meant me although he was looking at a fly, but I just stood there. Another fly came to rest on a paper in front of the general and began rubbing its hind legs together. The general lifted the swatter cautiously. I moved restlessly and the fly flew away. "You startled him!" barked General Littlefield, looking at me severely. I said I was sorry. "That won't help the situation!" snapped the General, with cold military logic. I didn't see what I could do except offer to chase some more flies toward his desk, but I didn't say anything. He stared out the window at the faraway figures of co-eds crossing the campus toward the library. Finally, he told me I could go. So I went. He either didn't know which cadet I was or else he forgot what he wanted to see me about. It may have been that he wished to apologize for having called me the main trouble with the university; or maybe he had decided to compliment me on my brilliant drilling of the day before and then at the last minute decided not to. I don't know. I don't think about it much any more.

❦ ❦ ❦

*Nathaniel Southgate Shaler*

# How Agassiz Taught Shaler[1]

AT THE time of my secession from the humanities, Agassiz was in Europe; he did not return, I think, until the autumn of 1859. I had, however, picked up several acquaintances among his pupils, learned what they were about, and gained some notion of his methods. After about a month he returned, and I had my first contact with the man who was to have the most influence on my life of any of the teachers to whom I am indebted. I shall never forget

[1] From *Autobiography of Nathaniel Southgate Shaler* (Boston: Houghton Mifflin Company, 1907), 93-100, with omissions. Reprinted by permission of Gabriella Shaler Webb.

even the lesser incidents of this meeting, for this great master by his presence gave an importance to his surroundings, so that the room where you met him and the furniture stayed with the memory of him.

When I first met Louis Agassiz, he was still in the prime of his admirable manhood; though he was then fifty-two years old, and had passed his constructive period, he still had the look of a young man. His face was the most genial and engaging that I had ever seen, and his manner captivated me altogether. But as I had been among men who had a free swing, and for a year among people who seemed to me to be cold and super-rational, hungry as I doubtless was for human sympathy, Agassiz's welcome went to my heart —I was at once his captive. It has been my good chance to see many men, of engaging presence and ways, but I have never known his equal. . . .

As my account of Agassiz's quality should rest upon my experiences with him, I shall now go on to tell how and to what effect he trained me.[2] In that day there were no written examinations on any subjects to which candidates for the Lawrence Scientific School had to pass. The professors in charge of the several departments questioned the candidates, and determined their fitness to pursue the course of study they desired to undertake. Few or none who had any semblance of an education were denied admission to Agassiz's laboratory. At that time, the instructors had, in addition to their meagre salaries—his was then $2,500 per annum,—the regular fees paid in by the students under his charge. So I was promptly assured that I was admitted. Be it said, however, that he did give me an effective oral examination, which, as he told me, was intended to show whether I could expect to go forward to a degree at the end of four years of study. On this matter of the degree he was obdurate, refusing to recommend some who had been with him for many years, and had succeeded in their special work, giving as reason for his denial that they were "too ignorant."

The examination Agassiz gave me was directed first to find that I knew enough Latin and Greek to make use of those languages; that I could patter a little of them evidently pleased him. He didn't care for those detestable rules for scanning. Then came German and French, which were also approved: I could read both, and spoke the former fairly well. He did not probe me in my weakest place, mathematics, for the good reason that, badly as I was off in that subject, he was in a worse plight. Then asking me concerning my reading, he found that I had read the *Essay on Classification*, and had noted in it the influence of Schelling's views. Most of his questioning related to this field, and the more than fair beginning of our relations then made was due to the fact that I had some enlargement on that side. So, too, he was pleased to find that I had managed a lot of Latin, Greek, and German poetry, and had been trained with the sword. He completed this inquiry by requiring that I bring my foils and masks for a bout. In this test he did not fare well, for, though not untrained, he evidently knew more of the *Schläger*

2 At this time Shaler was nineteen years old.

than of the rapier. He was heavy-handed, and lacked finesse. This, with my previous experience, led me to the conclusion that I had struck upon a kind of tutor in Cambridge not known in Kentucky.

While Agassiz questioned me carefully as to what I had read and what I had seen, he seemed in this preliminary going over in no wise concerned to find what I knew about fossils, rocks, animals, and plants; he put aside the offerings of my scanty lore. This offended me a bit, as I recall, for the reason that I thought I knew, and for a self-taught lad really did know, a good deal about such matters, especially as to the habits of insects, particularly spiders. It seemed hard to be denied the chance to make my parade; but I afterward saw what this meant—that he did not intend to let me begin my tasks by posing as a naturalist. The beginning was indeed quite different, and, as will be seen, in a manner that quickly evaporated my conceit. It was made and continued in a way I will now recount.

Agassiz's laboratory was then in a rather small two-storied building, looking much like a square dwelling-house, which stood where the College Gymnasium now stands . . . Agassiz had recently moved into it from a shed on the marsh near Brighton bridge, the original tenants, the engineers, having come to riches in the shape of the brick structure now known as the Lawrence Building. In this primitive establishment Agassiz's laboratory, as distinguished from the storerooms where the collections were crammed, occupied one room about thirty feet long and fifteen feet wide—what is now the west room on the lower floor of the edifice. In this place, already packed, I had assigned to me a small pine table with a rusty tin pan upon it. . . .

When I sat me down before my tin pan, Agassiz brought me a small fish, placing it before me with the rather stern requirement that I should study it, but should on no account talk to any one concerning it, nor read anything relating to fishes, until I had his permission so to do. To my inquiry, "What shall I do?" he said in effect: "Find out what you can without damaging the specimen; when I think that you have done the work I will question you." In the course of an hour I thought I had compassed that fish; it was rather an unsavory object, giving forth the stench of old alcohol, then loathsome to me, though in time I came to like it. Many of the scales were loosened so that they fell off. It appeared to me to be a case for a summary report, which I was anxious to make and get on to the next stage of the business. But Agassiz, though always within call, concerned himself no further with me that day, nor the next, nor for a week. At first, this neglect was distressing; but I saw that it was a game, for he was, as I discerned rather than saw, covertly watching me. So I set my wits to work upon the thing, and in the course of a hundred hours or so thought I had done much—a hundred times as much as seemed possible at the start. I got interested in finding out how the scales went in series, their shape, the form and placement of the teeth, etc. Finally, I felt full of the subject, and probably expressed it in my bearing; as for words about it then, there were none from my master except his cheery "Good morning." At length, on the seventh day, came the question, "Well?" and my disgorge of learning to him as he sat on the edge of my table puffing his cigar. At the end of the hour's telling, he swung off and away, saying: "That is not right." Here I began to think that, after all, perhaps the rules for scanning Latin verse were not the worst infliction in the world. Moreover, it was clear that he was playing a game with me to find if I were capable of doing hard, continuous work without the support of a teacher, and this stimulated me to labor. I went at the task anew, discarded my first notes, and in another week of ten hours a day labor I had results which astonished myself and satisfied him. Still there was no trace of praise in words or manner. He signified that it would do by placing before me about a half a peck of bones, telling me to see what I could make of them, with no further directions to guide me. I soon found that they were the skeletons of half a dozen fishes of different species; the jaws told me so much at a first inspection. The task evidently was to fit the separate bones together in their proper order. Two months or more went to this task with no other help than an occasional looking over my grouping with the stereotyped remark: "That is not right." Finally, the task was done, and I was again set upon alcoholic specimens—this time a remarkable lot of specimens representing, perhaps, twenty species of the side-swimmers or Pleuronectidae.

I shall never forget the sense of power in dealing with things which I felt in beginning the more extended work on a group of animals. I had learned the art of comparing objects, which is the basis of the naturalist's work. At this stage I was allowed to read, and to discuss my work with others about me. I did both eagerly, and acquired a considerable knowledge of the literature of ichthyology, becoming especially interested in the system of classification, then most imperfect. I tried to follow Agassiz's scheme of division into the order of ctenoids and ganoids, with the result that I found one of my species of side-swimmers had cycloid scales on one side and ctenoid on the other. This not only shocked my sense of the value of classification in a way that permitted of no full recovery of my original respect for the process, but for a time shook my confidence in my master's knowledge. At the same time I had a malicious pleasure in exhibiting my "find" to him, expecting to repay in part the humiliation which he had evidently tried to inflict on my conceit. To my question as to how the non-descript should be classified he said: "My boy, there are now two of us who know that."

This incident of the fish made an end of my novitiate. After that, with a suddenness of transition which puzzled me, Agassiz became very communicative; we passed indeed into the relation of friends of like age and purpose, and he actually consulted me as to what I should like to take up as a field of study. Finding that I wished to devote myself to geology, he set me to work on the Brachiopoda as the best group of fossils to serve as data in determining the Palaeozoic horizons. So far as his rather limited knowledge of the matter went, he guided me in the field about Cambridge, in my reading, and to acquaintances of his who were concerned with earth structures. I came thus to know Charles T. Jackson, Jules Marcou, and, later, the brothers Rogers, Henry and James. At the same time I kept up the study of zoology, undertaking to make myself acquainted with living organic forms as a basis for a knowledge of fossils.

❦ ❦ ❦

*Rollo Walter Brown*

# Kittredge of Harvard[1]

THERE could be no doubt about the matter: George Lyman Kittredge consisted of more than one man. Just how many men were required to constitute him, nobody seemed able to say. But that he was not less than two, everybody who knew him was ready to admit.

The first of these two—the one he was most widely thought of as being— was the "Kitty" of Harvard Hall. Undergraduates with vivid imaginations made sketches of the old building on the point of blowing up, with zigzag electric fragments of Shakespeare shooting from windows and roof, whenever "Kitty" held forth. To many of them for a lifetime the total meaning of Harvard Hall was "Kitty."

The sight of him as he came to the ten-o'clock class was in itself something that had to be recognized as dramatic. In the pleasant autumn or spring, men stood high on the steps or out on the turf in front and watched in the direction of Christ Church to see who could catch the first glimpse of him.

"There he comes!" somebody called, and then everybody who was in a position to see watched him as he hurried breezily along—a graceful, tallish man in very light gray suit and gray fedora hat, with a full square beard at least as white as his suit, who moved with energy, and smoked passionately at a big cigar. Students used to say that he smoked an entire cigar while he walked the short distance along the iron fence of the old burying ground and across the street to Johnston Gate. But as he came through the gate he tossed the remnant of his cigar into the shrubbery with a bit of a flourish, and the students still outside hurried in and scrambled up the long stairway in order to be in their places—as he liked—before he himself entered. If any of them were still on the stairway when he came in at the outer door like a gust, they gave way and he pushed up past them, and into the good-sized room and down the aisle to the front, threw his hat on the table in the corner, mounted the two steps to the platform, looked about with a commanding eye, and there was sudden silence and unrestrained expectancy.

[1] From *Harvard Yard in the Golden Age*, by Rollo Walter Brown. Copyright, 1948, by permission of Current Books, Inc., A. A. Wyn, Publisher, New York.

"Any questions?" he asked—meaning questions about matters considered at the last meeting of the course. After five minutes of these questions, he was ready to begin.

The play under consideration was *Macbeth*—let us say; and he was ready to take up Act III. Always his method was a meticulously careful examination of every line, every significant word, with a running commentary on problems of drama and theatre. At the end of the year we were supposed to know five plays—sometimes a sixth—so thoroughly that in the final examination we could spot any line or piece of line that he quoted (usually about sixty), tell what came just before and after, tell who said the words and to whom, and be able to comment on whatever was significant in the passage. Then there were somewhat more than six hundred lines of memory passages. And there were books of assigned reading. Even the least wise in the course filled the margins of his copy of the text, and pages of gummed interleaving paper, with notes against an oncoming evil day.

"Now," he said, after he had read and commented upon Banquo's opening speech, and had reminded us once more that *Macbeth* is a swift-moving play, "there are three very important questions on this next page. They are neatly imbedded, yet for the purposes of the play, they stand out in red ink. What are they?"—and he glanced up and down the class list—"Mr. Howard."

Mr. Howard—it might have been Cabot or Flynn or Jones—did not seem to be present.

"Mr. Howard?" "Kitty" repeated, with the slightest trace of irritation in his voice.

When there was still no response he suddenly exploded. "The college office had two ghost men on my list for two or three weeks before I could get them off! Is this Mr. Howard another?"

There was no response.

"Is there anybody in this room who knows anything about this spook Mr. Howard?"

There was not a murmur, seemingly not even a breath, among the hundred or more students.

He slapped the book down on his desk so sharply that some of the men in the front row jumped. "By heavens, this is not to be endured! I asked a perfectly decent question, and I am going to have an answer if I have to take a poll of the entire class!"

A man in the middle of the room hesitantly lifted a hand. "I am Mr. Howard."

"Then why didn't you answer?"

"I was not prepared."

"Kitty" flew into so vast a rage that even the top of his head was ruddy. "Well, couldn't you at least have identified yourself? Stand up, Mr. Howard" —and he made a movement as if to step down off the platform—"so that this class can see who you are. And"—after Mr. Howard had very promptly stood up—"you are to come over to Sever 3 at twelve o'clock and expostulate with me—in the Elizabethan sense."

He picked up the book and in a twinkling went on, quite as if nothing unusual had happened, to point out that the three questions down the page were the ones that Macbeth asked Banquo:

> Ride you this afternoon?
>
> Is't far you ride?
>
> Goes Fleance with you?

And then in an engaging smoothness of temper and in flowing brilliance he commented on one passage after another, made compact explanation of linguistic details, reminded us that it was not the words that had become obsolete that made the most trouble for us in understanding Shakespeare, but the words that had not become obsolete, and otherwise rounded out the whole scene until we felt as if we must be knowing the play somewhat as the audience knew it when it was originally produced.

He came to a very brief stage direction. "Note that Shakespeare is usually brief. If Mr. George Bernard Shaw had been writing that stage direction, he would have filled a page, at least."

There was a flutter of mirthfulness. It was the style then to laugh at any mention of this new playwright, as though of course he could not be much.

"Incidentally," he said, as he paced the platform, "there are other differences between William Shakespeare and Mr. Shaw."

There was greater mirthfulness still; and time flowed on harmoniously.

Some professor of economics had great charts and maps on rollers all over the front of the room, and there were two or three long, gracefully sloping pointers at hand. "Kitty" picked up one of these and used it as a stafflike cane as he paced back and forth and commented. He was magnificent. He was an Anglo-Saxon king speaking to his people.

Once in his march as he socked the royal staff down, it came in two where there was a knot in the wood, and he made a somewhat unkingly lurch. A few students snickered very cautiously.

He glowered upon them. "You have a fine sense of humor!" Then without taking his eyes off the humbled faces, he drew his arm back as if he were hurling a javelin, and drove the long remnant of the pointer into the corner of the room. "Now laugh!" he dared them.

When "Kitty" was having a run of bad days, an hour might be highly electric from beginning to end.

One wintry morning when he was late and the legitimate seven minutes of grace had ticked away, somebody called bravely, "All out!" There was much shuffling of feet and there were echoing cries all over the room, "Time up!" "Let's go!" But nobody moved. Finally one man arose and marched defiantly toward the door, to the accompaniment of whoops and cheers.

Soon there was a solid procession pushing out through the doorway. Just when the Arnolds and Bonbrights from down in front were approaching the door and the room suddenly looked deserted, somebody called from downstairs: "Here he is!"

There was a mad scramble to get back into the room. But he was moving faster than any crowd could move. On the long semicircular stairway he pushed through with his green bookbag and smart gray hat held high, and let everyone give way in the manner possible. He was in the front of the room, and had his hat and overcoat and bookbag on the table, and was mounting the platform all in readiness to begin before the last of the returning students were in their chairs.

He waited for a moment of silence before he spoke—with something of scorn in his voice. "When I was an undergraduate in this college, by thunder we never went back for a professor."

Then for an hour he treated us as if we were a bunch of softies. He commented on words, on lines, on entire speeches with lightning speed. He assumed vast historical and linguistic knowledge on our part which we did not possess. He fired questions in every direction. One of these he addressed to a thirty-eight-year-old graduate student—a professor on leave from a well-known institution—and gave him such a cross-examination that he never came back to the course.

And then, just before bell time when even the laziest student in the course had been stimulated by the charged atmosphere to make notes and otherwise try to keep up, "Kitty" broke off in the middle of a sentence with a terrifying shout that was also a roar, slapped his copy of the play down on the desk, hurried toward the door, nervously pushing his hand back through his white hair, and disappeared into the hallway.

A moment later he reappeared at the door, bowing a man in with extraordinary graciousness. The man was frightened almost beyond speech. "I b-beg your pardon," he stammered, "I am not a member of the course; I am a visitor."

"That does not excuse you from the rules of courtesy. You were disrespectful to me and to the young gentlemen of the class. Nobody leaves this room till the bell rings."

By the time he was back at his desk and had found the interrupted sentence in the play, the bell was ringing and he made a gesture of dismissal. As the men crowded toward the door they somehow felt sheepish, like schoolboys.

It was always a double experience. "Kitty" might suddenly step out of the Elizabethan world and pounce upon some man and scare him until he was unable to define the diaphragm—it once happened—and require him to come to the next meeting "prepared to discuss the diaphragm" as a preliminary to an hour of *King Lear*. No man might feel altogether sure that he would escape. Once "Kitty" read with such a poetic impression of reality that a man who was later to be widely known as a magazine editor sat lost in rapturous enjoyment. Suddenly "Kitty" stopped. "Now what is the commanding word in that passage"—and he picked up the printed class list and let his eye run down over the names—"Mr. . . . Smith?" Mr. Smith had been so rapturously lost that he did not even know where the passage was. A neighbor whispered the number of the line to him and he answered correctly: "Why—'God.' " "Don't you 'Why—God' me!" "Kitty" stormed back at him, and then gave him such a dressing down for using the unnecessary word as he had never known, so that he always had that to carry along with his memory of the perfect reading. On another occasion "Kitty" picked up the class list, started on the R's, became interested in one man's brilliant answers to his rapid-fire cross-examination, and left the rest of the R's dangling in suspense throughout the three remaining months of the year.

Men knew that he was a miracle man, and thought it worth accepting all hazards in order to possess some part of his basic richness of life. They completed the year, grumbled a little about the marks he gave them—there were few A's—and very probably came back the next year to study the alternating group of plays. In that case they had the thorough knowledge of ten or eleven plays, instead of five or six; they knew eleven or twelve hundred lines of good passages by heart; they had vast information about drama and theatre and sources and language and Elizabethan life, and they had interesting fragments of such a store of miscellaneous knowledge and wisdom as they had not supposed until last year could be the possession of any one human being.

That was one of the men in the total George Lyman Kittredge. That part of him could not be brushed aside as if it were not an essential part. It was. But it was the more external part. Many of the men in the course in Shakespeare knew this well enough. They saw that it was their irresponsibility, or laziness, or grotesque ignorance, that touched him off into his tantrums. His disgust and amazement and scorn were release for a sensitive mind—usually in need of sleep—whose everyday high level made it impossible for him not to suffer in the presence of unlimited imperfections. And his graduate students who had never taken the course in Shakespeare found it difficult to believe the wild stories about him. For to them he was a courteous gentleman who begged them to smoke some of his good cigars and know that they were potential scholars about to be admitted to the most honorable company of men on earth.

His courtesy did not prevent him from exercising the dominant mind. When a student explained somewhat fearfully that he had noticed in the dictionary that a certain word was accented on the second syllable, "Kitty" said, as he put the word down on the back of an envelope, "That's wrong; I'll see that that is changed." Through generations of Shakespeare students—and his place on the board of editors of one dictionary—he caused a shift in preference to the pronunciation of "Elizabethan" with an accented long e. But he could never establish "Shakspere" as a preferred spelling. Sometimes, too, his overpositiveness came back upon him in ironic ways. He insisted on with-holding a degree from a man for insufficient acquaintance with the drama who later became a national figure in play-writing. He once prevented a man from receiving honors in English with whom ten years later he marched down the aisle at a university commencement where both received honorary degrees—the young author and the white-haired professor.

Men who were chiefly concerned with the literature of the eighteenth and nineteenth centuries very justly felt that he placed heavy emphasis on the early centuries. But he insisted that the early centuries were of the utmost im-portance, and that they were full of interest. The age of Chaucer, he con-tended, was closer to us than the age of Pope. Always there were students who had looked upon Chaucer as some vague accident back there on the edge of the pure night of the Dark Ages, and for a time they sat skeptical, although they assumed that Chaucer was somebody about whom they should know a little.

But when they listened to Professor Kittredge—or "Mr. Kittredge"—they saw the age of Chaucer coming to such vividness of view that they had to admit that it outshone the nearer centuries in brightness. He invited them to see that

> the spirit of radicalism was abroad in the land. To describe as an era of dumb submissiveness the age of Wyclif, and John Huss, and the Great Schism, of the Jacquerie in France and Tyler and Ball in England, is to read both litera-ture and history with one's eyes shut. . . . It was a scambling and unquiet time when nobody was at rest but the dead. In a word, it was a good age to live in, and so Chaucer found it.[2]

And so they found it—and the heroic world of Beowulf, and the world of English and Scottish popular ballads, and all the other less familiar worlds to which he introduced them. Something of his own vividness had gone into his original exploring, and now something of it went into the revelation of what he had discovered.

But whatever the area in which he for the moment was occupied, he was engaged in perhaps the most difficult—and most desperately needed—of all educational endeavors in the United States; that is, in having pure scholarship recognized as a source of life for all men. Scholarship is the final high honesty. Men worked with Professor Kittredge—always the least bit awesomely—and came to feel how great was the disgrace of a human mind that let itself be content with anything short of the completest disinterested understanding.

From his fortunate position he all the while was sending out great numbers of men to important college and university posts. They were such men as John M. Manly, of the University of Chicago, one of his earliest students; Walter Morris Hart, of the University of California; John Samuel Kenyon, of Hiram College; Karl Young, of Yale; Carleton Brown, chiefly of Bryn Mawr;

[2] *Chaucer and His Poetry.* 1915. Harvard University Press. By permission.

John A. Lomax, of the field of American ballads and folk songs; John Livingston Lowes, who came back from Washington University to teach in the Yard
for the rest of his active life—and write *The Road to Xanadu*.

At times the objection made its way back to Cambridge that some of his
disciples were not important men of this kind, but only "little Kittredges."
And sometimes the reports were true. If men are basically small they are sure
to adopt the accessible mannerisms of anyone whose superior qualities are out
of reach. But Professor Kittredge's distinguished former students constituted a
great company. In Texas, in Iowa, in Pennsylvania, in California, men accustomed to the ax-to-grind sort of thinking in what they called the practical
world looked upon these honest scholars as an ultimate standard of excellence
to be applied in matters of every perplexing sort.

And in Professor Kittredge it was more than honesty; it was high faith in
honesty. His former students often traveled a thousand miles—sometimes farther—to have his counsel when they were in doubt. A young professor in a
Midwestern college had confided in an older man in one of the chief universities of America about an original project that he had in mind for the next
year, and then found that the older man had immediately hurried off a young
colleague to work at the idea and be first in the field. Sleepless, the young
professor went to consult someone who was wise.

Professor Kittredge sat erect and smoked at a great fragrant cigar and
listened in silence until the man was through. Then he said without a moment's hesitation: "Don't let the matter trouble you for one minute. And don't
modify your plans—not by as much as a hair. Scurvy business of that kind
doesn't work out—in the end. It is not the other man's idea; he is working
at it because his chief suggested it to him. He will make little of it. The idea
is yours, from the inside of you, and consequently you will be aware of all
sorts of possibilities in it that the other man, whoever he is, will never see."
And when it turned out precisely so, Professor Kittredge said with a trace of
a smile round his eyes and down into his white beard, "We have to count
on its being like that."

He gave his complete self to the world of the teacher. He required nothing
else. In it he had labor and recreation and profound joy—without end. For
forty-eight years (1888-1936) he taught at Harvard. He never took a year of
leave, nor a half year. He did not like to have breaks in his work. He did
not like to go off to other universities to lecture in term time. He made
a number of trips to Europe, but with one exception he made them in
the summer-vacation period. England was his great fascination east of the
Atlantic. When he was made an honorary fellow of Jesus College, Cambridge,
he was delighted and proud. When Oxford wished to confer on him an
honorary degree he felt highly honored, of course. But the great joy of work
was at home.

In this world of the teacher to which he was devoted, he carried on endless research. When he was confronted by the teacher's much-discussed choice between teaching and research, he said: "Thank you, I'll take both."

In his own explorations the range that he covered was so wide that some persons actually believed that there were at least two persons named G. L. Kittredge writing at the time. He was interested in such matters as Increase Mather's views on smallpox, the ballads of Kentucky, the vocabulary of the Australasians, the history of witchcraft, the history of words for popular reading, cowboy songs, the early Teutonic notions of immortality, the toad in folklore, Chaucer on marriage, the history of religion, and scores of subjects thought of as more strictly within the field of language and literature. And his books ranged from *Chaucer and His Poetry* to *The Old Farmer and His Almanack*— and manuals of grammar and composition for high school.

It was at Barnstable, down on the Cape, that he was able to do much of his own work. For there he had long summer weeks that were little interrupted. If one chanced to be at the house on Hilliard Street in Cambridge just when he was about to go away for the summer, one might well decide that he was leaving for all time, so completely did he seem to be transferring his scholarly effects. Eventually he built a study a little away from the house in Barnstable so that he might work in entire seclusion, with only the cheerful voices of his children and their friends on the tennis court to remind him pleasantly—if he heard them at all—that he was not completely isolated in time and space.

On the Cape, too, he could be elementally refreshed. On the Cape, he was happy to say, he—or his son—had come upon the perfect pessimist, a native who grew chickens. When it was suggested that a few chicks just outside a coop were sturdy youngsters, the native replied, "Yes, but the trouble is, the old hen hatched out six, and by God all of them have died on me but five."

The Cape was heaven for work; yet back in Cambridge in the autumn he carried his own work right along with his teaching—and thereby constantly gave his teaching enrichment. He moved briskly from his classroom to Gore Hall, and very quickly disappeared. Then one came upon him somewhere deep in the stacks, lost to the immediate world over a puzzling text or fat galleys of proofs. The library was nothing musty and dead for him. It was man recorded. When the great new Widener Memorial Library was spoken of as an elephant among the other buildings in the Yard, he asked, "What if it is? You could destroy all the other Harvard buildings to the northward, and with Widener left standing, still have a university."

If days were not long enough, always there were nights. Like Charles Péguy, he considered night as the part of existence that holds everything together that is sacred to man, "wherein he accomplishes his being." But for Professor Kittredge this was not to be done through sleep; it was to be done through work.

For many years one of his intimate friends walked from Boston to Cambridge on Sunday afternoon, had supper with the Kittredges, and then the two read Greek together till eleven o'clock—as relaxation. But that still left the body of the night ahead. So, too, was it when his "ballad course" met at his house in the evening, and some of the most enthusiastic lingered a little in the big study. It was when his own house had become quiet, and the lights in houses everywhere were beginning to disappear, and the roar of the city had lost its nearness, and the world was otherwise losing the last signs of its daytime confusion, that he knew freedom. In the enveloping quiet he could give himself to work without fear of distraction. If he felt the need of diversion, he could read one more detective story.

When Mrs. Kittredge chanced to know at two or two-thirty or three in the morning that he was still at work, she would slip down and remind him that it was time for him to be getting some sleep. Very obediently he would go off to bed for the rest of the night. In the course of years, Mrs. Kittredge wearied a little of making the trip downstairs and had an electric bell installed with a button by her bed. But he did not like it. In the perfect quiet of night it made him jump. Sometimes nobody reminded him that he ought to be in bed, and he did not think of the matter himself; and when Thomas the chore man slipped into the study at six in the morning to build a new fire, there sat Professor Kittredge peacefully asleep in his comfortable chair before the empty fireplace, with one hand clutching a book on the arm of the chair as firmly as if he were awake. On such a night he did not get to bed at all.

When a vivid man does a sufficient number of things that are unfailingly characteristic, legend begins to attach itself to his name. And when he lives on and on through one college generation after another until men who were in his classes almost a half century before come back to visit their grandsons in the freshman class and find him still teaching with the same old fire, the contributions of legendary instance mount till they constitute a kind of running supplemental biography.

Men argued over the original color of his hair and beard, for he was gray —or white—so early that nobody could quite remember him when he was not gray or white. They liked to speak, too, of the fact that Kitty never bothered with any degree except an A.B. They laughed over the gushing woman who asked in disappointment why he had never taken a Ph.D. and his supposed reply: "Who would have examined me?" Or they repeated the story of the famous woman college president who wished a Harvard man as an instructor in English, but said she could not consider anyone who lacked a Ph.D., and of Charles Townsend Copeland's stentorian reply to her: "Thank God, then we'll not lose Kittredge!"

Legend was helped, too, by the fact that in his highly charged life there was always unpredictable heartening for the less positive, the less courageous. When a frightened young candidate for honors in English had to say in reply to a question: "I'm afraid I can't answer: I have not read all of Wordsworth," Professor Kittredge brought him quickly to life and confidence by replying: "Neither have I! I couldn't be hired to!" When the efficiency experts were rising up everywhere in institutions, and one of them asked Professor Kittredge just how many hours and minutes it took him to prepare one of his "lectures" on Shakespeare, he replied: "I refuse to answer. It's one of my trade secrets." Then he relented and said, "Just a lifetime—can't you see that?" When graduate students in the field of English made their way to Professor K.G.T. Webster's house at Gerry's Landing for a relaxing great dinner and then a joyous session on the third floor in a room that some of the guests thought of as an Anglo-Saxon mead hall, Professor Kittredge was always so full of wit and generosity of spirit that the guests were stirred to believe they could face anything.

So there he was, about to be seventy-five, full of fiery power, and seemingly without a thought that he had already taught ten years past the usual retiring age. He walked energetically through the traffic of Harvard Square and the policeman said bravely but so that Professor Kittredge would be sure not to hear, "Be a little careful there, Santa Claus!" In the Yard the general assumption seemed to be that nobody quite dared to tell him that he must retire.

On his seventy-fifth birthday, when he went to his class at Radcliffe the girls had put seventy-five magnificent crimson roses on his desk.

What was this they had done? Often enough he had scolded them. Sometimes he had walked out on them when they did not come up to his expectations in brilliance. And now they had remembered him in this fashion. They had almost taken an unfair advantage of him—so startling was it all. He told them—and suddenly he was deeply touched—that he found it difficult to express his great appreciation. "If it would help, I'd declare a holiday. And I do hereby declare a holiday." Then quite as suddenly he recovered his usual manner, looked up, and said with a self-defiant kind of smile: "Now if only some of you will tell me how to get them home without looking like a bridegroom!"

At home he admitted modestly to his wife that not every man received that many roses from his girl students on his seventy-fifth birthday. In the afternoon when one of his former students and his wife dropped in to offer best wishes, he was in the happiest of moods. He told them how near he had come to being born on the twenty-ninth of February. He admitted in great joviality that undergraduates had at times led him to make "characteristic remarks" and do "characteristic things," and he drew out of the past a few instances himself. Yes, he supposed he would be giving up teaching sooner or later, for he had in mind finishing that annotated edition of such plays of Shakespeare as had interested him most, and that would keep him busy for a number of years ahead.

And so it did.

❦ ❦ ❦

*Edmund Wilson*

# Christian Gauss as a Teacher of Literature [1]

I HAVE been asked to write about Christian Gauss as an influence on my generation at Princeton. Since we knew him as a teacher of literature only— I was in the class of 1916, and he did not become dean of the college till 1925—I shall speak mainly of this side of his activity.

As a professor of French and Italian, then, one of the qualities that distinguished Gauss was the unusual fluidity of mind that he preserved through his whole career. A teacher like Irving Babbitt was a dogmatist who either imposed his dogma or provoked a strong opposition. Christian Gauss was a teacher of a different kind—the kind who starts trains of thought that he does not himself guide to conclusions but leaves in the hands of his students to be carried on by themselves. The student might develop, extend them, transpose them into different terms, build out of them constructions of his own. Gauss never imposed, he suggested; and his own ideas on any subject were always taking new turns: the light in which he saw it would be shifted, it would range itself in some new context. It bored him, in his course on French Romanticism, to teach the same texts year after year; and with the writers that he could not get away from, he would vary the works read. With the less indispensable ones, he would change the repertory altogether. If Alfred de Vigny, for example, had been featured in the course when you took it, you might come back a few years later and find that he had been pushed into the background by Stendhal. Christian would have been reading up Stendhal, and his interest in him would seem almost as fresh as if he had never read him before. He would have some new insights about him, and he would pass these on to you when you came to see him, as he was doing to his students in class. I know from my own experience how the lightly dropped seeds from his lectures could take root and unfold in another's mind; and, while occupied in writing this memoir, I have happened to find striking evidence of the persistence of this vital gift in the testimony of a student of Romance languages who sat under Gauss twenty years later, and who has told me that, in preparing his doctor's thesis, he had at first been exhilarated by an illusion of developing original ideas, only to find the whole thing in germ in his old notes on Gauss's lectures. But though his influence on his students was so penetrating, Gauss founded no school of teaching—not even, I suppose, an academic tradition—because, as one of his colleagues pointed out to me, he had

[1] From *The Shores of Light: A Literary Chronicle of the Twenties and Thirties* (New York: Farrar, Strauss and Young, Inc., 1952), pp. 3-26. Copyright, 1952, Edmund Wilson.

no communicable body of doctrine and no pedagogical method that other teachers could learn to apply. If one went back to Princeton to see him, as I more or less regularly did, after one had got out of college, one's memory of his old preceptorials (relatively informal discussions with groups of five or six students) would seem prolonged, without interruptions, into one's more recent conversations, as if it had all been a long conversation that had extended, off and on, through the years: a commentary that, on Christian's part, never seemed to be trying to prove anything in any overwhelming way, a voyage of speculation that aimed rather to survey the world than to fix a convincing vision. In his role of the least didactic of sages, the most accessible of talkers, he seemed a part of that good eighteenth-century Princeton which has always managed to flourish between the pressures of a narrow Presbyterianism and a rich man's suburbanism. It is probable that Christian was at home in Princeton as he would not have been anywhere else. He was delightful in the days of his deanship, in the solid and compact and ample yellow-and-white Joseph Henry house, built in 1837, where there was always, during the weekends, a constant going and coming of visitors, who could pick up with him any topic, literary, historical or collegiate, and pursue it till someone else came and the thread was left suspended. Though by this time so important a local figure, he seemed always, also, international. He had been born of German parents in Michigan, and German had been his first language. In his youth he had spent a good deal of time in France. He had no foreign accent in English, and, so far as I was able to judge, spoke all his languages correctly and fluently; but French, Italian and English, at any rate, with a deliberate articulation, never running the words together, as if they were not native to him. One did not learn a bad accent from him, but one did not learn to speak the Romance languages as they are spoken in their own countries. On the other hand, the very uniformity of his candid tone, his unhurried pace and his scrupulous precision, with his slightly drawling intonations, made a kind of neutral medium in which everything in the world seemed soluble. I have never known anyone like him in any academic community. He gave the impression of keeping in touch, without the slightest effort—he must have examined all the printed matter that came into the university library—with everything that was going on. It used to amuse me sometimes to try him out on unlikely subjects. If one asked him a question about the Middle Ages, one absolutely got the impression that he had lived in Europe then and knew it at firsthand.

This extreme flexibility and enormous range were, of course, a feature of his lectures. He was able to explain and appreciate almost any kind of work of literature from almost any period. He would show you what the author was aiming at and the methods he had adopted to achieve his ends. He was wonderful at comparative literature, for his reading had covered the whole of the West, ancient, medieval and modern, and his memory was truly Macaulayan (an adjective sometimes assigned too cheaply). He seemed to be able to summon almost anything he wanted in prose or verse, as if he were taking down the book from the shelf. (He told me once that, in his younger days, he had set out to write something about Rabelais and had presently begun to grow suspicious of what he saw coming out. On looking up Taine's essay on Rabelais, he found that he had been transcribing whole paragraphs from it, his unconscious doing the work of translation.) He was brilliant at revealing the assumptions, social, aesthetic and moral, implicit in, say, a scene from a romantic play as contrasted with a scene from a Greek tragedy, or in the significance of a character in Dante as distinguished from the significance of a character in Shakespeare. I remember his later quoting with approval A. N. Whitehead's statement, in *Science and the Modern World*, that, "when you are criticizing the philosophy of an epoch," you should "not chiefly direct your attention to those intellectual positions which its exponents feel it necessary to defend. There will be some fundamental assumptions which adherents of all the variant systems within the epoch unconsciously presuppose. Such assumptions appear so obvious that people do not know what they are assuming because no other way of putting things has ever occurred to them." Gauss had always had a special sense of this. But he was interested also in individuals and liked to bring out the traits of a literary personality. His commentary on a poem of Victor Hugo's—*Le Mendiant* from *Les Contemplations*—would run along something like this: "A poor man is passing in the frost and rain, and Victor Hugo asks him in. He opens the door *'d'une façon civile'* [2]—he is always democratic, of course. *'Entrez, brave homme,'* he says, and he tells the man to warm himself and has a bowl of milk brought him—as anybody, of course, would do. He makes him take off his cloak—*'tout mangé des vers, et jadis bleu'*—and he hangs it on a nail, where the fire shines through its holes, so that it looks like a night illumined by stars.

> Et, pendant qu'il séchait ce haillon désolé
> D'où ruisselaient le pluie et l'eau des fondrières,
> Je songeais que cet homme était plain de prières.
> Et je regardais, sourd à ce que nous disions,
> Sa bure où je voyais des constellations.

"This sounds impressive, but what does it mean? Not a thing. We have not been told anything that would indicate that the old man is full of prayers. It is a gratuitous assumption on the part of Hugo. That the cloak with its holes reminded him of a heaven with constellations has no moral significance whatever. Yet with his mastery of verse and his rhetoric, Victor Hugo manages to carry it off. —I don't mean," he would add, "that he was insincere. Rather

---

[2] In a courteous way. Do come in, my good man. All eaten up by worms, and once blue in color.
And while he dried these sad rags, dripping with rain and mud from the road-ditch, I thought that this man was full of prayers. And deaf to what we were saying, I was looking at his rough coat and I could see stars on it.

than live under Louis Napoleon, he went into voluntary exile—at considerable personal inconvenience—for almost twenty years. He lived up to his democratic principles, but he was always a bit theatrical, and he was not very profound."

I include such reminiscences of the classroom in the hope that they may be of interest in putting on record Gauss's methods as a teacher, for the work of a great teacher who is not, as Gauss was not, a great writer is almost as likely to be irrecoverable as the work of a great actor. Not that Christian was ever in the least histrionic, as some of the popular professors of the time were. On the contrary, for all the friendliness of one's relations with him outside class when one eventually got to know him, his tone was sober and quiet, his attitude detached and impersonal. This was partly due to shyness, no doubt; but the impression he made was formidable. He would come into the classroom without looking at us, and immediately begin to lecture, with his eyes dropped to his notes, presenting a mask that was almost Dantesque and levelling on us only occasionally the clear gaze that came through his eyeglasses. When he made us recite in Dante, he would sometimes pace to and fro between the desk and the window, with his hands behind his back, rarely consulting the text, which he apparently knew by heart. In the case of some appalling error, he would turn with a stare of ironic amazement and remonstrate in a tone of mock grief: "You thought that barretry was the same as banditry? O-o-oh, Mr. X, that's too-oo ba-a-ad!" This last exclamation, drawled out, was his only way of indicating disapproval. His voice was always low and even, except at those moments when he became aware that the class was falling asleep, when he would turn on another voice, loud, nasal, declamatory and pitilessly distinct, which would be likely to begin in the middle of a sentence for the sake of the shock-value, I think, and in order to dissociate this special effect from whatever he happened to be saying—which might be something no more blood-curdling than a statement that André Chénier had brought to the classical forms a nuance of romantic feeling. When this voice would be heard in the class next door—for it penetrated the partition like a fire-siren—it always made people laugh; but for the students in Gauss's own room, it seemed to saw right through the base of the spine and made them sit forward intently. When it had had this effect, it would cease. He was never sarcastic and never bullied; but the discipline he maintained was perfect. Any signs of disorder were silenced by one straight and stern look.

Nevertheless, though Christian's methods were non-dramatic, he had a knack of fixing in one's mind key passages and key facts. His handling of Rousseau, for example, was most effective in building up the importance of a writer whom we might otherwise find boring. (In this case, he *has* left something that can be used by his successors in his volume of *Selections* from Rousseau, published by the Princeton University Press—though, as usual with Gauss's writing, the introduction and notes have little of the peculiar effectiveness of his lecture-room presentation.) He would start off by planting, as it were, in our vision of the panorama of history that critical moment of Rousseau's life which, since he did not include it in the *Confessions*, having already described it in the first of his letters to M. de Malesherbes, is likely to be overlooked or insufficiently emphasized (compare Saintsbury's slurring-over of this incident and its consequences for Western thought, in his *Encyclopaedia Britannica* article): the moment, almost as momentous as that of Paul's conversion on the road to Damascus, when Jean-Jacques, then thirty-seven, was walking from Paris to Vincennes, where he was going to see Diderot in prison, and happened to read the announcement that the Academy of Dijon was offering a prize for the best essay on the question, "Has the progress of the arts and sciences contributed to corrupt or to purify society?" Such an incident Gauss made memorable, invested with reverberating significance, by a series of incisive strokes that involved no embroidery or dramatics. It was, in fact, as if the glamor of legend, the grandeur of history, had evaporated and left him exposed to our passing gaze, the dusty and sunstruck Jean-Jacques—the clockmaker's son of Geneva, the ill-used apprentice, the thieving lackey, the vagabond of the roads—sinking down under a tree and dazzled by the revelation that all the shames and misfortunes of his life had been the fault of the society that had bred him—that "man is naturally good and that it is only through institutions that men have become wicked." In the same way, he made us feel the pathos and the psychological importance of the moment when the sixteen-year-old apprentice, returning from a walk in the country, found for the third time the gates of Geneva locked against him, and decided that he would never go back.

Christian admired the romantics and expounded them with the liveliest appreciation; but the romantic ideal in literature was not his own ideal. In spite of his imaginative gift for entering into other people's points of view, he was devoted to a certain conception of art that inevitably asserted itself and that had a tremendous influence on the students with literary interests who were exposed to Gauss's teaching. Let me try to define this ideal. Christian had first known Europe at firsthand as a foreign correspondent in the Paris of the late nineties, and he had always kept a certain loyalty to the "aestheticism" of the end of the century. There was a legend that seemed almost incredible of a young Christian Gauss with long yellow hair—in our time he was almost completely bald—who had worn a green velvet jacket;* and he would surprise you from time to time by telling you of some conversation he had had with Oscar Wilde or describing some such bohemian character as Bibi-La-Purée. It was rumored—though I never dared ask him about this—that he had once set out to experiment one by one with all the drugs mentioned in Baudelaire's *Les Paradis Artificiels*. He rather admired Wilde, with whom he had talked in cafés, where the latter was sitting alone and running up high piles of saucers.

* I learn from Mrs. Gauss, who has shown me a photograph, that the realities behind this legend were a head of blond bushy hair and a jacket which, though green, was not velvet.

He had given Christian copies of his books, inscribed; and Christian used to tell me, with evident respect, that Wilde in his last days had kept only three volumes: a copy of Walter Pater's *The Renaissance* that had been given him by Pater, Flaubert's *La Tentation de Saint Antoine* and Swinburne's *Atalanta in Calydon*. And it was Gauss's great advantage over the school of Babbitt and More that he understood the artist's morality as something that expressed itself in different terms than the churchgoer's or the citizen's morality; the fidelity to a kind of truth that is rendered by the discipline of aesthetic form, as distinct from that of the professional moralist: the explicit communication of a "message." But there was nothing in his attitude of the truculent pose, the defiance of the bourgeoisie, that had been characteristic of the fin de siècle and that that other professor of the Romance languages, Gauss's near-contemporary, Ezra Pound, was to sustain through his whole career. How fundamental to his point of view, how much a thing to be taken for granted, this attitude had become, was shown clearly in a conversation I had with him, on some occasion when I had come back after college, when, in reply to some antinomian attitude of mine, or one that he imputed to me, he said, "But you were saying just now that you would have to rewrite something before it could be published. That implies a moral obligation." And his sense of the world and the scope of art was, of course, something very much bigger than was common among the aesthetes and the symbolists.

Partly perhaps as a heritage from the age of Wilde but, more deeply, as a logical consequence of his continental origin and culture, he showed a pronounced though discreet *parti pris* against the literature of the Anglo-Saxon countries. In our time, he carried on a continual feud—partly humorous, yet basically serious—with the canons of the English department. I remember his telling me, with sly satisfaction, about a visiting French professor, who had asked, when it was explained to him that someone was an authority on Chaucer, *"Il est intelligent tout de même?"* [3] Certain classical English writers he patronized—in some cases, rightly, I think. Robert Browning, in particular, he abominated. The author of *Pippa Passes* was one of the very few writers about whom I thought his opinions intemperate. "That Philistine beef-eating Englishman," he would bait his colleagues in English, "—what did he know about art? He writes lines like 'Irks care the crop-full bird? Frets doubt the maw-crammed beast?'" When I tried to find out once why Browning moved Christian to such special indignation, he told me, a little darkly, that he had greatly admired him in boyhood and had learned from him "a lot of bad doctrine." He said that the irregular love affairs in Browning were made to seem too jolly and simple, and insisted that the situation of the self-frustrated lovers of *The Statue and the Bust* had never been faced by Browning: If "the end in sight was a vice," the poet should not have wanted to have them get together; if he wanted them to get together, he ought not to have described it as a

[3] He is intelligent just the same?

vice, but, on the other hand, he ought to have foreseen a mess. "He is one of the most immoral poets because he makes moral problems seem easy. He tells you that the good is sure to triumph." He would suggest to you an embarrassing picture of a Browning offensively hearty—"not robust," he would say slily, "but robustious"—bouncing and booming in Italy, while the shades of Leopardi and Dante looked on, as Boccaccio said of the latter, *"con isdegnoso occhio."* [4] The kind of thing he especially hated was such a poem as the one, in *James Lee's Wife*, that begins, "O good gigantic smile o' the brown old earth." . . . Of Byron—though Byron's writing was certainly more careless than Browning's—he had a much better opinion, because, no doubt, of Byron's fondness for the Continent as well as his freer intelligence and his experience of the ills of the world. He accepted Byron's love affairs—he had nothing of the prig or the Puritan—because Byron knew what he was doing, and was not misleading about it. As for Shakespeare, though Christian was, of course, very far from the point of view of Voltaire, there was always just a suggestion of something of the kind in the background. He knew Shakespeare well and quoted him often, but Shakespeare was not one of the authors whom Christian had lived in or on; and he always made us feel that that sort of thing could never come up to literature that was polished and carefully planned and that knew how to make its points and the meaning of the points it was making. He was certainly unfair to Shakespeare in insisting that the Shakespearean characters all talk the same language, whereas Dante's all express themselves differently. For Christian, the great poet was Dante, and he gradually convinced you of this in his remarkable Dante course. He made us see the objectivity of Dante and the significance of his every stroke, so that even the geographical references have a moral and emotional force (the Po that finds peace with its tributaries in the Paolo and Francesca episode, the mountain in the Ugolino canto that prevents the Pisans from seeing their neighbors of Lucca); the vividness of the scenes and the characters (he liked to point out how Farinata's arrogant poise was thrown into dramatic relief by the passionate interruption of Cavalcanti); and the tremendous intellectual power by which all sorts of men and women exhibiting all sorts of passions have been organized in an orderly vision that implies, also, a reasoned morality. No Englishman, he made us feel, could ever have achieved this; it would never have occurred to Shakespeare. Nor could any English novelist have even attempted what Gustave Flaubert had achieved—a personal conception of the world, put together, without a visible seam, from apparently impersonal descriptions, in which, as in Dante, not a stroke was wasted. He admired the Russians, also, for their sober art of implication. I remember his calling our attention to one of the church scenes in Tolstoy's *Resurrection*, in which, as he pointed out, Tolstoy made no overt comment, yet caused you to loathe the whole thing by describing the ceremony step by step. This non-English, this classical and Latin ideal, became indissolubly associated in our minds with the summits of literature. We got from Gauss

4 with disdainful eve.

a good many things, but the most important things we got were probably Flaubert and Dante. John Peale Bishop, who came to Princeton intoxicated with Swinburne and Shelley, was concentrating, by the time he graduated, on hard images and pregnant phrases. Ezra Pound and the imagists, to be sure, had a good deal to do with this, but Gauss's courses were important, too, and such an early poem of Bishop's as *Losses*, which contrasts Verlaine with Dante, was directly inspired by them. Less directly, perhaps, but no less certainly, the development of F. Scott Fitzgerald from *This Side of Paradise* to *The Great Gatsby*, from a loose and subjective conception of the novel to an organized impersonal one, was also due to Christian's influence. He made us all want to write something in which every word, every cadence, every detail, should perform a definite function in producing an intense effect.

Gauss's special understanding of the techniques of art was combined, as is not always the case, with a highly developed sense of history, as well as a sense of morality (he admirably prepared us for Joyce and Proust). If he played down—as I shall show in a moment—the Thomist side of Dante to make us see him as a great artist, he brought out in Flaubert the moralist and the bitter critic of history. And so much, at that period, was all his thought pervaded by the *Divine Comedy* that even his own version of history had at moments a Dantesque touch. It would not have been difficult, for example, to transpose such a presentation as the one of Rousseau that I have mentioned above into the sharp concise self-description of a character in the *Divina Commedia*: "I am the lockmaker's son of Geneva who said that man has made man perverse. When for the third time the cruel captain closed the gates, I made the sky my roof, and found in Annecy the love Geneva had denied" . . .

With this sense of history of Christian's was involved another strain in his nature that had nothing to do with the aestheticism of the nineties and yet that lived in his mind with it quite comfortably. His father, who came from Baden—he was a relative of the physicist Karl Friedrich Gauss—had taken part in the unsuccessful German revolution of 1848 and come to the United States with the emigration that followed it. The spirit of '48 was still alive in Christian, and at the time of the first World War an hereditary hatred of the Prussians roused him to a passionate championship of the anti-German cause even before the United States declared war. Later on, when Prohibition was imposed on the nation, the elder Gauss, as Christian told me, was so much infuriated by what he regarded as an interference nothing short of Prussian with the rights of a free people that he could not talk calmly about it, and, even when dean of the college and obliged to uphold the law, the American-born Christian continued in public to advocate its repeal, which required a certain courage in Presbyterian Princeton. It was this old-fashioned devotion to liberty that led him to admire Hugo for his refusal to live under the Second Empire, and Byron for his willingness to fight for Italian and Greek liberation. "Everywhere he goes in Europe," Christian would say of Byron, "it is the places, such as the prison of Chillon, where men had been oppressed, that arouse him."

When he lectured on Anatole France, he would point out the stimulating contrast between the early France of *Sylvestre Bonnard,* who always wrote, as he said, like a kindly and bookish old man, and the France who defended Dreyfus, made a tour of the provinces to speak for him and remained for the rest of his life a social satirist and a radical publicist. In the years when I was first at Princeton, Gauss called himself, I believe, a socialist; and during the years of depression in the thirties, he gravitated again toward the Left and, in *A Primer for Tomorrow* (1934), he made some serious attempt to criticize the financial-industrial system. In an inscription in the copy he sent me, he said that my stimulation had counted for something in his writing the book. But I was never able to persuade him to read Marx and Engels at firsthand: he read Werner Sombart instead; and I noted this, like the similar reluctance of Maynard Keynes to look into Marx, as a curious confirmation of the theory of the Marxists that the "bourgeois intellectuals" instinctively shy away from Marxist thought to the extent of even refusing to find out what it really is. Yet Christian had read Spengler with excitement—it was from him that I first heard of *The Decline of the West*—immediately after the war; and he never, in these later years, hesitated, in conversation, to indulge the boldest speculations as to the destiny of contemporary society.

He was a member of the National Committee of the American Civil Liberties Union, and he made a point, after the second war, of speaking to Negro audiences in the South. On my last visit to Princeton when I saw him, in the spring of 1951, he talked to me at length about his adventures in the color-discrimination states—how the representatives of some Negro organization under whose auspices he had been speaking had been unable to come to see him in his white hotel, and how, as he told me with pride, he had succeeded, for the first time in the history of Richmond, in assembling—in a white church, to which, however, he found the Negroes were only admitted on condition of their sitting in the back pews—a mixed black and white audience. As he grew older, he became more internationalist. He foresaw, and he often insisted, at the end of the first World War, that nothing but trouble could come of creating more small European states, and, at the end of the second war, he was bitterly opposed to what he regarded as the development of American nationalism. He complained much, in this connection, of the intensive cultivation, in the colleges, of American literature, which had been carried on since sometime in the middle thirties with a zeal that he thought more and more menacing to sound international values. I did not, on the whole, agree with him in disapproving of the growth of American studies; but I could see that, with his relative indifference to English literature, he must have conceived, at the end of the century, an extremely low opinion of American. He took no interest in Henry James and not very much in Walt Whitman. He told me once that Henry Ford had said, "Cut your own wood and it will warm you twice," not knowing that Ford had been quoting Thoreau. For Christian, the level of American writing was more or less represented by William Dean

Howells, the presiding spirit of the years of his youth, for whom he felt hardly the barest respect. It was absolutely incredible to him—and in this I did agree with him—that *The Rise of Silas Lapham* should ever have been thought an important novel. "It wasn't much of a rise," he would say. Yet the "renaissance" of the twenties—unlike Paul Elmer More—he followed with sympathetic, if critical, interest.

Christian Gauss was a complex personality as well as a subtle mind, and one finds it in some ways difficult to sort out one's impressions of him. I want to try to deal now with the moral qualities which, combined with his unusual intellectual powers, gave him something of the stature of greatness. In some sense, he was a moral teacher as well as a literary one; but his teaching, in the same way as his criticism, was conveyed by throwing out suggestions and dropping incidental comments. In this connection, I want to quote here the tribute of Mr. Harold R. Medina, the distinguished federal judge, from the symposium in the *Alumni Weekly*. It expresses a good deal better than anything I was able to write myself, when I drafted this memoir for the first time, the penetrating quality of Gauss's power, and it is interesting to me in describing an experience that closely parallels my own on the part of an alumnus of an earlier class—1909—who was to work in a different field yet who had known Christian Gauss, as I had, not as dean of the college, but as teacher of literature.

"Of all the men whom I have met," Mr. Medina writes, "only four have significantly influenced my life. Dean Gauss was the second of these; the first, my father. From freshman year on I had many courses and precepts with Dean Gauss and during my senior year I was with him almost daily. He attracted me as he did everyone else; and I sensed that he had something to impart which was of infinitely greater importance than the mere content of the courses in French Literature. It was many years after I left Princeton before I realized that it was he who first taught me how to think. How strange it is that so many people have the notion that they are thinking when they are merely repeating the thoughts of others. He dealt in ideas without seeming to do so; he led and guided with so gentle a touch that one began to think almost despite oneself. The process once started, he continued in such fashion as to instil into my very soul the determination to be a seeker after truth, the elusive, perhaps never to be attained, complete and utter truth, no matter where it led or whom it hurt. How he did it I shall never know; but that it was he I have not the slightest doubt. His own intellectual integrity was a constant example for me to follow. And to this precious element he added another. He gave me the vision of language and literature as something representing the continuous and never-ending flow of man's struggle to think the thoughts which, when put into action, constitute in the aggregate the advance of civilization. Whatever I may be today or may ever hope to be is largely the result of the germination of the seeds he planted. The phenomena of cause and effect are not to be denied.

With Dean Gauss there were so many hundreds of persons, like myself, whom he influenced and whose innate talents he developed that the ripples he started in motion were multiplied again and again. In critical times I always wondered whether he approved or would approve of things I said and did. And this went on for over forty years."

"To instil into my very soul the determination to be a seeker after truth . . . no matter where it led or whom it hurt." I remember my own thrilled response when, in taking us through the seventeenth canto of the *Paradiso*, Christian read without special emphasis yet in a way that brought out their conviction a tercet that remained from that moment engraved, as they say, on my mind:

> E s'io al vero son timido amico,
>   Temo di perder viver tra coloro
>   Che questo tempo chiameranno antico.

—"If to the truth I prove a timid friend, I fear to lose my life [to fail of survival] among those who will call this time ancient." The truth about which Dante is speaking is his opinion of certain powerful persons, who will, as he has just been forewarned in Heaven, retaliate by sending him into exile—a truth which, as Heaven approves, he will not be deterred from uttering. Another moment in the classroom comes back to me from one of Christian's preceptorials. He had put up to us the issue created by the self-assertive type of romantic, who followed his own impulse in defiance of conventional morality and with indifference to social consequences; and he called upon me to supply him with an instance of moral conflict between social or personal duty and the duty of self-realization. I gave him the case of a problem with which I had had lately to deal as editor of the *Nassau Lit*, when I had not been able to bring myself to tell a friend who had set his heart upon contributing that the manuscripts he brought me were hopeless. "That's not an impulse," said Christian, "to do a humane thing: it's a temptation to do a weak thing." I was struck also by what seemed to me the unusual line that he took one day in class when one of his students complained that he hadn't been able to find out the meaning of a word. "What did you call it?" asked Christian. "Didn't you call it something?" The boy confessed that he hadn't. "That's bad intellectual form," said Christian. "Like going out in the morning with your face unwashed. In reading a foreign language, you must never leave a gap or a blur. If you can't find out what something means, make the best supposition you can. If it's wrong, the chances are that the context will show it in a moment or that you'll see, when the word occurs again, that it couldn't have meant that." This made such an impression on me that—just as Mr. Medina says he has been asking himself all his life whether Christian would approve of his actions—I still make an effort to live up to it.

I love to remember, too, how Christian began one of his lectures as follows: "There are several fundamental philosophies that one can bring to one's life in the world—or rather, there are several ways of taking life. One of these ways of taking the world is not to have any philosophy at all—that is the way most people take it. Another is to regard the world as unreal and God as the only reality; Buddhism is an example of this. Another may be summed up in the words *Sic transit gloria mundi*[5]—that is the point of view you find in Shakespeare." He then went on to an explanation of the eighteenth-century philosophy which assumed that the world was real and that we ourselves may find some sense in it and make ourselves happy in it. On another occasion, in preceptorial, Christian asked me, "Where do you think our ideals come from—justice, righteousness, beauty and so on?" I replied, "Out of the imaginations of men"; and he surprised me by answering, "That is correct." This made an impression on me, because he usually confined himself to a purely Socratic questioning, in which he did not often allow himself to express his own opinions. I felt that I had caught him off guard: what he had evidently been expecting to elicit was either Platonic idealism or Christian revelation.

It was only outside class and at secondhand that I learned that he said of himself at this time that his only religion was Dante; yet it could not escape us in the long run that the Dante we were studying was a secular Dante—or rather, perhaps, a Dante of the Reformation—the validity of whose art and morality did not in the least depend on one's acceptance or non-acceptance of the faith in the Catholic Church. Christian would remind us from time to time of Dante's statement, in his letter to Can Grande, that his poem, though it purported to describe a journey to the other world, really dealt with men's life in this, and we were shown that the conditions of the souls in Hell, Purgatory and Heaven were metaphors for our moral situation here. The principle of salvation that we learned from Dante was not the Catholic surrender to Jesus—who plays in the *Divine Comedy* so significantly small a role—but the vigilant cultivation of *"il ben del intelletto."* [6]

Some of those who had known Christian Gauss in his great days as a teacher of literature were sorry, after the war, to see him becoming involved in the administrative side of the University. I remember his saying to me one day, in the early stages of this, "I've just sent off a lot of letters, and I said to myself as I mailed them, 'There are seventeen letters to people who don't interest me in the least.' " But the job of the Dean's office did interest him—though it seemed to us that it did not take a Gauss to rule on remiss or refractory students. He had never liked repeating routine, and I suppose that his department was coming to bore him. He made, by all accounts, a remarkable dean—for his card-catalogue memory kept all names and faces on file even for decades after the students had left, and the sensitive feeling for character that had been hidden behind his classroom mask must have equipped him with a special

[5] Thus pass away the glories of the world.
[6] The gift of intellectual understanding.

tact in dealing with the difficult cases. His genius for moral values had also a new field now in which it could exercise itself in an immediate and practical way, and the responsibilities of his office—especially in the years just after the war, when students were committing suicide and getting into all sorts of messes—sometimes put upon him an obvious strain. Looking back since his death, it has seemed to me that the Gauss, who was dean of Princeton must have differed almost as much from the Gauss with whom I read French and Italian as this austere teacher had done from the young correspondent in Paris, who had paid for Oscar Wilde's drinks. The Gauss I had known in my student days, with his pale cheeks and shuttered gaze, his old raincoat and soft flat hat, and a shabby mongrel dog named Baudelaire which had been left with him by the Jesse Lynch Williamses and which sometimes accompanied him into class —the Gauss who would pass one on the campus without speaking, unless you attracted his attention, in an abstraction like that of Dante in Hell and who seemed to meet the academic world with a slightly constrained self-conscious- ness at not having much in common with it—this figure warmed up and filled out, became recognizably Princetonian in his neckties and shirts and a touch of that tone that combines a country-club self-assurance with a boyish country- town homeliness. He now met the college world, unscreened, with his humorous and lucid green eyes. He wore golf stockings and even played golf. He interested himself in the football team and made speeches at alumni ban- quets. Though I know that his influence as dean was exerted in favor of scholarships, higher admission requirements and the salvaging of the Humani- ties—I cannot do justice here to this whole important phase of his career—the only moments of our long friendship when I was ever at all out of sympathy with him occurred during these years of officialdom; for I felt that he had picked up a little the conventional local prejudices when I would find him pro- testing against the advent in Princeton of the Institute for Advanced Study or, on one occasion, censoring the *Lit* for publishing a "blasphemous" story. One was always impressed, however, by the way in which he seemed to have absorbed the whole business of the University.

We used to hope that he would eventually be president; but, with the domi- nation of business in the boards of trustees of the larger American colleges, it was almost as improbable that Christian would be asked to be president of Prince- ton as it would have been that Santayana should be asked to be president of Harvard. Not, of course, that it would ever have occurred to anyone to propose such a post for Santayana, but it was somehow characteristic of Christian's career that the idea should have entered the minds of his friends and that nothing should ever have come of it. There appeared in the whole line of Christian's life a certain diversion of purpose, an unpredictable ambiguity of aim, that corresponded to the fluid indeterminate element in his teaching and conversation. He had originally been a newspaper correspondent and a writer of reviews for the literary journals, who hoped to become a poet. He was later a college professor who had developed into a brilliant critic—by far the best, so far as I know, in our academic world of that period—and who still looked forward to writing books; I once found him, in one of his rare moments of leisure, beginning an historical novel. Then, as dean, in the late twenties and thirties, he came to occupy a position of intercollegiate distinction rather incongruous with that usually prosaic office. Was he a "power" in American education? I do not believe he was. That kind of role is possibly only for a theorist like John Dewey or an administrator like Charles W. Eliot. Though he was offered the presidency of another college, he continued at Princeton as dean and simply awaited the age of retirement. When that came, he seemed at first depressed, but later readjusted himself. I enjoyed him in these post-official years. He was no longer overworked and he no longer had to worry about the alumni. He returned to literature and started an autobiography, with which, however, he said he was unsatisfied. In October of 1951, he had been writing an introduction for a new edition of Machiavelli's *Prince*, and he was pleased with it when he had finished. He took Mrs. Gauss for a drive in the car, and they talked about a trip to Florida. He had seemed in good spirits and health, though he had complained the Saturday before, after going to the Cornell game, where he had climbed to one of the top tiers of seats, that he was feeling the effects of age—he was now seventy-three. The day after finishing his introduction, he took the manuscript to his publisher in New York and attended there a memorial service for the Austrian novelist Hermann Broch, whom he had known when the latter lived in Princeton. While waiting outside the gates for the train to take him back to Princeton, with the evening paper in his pocket, his heart failed and he suddenly fell dead.

One had always still expected something further from Christian, had hoped that his character and talents would arrive at some final fruition. But—what seems to one still incredible—one's long conversation with him was simply forever suspended. And one sees now that the career was complete, the achievement is all there. He has left no solid body of writing; he did not remake Princeton (as Woodrow Wilson in some sense was able to do); he was not really a public man. He was a spiritual and intellectual force—one does not know how else to put it—of a kind that it may be possible for a man to do any of those other things without in the least becoming. His great work in his generation was unorganized and unobtrusive; and *Who's Who* will tell you nothing about it; but his influence was vital for those who felt it.

> Chè in la mente m'è fitta, ed or m'accora,
> La cara e buona imagine paterna
> Di voi, quando nel mondo ad ora ad ora
> M'insegnavate come l'uom s'eterna. . . .[7]

[7] *Inferno*, XV, 82-85: For in my memory is fixed, and now goes to my heart, the dear and kind paternal image of you, when in the world, hour by hour, you taught me how man makes himself eternal.

❦ ❦ ❦

*Robert M. Hutchins*

# Gate Receipts and Glory[1]

THE football season is about to release the nation's colleges to the pursuit of education, more or less. Soon the last nickel will be rung up at the gate, the last halfback will receive his check, and the last alumnus will try to pay off those bets he can recall. Most of the students have cheered themselves into insensibility long ago.

This has been going on for almost fifty years. It is called "overemphasis on athletics," and everybody deplores it. It has been the subject of scores of reports, all of them shocking. It has been held to be crass professionalism, all the more shameful because it masquerades as higher education. But nobody has done anything about it. Why? I think it is because nobody wants to. Nobody wants, or dares, to defy the public, dishearten the students, or deprive alma mater of the loyalty of the alumni. Most emphatically of all, nobody wants to give up the gate receipts. The trouble with football is the money that is in it, and every code of amateurism ever written has failed for this reason.

Money is the cause of athleticism in the American colleges. Athleticism is not athletics. Athletics is physical education, a proper function of the college if carried on for the welfare of the students. Athleticism is not physical education but sports promotion, and it is carried on for the monetary profit of the colleges through the entertainment of the public. This article deals with athleticism, its cause, its symptoms and its cure.

Of all the crimes committed by athleticism under the guise of athletics, the most heinous is the confusion of the country about the primary purpose of higher education. The primary purpose of higher education is the development of the mind. This does not mean that colleges and universities should neglect the health of their students or should fail to provide them with every opportunity for physical development. The question is a question of emphasis. Colleges and universities are the only institutions which are dedicated to the training of the mind. In these institutions, the development of the body is important, but secondary.

The apologists of athleticism have created a collection of myths to convince the public that biceps is a substitute for brains. Athletics, we are told, produces well-rounded men, filled with the spirit of fair play. Athletics is good for the health of the players; it is also good for the morals of the spectators. Leadership on the playing fields means leadership in life. The Duke of Wellington said so. Athletes are red-blooded Americans, and the athletic colleges are bulwarks against Communism. Gate receipts are used to build laboratories and to

[1] From *The Saturday Evening Post*, Dec. 3, 1938. Reprinted by permission of the author.

pay for those sports that can't pay for themselves. Football is purely a supplement to study. And without a winning team a college cannot hope to attract the students or the gifts which its work requires.

These myths have about them a certain air of plausibility. They are widely accepted. But they are myths. As the Carnegie Foundation has said, "The fact that all these supposed advantages are tinged at one point or another with the color of money casts over every relaxation of standards a mercenary shadow." The myths are designed, consciously or unconsciously, to conceal the color of money and to surround a financial enterprise with the rosy glow of Health, Manhood, Public Spirit and Education.

Since the primary task of colleges and universities is the development of the mind, young people who are more interested in their bodies than in their minds should not go to college. Institutions devoted to the development of the body are numerous and inexpensive. They do not pretend to be institutions of learning, and there is no faculty of learned men to consume their assets or interfere with their objectives.

Athleticism attracts boys and girls to college who do not want and cannot use a college education. They come to college for "fun." They would be just as happy in the grandstand at the Yankee Stadium, and at less expense to their parents. They drop out of college after a while, but they are a sizable fraction of many freshman classes, and, while they last, they make it harder for the college to educate the rest. Even the earnest boys and girls who come to college for an education find it difficult, around the middle of November, to concentrate on the physiology of the frog or the mechanics of the price structure.

Worse yet, athleticism gives the student a mistaken notion of the qualities that make for leadership in later life. The ambition of the average student who grew up reading Stover at Yale is to imitate as closely as possible the attitude and manners of the current football hero. Since this country, like all others, needs brains more than brawn at the moment, proposing football heroes as models for the rising generation can hardly have a beneficial effect on the national future.

The exponents of athleticism tell us that athletics is good for a boy. They are right. But athleticism focuses its attention on doing good for the boys who least need it. Less than half of the undergraduate males—800 out of 1900 at the University of Chicago, for instance—are eligible for intercollegiate competition. But where athleticism reigns, as happily it does not at Chicago, 75 per cent of the attention of the physical-education staff must be lavished on that fraction of the student body who make varsity squads. The Carnegie Foundation found that 37 per cent of all undergraduates engage in no athletic activity, not even in intramural games. Since graduate and professional students are also eliminated from competition, we have more than half the college and university population of the country neglected because we devote ourselves, on the pretext that athletics is good for a boy, to overdeveloping a handful of stars.

And athletics, as it is conducted in many colleges today, is not even good for the handful. Since the fate of the coach sometimes depends on victory, players have sometimes been filled with college spirit through caffein tablets and strychnine. At least one case reached the public in which a coach removed a plaster cast from a star's ankle and sent him in "to win." The Carnegie Foundation found that 17.6 per cent of all football players in twenty-two colleges suffered serious injuries. The same report asserts that college athletes have about the same life expectancy as the average college man and not so good an expectancy as men of high scholarship rank.

Most athletes will admit that the combination of weariness and nervousness after a hard practice is not conducive to study. We can thus understand why athleticism does not contribute to the production of well-rounded men destined for leadership after graduation. In many American colleges it is possible for a boy to win twelve letters without learning how to write one. I need only suggest that you conjure up the name of the greatest college football star of fifteen years ago and ask yourself, "Where is he now?" Many of his contemporaries who made no ninety-yard runs enjoy at least as good health as our hero and considerably more esteem. The cheers that rock the stadium have a rapid depreciation rate.

The alleged connection between athletic experience and moral principles is highly dubious. At worst, the college athlete is led to believe that whatever he does, including slugging, is done for the sake of alma mater. He does not learn that it is sometimes better, both on and off the playing field, to lose than to win. At best, the college athlete acquires habits of fair play, but there is no evidence that he needs to join the football squad to acquire them; he can get them from the studies he pursues and from living in a college community which, since it is a community of comparatively idealistic people, is less tolerant of meanness than most. The football players who threw the campus "radicals" into the lake at the University of Wisconsin knew little of fair play, and incidents in which free speech in the colleges is suppressed have frequently shown the athletic group lined up on the side of suppression.

Even if it were true that athletics developed courage, prudence, tolerance and justice, the commercialism that characterizes amateur sport today would be sufficient to harden the purest young man. He is made to feel that his primary function in college is to win football games. The coach demands it, because the coach wants to hold his job. The college demands it, because the college wants the gate receipts. And the alumni demand it, because the test of a college is the success of its teams and they want to be alumni of a good college.

The university with which I am connected has a different kind of college and a different kind of alumni. I can make this statement because I am in no way responsible for its happy condition. When John D. Rockefeller founded the University of Chicago forty-five years ago, he told William Rainey Harper to run it as he pleased. It pleased Mr. Harper to appoint men of character and distinction. One of the men he appointed was Amos Alonzo Stagg. To the amazement of the country, Mr. Harper made Mr. Stagg a professor on life appointment. It was the first time such a thing had happened.

Secure in his position, whether he produced winning teams or not, Mr. Stagg for forty years kept Chicago an amateur university. Some of his teams were champions. Chicago still has the second best won-and-lost record in the Big Ten, although we are using it up pretty fast. But through all those years Chicago students learned that athletics is only one aspect, and a secondary one, of college education. The result is that today Chicago's alumni are loyal to their university and generous with their moral and financial support.

The prestige that winning teams confer upon a university, and the profits that are alleged to accompany prestige, are the most serious obstacles to reform. Alumni whose sole interest in their alma mater is its athletic standing lose their interest when its teams run on bad years. The result, which horrifies college presidents, is that the alumni do not encourage their children or their neighbors' children to attend the old college. The American public believes that there is a correlation between muscle and manliness. Poor teams at any college are supposed to mean that the character of its student body is in decay.

The myth that donors, like alumni and the public, are impressed by football victories collapses on examination of the report recently issued by the John Price Jones Corporation, showing gifts and bequests to colleges and universities between 1920 and 1937. Among the universities, Harvard, Yale and Chicago led the list, each having received more than $50,000,000. The records of these universities on the gridiron were highly irregular, to say the least; that of one of them was positively bad. Among the colleges, Williams, Wesleyan and Bowdoin led the list, each having received more than $5,000,000. Men of wealth were undeterred by the inconsequential athletic status of these colleges; it does not appear that philanthropists were attracted to their rivals by the glorious victories they scored over them.

If athleticism is bad for students, players, alumni and the public, it is even worse for the colleges and universities themselves. They want to be educational institutions, but they can't. The story of the famous halfback whose only regret, when he bade his coach farewell, was that he hadn't learned to read and write is probably exaggerated. But we must admit that pressure from trustees, graduates, "friends," presidents and even professors has tended to relax academic standards. These gentry often overlook the fact that a college should not be interested in a fullback who is a half-wit. Recruiting, subsidizing and the double educational standard cannot exist without the knowledge and the tacit approval, at least, of the colleges and universities themselves. Certain institutions encourage susceptible professors to be nice to athletes now admitted by paying them for serving as "faculty representatives" on the college athletic board.

We have the word of the famous Carnegie Report that the maxim "every athlete is a needy athlete" is applied up and down the land. Hard times have reduced the price of football players in conformity with the stock-market index. But when we get back to prosperity we may hope to see the resurrection of that phenomenon of the Golden Era, a corporation which tried to corner the market by signing up high-school athletes and auctioning them off to the highest bidder. The promoter of this interesting venture came to a bad end, and I regretted his fate, for he was a man of imagination and a friend of the football tramp, who has always been a victim of cutthroat competition.

Enthusiastic alumni find it hard to understand why a fine young man who can play football should be deprived of a college education just because he is poor. No young man should be deprived of an education just because he is poor. We need more scholarships, but athletic ability should have nothing to do with their award. Frequently the fine young man the alumnus has in mind can do nothing but play football. The alumnus should try hiring the young man and turning him loose in his factory. From the damage that would result he could gain some insight into the damage done his alma mater through admitting students without intellectual interests or capacity.

If the colleges and universities are to commend themselves to the public chiefly through their athletic accomplishments, it seems to me that they ought to be reorganized with that aim in view. Instead of looking for college presidents among educators, we should find them among those gentlemen who have a solid record of sports promotion behind them. Consider what Tex Rickard could have done for Harvard. I am rapidly approaching the retirement age, and I can think of no worthier successor, from the standpoint of athleticism, than Mr. Mike Jacobs, the sage of the prize ring. Mr. Jacobs has demonstrated his genius at selecting young men and developing them in such a way as to gather both gold and glory for the profession of which he is the principal ornament.

Another suggestion for elevating Chicago to the level of some of its sister institutions was advanced last year by Mr. William McNeill, editor of the student paper. Mr. McNeill proposed that instead of buying football players, the colleges should buy race horses. Alumni could show their devotion to alma mater by giving their stables to alma mater. For the time being, Yale would be way out in front, for both Mr. Jock Whitney and Mr. Cornelius Vanderbilt Whitney graduated there. But by a judicious distribution of honorary degrees horse fanciers who never went to college might be induced to come to the assistance of institutions which had not attracted students who had become prosperous enough to indulge in the sport of kings. Chicago could, for instance, confer the doctorate of letters upon that prominent turfman, Alderman Bathhouse John Coughlin, and persuade The Bath to change the color of his silks from green to maroon. The alumni could place their money on Chicago across the board. The students could cheer. Most important of all, the horses would not have to pass examinations.

The center of football strength has been moving, since the turn of the century, from the East to the Middle West, from the Middle West to the

Pacific Coast, and from the Pacific Coast to the South and Southwest. According to a recent analysis by Professor Eells, of Stanford, the leading educational institutions of the country are, in order of their eminence, Harvard, Chicago, Columbia, Yale, California, Johns Hopkins, Princeton, Michigan and Wisconsin. None of these universities, except California, is close to the top of Professor Dickinson's annual athletic ranking, and California's success has something to do with the fact that it has a male undergraduate enrollment of 7500 compared with Harvard's 3700 and Chicago's 1900. We used to say that Harvard enjoyed its greatest years as an educational institution when Ted Coy was playing at Yale. If football continues to move to the poorer colleges, the good ones may be saved. Meanwhile it is only fair to say that some inferior colleges are going broke attempting to get rich—and famous—at football.

Athleticism, like crime, does not pay. Last summer St. Mary's College, home of the Galloping Gaels, was sold at auction and bought in by a bondholders' committee. This was the country's most sensational football college. Since 1924 it has won eighty-six and tied seven of its 114 games. Its academic efforts were inexpensive and its gate receipts immense. The bondholders were surprised to learn that it was running $72,000 a year behind in its budget. They were even more surprised to find that football expenses were almost equal to football income.

To make big money in athletics you have to spend big money. Winning coaches come high. The head coaches in our larger colleges and universities receive, on the average, $611 a year more than the highest-ranking professors in the same institutions. One famous coach of a small college was found, not long ago, receiving $25,000 in a year, between his salary and his percentage of the receipts. This situation is not without its advantages to the members of my hard-pressed profession. The president of one celebrated university was paid $8000 a year. A coach qualified to direct the football destinies of the institution could not be found for less than $15,000. Since the trustees had to have the coach, and since they couldn't pay the president less than the coach, they raised the president's salary to $15,000 too.

Subsidizing is expensive. Equipment, travel, advertising and publicity are expensive. These things have been known to run to $10,000 or $15,000, even in the smaller colleges, for football alone. Some of the more glorious teams carry a Pullman full of newspapermen across the country with them, paying the reporters' expenses.

The myth that football receipts support research, education, or even other sports has just been exploded by President Wilkins, of Oberlin. His analysis of football costs in twenty-two typical colleges shows that only two have a surplus of football income over football expense. The twenty others spend on football all they get from football and $1743 apiece a year additional. This is the income on $45,000 of their endowment.

President Wilkins' investigation of the colleges raises an interesting question. If most of the colleges lose money at football, is it not likely that most of the universities, with their proportionately heavy expense, are also playing a losing game? I know of only one university that ever claimed to have built a laboratory out of excess gate receipts, but many of our larger institutions claim that football finances their so-called minor sports. Perhaps it does in a few universities and in the years of their great teams. But I should like to see a study made of the universities along the lines of President Wilkins' investigation of the colleges; and I might suggest to those who make the study that they scrutinize the accounting methods of some of our educators to see if they are charging up coaches and even trainers as "professors," the purchase of players to "contingent expense," and the debt on the stadium to "Real estate."

In 1925 the American Association of University Professors expressed the hope that colleges would in time publish the cost of stadiums. This hope has not been fulfilled, and for the most part the cost of stadiums remains one of the dark secrets of the athletic underworld. I understand that there are only two stadiums in the Big Ten which were not built with borrowed money, and that two have not yet been paid for. One cost $1,700,000.

Last fall I met a university president the day before his team was to play its opening game. All he could say was, "We've got to win tomorrow. We've got to pay off that $35,000 on the stadium this year." The necessity of packing these arenas has led colleges to schedule as many big games as possible. In order to establish the team's value as a spectacle as soon as possible, a big game must be played to open the season. The old scheme of playing easy games until the team is in shape has had to be abandoned. Consequently, practice must begin earlier to get the team in shape earlier. Harvard and Princeton have just extended pre-season practice and have given a bad example to the country.

The reason that college stadiums can't be paid off is plain. They are built for one sport, football. A great team year after year might, in fifteen or twenty years, pay off the bond issue. But there are no great teams year after year. Athletic eminence is cyclical. College A has a great team and decides to build a great stadium, so that the entire population can watch it. But the alumni of College B, which is the traditional rival of College A, are irritated because their alma mater is being beaten by those thugs across the river.

So the alumni go out and buy a great team for College B. Colleges C and D also have alumni who also like to win.

In a few years College A is being beaten regularly and the stadium, except for those local citizens who can't afford to get away to watch B, C, and D, is empty. Then College B builds a great new stadium to cash in on its great new record, and goes through the same routine.

There are several factors already operating to reduce athleticism, whether or not we decide to do anything about it. The rise of the junior colleges, which educate freshmen and sophomores only, is reducing the supply of athletic material for the four-year colleges and universities.

Professional football, which is attracting larger and larger crowds, may ultimately do for college football what professional baseball had done for college baseball. And the United States Supreme Court, in a case involving the taxation of gate receipts, has clarified the national mind to some extent by indicating that intercollegiate football is business.

But neither the Supreme Court, nor professional football, nor the junior colleges can be depended upon to reform us. We must reform ourselves. How? The committees which have studied the subject—and their name is legion— have suggested stricter eligibility rules, reduction of training periods, elimination of recruiting and subsidizing, easier schedules, limitation of each student's participation to one sport, and abandonment of the double scholastic standard for athletes. President-Emeritus Lowell, of Harvard, once proposed the Oxford and Cambridge system of limiting each sport to one game a season, and that one with the college's natural rival. Mr. Lowell's scheme might have the merit of enabling students and the public to work off their seasonal frenzy in one big saturnalia.

These reforms will never achieve reform. They may serve to offset athleticism at those few institutions which are already trying to be colleges instead of football teams. But it is too much to hope that they will affect the colleges and universities at large.

Since money is the cause of athleticism, the cure is to take the money out of athletics. This can be done only in defiance of the students, the alumni, the public, and, in many cases, the colleges themselves. The majority of the colleges and universities will not do it, because in the aggregate they dare not. Johns Hopkins, in Maryland, and Reed College, in Oregon, have dared, but nobody cares, athletically speaking, what Johns Hopkins or Reed does.

The task of taking the money out of athletics must be undertaken by those institutions which are leaders, institutions which can afford the loss of prestige and popularity involved. I suggest that a group of colleges and of universities composed, say, of Amherst, Williams, Dartmouth, Harvard, Yale, Chicago, Michigan, Stanford and California agree to take the following steps, to take them in unison and to take them at once:

1. Reduce admission to ten cents. This will cover the handling costs. For years prominent educators, all the way from Harper, of Chicago, to Butler, of Columbia, have insisted that college athletics should be supported from endowment like any other educational activity. Colleges should support athletics out of their budgets, or get out of athletics, or get out of education.

2. Give the director of athletics and the major coaches some kind of academic tenure, so that their jobs depend on their ability as instructors and their character as men and not on the gates they draw.

While these two steps are being taken, it might be well, for the sake of once more putting students instead of athletes on the college playing fields, to try to stimulate the urge to play for fun and health, instead of the urge to win at any cost. There are two ways to do this, and many colleges and universities are trying both with considerable satisfaction to their students:

1. Broaden the base of athletic participation, so that all students, graduate and undergraduate, big fellows and little fellows, can play. The development of intramural athletics, which costs less than the maintenance of present programs, is a step in this direction. The English system of selecting a varsity from the intramural teams toward the end of the season and then playing a limited number of intercollegiate games suggests itself at this point.

2. Emphasize games which students will play in later life, when they need recreation and physical fitness as much as in college. Such sports are tennis, handball, skating, swimming, softball, bowling, rackets, golf and touch football. Few college graduates are able to use football, baseball or basketball, except as topics of conversation.

In a word: More athletics, less athleticism.

I think that after the steps I have suggested have been taken by the colleges and universities I have named, the rest of the country's educational institutions will not long be able to ignore their example.

Nor will the public, once the break has been made, attempt for long to prevent reform. The public, in the last analysis, pays for the colleges and the universities. It wants something for its money. It has been taught to accept football. It can, I am confident, be taught to accept education.

The public will not like ten-cent football, because ten-cent football will not be great football. The task of the colleges and the universities, then, is to show the country a substitute for athleticism.

That substitute is light and learning. The colleges and universities, which taught the country football, can teach the country that the effort to discover truth, to transmit the wisdom of the race, and to preserve civilization is excit-ing and perhaps important too.

*Arthur Miller*

# University of Michigan[1]

MY FIRST affection for the University of Michigan was due, simply, to their accepting me. They had already turned me down twice because my academic record (I had flunked algebra three times in my Brooklyn high school) was so low as to be practically invisible, but the dean reversed himself after two letters in which I wrote that since working for two years—in a warehouse at $15 a week—I had turned into a much more serious fellow. He said he would give me a try, but I had better make some grades. I could not conceive of a dean at Columbia or Harvard doing that.

When I arrived in 1934, at the bottom of the depression, I fell in love with

[1] From *Holiday*, XIV (December, 1953), 68 *et passim*. © Copyright by *Holiday*, 1953, © copyright by Arthur Miller, 1956.

the place, groggy as I was from the bus ride, because I was out of the warehouse at last, and at least formally a part of a beautiful town, the college town of Ann Arbor. I resolved to make good for the dean, and studied so hard my first semester that in the history exam my mind went completely blank and the professor led me out of the class and told me to go to sleep and to come back and take the exam again.

I loved it also because of the surprises. Elmo Hamm, the son of a potato farmer in Upper Michigan, turned out to be as sharp a student as any of the myopic drudges who got the best grades in New York. I loved it because Harmon Remmel, the son of an Arkansas banker, lived in the room next to mine and from him I got a first glimpse of what the South meant to a Southerner, a Southerner who kept five rifles racked on the wall, and two .38's in his valise, and poured himself bullets in a little mold he kept on his desk. (In his sophomore year he disappeared, and I found out he had been unable to bear it any longer once duck-hunting time had rolled around again.)

I loved the idea of being separated from the nation, because the spirit of the nation, like its soil, was being blown by crazy winds. Friends of mine in New York, one of them a *cum laude* from Columbia, were aspiring to the city fireman's exam, but in Ann Arbor I saw that if it came to the worst a man could live on nothing for a long time. I earned $15 a month for feeding a building full of mice—the National Youth Administration footing the bill—and out of it I paid $1.75 a week for my room and squeezed the rest for my Granger tobacco (two packs for thirteen cents), my books, laundry and movies. For my meals I washed dishes in the co-op cafeteria. My eyeglasses were supplied by the Health Service, and my teeth were fixed for the cost of materials. The girls paid for themselves, including the one I married.

I think I sent more students to Michigan than anybody else who ever went there.

It was a great place for anybody who wanted to write. The Hopwood Awards, with prizes ranging from $250 to $1500, were an incentive, but there was something more. The English Department had, and still has, a serious respect for undergraduate writing efforts. Prof. Kenneth Rowe, who teaches playwriting, may not have created a playwright (no teacher ever did), but he surely read what we wrote with the urgency of one who actually had the power to produce the play. I loved the place, too, because it was just big enough to give one the feeling that his relative excellence or mediocrity had real meaning, and yet not so big as to drown one in numbers.

I remember the June of each year when the Hopwood Awards were announced, and the crowds would form to hear the featured speaker—some literary light from the book world—after which the presentations were made. How I hated those speakers for holding up the awards! And those prizes meant more than recognition. In my case at least, they meant the end of mouse-feeding and room-sharing, and the beginning of a serious plan to become a playwright. Avery Hopwood made millions by writing bedroom farces like *Getting Gertie's Garter* and *Up in Mabel's Room;* if my sense of it is correct, never was so much hope created in so many people by so modest an accomplishment. I have never sweated on an opening night the way I did at Hopwood time.

I do not know whether the same thing happened at Harvard or Columbia or Yale, but when I was at Ann Arbor I felt I was at home. It was a little world and it was man-sized. My friends were the sons of die-makers, farmers, ranchers, bankers, lawyers, doctors, clothing workers and unemployed relief recipients. They came from every part of the country and brought all their prejudices and special wisdoms. It was always so wonderful to get up in the morning. There was a lot learned every day. I recall going to hear Kagawa, the Japanese philosopher, and how, suddenly, half the audience stood up and walked out because he had used the word Manchukuo, which is Japanese, for the Chinese province of Manchuria. As I watched the Chinese students excitedly talking outside on the steps of Hill Auditorium, I felt something about the Japanese attack on China that I had not felt before.

It was a time when the fraternities, like the football team, were losing their glamour. Life was too earnest. But I remember glancing with sadness at the photographs of Newman, Oosterbaan and the other gridiron heroes and secretly wishing that the gladiatorial age had not so completely disappeared. Instead, my generation thirsted for another kind of action, and we took great pleasure in the sit-down strikes that burst loose in Flint and Detroit, and we gasped when Roosevelt went over the line with the TVA, and we saw a new world coming every third morning, and some of the old residents thought we had gone stark raving mad.

I tell you true, when I think of the Library I think of the sound of a stump speaker on the lawn outside because so many times I looked up from what I was reading to try to hear what issue they were debating now. The place was full of speeches, meetings and leaflets. It was jumping with Issues.

But political facts of life were not all I learned. I learned that under certain atmospheric conditions you could ice-skate up and down all the streets in Ann Arbor at night. I learned that toward June you could swim in a certain place without a suit on, and that the Arboretum, a tract of land where the botanists studied plants and trees, was also good for anatomical studies, especially in spring under a moon. I had come to school believing that professors were objective repositories of factual knowledge; I found that they were not only fallible but some of them were damn fools, and enough of them seekers and questioners to make talking with them a longlasting memory.

I left Ann Arbor in the spring of 1938 and in two months was on relief. But, whether the measurement was false or not, I felt I had accomplished something there. I knew at least how much I did not know. I had found many friends and had the respect of the ones that mattered to me. It had been a small world, gentler than the real one but tough enough. It was my idea of what a university ought to be.

What is it now? You can see at once, I hope, that my judgment is not objective if only because my memories of the place are sweet, and so many things that formed those memories have been altered. There are buildings now where I remembered lawn and trees. And yet, I told myself as I resented these intrusions, in the Thirties we were all the time calling for these dormitories and they are finally built. In my day bequests were used for erecting less useful things—the carillon tower whose bells woke us up in the morning, the Rackham Building, a grand mausoleum which seemed to have been designed for sitting around in a wide space.

There are certain facts about the University today that can be disposed of right off. In almost every field of study, a student will probably find no better training anywhere than at Michigan. Some say that in Forestry, Medicine, Creative Writing, and many other fields it is really the top. I wouldn't know, I never went to any other school.

The student will need about a thousand dollars a year, which is cheaper than a lot of places. He will get free medical care and hospitalization; he will be able to borrow money from the University if he needs it and may take nearly forever to pay it back; he will use modern laboratories in the sciences and an excellent library in the humanities; as a freshman he will live in new dormitories, and the girls will have to be in bed at ten-thirty; if he flies to school he will land at the Willow Run Airport, the safest in the country, owned now by the University; he will have a radio station and a television station to try his scripts, if he writes, and if he is more literary than that he can try for a Hopwood Award in poetry, drama, the essay and the novel.

He will meet students of many backgrounds. Two thirds will be from Michigan, and a large proportion of those from small towns. About nine hundred will be foreign, including Japanese, Turks, Chinese and Europeans. If he is Negro he will find little discrimination, except in a few Greek-letter fraternities. Most of his classes will be large in the first years, but his teachers have regular visiting hours and with a little push he can get to know them. He will not be permitted to drive a car or to keep liquor in his room.

On many winter mornings he will wake to find great snows, and there will be a serene hush upon the campus and the creaking of branches overhead as he walks to his class. In spring he will glance outside at a blossoming world and resolve to keep his eye away from the girl sitting beside him. By June, the heat of the prairies will threaten to kill him and he will leave just in time.

If he has the talent, he may join the *Michigan Daily* staff, and the *Daily* is as close to a real newspaper as he will find in any school. On its own press, it prints about 7500 copies a day, has the Associated Press wire service and syndicated columnists, and its student staff is paid $12 a month and up. The university athletic plant includes a stadium seating nearly 100,000 people, indoor and outdoor tennis courts, swimming pools, and so on.

If a figure can convey an idea of complexity and size—it costs about $40,000,000 a year to keep the place going. There are now better than 18,000 students and nearly 1200 faculty, and the figures will rise next year and the year after. The school has just bought 347 acres for new buildings. More facts may be had for the asking; but in any case, you couldn't do better for facilities.

Things seem to be getting *done* now. For instance, on the north side of the campus the Phoenix Project is going up, the only thing of its kind in the country. It was conceived by an alumnus in the advertising business who discovered, while traveling through Europe, that we were being accused of using the atom for war only. Returning here, he began a campaign for alumni contributions to create an institute which will accept no Government money, do no war work, and instead of operating in secrecy will attempt to discover and disperse the knowledge of the atom that will, some say, revolutionize human life. Research projects are under way, although the scientists are not yet housed in one building, and already a method has been found by which the dreaded trichina, often found in pork, is destroyed. One of the men in charge of the project told me that the implications of Phoenix will reach into every science, that it has already moved into botany, medicine, dentistry, and eventually will span them all.

There is an enormous growth in all kinds of theater since I was at Michigan. Somewhere, sometime this year on campus, you could have seen *Brigadoon*, Gilbert and Sullivan, a German play, a French play, Aristophanes, Pirandello, *Deep are the Roots*, *Faust*, *Madame Butterfly*, *Mister Roberts*, and more, all acted by students. A professional theater has done Camus, Bridie, Shakespeare, Saroyan, Yeats, Gertrude Stein, Sophocles, Synge and the Norwegian Krog. A symphony orchestra and a jazz band play student compositions frequently; there is a practically continuous art show going on with both traveling and local exhibitions on view; the best foreign and art films are shown once a week and the joint is jumping with concerts. All this is proof that a considerable number of people in Ann Arbor are looking for more than technology and are eager to feed their souls—a fact sometimes doubted by many in and out of the University.

The increase in students goes far to explain the impression of great activity, of building, of research, the scores of research projects, and of course the great increases in the faculty, especially in the English and Psychology departments. But the changes are also qualitative. As one small sign, the Music School has a few teachers who actually compose. The old idea of the University is not passing away, it is being worked away, it seems; the study of phenomena is giving way to the creation of useful things. *Generation*, the literary magazine, does not merely publish essays on music but new scores, as well as poetry, photographs and stories.

The University has the feel of a practical workshop these days. In my time a great deal of research and thesis writing was carried on by people who were simply hiding from the Depression. When you asked undergraduates what they intended to major in, and what career they meant to follow, you saw an oblong blur float across their eyes. These days nearly everybody seems to be quite sure. I knew graduate students who lived in an abandoned house with no electricity or heat, and never took the boardings off the windows for fear of discovery, and one of them had been around so long he had gone through every course in the Lit school but Roman Band Instruments. The lucky ones got an assistantship at $600 a year and even so looked like they had dropped out of a novel by Dostoevski. Now, in some departments, a man doing his dissertation hooks into a research project and earns $2400 a year and sometimes gets secretarial help in the bargain.

The Psychology Department, for instance, which used to have about a half-dozen members, and was year in year out trying to discover the learning processes of rats put through an enormous maze, now spreads out over a whole floor of offices, and spends tens of thousands investigating mass behavior of *people*, of all things, problems of industrial psychology, and in the words of one troubled researcher, "how to make people do what you want them to while thinking they are doing it because *they* want to."

From the physical, quantitative point of view, it seems to me that if by some magic this University of 1953 had suddenly materialized on a morning in 1935, let's say, we would have decided that the millennium had arrived. The mere fact that every morning the Michigan *Daily* displays two columns of invitations from corporations and Government bureaus to students to apply for positions would have been enough.

The millennium is here, and yet it isn't here. What's wrong, then? I have no proof for this, but I felt it many times in my stay and I'll say it: I did not feel any love around the place. I suspect that I resent the Detroit Modern architecture of the new Administration Building and the new Haven and Mason Halls, and the fluorescent lighting and the gray steel furniture in the teachers' office cubicles. Can steel furniture ever belong to anybody, or can anybody ever belong to steel furniture? Is it all right to need so much administration that you have to put up an office building with nothing but administrators in it? Maybe it's all right, but God, it's not a University, is it? Why not? I don't know why not, it just feels like an insurance company, that's all. And yet, with eighteen to twenty thousand students, I suppose you've got to have it. Somebody's got to count them. But there is no love in it.

There is a certain propriety around the place that I found quite strange. Or was it always that way and I didn't notice? I do not remember teachers lowering their voices when they spoke to you in the corridors, but they do that now. At first I thought it was my imagination, and I asked a few men about it, but they denied that they do it. Still, they are doing it. The place is full of comportment. Maybe I have been around theatrical folk too long but it seemed to me that everybody had turned into engineers—in my day all engineers wore black suits and short, antiseptic haircuts. The curious thing is that now the engineers affect buckskin shoes and dungarees or tan chino work pants.

The lists of help-wanted notices alone would have solved the problem of my generation. And yet in talking with a certain high administrative official, it quickly became evident that the millennium had not yet arrived. I found it hard to believe that this gentleman had been elevated to Administration, because when he was my teacher several hundred years ago he used to drop his coat on the floor sometimes and forget about tying his tie correctly, and his suits were usually rumpled. He just wasn't executive. Now his suits are pressed, and finished worsted not tweed, but the smile is still warm and the eyes crinkle with a great love for humanity. He is very proud of the school, but there is a cloud. There is a cloud over the whole place which is hard to define, and here is part of it. I do not quote him but summarize what he said:

There is less hanging around the lamppost than there used to be. The student now is very young and he has little background. He generally comes with high respect for Michigan's academic standards. The school takes the top half of the in-state students and the top 20 per cent of the out-staters. Fear of the competition is one reason why they absorb themselves in the pursuit of grades. Another is that they do not want to lose their Army deferments. Finally, in the old days a corporation would interview a C student because he might have other valuable qualities, while today the selections are almost statistical— they see the very top of the class and no others. The students know this and are more methodical about grades to the neglect of other interests.

The implication seemed to be that they are more machinelike and perhaps even duller. Or perhaps he meant only that some spirit had departed.

What spirit was he referring to? I think I know. The word University used to imply a place of gentle inquiry, an absorbing waste of time from the money point of view, a place where one "broadened" oneself. And I think he meant that everything is being *defined* now, it is all becoming so purposeful in the narrow sense of the trade school that some of the old separation between University and commerce, University and vocation, University and practicality in the narrow sense, is disappearing.

One symptom of this is the growing and dangerous rivalry with Michigan State College. In my day State was an agricultural college, and the University of Michigan was "The Harvard of the West." Today State is challenging the University for supremacy in all departments, even threatening to rename itself Michigan State *University*. Dr. John A. Hannah, State's vigorous president, has been able to raise enough funds to build a row of impressive dormitories along the main road. The public can see and count the things it is getting for its money. The University cannot compete for the public's appreciation—and support—on the basis of invisible accomplishments like culture and broadening. Consequently, a new and in my time unheard-of slogan is going around the faculty gatherings. Service to the State is the idea. Do things they can *see*. My friend spoke with startlingly serious irritation, real misgivings, about State's victories over Michigan in football. It has come even to that.

As in everything else, therefore, the competition must be carried through on the level of the lowest bidder. Michigan State has always been able to show that where one blade of corn had grown now there were two because of its new insecticides, and the cows were happier for its vaccines. Michigan State went on television, got its own station, so the University decided to win friends and acquire *its* station.

A professor of English was speaking to me in his office. I must note the incongruity of this particular man sitting in this particular office. In my time this man was, how shall I say, dusty. We were all afraid of him because in his classes you either knew your stuff or you didn't. His subject had made him pale and austerely exact. A great poem was a structure that had to be turned and turned until you understood its time, its place, its rhythms and the telling reference in every line. Only a powerful love for the poem itself could have generated his kind of energy in teaching it. He is the kind of man who just does not go with fluorescent lighting and long hallways with little cubicles opening off them, and rivalry toward Michigan State. Or so it seemed long ago.

I asked if he noticed any difference between the present student and school, and the student and school of fifteen years ago. A repressed anger crackled in his eyes.

"It's *all* different. Take the study of literature. Who are its judges? The psychologist is looked to for an analysis of motivations. But even that isn't as bad as looking at a book or a play to discover what kind of Oedipus complex the author had. The sociologists are deferred to as the only men who can really say how typical the situation is in society, and the anthropologist also has a few words handy. Now, I am only an amateur in these disciplines. They are the experts. And what about the literary people? They are becoming experts in their own way. We have what are called The New Critics. The poem to them is a thing in itself. If the diction is exact, the imagery consistent, the writing original and the form consonant with the breadth of the matter, that's the end of it. It is as though the values of humanity—"

The Values. A certain few themes kept coming up wherever I went, and The Values were in the center. The impression gained from certain quarters is that, in 1953, it is thought sufficient to have described a piece of existence, whether it is a book or an isotope. The conflict is being played around certain connected themes. One is The Values. Another is Apathy.

Another English teacher told me: "The student today has no spine. He thinks he is here to receive something that is wrapped up, easily digestible and complete. He is not really working anything *out.*"

The *Michigan Daily* keeps bewailing "apathy" among the students. One reason is that it cannot find enough men to man its positions. The Values and Apathy.

I went back to the *Daily* building and looked up the papers of my day, '34 to '38. I was surprised and amused to read that the Michigan student was a lizard, apathetic, uninterested in campus affairs.

So it gets more complicated. The student is apathetic, but the *Daily* thought he was apathetic in 1936. In those days we laughed at research-for-its-own-sake and now people are disturbed because everything has got so practical, provable and dangerously unvague.

A psychology professor told me: "The student *is* different. The back-talk is feeble. They *are* passive. Imagine a graduate student asking me to tell him what his dissertation subject should be. I couldn't believe my ears at first, but it is happening regularly now. And more than that, they expect me to lay out the lines of their research, and when I try not to do it they are astonished. They regard themselves as instruments. It is as though they thought it a waste of time to speculate, to move into unknown territory, which is just what they should be doing."

Another psychologist said: "The most embarrassing question you can ask a researcher is, 'Why are you doing this?' He can tell you its immediate application, but whether it is good or bad to apply it or whether it could be a disastrous power to put in the wrong hands either is not his business or else he is just hoping for the best."

I began to feel after a while that something was chasing everybody here. The Necessity to Keep Doing. A fantastic number of discoveries being made and a gnawing worry about What it is All For. I think the Phoenix Project is one answer, a statement of the University's conscience.

One example of this atmosphere of pursuit is the television question.

A professor of English: "Now we are going on television. Why? Allegedly to spread education among the people. But is that really why? It is not. It is because Michigan State is winning friends and influencing people, so we must. Did you know that they send out calendars reading, 'Come to Michigan State, The Friendly College'? We are now going to be 'friendly'! Can you really teach people on a University level through TV? My subject is hard. It requires that a student work to understand it. Isn't it inevitable that we will have to make it easier and easier, and lower our standards in order to compete? The TV audience is profoundly passive. It is looking for a massage, not a message. And in addition my subject has 'controversial' aspects. Can a teacher maintain the courage to speak his heart in the face of the pressure groups and the mass ignorance they can arouse against him? I don't believe it. We are being asked to become entertainers, and the time will come when a professor will be cast for voice, looks and camera manners. Oh, you can laugh, but it is absolutely in the cards. We are going to have to put ourselves over, we are going to have to sell Michigan. The neon age of education is upon us. And don't confuse this with Democracy. It is the triumph of the Leveler, and the man in charge is an advertising man."

I could go on endlessly because in nearly every conversation these themes kept cropping up. But there are many who deny their validity.

A physicist: "I know they are all beefing about passivity but I don't find it in my field. They are as hep and alive as they ever were. Some of this 'apathy' is really a kind of maturity. Kids don't join things so much now because they are more serious. There is, of course, the problem of values. The atomic boys found that out with a jolt. It is not enough to discover something, one must work on the problem of its use. And you can be sure that a scientist who has the brains to work in nuclear physics is intelligent enough to worry about values. So much so that some people risked a great deal and went to the Government to implore them to understand what the atom implied. Don't think for a minute that we are automatons without conscience. Nothing is farther from the truth."

Another English professor: "I can't tell any great difference between these kids and any peacetime class. I think what some of the others are complaining about is really based on our experience with the veterans who left here about 1948. It's true, they were thrilling people to teach. They were serious but inquisitive, they were after the facts but they knew that a philosophy, a standard of values, was of first importance. But the prewar classes didn't measure up to the veterans either."

I met students in the restaurants, in dormitories, classrooms, hallways, and in the Union, the center for nonfraternity students. If there were no two alike they nevertheless had certain common feelings that came up to the surface very quickly. Michigan means freedom to them. It has nothing to do with academic freedom but a release from home and the neighborhood or town they came from. This is as it always was, but I had forgotten what an adventure it was to leave home. One afternoon I sat with the girls on the veranda of the Martha Cook dormitory. Martha Cook is brick and ivy, lawns and old trees, and windows you remember as leaded but which are not, mellow wood and an outline of Tudor-out-of-Yale.

The Girl From Massachusetts: "Oh, gosh, yes. I would never dare do at home what I think nothing of doing here. What, exactly? Well, I don't know, but I go out with fellows my parents wouldn't approve of. You couldn't be friendly, really, with a Chinese or a Negro in my town. Not really, you couldn't. You can here."

The Girl From New York (the intellectual): "Well, that's not quite true. It's very complicated."

The Girl From Ohio (who will marry a law student after graduation and settle in Rio, where he will practice): "I think it's enormously freer. It's like, well, it's an explosion, almost. I started in literature, then I went to botany, and now I'm in music." And brother, she was. As they used to say, she was bursting with life, sitting there in blue jeans, her heels tucked against her buttocks, her knees up around her cheeks, and a sunburned face sucking in everything that was said and ever would be said. But the others thought she was hasty in planning to settle outside the country. I was surprised. I had thought they would all be thrilled at the prospect of foreign lands. It took a minute for them to say exactly why they thought her hasty.

"There might be a revolution there," they finally agreed. It would be better to stay home.

Maybe they were just envious. But they weren't apathetic, if that means dull, without thought. The Depression means to them what World War I meant to us; that is, an old-fashioned thing. Time after time I got the same image —"It couldn't happen that way again. The Government wouldn't let it, I don't think." They seem to feel that society is under control; it is so enormous, and it *is* operating, that there is just nothing to think about in that department. They feel there is enormous opportunity for anybody; that men are rewarded pretty much according to their abilities, and time and time again said the same line, "It's up to me."

The famous panty raids that swept the country started at Michigan last year and these girls had witnessed that strange crusade. It seems that some guy was blowing a trumpet in one of the men's dorms and somebody else yelled at him to stop, and the trumpet player dared the other guy to make him stop, but instead of fighting they decided to invade the women's dormitories and steal panties. A crowd gathered, and kept getting bigger all night as one dormitory after another was entered. Martha Cook was among those that "fell." The girls were quite gay about it and told the story as though they kind of wished more of the same would happen now and then.

The story sounded as though it might well have happened at any time, the Thirties included, but to my ear there was nevertheless a strange note in it. It did not sound like a simple sexual outburst. As the girls spoke, I had the feeling that the panty raids were one of those phenomena which are only superficially sexual and were directed more as a challenge to the atmosphere of paternal repression which is, and always was, quite strong at Michigan.

An administrative official arranged a luncheon for me with a dozen or so student leaders. I feared this would be a polite waste of time and it is no reflection on the man to say that they were under wraps in his presence. As they themselves told me later, the paternalism of the administration is not conducive to student expression. It was always a rather heavily administration-dominated school, but in the old days they had a fight for their money. I remember one hell of a racket when Fred Warner Neal, probably the most prolific reporter the paper ever had, resigned from the *Daily*—which gave him a full column on Page 1 to write his resignation—because the administration had forbidden him to write some story or other. And I remember he was reinstated. I remember committees demanding to see the president whenever they didn't like something, and I remember a few times when they won the argument, or half won it.

These dozen, being interested enough to head up the student legislature, the interfraternity council and so on, were the contemporary equivalents of the people who made the noise in my time. While the official was with us they weren't very noisy; it might have been a meeting of young bankers. But he had to leave soon and we were alone and it started coming.

"People are afraid to say anything."

Afraid of what?

"Well, for instance, a lot of people are tired of paying high prices for books. We want a University bookstore, but we know we'll never get one because the bookstores will raise hell and, besides, the Administration won't pay any attention to us."

But you're evidently not afraid to make the demand.

"No, not exactly afraid—"

What do you think would happen if you tried to rally support on campus for a demand like that?

"You mean, like to have a meeting or demonstrate?"

They all looked uncomfortable. Some laughed nervously.

One boy said, "We'd be called communists."

You mean that truly?

"Sure. But the worst thing would be that back home the papers would pick up our names and there might be trouble."

You mean they'd think you'd been turned into Reds here?

"Some people would think so, but it's not exactly being called communists, it's different."

What exactly is it?

"Well, it's that when you went to, let's say, the local plant for a job and if they found out about it they would—well, they wouldn't like you."

Oh.

A girl: "I live in a co-operative house." And really, she blushed. "I'm getting ashamed to mention it because people on campus ask me why do you live with those collectivists? But it's cheaper, and anyway they're not collectivists." They all laughed but they knew that what she was saying was true.

A boy hitherto silent: "I know for a fact that everything you do is being written down and sent to the authorities."

Like what?

"Never mind, I just know it."

I had, the day before, been sitting in the *Daily* building going through the 1934-38 papers. A middle-aged man with eyeglasses and a thick neck took out a file and after a while began noting things down. A reporter came over to me and whispered that this man was a state policeman, and his job was to check up on subversives in the school. The reporter said that he and the others on the paper were always trying to tell the man that the people he was listing were not Reds, but he went right on, in a very affable way, listing anyone who was connected with anything "controversial."

It is necessary to add that at the luncheon, the very broaching of this subject reddened some faces. They were bravely willing to discuss it, and really quite eager to, but if they were not in fear I do not understand anything.

"That's why everybody wants to get into Intelligence."

What's that?

"I'm telling you the facts."

"Oh, go on, they just feel they won't get shot in Intelligence."

"There's a lot of jobs in the Army where you don't get shot. I swear, they all want to get into Intelligence."

So that they can investigate other people?

"No, they don't want to investigate other people, but they feel once they get in there they won't be bothered any more."

Would you like to get into Intelligence?

Laughter. "Sure, I'd take it."

And he blushes. That is, he blushes, but he would take it although he's against it.

There are more evidences of gumshoeing around the campus, but it would be false to picture the place as being in fear of any specific thing. The important fact to me is that the gumshoeing is disliked, sometimes scorned, but accepted as perfectly natural. Sometimes the old liberalism will crop up, however. Not long ago the University prohibited a communist from speaking on campus, and Professor Slosson went to the hall where the man had to make his address, debated with him, and from all accounts slaughtered him.

Compared to my years at Michigan there does seem to be a blanket over the place now. The tone is more subdued, if one measures tone by the amount of discussion, argument and protest openly indulged in. In my day we were more likely to believe that what we thought and did would have an effect upon events, while the present student sees himself separated from the great engine that is manufacturing his and the country's fate.

But it would be inaccurate to think that these boys and girls are inert. I sat in on a graduate seminar in Political Science one afternoon at which five students and a professor were discussing the subtlest relationships between political ideologies over a span of three centuries. It is a long time since I witnessed such complete concentration upon essentials, sharpness of mind, and freedom from cant and sloganeering. In the Thirties such a discussion would have verged on partisanship after an hour, but it never did here, and that is a big change, I think.

They know now that the old easy solutions are suspect, and they are examining rather than exhorting each other. In this sense they are more mature than we were, yet they are also more separated and removed from the idea of action. But action is immensely more complicated than it was and more difficult to conceive—for instance, one of the heaviest loads they bear is the Army draft. In my day we could rally and vote against conscription because it was only a threat, while today there is nothing to be done about it, and it makes futile many of their plans and weakens as well the very idea of controlling their own destinies.

I do not know how things will work out at Michigan any more than the next man does. It may be the faculty men are correct who see a profound shift of values which will make of Michigan a place not unintelligent, not overtly browbeaten, but a school of obedient pragmatists where each individual walks in blinders toward his niche in government or giant corporation, his soul unswept by the hot blasts of new ideas and vast social concepts. The very bigness of Michigan, the size of the investment in it, and the mutual suspicion that is gripping so many people are forces that would help such a process along. And there is a deeper, less-noticed frame of mind which goes even farther to create such an atmosphere, and I think of the faculty man-of-good-will, in this context, who was talking to me about a certain administrator who paid no attention to the students' ideas or complaints or suggestions. "It's a pity," said this faculty man, "that X's public relations are not better." Whether X might in fact have *been* authoritarian and unheeding was evidently beside the point. The fault to remedy was X's inability to put himself over. It is in such remarks and attitudes that one sees the absence of an idealism I clearly remember at Michigan, and in its place a kind of pragmatism that threatens to create a race of salesmen in the tawdry sense of that word.

I cannot promise that it will not end this way—a chromium-plated silence, a highly organized, smoothly running factory for the production of conformism. I only know that in my time it was supposed to be a training ground for leftists or, from the opposite viewpoint, a cave of vigilantism, and it turned out to be neither. I know that when I recently sat with individual students they spoke like seekers, their clean, washed faces as avid for truth as I suppose we were so long ago. I know that they do not think of themselves as a "silent generation" or as a generation at all but simply as "me." I know that in their rooming houses and dormitories the old bull sessions go on into the mornings, but I also know that what so many of them really feel—and here, I think, lies the difference between the generations—they are not saying in public nowadays, if it seems to question that this is the best of all possible worlds. It is simply not done in 1953.

When I stood waiting for the plane at Willow Run I tried to summon up the memory of the other time I had left Ann Arbor, in the fall of 1938. I had had a ride to New York with a young salesman of saddles and riding equipment who had just passed through Ann Arbor. He had been in contact only with the upper echelons of the community—certain high officials, industrialists, a regent or two who owned horses. He had sold a lot of saddles in Ann Arbor. He was leaving with the impression of a fairly ritzy school. For myself, I had not known a single soul in four years who had mounted a horse.

As he started the engine I waved to a girl who was standing in front of the Women's League, a girl that I dared not dream I would ever have money enough, or security of soul enough, to marry. As we drove east, through Toledo, Ashtabula, the red-brick roads through the Ohio farmlands, I tried to tell him what Michigan really was. It was the professor who, with selected members of his class, held séances during which the spirits of Erasmus, Luther and other historical figures were summoned and listened to. It was the fraternity boys sitting on the porches of their mansions, singing nostalgic Michigan songs as in a movie, and it was three radicals being expelled. It was, in short, the testing ground for all my prejudices, my beliefs and my ignorance, and it helped to lay out the boundaries of my life. For me it had, above everything else, variety and freedom. It is probably the same today. If it is not, a tragedy is in the making.

❦ ❦ ❦

# Education

*Frederic E. Pamp, Jr.*

## Liberal Arts as Training for Business[1]

IT IS NOT hard to predict that the practice of management will be profoundly affected by the rapidly approaching forces of automation and statistical decision making.

Any company with a decent regard for its survival must be trying to forecast the terms of those forces, for it must recruit and promote today the executives who will be running the company tomorrow. Can we write the job description for a vice president of X Manufacturing Company for 1965, or 1975? What will he have to know? What new skills, what new sensitivities will he have to possess to deal successfully with the new elements in management and (what is perhaps more important) the new combinations of old elements?

There have been enough changes just since the end of World War II to make the job grow alarmingly. These changes have in fact been largely responsible for the feverish attention that has been paid to management development in recent years. As Frederick Lewis Allen describes the complicated nature of present executive requirements:

> The corporation executive today must be the captain of a smooth-working team of people who can decide whether the time has come to build a new polymerization plant, what the answer is to the unsatisfactory employe relations in a given unit of the business, how to cope with a new government regulation, how to achieve a mutually respectful understanding with union representatives and what position to take on price increases in order to maintain the good will of the public. In short, he is confronted with so many questions which require knowledge, intellectual subtlety, political insight and human flexibility that he desperately needs a mental equipment of the sort that the old-time tycoon could do without.

### NEW DEMANDS

Up to now most of the increased demands on management have been quantitative. An executive has had to know more about engineering, about accounting,

[1] From *Harvard Business Review*, XXXIII (May-June, 1955), 42-50, with omissions. Copyright, 1955, the President and Fellows of Harvard College.

about his industry, about the position of his company in the industry, about society and the world around him—all to the end of better control of masses of data and information, and better decision making on the basis of such material.

Now we are faced with the fact that many of the quantitative aspects of the executive's job are going to recede into the innards of a computer. Thus, in one company, dozens of clerks used to work laborious days on their slide rules to provide data for what were no more than calculated guesses, on top of which management built a whole pyramid of deliberate decisions. A computer can now take readings of the whole spectrum of data at any time desired, give the relevant figures their proper weights, and come up with production schedules, orders for materials, and financial budgets to ensure maximum efficiency of operation.

Nevertheless, the executive is not likely to join the ranks of the technologically unemployed, just because he will have shucked off many of the problems on which he formerly exercised his executive judgment and "feel." It is inevitable that new problems will crowd in to take the place of the old ones. And, in other than quantitative judgments, a new standard of accuracy and precision will be called for to match the level of accuracy displayed by the computer. A small fable for executives was played out before millions on television at the last election, when the computer performed faultlessly on faulty data and came out blandly with answers that could have ruined a company if they had concerned a gamble on marketing or capital investment.

In any event, the competitive edge acquired by one company by acquisition of a computer will not last long in any industry. Sooner or later all companies will be returned to the equilibrium defined recently by Albert L. Nickerson, Vice President and Director of Foreign Trade, Socony-Vacuum Oil Company:

> If one competitor has a material advantage today it—or a workable counterpart—is likely soon to become common property. An enterprise must rely for survival and progress on the personal qualifications of those who make up its ranks and direct its destinies.

### QUALITIES NEEDED

Management development has already shaken down from an early concentration on executive manning charts and development of logical succession to key jobs, through a period of sorties into specialized training groups, to a generally accepted set of principles for assessment and development of the candidate on the job under realistic standards of performance. All this prepares for the job as it has shaped up in the past decade and as it exists today (as military staffs are always alleged to prepare for the last war). It is time for the focus to shift again—to the building of the kind of executive quality which will be at a premium tomorrow.

Straight-line extension of the norm that has led the company this far will not necessarily suffice to lead it in the future. Top management cannot expect to pick its succession exactly in its own image and get away with it. Neither is it enough to take the pattern of executive personality that has succeeded in one company (or a thousand) under present conditions. The first question a company must now begin to ask of its candidates for executive responsibility is: "What can you do that a computer can't?"

In more and more companies, the decisive factor is going to be the breadth and depth of executive judgment. As vast areas of what used to be decision making become subject to mechanical computations which are all equally correct in all companies, the edge will be won by the company whose executives do a better job of handling the qualitative factors which remain after the measurable factors have been taken out, and then of putting all the pieces together into a single, dynamic whole—what Peter Drucker calls "seeing a business as a whole in conceptual synthesis."

## Breadth of Judgment

On one point all authorities have agreed. Narrow specialization is not enough; this is already responsible for most of the inability of middle management executives to be considered for promotion. John L. McCaffrey, President of International Harvester Company, puts it this way:

> . . . the world of the specialist is a narrow one and it tends to produce narrow human beings. The specialist usually does not see over-all effects on the business and so he tends to judge good and evil, right and wrong, by the sole standard of his own specialty.
>
> This narrowness of view, this judgment of all events by the peculiar standards of his own specialty, is the curse of the specialist from the standpoint of top management consideration for advancement. Except in unusual cases, it tends to put a road-block ahead of him after he reaches a certain level.

Thus, there has been a growing call for "breadth" in educational preparation for management, and a surprising degree of agreement on the need for more *liberal arts* in colleges.

Educators, especially those in state-supported colleges, may be forgiven a certain bewilderment if, after bending every effort—and many curricula—to answer insistent demands from business for more and more specialty and vocational courses on all levels, they are now abused for turning out graduates unprepared for the full scope of executive action in management for today, much less for tomorrow. They have responded by pointing out that the company recruiters still come to the colleges with many more demands for technicians than for liberal arts graduates.

Action has been taken to bring educators in the liberal arts and business executives together to discuss the desirable objectives of education for management. A new respect is developing on the part of businessmen for the standards which the privately endowed, liberal arts colleges have been defending for many years. Agreement on ends and, to some extent, on curricular means to these ends has been worked out in conferences such as those held by the College English Association at the University of Massachusetts in 1952, at the Corning Glass Center in 1953, at Michigan State College and the Kellogg Center in East Lansing in 1954, and the most recent one sponsored by General Electric at Schenectady this spring.

Viewed in these terms many subjects and disciplines can lay claim to a role in education for management. It is obvious that wider subject matter, more courses about more things in the contemporary world, will give the student more breadth.

## Depth of Judgment

But it is also apparent that in a day when the executive will be able to dial the electronic reference library and get all the facts about all the subjects he wants, mere accretion of facts will not warrant his putting in the time to prepare merely to know more facts. The call is for more than "breadth" alone; it is for the ability to move surely and with confidence on unfamiliar ground, to perceive central elements in situations and see how their consequences fall into line in many dimensions. Tomorrow's executive must be able to move surely from policy to action in situations that will be different from anything any generation has experienced before.

There have been developments in traditional educational disciplines within the liberal arts which, much to the surprise of those closest to them, will very likely turn out to be far more important to educational preparation for management than many of the flashy subjects that have seemingly been set up to serve business needs exclusively. The study of the *humanities*—of literature, art, and philosophy, and of the critical terms that these disciplines use to assess the world—is startlingly more pertinent and practical than the "practical" vocational preparation.

Executives should know that recent graduates in the humanities have had a much different experience from those who went through our better colleges ten years ago. They have experienced a much more closely disciplined course in the examination of literature and creative works—of the objectives and the tissue of meanings and symbols which make up the over-all theme of the writing or the painting or the composition, or other form of creative work.

These disciplines have of course other axes to grind than preparing executives to fill job descriptions. They are elements in our civilization which give it life beyond any technologies or economic systems. The arts, education, and management all serve a higher purpose, and business will do society no good if it demands, as do some business leaders, that education serve business directly and solely. That would be the same as insisting that a corporation be restricted only to working capital and forbidden to raise long-term funds.

But the very fact that the humanities serve a larger need than management training is one of the main reasons why they are so valuable for that purpose.

### THE EXECUTIVE'S JOB

At first glance, the importance of training in these fields hitherto considered peripheral, if not downright irrelevant, to management may be difficult to see.

The contribution of the physical sciences is obvious. Also, at long last, we have come to appreciate the significance of the social sciences, which appear to relate directly to business both because of their content and because of their disciplines. It is obvious that an executive must be able to interpret the social and political environment in which his company operates. Further, he must be familiar with as much of the growing body of knowledge of human behavior as possible. But the liberal arts have always been considered remote from the practical hurly-burly of daily decision making.

To demonstrate that precisely the reverse is true, let us examine the disciplines within which the executive moves. In so doing, we may alter our ideas of his job as it has traditionally been regarded, and bring into focus the parallels between the disciplines of the liberal arts and the disciplines of management.

If we analyze the central activity of the executive, his *process of decision,* we can see three kinds of disciplines which prepare directly for the skills and qualities needed:

(1) The executive must distinguish and define the possible lines of action among which a choice can be made. This requires imagination, the ability to catch at ideas, shape them into concrete form, and present them in terms appropriate to the problem.

(2) He must analyze the consequences of taking each line of action. Here the computer and operations research techniques can do much, but the executive must set the framework for the problems from his experience and imagination, and work with his own sensitivity and knowledge in the area of human beings where statistics and scientific prediction are highly fallible guides.

(3) Then in the decision he must have the grasp to know its implications in all areas of an organism which is itself far from being absolutely predictable: the company, the market, the economy, and the society.

## Beyond Science

Most executives act on the basis of a definite hypothesis about the nature of business, much as a scientist acts on a hypothesis about the universe. However, many of the elements subconsciously admitted to such a hypothesis are likely to be wrongheaded prejudices based on insufficient data. Indeed, one of the biggest contributions of operations research has been in identifying all the various factors that are involved and in establishing their net weighted relationships. The fact remains that a good proportion of business decisions have been proved pragmatically valid, to judge by the success of American management to date; and this casts real doubt on whether business is quite as "scientific" as many businessmen would like to think.

There has been a good deal of questioning for some time among more thoughtful management authorities whether management is or can be (or even ought to be) considered a science. . . . This question is important because of the possibility that much of top management's dissatisfaction with the executives available for promotion today has resulted from the educational and training assumption that management is a science or, worse, a collection of techniques, and can be prepared for in those terms alone.

There is the correlative danger that attempts to make management a science and only a science will destroy its essential nature and vigor in the American system. . . . Even if management were not faced with the great changes that are upon us, it would be essential to educate executives for the future who know how to ask impolite questions of the categories of science, just so as to avoid the danger that management as a body of knowledge will freeze into dangerously rigid controls on the whole enterprise system.

It is perhaps the most striking fact about the new techniques of management that when they have developed fully, we shall know much better how far the writ of science runs in management; we shall know how far beyond science a man must go to practice management.

## Added Dimensions

I do not mean to deny that management needs a strong measure of scientific ability. But in organizing and systematizing education for the practice of management it has perhaps been forgotten that more dimensions of hypothesis and experience are involved than are available to science. The practice of management can repeat Hamlet's words to science today: "There are more things in heaven and earth, Horatio, than are dreamed of in your philosophy." The exclusively technical or scientific man is on a tennis court as compared to the generalist who has the added dimensions more like those of a squash court available to him. The latter can get the ball of decision bouncing off more walls.

### APPROPRIATE DISCIPLINES

In view of all this, what can the humanities offer that is pertinent to the executive's job? For one thing, there is plenty of testimony that a common factor in executive success is the ability to express oneself in language. To illustrate:

> There have been many examinations of the background of executives to discover the secrets of success, which have pointed to other than technical accomplishment. In the most recent of these, by Wald and Doty in this magazine, which is more an examination in depth than any that have gone before, it is clear that the literary aptitude of the 33 executives examined was high compared to the scientific. These executives also felt that English was one of the most useful subjects they could take in college to help them toward success.

It is certainly true that the student in the humanities goes deeper into language, and must get more from it and do more with it. But to assume from this that language is only a tool is to stop far short of the possibilities.

Language is not only a tool; it is the person himself. He makes his language, but his language also makes him. "Speak that I may know thee" is the old saw. Any study of language that stops with "techniques of communication," that sees the relationship as one-directional, is stunting the student's growth as an individual. Thus the study of literature as communication only, and not also as experience, is short-changing the student. Study of literature for its own sake is an activity which widens and deepens the personality.

Arthur A. Houghton, Chairman of the Board of Corning Glass, poses the problem bluntly with his statement opening the College English Association Conference at Corning last year:

> The executive does not deal with physical matter. He deals exclusively with ideas and with men. . . . He is a skilled and practical humanist.

Human situations are controlling in a large proportion of business decisions. The executive, it is agreed, must be able to deal with these situations before all else. The instincts for plucking out the fullest implications and keys to human situations are not developed in technical courses of study, nor even in courses in human relations where the techniques pragmatically set the key for action.

There are numerical keys to situations, from accounting; there are quantitative keys, provided by operations research and other techniques drawn from the physical sciences; there are theoretical keys, such as those of Freudian analysis; and there are the keys of the social sciences, which claim to have no preconceptions or assumptions but which are guided by doctrines nonetheless. But none of these keys provides the executive with the ability to see situations as a whole after and above all the data that are available, to seize on the central elements and know where the entry of action can be made.

## Role of Creativity

The fullest kind of training for this ability can actually be given by the practice of reading and analyzing literature and art. In his function the executive must do pretty much what a critic of literature must do, i.e., seize upon the key, the theme of the situation and the symbolic structure that gives it life. The executive must, moreover, create his object for analysis by himself, combining the ingredients of people and data. He must develop insight of an analytic, subjective kind—something he will never get in terms of pure science, for people and things in management situations just will not behave themselves with the admirable regularity and predictability of gases in a test tube!

The fact is, of course, that science itself has had to reconsider its assumptions about the nature of creative activity in its own field. In place of the mechanical concept of the mind as a computer patiently turning over the whole range of possible solutions one by one until it lights on the right one, explanations of scientific discovery now sound more and more like artistic or literary creation —much like John Livingston Lowes's description of how Coleridge inspiredly fused his whole range of experience and impression into "The Ancient Mariner."

The creative element in management, as in the humanities, is developed by the disciplined imagination of a mind working in the widest range of dimensions possible. Some of those dimensions can be more precisely stated. As Clarence Randall has put it:

> My job today is in the realm of ideas. If I must delegate, I must delegate the things that are physical; the things that are material. . . .

Many others have agreed that the most valuable commodity in management is ideas. Yet those disciplines which explore ideas for their own sake, which treat ideas as having life and interaction of their own, have been set off by many as "impractical." Now that the range is widening for management problems, we shall do well to demand that the traditional disciplines, which have dealt in ideas as they interact, in situations as wide as the artist's view of life, become a major part of education for managers. The greater this range of resource for the minds of management, the more and better will be the ideas that emerge.

Because literature is the disciplined control and development of ideas, it deserves a prominent place in this educational plan. Furthermore, to deal with literature and the arts is to deal with ideas not in the stripped and bloodless way of science, but in the inclusive, pell-mell way that experience comes to us in real life—ideas and practice all muddled up.

## The Need for Order

Lyndall F. Urwick, in a lecture given a few years ago at the University of California, said:

> What the student needs is a universe of discourse, a frame of reference, so that when he encounters the raw material of practical life his mind is a machine which can work fruitfully upon that material, refer his own practical experience, which must be extremely limited, to general principles, and so develop an attitude, a guiding philosophy, which will enable him to cope with the immense responsibilities of business leadership in the twentieth century.

The executive's job, like life, is just one thing after another. The executive must be continually and instinctively making order and relation out of unrelated ideas—sorting, categorizing—to the end of action. The order he is able to impose on this mass of experience and the actions he initiates determine his success as an executive. He must find meanings for his company and his function, not only in control reports, balance sheets, market data, and forecasts, but also in human personalities, unpredictable human actions and reactions; and he must refer all to a scale of values. He must be prepared to answer the demand of the people who work for him: that their work contribute to the meaning of their lives. Without some awareness of the possibilities for meaning in human life he is not equipped for this central job of managing people. That awareness is a direct function of the humanities.

The key to the executive's situation and problem, then, is the fact and type of the network of meanings he must use and deal with. They are his stock in trade. He must remain aware of significance and meaning in the obvious: production rates, standards, absenteeism, and the rest. But today he must be acquiring more awarenesses to keep up. These can no longer be limited to the political and international. They are wider. Here the experience and criticism of the arts—especially literature—are direct preparation; for reading of this kind is above all a search for meanings. The mind that leads this search in literature and art—the author, the artist, the composer—is the most sensitive and aware. The mind that follows—the reader, the listener, the viewer—is itself stretched in the process; it too is going to grow more alert and aware.

Meanings on the widest possible level feed perception on a narrower one. The executive whose experience of meanings is thus widened has a suppleness of perception on narrower problems which can key them to effectiveness and coordination with policies and objectives on up the scale of management.

It is only prudent, then, that the executive's preparation include a participation (actual or vicarious) in the highest development of this process. Every novel and play and poem is an imposition of order in terms of human beings and of meaning in terms of a scale of values on the elements of experience that are found formless and pointless in any human experience. The terms by which this order is achieved over the whole scale of management action uses technology and science as tools, but it must have a sense of the whole and of values to be fully effective.

One of the most perceptive comments on the nature of the executive's job was made by Crawford H. Greenewalt, President of du Pont:

> . . . The basic requirement of executive capacity is the ability to create a harmonious whole out of what the academic world calls dissimilar disciplines.

This ability to see the whole of things is again a central function of the humanities. The sciences have flourished by acute concentration upon those elements of the universe that can be measured, but science itself will today admit that it is not a means to the knowledge of the whole of man or of the universe.

The whole of a play or a poem or a novel is the object of the studies of literature because the meaning and structure of each part of it make sense only in terms of the whole. Thus one can say that this feeling for completeness which must govern management even more in the future than it has in the past is directly served by the humanities.

## The Search for Values

Another, and perhaps the most important, aspect of the executive's job is the fact that he must operate in terms of values. Peter F. Drucker puts this at the center of the management job:

> Defining the situation always requires a decision on objectives, that is, on values and their relationship. It always requires a decision on the risk the

manager is willing to run. It always, in other words, requires judgment and a deliberate choice between values.

Only in the humanities are values inextricable from the materials that are studied. The significance of this is pointed up by a comment in the Yale Report on General Education:

> The arts are distinguished by the fact that their order already exists in the material studied. . . . The student who works with them learns to deal with intuitive symbolic ways of interpreting experience, ways which combine into one order the rational, the descriptive, and the evaluative.

If there is a better description of the basic elements of management decision than that last sentence, I have not seen it. Men who must deal with situations above all in terms of values must be prepared by being exposed to those disciplines which admit that they are the stuff of all human life. It is here too that the most obvious reason usually advanced for the advantage of the humanities to an executive gains a new significance. With this equipment he is more likely to have interests outside the business. Not only is he thus likely to be less feverishly possessive about his status in the company, but he has available a far more extensive range of values against which to set his relations with others in the company and the policies of the company itself as well (when he is in a position to set those policies).

The tendency on the part of some social scientists—and some professors of literature—to assert the relativity of values is now going out of academic style. Even the most coldly objective of them now agree that some assumption of at least a hierarchy of values is necessary for worthy social action. This concession is of course not enough. The humanities can themselves be explained as the attempt to work out values in the arts, in all the possible terms of human action. Just as every poem, novel, or play is a representation of a scale of values, and thus has a life independent of the society that produced it, so the most objective study of value systems must admit that there are values by which the value systems themselves can be judged. The difference can be simply stated: for the humanities the values are inextricably linked to the materials; the sciences and social sciences attempt to divorce the materials from the value patterns. . . .

Those disciplines in education which provide human and traditional perspective on the sciences and social sciences have always been of the highest importance in developing this ultimate management skill; they will become more important as time goes on, for, as President Nathan Pusey of Harvard has remarked, "The humanities draw things back together."

## CONCLUSION

The essence of the humanities, then, is meanings and value judgments on all levels. When they are well taught, they force the student to deal with things as a whole, with the gradations and expressions of meaning, worked out in terms of experience coordinated by values and communicated by the disciplined imagination of the artist or writer. These meanings, in a framework of fact, intellect, emotion, and social values, are pulled together in an essentially spiritual complex.

The key to management, and to the executives who make it up, is found in its very nature as an activity. It is easy to define management as a combination of resources, but the fact that the human resources in that combination are in a very special way unique is something that links the humanistic disciplines and management far more firmly than engineering links production to science. . . .

Participation as a student in the poetic process of turning vision into rhetoric is parallel basically to the central problem of the executive, when he works to get policy and company goals into action, integrating plans and objectifying them. And executive action in its own way is no less an art.

## A New Synthesis

There are levels of organization in intellectual disciplines as well as in people. On the level of composition, rhetoric, and communication the humanities offer useful tools for the technician in business. But there also are higher levels of organization and integration in work of literary art, which correspond to the integrated personality for which management is looking. Only by exposure to these can we hope to get the character which is essentially the organization of the personality on the highest level of values.

To neglect the humanities in education is to accept the doctrine of the educationalists as set by John Dewey: "The educational process has no end beyond itself." Management has already discovered that the corporation cannot long exist if it has no end beyond itself. It has now seen its error in giving education the impression that the end of education should be the service of the technical needs of business. There is a new synthesis now in the making through which the true ends of both can best be served. It remains only for management to put it into effect.

Businessmen can of course do the obvious, such as recruiting liberal arts graduates on an equal footing with engineers and technicians. But they can do more. They can ask impolite questions of those who teach the humanities. Do they as teachers produce clarifications of value judgments in their students? Are the students compelled to wrestle with values, as real things or *as if* they were real? Are they driven to see situations as a whole and to analyze them with all the elements in their experience, including their moral values? Businessmen can make it known that their standards for education are not merely technical or specialized. They can thus deeply affect educational policy to the benefit of management and American society.

A realization of these facts can also affect the atmosphere in which potential executives are trained on the job. The procedures which now devote the potential executive's most imaginative years to apprenticeship to figures and techniques can perhaps be changed to take advantage of the stimulated imagination, the taste for general ideas with which the graduate emerges from college, without losing the advantages of buckling down to work and getting a responsible job done. Multiple management no doubt owes a good deal of its success in the many companies using it to its ability thus to harness the most creative elements in the thinking of younger men. There are other ways of working out plans that will tap the liberating qualities of study of the humanities which will not interfere with the necessity for technical training. They should be investigated.

The humanities in the colleges are now struggling to put the pieces of the specialties back together again in order to make the integrated men that management can best use. If they get the sort of direct support already given by Corning Glass Works, General Motors, and General Electric as expressed in their sponsorship of the College English Association's conferences, and in the research projected by that organization, these disciplines can prove the most valuable single resource available for the management of the future.

❦ ❦ ❦

*The Harvard Committee*

# General and Special Education [1]

EDUCATION is broadly divided into general and special education; our topic now is the difference and the relationship between the two. The term, general education, is somewhat vague and colorless; it does not mean some airy education in knowledge in general (if there be such knowledge), nor does it mean education for all in the sense of universal education. It is used to indicate that part of a student's whole education which looks first of all to his life as a responsible human being and citizen; while the term, special education, indicates that part which looks to the student's competence in some occupation. These two sides of life are not entirely separable, and it would be false to imagine education for the one as quite distinct from education for the other—more will be said on this point presently. Clearly, general education has somewhat the meaning of liberal education, except that, by applying to high school as well as to college, it envisages immensely greater numbers of students and thus escapes the invidium which, rightly or wrongly, attaches to liberal education in the minds of some people. But if one cling to the root meaning of liberal as that which befits or helps to make free men, then general and liberal education have identical goals. The one may be thought of as an earlier stage of the other, similar in nature but less advanced in degree.

The opposition to liberal education—both to the phrase and to the fact—

[1] Reprinted by permission of the publishers from Paul H. Buck and others. *General Education in a Free Society:* The Report of the Harvard Committee, Cambridge, Mass.: Harvard University Press, 1945.

stems largely from historical causes. The concept of liberal education first appeared in a slave-owning society, like that of Athens, in which the community was divided into freemen and slaves, rulers and subjects. While the slaves carried on the specialized occupations of menial work, the freemen were primarily concerned with the rights and duties of citizenship. The training of the former was purely vocational; but as the freemen were not only a ruling but also a leisure class, their education was exclusively in the liberal arts, without any utilitarian tinge. The freemen were trained in the reflective pursuit of the good life; their education was unspecialized as well as unvocational; its aim was to produce a rounded person with a full understanding of himself and of his place in society and in the cosmos.

Modern democratic society clearly does not regard labor as odious or disgraceful; on the contrary, in this country at least, it regards leisure with suspicion and expects its "gentlemen" to engage in work. Thus we attach no odium to vocational instruction. Moreover, in so far as we surely reject the idea of freemen who are free in so far as they have slaves or subjects, we are apt strongly to deprecate the liberal education which went with the structure of the aristocratic ideal. Herein our society runs the risk of committing a serious fallacy. Democracy is the view that not only the few but that all are free, in that everyone governs his own life and shares in the responsibility for the management of the community. This being the case, it follows that all human beings stand in need of an ampler and rounded education. The task of modern democracy is to preserve the ancient ideal of liberal education and to extend it as far as possible to all the members of the community. In short, we have been apt to confuse accidental with fundamental factors, in our suspicion of the classical idea. To believe in the equality of human beings is to believe that the good life, and the education which trains the citizen for the good life, are equally the privilege of all. And these are the touchstones of the liberated man: first, is he free; that is to say, is he able to judge and plan for himself, so that he can truly govern himself? In order to do this, his must be a mind capable of self-criticism; he must lead that self-examined life which according to Socrates is alone worthy of a free man. Thus he will possess inner freedom, as well as social freedom. Second, is he universal in his motives and sympathies? For the civilized man is a citizen of the entire universe; he has overcome provincialism, he is objective, and is a "spectator of all time and all existence." Surely these two are the very aims of democracy itself.

But the opposition to general education does not stem from causes located in the past alone. We are living in an age of specialism, in which the avenue to success for the student often lies in his choice of a specialized career, whether as a chemist, or an engineer, or a doctor, or a specialist in some form of business or of manual or technical work. Each of these specialties makes an increasing demand on the time and on the interest of the student. Specialism is the means for advancement in our mobile social structure; yet we must envisage the fact that a society controlled wholly by specialists is not a wisely ordered society. We cannot, however, turn away from specialism. The problem is how to save general education and its values within a system where specialism is necessary.

The very prevalence and power of the demand for special training makes doubly clear the need for a concurrent, balancing force in general education. Specialism enhances the centrifugal forces in society. The business of providing for the needs of society breeds a great diversity of special occupations; and a given specialist does not speak the language of the other specialists. In order to discharge his duties as a citizen adequately, a person must somehow be able to grasp the complexities of life as a whole. Even from the point of view of economic success, specialism has its peculiar limitations. Specializing in a vocation makes for inflexibility in a world of fluid possibilities. Business demands minds capable of adjusting themselves to varying situations and of managing complex human institutions. Given the pace of economic progress, techniques alter speedily; and even the work in which the student has been trained may no longer be useful when he is ready to earn a living or soon after. Our conclusion, then, is that the aim of education should be to prepare an individual to become an expert both in some particular vocation or art and in the general art of the free man and the citizen. Thus the two kinds of education once given separately to different social classes must be given together to all alike.

In this epoch in which almost all of us must be experts in some field in order to make a living, general education therefore assumes a peculiar importance. Since no one can become an expert in all fields, everyone is compelled to trust the judgment of other people pretty thoroughly in most areas of activity. I must trust the advice of my doctor, my plumber, my lawyer, my radio repairman, and so on. Therefore I am in peculiar need of a kind of sagacity by which to distinguish the expert from the quack, and the better from the worse expert. From this point of view, the aim of general education may be defined as that of providing the broad critical sense by which to recognize competence in any field. William James said that an educated person knows a good man when he sees one. There are standards and a style for every type of activity—manual, athletic, intellectual, or artistic; and the educated man should be one who can tell sound from shoddy work in a field outside his own. General education is especially required in a democracy where the public elects its leaders and officials; the ordinary citizen must be discerning enough so that he will not be deceived by appearances and will elect the candidate who is wise in his field.

Both kinds of education—special as well as general—contribute to the task of implementing the pervasive forces of our culture. Two complementary forces are at the root of our culture: on the one hand, an ideal of man and society distilled from the past but at the same time transcending the past as a standard of judgment valid in itself, and, on the other hand, the belief that no existent expressions of this ideal are final but that all alike call for perpetual scrutiny and change in the light of new knowledge. Specialism is usually the vehicle of this second force. It fosters the open-mindedness and love of investigation which are the wellspring of change, and it devotes itself to the means by which change is brought about. The fact may not always be obvious. There is a sterile specialism which hugs accepted knowledge and ends in the bleakest conservatism. Modern life also calls for many skills which, though specialized, are repetitive and certainly do not conduce to inquiry. These minister to change but unconsciously. Nevertheless, the previous statement is true in the sense that specialism is concerned primarily with knowledge in action, as it advances into new fields and into further applications.

Special education comprises a wider field than vocationalism; and correspondingly, general education extends beyond the limits of merely literary preoccupation. An example will make our point clearer. A scholar—let us say a scientist (whether student or teacher)—will, in the laudable aim of saving himself from narrowness, take a course in English literature, or perhaps read poetry and novels, or perhaps listen to good music and generally occupy himself with the fine arts. All this, while eminently fine and good, reveals a misapprehension. In his altogether unjustified humility, the scientist wrongly interprets the distinction between liberal and illiberal in terms of the distinction between the humanities and the sciences. Plato and Cicero would have been very much surprised to hear that geometry, astronomy, and the sciences of nature in general, are excluded from the humanities. There is also implied a more serious contempt for the liberal arts, harking back to the fallacy which identifies liberal education with the aristocratic ideal. The implication is that liberal education is something only genteel. A similar error is evident in the student's attitude toward his required courses outside his major field as something to "get over with," so that he may engage in the business of serious education, identified in his mind with the field of concentration.

Now, a general education is distinguished from special education, not by subject matter, but in terms of method and outlook, no matter what the field. Literature, when studied in a technical fashion, gives rise to the special science of philology; there is also the highly specialized historical approach to painting. Specialism is interchangeable, not with natural science, but with the method of science, the method which abstracts material from its context and handles it in complete isolation. The reward of scientific method is the utmost degree of precision and exactness. But, as we have seen, specialism as an educational force has its own limitations; it does not usually provide an insight into general relationships.

A further point is worth noting. The impact of specialism has been felt not only in those phases of education which are necessarily and rightly specialistic; it has affected also the whole structure of higher and even of secondary education. Teachers, themselves products of highly technical disciplines, tend to reproduce their knowledge in class. The result is that each subject, being taught by an expert, tends to be so presented as to attract potential experts. This complaint is perhaps more keenly felt in colleges and universities, which naturally look to scholarship. The undergraduate in a college receives his teaching from professors who, in their turn, have been trained in graduate schools. And the latter are dominated by the ideal of specialization. Learning now is diversified and parceled into a myriad of specialties. Correspondingly, colleges and universities are divided into large numbers of departments, with further specialization within the departments. As a result, a student in search of a general course is commonly frustrated. Even an elementary course is devised as an introduction to a specialism within a department; it is significant only as the beginning of a series of courses of advancing complexity. In short, such introductory courses are planned for the specialist, not for the student seeking a general education. The young chemist in the course in literature and the young writer in the course in chemistry find themselves in thoroughly uncomfortable positions so long as the purpose of these courses is primarily to train experts who will go on to higher courses rather than to give some basic understanding of science as it is revealed in chemistry or of the arts as they are revealed in literature.

It is most unfortunate if we envisage general education as something formless—that is to say, the taking of one course after another; and as something negative, namely, the study of what is not in a field of concentration. Just as we regard the courses in concentration as having definite relations to one another, so should we envisage general education as an organic whole whose parts join in expounding a ruling idea and in serving a common aim. And to do so means to abandon the view that all fields and all departments are equally valuable vehicles of general education. It also implies some prescription. At the least it means abandoning the usual attitude of regarding "distribution" as a sphere in which the student exercises a virtually untrammeled freedom of choice. It may be objected that we are proposing to limit the liberty of the student in the very name of liberal education. Such an objection would only indicate an ambiguity in the conception of liberal education. We must distinguish between liberalism in education and education in liberalism. The former, based as it is on the doctrine of individualism, expresses the view that the student should be free in his choice of courses. But education in liberalism is an altogether different matter; it is education which has a pattern of its own, namely, the pattern associated with the liberal outlook. In this view, there are truths which none can be free to ignore, if one is to have that wisdom through which life can become useful. These are the truths concerning the structure of the good life and concerning the factual conditions by which it may be achieved, truths comprising the goals of the free society.

Finally, the problem of general education is one of combining fixity of aim with diversity in application. It is not a question of providing a general education which will be uniform through the same classes of all schools and colleges all over the country, even were such a thing possible in our decentralized system. It is rather to adapt general education to the needs and intentions of different groups and, so far as possible, to carry its spirit into special education. The effectiveness of teaching has always largely depended on this willingness to adapt a central unvarying purpose to varying outlooks. Such adaptation is as much in the interest of the quick as of the slow, of the bookish as of the unbookish, and is the necessary protection of each. What is wanted, then, is a general education capable at once of taking on many different forms and yet of representing in all its forms the common knowledge and the common values on which a free society depends.

❧ ❧ ❧

*David Riesman*

# Thoughts on Teachers and Schools[1]

PROGRESSIVE education in its initial American formulation (between about 1900 and 1925) was the product of highly intellectual teachers. These were men and women of marked individuality, talent, and enthusiasm, who became aware of the emotional shallowness and the rote learning of the traditional schools, and sought to found new schools which would not only encourage the arts, the education of the emotions, and group cooperativeness, but which would do an even better intellectual job because more individualized and more closely geared to the child's developing pattern of motivations. These pioneers (being in this like other reformers whose plans have to some degree miscarried) could take for granted their own cultivation and belief in learning, as well as their own zeal, and they could go on from that foundation to try to give the children in their care—as most of us want to give our own children—the things they had missed in their own schooling. I have myself interviewed children and observed classes at several progressive private schools, and I can testify that at their best they turn out interesting and interested children, some of whom their parents and later teachers may find glib and unruly, but not stuffy or deceitful. For many children from narrow or emotionally frozen families, such a school provides an opportunity to thaw out in a milieu at once therapeutic and stimulating.

The doctrinal tenets of such schools have filtered into many public schools with very mixed results. The filtering has not only been "downward" from the superior institutions (such as Teachers College at Columbia) to the junior colleges which have called themselves "teachers colleges" in the hinterland. There has also been a movement "upwards" from the nursery school model, where miracles appear to be accomplished by teachers unable to fall back on the drill of reading or writing in dealing with these preliterate tribes of fours, fives, and sixes: this demonstration of a happy school group, devoted to not much else than its being "happy" and being a "group," has influenced many primary and even high school teachers. It would not have done so to the same degree if the diffusion of progressive (and nursery model) education had

[1] From *The Anchor Review*, Number One (Garden City, N. Y.: Doubleday & Company, 1955), pp. 40-60. Reprinted by permission of the author.

not coincided with the growing emphasis on social skills in the community at large—an emphasis itself in part the product of the same social developments which freed millions to attend school and other millions to teach, transport, and feed them. As our society becomes more play-oriented and less work-oriented, more willing to admit personal sensitivity and warmth to the roster of prime virtues, more concerned with the mood of the group and perhaps less with the achievements of the individual, those goals which the original progressive educators wanted to add to traditional purposes tend in many public (and indeed some private) schools to become the only goals—goals, indeed, no longer so essential for the schools to aim at, since parents and the mass media, among many other social forces, are already active in securing them.

Listen, for instance, to a Massachusetts bread salesman describing to an interviewer what he hopes for in the high school education of one of his sons (and explaining incidentally why he is not sending the young man to college, though he is intelligent enough and the family could afford it):

> I tried to tell him where he isn't going to be a doctor or lawyer or anything like that, I told him he should learn English and learn to meet people. Then he could go out and sell something worthwhile where a sale would amount to something for him. . . . I took typing, shorthand, bookkeeping and we had Latin, French, geometry. We had everything. But anything I would know then I've forgotten now. . . . I don't think a high school diploma is important. I mean only in so far as you might apply for a job and if you can say, "I have a diploma," it might help get the job . . .

Or listen (as recorded by William Whyte, Jr.) to a parent in Park Forest, a suburb of Chicago:

> Janet is studying marketing and she's only in the sixth grade. She's studying ads and discounts, things I didn't get until college. The children are certainly getting a broad view of things.

Implicit in the attitude of both these parents is the belief that the school should prepare children for adult life by imitating that life; indeed, the same "child-centered" schools that would fear maladjustment through advancing an intellectually precocious child beyond his social age-mates often do their best to anticipate in the schoolroom the adult "here and now" of buying and selling, of parliamentary procedure and civic responsibility.

In this situation, some of our teachers are fighting a losing battle in defense of the traditional intellectual values and the classical curriculum. But others (including many school superintendents) have turned necessity into virtue and favor the sort of programs that the parents I have just quoted would themselves like to see installed. Thus, Eric Baber, the high school superintendent in Park Forest, tells his teachers and parents that American education is still "far too much concentrated on the intellectual aspect of education." As he said in a teachers workshop:

The so-called "bright student" is often one of the dumbest or least apt when he gets away from his textbooks and memory work. This is evidenced by the fact that many $20,000 to $100,000-a-year jobs in business, sales, sports, radio . . . are held by persons with I.Q.'s of less than ninety.

Baber is very proud of the "communication laboratory" his modern school plant includes; as he says, "ours is an age of group action," and one in which the children "must have actual experiences in solving problems that have meaning for *them*." No less explicit is the principal of a junior high school in Urbana, Illinois, speaking to a meeting of the National Association of Secondary-School Principals:

Through the years we've built a sort of halo around reading, writing and arithmetic. . . . The Three R's for All Children and All Children for the Three R's! That was it. We've made some progress in getting rid of that slogan. But every now and then some mother with a Phi Beta Kappa award or some employer who has hired a girl who can't spell stirs up a fuss about the schools . . . and the ground is lost. . . . When we come to the realization that not every child has to read, figure, write, and spell . . . that many of them either cannot or will not master these chores . . . then we shall be on the road to improving the junior high curriculum. Between this day and that a lot of selling must take place. But it's coming. We shall some day accept the thought that it is just as illogical to assume that every boy must be able to read as it is that each one must be able to perform on a violin, that it is no more reasonable to require that each girl shall spell well than it is that each one shall bake a good cherry pie. . . .
    When adults finally realize that fact, everyone will be happier . . . and schools will be nicer places in which to live. . . .

This official may well be convinced that he is heretical and ahead of his time for, after all, he does come from the same university town as does Arthur Bestor (Professor of History at the University of Illinois) whose *Educational Wastelands* quotes this gem. This book is one of the least intemperate of a number of recent slashing attacks on just these self-styled "progressive" tendencies in secondary school teaching, some of which blame all attenuation of standards on John Dewey. We professors and intellectuals are generally inclined to trace tendencies we do not like to the ideas of other intellectuals, and this may in the long run be legitimate, but I do feel that Bestor exaggerates the autonomous role of the schools, and hence of their mentors, in fostering a mindless pragmatism and vocationalism which they often simply absorb from their constituencies.

Indeed, so strong are these constituencies that teachers and school officials are today frequently harassed beyond endurance by outsiders who have more prestige or power than they and who therefore feel free to intervene. The result is that it is hard for many in the school system to distinguish between a Barzun or a Bestor (or a Riesman) who has made some effort to understand their problems from within, and that horde of uninformed and usually reactionary "taxpayer" critics of "new-fangled" notions in the schools. The latter are apt to urge that what was good enough for grandpappy is good enough for his descendants. Since the grandchildren will face stiffer competition in terms of formal educational credentials, this penny-pinching view (sometimes abetted by local commerce and industry) simply kicks away a ladder to mobility which the new generation needs if it is to keep step with the rising educational and living standards of the country as a whole. In contrast, my own view is that grandpappy's education was not good enough for him in a day when artistic and empathic skills were seldom transmitted, but it does have certain redeeming virtues which only become evident when the rest of the society has caught up with an outlook that was rare at the turn of the century. In other words, I feel that schools can perform something of a *counter-cyclical* (or "governor") function; within the limits of their weakness, they can fall back on older traditions with very contemporary purposes in mind.

When faced with such a plea coming from a university campus, the school teacher—beleaguered, as I have said, with a multiplicity of special pleading— is apt to appear to turn a deaf ear and to use a diplomatic tongue. She knows that males are apt to be abstract, idealistic, and impractical—and patronizing. There is also the awareness that university professors, like other people, often have vested interests of their own, in discipline and in their "disciplines," to protect. Yet the very democratizing tendencies we have been discussing, which have had such unanticipated regressive consequences, compel teachers and school personnel generally to be accessible. It is hard for them to be other than defensive toward criticism, or, like all professionals faced with troublesome clients, duplicitous in finding the semantics by which all comers can be fended off.

Still, would these teachers be so vulnerable to the many competing demands now made upon them if these demands did not awaken echoes within them of unsolved problems in their own lives?

In interviews with Kansas City high school teachers, the poignant note comes up again and again of a self-confessed adolescent shyness. They feel this was bad, that they should have been "more outgoing" (perhaps they would have found a husband); some indicated that in becoming teachers they had conquered their shyness. In their relations with other teachers, they have established a coterie that they missed in school (and one that protects them to some extent from the unflattering public image of the unmarried school teacher). More important, they want very much to appear vivacious, warm, and outgoing in class. (One could make an interesting comparison here with current models of appropriate behavior in social workers and clergymen.) They want very much to be liked by the children, as well as by their colleagues, and they are perhaps more aware than before whether or not they are liked, especially as the children, good little communicators that they are, include among their social skills the ability to exploit the teachers' need for approval.

Is it true, then, that the cultivated and intellectual teacher has lost her role as a model for other teachers? Not completely. Not a few, whatever their superintendents might sometimes prefer, do not wish to be merely "outgoing." There is the case of one high school drama teacher, the daughter of a very cosmopolitan newspaper editor; after a divorce she returned to the city of her birth and started teaching school there ("political pull," of the sort now waning, helped her get a certificate). This teacher, well-traveled and sophisticated, has a remarkable gift for exciting her pupils' interest in the theatre; she is proud of "graduates on Broadway and in Hollywood." But her fellow-teachers have grave misgivings about her. They complain that she cares "too much about the drama" and "too little about the children." They complain that her productions demand too much time and effort, that the children who get so enthusiastic about putting on plays have little time for other subjects and for sociability, and they feel that the plays should involve a greater number of the children in their production, even at the cost of making the performances less professional. It would be more democratic, they say, to "give everybody a chance," and the drama, like other activities, is seen as one more way to encourage group participation rather than as a way to encourage vocations in the theatre. (The new school principal, a younger man who believes that the duty of the school is to "cultivate the total personality" of the child, has made life difficult for the drama teacher. What he wants is a good working-team of teachers, not stars on the Broadway firmament . . . nor excessive demands on the school auditorium.) I suspect, however, that these teachers would be less critical of their colleague, less articulate about her allegedly disproportionate preoccupation with the theatre, if they did not themselves in some degree aspire to cosmopolitan ways. In taking on responsibility for the child's social and emotional development, they have not wholly relinquished the older responsibility for "culture"; and it is their very ambivalence about partially contending models of school teaching that makes them so angry with those teachers, holdovers from an earlier day, who represent not only unequivocally high and secure social status but also the not entirely downgraded status of intellectual discipline and urbanity.

And it is equally true that a great many, if not all, of the "old-fashioned" teachers have been influenced and even upset by the newer pressures for a more democratic school system—democratic in its attention to the less scholarly (i.e. the non-college-preparatory) group, and to the standards set by the children and their parents. Here is an elderly English teacher at a high school which once was proud of its high academic demands (it had been modeled on the "Latin schools" of New England):

> Mr. ——— believed so thoroughly in education as I really believe in it, yet I realize that it can't go on. I mean you can't go on pounding classical education into everybody's head as long as you are going to have everybody going to the same school. . . . Mr. ———, I am sure, felt that

there were a lot of people who couldn't learn. . . . But he never relaxed what he thought were necessary standards . . . and if they couldn't make it they couldn't make it and that was all. . . . The older teachers who grew up with that were hard put—they like Mr. ——— [the new principal], it's hard for anyone not to like him, but they just think everything is going to pot. . . . I think what he is trying to do is win over the student body to the idea that school administrators and school teachers aren't off there in another world. And then once he has their co-operation to let them make some of the rules and regulations they will be willing to abide by. . . . There have been so many educators and educators that have the theory that reading and writing and arithmetic are sort of overrated; that you must teach people how to be people. . . .

It is plain from such interviews that few teachers are so case-hardened as not to feel some ambivalence concerning the "battle of the books."

This conflict also emerges clearly in a series of group discussions with public school teachers in Chicago and Milwaukee which my colleague, Hedda Bolgar, a clinical psychologist, has been conducting. She finds that once the initial defensiveness of teachers against inquisitiveness is overcome, teachers are very eager to talk to an understanding outsider about their inner aims and external conflicts. Underneath a protective coating of cynicism and careerism these teachers frequently harbor a most grandiose and self-defeating expectation of omnicompetence in the classroom. They expect themselves to respond sympathetically to individual problem-children, even psychotic ones that would baffle an experienced psychologist. Partly aware of current mental-health emphases, they can no longer simply reject a child as "a troublemaker," or if they do they will feel guilty about it. In other words, the teachers have been exposed enough to psychiatric currents of thought to learn that children's aggressive behavior has to be explained and cannot be simply reacted to with counteraggression, but they do not often have sufficient knowledge to accept their own aggression.

Overtly, they may resist the expectation that there is no child they cannot handle, no child to whose needs they cannot minister while preventing it from dominating the group; they may say to one another, "Who does the School Board think we are, parking such little bastards with us?" Overtly, they may think they have done their job if they "keep the kids out of a messy home five hours a day," and they may, as we know, punish a teacher who does too much for the children, who is too enthusiastic—who is a scab or rate-buster in setting too high standards of performance. But underneath they seem to be demanding of themselves that they achieve therapeutic or motherly relations with all the children. Just because they no longer think of themselves as teachers of a subject but rather as teachers of an age-grade, they are at once tempted and betrayed by an ideal of omnicompetence. Though they are in fact in the position of the Old Woman Who Lived in a Shoe, they somehow accept the inner responsibility for making up in their own persons for all the deficiencies in the community. They feel badly if "their" children break windows or go to jail or drop out, no matter what the objective situation—much as many mothers feel.

I suggest that the cynicism with which many teachers talk among themselves is thus in part a defense against a still unextinguished (if often unconscious) ideal image of themselves as unruffled magnanimous individuals, at once motherly and wholly competent. If it were not for this, the teachers as a close-knit collegial group could cope somewhat better than they do with well-meant interferences by social workers, psychiatrists, superintendents, and educators, who directly and indirectly reinforce this extravagant image of what the teacher should be, pushing it always further from the traditional conception of the teacher as a subject-matter specialist, which is to say, a person of limited competence.

When it is pointed out to them that they are not, after all, psychiatrists and cannot expect themselves to cure problem-children, but only at best not to harm them, they react first with anger at the threat to their ideal of omnicompetence, but eventually with relief. And there is some evidence that they become better, less harassed teachers when they can fully realize that their function is limited—primarily, to teach a subject—and that they cannot as individuals compensate for all the ways in which our social organization now puts children in school because it doesn't want them in the labor force, or on the street corner, or because it has no other place for the disturbed child at the moment.

This relinquishment of claims, however, is easier said than done. What is a teacher to do when, as happened the other day in a Chicago elementary school, a lonely Negro girl comes to her to complain of the fact that she has "no friends in school," and that her mother will not allow her to make friends by inviting any children to her home? Is the teacher to send this twelve-year-old child back to her hopeless English lesson? What is the teacher to do as she watches a twelve-year-old boy, son of Jewish immigrant parents, develop an increasing contempt for children who have not raced through as many encyclopedias as he has in amassing an armory of unrelated facts with which, in quizkid style, he goes into battle? Is she to wait until the school, which needs a new building (though in general our school buildings are the cathedrals of our time) and more teachers, gets around to appointing a school psychologist? She would have to be more unequivocally devoted to learning for its own sake than are most of my university colleagues in order to be able to resist the appeal to her motherly, or clinical, sympathies. The result is that she pays less attention to the balanced and potentially gifted child who, she rationalizes, can look after himself.

In this situation, where the schools and the teachers cannot possibly meet all the demands they put on themselves, I think it would be helpful to develop a systematic theory of education as *counter-cyclical*. Just as Keynesian economics would have the government and the banks save in a time of inflation and spend in a time of depression, so teachers, in selecting among the expectations held out to them, have some modest opportunities to oppose "life" in its momentary excesses. A generation or so ago teachers were farsighted in being preoccupied with social skills, and in those many too many areas where underprivileged children still lack access to those skills, it remains important to emphasize them. In fact, to return to our theme at the beginning of the article, where the community continues to be production-minded, the schools can afford to emphasize the gentler arts of social and personal understanding; even today, the country is undoubtedly overplentifully supplied with sadistic teachers who employ their subject-matter superiorities to torment children in the Victorian manner. Increasingly, however, such settings would appear to be waning in frequency and impact; as the community becomes more consumption-minded, and as the out-of-school context helps cultivate the children's social skills, humaneness as such in the schools may on occasion be given a slightly lower priority and an emphasis on the teacher's own production-mindedness—whether with respect to French, football, or mathematics—is likely to be more beneficial and less traumatic. For in the middle-class homes of today children are listened to—they are no longer seen and not heard. The home is itself a "communication laboratory," at least in the middle class. Children can and do use the movies, TV, comics, and magazines like *Seventeen*, as well as each other's example, to learn proper social behavior, especially since they no longer have to do many chores around the house. No one should sneer at the children's social proficiencies: if one compares American young people with their counterparts a generation ago (or in Europe today) one is struck by their poise, their understanding of themselves, each other, and adults; they can often handle touchy questions with a tact and facility our diplomats might well envy. As in the comic strip *Penny*, it is often the adults, not the adolescents, who are the awkward ones. But this very discrepancy, as I have observed, leads both parents and teachers, often conscious of their own childhood inadequacies and gaucheries, to give many children what amounts to postgraduate education in sociability when what they need, for the most part, is something very different. What they need, I suggest, is protection for those long-term intellectual and humanistic interests that are momentarily under severe pressure from so many sides.

From this perspective, progressive education was undoubtedly a counter-cyclical force a generation ago (as it still is in many "backward" areas and for many individual children). It put pressure on conservative and conventional parents, and on their children. It involved the family in a dialetic which, if at times confusing, was frequently productive for all members—for the parents who strove to "keep up," and for the children who strove to understand and even sympathize with parents. Today, in many more prosperous suburbs, it is these children who presently are parents, and whose children are in turn attending schools that are no longer bucking the tide, are no longer experimental. No strong disagreements within the family, no tensions between family and school now require creative resolution. Yet the relaxed adjustment achieved in this way, while in some respects an undeniable advance over earlier miseries, means in terms of the life cycle less variety and less challenge.

This implies that, in many schools, where warm and outgoing teachers are present in sufficient number, effort should be directed to seeing that the children have contact with at least one teacher who cares profoundly about a subject matter like Latin or music which is at first sight remote from the concerns of everyday life. To be sure, such a teacher need not be indifferent to children. She may well come to be particularly attached to those pupils who are attached to her subject (as in Mary McCarthy's recent personal memoir). Such a person can do something to set up a competing model to the mediocrity that results from turning a school entirely over to teachers who have been shy and want to be personable and who hence care too much whether the children respond pleasantly to them and to each other; these are the teachers who have entered the profession to escape the farm or the working class and who come to be captivated by the paraphernalia of professionalism, such as "teacher talk" about classroom skills and audio-visual aids. If schools were to eliminate the difficult or eccentric teachers who present alternative models of good teaching, they would indeed become like life in 1955, only more so.

For truly high aims, whether they be occupational, personal, or intellectual, tend to contradict life as it is lived in any given place and time. Schools in the past, more by accident and even ignorance than design, have opened vistas to such aims (for at least a minority) by their very *un-lifelike* character. A student who, through a devoted teacher, could learn to live with Cicero or Mercutio, Joan of Arc or Jane Austen, might well succeed in discovering forms of existence transcending the observable in home or playground: transcending both the bread salesman and the idea salesman.

If children, tough and adaptable creatures that they are, can stand being confronted with a wider gamut of personal models than most public schools now make available, all I have said so far would imply that teachers—a group who reach a plateau of grown-upness early and stay on it long—are much less hardy and cannot be asked to face the personal consequences of counter-cyclical behavior. Indeed, in writing as I do I have the ironical misgiving that I, too, may only be adding to expectations for omnicompetence which, as I have contended, are already unrealistic. Just as I would not expect a banker who believed a depression was coming, and who had read Keynes, to invest his personal fortune as a way of increasing purchasing power, so I do not expect individual teachers to carry the whole system on their backs while beginning a counter-cyclical revolution. Still, I want to encourage some of them to give up trying to be psychiatrists, mothers, and moralists, to give up making citizens, demo-crats, and tolerant children. Could they not be persuaded to concentrate more than many now feel justified in doing on their roles as teachers of specific subjects? This is, after all, a job no one else is assigned or trained to do.

I am not arguing that the entire responsibility for counter-cyclical cultural activity must be borne by the secondary schools. The universities, the media, and the other makers of taste and opinion have a similar responsibility. Nor am I contending for a simple "middle way" between extremes, which can be discovered by a metaphorical thermostat or servo-mechanism. We lack at present the most elementary indices for telling, let us say, that the coming generation will possess "enough" social skills but not enough musical or mathematical ones. I am arguing that, for the foreseeable future, no agency with any leeway should make it its business to imitate "life" or to be "realistic" in the Philistine sense of that term, but rather that it should make a good guess as to where "life" is leading, and then proceed to criticize and correct it. Since in most quarters the dangers of intellectual arrogance are fast passing, school officials might make it a matter of professional pride to be as unpopular (short of dismissal) with the community as they can. It would help educate parents as well as children if a few principals and superintendents supported their teachers against any pressures for lowering of standards and insisted on high competence in subject matter in as many appointees as possible. This will occasionally involve them in defending and befriending someone like our drama teacher; eccentric as such teachers are apt to be in their devotion to a subject, they may not be quite the best "team players" in the teacher-colleague group.

Paradoxically, it is in a non-academic area that this is already standard practice. I refer to the sports coach, who is ordinarily expected to get his pupils to do their best (even, sometimes, at shocking cost to body and soul). In this field, "democracy" means a free way for talent and not, save in a few schools which are hostile to competition as such, that everyone must proceed at a medium pace, or be elected rather than selected for the team. Many of us— forgetting that before the days of organized sports our schools and colleges were locales of barely controlled roistering—tend to look down on the coach, though he may today be a better teacher than many of his colleagues by virtue of his more unequivocal aims: the excellence of his pupils is the answer to his prayers. Even while we moderate his zeal, we might use it as a model for teachers of painting and poetry, some of whom should unquestionably concern themselves with children's self-expression, but others with giving even the less gifted children the valuable sense that there are cultural continuities and standards of excellence.

Is there any chance for such a program? The same social developments which have put brakes on old-fashioned competition have made it possible to recruit a new sort of teacher and school official—a person whose eye is set not on money or social success but on leading a useful life of service. Perhaps the majority of these end up in private schools; and this will go on as long as, in a great many states, public school teachers most easily win a certificate by attending the teachers colleges or those university stepchildren, the education departments of state universities. These colleges and departments are not exactly centers of intellectual excitement or cultivation. Inasmuch as well-established private schools can withstand community pressures far better than most public schools they are therefore better prepared to experiment with counter-cyclical measures. Yet some teachers manage to shuttle between public and private schools, and it makes sense to encourage as many as possible to spend some time in a model school, even if not permanently retained there. A similar hope guided the Whitney Foundation to invite a group of public high school teachers from different states to spend a year at Columbia or Yale with no assignment to study education but simply to expand their personal as well as broad academic horizons. (When I met with the Columbia group I was reminded of how many enthusiastic and devoted teachers the public school system can still boast.) Not all of today's young people who (as they often put it) want to "work with children" are devoid of interest in a topic which is to be introduced to children. I am told that the Fellows who have already gone back to their former schools have in many instances taken the leadership in moves to strengthen the humanistic and intellectually challenging elements of the high school program.

A last word on one other important counter-cyclical possibility. Chicago research has indicated there are a few schools in slum districts from which teachers do not attempt to flee, even when entitled to by length of service. These turn out to be schools where the principal is of such caliber as to win the devotion of his teachers; as his reputation grows, he can even attract them. The principal therefore can, if he has talent and character, reverse the usual situation in which the most deprived children are taught either by the most inexperienced or by the most hardened and indifferent teachers. He can, in fact, reverse the vicious circle of mediocrity.

However, such principals are naturally scarce, and great changes in salaries and systems of recruitment are not in prospect. Indeed, I sometimes feel that even well-intended criticism of the schools serves, in the present climate of budget and opinion, only to make school officials and teachers still more nervous and fearful of community pressure than they already are, with inevitably baneful effects on them and on pupils. Must we then look for counter-cyclical measures outside the education industry entirely? Counter-cyclical strategy in general must be flexible. And I am inclined to ask, for instance, whether educational television may not provide a new opportunity for reaching children with challenging ideas and cultivated goals, either directly or by tie-ins with other community facilities such as libraries and museums. It is at least arguable that TV is at present open and experimental in a way that the public schools cannot possibly be—even though, like the schools, it is subject to enormous pressures to be pious and please everybody.

Even now, however, one finds children for whom the mass media have opened windows, and not only children whose addiction to a monotone of programming has simply made the schools' task appear more hopeless than heretofore. Keynesian theory leads one always to look for the "multiplier" effect—the relatively small increase in the rate of capital investment that can set off momentous economic dynamisms. In Williamsburg, a New York City slum of a generation ago, the public library served (as Alfred Kazin has poignantly recalled) as a storehouse of excitement for children bored to distraction at the run-down neighborhood school. If one looks at the little blue lights of TV that serve as compensation for an underprivileged existence in Harlem, or Chicago's Bronzeville, one cannot help but wonder what chances there are of a child's catching fire from a play, or a poem read aloud, or a concert. But could it be that, just as some TV dramas have followed the movies in making school teachers out to be "good guys" or "pin-ups," the public school teacher who now sees TV as one more enemy may conceivably find her roles clarified and her purposes supported by new images quite beyond the sabotage of the supervisor and the censorship of the school board?

🐾 🐾 🐾

*Robert M. Hutchins*

# The Meaning and Significance of Academic Freedom[1]

THE ARGUMENTS for academic freedom are the same as those for freedom of speech, and they rest on the same foundation. Here are the familiar words of John Stuart Mill:

> If all mankind minus one were of one opinion, and only one person were of the contrary opinion, mankind would be no more justified in silencing that one person, than he, if he had the power, would be justified in silencing mankind. . . . the peculiar evil of silencing the expression of an opinion is, that it is robbing the human race; posterity as well as the existing generation; those who dissent from the opinion, still more than those who hold it. If the opinion is right, they are deprived of the opportunity of exchanging error for truth: if wrong, they lose, what is almost as great a benefit, the clearer perception and livelier impression of truth, produced by its collision with error.

Man is a learning animal. The state is an association the primary aim of which is the virtue and intelligence of the people. Men learn by discussion, through the clash of opinion. The best and most progressive society is that in which expression is freest. Mill said, "There ought to exist the fullest liberty of professing and discussing, as a matter of ethical conviction, any doctrine, however immoral it may be considered." The civilization we seek is the civilization of the dialogue, the civilization of the logos.

In such a society the intelligent man and the good citizen are identical. The educational system does not aim at indoctrination in accepted values but at the

[1] From *The Annals of the American Academy of Political and Social Science*, XXX (July, 1955), 72-78. Copyright, 1955, The American Academy of Political and Social Science.

improvement of society through the production of the intelligent man and the good citizen. Education necessarily involves the critical examination of conflicting points of view; it cannot flourish in the absence of free inquiry and discussion.

In a democracy what the public needs to know about the teachers in the educational system is that they are competent. The competent teacher knows the subject he is teaching and how to communicate it to his pupils. Unlike the teacher in a totalitarian state, he is not supposed to purvey the prevailing dogma. He is supposed to encourage his students to use their own intelligence and to reach their own conclusions.

The definition of competence does not shift with every wind of prejudice, religious, political, racial, or economic. If competence had been the issue at Brown University during the free silver controversy, the President would not have been asked to resign because of his premature distaste for the Gold Standard. The modern note was struck there. What was requested of the President was "not a renunciation of his views, but a forbearance to promulgate them." And the reason was that these views were "injurious to the pecuniary interests of the University." On the other hand, the standard of competence did protect a professor at the University of Chicago who was a leading critic of Samuel Insull and the other local oligarchs of the time. He was doubtless injurious to the pecuniary interests of the university, but he and it lived through it, and he is today the senior Senator from Illinois.

## WRONG QUESTIONS

We have been stifling education in this country because we have been asking the wrong questions. If you are asking the right questions, you ask about a subject of discussion whether it is important. You do not forbid students to discuss a subject, like the entry of Red China into the United Nations, on the ground that it is too important. The right question about a subject of research and the methods of investigation is whether competent scholars believe that the subject should be investigated and that this is the way to investigate it. You do not permit the Post Office Department to protect the Johns Hopkins School of Advanced International Studies from *Izvestia* and *Pravda*. The right question about a textbook is whether competent people think it can make a contribution to education. You do not ask whether incompetent people are going to be offended by passages taken out of context. The right question about a research man on unclassified work is whether he is competent to do it. You do not act like the United States Public Health Service and weaken the country by withdrawing contracts from research workers on unstated grounds that can only be grounds of loyalty.

As I have said, the right question about a teacher is whether he is competent. If we had been asking about competence we should have had quite a different atmosphere in the case of teachers who were Communists or ex-Communists, who refused to testify about themselves, or who declined to discuss the political affiliations of others. We have been so busy being sophisticated anti-Communists, detecting the shifts and devices of Communist infiltration, that we have failed to observe that our educational responsibility is to have a good educational system. We do not discharge that responsibility by invading civil liberties, reducing the number of qualified teachers available, eliminating good textbooks, and intimidating the teaching staff. The standard of competence means that there must be some relation between the charges against a teacher and the quality of his teaching. The standard of competence would have protected us against teachers following a party line or conducting propaganda. If a teacher sought to indoctrinate his pupils, which is the only circumstance under which he could be dangerous as a teacher, he would be incompetent, and should be removed as such. The standard of competence would have saved us from the excesses of the silly season, such as the refusal of the University of Washington to let Professor Oppenheimer lecture there on physics, and from the consequences of concentrating on the negative task of preventing one particular unpopular variety of infiltration. If we had used the standard of competence we should have been free to fix our minds on the positive responsibility of building an educational system, and with half the energy we have put into being scared to death we might have built a great one.

Since our guilty conscience tells us that there ought to be some connection between what a man does and the punishment visited upon him, we often try to pretend that this is the rule we are following. The Attorney General of the United States, speaking in New York three weeks ago, said that schools should not be sanctuaries or proving grounds "for subversives shaping the minds of innocent children."

This picture of subversives shaping the minds of innocent children has nothing to do with the case. The teachers who have lost their jobs in the campaign against subversives have not been charged with doing anything to the minds of any children. The case of Goldie Watson here in Philadelphia is typical: testimony about the good she had done the minds of the children in her classes was rejected as impertinent. The only evidence allowed was as to whether she had declined to answer questions about her political affiliations. She had, and she was fired. The same procedure seems to be followed everywhere, even at Harvard. When a professor there is called on the carpet, the issue is whether he is a member of something or other, or whether he has lied or refused to answer questions about such membership. The matter of his competence in his field or what he has done to the innocent minds of the Harvard students is never referred to.

### FEAR OF IDEAS

We are getting so afraid of ideas that we are afraid of people who associate with people who are said to have ideas, even if they themselves have not expressed them. The State Curriculum Commission of California is now studying investigators' reports on the authors of twenty-three textbooks. Dr. C. C.

Trillingham, Los Angeles County Superintendent of Schools and a member of the commission, said, "If an author is aligned with the Communists, we don't want his textbook, even if there is no Red propaganda in it."

We regard what a man says as irrelevant in determining whether we will listen to him. What a man does in his job is irrelevant in determining whether he should continue in it. This amounts to a decision that people whose ideas or whose associates' ideas we regard as dangerous cannot be permitted to earn a living or to make a contribution in any capacity to the well-being of the community. The Supreme Court of California has just taken this logical next step: it has held, in effect, that a Communist can have no contractual rights that the rest of us are bound to respect.

Not long ago at a dinner of the senior members of the faculty of the University of Birmingham in England, I sat across the table from a professor who is a member of the executive committee of the Communist party of Great Britain. The British appear to be getting value out of a scholar whom none of the great American universities could appoint.

One of the more important advances in law and government effected by the struggles of our ancestors is that proclaimed by the Fifth Amendment. Why should the government demand that a man convict himself out of his own mouth instead of requiring the prosecution to make the effort to establish the charges that it has brought against him? All the Fifth Amendment means is: prove it. Injury is added to insult if there is no pretence that the questions asked must be relevant or proper. In some public school systems refusal to answer any questions by the Board of Education or any other public body is insubordination; insubordination justifies dismissal.

Surely the issue is whether the questions are legitimate. It cannot be insubordination to refuse to answer illegitimate questions. We have gone very far under the influence of one of the rollicking dicta of Mr. Justice Holmes, that there is no constitutional right to be a policeman; but not so far that public employment can be denied on a ground that has nothing to do with the duties to be performed. If the President were to refuse to employ baldheaded men in the federal establishment, the Supreme Court would find, I believe, that the bald had been deprived of their constitutional rights.

IS IT TOO LATE?

You may say that the issue I am discussing is academic in every sense: there is no use now in talking about the right of Communists, ex-Communists, or persons who decline to answer questions about their political affiliations to teach in the United States. Milton Mayer in his forthcoming book, *They Thought They Were Free*, tells the story of the way history passed Martin Niemoeller by. When the Nazis attacked the Communists, he was a little uneasy, but he was not a Communist, and he did nothing. When they attacked the Socialists, he was uneasy, but he was not a Socialist, and he did nothing. They went after the schools, the press, and the Jews, but he was not directly affected, and he did nothing. Then they attacked the Church. Pastor Niemoeller was a churchman. He tried to do something, but it was too late.

I hope it is not too late to point out where our preoccupation with public relations and our failure of courage and intelligence may take us. The New York *Times* on March 17 and the New York *Herald Tribune* on March 19 published editorials on the question whether teachers who decline to testify about others should be dismissed. The significant thing about the editorials is this: they both, perhaps unconsciously, extend the limits of the prevailing boycott. The *Times* condemns "adherence to Communist doctrine," thus adding theoretical Marxists to those automatically disqualified. The *Herald Tribune* comes out against Communists "or any other brands of subversives," thus opening vast new unmapped areas of investigation, recrimination, and confusion.

### REECE COMMITTEE

These two newspapers bitterly attacked the Reece committee, appointed in the House to investigate foundations; but they appear to have succumbed to its influence, which is another evidence that if you say something outrageous authoritatively, loudly, and often enough you will eventually find yourself quoted in the most respectable places. The Reece committee includes among the subversives almost anybody who differs with the two members of the committee who constitute the majority. Zechariah Chafee, Jr., said at the University of Oregon last October, "The word 'subversive' has no precise definition in American law. It is as vague as 'heretical' was in the medieval trials which sent men to the stake." Leading the list of Reece committee subversives are those who do not share its philosophical prejudices. The committee condemned a philosophical doctrine, empiricism, and those who hold it as the fountainhead of the subversive tendencies now engulfing the country. If a philosophical position can be treasonable, particularly one as harmless as a preference for fact over theory, and if two politicians can make it treasonable, freedom of thought, discussion, and teaching may not be with us long.

By repetition the Reece committee is obtaining unconscious acceptance of another proposition, which, coupled with the proposition that politicians may declare a doctrine and its adherents subversive, still further imperils freedom of teaching and inquiry. This is the proposition that tax-exempt money is public money and that a tax-exempt institution is therefore subject to a special variety of public surveillance. An extension of this proposition is found in the California statute requiring all claimants of tax exemption to take a nondisloyalty oath. If carried to the logical limits hinted at in the Reece Report, this notion of the public control of private, tax-exempt corporations could deprive the independent educational institutions of this country of their autonomy, that characteristic which has given them their value in the development of the American educational system.

Tax exemption is conferred for the purpose of facilitating the performance of a public task by a private agency. A corporation that carries on education and research to that extent relieves the taxpayers of their obligation to finance such work in state-supported institutions. Tax exemption imposes no duty on colleges and universities except that of conducting teaching and research according to their best judgment of what good teaching and research are. It does not impose the duty of making sure that the teaching and research conform to the views of the majority of a legislative committee.

### CALIFORNIA SENATE COMMITTEE ON UN-AMERICAN ACTIVITIES

Consider what those views might be. Richard E. Combs, Chief Counsel for the California Senate Committee on Un-American Activities, testified two years ago before a subcommittee of the United States Senate. He gave an account of how Communists reorient courses of instruction. He thought it worth while to report that the name of a course at a California university had been changed from public speaking to speech, and the books had been changed from Robert Louis Stevenson, Masefield, and Kipling to John Stuart Mill. The subversive nature of these changes may not be clear to you, but it was clear to Mr. Combs and, from all that appears, to the California committee that employs him and the committee of the United States Senate before which he testified. The appraisal of courses of study or of the performance of teachers is a professional job, not to be undertaken by the naïve and unskilled.

Consider the role of the California Senate Committee on Un-American Activities in the administration of California institutions of higher learning. The committee claims that a chain of security officers on campuses has been welded by its efforts. If its claims are correct—and they have been disputed—professors and students at eleven institutions are being continuously spied upon for the benefit of a legislative committee. The committee has an arrangement whereby it passes on the qualifications of members and prospective members of the faculties from the standpoint of their Americanism. The reason for this is said to be that the colleges and universities are not competent to assess the Americanism of their teachers, and the committee is. According to the committee at least a hundred members of these faculties have been forced to resign and at least one hundred prospective members have failed of appointment because of the committee's work. It is too bad that the committee has not disclosed the information that led to the interdiction of its victims. One shudders to think that it may have been enough to have been heard quoting John Stuart Mill.

### BEHIND ACADEMIC FREEDOM

But the issue of legal control is not basic. Academic freedom comes and goes because of some conviction about the purpose of education on the part of those who make the decisions in society. The Kaiser gave professors freedom of research because he believed that this was one way to make Germany strong and prosperous. This freedom did not extend to professors who wanted to engage actively in politics on the wrong side, the side of the Social Democratic party. The Kaiser did not set a high value on independent criticism.

In a democratic community the question is what do the people think education is and what do they think it is for? I once asked a former Minister of Education of the Netherlands what would have happened if he had exercised his undoubted legal authority and appointed professors of whom the faculties of the Dutch universities did not approve. He said, "My government would have fallen." He meant that the people of Holland would not tolerate political interference with the universities: they understood the universities well enough to recognize interference when they saw it and felt strongly enough about it to make their wishes effective.

The public officers and businessmen who are the trustees of the provincial universities in the United Kingdom have legal control over them, but would never think of exercising it in any matter affecting education and research. They limit themselves to business. The taxpayers now meet more than half the cost of Oxford and Cambridge, but no Englishman supposes that this entitles the government to exert any influence in their academic affairs.

If the people believe that independent thought and criticism are essential to the progress of society, if they think that universities are centers of such criticism and that the rest of the educational system is intended primarily to prepare the citizen to think for himself, then academic freedom will not be a problem, it will be a fact. Under these circumstances teachers would not be second-class citizens, subject to limitations of expression and behavior that show the public thinks the teacher of today is the nursemaid of yesterday. A teacher would be appointed because he was capable of independent thought and criticism and because he could help the rising generation learn to think for itself. He would be removed only if those who appointed him proved to be mistaken in these matters. The proof of their error would have to be made to persons who could understand the issue—an out-of-hand administrative removal approved by a board of laymen without participation by academic experts is a denial of academic freedom.

### ACADEMIC RESPONSIBILITY

The people of this country think that education is a perfectly splendid thing and have not the faintest idea of what it is about. The reason that they are in this condition is that educators have had no time and little inclination to explain. After all, the great desideratum of American education in the last thirty-five years has been money. If you want money, you do not talk about independent thought and criticism; you do not engage in it too obtrusively; you may even suppress it if it becomes too flagrant. To get money you must be popular. "He thinks too much" is a classical reference to an unpopular man. Or as a great industrialist once remarked to a friend of mine, "You are either a Communist or a thinker."

I have no doubt that much of the trouble of recent years about academic freedom has been the result of the cold war and our panic about it. As Professor Chafee has said, "Freedom of speech belongs to a people which is free from fear." But the basic issue is public understanding. If public understanding had been serious and complete, the cold war could not have thrown us off our balance.

I do not deny that many eloquent statements of the purpose of American education have been made. They cannot offset the impression created by the official propaganda of educational institutions, by their fatuous efforts to please everybody, and by their emphasis on the nonintellectual and even anti-intellectual activities associated with education in this country. Freedom of teaching and research will not survive unless the people understand why it should. They will not understand if there is no relation between the freedom that is claimed and the purpose it is supposed to serve. If the teacher of today is the nursemaid of yesterday, he does not need academic freedom—at least the nursemaid never did.

Academic freedom is indispensable to the high calling of the academic profession. If the profession is true to the calling, it will deserve the freedom, and it will get it.

❦ ❦ ❦

## A. E. Housman

# Introductory Lecture[1]

THE acquisition of knowledge needs no formal justification: its true sanction is a much simpler affair, and inherent in itself. People are too prone to torment themselves with devising far-fetched reasons: they cannot be content with the simple truth asserted by Aristotle: "all men possess by nature a craving for knowledge." πάντες ἄνθρωποι τοῦ εἰδέναι ὀρέγονται φύσει. This is no rare endowment scattered sparingly from heaven that falls on a few heads and passes others by: curiosity, the desire to know things as they are, is a craving no less native to the being of man, no less universal through mankind, than the craving for food and drink. And do you suppose that such a desire means nothing? The very definition of the good, says Aristotle again, is that which all desire. Whatever is pleasant is good, unless it can be shewn that in the long run it is harmful, or, in other words, not pleasant but unpleasant. Mr. Spencer himself on another subject speaks thus: "So profound an ignorance is there of the laws of life, that men do not even know that their sensations are their natural guides, and (when not rendered morbid by long continued disobedience) their trustworthy guides." The desire of knowledge does not need, nor

[1] From A. E. Housman, *Introductory Lecture*, 1937, pp. 26-36. By permission of Cambridge University Press

could it possibly possess, any higher or more authentic sanction than the happiness which attends its gratification.

Perhaps it will be objected that we see, every day of our lives, plenty of people who exhibit no pleasure in learning and experience no desire to know; people, as Plato agreeably puts it, who wallow in ignorance with the complacency of a brutal hog. We do; and here is the reason. If the cravings of hunger and thirst are denied satisfaction, if a man is kept from food and drink, the man starves to death, and there is an end of him. This is a result which arrests the attention of even the least observant mind; so it is generally recognised that hunger and thirst cannot be neglected with impunity, that a man ought to eat and drink. But if the craving for knowledge is denied satisfaction, the result which follows is not so striking to the eye. The man, worse luck, does not starve to death. He still preserves the aspect and motions of a living human being; so people think that the hunger and thirst for knowledge can be neglected with impunity. And yet, though the man does not die altogether, part of him dies, part of him starves to death: as Plato says, he never attains completeness and health, but walks lame to the end of his life and returns imperfect and good for nothing to the world below.

But the desire of knowledge, stifle it though you may, is none the less originally born with every man; and nature does not implant desires in us for nothing, nor endow us with faculties in vain. "Sure," says Hamlet,

> Sure, He that made us with such large discourse,
> Looking before and after, gave us not
> That capability and godlike reason
> To fust in us unused.

The faculty of learning is ours that we may find in its exercise that delight which arises from the unimpeded activity of any energy in the groove nature meant it to run in. Let a man acquire knowledge not for this or that external and incidental good which may chance to result from it, but for itself; not because it is useful or ornamental, but because it is knowledge, and therefore good for man to acquire. "Brothers," says Ulysses in Dante, when with his old and tardy companions he had left Seville on the right hand and Ceuta on the other, and was come to that narrow pass where Hercules assigned his landmarks to hinder man from venturing farther: "Brothers, who through a hundred thousand dangers have reached the West, deny not, to this brief vigil of your senses that remains, experience of the unpeopled world behind the sunset. Consider of what seed ye are sprung: ye were not formed to live like brutes, but to follow virtue and knowledge." For knowledge resembles virtue in this, and differs in this from other possessions, that it is not merely a means of procuring good, but is good in itself simply: it is not a coin which we pay down to purchase happiness, but has happiness indissolubly bound up with it. Fortitude and continence and honesty are not commended to us on the ground that they conduce, as on the whole they do conduce, to material success, nor yet on the ground that they will be rewarded hereafter: those whose office it is to exhort mankind to virtue are ashamed to degrade the cause they plead by proffering such lures as these. And let us too disdain to take lower ground in commending knowledge: let us insist that the pursuit of knowledge, like the pursuit of righteousness, is part of man's duty to himself, and remember the Scripture where it is written: "He that refuseth instruction despiseth his own soul."

I will not say, as Prof. Tyndall has somewhere said, that all happiness belongs to him who can say from his heart "I covet truth." Entire happiness is not attainable either by this or by any other method. Nay it may be urged on the contrary that the pursuit of truth in some directions is even injurious to happiness, because it compels us to take leave of delusions which were pleasant while they lasted. It may be urged that the light shed on the origin and destiny of man by the pursuit of truth in some directions is not altogether a cheerful light. It may be urged that man stands to-day in the position of one who has been reared from his cradle as the child of a noble race and the heir to great possessions, and who finds at his coming of age that he has been deceived alike as to his origin and his expectations, that he neither springs of the high lineage he fancied, nor will inherit the vast estate he looked for, but must put off his towering pride, and contract his boundless hopes, and begin the world anew from a lower level: and this, it may be urged, comes of pursuing knowledge. But even conceding this, I suppose the answer to be that knowledge, and especially disagreeable knowledge, cannot by any art be totally excluded even from those who do not seek it. Wisdom, said Aeschylus long ago, comes to men whether they will or no. The house of delusions is cheap to build, but draughty to live in, and ready at any instant to fall; and it is surely truer prudence to move our furniture betimes into the open air than to stay indoors until our tenement tumbles about our ears. It is and it must in the long run be better for a man to see things as they are than to be ignorant of them; just as there is less fear of stumbling or of striking against corners in the daylight than in the dark.

Nor again will I pretend that, as Bacon asserts, "the pleasure and delight of knowledge and learning far surpasseth all other in nature." This is too much the language of a salesman crying his own wares. The pleasures of the intellect are notoriously less vivid than either the pleasures of sense or the pleasures of the affections, and therefore, especially in the season of youth, the pursuit of knowledge is likely enough to be neglected and lightly esteemed in comparison with other pursuits offering much stronger immediate attractions. But the pleasure of learning and knowing, though not the keenest, is yet the least perishable of pleasures; the least subject to external things, and the play of chance, and the wear of time. And as a prudent man puts money by to serve as a provision for the material wants of his old age, so too he needs to lay up against the end of his days provision for the intellect. As the years go by, comparative values are found to alter: Time, says Sophocles, takes many things which once were pleasures and brings them nearer to pain. In the day when the strong men shall bow themselves, and desire shall fail, it will be a matter of yet more concern than now, whether one can say "my mind to me a kingdom is"; and whether the windows of the soul look out upon a broad and delightful landscape, or face nothing but a brick wall.

Well then, once we have recognised that knowledge in itself is good for man, we shall need to invent no pretexts for studying this subject or that; we shall import no extraneous considerations of use or ornament to justify us in learning one thing rather than another. If a certain department of knowledge specially attracts a man, let him study that, and study it because it attracts him; and let him not fabricate excuses for that which requires no excuse, but rest assured that the reason why it most attracts him is that it is best for him. The majority of mankind, as is only natural, will be most attracted by those sciences which most nearly concern human life; those sciences which, in Bacon's phrase, are drenched in flesh and blood, or, in the more elegant language of the *Daily Telegraph*, palpitate with actuality. The men who are attracted to the drier and the less palpitating sciences, say logic or pure mathematics or textual criticism, are likely to be fewer in number; but they are not to suppose that the comparative unpopularity of such learning renders it any the less worthy of pursuit. Nay they may if they like console themselves with Bacon's observation that "this same *lumen siccum* doth parch and offend most men's watery and soft natures," and infer, if it pleases them, that their natures are less soft and watery than other men's. But be that as it may, we can all dwell together in unity without crying up our own pursuits or depreciating the pursuits of others on factitious grounds. We are not like the Ottoman sultans of old time, who thought they could never enjoy a moment's security till they had murdered all their brothers. There is no rivalry between the studies of Arts and Laws and Science but the rivalry of fellow-soldiers in striving which can most victoriously achieve the common end of all, to set back the frontier of darkness.

It is the glory of God, says Solomon, to conceal a thing: but the honour of kings is to search out a matter. Kings have long abdicated that province; and we students are come into their inheritance: it is our honour to search out the things which God has concealed. In Germany at Easter time they hide coloured eggs about the house and the garden that the children may amuse themselves in hunting after them and finding them. It is to some such game of hide-and-seek that we are invited by that power which planted in us the desire to find out what is concealed, and stored the universe with hidden things that we might delight ourselves in discovering them. And the pleasure of discovery differs from other pleasures in this, that it is shadowed by no fear of satiety on the one hand or of frustration on the other. Other desires perish in their gratification, but the desire of knowledge never: the eye is not satisfied with seeing nor the ear filled with hearing. Other desires become the occasion of pain through dearth of the material to gratify them, but not the desire of knowledge: the sum of things to be known is inexhaustible, and how ever long we read we shall never come to the end of our story-book. So long as the mind of man is what it is, it will continue to exult in advancing on the unknown throughout the infinite field of the universe; and the tree of knowledge will remain for ever, as it was in the beginning, a tree to be desired to make one wise.

# ❧ ❧ ❧ II. Reading and Writing

# Reading

*Francis Bacon*

## Of Studies[1]

STUDIES serve for delight, for ornament, and for ability. Their chief use for delight is in privateness and retiring; for ornament, is in discourse; and for ability, is in the judgment and disposition of business; for expert men can execute, and perhaps judge of particulars, one by one; but the general counsels, and the plots and marshaling of affairs come best from those that are learned. To spend too much time in studies is sloth; to use them too much for ornament is affectation; to make judgment wholly by their rules is the humor of a scholar. They perfect nature, and are perfected by experience; for natural abilities are like natural plants, that need pruning by study; and studies themselves do give forth directions too much at large, except they be bounded in by experience. Crafty men contemn studies, simple men admire them, and wise men use them; for they teach not their own use; but that is a wisdom without them and above them, won by observation. Read not to contradict and confute, nor to believe and take for granted, nor to find talk and discourse, but to weigh and consider. Some books are to be tasted, others to be swallowed, and some few to be chewed and digested; that is, some books are to be read only in parts; others to be read but not curiously, and some few to be read wholly, and with diligence and attention. Some books also may be read by deputy, and extracts made of them by others; but that would be only in the less important arguments and the meaner sort of books; else distilled books are, like common distilled waters, flashy things. Reading maketh a full man; conference a ready man; and writing an exact man. And, therefore, if a man write little, he had need have a great memory; if he confer little, he had need have a present wit; and if he read little, he had need have much cunning, to seem to know that he doth not. Histories make men wise; poets, witty; the mathematics, subtle; natural philosophy, deep; moral, grave; logic and rhetoric, able to contend; *Abeunt studia in mores.*[2] Nay, there is no stand or impediment in the wit but

---

[1] From *The Essayes or Counsels, Civill and Morall* (enlarged ed., London, 1625), No. 50. The text has been somewhat modernized.

[2] Studies form manners.

may be wrought out by fit studies; like as diseases of the body may have appropriate exercises. Bowling is good for the stone and reins, shooting for the lungs and breast, gentle walking for the stomach, riding for the head and the like. So if a man's wit be wandering, let him study the mathematics; for in demonstrations, if his wit be called away never so little, he must begin again. If his wit be not apt to distinguish or find differences, let him study the schoolmen; for they are *cymini sectores*.[3] If he be not apt to beat over matters, and to call up one thing to prove and illustrate another, let him study the lawyers' cases; so every defect of the mind may have a special receipt.

🌢 🌢 🌢

*Chauncey B. Tinker*

# The Library[1]

SOON after the members of the Freshman Class are admitted to college, they are addressed by a series of upper-classmen who represent the various activities with which the place abounds. The post of honour is usually given to the captain of the football team, who pleads for a large squad and attendance at the games. The football player is succeeded by those who advertise the other sports; and they, in turn, by the representatives of the literary world: students are not to forget the importance of the college newspaper (be it daily or weekly is a matter of no consequence). There are often social and fraternity appeals added to the confusion; and, lastly, religious and scholarly activities—the class deacon and the president of Phi Beta Kappa—are given a belated hearing. But even then, when the newly-enrolled college-man has been shown all the rewards that may come from giving his allegiance to the world, it is doubtful whether any of the speakers will have mentioned the College Library.

This of course is because the Library has no outward and visible reward to offer to its devotees. Even to many who might become devotees it seems like a cold and dusty place, where the books are locked away in distant "stacks" which the student cannot visit, and which are too often presided over by male or female dragons whose obvious aim seems to be to protect them from those who wish to use them. There is an old story told of a triumphant librarian who, on a famous occasion, boasted that all the books save one were on the shelves, and, added he, "I know where that is, and to-morrow the library will be complete." In opposition to such a theory as this it would be wiser to contend that the ideal library is one in which the shelves are empty, since the books are all in circulation. Between these two contrary states, the College Library preserves a precarious life. The circulation of its books is like the

[3] Dividers of cuminseed, i.e., hairsplitters.

[1] From *On Going to College: A Symposium*, 1938, pp. 293-298. By permission of Oxford University Press, New York.

circulation of the blood, passing constantly back and forth from the heart to the members of the body.

The frequent assertion that the Library is the heart and center of the College is the simple truth. All scholarly work, and all undergraduate study as well, consists either of the reading and interpretation of the recorded thought of the past or of the setting down of new information for the guidance of posterity. This is true of science as well as of the "humanities." Experiments made in laboratories are recorded, first of all, in note-books and later in the learned publications of the science concerned. The results of all such work are promptly given to the world, so that others may use and profit by them. If the power of recording thought in writing, or print, which is only another form of writing, were taken from us,—by divine *fiat*, let us say,—all civilization would cease at once, and we should relapse into the state of beasts.

The average devotee of a library passes, commonly, through three stages. A man's first notion regarding a public library is that it is filled with books to amuse our leisure. It is very probable that the student coming to college has been in the habit of drawing from the town-library such fiction as he has read. If that library has been wisely administered, he has gradually learned that there are many other uses to which it may be put, if only he is so disposed. And this is, in general, a healthy notion at that time of life. A boy has gained a great deal if he merely realizes that sources of intellectual amusement are to be found within public library walls, and he should continue to derive such entertainment from the college library.

Meanwhile in his classes the student will have been required to purchase certain books for study, and the mastery of them will be demanded by his teachers; but, in addition to this, he will be sent to the college library to consult other books without any intimation from his instructors that he should purchase them. He is only to learn how to consult these books, how to bring the information that he will find there into relation with the subject as set forth in his text-book. He will then learn that no book can be adequately understood by itself alone, but will yield up its treasure only when its words are compared with those of other books, and its truths tested by the experience of other men. The student will find that some of the books to which his attention has been directed are to be quickly consulted and quickly laid aside, as containing but little—though that little may be of great importance—that is related to the subject which he is investigating. Others may well seem to him more important than his text-book, and he may indeed in certain cases come to realize that his text-book has been quarried out of some larger and grander treatise on the subject. Gradually he will come to understand the truth of Bacon's words, "Some books are to be tasted, others to be swallowed, and some few to be chewed and digested; that is some books are to be read only in parts; others to be read, but not curiously; and some few to be read wholly, and with diligence and attention." Such counsel as this of Bacon's implies the guidance of a teacher and the existence of a library to which the student may be sent.

No teacher will be content if his instruction ends in his class-room, and a student will have begun the educational process only when he carries away the lessons which he has received in the class-room, not as a body of dogma, to be received as *de fide*, but as an organic and growing thing to be constantly nourished by human intercourse and by private study.

After a student has thus used the library for many months, he will discover that his work there has constituted a kind of initiation into scholarship, or what is more narrowly described as "research." He will find that in his restless pursuit of elusive facts, his examination of sources, and his comparison of one man's view with another's, he has come into possession of information and of ideas which may fairly be termed *new*—in short, that he has entered the very narrow group of those who have a right to an opinion on the matter. He may even come to possess more knowledge of the subject than anybody else. His knowledge may be humble and remote from human interest; it may even be trifling information which he has uncovered; but the experience of thus acquiring it is not trifling, for in it he may see reflected the whole process and progress of learning. He will come to understand why scholars enclose themselves in libraries and scientists in laboratories; why lawyers must be perpetually concerned with precedents—the history—of their profession; and why physicians who aspire to excel must be always studying the latest developments of the art of healing. For every true exponent of a profession is interested not only in learning but in the progress of learning. And the student will come to see that the library or laboratory is a temple dedicated to a faith.

When he has been fully initiated as a scholar, he will also understand why professional practitioners are always talking of documents and of "original sources." He will understand why a scholar is peculiarly excited by written evidence coming to him out of the remote past, in words written long ago by a hand that has now crumbled to dust. *Litera scripta manet.*[2] Here is something that bears testimony to conditions of life which have long since passed away, and are to be rescued and made to live again only by the efforts of scholars. I cannot here do better than to quote the words of a collector of autograph letters, whose name I do not know, but who summarized very well what I am trying to put before the college student:

> An autograph is not only a rarity, but it is a unique rarity. You cannot duplicate it. And it is not only a unique rarity; it is, in a real sense, the embodiment of a human personality. One touches hands, so to speak, with the writer himself; and if the writer be a famous person who, by his genius, has won our hearts, the autograph becomes a veritable living thing. It speaks for the man in a way that no printed page can.

That is, I think, a happy expression of the delight which a scholar feels when, at last, he holds in his hand the written evidence on which a recorded fact reposes. Happy is the student who, while yet in college, has such an experience. It is only in a library that he can have it.

[2] The written word remains.

I must not conclude these remarks without some word regarding the value of a student's *private* library. Nothing can ever take the place of that. Not the British Museum, not the Bibliothèque Nationale can take the place of the books which the student has bought and read for their own beloved sake. They are like the twenty books clad in black or red, which were prized by Chaucer's Clerk above all the pleasures of the world. To live in the daily presence of a few great books is itself an education. There is something in their very physical presence which invites us to turn and to return to them, till at last old acquaintance begets in us a likeness to our ancient associates, the worthies of the world.

No personal library can ever discharge the function of a great college library, as no college library can ever be to a man what his own humble collection of well-worn books may be; but love of one begets a love of the other, and as there is distinction in a great college library, so there may be distinction in a private assemblage of books, however small.

There is an old and perhaps foolish query about the books which one would wish to take with him if he were to sojourn upon a desert island. But like some other foolish questions, the problem which it sets us is worth pondering. Upon the voyage of life there are few books of which we may hope to make lifelong companions; and, as in the other relations of life, it behoves us, if we hope to avoid calamity on our voyage, to choose our mates with discretion.

❧ ❧ ❧

*Irwin Edman*

# Unrequired Reading[1]

THE title of this essay may strike you as a typographical error. You may be saying to yourself that the writer really means required reading, and the phrase conjures up for you, I suspect, lists distributed on the first days of college courses: Volume One of this distinguished scholar's work on the Byzantine empire in the fourth century, that brochure on the economic interpretation of the Constitution, this pundit's principles of economics, that pedant's source book.

Or, perhaps, still under the apprehension that I mean required reading, you are reminded of what by now is one of the more maddening insolences of criticism, or at any rate of book reviewing. "This," says Mr. Notability, "is a

[1] *Saturday Review of Literature*, Nov. 4, 1950, pp. 9-10, 36-38. Copyright, The Saturday Review Associates, 25 W. 45th St., New York City. Reprinted by permission of the author and the publisher.

*must* book." This in the atomic age is compulsory reading. In a world of anxiety this uneasy novel is not to be passed by.

I beg of you to forget such obligations and responsibilities. To this day you have to forget that you *had* to read "Macbeth" in order to begin to remember how perturbingly moving a play it is. Hardly anyone would reread Burke's "Speech on Conciliation" if he recalled how he had to make an abstract of it in high school. For one forgets the delight in the obligation, the eloquence in the remembered pressure. In one way or another even the nonprofessional reader reads from some felt or alleged obligation, some illusion of responsibility. He reads to know or to be in the know, to acquire a mature mind, to insure peace of soul, to understand what to do when the bomb drops, or when peace breaks out. We read because we feel we must know what's what, who is who, why is why. We read because in some way it seems compulsory to know Gide and Proust and Kafka and Sartre, because existentialism is being talked about, first in the small worlds of the little reviews, and then in the larger domains of the gossip columns, the digests, the library forums at the women's lubs.

In the sociology of our culture reading has, in so far as it has at all survi ᵈ television and the comic strip, survived as a form of obligation. The student, ᴜhe publisher, the editor, the scholar, even those, including the ladies who feel only the obligation to be *au courant, à la page,* or knowledgeable, read, for the most part, because they have to or think they have to. Not that anyone in any of these groups has necessarily actually read all that the mandarins of literate society expect or enjoin. At college even the most industrious or conforming of us did not do, as we used to put it, all the assigned reading, despite the ominous final examinations as reasons for doing so.

Nor as adults do we read all the books we are supposed to read. We compromise by reading with care the leading book reviews. For purposes of dinnerparty conversation the latter method is not without its virtues. One's mind is not cluttered up with the actual details, one's imagination is not haunted by the actual flavor of the book, and one has a good lead and a good authority on what one is supposed to say and think. This obligation to read fashionable current works, to know this year's Hemingway and next year's Toynbee, to know —or to know about—cybernetics, all this makes it almost impossible even for those who have no professional commitments and concerns with books to retain the quality and status of amateurs and to read books for pleasure, to peruse a volume for pure enjoyment, to read not for food but for love.

The inability, including that of lack of time, to read for pleasure, is perhaps especially to be noticed among those whose professional concern *is* with books. The student, the scholar, the teacher, the editor, the publisher all have to do a good deal of reading for special purposes, in special areas, for special reasons. Even when a student enjoys his required reading in a course he still has in mind, if only half consciously, his responsibilities to a teacher and to an examination. An advanced scholar may enjoy a new monograph in his own field, but he cannot read it simply as a delighted dilettante. The chances are that if it is by a rival scholar his delight would in any case not be unqualified. Even, or particularly, if it is good he may not like it. The brochure is an instrument in his work and also a challenge to his own hypotheses and standards of criticism. He is alerted for errors, inconsistencies, and exaggerations. Even if it is good he cannot read it merely as a pastime. And to the specialist there is usually no time to read books outside the specialty.

The editor and the publisher are in much the same dilemma, even the most imaginative editor, and the type of publisher—not, I am told, too current—who likes books even when he doesn't like authors. He may, like Maxwell Perkins, be adventurously alert for new talent. He may be solicitously on the lookout for genius, but in reading a manuscript he has to read with the hunter's eye, the collector's zeal, rather than with the freedom of pleasure.

And yet somehow reading for the love of it persists, both among those who have to deal with books all the time and among those who read largely to keep up with the Joneses intellectually or earnestly to know the best that is being said and thought in the contemporary world or because they feel they have fallen into a rut of illiteracy, what with the demands of their children, canasta, and television. The man or woman who has to read professionally steals time, sometimes late at night, to recover the youthful and delicious pleasure of reading for its own sake. He has just read a novel of lust and pillage in the Deep South, or of neurosis in Newtown, Conn. His eyes are tired and his mind dulled. And suddenly on his shelves he sees a volume of George Borrow, and he is off selling Bibles in Spain, meeting a liberal mayor in a provincial town, who releases him from arrest because he comes from the land of the great Jeremy Bentham. He picks up Jane Austen and is in the Grand Pump Room at Bath.

To what books does one turn, what pleasures does one rediscover when one is too tired or too indolent or too rebellious to read what one must? I remember as a college student being somewhat shocked to learn that Woodrow Wilson— and, what to me at the time was worse, John Dewey—turned for relaxation to detective stories. Since that time so many eminent persons, including my own valued colleagues, have turned to detective stories, too (and written treatises on their hobby), that I have ceased to be shocked, although I have not arrived at being converted. The detective stories that are simply puzzles seem to me weariness compounded, or those tricked out with a whimsey of culture, pure drivel. There are other avenues of literature to turn to more liberating and enchanting.

The curious fact is that quite difficult books are a relaxation and a pleasure, and complex tomes a delight when one has no immediate responsibility whatever for them. I discovered this very early as have thousands of those who began their reading young. For me the insight came in a branch library of the New York Public Library, where a librarian, Miss Lawrence by name, seeing me somewhat nearsightedly exploring the shelves, came to help me. "Are you looking for anything special?" she asked. Somewhat ashamed, I said that I was not. I was wandering in what to me was a fresh and wonderful wilderness. But I began to discover that there it was a well-organized forest, in which trees of the same family stood beside each other and which some forester had labeled with mystical numbers that indicated relationship. It was naturally the Eight Hundreds that I first wandered among. Even in a small branch library in 1910 New York there were a surprising number of books classified under literature. Close by were the biographies, and the number of novels and lives-and-times I read while I was in my early teens is astonishing to myself now that I look back on it. It is the endlessness of the number of books that both appealed to me and appalled me. At the same age when one has a good appetite physically in a parallel way one is stimulated by quantity in print, and frightened that one may cease to be before one has read everything. I think that was one of the things that impressed me about the novels of William de Morgan and Arnold Bennett, not to add Dickens and Thackeray. These were wonderful vast realms to enter into, to lose one's self in. It was here, too, that one discovered quite by accident, as Henry Adams said he discovered Beethoven by accident in a German beer garden, volumes of history and biography often simply by their title.

It is difficult to know what is so attractive about the title "The Rise of the Dutch Republic" or why it should fascinate a fourteen-year-old boy. "The Oregon Trail" was another matter; any American boy would have his mind stirred by any glance at a page of that stunning work of imaginative history. Next to quantity and variety was the joy of discovering things that because I had heard no one mention them came to me with the force of discovery. I think Hamlin Garland was for me a genuine find. I don't know that I had ever heard anyone refer to him and suddenly I came across a dusty brown book about dusty country. It was called "Main-Travelled Roads," and it gave me a sense of the Middle West more profound, accurate, and touching, I think, than I was to get from "Main Street" years later. Was it (I am quite certain it was) in the same library that I came across "Looking Backward"? It made me a Socialist at the age of fifteen and gave me my first boy's dream of Utopia. But, best of all, I discovered the books in the One Hundreds: philosophy, which dealt with first and last things (there was actually H. G. Wells's book by that title), and psychology, with its books on the working of the human mind. To this day I can never pass a branch library without a thrill of memory. This is where I learnt to read for pleasure and where I discovered the lineaments of nature and life.

I continued to learn thus in college, too, for it is in wandering around the shelves and later among the stacks that one acquires the sense that at almost any random number of library classification one may run across something unexpected in the way of beauty and truth. For the pleasure in reading is far from being that simply of nibbling literary hors d'oeuvres. De Quincey divided books into those of knowledge and those of power, power over our hearts and imagination. But there are books of knowledge that have that power. There happened to be published in this country just at the time I was a freshman the series of volumes written mostly by Britons called the Home University Library. The little yellow volumes contained small masterpieces of exposition of important things, presented without either dullness or pomposity. Bertrand Russell's "Problems of Philosophy," Whitehead's "Introduction to Mathematics," Marett's "Anthropology"—all opened up vistas of unexplored possibility for me, and from H. N. Brailsford's "Shelley, Godwin, and Their Circle" I got more of a sense of the romantic movement in English poetry than from the more pretentious works of scholarship I was asked to read. Not that the book was better than those, but it was small, modest, intimate, and I had found it for myself. On the reading lists were always books that were merely suggested, and those seemed ever so much more inviting than those that were commanded. Conybeare's "Myth, Magic, and Morals"—I don't know whether it was as good as it then seemed—but I am sure Fustel de Coulanges's "The Ancient City" was.

As it turned out Fate or accident brought me into a life of professional dealing with books. I read them as a professional student of philosophy, I review them as a professional reviewer, occasionally I read them in manuscript to tell publishers with an intended mixture of shrewdness and academic responsibility whether they are worth publishing for themselves or for profit or for both. But all that reading I do not think really counts, not as entertainment, not as education. It is the unrequired reading one steals time for that is the reader's lifeblood.

The great thing about a book is having it in one's home like a medicine or an analgesic, a stimulus or a soporific when the drugstores are all closed. Late at night one's private library is like a medicine chest. One cannot tell what one will be in the mood for or what one's spirit will most urgently crave. Or if the analogy seems too medicinal, perhaps the refrigerator or the cookie jar will do. Who knows when suddenly, late at night when libraries and bookstores are tight shut, there will come into one's head the sudden passionate need to reread some Dickens? Or, if the truth be told, to read some of him for the first time? Somewhere one day, in a critic I greatly respected, I found a paranthetic clause which said, " 'Our Mutual Friend,' which is, of course, Dickens's masterpiece." I bridled a little at the "of course." I tried to think back to the book itself and to my discomfiture I realized I had never read it. That night I was happy that a year ago I had purchased a set of Dickens in big, clear type on a spacious page. After about fifty pages I began to see the plausibility of the easy dogmatism of my critical friend.

Again there may pop into one's head a passage which had bemused one many years ago, like the opening chapter on the London fog in "Bleak House" or the death of the Bishop's wife in Trollope's "Last Chronicles of Barset," that definitive portrait of a dominating woman in whose death scene, at once ironic and pathetic, one may find one of the places where it is impossible to condescend to Trollope. There are any number of books I should, I think, never have read had I not prudently bought them against the time I should have the time to read them, the letters of Edward Fitzgerald, for example, or those of Lady Mary Wortley Montagu or Kilvert's Diary, the journal of that gifted and obscure provincial English cleric whose tender and acute notes on life and nature, and on his life and nature, came to light only a few years ago. And there are works born to be read perennially like the essays of Emerson, the sermons of Donne.

Raiding the icebox is not half so much fun as raiding one's shelves, and sometimes one is surprised to find what books one has bought or received through the kind (or calculated thoughtfulness) of some publisher heaven knows when. When on earth and where did one pick up Henry James's "Notes of a Son and Brother" with its emotions recollected from boyhood of New York of a century ago? One recalls perhaps where one found "A Little Tour in France." There is the familiar paper-covered Tauchnitz edition of prewar memory found in a little bookshop at Nimes, along with other apparatus, like guide-books for English-speaking tourists visiting the magical landscape of Provence for the first time.

And that by a natural association leads me to consider the reading one has done, not only unrequiredly but unexpectedly largely because of the distributive enterprise of American publishers. The twenty-five-cent, now more likely the thirty-five-cent, book and the Modern Library found in small stationery shops or drugstores in remote prairie towns—what a boon these are to the traveler, how much they provide pleasure and enlightenment for hours that would otherwise be fretfully or dully passed in airports or railway stations waiting for delayed planes or trains. Often it is true that one can go through a whole sheaf of reprints to find nothing save "Blood on the Moon" or "Thunderbird on the Trail," but, especially lately, the foraging is better. Sometimes, because the choices worth consideration are few, one is happily constrained to light upon something that is not exactly in the mood one had been looking for but establishes another mood and opens another realm of gold or truth. What I was hoping for one day, marooned for hours in Great Falls, Montana, was a novel, say, by Virginia Woolf. What I found was George Gamow's "Life and Death of the Sun," a book calculated to give one a more stable sense of proportion, even of orientation on the Korean or any other crisis than could the most comprehensive picture weekly or the most thorough review of the week. These reprint series afford wonderful chances, at odd moments and at minimal expense, to take a look—often at the outset a prejudiced look—at books that have had an undignified popularity, and to discover that even if it isn't true in the phrase of a once-famous advertising slogan that such popularity must be deserved, at least there are reasons popularity is attained, reasons not altogether of high-pressure publicity.

I have written for the most part as if unrequired meant necessarily scattered or relatively trivial reading. There must be earnest souls among my readers who feel that it ought to be said that reading even for pleasure includes the pleasures of knowledge and of thought as well as those of imagination and of fancy. It does. I have been stressing the interest of the general or the common reader. But the general reader is with respect to specific fields always in some mild respect a specialist, even if only in the matter of taste; when Samuel Johnson used the term common reader he meant it as a compliment, and the common reader is often uncommonly serious in his literary pleasures. There are books of knowledge that give twin delights: first that of pleasure in exposition lucidly and persuasively done, and the larger joy of vision of the world—a wider and a more exact vision of the universe around us or some crucial, timely, or timeless aspect of it. There are volumes of the gravest history, the most severe speculative philosophy, poetry, the most concentrated and reflective, so long as they are read not because one feels one must fill in this gap in one's knowledge of medieval history or that hole in one's knowledge of the byways of metaphysics or that era or school of poetry. It is clear that the line between reading and study is not a sharp one. But there is a distinction. One does not just *read* Spinoza's "Ethics" (it is a work demanding the severest concentration) but also one does not always read late at night or when one is quite tired. It is possible to read for fun when one is full of energy and health, on a summer day at a mountain altitude, and on vacation, and it is at such times that such intellectually muscular exercise is a true pleasure. In music there are *divertimenti*, serenades, and bagatelles which are enjoyed simply for their delicious minor selves. In music, too, there are requiem masses, sonatas, and symphonies, and there are the late quartets of Beethoven that at least one serious writer has held to disclose whole other worlds or aspects of *our* whole world not expressible in any other way. Most of this article I have been discussing the *divertimenti* of literature. But there is no essential reason why the most demanding and profound of books should not provide along with the tension of effort the pleasures that one may, I think, without professional bias call philosophical.

The analogy with music is not merely fanciful. In music, too, especially when one is only half and dreamily listening or listening with the unthinking ear, it is in smaller incidental works that one may most acutely be aware of the delicacies of counterpoint and rhythms, of melody, color, and orchestration. But in listening to works on a scale grander both in size and in reference one is not listening simply to the surface of sounds but to the meaning and structure of a world, perhaps, as Schopenhauer thought, of *the* world. It is in the printed word and by way of it that these wider and more comprehensive delights, that the joys of contemplative insight as well as the athletic virtuosities of thought may be experienced. For centuries men have climbed mountains for the sheer arduous enterprising pleasure of it, as well as for the ultimate rewarding view. There are books the very reading of which by slow, ascending, total comprehension constitutes stringent but genuine joy. But to take Spinoza's "Ethics" again as an example. Through the careful mastery of it it comes to be enjoyable; the final joy is the achieved vision, the perspective opened upon the eternally glowing serenity that such a perspective yields.

I do not mean to imply that serious works in philosophy are always hard reading though they may demand, even to enjoy them as writing, intense and wakeful alertness. There is a spurious superstition, fortified I fear by the practice of many American scholars, that profound books must be difficult, that serious works must be written with awkward want of grace. It is true that nobody reads Aristotle's "Metaphysics" for its prose style nor, for that matter, works by John Dewey. But there is a long and splendid tradition in philosophy of books at once serious as to matter, distinguished and beguiling as to style; one has but to remember David Hume and Bishop Berkeley. There are in all conscience ultimate ambiguities about life and nature, but even the difficulties of understanding the world can be clearly stated, and it was Aristotle himself who suggested that to know anything was to be able to state it.

It therefore turns out that there are occasions in our reading when the joys of unrequired reading are matched by the profit of wisdom. Books read for pleasure turn out to be liberators of imagination, transmitters of insight, disclosures of life seen steadily and whole; books written out of the most serious concerns of existence turn out to be entrancing literature. There is an aftermath of Puritanism, of moral asceticism among us that makes us suspicious of reading done for the spontaneity or the devil of it. Especially in times of crisis (crisis now seems to have become the normal weather of the world) reading for fun seems to have the immorality of a holiday at the wrong time, an escape from things that urgently need doing. Such spare time as we have we are frequently asked to turn to useful reading. We must find out more about civil defense, about soil erosion, about the welfare or, as its opponents think, the illfare of the state. We need to be briefed at once concerning the history and culture of Korea. We have to know all about Indo-China, and now. Doubtless we do, if only to become armchair strategists.

But at the risk of being thrown to the Congressional Committees as a saboteur I would like to plead not only the intrinsic enjoyments but the timely social usefulness of unrequired reading. As we are often reminded (even at the wrong moment) there is slave labor in Russia. We need to beware lest, out of hysterical fear, we make standard among ourselves the habit of a slave labor of the mind. The freedom of joy, including the freedom to enjoy reading, the liberty for play of imagination, for roving over the whole domain of time and space and humanity—these will help keep freedom alive among us politically. It is not slaves who will be concerned about freedom, and it is only free minds that will keep the values of civilization fresh and growing among us. One of those values is the unrequired adventuring among books, the lifeblood of our civilization.

❦ ❦ ❦

*Henry David Thoreau*

# Reading[1]

WITH a little more deliberation in the choice of their pursuits, all men would perhaps become essentially students and observers, for certainly their nature and destiny are interesting to all alike. In accumulating property for ourselves or our posterity, in founding a family or a state, or acquiring fame even, we are mortal; but in dealing with truth we are immortal, and need fear no change nor accident. The oldest Egyptian or Hindoo philosopher raised a corner of the veil from the statue of the divinity; and still the trembling robe remains raised, and I gaze upon as fresh a glory as he did, since it was I in him that was then so bold, and it is he in me that now reviews the vision. No dust has settled on that robe; no time has elapsed since that divinity was revealed. That time which we really improve, or which is improbable, is neither past, present, nor future.

My residence was more favorable, not only to thought, but to serious reading, than a university; and though I was beyond the range of the ordinary circulating library, I had more than ever come within the influence of those books which circulate round the world, whose sentences were first written on bark, and are now merely copied from time to time onto linen paper. Says the poet Mîr Camar Uddîn Mast, "Being seated, to run through the region of the spiritual world; I have had this advantage in books. To be intoxicated by a single glass of wine; I have experienced this pleasure when I have drunk the liquor of the esoteric doctrines." I kept Homer's Iliad on my table through the summer, though I looked at his page only now and then. Incessant labor with my hands, at first, for I had my house to finish and my beans to hoe at the same time, made more study impossible. Yet I sustained myself by the prospect of such reading in future. I read one or two shallow books of travel in the intervals of my work, till that employment made me ashamed of myself, and I asked where it was then that *I* lived.

The student may read Homer or Æschylus in the Greek without danger of dissipation or luxuriousness, for it implies that he in some measure emulate their heroes, and consecrate morning hours to their pages. The heroic books, even if printed in the character of our mother tongue, will always be in a language dead to degenerate times; and we must laboriously seek the meaning of each word and line, conjecturing a larger sense than common use permits out of what wisdom and valor and generosity we have. The modern cheap and fertile press, with all its translations, has done little to bring us nearer to the heroic writers of antiquity. They seem as solitary, and the letter in which they are

[1] From *Walden*, ed. by Norman Holmes Pearson, "Rinehart Editions" (New York: Rinehart & Company, Inc., 1948), pp. 81-90. First printed in 1849.

printed as rare and curious, as ever. It is worth the expense of youthful days and costly hours, if you learn only some words of an ancient language, which are raised out of the trivialness of the street, to be perpetual suggestions and provocations. It is not in vain that the farmer remembers and repeats the few Latin words which he has heard. Men sometimes speak as if the study of the classics would at length make way for more modern and practical studies; but the adventurous student will always study classics, in whatever language they may be written and however ancient they may be. For what are the classics but the noblest recorded thoughts of man? They are the only oracles which are not decayed, and there are such answers to the most modern inquiry in them as Delphi and Dodona never gave. We might as well omit to study Nature because she is old. To read well, that is, to read true books in a true spirit, is a noble exercise, and one that will task the reader more than any exercise which the customs of the day esteem. It requires a training such as the athletes underwent, the steady intention almost of the whole life to this object. Books must be read as deliberately and reservedly as they were written. It is not enough even to be able to speak the language of that nation by which they were written, for there is a memorable interval between the spoken and the written language, the language heard and the language read. The one is commonly transitory, a sound, a tongue, a dialect merely, almost brutish, and we learn it unconsciously, like the brutes, of our mothers. The other is the maturity and experience of that; if that is our mother tongue, this is our father tongue, a reserved and select expression, too significant to be heard by the ear, which we must be born again in order to speak. The crowds of men who merely *spoke* the Greek and Latin tongues in the Middle Ages were not entitled by the accident of birth to *read* the works of genius written in those languages; for these were not written in that Greek or Latin which they knew, but in the select language of literature. They had not learned the nobler dialects of Greece and Rome, but the very materials on which they were written were waste paper to them, and they prized instead a cheap contemporary literature. But when the several nations of Europe had acquired distinct though rude written languages of their own, sufficient for the purposes of their rising literatures, then first learning revived, and scholars were enabled to discern from that remoteness the treasures of antiquity. What the Roman and Grecian multitude could not *hear*, after the lapse of ages a few scholars *read*, and a few scholars only are still reading it.

However much we may admire the orator's occasional bursts of eloquence, the noblest written words are commonly as far behind or above the fleeting spoken language as the firmament with its stars is behind the clouds. *There* are the stars, and they who can may read them. The astronomers forever comment on and observe them. They are not exhalations like our daily colloquies and vaporous breath. What is called eloquence in the forum is commonly found to be rhetoric in the study. The orator yields to the inspiration of a transient occasion, and speaks to the mob before him, to those who can *hear* him; but the writer, whose more equable life is his occasion, and who would be distracted by the event and the crowd which inspire the orator, speaks to the intellect and heart of mankind, to all in any age who can *understand* him.

No wonder that Alexander carried the Iliad with him on his expeditions in a precious casket. A written word is the choicest of relics. It is something at once more intimate with us and more universal than any other work of art. It is the work of art nearest to life itself. It may be translated into every language, and not only be read but actually breathed from all human lips;—not be represented on canvas or in marble only, but be carved out of the breath of life itself. The symbol of an ancient man's thought becomes a modern man's speech. Two thousand summers have imparted to the monuments of Grecian literature, as to her marbles, only a maturer golden and autumnal tint, for they have carried their own serene and celestial atmosphere into all lands to protect them against the corrosion of time. Books are the treasured wealth of the world and the fit inheritance of generations and nations. Books, the oldest and the best, stand naturally and rightfully on the shelves of every cottage. They have no cause of their own to plead, but while they enlighten and sustain the reader his common sense will not refuse them. Their authors are a natural and irresistible aristocracy in every society, and, more than kings or emperors, exert an influence on mankind. When the illiterate and perhaps scornful trader has earned by enterprise and industry his coveted leisure and independence, and is admitted to the circles of wealth and fashion, he turns inevitably at last to those still higher but yet inaccessible circles of intellect and genius, and is sensible only of the imperfection of his culture and the vanity and insufficiency of all his riches, and further proves his good sense by the pains which he takes to secure for his children that intellectual culture whose want he so keenly feels; and thus it is that he becomes the founder of a family.

Those who have not learned to read the ancient classics in the language in which they were written must have a very imperfect knowledge of the history of the human race; for it is remarkable that no transcript of them has ever been made into any modern tongue, unless our civilization itself may be regarded as such a transcript. Homer has never yet been printed in English, nor Æschylus, nor Virgil even,—works as refined, as solidly done, and as beautiful almost as the morning itself; for later writers, say what we will of their genius, have rarely, if ever, equalled the elaborate beauty and finish and the lifelong and heroic literary labors of the ancients. They only talk of forgetting them who never knew them. It will be soon enough to forget them when we have the learning and the genius which will enable us to attend to and appreciate them. That age will be rich indeed when those relics which we call Classics, and the still older and more than classic but even less known Scriptures of the nations, shall have still further accumulated, when the Vaticans shall be filled with Vedas and Zendavestas and Bibles, with Homers and Dantes and Shakespeares, and all the centuries to come shall have successively deposited their trophies in the forum of the world. By such a pile we may hope to scale heaven at last.

The works of the great poets have never yet been read by mankind, for only great poets can read them. They have only been read as the multitude read the stars, at most astrologically, not astronomically. Most men have learned to read to serve a paltry convenience, as they have learned to cipher in order to keep accounts and not be cheated in trade; but of reading as a noble intellectual exercise they know little or nothing; yet this only is reading, in a high sense, not that which lulls us as a luxury and suffers the nobler faculties to sleep the while, but what we have to stand on tip-toe to read and devote our most alert and wakeful hours to.

I think that having learned our letters we should read the best that is in literature, and not be forever repeating our a-b-abs, and words of one syllable, in the fourth or fifth classes, sitting on the lowest and foremost form all our lives. Most men are satisfied if they read or hear read, and perchance have been convicted by the wisdom of one good book, the Bible, and for the rest of their lives vegetate and dissipate their faculties in what is called easy reading. There is a work in several volumes in our Circulating Library entitled "Little Reading," which I thought referred to a town of that name which I had not been to. There are those who, like cormorants and ostriches, can digest all sorts of this, even after the fullest dinner of meats and vegetables, for they suffer nothing to be wasted. If others are the machines to provide this provender, they are the machines to read it. They read the nine thousandth tale about Zebulon and Sophronia, and how they loved as none had ever loved before, and neither did the course of their true love run smooth,—at any rate, how it did run and stumble, and get up again and go on! how some poor unfortunate got up on to a steeple, who had better never have gone up as far as the belfry; and then having needlessly got him up there, the happy novelist rings the bell for all the world to come together and hear, O dear! how he did get down again! For my part, I think that they had better metamorphose all such aspiring heroes of universal noveldom into man weather-cocks, as they used to put heroes among the constellations, and let them swing round there till they are rusty, and not come down at all to bother honest men with their pranks. The next time the novelist rings the bell I will not stir though the meeting-house burn down. "The Skip of the Tip-Toe-Hop, a Romance of the Middle Ages, by the celebrated author of 'Tittle-Tol-Tan,' to appear in monthly parts; a great rush; don't all come together." All this they read with saucer eyes, and erect and primitive curiosity, and with unwearied gizzard, whose corrugations even yet need no sharpening, just as some little four-year-old bencher his two-cent gilt-covered edition of Cinderella,—without any improvement, that I can see, in the pronunciation, or accent, or emphasis, or any more skill in extracting or inserting the moral. The result is dulness of sight, stagnation of the vital circulations, and a general deliquium and sloughing off of all the intellectual faculties. This sort of gingerbread is baked daily and more sedulously than pure wheat or rye-and-Indian in almost every oven, and finds a surer market.

The best books are not read even by those who are called good readers. What does our Concord culture amount to? There is in this town, with a very few exceptions, no taste for the best or for very good books even in English literature, whose words all can read and spell. Even the college-bred and so-called liberally educated men here and elsewhere have really little or no acquaintance with the English classics; and as for the recorded wisdom of mankind, the ancient classics and Bibles, which are accessible to all who will know of them, there are the feeblest efforts anywhere made to become acquainted with them. I know a woodchopper, of middle age, who takes a French paper, not for news as he says, for he is above that, but to "keep himself in practice," he being a Canadian by birth; and when I ask him what he considers the best thing he can do in this world, he says, beside this, to keep up and add to his English. This is about as much as the college-bred generally do or aspire to do, and they take an English paper for the purpose. One who has just come from reading perhaps one of the best English books will find how many with whom he can converse about it? Or suppose he comes from reading a Greek or Latin classic in the original, whose praises are familiar even to the so-called illiterate; he will find nobody at all to speak to, but must keep silence about it. Indeed, there is hardly the professor in our colleges, who, if he has mastered the difficulties of the language, has proportionally mastered the difficulties of the wit and poetry of a Greek poet, and has any sympathy to impart to the alert and heroic reader; and as for the sacred Scriptures, or Bibles of mankind, who in this town can tell me even their titles? Most men do not know that any nation but the Hebrews have had a scripture. A man, any man, will go considerably out of his way to pick up a silver dollar; but here are golden words, which the wisest men of antiquity have uttered, and whose worth the wise of every succeeding age have assured us of;—and yet we learn to read only as far as Easy Reading, the primers and class-books, and when we leave school, the "Little Reading," and story-books, which are for boys and beginners; and our reading, our conversation and thinking, are all on a very low level, worthy only of pygmies and manikins.

I aspire to be acquainted with wiser men than this our Concord soil has produced, whose names are hardly known here. Or shall I hear the name of Plato and never read his book? As if Plato were my townsman and I never saw him, —my next neighbor and I never heard him speak or attended to the wisdom of his words. But how actually is it? His Dialogues, which contain what was immortal in him, lie on the next shelf, and yet I never read them. We are under-bred and low-lived and illiterate; and in this respect I confess I do not make any very broad distinction between the illiterateness of my townsman who cannot read at all and the illiterateness of him who has learned to read only what is for children and feeble intellects. We should be as good as the worthies of antiquity, but partly by first knowing how good they were. We are a race of tit-men, and soar but little higher in our intellectual flights than the columns of the daily paper.

It is not all books that are as dull as their readers. There are probably words addressed to our condition exactly, which, if we could really hear and understand, would be more salutary than the morning or the spring to our lives, and possibly put a new aspect on the face of things for us. How many a man has dated a new era in his life from the reading of a book! The book exists for us, perchance, which will explain our miracles and reveal new ones. The at present unutterable things we may find somewhere uttered. These same questions that disturb and puzzle and confound us have in their turn occurred to all the wise men; not one has been omitted; and each has answered them, according to his ability, by his words and his life. Moreover, with wisdom we shall learn liberality. The solitary hired man on a farm in the outskirts of Concord, who has had his second birth and peculiar religious experience, and is driven as he believes into silent gravity and exclusiveness by his faith, may think it is not true; but Zoroaster, thousands of years ago, travelled the same road and had the same experience; but he, being wise, knew it to be universal, and treated his neighbors accordingly, and is even said to have invented and established worship among men. Let him humbly commune with Zoroaster then, and through the liberalizing influence of all the worthies, with Jesus Christ himself, and let "our church" go by the board.

We boast that we belong to the Nineteenth Century and are making the most rapid strides of any nation. But consider how little this village does for its own culture. I do not wish to flatter my townsmen, nor to be flattered by them, for that will not advance either of us. We need to be provoked,—goaded like oxen, as we are, into a trot. We have a comparatively decent system of common schools, schools for infants only; but excepting the half-starved Lyceum in the winter, and latterly the puny beginning of a library suggested by the State, no school for ourselves. We spend more on almost any article of bodily aliment or ailment than on our mental aliment. It is time that we had uncommon schools, that we did not leave off our education when we begin to be men and women. It is time that villages were universities, and their elder inhabitants the fellows of universities, with leisure—if they are, indeed, so well off—to pursue liberal studies the rest of their lives. Shall the world be confined to one Paris or one Oxford forever? Cannot students be boarded here and get a liberal education under the skies of Concord? Can we not hire some Abélard to lecture to us? Alas! what with foddering the cattle and tending the store, we are kept from school too long, and our education is sadly neglected. In this country, the village should in some respect take the place of the nobleman of Europe. It should be the patron of the fine arts. It is rich enough. It wants only the magnanimity and refinement. It can spend money enough on such things as farmers and traders value, but it is thought Utopian to propose spending money for things which more intelligent men know to be of far more worth. This town has spent seventeen thousand dollars on a town-house, thank fortune or politics, but probably it will not spend so much on living wit, the true meat to put into that shell, in a hundred years. The one hundred and twenty-five dollars annually subscribed for a Lyceum in the winter is better spent than any other equal sum raised in the town. If we live in the Nineteenth Century, why should we not enjoy the advantages which the Nineteenth Century offers? Why should our life be in any respect provincial? If we will read newspapers, why not skip the gossip of Boston and take the best newspaper in the world at once?—not be sucking the pap of "neutral family" papers, or browsing "Olive-Branches" here in New England. Let the reports of all the learned societies come to us, and we will see if they know anything. Why should we leave it to Harper & Brothers and Redding Co. to select our reading? As the nobleman of cultivated taste surrounds himself with whatever conduces to his culture,—genius—learning—wit—books—paintings—statuary—music— philosophical instruments, and the like; so let the village do,—not stop short at a pedagogue, a parson, a sexton, a parish library, and three selectmen, because our Pilgrim forefathers got through a cold winter once on a bleak rock with these. To act collectively is according to the spirit of our institutions; and I am confident that, as our circumstances are more flourishing, our means are greater than the nobleman's. New England can hire all the wise men in the world to come and teach her, and board them round the while, and not be provincial at all. That is the *uncommon* school we want. Instead of noblemen, let us have noble villages of men. If it is necessary, omit one bridge over the river, go round a little there, and throw one arch at least over the darker gulf of ignorance which surrounds us.

❦ ❦ ❦

*Leonard Q. Ross*

# Mr. K*a*p*l*a*n and Shakespeare[1]

IT WAS Miss Higby's idea in the first place. She had suggested to Mr. Parkhill that the students came to her class unaware of the *finer* side of English, of its beauty and, as she put it, "the glorious heritage of our literature." She suggested that perhaps poetry might be worked into the exercises of Mr. Parkhill's class. The beginner's grade had, after all, been subjected to almost a year of English and might be presumed to have achieved some linguistic sophistication. Poetry would make the students conscious of precise enunciation; it would make them read with greater care and an ear for sounds. Miss Higby, who had once begun a master's thesis on Coventry Patmore, *loved* poetry. And, it should be said in all justice, she argued her cause with considerable logic. Poetry *would* be excellent for the enunciation of the students, thought Mr. Parkhill.

So it was that when he faced the class the following Tuesday night, Mr.

1 From *The Education of Hyman Kaplan*, by Leonard Q. Ross, pp. 129-140. Copyright, 1937, by Harcourt, Brace & Company, Inc. Originally published in *The New Yorker*.

Parkhill had a volume of Shakespeare on his desk, and an eager, almost an expectant, look in his eye. The love that Miss Higby bore for poetry in general was as nothing compared to the love that Mr. Parkhill bore for Shakespeare in particular. To Mr. Parkhill, poetry meant Shakespeare. Many years ago he had played Polonius in his senior class play.

"Tonight, class," said Mr. Parkhill, "I am going to try an experiment."

The class looked up dutifully. They had come to regard Mr. Parkhill's pedagogical innovations as part of the natural order.

"I am going to introduce you  to poetry—great poetry. You see—" Mr. Parkhill delivered a modest lecture on the beauty of poetry, its expression of the loftier thoughts of men, its economy of statement. He hoped it would be a relief from spelling and composition exercises to use poetry as the subject matter of the regular Recitation and Speech period. "I shall write a passage on the board and read it for you. Then, for Recitation and Speech, you will give short addresses, using the passage as the general topic, telling us what it has brought to your minds, what thoughts and ideas."

The class seemed quite pleased by the announcement. Miss Mitnick blushed happily. (This blush was different from most of Miss Mitnick's blushes; there was aspiration and idealism in it.) Mr. Norman Bloom sighed with a businesslike air: you could tell that for him poetry was merely another assignment, like a speech on "What I Like to Eat Best" or a composition on "A Day at a Picnic." Mrs. Moskowitz, to whom any public performance was unpleasant, tried to look enthusiastic, without much success. And Mr. Hyman Kaplan, the heroic smile on his face as indelibly as ever, looked at Mr. Parkhill with admiration and whispered to himself: "Poyetry! Now is poyetry! My! Mus' be progriss ve makink awreddy!"

"The passage will be from Shakespeare," Mr. Parkhill announced, opening the volume.

An excited buzz ran through the class as the magic of that name fell upon them.

"Imachine!" murmured Mr. Kaplan. "Jakesbeer!"

"*Shake*speare, Mr. Kaplan!"

Mr. Parkhill took a piece of chalk and, with care and evident love, wrote the following passage on the board in large, clear letters:

> Tomorrow, and tomorrow, and tomorrow
> Creeps in this petty pace from day to day,
> To the last syllable of recorded time;
> And all our yesterdays have lighted fools
> The way to dusty death. Out, out, brief candle!
> Life's but a walking shadow, a poor player
> That struts and frets his hour upon the stage,
> And then is heard no more; it is a tale
> Told by an idiot, full of sound and fury,
> Signifying nothing.

A reverent hush filled the classroom, as eyes gazed with wonder on this passage from the Bard. Mr. Parkhill was pleased at this.

"I shall read the passage first," he said. "Listen carefully to my enunciation—and—er—let Shakespeare's thoughts sink into your minds."

Mr. Parkhill read: " 'Tomorrow, and tomorrow, and tomorrow . . .' " Mr. Parkhill read very well and this night, as if some special fire burned in him, he read with rare eloquence. "Out, out, brief candle!" In Miss Mitnick's eyes there was inspiration and wonder. "Life's but a walking shadow . . ." Mrs. Moskowitz sat with a heavy frown, indicating cerebration. "It is a tale told by an idiot . . ." Mr. Kaplan's smile had taken on something luminous; but his eyes were closed: it was not clear whether Mr. Kaplan had surrendered to the spell of the Immortal Bard or to that of Morpheus.

"I shall—er—read the passage again," said Mr. Parkhill, clearing his throat vociferously until he saw Mr. Kaplan's eyes open. " 'Tomorrow, and tomorrow, and tomorrow. . . .' "

When Mr. Parkhill had read the passage for the second time, he said: "That should be quite clear now. Are there any questions?"

There were a few questions. Mr. Scymzak wanted to know whether "frets" was "a little kind excitement." Miss Schneiderman asked about "struts." Mr. Kaplan wasn't sure about "cripps." Mr. Parkhill explained the words carefully, and several illustrative uses of each word. "No more questions? Well, I shall allow a few minutes for you all to—er—think over the meaning of the passage. Then we shall begin Recitation and Speech."

Mr. Kaplan promptly closed his eyes again, his smile beatific. The students sank into that revery miscalled thought, searching their souls for the symbols evoked by Shakespeare's immortal words.

"Miss Caravello, will you begin?" asked Mr. Parkhill at last.

Miss Caravello went to the front of the room. "Da poem isa gooda," she said slowly. "Itsa have—"

"It *has*."

"It hasa beautiful wordsa. Itsa lak Dante, Italian poet—"

"Ha!" cried Mr. Kaplan scornfully. "Shaksbeer you metchink mit Tante? *Shaksbeer?* Mein Gott!"

It was obvious that Mr. Kaplan had identified himself with Shakespeare and would tolerate no disparagement of his *alter ego*.

"Miss Caravello is merely expressing her own ideas," said Mr. Parkhill pacifically. (Actually, he felt completely sympathetic to Mr. Kaplan's point of view.)

"Hau Kay," agreed Mr. Kaplan, with a generous wave of the hand. "But to me is no comparink a high-cless man like Shaksbeer mit a Tante, dat's all."

Miss Caravello, her poise shattered, said a few more words and sat down.

Mrs. Yampolsky's contribution was brief. "This is full deep meanings," she said, her eyes on the floor. "Is hard for a person not so good in English to unnistand. But I like."

" '*Like!*' " cried Mr. Kaplan with a fine impatience. " '*Like?*' Batter *love*, Yampolsky. Mit Shaksbeer mus' be *love!*"

Mr. Parkhill had to suggest that Mr. Kaplan control his aesthetic passions. He did understand how Mr. Kaplan felt, however, and sensed a new bond between them. Mrs. Yampolsky staggered through several more nervous comments and retired.

Mr. Bloom was next. He gave a long declamation, ending: "So is passimistic ideas in the poem, and I am optimist. Like should be happy—so we should remember this is only a poem. Maybe is Shakespeare too passimistic."

"You wronk, Bloom!" cried Mr. Kaplan with prompt indignation. "Shaksbeer is passimist because is de *life* passimist also!"

Mr. Parkhill, impressed by this philosophical stroke, realized that Mr. Kaplan, afire with the glory of the Swan of Avon, could not be suppressed. Mr. Kaplan was the kind of man who brooked no criticism of his gods. The only solution was to call on Mr. Kaplan for his recitation at once. Mr. Parkhill was, indeed, curious about what fresh thoughts Mr. Kaplan would utter after his passionate defences of the Bard. When Mr. Parkhill had corrected certain parts of Mr. Bloom's speech, emphasizing Mr. Bloom's failure to use the indefinite article, he said: "Mr. Kaplan, will *you* speak next?"

Mr. Kaplan's face broke into a glow; his smile was like a rainbow. "Soitinly," he said, walking to the front of the room. Never had he seemed so dignified, so eager, so conscious of a great destiny.

"Er—Mr. Kaplan," added Mr. Parkhill, suddenly aware of the possibilities which the situation (Kaplan on Shakespeare) involved: "Speak *carefully.*"

"*Spacially* careful vill I be," Mr. Kaplan reassured him. He cleared his throat, adjusted his tie, and began: "Ladies an' gantleman, you hoid all kinds minninks abot dis piece poyetry, an'—"

"Poetry."

"—abot dis piece *poetry*. But to me is a difference minnink altogadder. Ve mus' tink abot Julius Scissor an' how *he* falt!"

Mr. Parkhill moved nervously, puzzled.

"In dese exact voids is Julius Scissor sayink—"

"Er—Mr. Kaplan," said Mr. Parkhill once he grasped the full import of Mr. Kaplan's error. "The passage is from 'Macbeth.' "

Mr. Kaplan looked at Mr. Parkhill with injured surprise. "*Not* fromm 'Julius Scissor'?" There was pain in his voice.

"No. And it's—er—'Julius *Cae*sar.' "

Mr. Kaplan waited until the last echo of the name had permeated his soul. "Podden me, Mr. Pockheel. Isn't '*seezor*' vat you cottink somting op mit?"

"That," said Mr. Parkhill quickly, "is 'scissor.' You have used 'Caesar' for 'scissor' and 'scissor' for 'Caesar.' "

Mr. Kaplan nodded, marveling at his own virtuosity.

"But go on with your speech, please." Mr. Parkhill, to tell the truth, felt a little guilty that he had not announced at the very beginning that the passage was from "Macbeth." "Tell us *why* you thought the lines were from 'Julius Caesar.' "

"Vell," said Mr. Kaplan to the class, his smile assuming its normal serenity. "I vas positif, becawss I can *see* de whole ting." He paused, debating how to explain this cryptic remark. Then his eyes filled with a strange enchantment. "I see de whole scinn. It's in a tant, on de night bafore dey makink Julius de Kink fromm Rome. So he is axcited an' ken't slip. He is layink in bed, tinking: 'Tomorrow an' tomorrow an' tomorrow. How slow dey movink! Almost cripps! Soch a pity de pace!' "

Before Mr. Parkhill could explain that "petty pace" did not mean "Soch a pity de pace!" Mr. Kaplan had soared on.

"De days go slow, fromm day to day, like leetle tsyllables on phonograph racords fromm time."

Anxiety and bewilderment invaded Mr. Parkhill's eyes.

" 'An' vat abot yestidday?' tinks Julius Scissor. Ha! 'All our yestiddays are only makink a good light for fools to die in de dost!' "

" 'Dusty death' doesn't mean—" There was no interrupting Mr. Kaplan.

"An' Julius Scissor is so tired, an' he vants to fallink aslip. So he hollers, mit fillink, 'Go ot! Go ot! Short candle!' So it goes ot."

Mr. Kaplan's voice dropped to a whisper. "But he ken't slip. Now is bodderink him de idea fromm life. 'Vat is de life altogadder?' tinks Julius Scissor. An' he gives answer, de pot I like de bast. 'Life is like a bum actor, strottink an' hollerink arond de stage for only vun hour bafore he's kicked ot. Life is a tale told by idjots, dat's all, full of fonny sonds an' phooey!' "

Mr. Parkhill could be silent no longer. " 'Full of sound and fury!' " he cried desperately. But inspiration, like an irresistible force, swept Mr. Kaplan on.

" 'Life is monkey business! It don' minn a ting. It signifies nottink!' An' den Julius Scissor closes his ice fest—" Mr. Kaplan demonstrated the Consul's exact ocular process in closing his "ice"—"an' falls dad!"

The class was hushed as Mr. Kaplan stopped. In the silence, a tribute to the fertility of Mr. Kaplan's imagination and the power of his oratory, Mr. Kaplan went to his seat. But just before he sat down, as if adding a postscript, he sighed: "Dat vas mine idea. But ufcawss is all wronk, becawss Mr. Pockheel said de voids ain't abot Julius Scissor altogadder. It's all abot an Irishman by de name Macbat."

Then Mr. Kaplan sat down.

It was some time before Mr. Parkhill could bring himself to criticize Mr. Kaplan's pronunciation, enunciation, diction, grammar, idiom, and sentence structure. For Mr. Parkhill discovered that he could not easily return to the world of reality. He was still trying to tear himself away from that tent outside Rome, where "Julius Scissor," cursed with insomnia, had thought of time and life—and philosophized himself to a strange and sudden death.

Mr. Parkhill was distinctly annoyed with Miss Higby.

❦ ❦ ❦

# Writing

*Donald J. Lloyd*

## Snobs, Slobs, and the English Language [1]

THERE IS at large among us today an unholy number of people who make it their business to correct the speech and writing of others. When Winston Churchill says "It's me" in a radio address, their lips purse and murmur firmly, "It is I," and they sit down and write bitter letters to the New York *Times* about What is Happening to the English Language. Reading "I only had five dollars," they circle *only* and move it to the right of *had*, producing "I had only five dollars" with a sense of virtue that is beyond the measure of man. They are implacable enemies of "different than," of "loan" and "contact" used as verbs, and of dozens of other common expressions. They put triumphant exclamation marks in the margins of library books. They are ready to tangle the thread of any discussion by pouncing on a point of grammar.

If these people were all retired teachers of high-school English, their weight in the community would be negligible; but unfortunately they are not. They are authors, scholars, businessmen, librarians—indeed, they are to be found wherever educated people read and write English. And they are moved by a genuine concern for the language. They have brought us, it is true, to a state in which almost anybody, no matter what his education or the clarity of his expression, is likely to find himself attacked for some locution which he has used. Yet their intentions are of the best. It is only that their earnest minds are in the grip of two curious misconceptions. One is that there is a "correct" standard English which is uniform and definite and has been reduced to rule. The other is that this "correct" standard can only be maintained by the vigilant attention of everybody concerned with language—indeed, by the whole body of educated men and women.

The enemy these self-appointed linguistic sentries see lurking in every expression which stirs the correcter's instinct in them is something they call illiteracy—which is not a simple state of being unlettered, but something more. This illiteracy is a willful and obstinate disregard for the standards of civilized expression. It stirs anger in them when they think they see it, because it seems to them a voluntary ignorance, compounded out of carelessness and sloth. When they think they find it in men who hold responsible positions in the community, they feel it to be a summation of all the decline of the graces of culture,

[1] From *The American Scholar*, XX (Summer, 1951), 279-288. Copyright, 1951, United Chapters of Phi Beta Kappa.

the last reaches of a great wave of vulgarity which is eroding the educated and literate classes. It seems to them to be a surge of crude populism; they hear in each solecism the faint, far-off cries of the rising mob. It is really a sort of ringing in their ears.

In view of the general agreement among the literate that a "correct" standard English exists, and in view of the vituperation directed at anyone suspected of corrupting it, one would expect some kind of agreement about what is correct. There is little to be found; the easy utterance of one educated man is the bane of another. "For all the fussiness about *which* and *that*," remarked Jacques Barzun in the *Nation*, "the combined editorial brass of the country have feebly allowed the word 'disinterested' to be absolutely lost in its original sense. One finds as careful a writer as Aldous Huxley using it to mean uninterested, so that by now a 'disinterested judge' is one that goes to sleep on the bench." And on the subject of what surely is a harmless word, *whom*, Kyle Crichton, associate editor of *Collier's*, is quoted in *Harper's*: "The most loathsome word (to me at least) in the English language is 'whom.' You can always tell a half-educated buffoon by the care he takes in working the word in. When he starts it I know I am faced with a pompous illiterate who is not going to have me long as company."

Probably only a cynic would conclude from the abundance of such comments that those who demand correct English do not know it when they meet it; but some students of language must have been led to wonder, for they have made up lists of disputed locutions and polled the literate on them. So far, the only agreement they have reached has to be expressed in statistical terms.

The latest of these surveys, a questionnaire containing nineteen disputed expressions, was reported by Norman Lewis in *Harper's* magazine for March, 1949. Lewis sent his list to 750 members of certain groups chosen mainly for their professional interest in the English language: lexicographers, high school and college teachers of English, authors, editors, journalists, radio commentators, and "a random sampling of *Harper's* subscribers."

If we count out two groups on the basis of extremely special knowledge and interest—the college professors of English and the lexicographers—we find all the others accepting about half the expressions. The authors and editors (book and magazine) were highest with about 56 per cent, and the editors of women's magazines lowest with about 45. (The expression which was least favored was *less* in the sense of *fewer*—"I encountered *less* difficulties than I had expected" —but even that received an affirmative vote of 23 per cent.) The distinguished electors seem individually to have played hop, skip and jump down the column, each finding among the nineteen expressions about ten he could approve of. If any two fell on the same ten, it was merely a coincidence.

A person innocent in the ways of this controversy, but reasonably well-informed about the English language, noticing that the disputants ignore the massive conformity of most writers in most of their language practices, in order to quibble about fringe matters, might assume that they would welcome the cold light of linguistic science. This is a naïve assumption. In response to an attempt of mine to correct some of the misapprehensions I found in Mr. Barzun's article—among them his curious notion that "detached" and not "uninterested" was the original meaning of "disinterested"—he replied by letter that I represented a misplaced and breezy scientism, and that what I said struck him as "the raw material of 'populism' and willful resistance to Mind. . . . All dictionaries to the contrary notwithstanding, the word disinterested is now prevailingly used in the meaning I deprecated. . . . The fact that an illiterate mistake may become the correct form . . . is no reason for not combating it in its beginnings. . . ." This rejection both of the professional student of language and of the dictionary, when they disagree with the opinions of the writer, has the effect of making each man his own uninhibited authority on language and usage—an effect which I do not believe was exactly what Mr. Barzun had in mind.

What he did have in mind he stated clearly in one distinguished paragraph:

A living culture in one nation (not to speak of one world) must insist on a standard of usage. And usage, as I need not tell you, has important social implications apart from elegance and expressiveness in literature. The work of communication in law, politics and diplomacy, in medicine, technology, and moral speculation depends on the maintenance of a medium of exchange whose values must be kept fixed, as far as possible, like those of any other reliable currency. To prevent debasement and fraud requires vigilance, and it implies the right to blame. It is not snobbery that is involved but literacy on its highest plane, and that literacy has to be protected from ignorance and sloth.

It is a pity that these sentiments, so deserving of approval, should receive it from almost all educated people except those who really know something about how language works. One feels like an uncultivated slob when he dissents—one of the low, inelegant, illiterate, unthinking mob. Yet as a statement about the English language, or about standard English, it is not merely partly true and partly false, but by the consensus of most professional students of language, totally false. It is one of those monstrous errors which gain their original currency by being especially plausible at a suitable time, and maintain themselves long after the circumstances which give rise to them have vanished. Mr. Barzun's remarks are an echo from the eighteenth century; they reek with an odor mustier than the lavender of Grandmother's sachet. They have little relevance to the use of the English language in America in our day.

In actual fact, the standard English used by literate Americans is no pale flower being overgrown by the weeds of vulgar usage: it is a strong, flourishing growth. Nor is it a simple, easily describable entity. Indeed, it can scarcely be called an entity at all, except in the loose sense in which we call the whole vast sum of all the dialects of English spoken and written throughout the world a single language. In this sense, standard American English is the sum of the language habits of the millions of educated people in this country. It is rooted in the intellectual life of this great and varied people. Its forms express what its users wish to express; its words mean what its users think they mean; it is correctly written when it is written by those who write it, and correctly spoken by those who speak it. No prim and self-conscious hoarding of the dead fashions of a superior class gives it its power, but its negligent use by minds intent on stubborn and important problems. There is no point in a tiresome carping about usage; the best thing to do is relax and enjoy it.

There are five simple facts about language in general which we must grasp before we can understand a specific language or pass judgment on a particular usage. It is a pity that they are not more widely known in place of the nonsense which now circulates, for they would relieve the native-born speaker of English of his present uncertainty, and give him a proper authority and confidence in his spontaneous employment of his mother tongue. They arise from a common-sense analysis of the nature of language and the conditions of its use.

In the first place, language is basically speech. Speech comes first in the life of the individual and of the race. It begins in infancy and continues throughout our lives; we produce and attend to a spoken wordage much greater than the written. Even the mass of writing which floods in upon us today is only the froth on an ocean of speech. In history, also, speech comes first. English has been written for only about fifteen hundred years; before this, it is of incalculable antiquity. In speech its grammar was developed; from changes in the sounds of speech, changes in its grammar come. The educated are inclined to feel that the most important aspect of language is the written form of it, and that the spoken language must and should take its standards from this. Actually, the great flow of influence is from speech to writing. Writing does influence speech somewhat, but its influence is like the interest a bank pays on the principal entrusted to it. No principal, no interest.

In the second place, language is personal. It is an experience and a pattern of habits of a very intimate kind. In the home, the family, the school and the neighborhood we learn the speechways of our community, learning to talk as those close to us talk in the give and take of daily life. We are at one with our nation in our easy command of the pitch, tune and phrase of our own home town. Language is personal, also, in that our grasp of it is no greater than our individual experience with it. The English we know is not that vast agglomeration of verbal signs which fills and yet escapes the largest lexicons and grammars, but what we have personally heard and spoken, read and written. The best-read man knows of his native language only a limited number of forms in a limited number of combinations. Outside of these, the wealth which a copious tongue has as its potential is out of his world, and out of everybody's, for no dictionary is so complete or grammar so compendious as to capture it.

The third fact about language is that it changes. It changes in its sounds, its meanings and its syntax. The transmission of sounds, words and meanings from generation to generation is always in some respects imprecise. Minute differences add up in time to perceptible changes, and changes to noticeable drifts.

Difference in changes and in rates of change make local speech sounds, pitches, tones and vocabularies draw subtly and persistently away from one another. And all it takes to produce an identifiable dialect is sufficient segregation over a sufficient length of time.

The fourth great fact about language, then, is that its users are, in one way or another, isolated. Each has with only a few others the sort of familiar relationships which join them in one language community. Yet there are upward of two hundred million native speakers of English in the world. Obviously they cannot all be in close touch with one another. They congeal in nuclei—some stable, some transitory—which by a kind of double-action draw them together and enforce isolation of many more-or-less shifting kinds: the isolation of distance, of education, of economic levels, of occupation, age and sex, of hobbies and political boundaries. Any one of these will be reflected in language habits; any two or three will bring about, in one community, speech differences as great as those caused by oceans and mountain ranges.

The fifth great fact about language is that it is a historical growth of a specific kind. The nature of English is one of the absolutes of our world, like air, water and gravity. Its patterns are not subject to judgment; they simply are. Yet they have not always been what they are; like the physical world, they have changed with time, but always in terms of what they have been. *Boy loves girl* means something different from *girl loves boy*. It is futile for us to prefer another way of conveying these meanings: that is the English way, and we must live with it. Yet students of the language see in this simple pattern the result of a cataclysmic change, great and slow like the geologic upheavals that have brought old salt beds to the very tops of mountain ranges, and as simple. Each is what it is because of what it has been before.

Language as a social instrument reflects all the tides which sweep society, reacting in a local or surface way easily and quickly—as a beach changes its contours to suit the waves—but it offers everywhere a stubborn rock core that only time and massive pressures can move. The whim of a girl can change its vocabulary, but no will of man can touch its essential structure; this is work for the long attrition of generations of human use. Ever lagging a little behind human needs, it offers a multitude of terms for the things men no longer care about, but keeps them improvising to say what has not been said before.

Spoken English is, then, by its own nature and the nature of man, a welter of divergences. The divergences of class and place are sharpest in Britain, where the same dialects have been spoken in the same shires and villages for more than a thousand years. Although these can be heard in America by any traveler, no matter how dull his ear, they are relatively slight, for our language is essentially and repeatedly a colonial speech. Each of the American colonies drew settlers from various parts of Britain; each worked out a common speech based mainly on the dialect of its most influential group of immigrants (which differed from colony to colony); each remained in relative isolation from the others for about a hundred years. Then many colonists began to move to the interior: wave after wave of settlers traveled along rather distinct lines of advance until the continent was covered. Everywhere there was a mingling of dialects, with a composite speech arising, based mainly on the speech of the dominant local group. And so we have a Northern speech fanning out from the Northeastern states, a Midland speech fanning out from the Mid-Atlantic states, and a Southern speech in the land of cottonraisers, all crossing and merging as the pioneers moved west. Local differences are greatest along the Atlantic coast.

Wherever our people settled, they worked out local ways of talking about the things of common experience, and found their own verbal symbols of class distinctions. Here and there are areas where foreign-speaking groups clung together and developed special exotically-flavored dialects, but otherwise most speech patterns in America can be traced back to the dialects of Britain. Everywhere there is a common speech used by the multitude which works with its hands, and a slightly different dialect spoken by the professional and leisure classes.

The standard English written by Americans is not, however, the written form of educated speech, which shows great local variation. Its spellings have only a rough equivalence to the sounds we make; its grammatical system, which has nationwide and even worldwide currency, had its origin in the educated speech of the Northeastern states, and before that in the dialect of London, England. The concentration of schools, colleges, publishing houses and print shops in early New England and New York had the same effect in this country as the concentration in England, for centuries, of political power, commercial activity and intellectual life in London: it established a written standard, native only to those who grew up near the Hudson River or east of it. Elsewhere in America this written standard has been a learned class dialect—learned in the schools as the property and distinguishing mark of an educated class. Like many of its spellings, it is itself a relic of the past, an heirloom handed down from the days when the whole nation looked to the schoolmasters of New England for its book-learning.

The present controversy about usage is simply a sign that times have changed. The several vast and populous regions of this country have grown self-sufficient and self-conscious, and have taken the education of their youth into their own hands. Where the young once had to travel to the East for a respectable education, they receive it now in local public systems of rapid growth and great size. From local schools they may go to local universities of fifteen to fifty thousand students, where they can proceed to the highest degrees. Yale University is overcrowded with some six thousand students; in the community colleges alone of California more than 150,000 are enrolled. Most of these young people take their diplomas and go to work among their own people. They form a literate class greater in numbers and in proportion to the total population than the world has ever seen before. Speaking the speech of their region, they mingle naturally and easily with its people. When they write, they write the language they know, and they print it, for the most part, in presses close at hand. Everywhere they speak a standard literate English—but with differences: a regional speech derived from the usages of the early settlers.

Standard written English is, after all, an abstraction—a group of forms rather arbitrarily selected from the multitude offered by the language as a whole—an abstraction which serves the peculiar needs of the intellect. It achieves its wide currency because the interests of its users are the common interests of the educated, which transcend frontiers and negate distances—law, literature, science, industry and commerce. It is the tool of intelligence. Any thinking person must use it, because only this form of the language provides the instruments of delicate intellectual discrimination. And it is not static. As the needs of the intellect change, standard English changes. Change is its life, as anyone can see who picks up a book written only a little time ago, or examines almost any old newspaper.

The common speech of the uneducated, on the other hand, is comparatively static. Though it varies greatly from place to place, it is everywhere conservative; far from corrupting the standard language, it follows slowly after, preserving old forms long ago given up by literate speakers. "Them things" was once standard, and so were "he don't," "giv," and "clumb" and "riz." Its patterns are archaic, its forms homely and local. Only its vocabulary is rich and daring in metaphor (but the best of this is quickly swiped by writers of standard English). Seldom written because its speakers seldom write, it is yet capable of great literary beauties, uncomplicated force, compact suggestion, and moving sentiment. But it will not bear the burden of heavy thinking, and anyhow, heavy thinkers have a better tool to use. It is about as much danger to the standard language as an old house cat.

I have often wondered at the fear of common English and its speakers which the cultural aristocracy display, at their curious definition of illiteracy, and at the intemperance of their terms, which verges on the pathological. A Freudian should have a picnic with them. They use such epithets as *illiteracies, crudities, barbarisms, ignorance, carelessness* and *sloth*. But who is not negligent in language, as in the mechanics of driving a car? They mutter darkly about "inchoate mob feelings." They confess themselves snobs by denying that their attitudes are snobbish. The stridency of their self-assurance puzzles the mind.

We might better adjust our minds to the divergences of usage in standard written English, for time, space and the normal drift of culture have put them here. We need not raise our eyebrows at a different twist of phrase, but enjoy it as an echo of a way of life somewhat different from our own, but just as good. We could do more than enjoy these things; we could recognize that the fixed forms of the language which do not come to our attention were developed in the past. We have come too late for the show. It is the changing forms that evidence the life in our language and in our society; we could learn much about our people and their ways by simply and objectively observing them.

If there is one thing which is the essence of language, it is its drive to adapt. In an expanding culture like ours, which is invading whole new realms of thought and experience, the inherited language is not wholly suited to what we have to say. We need more exact and expressive modes of utterance than we have; we are working toward finer tolerances. The fabric of our language is flexible, and it can meet our needs. Indeed, we cannot stop it from doing so. Therefore it would be well and wholesome for us to see, in the locutions of the educated which bring us up sharply as we read, not evidences of a rising tide of illiteracy (which they are not), but marks of a grand shift in modes of expression, a self-reliant regionalism, and a persistent groping toward finer distinctions and a more precise utterance.

❦ ❦ ❦

*Jacques Barzun*

# The Retort Circumstantial[1]

MR. LLOYD'S ARTICLE is the culmination of a lively correspondence between him and me, in the course of which I feel sure that I repeatedly cut the ground from under his feet. Since from the outset he hadn't a leg to stand on, my efforts were bound to be useless, but we were both having such a good time that neither of us noticed his plight. At my suggestion he has consented to display his miraculous position in public, and I must therefore return to the charge. The public will judge.

It seems clear in the first place that by preaching the attitude of the mere recorder, the *registrar* of linguistic fact, Mr. Lloyd disqualifies himself for remonstrating with me or anybody else. I, as a writer, am his source, his document, his *raison d'être*, and he can no more logically quarrel with me than he can with a piece of papyrus. Nevertheless, I am willing to concede his human (and very modern) right to inveigh against my moralism in the tones of an outraged moralist.

What then does his objection come to? That in seeking to criticize certain tendencies in current literary English, I am usurping an authority I do not possess, and interfering with the natural evolution of the language. This is the prime fallacy in his case, which rests on a chain of reasoning somewhat as follows: English has greatly changed through the ages; many of these changes were resisted by purists; but the evolution was irresistible, and the result is something we now consider correct and natural. Hence Mr. Barzun's attitude is *contra naturam*; he is an old fogey, a snob, and an ignoramus who thinks he can set his face against the future only because he is blind to the past.

The truth is, of course, that one does not obtain "nature" by merely removing opposition, wise or unwise. Nor can we know what is inevitable until we have tried good and hard to stop it. The whole analogy with nature is false

[1] From *The American Scholar*, XX (Summer, 1951), 289-293. Copyright, 1951, United Chapters of Phi Beta Kappa.

because language is an artificial product of social life, all of whose manifestations, even when regular, bear only a remote likeness to the course of nature. Being a social product, language is everybody's football, and that is precisely what gives me, as well as Mr. Lloyd, the right to push it this way or that by argument.

And here it is important to remember that resistance to change is by no means futile. The history of the language is not what the gallant liberals make out—a struggle between the dauntless Genius of English and a few misguided conservatives. It is a free-for-all. At this point it is usual for the advocates of the "Hands Off" policy to trot out the word "mob," which Swift attacked with several other curtailed forms, and pretend that it was ridiculous of the Dean to boggle at it, "in the light of what came after." Well, what came after is that we deodorized "mob," and abandoned altogether the other vulgarities he was deprecating: we no longer use *rep, pozz, phiz, hipps,* or *plenipo*. The future, in short, belonged as much to Dean Swift as to his opponents—and rather more if we count the hits and misses.

So much for the pseudo-naturalism of the linguistic registrars. Their vow not to judge among words and usages is a fine thing as long as it expresses a becoming sense of incapacity, but it must not turn into a union rule enforceable on those who have taken precisely opposite vows—namely, to exploit, preserve, and possibly enrich the language. This is the duty of the writer, it calls for judgment, and it brings us to that blessed word "disinterested," which seems to have acted on Mr. Lloyd like a whiff of mustard to the nose.

My simple and meritorious deed as regards "disinterested" was to draw attention to its widespread misuse as a duplicate of *un*interested. Examples abound, and the fight against the plague may already be lost without the confusion being anything like over. Every piece of printed matter exhibits it, and nearly every conversation. Just the other day I heard this sentence, spoken to identify a stranger: "He is an impresario, but when it comes to art, he's completely disinterested." Did the speaker mean, X has no interest in art? Or: he is so much interested in it that money is no object? According to current usage this is impossible to determine without questioning the speaker. Not even his presumed degree of education will settle the matter, for the wrong use has affected all ranks.

At the phrase "wrong use," Mr. Lloyd twitched his non-existent leg, and with his hands made the motions of a man taking to earth in a dictionary. A few American, and especially collegiate, dictionaries do give the meaning "uninterested" as a second choice—which is a sufficient reason for me to view with a lack-luster eye Mr. Lloyd's naïve faith in lexicographers. The one work that seems relevant to the argument is the O.E.D., which gives us the history of the word. It tells us that the meaning *un*interested is obsolete and it lists five separate earlier forms, going back to the French of Montaigne, all connected with the idea of "removing the self interest of a person in a thing." As an English adjective, examples are given from 1659 to Dr. Livingstone in 1865, with the meaning: "not influenced by interest, impartial, unbiased, unprejudiced." My original remark was to the effect that nowadays the "disinterested judge" is probably taken to mean one who sleeps on the bench. My final remark is: As a writer concerned with the precision and flexibility of the language I use, I cannot regard the return to an obsolete and ambiguous form as useful or in any other way justified.

I now carry the war into the enemy's camp. If instead of complacently taking notes on the growing confusion, and protecting under pretext of "science" the vagaries of modern usage, Mr. Lloyd and his compeers would reflect upon their data, they might be able to safeguard the complex instrument of our speech by telling us when and why these deplorable losses occur, and how they might be repaired—loss of clarity and exactness at large, absolute loss of meaning in a word such as "disinterested" and in another such as "connive." Everyone has seen this last used as a synonym for "conspire" and "contrive"; I have heard it in the intransitive sense of "manage" about some trivial business: "How did you connive?" Hitherto, when you escaped from the concentration camp because the guard deliberately looked the other way, it was he who *connived* at your escape, no one else. Can it be that the action is obsolete and we no longer need the word?

These instances are not isolated, and I shall accept statistical refutation only from someone who can show that he reads each year more written matter than I, and hears a greater variety of local uses from a larger body of students.

Meantime, the generality which I hazarded, and which Mr. Lloyd assails as undemocratic and tainted with ethical feeling, is that with the rapid extension of educational opportunities, many persons of otherwise simple hearts are snatching at words half understood in order to bedeck their thoughts. Only the other day I read in a "literary" review about a distinguished American critic who was so full of insight that he could be called a *voyeur*. The writer meant *voyant*, if anything, but he could certainly be sued for slander before an educated court.

Foreign words are always treacherous, but what of the newspaper editorial which states that Mr. So-and-so's election is "highly fortuitous" (meaning "fortunate"), or the college dean who tells parents that his institution gives the students "a fulsome education"? Then there are those who believe that "to a degree" means "to a certain extent," instead of just the opposite. Have not the oil and drug companies been forced to change their labels to "flammable" because many users of their products took "*inflammable*" to mean non-combustible? At that stage, the issue ceases to be comic or inconsequential. With the tremendous output of verbiage by air and print to which we are all subjected, the corruption of meaning is rapid and extensive. We are at the mercy of anyone who thinks the sense of a word is discoverable by inspection, and whose misuse consequently liberates an echoing error in the minds of his peers.

To put it differently, the danger to English today is not from bad grammar, dialect, vulgar forms, or native crudity, but from misused ornaments three syllables long. The enemy is not illiteracy but incomplete literacy—and since this implies pretension it justifies reproof. There is no defense against the depredations of the brash except vigilance and no quarter given. I am certain that in this regard Mr. Lloyd, who writes with so much felicity and force, does exactly this in his capacity as a college teacher of English. Why then does he not square his precepts with his practice? I cannot answer for him, but to help his amputated philosophy to its feet, I want by way of conclusion to quote from a writer who, being anonymous and attached to both journalism and business, can hardly be suspected of flaunting pedantry and preciosity. The extract is from *Fortune* for November, 1950:

"Language is not something we can disembody; it is an ethical as well as a mechanical entity, inextricably bound up in ourselves, our positions, and our relations with those about us."

*The Editors of* Fortune

# The Language of Business [1]

NOT so long ago, the businessman used to take his language pretty much for granted. He could afford to. His place was respected and his authority unquestioned. And so he bought, he sold, he collected his bills, made an occasional speech perhaps—and if the public, the workers, or the government didn't quite understand what he was up to, well, so much the better for all concerned.

But no longer. Acknowledging the fact—and the necessity—of others' scrutiny, he has made the interchange of facts and ideas with them one of his principal jobs. The house organ, the interoffice memo, the press release, the press conference, the annual report—the range of his efforts has grown enormous. So widespread, indeed, that business has become almost as extensive a publisher as the government itself.

Is the language of business up to the job? The news—and refreshing news it is—is that the American businessman himself has begun to conclude that it is not. Some, in fact, have gone so far as to assert that the pomposity of management prose is the "root ill of our communication troubles." While that may be an overexcited judgment, management's surveys have demonstrated that a large amount of its language has been not only incomprehensible to the people it is trying to reach, but enormously expensive in money, time, and misunderstanding as well. "It is high time the American businessman discovered the English language—it would be very useful to him" . . . "We've turned our offices into paper mills" . . . "We love curt clear correspondence—but damned few of us know how to write it." Everywhere the chorus of self-criticism is growing.

[1] Reprinted from the November, 1950 issue of *Fortune* Magazine by special permission of the Editors. Copyright, 1950, Time, Inc.

The positive results of this self-examination have been impressive. In company after company, executives have been setting up "writing clinics" to scour management copy, staging correspondence-improvement courses, holding school in conference and public-speaking techniques, and, at the very least, peppering subordinates with "For-God's-sake-won't-you-people-learn-to-use-English-around-here" memos. All of which is clearly to the good. At the same time—and not so clearly to the good—a school of experts has come forward to help the businessman by redesigning the language of industry. To accomplish this, the experts have developed a scientific method that, as we shall see later, has some disturbing implications. Meanwhile, a look at the anatomy of this language that is to be redesigned.

First, the written variety—and that infamous jargon, which, for want of a better term, we'll call businesese. Its signal characteristic, as the reader and all other critics of businesese will recognize, is its uniformity. Almost invariably, businesese is marked by the heavy use of the passive construction. Nobody ever *does* anything. Things *happen*—and the author of the action is only barely implied. Thus, one does not refer to something, reference is made to; similarly, while prices may rise, nobody *raises* them. To be sure, in businesese there is not quite the same anonymity as is found in federal prose, for "I" and "we" do appear often. Except when the news to be relayed is good, however, there is no mistaking that the "I" and "we" are merely a convenient fiction and that the real author isn't a person at all but that great mystic force known as the corporation.

Except for a few special expressions, its vocabulary is everywhere quite the same. Midwesterners are likely to dispute the latter point, but a reading of approximately 500,000 words of business prose indicates no striking differences —in the Midwest or anywhere else. Moreover, in sounding out a hundred executives on the subject, *Fortune* found that their views coincided remarkably, particularly so in the matter of pet peeves (principally: "please be advised," "in reference to yours of . . . ," "we wish to draw attention," "to acknowledge your letter"). The phrases of businesese are everywhere so uniform, in fact, that stenographers have a full set of shorthand symbols for them.

Because of this uniformity, defenders of businesese can argue that it doesn't make for misunderstanding. After all, everybody knows the symbols, and, furthermore, wouldn't a lot of people be offended by the terseness of more concise wording? There is something to this theory. Since businesese generally is twice as wordy as plain English, however, the theory is rather expensive to uphold. By the use of regular English the cost of the average letter—commonly estimated at 75 cents to $1—can be cut by about 20 cents. For a firm emitting a million letters a year, this could mean an annual saving of $200,000. Probably it would be even greater; for, by the calculations of correspondence specialist Richard Morris, roughly 15 per cent of the letters currently being written wouldn't be necessary at all if the preceding correspondence had been in regular English in the first place.

Where do the terms of businesese come from? Most, of course, are hand-me-downs from former generations of businessmen, but many are the fruit of cross-fertilization with other jargons. A businessman who castigates government bureaucrats, for example, is at the same time apt to be activating, expediting, implementing, effectuating, optimizing, minimizing, and maximizing—and at all levels and echelons within the framework of broad policy areas. Similarly, though he is amused by the long-hairs and the social scientists, he is beginning to speak knowingly of projective techniques, social dynamics, depth interviewing, and sometime soon, if he keeps up at this rate, he will probably appropriate that hallmark of the sound sociological paper, "insightful." Businesese, in fact, has very nearly become the great common meeting ground of the jargons.

Why do people who in private talk so pungently often write so pompously? There are many reasons: tradition, the demands of time, carelessness, the conservative influence of the secretary. Above all is the simple matter of status. Theorem: the less established the status of a person, the more his dependence on jargon. Examine the man who has just graduated from pecking out his own letters to declaiming them to a secretary and you are likely to have a man hopelessly intoxicated with the rhythm of businesese. Conversely, if you come across a blunt yes or no in a letter, you don't need to glance further to grasp that the author feels pretty firm in his chair.

The application of euphemism, a favored device of businesese, further illustrates this status principle. Take the field of selling. At the top of the ladder you will find a great many people in it: *sales* managers, vice presidents for *sales*, etc. As you go down the ranks, however, it becomes difficult to find people in this line of work. Field underwriters, estate planners, merchandising apprentices, social engineers, distribution analysts, and representatives of one kind or another, yes. But *sales*men? Rarely.

Not only does businesese confer status, it protects it as well, by its magnificent usefulness for buck passing and hedging. "All you have to remember," one executive says, "is the one basis which characterizes all such intracommunication: let the language be ambiguous enough that if the text be successfully carried out, all credit may be claimed; but if the text be unsuccessfully carried out, a technical alibi can be set up out of the text itself."

For this purpose there is a regular subglossary of businesese. Most notable terms: "in the process of," "at this time," "under consideration," "in the not-too distant future," "company policy," and, when one is unable to explain something properly, "obviously." People who have to submit periodic reports to their superiors are particularly dependent on such terms—salesmen, for example, would have a hard time if they couldn't report of some prospects that they were "very impressed." ("I am allergic to that word," says one sales manager. "It results in so few orders.")

The full application of businesese to hedging occurs when more than two heads are put to work on a problem. As the members of top management sit around the table, a relatively simple policy statement is introduced for discussion. This is kicked around a bit, as the saying goes, for though it certainly is a fine statement, couldn't agree with it more, there are just a few little angles and suggestions that maybe ought to be noted. Thereupon each executive, much as a baseball captain grasps a bat in choosing up sides, adds his qualification, until finally the original statement has been at once pointed up, toned down, given more dignity, made more forceful, altered to anticipate possible objections, concretized, amended, and resolved. Now no longer a mere statement but a philosophy, or collection of philosophies, it is turned over to the Public Relations Department to give to the waiting public. There is nothing, as so many people say, quite like what you get when everybody on the team works together.

Besides written businesese, there is another and far more influential category of business English. Generally, it is found in the spoken language of business—in particular, that brand to be heard at the banquet table, the convention, and the conference table.

It might best be called *reverse* gobbledegook, for in almost every outward respect it is the opposite of written jargon. Where written jargon is multisyllabic, the other is filled with short terse words; its sentences are short and their construction so much more active than passive that exclamation marks occur almost as frequently as periods. It is English that is on the beam, English with its feet on the ground; in short, *shirt-sleeve* English.

Thanks to reverse gobbledegook, the less you have to say, the more emphatically you can say it. All one has to do is use certain hard-hitting expressions, and refer as frequently as possible to the fact that these expressions are being used. A sure forewarning of its onrush, accordingly, is a prefatory announcement by the speaker that he is not going to beat around the bush, pull any punches, pussyfoot, use two-dollar words, or the like. The rest is inevitable; so standardized are the expressions of reverse gobbledegook that an audience would be stunned to attention were a single one of them altered by so much as a word. (One of these days a clever speaker is going to capitalize on this. "Gentlemen," he will say, "I offer a panacea.")

As a result, reverse gobbledegook can be self-defeating; that is, since its whole effect lies in the dynamic quality the words convey, their constant use tends to neutralize them. This can be overcome, however, by adding strengtheners—so that, in a very real sense of the word, it cannot be overemphasized that you sincerely, and unquestionably, meant what you said in the first place.

Like written businesese, reverse gobbledegook also confers status. For this purpose, it provides a sort of slang that, skillfully applied—particularly at the conference table—will impart to the user an appearance of savviness, cooniness, and general know-how. Want to mark yourself as a comer in the advertising field? Speak, then, of fun stories, sweet guys, the hard sell, straw men you set up to back into, and points you can hang your hat on.[2] For each field

2 Other current advertising favorites: "let's pull all the stops out on this one"; "let's noodle this one"; "let's sneak the message across"; "we'll touch all bases on this one";

you will find a subglossary, and, common to all of them, such universal terms as "play it by ear," "the pitch," "the deal," and the many expressions built on the suffix "wise." ("Budget-wise, Al, the pitch shapes up like this . . .")

Another characteristic of reverse gobbledegook is its dependence on analogy and metaphor. During a single banquet you may find business problems equated with an airplane, a broad highway, a boat being rocked, a river, a riverbank, a stream, a bridge, a train, a three-legged stool, and, sometimes, three or four of these things at once in which case the passage is generally summed up with something like "It's as simple as that," or "That's all there is to the problem." (From a recent speech: "So business enterprise of America is trying to hone a sales force into the cutting edge of an economy and there is a virus running rampant in the flock. Security-mindedness is a log across the stream when it comes to developing the optimistic salesman outlook.")

Outstanding is the great American football analogy. No figure of speech is a tenth as seductive to the businessman. Just why this should be so—baseball, curiously, is much less used—is generally explained by its adaptability to all sorts of situations. Furthermore, the football analogy is *satisfying*. It is bounded by two goal lines and is thus finite. There is always a solution. And that is what makes it so often treacherous.

For analogy and metaphor can be insidiously attractive substitutes for thought. They are not, of course, when fleetingly used, when, as H. W. Fowler puts it (in *Modern English Usage*), they "flash out for the length of a line or so and are gone," but this is rarely the case in reverse gobbledegook. The user starts innocuously enough; his policy is *like* a thingamajig in one respect. But only the stanchest mind can resist the analogy further. Before long he is entwined, and unconsciously operating on the premise that his policy *is* a thingamajig. The language, in short, has molded thinking, and the results can be a good bit more serious than a poor speech.

The mishaps of one consumer-goods corporation illustrate this hazard. Not so long ago, the men who owned the company were casting about for a Goal. Up to then it had been money. But now they had acquired a lot of it, they were getting on in years, and anyway it didn't sound good. And so, on this enlightened-goal problem, the Chief fell to pondering at the conference table. When you get right down to it, the company was just like a big football team. You don't win unless you have a good team, do you? You could say that again. Well, before he gets a good team, what does the coach have to

---

"means absolutely nothing to the lay mind"; "we'll get a plus value on this one"; "it was quite a hassle"; "let's not hassle over this."

Journalists laugh and laugh at this sort of thing. Just why, it is difficult to say, except possibly that being less inventive, they prefer to hang on to the old expressions rather than coin new ones. Terms now nearing the end of the run (including some of *Fortune's*): ambivalence, dichotomy, schizophrenic, "two hours and four martinis (beers, etc.) later"; "it's as difficult (easy, etc.) as it is complex (difficult, etc.)"; "their profits (feelings, etc.) are showing."

do? Very simple. He has to go out and find good players. Just thinking out loud, mind you, but wasn't the big job then to get the right recruits?

Almost automatically, this was mimeographed as the company's rationale— "The Touchdown Play" it was called—and before long executives were spending almost as much time on the new trainees as they were on their regular jobs, and when they weren't doing this, they were scouring the colleges for more. Everything went swimmingly; the policy was soon the wonder of the merchandising world; the top executives were suffused with a sense of enlightenment—and the place was jammed with eager young men.

In only one respect did the analogy break down. A year later practically all of the competition came out with a new product embodying a notable technical advance. Our company didn't. It was still getting the team ready.

Now with almost every use of the cliché and stereotype mentioned so far, a better case could be made out for the use of simple, unhackneyed English. It is a mistake, however, to be too rigorously critical on this score. Since the symbols of language convey emotion as well as communicate facts and ideas, many a prefabricated phrase has become inextricably tied with certain emotional responses. This infuriates the semanticists—"intensional thinking" is their cuss word for it—but a good part of business has been built on it. The American sales meeting, certainly, would be quite impossible otherwise.

Furthermore business, like many another occupation, is governed by a ritual as rigid as the steps of ballet, and while the efficient executive makes fun of all this, he has the good sense to know when to put it to use himself. The dinner for the retiring employee, for example; for years this has been prime fodder for short-story writers. But what if the toastmaster were to dispense with the timeworn expressions and thus tacitly concede what everyone knows to be nothing less than the truth: that old Charlie has been getting in everybody's hair for the last fifteen years and it'll be wonderful to see him go. Everyone, Charlie's worst enemies included, would be shocked, morale would suffer, and the usefulness of the executive to the organization would be lessened.

So with the interoffice memo about the man being horizontally promoted to some branch office. Again the ceremonial is unvarying: pillar of strength . . . larger responsibilities . . . Ed's invaluable experience in this field makes him the logical . . . know the whole staff will join me in wishing Ed good luck in his new job . . . Nobody is fooled in the slightest, of course, but what could have been a disagreeable, and for Ed a shattering, experience is smoothed over by the blessed analgesic of businesese. There is *something* of a case for timeworn expressions. But it is a case that needs no further making.

For all its faults, business language is the subject of plenty of good news. Over a third of top U.S. corporations, a *Fortune* sampling indicates, have set up some sort of program to improve it. Monsanto Chemical and Glidden Co. are working on both letters and interoffice memos. "In our campaign to simplify communications," reports Glidden's President Dwight Joyce, "we encourage 'Yes' and 'No' answers, which in turn makes for briefer, clearer questions." Montgomery Ward uses slide films to show its people how to write good-will-building letters. Numerous banks, insurance companies, and department stores have engaged experts to simplify and personalize their letters. And over the past two years the "Cy" Frailey business-correspondence courses sponsored by the Dartnell Corp. in major cities of the U.S. have attracted 25,000 executives.

Public-speaking courses are provided by such companies as SKF, Jones & Laughlin, and Johnson & Johnson. In the last two years General Motors has encouraged 2,000 of its management and supervisory people to express themselves better by taking Dale Carnegie speech courses. Business and management associations (e.g., National Association of Manufacturers, American Management Association, American Institute of Banking, National Association of Foremen) publish material on speech training. In one notable instance, at Bridgeport, Connecticut, an informal group of businessmen became so absorbed in the problem that they chipped in and hired a Yale professor to teach them how to address groups and conduct meetings. And evidently the crusade is more than a nine-to-five concern of businessmen. To judge from recent book sales, they are reading more "practical English" and vocabulary-building books than ever before.

Paralleling these better-business-English efforts has been a movement of even greater significance. It has been called the "plain talk" movement, but it is, in fact, a sort of prose-engineering program, for its core is the use of some newly refined scientific techniques to achieve readability. In only four years it has already produced a measurable effect on the English of business and, if it continues to thrive, it will have a profound effect not only on the English of business but on the English of advertising, journalism, and literature as well.

How did it happen? Such phenomena are usually hard to account for. This one, however, is not.

"My own contribution . . . has been quite modest," readability expert Dr. Rudolf Flesch recently told a convention of P.R. men, "but I think I can truthfully say that it has already had some effect." Dr. Flesch was unduly modest. Rarely have the man and the moment collided so effectively. Almost from the moment in 1946 when he turned his Columbia Ph.D. thesis on readability into the best-selling *The Art of Plain Talk*, Flesch's impact has been tremendous.

The scientific basis was not new; it was evolved by psychologists in the 1920's for the grading and writing of children's textbooks. But as developed by Flesch it gave a new form—and justification—to a movement that had been overtaking American prose. "It was as if," recalls one enthusiast, "we had just been waiting for someone to break the ice."

What Flesch teaches, briefly, is a scientific method of achieving plain, understandable prose. To this end we should write as we talk; eschew irony, rhythm, rhetorical sentences; substitute concrete for abstract words. Equally important, we should surcharge our prose with as much human interest as possible. Then, to measure how we are succeeding, we can apply two formulas. One, based on syllable and sentence count per 100 words, measures the "reading ease" of our writing. The other, based on the percentage of "personal" words and sentences, measures its "human interest." The reading-ease index is tied to the different levels of the U.S. adult population. Thus we can scientifically make sure that we are writing to the level of our particular audience —or better yet, as Flesch advises, somewhat below it.[3]

The first impact of this doctrine was on newspaper writing, but soon it was making itself felt in another field. For years industrial psychologists had been champing to apply scientific methods to employee-management communication material, but, what with cultural-lag troubles, they hadn't been able to get very far. And now here at last was the ideal wedge; "the effectiveness . . . [of] the Flesch formula," as one put it, "forces the issue." Enthusiastically they fell to work measuring house-organ prose, reconstructing information bulletins, and in general showing business just how terrible its stuff was and how much better it could be.

Before long another readability expert, Robert Gunning, was making studies for Borden's, the B. & O. Railroad, and other large companies. John McElroy (formerly head of Gunning's industrial division) set up Readability Associates, and was soon holding seminars on his "fog-count" system for such firms as Ford, Detroit Edison, and American Airlines. General Motors, making a broad attack on the readability problem, has at times employed all three experts, Gunning, McElroy, and Flesch.[4] The Psychological Corp. began four-day workshops, where, at $500 a head, company representatives could be instructed in the readability techniques so that they in turn could go back and teach them to others. Even the military joined in; in the most notable of such efforts the Air Matériel Command got out an official—and highly readable—manual on the Flesch approach and put psychologist A. O. England to work indoctrinating all hands in it.

What's been the effect of all this? The readability formulas have dramatized, as no subjective critique ever could, the needless obscurity and pomposity of much everyday language. Furthermore, the readability texts have been full of so much good sense on such matters as grammar and punctuation that they

[3] The reading-ease formula—statisticians call it "regression equation"—is 206.835 minus (1.015 times the average number of words per sentence) plus (.846 times the number of syllables per 100 words). Using this (simplified in chart form for quick use), we find that the reading-ease score of the two preceding text paragraphs is 53. This puts them on the "fairly difficult"—i.e., high school—reading level, and thus readable by 54 per cent of the adult population. Human-interest score: 30 ("interesting").

[4] G.M. has devised a "Reading-Ease Calculator"—a kind of wheel by which, with a minimum of mathematics, the prose in its twenty-seven employee publications can be measured. Also it has Purdue psychologists compiling a list of the words most frequently used by G.M. personnel, and is measuring the reading-ability levels of some of its employee groups.

have served to encourage the timid away from outworn do's and dont's of writing. Where the readability doctrines have been taught, there has been not only a decrease in the use of jargon, but a new enthusiasm and respect for the rhythm of colloquial speech.

So far, so good. But how much further, and then how good? The implications of the readability approach warrant careful thought. For if American "functional" English is to be homogenized more and more along these new lines, we should at least, before it all becomes official, have a hard look at what it is leading us to. In purest businesese, is there a danger that we'll jump out of a Pandora's box into a fire?

First, a look at some of the new rules. Most important, the advice that is the core of the movement: to write as we talk. Part of the "secret" of readable writing, we are told, lies in repetition and loosely built sentences—because that is the way we talk. Well, at least that's the way some people talk—haltings, back-trackings, and that sort of thing—they talk on forever sometimes—a lot of excelsior, that's what it adds up to—and it's not difficult at all, because it's certainly easier than the old-fashioned way of organizing your thoughts. In fact, there is only one real question to be raised. Are talking and writing the same thing? They are not—and to say that they should be allows and encourages us to rationalize sloppiness and faulty thinking.

In this colloquializing we are also adjured to make everything into a human-interest story. (Flesch: "There's nothing on earth that cannot be told through a hero or heroine who's trying to solve a problem in spite of a series of obstacles.") It is true, of course, that one who describes a problem in terms of the simple love of a man for his dog, a tale as old as time, will have a more *readable* piece than one who tends to somewhat more abstract treatment. But there are quite a number of things that *cannot* be explained by a human-interest tale, and to treat them as if they could be is to mislead the reader by oversimplifying.

Emphasis on the short word, naturally enough, is another feature of the plain-talk movement, and while the readability experts themselves caution people against applying this prescription too rigidly, it has reached a rather extreme point of veneration. Short words, certainly, need no defense. But there are times when the longer one is the *right* word, and if it were not used the writer would have to take up more space saying it another way. And even if the long word were unknown to such and such a percentage of the audience, it might be perfectly clear—or stimulating—to them in a context of sound, lucid English. The Elizabethans knew this well—and so, for that matter, do the pulp writers (e.g., the gibbous moon, the lambent rays, diaphanous dresses, etc.).

By now, if we have followed the above rules, our style should be understandable enough. Just to make sure, however, Flesch has a few more rules:

*Do not use rhythm (maybe your reader won't catch on).*

*Do not use periodic sentences.*

*Do not use rhetorical questions.*

*Do not use metaphors without an explanation.*
*Do not use contrast without an explanation.*
*Do not use irony (half the people won't get it).*

Now we are not to forswear these devices because they are bad; we are to discard them because somebody *might* possibly misunderstand us. The blood-toil-tears-and-sweat metaphor of Churchill, for example: "The reader gets a vague notion," says Flesch, "that Churchill used a little word picture of three wet things instead of saying *war*; and that's that." Flesch goes on to ask a rhetorical question: would "you must expect great suffering and hard work" have been a better way to put it? "Nobody, of course," he says, "can answer such a question." Nobody? We'll take a crack at it. NO!

If we have followed these rules, we are now able to talk the level of language the audience will be able to understand "without effort." But even this is not enough. *We must go one step below that level.* We must "shoot beneath the target"; we must "translate down the scale." And for this we don't even need the formulas, for, as Flesch correctly points out, this writing down should by now have become instinctive to us.

Let us imagine that over the next hundred years everyone followed this advice and deliberately wrote beneath the capabilities of his audience. What would happen? Theoretically, we would get ourselves into a sort of ever decreasing circle, and, as layer after layer of our language atrophied, eventually spiral our way back to the schoolbook level that got the whole readability doctrine under way in the first place. The "regression" equation would be complete.

And haven't we gone quite far enough as it is? Already we have turned the man in the street into a Frankenstein. We hand him an electric recorder to edit our movies; we watch his radio dial to predetermine what we will put on the air—and now we are to ape him to learn how to write.

We should long since have delivered ourselves of this oaf, for in reality he does not even exist. He is a self-perpetuating stereotype, the reflection of the lowest common denominators we have been looking for. In creating him we have done not only ourselves but our audiences a disservice, for though they will respond to the tawdry, they will also respond—as many a book, speech, ad, and movie has demonstrated—to the best we give them. But they cannot if we abdicate our moral obligation to give the best that is in us.

So what of the formulas? What do they really measure? Understandability? (And, if so, of what?) Simplicity? Or merely the number of things they are supposed to measure? For a practical experiment, *Fortune* selected thirteen out of a collection of 100 business speeches. The eight most fatuous of the speeches were put in one group; the five most lucid were put in another. Each speech was then evaluated by means of the two formulas to find its reading-ease and human-interest scores. The result: there was practically no *significant difference* between the average scores of the two groups. (Average reading-ease score: 61—eighth- and ninth-grade reading level; average human-

interest score: 40—"very interesting.") All, then, represented good "plain talk"
—and there was nothing in the scores to indicate the tremendous disparity
between the two types.

In thus ignoring the relationship between style and content, the formulas
have ignored the fundamentals of language. Language is not something we
can disembody; it is an ethical as well as mechanical matter, inextricably bound
up in ourselves, our positions, and our relations with those about us. When a
businessman doubletalks, for example, it is often for reasons deeper than mis-
handled prose—hypersensitivity to criticism, fear of the competition, fear of
getting out of line with trade-association policy, fear of a government suit, a
serious split in corporation policy—or, as is occasionally the case, the lack of
any policy to begin with. Is "plain talk" the answer here? It is not. It is a
fraud on the listener.

For it is only the illusion of simplicity that the manipulation of language
can win for us. Simplicity is an elusive, almost complex thing. It comes from
discipline and organization of thought, intellectual courage—and many other
attributes more hard won than by short words and short sentences. For plain
talk—honest plain talk—is the reward of simplicity, not the means to it. The
distinction may seem slight, but it is tremendously important.

In a sense, this whole prose-engineering movement is a measure of the
growing specialization of our society—for it is an attempt to provide a sort of
pidgin English by which we can intercommunicate over the gaps. So let us give
the readability people their due. At least they have tried to bridge the gaps
and, perhaps more important, they have called our attention to the necessity for
doing so. We owe them, then, a debt—and if their solution falls short in
many respects, the very avidity with which people have seized on it is
proof enough that there is a void to fill.

Thus the readability movement is also the measure of the failure of our
schools and colleges. Patently, something is very wrong with the teaching of
English when graduates so fail to grasp the fundamentals of good English that
they feel they must learn a separate kind for everyday life—and a rather bob-
tail one at that. The fault may be, as some have claimed, that our academic
English courses are still set up on the implicit assumption that their function
is to provide a schooling for those who are to be novelists, poets, and
scholars. Perhaps it is for this reason that the word "literary" is increasingly
used as a term of opprobrium.

Meanwhile the teaching of English in the non-liberal-arts courses has been
geared more and more to the "functional" kind of writing the graduate will
perform. "In my opinion," says Professor Edward Kilduff of N.Y.U.'s School
of Commerce, "the most effective kind of English composition being taught
today . . . is the realistic, practical non-literary American type that we find in
such courses as business writing, engineering writing, newspaper writing, publicity writing, and advertising writing."

True or not, is a further extension of this trend necessarily the answer?

Specialization in our colleges has already gone so far that it is hard to see how a further breakdown of the humanities would be anything but harmful. We do not need more "applied" English courses; what we need, first of all, is better basic ones. How this is to be achieved in our schools and colleges is a difficult problem, but it is time we were about it.

For somewhere, certainly, between the extremes of the "functional" and the "literary" there is a happy middle ground. Those firms who have pioneered in improving the language of their people seem to have reached the same conclusion. The great majority of their courses, seminars, and "clinics" have been concentrated not on supplying rules to be slavishly followed—but on provoking an *awareness* of good English. Their example is one that all of U.S. business can follow with great profit.

In the meantime let us not forswear all the richness of our language. Its misuse is not the root ill of our communication problem; it is only the signal of it. And if we make a real effort to win mutual understanding, we need have no fear of the infinite variety of our language—or the ability of our listeners to respond to it. All of which applies to businessmen no less than to everyone else in our society. When businessmen have something to say, and mean it, and feel it, their audience will understand.

❦ ❦ ❦

*From* The New Yorker

# Notes and Comment[1]

A PUBLISHER in Chicago has sent us a pocket calculating machine by which we may test our writing to see whether it is intelligible. The calculator was developed by General Motors, who, not satisfied with giving the world a Cadillac, now dream of bringing perfect understanding to men. The machine (it is simply a celluloid card with a dial) is called the Reading-Ease Calculator and shows four grades of "reading ease"—Very Easy, Easy, Hard, and Very Hard. You count your words and syllables, set the dial, and an indicator lets you know whether anybody is going to understand what you have written. An instruction book came with it, and after mastering the simple rules we lost no time in running a test on the instruction book itself, to see how *that* writer was doing. The poor fellow! His leading essay, the one on the front cover, tested Very Hard.

Our next step was to study the first phrase on the face of the calculator: "How to test Reading-Ease of written matter." There is, of course, no such thing as reading ease of written matter. There is the ease with

[1] *The New Yorker*, XXVII (Mar. 7, 1951), 21-22. Reprinted by permission. Copyright, 1951, The New Yorker Magazine, Inc.

which matter can be read, but that is a condition of the reader, not of the matter. Thus the inventors and distributors of this calculator get off to a poor start, with a Very Hard instruction book and a slovenly phrase. Already they have one foot caught in the brier patch of English usage.

Not only did the author of the instruction book score badly on the front cover, but inside the book he used the word "personalize" in an essay on how to improve one's writing. A man who likes the word "personalize" is entitled to his choice, but we wonder whether he should be in the business of giving advice to writers. "Whenever possible," he wrote, "personalize your writing by directing it to the reader." As for us, we would as lief Simonize our grandmother as personalize our writing.

In the same envelope with the calculator, we received another training aid for writers—a booklet called "How to Write Better," by Rudolf Flesch. This, too, we studied, and it quickly demonstrated the broncolike ability of the English language to throw whoever leaps cocksurely into the saddle. The language not only can toss a rider but knows a thousand tricks for tossing him, each more gay than the last. Dr. Flesch stayed in the saddle only a moment or two. Under the heading "Think Before You Write," he wrote, "The main thing to consider is your *purpose* in writing. Why are you sitting down to write?" And echo answered: Because, sir, it is more comfortable than standing up.

Communication by the written word is a subtler (and more beautiful) thing than Dr. Flesch or General Motors imagines. They contend that the "average reader" is capable of reading only what tests Easy, and that the writer should write at or below this level. This is a presumptuous and degrading idea. There is no average reader, and to reach down toward this mythical character is to deny that each of us is on the way up, is ascending. ("Ascending," by the way, is a word Dr. Flesch advises writers to stay away from. Too unusual.)

It is our belief that no writer can improve his work until he discards the dulcet notion that the reader is feeble-minded, for writing is an act of faith, not a trick of grammar. Ascent is at the heart of the matter. A country whose writers are following a calculating machine downstairs is not ascending —if you will pardon the expression—and a writer who questions the capacity of the person at the other end of the line is not a writer at all, merely a schemer. The movies long ago decided that a wider communication could be achieved by a deliberate descent to a lower level, and they walked proudly down until they reached the cellar. Now they are groping for the light switch, hoping to find the way out.

We have studied Dr. Flesch's instructions diligently, but we return for guidance in these matters to an earlier American, who wrote with more patience, more confidence. "I fear chiefly," he wrote, "lest my expression may not be *extra-vagant* enough, may not wander far enough beyond the narrow limits of my daily experience, so as to be adequate to the truth of which I

have been convinced. . . . Why level downward to our dullest perception always, and praise that as common sense? The commonest sense is the sense
of men asleep, which they express by snoring."

Run that through your calculator! It may come out Hard, it may come out
Easy. But it will come out whole, and it will last forever.

❧ ❧ ❧

*George Orwell*

# Politics and the English Language[1]

MOST people who bother with the matter at all would admit that the English language is in a bad way, but it is generally assumed that we cannot
by conscious action do anything about it. Our civilization is decadent, and
our language—so the argument runs—must inevitably share in the general
collapse. It follows that any struggle against the abuse of language is a sentimental archaism, like preferring candles to electric light or hansom cabs to
aeroplanes. Underneath this lies the half-conscious belief that language is a
natural growth and not an instrument which we shape for our own purposes.

Now, it is clear that the decline of a language must ultimately have political
and economic causes: it is not due simply to the bad influence of this or
that individual writer. But an effect can become a cause, reinforcing the original cause and producing the same effect in an intensified form, and so on
indefinitely. A man may take to drink because he feels himself to be a
failure, and then fail all the more completely because he drinks. It is rather
the same thing that is happening to the English language. It becomes ugly
and inaccurate because our thoughts are foolish, but the slovenliness of our
language makes it easier for us to have foolish thoughts. The point is that
the process is reversible. Modern English, especially written English, is full of
bad habits which spread by imitation and which can be avoided if one is
willing to take the necessary trouble. If one gets rid of these habits one
can think more clearly, and to think clearly is a necessary first step towards
political regeneration: so that the fight against bad English is not frivolous
and is not the exclusive concern of professional writers. I will come back to
this presently, and I hope that by that time the meaning of what I have
said here will have become clearer. Meanwhile, here are five specimens of
the English language as it is now habitually written.

These five passages have not been picked out because they are especially
bad—I could have quoted far worse if I had chosen—but because they illustrate
various of the mental vices from which we now suffer. They are a little

[1] From *Shooting An Elephant and Other Essays* by George Orwell, copyright, 1945,
1946, 1949, 1950, by Sonia Brownell Orwell. Reprinted by permission of Harcourt,
Brace and Company, Inc.

below the average, but are fairly representative samples. I number them so that I can refer back to them when necessary:

(1) I am not, indeed, sure whether it is not true to say that the Milton who once seemed not unlike a seventeenth-century Shelley had not become, out of an experience ever more bitter in each year, more alien (sic) to the founder of that Jesuit sect which nothing could induce him to tolerate. Professor Harold Laski (Essay in *Freedom of Expression*)

(2) Above all, we cannot play ducks and drakes with a native battery of idioms which prescribes such egregious collocations of vocables as. the Basic *put up with* for *tolerate* or *put at a loss* for *bewilder*.
Professor Lancelot Hogben (*Interglossa*)

(3) On the one side we have the free personality; by definition it is not neurotic, for it has neither conflict nor dream. Its desires, such as they are, are transparent, for they are just what institutional approval keeps in the forefront of consciousness; another institutional pattern would alter their number and intensity; there is little in them that is natural, irreducible, or culturally dangerous. But *on the other side*, the social bond itself is nothing but the mutual reflection of these self-secure integrities. Recall the definition of love. Is not this the very picture of a small academic? Where is there a place in this hall of mirrors for either personality or fraternity?
Essay on psychology in *Politics* (*New York*)

(4) All the "best people" from the gentlemen's clubs, and all the frantic fascist captains, united in common hatred of Socialism and bestial horror of the rising tide of the mass revolutionary movement, have turned to acts of provocation, to foul incendiarism, to medieval legends of poisoned wells, to legalize their own destruction of proletarian organizations, and rouse the agitated petty-bourgeoisie to chauvinistic fervor on behalf of the fight against the revolutionary way out of the crisis. Communist pamphlet

(5) If a new spirit *is* to be infused into this old country, there is one thorny and contentious reform which must be tackled, and that is the humanization and galvanization of the B.B.C. Timidity here will bespeak canker and atrophy of the soul. The heart of Britain may be sound and of strong beat, for instance, but the British lion's roar at present is like that of Bottom in Shakespeare's *Midsummer Night's Dream*—as gentle as any sucking dove. A virile new Britain cannot continue indefinitely to be traduced in the eyes, or rather ears, of the world by the effete languors of Langham Place, brazenly masquerading as "standard English." When the Voice of Britian is heard at nine o'clock, better far and infinitely less ludicrous to hear aitches honestly dropped than the present priggish, inflated, inhibited, school-ma'amish arch braying of blameless bashful mewing maidens.
Letter in *Tribune*

Each of these passages has faults of its own, but quite apart from avoidable ugliness, two qualities are common to all of them. The first is staleness of imagery; the other is lack of precision. The writer either has a meaning and cannot express it, or he inadvertently says something else, or he is almost indifferent as to whether his words mean anything or not. This mixture of vagueness and sheer incompetence is the most marked characteristic of modern English prose, and especially of any kind of political writing. As soon as certain topics are raised, the concrete melts into the abstract and no one seems able to think of turns of speech that are not hackneyed: prose consists less and less of *words* chosen for the sake of their meaning, and more and more of *phrases* tacked together like the sections of a prefabricated hen-house. I list below, with notes and examples, various of the tricks by means of which the work of prose-construction is habitually dodged:

*Dying metaphors.* A newly-invented metaphor assists thought by evoking a visual image, while on the other hand a metaphor which is technically "dead" (e.g., *iron resolution*) has in effect reverted to being an ordinary word and can generally be used without loss of vividness. But in between these two classes there is a huge dump of worn-out metaphors which have lost all evocative power and are merely used because they save people the trouble of inventing phrases for themselves. Examples are: *Ring the changes on, take up the cudgels for, toe the line, ride roughshod over, stand shoulder to shoulder with, play into the hands of, an axe to grind, grist to the mill, fishing in troubled waters, on the order of the day, Achilles' heel, swan song, hotbed.* Many of these are used without knowledge of their meaning (what is a "rift," for instance?), and incompatible metaphors are frequently mixed, a sure sign that the writer is not interested in what he is saying. Some metaphors now current have been twisted out of their original meaning without those who use them even being aware of the fact. For example, *toe the line* is sometimes written *tow the line*. Another example is *the hammer and the anvil*, now always used with the implication that the anvil gets the worst of it. In real life it is always the anvil that breaks the hammer, never the other way about: a writer who stopped to think what he was saying would be aware of this, and would avoid perverting the original phrase.

*Operators, or verbal false limbs.* These save the trouble of picking out appropriate verbs and nouns, and at the same time pad each sentence with extra syllables which give it an appearance of symmetry. Characteristic phrases are: *render inoperative, militate against, prove unacceptable, make contact with, be subjected to, give rise to, give grounds for, have the effect of, play a leading part* (role) *in, make itself felt, take effect, exhibit a tendency to, serve the purpose of, etc., etc.* The keynote is the elimination of simple verbs. Instead of being a single word, such as *break, stop, spoil, mend, kill,* a verb becomes a phrase, made up of a noun or adjective tacked on to some general-purposes verb such as *prove, serve, form, play, render.* In addition, the passive voice is wherever possible used in preference to the active, and noun constructions are used instead of gerunds (*by examination of* instead of *by examining*). The range of verbs is further cut down by means of the *-ize* and *de-* formations, and banal statements are given an appearance of profundity by means of the *not un-* formation. Simple conjunctions and prepositions are replaced by such phrases as *with respect to, having regard to, the fact that, by dint of, in view of, in the interests of, on the hypothesis that;* and the ends of sentences are saved from anti-climax by such resounding commonplaces as *greatly to be desired, cannot be left out of account, a development to be expected in the near future, deserving of serious consideration, brought to a satisfactory conclusion,* and so on and so forth.

*Pretentious diction.* Words like *phenomenon, element, individual* (as noun), *objective, categorical, effective, virtual, basis, primary, promote, constitute, exhibit, exploit, utilize, eliminate, liquidate,* are used to dress up simple statements and give an air of scientific impartiality to biased judgments. Adjectives like *epoch-making, epic, historic, unforgettable, triumphant, age-old, inevitable, inexorable, veritable,* are used to dignify the sordid processes of international politics, while writing that aims at glorifying war usually takes on an archaic color, its characteristic words being: *realm, throne, chariot, mailed fist, trident, sword, shield, buckler, banner, jackboot, clarion.* Foreign words and expressions such as *cul de sac, ancien régime, deus ex machina, mutatis mutandis, status quo, gleichschaltung, weltanschauung,* are used to give an air of culture and elegance. Except for the useful abbreviations *i.e., e.g.,* and *etc.,* there is no real need for any of the hundreds of foreign phrases now current in English. Bad writers, and especially scientific, political and sociological writers, are nearly always haunted by the notion that Latin or Greek words are grander than Saxon ones, and unnecessary words like *expedite, ameliorate, predict, extraneous, deracinated, clandestine, subaqueous* and hundreds of others constantly gain ground from their Anglo-Saxon opposite numbers.[2] The jargon peculiar to Marxist writing (*hyena, hangman, cannibal, petty bourgeois, these gentry, lackey, flunkey, mad dog, White Guard, etc.*) consists largely of words and phrases translated from Russian, German or French; but the normal way of coining a new word is to use a Latin or Greek root with the appropriate affix and, where necessary, the *-ize* formation. It is often easier to make up words of this kind (*de-regionalize, impermissible, extramarital, non-fragmentary* and so forth) than to think up the English words that will cover one's meaning. The result, in general, is an increase in slovenliness and vagueness.

*Meaningless words.* In certain kinds of writing, particularly in art criticism and literary criticism, it is normal to come across long passages which are almost completely lacking in meaning.[3] Words like *romantic, plastic, values,*

[2] An interesting illustration of this is the way in which the English flower names which were in use till very recently are being ousted by Greek ones, *snap-dragon* becoming *antirrhinum, forget-me-not* becoming *myosotis,* etc. It is hard to see any practical reason for this change of fashion: it is probably due to an instinctive turning-away from the more homely word and a vague feeling that the Greek word is scientific.

[3] Example: "Comfort's catholicity of perception and image, strangely Whitmanesque in range, almost the exact opposite in aesthetic compulsion, continues to evoke that trembling atmospheric accumulative hinting at a cruel, an inexorably serene timelessness . . . Wrey Gardiner scores by aiming at simple bullseyes with precision. Only they are

*human, dead, sentimental, natural, vitality,* as used in art criticism, are strictly meaningless, in the sense that they not only do not point to any discoverable object, but are hardly even expected to do so by the reader. When one critic writes, "The outstanding feature of Mr. X's work is its living quality," while another writes, "The immediately striking thing about Mr. X's work is its peculiar deadness," the reader accepts this as a simple difference of opinion. If words like *black* and *white* were involved, instead of the jargon words *dead* and *living,* he would see at once that language was being used in an improper way. Many political words are similarly abused. The word *Fascism* has now no meaning except in so far as it signifies "something not desirable." The words *democracy, socialism, freedom, patriotic, realistic, justice,* have each of them several different meanings which cannot be reconciled with one another. In the case of a word like *democracy,* not only is there no agreed definition, but the attempt to make one is resisted from all sides. It is almost universally felt that when we call a country democratic we are praising it: consequently the defenders of every kind of régime claim that it is a democracy, and fear that they might have to stop using the word if it were tied down to any one meaning. Words of this kind are often used in a consciously dishonest way. That is, the person who uses them has his own private definition, but allows his hearer to think he means something quite different. Statements like *Marshal Pétain was a true patriot, The Soviet Press is the freest in the world, The Catholic Church is opposed to persecution,* are almost always made with intent to deceive. Other words used in variable meanings, in most cases more or less dishonestly, are: *class, totalitarian, science, progressive, reactionary, bourgeois, equality.*

Now that I have made this catalogue of swindles and perversions, let me give another example of the kind of writing that they lead to. This time it must of its nature be an imaginary one. I am going to translate a passage of good English into modern English of the worst sort. Here is a well-known verse from *Ecclesiastes:*

> I returned, and saw under the sun, that the race is not to the swift, nor the battle to the strong, neither yet bread to the wise, nor yet riches to men of understanding, nor yet favor to men of skill; but time and chance happeneth to them all.

Here it is in modern English:

> Objective consideration of contemporary phenomena compels the conclusion that success or failure in competitive activities exhibits no tendency to be commensurate with innate capacity, but that a considerable element of the unpredictable must invariably be taken into account.

This is a parody, but not a very gross one. Exhibit (3), above, for instance, contains several patches of the same kind of English. It will be seen

---

not so simple, and through this contented sadness runs more than the surface bittersweet of resignation." (*Poetry Quarterly.*)

that I have not made a full translation. The beginning and ending of the sentence follow the original meaning fairly closely, but in the middle the concrete illustrations—race, battle, bread—dissolve into the vague phrase "success or failure in competitive activities." This had to be so, because no modern writer of the kind I am discussing—no one capable of using phrases like "objective consideration of contemporary phenomena"—would ever tabulate his thoughts in that precise and detailed way. The whole tendency of modern prose is away from concreteness. Now analyze these two sentences a little more closely. The first contains 49 words but only 60 syllables, and all its words are those of everyday life. The second contains 38 words of 90 syllables: 18 of its words are from Latin roots, and one from Greek. The first sentence contains six vivid images, and only one phrase ("time and chance") that could be called vague. The second contains not a single fresh, arresting phrase, and in spite of its 90 syllables it gives only a shortened version of the meaning contained in the first. Yet without a doubt it is the second kind of sentence that is gaining ground in modern English. I do not want to exaggerate. This kind of writing is not yet universal, and outcrops of simplicity will occur here and there in the worst-written page. Still, if you or I were told to write a few lines on the uncertainty of human fortunes, we should probably come much nearer to my imaginary sentence than to the one from *Ecclesiastes*.

As I have tried to show, modern writing at its worst does not consist in picking out words for the sake of their meaning and inventing images in order to make the meaning clearer. It consists in gumming together long strips of words which have already been set in order by someone else, and making the results presentable by sheer humbug. The attraction of this way of writing is that it is easy. It is easier—even quicker, once you have the habit—to say *In my opinion it is a not unjustifiable assumption that* than to say *I think*. If you use ready-made phrases, you not only don't have to hunt about for words; you also don't have to bother with the rhythms of your sentences, since these phrases are generally so arranged as to be more or less euphonious. When you are composing in a hurry—when you are dictating to a stenographer, for instance, or making a public speech—it is natural to fall into a pretentious, Latinized style. Tags like *a consideration which we should do well to bear in mind* or *a conclusion to which all of us would readily assent* will save many a sentence from coming down with a bump. By using stale metaphors, similes and idioms, you save much mental effort at the cost of leaving your meaning vague, not only for your reader but for yourself. This is the significance of mixed metaphors. The sole aim of a metaphor is to call up a visual image. When these images clash—as in *The Fascist octopus has sung its swan song, the jackboot is thrown into the melting pot*—it can be taken as certain that the writer is not seeing a mental image of the objects he is naming; in other words he is not really thinking. Look again at the examples I gave at the beginning of this essay. Professor Laski (1) uses five negatives in 53 words. One of these is superfluous, making nonsense of the whole passage, and in addition there is the slip *alien* for akin, making further nonsense, and several avoidable pieces of clumsiness which increase the general vagueness. Professor Hogben (2) plays ducks and drakes with a battery which is able to write prescriptions, and, while disapproving of the everyday phrase *put up with*, is unwilling to look *egregious* up in the dictionary and see what it means. (3), if one takes an uncharitable attitude towards it, is simply meaningless: probably one could work out its intended meaning by reading the whole of the article in which it occurs. In (4), the writer knows more or less what he wants to say, but an accumulation of stale phrases chokes him like tea leaves blocking a sink. In (5), words and meaning have almost parted company. People who write in this manner usually have a general emotional meaning—they dislike one thing and want to express solidarity with another—but they are not interested in the detail of what they are saying. A scrupulous writer, in every sentence that he writes, will ask himself at least four questions, thus: What am I trying to say? What words will express it? What image or idiom will make it clearer? Is this image fresh enough to have an effect? And he will probably ask himself two more: Could I put it more shortly? Have I said anything that is avoidably ugly? But you are not obliged to go to all this trouble. You can shirk it by simply throwing your mind open and letting the ready-made phrases come crowding in. They will construct your sentences for you—even think your thoughts for you, to a certain extent—and at need they will perform the important service of partially concealing your meaning even from yourself. It is at this point that the special connection between politics and the debasement of language becomes clear.

In our time it is broadly true that political writing is bad writing. Where it is not true, it will generally be found that the writer is some kind of rebel, expressing his private opinions and not a "party line." Orthodoxy, of whatever color, seems to demand a lifeless, imitative style. The political dialects to be found in pamphlets, leading articles, manifestoes, White Papers and the speeches of under-secretaries do, of course, vary from party to party, but they are all alike in that one almost never finds in them a fresh, vivid, home-made turn of speech. When one watches some tired hack on the platform mechanically repeating the familiar phrases—*bestial atrocities, iron heel, bloodstained tyranny, free peoples of the world, stand shoulder to shoulder*—one often has a curious feeling that one is not watching a live human being but some kind of dummy: a feeling which suddenly becomes stronger at moments when the light catches the speaker's spectacles and turns them into blank discs which seem to have no eyes behind them. And this is not altogether fanciful. A speaker who uses that kind of phraseology has gone some distance towards turning himself into a machine. The appropriate noises are coming out of his larynx, but his brain is not involved as it would be if he were choosing his words for himself. If the speech he is making is one that he is accustomed to make over and over again, he may be almost unconscious of what he is saying, as one is when one utters the responses in church. And this reduced state of consciousness, if not indispensable, is at any rate favorable to political conformity.

In our time, political speech and writing are largely the defense of the indefensible. Things like the continuance of British rule in India, the Russian purges and deportations, the dropping of the atom bombs on Japan, can indeed be defended, but only by arguments which are too brutal for most people to face, and which do not square with the professed aims of political parties. Thus political language has to consist largely of euphemism, question-begging and sheer cloudy vagueness. Defenseless villages are bombarded from the air, the inhabitants driven out into the countryside, the cattle machine-gunned, the huts set on fire with incendiary bullets: this is called *pacification*. Millions of peasants are robbed of their farms and sent trudging along the roads with no more than they can carry: this is called *transfer of population* or *rectification of frontiers*. People are imprisoned for years without trial, or shot in the back of the neck or sent to die of scurvy in Arctic lumber camps: this is called *elimination of unreliable elements*. Such phraseology is needed if one wants to name things without calling up mental pictures of them. Consider for instance some comfortable English professor defending Russian totalitarianism. He cannot say outright, "I believe in killing off your opponents when you can get good results by doing so." Probably, therefore, he will say something like this:

> While freely conceding that the Soviet régime exhibits certain features which the humanitarian may be inclined to deplore, we must, I think, agree that a certain curtailment of the right to political opposition is an unavoidable concomitant of transitional periods, and that the rigors which the Russian people have been called upon to undergo have been amply justified in the sphere of concrete achievement.

The inflated style is itself a kind of euphemism. A mass of Latin words falls upon the facts like soft snow, blurring the outlines and covering up all the details. The great enemy of clear language is insincerity. When there is a gap between one's real and one's declared aims, one turns, as it were instinctively, to long words and exhausted idioms, like a cuttlefish squirting out ink. In our age there is no such thing as "keeping out of politics." All issues are political issues, and politics itself is a mass of lies, evasions, folly, hatred and schizophrenia. When the general atmosphere is bad, language must suffer. I should expect to find—this is a guess which I have not sufficient knowledge to verify—that the German, Russian and Italian languages have all deteriorated in the last ten or fifteen years as a result of dictatorship.

But if thought corrupts language, language can also corrupt thought. A bad usage can spread by tradition and imitation, even among people who should and do know better. The debased language that I have been discussing is in some ways very convenient. Phrases like *a not unjustifiable assumption, leaves much to be desired, would serve no good purpose, a consideration which we should do well to bear in mind,* are a continuous temptation, a packet of aspirins always at one's elbow. Look back through this essay, and for certain you will find that I have again and again committed the very faults I am protesting against. By this morning's post I have received a pamphlet dealing with conditions in Germany. The author tells me that he "felt impelled" to write it. I open it at random, and here is almost the first sentence that I see: "[The Allies] have an opportunity not only of achieving a radical transformation of Germany's social and political structure in such a way as to avoid a nationalistic reaction in Germany itself, but at the same time of laying the foundations of a cooperative and unified Europe." You see, he "feels impelled" to write—feels, presumably, that he has something new to say—and yet his words, like cavalry horses answering the bugle, group themselves automatically into the familiar dreary pattern. This invasion of one's mind by ready-made phrases (*lay the foundations, achieve a radical transformation*) can only be prevented if one is constantly on guard against them, and every such phrase anesthetizes a portion of one's brain.

I said earlier that the decadence of our language is probably curable. Those who deny this would argue, if they produced an argument at all, that language merely reflects existing social conditions, and that we cannot influence its development by any direct tinkering with words and constructions. So far as the general tone or spirit of a language goes, this may be true, but it is not true in detail. Silly words and expressions have often disappeared, not through any evolutionary process but owing to the conscious action of a minority. Two recent examples were *explore every avenue* and *leave no stone unturned,* which were killed by the jeers of a few journalists. There is a long list of fly-blown metaphors which could similarly be got rid of if enough people would interest themselves in the job; and it should also be possible to laugh the *not un-* formation out of existence,[4] to reduce the amount of Latin and Greek in the average sentence, to drive out foreign phrases and strayed scientific words, and, in general, to make pretentiousness unfashionable. But all these are minor points. The defense of the English language implies more than this, and perhaps it is best to start by saying what it does *not* imply.

To begin with, it has nothing to do with archaism, with the salvaging of obsolete words and turns of speech, or with the setting-up of a "standard English" which must never be departed from. On the contrary, it is especially concerned with the scrapping of every word or idiom which has outworn its usefulness. It has nothing to do with correct grammar and syntax, which are of no importance so long as one makes one's meaning clear, or with the avoidance of Americanisms, or with having what is called a "good prose

---

[4] One can cure oneself of the *not un-* formation by memorizing this sentence: A *not unblack dog was chasing a not unsmall rabbit across a not ungreen field.*

style." On the other hand it is not concerned with fake simplicity and the attempt to make written English colloquial. Nor does it even imply in every case preferring the Saxon word to the Latin one, though it does imply using the fewest and shortest words that will cover one's meaning. What is above all needed is to let the meaning choose the word, and not the other way about. In prose, the worst thing one can do with words is to surrender them. When you think of a concrete object, you think wordlessly, and then, if you want to describe the thing you have been visualizing, you probably hunt about till you find the exact words that seem to fit it. When you think of something abstract you are more inclined to use words from the start, and unless you make a conscious effort to prevent it, the existing dialect will come rushing in and do the job for you, at the expense of blurring or even changing your meaning. Probably it is better to put off using words as long as possible and get one's meaning as clear as one can through pictures or sensations. Afterwards one can choose—not simply *accept*—the phrases that will best cover the meaning, and then switch round and decide what impressions one's words are likely to make on another person. This last effort of the mind cuts out all stale or mixed images, all prefabricated phrases, needless repetitions, and humbug and vagueness generally. But one can often be in doubt about the effect of a word or a phrase, and one needs rules that one can rely on when instinct fails. I think the following rules will cover most cases:

(i) Never use a metaphor, simile or other figure of speech which you are used to seeing in print.

(ii) Never use a long word where a short one will do.

(iii) If it is possible to cut a word out, always cut it out.

(iv) Never use the passive where you can use the active.

(v) Never use a foreign phrase, a scientific word or a jargon word if you can think of an everyday English equivalent.

(vi) Break any of these rules sooner than say anything barbarous.

These rules sound elementary, and so they are, but they demand a deep change of attitude in anyone who has grown used to writing in the style now fashionable. One could keep all of them and still write bad English, but one could not write the kind of stuff that I quoted in these five specimens at the beginning of this article.

I have not here been considering the literary use of language, but merely language as an instrument for expressing and not for concealing or preventing thought. Stuart Chase and others have come near to claiming that all abstract words are meaningless, and have used this as a pretext for advocating a kind of political quietism. Since you don't know what Fascism is, how can you struggle against Fascism? One need not swallow such absurdities as this, but one ought to recognize that the present political chaos is connected with the decay of language, and that one can probably bring about some improvement by starting at the verbal end. If you simplify your English, you are freed from the worst follies of orthodoxy. You cannot speak any of the necessary dialects, and when you make a stupid remark its stupidity will be obvious, even to yourself. Political language—and with variations this is true of all political parties, from Conservatives to Anarchists—is designed to make lies sound truthful and murder respectable, and to give an appearance of solidity to pure wind. One cannot change this all in a moment, but one can at least change one's own habits, and from time to time one can even, if one jeers loudly enough, send some worn-out and useless phrase—some *jackboot, Achilles' heel, hotbed, melting pot, acid test, veritable inferno* or other lump of verbal refuse—into the dustbin where it belongs.

❦ ❦ ❦

*Geoffrey T. Hellman*

## "Time" Lumbers On[1]

You can't always put your finger on what it is that makes a person attractive. The people in *Time* have long seemed unusually attractive to me, and I have sometimes wondered why this was so, since they are, by and large, the same bunch you find in the papers and in *Newsweek*, where they seem O.K. but not as compelling. I have gone to some pains to analyze the matter by studying *Time* carefully for the past several months, and I think the chief source of their charm is the way their voltage gets stepped up once they get into *Time*. Most of the people in *Time* are men. What steps up men's voltage? Girls. The biggest category on *Time's* masthead of two hundred and nineteen names is that of its sixty-two girl editorial researchers. I suspect that it's largely the presence of these ladies—especially the ones with the wonderful names, like Bernadine Beerheide, Harriet Ben Ezra, Quinera Sarita King, Danuta Reszke-Birk, Deirdre Mead Ryan, and Yi Ying Sung—that peps up *Time's* denizens. *Newsweek* has far fewer girls, and their names aren't quite as stimulating. No offense, I hope. Mrs. Reid is the only girl on the *Herald Tribune's* masthead, and as for the *Times*, it's Arthur Hays Sulzberger, Julius Ochs Adler, Orvil E. Dryfoos, Amory H. Bradford, Francis A. Cox all the way. Confidence-inspiring, but not pulse-quickening.

Be that as it may (and what isn't?), the people in *Time* are possessed of an unusual vigor, which is reflected in their gait, in the pace of their vehicles, and in their conversation. Take President Eisenhower, for example. He rarely walks in *Time*; he strides. "A smiling Dwight Eisenhower . . . strode to the rostrum" in the January 17th *Time*. More recently, in the February 28th issue, he "strode into the Congressional Room of Washington's Statler Hotel." To stride, according to Webster, means "to walk with long steps, esp. in a measured or pompous manner." *Time* is a patriotic magazine, and I have a feeling that when the President strides in its pages he is doing it in a meas-

[1] From *The New Yorker*, XXX (April 16, 1955), 34-36. Permission the author.
© 1955 The New Yorker Magazine, Inc.

ured rather than a pompous manner. Furthermore, when he writes a letter, he doesn't dictate it lackadaisically and then glue it up in an envelope with a lacklustre lick; he treats it like a fire-cracker, or a twenty-one-gun salute: "Last week Ike fired off a new letter to CAB."

Another February 28th *Time* strider, and a man whose vehicular pace is well calculated to make Quinera and Danuta sit up and take notice, is Colonel Marcos Pérez Jiménez, President of Venezuela. "Stopping the procession," *Time* states, "he strode over to the Mercedes-Benz." Pérez Jiménez is playing ball with us when it comes to oil, and I'm glad to learn that a strider rather than a sidler, he. It's good to know, too, that when he gets into a car he doesn't just drive; he snakes, streaks off, swerves along, speeds away, flashes by, hurries dustily on, and coasts. What a delightfully spirited Good Neighbor he is! "In gullied wastelands, the shriek of [his] tires and the stench of scorched rubber filled entire valleys." Can this be? Can one man stink up an entire valley? No matter. The concept is gargantuan; the Colonel is my boy.

Still another *Time* strider, and also a fast man on wheels, is Harlow H. Curtice, president of General Motors. "Into a large, cluttered Detroit studio one day 18 months ago strode a trim, lean man with the suave good looks of an ambassador and the cheery smile of a salesman," *Time* writes. Most people would pick their way in a cluttered studio, but not Curtice. As if striding, and looking as suave as Clare Boothe Luce, weren't enough to make you love the man, *Time* calls him "Red" seven times in one article. (Red is Harlow's nickname, not a crack.) When Red travels, he doesn't drive, or fly, or take a train; he swings. "Curtice swung around the country getting to know his harried dealers." This sounds as though he had a prehensile tail, which I, for one, find attractive, though I suppose it might harry a conventional Cadillac dealer. I don't mean to make a monkey out of Red; according to *Time*, he is closer to a Cadillac than to a marmoset:

> His bright blue eyes sparkle like a newly polished car [*Time* writes], his smile is as broad as a Cadillac grille. His voice is quiet, his manner calm. But under the Curtice hood there throbs a machine with the tireless power of one of his own 260-h.p. engines.

Curtice's voice may be quiet but his conversation is forceful. When he announces an expansion program, he does it "boldly"; his predictions are "right on the button"; "on weekends he likes to drop in on the nearby Buick division, shoot the breeze with anyone from a sweeper to a foreman."

*Time* gets a little mixed up about Red—he "never seems to be in a hurry," it says, and, two paragraphs later, "Curtice has a hot-rodder's feeling for cars . . . likes to dash around his home town of Flint in a sporty grey-blue Buick Skylark" —but, all in all, the picture of a bold, hooded, throbbing, breeze-shooting, skylarking president is an engaging one.

For a while after reading about Curtice, Eisenhower, and Pérez Jiménez, I had the idea that only presidents strode in *Time*. Not at all. Look at Scotland's Roman Catholic Father Sydney MacEwan, "a white-haired but boyish-looking priest in a knee-length clerical coat [who] strode to the dais in the Waldorf-Astoria's Jade Room." But I regret to state that striders don't always stay boyish-looking; sometimes their strides give out, and they are reduced to walking. "An old man climbed aboard United Air Lines flight 709 in New York . . . to fly to Los Angeles," *Time* writes of General Douglas MacArthur. "His famous stride had become a careful step, his hands looked transparent and his skin like parchment. . . ."

This brings me to another attractive locomotive trait of *Time's* cast of characters. They don't *get* into vehicles; they *climb* into them, which sounds more manly. They also climb out of them. When MacArthur got to Los Angeles, he "climbed out." John Foster Dulles is forever climbing in and out of planes in *Time,* and President René Coty, of France, "climbed from his bed to confer with pouchy-eyed politicians," while his wife, whose movements also eschew the humdrum, "padded about the palace kitchen . . . serving endless cups of coffee." Did Coty climb *up* from his bed or *down* from it? Up, I guess; those politicians were hanging from the ceiling, and were pouchy-eyed from looking down on their recumbent leader. My favorite *Time* climber is Coty's compatriot Pierre Mendès-France, who "climbed into his black Citroën." This is a real feat, even for a Frenchman who has stunted his growth by drinking milk.

I'm sorry that Mendès-France is out of office, and therefore presumably out, or relatively out, of the pages of *Time.* He will be missed. When he wasn't climbing in *Time,* he was hurrying out or walking briskly, and when he talked, he snapped. "*Eh bien,*" he once snapped in *Time,* "I seem to have plenty of friends but few supporters." His downfall is clearly attributable to overexercise. He got so bushed bustling about *Time's* Foreign News department that he was too exhausted to repair his political fences.

*Time's* snappers girdle the globe. " 'We are not prepared to accept the proposition that because the Soviet Union and the U.S. are agreed, all problems are solved,' snapped [India's Krishna] Menon," while the Americas abound in snappers:

"It's unanimous!" snapped Congressman William Dawson.

Private Schine snapped: "I have stopped speaking to newspapermen."

Joe [McCarthy] snapped back: "They have been shooting at me, and I've got to get back at them."

"I am here to apply the law and you ask me to break it!" snapped Café Filho [President of Brazil].

Asked by waiting newsmen about his intentions, [Marlon Brando] snapped: "It is not a publicity stunt, and I do intend to marry the girl."

Brando's girl, by the way, burbles, which makes for a nice combination. They can play burble-and-snap:

"I know I am going to start a new life with the help of Marlon, and it will be different from what I have done so far," burbled she.

When the two of them get into a vehicle in *Time*, they hop on and chug off, and when he leaves her, he speeds off.

McCarthy's snaps sometimes cause other Senators to gruff:

> But when he heard of McCarthy's statement, Colorado's tough, burly [Edwin C.] Johnson gruffed: "This is the first time I've ever been called a hand-maiden."

McCarthy not only snaps, he also ambles, lumbers, elbows, and careens:

> A scowling, puffy-eyed McCarthy . . . lumbered into the hearing room . . . then he ambled out. . . . McCarthy elbowed his way through the crowd . . .

> Careening about his old stamping grounds in his home town of Appleton, Wisconsin's Senator Joseph R. McCarthy . . .

McCarthy's closest locomotive parallel is Ernest Hemingway:

> Rolling to starboard like an old freighter, Ernest Hemingway lumbered about his weather-beaten manor. . . .

Not so peppy, perhaps, but a novelty. And when it comes to the girls on *Time's* masthead, Hemingway knows what he's doing; he married one of them.

A more athletic note is struck by Governor Craig of Indiana, Admiral Halsey, and Nehru:

> Having vaulted into the governor's office in a hurry, George Craig landed running, has been in a hurry ever since.

> After the game . . . Fleet Admiral (ret.) William F. ("Bull") Halsey . . . bounced around like a midshipman . . .

> A slender man with jodhpured legs and a rose-bud in his buttonhole scooted about the diplomatic conference rooms of London with whispered propositions on his lips. India's Jawaharlal Nehru wanted to be helpful.

But don't think that Nehru always scoots around whispering in *Time*; sometimes he croaks:

> "Since the dawn of history," croaked Nehru throatily . . .

As in the case of McCarthy's snaps, one colorful *Time* vocalization often begets another. Nehru's croaks are followed by conversational chuckles from his colleagues:

> Pudgy Rafi Ahmad Kidwai, 60, Minister of Food and Agriculture . . . chuckled: "That will make Nehru think twice."

And here's a pounce that flushed a weasel:

> His interrogator pounced: "But you did say it! Why?" Weaseled (Alfred) Hitchcock uneasily: "It depends what press it was."

Before going on to some of the other ways in which the people in *Time* exercise their vocal cords, let us observe how certain ladies among them move:

Mrs. George Malone . . . flounced from the banquet hall.

One day Oveta Culp Hobby clicked in with a bundle of charts.

Very well. Back to *Time's* conversationalists. In addition to snapping, snorting, burbling, chuckling, croaking, pouncing, weaseling, and shooting the breeze, they groan, coo, snarl, taunt, thunder, chortle, crack, intone, growl, drawl, sneer, grumble, rumble, blurt, smirk, purr, husk, rasp, bubble, beam, smile, grin, drone, roar amid guffaws, sigh, worry, and spit entire sentences and even paragraphs. I have all the documentation at hand, but suffice it to bellow that Billy Graham and Senator Irving M. Ives thunder; Frank Lloyd Wright chortles; Konrad Adenauer growls; Winston Churchill growls, rumbles, and worries (he is also a snapper); Georgia's Governor Marvin Griffin drawls genially; Montgomery Ward Chairman Sewell Avery smiles "Do you know anyone who has $600 million all wrapped up in a bundle?;" Nat (King) Cole, a singer, husks, while shrugging, "Dialogue is just lyrics that don't rhyme"; and a "disgruntled hotelman" sighs "That is a sight that Pondicherry will not again see."

Adenauer, incidentally, whistle-stops when he takes a train, while Senator Ives, in a Caddy, roars down (without guffaws) to Manhattan. I've found only one man in *Time* who makes a really poor vehicular showing—Senator Wayne Morse:

One jungle-hot afternoon a weathered Model T lurched down the 1600 block of Pennsylvania Avenue. . . . Out popped Wayne Morse.

*Time* is a Republican magazine, so perhaps Morse, who reneged on the Republicans, doesn't feel at home in it. He lurches and pops out, instead of roaring and climbing, because he's ill at ease.

Well, I think I'll gruff my analysis to a close, but first I want to point to a character trait that enhances the attractiveness of *Time* people all over the world: dutifulness. They do everything from talking dutifully to marrying dutifully:

Said Maurine [Neuberger, wife of the Senator from Oregon] dutifully: she will retire from politics to help her husband in Washington.

[Matyas] Rakosi [former Premier of Hungary] dutifully sent word that he agreed completely with the newest New Course.

Pérez Jiménez [remember the old strider, dusty hurrier, and stinker-upper?] dutifully put down a dozen or so minor uprisings.

Queen Elizabeth II's younger sister dutifully attended to the routine chores of visiting royalty.

On [the Queen Mother's] arrival at the center, bystanding neighborhood ragamoppets applauded her dutifully.

Crown Prince of Rumania . . . Carol Hohenzollern . . . dutifully married Princess Helen of Greece.

Dutifully, Faure tried.

Faure, of course, is Mendès-France's successor, and in *Time* he's dutifully trying to get the support of the Socialists for a left-center coalition. He didn't succeed (some ragamoppets grimaced him down), but what can you expect of a man who—so far, at any rate—hasn't stridden, vaulted, bounced, or *entrechatted* his way into a conference room? I never heard of a Frenchman who didn't want to get on the good side, or sides, of sixty-two girls. Faure is warming up. He sighed in the March 28th issue of *Time*, and as of April 4th he is credited with a seven-sentence snap. I hear he's hired a drive-yourself Renault, and that we may hope for a shrieking-tired ricochet any week.

❧ ❧ ❧

*Frank Sullivan*

# The Cliché Expert Reveals Himself in His True Colors [1]

Q:   MR. ARBUTHNOT, would you mind telling us today how you happened to become a cliché expert? Was it easy?

A:   Easy! Don't make me laugh, Mr. Crouse. It was an uphill climb. A cliché novitiate is no bed of roses, and if anyone ever tells you it is, do you know how I want you to take his statement?

Q:   How?

A:   With a grain of salt. I shall tell you about my career, since you insist, and as a special treat, I shall describe it to you entirely in terms of the seesaw cliché.

Q:   The seesaw cliché?

A:   You'll see what I mean. Before I made my mark as a cliché expert, I had my ups and downs. Sometimes, when everything was at sixes and sevens, it almost seemed as though my dearest ambitions were going to wrack and ruin. I had moments when I was almost tempted to believe that everything was a snare and a delusion. Even my own flesh and blood discouraged me, in spite of the fact that I was their pride and joy . . . You aren't listening, Mr. Crouse.

Q:   Yes I am. I just closed my eyes because the light hurt. You were saying that your own kith and kin discouraged you.

A:   I didn't say kith and kin, but it doesn't matter. For a considerable period of time it was nip and tuck whether I would sink or swim. If I had not been hale and hearty, and well equipped for a rough-and-tumble struggle, I wouldn't have come through. But I kept at it, hammer and tongs. I gave 'em tit for tat . . . Mr. Crouse, you *are* asleep.

[1] From *A Pearl in Every Oyster* (Boston: Little, Brown and Company, 1938), pp. 284-290. Reprinted by permission of the author.

Q: No, I'm not, Mr. Arbuthnot. You were saying you went after your goal hard and fast.

A: I did. I eschewed wine, woman, and song—

Q: Ah, but wine, woman, and song is not a seesaw cliché, Mr. Arbuthnot.

A: Yes it is, too. Woman is standing in the middle, balancing. I worked morning, noon, and night, and kept to the straight and narrow. The consequence was that in the due course of time—

Q: And tide?

A: Please! In the due course of time things began to come my way by fits and starts, and a little later by leaps and bounds. Now, I'm fine and dandy.

Q: High, wide, and handsome, eh?

A: I wish I had said that, Mr. Crouse.

Q: You—

A: Will, Oscar. Had you there, Mr. Crouse, didn't I, ha ha! When I started I was free, white, and twenty-one. Now I'm fat, fair, and forty, and I venture to predict that no man, without regard to race, creed, or color, is a better master of the cliché than your servant—your *humble* servant—Magnus Arbuthnot. So much for my life story in terms of the seesaw cliché.

Q: It certainly is an interesting story, Mr. Arbuthnot—by and large.

A: Well, in all due modesty, I suppose it is, although sometimes, to tell you the truth, I think there is neither rhyme nor reason to it.

Q: Where were you born, Mr. Arbuthnot?

A: In the altogether.

Q: I see. How?

A: On the impulse of the moment.

Q: And when?

A: In the nick of time.

Q: It is agreeable to find a man so frank about himself, Mr. Arbuthnot.

A: Why not? You asked me a question. You know what kind of question it was?

Q: Impertinent?

A: Oh, my dear man, no.

Q: Personal?

A: Civil. You asked me a civil question. I answered you by telling you the truth. I gave it to you, if I may be permitted to say so, straight from the shoulder. I revealed myself to you in my—

Q: True colors?

A: Ah, someone told you. Rather, someone *went* and told you.

Q: Were you ever in love, Mr. Arbuthnot, or am I out of order in asking that?

A: Not at all. I have had my romances.

Q: How nice.

A: Ah, you wouldn't say so if you knew what kind of romances they were.

Q: What kind were they?

A: Blighted romances, all of 'em. I kept trying to combine single blessedness with wedded bliss. It didn't work. I had a sweetheart in every port, and I worshiped the ground they walked on, each and every one of them. This ground amounts to a matter of 18,467 acres, as of my latest blighted romance.

Q: Hm! You must have been quite a pedestrian.

A: Well, those are the figures when the tide was out; only 16,468 acres at the neap. I was land-poor at the end. And you take the advice of a sadder—

Q: And a wiser man.

A: That's what I was going to say. And never trust the weaker sex, or you'll have an awakening. You seem to be so smart, interrupting me all the while, maybe you can tell me what kind of awakening.

Q: Awakening? Awakening? I'm afraid you have me.

A: Rude awakening.

Q: Oh, of course. Now, I don't think your story would be complete, Mr. Arbuthnot, without some statement from you regarding your material circumstances. Are you well-to-do, or are you—

A: Hard pressed for cash? No, I'm solvent. I'm well paid.

Q: You mean you get a handsome salary?

A: I prefer to call it a princely stipend. You know what kind of coin I'm paid in?

Q: No. What?

A: Coin of the realm. Not that I give a hoot for money. You know how I refer to money?

Q: As the root of all evil?

A: No, but you have a talking point there. I call it lucre—filthy lucre.

Q: On the whole, you seem to have a pretty good time, Mr. Arbuthnot.

A: Oh, I'm not complaining. I'm as snug as a bug in a rug. I'm clear as crystal—when I'm not dull as dishwater. I'm cool as a cucumber, quick as a flash, fresh as a daisy, pleased as Punch, good as my word, regular as clockwork, and I suppose at the end of my declining years, when I'm gathered to my ancestors, I'll be dead as a doornail.

Q: *Eh bien! C'est la vie!*

A: *Mais oui, mon vieux.* I manage. I'm the glass of fashion and the mold of form. I have a finger in every pie, all except this finger. I use it for pointing with scorn. When I go in for malice, it is always malice aforethought. My nods are significant. My offers are standing. I am at cross-purposes and in dire straits. My motives are ulterior, my circles are vicious, my retainers are faithful, and my hopefuls are young. My suspicions are sneaking, my glee is fiendish, my stories are likely. I am drunk.

Q: Drunk?

A: Yes, with power. You know where?

Q: Where?

A: Behind the throne. I am emotional. My mercies are tender, and when I cry, I cry quits. I am lost in thought and up in arms. I am a square shooter with my trusty revolver. My courage is vaunted and my shame is crying, but I don't care—a rap. I have been in the depths of despair, when a watery grave in the briny deep seemed attractive. Eventually I want to marry and settle down, but the woman I marry must be clever.

Q:   Clever?

A:   With the needle.

Q:   Well, I'd certainly call you a man who had led a full life, Mr. Arbuthnot, and a likable chap, too.

A:   Yes, I'm a peach of a fellow. I'm a diamond in the rough, all wool and a yard wide. I'm too funny for words and too full for utterance. I'm a gay dog, and I like to trip the light fantastic and burn the candle at both ends with motley throngs of boon companions. I may be foolish but my folly is at least sheer.

Q:   I think you certainly have run—

A:   I certainly have. The entire gamut of human emotions. I know the facts of life. I'm afraid I've got to go now, Mr. Crouse. I'm due back at my abode. Do you know what kind of abode I live in?

Q:   Humble, Mr. Arbuthnot?

A:   Certainly not. Palatial! Goodbye, my little periwinkle!

❦ ❦ ❦

*Geoffrey Moore*

# American Prose Today[1]

BUT IS there such a thing as an American prose? I refer here to nonfiction, the prose of exposition, the ordinary literary means of communication.

The sophist might answer: Yes, American prose is prose written by Americans. But, we persist: Is it different from English prose, and, if so, how? Or, alternatively: Is there "an American style"? The answer might be that there are a number of American styles and that they owe their nature to the circumstances of American development. Not merely racial, or religious, or social differences, but, as Mr. Wallace Stevens once said, physical ones too, have made the attitude of the people different, and the attitude of a people is reflected in its prose. Add to this the spirit which founded the United States, the early struggles, the theocratic art-banishing society of New England, the early establishment of a unique kind of democracy, the distrust of aristocratic virtues (elegance, propriety, mannered grace, intellect) and the acceptance of brotherhood-become-chumminess, and you have a taste of the brew which might be expected to make American prose different from British. From the first, the

[1] From *New World Writing*, Eighth Mentor Selection (New York: New American Library, 1955), pp. 47-70, with omissions. Copyright ©, 1955, by Geoffrey Moore.

American moved about a lot and so, despite the difference in accent between, say, South Carolina and New Hampshire, usage was sufficiently standard that he could be understood in any part of the country. In England, however, as Mr. Harold Whitehall has pointed out, the inhabitants of, for example, Howden in Yorkshire used to find it very difficult to understand the inhabitants of Dews- bury, forty miles away. And so, largely on the basis of aristocratic speech, Britain developed a *lingua franca*, Received Standard English, the rules of which could be laid down and accepted as gospel. H. W. Fowler could write a *Modern English Usage*, but no American ever either dared to write, or felt the necessity of writing, a *Modern American Usage*. Mr. Horwill, an Englishman, did, of course, produce one, but that was for the aid of the British. However, there seems, by this time, to have developed a generally accepted and, as it were, legitimate body of American usage which can be called Standard without fear of offending Americans' own susceptibilities. At least I take it to be so and, with this in mind, I should like to examine various examples of modern "expositional" American prose in an effort to discover whether they have the 'independence and vigour" which, in 1954, *The Times Literary Supplement* found so marked in American creative writing. Although this will involve commenting on usage, I do not propose to single out American usages which are now perfectly acceptable in Britain.

### POLITICAL PROSE

My purpose was to sketch the genesis and set in some crude historical perspective the present troubled world scene, and then to attempt to defrost a tiny segment of the opaque window through which we see others and others see us—and to do it briefly, having listened to many lectures myself!

This is from the foreword to Adlai Stevenson's *Call to Greatness*. Two things are immediately noticeable: first, the modest tone, and, second, the use of an original figure of speech which has been drawn naturally and unaffectedly from American experience. Almost all Americans, except those who live in the extreme Southern states, find it necessary at some time during the winter to "defrost," either manually or by aid of a device built into their cars, a driving window which has been made opaque by frost or frozen snow. The style might be described as "literary" (e.g., "genesis," "present troubled world scene"), yet it gives an impression of ease. It has the ring of sincerity and makes us feel that we can trust a man who is at once so unpretentious and yet so quietly convinced that he can clarify our vision of world affairs.

Having come to the above conclusion about this passage, I was surprised, on re-reading it, to find that it is actually ungrammatical. I say "surprised" since, as a teacher, my eye is, if anything, over-alert to such things. The fault is in the first line, in which, to make grammatical sense, there should be an "of" after "genesis." It gives a very awkward ring to the sentence, however, and the writer, being American, was led to reject it. An Englishman would probably either have put it in or re-worded the sentence. It is, I think, a good example of how even the most educated and highly literate of Americans have, when they feel like it, a cavalier attitude toward the niceties of grammar. I have noticed that in the *non solum, sed etiam* construction, for example, Americans rarely put in the "also."

### HISTORICAL PROSE

(a) As the sectional tension increased, the sense of irrepressible differences, long buried in the national consciousness, began to burst into the clear. The growing pressure on the North had finally persuaded many Northerners that the slavery system embodied a fundamental threat to free society.

(b) August gave way to September, September to October, and the clamor grew increasingly furious. Jackson men paraded the streets in the glare of torches, singing campaign songs, carrying hickory poles, gatherin around huge bonfires blazing high into the night.

These two extracts are both from Arthur M. Schlesinger, Jr.'s *The Age of Jackson*. Together they make a point better than one alone, and that point is that the methods and the vocabulary of the journalist have invaded the writing of history. (Cf. *Time*, April 22, 1955, "Warm in the April sunshine, London's upper-crust horseplayers crowded the club enclosure at Kempton Park Race Track. Peeresses in Dior tweeds appraised each other. . . ." etc.) The tone is different. *Time's* is not merely colourful; it is impertinent. Mr. Schlesinger is not writing sensationally, he is merely trying to "bring the scene to life." Although he is in no sense perverting the facts, he is nonetheless "popularising" history. And since he is not merely a famous historian, but also an academic one, approved of academically, the method is worth remarking on. It is not entirely new. Strachey was, of course, a populariser and, so to pick an example from a number of others, was Philip Guedalla; but the texture of these English writers was finer grained, more glittering. Mr. Schlesinger's style, although it is not bad, is without flair, bouncy yet workaday ("as sectional tension increased," "embodied a fundamental threat"), with an occasional, rather disconcerting vernacular phrase (e.g., "into the clear"). It is the style of a man who has not thought much about language. The four parts of Mr. Schlesinger's first sentence create four different effects. The first gives us the sense of *pulling*, the second of energy contained under *pressure*, like steam in a kettle, the third *buries* this steam kettle, the fourth allows it to "burst into the clear" which seems superficially to fit with the idea of "irrepressible differences," but is vaguely disconcerting until we realize that the stress is on "into the clear," which is a hunting term. There is, in other words, a confusion of different kinds of language. This is for me a most interesting discovery, since I did not pick Mr. Schlesinger invidiously, but in a spirit of enquiry, knowing him to be one of the most outstanding of the younger American historians.

CRITICAL PROSE

(a) Such an art when it pretends to measure life is essentially vicarious; it is a substitute for something that never was—like a tin soldier, or Peter Pan. It has all the flourish of life and every sentimental sincerity. Taken for what it is, it is charming and even instructive. Taken solemnly, as it is meant to be, the distortion by which it exists is too much for it, and it seems a kind of baby-talk.

(b) . . . aesthetic value has been defined as conformity to or expression of a culture. This is the side of formism most prevalent today. A work of art has aesthetic value in proportion as it gives expression to its age. This definition tends to run over into a cultural relativism very congenial to contemporary art historians, and in marked contrast to the universality of aesthetic values emphasized in the first formulation of aesthetic value for formism above as representation of the universal.

(c) There is nothing to do different from what we already do: if poets write poems and readers read them, each as best they can—if they try to live not as soldiers or voters or intellectuals or economic men, but as human beings—they are doing all that can be done. But to expect them (by, say, reciting one-syllable poems over the radio) to bring back that Yesterday in which people stood on chairs to look at Lord Tennsyon, is to believe that General Motors can bring back "the tradition of craftsmanship" by giving, as it does, prizes to Boy Scouts for their scale-models of Napoleonic coaches; to believe that the manners of the past can be restored by encouraging country-people to say *Grüss Gott* or *Howdy, stranger* to the tourists they meet along summer lanes.

The first extract is from R. P. Blackmur's essay on the verse of E. E. Cummings in *The Double Agent*; the second is from Stephen C. Pepper's *The Basis of Criticism in the Arts*; and the third from Randall Jarrell's *Poetry and the Age*. The field of criticism in the United States is so rich that I should have preferred to take at least two or three more examples—from Edmund Wilson, say, or Van Wyck Brooks, or the late F. O. Matthiessen. However, these three samples do at least reveal three important aspects of American criticism. The second passage is of the kind which is so often the target for British writers— jargon criticism. I could have quoted more extreme examples (from Kenneth Burke, for instance) for there is a great deal of this kind of thing, particularly in academic or semi-academic writing, of which there is so much more in the United States than anywhere else. I think of it sometimes as a Germanic derivation. "The side of formism," "cultural relativism," and the garbled mumble of the end of the final sentence—this is the antithesis of clarity. Perhaps it is the result of Coleridge's example; he learnt from Germany too. Perhaps it is the overseriousness and earnestness of the American commentator. Perhaps it is a little of the unconscious desire to blind the vulgar with science. Perhaps it is an attempt to order a frighteningly vast world of thought and feeling. Perhaps it is—as Marius Bewley suggested of Kenneth Burke—that these "methodological" critics have developed their jargon and their unreadable style in order to isolate them "against the shock of the work of art itself." But, whatever the reason, the effect is both exasperating and perturbing.

The Blackmur passage, on the other hand, is a good illustration of what we mean when we say that someone's writing "has style." The language is both elegant and precise, the manner judicious but not portentous, flavored by just the right amount of everyday reference ("tin soldier, or Peter Pan" and "baby-talk"). It is the writing of an acute sensibility. We cannot help feeling the force of the conviction behind the sentiments, not only because of what they say but because of the manner of their expression. The language is faintly Jamesian, ("all the flourish of life and every sentimental sincerity"). The final effect is of a man who respects literature too much to make it merely a stamping-ground for pseudo-scientific theories.

Mr. Jarrell, in his conversational ease, his common sense and his liveliness, is representative of the younger generation of American critics. He will not allow his individual perception and spirit to be subdued by the acceptances of academic style and theory. His is a style of wit and irony, which can sometimes approach the self-consciously brilliant but is anchored to earth (and this is why it is so effective for most readers) by the essential rightness of the sentiments. The style is more noticeably idiosyncratic than Mr. Blackmur's. It is perceptive, impressionistic, and opinionated. But in the last resort it obtains its effect by laying the cards on the table and saying, as it were, "Now, after all. . . ." Only a man with a wide cultural background and a sureness of judgment based on good taste can afford to do this. Finally, the style achieves a vividness and con-creteness by reference to manners and institutions well known in American life.

### LETTERS: OFFICIAL AND OTHERWISE

(a) Keeping company with these people in their notion is the man who gets a hard-to-understand Government letter. To be sure, he is peeved upon being muddled by a phrase such as "noncompensable evaluation heretofore assigned," but he is seldom really mad.

This is not from a letter but from an American government manual telling officials how to write letters more economically and less pretentiously (*Plain Letters*, published by the U. S. National Archives and Records Service in Washington, March, 1955). The writer, Miss Mona Sheppard, "staff specialist in correspondence management," has fallen, in her desire to avoid officialese and use what she calls, after Franklin K. Lane, "straightaway English," into another kind of jargon, the jargon of chumminess. Perhaps I am morbidly sensitive, but to read this passage chills my spine and raises my hackles. It is full of the kind of matey journalese which is found not only in the newspapers and on the radio but in bank circulars, advertising letters, exhortations from alumni associations, or invitations to Old Home Week with the Elks. My complaint is not with colloquial American, as such, which is extremely effective when used with skill and discrimination, by, say, Thurber, or Robert Benchley, or E. B. White, or the general run of *New Yorker* writers (or funny, in a sad sort of way, when used creatively by, say, Ring Lardner). My complaint is rather with the barbarous tone of this specimen, the absence of feeling for the values of words, the sheer lack of grace. "Keeping company with these people in their notion" is roundabout and ugly. "Hard-to-understand" is an example of the prostitution of English which is increasingly found in British as well as American daily journalism. But if I spend any longer on this passage I shall get mad too.

The language of the model letters which the Manual holds up for approval is not quite so ungraceful as the language of the instructions, but it is frequently inept, equally lacking in any sort of ear for the English language. And since, at this point, I anticipate cries of rage, and, possibly, of misunderstanding, from the direction of Washington, let me say that Style, as I understand it, is at the farthest possible remove from ornament, flourish, or affectation. It is, in Sir Arthur Quiller-Couch's words, "the power to touch with ease, grace, precision, any note in the gamut of human thought or emotion." "But essentially," Sir Arthur goes on, "it resembles good manners. It comes of endeavouring to understand others, of thinking for them rather than for yourself. . . ." (This is a point that the jargon critics could well bear in mind.)

> (b) You make me feel very much at home in Pittsburgh. I like the people I meet there; and I am enthusiastic about the job you are doing. But I would be showing rank favoritism if I were to move to go out there to start off your Institute. I have to catch up with my obligations in other parts of the country. I am, of course, flattered that you asked me to come.

This extract, from a letter held up as a good example for Government letter writers, breathes insincerity through its very heartiness. The punctuation and grammar (the placing of the semicolon and the use of "would" instead of "should") are the work of an imperfectly educated man, and the cliché, "showing rank favoritism," clashes horribly with the self-consciously colloquial "to move to go out there to start off. . . ." This is the literary equivalent of the glad hand, and just as distasteful.

The fact that the best letter in *Plain Letters* is by Abraham Lincoln is ominous. President Lincoln's letter is exact, entirely unaffected, and, through its very simplicity, a noble piece of writing, worthy to be quoted in full. It runs:

WASHINGTON, July 13, 1863

MAJOR GENERAL GRANT. My Dear General: I do not remember that you and I ever met personally. I write this now as a grateful acknowledgement for the almost inestimable service you have done the country. I wish to say a word further. When you first reached the vicinity of Vicksburg, I thought you should do what you finally did—march the troops across the neck, run the batteries with the transports, and thus go below; and I never had any faith, except a general hope that you knew better than I, that the Yazoo Pass expedition and the like could succeed. When you got below and took Port Gibson, Grand Gulf, and vicinity, I thought you should go down the river and join General Banks, and when you turned northward, east of the Big Black, I feared it was a mistake. I now wish to make the personal acknowledgement that you were right and I was wrong.

Yours very truly,

A. Lincoln

There is one last, interesting point about this American government manual. It concerns itself only with letters written by officials to the general public. The British Government publication, *The Complete Plain Words* (1954), written by Sir Ernest Gowers, (who is not a "staff specialist in correspondence management" but merely an educated man) is by comparison "pure," being concerned with the encouragement of good, clear prose in whatever kind of communication. The idea that clear prose ought to be encouraged *because* it establishes better communication, and relations, between the Government and the public, would, I am sure, be abhorrent to Sir Ernest, as it would to any man of principle.

### JOURNALISTIC PROSE

In a democratic country, in which almost everyone can read and in which everyone is supposed to have equal opportunities for education, or for anything else, one might expect to find a "typical" or "representative" American style, in the kind of publication which is read by the majority. According to figures taken from the polls of the Princeton Institute of Public Opinion and Mr. J. K. Wood's *Magazines of the United States*, although only approximately 20 per cent of Americans read books at all, 83 per cent regularly read newspapers and magazines.

### 1. Newspapers

(a) Secretary of Agriculture Ezra Taft Benson has called on western Kansas farmers to begin a day of "prayer and supplication to ask God in heaven to send rain." Well, that's one way of stopping the good Kansas dirt from blowing over to Russia. It's certainly not the best way. The secretary has made a tour; he's impressed. But first and foremost the secretary is a politician, not a conservationist. It will take a little more than politics to keep that western Kansas dirt on the ground.

This passage from a student newspaper editorial seems clear and direct— "conversational," "natural," in fact, yet not altogether or ingenuously so. The tone is cocky. "Secretary of Agriculture Ezra Taft Benson" is borrowed from *Time's* style, which was presumably invented to give the impression that everybody's time including *Time's*, was limited. Yet the saving of one three-letter word and two commas is not worth the ungracefulness of the usage. One feels that the writer is breathing down one's neck. A cliché slips in ("first and foremost"). "Impressed" gives one a feeling of inadequately describing Mr. Benson's possible reactions. Noticeable American usages are "called on," which has a Town Meeting ring, and "politician," which in England means someone in politics but in the United States is a bad word.

(b) Reed's number one problem is working capital. So in order to get money for equipment and to meet his payroll until he gets to rolling, he is incorporating the business and plans to sell stock. The telephone switchboard will be installed soon and within the next few weeks he plans to have a grand opening.

This is from an article in the *St. Louis Post-Dispatch*, and is sub-colloquial. It reads like a cross between the vernacular and the language of radio copy-writers—more the latter. Few in conversation talk about their "number one" problem, but writers of "commercials" do. "Meet his payroll" and "get to roll-ing" are examples of those vivid coinages which arise out of a forceful expand-ing society in which the tone of general prose is set by the majority, who have no ear for subtlety of language. They are designed to give an impressionistic pic-ture to people whose range of communication, understanding, and imagination is narrow. This kind of prose does not work through the intelligence but through the emotions. The repetition of "get" and "plan" emphasises the nar-rowness of the vocabulary. Within its limits it is a most effective kind of com-munication, and sufficiently hard-punching to penetrate the dullest mind capable of reading words on a page. It is an example of American pragmatism. It is probably inevitable in a democratic society in which the mass media have superseded the printed page as the chief means of communication. It reflects the speech and the habits of mind of the majority of people and it would be sentimental, ineffectual, and entirely unrealistic (not to say reactionary) for one to regret that this particular form of speech ever invaded prose. But one does.

(c) The Pakistan grain storage contract presents a flagrant case of official negligence and mismanagement. Any monkey business with government contracts can and should be a matter of public concern. So we have this rela-tively small item of grain elevators grown into a national story.

(d) For the present, and with all due consideration of both Soviet aims and motivations, it appears as if the Soviets are prepared to give ground at least in part and at least at one point—Austria. After stalling and sabotaging the Austrian treaty in more than 260 treaty meetings stretching over nearly a decade, they have now reached agreement with Austria on the terms of lib-eration which, barring new Soviet demands, the West is likely to accept.

These two passages are from editorials, the first in the *Kansas City Star* for May 4, 1955, the second from *The New York Times* for May 2, 1955. The most noticeable thing about the first is the way in which it combines an elevated and judicious style with colloquialisms. "Presents a flagrant case" in the first passage consorts oddly with "monkey business." The grave "can and should be a matter of public concern" is immediately followed by the colloquial "So we have this . . . ," as one might say, to a friend, "So we have this fellow (or car, or problem) on our hands." This lack of taste, of consistency of tone, of feeling for what is appropriate in the context may arise from the comparative lack of literary training in American, particularly Middle Western, schools. *The New York Times* passage is a much better piece of writing and much more of a piece. It is much less "literary" than a leader in the London *Times* would be, but more pompous. To some extent, "stalling," which is vivid and vernacular, conflicts with the high editorial style ("all due consideration").

2. *Magazines*

(a) The only comment on the American economy that can be made with perfect assurance is that nobody really understands it. On the whole, this is a good thing. An economy capable of being thoroughly understood would probably prove treacherous. Of course, there are always a few professionals who like to believe that they understand the American economy, and these people turn up at Congressional hearings to explain why the market acts the way it does, but it is quite obvious that they are just groping their way along, the same as everybody else.

This is from the editorial page of *The New Yorker* entitled "Talk of the Town," the nearest thing to the essay one can find in the United States today. It is highly intelligent and professionally polished, yet intimate and engaging in its manner. The man who wrote this passage did have an ear, and he did have taste. The short second sentence picks up an echo both of the New York Yiddish colloquialism "This is a good thing?" and the British (*1066 and All That*) "a Good Thing," and yet is simply effective without these probably unintended connotations. The third sentence is disarming. It is as sensitively balanced as a line of verse. "Treacherous" strikes one as being just the right word; no other will do. It is meaningful, connotative, and funny, yet not fancy. "Of course," "these people," and "the same as everybody else" keep the level down, an important thing in a milieu in which ceremony or over-refinement are quickly smelled out. This kind of prose mirrors the most attractive kind of American personality, that of a man who is polite but not deferential, droll, easy in manner, and responsive.

(b) Barsov went. At his own request, the U.S. authorities flew him to Linz. "Are you sure you want to go back?" they asked him at the end. He was.

The Soviets had a propaganda bonanza in Barsov; they pointed to him as an example of what happens to those who desert the Soviets and trust the West.

This quotation from an article in the *Reader's Digest* is an example of "bright" snappy journalism. The clipped style ("Barsov went," "He was.") probably owes something to the Walter Winchell manner of radio reporting. The American slang word "bonanza" (a rich strike) is a good choice since it adds, like a raccoon's tail to a streamlined car, a human touch to prose which is in danger of becoming cold through its professional terseness. This prose is tailored for "modern people" who, after a day in the office or the factory, believe that the best way to relax is by not mentally taxing themselves. It has, therefore, a "cat on the mat" simplicity and clarity, otherwise a number of readers (who knows how many?) would consider themselves too tired even to try to grasp its import. This kind of prose must also have a reasonable quota of direct speech and be sharply paragraphed, for unrelieved indirect speech and normal paragraphing would be too dull and difficult to lure the fickle attention of the new kind of reader. Such devices are, of course, used in other publications too, both inside and outside the United States. In Britain, for example, the *Daily Express*, which is much influenced by the fashions of the United States, is an extreme example of bright journalism. . . .

(c) The speaker rustled his notes, clinked a pocketful of keys and stared at the ceiling while he fumbled for words. Then his wife's voice cut through the jangle: "Put your keys down, honey." Meekly, irascible Columnist Westbrook Pegler obeyed. For once the foaming temper was in check. Mellow with memory, onetime Sportswriter Pegler had turned out for the Tucson, Ariz. Press Club dinner, greeting the new baseball season.

Peg. . . .

This passage is, of course, from *Time* (April 11, 1955). The formula is familiar and highly successful: first, the dramatic opening, the deliberate holding back of the name. Who can this Milquetoast be? To our surprise, it is none other than irascible Columnist Westbrook Pegler, who, having been introduced in a cloud of unknowing, soon becomes, in the democratic fashion, our friend, "Peg." This richly staged introduction, as designing as an advertiser's banquet, achieves its purpose admirably, again within the imaginative scope and vocabulary of the lowest common denominator of readers, although the level is, one suspects, rather higher than that of the *Reader's Digest*. It is the most lavish example so far of the presentation of factual material in an emotional way. It was prophesied by Tocqueville as a concomitant of the Age of Democracy. Everyone can read, but few can or want to read properly. Even to say "properly" is suspect in this time of the triumph of the mindless. Must democracy inevitably lead to the relaxing of standards and pandering to increasingly jaded palates? It is a nice question. The "average reader" cannot be expected to use his brain because he wants "relaxation" after his day's work, or because he has no time to spare, or because he wasn't taught properly in High School. So the writers of *Time* labour (and they probably have some fun doing it, too) to present him with ever more brightly written and attractively presented material. If they did not, their public would go off and read *Newsweek*, no doubt.

### ADVERTISING PROSE

(a) Yes, only Viceroy has this filter composed of 20,000 tiny filter traps. You cannot obtain the same filtering action in *any other cigarette*. . . . That's why more college men and women smoke Viceroys than any other filter cigarette. . . .

This passage, taken from an advertisement by the makers of Viceroy cigarettes in a student newspaper, is typical of nationwide current advertising technique for cigarettes, and of the kind of prose used in such advertisements.

The copywriters have apparently now reached their nadir, for they are using the same formula in print as on the radio. Perhaps this is significant in terms of the relationship of speech to literature in the United States, but I doubt it. The method is one of insidious hammering, as if with a little rubber hammer which the torturer wields tirelessly, so that, in the end, one's whole body is in tune with the nagging rhythmic blows. Four (at least four) things are constant: first, the meaningless and tiresome "yes," worn like a charm to scare away the advertising man's bogey (lack of smoothness, lack of a "friendly" yet authoritative, selling ring); second, the appeal to "science"; third, the "You cannot . . . in *any other cigarette*" (which varies in some cases to "No other cigarette made . . ." etc.); and fourth, the repetition on the same, though slightly modulated note ("That's why . . . than any other filter smoke"). Writers on the traditional ballad tell us that their anonymous authors used the device of "incremental repetition" in order that a rhythmic, memorable pattern might be retained in the minds of an audience which lived in an oral tradition. Here is incremental repetition today, serving other ends in another society.

> *Why Swelter? Just a Twist of the Wrist Changes*
> *Hot Misery . . . to Cool Comfort!*
> *Live and Work in G-E "Comfort-Conditioned Air"!*

> *Simply dial out swelter with this great new General Electric Room Air Conditioner! You can sleep dry and cool tonight in G-E "Comfort-Conditioned Air"—air that's always cool, dry and filtered to reduce dust, dirt and pollen.*
> *Why Not Call on Your General Electric Dealer Now?*

The most noticeable thing about this passage, which is taken from an advertisement in *Life*, is its colourful and highly sensory use of language. This, coupled with the exclamatory style, creates an effect of pseudo-momentousness. Nothing more, possibly, in the way of emotive effect, could have been crammed into the headline. The advertising copywriters are, as I believe Mr. Hayakawa once pointed out, the folk-poets of modern commercial civilisation. They know all the tricks of language that a poet or a short story writer knows, but they put them to the service, not of art, but of commercial persuasion. As Tocqueville said, "Democracy not only infuses a taste for letters among the trading classes, but introduces a trading spirit into literature." The writer of this copy ("Just a Twist of the Wrist") had an ear for the fundamental rhythms of the English language, a language which naturally and easily falls into patterns of rhyme, alliteration and onomatopoeia. These are patterns which can be found as easily in literature as in ordinary speech, from "A faire felde ful of folke / Fonde I there bytwene," of William Langland to "The breezes blew, the white foam flew, / The furrow follow'd free" of Coleridge, from Cockney rhyming slang to the "What's cookin', good-lookin' " of the American high school boy.

"Dial it out" is another example of verbal ingenuity devoted to the end of persuading. The effect is concentrated and dramatic. One can see oneself just dialling away "swelter," (i.e. the state of sweltering) by that "twist of the wrist."

The use of "swelter" here, incidentally, is an interesting illustration of the extreme grammatical flexibility of the English language in communicating sensations, and also of the streamlining tendency of American English.

Another interesting invention is "Comfort-Conditioned Air." Perhaps the copywriter, like Fleming with his moulds, made the discovery by sheer accident. At any rate, it seems to be a reversal of the familiar "Air-Conditioned Comfort." And the wonder of it is that it means something. The poet, fiddling with words, struck rich ore (a bonanza). The effect of it was so heady that when he came to compose the whole line he made the very air, now "cool, dry and filtered," the property of General Electric. What kind of air have you there, Mr. Jones? I have G.E. Comfort-Conditioned Air in here, Mr. Smith.

One last point calls for mention and that is the use of "great," which, second to "beautiful," seems to be the most overworked word in the English language. If this air-conditioner is "great," what then was the invention of the aeroplane or the propounding of the Theory of Relativity?

I trust that my own tone, in commenting on these examples, has not at times seemed like that of the Reverend John Witherspoon. The Reverend John was mild in comparison with later British commentators who were apt to report on the misuse of language in the United States with shouts of glee, thus arousing the animosity and eventually the triumphant counter-cries of H. L. Mencken. A pre-Revolutionary (immigrant) American, the Reverend John hoped for a specifically American style, to be watched over by some "center of learning and politeness." In the meantime he thought it his duty to point out the various misuses of the English language in America, which he listed under the headings of: (1) Americanisms, (2) vulgarisms in England and America, (3) vulgarisms in America alone, (4) local phrases or terms, (5) common blunders arising from ignorance, (6) cant phrases, (7) personal blunders, and (8) technical terms introduced into the language.

On subjects like America and Prose one's mind cannot be made a blank. One has impressions, and my impression, before examining the samples I have chosen, was that in spite of some obvious examples of excessive rhetoric, of ineptness in handling words, of crudeness, of a peculiarly American kind of inflation, American prose as a whole had more naturalness than the English and at its best a transparent sincerity and simplicity worthy of American ideals. I did not, however, choose my quotations to prove this point. I threw my net as wide as I could, examined the pieces as objectively as possible, and relied on my findings to provide me with some conclusions which might or might not prove what I had previously accepted

I find, on the whole, that my preconceptions are borne out only in so far as the best topical commentary, the best political writing, the best criticism and, above all, the best humorous writing is concerned. Elsewhere, there are great variations Of course. the reader might object that he could have chosen a whole set of other samples which would alter the emphasis, or alternatively, that the quotations were far too short for judgment. This might be true, but short of conducting a statistical survey I do not see what else could be done. Perhaps, before our time runs out, one of the great Foundations will have provided funds for such an enterprise. But since language cannot be gauged like physical reactions, and the value of the comments depends on the taste of the investigator, it would be a difficult task. In the meantime, and in the light of my own crude sampling, I offer, diffidently, some general conclusions.

In the first place, it seems to me that American "expositional prose" is much weaker than American creative prose. Only in the case of people of acute sensibility, at the highest level, do we find a kind of prose which, by its tasteful natural diction, its use of figures drawn from American life, and its ease of manner can be held up as an example of the use of English which is both good and distinctively American. The American temperament seems better fitted to explore the creative possibilities of language, and one can find all kinds of examples to support this from the ebullience but relative crudeness of Thomas Wolfe to the fine-grained yet almost overwhelmingly rhetorical "immediacy" of William Faulkner. In the hands of the modern American short story writer, particularly, American prose is both beautiful and exciting to read. Life leaps from the page: sights, colours, smells, all the multifarious aspects of common and uncommon human existence make an impact which British creative prose rarely achieves. But the cultural climate of the United States in the 20th century has apparently not been conducive to the development of a widespread and distinctively American instrument for conveying facts, ideas, and comment at the general level. Feelings and emotions get in the way, for one thing. There is too commonly an inability to express a logical sequence of thought with "ease, grace, precision," what I have called "having no ear" for the English language. One reason for this lies, I am sure, in the deep-seated American feeling that "style" is something ornamental, part of a way of life that is variously called "British" or "aristocratic." It does not matter that the reaction, which is an emotional one, is understandable. What matters is that it is bad for American prose. To quote Sir Arthur Quiller-Couch again:

> The editor of a mining paper in Denver, U.S.A., boldly the other day laid down this law, that niceties of language were mere "frills": all a man needed was "to get there," that is, to say what he wished in his own way. But just here . . . lies the mischief. You will not get there by hammering away on your own untutored impulse. You must first be your own reader, chiselling out the thought definitely for yourself: and, after that, must carve out the intaglio more sharply and neatly, if you would impress its image accurately upon the wax of other men's minds.

But there is another reason, I believe, for the comparative lack of literary ability in all but the exceptional in the United States and this lies in the tendency to "educate for life" and to relegate literature to an inferior place. A questionnaire sent out in 1949 for *Harper's Magazine* by Norman Lewis revealed what Mr. Lewis called a "linguistic liberalism" among those people in the United States who "use the English language as a direct means of earning a livelihood." This meant accepting such expressions as "His work is different *than* mine," "I encountered *less* difficulties than I had expected" (attributed to Mr. Arthur Schlesinger, Jr.), and "The reason I'm worried is *because* I think she's ill." If we substitute "sloppy English" for "linguistic liberalism" we are, I think, nearer the mark. Yet, as against ninety-three American College Professors of English who rejected the first expression there were sixty-two who accepted it as worthy of currency in educated speech. Forty-nine out of the one hundred and fifty-five even accepted the barbarous second example, and the astounding total of eighty-nine out of one hundred and fifty-five the third. This perhaps partly explains why college students' essays are such examples of bad prose. But what is far more perturbing than uneducated usage in educated exposition is the sheer muddle of the language, the lack of an ability, in the college group, to express ideas lucidly and coherently. Yet even those who seem on the page to be semi-literate morons can make good sense when they speak, be ready in comment, even advance ideas. One's conclusion cannot but be that American conditions, educational and otherwise, have militated against clear and graceful literary expression. Yet Abraham Lincoln, that self-educated man, could express himself simply, cogently, and with style. Could he have learnt it had he grown up in America today? Where would he find models? Well, he could find them for one thing in Mr. Stevenson's prose, or in Mr. Oppenheimer's, or Mr. Randall Jarrell's, or Mr. Thurber's. He could read *The New Yorker*, or the *Atlantic*, or *Harper's*. The compilers of college textbooks of exposition certainly seem to strive to put good examples of prose before their readers. One wonders what the 40 per cent of college professors of English who say "His work is different *than* mine" do with them. Point out their queer usage perhaps?

It seems, then, that "independence and vigour," which the United States has in abundance, may produce good novels and stories but does not make a good climate for expositional prose which, unlike creative writing, touches everybody. In fact, the outstanding exceptions which I have noted would be classified by some as outside the mainstream of American culture. It almost seems as if there were, as Disraeli said of 19th century English society, "two nations" in America, but instead of these two nations being the rich and the poor they are the educated and the uneducated, the literate and the semi-literate. One remembers some of Tocqueville's prophecies:

> The most common expedient employed by democratic nations to make an innovation in language consists in giving some unwonted meaning to an expression already in use. This method is very simple, prompt, and convenient; no learning is required to use it aright, and ignorance itself rather facilitates the practice; but that practice is most dangerous to the language.

There will always, I feel, be Americans to whom these practices will be abhorrent. They will uphold the standards of American prose to the end. But to whom will they make their communication, except to each other?

All this raises, no doubt, most interesting questions, some as basic as one could wish for, such as: Does literacy matter? It is true that one can be intelligent without being literate. But Western Civilisation is built upon such principles and traditions as demand literacy. To deny it is to deny Western Civilisation as an idea and to prepare the way for barbarism. Yet some years ago a Californian professor seriously suggested, not merely that the oral might eventually entirely supersede the written communication, but that it was a good thing that it should do so. Perhaps in the end it will be so. Perhaps the triumph of the mass media and the encouragement of "speech" rather than literature in schools has started a tide which cannot be turned. And what, when it is upon them, will the publishers and manufacturers of typewriters do then, poor things? If they are, like the rest of us, still here, that is.

❧ ❧ ❧

## H. L. Mencken

# The American Language [1]

THE first Englishman to notice an Americanism sneered at it aloofly, thus setting a fashion that many of his countrymen have been following ever since. He was one Francis Moore, a ruffian who came out to Georgia with Oglethorpe in 1735, and the word that upset him was *bluff*, in the sense of "a cliff or headland with a broad precipitous face." He did not deign to argue against it; he simply dismissed it as "barbarous," apparently assuming that all Englishmen of decent instincts would agree with him. For nearly a century they seem to have done so, and *bluff* lingered sadly below the salt. When it was printed at all in Great Britain it was set off by sanitary quotation marks, or accompanied by other hints of deprecation, as *rubberneck, hot spot* and *nerts* are accompanied today. But then, in 1830, the eminent Sir Charles Lyell used it shamelessly in the first volume of his monumental "Principles of Geology," and from that day to this it has been a perfectly respectable if somewhat unfamiliar word in England, with a place in every dictionary.

Its history is the history of almost countless other Americanisms. They have been edging their way into English since early colonial times, and, for more than a century past, in constantly increasing volume, but I can't recall one that didn't have to run a gauntlet of opposition in the motherland, at times verging upon the frantic. After the Revolution, that opposition took on the proportions of a holy war. Never an American book came out that the English reviewers did not belabor its vocabulary violently. The brunt of the attack, of course, had to be borne by the poetasters of the era—for example, Joel Barlow, whose "columbiad" (1807) loosed a really terrifying geyser of abuse. But even the most seri-

[1] "The American Language," *Yale Review*, XXV (March, 1936), 538-552, with omissions. Copyright Yale University Press.

ous writers got their share—among them, Jefferson, John Marshall, Noah Webster, and John Quincy Adams. Jefferson's crime was that he had invented the
verb to *belittle*. It was, one may argue plausibly, a very logical, useful, and perhaps even nifty word, and seventy-five years later the prissy Anthony Trollope
was employing it without apology. But when Jefferson ventured to use it in his
"Notes on Virginia" (1787) "The London Review" tossed and raged in a manner befitting the discovery of a brace of duelling pistols beneath the cope of the
Archbishop of Canterbury, and for several years following its dudgeon was
supported virtuously by most of the other reviews. "What an expression!"
roared the "London." "It may be an elegant one in Virginia, but for our part,
all we can do is to *guess* at its meaning. For shame, Mr. Jefferson! Freely, good
sir, will we forgive all your attacks, impotent as they are illiberal, upon our national character: but for the future spare—O spare, we beseech you, our
mother-tongue!"

The underscoring of *guess* was a fling in passing at another foul Americanism. It was the belief of most Englishmen then, as it is today, that the use of
the verb in the sense of *to suppose* or *assume* originated in this country. It is
actually to be found, in that meaning precisely, in "Measure for Measure" and
"Henry VI"; nay, in Chaucer, Wycliffe, and Gower. But such historical considerations have never daunted the more ardent preservers of the King's English.
When a word acquires an American flavor it becomes anathema to them, even
though it may go back to Boadicea. *To advocate* offers an instructive example.
It appeared in English in the dark backward and abysm of time, but during
the eighteenth century it seems to have dropped out of general use, though
Burke used it. Towards the end of the century it came into vogue in this country, and soon it made its way back to the land of its birth. It was received
with all the honors proper to an invasion of Asiatic cholera. The reviews denounced it as loutish, "Gothic," and against God, and lumped it with *to com-
promit* and *to happify* as proof that civilization was impossible in America, and
would be so forevermore. Even Benjamin Franklin, returning from England in
1789, was alarmed into begging Noah Webster to "reprobate" it, along with *to
notice, to progress*, and *to oppose*. There is no record of Noah's reply, but it is
most unlikely that he did any reprobating, for when he began to make dictionaries he included all four verbs, and they have been listed in every considerable dictionary published since, whether in this country or in England.

The leader of the heroic struggle to keep Americanisms out of Britain, in its
early stages, was the celebrated William Gifford, editor of "The Quarterly Review." Gifford was a killer in general practice, and his savage assaults on
Wordsworth, Shelley, and Keats are still unpleasantly remembered. He was the
first magazine editor in history to make the trade pay, and when he died in
1828 he left £25,000 and was buried in Westminster Abbey. One of his
major specialties was the villainousness of everything American, from politics to
table manners and from theology to speechways. Among the allegations that
he either made himself or permitted his contributors to make were these: (*a*)

that the Americans employed naked colored women to wait upon them at table, (b) that they kidnapped Scotsmen, Irishmen, Hollanders, and Welshmen and sold them into slavery, and (c) that they were planning to repudiate the English language altogether, and adopt Hebrew in its place. This last charge, as it flew from tongue to tongue, acquired variorum readings. One of them made the new American language an Indian dialect, another made it Greek, and a third was to the effect that the people of Britain would be forced to acquire Greek, thus leaving English to the wicked will of the barbaric Yankees. It all sounds idiotic today, but in 1814 it was taken quite seriously by many Englishmen. Gifford was a tyrannical editor and so vastly enjoyed slashing his contributors' copy that Southey once denounced him as "a butcherly review-gelder." But anything that was against the damyankee passed his eye unscathed, and he piled up accusations in a manner so shameless that "The North American Review" was moved to protest that if the tirade went on it would "turn into bitterness the last drops of good-will towards England that exist in the United States."

In the early Twenties of that century there was some amelioration, and when Gifford retired from the "Quarterly" in 1824, voices that were almost conciliatory began to be heard. They heaped praises on Niagara Falls, found something to commend in Cooper's "Spy," and even had kind words for the speed and luxuriousness of American canalboats. But my most diligent researches have failed to unearth anything complimentary to the American language. It continued to be treated as a grotesque and immoral gibberish, full of uncouth terms and at war with all the canons of English. Every British traveller who came to these shores between the War of 1812 and the Civil War had something to say about the neologisms his ears and eyes encountered on his tour, and nearly all were constrained to deplore them. Captain Basil Hall, who was here in 1827 and 1828, went about in a palpitating daze, confounded and outraged by the signs on American places of business. *Clothing Store* he interpreted after long thought, and *Flour and Feed Store* after prayer and soul-searching, but what on earth was a *Leather and Finding Store?* Captain Thomas Hamilton, who followed five years later, found it impossible to penetrate to "the precise import" of *Dry-Goods Store*, and when he encountered an establishment offering *Hollow Ware, Spiders, and Fire-Dogs* he gave up in despair.

Hall was not one to take it lying down. He decided to call upon Noah Webster, whose American Dictionary of the English Language had just come out, to find out what the Yankees meant by using the mother tongue so cruelly. Webster shocked him by arguing stoutly that "his countrymen had not only a right to adopt new words, but were obliged to modify the language to suit the novelty of the circumstances, geographical and political, in which they were placed." The great lexicographer "who taught millions to spell but not one to sin" went on to observe judicially that it was "quite impossible to stop the progress of language—it is like the course of the Mississippi, the motion of which, at times, is scarcely perceptible; yet even then it possesses a momentum quite irresistible. Words and expressions will be forced into use in spite of all the exertions of all the writers in the world."

"But surely," persisted Hall, "such innovations are to be deprecated?"

"I don't think that," replied old Noah. "If a word becomes universally current in America, where English is spoken, why should it not take its station in the language?"

"Because," declared Hall with magnificent pertinacity, "there are words enough already."

This heroic dogma is still heard in England, where even native novelties are commonly opposed violently, and not infrequently strangled at birth. There seems to be, in the modern Englishman, very little of that ecstasy in word-making which so prodigiously engrossed his Elizabethan forebears. Shakespeare alone probably put more new words into circulation than all the English writers since Carlyle, and they were much better ones. The ideal over there today is not picturesque and exhilarating utterance, but correct and reassuring utterance, and one of its inevitable fruits is that bow-wow jargon which Sir Arthur Quiller-Couch describes in "On the Art of Writing" as "the medium through which boards of government, county councils, syndicates, committees, commercial firms, express the processes as well as the conclusions of their thought, and so voice the reason of their being." It is, at its worst, at least in accord with what are taken to be the principles of English grammar, and at its best it shows excellent manners and even a kind of mellifluous elegance; indeed, the English, taking one with another, may be said to write much better than we do—at all events by the standards of the schoolmaster. But what they write is seldom animated by anything properly describable as bounce. It lacks novelty, variety, audacity. There is little juice in it. The reader confronted by it is treated politely and lulled pleasantly, but he seldom enjoys the enchantment of surprise. That diligent search for new and racy locutions which occupied so much of the work day of Walt Whitman and William Dean Howells alike, and is practised so assiduously by scores of saucy Andersons and Hemingways, Sandburgs and Saroyans today, is carried on across the ocean by only a few extravagant eccentrics, virtually all of whom—for example, James Joyce and Ezra Pound—are non- and even anti-Englishmen. The hundred-per-cent English writers, save when they stoop to conscious wickedness, seldom depart very far from the jargon of Quiller-Couch. It is by no means a monopoly of the classes he named, nor is it reserved for solemn occasions. I find it also in my favorite English weekly, the "News of the World," which is devoted principally to sports, the theatres, and the more scabrous varieties of crime, and is probably a far better mirror of England than the "Times." When the "News of the World" reports the downfall of a rural dean or a raid on a Mayfair night club, the thing is done in a style so tight and brittle that nothing to match it is discoverable in this country, at least outside the pages of "The Homiletic Review." "When we want to freshen our speech," Mrs. Virginia Woolf was lately saying, "we borrow from American—*poppycock, rambunctious, flip-flop, booster, good mixer.* All the expressive, ugly, vigorous slang which creeps into use among us, first in talk, later in writing, comes from across the Atlantic." . . .

Whenever an Americanism comes publicly into question in England, there are efforts to track down its etymology, and sometimes the theories offered are extremely bizarre. In January, 1935, for example, the London "Morning Post" opened its columns to a furious and fantastic discussion of the verb-phrase, *to get his goat.* I content myself with one of the explanations: "Among the Negroes in Harlem it is the custom for each household to keep a goat to act as general scavenger. Occasionally one man will steal another's goat, and the household débris then accumulates to the general annoyance." The truth is that *to get his goat* seems to be of French origin, and in the form of *prendre sa chèvre* philological genealogists have traced it back to the year 1585. But whatever is strange and upsetting is put down, in England, to the hellish ingenuity of Americans—save, of course, when genuine Americanisms are claimed as really English. This last happens often enough to give what may be called a cockeyed aspect to the perennial pother. In 1934 even the learned Dr. C. T. Onions, one of the editors of the great Oxford Dictionary, succumbed to the madness by offering to find in the dictionary any alleged Americanism that a reporter for the London "Evening News" could name. The reporter began discreetly with *fresh* (in the sense of *saucy*), *to figure* (in the sense of *to believe* or *conclude*), and *to grill* (in the sense of *to question*), and Dr. Onions duly found them all. But when the reporter proceeded to *bunkum,* the learned editor had to forget conveniently that its progenitor was the thoroughly American *buncombe,* when *rake-off* followed he had to admit that the earliest example in the dictionary was from an American work, and when *baloney* and *nerts* were hurled at him he blew up with a bang.

Here, of course, Dr. Onions and his interlocutor ended on the level of slang, but there is no telling where they would be if they could be translated to the year 2036. *Baloney,* like *to belittle,* has the imprimatur of an eminent tribune of the people, and is quite as respectable, philologically speaking, as *buncombe, gerrymander, pork barrel, filibuster, carpetbagger, gag rule,* or *on the fence.* All these came into American from the argot of politics, and got only frowns from the schoolmarm, but they are all quite sound American today, and most of them have gone into English. As for *nerts,* it seems to be but one more member of an endless dynasty of euphemisms, beginning with *zounds* and coming down to *son-of-a-gun, gee,* and *darn. Darn,* like *nerts,* is an Americanism, and Dr. Louise Pound has demonstrated that it descends from *eternal,* which first turned into *tarnal* and then lost its tail and borrowed the head of *damn.* I have heard a bishop use it freely in private discourse, with a waggish sprinkling of actual *damns. Son-of-a-gun* is now so feeble and harmless that the Italians in America use it as a satirical designation for native Americans, who seem to them to fall far behind the Italian talent for profanity and objurgation. It is, I believe, a just criticism. Some time ago I was engaged by a magazine to do an article on American and English swearwords. After two or three attempts I had to give it up, for I found that neither branch of our ancient Frisian tongue could show anything worthy of serious consideration. The antinomians of England stick to two or three banal obscenities, one of which, *bloody*, is obscene only formally, and we Americans seldom get beyond variations of *hell* and *damn*. A single Neapolitan boatman could swear down the whole population of Anglo-Saxondom.

*Bloody* is perfectly innocuous in the United States, and it may be innocuous in England also on some near tomorrow—or even more disreputable than it is today. There is no predicting the social career of words. Dr. Leonard Bloomfield says that even "our word *whore*, cognate with the Latin *carus* (dear), must have been at one time a polite substitute for some term now lost." Prophecy fails just as dismally when propriety does not come into question. Shakespeare's numerous attempts to introduce new words, some of them his own inventions and others borrowed from the slang of the Bankside, failed almost as often as they succeeded. He found ready takers for *courtship, lonely, sportive, multitudinous, hubbub* and *bump*, but his audiences would have none of *definement*, in the sense of description, or of *citizen* as an adjective, and both seem strange and uncouth to us today, though all the others are as familiar and as decorous as *cat* or *rat*. When John Marston used *strenuous* in 1599 it was attacked by Ben Jonson as barbarous, but a dozen years later it had got into Chapman's Homer, and by 1670 it was being used by Milton. It remained perfectly respectable until 1900, when Theodore Roosevelt announced the Strenuous Life. Both the idea and the term struck the American fancy, and in a little while the latter passed into slang, and was worn so threadbare that all persons of careful speech sickened of it. To this day it carries a faintly ridiculous connotation, and is seldom used seriously. But by 1975 it may be restored to the dignity of *psychopath* or *homoousian*. No one can say yes with any confidence, and no one can say no. "Even the greatest purist," observes Robert Lynd, "does not object to the inclusion of *bogus* in a literary English vocabulary, though a hundred years ago it was an American slang word meaning an apparatus for coining false money. *Carpetbagger* and *bunkum* are other American slang words that have naturalized themselves in English speech, and *mob* is an example of English slang that was once as vulgar as *photo*." . . .

One finds in current American all the characters and tendencies that marked the rich English of Shakespeare's time—an eager borrowing of neologisms from other languages, a bold and often very ingenious use of metaphor, and a fine disdain of the barricades separating the parts of speech. The making of new words is not carried on only, or even principally, to fill gaps in the vocabulary; indeed, one may well agree with Captain Hall that "there are words enough already." It is carried on because there survives in the American something that seems to have faded out of the Englishman: an innocent joy in word-making for its own sake, a voluptuous delight in the vigor and elasticity of the language. The search for the *mot juste* is an enterprise that is altogether too pedantic for him; he much prefers to solve his problem by non-Euclidian devices. *Hoosegow* was certainly not necessary when it appeared, for we already had a large repertory of synonyms for *jail*. But when the word precipitated itself from the Spanish *juzgado* somewhere along the Rio Grande it won quick currency, and in a little while it was on the march through the country, and soon or late, I suppose, it will produce its inevitable clipped forms, *hoose* and *gow*, and its attendant adjective and verb. *Corral*, which entered by the same route in the Forties of the last century, had hatched a verb before the Civil War, and that verb, according to Webster's New International (1934), now has four separate and distinct meanings. *Bummer*, coming in from the German, is now clipped to *bum*, and is not only noun, verb, and adjective but also adverb. *Buncombe*, borrowed by the English as *bunkum*, has bred *bunco* and *bunk* at home, both of which rove the parts of speech in a loose and easy way, and the last of which has issue in the harsh verb *to debunk*, still under heavy fire in England.

The impact of such lawless novelties upon the more staid English of the motherland is terrific. The more they are denounced as heathen and outlandish, the quicker they get into circulation. Nor do they prosper only on the level of the vulgate, and among careless speakers. There are constant complaints in the English newspapers about their appearance in the parliamentary debates, and even in discourses from the sacred desk, and they begin to show themselves also in *belles-lettres*, despite the English dislike of new ways of writing. Their progress, in fact, is so widespread and so insidious that they often pop up in the diatribes that revile them; the Englishman, conquered at last, can no longer protest against Americanisms without using them. Moreover, they are now supported actively by a definitely pro-American party of writers and scholars, and though it is still small in numbers, at least compared to the patriot band, it shows some distinguished names. The late Robert Bridges, Poet Laureate, was an active member of it, and among its other adherents are Wyndham Lewis, Edward Shanks, Richard Aldington, and Sir John Foster Fraser. Sir William Craigie, perhaps the first of living lexicographers, is so greatly interested in the American form of English that he has spent the years since 1925 in a scientific examination of it, and will presently begin the publication of an elaborate dictionary. If only because of the greater weight of the population behind it, it seems destined to usurp the natural leadership of British English, and to determine the general course of the language hereafter. But its chief advantage in this struggle is really not the numerical one, but the fact that its daring experiments and iconoclasms lie in the grand tradition of English, and are signs of its incurable normalcy and abounding vigor.

How far it will move away from the theorizing of grammarians and the policing of schoolmarms remains to be seen. They still make valiant efforts to curb its wayward spirit, but with gradually diminishing success. When, a few years ago, the late Sterling A. Leonard of the University of Wisconsin submitted a long series of their admonitions to a committee of educated Americans, including many philologians, he found that opinion was against them on that high

level almost as decidedly as it was on lower ones. His judges favored scores of
forms that the school grammars and popular handbooks of usage still condemn.
Since then a more direct attack upon the conservative position has been made
by Dr. Robert C. Pooley of the same university. He shows that some of the rules
laid down with most assurance by pedants have no support in either history or
logic, and are constantly violated by writers of unquestionable authority. There
have even been rumblings of revolt in the conservative camp. The late George
Philip Krapp of Columbia, who was surely anything but a radical, was of the
opinion that English would undergo profound changes in the United States,
and that many of them would be of such a character that its very grammatical
structure would be shaken. Dr. George O. Curme of Northwestern University
is another eminent grammarian who warns his colleagues that the rules they
cherish have no genuine authority, and must be overhauled from time to
time. Once they steel themselves to that sacrifice of their professional dignity,
he says, "it will give a thrill to English-speaking students to discover that the
English language does not belong to the schoolteacher but belongs to them, and
that its future destiny will soon rest entirely in their hands."

   Dr. Curme is always careful to think and speak of American as no more than
a variation of English. But it must be obvious that, in late years, the tail has begun a vigorous wagging of the dog. "The facts that we ought to realize," says
Edward Shanks to his fellow Britons, "and that we ignore when we talk loftily
about Americanisms, are that America is making a formidable contribution to
the development of our language, and that all our attempts to reject that contribution will in the long run be vain."

# ❧ ❧ ❧ III. Thinking

*Gilbert Highet*

## The Unpredictable Intellect [1]

YET WE cannot foresee the stages of this war in which we are all engaged—the war for the enslavement or liberation of the mind of humanity. The movement of the human intellect is impossible to prophesy: difficult even to record and analyze. Whether we shall ever be able to write a systematic history of thought, explaining the laws that govern its growth and movement, I know not; but at present those who have studied the migration of ideas find it far beyond their powers. Historians such as Sorokin and Toynbee and anthropologists such as Kroeber and Linton have found it hard enough to describe the manifold, the illimitably various stimuli that awaken the sleeping reason and the multiple channels through which thought flows from one mind to another, from one region to another. So far, scholars have been able to establish only the broadest and vaguest rules to assist us in understanding these processes. They are wonders. They are mysteries.

It is difficult, for instance, to see why a single nation should be able in one century to produce a thousand inventors, philosophers, poets, and statesmen, and then, within a few generations, become speechless and apparently thoughtless. Why should one country seethe with intellectual energy as long as it is poor and danger-ridden, only to fall into indolent stupor when it gets wealth and security, while its neighbor, long silent during centuries of poverty and humiliation, finds its voice only after acquiring power and riches? How is it that, within the same country at different times, scientists are now admired and now neglected, poets are sometimes blessed as benefactors and sometimes despised as eccentrics? We know well how often two men, or two groups in different parts of the world, will make the same discovery or think similar thoughts without knowing each other; and that is strange; but it is stranger still to roam through the history of genius, and watch, and see how often mighty minds have appeared in lonely lands and savage tribes and eras full of repression and of hateful violence.

### LONELY GENIUS

Sometimes, climbing among the western mountains, one crosses a long windlashed and snow-beaten shoulder of harsh broken rocks; and in a tiny hollow

[1] From *Man's Unconquerable Mind* (New York: Columbia University Press, 1954), pp. 29-45. Copyright, 1954, Columbia University Press.

halfway across it, see, there is a tuft of bright flowers. Sometimes, from higher up, one looks down into a barren canyon, whose stony walls echo with the dull roar of the torrent below and with the crash of crumbling slabs and pinnacles above: there is not a patch of green, not a visible handful of nourishing earth; but halfway down those precipitous walls, raising its gallant head and spreading its hopeful arms, there grows a pine tree rooted in an invisible notch, and the birds flicker around it.

No less delightful and wonderful is it to read the history of some bloody epoch, crusted with murder and torture, resounding with dull groans, choked hymns, and shouts of senseless violence, and in the midst of it to meet a serene and gracious mind, studying nature and making poetry; or to discover, among lazy bourgeois or glum earthbound peasants, a powerful intellect grappling with abstractions of number, producing unique inventions, or building a systematic interpretation of the universe.

Such was the Buddha. Such was Sequoyah, the Cherokee Indian who, alone, created a written language for his people. Such was the greatest philosopher of the Dark Ages, Johannes Scotus Eriugena—John the Celt from Ireland, as he emphatically called himself—who, almost alone in western Europe at that time, contrived to learn Greek, and created a vast philosophical vision of the spiritual world such as no thinker today could equal. Such was Gregor Mendel, the quiet monk who worked and thought patiently in his garden until he had discovered some of the fundamental laws of heredity. And such were many artists who lived obscurely and whose personalities are all but forgotten, but who made masterpieces of beauty. We may know the name of Aleijadinho, that pathetic figure who became the finest sculptor of Latin America; but the carvers of Chartres are known only by their work, and we cannot even guess the race of the artist who made the exquisite bronze heads from Benin in west Africa.

### NEW SYNTHESIS

Yet even apart from such lonely geniuses there are other surprises in the history of thought, phenomena almost as unexpected and almost as inexplicable. There are men who express the age and the milieu in which they were educated, but who, by the intensity of their imagination, the sweep of their knowledge, and their astounding versatility, rise high above their era and their neighbors, so that they inhabit both time and eternity at once. When we analyze their minds we can identify nearly all the component elements, tracing this to family and that to school and the other to social climate, and yet the compound is far more than the sum of all these elements: richer, intenser, different in quality as a diamond is different from carbon. Shallow thinkers often fail to understand that this qualitative difference occurs again and again in the realm of the intellect. That is what leads some critics to deny that Shakespeare could have written those plays because he was only a middle-class provincial youth who went from a small-town school to become an actor: they expect the real author to be someone calculable, like the university-trained lawyer and statesman Bacon, or a witty and graceful young nobleman with the learning and worldly experience of the Renaissance in his very blood. But they are wrong. They are making the elementary error of believing that, in the world of the mind, two and two make four.

Such people can never have taught. One of the few but great rewards of teaching is to see, not once but again and again, how one boy indistinguishable from the others in an average group, will, stimulated by a single remark of the teacher or excited by exploring a new subject, suddenly begin to change. He grows in wisdom; he throws out original ideas of his own; his very speech and handwriting become more mature; he lives on a new time-scale; he changes so rapidly that he distances all his friends and cannot remember or recognize his twelve-months-younger self. Somehow, some happy chance or providential effort has—what can we say? there are no images to describe the event, which is as mysterious as all vital processes—something has caused the energies of his mind, hitherto dissonant or unused, and the emotions with which he once played, or which played with him, to combine into a new, living, active, creative synthesis. This boy astonishes his friends and his parents: usually not himself, for he feels he is simply learning to use powers which are already his own; and never the teacher, who knows the almost limitless treasure of ability and creativity that every pupil carries about in the locked safe of his mind, and who always hopes and strives to unlock it.

And further, those who believe that forces and results in the field of the intellect are always calculable—those who think Bacon or Oxford ought to have written the Shakespearean dramas because that would be easier to understand —must know very little of the personal history of genius. In a touchingly awkward poem representing the shy self-encouragement of a lonely young man in a far country, John Masefield writes

> I have seen flowers come in stony places;
> And kindness done by men with ugly faces;
> And the gold cup won by the worst horse at the races;
>     So I trust, too.

And one certain truth about the great works of the mind—inventions, philosophical systems, poems and plays, pictures and music, scientific discoveries and political institutions—is that many of them were made by men who started life in ordinary, even in unfavorable, situations and then far outsoared their origins.

Isaac Newton was the son of a Lincolnshire farmer: unlike some mathematicians, he was not even bright in boyhood; he was a mediocre student when he went to Cambridge; and then within a few years, the spark descended. Gauss, one of the supreme geniuses of mathematics and electromagnetism, was a village boy like a million others. The founder of modern art-history, Winckelmann, was miserably poor and started as a hack schoolmaster, taking classes all day, sleeping in his schoolhouse, staying awake half the night to teach himself

Latin and Greek in preparation for the magnificent career he could only dimly foresee. The by-blow of an Italian gentleman and a country girl was apprenticed to the trade of painting, like many thousands before and after him: but this one was Leonardo da Vinci. Such handicaps hamper but do not crush the growth of the mind: they may even stimulate it. Even the general enemy, ordinariness and routine, cannot always spoil the seed. Loyola, founder of the Jesuits, was a brave ignorant soldier in an age full of stupid men with swords. Luther and Rabelais were monks indistinguishable from myriads of other monks in other lands and times. Socrates was a stonemason in a city crowded with builders. No, the whole history of human thought is as various, as marvelous, as unexpected, and as inexplicable as other mysteries of this universe. Science, with its search for laws, always oversimplifies. But the wise scientist always makes his way through the realm of law into the region of wonder. In a few years he can master the principles of plant and animal life, reproduction, and distribution—and then, for ever thereafter, he remains astounded by the incalculable multiplicity of animal forms, the unthinkable subtlety of plants, knowing that when new varieties are discovered they may contain something as unpredictable as a new divine creation. The complexities of human language, the intricate life of microorganisms, the invisible radiations that fill the universe, the power of mutation in living forms—all these can be faintly or crudely grasped, but never fully understood. One of the truest sayings of the medieval thinkers was OMNIA EXEVNT IN MYSTERIVM, *All things pass into mystery*. We are not intended only to diagnose and calculate, but also to wonder, to admire; to expect the unexpected.

### THE MIND A MYSTERY

Yes, the outer world—both visible and invisible—is ultimately a mystery. So too is the other world we inhabit—the inner world, the world of the mind. Not one of us knows what his own mind contains. Not one of us knows what his own mind can do, or will produce.

Some of the busy and complex activity of the mind is permanently hidden. We can scarcely ever see its vaguest outlines, except now and then in dreams or apparently purposeless actions. Priests at confession, psychoanalysts listening and probing, lawyers and judges analyzing acts of cunning and violence, ethnologists examining myths, and critics penetrating poems, yes, all of us when we listen to music, that wordless language of the soul, experience something of that powerful and terrible world, but can never know it fully. It means to hide itself. The pupils of Freud have sometimes made the problem too simple, saying that the inner activity of the mind was a ferment of "immoral" or rejected, censored, and repressed material—a living skeleton chained in our cupboard. But the true picture is far more complex. Much of our hidden life literally cannot be dominated, directly helped or impeded, or ever understood by our reasoning mind. The instincts, memory, invention, imagination—these and other activities lie largely outside the range of consciousness. The reason can observe them at work, occasionally intervene, and with constant and difficult effort learn to influence them; but their origins, their full power, their methods, all remain beyond its scope. Jesus once asked "Which of you, by thinking about it, can add a foot to his height?" But we might also ask ourselves whether any of us can forecast what ideas will be put up by his mind a year from now; a week from now; tomorrow; within the next hour.

We are all cave men. The cave we inhabit is our own mind; and consciousness is like a tiny torch, flickering and flaring, which can at best show us only a few outlines of the cave wall that stands nearest, or reflect a dangerous underground river flowing noiselessly at our feet, so that we start back in horror before we are engulfed; as we explore, we come often on shapes of beauty, glittering stalactites, jewel-encrusted pillars, delicate and trusting animals which befriend and follow us; sometimes we even find relics of an earlier time, a primitive statue with flowers still fresh at its feet, or shapes of beasts painted on the wall with bloody handprints beside them; now and then we stumble over a heap that crackles and mutters and moves, but we turn our light away and hurry on; the path we follow sometimes seems to trace an elaborate pattern, although our little flame shows us only a few lines, converging and then curving off into darkness; often its rays die down, threatening to go out altogether and leave us in the resounding gloom; at least thrice in our journey we must crouch down because the cave roof sinks low above us, so that we can go forward only on our knees; when we emerge, it is into another cavern larger than the last but more awesome, where we hear the beat of unseen wings above our head; there are side openings into which our light shines only faintly, to reveal glowing eyes and fearful teeth far in their recesses; the worst of all our trials is that when we venture to speak, the vast invisible walls and roof distort our words into formidable echoes, dying away in superhuman whispers or hateful growls; and, after many a year of wandering, when our torch gleams upon a silent pool and we bend over its calm surface, we do not recognize the face that stares up into our anxious and astonished eyes.

The self is hidden. We do not know ourselves, our brothers and sisters, husbands or wives or children. No friend knows his friend.

Yet all this mystery holds greatness as well as darkness. The cavern is dim, somber, unexplored; but it contains treasures. Every human brain is filled with unused power. Out of all the billions of men and women who have lived, only a few hundred thousand have been able to employ so much of that power as to change the world. The rest have been dutiful or lazy, good or bad, sensuous or self-denying, thrifty or wasteful, cowardly or brave. Those few hundred thousand, perhaps only a score of thousands in all, are the minds that have made our world. Scientists, strategists, industrialists, aesthetes, explorers, inventors, organizers, authors, musicians, philosophers, doctors and teachers, lawyers and statesmen, several thousand in each class, these are the minds who have given the rest of mankind incalculable benefits, or done it immeasurable damage. They are responsible for much of human history.

Consider the world, apart from mankind. It is either static or else changing in a gradual and apparently automatic rhythm. The planet swings around the sun, steadily slowing down. The tides flow back and forward with the retreating and returning moon. Weather wears the rocks, the sea eats at the shores, the polar ice advances and recedes. The air and land and water are filled with living things—but they scarcely ever change, or if they do, it is over vast spaces of time. Ferns grow and fish swim and micro-organisms vibrate in our world just as they did long before men walked upon the earth; the industrious ants continue with their routine of self-preservation and self-perpetuation as they did when the dinosaurs ruled. But man, in his brief history, has transformed both the world and himself. His specific quality is purposeful change through thought. He is most truly alive when he thinks.

There are only three secular explanations of history. One is that it is made by groups of people acting together. The second is that historical change is produced by blind impersonal "forces." The third is that it is decided and led by powerful individuals. Of course all these theories are true to some extent; and none is true exclusively. Climatic shifts and epidemic diseases move or destroy populations. Social, economic, religious, aesthetic patterns are worked out by successive generations; vast migrations occur without a single leader. Heroes and villains and geniuses preach, rebel, invent, govern. Yet in man's more recent history many of the most powerful and vital changes have been initiated by strong individuals. Not all of these were thinkers. Some were driven by passions of love or hatred or violence or pride. But the work of the thinking man has been more lasting.

Since it is all a mystery, we can never tell how great thinkers emerge. There are very few rules for producing them. They do not grow like trees; they cannot be bred like selected animals. People are not born thoughtless or thoughtful. Probably the surest way to grow up stupid is to be part of a large static population doing manual labor and living just on the level of subsistence; and the next best is to be born in a nice family with inherited wealth, brought up in an assured social position, and sent to a quiet and correct school. The young ploughboy and the young marquis are both in a mental prison, one following the furrow, the other set in his comfortable rut.

### TRAINING THE THINKER

No, we can never tell how great minds arise, and it is very hard to tell how to detect and encourage them when they do appear. But we do know two methods of feeding them as they grow.

One is to give them constant challenge and stimulus. Put problems before them. Make things difficult for them. They need to think. Produce things for them to think about and question their thinking at every stage. They are inventive and original. Propose experiments to them. Tell them to discover what is hidden.

The second method is to bring them into contact with other eminent minds.

It is not enough, not nearly enough, for a clever boy or girl to meet his fellows and his teachers and his parents. He (or she) must meet men and women of real and undeniable distinction. That is, he must meet the immortals. That brilliant and pessimistic scoundrel Plato died just over 2,300 years ago, but through his books he is still talking and thinking and leading others to think; and there is no better way, none, for a young man to start thinking about any kind of philosophical problem—human conduct, political action, logical analysis, metaphysics, aesthetics—than by reading Plato and trying to answer his arguments, detect his sophisms, resist his skillful persuasions, and become both his pupil and his critic. No one can learn to write music better than by studying *The Well-tempered Clavier* of Bach and the symphonies of Beethoven. A young composer who does so will not, if he is any good, write music like Bach and Beethoven. He will write music more like the music that he wanted to write. A man may become a routine diplomat by following the rule book and solving every problem as it comes up, but if he is to grow into a statesman he must read his Machiavelli and consider the lives of Bismarck and Lincoln and Disraeli. The best way toward greatness is to mix with the great.

Challenge and experiment; association with immortal minds: these are the two sure ways of rearing intelligent men and women. And these two opportunities for greatness are, or ought to be, provided by schools and colleges and universities. "But," you will ask, "do schools exist only to train geniuses?" No, but they do not exist only to train the average and to neglect or benumb the talented. They exist to make the best of both. One of the heaviest responsibilities in education is to do justice to exceptional minds, remembering that they may emerge in any place, at any time, and in any body—even a clumsy and misshapen frame may hold a brilliant mind. It must be a strange experience to teach in a little country school, the same subjects year after year to the same families, and then to find a gifted young engineer or a born dramatist among one's pupils. Disconcerting. Difficult. Difficult to know how to encourage without patronizing; difficult not to be a little jealous. Yet the history of knowledge is filled with true stories of teachers who recognized outstanding gifts in a pupil and gave him all he needed to set him on his way to eminence: touching and encouraging, these tales. Such is the story of the Spanish peasant boy who was drawing with charcoal on a plank when a teacher saw him, started training him, and helped to make the artist Goya. Such is the tale of the thin sensitive undersized London schoolboy whose schoolmaster's son gave him the run of his private library: it was among those shelves and as a result of that kindness that the youngster wrote a poem called "On First Looking into Chapman's Homer." Behind almost every great man there stands either a good parent or a good teacher.

Education in America and in the other countries of the West is an inspiriting achievement: all those light, healthy schools, those myriad colleges, so many youngsters having a fine time and not working too hard. Yet it has a couple of weaknesses. One is that education has become almost too easy to get. It is accepted like a supply of pure water: no one expects to get much stimulus or nourishment from it, but it is used to keep the tissues well filled and the outer surface clean. The other is that it does not often carry over into mature life. The average American would rather be driving a car along a crowded highway than reading a book and thinking. The average Frenchman would rather be drinking an extra bottle of wine than watching a play by Racine. The average Britisher would rather fill up a football-pool form than listen to Elgar's *Enigma*. Why this should be so, I cannot tell. It must be something wrong with education. Probably it is the cult of the average: the idea that schools exist in order to make everyone pretty much the same, and that happiness consists in sharing a group life, sweet, humming, undifferentiated, and crowded like bees in a hive.

Schools do exist for the average. They also exist to serve the distinguished. America was built both by a multitude of common men and women and also by a few eccentrics, heroes, and giants, those whom Stephen Spender exalts when he writes

> I think continually of those who were truly great.
> Who, from the womb, remembered the soul's history
> Through corridors of light where the hours are suns
> Endless and singing. Whose lovely ambition
> Was that their lips, still touched with fire,
> Should tell of the spirit clothed from head to foot in song.
>
> . . . .
>
> Born of the sun they travelled a short while towards the sun
> And left the vivid air signed with their honour.

The life of every teacher is partly dedicated to discovering and encouraging those few powerful minds who will influence our future, and the secret of education is never to forget the possibility of greatness.

We owe them reverence, the great minds of the past and present and future. It is inspiring and delightful even to scan their names. One shines on another, receiving light in return. It is like looking at the stars, when the eye travels from the Bear to Orion, from Aldebaran to Sirius and Vega, from glory to glory.

When we think of the most majestic mind of the Middle Ages, of Dante, our thought soon travels to his master and companion Vergil, who guided him through Hell and Purgatory until he attained the vision of the beloved; from Dante to the prose counterpart of his poem, the *Summa* of St. Thomas Aquinas; and back from St. Thomas to his master Aristotle. If we read an essay by Francis Bacon, we soon remember the earlier, kinder essayist Montaigne; and then, recalling that Bacon was a scientific thinker, we turn to Descartes, and from him to a kindred mind, Leibnitz, and so from greatness to greatness. Descartes and Newton both interpreted the universe: from Newton it is inevitable to travel back to Kepler and Brahe, forward to Laplace. Sometimes, again, great minds recall each other because, although they were strangers and

worked in different media, they saw similar aspects of the universe. It is difficult to play certain fugues by Bach (such as the E flat minor in Book II, full
of cold harmonies, meditative rhythms, and somber melancholy) without thinking of the wise old men with unsmiling wrinkled faces and deep eyes, who
watch us from the shadows of Rembrandt's last pictures. It is difficult to look
at Dürer's mystical etchings without thinking of Goethe's *Faust*.

Such men were not—as shallow historians try to tell us—creatures of their
time and place. Often they were eccentrics who ignored or preceded their
epoch; nearly always they were largely self-made; by giving their age a voice
and by teaching it, they helped to form it, to dominate it. To read the life of
even one such thinker is to renew one's faith in humanity, one's sense of duty
to the world. To move freely among the captain minds of any one great age—
say the seventeenth century, or the century that produced Cicero, Lucretius, Vergil, Horace, and Livy, or the nineteenth century—is to be perpetually astounded at the depth unplumbable, the infinite variety of the human mind, and
to repeat the words of the Greek tragedian:

> Wonders are many, but none,
> none is more wondrous than man.

❧ ❧ ❧

*William H. Whyte, Jr.*

# The Cadillac Phenomenon [1]

IF EVER a fat and happy group of businessmen foregathered, it was the Cadillac
executives and dealers who met at the Waldorf last November to talk over
strategy. At the climactic moment, the house lights dimmed, the curtains
parted, and there, slowly revolving under the spotlights, was the 1955 Sixty
Special Sedan ($5,292.07, f.o.b. Detroit). Like priests worshipping before
some ancient deity, the dealers gazed in rapt silence for a moment. Then, perhaps triggered by a highlight caught in the Florentine Curve of the rear window, or perhaps it was out of some common impulse of gratitude, suddenly,
spontaneously, they broke into an applause charged with genuine emotion.
There it was: nineteen gorgeous feet, two and a half solid tons of American
Dream—and all theirs!

What they were seeing, as well they knew, was not just a car but an institution. Probably never before has one material object become so much the focus
for so many of the aspirations that propel the American ego.

Polls have indicated that at least one out of two Americans would buy a
Cadillac before any other car if they had the money. G.M. itself is not sure just

---

[1] From *Fortune*, LI (February, 1955), 106-109 *et passim*. Reprinted by Special Permission from the February, 1955 issue of *Fortune Magazine*; © 1955 by Time, Inc.

what the potential market is; last year the Cadillac division built a record of 123,734 cars, yet at year end had 90,000 unfilled orders.

Of the million and a half cars sold in the $3,200-and-over class in the U.S. in the last five years, 30 to 40 per cent were Cadillacs. In the first eight months of last year, 73,715 Cadillacs were sold, practically as many as all the big Chryslers (41,074), Lincolns (25,583), and big Packards (8,298) put together. More of the popular Series 62 Cadillacs were sold (57,943) than Buick Roadmasters (44,111).

The 800,000 Cadillacs on the road constitute a gold standard for the nation's used-car lots. The poor man's Cadillac sometimes *is* a Cadillac, and in some working-class neighborhoods Cadillacs outnumber any other make.

"Cadillac" has been firmly integrated into the language as a symbol. Newspapers, despite the old taboo against using brand names in news columns, use this one all the time, e.g., JUST COULDN'T TRANSLATE HIS LOVE INTO CADILLACS.

The jokes about Cadillac are legion. (First man: What kind of car are you going to get? Second man: What else?) It has got to be such a staple of humor, as a matter of fact, that radio and TV programs sponsored by the competition are in constant peril from Cadillac jokes. "Some downfall that girl had," quipped a comedienne on the Ed Sullivan show. "Her downfall was a mink coat and a Cadillac!" Sponsor Lincoln-Mercury was not amused.

Finally, as dealers like to observe, almost everybody sooner or later will ride in a Cadillac whether he likes it or not; 90 per cent of the hearses sold in the U.S. are Cadillacs.

### THE SHOWMEN

How did it all happen? To make the obvious point that Cadillac is a magnificent hunk of machinery does not explain the phenomenon: it is clear that Cadillac's popularity is out of all proportion to the mechanical differences between it and other makes. Quality must precede prestige, of course, and part of Cadillac's popularity can be attributed to superb engineering. So, too, can it be attributed in part to coincidence and plain luck. But to a large degree Cadillac has become an institution because the Cadillac management has worked deliberately to make it one. In a marketing strategy beautifully attuned to the vast social changes that have been taking place in the U.S., Cadillac has perfected a wonderfully effective method of mass-merchandising a quality symbol. From the design of the car to the advertising of it, the Cadillac approach has been a triumph of selling and showmanship.

In this "mass" success, as will be seen, may lie pitfalls. With so many Cadillacs on the road, some observers think, the path is wide open for a less "ordinary" car. Significantly, the Ford Motor Co. plans to market within a year an elegant Continental with a price tag of about $10,000. Ford, in effect, is placing a $20-million bet that there is a vacuum to be filled in the prestige-car market.

But Cadillac General Manager Don Ahrens is bothered not at all by the "ordinary" tag. Why, he asks, should he be? Last year his dealers grossed $980 million, and since they had to give away none of the list price in "long" trade-ins, they enjoyed an operating profit of about $45 million—or 5 per cent, more than twice the rate for all auto dealers. The Cadillac division, with some $400 million to $500 million of gross sales, has been doing rather handsomely too—indeed, if it were an independent company, it would rank among the hundred largest corporations in the country. Not less production, but *more*, is in order, Ahrens figures; last November he put his Detroit plant on two shifts and announced that for 1955 he was going after 150,000, count them, Cadillac sales.

### FAREWELL TO THE "CLASSICS"

Twenty years ago neither Cadillac nor any other luxury-car maker would have dreamed of such a goal. In the early Thirties, the luxury-car merchandising was still aimed at a small upper-income class. Leaf through some old *Fortunes* of the era and the ads tell the story—there, next to the custom-tailoring ads, is the big Lincoln at the Maryland Hunt Cup, a Packard limousine coming out of the driveway of J. Pierpont somebody's estate; or there is the proud boast that "once again Cadillac announces that it is limiting production of the V-16 to two hundred cars." Occasionally the ads would beckon newcomers into the field, but generally they implied that their cars were reserved for the rich, and if anyone didn't get the point he had only to look at the price tag. Today the average price of all Cadillacs sold is only 1.7 that of the average price of all cars sold; in 1930 Cadillacs were four times as expensive.

In retrospect, the early Thirties were the Golden Age of the great "classic" cars. The economic underpinnings of that restricted market had already been knocked asunder, however, and one by one the big cars fell. Pierce-Arrow went out of business in 1935; Lincoln production dwindled to a few thousand cars a year, and the company turned to the cheaper Zephyr, dropping its big K line altogether in 1940. Packard kept on, but only at the price of downgrading the Packard name; where Cadillac had given a separate name, LaSalle, to its low-priced line, Packard bestowed its own name on a low-priced line of sixes and eights.

Cadillac hadn't been doing very well either, but in 1936, just about the time much of the competition was limping off the field, General Motors put Nick Dreystadt in charge of Cadillac. Dreystadt, a German-born ex-mechanic, set to work pruning the line of the V-12's and V-16's and invested heavily in cost-cutting production facilities. Meanwhile Cadillac's designers were getting in stride. In the 1938 Sixty Special (Cadillac's intermediate-price sedan) they had come up with a design that foreshadowed the postwar "hardtop" styling, and many of its features were subsequently fitted into the other Cadillacs. By late 1940 Dreystadt had his package; with the cheapest model down to $1,345, he discontinued the LaSalle and began merchandising Cadillac to a vastly expanded market. In 1941, the last full production year before World War II,

Dreystadt came out with another major model change. Sales, which had never exceeded 40,000, soared to 60,000.

After making tanks for four years, Cadillac picked up where it had left off. It was in a beautiful position. It had a large following of contented wartime owners talking up Cadillac durability, and a high-acceptance car with which to resume production. Well before the end of World War II Cadillac had set a postwar goal of 100,000 cars a year. Despite materials allocation, there would be enough steel, for General Motors had decided that if there were going to be more customers than cars, it might as well be generous with the division that could return the most dollars per pound of steel.

The competition was not prepared for the onslaught coming up. Selling cars in the postwar was easy, but at a time when the market would take anything, these companies largely missed their chance to build up an enthusiastic corps of owners. Chrysler, Packard, and Lincoln were saddled with designs that hadn't caused any noticeable stampede before the war, and they were slow to retool for new ones. In 1948 and 1949 they did bring out new models, but the public took no particular fancy to these either.

And Cadillac never gave them a chance to catch up. It brought out a completely redesigned car in 1948 and the public loved it. The following year Jack Gordon, who had succeeded Dreystadt as general manager in 1946, introduced his overhead-valve, high-compression engine and with it a persuasive "economy" story. When sales manager Don Ahrens succeeded Gordon in 1950, the pace continued. He had the benefit of such G.M. cost-spreading devices as the "C" body shell that Cadillac shares with Buick; on his own, however, he went on to spend as much on subtle changes as some manufacturers spent for complete change-overs. After laying out $32 million for a major model change in 1954, for example, Ahrens spent an additional $18 million on minor alterations for the '55s (cost of changing the side molding of the 1955 model: $3,500,000). All in all, between 1946 and 1955 Cadillac put out something like $160 million for tools, dies, and plant improvement.

### THE NEWCOMERS

So much for the management decisions that contributed to Cadillac's ascendancy. During all this time, however, a lot of things were happening outside Detroit that were equally important to Cadillac's success. Most important, a new kind of consumer market was emerging. The new big rich—butts of so many Cadillac jokes—attracted the public's attention, but the significant arrivals on the postwar scene were the new *well-to-do*. Each year additional thousands of consumers were being elevated into the $25,000-and-over income brackets. Furthermore, while taxes were siphoning off top-bracket incomes, they also stimulated a growth of "business expense" perquisites, and a further, if less traceable, increase in the number of people who were able to enjoy the good life.

For psychological as well as economic reasons, many of these people had an affinity for Cadillac. In a society where their own and others' positions had been shifting so rapidly, they needed a fix—a visible symbol that would affirm, to themselves as much as others, where they had got to, and how it would be from here on in.

Cadillac might have been a beneficiary of this need, whatever its advertising strategy; since the Cadillac seemed to many the best car around, people probably would have made a symbol of it whether Cadillac had asked them to or not. The point is that Cadillac *did*. Once it recognized the craving for a success symbol, it did more than accept this as a plus factor; it went on to make the exploitation of the craving the basis of its whole postwar market approach.

A great many people, of course, buy Cadillacs for other reasons than to prove they've just made the grade. But these people, Cadillac reasoned, are no great problem and once Cadillac gets them, they stay with Cadillac (74 per cent of all Cadillac sales are to previous Cadillac buyers). If the company was to widen its market, thought Jim Adams, head of its advertising agency, MacManus, John & Adams, the man to go after was someone else: the man on his way up. The Cadillac people agreed.

The psychological warfare began. Adams, a large, genial man who looks every inch the contented Cadillac owner, was a thoroughgoing elementalist. There would be no truck with motivation research; Adams already knew just where the belly was. He was going to merchandise Cadillac as "a way of life." He figured it might take an "incubation period" of about two years to warm up prospects, and, since production was still limited, possibly a lot of them wouldn't be able to get a Cadillac when they did get warm. But it was the long term that Adams was playing for, and the more people who drove themselves crazy for want of a Cadillac, the more fixed Cadillac would be as a symbol.

For some Madison Avenue tastes Adams' pitch to the American ego was much too blatant ("brutal," "inexpressibly vulgar"). Blatant or no, it was to be a virtual primer in the old-fashioned virtues of directness and consistency, and it helped define for the whole Cadillac organization the main line of attack. Adams indulged in practically no "factory talk" about mechanical features. Instead, he told a story. It was a simple story, and a man ambitious to show the Joneses where they could head in did not have to read between the lines for the moral of it.

Here, abridged from a collection of Adams' ads, is the way the Cadillac story goes.

Let's say it was thirty-one years ago, on a beautiful morning in June. A boy stood by a rack of papers on a busy street and heard the friendly horn of a Cadillac. "Keep the change," the driver smiled, as he took his paper and rolled out into the traffic. "There," thought the boy, as he clutched his coin, "is the car for me!"

And since this is America, where dreams make sense in the heart of a boy, he is now an industrialist. He has fought—without interruption—for the place in the world he wants his family to occupy. Few would deny him some taste of the fruits of labor. No compromise this time! The papers are all in order . . . and the car of his dreams is waiting for him. It's his!

It's Junetime—and the top is down—and he's going halfway up the hill, to a spot where a lane strays into the wildwood and he can glimpse the top of a fieldstone chimney above the trees. The family rushes out with the final voice of confirmation. "Hi there, neighbor, isn't it a lovely day?"

There's the first trip to the office with a waiting delegation to admire his choice. He'll get those quick glances of approval that tell him the dream he dreamed for so many years is still in the hearts of others.

Let him arrive at the door of a distinguished hotel or a famous restaurant . . . and he has the courtesy that goes with respect. "Here is a man," the Cadillac says—almost as plainly as the words are written here—"who has earned the right to sit at this wheel."

## PEACE OF MIND

Month after month, year after year, the ads have hammered away at the theme—reward, earned, dream; achievement, dream, June, earned, admiration, CADILLAC! Whatever the mixture, there is always one dominant thought: if you've earned it, don't hesitate! Occasionally the diet gets too rich for popular consumption and there have been flurries of mail saying don't pull that earned-it stuff on us, the biggest gangster in town owns a Cadillac. Adams confesses, "We lay low for a while then," but before long he is reaching for the needle again. (Tentative ads for '55: "Only Thirty-Five, But He's Earned It." "To the Class of 1984.")

Frequently Adams does dwell on such non-symbolic aspects of Cadillac as its ease of driving. Even here, however, the main theme is never very far away. Cadillac driving is *serene* driving. It is a *proved therapeutic*. It offers *peace of mind*. It makes you *feel good*. It even changes your personality. You tip better; you acquire a sense of *noblesse oblige*. Let the other fellow dash past at the light. The race is over. Relax. *You don't have to prove a thing.*

Lest this peace-of-mind pitch repel the young in heart, Adams builds into it two levels of meaning. In his ad "Tread Lightly, Proud Foot!" he writes with solemn mien that there is something Cadillac wishes to impress upon people. Under that hood is a juggernaut. Now it was put there for safety. It was *not* put there for dramatic displays on the getaway, for the ungracious purpose of dominating the highway, for blinding, exhilarating surges of speed—never, *never* push the pedal down the last, unbelievable half-inch. "I drive them crazy," Adams says, happily, "to get their foot on that accelerator."

## MAN ECONOMIZING

There is, of course, one large disadvantage in the symbol appeal: What would the neighbors think? *The man should own a Cadillac. His accomplishments entitle him to it. But he feels that if he purchased a Cadillac, some of his friends might think him ostentatious.* Several years ago the management was distressed to learn that the executives of a large insurance company were not driving Cadillacs out of fear of the stockholders. Similarly, reports went, executives in other firms were being constrained by fear of the boss.

To combat this, Adams took the offensive. Waving the white feather at the foolish and pusillanimous people who needlessly deprive themselves of a Cadillac, he tells them there are other cars that actually cost more. Furthermore, he says, making a significant detour into product copy, these non-Cadillac people may get less gas mileage. To someone who can pay $5,000 for a car a few dollars a year saved in gas would seem trifling. What the ads do, however, is provide the prospect with a minor premise that can be masqueraded as the major premise; don't get him wrong, he can tell his friends, that prestige stuff is strictly for the birds, the real reason he bought a Cadillac was economy, honestly.

### YOU, TOO, CAN JOIN THE CLUB

In this market approach Cadillac strikes a shrewd balance between the exclusive and the democratic. On the one hand, it merchandises the join-the-club idea, and what adman Adams promises, sales manager Jim Roche works to deliver. Dealers' salesmen may not break any legs running after customers these days, but once a man joins the club he is made the object of a great deal of carefully planned custom attention. He is counseled to look upon any Cadillac agency anywhere as a home away from home; any repairs done when he's on a trip can be charged to his home dealer and each dealer is supposed to stand ready to cash checks, get hotel reservations or theatre tickets for the itinerant club member. From Detroit the new owner gets a personal letter from Jim Roche; later, one from Ahrens along with a questionnaire to find out if he is completely satisfied. Says Ahrens, "It's all part of selling a guy peace of mind and pride."

But the club doors are wide open. Not only in its copy, but in the media it selects, Cadillac bends over backward to make the point that anyone is eligible. Some people wonder why Cadillac invests so much of its $8-million advertising budget in newspapers and thus pays to reach millions of people who could never afford the car. Cadillac does this because it believes that in the communication of prestige there is a *trickle-up* as well as a trickle-down effect, and that the filling-station attendant, the doorman, and all the other men on the street are stewards of the symbol as much as the Cadillac owner. The owner's image of Cadillac is in part what he thinks *their* image is. And who knows? You never can tell which man on the street will turn up with the $5,000 to buy a Cadillac. And if he has had to cross over the tracks to get there, Cadillac doesn't worry.

A number of prominent Negroes are Cadillac owners and though the company does not dwell on this in its advertising, it is proud of the fact that they singled out Cadillac—as an *Ebony* editorial asked, what better symbol for economic and social achievement? "You can get so hellishly exclusive," says

Adams, "only a few feel they should buy. The perfect compromise is our aim. While the right hand holds us up as a celestial symbol, the left should indicate that we are not too far above the earth. Tiptoe, we say, and you can reach us!"

## THE PEOPLE WHO EARNED IT

To see just how well attuned the "earned-it" approach has been to the market, take a look at who actually owns the Cadillacs. The first thing apparent is that the "aristocracy" has become an insignificant market for the luxury car. A study of Cadillac registrations in the Philadelphia area indicates that of approximately 6,500 Social Register households, only about 1.5 per cent own Cadillacs —less than the proportion of new Cadillac registrations in the U.S. population at large (1.98 per cent). The same is true, incidentally, for other luxury cars. Only about 2 per cent of the Social Register families in Philadelphia own Buick Roadmasters, Lincolns, big Chryslers, or big Packards.

Among Social Registerites there is now a kind of reverse snobbery. As they drive about in Ford station wagons, many like to look on the Cadillac in the same humor that they look on the new subdevelopments overrunning their golf courses. It is not so much the styling of the Cadillac that abrades them, though they make their critique in these terms. Cadillac has become too much a reward for achieved rather than passed-on wealth and thus an affront to a somewhat dispossessed gentry.

As the ads say, the typical Cadillac owner is the man who has worked hard. The entrepreneur heads the list. Many corporation executives own Cadillacs, but independent businessmen, with less protocol to worry about and often more "business expense" money to play around with, make up the largest single group of owners. A *Popular Mechanics* poll of Cadillac owners (September, 1954), for example, showed that 33 per cent of all Cadillacs are owned by independent businessmen. Twenty per cent are owned by executives, and 7 per cent by salesmen.

## THE COMPANY CADILLACS

Motor-vehicle-bureau registration lists reflect the "business expense" trend. A surprising proportion of Cadillacs are registered, not in the names of individuals, but of companies, and usually small ones. Of all Cadillac registrations in Manhattan, for example, 37 per cent are in firm names; in Philadelphia, 20 per cent.

Registrations also show a strong per capita concentration of Cadillacs in the urban Jewish business and professional world. In part this is due to Cadillac's affinity with upward mobility—in the dress industry area along Manhattan's Seventh Avenue, for example, there are probably more Cadillac jokes per square yard than anywhere else. But this is only part of the story. "You hear a lot of talk," one Jewish observer says, "about people on the way up buying Cadillacs because they are psychologically insecure. A lot of that is true but it is not all so psychological as that. Jews have a healthy love of good living and Cadillac seems the most comfortable and luxurious car. So if a man can afford it, why should he deny himself just because he is worried about what people might think?" Who, he asks, is being insecure?

Among professional owners, doctors predominate; roughly 7½ per cent of the Cadillac registrations in Philadelphia are held by doctors. The greatest concentration is usually assumed to be among specialists but the general practitioners have been coming up fast. "If we didn't drive Cadillacs, the patients would think less of us," says one practitioner, without twitching a muscle. "They figure something must be wrong with a doctor these days who can't afford one."

The hard core of the Cadillac market, in sum, is a group of fairly solid citizens. They are well off;—only 18 per cent of Cadillacs are sold on the installment plan vs. an average for all cars of over 60 per cent. Most Cadillac owners have a second car (69 per cent of the owners polled by *Popular Mechanics* had two or more cars, and 26 per cent had another Cadillac). But they are no spendthrifts: a lot of Cadillac owners *do* wash their own Cadillacs.

### THE CROSS-UP

In styling, Cadillac shows a genius for matching the "personality" of the car with that of its market. From the jutting "Dagmars" on the front bumper to the leviathan rear deck, the car itself breathes the same spirit as Jim Adams' copy. It is a *dominant* car. "It has a sort of raw prestige," a competitor puts it, "the kind that attracts the animalistic instincts."

While the latter is a somewhat envious judgment, Cadillac would not argue the basic point. Cadillac is a handsome car and its designers take great care with refinement of detail—it has, they like to say, "the Cellini look." They are very careful, however, not to get the basic design *too* refined.

Cadillac has managed to keep an unusual continuity of design—its car is never confused with somebody else's. Yet at the same time it has displayed an uncanny ability to come up with a feature that makes the bystander think to himself, the hell they say. G.M. stylist Bill Mitchell, who has had a lot to do with the design of the postwar Cadillacs, explains that "It takes a controversial design to be a success. If it is 'nice,' we don't like it. We like something gutty, something shocking. There's got to be a cross-up." Ahrens, who also has a keen eye for the right kind of dissonance, is entirely in accord: "You have to stretch it out somehow. You've got to be a little brutal about it."

### THE FISHTAIL

Cadillac, being Cadillac, can get away with it. Take, for example, the famous fishtail. When it was designing its first postwar model, Cadillac was on the verge of taking at face value requests for a "sensible" car—for a while Cadillac seriously considered dechroming the front grill. But the Cadillac people were showmen at heart. For the '43 model that never appeared, the designers had made a clay mock-up of a rear fender upswept like the tail of a P-38. After looking at it for several years, Cadillac executives had learned to live with it;

eventually to like it. This, they decided, taking a deep breath, would make a wonderful hallmark.

As soon as the '48 model appeared, the protests began to roll in, and the management noted uneasily that about 50 per cent of the spectators of the G.M. automobile shows also showed distaste for the fin. It has long been rumored that in desperation the company hurried up designs on a finless rear fender. The rumor is true; the company did. But somewhere along the line opinion began to change. The more fins that appeared on the road, the more people got used to them, and finally they began to like them. "We would have been murdered," a competitor says, in open admiration.

Then the rear deck. Too long, people complained when Cadillac stretched it out on the 1948 Sixty Special. Cadillac took the hint and stretched it out some more, until now there is almost as much car behind as there is in front.

Before long Cadillac slipped a piece of vertical chrome on the rear door. Again people protested that Cadillac had really gone too far; didn't they know the vertical line broke up the horizontal sweep of the car? As it happens, Cadillac did know it, but it figured this cross-up was in order, and with eighteen or nineteen feet of horizontal sweep, Cadillac could afford a break that, on smaller cars, would look a little silly.

In the 1952 model Cadillac's designers set dual exhausts in the rear bumpers and in the '54 model called more attention to them. For another cross-up, they enlarged the "Dagmars" on the front bumper. "This time," says a competitor's designer, somewhat hesitantly, "I think Cadillac has really gone too far."

Has Cadillac's success bred complacency? Certainly, the dealer organization might be a bit too contented. *Fortune* correspondents shopped the luxury cars in twelve cities across the U.S. and without a single exception the Cadillac salesmen in each city did the poorest job. While they could hardly be blamed for being contented, they made it a little too plain that they didn't give a damn whether the customer wanted a Cadillac or not. In contrast, the salesmen for the other top-price makes demonstrated that adversity can be stimulating. Quite aside from better trade-in offers, most of them did a good basic selling job— the Lincoln salesmen, in particular—and several got the customer behind the wheel posthaste.

Against the perils of contentment, however, must be set the fact that in fundamentals the Cadillac dealer organization is extremely strong. Nearly all dealers are in excellent financial shape, their plants are tiptop, and they are in fine rapport with sales manager Jim Roche and Don Ahrens.

So far as Cadillac management is concerned, complacency does not seem imminent. Ahrens has a strong killer instinct, and when he says it has pained him to give away business to the competition because of the limitations on Cadillac production there is not the slightest doubt that it has in fact pained him very much. He has already spent a lot to get capacity up to 150,000 cars a year and he has given chief engineer Fred Arnold a hefty budget for dies and tools for the upcoming '56 and '57 models.

In all this, the General Motors top management is a willing ally. Part of an increase in Cadillac's sales would undoubtedly come out of its sister division, Buick, which is G.M. boss Harlow Curtice's alma mater. Like Wilson and Sloan before him, however, Curtice recognizes Cadillac's importance to G.M. Even if it lost money, Cadillac would be valuable to the company as a style and engineering leader; if Cadillac can supply these benefits and make good profits too, who would deny it more facilities?

## THE CONTINENTAL TOUCH

If Cadillac's dominance is to be challenged, the competition will have to come up with something rather spectacular. Chrysler, Lincoln, and Packard each have strong engineering points to make, and in any objective comparison with Cadillac their 1955 models have a great deal to offer. They are competing, however, against a symbol: to beat Cadillac they can't be just a little better; the cars must in some way force themselves on the public's consciousness as demonstrably superior—at the very least have a "personality" in both design and advertising that makes an appeal Cadillac does not.

The first strikingly different "personality" will probably come from Ford. Under Bill Ford, youngest of the three Ford brothers, an enthusiastic group of designers and engineers is readying a new Continental. Their approach to the luxury market is considerably different from Cadillac's. For one thing, they plan to make the Continental a more hand-tooled affair and to promote it as such. Initially, they are thinking of an output of 2,000 to 5,000 cars a year. The car itself, in contrast to the boldness of the Cadillac, will have a European elegance and a conformation that will again emphasize the long hood. Then there is the price: roughly, $9,000 to $10,000.

The Continental promises to be a beautiful car and, somewhat like G.M.'s dream cars, may pay big dividends in the luster cast on the rest of the line. Will it be a commercially profitable operation as well? How it fares in this respect will tell a lot about the future of the luxury market.

Two questions are at issue. First, the economic one: are there enough people able—and willing—to pay the price demanded by small production? Cadillac, which sells its Eldorado for around $6,300, believes there is no market worth bothering about for a car over $7,000. It is sensitive to the fact that the big increase in consumer incomes has been in the middle-income group; it is also mindful that the percentage of high-priced-car sales to total cars sales has hovered fairly consistently around 5 per cent since 1948.

Bill Ford, however, does not care so much about the proportion of people able to pay $10,000 as the absolute number of them. And there are enough people making $50,000 and over after taxes to provide, in theory at least, a market for 25,000 or so $10,000 cars a year. For many of these people, it could further be argued, the very fact that the price of the car is about double that of Cadillac could be something of an attraction rather than a disadvantage.

The social aspect of the price, then, may well be the critical one. Since nothing quite like the Continental is now in the market, there are no ready analogies, but it can be noted that Rolls-Royce has been selling less than 150 cars a year in the U.S. since the war. Even rich Americans, it would seem, are pretty well sold on the advantages of the mass-produced product, and like anyone else, they are sensitive to the charge of conspicuousness that goes with a high price tag.

That there is a vacuum in the present car market may very well be true; certainly the postwar increase in sales of such foreign cars as the Jaguar and the proliferation of "classic" car clubs are clues to an unsated yearning for something different. Most people who buy special cars buy to satisfy a taste, and in each case they must sacrifice something to satisfy that taste—it could be a comfortable ride, for example, or passenger space, or economy—and the decision depends on whether the taste appeal outweighs the sacrifice. The people whose tastes will be most aroused by the Continental may not be the same as those most able to pay. Yet it may be those who have to reach—as much as the rich —who will spell the critical difference between success and failure.

### TOO MANY CADILLACS?

Which brings up the matter, finally, of the risks Cadillac is taking by *upping* production. Among used-car dealers there are fears that the passing of the hard-to-get phase may dim Cadillac's appeal. Says Irving Sachs, who boasts he is the country's "Largest Unauthorized Cadillac Dealer," "It's the only hot car around and the scarcity's one of the reasons. If Cadillacs get too easy to get, maybe people won't be so anxious to buy."

For all the ready agreement that quantity lessens a prestige car's appeal, however, there is no proof of the fact, and some to the contrary. For the past seven years *Fortune* has been making annual surveys of its readers, which, among other things, provide a running study of shifts in their attitude toward cars. In 1948, 44.8 per cent of the *Fortune* readers queried named Cadillac as the car in the high-priced field they would "most like to have." In the intervening years the number of Cadillacs on the road grew steadily—and so did the proportion of readers nominating Cadillac; by 1953 the number was up to 61 per cent. Preliminary returns from the '54 survey indicate about the same proportion. While people think the other fellow may dislike a car that is too popular, they don't necessarily act on that basis when they themselves buy.

For the immediate future, at any rate, Cadillac should be able to keep its vise grip on the American pulse, and, if it sells those 150,000, tighten it up a bit. The company has been earning the grip and like the Cadillac owner at the stoplight, its people can't help but smile just a little. Even at all those jokes about Cadillac: as long as the jokes aren't about Lincoln and Packard and Chrysler, Don Ahrens and his lieutenants couldn't chuckle more. The public has to yell uncle somehow.

🌱 🌱 🌱

*Susanne K. Langer*

# Language and Thought[1]

A SYMBOL is not the same thing as a sign; that is a fact that psychologists and philosophers often overlook. All intelligent animals use signs; so do we. To them as well as to us sounds and smells and motions are signs of food, danger, the presence of other beings, or of rain or storm. Furthermore, some animals not only attend to signs but produce them for the benefit of others. Dogs bark at the door to be let in; rabbits thump to call each other; the cooing of doves and the growl of a wolf defending his kill are unequivocal signs of feelings and intentions to be reckoned with by other creatures.

We use signs just as animals do, though with considerably more elaboration. We stop at red lights and go on green; we answer calls and bells, watch the sky for coming storms, read trouble or promise or anger in each other's eyes. That is animal intelligence raised to the human level. Those of us who are dog lovers can probably all tell wonderful stories of how high our dogs have sometimes risen in the scale of clever sign interpretation and sign using.

A sign is anything that announces the existence or the imminence of some event, the presence of a thing or a person, or a change in a state of affairs. There are signs of the weather, signs of danger, signs of future good or evil, signs of what the past has been. In every case a sign is closely bound up with something to be noted or expected in experience. It is always a part of the situation to which it refers, though the reference may be remote in space and time. In so far as we are led to note or expect the signified event we are making correct use of a sign. This is the essence of rational behavior, which animals show in varying degrees. It is entirely realistic, being closely bound up with the actual objective course of history—learned by experience, and cashed in or voided by further experience.

If man had kept to the straight and narrow path of sign using, he would be like the other animals, though perhaps a little brighter. He would not talk, but grunt and gesticulate and point. He would make his wishes known, give warnings, perhaps develop a social system like that of bees and ants, with such a wonderful efficiency of communal enterprise that all men would have plenty to eat, warm apartments—all exactly alike and perfectly convenient—to live in, and everybody could and would sit in the sun or by the fire, as the climate demanded, not talking but just basking, with every want satisfied, most of his life. The young would romp and make love, the old would sleep, the middle-aged would do the routine work almost unconsciously and eat a great deal. But that would be the life of a social, superintelligent, purely sign-using animal.

[1] From Susanne K. Langer, "The Lord of Creation." Reprinted from the January 1944 issue of *Fortune* Magazine by special permission of the Editors. Copyright, 1944, Time, Inc.

To us who are human, it does not sound very glorious. We want to go places and do things, own all sorts of gadgets that we do not absolutely need, and when we sit down to take it easy we want to talk. Rights and property, social position, special talents and virtues, and above all our ideas, are what we live for. We have gone off on a tangent that takes us far away from the mere biological cycle that animal generations accomplish; and that is because we can use not only signs but symbols.

A symbol differs from a sign in that it does not announce the presence of the object, the being, condition, or whatnot, which is its meaning, but merely *brings this thing to mind*. It is not a mere "substitute sign" to which we react as though it were the object itself. The fact is that our reaction to hearing a person's name is quite different from our reaction to the person himself. There are certain rare cases where a symbol stands directly for its meaning: in religious experience, for instance, the Host is not only a symbol but a Presence. But symbols in the ordinary sense are not mystic. They are the same sort of thing that ordinary signs are; only they do not call our attention to something necessarily present or to be physically dealt with—they call up merely a conception of the thing they "mean."

The difference between a sign and a symbol is, in brief, that a sign causes us to think or act *in face of* the thing signified, whereas a symbol causes us to think *about* the thing symbolized. Therein lies the great importance of symbolism for human life, its power to make this life so different from any other animal biography that generations of men have found it incredible to suppose that they were of purely zoological origin. A sign is always embedded in reality, in a present that emerges from the actual past and stretches to the future; but a symbol may be divorced from reality altogether. It may refer to what is *not* the case, to a mere idea, a figment, a dream. It serves, therefore, to liberate thought from the immediate stimuli of a physically present world; and that liberation marks the essential difference between human and nonhuman mentality. Animals think, but they think *of* and *at* things; men think primarily *about* things. Words, pictures, and memory images are symbols that may be combined and varied in a thousand ways. The result is a symbolic structure whose meaning is a complex of all their respective meanings, and this kaleidoscope of *ideas* is the typical product of the human brain that we call the "stream of thought."

The process of transforming all direct experience into imagery or into that supreme mode of symbolic expression, language, has so completely taken possession of the human mind that it is not only a special talent but a dominant, organic need. All our sense impressions leave their traces in our memory not only as signs disposing our practical reactions in the future but also as symbols, images representing our *ideas* of things; and the tendency to manipulate ideas, to combine and abstract, mix and extend them by playing with symbols, is man's outstanding characteristic. It seems to be what his brain most naturally and spontaneously does. Therefore his primitive mental function is not judging reality, but *dreaming his desires*.

Dreaming is apparently a basic function of human brains, for it is free and unexhausting like our metabolism, heartbeat, and breath. It is easier to dream than not to dream, as it is easier to breathe than to refrain from breathing. The symbolic character of dreams is fairly well established. Symbol mongering, on this ineffectual, uncritical level, seems to be instinctive, the fulfillment of an elementary need rather than the purposeful exercise of a high and difficult talent.

The special power of man's mind rests on the evolution of this special activity, not on any transcendently high development of animal intelligence. We are not immeasurably higher than other animals; we are different. We have a biological need and with it a biological gift that they do not share.

Because man has not only the ability but the constant need of *conceiving* what has happened to him, what surrounds him, what is demanded of him— in short, of symbolizing nature, himself, and his hopes and fears—he has a constant and crying need of *expression*. What he cannot express, he cannot conceive; what he cannot conceive is chaos, and fills him with terror.

If we bear in mind this all-important craving for expression we get a new picture of man's behavior; for from this trait spring his powers and his weaknesses. The process of symbolic transformation that all our experiences undergo is nothing more nor less than the process of *conception*, which underlies the human faculties of abstraction and imagination.

When we are faced with a strange or difficult situation, we cannot react directly, as other creatures do, with flight, aggression, or any such simple instinctive pattern. Our whole reaction depends on how we manage to conceive the situation—whether we cast it in a definite dramatic form, whether we see it as a disaster, a challenge, a fulfillment of doom, or a fiat of the Divine Will. In words or dreamlike images, in artistic or religious or even in cynical form, we must *construe* the events of life. There is great virtue in the figure of speech, "I can *make* nothing of it," to express a failure to understand something. Thought and memory are processes of *making* the thought content and the memory image; the pattern of our ideas is given by the symbols through which we express them. And in the course of manipulating those symbols we inevitably distort the original experience, as we abstract certain features of it, embroider and reinforce those features with other ideas, until the conception we project on the screen of memory is quite different from anything in our real history.

Conception is a necessary and elementary process; what we do with our conceptions is another story. That is the entire history of human culture—of intelligence and morality, folly and superstition, ritual, language, and the arts—all the phenomena that set man apart from, and above, the rest of the animal kingdom. As the religious mind has to make all human history a drama of sin and salvation in order to define its own moral attitudes, so a scientist wrestles with the mere presentation of "the facts" before he can reason about them. The process of *envisaging* facts, values, hopes, and fears underlies our whole behavior pattern; and this process is reflected in the evolution of an extraordinary phenomenon found always, and only, in human societies—the phenomenon of language.

Language is the highest and most amazing achievement of the symbolistic human mind. The power it bestows is almost inestimable, for without it anything properly called "thought" is impossible. The birth of language is the dawn of humanity. The line between man and beast—between the highest ape and the lowest savage—is the language line. Whether the primitive Neanderthal man was anthropoid or human depends less on his cranial capacity, his upright posture, or even his use of tools and fire, than on one issue we shall probably never be able to settle—whether or not he spoke.

In all physical traits and practical responses, such as skills and visual judgments, we can find a certain continuity between animal and human mentality. Sign using is an ever evolving, ever improving function throughout the whole animal kingdom, from the lowly worm that shrinks into his hole at the sound of an approaching foot, to the dog obeying his master's command, and even to the learned scientist who watches the movements of an index needle.

This continuity of the sign-using talent has led psychologists to the belief that language is evolved from the vocal expressions, grunts and coos and cries, whereby animals vent their feelings or signal their fellows; that man has elaborated this sort of communion to the point where it makes a perfect exchange of ideas possible.

I do not believe that this doctrine of the origin of language is correct. The essence of language is symbolic, not signific; we use it first and most vitally to formulate and hold ideas in our own minds. Conception, not social control, is its first and foremost benefit.

Watch a young child that is just learning to speak play with a toy; he says the name of the object, e.g.: "Horsey! horsey! horsey!" over and over again, looks at the object, moves it, always saying the name to himself or to the world at large. It is quite a time before he talks to anyone in particular; he talks first of all to himself. This is his way of forming and fixing the *conception* of the object in his mind, and around this conception all his knowledge of it grows. *Names* are the essence of language; for the *name* is what abstracts the conception of the horse from the horse itself, and lets the mere idea recur at the speaking of the name. This permits the conception gathered from one horse experience to be exemplified again by another instance of a horse, so that the notion embodied in the name is a general notion.

To this end, the baby uses a word long before he *asks for* the object; when he wants his horsey he is likely to cry and fret, because he is reacting to an actual environment, not forming ideas. He uses the animal language of *signs* for his wants; talking is still a purely symbolic process—its practical value has not really impressed him yet.

Language need not be vocal; it may be purely visual, like written language, or even tactual, like the deaf-mute system of speech; but it *must be denotative.*

The sounds, intended or unintended, whereby animals communicate do not constitute a language, because they are signs, not names. They never fall into an organic pattern, a meaningful syntax of even the most rudimentary sort, as all language seems to do with a sort of driving necessity. That is because signs refer to actual situations, in which things have obvious relations to each other that require only to be noted; but symbols refer to ideas, which are not physically there for inspection, so their connections and features have to be represented. This gives all true language a natural tendency toward growth and development, which seems almost like a life of its own. Languages are not invented; they grow with our need for expression.

In contrast, animal "speech" never has a structure. It is merely an emotional response. Apes may greet their ration of yams with a shout of "Nga!" But they do not say "Nga" between meals. If they could *talk about* their yams instead of just saluting them, they would be the most primitive men instead of the most anthropoid of beasts. They would have ideas, and tell each other things true or false, rational or irrational; they would make plans and invent laws and sing their own praises, as men do.

❦ ❦ ❦

*James Harvey Robinson*

# Four Kinds of Thinking[1]

W E DO not think enough about thinking, and much of our confusion is the result of current illusions in regard to it. Let us forget for the moment any impressions we may have derived from the philosophers, and see what seems to happen in ourselves. The first thing that we notice is that our thought moves with such incredible rapidity that it is almost impossible to arrest any specimen of it long enough to have a look at it. When we are offered a penny for our thoughts we always find that we have recently had so many things in mind that we can easily make a selection which will not compromise us too nakedly. On inspection we shall find that even if we are not downright ashamed of a great part of our spontaneous thinking it is far too intimate, personal, ignoble or trivial to permit us to reveal more than a small part of it. I believe this must be true of everyone. We do not, of course, know what goes on in other people's heads. They tell us very little and we tell them very little. The spigot of speech, rarely fully opened, could never emit more than driblets of the ever renewed hogshead of thought—*noch grösser wie's Heidelberger Fass*. We find it hard to believe that other people's thoughts are as silly as our own, but they probably are.

[1] From *The Mind in the Making*, by James Harvey Robinson. Copyright, 1921, by Harper & Brothers. Copyright, 1949, by Bankers Trust Company. Reprinted by permission of the publishers.

We all appear to ourselves to be thinking all the time during our waking hours, and most of us are aware that we go on thinking while we are asleep, even more foolishly than when awake. When uninterrupted by some practical issue we are engaged in what is now known as a *reverie*. This is our spontaneous and favorite kind of thinking. We allow our ideas to take their own course and this course is determined by our hopes and fears, our spontaneous desires, their fulfillment or frustration; by our likes and dislikes, our loves and hates and resentments. There is nothing else anything like so interesting to ourselves as ourselves. All thought that is not more or less laboriously controlled and directed will inevitably circle about the beloved Ego. It is amusing and pathetic to observe this tendency in ourselves and in others. We learn politely and generously to overlook this truth, but if we dare to think of it, it blazes forth like the noontide sun.

The reverie or "free association of ideas" has of late become the subject of scientific research. While investigators are not yet agreed on the results, or at least on the proper interpretation to be given to them, there can be no doubt that our reveries form the chief index to our fundamental character. They are a reflection of our nature as modified by often hidden and forgotten experiences. We need not go into the matter further here, for it is only necessary to observe that the reverie is at all times a potent and in many cases an omnipotent rival to every other kind of thinking. It doubtless influences all our speculations in its persistent tendency to self-magnification and self-justification, which are its chief preoccupations, but it is the last thing to make directly or indirectly for honest increase of knowledge.[2] Philosophers usually talk as if such thinking did not exist or were in some way negligible. This is what makes their speculations so unreal and often worthless.

The reverie, as any of us can see for himself, is frequently broken and interrupted by the necessity of a second kind of thinking. We have to make practical decisions. Shall we write a letter or no? Shall we take the subway or a bus? Shall we have dinner at seven or half-past? Shall we buy U. S. Rubber or a Liberty Bond? Decisions are easily distinguishable from the free flow of the reverie. Sometimes they demand a good deal of careful pondering and the recollection of pertinent facts; often, however, they are made impulsively. They are a more difficult and laborious thing than the reverie, and we resent

---

[2] The poet-clergyman, John Donne, who lived in the time of James I, has given a beautifully honest picture of the doings of a saint's mind: "I throw myself down in my chamber and call in and invite God and His angels thither, and when they are there I neglect God and His Angels for the noise of a fly, for the rattling of a coach, for the whining of a door. I talk on in the same posture of praying, eyes lifted up, knees bowed down, as though I prayed to God, and if God or His angels should ask me when I thought last of God in that prayer I cannot tell. Sometimes I find that I had forgot what I was about, but when I began to forget it I cannot tell. A memory of yesterday's pleasures, a fear of tomorrow's dangers, a straw under my knee, a noise in mine ear, a light in mine eye, an anything, a nothing, a fancy, a chimera in my brain troubles me in my prayer."—Quoted by Robert Lynd, *The Art of Letters*, pp. 46-47.

having to "make up our mind" when we are tired, or absorbed in a congenial reverie. Weighing a decision, it should be noted, does not necessarily add anything to our knowledge, although we may, of course, seek further information before making it.

A third kind of thinking is stimulated when any one questions our belief and opinions. We sometimes find ourselves changing our minds without any resistance or heavy emotion, but if we are told that we are wrong we resent the imputation and harden our hearts. We are incredibly heedless in the formation of our beliefs, but find ourselves filled with an illicit passion for them when anyone proposes to rob us of their companionship. It is obviously not the ideas themselves that are dear to us, but our self-esteem, which is threatened. We are by nature stubbornly pledged to defend our own from attack, whether it be our person, our family, our property, or our opinion. A United States Senator once remarked to a friend of mine that God Almighty could not make him change his mind on our Latin-America policy. We may surrender, but rarely confess ourselves vanquished. In the intellectual world at least peace is without victory.

Few of us take the pains to study the origin of our cherished convictions; indeed, we have a natural repugnance to so doing. We like to continue to believe what we have been accustomed to accept as true, and the resentment aroused when doubt is cast upon any of our assumptions leads us to seek every manner of excuse for clinging to them. *The result is that most of our so-called reasoning consists in finding arguments for going on believing as we already do.*

I remember years ago attending a public dinner to which the Governor of the state was bidden. The chairman explained that His Excellency could not be present for certain "good" reasons; what the "real" reasons were the presiding officer said he would leave us to conjecture. This distinction between "good" and "real" reasons is one of the most clarifying and essential in the whole realm of thought. We can readily give what seem to us "good" reasons for being a Catholic or a Mason, a Republican or a Democrat, an adherent or opponent of the League of Nations. But the "real" reasons are usually on a quite different plane. Of course the importance of this distinction is popularly, if somewhat obscurely, recognized. The Baptist missionary is ready enough to see that the Buddhist is not such because his doctrines would bear careful inspection, but because he happened to be born in a Buddhist family in Tokio. But it would be treason to his faith to acknowledge that his own partiality for certain doctrines is due to the fact that his mother was a member of the First Baptist church of Oak Ridge. A savage can give all sorts of reasons for his belief that it is dangerous to step on a man's shadow, and a newspaper editor can advance plenty of arguments against the Bolsheviki. But neither of them may realize why he happens to be defending his particular opinion.

The "real" reasons for our beliefs are concealed from ourselves as well as from others. As we grow up we simply adopt the ideas presented to us in regard to such matters as religion, family relations, property, business, our country, and the state. We unconsciously absorb them from our environment.

They are persistently whispered in our ear by the group in which we happen to live. Moreover, as Mr. Trotter has pointed out, these judgments, being the product of suggestion and not of reasoning, have the quality of perfect obviousness, so that to question them

> . . . is to the believer to carry skepticism to an insane degree, and will be met by contempt, disapproval, or condemnation, according to the nature of the belief in question. When, therefore, we find ourselves entertaining an opinion about the basis of which there is a quality of feeling which tells us that to inquire into it would be absurd, obviously unnecessary, unprofitable, undesirable, bad form, or wicked, we may know that that opinion is a nonrational one, and probably, therefore, founded upon inadequate evidence.[3]

Opinions, on the other hand, which are the result of experience or of honest reasoning do not have this quality of "primary certitude." I remember when as a youth I heard a group of business men discussing the question of the immortality of the soul, I was outraged by the sentiment of doubt expressed by one of the party. As I look back now I see that I had at the time no interest in the matter, and certainly no least argument to urge in favor of the belief in which I had been reared. But neither my personal indifference to the issue, nor the fact that I had previously given it no attention, served to prevent an angry resentment when I heard *my* ideas questioned.

This spontaneous and loyal support of our preconceptions—this process of finding "good" reasons to justify our routine beliefs—is known to modern psychologists as "rationalizing"—clearly only a new name for a very ancient thing. Our "good" reasons ordinarily have no value in promoting honest enlightenment, because, no matter how solemnly they may be marshaled, they are at bottom the result of personal preference or prejudice, and not of an honest desire to seek or accept new knowledge.

In our reveries we are frequently engaged in self-justification, for we cannot bear to think ourselves wrong, and yet have constant illustrations of our weaknesses and mistakes. So we spend much time finding fault with circumstances and the conduct of others, and shifting on to them with great ingenuity the onus of our own failures and disappointments. *Rationalizing is the self-exculpation which occurs when we feel ourselves, or our group, accused of misapprehension or error.*

The little word *my* is the most important one in all human affairs, and properly to reckon with it is the beginning of wisdom. It has the same force whether it is *my* dinner, *my* dog, and *my* house, or *my* faith, *my* country, and *my* God. We not only resent the imputation that our watch is wrong, or our car shabby, but that our conception of the canals of Mars, of the pronunciation of "Epictetus," of the medicinal value of salicine, or the date of Sargon I, is subject to revision.

Philosophers, scholars, and men of science exhibit a common sensitiveness in

[3] *Instincts of the Herd*, p. 44.

all decisions in which their *amour propre* is involved. Thousands of argumenta-tive works have been written to vent a grudge. However stately their reasoning, it may be nothing but rationalizing, stimulated by the most commonplace of all motives. A history of philosophy and theology could be written in terms of grouches, wounded pride, and aversions, and it would be far more instructive than the usual treatments of these themes. Sometimes, under Providence, the lowly impulse of resentment leads to great achievements. Milton wrote his treatise on divorce as a result of his troubles with his seventeen-year-old wife, and when he was accused of being the leading spirit in a new sect, the Di-vorcers, he wrote his noble *Areopagitica* to prove his right to say what he thought fit, and incidentally to establish the advantage of a free press in the promotion of Truth.

All mankind, high and low, thinks in all the ways which have been de-scribed. The reverie goes on all the time not only in the mind of the mill hand and the Broadway flapper, but equally in weighty judges and godly bishops. It has gone on in all the philosophers, scientists, poets, and theologians that have ever lived. Aristotle's most abstruse speculations were doubtless tempered by highly irrelevant reflections. He is reported to have had very thin legs and small eyes, for which he doubtless had to find excuses, and he was wont to in-dulge in very conspicuous dress and rings and was accustomed to arrange his hair carefully.[4] Diogenes the Cynic exhibited the impudence of a touchy soul. His tub was his distinction. Tennyson in beginning his "Maud" could not for-get his chagrin over losing his patrimony years before as the result of an un-happy investment in the Patent Decorative Carving Company. These facts are not recalled here as a gratuitous disparagement of the truly great, but to insure a full realization of the tremendous competition which all really exacting thought has to face, even in the minds of the most highly endowed mortals.

And now the astonishing and perturbing suspicion emerges that perhaps al-most all that had passed for social science, political economy, politics, and ethics in the past may be brushed aside by future generations as mainly rationalizing. John Dewey has already reached this conclusion in regard to philosophy.[5] Veblen[6] and other writers have revealed the various unperceived presupposi-tions of the traditional political economy, and now comes an Italian sociologist, Vilfredo Pareto, who, in his huge treatise on general sociology, devotes hun-dreds of pages to substantiating a similar thesis affecting all the social sci-ences.[7] This conclusion may be ranked by students of a hundred years hence as one of the several great discoveries of our age. It is by no means fully worked out, and it is so opposed to nature that it will be very slowly accepted by the

[4] Diogenes Laertius, book v.          [5] *Reconstruction in Philosophy.*

[6] *The Place of Science in Modern Civilization.*

[7] *Traité de Sociologie Générale, passim.* The author's term *"derivations"* seems to be his precise way of expressing what we have called the "good" reasons, and his *"residus"* correspond to the "real" reasons. He well says, *"L'homme éprouve le besoin de raisonner, et en outre d'étendre un voile sur ses instincts et sur ses sentiments"*—hence, rationaliza-tion. (P. 788.) His aim is to reduce sociology to the "real" reasons. (P. 791.)

great mass of those who consider themselves thoughtful. As a historical student I am personally fully reconciled to this newer view. Indeed, it seems to me inevitable that just as the various sciences of nature were, before the opening of the seventeenth century, largely masses of rationalizations to suit the religious sentiments of the period, so the social sciences have continued even to our own day to be rationalizations of uncritically accepted beliefs and customs.

*It will become apparent as we proceed that the fact that an idea is ancient and that it has been widely received is no argument in its favor, but should immediately suggest the necessity of carefully testing it as a probable instance of rationalization.*

This brings us to another kind of thought which can fairly easily be distinguished from the three kinds described above. It has not the usual qualities of the reverie, for it does not hover about our personal complacencies and humiliations. It is not made up of the homely decisions forced upon us by everyday needs, when we review our little stock of existing information, consult our conventional preferences and obligations, and make a choice of action. It is not the defense of our own cherished beliefs and prejudices just because they are our own—mere plausible excuses for remaining of the same mind. On the contrary, it is that peculiar species of thought which leads us to *change* our mind.

It is this kind of thought that has raised man from his pristine, subsavage ignorance and squalor to the degree of knowledge and comfort which he now possesses. On his capacity to continue and greatly extend this kind of thinking depends his chance of groping his way out of the plight in which the most civilized peoples of the world now find themselves. In the past this type of thinking has been called Reason. But so many misapprehensions have grown up around the word that some of us have become suspicious of it. I suggest, therefore, that we substitute a recent name and speak of "creative thought" rather than of Reason. *For this kind of meditation begets knowledge, and knowledge is really creative inasmuch as it makes things look different from what they seemed before and may indeed work for their reconstruction.*

In certain moods some of us realize that we are observing things or making reflections with a seeming disregard of our personal preoccupations. We are not preening or defending ourselves; we are not faced by the necessity of any practical decision, nor are we apologizing for believing this or that. We are just wondering and looking and mayhap seeing what we never perceived before.

Curiosity is as clear and definite as any of our urges. We wonder what is in a sealed telegram or in a letter in which some one else is absorbed, or what is being said in the telephone booth or in low conversation. This inquisitiveness is vastly stimulated by jealousy, suspicion, or any hint that we ourselves are directly or indirectly involved. But there appears to be a fair amount of personal interest in other people's affairs even when they do not concern us except as a mystery to be unraveled or a tale to be told. The reports of a divorce suit will have "news value" for many weeks. They constitute a story, like a novel or play or moving picture. This is not an example of pure curiosity, however, since we readily identify ourselves with others, and their joys and despair then become our own.

We also take note of, or "observe," as Sherlock Holmes says, things which have nothing to do with our personal interests and make no personal appeal either direct or by way of sympathy. This is what Veblen so well calls "idle curiosity." And it is usually idle enough. Some of us when we face the line of people opposite us in a subway train impulsively consider them in detail and engage in rapid inferences and form theories in regard to them. On entering a room there are those who will perceive at a glance the degree of preciousness of the rugs, the character of the pictures, and the personality revealed by the books. But there are many, it would seem, who are so absorbed in their personal reverie or in some definite purpose that they have no bright-eyed energy for idle curiosity. The tendency to miscellaneous observation we come by honestly enough, for we note it in many of our animal relatives.

Veblen, however, uses the term "idle curiosity" somewhat ironically, as is his wont. It is idle only to those who fail to realize that it may be a very rare and indispensable thing from which almost all distinguished human achievement proceeds, since it may lead to systematic examination and seeking for things hitherto undiscovered. For research is but diligent search which enjoys the high flavor of primitive hunting. Occasionally and fitfully idle curiosity thus leads to creative thought, which alters and broadens our own views and aspirations and may in turn, under highly favorable circumstances, affect the views and lives of others, even for generations to follow. An example or two will make this unique human process clear.

Galileo was a thoughtful youth and doubtless carried on a rich and varied reverie. He had artistic ability and might have turned out to be a musician or painter. When he had dwelt among the monks at Valambrosa he had been tempted to lead the life of a religious. As a boy he busied himself with toy machines and he inherited a fondness for mathematics. All these facts are of record. We may safely assume also that, along with many other subjects of contemplation, the Pisan maidens found a vivid place in his thoughts.

One day when seventeen years old he wandered into the cathedral of his native town. In the midst of his reverie he looked up at the lamps hanging by long chains from the high ceiling of the church. Then something very difficult to explain occurred. He found himself no longer thinking of the building, worshipers, or the services; of his artistic or religious interests; of his reluctance to become a physician as his father wished. He forgot the question of a career and even the *graziosissime donne*. As he watched the swinging lamps he was suddenly wondering if mayhap their oscillations, whether long or short, did not occupy the same time. Then he tested his hypothesis by counting his pulse, for that was the only timepiece he had with him.

This observation, however remarkable in itself, was not enough to produce a really creative thought. Others may have noticed the same thing and yet nothing came of it. Most of our observations have no assignable results. Galileo may have seen that the warts on a peasant's face formed a perfect isosceles triangle, or he may have noticed with boyish glee that just as the officiating priest was uttering the solemn words, *ecce agnus Dei*, a fly lit on the end of his nose. To be really creative, ideas have to be worked up and then "put over," so that they become a part of man's social heritage. The highly accurate pendulum clock was one of the later results of Galileo's discovery. He himself was led to reconsider and successfully to refute the old notions of falling bodies. It remained for Newton to prove that the moon was falling, and presumably all the heavenly bodies. This quite upset all the consecrated views of the heavens as managed by angelic engineers. The universality of the laws of gravitation stimulated the attempt to seek other and equally important natural laws and cast grave doubts on the miracles in which mankind had hitherto believed. In short, those who dared to include in their thought the discoveries of Galileo and his successors found themselves in a new earth surrounded by new heavens.

On the 28th of October, 1831, two hundred and fifty years after Galileo had noticed the isochronous vibrations of the lamps, creative thought and its currency had so far increased that Faraday was wondering what would happen if he mounted a disk of copper between the poles of a horseshoe magnet. As the disk revolved, an electric current was produced. This would doubtless have seemed the idlest kind of experiment to the stanch business men of the time who, it happened, were just then denouncing the child-labor bills in their anxiety to avail themselves to the full of the results of earlier idle curiosity. But should the dynamos and motors which have come into being as the outcome of Faraday's experiment be stopped this evening, the business man of to-day, agitated over labor troubles, might, as he trudged home past lines of "dead" cars, through dark streets to an unlighted house, engage in a little creative thought of his own and perceive that he and his laborers would have no modern factories and mines to quarrel about if it had not been for the strange, practical effects of the idle curiosity of scientists, inventors, and engineers.

The examples of creative intelligence given above belong to the realm of modern scientific achievement, which furnishes the most striking instances of the effects of scrupulous, objective thinking. But there are, of course, other great realms in which the recording and embodiment of acute observation and insight have wrought themselves into the higher life of man. The great poets and dramatists and our modern story-tellers have found themselves engaged in productive reveries, noting and artistically presenting their discoveries for the delight and instruction of those who have the ability to appreciate them.

The process by which a fresh and original poem or drama comes into being is doubtless analogous to that which originates and elaborates so-called scientific discoveries; but there is clearly a temperamental difference. The genesis and advance of painting, sculpture, and music offer still other problems. We really as yet know shockingly little about these matters, and indeed very few people have the least curiosity about them.[8] Nevertheless, creative intelligence in its various

---

[8] Recently a re-examination of creative thought has begun as a result of new knowledge which discredits many of the notions formerly held about "reason." See, for example, *Creative Intelligence*, by a group of American philosophic thinkers; John Dewey,

forms and activities is what makes man. Were it not for its slow, painful, and constantly discouraged operations through the ages man would be no more than a species of primate living on seeds, fruit, roots, and uncooked flesh, and wandering naked through the woods and over the plains like a chimpanzee.

The origin and progress and future promotion of civilization are ill understood and misconceived. These should be made the chief theme of education, but much hard work is necessary before we can reconstruct our ideas of man and his capacities and free ourselves from innumerable persistent misapprehensions. There have been obstructionists in all times, not merely the lethargic masses, but the moralists, the rationalizing theologians, and most of the philosophers, all busily if unconsciously engaged in ratifying existing ignorance and mistakes and discouraging creative thought. Naturally, those who reassure us seem worthy of honor and respect. Equally naturally, those who puzzle us with disturbing criticisms and invite us to change our ways are objects of suspicion and readily discredited. Our personal discontent does not ordinarily extend to any critical questioning of the general situation in which we find ourselves. In every age the prevailing conditions of civilization have appeared quite natural and inevitable to those who grew up in them. The cow asks no questions as to how it happens to have a dry stall and a supply of hay. The kitten laps its warm milk from a china saucer, without knowing anything about porcelain; the dog nestles in the corner of a divan with no sense of obligation to the inventors of upholstery and the manufacturers of down pillows. So we humans accept our breakfasts, our trains and telephones and orchestras and movies, our national Constitution, our moral code and standards of manners, with the simplicity and innocence of a pet rabbit. We have absolutely inexhaustible capacities for appropriating what others do for us with no thought of a "thank you." We do not feel called upon to make any least contribution to the merry game ourselves. Indeed, we are usually quite unaware that a game is being played at all.

We have now examined the various classes of thinking which we can readily observe in ourselves and which we have plenty of reasons to believe go on, and always have been going on, in our fellow-men. We can sometimes get quite pure and sparkling examples of all four kinds, but commonly they are so confused and intermingled in our reverie as not to be readily distinguishable. The reverie is a reflection of our longings, exultations, and complacencies, our fears, suspicions, and disappointments. We are chiefly engaged in struggling to maintain our self-respect and in asserting that supremacy which we all crave and which seems to us our natural prerogative. It is not strange, but rather quite inevitable, that our beliefs about what is true and false, good and bad, right and wrong, should be mixed up with the reverie and be influenced by the same considerations which determine its character and course. We resent criticisms of

*Essays in Experimental Logic* (both pretty hard books); and Veblen, *The Place of Science in Modern Civilization*. Easier than these and very stimulating are Dewey, *Reconstruction in Philosophy*, and Woodworth, *Dynamic Psychology*.

our views exactly as we do of anything else connected with ourselves. Our notions of life and its ideals seem to us to be *our own* and as such necessarily true and right, to be defended at all costs.

*We very rarely consider, however, the process by which we gained our convictions.* If we did so, we could hardly fail to see that there was usually little ground for our confidence in them. Here and there, in this department of knowledge or that, some one of us might make a fair claim to have taken some trouble to get correct ideas of, let us say, the situation in Russia, the sources of our food supply, the origin of the Constitution, the revision of the tariff, the policy of the Holy Roman Apostolic Church, modern business organization, trade unions, birth control, socialism, the League of Nations, the excess-profits tax, preparedness, advertising in its social bearings; but only a very exceptional person would be entitled to opinions on all of even these few matters. And yet most of us have opinions on all these, and on many other questions of equal importance, of which we may know even less. We feel compelled, as self-respecting persons, to take sides when they come up for discussion. We even surprise ourselves by our omniscience. Without taking thought we see in a flash that it is most righteous and expedient to discourage birth control by legislative enactment, or that one who decries intervention in Mexico is clearly wrong, or that big advertising is essential to big business and that big business is the pride of the land. As godlike beings, why should we not rejoice in our omniscience?

It is clear, in any case, that our convictions on important matters are not the result of knowledge or critical thought, nor, it may be added, are they often dictated by supposed self-interest. Most of them are *pure prejudices* in the proper sense of that word. We do not form them ourselves. They are the whispering of "the voice of the herd." We have in the last analysis no responsibility for them and need assume none. They are not really our own ideas, but those of others no more well informed or inspired than ourselves, who have got them in the same careless and humiliating manner as we. It should be our pride to revise our ideas and not to adhere to what passes for respectable opinion, for such opinion can frequently be shown to be not respectable at all. We should, in view of the considerations that have been mentioned, resent our supine credulity. As an English writer has remarked:

> If we feared the entertaining of an unverifiable opinion with the warmth with which we fear using the wrong implement at the dinner table, if the thought of holding a prejudice disgusted us as does a foul disease, then the dangers of man's suggestibility would be turned into advantages.[9]

The purpose of this essay is to set forth briefly the way in which the notions of the herd have been accumulated. This seems to me the best, easiest, and least invidious educational device for cultivating a proper distrust for the older notions on which we still continue to rely.

[9] Trotter, *op. cit.*, p. 45. The first part of this little volume is excellent.

The "real" reasons, which explain how it is we happen to hold a particular belief, are chiefly historical. Our most important opinions—those, for example, having to do with traditional, religious, and moral convictions, property rights, patriotism, national honor, the state, and indeed all the assumed foundations of society—are, as I have already suggested, rarely the result of reasoned consideration, but of unthinking absorption from the social environment in which we live. Consequently, they have about them a quality of "elemental certitude," and we especially resent doubt or criticism cast upon them. So long, however, as we revere the whisperings of the herd, we are obviously unable to examine them dispassionately and to consider to what extent they are suited to the novel conditions and social exigencies in which we find ourselves to-day.

The "real" reasons for our beliefs, by making clear their origins and history, can do much to dissipate this emotional blockade and rid us of our prejudices and preconceptions. Once this is done and we come critically to examine our traditional beliefs, we may well find some of them sustained by experience and honest reasoning, while others must be revised to meet new conditions and our more extended knowledge. But only after we have undertaken such a critical examination in the light of experience and modern knowledge, freed from any feeling of "primary certitude," can we claim that the "good" are also the "real" reasons for our opinions.

I do not flatter myself that this general show-up of man's thought through the ages will cure myself or others of carelessness in adopting ideas, or of unseemly heat in defending them just because we have adopted them. But if the considerations which I propose to recall are really incorporated into our thinking and are permitted to establish our general outlook on human affairs, they will do much to relieve the imaginary obligation we feel in regard to traditional sentiments and ideals. Few of us are capable of engaging in creative thought, but some of us can at least come to distinguish it from other and inferior kinds of thought and accord to it the esteem that it merits as the greatest treasure of the past and the only hope of the future.

❧ ❧ ❧

*Graham Wallas*

# The Four Stages of Thought[1]

WHAT I wish to investigate is at what stages in the thought-process the thinker should bring the conscious and voluntary effort of his art to bear. Here we at once meet the difficulty that unless we can recognize a psychological event, and distinguish it from other events, we cannot bring conscious effort

[1] From *The Art of Thought* by Graham Wallas, copyright, 1936, by Harcourt, Brace and Company, Inc.; renewed, 1953, by May Graham Wallas. Reprinted by permission of the publishers.

to bear directly upon it; and that our mental life is a stream of intermingled psychological events, all of which affect each other, any of which, at any given moment, may be beginning or continuing or ending, and which, therefore, are extremely hard to distinguish from each other.

We can, to some degree, avoid this difficulty if we take a single achievement of thought—the making of a new generalization or invention, or the poetical expression of a new idea—and ask how it was brought about. We can then roughly dissect out a continuous process, with a beginning and a middle and an end of its own. Helmholtz, for instance, the great German physicist, speaking in 1891 at a banquet on his seventieth birthday, described the way in which his most important new thoughts had come to him. He said that after previous investigation of the problem "in all directions . . . happy ideas come unexpectedly without effort, like an inspiration. So far as I am concerned, they have never come to me when my mind was fatigued, or when I was at my working table. . . . They came particularly readily during the slow ascent of wooded hills on a sunny day." [2] Helmholtz here gives us three stages in the formation of a new thought. The first in time I shall call Preparation, the stage during which the problem was "investigated . . . in all directions"; the second is the stage during which he was not consciously thinking about the problem, which I shall call Incubation; the third, consisting of the appearance of the "happy idea" together with the psychological events which immediately preceded and accompanied that appearance, I shall call Illumination.

And I shall add a fourth stage, of Verification, which Helmholtz does not here mention. Henri Poincaré, for instance, in the book *Science and Method*, describes in vivid detail the successive stages of two of his great mathematical discoveries. Both of them came to him after a period of Incubation (due in one case to his military service as a reservist, and in the other case to a journey), during which no conscious mathematical thinking was done, but, as Poincaré believed, much unconscious mental exploration took place. In both cases Incubation was preceded by a Preparation stage of hard, conscious, systematic, and fruitless analysis of the problem. In both cases the final idea came to him "with the same characteristics of conciseness, suddenness, and immediate certainty." Each was followed by a period of Verification, in which both the validity of the idea was tested, and the idea itself was reduced to exact form. "It never happens," says Poincaré, in his description of the Verification stage, "that unconscious work supplies *ready-made* the result of a lengthy calculation in which we have only to apply fixed rules. . . . All that we can hope from these inspirations, which are the fruit of unconscious work, is to obtain points

2 See Rignano, *Psychology of Reasoning* (1923), pp. 267-268. See also Plato, *Symposium* (210): "He who has been instructed thus far in the things of love, and has learned to see beautiful things in due order and succession, when he comes to the end, will suddenly perceive a beauty wonderful in its nature"; and Rémy de Goncourt: "My conceptions rise into the field of consciousness like a flash of lightning or the flight of a bird" (quoted by H. A. Bruce, *Psychology and Parenthood*, 1919, p. 89).

of departure for such calculations. As for the calculations themselves, they must be made in the second period of conscious work which follows the inspiration, and in which the results of the inspiration are verified and the consequences deduced. The rules of these calculations are strict and complicated; they demand discipline, attention, will, and consequently, consciousness." In the daily stream of thought these four different stages constantly overlap each other as we explore different problems. An economist reading a Blue Book, a physiologist watching an experiment, or a business man going through his morning's letters, may at the same time be "incubating" on a problem which he proposed to himself a few days ago, be accumulating knowledge in "preparation" for a second problem, and be "verifying" his conclusions on a third problem. Even in exploring the same problem, the mind may be unconsciously incubating on one aspect of it, while it is consciously employed in preparing for or verifying another aspect. And it must always be remembered that much very important thinking, done for instance by a poet exploring his own memories, or by a man trying to see clearly his emotional relation to his country or his party, resembles musical composition in that the stages leading to success are not very easily fitted into a "problem and solution" scheme. Yet, even when success in thought means the creation of something felt to be beautiful and true rather than the solution of a prescribed problem, the four stages of Preparation, Incubation, Illumination, and the Verification of the final result can generally be distinguished from each other.

If we accept this analysis, we are in a position to ask to what degree, and by what means, we can bring conscious effort, and the habits which arise from conscious effort, to bear upon each of the four stages. I shall not deal at any length with the stage of Preparation. It includes the whole process of intellectual education. Men have known for thousands of years that conscious effort and its resulting habits can be used to improve the thought-processes of young persons, and have formulated for that purpose an elaborate art of education. The "educated" man can, in consequence, "put his mind on" to a chosen subject, and "turn his mind off" in a way which is impossible to an uneducated man. The educated man has also acquired, by the effort of observation and memorizing, a body of remembered facts and words which gives him a wider range in the final moment of association, as well as a number of those habitual tracks of association which constitute "thought-systems" like "French policy" or "scholastic philosophy" or "biological evolution," and which present themselves as units in the process of thought.

The educated man has, again, learned, and can, in the Preparation stage, voluntarily or habitually follow out, rules as to the order in which he shall direct his attention to the successive elements in a problem. Hobbes referred to this fact when in the *Leviathan* he described "regulated thought," and contrasted it with that "wild ranging of the mind" which occurs when the thought process is undirected. Regulated thought is, he says, a "seeking." "Sometimes," for instance, "a man seeks what he has lost. . . . Sometimes a man knows a place determinate, within the compass whereof he is to seek; and then his thoughts run over all the parts thereof, in the same manner as one would sweep a room to find a jewel; or as a spaniel ranges the field, till he find a scent; or as a man should run over the alphabet, to start a rhyme." A spaniel with the brain of an educated human being could not, by a direct effort of will, scent a partridge in a distant part of the field. But he could so "quarter" the field by a preliminary voluntary arrangement that the less-voluntary process of smelling would be given every chance of successfully taking place.

Included in these rules for the preliminary "regulation" of our thought, are the whole traditional art of logic, the mathematical forms which are the logic of the modern experimental sciences, and the methods of systematic and continuous examination of present or recorded phenomena which are the basis of astronomy, sociology and the other "observational" sciences. Closely connected with this voluntary use of logical methods is the voluntary choice of a "problem-attitude" (*Aufgabe*). Our mind is not likely to give us a clear answer to any particular problem unless we set it a clear question, and we are more likely to notice the significance of any new piece of evidence, or new association of ideas, if we have formed a definite conception of a case to be proved or disproved. A very successful thinker in natural science told me that he owed much of his success to his practice of following up, when he felt his mind confused, the implications of two propositions, both of which he had hitherto accepted as true, until he had discovered that one of them *must* be untrue. Huxley on that point once quoted Bacon, "Truth comes out of error much more rapidly than it comes out of confusion," and went on, "If you go buzzing about between right and wrong, vibrating and fluctuating, you come out nowhere; but if you are absolutely and thoroughly and persistently wrong you must some of these days have the extreme good fortune of knocking your head against a fact, and that sets you all right again." This is, of course, a production, by conscious effort, of that "dialogue form" of alternate suggestion and criticism which Varendonck describes as occurring in the process of uncontrolled thought. It is, indeed, sometimes possible to observe such an automatic "dialogue" at a point where a single effort of will would turn it into a process of preparatory logical statement. On July 18, 1917, I passed on an omnibus the fashionable church of St. Margaret's, Westminster. Miss Ashley, the richest heiress of the season, was being gorgeously married, and the omnibus conductor said to a friend, "Shocking waste of money! But, there, it does create a lot of labour, I admit that." Perhaps I neglected my duty as a citizen in that I did not say to him, "Now make one effort to realize that inconsistency, and you will have prepared yourself to become an economist."

And though I have assumed, for the sake of clearness, that the thinker is preparing himself for the solution of a single problem, he will often (particularly if he is working on the very complex material of the social sciences) have several kindred problems in his mind, on all of which the voluntary work of preparation has been, or is being done, and for any of which, at the Illumination stage, a solution may present itself.

The fourth stage, of Verification, closely resembles the first stage, of Preparation. It is normally, as Poincaré points out, fully conscious, and men have worked out much the same series of mathematical and logical rules for controlling Verification by conscious effort as those which are used in the control of Preparation.

There remain the second and third stages, Incubation and Illumination. The Incubation stage covers two different things, of which the first is the negative fact that during Incubation we do not voluntarily or consciously think on a particular problem, and the second is the positive fact that a series of unconscious and involuntary (or foreconscious and forevoluntary) mental events may take place during that period. It is the first fact about Incubation which I shall now discuss, leaving the second fact—of subconscious thought during Incubation, and the relation of such thought to Illumination—to be more fully discussed in connection with the Illumination stage. Voluntary abstention from conscious thought on any particular problem may, itself, take two forms: the period of abstention may be spent either in conscious mental work on other problems, or in a relaxation from all conscious mental work. The first kind of Incubation economizes time, and is therefore often the better. We can often get more result in the same time by beginning several problems in succession, and voluntarily leaving them unfinished while we turn to others, than by finishing our work on each problem at one sitting. A well-known academic psychologist, for instance, who was also a preacher, told me that he found by experience that his Sunday sermon was much better if he posed the problem on Monday, than if he did so later in the week, although he might give the same number of hours of conscious work to it in each case. It seems to be a tradition among practising barristers to put off any consideration of each brief to the latest possible moment before they have to deal with it, and to forget the whole matter as rapidly as possible after dealing with it. This fact may help to explain a certain want to depth which has often been noticed in the typical lawyer-statesman, and which may be due to his conscious thought not being sufficiently extended and enriched by subconscious thought.

But, in the case of the more difficult forms of creative thought, the making, for instance, of a scientific discovery, or the writing of a poem or play or the formulation of an important political decision, it is desirable not only that there should be an interval free from conscious thought on the particular problem concerned, but also that that interval should be so spent that nothing should interfere with the free working of the unconscious or partially conscious processes of the mind. In those cases, the stage of Incubation should include a large amount of actual mental relaxation. It would, indeed, be interesting to examine, from that point of view, the biographies of a couple of hundred original thinkers and writers. A. R. Wallace, for instance, hit upon the theory of evolution by natural selection in his berth during an attack of malarial fever at sea; and Darwin was compelled by ill-health to spend the greater part of his waking hours in physical and mental relaxation. Sometimes a thinker has been able to get a sufficiency of relaxation owing to a disposition to idleness, against which he has vainly struggled. More often, perhaps, what he has thought to be idleness, is really that urgent craving for intense and uninterrupted day-dreaming which Anthony Trollope describes in his account of his boyhood.

One effect of such a comparative biographical study might be the formulation of a few rules as to the relation between original intellectual work and the virtue of industry. There are thousands of idle "geniuses" who require to learn that, without a degree of industry in Preparation and Verification, of which many of them have no conception, no great intellectual work can be done, and that the habit of procrastination may be even more disastrous to a professional thinker than it is to a man of business. And yet a thinker of good health and naturally fertile mind may have to be told that mere industry is for him, as it was for Trollope in his later years, the worst temptation of the devil. Cardinal Manning was a man of furious industry, and the suspension of his industry as an Anglican archdeacon during his illness in 1847 was, for good or evil, an important event in the history of English religion. Some of those who, like myself, live in the diocese of London, believe that we have reason to regret an insufficiency of intellectual leadership from our present bishop. The bishop himself indicated one of the causes of our discontent in a letter addressed, in September, 1922, to his clergy. "I come back to an autumn of what, from a human point of view, is unrelieved toil. October 1st to Christmas Day is filled every day, except for the one day off every week, from 10 A.M. to 6 P.M." Then comes a long list of administrative and pastoral engagements, including "three days interviewing 110 Harrow boys to be confirmed," "a critical Bill to see through the House of Lords," and "some sixty sermons and addresses already arranged in the diocese, besides the daily letters and interviews." "All this," he says, "might justify the comment of a kindly man of the world, 'Why, Bishop, you live the life of a dog! But this is precisely, though on a larger scale, the life of every one of you.' " It is clear that the bishop considers that he and his clergy ought to be admired for so spending their time; and that he conceives the life of a turn-spit dog to be the most likely to enable them to be successful in the exercise of their office. One sometimes, however, wonders what would be the result if our bishop were kept for ten weeks in bed and in silence, by an illness neither painful nor dangerous, nor inconsistent with full mental efficiency.

Mental relaxation during the Incubation stage may of course include, and sometimes requires, a certain amount of physical exercise. I have already quoted Helmholtz's reference to "the ascent of wooded hills on a sunny day." A. Carrel, the great New York physiologist, is said to receive all his really important thoughts while quietly walking during the summer vacation in his native Brittany. Jastrow says that "thinkers have at all times resorted to the restful inspiration of a walk in the woods or a stroll over hill and dale." When I once discussed this fact with an athletic Cambridge friend, he expressed his gratitude for any evidence which would prove that it was the duty of all intellectual workers to spend their vacations in Alpine climbing. Alpine climbing has undoubtedly much to give both to health and to imagination, but it would be an interesting quantitative problem whether Goethe, while riding a mule over the Gemmi Pass, and Wordsworth, while walking over the Simplon, were in a more or in a less fruitful condition of Incubation than are a modern Alpine Club party ascending, with hands and feet and rope and ice-axe, the Finster-Aarhorn. In this, however, as in many other respects, it may be that the human organism gains more from the alternation of various forms of activity than from a consistent devotion to one form. In England, the administrative methods of the older universities during term-time may, I sometimes fear, by destroying the possibility of Incubation, go far to balance any intellectual advantages over the newer universities which they may derive from their much longer vacations. At Oxford and Cambridge, men on whose powers of invention and stimulus the intellectual future of the country may largely depend, are made personally responsible for innumerable worrying details of filling up forms and sending in applications. Their subconscious minds are set on the duty of striking like a clock at the instant when Mr. Jones's fee must be paid to the Registrar. In the newer English universities, the same duties are rapidly and efficiently performed by a corps of young ladies, with card-catalogues, typewriters, and diaries.

But perhaps the most dangerous substitute for bodily and mental relaxation during the stage of Incubation is neither violent exercise nor routine administration, but the habit of industrious passive reading. Schopenhauer wrote that "to put away one's own original thoughts in order to take up a book is the sin against the Holy Ghost." During the century from 1760 to 1860, many of the best brains in England were prevented from acting with full efficiency by the way in which the Greek and Latin classics were then read. It is true that Shelley's imagination was stung into activity by Plato and Æschylus, and that Keats won a new vision of life from Chapman's translation of Homer; but even the ablest of those who then accepted the educational ideals of Harrow and Eton and Oxford and Cambridge did not approach the classical writers with Shelley's or Keats's hunger in their souls. They plodded through Horace and Sophocles and Virgil and Demosthenes with a mild conscious aesthetic feeling, and with a stronger and less conscious feeling of social, intellectual and moral superiority; any one who was in the habit of reading the classics with his feet on the fender must certainly, they felt, be not only a gentleman and a scholar but also a good man.

Carlyle once told Anthony Trollope that a man, when travelling, "should not read, but sit still and label his thoughts." On the other hand, Macaulay, before he went out to India in 1834 to be Legislative Member of the Supreme Council, wrote to his sister: "The provision which I design for the voyage is Richardson, Voltaire's works, Gibbon, Sismondi's *History of the French*, Davila, *Orlando* in Italian, *Don Quixote* in Spanish, Homer in Greek, Horace in Latin. I must also have some books of jurisprudence, and some to initiate me in Persian and Hindustane"; and, at the end of the four months' voyage, he wrote: "Except at meals, I hardly exchanged a word with any human being. . . . During the whole voyage I read with keen and increasing enjoyment. I devoured Greek, Latin, Spanish, Italian, French, and English; folios, quartos, octavos, and duo-decimos." If he had followed Carlyle's advice, he would have had a better chance of thinking out a juristic and educational policy for India which would not have been a mere copy of an English model. One understands why Gladstone's magnificent enthusiasm and driving force was never guided by sufficient elasticity or originality of mind, when one reads, in Mrs. Gladstone's *Life* how she and her sister married the two most splendid Etonians of their time—Gladstone and his friend Lord Lyttelton—and spent a honeymoon of four in Scotland. "Any little waiting time as at the railway stations," says her daughter, Mrs. Drew, "was now spent in reading—both husbands carrying the inevitable little classics in their pockets." During the days when new knowledge, new forms of thought, new methods in industry and war and politics, and the rise of new nations were transforming Western civilization, "Lord Lyttelton was to be seen at cricket-matches in the playing field at Eton, lying on his front, reading between the overs, but never missing a ball."

So far I have inquired how far we can voluntarily improve our methods of thought at those stages—Preparation, Incubation (in its negative sense of abstention from voluntary thought on a particular problem), and Verification—over which our conscious will has comparatively full control. I shall now discuss the much more difficult question of the degree to which our will can influence the less controllable stage which I have called Illumination. Helmholtz and Poincaré, in the passages which I quoted above, both speak of the appearance of a new idea as instantaneous "flash," it is obvious that we cannot influence it by a direct effort of will; because we can only bring our will to bear upon psychological events which last for an appreciable time. On the other hand, the final "flash," or "click," is the culmination of a successful train of association, which may have lasted for an appreciable time, and which has probably been preceded by a series of tentative and unsuccessful trains. The series of unsuccessful trains of association may last for periods varying from a few seconds to several hours. H. Poincaré, who describes the tentative and unsuccessful trains as being, in his case, almost entirely unconscious, believed that they occupied a considerable proportion of the whole Incubation stage. "We might," he wrote, "say that the conscious work [i.e., what I have called the Preparation stage] proved more fruitful because it was interrupted [by the Incubation stage], and that the rest restored freshness to the mind. But it is more probable that the rest was occupied with unconscious work, and that the result of this work was afterwards revealed." [3]

---

[3] H. Poincaré, *Science and Method* (trans., pp. 54 and 55). On the other hand, one of the ablest of modern mathematical thinkers told me that he believed that his Incubation period was, as a rule, spent in a state of actual mental repose for all or part of his brain, which made the later explosion of intense and successful thought possible. His belief may have been partly due to the fact that his brain started fewer unsuccessful and more successful association-trains than the brains of other men.

Different thinkers, and the same thinkers at different times, must, of course, vary greatly as to the time occupied by their unsuccessful trains of association; and the same variation must exist in the duration of the final and successful train of association. Sometimes the successful train seems to consist of a single leap of association, or of successive leaps which are so rapid as to be almost instantaneous. Hobbes's "Roman penny" train of association occurred between two remarks in an ordinary conversation, and Hobbes, as I have said, ends his description of it with the words, "and all this in a moment of time, for thought is quick" (*Leviathan*, Chap. III). Hobbes himself was probably an exceptionally rapid thinker, and Aubrey may have been quoting Hobbes's own phrase when he says that Hobbes used to take out his note-book "as soon as a thought darted."

But if our will is to control a psychological process, it is necessary that that process should not only last for an appreciable time, but should also be, during that time, sufficiently conscious for the thinker to be at least aware that something is happening to him. On this point, the evidence seems to show that both the unsuccessful trains of association, which might have led to the "flash" of success, and the final and successful train are normally either unconscious, or take place (with "risings" and "fallings" of consciousness as success seems to approach or retire), in that periphery or "fringe" of consciousness which surrounds our "focal" consciousness as the sun's "corona" surrounds the disk of full luminosity. This "fringe-consciousness" may last up to the "flash" instant, may accompany it, and in some cases may continue beyond it. But, just as it is very difficult to see the sun's corona unless the disk is hidden by a total eclipse, so it is very difficult to observe our "fringe-consciousness" at the instant of full Illumination, or to remember the preceding "fringe" after full Illumination has taken place. As William James says, "When the conclusion is there, we have always forgotten most of the steps preceding its attainment" (*Principles*, Volume I, p. 260).

It is obvious that both Helmholtz and Poincaré had either not noticed, or had forgotten any "fringe-conscious" psychological events which may have preceded and have been connected with the "sudden" and "unexpected" appearance of their new ideas. But other thinkers have observed and afterwards remembered their "fringe-conscious" experiences both before and even at the moment of full Illumination. William James himself, in that beautiful and touching, though sometimes confused introspective account of his own thinking which forms Chapter IX of his *Principles*, says: "Every definite image in the mind is steeped and dyed in the free water that flows round it. With it goes the sense of its relations, near and remote, the dying echo of whence it came to us, the dawning sense of whither it is to lead. The significance, the value, of the image is all in this halo or penumbra that surrounds and escorts it" (*Principles*, Vol. I, p. 255).

I find it convenient to use the term "Intimation" for that moment in the Illumination stage when our fringe-consciousness of an association-train is in the state of rising consciousness which indicates that the fully conscious flash of success is coming. A high English civil servant described his experience of Intimation to me by saying that when he is working at a difficult problem, "I often know that the solution is coming, though I don't know what the solution will be," and a very able university student gave me a description of the same fact in his case almost in the same words. Many thinkers, indeed, would recognize the experience which Varendonck describes when he says that on one occasion: "When I became aware that my mind was simmering over something, I had a dim feeling which is very difficult to describe; it was like a vague impression of mental activity. But when the association had risen to the surface, it expanded into an impression of joy." His phrase "expanded into an impression of joy," clearly describes the rising of consciousness as the "flash" approaches.

Most introspective observers speak, as I have done, of Intimation as a "feeling," and the ambiguity of that word creates its usual crop of difficulties. It is often hard to discover in descriptions of Intimation whether the observer is describing a bare awareness of mental activity with no emotional colouring, or an awareness of mental activity coloured by an emotion which may either have originally helped to stimulate the train of thought, or may have been stimulated by the train of thought during its course. Mr. F. M. McMurry seems to refer to little more than awareness when he says, in his useful text-book, *How to Study*, "Many of the best thoughts, probably most of them, do not come, like a flash, fully into being but find their beginnings in dim feelings, faint intuitions that need to be encouraged and coaxed before they can be surely felt and defined." Dewey, on the other hand, is obviously describing awareness coloured by emotion when he says that a problem may present itself "as a more or less vague feeling of the unexpected, of something queer, strange, funny, or disconcerting." Wundt was more ambiguous when he said (in perhaps the earliest description of Intimation) that feeling is the pioneer of knowledge, and that a novel thought may come to consciousness first of all in the form of a feeling. My own students have described the Intimation preceding a new thought as being sometimes coloured by a slight feeling of discomfort arising from a sense of separation from one's accustomed self. A student, for instance, told me that his first recognition that he was reaching a new political outlook came from a feeling, when, in answer to a question, he was stating his habitual political opinions, that he "was listening to himself." I can just remember that a good many years ago, in a period preceding an important change of my own political position, I had a vague, almost physical, recurrent feeling as if my clothes did not quite fit me. If this feeling of Intimation lasts for an appreciable time, and is either sufficiently conscious, or can by an effort of attention be made sufficiently conscious, it is obvious that our will can be brought directly to bear on it. We can at least attempt to inhibit, or prolong, or divert, the brain-activity which Intimation shows to be going on. And, if Intimation accompanies a rising train of association which the brain accepts, so to speak, as plausible, but would not, without the effort of attention, automatically push to the "flash" of conscious success, we can attempt to hold on to such a train on the chance that it may succeed.

It is a more difficult and more important question whether such an exercise of will is likely to improve our thinking. Many people would argue that any attempt to control the thought-process at this point will always do more harm than good. A schoolboy sitting down to do an algebra sum, a civil servant composing a minute, Shakespeare re-writing a speech in an old play, will, they would say, gain no more by interfering with the ideas whose coming is vaguely indicated to them, before they come, than would a child by digging up a sprouting bean, or a hungry man in front of a good meal, by bringing his will to bear on the intimations of activity in his stomach or his salivary glands. A born runner, they would say, achieves a much more successful co-ordination of those physiological and psychological factors in his organism which are concerned in running, by concentrating his will on his purpose of catching the man in front of him, than by troubling about the factors themselves. And a born orator will use better gestures if, as he speaks, he is conscious of his audience than if he is conscious of his hands. This objection might be fatal to the whole conception of an art of thought if it did not neglect two facts, first that we are not all "born" runners or orators or thinkers, and that a good deal of the necessary work of the world has to be done by men who in such respects have to achieve skill instead of receiving it at birth; and, secondly, that the process of learning an art should, even in the case of those who have the finest natural endowment for it, be more conscious than its practice. Mr. Harry Vardon, when he is acquiring a new grip, is wise to make himself more conscious of the relation between his will and his wrists than when he is addressing himself to his approach-shot at the decisive hole of a championship. The violinist with the most magnificent natural temperament has to think of his fingers when he is acquiring a new way of bowing; though on the concert-platform that acquirement may sink beneath the level of full consciousness. And, since the use of our upper brain for the discovery of new truth depends on more recent and less perfect evolutionary factors than does the use of our wrists for hitting small objects with a stick, or for causing catgut to vibrate in emotional patterns, conscious art may prove to be even more important, as compared to spontaneous gift, in thought than in golf or violin-playing. Here, again, individual thinkers, and the same thinker at different times and when engaged on different tasks, must differ greatly. But my general conclusion is that there are few or none among those whose work in life is thought who will not gain by directing their attention from time to time to the feeling of Intimation, and by bringing their will to bear upon the cerebral processes which it indicates.

On this point the most valuable evidence that I know of is that given by the poets. Poets have, more constantly than other intellectual workers, to "make use" (as Varendonck says) "of foreconscious processes for conscious ends." The production of a poem is a psychological experiment, tried and tested under severer conditions than those of a laboratory, and the poet is generally able to describe his "fringe-consciousness" during the experiment with a more accurate and sensitive use of language than is at the command of most laboratory psychologists. Several of the younger living English poets have given admirable descriptions of Intimation, often using metaphors derived from our experience in daily life of a feeling that there is something which we have mislaid, and which we cannot find because we have forgotten what it is. Mr. John Drinkwater, for instance, says:

> Haunting the lucidities of life
> That are my daily beauty, moves a theme
> Beating along my undiscovered mind.

And Mr. James Stephens says:

> I would think until I found
>     Something I can never find,
> Something lying on the ground
>     In the bottom of my mind.

Mr. J. Middleton Murry, in his *Problem of Style* (1922, p. 93), points out the psychological truth of Shakespeare's well-known description of the poet's work:

> . . . as imagination bodies forth
> The forms of things unknown, the poet's pen
> Turns them to shapes and gives to airy nothings
> A local habitation and a name.

"Forms of things unknown" and "airy nothings" are vivid descriptions of the first appearance of Intimation; and "local habitation and a name" indicates the increasing verbal clearness of thought as Intimation approaches the final moment of Illumination; and may also indicate that Shakespeare was a much more conscious artist than many of his admirers believe.

Some English poets and students of poetry have given descriptions not only of the feeling of Intimation, but also of the effort of will by which a poet may attempt to influence the mental events indicated by Intimation, and the dangers to the thought itself involved in such an effort. In these descriptions they often use metaphors drawn from a boy's attempts to catch in his hand an elusive fish, or a bird which will dart off if the effort is made a fraction of a second too soon or too late. . . .

In this respect, the most obvious danger against which the thinker has to guard is that the association-train which the feeling of Intimation shows to be going on may either drift away of itself, as most of our dreams and daydreams do, into mere irrelevance and forgetfulness, or may be interrupted by the intrusion of other trains of association. All thinkers know the effect of the ringing of the telephone bell, or the entrance of some one with a practical question which must be answered, during a promising Intimation. Aristophanes, when in the Clouds he makes Socrates complain that his disciple by asking him a question had caused a valuable thought to "miscarry," was probably quoting some saying of Socrates himself, whose mother was a midwife, and who was fond of that metaphor. If, therefore, the feeling of Intimation presents itself while one is reading, it is best to look up from one's book and so avoid the danger that the next printed sentence may "start a new hare." Varendonck describes how, in one of his day-dreams, "The idea that manifested itself ran thus: *'There is something going on in my foreconsciousness which must be in direct relation to my subject. I ought to stop reading for a little while, and let it come to the surface.'* " And, besides such negative precautions against the interruption of an association-train, it is often necessary to make a conscious positive effort of attention to secure success. Vincent d'Indy, speaking of musical creation, said that he "often has on waking, a fugitive glimpse of a musical effect which—like the memory of a dream—needs a strong immediate concentration of mind to keep it from vanishing." But even the effort of attention to a train of association may have the effect of interrupting or hindering it. Schiller is reported by Vischer to have said that when he was fully conscious of creation his imagination did not function "with the same freedom as it had done when nobody was looking over my shoulder."

To a modern thinker, however, the main danger of spoiling a train of association occurs in the process of attempting—perhaps before the train is complete —to put its conclusion into the words. Mr. Henry Hazlitt, in his *Thinking as a Science* (1916), p. 82, says, "Thoughts of certain kinds are so elusive that to attempt to articulate them is to scare them away, as a fish is scared by the slightest ripple. When these thoughts are in embryo, even the infinitesimal attention required for talking cannot be spared"; and a writer on Montaigne in *The Times Literary Supplement* for January 31, 1924, says, "We all indulge in the strange pleasant process called thinking, but when it comes to saying, even to some one opposite, what we think, then how little we are able to convey! The phantom is through the mind and out of the window before we can lay salt on its tail, or slowly sinking and returning to the profound darkness which it has lit up momentarily with a wandering light." In the case of a poet, this danger is increased by the fact that for the poet the finding of expressive words is an integral part of the more or less automatic thought-process indicated by Intimation. The little girl had the making of a poet in her who, being told to be sure of her meaning before she spoke, said, "How can I know what I think till I see what I say?" A modern professed thinker must, however, sooner or later in the process of thought, make the conscious effort of expression, with all its risks. A distant ancestor of ours, some Aurignacian Shelley, living in the warm spell between two ice ages, may have been content to lie on the hillside, and allow the songs of the birds and the loveliness of the clouds to mingle with his wonder as to the nature of the universe in a delightful uninterrupted stream of rising and falling reverie, enjoyed and forgotten as it passed. But the modern thinker has generally accepted, willingly or unwillingly, the task of making permanent his thought for the use of others, as the only justification of his position in a society few of whose members have time or opportunity for anything but a life of manual labour.

The interference of our will should, finally, vary—with the variations of the subject-matter of our thought—not only in respect of the point in time at which it should take place, but also in respect to the element in a complex thought-process with which we should interfere. A novelist who had just finished a long novel, and who must constantly have employed his conscious will while writing it, to make sure of a good idea or phrase, or to improve a sentence, or rearrange an incident, told me that he had spoilt his book by interfering with the automatic development of his main story and of its chief characters, in order to follow out a preconceived plot. Dramatists and poets constantly speak of the need of allowing their characters to "speak for themselves"; and a creative artist often reaches maturity only when he has learned so to use his conscious craftsmanship in the expression of his thought as not to silence the promptings of that imperfectly co-ordinated whole which is called his personality. It is indeed at the stage of Illumination with its fringe of Intimation that the thinker should most constantly realize that the rules of his art will be of little effect unless they are applied with artistic delicacy of apprehension.

❦ ❦ ❦

## S. I. Hayakawa

# Contexts[1]

> Dictionary definitions frequently offer verbal substitutes for an unknown term which only conceal a lack of real understanding. Thus a person might look up a foreign word and be quite satisfied with the meaning "bullfinch" without the slightest ability to identify or describe this bird. Understanding does not come through dealings with words alone, but rather with the things for which they stand. Dictionary definitions permit us to hide from ourselves and others the extent of our ignorance.—H. R. HUSE

### HOW DICTIONARIES ARE MADE

IT IS an almost universal belief that every word has a "correct meaning," that we learn these meanings principally from teachers and grammarians (except that most of the time we don't bother to, so that we ordinarily speak "sloppy English"), and that dictionaries and grammars are the "supreme authority" in matters of meaning and usage. Few people ask by what authority the writers of dictionaries and grammars say what they say. The docility with which most

[1] From *Language in Thought and Action* by S. I. Hayakawa, copyright, 1941, 1949, by Harcourt, Brace and Company, Inc.

people bow down to the dictionary is amazing, and the person who says, "Well, the dictionary is wrong!" is looked upon with smiles of pity and amusement which say plainly, "Poor fellow! He's really quite sane otherwise."

Let us see how dictionaries are made and how the editors arrive at definitions. What follows applies, incidentally, only to those dictionary offices where first-hand, original research goes on—not those in which editors simply copy existing dictionaries. The task of writing a dictionary begins with the reading of vast amounts of the literature of the period or subject that it is intended to cover. As the editors read, they copy on cards every interesting or rare word, every unusual or peculiar occurrence of a common word, a large number of common words in their ordinary uses, *and also the sentences in which each of these words appears,* thus:

> pail
> The dairy *pails* bring home increase of milk
> Keats, *Endymion*
> I, 44-45

That is to say, the *context* of each word is collected, along with the word it-self. For a really big job of dictionary writing, such as the *Oxford English Dictionary* (usually bound in about twenty-five volumes), millions of such cards are collected, and the task of editing occupies decades. As the cards are collected, they are alphabetized and sorted. When the sorting is completed, there will be for each word anywhere from two or three to several hundred illustrative quotations, each on its card.

To define a word, then, the dictionary editor places before him the stack of cards illustrating that word; each of the cards represents an actual use of the word by a writer of some literary or historical importance. He reads the cards carefully, discards some, re-reads the rest, and divides up the stack according to what he thinks are the several senses of the word. Finally, he writes his definitions, following the hard-and-fast rule that each definition *must* be based on what the quotations in front of him reveal about the meaning of the word. The editor cannot be influenced by what *he* thinks a given word *ought* to mean. He must work according to the cards, or not at all.

The writing of a dictionary, therefore, is not a task of setting up authoritative statements about the "true meanings" of words, but a task of *recording,* to the best of one's ability, what various words *have meant* to authors in the distant or immediate past. *The writer of a dictionary is a historian, not a law-giver.* If, for example, we had been writing a dictionary in 1890, or even as late as 1919, we could have said that the word "broadcast" means "to scatter," seed and so on; but we could not have decreed that from 1921 on, the commonest meaning of the word should become "to disseminate audible messages, etc., by wireless telephony." To regard the dictionary as an "authority," therefore, is to credit the dictionary writer with gifts of prophecy which neither he nor anyone else possesses. In choosing our words when we speak or write, we can be *guided* by the historical record afforded us by the dictionary, but we cannot be *bound* by it, because new situations, new experiences, new inventions, new feelings, are always compelling us to give new uses to old words. Looking under a "hood," we should ordinarily have found, five hundred years ago, a monk; today, we find a motorcar engine.

### VERBAL AND PHYSICAL CONTEXTS

The way in which the dictionary writer arrives at his definitions is merely the systematization of the way in which we all learn the meanings of words, beginning at infancy, and continuing for the rest of our lives. Let us say that we have never heard the word "oboe" before, and we overhear a conversation in which the following sentences occur:

> He used to be the best *oboe* player in town. . . . Whenever they came to that *oboe* part in the third movement, he used to get very excited. . . . I saw him one day at the music shop, buying a new reed for his *oboe*. . . . He never liked to play the clarinet after he started playing the *oboe*. He said it wasn't so much fun, because it was too easy.

Although the word may be unfamiliar, its meaning becomes clear to us as we listen. After hearing the first sentence, we know that an "oboe" is "played," so that it must be either a game or a musical instrument. With the second sentence the possibility of its being a game is eliminated. With each succeeding sentence the possibilities as to what an "oboe" may be are narrowed down until we get a fairly clear idea of what is meant. This is how we learn by *verbal context*.

But even independently of this, we learn by *physical and social context*. Let us say that we are playing golf and that we have hit the ball in a certain way with certain unfortunate results, so that our companion says to us, "That's a bad *slice*." He repeats this remark every time our ball fails to go straight. If we are reasonably bright, we learn in a very short time to say, when it happens again, "That's a bad slice." On one occasion, however, our friend says to us, "That's not a *slice* this time; that's a *hook*." In this case we consider what has happened, and we wonder what is different about the last stroke from those previous. As soon as we make the distinction, we have added still another word to our vocabulary. The result is that after nine holes of golf, we can use both these words accurately—and perhaps several others as well, such as "divot," "number-five iron," "approach shot," *without ever having been told what they mean*. Indeed, we may play golf for years without ever being able to give a dictionary definition of "to slice": "To strike (the ball) so that the face of the club draws inward across the face of the ball, causing it to curve toward the right in flight (with a right-handed player)" (*Webster's New International*

*Dictionary*). But even without being able to give such a definition, we should still be able to use the word accurately whenever the occasion demanded.

We learn the meanings of practically all our words (which are, it will be remembered, merely complicated noises), not from dictionaries, not from definitions, but from hearing these noises as they accompany actual situations in life and learning to associate certain noises with certain situations. Even as dogs learn to recognize "words," as for example by hearing "biscuit" at the same time as an actual biscuit is held before their noses, so do we all learn to interpret language by being aware of the happenings that accompany the noises people make at us—by being aware, in short, of contexts.

The "definitions" given by little children in school show clearly how they associate words with situations; they almost always define in terms of physical and social contexts: "Punishment is when you have been bad and they put you in a closet and don't let you have any supper." "Newspapers are what the paper boy brings and you wrap up the garbage with it." These are good definitions. The main reason that they cannot be used in dictionaries is that they are *too* specific; it would be impossible to list the myriads of situations in which every word has been used. For this reason, dictionaries give definitions on a high level of abstraction; that is, with particular references left out for the sake of conciseness. This is another reason why it is a great mistake to regard a dictionary definition as "telling us all about" a word.

### EXTENSIONAL AND INTENSIONAL MEANING

From this point on, it will be necessary to employ some special terms in talking about meaning: *extensional meaning*, which will also be referred to as *denotation*, and *intensional meaning*—note the *s*—which will also be referred to as *connotation*.[2] Briefly explained, the extensional meaning of an utterance is that which it *points to* or denotes in the extensional world. . . . That is to say, the extensional meaning is something that *cannot be expressed in words*, because it is that which words stand for. An easy way to remember this is to put your hand over your mouth and point whenever you are asked to give an extensional meaning.

The *intensional meaning* of a word or expression, on the other hand, is that which is *suggested* (connoted) inside one's head. Roughly speaking, whenever we express the meaning of words by uttering more words, we are giving intensional meaning, or connotations. To remember this, put your hand over your eyes and let the words spin around in your head.

Utterances may have, of course, both extensional and intensional meaning. If they have no intensional meaning at all—that is, if they start no notions whatever spinning about in our heads—they are meaningless noises, like for-

---

[2] The words *extension* and *intension* are borrowed from logic; *denotation* and *connotation* are borrowed from literary criticism. The former pair of terms will ordinarily be used, therefore, when we are talking about people's "thinking habits"; the latter, when we are talking about words themselves.

eign languages that we do not understand. On the other hand, it is possible for utterances to have no extensional meaning at all, in spite of the fact that they may start many notions spinning about in our heads. Since this point will be discussed more fully . . . , perhaps one example will be enough: the statement, "Angels watch over my bed at night," is one that has intensional but no extensional meaning. This does not mean that there are no angels watching over my bed at night. When we say that the statement has no extensional meaning, we are merely saying that we cannot see, touch, photograph, or in any scientific manner detect the presence of angels. The result is that, if an argument begins on the subject whether or not angels watch over my bed, *there is no way of ending the argument to the satisfaction of all disputants*, the Christians and the non-Christians, the pious and the agnostic, the mystical and the scientific. Therefore, whether we believe in angels or not, knowing in advance that any argument on the subject will be both endless and futile, we can avoid getting into fights about it.

When, on the other hand, statements have extensional content, as when we say, "This room is fifteen feet long," arguments can come to a close. No matter how many guesses there are about the length of the room, all discussion ceases when someone produces a tape measure. This, then, is the important difference between extensional and intensional meanings: namely, when utterances have extensional meanings, discussion can be ended and agreement reached; when utterances have intensional meanings only and no extensional meanings, arguments may, and often do, go on indefinitely. Such arguments can result only in irreconcilable conflict. Among individuals, they may result in the breaking up of friendships; in society, they often split organizations into bitterly opposed groups; among nations, they may aggravate existing tensions so seriously as to become contributory causes of war.

Arguments of this kind may be termed "non-sense arguments," because they are based on utterances about which no sense data can be collected. Needless to say, there are occasions when the hyphen may be omitted—that depends on one's feelings toward the particular argument under consideration. The reader is requested to provide his own examples of "non-sense arguments." Even the foregoing example of the angels may give offense to some people, in spite of the fact that no attempt is made to deny or affirm the existence of angels. He can imagine, therefore, the uproar that might result from giving a number of examples, from theology, politics, law, economics, literary criticism, and other fields in which it is not customary to distinguish clearly sense from non-sense.

### THE "ONE WORD, ONE MEANING" FALLACY

Everyone, of course, who has ever given any thought to the meanings of words has noticed that they are always shifting and changing in meaning. Usually, people regard this as a misfortune, because it "leads to sloppy thinking" and "mental confusion." To remedy this condition, they are likely to suggest that we should all agree on "one meaning" for each word and use it onl with that meaning. Thereupon it will occur to them that we simply cannot make people agree in this way, even if we could set up an ironclad dictatorship under a committee of lexicographers who could place censors in every newspaper office and dictaphones in every home. The situation, therefore, appears hopeless.

Such an impasse is avoided when we start with a new premise altogether— one of the premises upon which modern linguistic thought is based: namely, *that no word ever has exactly the same meaning twice.* The extent to which this premise fits the facts can be demonstrated in a number of ways. First, if we accept the proposition that the contexts of an utterance determine its meaning, it becomes apparent that since no two contexts are ever *exactly* the same, no two meanings can ever be exactly the same. How can we "fix the meaning" even for as common an expression as "to believe in" when it can be used in such sentences as the following?

> *I believe in* you (I have confidence in you).
> *I believe in* democracy (I accept the principles implied by the term democracy).
> *I believe in* Santa Claus (It is my opinion that Santa Claus exists).

Secondly, we can take for example a word of "simple" meaning like "kettle."

But when John says "kettle," its intensional meanings to him are the common characteristics of all the kettles John remembers. When Peter says "kettle," however, its intensional meanings to him are the common characteristics of all the kettles he remembers. *No matter how small or how negligible the differences may be between John's "kettle" and Peter's "kettle," there is some difference.*

Finally, let us examine utterances in terms of extensional meanings. If John, Peter, Harold, and George each say "my typewriter," we would have to point to *four different typewriters* to get the extensional meaning in each case: John's new Underwood, Peter's old Corona, Harold's L. C. Smith, and the undenotable intended "typewriter" that George plans some day to buy: "My typewriter, when I buy one, will be a noiseless." Also, if John says "my typewriter" today, and again "my typewriter" tomorrow, the extensional meaning is different in the two cases, because the typewriter is not *exactly* the same from one day to the next (nor from one minute to the next): slow processes of wear, change, and decay are going on constantly. Although we can say, then, that the differences in the meanings of a word on one occasion, on another occasion a minute later, and on still another occasion another minute later, are *negligible*, we cannot say that the meanings are *exactly* the same.

To say dogmatically that we "know what a word means" *in advance of its utterance* is nonsense. All we can know in advance is *approximately* what it *will* mean. After the utterance, we interpret what has been said in the light of both verbal and physical contexts, and act according to our interpretation. An examination of the verbal context of an utterance, as well as the examination of the utterance itself, directs us to the intensional meanings; an examination of the physical context directs us to the extensional meanings. When John says to James, "Bring me that book, will you?" James looks in the direction of John's pointed finger (physical context) and sees a desk with several books on it (physical context); he thinks back over their previous conversation (verbal context) and knows which of those books is being referred to.

Interpretation *must* be based, therefore, on the totality of contexts. If it were otherwise, we should not be able to account for the fact that even if we fail to use the right (customary) words in some situations, people can very frequently understand us. For example:

A. Gosh, look at that second baseman go!
B. (looking). You mean the shortstop?
A. Yes, that's what I mean.
A. There must be something wrong with the oil line; the engine has started to balk.
B. Don't you mean "gas line"?
A. Yes—didn't I say gas line?

Contexts sometimes indicate so clearly what we mean that often we do not even have to say what we mean in order to be understood.

### THE IGNORING OF CONTEXTS

It is clear, then, that the ignoring of contexts in any act of interpretation is at best a stupid practice. At its worst, it can be a vicious practice. A common example is the sensational newspaper story in which a few words by a public personage are torn out of their context and made the basis of a completely misleading account. There is the incident of an Armistice Day speaker, a university teacher, who declared before a high-school assembly that the Gettysburg Address was "a powerful piece of propaganda." The context clearly revealed that "propaganda" was being used according to its dictionary meanings rather than according to its popular meanings; it also revealed that the speaker was a very great admirer of Lincoln's. However, the local newspaper, completely ignoring the context, presented the account in such a way as to convey the impression that the speaker had called Lincoln a liar. On this basis, the newspaper began a campaign against the instructor. The speaker remonstrated with the editor of the newspaper, who replied, in effect, "*I don't care what else you said*. You said the Gettysburg Address was propaganda, didn't you?" This appeared to the editor complete proof that Lincoln had been maligned and that the speaker deserved to be discharged from his position at the university. Similar practices may be found in advertisements. A reviewer may be quoted on the jacket of a book as having said, "A brilliant work," while reading of the context may reveal that what he really said was, "It just falls short of being a brilliant work." There are some people who will always be able to find a defense for such a practice in saying, "But he did use the words, 'a brilliant work,' didn't he?"

People in the course of argument very frequently complain about words meaning different things to different people. Instead of complaining, they should accept it as a matter of course. It would be startling indeed if the word "justice," for example, were to have the same meaning to the nine justices of the United States Supreme Court; we should get nothing but unanimous decisions. It would be even more startling if "justice" meant the same to Fiorello La Guardia as to Josef Stalin. If we can get deeply into our consciousness the principle that no word ever has the same meaning twice, we will develop the habit of automatically examining contexts, and this enables us to understand better what others are saying. As it is, however, we are all too likely to have signal reactions to certain words and read into people's remarks meanings that were never intended. Then we waste energy in angrily accusing people of "intellectual dishonesty" or "abuse of words," when their only sin is that they use words in ways unlike our own, as they can hardly help doing, especially if their background has been widely different from ours. There are cases of intellectual dishonesty and of the abuse of words, of course, but they do not always occur in the places where people think they do.

In the study of history or of cultures other than our own, contexts take on special importance. To say, "There was no running water or electricity in the house," does not condemn an English house in 1570, but says a great deal against a house in Chicago in 1941. Again, if we wish to understand the Constitution of the United States, it is not enough, as our historians now tell us, merely to look up all the words in the dictionary and to read the interpretations written by Supreme Court justices. We must see the Constitution in its *historical context:* the conditions of life, the current ideas, the fashionable prejudices, and the probable interests of the people who drafted the Constitution. After all, the words "The United States of America" stood for quite a different-sized nation and a different culture in 1790 from what they stand for today. When it comes to very big subjects, the range of contexts to be examined, verbal, social, and historical, may become very large indeed.

THE INTERACTION OF WORDS

All this is not to say, however, that the reader might just as well throw away his dictionary, since contexts are so important. Any word in a sentence—any sentence in a paragraph, any paragraph in a larger unit—whose meaning is revealed by its context, *is itself part of the context of the rest of the text.* To look up a word in a dictionary, therefore, frequently explains not only that word itself, but the rest of the sentence, paragraph, conversation, or essay in which it is found. *All words within a given context interact upon one another.*

Realizing, then, that a dictionary is a historical work, we should understand the dictionary thus: "The word *mother* has most frequently been used in the past among English-speaking people to indicate *a female parent.*" From this we can safely infer, "If that is how it has been used, that is what it probably means in the sentence I am trying to understand." This is what we normally do, of course; after we look up a word in the dictionary, *we re-examine the context to see if the definition fits.*

A dictionary definition, therefore, is an invaluable guide to interpretation. Words do not have a single "correct meaning"; they apply to *groups* of similar situations, which might be called *areas of meaning.* It is for definition in terms of areas of meaning that a dictionary is useful. In each use of any word, we examine the particular context and the extensional events denoted (if possible) to discover the *point* intended within the area of meaning.

❦ ❦ ❦

*Philip Wheelwright*

# The Limits of Plain Sense [1]

*When people stammer together that is thinking.* GERTRUDE STEIN

THERE IS no more ironic illusion than to suppose that one has escaped from illusions. So subtly do the real and the illusory interpenetrate that their difference is never finally clear. Mind is by nature a meddler, and there are no self-evident criteria by which to discriminate its insights from its commentaries. Still, the quest for certainty persists. The history of philosophy, save for sceptical interludes, is a record of men's shifting intellectual stratagems by which to secure some firm line of demarcation between truth and error.

In the everyday business of living we do indeed establish convenient rules of thumb to indicate, for practical convenience, what can be handled and by what laws it may be expected to operate. Such public operables, actual and potential, constitute our physical world; the study of their regularities of operation is empirical science, and the practical exploitation of those regularities is technology. From time to time, but especially in our day, certain theorists, impressed by the science and technology and wishing a short-cut to first principles, advance this study of public operables as the one valid form of cognition, the sole way of escape from illusionistic muddle, and the system of public operables themselves as the only genuine kind of reality. Such postulation generates the philosophy known variously as materialism, naturalism, and positivism. The last name, positivism, being freest of adventitious connotations, is the one I shall mainly employ: it may be defined precisely as the philosophy which identifies "reality" with the public operables which can be scientifically determined (space-time events and their correlations), and "truth" with the sys-

[1] From *The Burning Fountain: A Study in the Language of Symbolism* (Bloomington: Indiana University Press, 1954), pp. 30-51, with omissions. Copyright, 1954, Indiana University Press. Reprinted by permission.

tem of empirically verified propositions about such operables and their inter-relations, together perhaps with propositions established by deduction from mathematical and logical axioms.

Positivism in the twentieth century goes beyond older forms of materialism: not only because of its recognition of revolutionary new scientific develop-ments, but also—what pertains to the theme of this book—by virtue of having worked out a semantic, which is to say a theory of meaning, of its own. Positiv-ism in this guise may be called *semantic positivism*. Whereas a positivist in general is anyone who identifies reality with the system of public operables that constitutes the physical world, and truth with the system of verifiable propositions describing that reality, a semantic positivist takes the yet more drastic step of identifying *meaning* with such terms and propositions as denote such operables. In other words, the semantic positivist starts off with a judg-ment about *language*. The only language that really means anything, he declares, is language which refers to things, events, and relations in the physical world. If it does not refer to the physical world, it does not refer to anything (for nothing else exists), and is therefore, strictly speaking, meaningless. By this bold stratagem the positivist gains an enviable advantage: instead of having to argue with dissenters he need only declare that the terms in which they formu-late their opposition do not conform to the conditions of meaningfulness which he has set up; in short, he dismisses them as talking nonsense.

As a matter of fact, semantic positivism only puts in plainer and more uncompromising form, with a more explicit statement of its postulates, an atti-tude which is shared by many so-called hard-headed realists—people who are fond of saying, "It all boils down to this"—and which may be called the Dogma of Plain Sense. Such an attitude represents, on its affirmative side, the excellent intention of promoting intelligibility and avoiding confusion. It proceeds from the principle that we ought to be as clear as possible about the meaning of our utterances, and be able to know when we are speaking sense and when we are just vaporizing. With this general aim every candid thinker will agree. The question is, where the line between sense and vaporizing is to be drawn. Semantic positivists have no difficulty in drawing it. Language may, on the one hand, they declare, assert something in the form of a proposition about what is "actually the case"; on the other it may, in the words of Rudolf Carnap, "express the emotions, fancies, images, or wishes of the speaker, and under proper conditions evoke emotions, wishes, or resolutions in the hearer."

It is instructive in this connection to have another look at the much dis-cussed theory once espoused by I. A. Richards. Since Professor Richards is one of the most alert of contemporary thinkers, it might not seem fair to saddle his present reputation with views which he expressed over twenty-five years ago. His more recent writings have shown a tendency to liberalize and soften the hard semantic postulates which he advocated during the 'twenties. Nevertheless the influence of those early books has persisted, and the point of view which they advocate is still very much alive. Inasmuch as that point of view, consistently developed, destroys the very basis of that poetic vision of the world which alone can give human life its transcendental significance, there is as much pertinence now as there ever was in subjecting it to critical scrutiny.

In *The Meaning of Meaning* (written in collaboration with C. K. Ogden), *Principles of Literary Criticism*, and *Science and Poetry* Richards struck virtually the same note of semantic positivism which receives fuller technical development in writers like Carnap:

> A statement may be used for the sake of the *reference*, true or false, which it causes. This is the *scientific* use of language. But it may also be used for the sake of the effects in emotion and attitude produced by the reference it occasions. This is the *emotive* use. The distinction once clearly grasped is simple. We may either use words for the sake of the reference they promote, or we may use them for the sake of the attitudes and emotions which ensue.

The distinction is simple enough, to be sure; indeed, far too over-simple. What follows from so uncompromising an "either-or"? The consequences for poetry and religion had been stated frankly enough in *The Meaning of Meaning* a few years earlier, where it was argued that as poetry and religion do not employ words scientifically, so neither of them employs words referentially— that is to say, neither of them is capable of speaking *about* anything: the one plain test of whether a given use of words is essentially symbolic and referential or essentially emotive being the question, "Is it true or false in the ordinary strict scientific sense?"

The ontological basis of Richards' semantic position became clarified in his article, "Between Truth and Truth," published in 1931. Two years earlier, in *Practical Criticism*, he had pursued more fully the question of communication in literature. From that standpoint he now reformulated his position. A poem, he now declared, describes and communicates something, but what? "Two alternatives, and not more I think, are before us, two main senses of 'describe' and 'communicate.' . . . The first sense is that in which a form of words describes or communicates the state of mind or experience of the speaker; the second is that in which it describes or communicates some state of affairs or fact which the speaker is thinking of or knowing (something in all but one case, that of introspection, *other than* the experience which is his thinking of it or knowing it). . . . To take an extreme instance, when a man says 'I'm damned!' he may be saying that eternal judgment has gone against him or showing that he is surprised or annoyed."

Richards then turns to John Clare's description of the primrose—

> With its crimp and curdled leaf
> And its little brimming eye,

about which, in a previous article, J. Middleton Murry had remarked that it "is surely an accurate description, but accurate with an accuracy unknown to and unachievable by science." Richards complains: Mr. Murry "does not say explicitly whether he takes it as a description of an object (the primrose) or of the experience of seeing one." And he adds: "It seems to me not likely that there will be widespread disagreement with the view that the description applies to the experience of seeing or imagining a primrose rather than to actual primroses."

But how absurd! Surely any observant flower lover, unless constrained by loyalty to a preconceived theory, will disagree. Neither the lexicographer's definition of the primrose as a "plant or flower of the genus Primula" nor a botanist's or biochemist's analysis of it into scientifically discoverable elements and processes can describe the perceived primrose in its full living actuality as adequately as Clare's lines have done. If we are willing to consider such words as "crimp" and "curdled" in their descriptive function (as Richards has done in formulating his complaint against Murry above), then clearly it is not the *experience* of a primrose that is being described (for it is not my experience that is crimp and curdled!) but *the primrose as experienced*.

The trouble is that Professor Richards had fallen here without realizing it into the trap of metaphysics. The defection is particularly noticeable in a footnote to the article just mentioned, where he distinguishes the "sensed or imagined primrose" from the "inferred or constructed common or gardener's primrose" on the ground that the former lacks such scientifically determinable characteristics as weight! The distinction does not stand up under examination. The very same primrose which I see as crimp and curdled I can also pick up and feel as having a trifling bit of weight. Such visual and such kinaesthetic experiences refer to what I naturally and reasonably regard as constituting a single object. So, too, but less directly, do the experiences of looking at the notches of a scale on which the primrose is being weighed. On the basis of this latter type of experience (mine or another's) the primrose is assigned a numerical figure which we call its "objective weight"—bearing some relation no doubt, but not a strictly determinable one, to the kinaesthetic experience of lightness which I feel when I take the flower in my hand. Now the fallacy of the semantic positivist is to reject the "crimp and curdled" kind of experience, and the kinaesthetic kind of experience ("Why, this flower weighs practically nothing!") for the kind of experience which consists in looking at notches on a scale or some other measuring instrument. For the notch on the scale to which the pointer turns can be securely agreed on by everyone who is not blind; and such agreement is unlikely in the case of the other qualities mentioned.

When I say "reject," of course I do not mean that a semantic positivist wants nothing to do with the more colorful and feelingful qualities of things. He may indeed, as Mr. Richards explicitly does, consider them more "valuable" for the larger human purposes than a knowledge of such abstract properties as length and weight. His rejection is not practical but ontological. He asserts that only *abstract objects*, like the scientist's primrose with its numerical length and weight and its chemical properties, have real existence whereas concrete objects, like Clare's primrose with its plenitude of warmly experienced qualities, are not really objects at all. He asserts, therefore, that when a poet or anyone else appears to be speaking about such qualities he is not really speaking *about* anything, but is merely ejaculating the history of his mind, "his feelings and attitudes in the moment of speaking, and conditions of their governance in the future." Naturally I do not deny that poetry does and should express in some degree the poet's feelings, nor that it may and should have for a reader the beneficial and equilibrating effects described in Richards' *Principles of Literary Criticism*. These things have their own kind of importance, but from the standpoint of interpreting what the poem *says* they are strictly secondary and sometimes quite irrelevant. Every science has its proper object; and the object of poetic interpretation, rightly conceived, is the poem under consideration, and not either the poet's supposed feelings or the reader's expected benefits. An adequate study of the meaning of poetry, then—what I shall call *the semantics of poetry*—must first establish unhampering postulates and find a suitable language whereby the nature and reference of poetic utterance can be indicated, without evasion into fields of discourse peripheral and sometimes alien to poetry. . . .

Nor does the problem of poetry stand alone. For the issue which I have been discussing amounts to this: whether there is such a thing as *poetic vision*, or whether the only true vision of things must be ultimately scientific. If you accept the latter alternative—the position of semantic positivism—then the consequences, provided you carry them out vigorously, will be utterly destructive for religion, for metaphysics, and even for ethics as independent disciplines; and that is to say, for the very mainsprings of significant human living. The truth-claims of these three disciplines necessarily transcend the reach of scientific methods of validation; therefore (so the positivist's argument runs) they cannot be validated at all, and so have a merely subjective status. Metaphysics is either preëmpted as an organon of the sciences—a critical instrument by which the methods of the individual sciences may be brought into greater unity with one another—or else is dismissed as presumptuous vaporizing and word-play. Religion and ethics are explained away as mere projections of personal or group emotions; and, when they seem to give any real insight into the nature of reality, they are denounced as shams.

Now ethics is important for everybody; for while there are individuals who think they are able to do without religion, metaphysics, and poetry (I am not now discussing whether they are self-deceived), it is obvious that human life cannot be lived in anything like a human way without some implicit acknowledgment of moral principles. The alternative, as Hobbes has memorably said, is a life "nasty, brutish, and short." Yet as we ponder the assumptions of positivism we are forced to the realization that on the basis which they set up there are no real moral issues. At least one eminent positivist, Alfred Ayer, faces the consequence frankly, and accepts it. An apparent moral statement, such as "You acted wrongly in stealing that money," is really, he maintains, nothing more than the simple factual statement, "You stole that money." The first sentence does not *mean* anything different from the second; it merely "evinces" the speaker's emotional disapproval—as if one had said "You stole that money" in a peculiar tone of horror.

So extreme a form of positivism as Ayer's is not hard to refute. Two weaknesses are quickly apparent. We might first appeal to the testimony of reflective experience that moral issues do exist. We might argue that deliberations, disputes, and decisions about right and wrong, good and evil, are at least as real a part of human life as any of the sensory and the scientifically determined data on which Ayer bases his position. We might conclude that a philosophy which writes off the evidence of mankind's experience in such a high-handed manner is grossly over-simplified and rather foolishly naïve. But we can also attack Ayer's argument on its home territory. If the ethical element in the sentence, "You did wrong in stealing that money"—i.e., the element which differentiates it from the factual statement, "You stole that money"—were *nothing more than* an expression of horror, it would follow that our judgment of the immorality of the act must increase and diminish in exact ratio to the changes in the feeling-tone of horror. This, however, is obviously not what actually happens. Horror or no horror, we can still raise and consider the moral issue. We can ask, "Is our horror or repugnance in this case *morally justified?*" Ayer would have to take this to mean, "How much horror do I feel at myself for feeling horror?"—which is plainly not what we mean when asking whether the original horror is justified. Ayer's theory of meaning is too black-and-white an affair to be capable of handling the moral dimension of human experience. . . .

My objection to the theory which I have been examining under the general name of "semantic positivism" may now be summed up. It requires, in effect, that the truth of a poem, or of a religious belief, or of a philosophical insight—of anything, in short, which is not a scientific statement of verifiable fact—be judged ultimately by its emotive and conative affects. Hence it may be aptly spoken of as the Affective Theory of poetic, religious, and philosophical truth. From its standpoint the existence of poetry can be justified only on one or other of two grounds: either on the hedonistic ground that it gives pleasure to those who like it, or on the clinical grounds defended by the earlier Richards and implicit in Morris that it tends to promote a healthier equilibrium of attitudes in the reader and therefore possibly in the society wherein he moves. Even religion can be given no firmer justification than one or the other of these, if the Affective Theory is true. There are, however, two grave flaws in that theory, one in the flower and one in the root. Experientially, the theory does not do justice to the full nature of either poetic or religious experience; and logically, it rests upon an arbitrary (and I believe false) presupposition.

On the first count let it be considered that neither the pleasurable nor the therapeutic effects of poetry or religion are fortuitous. While those of poetry may partly proceed from the direct propulsions of rhythm and imagery upon the physio-psychic organism, they most characteristically involve something more. A poem affects a mature reader as it does partly because it seems to him, notwithstanding its fantasies and pseudo-statements, to be offering a kind of genuine insight and thereby to be revealing, however obscurely and elusively, a kind of truth. In *King Lear*, for example, the language and imagery and character developments and story are inseparable aspects of the total poem and legitimate factors in its appeal. But *King Lear's* principal claim to greatness transcends these components: it is great because in and through such poetic devices it reveals depth-meaning—it adumbrates truths and quasi-truths of high importance about such matters as human nature, old age, false seeming, and self-confrontation through suffering. The depth-meaning of *Lear*—the "poetic truth" to be discovered in the play—is what mainly accounts for and justifies the Fit Reader's full response, an inseparable blending of emotive and intellectual. If the depth-meaning is not at least dimly and subconsciously adumbrated—and perhaps too sharp a focus of it is generally undesirable—the reader's response will hardly be the same. Impoverishment or distortion of the intellectual response will involve some impoverishment or distortion of the emotive. To regard the specifically poetic response as purely emotive, then, is a naïve way of psychologizing.

The shallowness of the positivistic interpretation of religion is even more evident. For in religion the depth-meaning is *all* that matters. If you ignore the depth-meanings of Sophocles or Dante or Shakespeare, something of the nature of poetry still remains in them; and those whose response is limited to story, imagery, and versification may still be responding in a way proper to poetry, though but limitedly so. But if you ignore the depth-meanings of religion, what you have left is not religion at all, but sabbatical play-acting. Prayer and worship can be justified as psychic therapy only if the postulant and worshiper believes that his utterance is somehow heard and somehow responded to. Now it is possible of course—I mean it is *logically* possible—that the religious believer is mistaken, and that his conviction of entering into a responsive relationship with a Power or Powers transcending the human condition is illusory. Whether transcendental existence and men's intercommunication with it are real or illusory is, as Pascal demonstrated, the most important question of all; and it cannot be settled by ruling out all answers but one as "meaningless." An adequate semantic organon should make it possible to formulate *both* theses—the religious and the anti-religious—intelligibly. A semantic theory which denies meaning to any and all specifically religious affirmations thereby prevents us from inquiring and discussing whether particular religious affirmations are true or false. Its denial of their meaning is a disguised way of rejecting their truth—claims *a priori*, and thus of prejudging the question of religious truth wholesale.

The other and more analytic objection to the Affective Theory concerns the presumed dichotomy on which it rests. Two types or modes or uses of discourse are sharply distinguished: typically called the referential and the emotive. Referential statements, as the previous exposition has shown, are postulated or defined to be true insofar as they correspond with, and truly describe, what is actually the case, false insofar as they do the contrary; and it is further postulated that in all instances of a referential statement it is possible to specify the empirical conditions under which it could be verified or disproved. Emotive discourse, on the other hand, is taken as expressing some emotive-conative state of the writer (or speaker) or as aiming to arouse such a state in the reader (or hearer), and therefore as not being intrinsically referential. The unguarded inference from "intrinsically emotive" to "not intrinsically referential" reveals the main logical presupposition of the Affective Theory: that language which is intrinsically the one cannot be intrinsically the other; that the terms "referential" and "emotive" (or their synonyms) constitute a natural dichotomy. This is a presupposition which must now be challenged.

For clarity it should be noted that ordinary "mixed discourse," which semanticists of all schools admit as a familiar possibility, is not what I am speaking about. A cry of "Fire!" for instance simultaneously conveys information—i.e., refers to an actual state of affairs—and expresses and communicates an emotive attitude. But the relation here between the two functions is extrinsic. The test of its extrinsicality is a simple one: the referential meaning can be explicated in propositional non-emotive form without loss. "A fire has broken out in this building," perhaps with some such corollary as "There is danger" or "There is need of immediate action"—this conveys virtually the same information as the original outcry, and indeed conveys it more exactly. In the case of poetic, and more generally of expressive discourse, on the contrary, such prosaic restatement is not possible without essential loss. My thesis is that truly expressive symbolism—in a poem, for example—means, refers, awakens insight, *in and through* the emotions which it engenders, and that so far as the emotion is not aroused the full insight is correspondingly not awakened. Granted that irrelevant emotions may be aroused, still the problem of learning to know and understand a poem is largely also the problem of distinguishing the relevant from the irrelevant—of distinguishing, that is to say, the responses aroused by the whole poem's intrinsic emotivity from the incidental responses aroused by isolated parts and fortuitous associations. In religious insight, too, (as distinguished from blind acceptance on the one hand and from theological ratiocination on the other) emotion may play a legitimate role. But it is of utmost importance to distinguish the quality of emotion which reveals some aspect of the Divine from the quality of emotion which obscures and confuses; the clarifying act of self-transcending reverence from the muck and muddle of self-deluding religiosity. In short, I am asserting that poetic and religious emotions, when they are depth-oriented, may have or come to have distinctively ontological bearings of their own. Whether one agrees or disagrees with this thesis, it is not a new or trifling one, and it ought not to be ruled out by the apriori maneuver of setting up a dichotomy that leaves no room for it.

Let us therefore reopen the logical possibilities of the situation by conceiving "referential" and "emotive" not as contraries but as independent variables.

The negative of *referential* is not emotive but *non-referential*; the negative of *emotive* is not referential but *non-emotive*. This logical truism enables us to construct a two-dimensional graph in which the vertical axis has "referential" (R) and "non-referential" (non-R) as its poles, the horizontal axis "emotive" (E) and "non-emotive" (non-E).

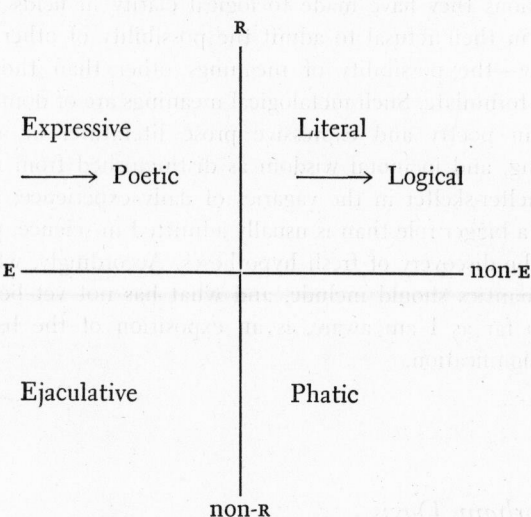

MODES OF DISCOURSE

Four areas are thus established, representing four modes of discourse:

R, non-E: *Literal discourse:* ordinary everyday language in its referential mode. *Logical discourse* is its ideally perfected form.

Non-R, non-E: *Phatic discourse:* "good morning," etc.

Non-R, E: *Ejaculative discourse:* "damn!" etc.—where, as distingushed from phatic discourse, something is really felt. For clarity's sake we must avoid the practice of some semanticists, of applying the word "expressive" in this connection.

R, E: *Expressive discourse:* language which is referential and emotive at once —not by incidental conjunction as in the cry of "Fire!" but in the more organic sense that the referential function, the proper meaning, takes at least some of its essential character from the emotivity of the language, and changes therefore as the emotivity changes. *Poetic discourse* is a species of expressive discourse, in which the main part of the meaning is controlled by the poet's art rather than by social custom and fortuitous association.

What I am proposing, in short, is a sort of Copernican Revolution in semantics. Or perhaps non-Euclidean, or trans-Euclidean, would offer an apter analogy. For whereas Euclidean geometry was once regarded as the be-all and end-all of geometrical truth, modern mathematicians are able to regard a world in which the postulate of parallels holds true, as merely a *limiting case* (perhaps also an actual one) in the universe of possibilities. Analogously, we may regard the semantic positivists as residing too doggedly in a Euclidean-like world. The aim, the instrument, and the presuppositions of logical discourse, as developed by the formal and experimental sciences, they accept without serious question. And my belief is that they are wrong, dead wrong—not of course in the contributions they have made to logical clarity in fields where it suitably belongs, but in their refusal to admit the possibility of other kinds of semantic objectivity—the possibility of meanings other than those which logical language can formulate. Such metalogical meanings are of dominant importance in religion, in poetry and expressive prose literature, in all the arts that "say" anything, and in moral wisdom as distinguished from moral rules; they are present helter-skelter in the vagaries of daily experience; and they even, I suspect, play a bigger role than is usually admitted in science, particularly when it comes to the discovery of fresh hypotheses. Accordingly, what any adequate theory of semantics should include, and what has not yet been systematically attempted so far as I am aware, is an exposition of the basic principles of metalogical signification.

❧ ❧ ❧

*Robert Gorham Davis*

# Logical Fallacies [1]

## UNDEFINED TERMS

THE first requirement for logical discourse is knowing what the words you use actually mean. Words are not like paper money or counters in a game. Except for technical terms in some of the sciences, they do not have a fixed face value. Their meanings are fluid and changing, influenced by many considerations of context and reference, circumstance and association. This is just as true of common words such as *fast* as it is of literary terms such as *romantic*. Moreover, if there is to be communication, words must have approximately the same meaning for the reader that they have for the writer. A speech in an unknown language means nothing to the hearer. When an adult speaks to a small child or an expert to a layman, communication may be seriously limited by lack of a mature vocabulary or ignorance of technical terms. Many arguments are meaningless because the speakers are using important words in quite different senses.

Because we learn most words—or guess at them—from the contexts in which we first encounter them, our sense of them is often incomplete or wrong. Read-

[1] From *Handbook for English A*, Harvard University, 1941, pp. 58-66. Reprinted by permission of Theodore Morrison and Robert Gorham Davis.

ers sometimes visualize the Assyrian who comes down like the wolf on fold as an enormous man dressed in cohorts (some kind of fancy armor, possibly) gleaming in purple and gold. "A rift in the lute" suggests vaguely a cracked mandolin. Failure to ascertain the literal meaning of figurative language is a frequent reason for mixed metaphors. We are surprised to find that the "devil" in "the devil to pay" and "the devil and the deep blue sea" is not Old Nick, but part of a ship. Unless terms mean the same thing to both writer and reader, proper understanding is impossible.

## ABSTRACTIONS

The most serious logical difficulties occur with abstract terms. An abstraction is a word which stands for a quality found in a number of different objects or events from which it has been "abstracted" or taken away. We may, for instance, talk of the "whiteness" of paper or cotton or snow without considering qualities of cold or inflammability or usefulness which these materials happen also to possess. Usually, however, our minds carry over other qualities by association. See, for instance, the chapter called "The Whiteness of the Whale" in *Moby Dick*.

In much theoretic discussion the process of abstraction is carried so far that although vague associations and connotations persist, the original objects or events from which the qualities have been abstracted are lost sight of completely. Instead of thinking of words like *sincerity* and *Americanism* as symbols standing for qualities that have to be abstracted with great care from examples and test cases, we come to think of them as real things in themselves. We assume that Americanism is Americanism just as a bicycle is a bicycle, and that everyone knows what it means. We forget that before the question, "Is Father Coughlin sincere?" can mean anything, we have to agree on the criteria of sincerity.

When we try to define such words and find examples, we discover that almost no one agrees on their meaning. The word *church* may refer to anything from a building on the corner of Spring Street to the whole tradition of institutionalized Christianity. *Germany* may mean a geographical section of Europe, a people, a governing group, a cultural tradition, or a military power. Abstractions such as *freedom, courage, race, beauty, truth, justice, nature, honor, humanism, democracy,* should never be used in a theme unless their meaning is defined or indicated clearly by the context. Freedom for whom? To do what? Under what circumstances? Abstract terms have merely emotional value unless they are strictly defined by asking questions of this kind. The study of a word such as *nature* in a good unabridged dictionary will show that even the dictionary, indispensable though it is, cannot determine for us the sense in which a word is being used in any given instance. Once the student understands the importance of definition, he will no longer be betrayed into fruitless arguments over such questions as whether free verse is "poetry" or whether you can change "human nature."

## NAME-CALLING

It is a common unfairness in controversy to place what the writer dislikes or opposes in a generally odious category. The humanist dismisses what he dislikes by calling it *romantic;* the liberal, by calling it *fascist;* the conservative, by calling it *communistic.* These terms tell the reader nothing. What is *piety* to some will be *bigotry* to others. *Non-Catholics* would rather be called *Protestants* than *heretics.* What is *right-thinking* except a designation for those who agree with the writer? Labor leaders become *outside agitators;* industrial organizations, *forces of reaction;* the Child Labor Amendment, the *youth control bill;* prison reform, *coddling;* progressive education, *fads and frills.* Such terms are intended to block thought by an appeal to prejudice and associative habits. Three steps are necessary before such epithets have real meaning. First, they must be defined; second, it must be shown that the object to which they are applied actually possesses these qualities; third, it must be shown that the possession of such qualities in this particular situation is necessarily undesirable. Unless a person is alert and critical both in choosing and in interpreting words, he may be alienated from ideas with which he would be in sympathy if he had not been frightened by a mere name.

### GENERALIZATION

Similar to the abuse of abstract terms and epithets is the habit of presenting personal opinions in the guise of universal laws. The student often seems to feel that the broader the terms in which he states an opinion, the more effective he will be. Ordinarily the reverse is true. An enthusiasm for Thomas Wolfe should lead to a specific critical analysis of Wolfe's novels that will enable the writer to explain his enthusiasm to others; it should not be turned into the argument that Wolfe is "the greatest American novelist," particularly if the writer's knowledge of American novelists is somewhat limited. The same questions of *who* and *when* and *why* and under what *circumstances* which are used to check abstract terms should be applied to generalizations. Consider how contradictory proverbial wisdom is when detached from particular circumstances. "Look before you leap," but "he who hesitates is lost."

Superlatives and the words *right* and *wrong, true* and *untrue, never* and *always* must be used with caution in matters of opinion. When a student says flatly that X is true, he often is really saying that he or his family or the author of a book he has just been reading, persons of certain tastes and background and experience, *think* that X is true. Unless these people are identified and their reasons for thinking so explained, the assertion is worthless. Because many freshmen are taking survey courses in which they read a single work by an author or see an historical event through the eyes of a single historian whose bias they may not be able to measure, they must guard against this error.

## SAMPLING

Assertions of a general nature are frequently open to question because they are based on insufficient evidence. Some persons are quite ready, after meeting one Armenian or reading one medieval romance, to generalize about Armenians and medieval romances. One ought, of course, to examine objectively as many examples as possible before making a generalization, but the number is less important than the representativeness of the examples chosen. The Literary Digest Presidential Poll, sent to hundreds of thousands of people selected from telephone directories, was far less accurate than the Gallup Poll which questioned far fewer voters, but selected them carefully and proportionately from all different social groups. The "typical" college student, as portrayed by moving pictures and cartoons, is very different from the "representative" college student as determined statistically. We cannot let uncontrolled experience do our sampling for us; instances and examples which impress themselves upon our minds do so usually because they are exceptional. In propaganda and arguments extreme cases are customarily treated as if they were characteristic.

If one is permitted arbitrarily to select some examples and ignore others, it is possible to find convincing evidence for almost any theory, no matter how fantastic. The fact that the mind tends naturally to remember those instances which confirm its opinions imposes a duty upon the writer, unless he wishes to encourage prejudice and superstition, to look carefully for exceptions to all generalizations which he is tempted to make. We forget the premonitions which are not followed by disaster and the times when our hunches failed to select the winner in a race. Patent medicine advertisements print the letters of those who survived their cure, and not of those who died during it. All Americans did not gamble on the stock exchange in the twenties, and all Vermonters are not thin-lipped and shrewd. Of course the search for negative examples can be carried too far. Outside of mathematics or the laboratory, few generalizations can be made airtight, and most are not intended to be. But quibbling is so easy that resort to it is very common, and the knowledge that people can and will quibble over generalizations is another reason for making assertions as limited and explicitly conditional as possible.

## FALSE ANALOGY

Illustration, comparison, analogy are most valuable in making an essay clear and interesting. It must not be supposed, however, that they prove anything or have much argumentative weight. The rule that what is true of one thing in one set of circumstances is not necessarily true of another thing in another set of circumstances seems almost too obvious to need stating. Yet constantly nations and businesses are discussed as if they were human beings with human habits and feelings; human bodies are discussed as if they were machines; the universe, as if it were a clock. It is assumed that what held true for seventeenth century New England or the thirteen Atlantic colonies also holds true for an industrial nation of 130,000,000 people. Carlyle dismissed the arguments for representative democracy by saying that if a captain had to take a vote among his crew every time he wanted to do something, he would never get around Cape Horn. This analogy calmly ignores the distinction between the lawmaking and the executive branches of constitutional democracies. Moreover, voters may be considered much more like the stockholders of a merchant line than its hired sailors. Such arguments introduce assumptions in a metaphorical guise in which they are not readily detected or easily criticized. In place of analysis they attempt to identify their position with some familiar symbol which will evoke a predictable, emotional response in the reader. The revival during the 1932 presidential campaign of Lincoln's remark, "Don't swap horses in the middle of the stream," was not merely a picturesque way of saying keep Hoover in the White House. It made a number of assumptions about the nature of depressions and the function of government. This propagandist technique can be seen most clearly in political cartoons.

## DEGREE

Often differences in degree are more important than differences in kind. By legal and social standards there is more difference between an habitual drunkard and a man who drinks temperately, than between a temperate drinker and a total abstainer. In fact differences of degree produce what are regarded as differences of kind. At known temperatures ice turns to water and water boils. At an indeterminate point affection becomes love and a man who needs a shave becomes a man with a beard. The fact that no men or systems are perfect makes rejoinders and counter-accusations very easy if differences in degree are ignored. Newspapers in totalitarian states, answering American accusations of brutality and suppression, refer to lynchings and gangsterism here. Before a disinterested judge could evaluate these mutual accusations, he would have to settle the question of the degree to which violent suppression and lynching are respectively prevalent in the countries under consideration. On the other hand, differences in degree may be merely apparent. Lincoln Steffens pointed out that newspapers can create a "crime wave" any time they wish, simply by emphasizing all the minor assaults and thefts commonly ignored or given an inch or two on a back page. The great reported increases in insanity may be due to the fact that in a more urban and institutionalized society cases of insanity more frequently come to the attention of authorities and hence are recorded in statistics.

## CAUSATION

The most common way of deciding that one thing causes another thing is the simple principle: *post hoc, ergo propter hoc,* "After this, therefore because of this." Rome fell after the introduction of Christianity; therefore Christianity was responsible for the fall of Rome. Such reasoning illustrates another kind of faulty generalization. But even if one could find ten cases in which a nation "fell" after the introduction of Christianity, it still would not be at all certain that Christianity caused the fall. Day, it has frequently been pointed out, follows night in every observable instance, and yet night cannot be called the cause of day. Usually a combination of causes produces a result. Sitting in a draught may cause a cold, but only given a certain physical condition in the person sitting there. In such instances one may distinguish between necessary and sufficient conditions. Air is a necessary condition for the maintenance of plant life, but air alone is not sufficient to produce plant life. And often different causes at different times may produce the same result. This relation is known as plurality of causes. If, after sitting in a stuffy theatre on Monday, and then again after eating in a stuffy restaurant on Thursday, a man suffered from headaches, he might say, generalizing, that bad air gave him headaches. But actually the headache on Monday may have been caused by eye-strain and on Thursday by indigestion. To isolate the causative factor it is necessary that all other conditions be precisely the same. Such isolation is possible, except in very simple instances, only in the laboratory or with scientific methods. If a picture falls from the wall every time a truck passes, we can quite certainly say that the truck's passing is the cause. But with anything as complex and conditional as a nation's economy or human character, the determination of cause is not easy or certain. A psychiatrist often sees a patient for an hour daily for a year or more before he feels that he understands his psychosis.

Ordinarily when we speak of cause we mean the proximate or immediate cause. The plants were killed by frost; we had indigestion from eating lobster salad. But any single cause is one in an unbroken series. When a man is murdered, is his death caused by the loss of blood from the wound, or by the firing of the pistol, or by the malice aforethought of the murderer? Was the World War "caused" by the assassination at Sarajevo? Were the Navigation Acts or the ideas of John Locke more important in "causing" the American Revolution? A complete statement of cause would comprise the sum total of the conditions which preceded an event, conditions stretching back indefinitely into the past. Historical events are so interrelated that the isolation of a causative sequence is dependent chiefly on the particular preoccupations of the historian. An economic determinist can "explain" history entirely in terms of economic developments; an idealist, entirely in terms of the development of ideas.

### SYLLOGISTIC REASONING

The formal syllogism of the type,

> All men are mortal
> John is a man
> Therefore John is mortal,

is not so highly regarded today as in some earlier periods. It merely fixes an individual as a member of a class, and then assumes that the individual has the given characteristics of the class. Once we have decided who John is, and what "man" and "mortal" mean, and have canvassed all men, including John, to make sure that they are mortal, the conclusion naturally follows. It can be seen that the chief difficulties arise in trying to establish acceptable premises. Faults in the premises are known as "material" fallacies, and are usually more serious than the "formal" fallacies, which are logical defects in drawing a conclusion from the premises. But although directly syllogistic reasoning is not much practiced, buried syllogisms can be found in all argument, and it is often a useful clarification to outline your own or another writer's essay in syllogistic form. The two most frequent defects in the syllogism itself are the undistributed and the ambiguous middle. The middle term is the one that appears in each of the premises and not in the conclusion. In the syllogism,

> All good citizens vote
> John votes
> Therefore John is a good citizen,

the middle term is not "good citizens," but "votes." Even though it were true that all good citizens vote, nothing prevents bad citizens from voting also, and John may be one of the bad citizens. To distribute the middle term "votes" one might say (but only if that is what one meant),

> All voters are good citizens
> John is a voter
> Therefore John is a good citizen.

The ambiguous middle term is even more common. It represents a problem in definition, while the undistributed middle is a problem in generalization. All acts which benefit others are virtuous, losing money at poker benefits others, therefore losing at poker is a virtuous act. Here the middle term "act which benefits others" is obviously used very loosely and ambiguously.

## NON-SEQUITUR

This phrase, meaning "it does not follow," is used to characterize the kind of humor found in pictures in which the Marx Brothers perform. It is an amusing illogicality because it usually expresses, beneath its apparent incongruity, an imaginative, associative, or personal truth. "My ancestors came over on the Mayflower; therefore I am naturally opposed to labor unions." It is not logically necessary that those whose ancestors came over on the Mayflower should be opposed to unions; but it may happen to be true as a personal fact in a given case. Contemporary psychologists have effectively shown us that there is often such a wide difference between the true and the purported reasons for an attitude that, in rationalizing our behavior, we are often quite unconscious of the motives that actually influence us. A fanatical antivivisectionist, for instance, may have temperamental impulses toward cruelty which he is suppressing and compensating for by a reasoned opposition to any kind of permitted suffering. We may expect, then, to come upon many conclusions which are psychologically interesting in themselves, but have nothing to do with the given premises.

### IGNORATIO ELENCHI

This means, in idiomatic English, "arguing off the point," or ignoring the question at issue. A man trying to show that monarchy is the best form of government for the British Empire may devote most of his attention to the character of George V and the affection his people felt for him. In ordinary conversational argument it is almost impossible for disputants to keep to the point. Constantly turning up are tempting side-issues through which one can discomfit an opponent or force him to irrelevant admissions that seem to weaken his case.

### BEGGING THE QUESTION; ARGUING IN A CIRCLE

The first of these terms means to assume in the premises what you are pretending to prove in the course of your argument. The function of logic is to demonstrate that because one thing or group of things is true, another must be true as a consequence. But in begging the question you simply say in varying language that what is assumed to be true is assumed to be true. An argument which asserts that we shall enjoy immortality because we have souls which are immaterial and indestructible establishes nothing, because the idea of immortality is already contained in the assumption about the soul. It is the premise which needs to be demonstrated, not the conclusion. Arguing in a circle is another form of this fallacy. It proves the premise by the conclusion and the conclusion by the premise. The conscience forbids an act because it is wrong; the act is wrong because the conscience forbids it.

### ARGUMENTS AD HOMINEM AND AD POPULUM

It is very difficult for men to be persuaded by reason when their interest or prestige is at stake. If one wishes to preach the significance of physiognomy, it is well to choose a hearer with a high forehead and a determined jaw. The arguments in favor of repealing the protective tariff on corn or wheat in England were more readily entertained by manufacturers than by landowners. The cotton manufacturers in New England who were doing a profitable trade with the South were the last to be moved by descriptions of the evils of slavery. Because interest and desire are so deeply seated in human nature, arguments are frequently mingled with attempts to appeal to emotion, arouse fear, play upon pride, attack the characters of proponents of an opposite view, show that their practice is inconsistent with their principles; all matters which have, strictly speaking, nothing to do with the truth or falsity, the general desirability or undesirability, of some particular measure. If men are desperate enough they will listen to arguments proper only to an insane asylum but which seem to promise them relief.

After reading these suggestions, which are largely negative, the student may feel that any original assertion he can make will probably contain one or several logical faults. This assumption is not true. Even if it were, we know from reading newspapers and magazines that worldly fame is not dimmed by the constant and, one suspects, conscious practice of illogicality. But generalizations are not made only by charlatans and sophists. Intelligent and scrupulous writers also have a great many fresh and provocative observations and conclusions to express and are expressing them influentially. What is intelligence but the ability to see the connection between things, to discern causes, to relate the particular to the general, to define and discriminate and compare? Any man who thinks and feels and observes closely will not want for something to express.

And in his expression a proponent will find that a due regard for logic does not limit but rather increases the force of his argument. When statements are not trite, they are usually controversial. Men arrive at truth dialectically; error is weeded out in the course of discussion, argument, attack, and counter-attack. Not only can a writer who understands logic show the weaknesses of arguments he disagrees with, but also, by anticipating the kind of attack likely to be made on his own ideas, he can so arrange them, properly modified with qualifications and exceptions, that the anticipated attack is made much less effective. Thus, fortunately, we do not have to depend on the spirit of fairness and love of truth to lead men to logic; it has the strong support of argumentative necessity and of the universal desire to make ideas prevail.

🌣 🌣 🌣

*Francis Bacon*

# Idols of the Mind[1]

### XXXVIII

THE idols and false notions which are now in possession of the human understanding, and have taken deep root therein, not only so beset men's minds that truth can hardly find entrance, but even after entrance obtained, they will again in the very instauration of the sciences meet and trouble us, unless men being forewarned of the danger fortify themselves as far as may be against their assaults.

[1] From *The Works of Francis Bacon*, ed. by James Spedding, Robert Ellis, and Douglas Heath (New York: Hurd and Houghton, 1869), VIII, 76-90, "Novum Organum" (London, 1620).

XXXIX

There are four classes of Idols which beset men's minds. To these for distinction's sake I have assigned names,—calling the first class *Idols of the Tribe*; the second, *Idols of the Cave*; the third, *Idols of the Marketplace*; the fourth, *Idols of the Theatre*.

XL

The formation of ideas and axioms by true induction is no doubt the proper remedy to be applied for the keeping off and clearing away of idols. To point them out, however, is of great use; for the doctrine of Idols is to the Interpretation of Nature what the doctrine of the refutation of Sophisms is to common Logic.

XLI

The Idols of the Tribe have their foundation in human nature itself, and in the tribe or race of men. For it is a false assertion that the sense of man is the measure of things. On the contrary, all perceptions as well of the sense as of the mind are according to the measure of the individual and not according to the measure of the universe. And the human understanding is like a false mirror, which, receiving rays irregularly, distorts and discolours the nature of things by mingling its own nature with it.

XLII

The Idols of the Cave are the idols of the individual man. For every one (besides the errors common to human nature in general) has a cave or den of his own, which refracts and discolours the light of nature; owing either to his own proper and peculiar nature; or to his education and conversation with others; or to the reading of books, and the authority of those whom he esteems and admires; or to the differences of impressions, accordingly as they take place in a mind preoccupied and predisposed or in a mind indifferent and settled; or the like: So that the spirit of man (according as it is meted out to different individuals) is in fact a thing variable and full of perturbation, and governed as it were by chance. Whence it was well observed by Heraclitus that men look for sciences in their own lesser worlds, and not in the greater or common world.

XLIII

There are also Idols formed by the intercourse and association of men with each other, which I call Idols of the Marketplace, on account of the commerce and consort of men there. For it is by discourse that men associate; and words are imposed according to the apprehension of the vulgar. And therefore the ill and unfit choice of words wonderfully obstructs the understanding. Nor do the definitions or explanations wherewith in some things learned men are wont to guard and defend themselves, by any means set the matter right. But words plainly force and overrule the understanding, and throw all into confusion, and lead men away into numberless empty controversies and idle fancies.

## XLIV

Lastly, there are Idols which have immigrated into men's minds from the various dogmas of philosophies, and also from wrong laws of demonstration. These I call Idols of the Theatre; because in my judgment all the received systems are but so many stage-plays, representing worlds of their own creation after an unreal and scenic fashion. Nor is it only of the systems now in vogue, or only of the ancient sects and philosophies, that I speak; for many more plays of the same kind may yet be composed and in like artificial manner set forth; seeing that errors the most widely different have nevertheless causes for the most part alike. Neither again do I mean this only of entire systems, but also of many principles and axioms in science, which by tradition, credulity, and negligence have come to be received.

But of these several kinds of Idols I must speak more largely and exactly, that the understanding may be duly cautioned.

## XLV

The human understanding is of its own nature prone to suppose the existence of more order and regularity in the world than it finds. And though there be many things in nature which are singular and unmatched, yet it devises for them parallels and conjugates and relatives which do not exist. Hence the fiction that all celestial bodies move in perfect circles; spirals and dragons being (except in name) utterly rejected. Hence too the element of Fire with its orb is brought in, to make up the square with the other three which the sense perceives. Hence also the ratio of density of the so-called elements is arbitrarily fixed at ten to one. And so on of other dreams. And these fancies affect not dogmas only, but simple notions also.

## XLVI

The human understanding when it has once adopted an opinion (either as being the received opinion or as being agreeable to itself) draws all things else to support and agree with it. And though there be a greater number and weight of instances to be found on the other side, yet these it either neglects and despises, or else by some distinction sets aside and rejects; in order that by this great and pernicious predetermination the authority of its former conclusions may remain inviolate. And therefore it was a good answer that was made by one who when they showed him hanging in a temple a picture of those who had paid their vows as having escaped shipwreck, and would have him say whether he did not now acknowledge the power of the gods,——— "Aye," asked he again, "but where are they painted that were drowned after their vows?" And such is the way of all superstition, whether in astrology, dreams, omens, divine judgments, or the like; wherein men, having a delight in such vanities, mark the events where they are fulfilled, but where they fail, though this happen much oftener, neglect and pass them by. But with far more subtlety does this mischief insinuate itself into philosophy and the sciences; in which the first conclusion colours and brings into conformity with itself all that come after, though far sounder and better. Besides, independently of that delight and vanity which I have described, it is the peculiar and perpetual error of the human intellect to be more moved and excited by affirmatives than by negatives; whereas it ought properly to hold itself indifferently disposed towards both alike. Indeed in the establishment of any true axiom, the negative instance is the more forcible of the two.

### XLVII

The human understanding is moved by those things most which strike and enter the mind simultaneously and suddenly, and so fill the imagination; and then it feigns and supposes all other things to be somehow, though it cannot see how, similar to those few things by which it is surrounded. But for that going to and fro to remote and heterogeneous instances, by which axioms are tried as in the fire, the intellect is altogether slow and unfit, unless it be forced thereto by severe laws and overruling authority.

### XLVIII

The human understanding is unquiet; it cannot stop or rest, and still presses onward, but in vain. Therefore it is that we cannot conceive of any end or limit to the world; but always as of necessity it occurs to us that there is something beyond. Neither again can it be conceived how eternity has flowed down to the present day; for that distinction which is commonly received of infinity in time past and in time to come can by no means hold; for it would thence follow that one infinity is greater than another, and that infinity is wasting away and tending to become finite. The like subtlety arises touching the infinite divisibility of lines, from the same inability of thought to stop. But this inability interferes more mischievously in the discovery of causes; for although the most general principles in nature ought to be held merely positive, as they are discovered, and cannot with truth be referred to a cause; nevertheless the human understanding being unable to rest still seeks something prior in the order of nature. And then it is that in struggling towards that which is further off it falls back upon that which is more nigh at hand; namely, on final causes: which have relation clearly to the nature of man rather than to the nature of the universe; and from this source have strangely defiled philosophy. But he is no less an unskilled and shallow philosopher who seeks causes of that which is most general, than he who in things subordinate and subaltern omits to do so.

## XLIX

The human understanding is no dry light, but receives an infusion from the will and affections; whence proceed sciences which may be called "sciences as one would." For what a man had rather were true he more readily believes. Therefore he rejects difficult things from impatience of research; sober things, because they narrow hope; the deeper things of nature, from superstition; the light of experience, from arrogance and pride, lest his mind should seem to be occupied with things mean and transitory; things not commonly believed, out of deference to the opinion of the vulgar. Numberless in short are the ways, and sometimes imperceptible, in which the affections colour and infect the understanding.

## L

But by far the greatest hindrance and aberration of the human understanding proceeds from the dullness, incompetency, and deceptions of the senses; in that things which strike the sense outweigh things which do not immediately strike it, though they be more important. Hence it is that speculation commonly ceases where sight ceases; insomuch that of things invisible there is little or no observation. Hence all the working of the spirits inclosed in tangible bodies lies hid and unobserved of men. So also all the more subtle changes of form in the parts of coarser substances (which they commonly call alteration, though it is in truth local motion through exceedingly small spaces) is in like manner unobserved. And yet unless these two things just mentioned be searched out and brought to light, nothing great can be achieved in nature, as far as the production of works is concerned. So again the essential nature of our common air, and of all bodies less dense than air (which are very many), is almost unknown. For the sense by itself is a thing infirm and erring; neither can instruments for enlarging or sharpening the senses do much; but all the truer kind of interpretation of nature is effected by instances and experiments fit and apposite; wherein the sense decides touching the experiment only, and the experiment touching the point in nature and the thing itself.

## LI

The human understanding is of its own nature prone to abstractions and gives a substance and reality to things which are fleeting. But to resolve nature into abstractions is less to our purpose than to dissect her into parts; as did the school of Democritus, which went further into nature than the rest. Matter rather than forms should be the object of our attention, its configurations and changes of configuration, and simple action, and law of action or motion; for forms are figments of the human mind, unless you will call those laws of action forms.

## LII

Such then are the idols which I call *Idols of the Tribe*; and which take their rise either from the homogeneity of the substance of the human spirit, or from its preoccupation, or from its narrowness, or from its restless motion, or from an infusion of the affections, or from the incompetency of the senses, or from the mode of impression.

## LIII

The *Idols of the Cave* take their rise in the peculiar constitution, mental or bodily, of each individual; and also in education, habit, and accident. Of this kind there is a great number and variety; but I will instance those the pointing out of which contains the most important caution, and which have most effect in disturbing the clearness of the understanding.

## LIV

Men become attached to certain particular sciences and speculations, either because they fancy themselves the authors and inventors thereof, or because they have bestowed the greatest pains upon them and become most habituated to them. But men of this kind, if they betake themselves to philosophy and contemplations of a general character, distort and colour them in obedience to their former fancies; a thing especially to be noticed in Aristotle, who made his natural philosophy a mere bond-servant to his logic, thereby rendering it contentious and well nigh useless. The race of chemists again out of a few experiments of the furnace have built up a fantastic philosophy, framed with reference to a few things; and Gilbert also, after he had employed himself most laboriously in the study and observation of the loadstone, proceeded at once to construct an entire system in accordance with his favourite subject.

## LV

There is one principal and as it were radical distinction between different minds, in respect of philosophy and the sciences; which is this: that some minds are stronger and apter to mark the differences of things, others to mark their resemblances. The steady and acute mind can fix its contemplations and dwell and fasten on the subtlest distinctions: the lofty and discursive mind recognises and puts together the finest and most general resemblances. Both kinds however easily err in excess, by catching the one at gradations the other at shadows.

## LVI

There are found some minds given to an extreme admiration of antiquity, others to an extreme love and appetite for novelty; but few so duly tempered that they can hold the mean, neither carping at what has been well laid down by the ancients, nor despising what is well introduced by the moderns.

This however turns to the great injury of the sciences and philosophy; since these affectations of antiquity and novelty are the humours of partisans rather than judgments; and truth is to be sought for not in the felicity of any age, which is an unstable thing, but in the light of nature and experience, which is eternal. These factions therefore must be abjured, and care must be taken that the intellect be not hurried by them into assent.

## LVII

Contemplations of nature and of bodies in their simple form break up and distract the understanding, while contemplations of nature and bodies in their composition and configuration overpower and dissolve the understanding: a distinction well seen in the school of Leucippus and Democritus as compared with the other philosophies. For that school is so busied with the particles that it hardly attends to the structure; while the others are so lost in admiration of the structure that they do not penetrate to the simplicity of nature. These kinds of contemplation should therefore be alternated and taken by turns; that so the understanding may be rendered at once penetrating and comprehensive, and the inconveniences above mentioned, with the idols which proceed from them, may be avoided.

## LVIII

Let such then be our provision and contemplative prudence for keeping off and dislodging the *Idols of the Cave*, which grow for the most part either out of the predominance of a favourite subject, or out of an excessive tendency to compare or to distinguish, or out of partiality for particular ages, or out of the largeness or minuteness of the objects contemplated. And generally let every student of nature take this as a rule,—that whatever his mind seizes and dwells upon with peculiar satisfaction is to be held in suspicion, and that so much the more care is to be taken in dealing with such questions to keep the understanding even and clear.

## LIX

But the *Idols of the Marketplace* are the most troublesome of all: idols which have crept into the understanding through the alliances of words and names. For men believe that their reason governs words; but it is also true that words react on the understanding; and this it is that has rendered philosophy and the sciences sophistical and inactive. Now words, being commonly framed and applied according to the capacity of the vulgar, follow those lines of division which are most obvious to the vulgar understanding. And whenever an understanding of greater acuteness or a more diligent observation would alter those lines to suit the true divisions of nature, words stand in the way and resist the change. Whence it comes to pass that the high and formal discussions of learned men end oftentimes in disputes about words and names; with which (according to the use and wisdom of the mathematicians) it would be more prudent to begin, and so by means of definitions reduce them to order. Yet even definitions cannot cure this evil in dealing with natural and material things; since the definitions themselves consist of words, and those words beget others: so that it is necessary to recur to individual instances, and those in due series and order; as I shall say presently when I come to the method and scheme for the formation of notions and axioms.

## LX

The idols imposed by words on the understanding are of two kinds. They are either names of things which do not exist (for as there are things left unnamed through lack of observation, so likewise are there names which result from fantastic suppositions and to which nothing in reality corresponds), or they are names of things which exist, but yet confused and ill-defined, and hastily and irregularly derived from realities. Of the former kind are Fortune, the Prime Mover, Planetary Orbits, Element of Fire, and like fictions which owe their origin to false and idle theories. And this class of idols is more easily expelled, because to get rid of them it is only necessary that all theories should be steadily rejected and dismissed as obsolete.

But the other class, which springs out of a faulty and unskilful abstraction, is intricate and deeply rooted. Let us take for example such a word as *humid*; and see how far the several things which the word is used to signify agree with each other; and we shall find the word *humid* to be nothing else than a mark loosely and confusedly applied to denote a variety of actions which will not bear to be reduced to any constant meaning. For it both signifies that which easily spreads itself round any other body; and that which in itself is indeterminate and cannot solidise; and that which readily yields in every direction; and that which easily divides and scatters itself; and that which easily unites and collects itself; and that which readily flows and is put in motion; and that which readily clings to another body and wets it; and that which is easily reduced to a liquid, or being solid easily melts. Accordingly when you come to apply the word,—if you take it in one sense, flame is humid; if in another, air is not humid; if in another, fine dust is humid; if in another, glass is humid. So that it is easy to see that the notion is taken by abstraction only from water and common and ordinary liquids, without any due verification.

There are however in words certain degrees of distortion and error. One of the least faulty kinds is that of names of substances, especially of lowest species and well-deduced (for the notion of *chalk* and of *mud* is good, of *earth* bad); a more faulty kind is that of actions, as *to generate, to corrupt, to alter*; the most faulty is of qualities (except such as are the immediate objects of the sense) as *heavy, light, rare, dense,* and the like. Yet in all these cases some notions are of necessity a little better than others, in proportion to the greater variety of subjects that fall within the range of the human sense.

But the *Idols of the Theatre* are not innate, nor do they steal into the understanding secretly, but are plainly impressed and received into the mind from the play-books of philosophical systems and the perverted rules of demonstration. To attempt refutations in this case would be merely inconsistent with what I have already said: for since we agree neither upon principles nor upon demonstrations there is no place for argument. And this is so far well, inasmuch as it leaves the honour of the ancients untouched. For they are no wise disparaged—the question between them and me being only as to the way. For as the saying is, the lame man who keeps the right road outstrips the runner who takes a wrong one. Nay it is obvious that when a man runs the wrong way, the more active and swift he is the further he will go astray.

But the course I propose for the discovery of sciences is such as leaves but little to the acuteness and strength of wits, but places all wits and understandings nearly on a level. For as in the drawing of a straight line or a perfect circle, much depends on the steadiness and practice of the hand, if it be done by aim of hand only, but if with the aid of rule or compass, little or nothing: so is it exactly with my plan. But though particular confutations would be of no avail, yet touching the sects and general divisions of such systems I must say something; something also touching the external signs which show that they are unsound; and finally something touching the causes of such great infelicity and of such lasting and general agreement in error; that so the access to truth may be made less difficult, and the human understanding may the more willingly submit to its purgation and dismiss its idols.

# ❧ ❧ ❧ IV. The Arts

# The Fine Arts

*Susanne K. Langer*

## The Cultural Importance of the Arts[1]

EVERY CULTURE develops some kind of art as surely as it develops language. Some primitive cultures have no real mythology or religion, but all have some art—dance, song, design (sometimes only on tools or on the human body). Above all, dance; that seems to be the oldest elaborated art.

The ancient ubiquitous character of art contrasts sharply with the prevalent idea that art is a luxury product of civilization, a cultural frill, a piece of social veneer.

It fits better with the conviction held by most artists, that art is the epitome of human life, the truest record of insight and feeling, and that the strongest military or economic society without art is poor in comparison with the most primitive tribe of savage painters, dancers, or idol-carvers. Wherever a society has really achieved culture (in the ethnological, not the popular sense of social form) it has begotten art, not late in its career, but at the very inception of it.

Art is, indeed, the spearhead of human development, social and individual. The vulgarization of art is the surest symptom of ethnic decline. The growth of a new art or even a great and radically new style always bespeaks a young and vigorous mind, whether collective or single.

What sort of thing is art, that it should play such a leading role in human development? It is not an intellectual pursuit, but is necessary to intellectual life; it is not religion, but grows up with religion, serves it and in large measure determines it (as Herodotus said, "Homer made the gods," and surely the Egyptian deities grew under the chisels of sculptors in strangely solemn forms).

We cannot enter here on a long discussion of what has been claimed as the essence of art, the true nature of art, or its defining function; in a single lecture dealing with one aspect of art, namely its cultural influence, I can only give you by way of preamble my own definition of art, with categorical

[1] From *Problems of Art: Ten Philosophical Lectures* by Susanne Langer, copyright 1957 by Susanne Langer. Used by permission of Charles Scribner's Sons.

brevity. That does not mean that I set up this definition in a categorical spirit, but only that we have no time to debate it, so you are asked to accept it as an assumption underlying these reflections.

Art, in the sense here intended—that is, the generic term subsuming painting, sculpture, architecture, music, dance, literature and drama—may be defined as the practice of creating perceptible forms expressive of human feeling. I say "perceptible" rather than "sensuous" forms because some works of art are given to imagination rather than to the outward senses. A novel, for instance, usually is read silently with the eye, but is not made for vision, as a painting is; and though sound plays a vital part in poetry, words even in poetry are not essentially sonorous structures like music. Dance requires to be seen, but its appeal is to deeper centers of sensation. The difference between dance and mobile sculpture makes this immediately apparent. But all works of art are purely perceptible forms that seem to embody some sort of feeling.

"Feeling" as I am using it here covers much more than it does in the technical vocabulary of psychology, where it denotes only pleasure and pain, or even in the shifting limits of ordinary discourse, where it sometimes means sensation (as when one says a paralyzed limb has no feeling in it), sometimes sensibility (as we speak of hurting someone's feelings), sometimes emotion (e.g., as a situation is said to harrow your feeling, or to evoke tender feeling), or a directed emotional attitude (we say we feel strongly *about* something), or even our general mental or physical condition, feeling well or ill, blue, or a bit above ourselves. As I use the word, in defining art as the creation of perceptible forms expressive of human feeling, it takes in all those meanings; it applies to *everything that may be felt.*

Another word in the definition that might be questioned is "creation." I think it is justified, not pretentious, as perhaps it sounds; but that issue is slightly beside the point here, so let us shelve it. If anyone prefers to speak of the "making" or "construction" of expressive forms that will do here just as well.

What does have to be understood is the meaning of "form," and more particularly "expressive form"; for that involves the very nature of art and therefore the question of its cultural importance.

The word "form" has several current uses; most of them have some relation to the sense in which I am using it here, though a few, such as: "a *form* to be filled in for tax purposes," or "a mere matter of form," are fairly remote, being quite specialized. Since we are speaking of art, it might be good to point out that the meaning of *stylistic patter*—"the sonata form," "the sonnet form"—is not the one I am assuming here. I am using the word in a simpler sense, which it has when you say, on a foggy night, that you see dimly moving forms in the mist; one of them emerges clearly, and is the form of a man. The trees are gigantic forms; the rills of rain trace sinuous forms on the window pane. The rills are not fixed things; they are forms of motion.

When you watch gnats weaving in the air, or flocks of birds wheeling over-head, you see dynamic forms—forms made by motion.

It is in this sense of an apparition given to our perception, that a work of art is a form. It may be a permanent form like a building or a vase or a picture, or a transient, dynamic form like a melody or a dance, or even a form given to imagination, like the passage of purely imaginary, apparent events that con-stitutes a literary work. But it is always a perceptible, self-identical whole; like a natural being, it has a character of organic unity, self-sufficiency, individual reality. And it is thus, as an appearance, that a work of art is good or bad or perhaps only rather poor; as an appearance, not as a comment on things beyond it in the world, nor as a reminder of them.

This, then, is what I mean by "form"; but what is meant by calling such forms "expressive of human feeling"? How do apparitions "express" any-thing—feeling, or anything else? First of all, let us ask just what is meant here by "express"; what sort of "expression" we are talking about.

Most people believe that music and poetry are expressions of emotion, and will further agree that a picture is a glimpse of reality seen through a temperament. Even a Gothic cathedral is supposed to express the religious emotions of its countless, anonymous builders. Its age makes the process indistinct enough to put it beyond very searching question. But it is harder to imagine how a modern office building or a fine, flung-out overpass across a highway—an architectural work of art, as many of our offices and ramps and bridges are—could be, in any essential way, an expression of its designer's emotion or state of mind. To treat it just like a lyric or an easel picture seems a bit silly.

The incongruity, however, points to a misunderstanding that becomes ap-parent only when we try to conceive the skyscraper as an emotional exhibi-tion, but that really confuses our judgment of the lyric and the picture as well. It is a misconception of what is meant by "expression" in art.

The word "expression" has two principal meanings: in one sense it means *self*-expression—giving vent to our feelings. In this sense it refers to a *symptom* of what we feel. Self-expression is a spontaneous reaction to a situation, an event, the company we are in, things people say, or what the weather does to us; it bespeaks the physical and mental state we are in and the emotions that stir us. In another sense, however, "expression" means the presentation of an idea, usually by the proper and apt use of words. But a device for the presentation of an idea is what we call a *symbol*, not a symptom. Thus a *word* is a symbol, and so is a meaningful combination of words. A common word, such as "horse," conveys an idea even when no one is exclaiming over the presence of a horse, or offering his kingdom for one—for instance, in the phrase "White Horse Whiskey," or in the dictionary, somewhere between "horror" and "horticulture."

A sentence, which is a special combination of words, expresses the idea of some state of affairs, real or imagined. Sentences are complicated symbols—

so complicated, sometimes, that we have to consider them word by word and analyze the way they are put together to understand the meanings they convey. And sometimes the meaning is an idea we never had before, or concerns something we have never seen—a new animal, a foreign place, or what not. Language will formulate new ideas as well as communicate old ones, so that all people know a lot of things that they have merely heard or read about. Symbolic expression, therefore, extends our knowledge beyond the scope of our actual experience.

If an idea is clearly conveyed by means of symbols we say it is *well expressed*. A person may work for a long time to give his statement the best possible form, to find the exact words for what he means to say and to carry his account or his argument most directly from one point to another. But a discourse so worked out is certainly not a spontaneous reaction. Giving expression to an idea is obviously a different thing from giving expression to feelings by laughing, crying, blushing, or quivering. You do not say of a man in a rage that his anger is well expressed; you either try to calm him down, or you rage back at him, but in either case you understand quite well that he is furious. The symptoms just are what they are, there is no critical standard for symptoms. If, on the other hand, the angry man tries to tell you what he is fuming about, he will have to collect himself, curtail his emotional expression, and find words to express his ideas. For to tell a story coherently involves "expression" in quite a different sense: this sort of expression is not "self-expression," but may be called "conceptual expression."

Language, of course, is our prime instrument of conceptual expression. The things we can say are in effect the things we can think. Words are the terms of our thinking as well as the terms in which we present our thoughts, because they present the objects of thought to the thinker himself. Before language communicates ideas, it gives them form, makes them clear, and in fact makes them what they are. Whatever has a name is an object for thought. Without words, sense experience is only a flow of impressions, as subjective as our feelings; words make it objective, and carve it up into *things* and *facts* that we can note, remember, and think about. Language gives outward experience its form, and makes it definite and clear.

There is, however, an important part of reality that is quite inaccessible to the formative influence of language: that is the realm of so-called "inner experience," the life of feeling and emotion. The reason why language is so powerless here is not, as many people suppose, that feeling and emotion are irrational; on the contrary, they seem irrational because language does not help to make them conceivable, and most people cannot conceive anything without the logical scaffolding of words. The unfitness of language to convey subjective experience is a somewhat technical subject, easier for logicians to understand than for artists; but the gist of it is that the form of language does not reflect the natural form of feeling, so we cannot shape any concepts of feeling with the help of ordinary, discursive language. Therefore the words whereby we refer to feeling only name very general kinds of inner experience—excitement, calm, joy, sorrow, love, hate, etc. But there is no language to describe just how one joy differs so radically from another, or what the experience of hate is really like, how it can interplay with feelings usually called love, how it burns and then goes cold in almost the same moment. The real nature of feeling is something language as such—as discursive symbolism—cannot render.

For this reason, the phenomena of feeling and emotion are usually treated by philosophers as irrational. The only pattern discursive thought can find in them is the pattern of outward events that occasion them. There are different degrees of fear, but they are thought of as so many degrees of the same simple feeling.

But human feeling is a fabric, not a vague mass. It has an intricate dynamic pattern, possible combinations and new emergent phenomena. It is a pattern of organically interdependent and interdetermined tensions and resolutions; a pattern of almost infinitely complex activation and cadence. To it belongs the whole gamut of our sensibility, the sense of straining thought, all mental attitude and motor set. Those are the deeper reaches that underlie the surface waves of our emotion, and make human life a *life of feeling* instead of an unconscious metabolic existence interrupted by feelings.

It is, I think, this dynamic pattern that finds its formal expression in the arts. The expressiveness of art is like that of a symbol, not that of an emotional symptom; it is as a formulation of feeling for our conception that a work of art is properly said to be expressive. It may serve somebody's need of self-expression besides; but that is not what makes it good or bad art. In a special sense one may call a work of art a symbol of feeling, for, like a symbol, it formulates our ideas of inward experience, as discourse formulates our ideas of things and facts in the outside world. A work of art differs from a genuine symbol—that is, a symbol in the full and usual sense—in that it does not point beyond itself to something else. The word "symbol" does not originally connote any representative function, or reference to something beyond itself; it means "thrown together"—συμβαλλειν. But in English usage it has come to mean a sign that stands for something else to which it directs our attention. This is something a work of art does not do. Its relation to feeling is a rather special one that we cannot undertake to analyze here; in effect, the feeling it expresses appears to be directly given with it, as the sense of a true metaphor, or the value of a religious myth, is not separable from its expression. We speak of the feeling *of*, or the feeling *in*, a work of art, not the feeling it means. And we speak truly; a work of art presents something like a direct vision of vitality, emotion, subjective reality.

The primary function of art is to objectify feeling so we can contemplate and understand it. It is the formulation of so-called "inward experience," the "inner life," that is impossible to achieve by discursive thought, because its forms are incommensurable with the forms of language and all its derivatives (e.g. mathematics, symbolic logic). Art objectifies the sentience and desire, self-consciousness and world-consciousness, emotions and moods that are generally regarded as irrational because words cannot give us clear ideas of them. But the premise tacitly assumed in such a judgment—namely, that anything language cannot express is formless and irrational—seems to me to be an error. I believe the life of feeling is not irrational; its logical forms are merely very different from the structures of discourse. But they are so much like the dynamic forms of art that art is their natural symbol. Through plastic works, music, fiction, dance, or dramatic forms we can conceive what vitality and emotion feel like.

All this time I have been expounding, word by word, what I mean by the definition of art proposed at the beginning of this lecture: Art is the practice of creating perceptible forms expressive of human feeling. We have dwelt on the exact sense of "form," and "expressive," and "feeling." Form in this context means a configuration, something seen or heard or imaginatively grasped as an entity, an integral whole given to perception like an apparition. Every work of art is a form in this sense. It may be a solid form, or a dynamic form like a whirl or a stream, or it may be a sounding form like a melody, or even the image of events known as a story, that, like dreams or memory, presents its form to imagination alone. "Expression" is here taken to mean articulation, not self-expression or venting of one's feeling. And "feeling," finally, is used in the broadest sense, denoting anything that can or could be felt—sensation, emotion, every tension in a sentient organism, from the feeling of vitality itself to the highest development of personal or even transcendent consciousness. The reason why works of art can express the nature of feeling, which language cannot present, is that artistic forms and the forms of feeling, or subjective reality, are logically similar, so that our directly felt life is reflected, symbolically articulated, and objectively presented to our understanding in works of art.

This brings us, at last, to the question of the cultural importance of the arts. Why is it so apt to be the vanguard of cultural advance, as it was in Egypt, in Greece, in Christian Europe (think of Gregorian music and Gothic architecture), in Renaissance Italy—not to speculate about ancient cavemen, whose art is all that we know of them? One thinks of culture as economic increase, social organization, the gradual ascendancy of rational thinking and scientific control of nature over superstitious imagination and magical practices. But art is not practical; it is neither philosophy nor science; it is not religion, morality, nor even social comment (as many drama critics take comedy to be). What does it contribute to culture that could be of major importance?

It merely presents forms—sometimes intangible forms—to imagination. Its direct appeal is to that faculty, or function, that Lord Bacon considered the chief stumbling block in the way of reason, that enlightened writers like Stuart. Chase never tire of condemning as the source of all nonsense and bizarre erroneous beliefs. And so it is; but it is also the source of all insight and true beliefs. Imagination is probably the oldest mental trait that is typically human— older than discursive reason; it is probably the common source of dream, reason, religion, and all true general observation. It is this primitive human power—imagination—that engenders the arts and is in turn directly affected by their products.

Somewhere at the animalian starting line of human evolution lie the beginnings of that supreme instrument of the mind, language. We think of it as a device for communication among the members of a society. But communication is only one, and perhaps not even the first, of its functions. The first thing it does is to break up what William James called the "blooming, buzzing confusion" of sense perception into units and groups, events and chains of events—things and relations, causes and effects. All these patterns are imposed on our experience by language. We think, as we speak, in terms of objects and their relations.

But the process of breaking up our sense experience in this way, making reality conceivable, memorable, sometimes even predictable, is a process of imagination. Primitive conception is imagination. Language and imagination grow up together in a reciprocal tutelage.

What discursive symbolism—language in its literal use—does for our awareness of things about us and our own relation to them, the arts do for our awareness of subjective reality, feeling and emotion; they give inward experiences form and thus make them conceivable. The only way we can really envisage vital movement, the stirring and growth and passage of emotion, and ultimately the whole direct sense of human life, is in artistic terms. A musical person thinks of emotions musically. They cannot be discursively talked about above a very general level. But they may none the less be known—objectively set forth, publicly known—and there is nothing necessarily confused or formless about emotions.

As soon as the natural forms of subjective experience are abstracted to the point of symbolic presentation, we can use those forms to *imagine* feeling and understand its nature. Self-knowledge, insight into all phases of life and mind, springs from artistic imagination. That is the cognitive value of the arts.

But their influence on human life goes deeper than the intellectual level. As language actually gives form to our sense-experience, grouping our impressions around those things which have names, and fitting sensations to the qualities that have adjectival names, and so on, the arts we live with—our picture books and stories and the music we hear—actually form our emotive experience. Every generation has its styles of feeling. One age shudders and blushes and faints, another swaggers, still another is godlike in a universal indifference. These styles in actual emotion are not insincere. They are largely unconscious—determined by many social causes, but *shaped* by artists, usually popular artists of the screen, the juke-box, the shop window and the picture magazine. (That, rather than incitement to crime, is my objection to the comics.) Irwin Edman remarks in one of his books that our emotions are largely Shakespeare's poetry.

This influence of art on life gives us an indication why a period of efflorescence in the arts is apt to lead a cultural advance: it formulates a new way of feeling, and that is the beginning of a cultural age. It suggests another matter for reflection, too: that a wide neglect of artistic education is a neglect in the education of feeling. Most people are so imbued with the idea that feeling is a formless total organic excitement in humans as in animals, that the idea of educating feeling, developing its scope and quality, seems odd to them, if not absurd. It is really, I think, at the very heart of personal education.

There is one other function of the arts that benefits not so much the advance of culture as its stabilization; an influence on individual lives. This function is the converse and complement of the objectification of feeling, the driving force of creation in art: it is the education of vision that we receive in seeing, hearing, reading works of art—the development of the artist's eye, that assimilates ordinary sights (or sounds, motions, or events) to inward vision, and lends expressiveness and emotional import to the world. Wherever art takes a motif from actuality—a flowering branch, a bit of landscape, a historic event or a personal memory, any model or theme from life—it transforms it into a piece of imagination, and imbues its image with artistic vitality. The result is an impregnation of ordinary reality with the significance of created form. This is the *subjectification of nature*, that makes reality itself a symbol of life and feeling.

I cannot say much about this last point because I am just working with the idea myself. One of my students gave it to me, in a criticism of my own theory. But it seems to me to be of great significance.

Let us sum up briefly, then, why the arts, which many people regard as a cultural frill, are actually never a late addition to civilized life, an ornament gracing society like tea ceremonies or etiquette, but are born during the rise and the primitive phases of cultures, and often outrun all other developments in achieving mature character and technical competence. Cultures begin with the development of personal and social and religious feeling. The great instrument of this development is art. For, (1) art makes feeling apparent, objectively given so we may reflect on it and understand it; (2) the practice and familiar knowledge of any art provides forms for actual feeling to take, as language provides forms for sensory experience and factual observation; and (3) art is the education of the senses to see nature in expressive form. Thereby the actual world becomes in some measure symbolic of feeling (without being "anthropomorphized," supposed to *have* feelings) and personally significant.

The arts objectify subjective reality, and subjectify outward experience of nature. Art education is the education of feeling, and a society that neglects it gives itself up to formless emotion. Bad art is corruption of feeling. This is a large factor in the irrationalism which dictators and demagogues exploit.

❧ ❧ ❧

*Hilaire Hiler*

# Why Abstract? [1]

ONE night I was sitting in a barroom with a couple of young Canadians who were very much interested in literature. They said that painting was a childish way of wasting one's time and that there were no first rate minds or even second rate minds interested in painting today. I had had a few drinks, and their attitude irritated me pretty considerably. I said, "Let's chew this business over a little." I took another brandy and soda and told them that they were a couple of damned little *parvenus*. Men were painting, I said, before any alphabets were thought of. Before they were farming, probably before they ever got self-conscious enough to get up and shout poetry. Perhaps there were no first rate minds but some very first rate feelings mixed up in the thing. In my opinion there was too much thinking, or what passed for thinking, going on now, and entirely too little feeling. Moreover . . . the wonderful haptic language of painting was still perfectly comprehensible by everyone who could understand it at all, after tens of thousands of years. We needed no glossary, no dictionary, no translation. Whereas . . . that after a few years it was difficult to understand the real meaning of a man of our own tongue like Shakespeare, and almost impossible to understand such relatively recent writings as those of Chaucer.

I could also study my subject freely as to space as well as time. I could feel and understand the design of ancient Persia or ancient China without benefit of university, language courses, or clergy. I had made sufficient progress in graphic language to understand and appreciate the design of the Ming vase which stood in the Louvre and quietly laughed off a few more generations.

I must say here that it seems tragic to me that this beautiful non-verbal language so universally human as to time and space should ever be cramped into regional forms or local or yokel confused idioms.

Thus we get to a point where we can begin to see the difference between a *picture* and a *painting*. The French and German terms for these two different things have clearer implications.

If these literary friends had such ideas—what ideas might a couple of much less literary people have? A story Miguel Covarrubias told me about the Mexican painter, Manuel Zarraga, might give us some idea.

Zarraga was working on a mural in the street or in a patio. While he was working he felt someone looking at his back, or over his shoulder. He continued painting for some time, and then looking around saw that two Indians were squatting down silently watching him paint.

[1] From *Why Abstract?* (Norfolk, Conn.: New Directions, 1945), pp. 15-29, with omissions. Reprinted by permission of the publisher.

After a long time one of them said in their own dialect, which Zarraga happened to understand very well, "Why does he make the machete so big?"

There was another lapse of time and then the other one said, "To go with the sombrero."

These two unverbalized fellows had not lost their feeling or knowledge of design. They expressed themselves in terms of design and were not worried about the picture but about the *painting*. They were not worried about the literary side of it for they could neither read nor write. They could feel.

The machete had to balance the sombrero. The Mexican mural went with the house, and the wall, and the hats, and the bowls, and the saddles, and the blankets. The basic design feeling for all these things was the same.

Form has something to do with style. Not stylization, which as I mentioned somewhere was a self-conscious and superficial thing, not prompted by any inner necessity or plastic necessity.

Form has a plastic significance. The word plastic, as I may have said before —and feel that I have to say again, means, as it is used here, the interrelationships of form and of color *as design* in a painting.

Form is a shape which has meaning, one might say resign meaning, in a given plastic set up. Every form in a design must have a definite geometric relationship to every other form in that design. This is what my friend Danz calls its "geomathic" quality. If we don't feel that fitness and relationship, it's no form at all but only a shape. The sort of relationship mentioned by the peons about the curve and the size of the machete and the curve and the size of the sombrero.

Form may be compared to the quality of dhythm in music and color to the quality of harmony. Form and color are definitely related, a fact which is not only accepted by contemporary artists, but also pretty well by psychologists.

It seems to me that certain types of color and certain types of form are interdependent, and that only the sort of freedom and the sort of discipline inherent in abstract design make it possible to utilize this profound and interesting consonance.

Another thought comes up quite naturally here and that is the one which must be used as the basic premise for all form in design: Everything that man constructs is based on the right angle. This angle is constant and static and classic, and influences fundamentally every design which I do.

In the house in which I am at present living, I must have the sort of painting that I like. It so happens that this painting is of and for, now.

I have a painting of Carl Holty's which fits into the living room. That painting can't live with certain furniture, rugs, draperies, or wallpaper, or, to put it a much better way, the sort of order which it represents can't stand the company of a different order of a different epoch. The painting of the last two or three decades determines the design of my house and everything in it. The architect agrees with me. The cabinet makers, and ceramists, and weavers who have to do with this contemporary thing agree with me. We're getting a little nearer to Emerson. Change your house and you change your thought and life.

Dr. Ernest Jones of London, who cured George VI of stammering, says that the important timeless element in a painting is not to be translated into literary or verbal terms. It speaks directly to and from the unapprehended subverbal portions of the mind in another symbolic language. The language of geometric form—design, is what I feel he must mean.

This is as good a time as any to explain another element in pictures which can be disposed of now and lead us further towards abstraction. This element, which is at present very popular, is known as "stylization." It usually, if not always, takes the form of exaggeration of one sort or another. Extra rough, extra smooth, extra straight, or extra rounded. The thick is made thicker or the thin thinner; or the whole thing is "streamlined."

Stylization has been tried at one time or another in some form or another in the life of almost every serious painter. It is not a solution. It is only skin deep. If I had an architect for my house who would build it in "modern style" without a thorough knowledge of why—(and so many architects here do just that with modern style or any other style)—I would have, not a modern or contemporary house intended as a "machine for living" because of contemporary limitations, materials and functions; I would have a "modernistic" house which I don't think either you or I would like any better than we like the word itself.

Now the paintings and everything else in the house would have to be constructed geometrically just as soundly and mathematically as the house itself. The geometry of our mechanical time would be the only way, since actually we are unable to genuinely feel or use any other one. To think this is possible, to try to do so, is in my opinion a somewhat pathetic form of wishful thinking. We see the results of this on all sides. At best, a little self-consciously inoffensive; at worst, pretty hideously tragic-comic.

I hope that these considerations may make the next thing I'm about to try to say a little clearer. It has to do with compromise.

The pictures you saw and admired at the Perls' Gallery were all more or less in the nature of serious, perhaps almost desperate, attempts to compromise. . . .

In the case of *Mediterranée*, the design is pretty easy to see. It is based on what is justly called the "folded envelope." If you care to look at the reproduction of the picture in the little book by Waldemar George, you'll see that the picture is based on a double pyramid (the one at the base with the point up and the one at the top with the point down) just about the way they are on the back of an envelope.

In the picture of the Chinamen and Negroes the design is a little more difficult to see but the color relationships are much more obvious. The third picture, the *Domino Players*, is still more obviously geometrical. It was painted with three colors, red ochre, cobalt blue, and yellow ochre—an unfortunate combination. An Indo-Chinese noble who happened to visit my studio described it well when he said "very interesting attempt to make cubism comprehensible." It is about the most successful compromise that I ever achieved.

These pictures were all painted somewhat over ten years ago. They were done with an approach which I called "Neonaturism," a word I was forced to coin when people asked me what sort of painting it was. I called it "Neonaturism" because I thought that I could combine design with representation when I made the objects perceived subservient to the basic design of the painting. This I tried to do by committing any required violences on their natural forms which I deemed necessary to force them into the design. Franz Marc must have had some such idea in mind when he did his famous, but I believe unsuccessful, picture with the blue horse.

That blue horse of his brings us to the crux of the reason why I now paint abstractly. You could tell me that geometrical design and composition are not incompatible with more or less representational painting. You could cite masterpieces from Giotto and before him, or from Picasso, to bolster your case. I would have a very hard time getting around such evidence. It's better therefore that I shouldn't try it, or risk boring you by a technical and somewhat involved discussion of the rules and means of design and composition as I see them. I feel that I'll still be able to explain to you why I now paint abstractly and leave these things, basically important though they may be, out of the discussion. . . .

Let me retrace my steps a little and tell you about the time I really began to paint abstractly and why I had to.

I was working in the Aquatic Park Building in San Francisco, where I had charge of the decoration of the interior of the building. There were a number of house painters working there and my work naturally brought me into contact with them. First I found out that they knew a lot more about their trade than most artists know about theirs. This was no news, nor is it very sensational, because after all house painting is a much simpler activity than picture painting. Still it's by no means as simple as most people think.

We talked a lot about color. I associated house painters and color in my mind. One day I saw a couple of them eating their lunch. They'd been painting a wall which was about half finished and they were putting on the second coat and hadn't finished a great deal of that. The first coat was white: the second coat was whiter. As you know, they dress in white overalls and wear white caps. They had a white drop cloth spread out under them to protect the floor. Two or three buckets of white paint were standing on the white drop cloth where they were sitting on a couple of boxes and very unhygienically eating sandwiches. The paper these lunches had been wrapped in was lying where they'd thrown it on the drop cloth.

This is the thing that caught me and intrigued me and the thing that I got such a kick out of. House painters use a great deal of very light colors which they properly call "tints." That is to say, for most painting they use mostly white, which is colored a very little bit by the addition of some pigment or other, depending on whether they want a very light gray, light blue, cream, etc.

These two painters were all in white and surrounded by white and all these whites were different! The first coat on the wall was not as white as was the white of the second coat. The overalls were a different white from the drop cloth, and the white paint was the whitest white where it was still in the pot or running down the sides of it. The paper was a little, not much, on the cream side. The drop cloth was a little on the gray side.

If you catch the picture you'll see how delicate and how interesting it was and what a problem for an artist it presented.

I went home as soon as I could and tried to paint it. I painted the whole thing just as I described it here and naturally put in the two house painters. They spoiled it. The thing about them that spoiled it was the natural color of their hands and faces.

Flesh color is not by any means white. The little areas of it broke up my color sequence and relationship. They had nothing to do with the particular thing I was interested in putting over. When I took the most obvious solution and painted the hands and faces white also, that was even more disturbing.

People who saw the picture with the house painters sitting there eating their lunch with their white hands and faces said:

a. "The poor men contracted painters' colic from not washing their hands before eating lunch. Very informative!"
b. "He's making out the proletariat as clowns!"
c. "Modern working conditions lead to T.B."

In short I found out in the long run that the only way I could use these different whites and not completely distract attention from what I considered and still consider their beautiful and subtle relationship to one another, was to leave out the hands and faces, and the painters, and there I was—as abstract as hell!

Or, to put it still another way! I found out that if I was so interested in all this wonderful color and wanted to handle it for its own sake, and in its relation to form, I'd better let myself be as free as possible from the associations and limitations of representation. The white face won't work any better than the blue horse or the pink tree.

Ten years or so ago I'd made a similar discovery, partially by accident and partially by knowledge which I came by somehow in a way I no longer remember. Maybe a good friend of mine, now deceased, hinted to me about it.

Suddenly, or so it seems now, I thought that I'd put some green into all the colors on the picture. I got very excited. I took Viridian, a green pigment we used, and put it into the blue of the sky, and the pond, and into the white walls of the houses, and the brown of the tree trunks, and the grayish brown of the paths, and I did nothing but this all that day. ("Adjusting," I now call it.) I was very excited. Just before I had to go and keep a date with a nice French girl I knew, I got the thing far enough along to know that I'd pulled it together and that as far as I was concerned there was no longer any question of destroying it. That it had taken on a sort of green glow and it looked pretty good.

I rushed out to my date and told Laurette all about it and she shared my excitement, and my enthusiasm, when she saw the picture (which, by the way, is now in Chicago).

Of course the trouble ten years ago was that the trunks of the trees were still psychologically brown, and the houses still white and so forth, even with the green pigment mixed in pretty liberally. The sky, because it was less green, was still blue.

The Park painting then, although probably the most successful thing from a standpoint of color I had accomplished up to that time, did not exploit the full possibilities of color because I still was unable to take that final step, which would enable me to have freedom from the aesthetic chaos of my surroundings and consequent plastic independence in the problem bounded by the four edges of my canvas—the microcosmic problem of creating a painting as an autonomous entity with its own exigencies, its own rules, its particular construction, etc., in and of itself.

Sometimes a happy combination of circumstances permits the full realization of the plastic problem, while leaving the possibility, I might say the natural possibility, of more or less representation. The rock may still resemble a rock. The forms of two dancers may still be recognizably two dancers. How often this may happen, I don't as yet know. Not often enough to be of very much importance, I should say.

The point to be stressed here is simply that when these forms do not happen to fit into the design, they must be modified from rocks or dancers and made to fit into the painting as form-color, for it is only as form-color that they are of any importance in and of the painting. In other words, as they're related to the other forms and colors in the concept of it.

So we're back to design again, and to repeat, I find that if a form which happens to be recognizable as an object does not interfere with the design— O.K.; if it does interfere with it, plastically or psychologically, it must be rebuilt, whittled down, appropriately colored, or fittingly modified in any way necessary to preserve the plastic unity of the painting. This is supposed to explain why some of the paintings are abstract, some partially abstract, and some quite representational. In other words, they are not abstract just for the sake of the word, but in direct ratio to the inherent design requirements.

Hitherto, I didn't know and I didn't care. I used to sell pictures . . . as long as they looked like things people liked or were interested in or had pleasant associations with. Ashamed as I may feel to admit it, this fact had an effect on my painting for a long time. Naturally, like everyone else I also had certain responsibilities to a number of other people. I liked to remain as comfortable mentally and physically as possible and to be as well thought of as possible.

Now for a number of reasons I'm more interested in painting for its own sake than I was then.

So many things have come up that I don't give a damn about a lot of things I used to care about, and I do give more of a damn about a lot of things I didn't dare care about.

These are the kind of reasons why I now paint abstractly and I hope that you'll understand, at least partially, why it can't be helped. It seems that that's the sort of thing that happens to some people who have reached certain points in their pokings about and their investigations. The sort of things which direct that feeling I was discussing and bring it into contact with factors which seem to make a new illusion and a new reality. These at least have the virtue of being fresher and less redundant than the ones they went through before.

Some of the conclusions implied here were reached, as seen upon examination, many years ago. For instance, I might claim the distinction, if distinction it is, of never having painted a nude, portrait, still life, landscape, or marine, in the classic sense of these terms.

Having looked at thousands of paintings (during and between the wars), most of which were certainly bad ones, a strong suspicion made itself felt that by and large the whole affair was getting pretty boring. A great many of my colleagues seemed not only to bore the public quite exquisitely, but even themselves, as they would freely admit in their more lucid or uninhibited moments.

Painting as an exercise of skill or dexterity à la Munich, an implication of refined "good taste," atmospheric, poetic or literary ideas in the passing mood, or prettily executed realisms of some one's tortured or suffering unconscious mind, seemed isolated from life and self-respecting construction in general.

Some of it was illustration, some of it—I was repeatedly informed—was pure painting, though it looked to me as though this viewpoint might really mean "pure brush stroke" or sometimes, merely, pure sloppiness. Whatever it was, I was no longer interested in it. I could no longer understand it very well or appreciate it in a lively fashion even when I thought I understood it. In fact, whether it was painting or not mattered little.

Color first and then design have come to interest me to the exclusion of practically all the considerations which are apparently taken as premises for the great majority of pictures hung in exhibitions at this time. It no longer seems relevant whether these two elements are accepted as painting or not. It seems that they're of sufficient interest and importance to stand for their own sakes in whatever field their exploitation happens to lead one.

Carl Holty wrote me a letter the other day about a visit he had with Piet Mondrian. Piet paints more abstractly than I do (in case you don't happen to know it). I was a little shocked to learn that Mondrian is now in his seventies. He paints so much younger than a lot of our "young painters." Well, anyway, he and Holty were discussing abstract painting and Mondrian very calmly said to Holty:

"To us this approach to painting is the only realistic one so that we can't change even if we wanted to, no matter how much our well-wishers think we should."

❧ ❧ ❧

*Frank Jewett Mather, Jr.*

## Botticelli's *Primavera*[1]

IN THE year 1477, Lorenzo di Pierfrancesco de' Medici having bought a villa at Castello, on the Prato road, commissioned a young Florentine painter, Sandro Botticelli, to paint a decorative panel for his villa. The dimensions, about seven by ten feet, and the subject, the "Coming of Spring," were prescribed. Lorenzo, not to be confused with his cousin and more illustrious namesake, was himself a minor poet and in touch with the great humanist poet Angelo Poliziano. Thus he was a patron of a kind to feel the loveliness of a Tuscan springtime. Botticelli accepted the theme with enthusiasm and cast about for its embodiment.

Instantaneously the general decorative arrangement flashed into Botticelli's mind, for a pattern is already there, waiting for a subject. He has admired the great new engraving of ten fighting men by one of his masters, Antonio Pollaiolo—a fine arabesque of tensely constructed white bodies effectively contrasting with the formal verticals of a grove in the background. Sometime Sandro meant to use the motive more exquisitely. This is his opportunity. His figures shall show a greater variety in drapery and semi-nudity.

It was perhaps at this stage some humanist friend called Sandro's attention to the beautiful lines in which Lucretius described the coming of spring.

> It ver et Venus, et Veneris praenuntius ante
> Pennatus graditur, zephyri vestigia propter
> Flora quibus mater praespargens ante viai
> Cuncta coloribus egregiis et odoribus opplet.

Spring and Venus move by, and the winged herald of Venus goes before; and close upon the track of the West Wind Flora, their mother, strews flowers ahead, covering all the paths with fairest colors and odors.

A group of five figures begins to order itself in Botticelli's mind; the composition now has found its main theme, but he consciously transforms the processional order of Lucretius. Spring no longer leads with Venus, but is blown and chased in by Zephyr at the rear of the line. And the trees shall bend as

[1] *Concerning Beauty* (Princeton: Princeton University Press, 1935), pp. 70-76. Copyright, 1935, Princeton University Press.

WALT                                                    *Carl* **Holty**

*An abstract portrait of the American poet,* **Walt Whitman,** *by a present-day artist.*

"Walt" by permission of Mr. Holty and Addison Gallery of American Art, Phillips Academy
(Reverse) "Primavera" by permission of David Ashley, Inc.

Zephyr passes, admitting his gentle power. As for Zephyr, Poliziano, in the *"Stanze"* is better than Lucretius. He represents Zephyr as lustful and flying behind Flora. Such shall be his relation to Spring. Flora does not follow Zephyr, but treads daintily ahead of him, behind Venus. Cupid's place as herald is above Venus and a little before her, and since he has wings, shall he not fly rather than walk? In its essentials the group at the right-hand side of the panel, the group that carries the meaning, is now established.

The carpet of spring flowers is obvious. Does not Lucretius suggest it? The flowers shall be so truthful that you could pluck them. They will contrast effectively with the formality of the paling of orange trees which he will pick out decoratively and conventionally with gold. But he will not stand on the somewhat monotonous verticalities of Pollaiolo's paling of trees. His paling shall be interspersed with olive branches delicately sharp against the sky. Everything shall be as fine and precise as any goldsmith's work.

So far everything has gone swimmingly. Presumably sketches have been made of the five figures, the group has taken on organization, at least mentally. Enrichments and refinements have occurred. Out of Spring's lovely mouth roses shall grow; the flowers woven in Flora's frock shall proclaim her function; Venus shall be gravid and heavily draped, for contrast with the semi-nude figures and because spring is the birthday of the year. But now comes an unforeseen difficulty; on the small scale customary at the time, the five figures will never make out a composition for the big, oblong panel. Some filling figures of a congruous kind are indispensable. What figures?

Sandro is reasonably educated, but no scholar. He consults a humanist friend who has the ready answer. Of course Mercury and the Three Graces are the fitting attendants for Venus. Did not Horace, Book I, Ode xxx, when he bid Venus visit the home of his mistress Glycera, summon also the Graces with girdles loosed and Mercury, who withal is a minor cloud-dispeller? Witness *Aeneid*, IV, 245. As for the Graces, Sandro's own fellow Florentine, Leonbattista Alberti, in his treatise *Della Pittura*, which Sandro has doubtless duly read, tells us that their hands should be intertwined, and they themselves clothed in ungirt and transparent veils—quoting Seneca, "implexis inter se manibus, ridentes, solutaque, perlucida veste ornatas." So the humanist counsellor.

Sandro thinks it over. Here are the needed filling figures, and excellent figures for the purpose. Mercury shall be fanning the mists from an orange tree with his caduceus. That will carry the processional rhythm across the picture up to a high finish. He shall then be the terminal figure of the group. But the Graces shall be treading a solemn measure and not smiling. Only the hoyden Spring with the rose in her mouth shall be joyous.

The rest shall be pensive, or like Flora, enigmatically detached, for if spring is the beginning of new life in the world, is it not also the beginning of new death? The flowers and love itself are but for a moment between budding and withering.

Something like this is in Sandro's mind as he sketches the four new figures and considers the organization of the two groups into one. Here the general cadence is clear. The onrush of Zephyr and Spring shall be retarded into the dainty treading of Flora, shall come to a monitory full pause in the heavily clad figure of gravid Venus, shall be resumed in a moderate and more subtle fashion in the dance of the Graces, shall end with the resolutely poised figure of Mercury with his back turned while his hand and magic wand make on high a closing repetend of the right to left motion.

The composition of the picture is now mentally complete. Remains a task of some days to set it down in all its details in a working drawing—a drawing unhappily lost, for which any sensible collector would mortgage his house to the limit. Remained still a task of many months to paint it through on the panel. Rapturous work, work under highest tension, nothing lost of the freshness of the primal vision, much added by way of fit enrichment; fastidiousness in choice of shapes and tints never relaxing, never overasserting itself; a marvel of taste, a miracle of executive prowess.

When it was set in the wall at Castello, Botticelli, unless he was entirely unlike any other painters, relatively lost interest in it. He was now at work on his nobly tragic "St. Augustine" for Ognissanti in competition with the formidably popular Ghirlandaio's "St. Jerome," he was already thinking of great frescoes to be made in Pope Sixtus's new chapel at Rome. Botticelli's part of the esthetic transaction connected with the "Allegory of Spring" was completed and well completed. That the transaction should continue was now the responsibility of others.

The painting is now ready to play its part in the esthetic transaction. Let me imagine myself before it. First at a distance I perceive the general design—a very varied processional advance of clothed and lightly draped forms from right to left across a quite formal paling of orange trees. Here I have repeated the primal vision of Botticelli as elaborated by trial and error. Of this trial and error virtually nothing comes to my attention, though I may note that the four figures on the left are out of the main action, may divine that they were an afterthought.

On nearer approach I grasp the exquisiteness of the detail without losing the sense of the whole picture. This detail, the ripe oranges on the trees, the iris, larkspurs, daisies, wild orchid, wood-strawberry daintily balancing in the grass tell me that it is early springtime. Herewith comes the meaning of the figures. Gravid Venus is identified by her winged son. The fantastic figure with a beflowered frock, and strewing flowers must be Flora. An associational item confirms and extends the identifications. I have read Herbert Horne's happy citation of the lines from Lucretius which names all five figures for me. This literary association is legitimately part of my appreciation, for it guided Botticelli in creation. Since it was important for him, it is important for me.

As I identify the main figures I sense their fastidiously distinguished character and the loveliness of the postures, actions and details which represent and delicately emphasize their functions. What a cadence it is, rising from the solemn boisterousness of Zephyr, through the adorable awkward twist of escaping Spring, to the mincing elegance of Flora's measured stride, and the full stop where Venus stands in undulating repose. It is also an undulation in depth, coming forward with Flora and the Graces at the ends, receding with Venus at the center. My sense of the whole picture is being constantly deepened and enriched as I make these explorations of details, and continue then through the flowery sward, the grove, the group of Mercury and the Graces. Here in appreciation I am perceiving that infinite delicate elaboration and richness which arising in Botticelli's imagination commanded his nervous and fastidious hand. These observations gradually tell me of the language in which Botticelli's meaning is expressed. While there is a lovely accompaniment of muted color, it is primarily a language of line—line that races, slows, darts, turns, stops, resumes, always giving assurance of form in implied motion. My soul has echoed the controlled sweep of Botticelli's hand. The sense of the pervading wistful, tranquil melancholy that surrounds and almost denies the high spirits of romping Spring grows deeper as I look.

The experiences which words can only enumerate as successive, have actually overlapped, interwoven, blended, and have uninterruptedly built up that psychical volume which is my appreciation of this lively picture, my virtual if also approximate repetition of what was essential in Botticelli's creative processes—my complete *geniessen*,[2] my partial but sufficient *nachschaffen*.[3]

❦ ❦ ❦

*Frank Lloyd Wright*

# Modern Architecture: The Cardboard House[1]

LET us take for text on this, our fourth afternoon, the greatest of all references to simplicity, the inspired admonition: *"Consider the lilies of the field—they toil not, neither do they spin, yet verily I say unto thee—Solomon in all his glory was not arrayed like one of these."* An inspired saying—attributed to an humble Architect in ancient times, called Carpenter, who gave up Architecture nearly two thousand years ago to go to work upon its Source.

And if the text should seem to you too far away from our subject this afternoon—

## "The Cardboard House"

—consider that for that very reason the text has been chosen. The cardboard house needs an antidote. The antidote is far more important than the house. As antidote—and as practical example, too, of the working out of an ideal of

---

[2] Enjoying.        [3] Re-creating.

[1] *Modern Architecture, Being the Kahn Lecture for 1930* (Princeton: Princeton University Press, 1931), pp. 68-80. Copyright, 1931, by Frank Lloyd Wright. Reprinted by permission of author and the Princeton University Press.

organic simplicity that has taken place here on American soil, step by step, under conditions that are your own—could I do better than to take apart for your benefit the buildings I have tried to build, to show you how they were, long ago, dedicated to the Ideal of Organic Simplicity? It seems to me that while another might do better than that, I certainly could not—for that is, truest and best, what I know about the Subject. What a man *does, that* he has.

When, "in the cause of Architecture," in 1893, I first began to build the houses, sometimes referred to by the thoughtless as "The New School of the Middle West" (some advertiser's slogan comes along to label everything in this our busy woman's country), the only way to simplify the awful building in vogue at the time was to conceive a finer entity—a better building—and get it built. The buildings standing then were all tall and all tight. Chimneys were lean and taller still, sooty fingers threatening the sky. And beside them, sticking up by way of dormers through the cruelly sharp, saw-tooth roofs, were the attics for "help" to swelter in. Dormers were elaborate devices, cunning little buildings complete in themselves, stuck to the main roof slopes to let "help" poke heads out of the attic for air.

Invariably the damp sticky clay of the prairie was dug out for a basement under the whole house, and the rubblestone walls of this dank basement always stuck up above the ground a foot or more and blinked, with half-windows. So the universal "cellar" showed itself as a bank of some kind of masonry running around the whole house, for the house to sit up on—like a chair. The lean, upper house-walls of the usual two floors above this stone or brick basement were wood, set on top of this masonry-chair, clapboarded and painted, or else shingled and stained, preferably shingled and mixed, up and down, all together with mouldings crosswise. These overdressed wood house-walls had, cut in them—or cut out of them, to be precise—big holes for the big cat and little holes for the little cat to get in and out or for ulterior purposes of light and air. The house-walls were be-corniced or bracketed up at the top into the tall, purposely profusely complicated roof, dormers plus. The whole roof, as well as the roof as a whole, was scalloped and ridged and tipped and swanked and gabled to madness before they would allow it to be either shingled or slated. The whole exterior was be-deviled—that is to say, mixed to puzzle-pieces, with corner boards, panel-boards, window-frames, corner-blocks, plinth-blocks, rosettes, fantails, ingenious and jigger work in general. This was the only way they seemed to have, then, of "putting on style." The scroll-saw and turning-lathe were at the moment the honest means of this fashionable mongering by the wood-butcher and to this entirely "moral" end. Unless the householder of the period were poor indeed, usually an ingenious corner-tower on his house eventuated into a candle-snuffer dome, a spire, an inverted rutabaga or radish or onion or—what is your favorite vegetable? Always elaborate bay-windows and fancy porches played "ring around a rosy" on this "imaginative" corner feature. And all this the building of the period could do equally well in brick or stone. It was an impartial society. All material looked pretty much alike in that day.

Simplicity was as far from all this scrap-pile as the pandemonium of the barn-yard is far from music. But it was easy for the Architect. All he had to do was to call: "Boy, take down No. 37, and put a bay-window on it for the lady!"

So—the first thing to do was to get rid of the attic and, therefore, of the dormer and of the useless "heights" below it. And next, get rid of the unwholesome basement, entirely—yes, absolutely—in any house built on the prairie. Instead of lean, brick chimneys, bristling up from steep roofs to hint at "judgment" everywhere, I could see necessity for one only, a broad generous one, or at most, for two, these kept low down on gently sloping roofs or perhaps flat roofs. The big fireplace below, inside, became now a place for a real fire, justified the great size of this chimney outside. A real fireplace at that time was extraordinary. There were then "mantels" instead. A mantel was a marble frame for a few coals, or a piece of wooden furniture with tiles stuck in it and a "grate," the whole set slam up against the wall. The "mantel" was an insult to comfort, but the *integral* fireplace became an important part of the building itself in the houses I was allowed to build out there on the prairie. It refreshed me to see the fire burning deep in the masonry of the house itself.

Taking a human being for my scale, I brought the whole house down in height to fit a normal man; believing in no other scale, I broadened the mass out, all I possibly could, as I brought it down into spaciousness. It has been said that were I three inches taller (I am 5 feet 8½ inches tall), all my houses would have been quite different in proportion. Perhaps.

House-walls were not to be started at the ground on a cement or stone water-table that looked like a low platform under the building, which it usually was, but the house-walls were stopped at the second story window-sill level, to let the rooms above come through in a continuous window-series, under the broad eaves of a gently sloping, overhanging roof. This made enclosing screens out of the lower walls as well as light screens out of the second story walls. Here was true *enclosure of interior space*. A new sense of building, it seems.

The climate, being what it was, a matter of violent extremes of heat and cold, damp and dry, dark and bright, I gave broad protecting roof-shelter to the whole, getting back to the original purpose of the "Cornice." The undersides of the roof projections were flat and light in color to create a glow of reflected light that made the upper rooms not dark, but delightful. The overhangs had double value, shelter and preservation for the walls of the house as well as diffusion of reflected light for the upper story, through the "light screens" that took the place of the walls and were the windows.

At this time, a house to me was obvious primarily as interior space under fine shelter. I liked the sense of *shelter*. I liked the sense of shelter in the "look of the building." I achieved it, I believe. I then went after the variegated bands of material in the old walls to eliminate odds and ends in favor of one material and a single surface from grade to eaves, or grade to second story sill-cope, treated as simple enclosing screens,—or else made a plain screen band around the second story above the window-sills, turned up over on to the ceiling beneath the eaves. This screen band was of the same material as the under side of the eaves themselves, or what architects call the "soffit." The planes of the building parallel to the ground were all stressed, to grip the whole to earth. Sometimes it was possible to make the enclosing wall below this upper band of the second story, from the second story window-sill clear down to the ground, a heavy "wainscot" of fine masonry material resting on the cement or stone platform laid on the foundation. I liked that wainscot to be of masonry material when my clients felt they could afford it.

As a matter of form, too, I liked to see the projecting base, or water-table, set out over the foundation walls themselves—as a substantial preparation for the building. This was managed by setting the studs of the walls to the inside of the foundation walls, instead of to the outside. All door and window tops were now brought into line with each other with only comfortable head-clearance for the average human being. Eliminating the sufferers from the "attic" enabled the roofs to lie low. The house began to associate with the ground and become natural to its prairie site. And would the young man in architecture ever believe that this was all "new" then? Not only new, but destructive heresy—or ridiculous eccentricity. So New that what little prospect I had of ever earning a livelihood by making houses was nearly wrecked. At first, "they" called the houses "dress-reform" houses, because Society was just then excited about that particular "reform." This simplification looked like some kind of "reform" to them. Oh, they called them all sorts of names that cannot be repeated, but "they" never found a better term for the work unless it was "Horizontal Gothic," "Temperance Architecture" (with a sneer), etc., etc. I don't know how I escaped the accusation of another "Renaissance."

What I have just described was all on the *outside* of the house and was there chiefly because of what had happened *inside*. Dwellings of that period were "cut-up," advisedly and completely, with the grim determination that should go with any cutting process. The "interiors" consisted of boxes beside or inside other boxes, called *rooms*. All boxes inside a complicated boxing. Each domestic "function" was properly box to box. I could see little sense in this inhibition, this cellular sequestration that implied ancestors familiar with the cells of penal institutions, except for the privacy of bed-rooms on the upper floor. They were perhaps all right as "sleeping boxes." So I declared the whole lower floor as one room, cutting off the kitchen as a laboratory, putting servants' sleeping and living quarters next to it, semi-detached, on the ground floor, screening various portions in the big room, for certain domestic purposes —like dining or reading, or receiving a formal caller. There were no plans like these in existence at the time and my clients were pushed toward these ideas as helpful to a solution of the vexed servant-problem. Scores of doors disappeared and no end of partition. They liked it, both clients and servants. The house became more free as "space" and more liveable, too. Interior spaciousness began to dawn.

Having got what windows and doors that were left lined up and lowered to convenient human height, the ceilings of the rooms, too, could be brought over on to the walls, by way of the horizontal, broad bands of plaster on the walls above the windows, the plaster colored the same as the room ceilings. This would bring the ceiling-surface down to the very window tops. The ceilings thus expanded, by extending them downward as the wall band above the windows, gave a generous overhead to even small rooms. The sense of the whole was broadened and made plastic, too, by this expedient. The enclosing walls and ceilings were thus made to flow together.

Here entered the important element of Plasticity—indispensable to successful use of the Machine, for true expression of Modernity. The outswinging windows were fought for because the casement window associated the house with out-of-doors—gave free openings, outward. In other words the so-called "casement" was simple and more human. In use and effect, more natural. If it had not existed I should have invented it. It was not used at that time in America, so I lost many clients because I insisted upon it when they wanted the "guillotine" or "double-hung" window then in use. The Guillotine was not simple nor human. It was only expedient. I used it once in the Winslow House—my first house—and rejected it thereafter—forever. Nor at that time did I entirely eliminate the wooden trim. I did make it "plastic," that is, light and continuously flowing instead of the heavy "cut and butt" of the usual carpenter work. No longer did the "trim," so called, look like carpenter work. The machine could do it perfectly well as I laid it out. It was all after "quiet." This plastic trim, too, with its running "back-hand" enabled poor workmanship to be concealed. It was necessary with the field resources at hand at that time to conceal much. Machinery versus the union had already demoralized the workmen. The Machine resources were so little understood that extensive drawings had to be made merely to show the "mill-man" what to leave off. But the "trim" finally became only a single, flat, narrow, horizontal wood-band running around the room, one at the top of the windows and doors and another next to the floors, both connected with narrow, vertical, thin wood-bands that were used to divide the wall-surfaces of the whole room smoothly and flatly into folded color planes. The trim merely completed the window and door openings in this same plastic sense. When the interior had thus become wholly plastic, instead of structural, a New element, as I have said, had entered Architecture. Strangely enough an element that had not existed in Architectural History before. Not alone in the trim, but in numerous ways too tedious to describe in words, this revolutionary sense of the plastic whole, an instinct with me at first, began to work more and more intelligently and have fascinating, unforeseen consequences. Here was something that began to organize itself. When several houses had been finished and compared with the house of the period, there was very little of that house left standing. Nearly every one had stood the house of the period as long as he could stand it, judging by appreciation of the change. Now all this probably tedious description is intended to indicate directly in bare outline how thus early there *was* an ideal of organic simplicity put to work, with historical consequences, here in your own country. The main motives and indications were (and I enjoyed them all):

First—to reduce the number of necessary parts of the house and the separate rooms to a minimum, and make all come together as enclosed space—so divided that light, air and vista permeated the whole with a sense of unity.

Second—To associate the building as a whole with its site by extension and emphasis of the planes parallel to the ground, but keeping the floors off the best part of the site, thus leaving that better part for use in connection with the life of the house. Extended level planes were found useful in this connection.

Third—To eliminate the room as a box and the house as another by making all walls enclosing screens—the ceilings and floors and enclosing screens to flow into each other as one large enclosure of space, with minor subdivisions only.

Make all house proportions more liberally human, with less wasted space in structure, and structure more appropriate to material, and so the whole more liveable. *Liberal* is the best word. Extended straight lines or streamlines were useful in this.

Fourth—To get the unwholesome basement up out of the ground, entirely above it, as a low pedestal for the living-portion of the home, making the foundation itself visible as a low masonry platform, on which the building should stand.

Fifth—To harmonize all necessary openings to "outside" or to "inside" with good human proportions and make them occur naturally—singly or as a series in the scheme of the whole building. Usually they appeared as "lightscreens" instead of walls, because all the "Architecture" of the house was chiefly the way these openings came in such walls as were grouped about the rooms as enclosing screens. The *room* as such was now the essential architectural expression, and there were to be no holes cut in walls as holes are cut in a box, because this was not in keeping with the ideal of "plastic." Cutting holes was violent.

Sixth—To eliminate combinations of different materials in favor of monomaterial so far as possible; to use no ornament that did not come out of the nature of materials to make the whole building clearer and more expressive as a place to live in, and give the conception of the building appropriate revealing emphasis. Geometrical or straight lines were natural to the machinery at work in the building trades then, so the interiors took on this character naturally.

Seventh—To incorporate all heating, lighting, plumbing so that these systems became constituent parts of the building itself. These service features became architectural and in this attempt the ideal of an organic architecture was at work.

Eighth—To incorporate as organic Architecture—so far as possible—furnishings, making them all one with the building and designing them in simple terms for machine work. Again straight lines and rectilinear forms.

Ninth—Eliminate the Decorator. He was all curves and all efflorescence, if not all "period."

This was all rational enough so far as the thought of an organic architecture went. The particular forms this thought took in the feeling of it all could only be personal. There was nothing whatever at this time to help make them what they were. All seemed to be the most natural thing in the world and grew up out of the circumstances of the moment. Whatever they may be worth in the long run is all they are worth.

Now *simplicity* being the point in question in this early constructive effort, organic simplicity I soon found to be a matter of true coordination. And Beauty I soon felt to be a matter of the sympathy with which such coordination was affected. Plainness was not necessarily simplicity. Crude furniture of the Roycroft-Stickley-Mission Style, which came along later, was offensively plain, plain as a barn door—but never was simple in any true sense. Nor, I found, were merely machine-made things in themselves simple. To think "in simple," is to deal in simples, and that means with an eye single to the altogether. This, I believe, is the secret of simplicity. Perhaps we may truly regard nothing at all as simple in itself. I believe that no one thing in itself is ever so, but must achieve simplicity (as an Artist should use the term) as a perfectly realized part of some organic whole. Only as a feature or any part becomes an harmonious element in the harmonious whole does it arrive at the estate of simplicity. Any wild flower is truly simple, but double the same wild flower by cultivation, it ceases to be so. The *scheme* of the original is no longer clear. Clarity of design and perfect significance both are first essentials of the spontaneously born simplicity of the lilies of the field who neither toil nor spin, as contrasted with Solomon who had "toiled and spun"—that is to say, no doubt had put on himself and had put on his temple, properly "composed," everything in the category of good things but the cook-stove.

Five lines where three are enough is stupidity. Nine pounds where three are sufficient is stupidity. But to eliminate expressive words that intensify or vivify meaning in speaking or writing is not simplicity; nor is similar elimination in Architecture simplicity—it, too, may be stupidity. In Architecture, expressive changes of surface, emphasis of line and especially textures of material, may go to make facts eloquent, forms more significant. Elimination, therefore, may be just as meaningless as elaboration, perhaps more often so. I offer any fool, for an example.

To know what to leave out and what to put in, just where and just how—Ah, *that* is to have been educated in knowledge of SIMPLICITY.

As for Objects of Art in the house even in that early day they were the "bête noir" of the new simplicity. If well chosen, well enough in the house, but only if each was properly digested by the whole. Antique or modern sculpture, paintings, pottery, might become objectives in the Architectural scheme and I accepted them, aimed at them, and assimilated them. Such things may take their places as elements in the design of any house. They are then precious things, gracious and good to live with. But it is difficult to do this well. Better, if it may be done, to design all features together. At that time, too, I tried to make my clients see that furniture and furnishings, not built in as integral features of the building, should be designed as attributes of whatever furniture was built in and should be seen as minor parts of the building itself, even if detached or kept aside to be employed on occasion. But when the building itself was finished, the old furniture the clients already possessed went in with them to await the time when the interior might be completed. Very few of the houses were, therefore, anything but painful to me after the clients moved in and, helplessly, dragged the horrors of the old order along after them.

But I soon found it difficult, anyway, to make some of the furniture in the "abstract"; that is, to design it as architecture and make it "human" at the same time—fit for human use. I have been black and blue in some spot, somewhere, almost all my life from too intimate contacts with my own furniture. Human beings must group, sit or recline—confound them—and they must dine, but dining is much easier to manage and always was a great artistic opportunity. Arrangements for the informality of sitting comfortably, singly or in groups, where it is desirable or natural to sit, and still to belong in disarray to the scheme as a whole—that is a matter difficult to accomplish. But it can be done now, and should be done, because only those attributes of human comfort and convenience, made to belong in this digested or integrated sense to the architecture of the home as a whole, should be there at all, in Modern Architecture. For that matter about four-fifths of the contents of nearly every home could be given away with good effect to that home. But the things given away might go on to poison some other home. So why not at once destroy undesirable things . . . make an end of them?

Here then, in foregoing outline, is the gist of America's contribution to Modern American Architecture as it was already under way in 1893. But the gospel of elimination is one never preached enough. No matter how much preached, Simplicity is a spiritual ideal seldom organically reached. Nevertheless, by assuming the virtue by imitation—or by increasing structural makeshifts to get superficial simplicity—the effects may cultivate a taste that will demand the reality in course of time, but it may also destroy all hope of the real thing.

Standing here, with the perspective of long persistent effort in the direction of an organic Architecture in view, I can again assure you out of this initial experience that Repose is the reward of true simplicity and that organic simplicity is sure of Repose. Repose is the highest quality in the Art of Architecture, next to integrity, and a reward for integrity. Simplicity may well be held to the fore as a spiritual ideal, but when actually achieved, as in the "lilies of the field," it is something that comes of itself, something spontaneously born out of the nature of the doing whatever it is that is to be done. Simplicity, too, is a reward for fine feeling and straight thinking in working a principle, well in hand, to a consistent end. Solomon knew nothing about it, for he was only wise. And this, I think, is what Jesus meant by the text we have chosen for this discourse—"Consider the lilies of the field," as contrasted, for beauty, with Solomon.

Now, a chair *is* a machine to sit in.

A home *is* a machine to live in.

The human body *is* a machine to be worked by will.

A tree *is* a machine to bear fruit.

A plant *is* a machine to bear flowers and seeds.

And, as I've admitted before somewhere, a heart *is* a suction-pump. Does that idea thrill you?

Trite as it is, it may be as well to think it over because the *least* any of these things may be, *is* just that. All of them are that before they are anything else. And to violate that mechanical requirement in any of them is to finish before anything of higher purpose can happen. To ignore the fact is either sentimentality or the prevalent insanity. Let us acknowledge in this respect, that this matter of mechanics is just as true of the work of Art as it is true of anything else. But, were we to stop with that trite acknowledgment, we should only be living in a low, rudimentary sense. This skeleton rudiment accepted, *understood*, is the first condition of any fruit or flower we may hope to get from ourselves. Let us continue to call this flower and fruit of ourselves, even in this Machine Age, ART. Some Architects, as we may see, now consciously acknowledge this "Machine" rudiment. Some will eventually get to it by circuitous mental labor. Some *are* the thing itself without question and already in need of "treatment." But "Americans" (I prefer to be more specific and say "Usonians") have been educated "blind" to the higher human uses of it all—while actually in sight of this higher human use all the while.

Therefore, now let the declaration that "all is machinery" stand nobly forth for what it is worth. But why not more profoundly declare that "Form follows Function" and let it go at that? Saying, "Form follows Function," is not only deeper, it is clearer, and it goes further in a more comprehensive way to say the thing to be said, because the implication of this saying includes the heart of the whole matter. It may be that Function follows Form, as, or if, you prefer, but it is easier thinking with the first proposition just as it is easier to stand on your feet and nod your head than it would be to stand on your head and nod your feet. Let us not forget that Simplicity of the Universe is very different from the Simplicity of a Machine.

New significance in Architecture implies new materials qualifying form and textures, requires fresh feeling, which will eventually qualify both as "ornament." But "Decoration" must be sent on its way or now be given the meaning that it has lost, if it is to stay. Since "Decoration" became acknowledged as such, and ambitiously set up for itself as Decoration, it has been a make-shift, in the light of this ideal of Organic Architecture. Any House Decoration, as such, is an architectural makeshift, however well it may be done, unless the decoration, so called, is part of the Architect's design in both concept and execution.

Since Architecture in the old sense died and Decoration has had to shift for itself more and more, all so-called Decoration has become *ornamental*, therefore no longer *integral*. There can be no true simplicity in either Architecture or Decoration under any such condition. Let Decoration, therefore, die for Architecture, and the Decorator become an Architect, but not an "Interior Architect."

Ornament can never be applied to Architecture any more than Architecture should ever be applied to Decoration. All ornament, if not developed within the nature of Architecture and as organic part of such expression, vitiates the whole fabric no matter how clever or beautiful it may be as something in itself.

Yes—for a century or more Decoration has been setting up for itself, and in our prosperous country has come pretty near to doing very well, thank you. I think we may say that it is pretty much all we have now to show as Domestic Architecture, as Domestic Architecture still goes with us at the present time. But we may as well face it. The Interior Decorator thrives with us because we have no Architecture. Any Decorator is the natural enemy of organic simplicity in Architecture. He, persuasive Doctor-of-Appearances that he *must* be when he becomes Architectural substitute, will give you an imitation of anything, even an imitation of imitative simplicity. Just at the moment, May 1930, he is expert in this imitation. France, the born Decorator, is now engaged with "Madame," owing to the good fortune of the French market, in selling us this ready-made or made-to-order simplicity. Yes, Imitation Simplicity is the latest addition to imported "stock." The Decorators of America are now equipped to furnish *especially* this. Observe. And how very charming the suggestions conveyed by these imitations sometimes are!

Would you have again the general principles of the spiritual-ideal of organic simplicity at work in our Culture? If so, then let us reiterate: First, Simplicity is Constitutional Order. And it is worthy of note in this connection that 9 times 9 equals 81 is just as simple as 2 plus 2 equals 4. Nor is the obvious more simple necessarily than the occult. The obvious is obvious simply because it falls within our special horizon, is therefore easier for us to *see*; that is all. Yet all simplicity near or far has a countenance, a visage, that is characteristic. But this countenance is visible only to those who can grasp the whole and enjoy the significance of the minor part, as such, in relation to the whole when in flower. This is for the critics.

This characteristic visage may be simulated—the real complication glossed over, the internal conflict hidden by surface and belied by mass. The internal complication may be and usually is increased to create the semblance of and get credit for—simplicity. This is the Simplicity-lie usually achieved by most of the "surface and mass" architects. This is for the young architect.

Truly ordered simplicity in the hands of the great artist may flower into a bewildering profusion, exquisitely exuberant, and render all more clear than ever. Good William Blake says exuberance is *beauty*, meaning that it is so in this very sense. This is for the Modern Artist with the Machine in his hands. False Simplicity—Simplicity as an affectation, that is Simplicity constructed as a Decorator's outside put upon a complicated, wasteful engineer's or carpenter's "Structure," outside or inside—is not good enough Simplicity. It cannot be simple at all. But that is what passes for Simplicity, now that startling Simplicity-effects are becoming the *fashion*. That kind of Simplicity is *violent*. This is for "Art and Decoration."

Soon we shall want Simplicity inviolate. There is one way to get that Simplicity. My guess is, there is *only* one way really to get it. And that way is, on principle, by way of *Construction* developed as Architecture. That is for us, one and all.

*Lewis Mumford*

# The Imperial Façade[1]

THE decade between 1890 and 1900 saw the rise of a new period in American architecture. This period had, it is true, been dimly foreshadowed by the grandiose L'Enfant, but if the superficial forms resembled those of the early republic, and if the precedents of classic architecture again became a guide, the dawning age was neither a revival nor a continuation.

In the meanwhile, fresh influences had entered. The generation of students who had studied in the Ecole des Beaux Arts after the Civil War was ready, at last, to follow the lone trail which Richard H. Hunt had blazed. Richardson's most intimate disciples reacted against the stamp of his personality and sought a more neutral mode of expression, consecrated by established canons of good taste. On top of this, the introduction of steel-cage construction removed the necessity for solid masonry, and placed a premium upon the mask. The stage was set for a new act of the drama.

All these influences shaped the style of our architecture when it arose; but the condition that gave it a substantial base was the rise of a new order in America's economic life. Up to this time, the chief industrial problem had been to improve the processes of mechanical production and to stake out new areas for exploitation. One may compare these economic advances to the separate

[1] From *Sticks and Stones* (New York: Boni & Liveright, 1924), pp. 123-151, with minor changes in the text made by the author. Reprinted by permission of the author.

sorties of an army operating on a wide front: any lone adventurer might take his courage in his hands and exploit an invention, or sink an oil well, if he could find it. By 1890 the frontier had closed; the major resources of the country were under the control of the monopolist; it became more important to consolidate gains than freshly to achieve them. Separate lines of railroads were welded into systems; separate steel plants and oil plants were wrought into trusts; and where monopoly did not rest upon a foundation of natural advantage, the "gentleman's agreement" began its service as a useful substitute. The popular movements which sought to challenge the forces of this new regime—the labor movement, socialism, populism—had neither analyzed the situation with sufficient care nor attracted the adherence of the majority. The defeat of Henry George as a local political candidate was symbolic: by 1888 a humane thinker like Edward Bellamy had already accepted the defeat, had embraced the idea of the trust, and had conceived a comprehensive utopia on the basis of letting the process of monopoly go the limit, so that finally, by a mere yank of the levers, the vast economic organizations of the country would become the "property" of the people.

The drift to the open lands came to a full pause. The land-empire had been conquered, and its overlords were waxing in power and riches: the name "millionaire" became the patent of America's new nobility. With the shift from industry to finance went a shift from the producing towns to the spending towns: architecture came to dwell in the stock exchanges, the banks, the shops, and the clubs of the metropolis; if it sought the countryside at all, it established itself in the villas that were newly laid out on hill and shore in the neighborhood of the great cities. The keys to this period are opulence and magnitude: "money to burn."

These years witnessed what the Roman historian, Ferrero, has called a *"véritable recommencement d'histoire."* In the new centers of privilege there arose a scale of living and a mode of architecture which, with all its attendant miseries, depletions, and exploitations, recalled the Rome of the first and second centuries after Christ. It is needless to say that vast acres of buildings, factories, shops, homes, were erected which had no relation at all to the imperial regime; for not everyone participated in either the benefits or the depressions that attended the growth of monopoly; but the accent of this period, the dominant note, was an imperial one. While the commonplace building of the time cannot be ignored, it remains, so to say, out of the picture.

Hardly had the process of concentration and consolidation begun before the proper form manifested itself. The occasion for its appearance was the World's Columbian Exposition, opened in 1893. In creating this fair, the enterprise and capacity for organization which the architects of Chicago had applied to the construction of the skyscraper transformed the unkempt wilderness of Jackson Park into the Great White City in the space of two short years. Here the architects of the country, particularly of New York and Chicago, appeared for the first time as a united profession, or, to speak more accurately, as a college.

Led by the New Yorkers, who had come more decisively under European influence, they brought to this exposition the combination of skill and taste in all the departments of the work that had, two centuries earlier, created the magnificent formalities of Versailles. There was unity of plan in the grouping of the main buildings about the lagoon; there was unity of tone and color in the gleaming white façades; there was unity of effect in the use of classic orders and classic forms of decoration. Lacking any genuine unity of ideas and purposes—for Root had initially conceived of a variegated oriental setting—the architects of the exposition had achieved the effects of unity by subordinating their work to an established precedent. They chanted a Roman litany above the Babel of individual styles. It was a capital triumph of the academic imagination. If these main buildings were architecture, America had never seen so much of it at one time before. Even that belated Greco-Puritan, Mr. Charles Eliot Norton, was warm in praise.

It would be foolish to quarrel with the style that was chosen for these exposition buildings, or to deny its propriety. Messrs. McKim, White, Hunt, and Burnham divined that they were fated to serve Renaissance despots and emperors with more than Roman power, and unerringly they chose the proper form for their activities. Whereas Rome had cast its spell over the architects of the early Renaissance because they wished once more to enter into its life, the life of its sages and poets and artists, it attracted the architects of the White City because of its external features—because of its stereotyped canons and rules—because of the relatively small number of choices it offered for a lapse in taste—because of its skill in conspicuous waste, and because of that very noncommittal quality in its massive forms which permitted the basilica to become a church, or the temple to become a modern bank.

Of all the Renaissance architects, their impulses and interests were nearest, perhaps, to Robert Adam, whose church at West Wycombe could be turned into a ballroom by the simple act of removing the pews, and permitting the gay walls and decorations to speak for themselves. Behind the white stiff façade of the World's Fair buildings was the steel and glass structure of the engineer: the building spoke one language and the "architecture" another. If the coming of the skyscraper had turned masonry into veneer, here was a mode of architecture which was little but veneer.

In their place, at the Fair, these classic buildings were all that could be demanded: Mr. Geoffrey Scott's defense of the Baroque, in The Architecture of Humanism, applies particularly to its essential manifestations in the Garden and the Theater—and why not in the Fair? Form and function, ornament and design, have no inherent relation, one with the other, when the mood of the architect is merely playful: there is no use in discussing the anatomy of architecture when its only aim is fancy dress. As a mask, as a caprice, the classic orders are as justifiable as the icing on a birthday cake: they divert the eye without damaging the structure that they conceal. Unfortunately, the architecture of the Renaissance has a tendency to imitate the haughty queen who advised the commons to eat cake. Logically, it demands that a Wall Street clerk shall live like a Lombardy prince, that a factory should be subordinated to esthetic contemplation; and since these things are impossible, it permits "mere building" to become illiterate and vulgar below the standards of the most debased vernacular. Correct in proportion, elegant in detail, courteous in relation to each other, the buildings of the World's Fair were, nevertheless, only the simulacra of a living architecture: they were the concentrated expression of an age which sought to produce "values" rather than goods. In comparison with this new style, the romanticism of the Victorian Age, with its avid respect for the medieval building traditions, was honesty and dignity itself.

The Roman precedent, modified by the work of Louis XIV and Napoleon III, by Le Nôtre and Haussmann, formed the basis not merely for the World's Fair, but for the host of city plans that were produced in the two decades that followed. It seemed for a while as if the architect might take the place of the engineer as city planner, and that the mangled regularity of the engineer's gridiron plan, laid down without respect to topographic advantage or to use, might be definitely supplanted in the remodeled central districts and in the new extensions and suburbs of the American city. The evil of the World's Fair triumph was that it suggested to the civic enthusiast that every city might become a fair: it introduced the notion of the City Beautiful as a sort of municipal cosmetic, and reduced the work of the architect to that of putting a pleasing front upon the scrappy building, upon the monotonous streets and the mean houses, that characterized vast areas in the newer and larger cities.

If the engineer who had devoted himself to sewers and street-plans alone had been superficial, the architectural city planner who centered attention upon parkways alone, grand avenues alone, and squares like the Place de l'Etoile alone, was equally superficial. The civic center and the parkway represented the better and more constructive side of this effort: in Cleveland, in Pittsburgh, in Springfield, Mass., harmonious groups of white buildings raised their heads above the tangle of commercial traffic, and in the restoration of L'Enfant's plan for Washington, the realities of the imperial regime at length caught up with the dreamer born out of his due time. A good many of these plans, however, were pathetically immature. One of the reports for Manhattan, for example, devoted pages and pages to showing the improvement that would follow the demolition of the wall around Central Park—and the importance of clipped trees in the design of grand avenues!

Plainly, the architect did not face with sufficient realism the colossal task with which he was confronted in the renovation of the city. He accepted his improvements too much at the value placed upon them by the leaders of Big Business—as a creator of land-values, as an element in increasing the commercial attractiveness of the city. Did not Mr. Daniel Burnham himself point to the improvements in Periclean Athens, not as the embodiment of Athenian citizenship and religion at its highest point, but as a measure for increasing the attractiveness of the city to visitors from abroad? Cut off from his true function to serve and beautify the community, made an accessory of business itself, like the merest salesman or advertising agent, it is no wonder that the architect speedily lost his leadership; and that the initiative went once again into the hands of the engineer.

The main merit of all these efforts to perpetuate the World's Fair is that they sought to achieve some of the dignity and decisiveness of the formal plan. Their weakness was that they neglected new elements, like the billboard, the skysign, the subway, the tall building, which undermined the effects of the plan even when it was achieved. In their efforts to escape from the welter of misguided commercial enterprise, the advocates of the city beautiful placed too great reliance upon spots of outward order and decency; they took refuge in the paper symmetry of axial avenues and round-points, as one finds them in Haussmann's Paris, and neglected the deeper and more genuine beauties of, let us say, the High Street in Oxford or Chipping Camden, or of many another European town that had achieved completion in its essentials before the nineteenth century.

In short, the advocates of the city beautiful sought a remedy on paper which could be purchased only by a thorough reorganization of the community's life. If all this applies to the better side of the World's Fair, it touches even more emphatically the worse.

The twenty years between 1890 and 1910 saw the complete rehabilitation of the Roman mode, as the very cloak and costume of imperial enterprise. The main effort of architecture was to give an effect of dignity and permanence to the façades of the principal thoroughfares: the public buildings must dominate the compositions, numerous boulevards and avenues must concentrate the traffic at certain points and guide the stranger to the markets and amusements: where possible, as in the Chicago plan, by Messrs. Burnham and Bennett, avenues must be cut through the gridiron pattern of blocks in order to achieve these effects. If this imperial street system is somewhat arbitrary, and if the necessary work of grading, filling, demolishing, and purchasing existing property rights is extremely costly, the end, nevertheless, justifies the means—the architecture impresses and awes a populace that shares vicariously in its glories. Should the effect prove a little too austere and formidable, the monuments will be offset with circuses and hippodromes.

In all this, the World's Fair was a precise and classic example, for it reproduced in miniature the imperial order. When the panic of 1893 kept people away from the exhibitions of art, industry, and culture, sideshows were promptly introduced by the astute organizers. Beyond the serene classic façades, which recalled the elevation of a Marcus Aurelius, sprawled the barkers, the freaks, and the tricksters, whose gaudy booths might have reminded the spectator of the other side of the imperial shield—the gaminism of Petronius Arbiter. The transformation of these white façades into the Gay White Ways came during the next decade; whilst the sideshows achieved a separate existence as "Coney Island." On top of this came the development of the mildly gladiatorial spectacles of football and baseball: at first invented for playful exercise, they became a standard means of exhibition by more or less professional performers. The erection of numerous amphitheaters and arenas, such as the Yale Bowl, the Harvard Stadium, the Lewisohn Stadium, and their counterparts in the West, rounded out the imperial spectacle.

By a happy congruence of forces, the large-scale manufacture of Portland cement, and the reintroduction of the Roman method of concrete construction, came during the same period. Can anyone contemplate this scene and still fancy that imperialism was nothing more than a move for foreign markets and territories of exploitation? On the contrary, it was a tendency that expressed itself in every department of Western civilization, and if it appears most naked, perhaps, in America, that is only because, as in the earlier periods, there was so little here to stand in its way. Mr. Louis Sullivan might well complain, in The Autobiography of an Idea, that imperialism stifled the more creative modes of architecture which might have derived from our fine achievements in science, from our tentative experiments in democracy. It seems inevitable, however, that the dominant fact in our civilization should stamp the most important monuments and buildings with its image. In justice to the great professors of the classic style, Messrs. McKim and Burnham and Carrere and Hastings, one must admit that the age shaped them and chose them and used them for its ends. Their mode of building was almost unescapably determined by the milieu in which they worked.

The change in the social scene which favored an imperial setting was not without its effects upon the industries that supplied the materials for architecture, and upon the processes of building itself. Financial concentration in the stone quarries, for example, was abetted by the creation of a national system of rail transportation, and partly, perhaps, by the elaboration of the mechanical equipment for cutting and trimming stone beyond a point where a small plant could work economically. The result was that during this period numerous small local quarries, which had been called into existence by Richardson's fine eye for color contrasts, were allowed to lapse. Vermont marble and Indiana limestone served better the traditions that had been created in the White City.

The carrying of coals to Newcastle is always a pathetic practice; it remained for the imperial age to make it a subject for boasting. Just as many Connecticut towns whose nearby fields are full of excellent granite boulders, boast a bank or a library of remote marble, so New York City, which has a solid foundation of schist, gneiss, and limestone, can point to only a handful of buildings, notably the College of the City of New York and Mr. Goodhue's Church of the Intercession, in which these excellent local materials were used. The curious result of being able by means of railway transportation to draw upon the ends of the earth for materials has been, not variety, but monotony. Under the imperial order the architect was forced to design structures that were identical in style, treatment, and material, though they were placed thousands of miles apart and differed in every important function. This ignorance of regional resources is not incompatible with grand effects, or even on occasion with decently good architecture. But it does not profit by that fine adaptation to site, that justness of proportion in the size of window and slope of roof, which is an earnest of the architect's mastery of the local situation. Substitute Manila for the military colony of Timgad, or Los Angeles for Alexandria, and it is plain that we have here another aspect of Ferrero's generalization. Even architects whose place of work was nearer to the site of their buildings were, nevertheless, compelled to copy the style of the more successful practitioners in New York and Chicago.

In government, in industry, in architecture, the imperial age was one. The underlying policy of imperialism is to exploit the life and resources of separate regions for the benefit of the holders of privilege in the capital city. Under this rule, all roads lead literally to Rome. While, as the German historian, W. H. Riehl, points out, the provincial highroads served to bring the city out into the countryside, the railroads served to bring the major cities together and to drain the products of rural regions into the metropolis. It was no accident that the great triumphs of American architecture during the imperial period were the railroad stations; particularly the Pennsylvania and the Grand Central in New York, and the Union Station in Washington. Nor is it by mere chance that the Washington and the Pennsylvania stations are the monuments to two architects, McKim and Burnham, who worshiped most whole-heartedly at the imperial shrine. With capital insight, these men established the American Academy at Rome: they recognized their home.

Esthetically considered, it is true, perhaps, that the finest element in the Pennsylvania station is the train hall, where the architect has dealt sincerely with his steel elements and has not permitted himself to cast a fond, retrospective eye upon the Roman baths. When all allowances are made, however, there remains less for criticism in the railway stations and the stadiums—those genuinely Roman bequests—than in any of the other imperial monuments. Indeed, so well does Roman architecture lend itself to the railroad station that one of the prime virtues of such a building, namely ease of circulation, was even communicated to the New York Public Library, where it is nothing but a nuisance, since it both increases the amount of noise and diminishes the amount of space for reading rooms that are already overcrowded.

Here, indeed, is the capital defect of an established and formalized mode: it tends to make the architect think of a new problem in terms of an old solution for a different problem. Mr. Charles McKim, for example, found himself hampered in the competition over the New York Public Library because the demands of the librarian for a convenient and expeditious administration of his business interfered with the full-blown conception which Mr. McKim had in mind. All this happened after years of demonstration in the Boston Library of Messrs. McKim and White's failure to meet that problem squarely; and it apparently was not affected by Mr. McKim's experience with the great Columbia Library, which has ample space for everything except books. In short, the classic style served well enough only when the building to be erected had some direct relation to the needs and interests of the Roman world—the concourse of idlers in the baths or the tiers of spectators in the circuses and hippodromes. When it came face to face with our own day, it had but little to say, and it said that badly, as anyone who will patiently examine the superimposed orders on the American Telegraph Building in New York will discover for himself.

With the transition from republican to imperial Rome, numerous monuments were erected to the Divine Caesar. Within a much shorter time than marked the growth of the imperial tradition in America, a similar edification of patriotic memories took place.

In the restoration of the original plan of Washington, which began in 1901, the axis of the plan was so altered as to make it pass through the Washington Monument; and at the same time the place of the Lincoln Memorial, designed by the late Mr. Henry Bacon, a pupil of Mr. McKim's, was assigned. This was the first of a whole series of temples devoted to the national deities. In the Lincoln Memorial, in the McKinley Memorial at Niles, Ohio, in the Hall of Fame at New York University, and in their prototype, Grant's Tomb, one feels not the living beauty of our American past, but the mortuary air of archaeology. The America that Lincoln was bred in, the homespun and humane and humorous America that he wished to preserve, has nothing in common with the sedulously classic monument that was erected to his memory. Who lives in that shrine, I wonder—Lincoln, or the men who conceived it: the leader who beheld the mournful victory of the Civil War, or the generation that took pleasure in the mean triumph of the Spanish-American exploit, and placed the imperial standard in the Philippines and the Caribbean?

On the plane of private citizenship, a similar movement took place: while before 1890 one can count the tombs in our cemeteries that boast loudly of the owner's earthly possessions and power, from that time onward the miniature temple-mausoleum becomes more and more frequent. In fact, an entire history of architecture could be deduced from our cemeteries; all that has so far been described could be marked in the progress from the simple slab, carved in almost Attic purity with a weeping willow or a cubistic cherub, that characterized the eighteenth century, to the bad lettering and the more awkward headstones of the early nineteenth century; and from this to the introduction of polished granite and iron ornament in the post-Civil War cemetery, down to the mechanically perfect mausoleum, where the corpses are packed like the occupants of a subway train, that some of our more effusively progressive communities boast of today. As we live, so we die: no wonder Shelley described Hell as a place much like London.

The Roman development of New York, Chicago, Washington, and the lesser metropolises, had an important effect upon the homes of the people. Historically, the imperial monument and the slum-tenement go hand in hand. The same process that creates an unearned increment for the landlords who possess favored sites, contributes a generous quota—which might be called the unearned excrement—of depression, overcrowding, and bad living, in the dormitory districts of the city. This had happened in imperial Rome; it had happened again in Paris under Napoleon III, where Haussmann's sweeping reconstructions created new slums in the districts behind the grand avenues, quite as bad, if far less obvious, as those that had been cleared away; and it happened once again in our American cities. Whereas in Rome a certain limit, however, was placed upon the expansion of the city because of the low development of vehicular traffic, the rise of mechanical transportation placed no bounds at all on the American city. If Rome was forced to create huge engineering projects like aqueducts and sewers in order to cleanse the inhabitants and remove the offal of its congested districts, the American city followed the example of the modern Romes like London and Paris by devising man-sewers, in which the mass of plebeians could be daily drained back and forth between their dormitories and their factories.

So far from relieving congestion, these colossal pieces of engineering only made more of it possible: by pouring more feeder lines into the central district of New York, Boston, Chicago, or where you will, rapid transit increased the housing congestion at one end and the business-congestion at the other. As for the primary sewer system devised for the imperial metropolis, it could scarcely even claim, with rapid transit, that it was a valuable commercial investment. The water outlets of New York are so thoroughly polluted that not merely have the shad and the oyster beds vanished from the Hudson River, where both once flourished, but it is a serious question whether the tides can continue to transport their vast load of sewage without a preliminary reduction of its content. Like the extension of the water conduits into the Adirondacks, all these necessary little improvements add to the per capita cost of living in an imperial metropolis, without providing a single benefit that a smaller city with no need for such improvements does not enjoy. In the matter of public parks, for example, the Committee on Congestion in New York, in 1911, calculated that the park space needed for the East Side alone, on the scale provided by the city of Hartford, would be greater than the entire area of Manhattan Island. In short, even for its bare utilitarian requirements, the mass-city, as the Germans call it, costs more and gives less than communities which have not had imperial greatness inflicted upon them.

As to the more positive improvements under the imperial regime, history leaves no doubt as to their dubious character, and current observation only reinforces history's lesson. In discussing the growth of the tenement in Rome after the Great Fire, Friedlander says:

"The motives for piling up storeys were as strong as ever: the site for Caesar's Forum had cost over £875,000 compensation to tenants and ground landlords. Rome had loftier houses than modern capital. A disproportionately large part of the area available for building was monopolized by the few, in consequence of the waste of space in the plethoric architecture of the day, and a very considerable portion was swallowed up by the public places, such as the imperial forums, which took up six hectares, as well as by the traffic regulations and extensions of the streets. The transformation and decoration of Rome by the Caesars enhanced the scarcity of housing, as did Napoleon III's improvements in Paris. A further adjutory cause of the increase in the price of dwellings was the habit of speculation in house property (which Crassus had practiced in great style) and the monopoly of the proprietors, in consequence of which houses were let and sublet."

It would be tedious to draw out the parallel: given similar social conditions in America we have not been able to escape the same social results, even down to the fact that the palliatives of private philanthropy flourish here again as they had not flourished anywhere on the same scale since the Roman Empire. So much for imperial greatness. When an architect like Mr. Edward Bennett can say, as he did in The Significance of the Fine Arts: "House the people densely, if necessary, but conserve great acres for recreation," we need not be in doubt as to who will profit by the density and who will profit, at the other end, by the recreation. It is not merely that the park must be produced to remedy the congestion: it is even more that the congestion must be produced in order to provide for the park. To profit by both the disease and the remedy is one of the masterstrokes of imperialist enterprise. Mr. Daniel Burnham said of the World's Fair, according to Mr. Bennett and Mr. Charles Moore, "that it is what the Romans would have wished to create in permanent form." One may say of our imperial cities that they are what the Romans did create—but whether the form will be permanent or not is a matter we may leave to the sardonic attentions of history.

For my own part, I think we have at last acquired a criterion which will enable us to sum up the architecture of the imperial age, and deal justly with these railroad stations and stadiums, these sewers and circuses, these aqueducts and parkways and grand avenues. Our imperial architecture is an architecture of compensation: it provides grandiloquent stones for people who have been deprived of bread and sunlight and all that keeps man from becoming vile. Behind the monumental façades of our metropolises trudges a landless proletariat, doomed to the servile routine of the factory system; and beyond the great cities lies a countryside whose goods are drained away, whose children are uprooted from the soil on the prospect of easy gain and endless amusements, and whose remaining cultivators are steadily drifting into the ranks of an abject tenantry. This is not a casual observation: it is the translation of the last three census reports into plain English. Can one take the pretensions of this architecture seriously; can one worry about its esthetics or take delight in such forms as Mr. Pope's Temple of the Scottish Rite in Washington, or Mr. Bacon's Lincoln Memorial? Yes, perhaps—if one refuses to look beyond the mask.

Even in some of its proudest buildings, the imperial show wears thin; and one need not peer into the slums beyond in order to realize its defects. The rear of the Metropolitan Museum or the Brooklyn Museum, for example, might be the rear of a row of Bronx tenements or Long Island City factories, so gaunt and barren and hideous is their aspect. If the imperial age was foreshadowed in the World's Fair, it has received its apotheosis in the museum. In contrast to the local museums one still finds occasionally in Europe, which are little more than extensions of the local curio cabinet, the imperial museum is essentially a loot-heap, a comprehensive repository for plunder. The sage Viollet-le-Duc once patly said that he preferred to see his apples hanging on a tree, rather than arranged in rows in the fruit shops; but the animus of the museum is to value the plucked fruit more than the tree that bore it.

Into the museum come the disjecta membra of other lands, other cultures, other civilizations. All that had once been a living faith and practice is here reduced to a separate specimen, pattern, or form. For the museum, the world of art has already been created: the future is restricted to a duplication of the perfected past. This animus is identic with that which made the Romans so skillful in copying Greek statues and so dull in carving their own; a desirable habit of humility were it not for the fact that the works of art in the past could not have been created had our ancestors been so punctual in respect to finished designs. The one thing the museum cannot attempt to do is to supply a soil for living art: all that it can present is a pattern for reproduction. To the extent that an insincere or imitative art is better than no art at all, the Imperial Age marked an advance: to the extent, however, that a living art is a fresh gesture of the spirit, the museum confessed all too plainly that the age had no fresh gestures to make; on that score, it was a failure, and the copying of period furniture and the design of period architecture were the livid proofs of that failure.

The museum is a manifestation of our curiosity, our acquisitiveness, our essentially predatory culture; and these qualities were copiously exhibited in the architecture of imperialism. It would be foolish to reproach the great run of architects for exploiting the characteristics of their age; for even those who in belief and design have remained outside the age—such resolute advocates of a medieval polity as Dr. Ralph Adams Cram—have not been able to divert its currents. In so far as we have learned to care more for empire than for a community of freemen living the good life, more for dominion over palm and pine than for the humane discipline of ourselves, the architect has but enshrined our desires. The opulence, the waste of resources and energies, the perversion of human effort represented in this architecture are but the outcome of our general scheme of working and living. Architecture, like government, is about as good as a community deserves. The shell that we create for ourselves marks our spiritual development as plainly as that of a snail denotes its species. If sometimes architecture becomes frozen music, we have ourselves to thank when it is a pompous blare of meaningless sounds.

❦ ❦ ❦

*Bernard Shaw*

# Handel's Messiah and Beethoven's Centenary[1]

## HANDEL'S MESSIAH

CHRISTMAS being the season of mirth, music, the great English killjoy, with its intolerable hypocrisies, is gladly put away until it is time to return to work and duty and mental improvement and other unpleasantnesses; consequently my critical machinery has got out of gear somewhat. I might have kept off the rust by attending the regulation Christmas performance of *The Messiah*; but I have long since recognized the impossibility of obtaining justice for that work in a Christian country. Import a choir of heathens, restrained by no considerations of propriety from attacking the choruses with unembarrassed sincerity of dramatic expression, and I would hasten to the performance if only to witness the delight of the public and the discomfiture of the critics. That is, if anything so indecent would be allowed here. We have all had our Handelian training in church, and the perfect churchgoing mood is one of pure abstract reverence. A mood of active intelligence would be scandalous. Thus we get broken in to the custom of singing Handel as if he meant nothing; and as it happens that he meant a great deal, and was tremendously in earnest about it, we know rather less about him in England than they do in the Andaman Islands, since the Andamans are only unconscious of him, whereas we are misconscious. To hear a thousand respectable young English persons jogging through *For He shall purify the sons of Levi* as if every group of semiquavers were a whole bar of four crotchets a capella, or repeating *Let Him deliver Him if He delight in Him* with exactly the same subdued and uncovered air as in *For with His stripes we are healed*, or lumbering along with *Hallelujah* as if it were a superior sort of family coach: all this is ludicrous enough; but when the nation proceeds to brag of these unwieldy choral impostures, these attempts to make the brute force of a thousand throats do what can only be done by artistic insight and skill, then I really lose patience. Why, instead of wasting huge sums on the multitudinous dullness called a Handel Festival does not somebody set up a thoroughly rehearsed and exhaustively studied performance of *The Messiah* in St. James's Hall with a chorus of twenty capable artists? Most of us would be glad to hear the work seriously performed once before we die.

However, if I did not go to *The Messiah*, I ventured on a pantomime, although in London we are unable to produce an endurable pantomime for exactly the same reasons that prevent us from achieving an endurable performance of *The Messiah*. Therefore I did not make the experiment in London. I

[1] From *Shaw on Music: A Selection from the Music Criticism of Shaw*, by Eric Bentley (New York: Anchor Books, Doubleday & Company, Inc., 1955), pp. 245-252, 83-89. Reprinted by permission of The Public Trustee and The Society of Authors.

found myself one evening in Bristol with nothing better to do than to see whether pantomime is really moribund. I am bound to say that it seems to me to be as lively as it was twenty-five years ago. The fairy queen, singing In Old Madrid with reckless irrelevance at the entrance to the cave where Aladdin found the lamp, was listened to with deep respect as an exponent of the higher singing; and in the cave itself The Bogie Man, in about fifty verses, took immensely. A street scene at night, with Chinese lanterns and a willow-pattern landscape, were stage pictures with just the right artistic quality for the occasion; and the absurdity of the whole affair on the dramatic side was amusing enough from an indulgent holiday point of view. There were no processions presenting one silly idea over and over again in different colored tights, until a thousand pounds had been wasted in boring the audience to distraction. And—though here I hardly expect to be believed—there was not a single child under ten on the stage. I told Mr. Macready Chute, the manager, that he should come to London to learn from our famous stage-managers here how to spend ten times as much money on a pantomime for one-tenth of the artistic return. I bade him, if he thirsted for metropolitan fame, to take for his triple motto, Expenditure, inanity, vulgarity, and that soon no spectacular piece would be deemed complete without him. With these precepts I left him, assuring him that I felt more than ever what a privilege it was to live in a convenient art-centre like London, where the nearest pantomime is at Bristol, and the nearest opera at Bayreuth.

*21 January 1891*

### THE MESSIAH AGAIN

Fundamentally my view of the Handel Festival is that of a convinced and ardent admirer of Handel. My favorite oratorio is *The Messiah*, with which I have spent many of the hours which others give to Shakespeare, or Scott, or Dickens. But for all this primary bias in favor of Handel, my business is still to be that of the critic, who, invited to pronounce an opinion on the merits of a performance by four thousand executants, must judge these abnormal conditions by their effect on the work as open-mindedly as if there were only four hundred, or forty, or four. And I am bound to add that he who, so judging, delivers a single and unqualified verdict on the Festival, stultifies himself. The very same conditions which make one choral number majestic, imposing, even sublime, make another heavy, mechanical, meaningless. For instance, no host could be too mighty for the Hallelujah Chorus, or See the Conquering Hero. In them every individual chorister knows without study or instruction what he has to do and how he has to feel. The impulse to sing spreads even to the audience; and those who are old hands at choral singing do not always restrain it.

I saw more than one of my neighbors joining in the Hallelujah on the first day; and if my feelings at that moment had permitted me to make a properly controlled artistic effort, I think I should have been no more able to remain silent than Santley was. Under the circumstances, however, I followed the example of Albani, who, knowing that she had to save her voice for *I know that my Redeemer liveth*, kept a vocal score tightly on her mouth the whole time, and looked over it with the expression of a child confronted with some intolerably tempting sweetmeat which it knows it must not touch.

But *The Messiah* is not all Hallelujah. Compare such a moment as I have just described with the experience of listening to the fiercely tumultuous *He trusted in God*, with its alternations of sullen mockery with high-pitched derision, and its savage shouts of *Let Him deliver Him if He delight in Him*, jogging along at about half the proper speed, with an expression of the deepest respect and propriety, as if a large body of the leading citizens, headed by the mayor, were presenting a surpassingly dull address to somebody. There may be, in the way of the proper presentation of such a chorus as this, something of the difficulty which confronted Wagner at the rehearsals of Tannhäuser in Paris in 1861, when he asked the ballet master to make his forces attack the Bacchanal in a bacchanalian way. "I understand perfectly what you mean," said the functionary; "but only to a whole ballet of *premiers sujets* dare I breathe such suggestions."

No doubt Mr. Manns's three thousand five hundred choristers might better his instructions so heartily as to go considerably beyond the utmost licence of art if he told them that unless they sang that chorus like a howling bloodthirsty mob, the utter loneliness of *Thy rebuke hath broken his heart*, and *Behold and see*, must be lost, and with it the whole force of the tragic climax of the oratorio. Besides which, there is the physical difficulty, which only a skilled and powerful orator could fully surmount, of giving instruction of that kind to such a host. But I see no reason why matters should not be vastly improved if Mr. Manns would adopt throughout the bolder policy as to speed which was forced on him after four on Selection day by the silent urgency of the clock, and persisted in to some extent—always with convincing effect—in Israel. Increased speed, however, is not all that is wanted. To get rid completely of the insufferable lumbering which is the curse of English Handelian choral singing, a spirited reform in style is needed.

For instance, Handel, in his vigorous moods, is fond of launching the whole mass of voices into florid passages of great brilliancy and impetuosity. In one of the most splendid choruses in *The Messiah, For He shall purify the sons of Levi*, the syllable "fy" comes out in a single trait consisting of no less than thirty-two semiquavers. That trait should be sung with one impulse from end to end without an instant's hesitation. How is it actually done in England? Just as if the thirty-two semiquavers were eight bars of crotchets taken alla breve in a not very lively tempo. The effect, of course, is to make the chorus so dull that all the reputation of Handel is needed to persuade Englishmen that they ought to enjoy it, whilst Frenchmen go away from our festivals confirmed in their skepticism as to our pet musical classic. When I had been listening for some minutes on Wednesday to the festival choristers trudging with ludicrous gravity through what they called *Tellit Outa Mongthe Hea-ea Then*, I could not

help wishing that Santley, who roused them to boundless enthusiasm by his
singing of Why do the nations, had given them a taste of their own quality by
delivering those chains of triplets on the words "rage" and "counsel," as
quavers in twelve-eight time in the tempo of the Pastoral Symphony. The
celestial Lift up your heads, O ye gates, lost half its triumphant exultation
from this heaviness of gait.

Again, in the beginning of For unto us, the tenors and basses told each
other the news in a prosaic, methodical way which made the chorus quite comic
until the thundering Wonderful, Counsellor, one of Handel's mightiest strokes,
was reached; and even here the effect was disappointing, because the chorus,
having held nothing in reserve, could make no climax. The orchestra needed at
that point about twenty more of the biggest of big drums. Another lost
opportunity was the pathetically grand conclusion of All we like sheep. Nothing in the whole work needs to be sung with more intense expression than
But the Lord hath laid on Him the iniquity of us all. Unless it sounds as if the
singers were touched to their very hearts, they had better not sing it at all. On
that Monday it came as mechanically as if the four entries of the voices had
been produced by drawing four stops in an organ. This was the greater pity,
because it must be conceded to our young Handel-sceptics that the preceding
musical portraiture of the sheep going astray has no great claims on their
reverence.

I am aware that many people who feel the shortcomings of our choral style
bear with it under the impression, first, that the English people are naturally
too slow and shy in their musical ways, and, second, that bravura vocalization
and impetuous speed are not possible or safe with large choruses. To this I
reply, first, that the natural fault of the English when they are singing with
genuine feeling is not slowness, but rowdiness, as the neighbors of the Salvation Army know; second, that it would undoubtedly be as risky to venture far
in the bravura direction with a very small chorus as to attempt the Walküre
fire-music or Liszt's Mazeppa in an ordinary theatre orchestra with its little
handful of strings. But both these compositions are safe with sixteen first and
sixteen second violins, because, though notes are dropped and mistakes made,
they are not all made simultaneously, and the result is that at any given instant
an overwhelming majority of the violins are right. For the same reason, I do
not see why nine hundred basses, even if they were the stiffest and slowest in
the world, could not be safely sent at full speed in the bravura style through
Handel's easy diatonic semiquaver traits, as safely as our violinists are now sent
through Wagner's demisemiquavers.

So much for the compatibility of speed with accuracy. As to safety, I need
only appeal to the results achieved by Mr. Manns on Friday, when he got away
from The Messiah, which is too sentimental for him, to Israel, which is far
more congenial to his temperament. The only choral number in this which was
quite unsatisfactory was I will exalt Him; and here the shortcoming was made
unavoidable by the peculiar style of the chorus, since it—like And with His

*stripes* in *The Messiah*—requires a beauty of execution which would suffice for a mass by Palestrina, and which is out of the question under Handel Festival conditions. The other choruses were spirited and forcible—some of them magnificent. *He gave them hailstones, But the waters overwhelmed,* and *The horse and his rider* were tremendous: one felt after them that the festival had justified its existence beyond all cavil.

If these criticisms are to bear any fruit in raising the festival performances of *The Messiah* to a typical artistic perfection—a result which I believe to be quite possible, and certainly well worth striving for—they must be weighed, not by Mr. Manns or the Crystal Palace authorities, but by the local conductors throughout the country, who coach their contingents in the work, and send them up with preconceived ideas as to its execution which Mr. Manns is powerless to change or even greatly to modify. Every contingent trained by a mere organist, to whom *The Messiah* is but a part of the drudgery of his professional routine, is simply a nuisance on the Handel orchestra. And every contingent trained by an artist who ranks the work among his treasures, and part of whose artistic ambition it is to hear at last in England a really adequate performance of it, is, as Judas Maccabeus says, "a thousand men."

*1 July 1891*

### BEETHOVEN'S CENTENARY

A hundred years ago a crusty old bachelor of fifty-seven, so deaf that he could not hear his own music played by a full orchestra, yet still able to hear thunder, shook his fist at the roaring heavens for the last time, and died as he had lived, challenging God and defying the universe. He was Defiance Incarnate: he could not even meet a Grand Duke and his court in the street without jamming his hat tight down on his head and striding through the very middle of them. He had the manners of a disobliging steamroller (most steamrollers are abjectly obliging and conciliatory); and he was rather less particular about his dress than a scarecrow: in fact he was once arrested as a tramp because the police refused to believe that such a tatterdemalion could be a famous composer, much less a temple of the most turbulent spirit that ever found expression in pure sound. It was indeed a mighty spirit; but if I had written the mightiest, which would mean mightier than the spirit of Handel, Beethoven himself would have rebuked me; and what mortal man could pretend to a spirit mightier than Bach's? But that Beethoven's spirit was the most turbulent is beyond all question. The impetuous fury of his strength, which he could quite easily contain and control, but often would not, and the uproariousness of his fun, go beyond anything of the kind to be found in the works of other composers. Greenhorns write of syncopation now as if it were a new way of giving the utmost impetus to a musical measure; but the rowdiest jazz sounds like *The Maiden's Prayer* after Beethoven's third *Leonora* overture; and certainly no negro corobbery that I ever heard could inspire the blackest dancer with such *diable au corps* as the last movement of the *Seventh Symphony*. And no other composer has ever melted his hearers into complete sentimentality by the tender beauty of his music, and then suddenly turned on them and mocked them with derisive trumpet blasts for being such fools. Nobody but Beethoven could govern Beethoven; and when, as happened when the fit was on him, he deliberately refused to govern himself, he was ungovernable.

It was this turbulence, this deliberate disorder, this mockery, this reckless and triumphant disregard of conventional manners, that set Beethoven apart from the musical geniuses of the ceremonious seventeenth and eighteenth centuries. He was a giant wave in that storm of the human spirit which produced the French Revolution. He called no man master. Mozart, his greatest predecessor in his own department, had from his childhood been washed, combed, splendidly dressed, and beautifully behaved in the presence of royal personages and peers. His childish outburst at the Pompadour, "Who is this woman who does not kiss me? The Queen kisses me," would be incredible of Beethoven, who was still an unlicked cub even when he had grown into a very grizzly bear. Mozart had the refinement of convention and society as well as the refinement of nature and of the solitudes of the soul. Mozart and Gluck are refined as the court of Louis XIV was refined: Haydn is refined as the most cultivated country gentlemen of his day were refined: compared to them socially Beethoven was an obstreperous Bohemian: a man of the people. Haydn, so superior to envy that he declared his junior, Mozart, to be the greatest composer that ever lived, could not stand Beethoven: Mozart, more farseeing, listened to his playing, and said "You will hear of him some day"; but the two would never have hit it off together had Mozart lived long enough to try. Beethoven had a moral horror of Mozart, who in *Don Giovanni* had thrown a halo of enchantment round an aristocratic blackguard, and then, with the unscrupulous moral versatility of a born dramatist, turned round to cast a halo of divinity round Sarastro, setting his words to the only music yet written that would not sound out of place in the mouth of God.

Beethoven was no dramatist: moral versatility was to him revolting cynicism. Mozart was still to him the master of masters (this is not an empty eulogistic superlative: it means literally that Mozart is a composer's composer much more than he has ever been a really popular composer); but he was a court flunkey in breeches whilst Beethoven was a Sansculotte; and Haydn also was a flunkey in the old livery: the Revolution stood between them as it stood between the eighteenth and nineteenth centuries. But to Beethoven Mozart was worse than Haydn because he trifled with morality by setting vice to music as magically as virtue. The Puritan who is in every true Sansculotte rose up against him in Beethoven, though Mozart had shewn him all the possibilities of nineteenth-century music. So Beethoven cast back for a hero to Handel, another crusty old bachelor of his own kidney, who despised Mozart's hero Gluck, though the pastoral symphony in *The Messiah* is the nearest thing in music to the scenes in which Gluck, in his Orfeo, opened to us the plains of Heaven.

Thanks to broadcasting, millions of musical novices will hear the music of Beethoven this anniversary year for the first time with their expectations raised to an extraordinary pitch by hundreds of newspaper articles piling up all the conventional eulogies that are applied indiscriminately to all the great composers. And like his contemporaries they will be puzzled by getting from him not merely a music that they did not expect, but often an orchestral hurlyburly that they may not recognize as what they call music at all, though they can appreciate Gluck and Haydn and Mozart quite well. The explanation is simple enough. The music of the eighteenth century is all dance music. A dance is a symmetrical pattern of steps that are pleasant to move to; and its music is a symmetrical pattern of sound that is pleasant to listen to even when you are not dancing to it. Consequently the sound patterns, though they begin by being as simple as chessboards, get lengthened and elaborated and enriched with harmonies until they are more like Persian carpets; and the composers who design these patterns no longer expect people to dance to them. Only a whirling Dervish could dance a Mozart symphony: indeed, I have reduced two young and practised dancers to exhaustion by making them dance a Mozart overture. The very names of the dances are dropped: instead of suites consisting of sarabands, pavanes, gavottes, and jigs, the designs are presented as sonatas and symphonies consisting of sections called simply movements, and labelled according to their speed (in Italian) as allegros, adagios, scherzos, and prestos. But all the time, from Bach's preludes to Mozart's *Jupiter Symphony*, the music makes a symmetrical sound pattern, and gives us the dancer's pleasure always as the form and foundation of the piece.

Music, however, can do more than make beautiful sound patterns. It can express emotion. You can look at a Persian carpet and listen to a Bach prelude with a delicious admiration that goes no further than itself; but you cannot listen to the overture to *Don Giovanni* without being thrown into a complicated mood which prepares you for a tragedy of some terrible doom overshadowing an exquisite but Satanic gaiety. If you listen to the last movement of Mozart's *Jupiter Symphony*, you hear that it is as much a riotous corobbery as the last movement of Beethoven's *Seventh Symphony*: it is an orgy of ranting drumming tow-row-row, made poignant by an opening strain of strange and painful beauty which is woven through the pattern all through. And yet the movement is a masterpiece of pattern designing all the time.

Now what Beethoven did, and what made some of his greatest contemporaries give him up as a madman with lucid intervals of clowning and bad taste, was that he used music altogether as a means of expressing moods, and completely threw over pattern designing as an end in itself. It is true that he used the old patterns all his life with dogged conservatism (another Sansculotte characteristic, by the way); but he imposed on them such an overwhelming charge of human energy and passion, including that highest passion which accompanies thought, and reduces the passion of the physical appetites to mere animalism, that he not only played Old Harry with their symmetry but often made it impossible to notice that there was any pattern at all beneath the storm of emotion. *The Eroica Symphony* begins by a pattern (borrowed from an overture which Mozart wrote when he was a boy), followed by a couple more very pretty patterns; but they are tremendously energized, and in the middle of the movement the patterns are torn up savagely; and Beethoven, from the point of view of the mere pattern musician, goes raving mad, hurling out terrible chords in which all the notes of the scale are sounded simultaneously, just because he feels like that, and wants you to feel like it.

And there you have the whole secret of Beethoven. He could design patterns with the best of them; he could write music whose beauty will last you all your life; he could take the driest sticks of themes and work them up so interestingly that you find something new in them at the hundredth hearing: in short, you can say of him all that you can say of the greatest pattern composers; but his diagnostic, the thing that marks him out from all the others, is his disturbing quality, his power of unsettling us and imposing his giant moods on us. Berlioz was very angry with an old French composer who expressed the discomfort Beethoven gave him by saying *"J'aime la musique qui me berce,"* "I like music that lulls me." Beethoven's is music that wakes you up; and the one mood in which you shrink from it is the mood in which you want to be let alone.

When you understand this you will advance beyond the eighteenth century and the old-fashioned dance band (jazz, by the way, is the old dance band Beethovenized), and understand not only Beethoven's music, but what is deepest in post-Beethoven music as well.

*From the Radio Times*
*18 March 1927*

*Roger Sessions*

# The Listener[1]

WE ARE all very much concerned, these days, with the listener—the person who neither makes music nor performs it, but simply listens to it. The market is flooded with books of all sorts, fulfilling all sorts of functions for all sorts of listeners, from the child to "the man who enjoys *Hamlet*" and even "the intelligent listener"—analyses to edify him, critical chit-chat to flatter him, and gossip to amuse him. We have grade school, high school, and university courses designed to inform him and, if possible, to educate him in "appreciation," in "intelligent listening," and even "creative listening." On the radio he may find quiz programs, interviews with personalities, broadcast orchestra rehearsals, and

[1] From *The Musical Experience of Composer, Performer, Listener* (Princeton: Princeton University Press, 1950), pp. 87-106. Copyright, 1950, Princeton University Press.

spoken program notes, which have been known on occasion to be so long that there is not enough time for the broadcast of the music. Surely we are leaving no stone unturned in the effort to prepare the listener fully for the strenuous task of listening to music.

This is actually a peculiar state of affairs. Music, and in fact art in general, is not one of the so-called necessities of life, nor does it yield us any of the creature comforts associated with the standard of living of which we are so proud. Why then should we be so concerned about the listener? Is not music available to him, if he wants it? Should we not rather demand simply that the listener be given the best products available? Should we not rather concern ourselves with the quality of our music, and with ways of producing the highest quality, with providing the best possible education for our young musicians, and with creating opportunities for them to function according to their merits? In truth, should we not rather devote ourselves to improving the quality of our music, and to seeing that music of the highest quality is available for all that wish to hear it?

Of course, we have no such choice of alternatives; and the concern that is felt for the listener today is no chance development but the result of the situation in which music finds itself in our contemporary world. Possibly still more than this it is the result of these conditions as they have developed in the United States. In saying that it is "a peculiar state of affairs" I certainly do not wish to imply that it is one to be, if possible, abolished or even, in any fundamental sense, corrected. It is rather a phenomenon to be noted and one which, I think, must be thoroughly understood if our culture is to achieve, as we all wish, a healthy growth. It is not a condition in any basic respect characteristic only of our musical or even our artistic life; it lies at the very core of the situation created by technology and all of its various ramifications; by repercussions, that is, of technology upon the economic, the political, the social and therefore upon the whole cultural world. This situation is a fact to be dealt with, intelligently, let us hope. And while we may smile at some of its manifestations and raise our eyebrows at others, we will certainly be wasting both time and energy if we spend them deploring it. We should also be pursuing cultural mirages if we either ignored it or remained unaware of the questions it poses.

The point is that we are trying with all our means to increase the number of listeners to music, and that not just because we believe culture to be a good thing which should be made available to all members of a democratic society, though we believe this too, of course. It is a part of our tradition, and we have been at pains to educate ourselves. We have even covered a great deal of ground very rapidly; and though we sometimes let ourselves be unduly impressed by mere statistics which mean actually less than we think they do, there is nevertheless a residue of quite genuine achievement not to be gainsaid.

But the condition I have been speaking of—that is, our preoccupation with the listener, and our solicitude for his problems—has quite other causes. The crucial fact is that within a space of approximately twenty-five years the musical public has grown in size from some thousands, mostly in the larger centers, to a so-called "mass audience" numbering many millions. The development of the radio, plus the expansion of the gramophone business, more than any other factors, have brought this about and have undoubtedly played a major role in stimulating interest, not only in concerts and operatic performances, but in musical activity of all sorts.

Thus a far greater quantity of music must be furnished, for so large a public, than was ever dreamed of before. I am of course speaking of performances rather than compositions, and am taking into account the facts both of recorded broadcasts and the nation-wide broadcasts of the large networks. The point is that both the entrepreneurs and the musicians, those who purvey and those who produce, become thus necessarily involved in business enterprise on a large scale. Even before the radio and the gramophone had begun to play the decisive part they do in our musical economy today, various factors, economic and otherwise, had already greatly restricted the role of private patronage in our public musical life. The purveyors of music, however disinterested, found themselves obliged to count costs and to concern themselves with profits. I say "however disinterested," and indeed I feel that in order to understand the situation as it has developed it is necessary to assume this disinterestedness. For the situation I am describing has not been made by individuals at all. It is the result of economic facts the like of which have never existed before; and the facts in question are far too large in scope, too intricately interwoven with the very bases of contemporary life, to be influenced one way or the other by the decisions of individuals.

When music or any other product is furnished to millions of individuals, it is bound to become necessary to consider the tastes of those individuals in relation to the product offered them. Those who furnish the product are obliged to produce as efficiently and as cheaply as possible the goods which they can sell to the most people; they are obliged, furthermore, to try to persuade the people to whom they sell that it is preferable to buy the goods that are most cheaply produced; it is furthermore necessary to do everything possible to enhance the value of the goods sold. If they fail to do these things they are taking foolish economic risks. The larger the quantities involved, the greater the potential profits; but while this is true, it is also true that the risks of possible catastrophic loss are greater. These facts are elementary; not only do they apply vitally to the situation of music today, but I believe that an understanding of them is absolutely indispensable if we are to understand any economic, political, or social aspects whatever of the contemporary world.

In brief, the "listener" has become, in relation to these facts, the "consumer," and however unaware we as individuals are of this, it is nevertheless the basic explanation of our interest in him. Though neither he nor we have chosen this role for him, circumstances have made it inevitable. In relation to the same facts (and please note the phrase carefully, for I shall try to show later that these are not the only facts), the status of the artist in our society has undergone a remarkable change. He has become (in relation to the same facts) no longer a cultural citizen, one of the cultural assets of the community with purely cultural responsibilities, but what is sometimes called a cog in the economic machine. He is asked and even in a sense required to justify his existence as a plausible economic risk; to, as we say, "sell" himself as a possible source of economic profit. Then, having done so, he must produce what is required of him in this sense. He, too, has an interest in the listener; it is the listener who buys his wares and therefore justifies his continued existence as an efficient cog. He has to be constantly aware, in fact, of the requirements of the machinery in approximately the terms I have outlined above. For the aims of business are essentially short-range aims, and it is doubtful whether business, as such, can conceivably operate on any other basis. It can allow itself the luxury of the long-range view only to the extent that it builds up enormous surpluses which make risks economically possible, and even then only under circumstances offering reasonable hope of long-range rewards.

Let me say once again that I do not consider this the entire picture of our cultural situation or of our cultural prospects. I shall later try to show why I do not believe it to be so. Furthermore, these remarks are generalizations, and subject to elaboration, with intricate scoring and with many subtleties of nuance. I do not intend to score them for you here. But we cannot understand the listener unless we know who he is in terms of the conditions actually prevalent. We must see him, in other words, not as an abstraction but as an existing and concrete figure in our musical society.

But it is not mainly in his role of consumer that I wish to speak of the listener. The question for us is rather his own experience of music—what hearing and understanding consist in, and, finally, what discrimination involves. What, in other words, is his relationship to music? How can he get the most from it? How can music mean the most to him? In what does his real education consist? Finally, how can he exercise his powers of discrimination in such a way as to promote valid musical experience in others and, so to speak, in the world in general?

I think we can distinguish four stages in the listener's development. First, he must hear; I have already indicated what I mean by this. It is not simply being present when music is performed, nor is it even simply recognized bits of the music—leit-motifs, or themes, or salient features in a score. It is rather, as it were, opening one's ears to the sounds as they succeed each other, discovering whatever point of contact one can find, and in fact following the music as well as one can in its continuity. We perhaps tend to ignore the fact that listeners are, like composers and performers, variously endowed, and also that they differ very widely in experience. But this initial stage in listening to music is an entirely direct one; the listener brings to the music whatever he can bring, with no other preoccupation than that of hearing. This is of course what is to be desired; it is the condition of his really hearing. He will hear the music only to the extent that he identifies himself with it, establishing a fresh and essentially naïve contact with it, without preconceived ideas and without strained effort.

The second stage is that of enjoyment, or shall we say the primary response. It is perhaps hardly discernible as a "second stage" at all: the listener's reaction is immediate and seems in a sense identical with the act of hearing. Undoubtedly this is what many listeners expect. And yet, on occasion, one may listen to music attentively, without any conscious response to it until afterwards; one's very attention may be so absorbed that a vivid sense of the sound is retained but a sense of communication is experienced only later. It is this sense of communication to which I refer under the term "enjoyment"; obviously, one may not and often does not, in any real sense, "enjoy" what is being communicated. There is certainly some music that we never "enjoy"; experience inevitably fosters discrimination, and there is certainly some truth even in the frequent, seemingly paradoxical, statement that "the more one loves music, the less music one loves." The statement is true in a sense if we understand it as applying to the experience of the individual, and not as a general rule. But if our relation to music is a healthy one—that is to say, a direct and simple one—our primary and quite spontaneous effort will be to enjoy it. If this effort becomes inhibited it will be by reason of experience and the associations that inevitably follow in its train. We shall in that case have acquired a sense of musical values, and our specific response will be curtailed in deference to the more general response which our musical experience has given us.

The third of the four phases I have spoken of consists in what we call "musical understanding." I must confess that I am not altogether pleased with this term. To speak quite personally if not too seriously, a composer will certainly have every right to feel pleased, but he may not feel entirely flattered, when he is told "I love your music, but of course I have no right to an opinion—I don't really understand it." In what does "musical understanding" consist? The difficulty, I think, comes from the fact that while, as I tried to show in the first chapter, the instinctive bases of music, the impulses which constitute its raw materials, are essentially of the most primitive sort, yet the organization of these materials, the shaping of them into a means of communication and later into works of art, is, and historically speaking has been, a long and intricate process and one which has few obvious contacts with the world of ordinary experience. The technique of every art has, of course, its esoteric phases; but in the case of visual art even these phases are relatively accessible to the layman, since he can, if he is really interested, grasp them in terms of quite ordinary practical activity. He will have learned early in his life to be aware of the basic facts of size, contour, color, and perspective on very much the same terms as are required for his perception of visual art. He can to a certain extent appreciate the artist's problems in these terms and can define his response, at least on an elementary level, in terms satisfactory to himself. This is even truer in the case of literary art, since he constantly uses words and to a greater or a lesser degree expresses himself by their means. Like Molière's "bourgeois gentleman," he has talked in prose all his life. His feeling for the values of both visual and literary art consists therefore in a high degree of refinement, and an extension, of experiences which are thoroughly familiar to him, through analogies constantly furnished by his ordinary life.

In the case of music there are no such clear analogies. The technical facts which are commonplace to the composer, and even many of those proper to the performer, have no clear analogies in the ordinary experience of the non-musician. The latter finds them quite mysterious and, as I have already pointed out, tends to exaggerate both their uniqueness and their inaccessibility to the layman. And if the latter finds it difficult to conceive of the mere fact of inner hearing and auditory imagination, how much more difficult will he find such a conception as, for instance, tonality, or the musical facts on which the principles of what we call "musical form" are based. He is likely not only to regard music *per se* as a book in principle closed to him, but, through the impressive unfamiliarity of whatever technical jargon he chances to hear, to misunderstand both the nature and the role of musical technique. It is likely to seem to him something of an abstraction, with an existence of its own, to which the sensations and impressions he receives from music are only remotely related, as by-products. How often, for instance, have I been asked whether the study and mastery of music does not involve a knowledge of higher mathematics! The layman is only too likely to react in either one of two ways, or in a combination of both. He is likely, that is, either to regard music as something to which he is essentially a stranger, or else to regard its generally accepted values as arbitrary, pretentious, and academic, and both to give to it and to receive from it far less than his aptitudes warrant.

The surprising thing is that all of these conclusions are based on a mistaken idea as to the real meaning of musical "understanding." Technique is certainly useful, not to say indispensable, to the composer or the performer; a knowledge of musical theory is certainly an advantage to the performer and practically inescapable for the composer. But theory, in the sense of generalization, is not of the least use to the listener; in practice it is a veritable encumbrance if he allows preoccupation with it to interfere with his contact with the music as such. He can certainly derive both interest and help from whatever can be pointed out to him in connection with the specific content of a piece of music; but he will be only misled if he is persuaded to listen in an exploratory rather than a completely receptive spirit. Any effort to help him must be in the direction of liberating, not of conditioning, his ear; and the generalizations of which musical theory consists demonstrably often lead him to strained efforts which are a positive barrier to understanding. The "technique" of a piece of music is essentially the affair of the composer; it is largely even subconscious, and composers frequently are confronted by perfectly real technical facts, present in their music, of which they had no conscious inkling. And do we seriously believe that understanding of Shakespeare, or James Joyce, or William Faulkner has anything to do with the ability to parse the sentences and describe the functions of the various words in *Hamlet* or *Ulysses*?

Of course not. Understanding of music, as relevant for the listener, means the ability to receive its full message. . . . In the primary sense, the listener's real and ultimate response to music consists not in merely hearing it, but in inwardly reproducing it, and his understanding of music consists in the ability to do this in his imagination. This point cannot be too strongly emphasized. The really "understanding" listener takes the music into his consciousness and remakes it actually or in his imagination, for his own uses. He whistles it on the street, or hums it at his work, or simply "thinks" it to himself. He may even represent it to his consciousness in a more concentrated form—as a condensed memory of sounds heard and felt, reproduced for his memory by a vivid sensation of what I may call character in sound, without specific details but in terms of sensations and impressions remembered.

It is for this reason that I am somewhat skeptical of the helpfulness of the kind of technical tid-bits and quasi-analyses sometimes offered to the listener as aids to understanding. The trouble with them, as so often presented, seems to me that the essential facts of musical technique cannot really be conveyed in this way. To give one instance, musicians talk, for convenience, about what we call the "sonata form." But they know, or should know, that the conception "sonata form" is a rough generalization and that in practice sonatas, at least those written by masters, are individual and that each work has its own form. To speak of "sonata form" without making clear what constitutes "form" in music, as such, is to falsify, not to illuminate. It is to imply that the composer adapts his ideas to a mold into which he then pours the music. It is also to lay far too much emphasis on what are called "themes," to the detriment of the musical flow in its entirety. What the layman needs is not to acquire facts but to cultivate senses: the sense of rhythm, of articulation, of contrast, of accent. He needs to be aware of the progression of the bass as well as the treble line; of a return to the principal or to a subsidiary key, of a far-flung tonal span. He needs to be aware of all these things as events which his ear witnesses and appreciates as a composition unfolds. Whether or not it is a help to have specific instances pointed out to him, it is certain in any case that his main source of understanding will be through hearing music in general, and specific works in particular, repeatedly, and making them his own through familiarity, through memory, and through inner re-elaboration.

I hardly need point out the fact that this is as true in regard to so-called "modern" music as it is to old. Where the music is radically unfamiliar the three processes I have described are slower. It must therefore be heard more often than the older music needs to be heard. At the beginning the impressions will be chaotic—much more chaotic than impressions produced by purely fortuitous sounds. The impression of chaos comes simply from the fact that the sounds and relationships are unfamiliar; their very consistency—since it, too, is based on contexts which are unfamiliar—seems like a denial of logic. As long as this impression prevails the listener has not yet made contact with the music. In connection with contemporary music, I have often observed the first sensations of real contact, while the musical language in question is still essentially unfamiliar but beginning to be intelligible. These first sensations may be acutely pleasurable; the work becomes highly exciting, conveying a kind of superficial excitement which disappears when the stage of real understanding is reached and gives way to an appreciation for the real "message" of the work. Once more, the key to the "understanding" of contemporary music lies in repeated hearing; one must hear it till the sounds are familiar, until one begins to notice false notes if they are played. One can make the effort to retain it in one's head, and one will always find that the accurate memory of sounds heard coincides with the understanding of them. In fact, the power to retain sounds by memory implies that they have been mastered. For the ear by its nature seeks out patterns and relationships, and it is only these patterns that we can remember and that make music significant for us.

The listener's final stage is that of discrimination. It is important that it should be the final stage since real discrimination is possible only with understanding; and both snobbery and immaturity at times foster prejudices which certainly differ from discrimination in any real sense. Actually it is almost impossible not to discriminate if we persist in and deepen our musical experience. We will learn to differentiate between lasting impressions and those which are fleeting, and between the musical experiences which give full satisfaction and those which only partly satisfy us. We will learn to differentiate between our impressions, too, in a qualitative sense. In this way, we cultivate a sense of values to which to refer our later judgment. We will learn that music is unequal in quality; we will possibly learn that instead of speaking of "immortality" in the case of some works and of the ephemeral quality of others, we must conceive of differences in the life span of works—that some works last in our esteem longer than others without necessarily lasting forever. We will learn finally to differentiate in the matter of character, to be aware of the differences between works in ways which have no relation to intrinsic worth. In other words, we will become critics.

The critic is, in fact, the listener who has become articulate, who has learned to put his judgments and his values into words. I am not, for the moment, speaking of him in his professional capacity but as what I may call the end-product of the listening process. It is important that we understand that he is the end-product, because otherwise we will, I think, understand correctly neither the listener nor the critic. I spoke earlier of the speed with which we, in the United States, have developed our culture and of the constant danger of producing a type of artistic culture in which the critic rather than the productive artist is the central figure. Lest this particular turn of phrase seem to indicate a prejudice against critics, which I do not feel, let me put it a little differently. The danger, and a very real one, is that we allow ourselves to cultivate, on the first level, a predominantly critical attitude toward art in precedence over a love for it; that in our overeagerness to produce what we consider mature results, we make of judgment an end in itself instead of the natural and full-grown by-product of a total artistic experience.

For as a growing culture, and possibly in regard to music more than anything else, we still have a strong residue of the diffidence and the self-distrust which results from the consciousness that we have not a thousand-year-old tradition behind us. In cultural matters we tend to question ourselves, our feelings, and our judgment, at every turn. This is, I believe, a deep-seated attitude, and one not always apparent on the surface of things. It expresses itself in a variety of attitudes, each of them potentially dangerous to our musical development, and still present in spite of the achievements of the past half-century. These achievements are real, even after we have dismissed all of the spurious claims resulting from the fact that we have money to buy goods produced elsewhere, and the fact that we often buy not wisely but too well, and that we possess not only the technique of salesmanship but a tremendous territory in which sales are possible. After we have looked beyond these claims and tried conscientiously to appraise the situation in an objective manner, our achievements are still impressive. But they will be in the last analysis sterile unless we overcome our tendency to self-questioning and learn to give ourselves freely to musical experience, and to recognize that mature artistic judgment can result only from the love of art; that any judgment in the absence of love is sterile and therefore false.

A healthy musical culture is one in which the creative function, the function arising from a strong and prevalent love for music, is the primary one, and in which the activities of the composer, the performer, and the listener (and in the category of listener I include the critic) are in their several ways embodiments of that love. It is obvious that real love for music, as for anything else, depends on inner security; but it is also true that inner security depends on the strength of love. What I have described as the critical attitude, the attitude which implies a forced or premature attempt to arrive at artistic judgment, is in reality only the result of basic insecurity; and there is some evidence that such insecurity threatens to become endemic to our culture. Are we not all familiar with the type of pseudo-sophistication that gives more importance to aversions than to preferences, that is more afraid of loving what is bad than of disliking what is good? Do we not all know too well the type of artistic talent which we see embodied in an essentially divided or imperfectly integrated personality—a personality which, like all mature personalities, contains both creative and critical elements, but in this instance divided through the fact that the two faculties are distrustful both of each other and of themselves? In such cases the creator-personality is inhibited through fears for the soundness of his artistic judgment, and the critic-personality is inhibited through fears that its mere existence may indicate a lack of creative force. Finally, there is always the danger that the young and gifted composer may be thrown into self-doubt, and his development seriously threatened, by excessive self-consciousness at exactly the moment when he should rightly be finding his own inner security, through the discovery of his own creative nature by means of constant and untroubled experimentation and productiveness.

The critic, then, finds his true function as an experienced listener, one who has made a vital contact with music and who has developed powers of discrimination through following up this contact to the point where he becomes conscious of values in a generalized sense. His importance in our total musical economy is obvious. I mean our musical economy, and not the economics of our musical life, where his professional role is considerable but more problematical in effect. For in accordance with his gifts he has the power to contribute strongly to musical life, through illumination of the real issues which are vital in any particular time and place. What these issues are for our contemporary world, I shall discuss more fully later. I wish to emphasize here simply that the true role of the critic is precisely to throw these issues into the clearest possible relief. His true role is that of collaborator, so to speak, in a common cultural effort in which composer and performer and listener all participate.

His role is, in a limited sense, a particularly crucial one, owing to our special history and the conditions under which music developed here. For many years, as it were, we imported all our music. It was a product of a tradition developed elsewhere, and our problem was to gain for ourselves the fruits of this tradition. The critic had the task of interpreting the tradition to the American public, and in consequence there was very little he could do except to take due note of judgments and values that had already reached maturity elsewhere. Today, with the ever-increasing development of a rich musical life of our own, he is forced to swim in more perilous waters and to discover values of his own. It is small wonder that he often shows a certain reluctance to do this, and takes refuge in writing long columns on the season's sixth performance of Tristan, or indulging, to cite a ghastly example I shall never forget, in vituperation of Critic B because the latter had written an unfavorable review of a book by Critic C, of whom Critic A (the author of the review in question) approved because he (Critic C) had written disparagingly of Critic D's book on Mozart. A veritable tangle of critics, with poor Mozart, in this case representing the only actual music involved in the whole matter, four steps away! All this is the result of an inherited habit of regarding music as a commodity to be bought and enjoyed, but in the production of which we have no part. I would like to suggest that this is not criticism at all; it is basically irrelevant chit-chat which can have no constructive consequence whatever. Because criticism, like composing, like performance, must spring out of a genuine culture; that is, a pervasive musical impulse, a living and shared relationship to music, which communicates itself within the framework of some kind of common experience. Our musical culture cannot exist, in fact, on any other terms; and the critic will properly fulfill his function only in energetic awareness of the issues and personalities immediate to the cultural situation in which he, too, lives and of which he, too, is inexorably a part. For even what we call the past is for us a part of our present experience, and our relationship to it is false unless we derive living experience from contact with it; and we cannot have that unless we are aware of ourselves and the forces that have gone into our own making. I am not suggesting that the critic should invariably praise contemporary music or even that he should necessarily ever do so. But it seems to me clear that his central task, as a critic, is to be aware of it and to understand it, and to become fully conscious of the issues that have brought it into being. These bring into play his real powers as a critic, make the greatest demands on his powers of discrimination and offer a truly exciting challenge to his gifts. They are certainly, as I have said, the most dangerous, and yet they are also the most stimulating, waters in which he is called upon to swim.

Finally, to conclude our discussion of the listener, let us ask what he demands of the composer. The question has been asked frequently in our time; it has been given tragic power in dictatorships where the effort has been made, sometimes as in Nazi Germany with ruthless force, to coordinate the artist to the purposes of those in power. Less ruthless, less consistently, and even less consciously applied, but none the less real, are the pressures which arise in such large-scale economy as I described at the beginning of this chapter—pressures such as those summarized for the theatrical world in the words "Broadway" or "Hollywood." The slogan, sometimes couched in more refined and even quasi-intellectual terms, is "Give the public what it wants;" but as I have pointed out, there is strong pressure on the public, too, to want what it is cheapest and most generally economical to give.

Let us phrase the question in more general terms: What does the listener demand from music? The answer will inevitably be that a variety of listeners want a variety of things. But on any level it may be taken for granted that the listener wants vital experience, whether of a deeply stirring, brilliantly stimulating, or simply entertaining type. If we understand this we should understand, too, that the composer can effectively furnish it only on his own terms. He can persuade others to love only what he loves himself, and can convince only by means of what fully convinces him. It is for this reason that the artist must be completely free, that such a question as I have stated here can ultimately have no importance to him. His obligation is to give the best he can give, wherever it may lead, and to do so without compromise and with complete conviction. This is in fact natural to him; if he is a genuine artist he cannot do otherwise. He can be sure that if he fully achieves his artistic goals, he will find listeners, and that if he has something genuine to say, the number of his listeners will increase, however slowly. This, in any case, will never be for him an artistic preoccupation, however much it may prove to be a practical one.

Composers, like poets, are born, not made; but once born, they have to grow. It is in this sense that a culture will, generally speaking, get the music that it demands. The question, once more, is what we demand of the composer. Do we demand always what is easiest, music that is primarily and invariably entertainment, or do we seriously want from him the best that he has to give?

In the latter case, are we willing to come to meet him, to make whatever effort is demanded of us as listeners, in order to get from his music what it has to give us? Once more, it is for the listener and not for the composer, as an individual, that the answer is important. On the answer we ultimately give depends the future of music in the United States.

❧ ❧ ❧

*Arthur Koestler*

# Cultural Snobbery [1]

2

A FRIEND of mine, whom I shall call Brenda, was given for her birthday by one of her admirers a Picasso line drawing in a simple modern frame. It was an admirable and typical sample of Picasso's "classical" period: a Greek youth carrying a girl in his arms, the contours of the two figures somehow mixed up and partly indistinguishable like those of Siamese twins with shared limbs, yet adding up to a charming and harmonious total effect. It looked like a lithograph, but it bore no serial number, so Brenda took it to be a reproduction and hung it, somewhat disappointed with the gift, over her staircase. On my next visit, several weeks later, it was hanging over her drawing room mantelpiece. "I see the Picasso reproduction has been promoted," I said. "*Reproduction!*" she cried indignantly. "It turned out it's an *original!* Isn't it lovely? Look at that line along the girl's hip . . . ," etc.

As a matter of fact, it *was* an original—a shyly understated gift of the mumbling and devoted admirer. But as it was a line drawing consisting of nothing but black contour on white paper, it needed an expert, or at least a good magnifying lens, to decide whether it was an original, a lithograph, or a reproduction. Neither Brenda nor any of her visitors could tell the difference. But they took it for granted, as we all do, that an original deserves a proud display, whereas a reproduction belongs, at best, over the staircase.

I shall now try to analyze, in a pedantic way, the reason for this apparently so natural attitude. The original is of course many times more expensive than a reproduction; but we would indignantly reject the idea of displaying a picture simply because it is expensive; we pretend to be guided in these matters by purely aesthetic considerations. Next, one might surmise that our contempt for reproductions originates in the poor quality and even poorer choice of subjects of the Victorian print. But modern printing techniques have achieved miracles, and some Ganymede reproductions are almost indistinguishable from the original. In the extreme case of the line drawing, we have complete aesthetic equivalence between original and reproduction.

[1] From *The Anchor Review Number One*, ed. Melvin J. Lasky, Doubleday Anchor Books, Garden City, 1955. Pp. 3-14. Reprinted by permission of A. D. Peters.

And yet there is something revolting in this equivalence. It even takes a certain courage to admit to oneself that the aesthetic effect of a copy might be indistinguishable from that of the original. We live in an age of stereotyped mass production; and after mass-produced furniture, mass-produced and prefabricated houses, the idea of mass-produced Piero della Francescas is indeed revolting. But then, we have no similar objection to mass-produced gramophone records. Nor to mass-produced books, and yet they too fall into the category of "reproductions." Why then do you prefer, according to your income, a more or less second-rate original picture on the wall to a first-rate reproduction of a masterpiece? Would you rather read a mediocre young poet in manuscript than Shakespeare in a paper-cover edition?

Our argument seems to have become bogged down. Let us find out what Brenda herself has to say to explain her behavior, in a dialogue with the writer:

BRENDA: "I simply can't understand what all this fuss and talk is about. But *of course* my attitude to the drawing has changed since I know that Picasso himself did it. That's nothing to do with snobbery—it's just that I wasn't told before."

K: "Your attitude has changed—but has that thing on the wall changed?"

B: "Of course it hasn't, but now I *see* it differently!"

K: "I would like to understand what it is that determines your attitude to a picture in general."

B: "Its quality, of course."

K: "And what determines its quality?"

B: "Oh, don't be such a pedant. Color, composition, balance, harmony, power, what have you."

K: "So, in looking at a picture, you are guided by purely aesthetic value judgments, depending on the qualities you mentioned?"

B: "Of course I am."

K: "Now, as that picture hasn't changed, and its qualities haven't changed, how can your attitude have changed?"

B: "But I have told you before, you idiot. Of course my attitude to it is now different, since I know it isn't one reproduction in a million, but done by Picasso himself. Can't you see?"

K: "No, I can't; you are contradicting yourself. The rarity of the object, and your knowledge of the manner in which it came into being, do not alter the qualities of that object, and accordingly should not alter your judgment of it, if it were really based on purely aesthetic criteria—as you believe it to be. But it isn't. Your judgment is not based on what you *see*, but on a purely accidental bit of information, which might be right or wrong and is entirely extraneous to the issue."

B: "Wrong? How *dare* you insinuate that my Picasso isn't an original? And how *dare* you say that the question whether he drew it himself is 'extraneous' to the issue?"

And so it will go on indefinitely. Yet Brenda is not stupid; she is merely confused in believing that her attitude to an object of art is determined by purely aesthetic considerations, whereas in fact it is decisively influenced by factors of a quite different order. She is unable to see her picture isolated from the context of her knowledge of its origin. For, in our minds, the question of origin, authorship, or authenticity, *though in itself extraneous to aesthetic value*, is so intimately and indistinguishably fused with our attitude to the object that we find it well-nigh impossible to isolate the two. Thus, Brenda unconsciously projects one scale of values onto a system of quite different values.

Is Brenda, then, a snob? It depends on the definition of snobbery at which we hope to arrive at the end. But as a working hypothesis, I would like to suggest that this process of unconsciously applying to any given field a judgment derived from an alien system of values constitutes the essence of the phenomenon of snobbery. By these standards Brenda would *not* be a snob if she had said: "The reproduction in this case is just as beautiful as the original. But one gives me a greater thrill than the other for reasons which have nothing to do with beauty." She is an unconscious snob because she is unable to distinguish between the two elements of her experience, unable to name the extraneous cause of her biased aesthetic judgment, or to see that it is biased.

I am aware of pedantically laboring an apparently obvious point. But it will become at once less obvious if we turn to a different yet related problem.


3

In 1948, a German art restorer named Dietrich Fey, engaged in reconstruction work on Lübeck's ancient St. Marien Church, stated that his workmen had discovered traces of old Gothic wall paintings dating back to the thirteenth century, under a coating of chalk on the church walls. The restoration of the paintings was entrusted to Fey's assistant, Lothar Malskat, who finished the job two years later. In 1950, Chancellor Adenauer presided over the ceremonies marking the completion of the restoration work in the presence of art experts from all parts of Europe. Their unanimous opinion, voiced by Chancellor Adenauer, was that the twenty-one thirteenth-century Gothic saints on the church walls were "a valuable treasure and a fabulous discovery of lost masterpieces."

None of the experts on that or any later occasion expressed doubt as to the authenticity of the frescoes. It was Herr Malskat himself who, two years later, disclosed the fraud. He presented himself on his own initiative at Lübeck police headquarters, where he stated that the frescoes were entirely his own work, undertaken by order from his boss, Herr Fey, and asked to be tried for forgery. The leading German art experts, however, stuck to their opinion: the frescoes, they said, were no doubt genuine, and Herr Malskat was merely seeking cheap publicity. An official Board of Investigation was appointed which came to the conclusion that the restoration of the wall paintings was a hoax—but only after

Herr Malskat had confessed that he had also manufactured hundreds of Rembrandts, Watteaus, Toulouse-Lautrecs, Picassos, Henri Rousseaus, Corots, Chagalls, Vlamincks, and other masters, and sold them as originals—some of which were actually found by the police in Herr Fey's house. Without this evidence, it is doubtful whether the German experts would ever have admitted having been fooled.

My point is not the fallibility of the experts. Herr Malskat's exploit is merely the most recent of a number of similarly successful hoaxes and forgeries—of which the most fabulous were probably van Megeeren's false Vermeers. The disturbing question which they raise is whether the Lübeck saints are less beautiful, and have ceased to be "a valuable treasure of masterpieces," simply because they had been painted by Herr Malskat and not by somebody else?

There are several answers to this line of argument, but before going into them I want to continue in the part of *advocatus diaboli* by considering an example of a forgery in a different field: Macpherson's *Ossian*. The case is so notorious that the facts need only be briefly mentioned. James Macpherson (1736-96), a Scottish poet and adventurer, alleged that in the course of his wanderings in the Highlands he had discovered some ancient Gaelic manuscripts. Enthusiastic Scottish littérateurs put up a subscription to enable Macpherson to pursue his researches, and in 1761 he published *Fingal, an Ancient Epic Poem in Six Books, together with Several Other Poems composed by Ossian, the Son of Fingal*. Ossian is the legendary third-century hero and bard of Celtic literature. *Fingal* was soon followed by the publication of a still larger Ossianic epic called *Temora*, and this by a collected edition, *The Works of Ossian*. The authenticity of Macpherson's text was at once questioned in England, particularly by Dr. Johnson (whom Macpherson answered by sending him a challenge to a duel), and to his death Macpherson refused, under various unconvincing pretexts, to publish his alleged Gaelic originals. By the turn of the century the controversy was settled and it was established that, while Macpherson had used fragments of ancient Celtic lore, most of the "Ossianic" texts were of his own making.

Yet here again the question arises whether the poetic quality of the work itself is altered by the fact that it was written not by Ossian, the son of Fingal, but by James Macpherson? The "Ossianic" texts were translated into many languages, and had a considerable influence on the literature and cultural climate of Europe at the late eighteenth and early nineteenth centuries. This is how the *Encyclopedia Britannica* sums up its evaluation of Macpherson:

> The varied sources of his work and its worthlessness as a transcript of actual Celtic poems do not alter the fact that he produced a work of art which . . . did more than any single work to bring about the romantic movement in European, and especially in German, literature. . . . Herder and Goethe . . . were among its profound admirers.

These examples could be continued indefinitely. Antique furniture, Roman statuary, Greek tanagra figures, and Italian madonnas are being forged, copied, counterfeited all the time, and the value we set on them is not determined by aesthetic appreciation and pleasure to the eye, but by the precarious and often uncertain judgment of experts. A mediocre but authenticated picture by a known master is held in higher esteem than an artistically superior work of his unknown pupil or "school"—not only by art dealers guided by "investment," but by all of us, including this writer. Are we, then, all snobs to whom a signature, an expert testimonial, or the postmark of a given period is more important than the intrinsic beauty of the object itself?

4

I now propose to present the case for the defense. It can be summed up in a single sentence: our appraisal of any work of literature or art is never a unitary act, but the result of two independent and simultaneous processes which tend to distort each other.

When we look at an Egyptian fresco, we do not enjoy the painting at its face value, but by means of an unconscious reattunement of the mind to the values of the period. We know, for instance, that the Egyptians had not discovered the technique of perspective in depth. We know that on certain Egyptian murals the size of the figures is determined by their relative social rank. Similarly, we look at every picture through a double frame: the solid frame which isolates it from its surroundings and creates for it a hole in space, as it were; and the unconscious frame of reference in our minds which creates for it a hole in time and locates it in its period and cultural climate. Every time we think that we are making a purely aesthetic judgment based on pure sensory perception, we are in fact judging relative to this second frame or context or mental field.

Any work of art, or literature, or music, can only be appreciated against the background of its period, and that is what we unconsciously do: when we naively believe that we are applying absolute criteria, we are in fact applying relative ones. When we contemplate the false Vermeer the first time believing it to be authentic and the second time knowing that it is a fake, our aesthetic experience will indeed completely change, though the picture has remained the same. For it is now seen in a different frame of reference and therefore, in fact, differently. The same considerations apply to the perpetrator of the fake. He may be able to imitate the technique of the eighteenth-century Flemish School, but he could not spontaneously start painting like Vermeer—because his visual organization is different, his perception of reality is different, and because he cannot, except by an artificial effort, erase from his mind the accumulated experience of everything that happened in painting since Vermeer. And if, by a tour de force, a contemporary artist succeeded in reconditioning his own vision to that of the Flemish eighteenth century or the Italian *quattro-*

*cento*, he would have to use mass hypnosis to recondition the vision of his customers in a similar manner.

We can add to our knowledge and experience, but we cannot subtract from it. When Picasso decides to disregard the laws of perspective, that means that he has passed through and beyond a certain technique—unlike the Egyptian painter, who has never acquired it. Evolution is an irreversible process; the culture of a period might apparently point into the same direction as an earlier one, but it does so from a different turn of the spiral. A modern primitive is different from a primitive primitive; contemporary classicism is different from any classical classicism; only the mentally insane are able to amputate part of their past.

And yet when we contemplate works of the past, we must perform just such a process of mental subtraction, by attuning our minds to the climate and experience of the period. In order to appreciate them, we must enter into their spirit, by forgetting our modern experience and all that we have learnt since that Homeric epic or Byzantine mosaic was created. We must descend into the past, making our mind a blank; and as we do so, we unconsciously condescend. We close our eyes to crudities of technique, naiveties of perception, prevailing superstitions, limitations of knowledge, factual errors. We make allowances. A little honest introspection will always reveal the element of condescension contained in our admiration for the classics; and part of our enjoyment when listening to the voices of the past is derived from this half-consciously patronizing attitude—"how clever of them to know that at their age." We feel that we have descended a turn of the spiral; we are looking up in awe and wonder at Dante's dreadful Paradise, but at the same time we seem to be bending down, with a tender, antiquarian stoop.

This legitimate kind of aesthetic double-think degenerates into snobbery at the point where the frame of reference becomes more important than the picture, when the thrill derived from the gesture of bending over the past dominates the aesthetic experience. The result is a widespread confusion of critical judgment—overestimation of the dead and belittlement of the living, indiscriminate reverence for anything that is "classical," "antique," "primitive," or simply old. In its extreme form this tendency prompts people to have their wall brackets and picture frames artificially dirtied to lend them the patina of age; so let us call it the "patina snobbery."

The process that leads to these distortions of judgment is basically the same as outlined before: the projection of one scale of values to a psychologically related but objectively alien field of experience. The essence of snobbery is to assess value according to a wrong type of scale; the snob is always trying to measure beauty with a thermometer or weight with a clock.

## 5

The thirteen-year-old daughter of a friend was recently taken to the Greenwich Museum. When she was asked which was the most beautiful thing she

had seen in the Museum, she said unhesitatingly: "Nelson's shirt." When asked
what was so beautiful about it, she explained: "That shirt with the blood on it
was jolly nice. Fancy real blood on a real shirt, which belonged to somebody
really historic!"

The child's thrill is obviously derived from the same source as the magic that
emanates from Napoleon's inkpot, the lock of hair on the Egyptian mummy's
head, the relic of the saint carried in annual procession, the strand of the rope
by which a famous murderer was hanged, and from Tolstoi's laundry bill. In the
mentality of the primitive, an object which had been in contact with a person
is not merely a souvenir: it becomes magically imbued with the substance of
that personality and in turn magically emanates something of that substance.

"There is, I am sure, for most of us, a special pleasure in sinking your teeth
into a peach produced on the estate of an earl who is related to the Royal
Family," a London columnist wrote recently in the Daily Express.

Primitive magic survives in the subconscious; the strand of hair carried in the
locket, grandmother's wedding dress, the faded fan of the first ball, the regimental badge, all have a half-conscious fetish character. The bobby-soxers who tear
shreds off the crooner's garb are the vulgarized twentieth-century version of the
worshipers cherishing a splinter from a saint's bone. The value that we set on
original manuscripts, on "signed" pieces of furniture, on Dickens' quill and
Kepler's telescope, are more dignified manifestations of the same unconscious
tendency. It is, as the child said, "jolly nice" to behold a fragment of a marble
by Praxiteles—even if it is battered out of human shape, with a leper's nose
and broken ears. The contact with the master's hand has imbued it with a magic
quality which has lingered on and radiates at us, conveying the same thrill as
"the real blood on Nelson's real shirt."

The change in our attitude—and in the art dealer's price—when it is learned
that a cracked and blackened piece of canvas is an "authenticated" work by X
has nothing to do with beauty, aesthetics, or what have you—it is the working
of sympathetic magic in us. (See Brenda and her Picasso drawing.) The inordinate importance that we attribute to the original, the authenticated, in those
borderline cases where only the expert could tell the difference, is a derivative
from primitive fetishism. And as every honest art dealer will admit, these borderline cases are so frequent as to be almost the rule. Moreover, it was a general
practice in the past for the master to let his pupils assist in the execution of
larger undertakings. It is not the eye that guides the average museum visitor,
but the magic of names and the magic of age. The bedevilment of aesthetic experience by unconscious fetish worship and patina snobbery is so general that it
has become a major factor in our attitude to the art of past epochs—an attitude
as remote from spontaneous appreciation as the "Emperor's Clothes" fallacy regarding hyper-modern art forms.

❦ ❦ ❦

# The Popular Arts

*Hollis Alpert*

## Movies Are Better Than the Stage[1]

*There is no such thing as photography in depth; a picture cannot record more than meets the camera's eye. A succession of cannily related shots can suggest an impression of depth, can burrow by implication a few inches beneath the surface; but it cannot dig so deep as a brilliantly related succession of words can. Words are subtler than pictures, capable of connoting a greater complexity than pictures. Inventively combined, they can cut closer to the heart's core; an imagined contest between the finest film ever made and the finest play ever written must inevitably end in victory for the play, by virtue of its verbal profundity.*—Walter Kerr, in "How Not to Write a Play."

*One picture is worth a thousand words.*—Fred R. Barnard, who in *Printer's Ink* credited the statement to Confucius, who, of course, said no such thing.

THERE is a school of thought—evidences of it are encountered at cocktail parties, in esoteric film journals, at the M-G-M commissary, and, occasionally, in books written by drama critics—that the movies as a possible art form came to a halt when the soundtrack was invented. The cinematic medium thereafter proceeded to limp along, impeded and cluttered by this thing called words. In these elegant circles, which consider the theatre to be a privileged (and embattled) sanctuary, movies have never been admitted to be a branch of the drama, and only so long as the cinema maintained its freakish character (showing people moving their lips soundlessly, expressing only mute passion) was it allowed a place in the scheme of things at all. Theatre geared to a stream of words was to be found only on the stage.

But movies refused to stay silent, and now and then they can be found talking very well indeed. It's even time to consider the possibility that the film, with its newly expanded screen and its superior resources for staging, is not only a form of theatre, but—in almost all ways—by far the best form.

This, however, is seldom admitted. One film historian upon being asked recently to list the ten best movies of all time quickly named ten pictures made

[1] From *The Saturday Review of Literature* (July 23, 1955), pp. 5-6, 31-32. Reprinted by permission of the author and *The Saturday Review*.

before 1928. The list was a familiar one, including such movies as *Potemkin*, *The Cabinet of Dr. Caligari*, *City Lights*, and *Variety*. Nothing made after the era of sound came into being seemed, in his view, the equal of these silent classics. There are little cinema societies, all across the land, which meet periodically to worship before the altar of the silent screen. The prints are dark, scratched, nearly eroded away, but still they flicker on for rapt audiences of ten or twenty.

The theory held by many who attend these showings is that the cinema, first and last, is a visual medium and that its primary language is movement. The movement is created by a change in the image, or by a succession of images. The images can be made meaningful by clever juxtaposition, and by technical tricks such as the dissolve. Walter Kerr, in his recent book *How Not to Write a Play*, puts it as follows: "The silence—or comparative silence—of the screen was an inherent condition of the medium. The function of the moving-picture camera is to take moving pictures." Later on he says, "The good motion picture of today remains a cut-and-flash unreeling of meaningful pictures (the recurring railroad tracks, the clock, the deserted street of *High Noon*) helped along the way by verbal fragments but depending not at all upon these fragments for basic excitement."

Without wishing to belittle the accomplishment in *High Noon* I would nevertheless like to quarrel with the theory. I have found my enjoyment of a picture like *Roman Holiday* or *From Here to Eternity* unimpaired by the fact that the actors in them took a good deal of time out, now and then, to talk to each other. I have seen the camera hold still for quite a while to give an actor the opportunity to make an impassioned speech, and have felt some basic excitement.

Movies did not talk from the very beginning because they did not know how to. It is true that a silent movie technique developed and that it was often used beautifully, but why should silence be the language of the movies for all time? The reason the movies developed a language separate from speech was because of the need for a substitute. That movies have been enriched as a result goes without question, but to confine the movies to the silent technique would be like confining acting to pantomime.

To stay with the theoretical a bit longer—the movie camera does not, as Mr. Kerr would have it, necessarily take moving pictures, nor is the taking of moving pictures its prime function. The camera is but one step in an operation that has the object of deceiving the eye and creating an illusion. The reason that fifty or sixty million Americans go each week to the movies is not to have their eyes washed (as is sometimes assumed) but to see lifelike illusions, and, more than anything else, to be told dramatic stories. *The film is not so much an art form as it is modern theatre*. Whether a story is presented to us on a screen or on a stage it is still a theatrical presentation. The movies are, in essence, popular theatre. When the mass audience goes to the movies rather than to a stage play it is not only because tickets are cheaper or because the material is more easily comprehended (something that was probably true thirty or forty years ago) but because it is getting, in many ways, a better show.

This mass audience, from year to year, has come in for some extraordinary lambasting. The movie public is derided as being made up largely of adolescents, or of having a twelve-year-old mentality, of lacking taste and discrimination, of being fickle, capricious, ignorant, and vulgar. It is supposed to be an audience that punishes thought, that shies from the controversial, that laps up cheesecake, puerility, foolishness, the sensational, and the saccharine. Periodically on the stage will appear a play showing Hollywood to be a hotbed of asininity and cynicism, making products for the entertainment of morons. The movies, either out of courage or abject humility (I'm not sure which), will then buy the play and make a movie showing the same point.

On the other hand, the theatre audience is something else again. It is assumed to have taste, discrimination, a mature mentality, background, breeding, and, above all, a feeling for Theatre. As one young lady said to me as we passed through the lobby on our way to some bad seats to see a mediocre murder melodrama: "Isn't there something exciting about just *going* to the theatre?" It is possible to attend any lunatic Broadway farce, an off-Broadway exercise in neurotica, or an inept summer-theatre performance and immediately be crowned with a distinction, that of being in the upper, or egghead, level of society.

Meanwhile, in spite of a passionate love for Theatre on the part of a good many who faithfully buy tickets to three hit shows per year, the theatre continues its decline. There are now about seventy Broadway productions a year, in contrast to the more than 200 shows on the boards twenty-five years ago. There are fewer theatres, fewer hits. Hits are made only when a majority of the drama critics agree with each other. The discriminating theatregoer has shown an increasing tendency to be led by the nose. The truth of the matter is that the theatre has seldom more than mild entertainment to offer us these days; it has little or no profundity. To intrigue the audience it has left to it the theatre must perforce go in for sensationalism, sex farces, and near-nudity.

That there are occasional good plays still to be seen is a tribute to the devotion and courage of our playwrights, who must fight their way through a maze of obstacles: the current "hit" psychosis, the heavy cost of production, the backer system, and eventually the critics—who generally recognize only two types of plays: hits and failures. What the theatre has left to it (spontaneity, wit, loftiness, topicality) becomes harder and harder to find.

Luckily, the movies, more through accident than by design, are currently filling the gap, and providing us with theatre—good, bad, and indifferent, but theatre nevertheless.

While dozens of sleazy horse operas and crime melodramas emerge each year from the movie factories, the moviegoer, should he wish to be discriminating, can pick himself some movie entertainment that will stack up very nicely against what the theatre has to offer him. By selecting from the best of Hollywood, and the choice items sent here from abroad, he will be able, at least once a week, to find something of superior quality. On view at this time are several that should prove the point. Their origins are diverse—some are from books, some from plays, others were written directly for the screen—what matters is that they are interesting, and available. The moviegoer must be brave, however, and not overlook the M-G-M musical *Love Me or Leave Me*. He must find his way to the Japanese film *Gate of Hell* and the Italo-English *Romeo and Juliet*. He will of course want to see *Summertime*, with Katharine Hepburn, and a remarkable experiment, *The Night of the Hunter*. Julie Harris will be found in *East of Eden*, and in *I Am a Camera*. *Violent Saturday* is a taut exercise in melodrama. *Mr. Roberts* will soon be around with an excellent cast, so will *The Rose Tattoo*. The list can easily be extended. I am only offering a sample.

Now, cast an eye over the list of plays currently running on Broadway. At last count there were nineteen shows on hand. Eight are musicals, a few of which we might term best bets; we must give Broadway its due, and acknowledge that it is often at its liveliest and best in its musicals. And you could hardly term them egghead fare. Neither is *Anniversary Waltz* nor *Anastasia*. The most pretentious item on Broadway at the moment is *Cat on a Hot Tin Roof*, a murky, unsatisfying play, woefully over-praised, that might eventually provide material for a good movie. (I keep remembering how beautifully *A Streetcar Named Desire* was adapted to its movie form.)

It took Laurence Olivier's *Henry V* to make a good many of us realize that a Shakespeare play could come to a stunning life, on film, never possible on the stage. Olivier's subsequent *Hamlet*, the Mankiewicz-Houseman *Julius Caesar*, Castellani's *Romeo and Juliet* have made the realization clearer. All the cumbersome and obsolete state trappings were thrown in the discard; the Elizabethan speech was able to shine amidst new, but quite proper settings. Interpretations may always be quarreled with; in staged Shakespeare as well as filmed Shakespeare. In the films there were cuts, excisions, even the elimination of a character here and there. When someone complains gloomily about the cuts in *Romeo and Juliet* it is considered only polite not to ask which of the speeches were most sorely missed, and to assume, instead, that every cultivated person reads the play at least once every two weeks. I, for one, will not look the gift horse in the mouth too closely. I would rather recognize the fact that Shakespeare now has a popular audience no one prior to 1930 could ever have dreamed of. I am also prepared to accept the conclusion that today's stage is a poorer medium for Shakespeare than the film.

This isn't only because the movies can stage the Battle of Agincourt when the theatre cannot. In the cases I have mentioned above the lines come out clearer and more richly. They are, after all, spoken under optimum conditions;

they can be heard as well by the pauper as by the rich man. In the Mankiewicz *Julius Caesar* millions have seen a magnificent—even fabulous—portrayal of Cassius, now also the possession of generations to come, as Booth's *Hamlet* was not. Part of the success of the Gielgud interpretation was made possible by the use of the close-up, a tool (and a handy one) unavailable to the stage.

Walter Kerr called this movie "an excellent reading of the play, carefully photographed." He went on to thank the producers "for making such a reading available (the stage at this time could not have afforded the cast)." He failed to mention the massive sets, the fluid change of scene, the hundreds of extras for the crowd scenes, the special effects used nicely for mood and atmosphere—all not only not affordable by the theatre, but not possible. As a *movie*, however, Mr. Kerr thought it inferior to the lowliest Chaplin two-reeler.

This notion, that the theatre is one thing and the film quite another, has been widespread for a long time. It has failed to take into account the continual development of the motion-picture form, from silence (and the eerie acting style the silence engendered) to the full use of modern screen *and* stage techniques. So astute a critic as the late James Agate put himself on record as follows: "I regard theatregoing as one thing, and filmgoing as quite another, and do not allow my films to impinge upon my plays. It is in the spectacular as opposed to the dramatic category that I place the films. The theatre, which talks about things rather than shows them, necessarily calls for a certain amount of imagination on the part of the playgoer, whereas the film, by showing everything, calls for no imagination at all."

I enjoy reading Agate, but on the above point I am afraid he was seeing through the mirror very darkly. It is axiomatic that, for dramatic effect, it is far more efficient to show something happening rather than to talk about it. Dialogue on the stage, the screen, or in fiction has its best use when it advances the action and characterizes. That the movies were able to eliminate that opening scene in which the maid and the butler talked about how late the master came home last night has been a relief to all of us. And when it is necessary, for the sake of subsequent action, to explain why Aunt Sadie behaves so curiously it is sometimes better not to have a friend of the family explain it for five minutes while sitting on a couch, but instead to backflash and show the significant moment that changed Aunt Sadie. The movies in this respect have the freedom of the novelist, a freedom playwrights have always envied. The flashback, of course, can be used on the stage, too—but how cumbersome the device seemed when Arthur Miller used it in *Death of a Salesman*. Talking about things on the stage all too often brings on boredom, instead of stimulating the imagination.

But good dialogue—talk that interests and that also advances the action—can occur in movies as in plays. *All About Eve*, for instance, had a lot of refreshing, literate, satiric talk. We all listened, quite unconcerned about whether the movie was moving or not. Films stimulate the imagination if the stories they tell are imaginatively stimulating. The limitation is not in the form, but in the material.

Recently I had occasion to see some movies made from Broadway plays of a couple of seasons ago. How much more satisfying, it struck me, to see I Am a Camera in its film version. The screenwriter (John Collier) seemed to have decided that he might as well use some material in the Isherwood story "Sally Bowles" that John van Druten didn't utilize in the play. Atmosphere can be easily established with the camera, and here it is a great help to a subtle and not too substantial story. No need to confine the action to a single box set, and if Sally Bowles and Herr Issyvoo were to visit a restaurant off they went and entered it, not from the wings, as stage people do, but from a street, as real people do. There is no need to complain, after all, if the reality of an illusion can be heightened by realistic settings.

An even better case in point is Summertime (made from The Time of the Cuckoo.) Instead of a stage Venice, we have a real Venice. Extraordinary color photography has made this Venice glow, but not because the writer and director had a travelogue in mind. The playwright wanted to show how the very atmosphere of Venice caused a spinsterish American woman to drop her scruples for a fling with a married Venetian. The movie is the most natural medium for the story. There before Miss Hepburn, and before us, is Venice. How else would she behave?

The stage versions, it is true, could speak somewhat more freely. Poor Sally was allowed her abortion in the play; the movie only allowed her to consider the idea. I'm not too unhappy that it worked out that way for her, but there is no denying that the stage can speak as adultly as it wishes to, while the movies must keep within the bounds of a concept known as "family entertainment." The existence of a network of censorship forces, keeping vigilant watch over the movies, is, in its way, a perverse tribute to the compelling power of the medium.

Yet, it's astonishing how, in spite of a constantly worn straitjacket, movies of mature content appear more and more frequently. The Country Girl (enhanced considerably in its transition from stage to screen) makes a profit, catapults its star to an Academy Award, and sets the producers to wondering which of its many ingredients caused its success. Was it the stars, Bing Crosby and Grace Kelly? Then Marty, without name stars, comes along, a low-budget film that is expected to bring in one of the biggest net profits, in terms of percentages, ever achieved by a movie. The writing is of a high order in both these pictures, the characterizations sound and sensitive. It is no wonder that Hollywood currently has a low regard for the hack-written screen "original," and is bidding instead for plays, the best TV scripts, novels, and short stories. The audience, having grown increasingly more selective in recent years, is showing a yen for the intelligent motion picture.

The Legion of Decency is again on the warpath, but it is noticeable that Hollywood isn't scaring quite so easily this time. For one thing, it's been found to be good publicity and financially rewarding to defy the censors. It happened with *The Moon Is Blue*. Observers have noticed a certain amount of loosening, lately, in the Production Code. Adultery, which mustn't be shown "explicitly, or justified, or presented attractively," seems to be getting increasingly hard to define. The Code seal has been given *Summertime*, in which Katharine Hepburn commits it, not unattractively.

Meanwhile, the stage has the edge in sophistication. It has a wider latitude of subjects that can be treated. There is a large audience still available to the theatre because of these ingredients. The pity is that the stage doesn't make better use of its artistic freedom. The theatrical series of four-letter words tossed, with excellent timing, at the audience in *Cat on a Hot Tin Roof* is a successful stunt, but hardly sensitive and illuminating theatre.

But Hollywood is feeling its oats. It's as though it wants to demonstrate that it can do anything the stage can do, and better. M-G-M has announced that it will go ahead with its plans to make *Tea and Sympathy*, a play that treats homosexuality with some explicitness. It seems to be blandly overlooking the Code provision that says: "Sex perversion or any inference of it is forbidden." The Code is, without doubt, beginning to rock slightly from pressures put upon it. The much maligned movie audience is, in the long run, responsible for this development.

There is a significant story that lies behind the fortunes of United Artists, a motion-picture company that, in a few years, has risen from near bankruptcy to a healthy financial position. United Artists has a policy of what it terms "creative autonomy." In practice it is largely a financing and distributing corporation. A producer such as Stanley Kramer, a writer such as Joseph L. Mankiewicz, can get the necessary backing to make a movie and be allowed a free hand in the making of it. A tight control is kept on the budget, but not on content or treatment. *Marty, Summertime, The Night of the Hunter*, are all the result of this policy. It has been noticed by other companies that United Artists has been giving some of the more staple studio products hot competition with its methods. As a result, there is no major studio that has not gone in for what is virtually independent production.

All around the world, at this time, are camped production teams making movies that wouldn't have been possible under the old studio assembly-line system. They are being made against natural backgrounds; they are giving talented film people the opportunity to make the kind of pictures they want to make. They won't all be good, but they will bring continued freshness to the screen, which obviously hasn't yet explored all its horizons. The stage, confined to Broadway, a hit psychology, and economic problems it finds harder and harder to solve, has less and less to offer the popular audience. That audience is elsewhere, seeing theatre at popular prices, with no wait for tickets, at the movies.

❦ ❦ ❦

*Robert Herridge*

# TV: Journey's Beginning[1]

THERE IS an old saying: "We don't know where we're going, but we're on our way." Someone, I think it was Carl Sandburg, said of this phrase that it was one of the emotional slogans that settled the West. I think it applies also in a very real sense to the most recent settlement of a wilderness—television.

At the moment television appears to be a kind of mass movement heading vaguely somewhere, and that "somewhere" is defined in as many ways as there are people in the medium. Television is expected to be many things; it is put to a number of uses; for the most part it is allowed to be everything except itself. And by itself, I mean television defined according to its own proper elements, its limitations, its potential—television as an art form, standing on its own feet and expressing itself in its own language with its own proper aesthetic for creator and judge, its makers and the audience.

I would like to suggest an approach to television: first, as an art form, and potentially a major art form; and secondly, as a theatre, which is neither a movie nor a Broadway playhouse, a theatre having its own dramatic form, rich, compelling and human, a theatre which functions in the market place, the place where Shakespeare's theatre functioned—in short, television as a theatre art form—its audience, potentially everybody.

This suggestion is based on my own experience as writer and producer of "Camera Three," 130 programs old this next week. We have on this program experimented extensively with this approach in what we call "the theatre of the imagination"—an experimentation, which, incidentally, would not have been possible without the wholehearted support of Clarence Worden, Assistant General Manager, and Sam Digges, General Manager of WCBS-TV.

We have experimented; and in the process of experimenting, we have learned certain things about that most elusive of all marriages, the marriage of form and substance—or in television terms, program format and subject material.

Again, television is many things to many people. Most generally, it is a complex mixture of mechanics, electronics, of people and purposes; it is largely what people make it. It is a kind of ubiquitous arena, a traveling stage upon which here comes everybody, or what you will—a stage to be set up anywhere and at any time man chooses to press the button of a television set. It is free for all—its audience is everyone, the entire community.

This establishes a very important fact and a profound responsibility. It establishes through form—the format of a program—a direct relationship between material and audience. What is done on the studio side of the camera is di-

[1] From *Variety* (January 4, 1956), p. 158. Copyright 1956 by Variety, Inc. Reprinted by permission of the author.

rectly communicated to the whole of a community. A television program ideally is an experience that involves each and all members of a society—some more, some less. The form of that experience, therefore—the television program form —is *communal* in nature. And while to many this has its drawbacks, I think it is a healthy situation.

For cultural-technological changes of the past half century have widened immeasurably those areas in which art forms are directly related to mass audiences. The arts are inseparably linked to various media of communication—mass communication. And it is a healthy situation when art is directly related to the whole of a community, and care should be taken on both sides of the camera that it develop in a healthy way. There are those who shudder at the idea of a whole nation or of 65 million people gathering at a certain time to witness a television program. Let them shudder—it keeps them occupied.

In Athens the entire population of the city gathered to witness and be a part of plays by Aeschylus and Sophocles. The differences are great, but the analogies are important and compelling to anyone thinking of television as a creative medium. I think of how this situation affects our conceptions and our working to create a television art form: a public, a communal form working with universal patterns and symbols as opposed to the highly individual and private forms working with private symbols and patterns.

All of this suggests forms that do not need footnotes nor program notes or any other extensive translating devices on their way to the heart, mind, and lives of the spectator.

It suggests a form and pattern which is, on the surface at least, immediately communicative, leading us deeper and deeper into the meaning of things which concern us all—the human situation, with life, birth and death, with conflict and suffering, with hope, dignity, and courage, and with something larger of which these are but a part.

Now, there is a thin ghostlike figure that haunts radio, television, motion pictures, and he says art is not for the mass audience. You are dealing with a mentality of 14 years, etc. My hope is that this figure will vanish into the thin air of the World War I Benet IQ tests from which he came.

And if anyone thinks that this would limit what might be called "the expression of profundities"—I refer him to the proper playing of the plays of Shakespeare. There is a broad surface communication either of joy or terror to the simplest spectator; there are depths enough to satisfy the most profound. Falstaff, for example, is as profoundly created a figure as I know; yet he is as broadly comic as W. C. Fields—as much a joy to children as to the Shakespearian scholar—and sometimes, as with great scholars, I am not sure it is for different reasons. Or take the lyric, "Full fathom five thy father lies, of his bones are coral made." Here is an apple for a child. It is also meat upon which we can chew for a lifetime.

The form I am thinking of—public, communal, will work at a number of levels of significance . . . spectacle, ceremony, character and conflict, tragic or comic rhythms, and deepest—a gradually revealed understanding of the meaning of human experience. All this is to suggest a kind of art form possible to a medium of mass communication—a kind of creativeness.

One may approach television with the same seriousness, the same strictness of attitude, that one approaches any major art form. The same basic aesthetic principles—pace, proportion, dominance, rhythm, unity, etc.—apply. Since like music, poetry, and drama as distinct from architecture, sculpture, and painting, time is a basic element in the form—the television form is dynamic (a better word perhaps is organic); it has a beginning, a middle, and an end with each part of its structure dependent upon the other and upon the function of the whole. This function is equivalent to the effect which the form produces on the spectator. It is an interpretation or illumination of some basic truth concerning reality, an audio-visual composition working on various levels of meaning. At its best it is for the spectator an experience—comic, tragic, lyric, episodic, etc. —that wholly involves the spectator in a kind of journey or experience through which he may pass from ignorance to knowledge concerning some aspect of the human experience.

For two and one-half years now, "Camera Three" has been this kind of an experiment—an attempt to work from this as a basic conception. We have tried, and the try has always been exciting. How well we have succeeded even in part is for others to say. But more and more, achievement seems possible—I mean the achievement of television as an art form and a theatre; I mean finding the right patterns and associations of words, music, movement, light patterns, objects, symbols—the proper language to write for television as a poet writes a poem or a painter paints a picture—the language to express deeply the human experience with a full sense of its reality.

When this happens, we will realize the potential of television as a creative medium—an art form for everybody that will be at once simple and profound, that will take an audience on a vital, dramatic, and deeply beautiful journey through the world of time and man, a journey that will deeply feed their lives with a sense of life, a journey they will not soon forget.

❧ ❧ ❧

S. J. Perelman

# Strictly from Mars, or, How to Philander in Five Easy Colors[1]

SOME love Van Johnson, some van Gogh; for every youth who pins up a photograph of Alexis Smith, there is another who does the same for Betty. Sneer if you will at the veal-faced adolescent haunting Grand Central for a glimpse of

[1] Permission of the author. Copyright 1946 The New Yorker Magazine, Inc. (Formerly The F-R. Publishing Corporation.)

Perry Como; one of these evenings you will claw your way through the lobby at a first-night intermission to genuflect before Evelyn Waugh or Shostakovich. Everyone, no matter how case-hardened, has his joss. I know a poised and cultivated woman whose contempt for her husband is infinite because he spent two years maneuvering an introduction to Bill Dickey. Last summer, she crouched for a whole afternoon in a bog on Martha's Vineyard to beg an autograph of Katharine Cornell. I, too, have my idol, and if he is neither toreador nor tenor, philosopher nor clown, he is nonetheless romantic for being a plain businessman. Paradoxically enough, I have never heard his name, and I wouldn't be at all sure he exists, except for the indisputable evidence of his handiwork. He is the man who dreams up the dialogue in those advertising comic strips.

The general story pattern of these strips, while elementary, has the rugged simplicity of a piece of pre-Columbian sculpture or the Jupiter Symphony. The hero, a small boy or a creature from outer space, stumbles on various simple or compound disasters and averts them through superhuman strength derived from eating a given cereal or sandwich spread. Though never conveyed in so many words, there is usually a sly implication that the purchaser will acquire similar prowess the instant he lays his money on the barrelhead.

A convenient specimen appeared in a recent Sunday *Herald Tribune*. It shows Peter Pan, a strangely mammiferous teen-ager in a Lincoln green jerkin, stepping out of the trademark on a jar of peanut butter and beguiling a boy to the circus. The pair breathlessly watches the star trapeze act, in which a girl aerialist shuttles between her own flimsy perch and the hands of her catcher. Suddenly, a rope frays and the girl dangles perilously beyond the catcher's reach. "Hang on!" encourages the ringmaster, who evidently has seen peanut butter save the day in many a crisis. "Peter Pan's on the way!" His faith is vindicated forthwith, when Peter, her ankles gripped by the catcher, swings out and snatches the girl back to safety. "Thanks for saving my life, Peter Pan," the latter observes somewhat lymphatically. "Yes," adds the ringmaster, a man obviously accustomed to deal with any social situation. "And I'm treating everybody to these swell peanut-butter sandwiches. Take all you want, folks!" By my limited standards, such munificence is roughly synonymous with a left to the kidneys, but circus people have their own curious code. With the final terse announcement *"It does not stick to the roof of your mouth!,"* Peter Pan steps back in the label and the reader presumably rushes to the nearest grocer. I started to, but my head was wedged between a couple of sofa pillows, and as it would have meant cutting it away with an acetylene torch, I decided to string out the autumn on margarine.

"How Thom McAn Foiled the Flood," a strip decorating the back cover of a comic book called "Wonder Woman," also has its moments of rare verbal beauty. Thom, a red-headed lad of Herculean vitality, is introduced lounging with three friends "outside the clubhouse of the Thom McAn Shoes-True Pals," surely the most neuralgic collection of words ever yoked together in English.

Informed by a radio flash that the town dam has broken, he hastily dons a pair of weird red Juliets, which he refers to as "bazooka-shoes," and whizzes to the scene. "Wow!" he shudders as he sees the torrent about to engulf the town. "Not a second to spare! And I can't move the town—so I have to move the flood!" Employing his shoes as a bulldozer, Thom rips a channel through the mountain, thus enabling the river to bypass the town, and returns to the club to receive the plaudits of his friends. "These 'bazooka-shoes' are O.K. for emergencies," he comments wryly. "But for everyday comfort and fun, I'll take good ol' Thom McAn shoes!" His jubilant comrades suggest a feast to celebrate his exploit, but Thom suddenly stands on protocol: "Wait, Jimmy here can't enter. He's not 'shoe-true to Thom McAn!' " After humiliating Jimmy so thoroughly that they lay the foundation for a whopping psychic trauma, his chums agree to let the outlaw participate, on condition he dig up a pair of Thom McAns. An hour later, Thom greets him at the clubhouse door. "Enter, pal," he says with greasy affability. "Your shoes are the key. Now you are officially a 'Thom McAn Shoe-True Pal!' " This piquant hash of child psychology and salesmanship, incidentally, appeared in a publication whose advisory board includes an assistant professor of education at Columbia, a professor of psychiatry and one of English literature at New York University, Pearl Buck, and Gene Tunney. The names of Captain Bligh and Torquemada were missing from the masthead, but I guess they happened to be out of town.

The most captivating example of this sort of moonshine I have met, however, is the strip called "Volto, He Comes from Mars Possessing Strange Magnetic Powers!," in a journal named *Star Spangled Comics*, which I found stashed in my son's bed a few days ago. We first encounter Volto, an interplanetary version of the late Lou Tellegen, on a roller coaster with a small boy. Suddenly, down the incline toward them hurtles another car. "What a way to run a roller coaster!" exclaims Volto pettishly. "I better get busy!" He extends his left hand, repelling the car, but the ensuing jolt dislodges one of the passengers, a reasonably well-stacked brunette. As she falls headlong, Volto extends his right hand and she is magically swept into his arms. A concessionaire hurries up to offer Volto a hundred dollars for the secret of his stunt. "It's no trick for Volto!" announces his young companion. "He's from Mars, where everybody gets that magnetism from eating whole-grain cereals!" Volto, plainly reluctant, looses his hold on the maiden. "And I must have some right now to recharge my power!" he chimes in with a wolfish grin. Simpering, the brunette tucks back a stray wisp of hair. "Then," she proposes, "let me repay you with the tastiest whole-grain cereal in this world—Grape-Nuts Flakes!" In the final tableau, Volto has apparently whisked the girl away to a quiet little cafeteria for a few rounds of flakes, and the strip concludes with the boy exalting the virtues of the cereal.

An electric climax to a thrilling episode—and yet, somehow, the whole affair leaves one frustrated. What *did* become of Volto and his little pigeon after they left the park? What about Volto's home life—did Mrs. Volto know where he was? Why was he bumming around an amusement park on Earth when he should have been tending to business on Mars? Obviously, Grape-Nuts is playing its cards very close to the vest indeed, and if we are to have an explanation, we shall have to evolve it ourselves. I'll go first:

Alice Volto stirred sleepily on her chaise longue, her ear cocked at the sound of her husband's tread in the corridor. She heard him fumble unsteadily at the keyhole; after a moment the door slammed and a penetrating odor of oatmeal wafted out of the foyer, punctuated by a stifled belch. "Oh, damnation," she thought hopelessly. "Another toot. And after all his promises, too." She held up her wristwatch to the back of her head, where the best of her eyes was located, and peered at the time. Nine-fifteen—two hours late. He would probably have some overplausible yarn about being detained by a client from Betelgeuse or Charles's Wain. She arose with weary resignation, flicked a suède buffer across her nose to accent its patrician metallic gleam, and issued into the living room.

"Hi, sweet," Volto mumbled from behind his evening paper. He was aware that he was holding it upside down, but he didn't care; he felt ghastly. If only he hadn't let that little tramp cajole him into a final dish of Crispies.

"Everything all right at the office?" asked Alice, casually levitating herself to the mantelpiece and lighting a cigarette. She had long since learned the value of forbearance and cunning with her husband.

"Oh, tiptop!" said Volto, assuming a grimace intended to convey sunny insouciance. "I blew out a sprocket this morning, but the nurse at the infirmary welded it."

"Better stop around at the plumber's in the morning and have a checkup," his wife advised. "You may still have a little steam in your gauge from last winter."

"No, I—I feel great," Volto assured her, nimbly brushing an ashtray to the floor and strewing the rug with butts. His red-lacquered neck turned a deeper shade. Alice, her lip curling in amused contempt, extended her right hand and the ashtray leaped back to the table. In the short, meaningful silence that followed, a fine perspiration mantled her husband's forehead.

"You must be famished, darling," remarked Alice, at last. "Your dinner's in the alcove."

"Why—er—uh, I don't think I want anything right now," said Volto, with a sickly grin. "I had a rather late lunch—"

"But it's your favorite dish!" Alice objected. "I made you a great big bowl of Wheaties mixed with Kix and shredded bran. You adore it."

"I know," Volto admitted unhappily. "But you see, I—well, this small goy I met on the midway—er, I mean to say *boy*—"

"What midway?" Alice interrupted.

"Why, the amusement park," he faltered. "The one down there on the Earth. Say, you wouldn't believe the way they run their roller coasters! Irresponsible— yes, sir, absolutely insane!"

"Really?" Alice's voice abruptly turned glacial. "What were you doing on the roller coaster?"

"Who, me?" asked Volto innocently. "Nothing. I was just riding in the front seat with this boy."

"I thought you were at the office all afternoon," said Alice.

"What's the matter with you—don't you understand Martian?" shouted Volto. "I told you I was down on Earth, didn't I?"

"I'm sorry," said Alice. "Well, go on."

"I *am* going on!" he screamed. "Only, for God's sake, stop yelling 'Go on, go on' at me! It's enough to drive a man crazy." He paused, drew some steel wool from his pocket, and sponged his brow. "Well, we were zooming along like anything, when a girl fell out of the other car—"

"Oh," said Alice. "Was she pretty?"

"What's that got to do with it?" demanded Volto savagely.

"Nothing," said Alice. "I was just curious."

"Well, don't start reading double meanings into everything," snapped her husband. "When I see a party in mortal peril, I don't ask if they're a Conover model before I go to their aid."

"No, but it comes in handy afterward," commented Alice. "What happened then?"

"Nothing," replied Volto. "I used my strange magnetic powers, that's all."

"I bet you did," said his wife. "Was she grateful?"

"How do you mean?" asked Volto cautiously.

"Well, you saved her life, if I interpret your story correctly."

"Too damn grateful," returned Volto. "You never saw such a nuisance. I wanted to come home, but she made me go and have some whole-grain cereals with her."

"Where—in a restaurant?" inquired Alice.

"Well—uh, not exactly." Volto hesitated. "You see, all the restaurants down there close by three in the afternoon. We tried 'em."

"But then she remembered she had some cereal up at her place, I suppose," suggested Alice.

"Why, how did you know?" asked Volto, taken aback.

"Oh, I just guessed," smiled his wife. "I always kept some on hand for emergencies before I knew you."

"Well, it was pretty white of her, all the same," said Volto defensively. "If I hadn't found some way to recharge, I might never have come back to this planet."

"My goodness," said Alice with a certain degree of composure. "Whatever would have become of me?"

"That's what I was afraid of," explained Volto. "It had me plenty worried for a spell."

"Well, dear," said Alice, descending from her perch, "you've had a full day, haven't you? Why don't you run along to bed?"

"Think I will," yawned her husband. "You going to sit up and read awhile?"

"No, I believe I'll take a spin," said Alice thoughtfully. "Did you leave the rocket out?"

Volto nodded. "Going over to your mother's?" he asked.

"Uh-uh," smiled Alice. "Coney Island."

❧ ❧ ❧

# E. J. Kahn, Jr.

# Ooff!! (Sob!) Eep!! (Gulp!) Zowie!!![1]

A FEW years ago, the Boston *Globe*, perhaps hoping to evoke a handsome testimonial to the influence of its editorial page, asked some of its readers who were attending college, and were thus possibly a cut above the intellectual average, to tell why they preferred the *Globe* to its competitors. Ninety per cent of the students said that they favored the *Globe* because it carried "Li'l Abner," a comic strip that is more or less concerned with the diverting antics of a singular tribe of hillbillies native to Dogpatch, a community situated somewhere in the mountains of the southeastern United States. The results of the *Globe's* survey were conveyed, in due course, to Al Capp, the man who draws and writes "Li'l Abner." Capp is a dark, heavy-set, brash, exuberant, witty, rowdy, and inventive man of thirty-eight, who sometimes professes to despise comic strips and might take a firmer stand against them than he does were it not for the fact that they earn him, before taxes, nearly a quarter of a million dollars a year, a sum that he cannot bring himself to despise. His first reaction to the *Globe's* findings, when a friend told him the news, was commendably objective. "This is deplorable," said Capp. "Is the younger generation utterly without taste?" A moment later, partly disengaging his teeth from the hand that so royally feeds him, he added, "Still, think how much more deplorable it would have been if those imbeciles had said they read the *Globe* because of 'Jane Arden.' "

Capp's full name is Alfred Gerald Caplin, but since the summer of 1934, when he introduced "Li'l Abner" to what he has grown fond of describing as a horrified public, he has been using the sawed-off version, being convinced that many readers of comics are apt to become restless and irritable when confronted with polysyllabic words. Last year, at the invitation of the Encyclopædia Britannica, Capp wrote a critical essay about the American comic strip for a

four-volume supplement called "Ten Eventful Years." Capp noticed delightedly
that he had been identified as "A. Cp.," a signature far outdoing in economy his
own effort. He was about to write the Britannica editors a congratulatory note
when a learned acquaintance explained that these scholars abbreviate all their
contributors' names, even those never previously cropped. According to Capp's
article, "The comic strip during the decade 1937-1946 became, in terms of the
constancy of the devotion of its followers, the most popular U.S. entertainment,
surpassing radio and the motion picture." In any terms, the comics are thriving.
Every month, nearly forty million comic books are bought and presumably read.
Every day, seventy million people, or half the population of the country, are
reputed to read, openly or furtively, comic strips in the newspapers. It is difficult to arrive at the exact number of readers of any given strip, since the syndicates that distribute these profitable features are partial to dealing in round, if
not downright puffy, figures. The United Feature Syndicate, which transmits
Capp's work to a waiting world, computed recently, with exceptional precision,
that "Li'l Abner" was printed in 30,189,151 copies of daily newspapers in this
country, as well as in a large but indeterminable quantity abroad. Any analysis
of such statistics is apt to bring on a headache. In the fall of 1944, for instance, United Feature, then dealing in conventional globular figures, announced that Capp had twenty-seven million readers and that he had acquired
them at the rate of seventy-five hundred a day. In the fall of 1945, the syndicate announced that in the preceding twelve months he had picked up 77,923
readers. This amounted to a daily gain for that year of a mere two hundred and
thirteen and a half readers, but the syndicate, instead of apologizing for this sudden diminution of converts per day, deftly shifted its ground and let it be
known that Capp habitually ensnared new readers at the rate of four and a half
a minute. It is agreed by people who ponder such matters that the field is led
today by five comic strips—"Blondie," "Dick Tracy," "Joe Palooka," "Little
Orphan Annie," and "Li'l Abner," though not necessarily in that order. Each
one appears in over twenty-five million copies of newspapers a week, and each
copy probably has at least one reader, or, in round figures, each strip has fifty
readers per second, day or night, rain or shine, dead or alive.

Partisans of each of the five most illustrious serials, including the men who
turn them out, are inclined to think that their own favorite is coincidentally the
national favorite. "More Americans give me a piece of their day," Capp recently
told a friend, "than anyone else in the country." He is not alone in viewing
himself as top dog. The *Illinois State Journal*, published in Springfield, observed last year that "Al Capp, more than any other comic strip artist, has won
the complete confidence and genuine affection of the American people. . . .
Li'l Abner [has] become an American institution." The Charlotte, North Carolina, *News*, further defining the strip's institutional status, called it "as much a
part of the national life as ice cream cones and taxes." These periodicals are
among the four hundred and twenty-seven daily and one hundred and seventy-
nine Sunday papers in the United States that carry "Li'l Abner." They pay, de-

pending on their size and other factors, from seventy-five cents to six hundred dollars a week for the privilege. Tributes to Capp's eminence have not come only from publications that contentedly serve as the oysters for his pearls. A federal law-enforcement officer in San Antonio once wrote Capp that in the course of his duties he had met up with people suffering from the stings of scorpions, from overdoses of marijuana, and from hydrophobia, but that he had never encountered anybody "who spouted more varied and distorted ideas than you do."

When Capp started "Li'l Abner," comic strips were around forty years old. The early comics were unpretentious illustrated gags; they were comical, or tried to be. By the thirties, according to the Britannica's Mr. Cp., "The clowns had been pushed off the comic page by the misery-vendors, the horror-vendors, the blood-merchants. The hilarious 'Bam!!!' or 'Zowie!!!!' ending of the comic simpleton overcome by the brutality, misunderstanding, avariciousness, or bad temper of his fellowman had been supplanted by the 'Help!! The rattlesnake is strangling me, Mother, dear!!!'—or—'Take dat, you copper—right t'roo de head!!!' type of ending wherein the comic simpleton was supplanted by a pathetic, golden-haired little girl simpleton or a blue-eyed, white-lipped, red-blooded detective simpleton, whose perils never ended—in fact, increased each day in violence and intricacy. . . . The comic strips, with a few die-hard, hard-fighting exceptions, were no longer comic. . . . The word went out from circulation departments that anxiety about the fate of Orphan Annie's dog sold far more papers than did joy over the foolishness of Boob McNutt." Capp is the hardest-fighting exception to the trend he disapproves of. His principal character, a young man named Li'l Abner Yokum, is a simpleton of inimitable foolishness, and practically everybody he meets up with is brutal, misunderstanding, avaricious, or bad-tempered. Abner is a handsome youth with an impressive physique, and he is constantly being troubled by the advances of highly attractive young ladies, but he admits to being in love only with such things as a dressmaker's dummy and a cockroach. Male readers of "Li'l Abner," contemplating this grotesque state of affairs, presumably indulge in a smug, self-satisfied smile, fairly certain that if *they* were ever to be pursued by a host of beautiful women, they would know what to do about it. Capp, working on the popular assumption that people of either sex derive immense satisfaction from laughing at the misadventures of creatures to whom they feel superior, has endowed his characters with such nonsensical traits that it is impossible for the most backward citizen of this country not to consider them inferior to himself. Capp's hillbillies are not all in love with cockroaches, but they are thoroughly individualistic in one way or another. They are uneducated, uninhibited, unsanitary, unconventional, and uncompromising, and it always surprises them that the rest of the world is out of step. By continually enmeshing these rural folk in the complexities of organized society, Capp produces the same kind of laughter aroused, in other fields, by the nonconformist struggles of Charlie Chaplin and Groucho Marx. Capp, an exceptionally worldly fellow, has a low opinion of the present state of organized society, and the fantasies he creates often touch upon current events and are heavily flavored with satire. "It's hard to know just how to sum up Al," a friend of Capp's said recently. "If you rule out the possibility that he is a madman, I guess I would call him an outrageously talented author of terribly funny illustrated topical fairy tales—with social significance."

Capp is perhaps without an equal among contemporary fairy-tale composers in his ability to proceed with engaging plausibility from a ludicrous premise to a preposterous conclusion. "My readers have a hard time," he said a while ago. "They have to learn to accept the incredible as the normal run of things." His readers can be divided into three categories, corresponding to the three levels upon which "Li'l Abner" is constructed. The base level is in the Bam!!!-and-Zowie!!!! tradition, a broad, slapstick foundation of frenzied adventure, such as hair-raising chases, violent fights, and people hanging by their finger-tips from the edges of precipitous cliffs. Readers of all ages who like to browse on this level are apt to be quite concerned about the outcome of Capp's elaborate and giddy plots, and those who get a chance always ask him whether Li'l Abner is ever going to marry the heroine of the strip, a handsome but vacuous young lady named Daisy Mae Scragg, whose love for Abner is equalled only by his distaste for her entire sex. Capp is sometimes tolerant of, but always bored with, people who make this inquiry about this foolish young couple, and he refers to them brusquely as "Abner fans." Readers who indicate to him that they are especially pleased with the middle, or socially significant, level of his work, and who ask him when he is going to take another poke at radio commercials or the United States Senate, are, he thinks, much more estimable citizens, and he calls them, approvingly, "disgusting Abner fans." The third level, sometimes of microscopic dimensions, consists of bits of Rabelaisian humor, often so adroitly covered up that, like rare archeological treasures, they are less likely to be spotted by children at play than by people who set out looking for them. These mischievous escapades in print amuse Capp more than anything else about his work, and the thought that few of his readers share this enjoyment with him depresses him. If, however, he were to make these touches more obvious, it is possible that his strip might be banned not only in Boston but in Springfield, Charlotte, and San Antonio as well.

When Capp encounters a reader who enjoys not only the two lower levels but the nuances on Level Three, he confers on the fellow the highest possible token of his esteem, the designation of "slobbering Abner fan." People who have thus been honored realize that the title is a compliment, since "slob" is one of Capp's favorite nouns. "To me, the word 'slob' has a great deal of force and humor," he has said. "It's one of those really choice and charming words." It is not regarded with the same fervor by the United Feature Syndicate, whose editors feel obliged to tone down Capp's material when they detect something that particularly worries them. (A United Feature man was once described by a sympathetic friend as a "quivering Abner fan," and a piece of promotional literature that the syndicate issued a couple of years ago said, with perhaps unconscious wistfulness, "You never know what's coming next when it comes off the pen of the creator of 'Li'l Abner.'") One of Capp's favorite characters is a Dogpatch girl called Moonbeam McSwine, whose name indicates her paradoxical nature, since although she is uncommonly good-looking, she detests bathing and prefers the company of hogs to that of men. Six years ago, Capp had her say, "Ah is a lazy good-fo'-nothin' slob!" Somebody in the United Feature offices gave this confessional a scrubbing on its way to the public, and when it finally appeared in print it read, "Ah is a lazy good-fo'-nothin'!" Capp was distressed by the disappearance of what to him had been the only really charming word in the sentence, but he cheered up a few years later when he succeeded in having Daisy Mae, a girl of profound delicacy, call Moonbeam McSwine a slob.

Capp is not a self-effacing man, but he has stubbornly resisted the temptation to consider himself, as many of his fellow-citizens do, the world's greatest contemporary comic-strip artist. He feels that he is merely one of the two greatest, the other being Milton Caniff, the gifted inventor of "Terry and the Pirates" (now being done by another man) and at present the shepherd of "Steve Canyon." Capp's estimate seems to be shared by the School of Education of New York University, which, when it revealed, not long ago, that it planned to conduct a study of "the cartoon narrative as a medium of communication," said that Caniff and Capp were the only two cartoon narrators who were slated to take part in the inquiry. Caniff does not share Capp's shy reluctance to put one man at the top of the list; Caniff puts Capp there. "Al's the best of us all," he said recently. "To me, he is the only really funny man in the funnies business." Capp's professional honors are numerous. For one thing, he was the first comic-strip creator (a noun used in the business to describe anyone who both writes and draws a strip) to introduce parodies of other comic strips into his own. For another, he was the first comic-strip man to effect a profitable tieup, in his strip, with commercial broadcasting. Last year, he collaborated on a song about Li'l Abner and, after persuading several important radio vocalists to plug it, worked them into the plot of his strip. Then, on whatever day they were scheduled to sing the number, caricatures of them appeared in "Li'l Abner" and mentioned their broadcasts. Considering that comic strips have to be put together several weeks before publication and that radio programs are often torn apart at the last minute, the fact that Capp managed to synchronize events in the two media was impressive.

Capp has done a great many things other comic-strip artists might well be afraid to attempt. "The funnies have always avoided the enormous comic gold mine of sex," he once said. He was not referring to his own strip. When a song entitled "Six Lessons from Madame La Zonga," which he did not help compose, was at its height, Capp introduced into "Li'l Abner" an engaging and romantic character named Adam Lazonga. "He was a perilous experiment," Capp wrote to a friend, "because he was the master of how to woo, Dogpatch style—a kinda wooing the details of which were never very clear to the reader or to me, but which was superior to all other styles—and because he had won loving cups in exhibitions of Dogpatch-style wooing the world over. It was a nervous moment when I let him loose in the nation's family newspapers. Readers were shocked as it dawned on them what he was famous for doing, but delighted by his courtly and genteel way of doing it, and his dignified attitude toward his work."

Capp has many distinctions besides that of digging pay dirt out of the gold mine of sex. Most comic-strip creators are sedentary folk. Capp is wildly peripatetic. He lives with his wife and their three children on a farm in New Hampshire, has a studio apartment in Boston, and spends from ten days to two weeks of every month relaxing, with indefatigable intensity, in New York. Moreover, he is the only major practitioner of his art involved in two richly rewarding strips. He does the plotting and writes the dialogue for "Abbie an' Slats," which appears in a hundred and thirty daily and eighty Sunday papers in this country. "Abbie" is officially the handiwork of Raeburn Van Buren, who draws it and signs it, but Capp thought up the idea for it eleven years ago, sold it to United Feature, has done all the writing for it ever since, and receives half the net proceeds from it. Neither Capp nor United Feature has ever publicly admitted his connection with "Abbie," perhaps out of consideration for the feelings of comic-strip creators who have barely enough imagination and energy to keep one serial going. Capp enjoys pretending that he has no stake in "Abbie," and when asked by interviewers from high-school papers, as he often is, to name his favorite strip next to "Li'l Abner," he usually pauses, seems to think hard for a moment, and then solemnly plumps for "Abbie an' Slats." In his Britannica article, he modestly mentions "Abner" only once, but he twice praises "Abbie." Just a week ago, Capp established some kind of precedent by reviving, in "Abbie," a character who had been unequivocally killed off several months before. "In comic strips," Capp wrote in a note to his readers that was signed "R.V.B.," "if *you* want it hard enough and if the cartoonist has *nerve* enough, we can get together, remake the make-believe world in which, for a few moments each day, we all meet." Having the continuities of two major comic strips at his mercy, Capp has been able to indulge in a good deal of horseplay. Among the characters who have turned up in "Li'l Abner" are Raeburn Van Huron, an Indian chief, and Bullseye Van Suren, a champion dart-thrower; "Abbie an' Slats" was once given over for several weeks to the story of a conceited, gluttonous, drunken, disorderly, and untalented comic-strip artist named Hal Yapp, the creator of a strip called "Li'l Ebenezer." Yapp worked—at a time when the late George Carlin was managing United Feature —for a syndicate run by George Garlic. Capp often ridicules public figures, and he receives a lot of indignant letters of protest from people who admire his victims. When the Hal Yapp continuity appeared in "Abbie an' Slats," a great many alert Al Capp fans addressed vituperative letters to Raeburn Van Buren, who has since been regarded in the profession as the most stoical member of the human race since Sparta.

Capp's best-known victim is Chester Gould, creator of "Dick Tracy." Three years ago, in "Li'l Abner," Capp unveiled a cartoonist named Lester Gooch, creator of a gory strip entitled "Fearless Fosdick." The title character of this strip-within-a-strip is a detective of immense stupidity and is the idol of Li'l Abner Yokum, whom Capp has described as an individual of average comic-strip-reading mentality. "When Yokum speaks," Capp once wrote in "Li'l Abner," in a further explanation of his hero's mentality, "he speaks for millions of morons." In the lampoons of "Dick Tracy" that Capp has turned out, he has made some sharp observations upon the effect of comics on the American mind. A year and a half ago, Capp began a "Fearless Fosdick" sequence with a letter to Gooch written by Yokum, who was probably speaking not only for millions but for Capp, too. "Yore drawrins cood allus be dependid on to frigten li'l chillun an ole ladys into fitts on account they was so ugly yore drawrins I meen," wrote Abner, the only member of his family, aside from a small pig, who is literate. "Yo has allus bin the leeder of yore profeshun naimly skeerin the liver out of yore fateful reeders. But, laitly, things has changed, Gooch. Lately, *other* comical stripp cree-ay-ters bin cree-ay-tin even *more* horibul cree-ay-shuns then *yo!* Like ladys wif gravel in thar hare, mudd in thar eyes and who smells badd. Natcherly, the Americun public injoys this vurry much, Gooch. The trubble, Gooch, is all *yo* drawrs is horribul *gennulmin!!* Oh, Gooch, don't lett yore galentry hold yo back! Yo kin drawr worse than any of 'em. Go to it, Gooch, whomp up a lady thet is *so* itchy, *so* shakey, *so* smelly, and *so* onbarubbly disgustin that once agin you will be the king of the funny page."

Shortly thereafter, Capp, who, naturally, aspires to be the king of the funny page himself, took his own advice and whomped up a lady named Lena the Hyena, an inhabitant of a country he called, to show what he thought of it, Lower Slobbovia. Lena had a face so unbearably disgusting that a coal-black shark, happening to glimpse and then to swallow a photograph of it, shrieked, turned white, and sank to the bottom of the sea. Capp did not, however, plan to frighten little children and old ladies into fits by letting them see Lena's face—or so he insists today. He left the space above her neck blank and wrote "Deleted by Editor" across it. Immediately, some of his readers, eager to have the livers scared out of them, wrote to him pleading for a look at the lady's features. Capp then announced, in "Li'l Abner," that only a morbid horror seeker could be interested in the sight. This provoked more letters from confessed morbid horror seekers. Capp, delighted, decided to open a contest for drawings of the worst-looking woman in the world, the winning picture to be used in the strip and the winning artist to receive a prize of five hundred dollars. Three hundred and eighty-one of the newspapers that run "Li'l Abner" joined in, and most of them offered additional awards. Close to a million entries were submitted. On the periphery of the big contest, people all over the country—including a group of adult members of the First Congregational Church of Toledo—banded together to hold elimination contests of their own. A schoolboy who said he owned an authentic likeness of Lena grew rich, by charging his classmates a nickel a peek, before his teacher took it away from him. The annual Homecoming Queen beauty contest of the University of Colorado was disrupted by a write-in movement for Lena, who did so much better than any of the six attractive live candidates that the president of the university hastily called off the competition. Just before Election Day, a California paper that was participating in the contest asked its readers to send in questions they wished to have answered by prospective office holders. The paper got a total of thirty political questions and seven thousand drawings of Lena the Hyena.

There has been only the one Lena contest. For the last ten years, however, every November has been brightened by the celebration, on hundreds of campuses and in other arenas, of an as yet unofficial holiday known as Sadie Hawkins Day, which, according to the Birmingham, Alabama, *Post*, a paper that publishes "Li'l Abner," has become "so firmly entrenched as part of the American way of life that it would take an act of Congress to wipe it off the books." In Dogpatch, Sadie Hawkins Day provides unmarried women with an opportunity to obtain husbands by catching the community's eligible men in a foot race. In the rest of the country, the day is a less forthright variation of the leap-year idea. At many academies where it is observed, it is simply an excuse for the temporary reversal of normal social relationships: girls date boys. On some campuses the holiday lasts for a week or more, usually ending with a costume party, for which the guests dress in the fashion of "Li'l Abner" characters, a most scantily clad crew. Every year, Capp is invited to take in a couple of thousand of these parties. Last November, after consenting to look in on eighteen of them, he said to a friend, "Aren't they a wonderful idea? A girl can look charming for nothing!" Halfway through his tour, when he entered an armory where twelve thousand young people, dressed charmingly in rags, had gathered to do him homage, he appeared to have lost some of his enthusiasm. "What have I wrought!" he was heard to mutter. After the eighteenth party, he retired to his studio, sat down, and dashed off a snarling "Li'l Abner" sequence about the kind of people who go to Sadie Hawkins Day parties. Half the girls who attend these functions come dressed as Daisy Mae, and usually they participate in a beauty contest, the winner of which is designated the Daisy Mae of her community. Capp is often invited to serve as a judge. A year ago, he was chief judge and guest of honor at a Sadie Hawkins Day frolic at a large state university. The governor of the state was also present. For several weeks, there had been primary elections to winnow out hundreds of aspiring Daisy Maes. Finally, one chilly night, ten attractive survivors were lined up in a gymnasium for Capp's scrutiny. He is often lax about keeping appointments, and in this instance he was a full hour late. "There were the ten Daisy Maes," he told a friend afterward, "waiting for me, shivering. Usually, when I handle the finals, I spot a couple of standouts right away, either one of whom would be all right to pick. But every now and then it's just no contest. This was one of those cases. One little girl in the line was the loveliest thing I had ever seen. As I was looking them all over, I couldn't help grinning at her. She smiled back. She knew she'd win. Well, there were a lot of photographers hanging around, as always, and I thought I'd be polite and let the governor, who was also hanging around, into the act. I gave him a loving cup and whispered to him, 'The third from the left.' I should have known better than to entrust something like that to a politician. The governor stepped forward and handed the cup to the second from the left, and before I could do anything about it, flash bulbs began popping all over the place and the audience was clapping and cheering. I was stupefied with horror. That poor little third from the left! I couldn't even tell her later about the mistake. It would have created too much of a furor on the campus."

Capp's success in arousing interest in the subject matter of his strip has been thoughtfully noted by many people with axes to grind, and press agents buzz around him as enthusiastically as if he were a syndicated columnist instead of a syndicated cartoonist. When the American Heritage Foundation, sponsor of the Freedom Train, wanted some extra-special publicity for the beginning of its journey, an appeal was made to Capp. He obliged by turning "Li'l Abner," for two weeks, into a dramatization of the Bill of Rights. Some weeks ago, he received a request from Albert Einstein for assistance in disseminating the solemn propaganda of the Emergency Committee of Atomic Scientists. "Will handle in Slobbovia sequence," Capp wrote on the margin of Einstein's letter, and there is no reason to believe that he will not. Capp does not have to be nudged to espouse a cause. Entirely on his own, he has worked up spirited campaigns against, for instance, zoot suits, Southern congressmen, big business, intolerance, and outdoor advertising signs. Once he put Li'l Abner and Daisy Mae in an automobile and sent them off on a sightseeing trip during which, to view the scenery, Abner was compelled to uproot a hundred and fifty obstructive billboards along a ten-mile stretch of otherwise scenic highway. "Gosh!!" said Daisy Mae afterward. "Hain't America a *bootiful* country—it's even more *bootiful* than billboards advertisin' pork, beans, girdles, shoes, cheese, an' crackers!!" Advertising men have tried to dissuade Capp from this particular crusade. "The implications of such an act," the president of the Outdoor Advertising Association of North Carolina wrote him after Abner's prodigious feats of upheaving, "can hardly remain unnoticed by . . . law-abiding citizens of the United States. . . . If, in the immediate future, a wave of vandalism or property destruction of panels occurs typifying your hero's actions, it will not be a difficult matter to place the blame in the proper quarter." The wave never broke, perhaps because most Americans cannot pull up billboards barehanded. Sometimes, when Capp gets mad, he merely threatens people or institutions with notoriety. During the war, he made a short journey in a day coach and didn't care for it. "I'd never seen anything like the stinking, screaming horror of the whole set-up," he said to an acquaintance. "The poor passengers were treated like prisoners of war. I wrote a letter to the president of the railroad saying that I was planning to have some Dogpatchers take that same trip and that I was going to have them insulted and reviled and knocked about like Polish Jews on a German train on the way to a crematorium. 'I'm going to make it like Dante's "Inferno," ' I told him, 'and I want no protest out of you!' I hadn't drawn a line of any such sequence and didn't intend to, but that railroad president called me up every half hour for four days, conducted a long investigation, discharged two employees, suspended fourteen others, and undoubtedly hasn't had a good night's sleep since."

Some citizens are as eager to get into Capp's strip as others are to stay out. Four years ago, he started using his space on Christmas Day to extend holiday greetings to his friends. Along Broadway, it is now considered even more desirable to get on Capp's December honors list than to be wished happy birthday by Nick Kenny. "You made me the happiest man in the world," a prominent comedian who got mentioned wired Capp last December 26th. As early as the Fourth of July, Capp begins receiving telegrams from press agents reminding him how friendly he feels towards their clients. "It's getting so that if I leave off anybody who was on the year before, he fires his press agent," Capp says. "Why, a music publisher I know called me up the other day and said, 'Al, if you don't include Dick Haymes the way I promised him, I may lose him entirely as a plugger of my songs.' " Capp likes to live well, and he includes on his Christmas list the names of the managers of whatever hotels and night clubs he expects to be spending a substantial amount of time in. Last year he ended his list with the Hampshire House, where he has never since had any trouble reserving a suite. The year before, he extended seasonal wishes to "Halifax." A friend asked him whether he meant the British Ambassador or the city. "I wasn't sure at the time I put it in," Capp replied, "but I got a nice letter of thanks from both." Throughout the year, Capp is offered small gifts if he will make even a casual mention in "Li'l Abner" of something or somebody with a commercial angle, but he has always refused. Once, he was oddly penalized for giving a free plug. The occasion was the opening in New York, in April, 1944, of a musical comedy, "Allah Be Praised!," whose producer, Alfred Bloomingdale, is a friend of Capp's. The cartoonist regards himself as an astute theatrical critic, especially of musical comedies. He attended several rehearsals of "Allah Be Praised!," was delighted with what he saw, and decided to give the show a helping hand. In the strips to be published during the month after the show opened, he decorated a number of walls and fences with placards saying, "Allah Bloomingdale Presents 'Allah Bloomingdale Be Praised.' " The show folded after twenty performances, by which time Capp's outdoor advertising on its behalf had long since been distributed to his newspapers, so it kept coming out for another ten days. Capp was annoyed that "Allah Be Praised!" closed with such inconvenient celerity, and he immediately began writing the book of a musical comedy of his own, an adaptation of "Li'l Abner," which he is still working on.

Outspoken admirers of Capp's work have hailed him as a writer comparable to Lewis Carroll, Mark Twain, Dickens, and Dostoevski, and as an artist comparable to Hogarth, Daumier, and Low. Capp is embarrassed by such accolades. He prefers to think of himself as a simple, incomparable entertainer who specializes in the art of imaginative storytelling. "Practically any artist is better than I am," he once said. "As an artist, I'm just capable." He had such doubts about his capabilities as a writer that three years after starting "Li'l Abner," he took a short-story course at Harvard. His instructor told him that he was not without promise and gave him a B-minus. Technological improvements in communications have given Capp many advantages over earlier storytellers. Homer, for instance, was unable to make himself heard beyond the range of his voice. Capp, without having to raise his voice, can almost simultaneously tell the story of "Li'l Abner" in five languages, in eighteen countries, including Sweden and Venezuela. For telling a black-and-white Monday-through-Saturday continued story and a four-color Sunday-to-Sunday story, he receives around thirty-five hundred dollars a week. His yarns have become so popular in the thirteen years he has been spinning them that he takes in an additional twelve thousand or so a year from royalties on the sales of comic books, toys, costume jewelry, ladies' blouses, cosmetics, and music that have something to do with his comic strip. On behalf of Cream of Wheat, he does six "Li'l Abner" advertisements a year, for which he gets two thousand dollars apiece. "Abbie an' Slats" is good for another twenty thousand annually. Capp has a couple of assistants who do some of his drawing, but even before he took the course at Harvard he declined all offers of assistance in writing. "Li'l Abner" requires an average of a hundred words a day. A fellow-author, arbitrarily assigning half of Capp's gross income from the syndication of "Abner" to its text, has computed that each word, including "Eep" and "Ooff," brings its author three dollars. Capp is not satisfied with this word rate. Most syndicated comic-strippers receive fifty per cent of the gross. Capp now gets sixty-five per cent and is due to get an increase to seventy in 1949. Nevertheless, he is suing United Feature for fourteen and a half million dollars, which he contends the syndicate has deprived him of, in one way or another, since 1934. This may well be the largest claim ever filed by a single literary man against a corporate patron of the arts. The case is an extremely complex one, and unless it is settled out of court, as it may well be, it could drag on for two or three years, like some comic-strip sequences. In the meantime, Capp and United Feature are still working together, in a tight-lipped way.

The success of any storyteller can be measured at least in part by the extent to which his inventions become idiom. Who can utter the words "wine-dark sea" without recalling Homer? Capp's literary achievements, although they have yet to appear in an anthology of quotations, have become a part of the language. He has persuaded a great many of his fellow-citizens that "gulp" and "sob" are expressions that can be legitimately inserted at any point in any sentence. He is responsible for the fact that "oh, happy day!," "amoozin' but confoozin'," "writ by hand," and "as any fool can plainly see" are now used with merciless persistence by millions of Americans. The current enormous popularity of the adverb "naturally" and its variants "natcherly" and "natch" may well be the result of his devotion to them. His nonchalant approach to grammar, punctuation, and spelling has been a stimulating challenge to teachers of English composition, many of whose pupils have indicated a determination to pattern their prose after Al Capp's rather than Dr. Samuel Johnson's. A high-school junior in Lake Bluff, Illinois, assigned to three weeks of earnest study of "some great poet, author, or other writer who symbolizes American literature," chose Capp. In halls of higher learning, too, Capp is a man to reckon with. A year ago, at the College of William and Mary, a debate was held on the subject "Resolved: That 'Dick Tracy' means more to the American public than 'Li'l Abner.' " Two teams, each made up of an undergraduate and a professor, declaimed their arguments. A jury of three other faculty members unanimously returned a verdict in favor of "Li'l Abner."

Some, though by no means all, educators have come to assume that comic strips are read mostly by children and that it is harmful for young and impressionable minds to be continually exposed to characters like Moonbeam McSwine, whose distaste for soap, except as food, has never visibly impaired her physical well-being. The creators of comics, however, long ago abandoned the notion that their readers are all, or even predominantly, children. In a recent survey of adult readers of a number of metropolitan papers that print "Li'l Abner," seventy per cent of the men and sixty per cent of the women questioned said that they followed the strip. Most of the members of our war-time armed forces were of voting age, and their allegiance to "Li'l Abner" seemed at times second only to the one they had pledged to the flag. When the Paris edition of Stars & Stripes was unable, for a brief spell, to publish "Abner," it ran an apologetic note saying, "We admit that no newspaper is much good without 'Li'l Abner,' but you'll have to read the rest of the paper for a few days." When "Li'l Abner" failed to appear for three days running in the Vancouver Sun, its editors made a great to-do over its absence, which they treated as a news event. Actually, the Sun could have published the strip on the second and third day—a delay in the mails had caused a week's worth of "Abner" to arrive twenty-four hours late—but the editors withheld the strip, on the theory, which proved correct, that the despair and then the relief of their readers would be enormously increased. Like many prominent providers of mass-distributed entertainment in an era notable for the affection consumers of this commodity lavish upon its manufacturers, Capp has a vast supply of fervent admirers who aspire to touch or at least to ogle him, and he enjoys his celebrity. He does not, however, receive all the adulation stored up for him, because, unlike most celebrities, his face is not known to all his fans. Some of them aren't even sure of his name: to them he is only that fellow who does "Li'l Abner." At that, his face and name are perhaps better known than are the faces and names of most comic-strip creators, owing to his repeated use of caricatures of the face and variations of the name in the body of his strip. He has always been fond of devising names such as J. P. Gorganfeller, for a millionaire, and

Southbrook Juggler, for a columnist, and he is particularly happy when he concocts something like Al Capricorn, for an astrologist, or George Cappley, for a late Bostonian. Connoisseurs of "Li'l Abner" are inclined to the belief that Capp has never got a bigger laugh out of anybody's name than he did out of his own in the fall of 1945, when he had one Westbrook P. Buckingham, the wealthy distiller of a soft drink called Burpsi-Booma, discuss the financing of a proposed new elixir, Eleven Urp, with a pair of Indians belonging to the Seegarstor tribe. "I need capital," said Buckingham. "Capital in Washin'ton. No can move um. Too big," said one of the Indians. "Me once scalp paleface name of 'Al Capital,'" remarked the other Indian triumphantly. There is no evidence that Dickens, Twain, Carroll, or Dostoevski ever contrived anything comparable.

Capp is also working on the project of enabling his admirers to recognize him in the flesh. His calling cards, of which he always carries a bountiful supply, bear on them not merely his name but Li'l Abner's easily recognizable features. When Capp travels, it is usually in a brand-new Cadillac convertible coupé, with the words "Al Capp," in a reproduction of the script in which he signs the strip, painted on the door. At present, he has two 1947 Cadillac convertible coupés, both painted in eye-catching colors and both autographed. While he is riding in either of them, his movements are characterized by a refreshing disdain for the traffic regulations devised by a hundred and forty million other people simply to inconvenience him, and also for policemen churlish enough to wish to enforce them. Some of his friends think that he is, in the vulgar phrase, a cop-hater, but he disagrees. Once, though, he depicted Li'l Abner being mauled by five loutish policemen simply for having picked a flower near a "Keep Off the Grass" sign; this assault occurred immediately after the same officers had unconcernedly watched a couple of thugs spend half an hour beating up an old man. Another time, while Abner and his parents were in London, Capp had them severely dress down a bobby for being polite to them, an attitude that, they told him, was, in a policeman, un-American. Capp himself rarely has any trouble with the police. Whenever a cop does wander across the street to argue with him as he sits in his car, the officer is usually disarmed either by the signature on the car door or, if he doesn't notice that, by the illustrated calling card Capp thrusts upon him. Practically all policemen, it seems, are "Li'l Abner" fans and cannot bring themselves, even after seeing Abner's creator execute a double U turn on a crowded parkway, to be Capp-haters. Capp is usually glad that his prominence can save him from difficulties, but there are moments when he wonders whether it might not be nice to be—instead of a widely acclaimed, splendidly motorized funny man—plain Alfred G. Caplin, a travelling salesman, say, in an unsigned Chevrolet. "My God," he once said, "if only you could imagine the sheer, soul-racking horror of knowing that whenever you are introduced to a stranger as the creator of—gulp—'Li'l Abner,' he'll respond by saying not 'How do you do' but 'Ha ha.'"

❧ ❧ ❧

*Barry Ulanov*

# What Is Jazz? [1]

In *The American Scene,* Henry James said of American cities, "So there it all is; arrange it as you can. Poor dear bad bold beauty; there must indeed be something about her . . . !" The same thing can be said of American jazz.

On the surface there is disorder and conflict in jazz. No common definition of this music has been reached. It resists dictionary definition, and its musicians splutter nervously and take refuge in the colorful ambiguities of its argot. Nonetheless, its beauty can be probed; its badness can be separated from its boldness. The process is a difficult one, as it is in any art, and in jazz two arts, the composing and the performing arts, are joined together. But if one goes beneath the surface and does not allow the contradictions and the confusions of appearances to put one off, much becomes clear, and the mystery at the center is seen to be the central mystery of all the arts.

The cortex of jazz consists of several layers, alternately hard and soft, complex in structure, and hard to take apart. It is compounded of the history of the music and of the many styles of jazz. At first the history seems disjointed and the styles contradictory. One marks a confounding series of shifts in place and person and style. One finds a music dominated by Negroes in New Orleans, by white musicians in Chicago, by important but apparently unrelated figures in New York. One discovers a disastrous split in jazz inaugurated by the swing era and intensified during the days of bebop and so-called progressive jazz. But then one looks and listens more closely, and order and continuity appear.

Americans have long been wedded to the boom-and-bust cycle, and their culture reflects that dizzying course. Jazz is not like that; it has no cycles; it doesn't spiral. Whether you adopt the approach of the economic historian, the cultural anthropologist, or the aesthetic philosopher, you will not find an easy reflection of a theory in jazz. While much of America—crises and ecstasies and even a moment or two of exaltation—has found its way into jazz, the history of jazz is a curiously even one, chaotic at any instant, but always moving ahead in what is for an art form almost a straight line.

For most of its history, jazz, rejected in its homeland, has had consciously to seek survival, conscientiously to explain and defend its existence. From its early homes, the Ozark hills, the Louisiana bayous, the Carolina cotton fields, the Virginia plantations, through the New Orleans bordellos and barrelhouses to its latter-day efflorescence it has been alternately condemned and misunderstood. Variously banned and bullied and sometimes cheered beyond its merits,

[1] From *A History of Jazz in America* by Barry Ulanov (New York: The Viking Press, Inc., 1954), chap. 1. Copyright 1952 by Barry Ulanov. Reprinted by permission of the Viking Press, Inc.

jazz has led a lonely life but a full one. It is still with us and looks to be around for quite a while.

No matter what the fortunes of jazz, its nucleus has remained constant, little touched by extravagances of opinion, sympathetic or unsympathetic. The nucleus of jazz—as differentiated from its cortex—contains its nerve center, its source of life, and here are its mystery and meaning. The nucleus of jazz is made up of melody, harmony, and rhythm, the triune qualities of the art of music which, as everybody knows, can be fairly simply defined. In bare definition, melody is any succession of notes, harmony any simultaneity of tones, rhythm the arithmetic measure of notes or tones. In closer examination, melody appears as a vast variety of things, ranging from so simple a tune as "Yankee Doodle" to the complexity of one of Arnold Schoenberg's constructions. In more detailed analysis, harmony shows up as a vertical ordering of a Bach fugue, or a tight structuring based entirely on whole tones in the impressionism of Debussy. But bewildering as the complications of melody and harmony can be, they are easier to analyze and verbalize than rhythm or any of its parts, and rhythm is the most important of the three in jazz.

Before attempting a synoptic definition of jazz as a noun (or discussing the misuse of "jazz" as a verb and "jazzy" as an adjective), and of the various corollary terms that explain the meaning of this music, it might be instructive to examine definitions by musicians themselves. The following definitions were made by jazz musicians in 1935, when their music was undergoing a revival as a result of the then current vogue for the jazz that went by the new name of swing. Benny Goodman was a great success, and jam sessions had become public again. Musicians themselves found it difficult to define "swing," by which of course they merely meant the 1935 version of jazz, which wasn't very different from the 1930 or 1925 music. Let us examine the definitions.

WINGY MANONE: "Feeling an increase in tempo though you're still playing at the same tempo."

MARSHALL STEARNS AND JOHN HAMMOND (jazz authorities) AND BENNY GOODMAN: "A band swings when its collective improvisation is rhythmically integrated."

GENE KRUPA: "Complete and inspired freedom of rhythmic interpretation."

JESS STACY: "Syncopated syncopation."

MORTON KAHN AND PAYSON RE: "Feeling a multitude of subdivisions in each beat and playing or implying the accents that you feel; that is, if the tune is played at the proper tempo, so that when you're playing it, you'll feel it inside."

GLENN MILLER: "Something that you have to feel; a sensation that can be conveyed to others."

FRANKIE FROEBA: "A steady tempo, causing lightness and relaxation and a feeling of floating."

TERRY SHAND: "A synthetic cooperation of two or more instruments helping along or giving feeling to the soloist performing."

OZZIE NELSON: "A vague something that you seem to feel pulsating from a danceable orchestra. To me it is a solidity and compactness of attack by which the rhythm instruments combine with the others to create within the listeners the desire to dance."

CHICK WEBB: "It's like lovin' a gal, and havin' a fight, and then seein' her again."

LOUIS ARMSTRONG: "My idea how a tune should go."

ELLA FITZGERALD: "Why, er—swing is—well, you sort of feel—uh—uh—I don't know—you just swing!"

These musicians were looking for a new set of terms that would catch the beat so basic to jazz; they were stumped for the words to describe the kind of improvisation necessary to jazz.

In the simple, compressed, sometimes too elliptic vocabulary of the jazz musician, one learns a great deal about the music he plays. One learns that "jazz" is a noun, that it is not American popular music (as it has often been thought to be), that the jazz musician is most interested in the rhythmic connotation of the word and in little else. If you tell him that some say the term comes from the phonetic spelling of the abbreviation of a jazz musician named Charles (Charles, Chas., Jass, Jazz), he is not in the least interested. If you tell him that there is a great deal of substance to the claim that the word comes from the French word *jaser*—to pep up, to exhilarate—he may nod his head with a degree of interest but ask you, "What about the beat?" You will learn from the jazz musician that "swing" is no longer a noun, in spite of the fact that it was first so used in the title of a Duke Ellington recording in 1931, "It Don't Mean a Thing if It Ain't Got that Swing," which gives it a kind of ex cathedra endorsement. You will learn that "swing" is a verb, a way of describing the beat, even as Ellington's title for another tune, "Bouncing Buoyancy," is a description of the same beat, even as the term "jump" is, even as "leaps" is, even as the description of jazz as "music that goes" is, even as in the thirties the compliment of "solid" to performer or performance was like "gone," "crazy," "craziest," "the end," and "cool" today. They are descriptions of the beat.

From an examination of jazz musicians' own words, it is possible to glean the subtle, unruly, and almost mystical concept of the jazz spirit, or feeling, or thinking—it is all these things and is so understood by the jazz musician himself. The jazzman has his own way of getting at the center of his music, and thus he formulates his own musical language. Also he converts the musical language into a verbal dialect of his own. In his own set of terms, musical and verbal, he thinks, he feels; he rehearses, he performs; he scores, he improvises; he gets a beat.

To get that elusive beat, a jazzman will do anything. Without it, he cannot do anything. With it, he is playing jazz, and that is a large and satisfying enough accomplishment. When a jazzman picks up a familiar tune, banal or too well-known through much repetition, and alters its rhythmic pattern in favor of a steady if sometimes monotonous beat, and varies its melodies and maybe even changes its chords, he is working freely, easily, and with as much spontaneity as he can bring to his music. That freedom, ease, and spontaneity brought him to jazz; within those determining limits he will find a place for himself or get out, or join one of the bands whose frightening parodies of jazz are so often more popular than the real thing. It is by his formal understanding of certain definite values that the jazz musician has conceived, organized, and developed his art. It has been hot; it has become cool. It has jumped and swung; it has sauntered. It has borrowed; it has originated. It has effected a change, a literal transformation; inherited conventions have gradually been restated, reorganized, and ultimately restructured as a new expression. It may be that jazz musicians have simply rediscovered a controlling factor in music, the improvising performer. Without any awareness of what he has done, the jazzman may have gone back to some of the beginnings of music, tapping once more the creative roots which nourished ancient Greek music, the plain chant, the musical baroque and its immediate successors and predecessors. We know that seventeenth- and eighteenth-century composers were improvisers and that when they brought their scores to other musicians they left the interpretation of parts to the discretion of the performers, even as an arranger for a jazz band does today.

But the jazz musician has brought more than procedures, composing conceptions, and improvisation to his music. Techniques have been developed that have broadened the resources and intensified the disciplines of certain instruments far beyond their use in other music. Colors have been added to solo instruments and to various combinations and numbers of instruments that are utterly unlike any others in music. New textures have emerged from a conception of tonality and of pitch that is not original but is entirely fresh in its application. The improvising jazz musician has a different and more responsible and rewarding position from that of his counterparts in earlier art and folk music. The rhythmic base of music has been reinterpreted, making the central pulse at once more primitive than it has been before in Western music, and more sophisticated in its variety.

This, then, is how one might define jazz: it is a new music of a certain distinct rhythmic and melodic character, one that constantly involves improvisation—of a minor sort in adjusting accents and phrases of the tune at hand, of a major sort in creating music extemporaneously, on the spot. In the course of creating jazz, a melody or its underlying chords may be altered. The rhythmic valuations of notes may be lengthened or shortened according to a regular scheme, syncopated or not, or there may be no consistent pattern of rhythmic variations so long as a steady beat remains implicit or explicit. The beat is usually four quarter-notes to the bar, serving as a solid rhythmic base for the improvisation of soloists or groups playing eight or twelve measures, or some multiple or dividend thereof.

These things are the means. The ends are the ends of all art, the expression of the universal and the particular, the specific and the indirect and the intangible. In its short history, jazz has generally been restricted to short forms and it has often been directed toward the ephemeral and the trivial, but so too has it looked toward the lasting perception and the meaningful conclusion. Much of the time jazz musicians have sought and obtained an unashamed aphrodisiac effect; they have also worshiped in their music, variously devout before the one God and the unnamed gods. Like poets and painters, they are of all faiths, their doctrines are many; but they are united in one conviction, that they have found a creative form for themselves, for their time, for their place.

At the opening of the *Gradus ad Parnassum*, the dialogue offered as a study of counterpoint by Johann Josef Fux in 1725, the music master Aloysius warns the student Josef: "You must try to remember whether or not you felt a strong natural inclination to this art even in childhood." The student answers: "Yes, most deeply. Even before I could reason, I was overcome by the force of this strange enthusiasm and I turned all my thoughts and feelings to music. And now the burning desire to understand it possesses me, drives me almost against my will, and day and night lovely melodies seem to sound around me. Therefore I think I no longer have reason to doubt my inclination. Nor do the difficulties of the work discourage me, and I hope that with the help of good health I shall be able to master it." Several jazz musicians have read Fux, even as Haydn and Beethoven did, though perhaps with less immediate application. They have, however, echoed the pupil's "strange enthusiasm"; that, these jazz-men said, was their experience, their "burning desire." Following the "inclina-tion," jazz musicians have not had much of the help of good health; some of them have flaunted their doggedly unreasonable living habits and suffered the personal and public consequences of the habits and of the flaunting. All this their music has reflected, and sometimes it is noisy and grotesque as a result. More often it has a fullness and richness of expression. Slowly, clearly, the music is maturing, and, for it and with it and by it, so are the musicians.

❧ ❧ ❧

# Literature and Criticism

*Matthew Arnold*

## Dover Beach

The sea is calm to-night.
The tide is full, the moon lies fair
Upon the straits; on the French coast, the light
Gleams and is gone; the cliffs of England stand,
Glimmering and vast, out in the tranquil bay.
Come to the window, sweet is the night-air!

Only, from the long line of spray
Where the sea meets the moon-blanched land,
Listen! you hear the grating roar
Of pebbles which the waves draw back, and fling,
At their return, up the high strand,
Begin and cease, and then again begin,
With tremulous cadence slow, and bring
The eternal note of sadness in.

Sophocles long ago
Heard it on the Aegean, and it brought
Into his mind the turbid ebb and flow
Of human misery: we
Find also in the sound a thought,
Hearing it by this distant northern sea.

The sea of faith
Was once, too, at the full, and round earth's shore
Lay like the folds of a bright girdle furled.
But now I only hear
Its melancholy, long, withdrawing roar,
Retreating, to the breath
Of the night-wind, down the vast edges drear
And naked shingles of the world.

Ah, love, let us be true
To one another! for the world, which seems
To lie before us like a land of dreams,
So various, so beautiful, so new,
Hath really neither joy, nor love, nor light,
Nor certitude, nor peace, nor help for pain;
And we are here as on a darkling plain
Swept with confused alarms of struggle and flight,
Where ignorant armies clash by night.

*Theodore Morrison*

# Dover Beach Revisited: A New Fable for Critics [1]

EARLY in the year 1939 a certain Professor of Educational Psychology, occupying a well-paid chair at a large endowed university, conceived a plot.
From his desk in the imposing Hall of the Social Sciences where the Research

[1] "Dover Beach Revisited: A New Fable for Critics," *Harper's Magazine*, CLXXX
(February, 1940), 235-244. Reprinted by permission of the author.

Institute in Education was housed he had long burned with resentment against teachers of literature, especially against English departments. It seemed to him that the professors of English stood square across the path of his major professional ambition. His great desire in life was to introduce into the study, the teaching, the critical evaluation of literature some of the systematic method, some of the "objective procedure" as he liked to call it, some of the certainty of result which he believed to be characteristic of the physical sciences. "You make such a fetish of science," a colleague once said to him, "why aren't you a chemist?"—a question that annoyed him deeply.

If such a poem as Milton's "Lycidas" has a value—and most English teachers, even to-day, would start with that as a cardinal fact—then that value must be measurable and expressible in terms that do not shift and change from moment to moment and person to person with every subjective whim. They would agree, these teachers of literature, these professors of English, that the value of the poem is in some sense objective; they would never agree to undertake any objective procedure to determine what that value is. They would not clearly define what they meant by achievement in the study of literature, and they bridled and snorted when anyone else attempted to define it. He remembered what had happened when he had once been incautious enough to suggest to a professor of English in his own college that it might be possible to establish norms for the appreciation of Milton. The fellow had simply exploded into a peal of histrionic laughter and then had tried to wither him with an equally histrionic look of incredulity and disgust.

He would like to see what would happen if the teachers of English were forced or lured, by some scheme or other, into a public exposure of their position. It would put them in the light of intellectual charlatanism, nothing less . . . and suddenly Professor Chartly (for so he was nicknamed) began to see his way.

It was a simple plan that popped into his head, simple yet bold and practical. It was a challenge that could not be refused. A strategically placed friend in one of the large educational foundations could be counted on: there would be money for clerical expenses, for travel if need be. He took his pipe from his pocket, filled it, and began to puff exultantly. To-morrow he must broach the scheme to one or two colleagues; to-night, over cheese and beer, would not be too soon. He reached for the telephone.

The plan that he unfolded to his associates that evening aroused considerable skepticism at first, but gradually they succumbed to his enthusiasm. A number of well-known professors of literature at representative colleges up and down the land would be asked to write a critical evaluation of a poem prominent enough to form part of the standard reading in all large English courses. They would be asked to state the criteria on which they based their judgment. When all the answers had been received the whole dossier would be sent to a moderator, a trusted elder statesman of education, known everywhere for his dignity, liberality of intelligence, and long experience. He would be asked to make a preliminary examination of all the documents and to determine from the point of view of a teacher of literature whether they provided any basis for a common understanding. The moderator would then forward all the documents to Professor Chartly, who would make what in his own mind he was frank to call a more scientific analysis. Then the jaws of the trap would be ready to spring.

Once the conspirators had agreed on their plot their first difficulty came in the choice of a poem. Suffice it to say that someone eventually hit on Arnold's "Dover Beach," and the suggestion withstood all attack. "Dover Beach" was universally known, almost universally praised; it was remote enough so that contemporary jealousies and cults were not seriously involved, yet near enough not to call for any special expertness, historical or linguistic, as a prerequisite for judgment; it was generally given credit for skill as a work of art, yet it contained also, in its author's own phrase, a "criticism of life."

Rapidly in the days following the first meeting the representative teachers were chosen and invited to participate in the plan. Professional courtesy seemed to require the inclusion of an Arnold expert. But the one selected excused himself from producing a value judgment of "Dover Beach" on the ground that he was busy investigating a fresh clue to the identity of "Marguerite." He had evidence that the woman in question, after the episode hinted at in the famous poems, had married her deceased sister's husband, thus perhaps affecting Arnold's views on a social question about which he had said a good deal in his prose writings. The expert pointed out that he had been given a half-year's leave of absence and a research grant to pursue the shadow of Marguerite through Europe, wherever it might lead him. If only war did not break out he hoped to complete this research and solve one of the vexing problems that had always confronted Arnold's biographers. His energies would be too much engaged in this special investigation to deal justly with the more general questions raised by Professor Chartly's invitation. But he asked to be kept informed, since the results of the experiment could not fail to be of interest to him.

After a few hitches and delays from other quarters, the scheme was ripe. The requests were mailed out, and the Professor of Educational Psychology sat back in grim confidence to await the outcome.

## II

It chanced that the first of the representative teachers who received and answered Professor Chartly's letter was thought of on his own campus as giving off a distinct though not unpleasant odor of the ivory tower. He would have resented the imputation himself. At forty-five Bradley Dewing was handsome in a somewhat speciously virile style, graying at the temples, but still well-knit and active. He prided himself on being able to beat most of his students at tennis; once a year he would play the third or fourth man on the varsity and go down to creditable defeat with some elegiac phrases on the ravages of

time. He thought of himself as a man of the world; it was well for his contentment, which was seldom visibly ruffled, that he never heard the class
mimic reproducing at a fraternity house or beer parlor his manner of saying:
"After all, gentlemen, it is pure poetry that lasts. We must never forget the
staying power of pure art." The class mimic never represents the whole of
class opinion but he can usually make everyone within earshot laugh.

Professor Dewing could remember clearly what his own teachers had said
about "Dover Beach" in the days when he was a freshman in college himself, phrases rounded with distant professorial unction: faith and doubt in the
Victorian era; disturbing influence of Darwin on religious belief; Browning the
optimist; Tennyson coming up with firm faith after a long struggle in the waters of doubt; Matthew Arnold, prophet of skepticism. How would "Dover
Beach" stack up now as a poem? Pull Arnold down from the shelf and find
out.

Ah, yes, how the familiar phrases came back. The sea is calm, the tide is
full, the cliffs of England stand. . . . And then the lines he particularly liked:

> Come to the window, sweet is the night air!
> Only, from the long line of spray
> Where the ebb meets the moon-blanch'd sand,
> Listen! you hear the grating roar
> Of pebbles which the waves draw back, and fling,
> At their return, up the high strand,
> Begin, and cease, and then again begin,
> With tremulous cadence slow . . .

Good poetry, that! No one could mistake it. Onomatopoeia was a relatively
cheap effect most of the time. Poe, for instance: "And the silken sad uncertain rustling of each purple curtain." Anyone could put a string of s's together
and make them rustle. But these lines in "Dover Beach" were different. The
onomatopoeia was involved in the whole scene, and it in turn involved the
whole rhythmical movement of the verse, not the mere noise made by the
consonants or vowels as such. The pauses—only, listen, draw back, fling, begin,
cease—how they infused a subdued melancholy into the moonlit panorama
at the same time that they gave it the utmost physical reality by suggesting the
endless iteration of the waves! And then the phrase "With tremulous cadence slow" coming as yet one more touch, one "fine excess," when it seemed
that every phrase and pause the scene could bear had already been lavished on
it: that was Miltonic, Virgilian.

But the rest of the poem?

> The sea of Faith
> Was once, too, at the full, and round earth's shore
> Lay like the folds of a bright girdle furl'd . . .

Of course Arnold had evoked the whole scene only to bring before us this
metaphor of faith in its ebb-tide. But that did not save the figure from triteness

and from an even more fatal vagueness. Everything in second-rate poetry is compared to the sea: love is as deep, grief as salty, passion as turbulent. The sea may look like a bright girdle sometimes, though Professor Dewing did not think it particularly impressive to say so. And in what sense is *faith* a bright girdle? Is it the function of faith to embrace, to bind, to hold up a petticoat, or what? And what is the faith that Arnold has in mind? The poet evokes no precise concept of it. He throws us the simple, undifferentiated word, unites its loose emotional connotations with those of the sea, and leaves the whole matter there. And the concluding figure of "Dover Beach":

> we are here as on a darkling plain
> Swept with confused alarms of struggle and flight,
> Where ignorant armies clash by night.

Splendid in itself, this memorable image. But the sea had been forgotten now; the darkling plain had displaced the figure from which the whole poem tacitly promised to evolve. It would not have been so if John Donne had been the craftsman. A single bold yet accurate analogy, with constantly developing implications, would have served him for the whole poem.

Thus mused Professor Dewing, the lines of his verdict taking shape in his head. A critic of poetry of course was not at liberty to pass judgment on a poet's thought; he could only judge whether, in treating of the thought or sensibility he had received from his age, the poet had produced a satisfactory work of art. Arnold, Professor Dewing felt, had not been able to escape from the didactic tone or from a certain commonness and vagueness of expression. With deep personal misgivings about his position in a world both socially and spiritually barbarous, he had sought an image for his emotion, and had found it in the sea—a natural phenomenon still obscured by the drapings of conventional beauty and used by all manner of poets to express all manner of feelings. "Dover Beach" would always remain notable, Professor Dewing decided, as an expression of Victorian sensibility. It contained lines of ever memorable poetic skill. But it could not, he felt, be accepted as a uniformly satisfactory example of poetic art.

### III

It was occasionally a source of wonder to those about him just why Professor Oliver Twitchell spent so much time and eloquence urging that man's lower nature must be repressed, his animal instincts kept in bounds by the exertion of the higher will. To the casual observer, Professor Twitchell himself did not seem to possess much animal nature. It seemed incredible that a desperate struggle with powerful bestial passions might be going on at any moment within his own slight frame, behind his delicate white face in which the most prominent feature was the octagonal glasses that focused his eyes on the outside world. Professor Twitchell was a good deal given to discipleship but not much to friendship. He had himself been a disciple of the great Irving Babbitt, and he attracted a small number of disciples among his own more earnest students. But no one knew him well. Only one of his colleagues, who took a somewhat sardonic interest in the mysteries of human nature, possessed a possible clue to the origin of his efforts to repress man's lower nature and vindicate his higher. This colleague had wormed his way sufficiently into Oliver Twitchell's confidence to learn about his family, which he did not often mention. Professor Twitchell, it turned out, had come of decidedly unacademic stock. One of his brothers was the chief salesman for a company that made domestic fire-alarm appliances. At a moment's notice he would whip out a sample from his bag or pocket, plug it into the nearest electric outlet, and while the bystanders waited in terrified suspense, would explain that in the dead of night, if the house caught fire, the thing would go off with a whoop loud enough to warn the soundest sleeper. Lined up with his whole string of brothers and sisters, all older than he, all abounding in spirits, Professor Twitchell looked like the runt of the litter. His colleague decided that he must have had a very hard childhood, and that it was not his own animal nature that he needed so constantly to repress, but his family's.

Whatever the reasons, Professor Twitchell felt no reality in the teaching of literature except as he could extract from it definitions and illustrations of man's moral struggle in the world. For him recent history had been a history of intellectual confusion and degradation, and hence of social confusion and degradation. Western thought had fallen into a heresy. It had failed to maintain the fundamental grounds of a true humanism. It had blurred the distinction between man, God, and nature. Under the influence of the sciences, it had set up a monism in which the moral as well as the physical constitution of man was included within nature and the laws of nature. It had, therefore, exalted man as naturally good, and exalted the free expression of all his impulses. What were the results of this heresy? An age, complained Professor Twitchell bitterly, in which young women talked about sexual perversions at the dinner table; an age in which everyone agreed that society was in dissolution and insisted on the privilege of being dissolute; an age without any common standards of value in morals or art; an age, in short, without discipline, without self-restraint in private life or public.

Oliver Twitchell when he received Professor Chartly's envelope sat down with a strong favorable predisposition toward his task. He accepted wholeheartedly Arnold's attitude toward literature: the demand that poetry should be serious, that it should present us with a criticism of life, that it should be measured by standards not merely personal, but in some sense *real*.

"Dover Beach" had become Arnold's best-known poem, admired as his masterpiece. It would surely contain, therefore, a distillation of his attitude. Professor Twitchell pulled down his copy of Arnold and began to read; and as he read he felt himself overtaken by surprised misgiving. The poem began well enough. The allusion to Sophocles, who had heard the sound of the retreating tide by the Ægean centuries ago, admirably prepared the groundwork of high seriousness for a poem which would culminate in a real criticism of human experience. But did the poem so culminate? It was true that the world

> Hath really neither joy, nor love, nor light, . . .
> Nor certitude, nor peace, nor help for pain

if one meant the world as the worldling knows it, the man who conducts his life by unreflective natural impulse. Such a man will soon enough encounter the disappointments of ambition, the instability of all bonds and ties founded on nothing firmer than passion or self-interest. But this incertitude of the world, to a true disciple of culture, should become a means of self-discipline. It should lead him to ask how life may be purified and ennobled, how we may by wisdom and self-restraint oppose to the accidents of the world a true human culture based on the exertion of a higher will. No call to such a positive moral will, Professor Twitchell reluctantly discovered, can be heard in "Dover Beach." Man is an ignorant soldier struggling confusedly in a blind battle. Was this the culminating truth that Arnold the poet had given men in his masterpiece? Professor Twitchell sadly revised his value-judgment of the poem. He could not feel that in his most widely admired performance Arnold had seen life steadily or seen it whole; rather he had seen it only on its worldly side, and seen it under an aspect of terror. "Dover Beach" would always be justly respected for its poetic art, but the famous lines on Sophocles better exemplified the poet as a critic of life.

IV

As a novelist still referred to in his late thirties as "young" and "promising," Rudolph Mole found himself in a curious relation toward his academic colleagues. He wrote for the public, not for the learned journals; hence he was spared the necessity of becoming a pedant. At the same time the more lucrative fruits of pedantry were denied to him by his quiet exclusion from the guild. Younger men sweating for promotion, living in shabby genteel poverty on yearly appointments, their childless wives mimicking their academic shop-talk in bluestocking phrases, would look up from the stacks of five-by-three cards on which they were constantly accumulating notes and references, and would say to him, "You don't realize how lucky you are, teaching composition. You aren't expected to know anything." Sometimes an older colleague, who had passed through several stages of the mysteries of preferment, would belittle professional scholarship to him with an elaborate show of graciousness and envy. "We are all just pedants," he would say. "You teach the students what they really want and need." Rudolph noticed that the self-confessed pedant went busily on publishing monographs and being promoted, while he himself remained, year by year, the English Department's most eminent poor relation. He was not embittered. His dealings with students were pleasant and interesting. There was a sense of reality and purpose in trying to elicit from them a better expression of their thoughts, trying to increase their understanding of the literary crafts. He could attack their minds on any front he chose, and he could follow his intellectual hobbies as freely as he liked, without being confined to the artificial boundaries of a professional field of learning.

Freud, for example. When Professor Chartly and his accomplices decided that a teacher of creative writing should be included in their scheme and chose Rudolph Mole for the post, they happened to catch him at the height of his enthusiasm for Freud. Not that he expected to psychoanalyze authors through their works; that, he avowed, was not his purpose. You can't deduce the specific secrets of a man's life, he would cheerfully admit, by trying to fit his works into the text-book patterns of complexes and psychoses. The critic, in any case, is interested only in the man to the extent that he is involved in his work. But everyone agrees, Rudolph maintained, that the man is involved in his work. Some part of the psychic constitution of the author finds expression in every line that he writes. We can't understand the work unless we can understand the psychic traits that have gained expression in it. We may never be able to trace back these traits to their ultimate sources and causes, probably buried deep in the author's childhood. But we need to gain as much light on them as we can, since they appear in the work we are trying to apprehend, and determine its character. This is what criticism has always sought to do. Freud simply brings new light to the old task.

Rudolph was fortunate enough at the outset to pick up at the college bookstore a copy of Mr. Lionel Trilling's recent study of Matthew Arnold. In this volume he found much of his work already done for him. A footnote to Mr. Trilling's text, citing evidence from Professors Tinker and Lowry, made it clear that "Dover Beach" may well have been written in 1850, some seventeen years before it was first published. This, for Rudolph's purposes, was a priceless discovery. It meant that all the traditional talk about the poem was largely null and void. The poem was not a repercussion of the bombshell that Darwin dropped on the religious sensibilities of the Victorians. It was far more deeply personal and individual than that. Perhaps when Arnold published it his own sense of what it expressed or how it would be understood had changed. But clearly the poem came into being as an expression of what Arnold felt to be the particular kind of affection and passion he needed from a woman. It was a love poem, and took its place with utmost naturalness, once the clue had been given, in the group of similar and related poems addressed to "Marguerite." Mr. Trilling summed up in a fine sentence one strain in these poems, and the principal strain in "Dover Beach," when he wrote that for Arnold "fidelity is a word relevant only to those lovers who see the world as a place of sorrow and in their common suffering require the comfort of constancy."

> Ah, love, let us be true
> To one another! for the world . . .
> Hath really neither joy, nor love, nor light . . .

The point was unmistakable. And from the whole group of poems to which "Dover Beach" belonged, a sketch of Arnold as an erotic personality could be derived. The question whether a "real Marguerite" existed was an idle one, for the traits that found expression in the poems were at least "real" enough to produce the poems and to determine their character.

And what an odd spectacle it made, the self-expressed character of Arnold as a lover! The ordinary degree of aggressiveness, the normal joy of conquest and possession, seemed to be wholly absent from him. The love he asked for was essentially a protective love, sisterly or motherly; in its unavoidable ingredient of passion he felt a constant danger, which repelled and unsettled him. He addressed Marguerite as "My sister!" He avowed and deplored his own womanish fits of instability:

> I too have wish'd, no woman more,
> This starting, feverish heart, away.

He emphasized his nervous anguish and contrary impulses. He was a "teas'd o'erlabour'd heart," "an aimless unallay'd Desire." He could not break through his fundamental isolation and submerge himself in another human soul, and he believed that all men shared this plight:

> Yes: in the sea of life enisl'd,
> With echoing straits between us thrown,
> Dotting the shoreless watery wild,
> We mortal millions live *alone*.

He never "without remorse" allowed himself

> To haunt the place where passions reign,

yet it was clear that whether he had ever succeeded in giving himself up wholeheartedly to a passion, he had wanted to. There could hardly be a more telltale phrase than "Once-long'd-for storms of love."

In short much more illumination fell on "Dover Beach" from certain other verses of Arnold's than from Darwin and all his commentators:

> Truth—what is truth? Two bleeding hearts
> Wounded by men, by Fortune tried,
> Outwearied with their lonely parts,
> Vow to beat henceforth side by side.

> The world to them was stern and drear;
> Their lot was but to weep and moan.
> Ah, let them keep their faith sincere,
> For neither could subsist alone!

Here was the nub. "Dover Beach" grew directly from and repeated the same emotion, but no doubt generalized and enlarged this emotion, sweeping into one intense and far-reaching conviction of insecurity not only Arnold's per-

sonal fortunes in love, but the social and religious faith of the world he lived
in. That much could be said for the traditional interpretation.

Of course, as Mr. Trilling did not fail to mention, anguished love affairs,
harassed by mysterious inner incompatibilities, formed a well-established literary convention. But the fundamental sense of insecurity in "Dover Beach"
was too genuine, too often repeated in other works, to be written off altogether
to that account. The same sense of insecurity, the same need for some rock of
protection, cried out again and again, not merely in Arnold's love poems but in
his elegies, reflective pieces, and fragments of epic as well. Whenever Arnold produced a genuine and striking burst of poetry, with the stamp of true
self-expression on it, he seemed always to be in the dumps. Everywhere dejec-
tion, confusion, weakness, contention of soul. No adequate cause could be
found in the events of Arnold's life for such an acute sense of incertitude; it
must have been of psychic origin. Only in one line of effort this fundamental
insecurity did not hamper, sadden, or depress him, and that was in the free play
of his intelligence as a critic of letters and society. Even there, if it did not
hamper his efforts, it directed them. Arnold valiantly tried to erect a barrier of
culture against the chaos and squalor of society, against the contentiousness
of men. What was this barrier but an elaborate protective device?

The origin of the psychic pattern that expressed itself in Arnold's poems
could probably never be discovered. No doubt the influence that Arnold's father exercised over his emotions and his thinking, even though Arnold re-
belled to the extent at least of casting off his father's religious beliefs, was of
great importance. But much more would have to be known to give a definite
clue—more than ever could be known. Arnold was secure from any attempt to
spy out the heart of his mystery. But if criticism could not discover the cause, it
could assess the result, and could do so (thought Rudolph Mole) with greater
understanding by an attempt, with up-to-date psychological aid, to delve a little
deeper into the essential traits that manifested themselves in that result.

V

In 1917 Reuben Hale, a young instructor in a Western college, had lost his
job and done time in the penitentiary for speaking against conscription and
for organizing pacifist demonstrations. In the twenties he had lost two more
academic posts for his sympathies with Soviet Russia and his inability to forget his Marxist principles while teaching literature. His contentious, eager,
lovable, exasperating temperament tried the patience of one college administration after another. As he advanced into middle age, and his growing family
suffered repeated upheavals, his friends began to fear that his robust quarrels
with established order would leave him a penniless outcast at fifty. Then he
was invited to take a flattering post at a girls' college known for its liberality of
views. The connection proved surprisingly durable; in fact it became Professor
Hale's turn to be apprehensive. He began to be morally alarmed at his own
security, to fear that the bourgeois system which he had attacked so valiantly

had somehow outwitted him and betrayed him into allegiance. When the C.I.O. made its initial drive and seemed to be carrying everything before it, he did his best to unseat himself again by rushing joyfully to the nearest picket lines and getting himself photographed by an alert press. Even this expedient failed, and he reconciled himself, not without wonder, to apparent academic permanence.

On winter afternoons his voice could be heard booming out through the closed doors of his study to girls who came to consult him on all manner of subjects, from the merits of Plekhanov as a Marxist critic to their own most personal dilemmas. They called him Ben; he called them Smith, Jones, and Robinson. He never relaxed his cheerful bombardment of the milieu into which they were born, and of the larger social structure which made bourgeois wealth, bourgeois art, morals, and religion possible. But when a sophomore found herself pregnant it was to Professor Hale that she came for advice. Should she have an abortion or go through with it and heroically bear the social stigma? And it was Professor Hale who kept the affair from the Dean's office and the newspapers, sought out the boy, persuaded the young couple that they were desperately in love with each other, and that pending the revolution a respectable marriage would be the most prudent course, not to say the happiest.

James Joyce remarks of one of his characters that she dealt with moral problems as a cleaver deals with meat. Professor Hale's critical methods were comparably simple and direct. Literature, like the other arts, is in form and substance a product of society, and reflects the structure of society. The structure of society is a class structure: it is conditioned by the mode of production of goods, and by the legal conventions of ownership and control by which the ruling class keeps itself in power and endows itself with the necessary freedom to exploit men and materials for profit. A healthy literature, in a society so constituted, can exist only if writers perceive the essential economic problem and ally themselves firmly with the working class.

Anyone could see the trouble with Arnold. His intelligence revealed to him the chaos that disrupted the society about him; the selfishness and brutality of the ruling class; the ugliness of the world which the industrial revolution had created, and which imperialism and "liberalism" were extending. Arnold was at his best in his critical satire of this world and of the ignorance of those who governed it. But his intelligence far outran his will, and his defect of will finally blinded his intelligence. He was too much a child of his class to disown it and fight his way to a workable remedy for social injustice. He caught a true vision of himself and of his times as standing between "two worlds, one dead, one powerless to be born." But he had not courage or stomach enough to lend his own powers to the birth struggle. Had he thrown in his sympathies unreservedly with the working class, and labored for the inescapable revolution, "Dover Beach" would not have ended in pessimism and confusion. It would have ended in a cheerful, strenuous, and hopeful call to action. But Arnold could not divorce himself from the world of polite letters, of education, of culture, into which he had been born. He did his best to purify them, to make them into an instrument for the reform of society. But instinctively he knew that "culture" as he understood the term was not a social force in the world around him. Instinctively he knew that what he loved was doomed to defeat. And so "Dover Beach" ended in a futile plea for protection against the hideousness of the darkling plain and the confused alarms of struggle and flight.

Professor Chartly's envelope brought Reuben Hale his best opportunity since the first C.I.O picket lines to vindicate his critical and social principles. He plunged into his answer with complete zest.

VI

When Peter Lee Prampton agreed to act as moderator in Professor Chartly's experiment he congratulated himself that this would be his last great academic chore. He had enjoyed his career of scholarship and teaching, no man ever more keenly. But now it was drawing to an end. He was loaded with honors from two continents. The universities of Germany, France, and Britain had first laid their formative hands on his learning and cultivation, then given their most coveted recognition to its fruits. But the honor and the glory seemed a little vague on the June morning when the expressman brought into his library the sizable package of papers which Professor Chartly had boxed and shipped to him. He had kept all his life a certain simplicity of heart. At seventy-four he could still tote a pack with an easy endurance that humiliated men of forty. Now he found himself giving in more and more completely to a lust for trout. Half a century of hastily snatched vacations in Cape Breton or the Scottish Highlands had never allowed him really to fill up that hollow craving to find a wild stream and fish it which would sometimes rise in his throat even in the midst of a lecture.

Well, there would be time left before he died. And meanwhile here was this business of "Dover Beach." Matthew Arnold during one of his American lecture tours had been entertained by neighbors of the Pramptons. Peter Lee Prampton's father had dined with the great man, and had repeated his conversation and imitated his accent at the family table. Peter himself, as a boy of nineteen or so, had gone to hear Arnold lecture. That, he thought with a smile, was probably a good deal more than could be said for any of these poor hacks who had taken Professor Chartly's bait.

At the thought of Arnold he could still hear the carriage wheels grate on the pebbly road as he had driven, fifty odd years ago, to the lecture in town, the prospective Mrs. Prampton beside him. His fishing rod lay under the seat. He chuckled out loud as he remembered how a pound-and-a-half trout had jumped in the pool under the clattering planks of a bridge, and how he had pulled up the horse, jumped out, and tried a cast while Miss Osgood sat scolding in the carriage and shivering in the autumn air. They had been just a little late reaching the lecture, but the trout, wrapped in damp leaves, lay safely beside the road.

It was queer that "Dover Beach" had not come more recently into his mind. Now that he turned his thoughts in that direction the poem was there in its entirety, waiting to be put on again like a coat that one has worn many times with pleasure and accidentally neglected for a while.

The sea of faith was once, too, at the full.

How those old Victorian battles had raged about the Prampton table when he was a boy! How the names of Arnold, Huxley, Darwin, Carlyle, Morris, Ruskin had been pelted back and forth by the excited disputants! *Literature and Dogma, God and the Bible, Culture and Anarchy.* The familiar titles brought an odd image into his mind: the tall figure of his father stretching up to turn on the gas lamps in the evening as the family sat down to dinner; the terrific pop of the pilot light as it exploded into a net of white flame, shaped like a little beehive; the buzz and whine of a jet turned up too high.

> Ah, love, let us be true
> To one another! for the world, which seems
> To lie before us like a land of dreams,
> So various, so beautiful, so new,
> Hath really neither joy, nor love, nor light,
> Nor certitude, nor peace, nor help for pain . . .

Peter Lee Prampton shivered in the warmth of his sunny library, shivered with that flash of perception into the past which sometimes enables a man to see how all that has happened in his life, for good or ill, turned on the narrowest edge of chance. He lived again in the world of dreams that his own youth had spread before him, a world truly various, beautiful, and new; full of promise, adventure, and liberty of choice, based on the opportunities which his father's wealth provided, and holding out the prospect of a smooth advance into a distinguished career. Then, within six months, a lavish demonstration that the world has neither certitude, nor peace, nor help for pain: his mother's death by cancer, his father's financial overthrow and suicide, the ruin of his own smooth hopes and the prospect instead of a long, hampered, and obscure fight toward his perhaps impossible ambition. He lived again through the night hours when he had tramped out with himself the youthful question whether he could hold Miss Osgood to her promise in the face of such reversals. And he did not forget how she took his long-sleepless face between her hands, kissed him, and smiled away his anxiety with unsteady lips. Surely everyone discovers at some time or other that the world is not a place of certitude; surely everyone cries out to some other human being for the fidelity which alone can make it so. What more could be asked of a poet than to take so profound and universal an experience and turn it into lines that could still speak long after he and his age were dead?

The best of it was that no one could miss the human feeling, the cry from the heart, in "Dover Beach"; it spoke so clearly and eloquently, in a language everyone could understand, in a form classically pure and simple. Or did it? Who could tell what any job-lot of academicians might be trusted to see or fail to see? And this assortment in Chartly's package might be a queer kettle of fish! Peter Lee Prampton had lived through the *Yellow Book* days of Art for Art's sake; he had read the muckrakers, and watched the rise of the Marxists and the Freudians. Could "Dover Beach" be condemned as unsympathetic with labor? Could a neurosis or a complex be discovered in it? His heart sank at the sharp sudden conviction that indeed these and worse discoveries about the poem might be seriously advanced. Well, he had always tried to go on the principle that every school of criticism should be free to exercise any sincere claim on men's interest and attention which it could win for itself. When he actually applied himself to the contents of Professor Chartly's bale he would be as charitable as he could, as receptive to light from any quarter as he could bring himself to be.

But the task could wait. He felt the need of a period of adjustment before he could approach it with reasonable equanimity. And in the meanwhile he could indulge himself in some long-needed editorial work on his dry-fly book.

❧ ❧ ❧

*Aristotle*

# Poetics [1]

TRANSLATED BY INGRAM BYWATER

1    Our subject being Poetry, I propose to speak not only of the art in general but also of its species and their respective capacities; of the structure of plot required for a good poem; of the number and nature of the constituent parts of a poem; and likewise of any other matters in the same line of inquiry. Let us follow the natural order and begin with the primary facts.

Epic poetry and Tragedy, as also Comedy, Dithyrambic poetry, and most flute-playing and lyre-playing, are all, viewed as a whole, modes of imitation. But at the same time they differ from one another in three ways, either by a difference of kind in their means, or by differences in the objects, or in the manner of their imitations.

Just as colour and form are used as means by some, who (whether by art or constant practice) imitate and portray many things by their aid, and the voice is used by others; so also in the above-mentioned group of arts, the means with them as a whole are rhythm, language, and harmony—used, however, either singly or in certain combinations. A combination of harmony and rhythm

[1] From Richard McKeon, ed., *The Basic Works of Aristotle*, Random House, New York, 1941, pp. 1455-1487 with omissions.

alone is the means in flute-playing and lyre-playing, and any other arts there
may be of the same description, e.g. imitative piping. Rhythm alone, without
harmony, is the means in the dancer's imitations; for even he, by the rhythms
of his attitudes, may represent men's characters, as well as what they do and
suffer. There is further an art which imitates by language alone, without harmony, in prose or in verse, and if in verse, either in some one or in a plurality
of metres. This form of imitation is to this day without a name. We have no
common name for a mime of Sophron or Xenarchus and a Socratic Conversation; and we should still be without one even if the imitation in the two instances were in trimeters or elegiacs or some other kind of verse—though it is
the way with people to tack on 'poet' to the name of a metre, and talk of elegiac-
poets and epic-poets, thinking that they call them poets not by reason of the
imitative nature of their work, but indiscriminately by reason of the metre they
write in. Even if a theory of medicine or physical philosophy be put forth in a
metrical form, it is usual to describe the writer in this way; Homer and Em-
pedocles, however, have really nothing in common apart from their metre; so
that, if the one is to be called a poet, the other should be termed a physicist
rather than a poet. We should be in the same position also, if the imitation in
these instances were in all the metres, like the *Centaur* (a rhapsody in a medley of all metres) of Chaeremon; and Chaeremon one has to recognize as a
poet. So much, then, as to these arts. There are, lastly, certain other arts, which
combine all the means enumerated, rhythm, melody, and verse, e.g. Dithyrambic and Nomic poetry, Tragedy and Comedy; with this difference, however,
that the three kinds of means are in some of them all employed together, and
in others brought in separately, one after the other. These elements of difference in the above arts I term the means of their imitation.

2    The objects the imitator represents are actions, with agents who are
necessarily either good men or bad—the diversities of human character being
nearly always derivative from this primary distinction, since the line between
virtue and vice is one dividing the whole of mankind. It follows, therefore,
that the agents represented must be either above our own level of goodness, or
beneath it, or just such as we are; in the same way as, with the painters, the
personages of Polygnotus are better than we are, those of Pauson worse, and
those of Dionysius just like ourselves. It is clear that each of the above-mentioned arts will admit of these differences, and that it will become a separate
art by representing objects with this point of difference. Even in dancing, flute-
playing, and lyre-playing such diversities are possible; and they are also possible in the nameless art that uses language, prose or verse without harmony,
as its means; Homer's personages, for instance, are better than we are; Cleophon's are on our own level; and those of Hegemon of Thasos, the first
writer of parodies, and Nicochares, the author of the *Diliad*, are beneath it.
The same is true of the Dithyramb and the Nome: the personages may be presented in them with the difference exemplified in the . . . of . . . and

Argas, and in the Cyclopses of Timotheus and Philoxenus. This difference it is that distinguishes Tragedy and Comedy also; the one would make its personages worse, and the other better, than the men of the present day.

3    A third difference in these arts is in the manner in which each kind of object is represented. Given both the same means and the same kind of object for imitation, one may either (1) speak at one moment in narrative and at another in an assumed character, as Homer does; or (2) one may remain the same throughout, without any such change; or (3) the imitators may represent the whole story dramatically, as though they were actually doing the things described. .

As we said at the beginning, therefore, the differences in the imitation of these arts come under three heads, their means, their objects, and their manner.

So that as an imitator Sophocles will be on one side akin to Homer, both portraying good men; and on another to Aristophanes, since both present their personages as acting and doing. This in fact, according to some, is the reason for plays being termed dramas, because in a play the personages act the story. Hence too both Tragedy and Comedy are claimed by the Dorians as their discoveries; Comedy by the Megarians—by those in Greece as having arisen when Megara became a democracy, and by the Sicilian Megarians on the ground that the poet Epicharmus was of their country, and a good deal earlier than Chionides and Magnes; even Tragedy also is claimed by certain of the Peloponnesian Dorians. In support of this claim they point to the words 'comedy' and 'drama'. Their word for the outlying hamlets, they say, is *comae*, whereas Athenians call them *demes*—thus assuming that comedians got the name not from their *comoe* or revels, but from their strolling from hamlet to hamlet, lack of appreciation keeping them out of the city. Their word also for 'to act', they say, is *dran*, whereas Athenians use *prattein*.

So much, then, as to the number and nature of the points of difference in the imitation of these arts.

4    It is clear that the general origin of poetry was due to two causes, each of them part of human nature. Imitation is natural to man from childhood, one of his advantages over the lower animals being this, that he is the most imitative creature in the world, and learns at first by imitation. And it is also natural for all to delight in works of imitation. The truth of this second point is shown by experience: though the objects themselves may be painful to see, we delight to view the most realistic representations of them in art, the forms for example of the lowest animals and of dead bodies. The explanation is to be found in a further fact: to be learning something is the greatest of pleasures not only to the philosopher but also to the rest of mankind, however small their capacity for it; the reason of the delight in seeing the picture is that one is at the same time learning—gathering the meaning of things, e.g. that the man there is so-and-so; for if one has not seen the thing before, one's pleasure

will not be in the picture as an imitation of it, but will be due to the execution or colouring or some similar cause. Imitation, then, being natural to us—as also the sense of harmony and rhythm, the metres being obviously species of rhythms—it was through their original aptitude, and by a series of improvements for the most part gradual on their first efforts, that they created poetry out of their improvisations.

Poetry, however, soon broke up into two kinds according to the differences of character in the individual poets; for the graver among them would represent noble actions, and those of noble personages; and the meaner sort the actions of the ignoble. The latter class produced invectives at first, just as others did hymns and panegyrics. We know of no such poem by any of the pre-Homeric poets, though there were probably many such writers among them; instances, however, may be found from Homer downwards, e.g. his *Margites*, and the similar poems of others. In this poetry of invective its natural fitness brought an iambic metre into use; hence our present term 'iambic', because it was the metre of their 'iambs' or invectives against one another. The result was that the old poets became some of them writers of heroic and others of iambic verse. Homer's position, however, is peculiar: just as he was in the serious style the poet of poets, standing alone not only through the literary excellence, but also through the dramatic character of his imitations, so too he was the first to outline for us the general forms of Comedy by producing not a dramatic invective, but a dramatic picture of the Ridiculous; his *Margites* in fact stands in the same relation to our comedies as the *Iliad* and *Odyssey* to our tragedies. As soon, however, as Tragedy and Comedy appeared in the field, those naturally drawn to the one line of poetry became writers of comedies instead of iambs, and those naturally drawn to the other, writers of tragedies instead of epics, because these new modes of art were grander and of more esteem than the old.

If it be asked whether Tragedy is now all that it need be in its formative elements, to consider that, and decide it theoretically and in relation to the theatres, is a matter for another inquiry.

It certainly began in improvisations—as did also Comedy; the one originating with the authors of the Dithyramb, the other with those of the phallic songs, which still survive as institutions in many of our cities. And its advance after that was little by little, through their improving on whatever they had before them at each stage. It was in fact only after a long series of changes that the movement of Tragedy stopped on its attaining to its natural form. (1) The number of actors was first increased to two by Aeschylus, who curtailed the business of the Chorus, and made the dialogue, or spoken portion, take the leading part in the play. (2) A third actor and scenery were due to Sophocles. (3) Tragedy acquired also its magnitude. Discarding short stories and a ludicrous diction, through its passing out of its satyric stage, it assumed, though only at a late point in its progress, a tone of dignity; and its metre changed then from trochaic to iambic. The reason for their original use of the trochaic tetrameter was that their poetry was satyric and more connected with dancing than it now is. As soon, however, as a spoken part came in, nature herself found the appropriate metre. The iambic, we know, is the most speakable of metres, as is shown by the fact that we very often fall into it in conversation, whereas we rarely talk hexameters, and only when we depart from the speaking tone of voice. (4) Another change was a plurality of episodes or acts. As for the remaining matters, the superadded embellishments and the account of their introduction, these must be taken as said, as it would probably be a long piece of work to go through the details.

5     As for Comedy, it is (as has been observed) an imitation of men worse than the average; worse, however, not as regards any and every sort of fault, but only as regards one particular kind, the Ridiculous, which is a species of the Ugly. The Ridiculous may be defined as a mistake or deformity not productive of pain or harm to others; the mask, for instance, that excites laughter, is something ugly and distorted without causing pain.

Though the successive changes in Tragedy and their authors are not unknown, we cannot say the same of Comedy; its early stages passed unnoticed, because it was not as yet taken up in a serious way. It was only at a late point in its progress that a chorus of comedians was officially granted by the archon; they used to be mere volunteers. It had also already certain definite forms at the time when the record of those termed comic poets begins. Who it was who supplied it with masks, or prologues, or a plurality of actors and the like, has remained unknown. The invented Fable, or Plot, however, originated in Sicily with Epicharmus and Phormis; of Athenian poets Crates was the first to drop the Comedy of invective and frame stories of a general and nonpersonal nature, in other words, Fables or Plots.

Epic poetry, then, has been seen to agree with Tragedy to this extent, that of being an imitation of serious subjects in a grand kind of verse. It differs from it, however, (1) in that it is in one kind of verse and in narrative form; and (2) in its length—which is due to its action having no fixed limit of time, whereas Tragedy endeavours to keep as far as possible within a single circuit of the sun, or something near that. This, I say, is another point of difference between them, though at first the practice in this respect was just the same in tragedies as in epic poems. They differ also (3) in their constituents, some being common to both and others peculiar to Tragedy—hence a judge of good and bad in Tragedy is a judge of that in epic poetry also. All the parts of an epic are included in Tragedy; but those of Tragedy are not all of them to be found in the Epic.

6     Reserving hexameter poetry and Comedy for consideration hereafter,[1] let us proceed now to the discussion of Tragedy; before doing so, however,

[1] For hexameter poetry cf. chap. 23 f.; comedy was treated of in the lost Second Book.

we must gather up the definition resulting from what has been said. A tragedy, then, is the imitation of an action that is serious and also, as having magnitude, complete in itself; in language with pleasurable accessories, each kind brought in separately in the parts of the work; in a dramatic, not in a narrative form; with incidents arousing pity and fear, wherewith to accomplish its catharsis of such emotions. Here by 'language with pleasurable accessories' I mean that with rhythm and harmony or song superadded; and by 'the kinds separately' I mean that some portions are worked out with verse only, and others in turn with song.

I.   As they act the stories, it follows that in the first place the Spectacle (or stage-appearance of the actors) must be some part of the whole; and in the second Melody and Diction, these two being the means of their imitation. Here by 'Diction' I mean merely this, the composition of the verses; and by 'Melody', what is too completely understood to require explanation. But further: the subject represented also is an action; and the action involves agents, who must necessarily have their distinctive qualities both of character and thought, since it is from these that we ascribe certain qualities to their actions. There are in the natural order of things, therefore, two causes, Thought and Character, of their actions, and consequently of their success or failure in their lives. Now the action (that which was done) is represented in the play by the Fable or Plot. The Fable, in our present sense of the term, is simply this, the combination of the incidents, or things done in the story; whereas Character is what makes us ascribe certain moral qualities to the agents; and Thought is shown in all they say when proving a particular point or, it may be, enunciating a general truth. There are six parts consequently of every tragedy, as a whole (that is) of such or such quality, viz. a Fable or Plot, Characters, Diction, Thought, Spectacle, and Melody; two of them arising from the means, one from the manner, and three from the objects of the dramatic imitation; and there is nothing else besides these six. Of these, its formative elements, then, not a few of the dramatists have made due use, as every play, one may say, admits of Spectacle, Character, Fable, Diction, Melody, and Thought.

II.   The most important of the six is the combination of the incidents of the story. Tragedy is essentially an imitation not of persons but of action and life, of happiness and misery. All human happiness or misery takes the form of action; the end for which we live is a certain kind of activity, not a quality. Character gives us qualities, but it is in our actions—what we do—that we are happy or the reverse. In a play accordingly they do not act in order to portray the Characters; they include the Characters for the sake of the action. So that it is the action in it, i.e. its Fable or Plot, that is the end and purpose of the tragedy; and the end is everywhere the chief thing.   Besides this, a tragedy is impossible without action, but there may be one without Character. The tragedies of most of the moderns are characterless—a defect common among poets of all kinds, and with its counterpart in painting in Zeuxis as compared with Polygnotus; for whereas the latter is strong in char-

acter, the work of Zeuxis is devoid of it. And again: one may string together a series of characteristic speeches of the utmost finish as regards Diction
and Thought, and yet fail to produce the true tragic effect; but one will
have much better success with a tragedy which, however inferior in these
respects, has a Plot, a combination of incidents, in it. And again: the most
powerful elements of attraction in Tragedy, the Peripeties and Discoveries,
are parts of the Plot. A further proof is in the fact that beginners succeed
earlier with the Diction and Characters than with the construction of a story;
and the same may be said of nearly all the early dramatists. We maintain,
therefore, that the first essential, the life and soul, so to speak, of Tragedy is
the Plot; and that the Characters come second—compare the parallel in painting, where the most beautiful colours laid on without order will not give one
the same pleasure as a simple black-and-white sketch of a portrait. We maintain that Tragedy is primarily an imitation of action, and that it is mainly
for the sake of the action that it imitates the personal agents. Third comes
the element of Thought, i.e. the power of saying whatever can be said, or
what is appropriate to the occasion. This is what, in the speeches in Tragedy,
falls under the arts of Politics and Rhetoric; for the older poets make their
personages discourse like statesmen, and the modern like rhetoricians. One
must not confuse it with Character. Character in a play is that which reveals
the moral purpose of the agents, i.e. the sort of thing they seek or avoid,
where that is not obvious—hence there is no room for Character in a speech
on a purely indifferent subject. Thought, on the other hand, is shown in all
they say when proving or disproving some particular point, or enunciating
some universal proposition. Fourth among the literary elements is the Diction
of the personages, i.e., as before explained, the expression of their thoughts in
words, which is practically the same thing with verse as with prose. As for
the two remaining parts, the Melody is the greatest of the pleasurable accessories of Tragedy. The Spectacle, though an attraction, is the least artistic of
all the parts, and has least to do with the art of poetry. The tragic effect is
quite possible without a public performance and actors; and besides, the get-
ting-up of the Spectacle is more a matter for the costumier than the poet.

7    Having thus distinguished the parts, let us now consider the proper
construction of the Fable or Plot, as that is at once the first and the most
important thing in Tragedy. We have laid it down that a tragedy is an imitation of an action that is complete in itself, as a whole of some magnitude;
for a whole may be of no magnitude to speak of. Now a whole is that which
has beginning, middle, and end. A beginning is that which is not itself necessarily after anything else, and which has naturally something else after it; an
end is that which is naturally after something itself, either as its necessary or
usual consequent, and with nothing else after it; and a middle, that which is
by nature after one thing and has also another after it. A well-constructed
Plot, therefore, cannot either begin or end at any point one likes; beginning
and end in it must be of the forms just described. Again: to be beautiful,

a living creature, and every whole made up of parts, must not only present a certain order in its arrangement of parts, but also be of a certain definite magnitude. Beauty is a matter of size and order, and therefore impossible either (1) in a very minute creature, since our perception becomes indistinct as it approaches instantaneity; or (2) in a creature of vast size—one, say, 1,000 miles long—as in that case, instead of the object being seen all at once, the unity and wholeness of it is lost to the beholder.

Just in the same way, then, as a beautiful whole made up of parts, or a beautiful living creature, must be of some size, but a size to be taken in by the eye, so a story or Plot must be of some length, but of a length to be taken in by the memory. As for the limit of its length, so far as that is relative to public performances and spectators, it does not fall within the theory of poetry. If they had to perform a hundred tragedies, they would be timed by water-clocks, as they are said to have been at one period. The limit, however, set by the actual nature of the thing is this: the longer the story, consistently with its being comprehensible as a whole, the finer it is by reason of its magnitude. As a rough general formula, 'a length which allows of the hero passing by a series of probable or necessary stages from misfortune to happiness, or from happiness to misfortune', may suffice as a limit for the magnitude of the story.

8    The Unity of a Plot does not consist, as some suppose, in its having one man as its subject. An infinity of things befall that one man, some of which it is impossible to reduce to unity; and in like manner there are many actions of one man which cannot be made to form one action. One sees, therefore, the mistake of all the poets who have written a *Heracleid*, a *Theseid*, or similar poems; they suppose that, because Heracles was one man, the story also of Heracles must be one story. Homer, however, evidently understood this point quite well, whether by art or instinct, just in the same way as he excels the rest in every other respect. In writing an *Odyssey*, he did not make the poem cover all that ever befell his hero—it befell him, for instance, to get wounded on Parnassus and also to feign madness at the time of the call to arms, but the two incidents had no necessary or probable connexion with one another—instead of doing that, he took as the subject of the *Odyssey*, as also of the *Iliad*, an action with a Unity of the kind we are describing. The truth is that, just as in the other imitative arts one imitation is always of one thing, so in poetry the story, as an imitation of action, must represent one action, a complete whole, with its several incidents so closely connected that the transposal or withdrawal of any one of them will disjoin and dislocate the whole. For that which makes no perceptible difference by its presence or absence is no real part of the whole.

9    From what we have said it will be seen that the poet's function is to describe, not the thing that has happened, but a kind of thing that might happen, i.e. what is possible as being probable or necessary. The distinction

between historian and poet is not in the one writing prose and the other verse—you might put the work of Herodotus into verse, and it would still be a species of history; it consists really in this, that the one describes the thing that has been, and the other a kind of thing that might be. Hence poetry is something more philosophic and of graver import than history, since its statements are of the nature rather of universals, whereas those of history are singulars. By a universal statement I mean one as to what such or such a kind of man will probably or necessarily say or do—which is the aim of poetry, though it affixes proper names to the characters; by a singular statement, one as to what, say, Alcibiades did or had done to him. In Comedy this has become clear by this time; it is only when their plot is already made up of probable incidents that they give it a basis of proper names, choosing for the purpose any names that may occur to them, instead of writing like the old iambic poets about particular persons. In Tragedy, however, they still adhere to the historic names; and for this reason: what convinces is the possible; now whereas we are not yet sure as to the possibility of that which has not happened, that which has happened is manifestly possible, else it would not have come to pass. Nevertheless even in Tragedy there are some plays with but one or two known names in them, the rest being inventions; and there are some without a single known name, e.g. Agathon's *Antheus,* in which both incidents and names are of the poet's invention; and it is no less delightful on that account. So that one must not aim at a rigid adherence to the traditional stories on which tragedies are based. It would be absurd, in fact, to do so, as even the known stories are only known to a few, though they are a delight none the less to all.

It is evident from the above that the poet must be more the poet of his stories or Plots than of his verses, inasmuch as he is a poet by virtue of the imitative element in his work, and it is actions that he imitates. And if he should come to take a subject from actual history, he is none the less a poet for that; since some historic occurrences may very well be in the probable and possible order of things; and it is in that aspect of them that he is their poet.

Of simple Plots and actions the episodic are the worst. I call a Plot episodic when there is neither probability nor necessity in the sequence of its episodes. Actions of this sort bad poets construct through their own fault, and good ones on account of the players. His work being for public performance, a good poet often stretches out a Plot beyond its capabilities, and is thus obliged to twist the sequence of incident.

Tragedy, however, is an imitation not only of a complete action, but also of incidents arousing pity and fear. Such incidents have the very greatest effect on the mind when they occur unexpectedly and at the same time in consequence of one another; there is more of the marvellous in them than if they happened of themselves or by mere chance. Even matters of chance seem most marvellous if there is an appearance of design as it were in them; as for instance the statue of Mitys at Argos killed the author of Mitys'

POETICS 379

death by falling down on him when a looker-on at a public spectacle; for
incidents like that we think to be not without a meaning. A Plot, therefore,
of this sort is necessarily finer than others.

10     Plots are either simple or complex, since the actions they represent are
naturally of this twofold description. The action, proceeding in the way defined, as one continuous whole, I call simple, when the change in the hero's
fortunes takes place without Peripety or Discovery; and complex, when it
involves one or the other, or both. These should each of them arise out of
the structure of the Plot itself, so as to be the consequence, necessary or
probable, of the antecedents. There is a great difference between a thing
happening *propter hoc* and *post hoc*.

11     A Peripety is the change of the kind described from one state of
things within the play to its opposite, and that too in the way we are saying,
in the probable or necessary sequence of events; as it is for instance in
*Oedipus:* here the opposite state of things is produced by the Messenger, who,
coming to gladden Oedipus and to remove his fears as to his mother, reveals
the secret of his birth. And in *Lynceus:* just as he is being led off for execution, with Danaus at his side to put him to death, the incidents preceding
this bring it about that he is saved and Danaus put to death. A Discovery is,
as the very word implies, a change from ignorance to knowledge, and thus to
either love or hate, in the personages marked for good or evil fortune. The
finest form of Discovery is one attended by Peripeties, like that which goes
with the Discovery in *Oedipus*. There are no doubt other forms of it; what
we have said may happen in a way in reference to inanimate things, even
things of a very casual kind; and it is also possible to discover whether some
one has done or not done something. But the form most directly connected
with the Plot and the action of the piece is the first-mentioned. This, with a
Peripety, will arouse either pity or fear—actions of that nature being what
Tragedy is assumed to represent; and it will also serve to bring about the
happy or unhappy ending. The Discovery, then, being of persons, it may be
that of one party only to the other, the latter being already known; or both
the parties may have to discover themselves. Iphigenia, for instance, was discovered to Orestes by sending the letter; and another Discovery was required
to reveal him to Iphigenia.
    Two parts of the Plot, then, Peripety and Discovery, are on matters of this
sort. A third part is Suffering; which we may define as an action of a destructive or painful nature, such as murders on the stage, tortures, woundings,
and the like. The other two have been already explained.

12     The parts of Tragedy to be treated as formative elements in the whole
were mentioned in a previous Chapter.[2]
From the point of view, however, of its quantity, i.e. the separate sections

    ² Ch. 6.

into which it is divided, a tragedy has the following parts: Prologue, Episode, Exode, and a choral portion, distinguished into Parode and Stasimon; these two are common to all tragedies, whereas songs from the stage and *Commoe* are only found in some. The Prologue is all that precedes the Parode of the chorus; an Episode all that comes in between two whole choral songs; the Exode all that follows after the last choral song. In the choral portion the Parode is the whole first statement of the chorus; a Stasimon, a song of the chorus without anapaests or trochees; a *Commos*, a lamentation sung by chorus and actor in concert. The parts of Tragedy to be used as formative elements in the whole we have already mentioned; the above are its parts from the point of view of its quantity, or the separate sections into which it is divided.

13    The next points after what we have said above will be these: (1) What is the poet to aim at, and what is he to avoid, in constructing his Plots? and (2) What are the conditions on which the tragic effect depends?

We assume that, for the finest form of Tragedy, the Plot must be not simple but complex; and further, that it must imitate actions arousing fear and pity, since that is the distinctive function of this kind of imitation. It follows, therefore, that there are three forms of Plot to be avoided. (1) A good man must not be seen passing from happiness to misery, or (2) a bad man from misery to happiness. The first situation is not fear-inspiring or piteous, but simply odious to us. The second is the most untragic that can be; it has no one of the requisites of Tragedy; it does not appeal either to the human feeling in us, or to our pity, or to our fears. Nor, on the other hand, should (3) an extremely bad man be seen falling from happiness into misery. Such a story may arouse the human feeling in us, but it will not move us to either pity or fear; pity is occasioned by undeserved misfortune, and fear by that of one like ourselves; so that there will be nothing either piteous or fear-inspiring in the situation. There remains, then, the intermediate kind of personage, a man not preeminently virtuous and just, whose misfortune, how-ever, is brought upon him not by vice and depravity but by some error of judgment, of the number of those in the enjoyment of great reputation and prosperity; e.g. Oedipus, Thyestes, and the men of note of similar families. The perfect Plot, accordingly, must have a single, and not (as some tell us) a double issue; the change in the hero's fortunes must be not from misery to happiness, but on the contrary from happiness to misery; and the cause of it must lie not in any depravity, but in some great error on his part; the man himself being either such as we have described, or better, not worse, than that. Fact also confirms our theory. Though the poets began by accepting any tragic story that came to hand, in these days the finest tragedies are always on the story of some few houses, on that of Alcmeon, Oedipus, Orestes, Meleager, Thyestes, Telephus, or any others that may have been involved, as either agents or sufferers, in some deed of horror. The theoretically best trag-edy, then, has a Plot of this description. The critics, therefore, are wrong who blame Euripides for taking this line in his tragedies, and giving many of them an unhappy ending. It is, as we have said, the right line to take. The best proof is this: on the stage, and in the public performances, such plays, properly worked out, are seen to be the most truly tragic; and Euripides, even if his execution be faulty in every other point, is seen to be nevertheless the most tragic certainly of the dramatists. After this comes the construction of Plot which some rank first, one with a double story (like the *Odyssey*) and an opposite issue for the good and the bad personages. It is ranked as first only through the weakness of the audiences; the poets merely follow their public, writing as its wishes dictate. But the pleasure here is not that of Tragedy. It belongs rather to Comedy, where the bitterest enemies in the piece (e.g. Arestes and Aegisthus) walk off good friends at the end, with no slaying of any one by any one.

14     The tragic fear and pity may be aroused by the Spectacle; but they may also be aroused by the very structure and incidents of the play—which is the better way and shows the better poet. The Plot in fact should be so framed that, even without seeing the things take place, he who simply hears the account of them shall be filled with horror and pity at the incidents; which is just the effect that the mere recital of the story in *Oedipus* would have on one. To produce this same effect by means of the Spectacle is less artistic, and requires extraneous aid. Those, however, who make use of the Spectacle to put before us that which is merely monstrous and not productive of fear, are wholly out of touch with Tragedy; and not every kind of pleasure should be required of a tragedy, but only its own proper pleasure.

The tragic pleasure is that of pity and fear, and the poet has to produce it by a work of imitation; it is clear, therefore, that the causes should be included in the incidents of his story. Let us see, then, what kinds of incident strike one as horrible, or rather as piteous. In a deed of this description the parties must necessarily be either friends, or enemies, or indifferent to one another. Now when enemy does it on enemy, there is nothing to move us to pity either in his doing or in his meditating the deed, except so far as the actual pain of the sufferer is concerned; and the same is true when the parties are indifferent to one another. Whenever the tragic deed, however, is done within the family—when murder or the like is done or meditated by brother on brother, by son on father, by mother on son, or son on mother—these are the situations the poet should seek after. The traditional stories, accordingly, must be kept as they are, e.g. the murder of Clytaemnestra by Orestes and of Eriphyle by Alcmeon. At the same time even with these there is something left to the poet himself; it is for him to devise the right way of treating them. Let us explain more clearly what we mean by 'the right way'. The deed of horror may be done by the doer knowingly and consciously, as in the old poets, and in Medea's murder of her children in Euripides. Or he may do it, but in ignorance of his relationship, and discover that afterwards, as does the Oedipus in Sophocles. Here the deed is outside the play; but it may be within it, like the act of the Alcmeon in Astydamas, or that of the Telegonus in *Ulysses Wounded*. A third possibility is for one meditating some deadly injury to another, in ignorance of his relationship, to make the discovery in time to draw back. These exhaust the possibilities, since the deed must necessarily be either done or not done, and either knowingly or unknowingly.

The worst situation is when the personage is with full knowledge on the point of doing the deed, and leaves it undone. It is odious and also (through the absence of suffering) untragic; hence it is that no one is made to act thus except in some few instances, e.g. Haemon and Creon in *Antigone*. Next after this comes the actual perpetration of the deed meditated. A better situation than that, however, is for the deed to be done in ignorance, and the relationship discovered afterwards, since there is nothing odious in it, and the Discovery will serve to astound us. But the best of all is the last; what we have in *Cresphontes*,[3] for example, where Merope, on the point of slaying her son, recognizes him in time; in *Iphigenia*, where sister and brother are in a like position; and in *Helle*,[4] where the son recognizes his mother, when on the point of giving her up to her enemy.

This will explain why our tragedies are restricted (as we said just now) to such a small number of families. It was accident rather than art that led the poets in quest of subjects to embody this kind of incident in their Plots. They are still obliged, accordingly, to have recourse to the families in which such horrors have occurred.

On the construction of the Plot, and the kind of Plot required for Tragedy, enough has now been said.

15    In the Characters there are four points to aim at. First and foremost, that they shall be good. There will be an element of character in the play, if (as has been observed) what a personage says or does reveals a certain moral purpose; and a good element of character, if the purpose so revealed is good. Such goodness is possible in every type of personage, even in a woman or a slave, though the one is perhaps an inferior, and the other a wholly worthless being. The second point is to make them appropriate. The Character before us may be, say, manly; but it is not appropriate in a female Character to be manly, or clever. The third is to make them like the reality, which is not the same as their being good and appropriate, in our sense of the term. The fourth is to make them consistent and the same throughout; even if inconsistency be part of the man before one for imitation as presenting that form of character, he should still be consistently inconsistent. We have an instance of baseness of character, not required for the story, in the Menelaus in *Orestes*; of the incongruous and unbefitting in the lamentation of Ulysses in *Scylla*,[5] and in the (clever) speech of Melanippe;[6] and of incon-

[3] By Euripides. [4] Authorship unknown. [5] A dithyramb by Timotheus. [6] (Euripides)

sistency in *Iphigenia at Aulis*, where Iphigenia the suppliant is utterly unlike the later Iphigenia. The right thing, however, is in the Characters just as in the incidents of the play to endeavour always after the necessary or the probable; so that whenever such-and-such a personage says or does such-and-such a thing, it shall be the necessary or probable outcome of his character; and whenever this incident follows on that, it shall be either the necessary or the probable consequence of it. From this one sees (to digress for a moment) that the Dénouement also should arise out of the plot itself, and not depend on a stage-artifice, as in *Medea*, or in the story of the (arrested) departure of the Greeks in the *Iliad*. The artifice must be reserved for matters outside the play—for past events beyond human knowledge, or events yet to come, which require to be foretold or announced; since it is the privilege of the Gods to know everything. There should be nothing improbable among the actual incidents. If it be unavoidable, however, it should be outside the tragedy, like the improbability in the *Oedipus* of Sophocles. But to return to the Characters. As Tragedy is an imitation of personages better than the ordinary man, we in our way should follow the example of good portrait-painters, who reproduce the distinctive features of a man, and at the same time, without losing the likeness, make him handsomer than he is. The poet in like manner, in portraying men quick or slow to anger, or with similar infirmities of character, must know how to represent them as such, and at the same time as good men, as Agathon and Homer have represented Achilles.

All these rules one must keep in mind throughout, and, further, those also for such points of stage-effect as directly depend on the art of the poet, since in these too one may often make mistakes. Enough, however, has been said on the subject in one of our published writings.[7]

16      Discovery in general has been explained already. As for the species of Discovery, the first to be noted is (1) the least artistic form of it, of which the poets make most use through mere lack of invention, Discovery by signs or marks. Of these signs some are congenital, like the 'lance-head which the Earth-born have on them',[8] or 'stars', such as Carcinus brings in his *Thyestes*; others acquired after birth—these latter being either marks on the body, e.g. scars, or external tokens, like necklaces, or (to take another sort of instance) the ark in the *Discovery of Tyro*.[9] Even in these, however, admit of two uses, a better and a worse; the scar of Ulysses is an instance; the Discovery of him through it is made in one way by the nurse[10] and in another by the swineherds.[11] A Discovery using signs as a means of assurance is less artistic, as indeed are all such as imply reflection; whereas one bringing them in all of a sudden, as in the *Bath-story*,[12] is of a better order. Next after these are (2) Discoveries made directly by the poet; which are inartistic for that very reason; e.g. Orestes' Discovery of himself in *Iphigenia*: whereas his sister re-

7 In the lost dialogue *On Poets*.      8 Authorship unknown.      9 By Euripides.
10 *Od*. xix. 386-475.          11 *Od*. xxi. 205-25.          12 *Od*. xix. 392.

veals who she is by the letter,[13] Orestes is made to say himself what the poet
rather than the story demands.[14] This, therefore, is not far removed from the
first-mentioned fault, since he might have presented certain tokens as well.
Another instance is the 'shuttle's voice' in the *Tereus* of Sophocles. (3) A
third species is Discovery through memory, from a man's consciousness being
awakened by something seen. Thus in *The Cyprioe of Dicaeogenes*, the sight
of the picture makes the man burst into tears; and in the *Tale of Alcinous*,[15]
hearing the harper Ulysses is reminded of the past and weeps; the Discovery
of them being the result. (4) A fourth kind is Discovery through reasoning;
e.g. in *The Choephoroe*;[16] 'One like me is here; there is no one like me but
Orestes; he, therefore, must be here.' Or that which Polyidus the Sophist suggested for *Iphigenia*; since it was natural for Orestes to reflect: 'My sister was
sacrificed, and I am to be sacrificed like her.' Or that in the *Tydeus* of
Theodectes: 'I came to find a son, and am to die myself.' Or that in *The
Phinidae*:[17] on seeing the place the women inferred their fate, that they were
to die there, since they had also been exposed there. (5) There is, too, a
composite Discovery arising from bad reasoning on the side of the other party.
An instance of it is in *Ulysses the False Messenger*[17] he said he should
know the bow—which he had not seen; but to suppose from that that he
would know it again (as though he had once seen it) was bad reasoning.
(6) The best of all Discoveries, however, is that arising from the incidents
themselves, when the great surprise comes about through a probable incident,
like that in the *Oedipus* of Sophocles; and also in Iphigenia;[18] for it was not
improbable that she should wish to have a letter taken home. These last
are the only Discoveries independent of the artifice of signs and necklaces.
Next after them come Discoveries through reasoning.

17   At the time when he is constructing his Plots, and engaged on the
Diction in which they are worked out, the poet should remember (1) to put
the actual scenes as far as possible before his eyes. In this way, seeing everything with the vividness of an eye-witness as it were, he will devise what is
appropriate, and be least likely to overlook incongruities. This is shown by
what was censured in Carcinus, the return of Amphiaraus from the sanctuary;
it would have passed unnoticed, if it had not been actually seen by the audience; but on the stage his play failed, the incongruity of the incident offending the spectators. (2) As far as may be, too, the poet should even act
his story with the very gestures of his personages. Given the same natural
qualifications, he who feels the emotions to be described will be the most convincing; distress and anger, for instance, are portrayed most truthfully by one
who is feeling them at the moment. Hence it is that poetry demands a man
with a special gift for it, or else one with a touch of madness in him; the
former can easily assume the required mood, and the latter may be actually
beside himself with emotion. (3) His story, again, whether already made or

[13] *Iph. Taur.* 727 ff.    [14] Ib., 800 ff.    [15] *Od.* viii. 521 ff. (Cf. viii, 83 ff.)
[16] 11. 168-234.    [17] Authorship unknown.    [18] *Iph. Taur.* 582.

of his own making, he should first simplify and reduce to a universal form, before proceeding to lengthen it out by the insertion of episodes. The following will show how the universal element in *Iphigenia*, for instance, may be viewed: A certain maiden having been offered in sacrifice, and spirited away from her sacrificers into another land, where the custom was to sacrifice all strangers to the Goddess, she was made there the priestess of this rite. Long after that the brother of the priestess happened to come; the fact, however, of the oracle having for a certain reason bidden him go thither, and his object in going, are outside the Plot of the play. On his coming he was arrested, and about to be sacrificed, when he revealed who he was—either as Euripides puts it, or (as suggested by Polyidus) by the not improbable exclamation, 'So I too am doomed to be sacrificed, as my sister was'; and the disclosure led to his salvation. This done, the next thing, after the proper names have been fixed as a basis for the story, is to work in episodes or accessory incidents. One must mind, however, that the episodes are appropriate, like the fit of madness[19] in Orestes, which led to his arrest, and the purifying,[20] which brought about his salvation. In plays, then, the episodes are short; in epic poetry they serve to lengthen out the poem. The argument of the *Odyssey* is not a long one. A certain man has been abroad many years; Poseidon is ever on the watch for him, and he is all alone. Matters at home too have come to this, that his substance is being wasted and his son's death plotted by suitors to his wife. Then he arrives there himself after his grievous sufferings; reveals himself, and falls on his enemies; and the end is his salvation and their death. This being all that is proper to the *Odyssey*, everything else in it is episode.

18    (4)    There is a further point to be borne in mind. Every tragedy is in part Complication and in part Dénouement; the incidents before the opening scene, and often certain also of those within the play, forming the Complication; and the rest the Dénouement. By Complication I mean all from the beginning of the story to the point just before the change in the hero's fortunes; by Dénouement, all from the beginning of the change to the end. In the *Lynceus* of Theodectes, for instance, the Complication includes, together with the presupposed incidents, the seizure of the child and that in turn of the parents; and the Dénouement all from the indictment for the murder to the end. Now it is right, when one speaks of a tragedy as the same or not the same as another, to do so on the ground before all else of their Plot, i.e. as having the same or not the same Complication and Dénouement. Yet there are many dramatists who, after a good Complication, fail in the Dénouement. But it is necessary for both points of construction to be always duly mastered. (5) There are four distinct species of Tragedy—that being the number of the constituents also that have been mentioned:[21] first, the complex Tragedy, which is all Peripety and Discovery; second, the Tragedy of suffering, e.g. the

---

[19] *Iph. Taur.* 281 ff.                    [20] Ib., 1163 ff.
[21] This does not agree with anything actually said before.

*Ajaxes* and *Ixions*; third, the Tragedy of character, e.g. *The Phthiotides*[22] and Peleus.[23] The fourth constituent is that of "Specatcle', exemplified in *The Phorcides*,[24] in *Prometheus*,[25] and in all plays with the scene laid in the nether world. The poet's aim, then, should be to combine every element of interest, if possible, or else the more important and the major part of them. This is now especially necessary owing to the unfair criticism to which the poet is subjected in these days. Just because there have been poets before him strong in the several species of tragedy, the critics now expect the one man to surpass that which was the strong point of each one of his predecessors. (6) One should also remember what has been said more than once, and not write a tragedy on an epic body of incident (i.e. one with a plurality of stories in it), by attempting to dramatize, for instance, the entire story of the *Iliad*. In the epic owing to its scale every part is treated at proper length; with a drama, however, on the same story the result is very disappointing. This is shown by the fact that all who have dramatized the fall of Ilium in its entirety, and not part by part, like Euripides, of the whole of the Niobe story, instead of a portion, like Aeschylus, either fail utterly or have but ill success on the stage; for that and that alone was enough to ruin even a play by Agathon. Yet in their Peripeties, as also in their simple plots, the poets I mean show wonderful skill in aiming at the kind of effect they desire—a tragic situation that arouses the human feeling in one, like the clever villain (e.g. Sisyphus) deceived, or the brave wrongdoer worsted. This is probable, however, only in Agathon's sense, when he speaks of the probability of even improbabilities coming to pass. (7) The Chorus too should be regarded as one of the actors; it should be an integral part of the whole, and take a share in the action—that which it has in Sophocles, rather than in Euripides. With the later poets, however, the songs in a play of theirs have no more to do with the Plot of that than of any other tragedy. Hence it is that they are now singing intercalary pieces, a practice first introduced by Agathon. And yet what real difference is there between singing such intercalary pieces, and attempting to fit in a speech, or even a whole act, from one play into another?

19    The Plot and Characters having been discussed, it remains to consider the Diction and Thought. As for the Thought, we may assume what is said of it in our Art of Rhetoric, as it belongs more properly to that department of inquiry. The Thought of the personages is shown in everything to be effected by their language—in every effort to prove or disprove, to arouse emotion (pity, fear, anger, and the like), or to maximize or minimize things. It is clear, also, that their mental procedure must be on the same lines in their actions likewise, whenever they wish them to arouse pity or horror, or to have a look of importance or probability. The only difference is that with the act

[22] By Sophocles.                    [23] Probably Sophocles' *Peleus* is incorrect.
[24] By Aeschylus.                    [25] Probably a satyric drama by Aeschylus.

the impression has to be made without explanation; whereas with the spoken word it has to be produced by the speaker, and result from his language. What, indeed, would be the good of the speaker, if things appeared in the required light even apart from anything he says? . . .

21      . . . Metaphor consists in giving the thing a name that belongs to something else; the transference being either from genus to species, or from species to genus, or from species to species, or on the grounds of analogy. That from genus to species is exemplified in 'Here stands my ship'; for lying at anchor is the 'standing' of a particular kind of thing. That from species to genus in 'Truly ten thousand good deeds has Ulysses wrought', where 'ten thousand', which is a particular large number, is put in place of the generic 'a large number'. That from species to species in 'Drawing the life with the bronze', and in 'Severing with the enduring bronze'; where the poet uses 'draw' in the sense of 'sever' and 'sever' in that of 'draw', both words meaning to 'take away' something. That from analogy is possible whenever there are four terms so related that the second (B) is to the first (A), as the fourth (D) to the third (C); for one may then metaphorically put D in lieu of B, and B in lieu of D. Now and then, too, they qualify the metaphor by adding on to it that to which the word it supplants is relative. Thus a cup (B) is in relation to Dionysus (A) what a shield (D) is to Ares (C). The cup accordingly will be metaphorically described as the 'shield of *Dionysus*' (D+A), and the shield as the 'cup *of Ares*' (B+C). Or to take another instance: As old age (D) is to life (C), so is evening (B) to day (A). One will accordingly describe evening (B) as the 'old age *of the day*' (D+A)—or by the Empedoclean equivalent; and old age (D) as the 'evening' or 'sunset *of life*' (B+C). It may be that some of the terms thus related have no special name of their own, but for all that they will be metaphorically described in just the same way. Thus to cast forth seed-corn is called 'sowing'; but to cast forth its flame, as said of the sun, has no special name. This nameless act (B), however, stands in just the same relation to its object, sunlight (A), as sowing (D) to the seed-corn (C). Hence the expression in the poet, 'sowing around a god-created *flame*' (D+A). There is also another form of qualified metaphor. Having given the thing the alien name, one may by a negative addition deny of it one of the attributes naturally associated with its new name. An instance of this would be to call the shield not the 'cup *of Ares*,' as in the former case, but a 'cup *that holds no wine*' . . . .

22      The perfection of Diction is for it to be at once clear and not mean. The clearest indeed is that made up of the ordinary words for things, but it is mean, as is shown by the poetry of Cleophon and Sthenelus. On the other hand the Diction becomes distinguished and non-prosaic by the use of unfamiliar terms, i.e. strange words, metaphors, lengthened forms, and everything that deviates from the ordinary modes of speech.—But a whole statement

in such terms will be either a riddle or a barbarism, a riddle, if made up of metaphors, a barbarism, if made up of strange words. . . . It is a great thing, indeed, to make a proper use of these poetical forms, as also of compounds and strange words. But the greatest thing by far is to be a master of metaphor. It is the one thing that cannot be learnt from others; and it is also a sign of genius, since a good metaphor implies an intuitive perception of the similarity in dissimilars. . . .

Let this, then, suffice as an account of Tragedy, the art imitating by means of action on the stage.

23     As for the poetry which merely narrates, or imitates by means of versified language (without action), it is evident that it has several points in common with Tragedy.

I. The construction of its stories should clearly be like that in a drama; they should be based on a single action, one that is a complete whole in itself, with a beginning, middle, and end, so as to enable the work to produce its own proper pleasure with all the organic unity of a living creature. Nor should one suppose that there is anything like them in our usual histories. A history has to deal not with one action, but with one period and all that happened in that to one or more persons, however disconnected the several events may have been. Just as two events may take place at the same time, e.g. the sea-fight off Salamis and the battle with the Carthaginians in Sicily, without converging to the same end, so too of two consecutive events one may sometimes come after the other with no one end as their common issue. Nevertheless most of our epic poets, one may say, ignore the distinction.

Herein, then, to repeat what we have said before, we have a further proof of Homer's marvellous superiority to the rest. He did not attempt to deal with the Trojan war in its entirety, though it was a whole with a definite beginning and end—through a feeling apparently that it was too long a story to be taken in in one view, or if not that, too complicated from the variety of incident in it. As it is, he has singled out one section of the whole; many of the other incidents, however, he brings in as episodes, using the Catalogue of the Ships, for instance, and other episodes to relieve the uniformity of his narrative. As for the other epic poets, they treat of one man, or one period; or else of an action which, although one, has a multiplicity of parts in it. This last is what the authors of the *Cypria*[26] and *Little Iliad* [26] have done. And the result is that, whereas the *Iliad* or *Odyssey* supplies materials for only one, or at most two tragedies, the *Cypria* does that for several and the *Little Iliad* for more than eight: for an *Adjudgment of Arms*, a *Philoctetes*, a *Neoptolemus*, a *Eurypylus*, a *Ulysses as Beggar*, a *Laconian Women*, a *Fall of Ilium*, and a *Departure of the Fleet*; as also a *Sinon*, and a *Women of Troy*.

24     II. Besides this, Epic poetry must divide into the same species as Tragedy; it must be either simple or complex, a story of character or one of

[26] Authorship unknown.

suffering. Its parts, too, with the exception of Song and Spectacle, must be the same, as it requires Peripeties, Discoveries, and scenes of suffering just like Tragedy. Lastly, the Thought and Diction in it must be good in their way. All these elements appear in Homer first; and he has made due use of them. His two poems are each examples of construction, the *Iliad* simple and a story of suffering, the *Odyssey* complex (there is Discovery throughout it) and a story of character. And they are more than this, since in Diction and Thought too they surpass all other poems.

There is, however, a difference in the Epic as compared with Tragedy, (1) in its length, and (2) in its metre. (1) As to its length, the limit already suggested will suffice: it must be possible for the beginning and end of the work to be taken in in one view—a condition which will be fulfilled if the poem be shorter than the old epics, and about as long as the series of tragedies offered for one hearing. For the extension of its length epic poetry has a special advantage, of which it makes large use. In a play one cannot represent an action with a number of parts going on simultaneously; one is limited to the part on the stage and connected with the actors. Whereas in epic poetry the narrative form makes it possible for one to describe a number of simultaneous incidents; and these, if germane to the subject, increase the body of the poem. This then is a gain to the Epic, tending to give it grandeur, and also variety of interest and room for episodes of diverse kinds. Uniformity of incident by the satiety it soon creates is apt to ruin tragedies on the stage. (2) As for its metre, the heroic has been assigned it from experience; were any one to attempt a narrative poem in some one, or in several, of the other metres, the incongruity of the thing would be apparent. The heroic in fact is the gravest and weightiest of metres—which is what makes it more tolerant than the rest of strange words and metaphors, that also being a point in which the narrative form of poetry goes beyond all others. The iambic and trochaic, on the other hand, are metres of movement, the one representing that of life and action, the other that of the dance. Still more unnatural would it appear, if one were to write an epic in a medley of metres, as Chaeremon did.[27] Hence it is that no one has ever written a long story in any but heroic verse; nature herself, as we have said, teaches us to select the metre appropriate to such a story.

Homer, admirable as he is in every other respect, is especially so in this, that he alone among epic poets is not unaware of the part to be played by the poet himself in the poem. The poet should say very little *in propria persona*, as he is no imitator when doing that. Whereas the other poets are perpetually coming forward in person, and say but little, and that only here and there, as imitators, Homer after a brief preface brings in forthwith a man, a woman, or some other Character—no one of them characterless, but each with distinctive characteristics.

The marvellous is certainly required in Tragedy. The Epic, however, affords more opening for the improbable, the chief factor in the marvellous, because

[27] *Centaur.*

in it the agents are not visibly before one. The scene of the pursuit of Hector would be ridiculous on the stage—the Greeks halting instead of pursuing him, and Achilles shaking his head to stop them;[28] but in the poem the absurdity is overlooked. The marvellous, however, is a cause of pleasure, as is shown by the fact that we all tell a story with additions, in the belief that we are doing our hearers a pleasure.

Homer more than any other has taught the rest of us the art of framing lies in the right way. I mean the use of paralogism. Whenever, if A is or happens, a consequent, B, is or happens, men's notion is that, if the B is, the A also is—but that is a false conclusion. Accordingly, if A is untrue, but there is something else, B, that on the assumption of its truth follows as its consequent, the right thing then is to add on the B. Just because we know the truth of the consequent, we are in our own minds led on to the erroneous inference of the truth of the antecedent. Here is an instance, from the *Bath-story* in the *Odyssey*.[29]

A likely impossibility is always preferable to an unconvincing possibility. The story should never be made up of improbable incidents; there should be nothing of the sort in it. If, however, such incidents are unavoidable, they should be outside the piece, like the hero's ignorance in *Oedipus* of the circumstances of Laius' death; not within it, like the report of the Pythian games in *Electra*,[30] or the man's having come to Mysia from Tegea without uttering a word on the way, in *The Mysians*.[31] So that it is ridiculous to say that one's Plot would have been spoilt without them, since it is fundamentally wrong to make up such Plots. If the poet has taken such a Plot, however, and one sees that he might have put it in a more probable form, he is guilty of absurdity as well as a fault of art. Even in the *Odyssey* the improbabilities in the setting-ashore of Ulysses[32] would be clearly intolerable in the hands of an inferior poet. As it is, the poet conceals them, his other excellences veiling their absurdity. Elaborate Diction, however, is required only in places where there is no action, and no Character or Thought to be revealed. Where there is Character or Thought, on the other hand, an over-ornate Diction tends to obscure them.

25    As regards Problems and their Solutions, one may see the number and nature of the assumptions on which they proceed by viewing the matter in the following way. (1) The poet being an imitator just like the painter or other maker of likenesses, he must necessarily in all instances represent things in one or other of three aspects, either as they were or are, or as they are said or thought to be or to have been, or as they ought to be. (2) All this he does in language, with an admixture, it may be, of strange words and metaphors, as also of the various modified forms of words, since the use of these is conceded in poetry. (3) It is to be remembered, too,

---

[28] *Il.* xxii. 205.          [29] xix. 164-260.          [30] Soph. *El.* 660 ff.
[31] Probably by Aeschylus.                    [32] xiii. 116 ff.

that there is not the same kind of correctness in poetry as in politics, or indeed any other art. There is, however, within the limits of poetry itself a possibility of two kinds of error, the one directly, the other only accidentally connected with the art. If the poet meant to describe the thing correctly, and failed through lack of power of expression, his art itself is at fault. But if it was through his having meant to describe it in some incorrect way (e.g. to make the horse in movement have both legs thrown forward) that the technical error (one in a matter of, say, medicine or some other special science), or impossibilities of whatever kind they may be, have got into his description, his error in that case is not in the essentials of the poetic art. These, therefore, must be the premises of the Solutions in answer to the criticisms involved in the Problems.

I. As to the criticisms relating to the poet's art itself. Any impossibilities there may be in his descriptions of things are faults. But from another point of view they are justifiable, if they serve the end of poetry itself—if (to assume what we have said of that end) they make the effect of either that very portion of the work or some other portion more astounding. The Pursuit of Hector is an instance in point. If, however, the poetic end might have been as well or better attained without sacrifice of technical correctness in such matters, the impossibility is not to be justified, since the description should be, if it can, entirely free from error. One may ask, too, whether the error is in a matter directly or only accidentally connected with the poetic art; since it is a lesser error in an artist not to know, for instance, that the hind has no horns, than to produce an unrecognizable picture of one.

II. If the poet's description be criticized as not true to fact, one may urge perhaps that the object ought to be as described—an answer like that of Sophocles, who said that he drew men as they ought to be, and Euripides as they were. If the description, however, be neither true nor of the thing as it ought to be, the answer must be then, that it is in accordance with opinion. The tales about Gods, for instance, may be as wrong as Xenophanes thinks, neither true nor the better thing to say; but they are certainly in accordance with opinion. Of other statements in poetry one may perhaps say, not that they are better than the truth, but that the fact was so at the time; e.g. the description of the arms: 'their spears stood upright, butt-end upon the ground';[33] for that was the usual way of fixing them then, as it is still with the Illyrians. As for the question whether something said or done in a poem is morally right or not, in dealing with that one should consider not only the intrinsic quality of the actual word or deed, but also the person who says or does it, the person to whom he says or does it, the time, the means, and the motive of the agent—whether he does it to attain a greater good, or to avoid a greater evil.

III. . . . . Speaking generally, one has to justify (1) the Impossible by reference to the requirements of poetry, or to the better, or to opinion. For the pur-

33 *Il.* x. 152.

poses of poetry a convincing impossibility is preferable to an unconvincing possibility; and if men such as Zeuxis depicted be impossible, the answer is that it is better they should be like that, as the artist ought to improve on his model. (2) The Improbable one has to justify either by showing it to be in accordance with opinion, or by urging that at times it is not improbable; for there is a probability of things happening also against probability. (3) The contradictions found in the poet's language one should first test as one does an opponent's confutation in a dialectical argument, so as to see whether he means the same thing, in the same relation, and in the same sense, before admitting that he has contradicted either something he has said himself or what a man of sound sense assumes as true. But there is no possible apology for improbability of Plot or depravity of character, when they are not necessary and no use is made of them, like the improbability in the appearance of Aegeus in Medea[34] and the baseness of Menelaus in Orestes.

The objections, then, of critics start with faults of five kinds: the allegation is always that something is either (1) impossible, (2) improbable, (3) corrupting, (4) contradictory, or (5) against technical correctness. The answers to these objections must be sought under one or other of the above-mentioned heads, which are twelve in number.

26    The question may be raised whether the epic or the tragic is the higher form of imitation. It may be argued that, if the less vulgar is the higher, and the less vulgar is always that which addresses the better public, an art addressing any and every one is of a very vulgar order. It is a belief that their public cannot see the meaning, unless they add something themselves, that causes the perpetual movements of the performers—bad flute-players, for instance, rolling about, if quoit-throwing is to be represented, and pulling at the conductor, if Scylla is the subject of the piece. Tragedy, then, is said to be an art of this order—to be in fact just what the later actors were in the eyes of their predecessors; for Mynniscus used to call Callippides 'the ape', because he thought he so overacted his parts; and a similar view was taken of Pindarus also. All Tragedy, however, is said to stand to the Epic as the newer to the older school of actors. The one, accordingly, is said to address a cultivated audience, which does not need the accompaniment of gesture; the other, an uncultivated one. If, therefore, Tragedy is a vulgar art, it must clearly be lower than the Epic.

The answer to this is twofold. In the first place, one may urge (1) that the censure does not touch the art of the dramatic poet, but only that of his interpreter; for it is quite possible to overdo the gesturing even in an epic recital, as did Sosistratus, and in a singing contest, as did Mnasitheus of Opus. (2) That one should not condemn all movement, unless one means to condemn even the dance, but only that of ignoble people—which is the point of the criticism passed on Callippides and in the present day on others, that their

[34] 1. 663.

women are not like gentlewomen. (3) That Tragedy may produce its effect even without movement or action in just the same way as Epic poetry; for from the mere reading of a play its quality may be seen. So that, if it be superior in all other respects, this element of inferiority is no necessary part of it.

In the second place, one must remember (1) that Tragedy has everything that the Epic has (even the epic metre being admissible), together with a not inconsiderable addition in the shape of the Music (a very real factor in the pleasure of the drama) and the Spectacle. (2) That its reality of presentation is felt in the play as read, as well as in the play as acted. (3) That the tragic imitation requires less space for the attainment of its end; which is a great advantage, since the more concentrated effect is more pleasurable than one with a large admixture of time to dilute it—consider the *Oedipus* of Sophocles, for instance, and the effect of expanding it into the number of lines of the *Iliad*. (4) That there is less unity in the imitation of the epic poets, as is proved by the fact that any one work of theirs supplies matter for several tragedies; the result being that, if they take what is really a single story, it seems curt when briefly told, and thin and waterish when on the scale of length usual with their verse. In saying that there is less unity in an epic, I mean an epic made up of a plurality of actions, in the same way as the *Iliad* and *Odyssey* have many such parts, each one of them in itself of some magnitude; yet the structure of the two Homeric poems is as perfect as can be, and the action in them is as nearly as possible one action. If, then, Tragedy is superior in these respects, and also, besides these, in its poetic effect (since the two forms of poetry should give us, not any or every pleasure, but the very special kind we have mentioned), it is clear that, as attaining the poetic effect better than the Epic, it will be the higher form of art.

So much for Tragedy and Epic poetry—for these two arts in general and their species; the number and nature of their constituent parts; the causes of success and failure in them; the Objections of the critics, and the Solutions in answer to them.

❦ ❦ ❦

## S. I. Hayakawa

# Poetry and Advertising[1]

ONE does not often mention poetry and advertising in the same breath. Poetry is universally conceded to be the loftiest attainment of the verbal arts; its merits are attested to by the wise of all ages. Advertising, on the other hand, is not even an autonomous art; it is the handmaiden of commercial motives; its

[1] "Poetry and Advertising," *Poetry: A Magazine of Verse*, LXVII (January, 1946), 204-212. A Paper given at the Sixth Conference on Science, Philosophy, and Religion. Reprinted by permission of the author.

name carries connotations (well earned, one might add) of half-truths, deception, and outright fraud, of appeals to vanity, fear, snobbery, and false pride, of
radio programs hideous with wheedling voices.

There are many more contrasts. The best poetry seems to be fully appreciated only by the few and to be beyond the comprehension of the many. Advertising, however, is considered best when it is laughed over, thought about,
and acted upon by multitudes. Poetry is, in the general apprehension, something special to be studied in schools, to be enjoyed by cultivated people who
have time for that sort of thing, to be read on solemn or momentous occasions.
Advertising is a part of everyday life.

But poetry and advertising have much in common. They both make every
possible use of rhyme and rhythm, of words chosen for their connotative
rather than their denotative values, of ambiguities that strike the level of unconscious responses as well as the conscious. Furthermore, they both strive to
give meaning and overtones to the innumerable data of everyday experience;
they both attempt to make the objects of experience symbolic of something beyond themselves. A primrose by the river's brim ceases to be "nothing more"
because the poet invests it with meanings; it comes to symbolize the insensi-
tiveness of Peter Bell, the benevolence of God, or anything else he wants it
to symbolize. The advertiser is concerned with the primrose only if it happens
to be for sale. Once it is on the national market, the advertiser can increase its
saleability by making it thrillingly reminiscent of gaiety, romance, and aristocratic elegance, or symbolic of solid, traditional American virtues, or suggestive
of glowing health and youth, depending upon his whim. This is what the writer
of advertising does with breakfast food, toothpaste, laxatives, whisky, perfume,
toilet bowl cleaners. Indeed almost all advertising directed to the general public
is the *poetizing of consumer goods*.

Poetry and advertising are similar too in that they invite the reader to put
himself in a role other than his own. In reading poetry we identify ourselves
with the characters that a poet creates or with the poet himself. In the course of
the experiences that a poet puts us through during these identifications, we
feel as others have felt, we see as others have seen, we discover new ways of
looking upon ourselves in our relationships with fellow human beings. Advertisers also invite us to make identifications of ourselves in new roles, although
the roles are simpler, pleasanter, and more easily within reach. Readers are
invited to look upon themselves as "smart housewives and hostesses" (who
serve Spam), as "men of distinction" (who drink Calvert's), as responsible
and prudent fathers (who protect their dependents with Metropolitan insurance policies), as well-regulated families (who take Ex-Lax).

The identifications to which poets invite us require some imaginative strenu-
ousness on the part of the reader; those to which advertisers invite us require
no more than a disposition to daydream and the ability to remember a brand-
name that is repeated eight times in sixty-five seconds in spot announcements
at half-hour intervals sixteen hours a day. In spite of this marked contrast in the
demands made upon the audience, both have the common function of entering

into our imaginations and shaping those idealizations of ourselves that determine, in large measure, our conduct. "Life," said Oscar Wilde, "is an imitation of art," and in so far as both poetry and advertising exact this tribute of imitation, they are both, in a real sense, "creative."

Let us call this use of verbal magic (or skulduggery) for the purpose of giving an imaginative, or symbolic, or "ideal" dimension to life and all that is in it, *poetry*. If we speak separately of what are ordinarily called poetry and advertising, let us speak of the former as *disinterested poetry*, of the latter as *venal poetry*, the word *venal* being used in the sense of being available for hire.

Using our terms in this way, we see that our age is by no means deficient in poetry as is often charged. We have more access to poetry (or perhaps we should say poetry has more access to us) than has been the case at any other time in history. One hundred and thirty out of the two hundred pages of each issue of *Harper's Bazaar* are devoted to venal poetry; a similar proportion of poetry to text occurs in most mass circulation magazines. This poetry is written by the highest paid writers in the country, organized into companies of poets, rhapsodists, sub-poets, and sub-rhapsodists, known as "agencies." It is supplemented and reinforced by vast amounts of illustration on which the most expensive and most advanced methods of color reproduction are lavished. It is chanted into national hook-ups night and day at the cost of thousands of dollars an hour, and there it is tied into drama, music, satire, humor, social and political discussion, and news. Product and producer it sings—in unending paeans of praise.

None of the corrupt and vain emperors of history exacted of the sycophant poets in their retinues anything like the discipline imposed upon the poets of Procter and Gamble and Ford Motors. The copy-writer is immeasurably more restricted in his choice of subject-matter than a court poet ever was. Moreover, the merit of his poetry is not measured by the pleasure it gives a single patron; it is measured by its influence on sales statistics. Like the court poet, the copy-writer must praise not only his patron, but also the entire socio-economic system which keeps his patron rich and powerful. Milton was eloquent in his contempt for the "trencher fury of the riming parasite." A contemporary prophet able to look into the twentieth century might well have said to him, "You haven't seen anything yet. Wait until you see the institutional ads of the great corporations during World War II!"

Let us turn from venal poetry to disinterested poetry. Mr. Robert Hillyer in a recent article in *Saturday Review of Literature* entitled "Modern Poetry *versus* the Common Reader" speaks of modern poets as being in a "welter of confusion and frustration." He is distressed by the obscurity of their language— "the flight from clarity," as he calls it. He is certain that both the unintelligibility and the general tone of despair characteristic of much modern verse are due to the moral defects of poets. "Their confusion," says he, "is a sign of artistic effeminacy and egotism."

Mr. Douglas Bush has said in his paper for the Sixth Conference on Science,

Philosophy and Religion, that "the modern poet is not altogether fulfilling his traditional function. From antiquity up through the nineteenth century, the poet was regarded as a teacher and leader of his age, and nearly all the greatest poets have been more or less popular; they have counted in the general spiritual life of their times." "Since the romantic age and the industrial revolution," he adds, "the artist has been given to conceiving of himself, not as a normal active member of society, but as a detached, lonely, and hostile observer; and the breach was never wider than it is today, in spite of the poet's concern with the world's ills."

What is responsible for this condition? It is customary, I should say too customary, to blame the shortcomings of modern disinterested poetry on the poets. A great deal of the critical literature of our times is devoted to scolding poets for their excessive compression of images, their oddities of syntax, and their unhappy states of mind. They are constantly being told to buck up and be men, to utter brave and positive affirmations. Very few poets respond to the call, and those who do are seldom praised, even by those who do the calling.

The difficulties of modern poetry, although often exaggerated, are real. As we have been told, it is due in part to the complexity of the modern consciousness; it is due in part to the lack of a widely accepted and recognized poetic tradition; it is no doubt due in part also to the special threats to individuality offered in an industrial age. In addition to the reasons others have given, I should like to add another, namely, that in a world so filled with the clamor of venal writing (of which venal poetry is only the most offensive example), all poetry has come to sound suspicious, so that disinterested poets are practically compelled not to sound poetic (as people ordinarily understand the term poetic) lest suggestions of venal purpose creep into their writing.

In other words, never in history has it been so difficult to say anything with enthusiasm or joy or conviction without running into the danger of sounding as if you were trying to sell something. I shall not say that it is impossible today to make affirmations in verse about the more or less universal facts of human experience that poetry has traditionally been concerned with. But of the vastly increased difficulty of doing so there can be no doubt, and the difficulty continues to increase with the increasing skill, talent, and ingenuity that are constantly being enlisted into advertising, publicity, and public relations as a result of the material rewards offered in those professions.

It is difficult to describe scenery without sounding as if you were promoting a summer-resort, although past ages have done it without compunction:

> To one who has been long in city pent
> 'Tis very sweet to look into the fair
> And open face of heaven,—to breathe in prayer
> Full in the smile of the blue firmament . . .

It is difficult to take delight in a woman's beauty without sounding like an advertisement, although it used to be possible:

Whenas in silks my Julia goes,
Then, then, methinks, how sweetly flows
The liquefaction of her clothes . . .

She was a Phantom of delight
When first she gleamed upon my sight . . .

It is difficult to become inspired by those facets of American life familiar and dear to all of us without sounding as if you were leading into a message from the National Association of Manufacturers on the necessity of maintaining the free enterprise system. Indeed, it is even difficult to speak reverently of the courage of our soldiers and the debt we owe the dead without sounding as if you were shortly going to remind the reader how much he also owes to Nash-Kelvinator's contribution to the war effort.

In 1940, Mr. Archibald MacLeish in his controversial essay, "Post-War Writers and Pre-War Readers" (*New Republic,* June 10, 1940), described the younger generation as being "distrustful of all words, distrustful of all moral judgments of better and worse." He continued, "If all words are suspect, all judgments phony, all conviction of better and worse fake, then there is nothing real and permanent for which men are willing to fight, and the moral and spiritual unpreparedness of the country is worse than its unpreparedness in arms." The condition he described was not as bad as he feared, but there is no denying that to a large degree it still exists—perhaps, after the experience of war, youthful cynicism is even more intense now than then.

But Mr. MacLeish was entirely wrong, it seems to me, in ascribing this youthful scepticism to the influence of the disillusioned authors who followed the first World War: such men as Dos Passos, Hemingway, Barbusse, and Remarque. For every one person reached by such authors, advertisers and publicity men and economic propagandists with goods or ideas to sell reached tens of thousands. The distrust of words does not come from reading writers who honestly state their feelings and convictions, even if those feelings and convictions are extremely gloomy. The distrust arises from long experience with an unending stream of venal poetry, venal speech, venal writing. People are hardly to be blamed, when they encounter so much of it, if they begin to wonder if there is any other kind. The pre-emption by the venal poet of the common value-symbols of our culture, the symbols of courage, of beauty, of domesticity, of patriotism, of happiness, and even of religion, for the purposes of *selling,* that is, of *advantaging the speaker at the expense of the hearer,* has left the disinterested poet with practically no unsullied symbols to work with other than obscure ones hauled up out of *The Golden Bough* or the *Upanishads,* and practically nothing in common human experience to write about except those negative moods that the ghastly cheerfulness of the advertising pages of the *Ladies' Home Journal* has no use for.

The restoration of poetry to its traditional state as one of the most important of the communicators and creators of the values a civilization lives by awaits, therefore, a time when something less than 98 percent of radio time and 85 percent of space in mass-circulation magazines is devoted to selling something.[2] It awaits an economic change profound enough to relieve advertisers of the necessity of invoking all the symbols of home, of mother, of the American way of life, of morality, and of the Christian religion in order to sell a box of soap-flakes. It awaits the dissemination of semantic wisdom, which can be equally well given by departments of history, political science, chemistry, English, or home economics as by teachers of semantics, sufficient to restore insight into the often subtle differences between venal and disinterested utterance, between statements rich with meaning and other statements, equally resonant, containing only sound and fury. It awaits a vision large enough on the part of students of poetry to see that the problems of modern poetry are inextricably interwoven with the character of the *semantic environment* in which the disinterested poet is compelled to work, which in turn compels an examination of the technological, the sociological, the economic beliefs and practices that create that environment. In short, it awaits the time when students of poetry cease to treat their subject as a separate and isolated discipline and begin to look about them at the worlds of science, of commerce, of journalism, of public affairs, and find out what is going on. Then they will be able to do something more than deplore the state of modern poetry.

❧ ❧ ❧

*Arthur Miller*

## The Family in Modern Drama[1]

1

Most people, including the daily theater reviewers, have come to assume that the forms in which plays are written spring either from nowhere or from the temperamental choice of the playwrights. I am not maintaining that the selec-

[2] Eighty-five percent is perhaps a conservative estimate of the amount of venal writing in many popular magazines, since advertising by no means stops with the advertising pages. Indeed, *Cosmopolitan*, a Hearst publication, appears quite proud of the fact that its editorial content, including its fiction, is as venal in its intent as its paid advertising. The following is quoted from *Cosmopolitan's* advertisement in a trade journal, *Advertising Age*: "Paul Gallico has just told her a dramatic tale. Pepsi Cola is reaching her at the right moment! Because she's young—she's emotional! She responds easily, quickly, wholeheartedly. . . . And Gallico's fiction is just one example of the kind of brilliant entertainment that crowds the pages of *Cosmopolitan*. Great writing makes great reading. It exercises the emotions. It whets the appetite for gracious living. . . . Good going, Pepsi Cola! You've caught her in an emotional mood. She's just been through the make-believe world of Paul Gallico. She's been living the glamorous life so temptingly traced by Ursula Parrott, Sinclair Lewis and the other great *Cosmopolitan* writers. Emotion makes wars. Emotion makes marriages. Emotion makes SALES!"

tion of a form is as objective a matter as the choice of let us say a raincoat instead of a linen suit for a walk on a rainy day; on the contrary, most playwrights, including myself, reach rather instinctively for that form, that way of telling a play, which seems inevitably right for the subject at hand. Yet I wonder whether it is all as accidental, as "free" a choice, as it appears to be at a superficial glance. I wonder whether there may not be within the ideas of family on the one hand, and society on the other, primary pressures which govern our notions of the right form for a particular kind of subject matter.

It has gradually come to appear to me over the years that the spectrum of dramatic forms, from Realism over to the Verse Drama, the Expressionistic techniques, and what we call vaguely the Poetic Play, consists of forms which express human relationships of a particular kind, each of them suited to express either a primarily familial relation at one extreme, or a primarily social relation at the other.

When we think of Realism we think of Ibsen—and if we don't we ought to, because in his social plays he not only used the form but pressed it very close to its ultimate limits. What are the main characteristics of this form? We know it by heart, of course, since most of the plays we see are realistic plays. It is written in prose; it makes believe it is taking place independently of an audience which views it through a "fourth wall," the grand objective being to make everything seem true to life in life's most evident and apparent sense. In contrast, think of any play by Aeschylus. You are never under an illusion in his plays that you are watching "life"; you are watching a play, an art work.

Now at the risk of being obvious I must remind you that Realism is a style, an artful convention, and not a piece of reportage. What, after all, is real about having all the furniture in a living room facing the footlights? What is real about people sticking to the same subject for three consecutive hours? Realism is a style, an invention quite as consciously created as Expressionism, Symbolism, or any of the other less familiar forms. In fact, it has held the stage for a shorter period of time than the more poetic forms and styles which dominate the great bulk of the world repertoire, and when it first came into being it was obvious to all as a style, a poet's invention. I say this in order to make clear that Realism is neither more nor less "artistic" than any other form. The only trouble is that it more easily lends itself in our age to hack work, for one thing because more people can write passable prose than verse. In other ages, however, as for instance in the lesser Elizabethan playwrights, hack work could also make of the verse play a pedestrian and uninspired form.

As with any artist, Ibsen was writing not simply to photograph scenes from life. After all, at the time he wrote A *Doll's House* how many Norwegian or European women had slammed the door upon their hypocritical relations with their husbands? Very few. So there was nothing, really, for him to photograph. What he was doing, however, was projecting through his personal interpretation of common events what he saw as their concealed significance for society. In other words, in a perfectly "realistic" way he did not report so much as project or even prophesy a meaning. Put in playwriting terms, he created a symbol on the stage.

We are not ordinarily accustomed to juxtaposing the idea of a symbol with the idea of Realism. The symbolic action, symbolic speech, have come to be reserved in our minds for the more poetic forms. Yet Realism shares equally with all other ways of telling a play this single mission. It must finally arrive at a meaning symbolic of the underlying action it has set forth. The difference lies in its method of creating its symbol as opposed to the way the poetic forms create theirs.

Now, then, the question arises: Why, if Ibsen and several other playwrights could use Realism so well to make plays about modern life, and if in addition the modern American audience is so quickly at home with the form—why should playwrights over the past thirty years be so impatient with it? Why has it been assaulted from every side? Why do so many people turn their backs on it and revere instead any kind of play which is fanciful or poetic? At the same time, why does Realism always seem to be drawing us all back to its arms? We have not yet created in this country a succinct form to take its place. Yet it seems that Realism has become a familiar bore; and by means of cutout sets, revolving stages, musical backgrounds, new and more imaginative lighting schemes, our stage is striving to break up the old living room. However, the perceiving eye knows that many of these allegedly poetic plays are Realism underneath, tricked up to look otherwise. I am criticizing nobody, only stating that the question of form is a deeper one, perhaps, than we have been willing to admit.

As I have indicated, I have come to wonder whether the force or pressure that makes for Realism, that even requires it, is the magnetic force of the family relationship within the play, and the pressure which evokes in a genuine, unforced way the un-realistic modes is the social relationship within the play. In a generalized way we commonly recognize that forms do have some extra-theatrical, common-sense criteria; for instance, one of the prime difficulties in writing modern opera, which after all is lyric drama, is that you cannot rightly sing so many of the common thoughts of common life. A line like "Be sure to take your bath, Gloria," is difficult to musicalize, and impossible to take seriously as a sung concept. But we normally stop short at recognition of the ridiculous in this problem. Clearly, a poetic drama must be built upon a poetic idea, but I wonder if that is the whole problem. It is striking to me, for instance, that Ibsen, the master of Realism, while writing his realistic plays in quite as serious a frame of mind as in his social plays, suddenly burst out of the realistic frame, out of the living room, when he wrote *Peer Gynt*. I think that it is not primarily the living room he left behind, in the sense that this factor had made a poetic play impossible for him, but rather the family context. For Peer Gynt is first of all a man seen alone; equally, he is a man confronting non-familial, openly social relationships and forces.

I warn you not to try to apply this rule too mechanically. A play, like any human relationship, has a predominant quality, but it also contains powerful elements which although secondary may not be overlooked, and may in fact be crucial in the development of that relationship. I offer this concept, therefore, as a possible tool and not as a magic key to the writing or understanding of plays and their forms.

I have used Ibsen as an example because he wrote in several forms; another equally experimental dramatist was O'Neill. It ought to be noted that O'Neill himself described his preoccupation as being not with the relations between man and man, but with those between man and God. What has this remark to do with dramatic form? Everything, I think. It is obvious, to begin with, that Ibsen's mission was to create not merely characters, but a context in which they were formed and functioned as people. That context, heavily and often profoundly delineated, was his society. His very idea of fate, for instance, was the inevitability residing in the conflict between the life force of his characters struggling with the hypocrisies, the strangling and abortive effects of society upon them. Thus, if only to create a climax, Ibsen had to draw society in his plays as a realistic force embodied in money, in social mores, in taboos, and so on, as well as an internal, subjective force within his characters.

O'Neill, however, seems to have been seeking for some fate-making power behind the social force itself. He went to ancient Greece for some definition of that force; he reached toward modern religion and toward many other possible sources of the poetic modes. My point here, however, is that so long as the family and family relations are at the center of his plays his form remains—indeed, it is held prisoner by—Realism. When, however, as for instance in *The Hairy Ape* and *Emperor Jones*, he deals with men out in society, away from the family context, his forms become alien to Realism, more openly and self-consciously symbolic, poetic, and finally heroic.

2

Up to this point I have been avoiding any question of content except that of the family relation as opposed to relations out in the world—social relations. Now I should like to make the bald statement that all plays we call great, let alone those we call serious, are ultimately involved with some aspect of a single problem. It is this: How may a man make of the outside world a home? How and in what ways must he struggle, what must he strive to change and overcome within himself and outside himself if he is to find the safety, the surroundings of love, the ease of soul, the sense of identity and honor which, evidently, all men have connected in their memories with the idea of family?

One ought to be suspicious of any attempt to boil down all the great themes to a single sentence, but this one—"How may a man make of the outside world a home?"—does bear watching as a clue to the inner life of the great plays. Its aptness is most evident in the modern repertoire; in fact, where it is not the very principle of the play at hand we do not take the play quite seriously. If, for instance, the struggle in *Death of a Salesman* were simply between father and son for recognition and forgiveness it would diminish in importance. But when it extends itself out of the family circle and into society, it broaches those questions of social status, social honor and recognition, which expand its vision and lift it out of the merely particular toward the fate of the generality of men.

The same is true—although achieved in different ways—of a play like *A Streetcar Named Desire*, which could quite easily have been limited to a study of psychopathology were it not that it is placed clearly within the wider bounds of the question I am discussing. Here Blanche Dubois and the sensitivity she represents has been crushed by her moving out of the shelter of the home and the family into the uncaring, anti-human world outside it. In a word, we begin to partake of the guilt for her destruction, and for Willy's, because the blow struck against them was struck outside the home rather than within it—which is to say that it affects us more because it is a social fact we are witnessing.

The crucial question has an obverse side. If we look at the great plays—at *Hamlet, Oedipus, Lear*—we must be impressed with one fact perhaps above all others. These plays are all examining the concept of loss, of man's deprivation of a once-extant state of bliss unjustly shattered—a bliss, a state of equilibrium, which the hero (and his audience) is attempting to reconstruct or to recreate with new, latter-day life materials. It has been said often that the central theme of the modern repertoire is the alienation of man, but the idea usually halts at the social alienation—he cannot find a satisfying role in society. What I am suggesting here is that while this is true of our plays, the more or less hidden impulse antedating social alienation, the unsaid premise of the very idea of "satisfaction," is the memory of both playwright and audience of an enfolding family and of childhood. It is as though both playwright and audience believed that they had once had an identity, a *being*, somewhere in the past which in the present has lost its completeness, its definitiveness, so that the central force making for pathos in these large and thrusting plays is the paradox which Time bequeaths to us all: we cannot go home again, and the world we live in is an alien place.

One of the forms most clearly in contrast to Realism is Expressionism. I should like now to have a look at its relevancy to the family-social complex.

3

The technical arsenal of Expressionism goes back to Aeschylus. It is a form of play which manifestly seeks to dramatize the conflict of either social, religious, ethical, or moral forces *per se*, and in their own naked roles, rather than to present psychologically realistic human characters in a more or less realistic environment. There is, for instance, no attempt by Aeschylus to create the psychology of a violent "character" in *Prometheus Bound*, or of a powerful one; rather he brings on two figures whose names are Power and Violence, and they behave as the *idea* of Power and the *idea* of Violence ought to behave, according to the laws of Power and Violence. In Germany after the First World War, playwrights sought to dramatize and unveil the social condition of man with similar means. For instance, in *Gas I* and *Gas II* Georg Kaiser placed the figure of man against an image of industrial society but without the slightest attempt to characterize the man except as a representative of one or the other of the social classes vying for control of the machine. There are, of course, numerous other examples of the same kind of elimination of psychological characterization in favor of what one might call the presentation of forces. In *The Great God Brown*, for instance, as well as in *The Hairy Ape*, O'Neill reached toward this very ancient means of dramatization without psychology—without, one might say, behavior as we normally know it. *Everyman* is another work in that long line.

In passing, I must ask you to note that expressionist plays—which is to say plays preoccupied with the open confrontation of moral, ethical, or social forces —seem inevitably to cast a particular kind of shadow. The moment realistic behavior and psychology disappear from the play all the other appurtenances of Realism vanish too. The stage is stripped of knickknacks; instead it reveals symbolic *designs* which function as overt pointers toward the moral to be drawn from the action. We are no longer under quite the illusion of watching through a transparent fourth wall. Instead we are constantly reminded, in effect, that we are watching a theater piece. In short, we are not bidden to lose our consciousness of time and place, the consciousness of ourselves, but are appealed to through our intelligence, our faculties of knowing rather than of feeling.

This difference in the area of appeal is the difference between our familial emotions and our social emotions. The two forms not only spring from different sectors of human experience but end up by appealing to different areas of receptivity within the audience. Nor is this phenomenon confined to the play.

When one is speaking to one's family, for example, one uses a certain level of speech, a certain plain diction perhaps, a tone of voice, an inflection, suited to the intimacy of the occasion. But when one faces an audience of strangers, as a politician does, for instance—and he is the most social of men—it seems right and proper for him to reach for the well-turned phrase, even the poetic word, the aphorism, the metaphor. And his gestures, his stance, his tone of voice, all become larger than life; moreover, his character is not what gives him these prerogatives, but his role. In other words, a confrontation with society permits us, or even enforces upon us, a certain reliance upon ritual. Similarly with the play.

The implications of this natural wedding of form with inner relationships are many, and some of them are complex. It is true to say, I think, that the language of the family is the language of the private life—prose. The language of society, the language of the public life, is verse. According to the degree to which the play partakes of either relationship, it achieves the right to move closer or further away from either pole. I repeat that this "right" is given by some common consent which in turn is based upon our common experience in life.

It is interesting to look at a couple of modern plays from this viewpoint and to see whether critical sense can be made of them. T. S. Eliot's *The Cocktail Party*, for instance, drew from most intelligent auditors a puzzled admiration. In general, one was aware of a struggle going on between the apparencies of the behavior of the people and what evidently was the preoccupation of the playwright. There were a Husband and a Wife whom we were evidently expected to accept in that commonly known relationship, especially since the setting and the mode of speech and much of its diction were perfectly real if inordinately cultivated for a plebeian American audience. Even the theme of the play was, or should have been, of importance to most of us. Here we were faced with the alternative ways of giving meaning to domestic existence, one of them being through the cultivation of self, partly by means of the psychoanalytic ritual; the other and victorious method being the martyrization of the self, not for the sake of another, or as a rebuke to another, as martyrdom is usually indulged in in family life, but for the sake of martyrdom, of the disinterested action whose ultimate model was, according to the author, Jesus Christ. The heroine is celebrated for having been eaten alive by ants while on a missionary work among savages, and the very point is that there was no point—she converted nobody at all. Thus she gained her self by losing self or giving it away. Beyond the Meaningless she found Meaning at last.

To say the least, Eliot is manifestly an apt writer of verse. The inability of this play to achieve a genuine poetic level cannot therefore be laid to the usual cause—the unpoetic nature of the playwright's talent. Indeed, *Murder in the Cathedral* is a genuine poetic play, so he had already proved that he could achieve a wholeness of poetic form. I believe that the puzzlement created by *The Cocktail Party*, the sense of its being drawn in two opposite directions, is the result of the natural unwillingness of our minds to give to the Husband-Wife relation—a family relation—the prerogatives of the poetic mode, especially when the relationship is originally broached, as it is in this play, through any means approaching Realism.

Whether consciously or not, Eliot himself was aware of this dichotomy and wrote, and has said that he wrote, a kind of line which would not seem obtrusively formal and poetic to the listening ear. The injunction to keep it somehow unpoetic was issued by the central family situation, in my opinion. There was no need to mask his poetry at all in *Murder in the Cathedral*, because the situation is social, the conflict of a human being with the world. That earlier play had the unquestioned right to the poetic because it dealt with man as a public figure and could use the public man's style and diction.

### 4

We recognize now that a play can be poetic without verse, and it is in this middle area that the complexities of tracing the influence of the family and social elements upon the form become more troublesome. *Our Town* by Thornton Wilder is such a play, and it is important not only for itself but because it is the progenitor of many other works.

This is a family play which deals with the traditional family figures, the father, mother, brother, sister. At the same time it uses this particular family as a prism through which is reflected the author's basic idea, his informing principle —which can be stated as the indestructibility, the everlastingness, of the family and the community, its rhythm of life, its rootedness in the essentially safe cosmos despite troubles, wracks, and seemingly disastrous, but essentially temporary, dislocations.

Technically it is not arbitrary in any detail. Instead of a family living room or a house, we are shown a bare stage on which actors set chairs, a table, a ladder to represent a staircase or an upper floor, and so on. A narrator is kept in the foreground as though to remind us that this is not so much "real life" as an abstraction of it—in other words, a stage. It is clearly a poetic rather than a realistic play. What makes it that? Well, let us first imagine what would make it more realistic.

Would a real set make it realistic? Not likely. A real set would only discomfit us by drawing attention to what would then appear to be a slightly unearthly quality about the characterizations. We should probably say, "People don't really act like that." In addition, the characterization of the whole town could not be accomplished with anything like its present vividness if the narrator were removed, as he would have to be from a realistic set, and if the entrances and exits of the environmental people, the townspeople, had to be justified with the usual motives and machinery of Realism.

The preoccupation of the entire play is quite what the title implies—the town, the society, and not primarily this particular family—and every stylistic means used is to the end that the family foreground be kept in its place, merely as a foreground for the larger context behind and around it. In my opinion, it is this larger context, the town and its enlarging, widening significance, that is the bridge to the poetic for this play. Cut out the town and you will cut out the poetry.

The play is worth examining further against the Ibsen form of Realism to which it is inevitably related if only in contrast. Unlike Ibsen, Wilder sees his characters in this play not primarily as personalities, as individuals, but as forces, and he individualizes them only enough to carry the freight, so to speak, of their roles as forces. I do not believe, for instance, that we can think of the brother in this play, or the sister or the mother, as having names other than Brother, Sister, Mother. They are not given that kind of particularity or interior life. They are characterized rather as social factors, in their roles of Brother, Sister, Mother, in Our Town. They are drawn, in other words, as forces to enliven and illuminate the author's symbolic vision and his theme, which is that of the family as a timeless, stable quantity which has not only survived all the turmoil of time but is, in addition, beyond the possibility of genuine destruction.

The play is important to any discussion of form because it has achieved a largeness of meaning and an abstraction of style that created that meaning, while at the same time it has moved its audiences subjectively—it has made them laugh and weep as abstract plays rarely if ever do. But it would seem to contradict my contention here. If it is true that the presentation of the family on the stage inevitably forces Realism upon the play, how did this family play manage to transcend Realism to achieve its symbolistic style?

Every form, every style, pays its price for its special advantages. The price paid by *Our Town* is psychological characterization forfeited in the cause of the symbol. I do not believe, as I have said, that the characters are identifiable in a psychological way, but only as figures in the family and social constellation, and this is not meant in criticism, but as a statement of the limits of this form. I would go further and say that it is not *necessary* for every kind of play to do every kind of thing. But if we are after ultimate reality we must make ultimate demands.

I think that had Wilder drawn his characters with a deeper configuration of detail and with a more remorseless quest for private motive and self-interest, for instance, the story as it stands now would have appeared oversentimental and even sweet. I think that if the play tested its own theme more remorselessly, the world it creates of a timeless family and a rhythm of existence beyond the disturbance of social wracks would not remain unshaken. The fact is that the juvenile delinquent is quite directly traced to the breakup of family life and, indeed, to the break in that ongoing, steady rhythm of community life which the play celebrates as indestructible.

I think, further, that the close contact which the play established with its audience was the result of its coincidence with the deep longing of the audience for such stability, a stability which in daylight out on the street does not truly exist. The great plays pursue the idea of loss and deprivation of an earlier state of bliss which the characters feel compelled to return to or to re-create. I think this play forgoes the loss and suffers thereby in its quest for reality, but that the audience supplies the sense of deprivation in its own life experience as it faces what in effect is an idyl of the past. To me, therefore, the play falls short of a form that will press into reality to the limits of reality, if only because it could not plumb the psychological interior lives of its characters and still keep its present form. It is a triumph in that it does open a way toward the dramatization of the larger truths of existence while using the common materials of life. It is a truly poetic play.


5

Were there space, I should like to go into certain contemporary works with a view to the application in them of the forces of society and family—works by Clifford Odets, Tennessee Williams, Lillian Hellman, William Saroyan, and others. But I will jump to the final question I have in mind. If there is any truth in the idea of a natural union of the family and Realism as opposed to society and the poetic, what are the reasons for it?

First, let us remind ourselves of an obvious situation, but one which is often overlooked. The man or woman who sits down to write a play, or who enters a theater to watch one, brings with him in each case a common life experience which is not suspended merely because he has turned writer or become part of an audience. We—all of us—have a role anteceding all others: we are first sons, daughters, sisters, brothers. No play can possibly alter this given role.

The concepts of Father, Mother, and so on were received by us unawares before the time we were conscious of ourselves as selves. In contrast, the concepts of Friend, Teacher, Employee, Boss, Colleague, Supervisor, and the many other social relations came to us long after we gained consciousness of ourselves, and are therefore outside ourselves. They are thus in an objective rather than a subjective category. In any case, what we feel is always more "real" to us than what we know, and we feel the family relation while we only know the social one. Thus the former is the very apotheosis of the real and has an inevitability and a foundation indisputably actual, while the social relation is always relatively mutable, accidental, and consequently of a profoundly arbitrary nature to us.

Today the difficulty in creating a form that will unite both elements in a full rather than partial onslaught on reality is the reflection of the deep split between the private life of man and his social life. Nor is this the first time in history that such a separation has occurred. Many critics have remarked upon it, for instance, as a probable reason for the onset of Realism in the later Greek plays, for it is like a rule of society that, as its time of troubles arrives, its citizens revert to a kind of privacy of life that excludes society, as though man at such times would like to banish society from his mind. When this happens, man excludes poetry too.

All of which, while it may provide a solution, or at least indicate the mansion where the solution lives, only serves to point to the ultimate problem more succinctly. Obviously, the playwright cannot create a society, let alone one so unified as to allow him to portray man in art as a monolithic creature. The playwright is not a reporter, but in a serious work of art he cannot set up an image of man's condition so distant from reality as to violate the common sense of what reality is. But a serious work, to say nothing of a tragic one, cannot hope to achieve truly high excellence short of an investigation into the whole gamut of causation of which society is a manifest and crucial part. Thus it is that the common Realism of the past forty or fifty years has been assaulted—because it could not, with ease and beauty, bridge the widening gap between the private life and the social life. Thus it is that the problem was left unsolved by Expressionism, which evaded it by forgoing psychological realism altogether and leaping over to a portrayal of social forces alone. Thus it is that there is now a certain decadence about many of our plays; in the past ten years they have come more and more to dwell solely upon psychology, with little or no attempt to locate and dramatize the social roles and conflicts of their characters. For it is proper to ascribe decay to that which turns its back upon society when, as is obvious to any intelligence, the fate of mankind is social.

6

Finally, I should say that the current quest after the poetic as poetic is fruitless. It is the attempt to make apples without growing trees. It is seeking poetry precisely where poetry is not: in the private life viewed entirely within the bounds of the subjective, the area of sensation, or the bizarre and the erotic. From these areas of the private life have sprung the mood plays, the plotless plays for which there is much admiration as there is much relief when one turns from a problem to a ramble in the woods. I do not ask you to disdain such plays, for they are within the realm of art; I say only that the high work, the tragic work, cannot be forged waywardly, while playing by ear. There is a charm in improvisation, in letting one chord suggest the other and ending when the moment wanes. But the high order of art to which drama is fated will come only when it seeks to account for the total condition of man, and this cannot be improvised.

Whatever is said to describe a mood play, one point must be made: such plays all have in common an air of self-effacement—which is to say that they wish to seem as though they had not only no plot but no writer. They would convince us that they "just happen," that no directing hand has arranged matters—contrary to the Ibsen plays, for instance, or, for that matter, the Shakespearean play or the Greek.

Furthermore, the entire operation is most moody when the characters involved have the least consciousness of their own existence. The mood play is a play in hiding. A true plot is an assertion of meaning. The mood play is not, as it has been mistaken for, a rebellion of any kind against the so-called well-made play, especially when Ibsen is widely held to be a writer of well-made plays. For there is as much subjectivity and inner poetry in *Hedda Gabler*—I daresay a lot more—as in any of these mood plays. What is really repulsive in Ibsen to one kind of contemporary mind is not openly mentioned: it is his persistent search for an organizing principle behind the "moods" of existence and not the absence of mood in his work.

An art form, like a person, can achieve greatness only as it accepts great challenges. Over the past few decades the American theater, in its best moments, has moved courageously and often beautifully into the interior life of man, an area that had most often been neglected in the past. But now, I think, we are in danger of settling for tears, as it were—for any play that "moves" us, quite as though the ultimate criterion of the art were lachrymosity. For myself, I find that there is an increasing reliance upon what pass for realistic, even tough, analytical picturizations of existence, which are really quite sentimental underneath; and the sentiment is getting thicker, I think, and an end in itself. Sentimentalism is perfectly all right, but it is nowhere near a great challenge, and to pursue it, even under the guide of the exotic atmosphere and the celebration of the sensuous, is not going to bring us closer to the fated mission of the drama.

What, after all, is that mission? I may as well end with such a question because it underlies and informs every word I have written. I think of it so: Man has created so many specialized means of unveiling the truth of the world around him and the world within him—the physical sciences, the psychological sciences, the disciplines of economic and historical research and theory. In effect, each of these attacks on the truth is partial. It is within the rightful sphere of the drama—it is, so to speak, its truly just employment and its ultimate design—to embrace the many-sidedness of man. It is as close to being a total art as the race has invented. It can tell, like science, what is—but more, it can tell what ought to be. It can depict, like painting, in designs and portraits, in the colors of the day or night; like the novel it can spread out its arms and tell the story of a life, or a city, in a few hours—but more, it is dynamic, it is always on the move as life is and it is perceived like life through the motions, the gestures, the tones of voice, and the gait and nuance of living people. It is the singer's art and the painter's art and the dancer's art, yet it may hew to fact no less tenaciously than does the economist or the physician. In a word, there lies within the dramatic form the ultimate possibility of raising the truth-consciousness of mankind to a level of such intensity as to transform those who observe it.

The problem, therefore, is not simply an aesthetic one. As people, as a society, we thirst for clues to the past and the future; least of all, perhaps, do we know about the present, about what *is*. It is the present that is always most evasive and slippery, for the present always threatens most directly our defenses against seeing what we are, and it is the present, always the present, to which the dramatic form must apply or it is without interest and a dead thing, and forms do die when they lose their capacity to open up the present. So it is its very nature to bring us closer to ourselves if only it can grow and change with the changing world.

In the deepest sense, I think, to sophisticated and unsophisticated alike, nothing is quite so real to us, so extant, as that which has been made real by art. Nor is this ironical and comic. For the fact is that art is a function of the civilizing act quite as much as is the building of the water supply. American civilization is only recently coming to a conscious awareness of art not as a luxury but as a necessity of life. Without the right dramatic form a genuine onslaught upon the veils that cloak the present is not possible. In the profoundest sense I cannot create that form unless, somewhere in you, there is a wish to know the present and a demand upon me that I give it to you.

For at bottom what is that form? It is the everlastingly sought balance between order and the need of our souls for freedom; the relatedness between our vaguest longings, our inner questions, and private lives and the life of the generality of men which is our society and our world. How may man make for himself a home in that vastness of strangers and how may he transform that vastness into a home? This, as I have repeated, is the question a form must solve anew in every age. This, I may say, is the problem before you too.

❦ ❦ ❦

*Robert Penn Warren*

# A Lesson Read in American Books[1]

ONCE upon a time there was a nation, which we shall call X. At the time of which we write this nation stood at a moment of great power and great promise. A few generations earlier it had concluded a long and bloody civil war to achieve unity. More recently, in that unity, it had won a crashing victory over foreign foes. It had undergone, and was undergoing, a social revolution; there was unparalleled prosperity, a relaxing of old sanctions and prejudices, a widening of opportunity for all classes, great rewards for energy and intelligence. Its flag was on strange seas; its power was felt in the world. It was, even, producing a famous literature.

But—and here is the strange thing in that moment of energy and optimism —a large part, the most famous part, of that literature exhibited violence, degradation and despair as part of the human condition: tales of the old time of the civil war, tales of lust and horror, brother pimping for sister, father lusting for daughter, a head of the state doting on a fair youth, an old man's eyes plucked out, another old man killed in his sleep, friendship betrayed, obligations foregone, good men cursing the gods, and the whole scene drenched in blood. Foreigners encountering this literature might well conclude that the Land of X was peopled by degenerates sadly lacking in taste, manners and principle.

This is England, Elizabethan England, that we are talking about, and not the United States in this year of Our Lord and the Great Prosperity. But *mutatis mutandis,* and with proper recognition of the fact that we can scarcely claim a William Shakespeare, only John Fords and John Websters, we can talk about the United States in this connection, and join in conversation with Father Bruckberger, who has lately appeared in these pages, and with the editorial writer of *Life* magazine for Sept. 12.

These writers are concerned, as we must all be concerned, with America's image in the eyes of the world. "Is it right," asks Father Bruckberger, a sympathetic Frenchman visiting our shores, "that the great *flowering* of the American novel should hamper . . . America's leadership of the free world?" And the editorial writer in *Life:* "Europeans are already prejudiced against America by savage animadversions in their own classics against our 'vulgar' democracy. . . . Small wonder that our own self-depreciation helps them enlarge the evil image. . . ."

These two quotations raise a question, vexed and vexing, a question already old, no doubt, when the Greeks worried about it: how should esthetic value be

---

[1] From *The New York Times Book Review,* December 11, 1955. Reprinted by permission of the author and *The New York Times Book Review.*

related to prudential considerations? Presumably some of our literature has
esthetic value (Father Bruckberger handsomely calls it a "flowering"), but it
confirms some Europeans in their inherited low opinion of America, the country of "the almighty dollar," and of "respect to ordinary artisans," as Stendhal
puts it, and the "land of money and selfishness, where souls are cold," as Balzac
puts it. What do we do, then, when esthetic value is in conflict, or in apparent
conflict, with political values?

Father Bruckberger does not undertake to answer this for us. On the one
hand, he says that the "honor" of a literature is that it creates and sustains
"a great quarrel within the national consciousness." But on the other hand, he
bewails the effect abroad of this very quarrel within our national consciousness.
Certainly, he is too informed to attempt to resolve the difficulty along the lines
laid down by the editorial writer in *Life*, who, with certain ritualistic reservations, says that because America is now enjoying a boom, our literature should
be optimistic, and applauds the current success of *The Man in the Gray
Flannel Suit* because, though "flimsy art," it is "at least affirmative."

In fact, the editorial writer of *Life* takes as his golden text a quotation from
Sloan Wilson, the author of *The Man in the Gray Flannel Suit:* "The world's
treated me awfully well, and I guess it's crept into my work. . . . These are,
we forget, pretty good times. Yet too many novelists are still writing as if we
were back in the Depression years."

Though I have not yet read *The Man in the Gray Flannel Suit*, I should
venture to doubt that the world is going to treat its author quite as well as it
has treated Ernest Hemingway, William Faulkner, Theodore Dreiser, Sinclair
Lewis, T. S. Eliot, Robert Frost, and quite a few other American writers who
never found such a ready equation between bank balance and philosophy.
What is really at stake in this is a question of freedom. If the creative act is of
any value it is, in its special way, an act of freedom. It is, of course, conditioned
by a thousand factors, but study of its conditions—economic, biologic, or
whatever—has yet to reveal the secret of how that new intuition, the truly
created object whose *newness* is the mark of freedom, comes to be. But Mr.
Wilson, and presumably the approving editorial writer in *Life*, would deny this
freedom, would, in fact, go even farther than Karl Marx in asserting the economic determinism of literature. If you are not making dough, you will not be
a booster. Literature is a reflex of the stock market.

The philosophers of the Age of Conformism grant, however, that criticism
was once all right, long back. As the *Life* editorial puts it: "*The Great Gatsby*
still speaks eloquently of Prohibition's frauds and deceits, *Main Street* of the
high tide of provincial self-satisfaction, *The Grapes of Wrath* with a just anger
for the unnecessary humiliations of Depression. . . ." But criticism isn't all
right in this day and time, for there is nothing really wrong now to be criticized, and anybody who is critical, who isn't "affirmative," is a fool or knave, a
traitor or a sexual deviant, or a failure. May we not, however, in some chill
hour between dark and dawn, have the thought that our own age may—just

possibly—have its own frauds and deceits, deeper and more ambiguous than those anatomized in *The Great Gatsby*, that though this is not the age of provincial self-satisfaction, it may be the age of national self-righteousness and require a sharper scalpel than even *Main Street*, and that Divine Providence has given no written guarantee that It will not rebuke the smuggery of the Great Boom?

I do not think that the novel has yet been written to anatomize adequately this moment of our history, and I share the distaste of the editorial writer in *Life* for some of the works he alludes to, but the "American novel" which we should call for would not be less, but more, critical than those now current. At the same time I should hope that the literature to come will be more "affirmative," to use the word of the editorial. But the paradox here is that the literature that is most truly and profoundly critical is always the most profoundly affirmative.

In so far as a literature struggles to engage the deep, inner issues of life, the more will that literature be critical—the more, that is, will it engender impatience with the compromises, the ennui, the materialism, the self-deception, the complacency, and the secret, unnamable despairs that mark so much of ordinary life. Such a critical literature is at the same time affirmative because it affirms the will and courage to engage life at fundamental levels: the rock, if struck hard enough, will give forth the living waters.

The editorial writer in *Life* would not, I suppose, find these kinds of affirmation significant. He is concerned with doctrine, more or less explicitly put. But sometimes, even when doctrine is explicitly put, he has not, cannot, or does not, read it. Faulkner, he says, "for all his enormous gifts, can be searched in vain for that quality of redemption, through love and brotherhood, which always shines amid Dostoevsky's horrors." That very redemption, and its cost, is a recurrent theme of Faulkner's work. There is, for example, *The Bear*, with old Ike's vision of man's place in creation: God created man to hold suzerainty over the earth in His name, "not to hold for himself and his descendants' inviolable title forever, generation after generation, to the oblongs and squares of the earth, but to hold the earth mutual and intact in the communal anonymity of brotherhood, and all the fee He asked was pity and humility and sufferance and endurance and the sweat of his face for bread."

But let us go back where we started: the bad political impression which some of our literature presumably gives abroad. What are we to do? If we can't get writers to write the kind of literature we think useful for foreign consumption—if there really isn't such a thing as literature to specification—what then?

The answer is, I think, simple—and appalling. We must trust in our humility, and in our strength.

We must trust in our humility, because only by humility, the recognition that we have not fulfilled our best possibilities, can we hope to fulfill those possibilities. Some day, far-called, our navies may melt away, and on that day we may need the wisdom of ultimate humility. Meanwhile, in our moment of strength we hope that our strength is more than a historical accident, an index of the weakness of others. We hope that it has a moral grounding. But if that hope is to be more than a hope, it must be subjected to the test of conscience, and literature is one of the voices of our national conscience, however faltering and defective that voice may sometimes be. We must rebuke our *hubris,* not out of fear, but from love of a truth that we hope is within us.

We must trust in our strength, because only the strong can afford the luxury of radical self-criticism. Only if we believe in our strength can we take the risks of our full political and cultural development, with all the disintegrative and paradoxical possibilities in that dialectic. We should trust our strength, because America has a secret weapon, if we choose to use it: the weapon of not having a secret. It is the weapon of radical self-criticism—*radical* in the non-political and literal sense of the word. There was an old name for this, a name not often now used in this connection. That name was *democracy.*

So much for ourselves. But what of those poor foreigners who are so readily deceived by our literature? Are they, in the long run, quite so trapped in their prejudice, quite so incapable of the imaginative act, as Father Bruckberger seems to think? If so, why do they find our literature so fascinating, and why do they honor it? Can it be that, in a measure, they find in it a vital image of man, and some comment on his condition? Do they find in it, in the very fact of its existence, some mark of freedom?

I shall tell a story. A little while after the war in Europe I became acquainted with a young Italian who, in the first year of the war, as an officer in the Fascist Army, had deserted and taken to the mountains, to fight on our side. I once asked him what led him to this drastic step. He replied that American novelists had converted him. How, I asked. "Well," he said, "the Fascists used to let us read American fiction because it gave, they thought, a picture of a decadent America. They thought it was good propaganda for fascism to let us read Dreiser, Faulkner, Sinclair Lewis. But you know, it suddenly occurred to me that if democracy could allow that kind of criticism of itself, it must be very strong and good. So I took to the mountains."

❦ ❦ ❦

*Lionel Trilling*

# Manners, Morals, and the Novel [1]

THE INVITATION that was made to me to address you this evening was couched in somewhat uncertain terms. Time, place, and cordiality were perfectly clear, but when it came to the subject our hosts were not able to specify just what they wanted me to talk about. They wanted me to consider

---

[1] From *The Liberal Imagination,* by Lionel Trilling. Copyright, 1948, 1950, by Lionel Trilling. Reprinted by permission of The Viking Press, Inc., New York.

literature in its relation to manners—by which, as they relied on me to understand, they did not really mean *manners*. They did not mean, that is, the rules of personal intercourse in our culture; and yet such rules were by no means irrelevant to what they did mean. Nor did they quite mean manners in the sense of *mores*, customs, although, again, these did bear upon the subject they had in mind.

I understood them perfectly, as I would not have understood them had they been more definite. For they were talking about a nearly indefinable subject.

Somewhere below all the explicit statements that a people makes through its art, religion, architecture, legislation, there is a dim mental region of intention of which it is very difficult to become aware. We now and then get a strong sense of its existence when we deal with the past, not by reason of its presence in the past but by reason of its absence. As we read the great formulated monuments of the past, we notice that we are reading them without the accompaniment of something that always goes along with the formulated monuments of the present. The voice of multifarious intention and activity is stilled, all the buzz of implication which always surrounds us in the present, coming to us from what never gets fully stated, coming in the tone of greetings and the tone of quarrels, in slang and humor and popular songs, in the way children play, in the gesture the waiter makes when he puts down the plate, in the nature of the very food we prefer.

Some of the charm of the past consists of the quiet—the great distracting buzz of implication has stopped and we are left only with what has been fully phrased and precisely stated. And part of the melancholy of the past comes from our knowledge that the huge, unrecorded hum of implication was once there and left no trace—we feel that because it is evanescent it is especially human. We feel, too, that the truth of the great preserved monuments of the past does not fully appear without it. From letters and diaries, from the remote, unconscious corners of the great works themselves, we try to guess what the sound of the multifarious implication was and what it meant.

Or when we read the conclusions that are drawn about our own culture by some gifted foreign critic—or by some stupid native one—who is equipped only with a knowledge of our books, when we try in vain to say what is wrong, when in despair we say that he has read the books "out of context," then we are aware of the matter I have been asked to speak about tonight.

What I understand by manners, then, is a culture's hum and buzz of implication. I mean the whole evanescent context in which its explicit statements are made. It is that part of a culture which is made up of half-uttered or unuttered or unutterable expressions of value. They are hinted at by small actions, sometimes by the arts of dress or decoration, sometimes by tone, gesture, emphasis, or rhythm, sometimes by the words that are used with a special frequency or a special meaning. They are the things that for good or bad draw the people of a culture together and that separate them from the people of another culture. They make the part of a culture which is not art, or religion, or morals, or politics, and yet it relates to all these highly formulated departments of culture. It is modified by them; it modifies them; it is generated by them; it generates them. In this part of culture assumption rules, which is often so much stronger than reason.

The right way to begin to deal with such a subject is to gather together as much of its detail as we possibly can. Only by doing so will we become fully aware of what the gifted foreign critic or the stupid native one is not aware of, that in any complex culture there is not a single system of manners but a conflicting variety of manners, and that one of the jobs of a culture is the adjustment of this conflict.

But the nature of our present occasion does not permit this accumulation of detail and so I shall instead try to drive toward a generalization and an hypothesis which, however wrong they turn out to be, may at least permit us to circumscribe the subject. I shall try to generalize the subject of American manners by talking about the attitude of Americans toward the subject of manners itself. And since in a complex culture there are, as I say, many different systems of manners and since I cannot talk about them all, I shall select the manners and the attitude toward manners of the literate, reading, responsible middle class of people who are ourselves. I specify that they be reading people because I shall draw my conclusions from the novels they read. The hypothesis I propose is that our attitude toward manners is the expression of a particular conception of reality.

All literature tends to be concerned with the question of reality—I mean quite simply the old opposition between reality and appearance, between what really is and what merely seems. "Don't you *see?*" is the question we want to shout at Oedipus as he stands before us and before fate in the pride of his rationalism. And at the end of *Oedipus Rex* he demonstrates in a particularly direct way that he now sees what he did not see before. "Don't you *see?*" we want to shout again at Lear and Gloucester, the two deceived, self-deceiving fathers: blindness again, resistance to the clear claims of reality, the seduction by mere appearance. The same with Othello—reality is right under your stupid nose, how *dare* you be such a gull? So with Molière's Orgon—my good man, my honest citizen, merely *look* at Tartuffe and you will know what's what. So with Milton's Eve—"Woman, watch out! Don't you see—anyone can see— that's a *snake!*"

The problem of reality is central, and in a special way, to the great forefather of the novel, the great book of Cervantes, whose four-hundredth birthday was celebrated in 1947. There are two movements of thought in *Don Quixote*, two different and opposed notions of reality. One is the movement which leads toward saying that the world of ordinary practicality *is* reality in its fulness. It is the reality of the present moment in all its powerful immediacy of hunger, cold, and pain, making the past and the future, and all ideas, of no account. When the conceptual, the ideal, and the fanciful come into conflict with this, bringing their notions of the past and the future, then disaster results. For one thing, the ordinary proper ways of life are upset—the chained prisoners are understood to be good men and are released, the whore is taken for a lady. There is general confusion. As for the ideal, the conceptual, the fanciful, or romantic—whatever you want to call it—it fares even worse: it is shown to be ridiculous.

Thus one movement of the novel. But Cervantes changed horses in midstream and found that he was riding Rosinante. Perhaps at first not quite consciously—although the new view is latent in the old from the very beginning—Cervantes begins to show that the world of tangible reality is not the real reality after all. The real reality is rather the wildly conceiving, the madly fantasying mind of the Don: people change, practical reality changes, when they come into its presence.

In any genre it may happen that the first great example contains the whole potentiality of the genre. It has been said that all philosophy is a footnote to Plato. It can be said that all prose fiction is a variation on the theme of *Don Quixote*. Cervantes sets for the novel the problem of appearance and reality: the shifting and conflict of social classes becomes the field of the problem of knowledge, of how we know and of how reliable our knowledge is, which at that very moment of history is vexing the philosophers and scientists. And the poverty of the Don suggests that the novel is born with the appearance of money as a social element—money, the great solvent of the solid fabric of the old society, the great generator of illusion. Or, which is to say much the same thing, the novel is born in response to snobbery.

Snobbery is not the same thing as pride of class. Pride of class may not please us but we must at least grant that it reflects a social function. A man who exhibited class pride—in the day when it was possible to do so—may have been puffed up about what he *was*, but this ultimately depended on what he *did*. Thus, aristocratic pride was based ultimately on the ability to fight and administer. No pride is without fault, but pride of class may be thought of as today we think of pride of profession, toward which we are likely to be lenient.

Snobbery is pride in status without pride in function. And it is an uneasy pride of status. It always asks, "Do I belong—do I really belong? And does he belong? And if I am observed talking to him, will it make me seem to belong or not to belong?" It is the peculiar vice not of aristocratic societies which have their own appropriate vices, but of bourgeois democratic societies. For us the legendary strongholds of snobbery are the Hollywood studios, where two thousand dollars a week dare not talk to three hundred dollars a week for fear he be taken for nothing more than fifteen hundred dollars a week. The dominant emotions of snobbery are uneasiness, self-consciousness, self-defensiveness, the sense that one is not quite real but can in some way acquire reality.

Money is the medium that, for good or bad, makes for a fluent society. It does not make for an equal society but for one in which there is a constant shifting of classes, a frequent change in the personnel of the dominant class. In a shifting society great emphasis is put on appearance—I am using the word now in the common meaning, as when people say that "a good appearance is very important in getting a job." To appear to be established is one of the ways of becoming established. The old notion of the solid merchant who owns far more than he shows increasingly gives way to the ideal of signalizing status by appearance, by showing more than you have: status in a democratic society is presumed to come not with power but with the tokens of power. Hence the development of what Tocqueville saw as a mark of democratic culture, what he called the "hypocrisy of luxury"—instead of the well-made peasant article and the well-made middle-class article, we have the effort of all articles to appear as the articles of the very wealthy.

And a shifting society is bound to generate an interest in appearance in the philosophical sense. When Shakespeare lightly touched on the matter that so largely preoccupies the novelist—that is, the movement from one class to another—and created Malvolio, he immediately involved the question of social standing with the problem of appearance and reality. Malvolio's daydreams of bettering his position present themselves to him as reality, and in revenge his enemies conspire to convince him that he is literally mad and that the world is not as he sees it. The predicament of the characters in A *Midsummer Night's Dream* and of Christopher Sly seems to imply that the meeting of social extremes and the establishment of a person of low class in the privileges of a high class always suggested to Shakespeare's mind some radical instability of the senses and the reason.

The characteristic work of the novel is to record the illusion that snobbery generates and to try to penetrate to the truth which, as the novel assumes, lies hidden beneath all the false appearances. Money, snobbery, the ideal of status, these become in themselves the objects of fantasy, the support of the fantasies of love, freedom, charm, power, as in *Madame Bovary*, whose heroine is the sister, at a three-centuries' remove, of Don Quixote. The greatness of *Great Expectations* begins in its title: modern society bases itself on great expectations which, if ever they are realized, are found to exist by reason of a sordid, hidden reality. The real thing is not the gentility of Pip's life but the hulks and the murder and the rats and decay in the cellarage of the novel.

An English writer, recognizing the novel's central concern with snobbery, recently cried out half-ironically against it. "Who cares whether Pamela finally exasperates Mr. B. into marriage, whether Mr. Elton is more or less than moderately genteel, whether it is sinful for Pendennis nearly to kiss the porter's daughter, whether young men from Boston can ever be as truly refined as middle-aged women in Paris, whether the District Officer's fiancée ought to see so much of Dr. Aziz, whether Lady Chatterly ought to be made love to by the gamekeeper, even if he was an officer during the war? Who cares?"

The novel, of course, tells us much more about life than this. It tells us about the look and feel of things, how things are done and what things are worth and what they cost and what the odds are. If the English novel in its special concern with class does not, as the same writer says, explore the deeper layers of personality, then the French novel in exploring these layers must start and end in class, and the Russian novel, exploring the ultimate possibilities of spirit, does the same—every situation in Dostoevski, no matter how spiritual, starts with a point of social pride and a certain number of rubles. The great novelists knew that matters indicate the largest intentions of men's souls as well as the smallest and they are perpetually concerned to catch the meaning of every dim implicit hint.

The novel, then, is a perpetual quest for reality, the field of its research being always the social world, the material of its analysis being always manners as the indication of the direction of man's soul. When we understand this we can understand the pride of profession that moved D. H. Lawrence to say, "Being a novelist, I consider myself superior to the saint, the scientist, the philosopher and the poet. The novel is the one bright book of life."

Now the novel as I have described it has never really established itself in America. Not that we have not had very great novels but that the novel in America diverges from its classic intention, which, as I have said, is the investigation of the problem of reality beginning in the social field. The fact is that American writers of genius have not turned their minds to society. Poe and Melville were quite apart from it; the reality they sought was only tangential to society. Hawthorne was acute when he insisted that he did not write novels but romances—he thus expressed his awareness of the lack of social texture in his work. Howells never fulfilled himself because, although he saw the social subject clearly, he would never take it with full seriousness. In America in the nineteenth century, Henry James was alone in knowing that to scale the moral and aesthetic heights in the novel one had to use the ladder of social observation.

There is a famous passage in James's life of Hawthorne in which James enumerates the things which are lacking to give the American novel the thick social texture of the English novel—no state; barely a specific national name; no sovereign; no court; no aristocracy; no church; no clergy; no army; no diplomatic service; no country gentlemen; no palaces; no castles; no manors; no old country houses; no parsonages; no thatched cottages; no ivied ruins; no cathedrals; no great universities; no public schools; no political society; no sporting class—no Epsom, no Ascot! That is, no sufficiency of means for the display of a variety of manners, no opportunity for the novelist to do his job of searching out reality, not enough complication of appearance to make the job interesting. Another great American novelist of very different temperament had said much the same thing some decades before: James Fenimore Cooper found that American manners were too simple and dull to nourish the novelist.

This is cogent but it does not explain the condition of the American novel at the present moment. For life in America has increasingly thickened since the nineteenth century. It has not, to be sure, thickened so much as to permit our undergraduates to understand the characters of Balzac, to understand, that is, life in a crowded country where the competitive pressures are great, forcing intense passions to express themselves fiercely and yet within the limitations set by a strong and complicated tradition of manners. Still, life here has become more complex and more pressing. And even so we do not have the novel that touches significantly on society, on manners. Whatever the virtues of Dreiser may be, he could not report the social fact with the kind of accuracy it needs. Sinclair Lewis is shrewd, but no one, however charmed with him as a social satirist, can believe that he does more than a limited job of social understanding. John Dos Passos sees much, sees it often in the great way of Flaubert, but can never use social fact as more than either backdrop or "condition." Of our novelists today perhaps only William Faulkner deals with society as the field of tragic reality and he has the disadvantage of being limited to a provincial scene.

It would seem that Americans have a kind of resistance to looking closely at society. They appear to believe that to touch accurately on the matter of class, to take full note of snobbery, is somehow to demean themselves. It is as if we felt that one cannot touch pitch without being defiled—which, of course, may possibly be the case. Americans will not deny that we have classes and snobbery, but they seem to hold it to be indelicate to take precise cognizance of these phenomena. Consider that Henry James is, among a large part of our reading public, still held to be at fault for noticing society as much as he did. Consider the conversation that has, for some interesting reason, become a part of our literary folklore. Scott Fitzgerald said to Ernest Hemingway, "The very rich are different from us." Hemingway replied, "Yes, they have more money." I have seen the exchange quoted many times and always with the intention of suggesting that Fitzgerald was infatuated by wealth and had received a salutary rebuke from his democratic friend. But the truth is that after a certain point quantity of money does indeed change into quality of personality: in an important sense the very rich *are* different from us. So are the very powerful, the very gifted, the very poor. Fitzgerald was right, and almost for that remark alone he must surely have been received in Balzac's bosom in the heaven of novelists.

It is of course by no means true that the American reading class has no interest in society. Its interest fails only before society as it used to be represented by the novel. And if we look at the commercially successful serious novels of the last decade, we see that almost all of them have been written from an intense social awareness—it might be said that our present definition of a serious book is one which holds before us some image of society to consider and condemn. What is the situation of the dispossessed Oklahoma farmer and whose fault it is, what situation the Jew finds himself in, what it means to be a Negro, how one gets a bell for Adano, what is the advertising business really like, what it means to be insane and how society takes care of you or fails to do so—these are the matters which are believed to be most fertile for the novelist, and certainly they are the subjects most favored by our reading class.

The public is properly not deceived about the quality of most of these books. If the question of quality is brought up, the answer is likely to be: no, they are not great, they are not imaginative, they are not "literature." But there is an unexpressed addendum: and perhaps they are all the better for not being imaginative, for not being literature—they are not literature, they are reality, and *in a time like this* what we need is reality in large doses.

When, generations from now, the historian of our times undertakes to describe the assumptions of our culture, he will surely discover that the word *reality* is of central importance in his understanding of us. He will observe that for some of our philosophers the meaning of the word was a good deal in doubt, but that for our political writers, for many of our literary critics, and for most of our reading public, the word did not open discussion but, rather, closed it. Reality, as conceived by us, is whatever is external and hard, gross, unpleasant. Involved in its meaning is the idea of power conceived in a particular way. Some time ago I had occasion to remark how, in the critical estimates of Theodore Dreiser, it is always being said that Dreiser has many faults but that it cannot be denied that he has great power. No one ever says "a kind of power." Power is assumed to be always "brute" power, crude, ugly, and undiscriminating, the way an elephant appears to be. It is seldom understood to be the way an elephant actually is, precise and discriminating; or the way electricity is, swift and absolute and scarcely embodied.

The word *reality* is an honorific word and the future historian will naturally try to discover our notion of its pejorative opposite, appearance, mere appearance. He will find it in our feeling about the internal; whenever we detect evidences of style and thought we suspect that reality is being a little betrayed, that "mere subjectivity" is creeping in. There follows from this our feeling about complication, modulation, personal idiosyncrasy, and about social forms, both the great and the small.

Having gone so far, our historian is then likely to discover a puzzling contradiction. For we claim that the great advantage of reality is its hard, bedrock, concrete quality, yet everything we say about it tends toward the abstract and it almost seems that what we want to find in reality is abstraction itself. Thus we believe that one of the unpleasant bedrock facts is social class, but we become extremely impatient if ever we are told that social class is indeed so real that it produces actual differences of personality. The very people who talk most about class and its evils think that Fitzgerald was bedazzled and Hemingway right. Or again, it might be observed that in the degree that we speak in praise of the "individual" we have contrived that our literature should have no individuals in it—no people, that is, who are shaped by our liking for the interesting and memorable and special and precious.

Here, then, is our generalization: that in proportion as we have committed ourselves to our particular idea of reality we have lost our interest in manners. For the novel this is a definitive condition because it is inescapably true that in the novel manners make men. It does not matter in what sense the word manners is taken—it is equally true of the sense which so much interested Proust or of the sense which interested Dickens or, indeed, of the sense which interested Homer. The Duchesse de Guermantes unable to delay departure for the dinner party to receive properly from her friend Swann the news that he is dying but able to delay to change the black slippers her husband objects to; Mr. Pickwick and Sam Weller; Priam and Achilles—they exist by reason of their observed manners.

So true is this, indeed, so creative is the novelist's awareness of manners, that we may say that it is a function of his love. It is some sort of love that Fielding has for Squire Western that allows him to note the great, gross details which bring the insensitive sentient man into existence for us. If that is true, we are forced to certain conclusions about our literature and about the particular definition of reality which has shaped it. The reality we admire tells us that the observation of manners is trivial and even malicious, that there are things much more important for the novel to consider. As a consequence our social sympathies have indeed broadened, but in proportion as they have done so we have lost something of our power of love, for our novels can never create characters who truly exist. We make public demands for love, for we know that broad social feeling should be infused with warmth, and we receive a kind of public product which we try to believe is not cold potatoes. The reviewers of Helen Howe's novel of a few years ago, We Happy Few, thought that its satiric first part, an excellent comment on the manners of a small but significant segment of society, was ill-natured and unsatisfactory, but they approved the second part, which is the record of the heroine's self-accusing effort to come into communication with the great soul of America. Yet it should have been clear that the satire had its source in a kind of affection, in a real community of feeling, and told the truth, while the second part, said to be so "warm," was mere abstraction, one more example of our public idea of ourselves and our national life. John Steinbeck is generally praised both for his reality and his warmheartedness, but in The Wayward Bus the lower-class characters receive a doctrinaire affection in proportion to the suffering and sexuality which define their existence, while the ill-observed middle-class characters are made to submit not only to moral judgment but to the withdrawal of all fellow-feeling, being mocked for their very misfortunes and almost for their susceptibility to death. Only a little thought or even less feeling is required to perceive that the basis of his creation is the coldest response to abstract ideas.

Two novelists of the older sort had a prevision of our present situation. In Henry James's The Princess Casamassima there is a scene in which the heroine is told about the existence of a conspiratorial group of revolutionaries pledged to the destruction of all existing society. She has for some time been drawn by a desire for social responsibility; she has wanted to help "the people," she has longed to discover just such a group as she now hears about, and she exclaims in joy, "Then it's real, it's solid!" We are intended to hear the Princess's glad cry with the knowledge that she is a woman who despises herself, "that in the

darkest hour of her life she sold herself for a title and a fortune. She regards
her doing so as such a terrible piece of frivolity that she can never for the rest
of her days be serious enough to make up for it." She seeks out poverty, suffering, sacrifice, and death because she believes that these things alone are real;
she comes to believe that art is contemptible; she withdraws her awareness and
love from the one person of her acquaintance who most deserves them, and she
increasingly scorns whatever suggests variety and modulation, and is more and
more dissatisfied with the humanity of the present in her longing for the more
perfect humanity of the future. It is one of the great points that the novel
makes that with each passionate step that she takes toward what she calls the
real, the solid, she in fact moves further away from the life-giving reality.

In E. M. Forster's *The Longest Journey* there is a young man named
Stephen Wonham who, although a gentleman born, has been carelessly brought
up and has no real notion of the responsibilities of his class. He has a friend,
a country laborer, a shepherd, and on two occasions he outrages the feelings of
certain intelligent, liberal, democratic people in the book by his treatment of
his friend. Once, when the shepherd reneges on a bargain, Stephen quarrels
with him and knocks him down; and in the matter of the loan of a few
shillings he insists that the money be paid back to the last farthing. The intelligent, liberal, democratic people know that this is not the way to act to the
poor. But Stephen cannot think of the shepherd as the poor nor, although he
is a country laborer, as an object of research by J. L. and Barbara Hammond;
he is rather a reciprocating subject in a relationship of affection—as we say, a
friend—and therefore liable to anger and required to pay his debts. But this
view is held to be deficient in intelligence, liberalism, and democracy.

In these two incidents we have the premonition of our present cultural and
social situation, the passionate self-reproachful addiction to a "strong" reality
which must limit its purview to maintain its strength, the replacement by abstraction of natural, direct human feeling. It is worth noting, by the way, how
clear is the line by which the two novels descend from *Don Quixote*—how
their young heroes come into life with large preconceived ideas and are
knocked about in consequence; how both are concerned with the problem of
appearance and reality, *The Longest Journey* quite explicitly, *The Princess
Casamassima* by indirection; how both evoke the question of the nature of reality by contriving a meeting and conflict of diverse social classes and take
scrupulous note of the differences of manners. Both have as their leading characters people who are specifically and passionately concerned with social injustice and both agree in saying that to act against social injustice is right and
noble but that to choose to act so does not settle all moral problems but on
the contrary generates new ones of an especially difficult sort.

I have elsewhere given the name of moral realism to the perception of the
dangers of the moral life itself. Perhaps at no other time has the enterprise of
moral realism ever been so much needed, for at no other time have so many
people committed themselves to moral righteousness. We have the books that

point out the bad conditions, that praise us for taking progressive attitudes. We have no books that raise questions in our minds not only about conditions but about ourselves, that lead us to refine our motives and ask what might lie behind our good impulses.

There is nothing so very terrible in discovering that something does lie behind. Nor does it need a Freud to make the discovery. Here is a publicity release sent out by one of our oldest and most respectable publishing houses. Under the heading "What Makes Books Sell?" it reads, "Blank & Company reports that the current interest in horror stories has attracted a great number of readers to John Dash's novel . . . because of its depiction of Nazi brutality. Critics and readers alike have commented on the stark realism of Dash's handling of the torture scenes in the book. The publishers originally envisaged a woman's market because of the love story, now find men reading the book because of the other angle." This does not suggest a more than usual depravity in the male reader, for "the other angle" has always had a fascination, no doubt a bad one, even for those who would not themselves commit or actually witness an act of torture. I cite the extreme example only to suggest that something may indeed lie behind our sober intelligent interest in moral politics. In this instance the pleasure in the cruelty is protected and licensed by moral indignation. In other instances moral indignation, which has been said to be the favorite emotion of the middle class, may be in itself an exquisite pleasure. To understand this does not invalidate moral indignation but only sets up the conditions on which it ought to be entertained, only says when it is legitimate and when not.

But, the answer comes, however important it may be for moral realism to raise questions in our minds about our motives, is it not at best a matter of secondary importance? Is it not of the first importance that we be given a direct and immediate report on the reality that is daily being brought to dreadful birth? The novels that have done this have effected much practical good, bringing to consciousness the latent feelings of many people, making it harder for them to be unaware or indifferent, creating an atmosphere in which injustice finds it harder to thrive. To speak of moral realism is all very well. But it is an elaborate, even fancy, phrase and it is to be suspected of having the intention of sophisticating the simple reality that is easily to be conceived. Life presses us so hard, time is so short, the suffering of the world is so huge, simple, unendurable—anything that complicates our moral fervor in dealing with reality as we immediately see it and wish to drive headlong upon it must be regarded with some impatience.

True enough: and therefore any defense of what I have called moral realism must be made not in the name of some highflown fineness of feeling but in the name of simple social practicality. And there is indeed a simple social fact to which moral realism has a simple practical relevance, but it is a fact very difficult for us nowadays to perceive. It is that the moral passions are even more willful and imperious and impatient than the self-seeking passions. All history is at one in telling us that their tendency is to be not only liberating but also restrictive.

It is probable that at this time we are about to make great changes in our social system. The world is ripe for such changes and if they are not made in the direction of greater social liberality, the direction forward, they will almost of necessity be made in the direction backward, of a terrible social niggardliness. We all know which of those directions we want. But it is not enough to want it, not even enough to work for it—we must want it and work for it with intelligence. Which means that we must be aware of the dangers which lie in our most generous wishes. Some paradox of our natures leads us, when once we have made our fellow men the objects of our enlightened interest, to go on to make them the objects of our pity, then of our wisdom, ultimately of our coercion. It is to prevent this corruption, the most ironic and tragic that man knows, that we stand in need of the moral realism which is the product of the free play of the moral imagination.

For our time the most effective agent of the moral imagination has been the novel of the last two hundred years. It was never, either aesthetically or morally, a perfect form and its faults and failures can be quickly enumerated. But its greatness and its practical usefulness lay in its unremitting work of involving the reader himself in the moral life, inviting him to put his own motives under examination, suggesting that reality is not as his conventional education has led him to see it. It taught us, as no other genre ever did, the extent of human variety and the value of this variety. It was the literary form to which the emotions of understanding and forgiveness were indigenous, as if by the definition of the form itself. At the moment its impulse does not seem strong, for there never was a time when the virtues of its greatness were so likely to be thought of as weaknesses. Yet there never was a time when its particular activity was so much needed, was of so much practical, political, and social use—so much so that if its impulse does not respond to the need, we shall have reason to be sad not only over a waning form of art but also over our waning freedom.

❧ ❧ ❧

*William Faulkner*

# Man Will Prevail[1]

*Speech of Acceptance upon the award of the Nobel Prize for Literature, delivered in Stockholm on the tenth of December, nineteen hundred fifty.*

I FEEL that this award was not made to me as a man, but to my work—a life's work in the agony and sweat of the human spirit, not for glory and least of all for profit, but to create out of the materials of the human spirit something

[1] Reprinted by courtesy of Random House, Inc.

which did not exist before. So this award is only mine in trust. It will not be difficult to find a dedication for the money part of it commensurate with the purpose and significance of its origin. But I would like to do the same with the acclaim too, by using this moment as a pinnacle from which I might be listened to by the young men and women already dedicated to the same anguish and travail, among whom is already that one who will some day stand here where I am standing.

Our tragedy today is a general and universal physical fear so long sustained by now that we can even bear it. There are no longer problems of the spirit. There is only the question: When will I be blown up? Because of this, the young man or woman writing today has forgotten the problems of the human heart in conflict with itself which alone can make good writing because only that is worth writing about, worth the agony and the sweat.

He must learn them again. He must teach himself that the basest of all things is to be afraid; and, teaching himself that, forget it forever, leaving no room in his workshop for anything but the old verities and truths of the heart, the old universal truths lacking which any story is ephemeral and doomed— love and honor and pity and pride and compassion and sacrifice. Until he does so, he labors under a curse. He writes not of love but of lust, of defeats in which nobody loses anything of value, of victories without hope and, worst of all, without pity or compassion. His griefs grieve on no universal bones, leaving no scars. He writes not of the heart but of the glands.

Until he relearns these things, he will write as though he stood among and watched the end of man. I decline to accept the end of man. It is easy enough to say that man is immortal simply because he will endure: that when the last ding-dong of doom has clanged and faded from the last worthless rock hanging tideless in the last red and dying evening, that even then there will still be one more sound: that of his puny inexhaustible voice, still talking. I refuse to accept this. I believe that man will not merely endure: he will prevail. He is immortal, not because he alone among creatures has an inexhaustible voice, but because he has a soul, a spirit capable of compassion and sacrifice and endurance. The poet's, the writer's, duty is to write about these things. It is his privilege to help man endure by lifting his heart, by reminding him of the courage and honor and hope and pride and compassion and pity and sacrifice which have been the glory of his past. The poet's voice need not merely be the record of man, it can be one of the props, the pillars to help him endure and prevail.

# ❧ ❧ ❧ V. Science

# The Nature of Science

*James B. Conant*

## Concerning Electricity and Combustion[1]

THIS BOOK is in no sense a presentation of the history of science or of any branch of science. The objective is to indicate how certain principles might be taught by illustrations drawn from the development of science. . . . In this chapter two case histories are presented both drawn from the end of the eighteenth century. The first concerns the discovery of the electric battery, the second concerns the chemical revolution which placed our knowledge of combustion on a sound basis. . . .

### THE ROLE OF THE ACCIDENTAL DISCOVERY

The layman is frequently confused in regard to the role of the accidental discovery on the one hand and the planned experiment on the other. This is particularly true in connection with the development of new techniques and the evolution of new concepts from experiment. The case history which I recommend for a study of these topics is the work of Galvani and Volta on the electric current. This case history illustrates the fact that an accidental discovery may lead by a series of experiments (which must be well planned) to a new technique or a new concept or both; it also shows that in the exploration of a new phenomenon the experiments may be well planned without any "working hypothesis" as to the nature of the phenomenon, but that shortly an explanation is sure to arise. A new conceptual scheme will be evolved. This may be on a grand scale and have wide applicability, or may be strictly limited to the phenomenon in question. A test of the new concept or group of concepts in either instance will probably lead to new discoveries and the eventual establishment, modification, or overthrow of the conceptual scheme in question.

### GALVANI'S DISCOVERIES

The case history begins with certain observations made by Luigi Galvani, an Italian physician, a professor at Bologna, some time before 1786. This investi-

[1] From James B. Conant, *On Understanding Science: An Historical Approach* (New Haven: Yale University Press, 1947), pp. 65-97, with omissions. Reprinted by permission of the publishers.

gator noted the twitching of a frog's leg when the crural nerves were touched by a metallic scalpel in the neighborhood of an electrostatic machine from which sparks were drawn. *He followed up his observation.* At this point in a course on the Tactics and Strategy of Science the instructor would wax eloquent. He would remind the class that time and time again throughout the history of science the consequences of following up or not following up accidental discoveries have been very great. The analogy of a general's taking advantage of an enemy's error or a lucky break, like the capture of the Remagen bridge, could hardly fail to enter the discussion. Pasteur once wrote that "chance favors only the prepared mind." This is excellently illustrated by the case history at hand. The Dutch naturalist, Swammerdam, had previously discovered that if you lay bare the muscle of a frog in much the same way as Galvani did, grasp a tendon in one hand and touch the frog's nerve with a scalpel held in the other hand, a twitching will result. But Swammerdam never followed up his work. Galvani did. In his own words, "I had dissected and prepared a frog . . . and while I was attending to something else, I laid it on a table on which stood an electrical machine at some distance. . . . Now when one of the persons who were present touched accidentally and lightly the inner crural nerves of the frog with the point of a scalpel all the muscles of the legs seemed to contract again and again. . . . Another one who was there, who was helping us in electrical researches, thought that he had noticed that the action was excited when a spark was discharged from the conductor of the machine. Being astonished by this new phenomenon he called my attention to it, who at that time had something else in mind and was deep in thought. Whereupon I was inflamed with an incredible zeal and eagerness to test the same and to bring to light what was concealed in it."

Galvani did not succeed in bringing to light all that was concealed in the new phenomenon. But he proceeded far enough to make the subsequent discoveries inevitable. In a series of well-planned experiments he explored the obvious variables, but without a clear-cut, over-all hypothesis. This is the usual situation when a new phenomenon is encountered by a gifted experimenter. A series of working hypotheses spring to mind, are tested and either discarded or incorporated into a conceptual scheme which gradually develops. For example, Galvani first determined whether or not sparks had to be drawn from the electrical machine in order to occasion twitching. He found "Without fail there occurred lively contractions . . . at the same instant as that in which the spark jumped. . . ."

The nerves and muscles of the frog's leg constituted a sensitive detector of an electric charge. Galvani found that not only must a spark be passing from the electrostatic machine but the metallic blade of the scalpel must be in contact with the hand of the experimenter. In this way a small charge originating from the electrical disturbance, namely the spark, passed down the conducting human body through the scalpel to the nerve. So far the physician was on sound and fruitful ground. There now occurred one of those coincidences which more than once has initially baffled an investigator but eventually led to great advances. The frog's leg could under certain circumstances act not only as a sensitive electrical detector but as a source of electricity as well. When this happened, the electricity self-generated so to speak actuated the detector. One can readily see that the superposition of these two effects could be most bewildering and misleading. This was particularly so since the conditions under which the frog's leg became a source of electricity were totally unconnected with any electrical phenomena then known. The variable was the nature of the metal or I should say metals used. For Galvani discovered and duly recorded that the electrostatic machine could be dispensed with if the leg and the nerve were connected together by two *different* metals. Under these conditions the twitching occurred. (The experiment was usually performed as follows: a curved rod was made to touch simultaneously both a hook passing through the spinal cord of the frog and the "muscles of the leg or the feet.") "Thus, for example," wrote Galvani, "if the whole rod was iron or the hook was iron . . . the contractions either did not occur or were very small. But if one of them was iron and the other brass, or better if it was silver (silver seems to us the best of all the metals for conducting animal electricity) there occur repeated and much greater and more prolonged contractions."

Galvani had discovered the principle of the electric battery without knowing it. His two metals separated by the moist animal tissue were a battery, the frog's leg the detector. Every reader can perform the equivalent of Galvani's experiment himself. A copper coin and a silver one placed above and below the tongue when touched together produce in the tongue a peculiar "taste." A very small electric current flows and our tongue records the fact through a series of interactions of electricity and nerves much in the same way as did Galvani's "prepared" frogs. Not having a suspicion of all this, however, Galvani developed a conceptual scheme (an hypothesis on the grand scale, we might say) to account for all the phenomena in terms of what was then known about electricity which was derived entirely from experiment with electrostatic machines. Having found outside electrical disturbances unnecessary (when he unwittingly used the *right* metallic combination!) the experiments, he says, "cause us to think that possibly the electricity was present in the animal itself." Galvani's following up of an accidental discovery by a series of controlled experiments had led to a recording of the significant facts, but it was to be another Italian who developed the fruitful concept. It was Volta who in the late 1790's, continuing the study of the production of electricity by the contact of two different metals, invented the electric battery as a source of what we now often call Galvanic electricity.

### VOLTA'S INVENTION OF THE ELECTRIC BATTERY

Alessandro Volta (1745-1827) of Padua had earlier invented a new form of instrument for detecting small charges of electricity. He began by agreeing with Galvani about animal electricity and went about studying it. With his new instrument, a sensitive condensing electrometer, Volta explored various combinations of variables related to Galvani's early experiments and found that the frog could be eliminated in favor of almost any moist material. This discovery might be considered an example of the accidental discovery, but if so it is of a different order from that of Galvani. Explorations with new techniques and tools, if undertaken in a more or less orderly fashion, almost always turn up unexpected facts. In this sense a great majority of new facts of science are accidental discoveries. But the difference between this sort of experience and the example afforded by Galvani's work is obvious. Volta's new discovery amounted, of course, to the invention of the electric battery; for he showed that electricity was produced when two different metals were separated by water containing salt or lye. This was most conveniently done by using moistened paper. In a letter to the President of the Royal Society of London in 1800 Volta wrote "30, 40, 60 or more pieces of copper, or rather of silver, each in contact with a piece of tin, or of zinc, which is much better, and as many layers of water or of some other liquid which is a better conductor than pure water, such as salt-water or lye and so forth, or pieces of pasteboard or of leather, etc. well soaked with these liquids; . . . such an alternative series of these three sorts of conductors always in the same order, constitutes my new instrument; which imitates . . . the effects of Leyden jars. . . ." (see Figure 1). This new battery was a

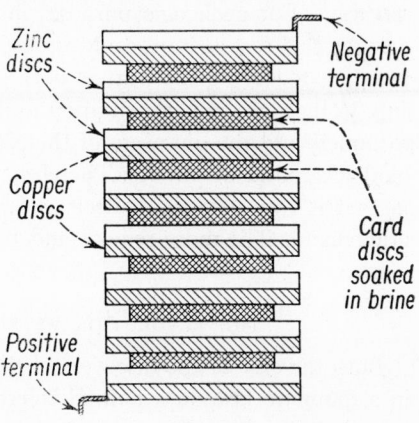

FIG. 1. *One form of Volta's battery or pile.*

source of electricity different from the electrostatic generator already known in 1800; it was the first source of continuous current. The battery produced electricity of low potential but of considerable quantity (low voltage, relatively high amperage); the sparks from a frictional machine are brief spasms of current of high potential but very low amperage.

There was a hot controversy between Galvani's disciples (Galvani died in 1798) and Volta about whether or not there was such a thing as animal electricity, and what caused the twitching of the frog's leg in the first experiments. Volta soon lost interest in the quarrel and devoted his attention to the study of his new battery. Today we have a rather complete and highly satisfactory conceptual scheme in which all the facts about electric batteries find their place. This is not the case, however, with observations about muscles, nerves, and electric currents in animal tissue. In this field one working hypothesis still replaces another and new experiments are still throwing new light on an ancient phenomenon. In a sense, we have not yet finished with Galvani's very first observation, but have finished with Volta's discovery. The original controversy centered on the question, is there animal electricity? This has now become largely a meaningless question, but in attempting to find an answer Volta discovered the electric battery. Such is often the course of scientific history. We end by solving a problem other than the one first at issue.

Another case history which illustrates the role of the accidental discovery, the well-planned experiments by which it may be followed up, the role of the working hypothesis, the development of an hypothesis on the grand scale, and the rapid emergence of both a new technique and a new concept is furnished by a study of the discovery of X rays. The story is familiar to all scientists though perhaps it is not generally known that before Roentgen announced his discovery, several other investigators had noticed the fogging of photographic plates near an electric discharge tube. Roentgen followed up his accidental observation. For pedagogic purposes in a course on the Tactics and Strategy of Science this case history could be used to supplement the one just given or in place of it. Roentgen's work is both simpler and more complex than Galvani's and Volta's; the experimentation and reasoning are more straightforward, but to understand the discovery of the X rays the student should have a considerable background of physics. Therefore, the eighteenth-century example is better in that it almost explains itself as far as technical terms are involved. On the other hand, it is more remote and perhaps less interesting to the average layman.

### THE REVOLUTIONARY EFFECT OF NEW TECHNIQUES

Both the case of the discovery of the electric battery and that of X rays show in a dramatic fashion a point I referred to in the last chapter, namely, that a new technique may have an almost revolutionary effect. With the new electric battery in the beginning of the nineteenth century. Humphry Davy and many others discovered all sorts of new electrochemical and physical phenomena; from them in turn came in rapid succession new techniques and new concepts. Likewise in our own day after the publication of an account of the X-ray tube, new experimental facts came forth in torrents. Tremendous spurts in the progress of the various sciences are almost always connected with the development of a new technique or the sudden emergence of a new concept. It is as though a group of prospectors were hunting in barren ground and suddenly struck a rich vein of ore. All at once everyone works feverishly and the gold begins to flow.

### TWO FURTHER PRINCIPLES IN THE TACTICS AND
### STRATEGY OF SCIENCE

Let us now turn to the second case history to be considered in this chapter. It is an example drawn from the history of chemistry in the second half of the eighteenth century, and, it is only fair to warn the reader, a most complicated case. Perhaps too much effort is required to master the facts involved to make this a good example for the layman. But I believe it should be included in the course I am proposing because in it two important principles in the Tactics and Strategy of Science are illustrated in a peculiarly striking fashion. These principles are as follows:

First, a useful concept may be a barrier to the acceptance of a better one if long-intrenched in the minds of scientists.

Second, experimental discoveries must fit the time; facts may be at hand for years without their significance being realized; the total scientific situation must be favorable for the acceptance of new views.

### THE OVERTHROW OF THE PHLOGISTON THEORY

The case history which illustrates excellently these two important points might be entitled "the overthrow of the phlogiston theory" or "Lavoisier's work on combustion in the 1770's." As indicated by the first phrase the case also affords a classic example of the mustering of evidence pro and con when two rival concepts are in collision. This phenomenon though frequent is usually so transient in the history of science as to be hard to capture for purposes of historical study. In the investigation of combustion the normal progress of science was, so to speak, delayed; this fact, in a sense, accounts for why a study of this difficult passage in scientific history is of special significance to those interested in the Tactics and Strategy of Science.

The easiest way to understand the revolution in chemistry associated with the name of Lavoisier is first to describe the phenomena in question in terms of modern concepts; then to show how for nearly a hundred years everyone was thoroughly confused. This pedagogic device would have to be used by the instructor in the course I am suggesting. It involves the dogmatic statement of a certain amount of popularized physics and chemistry, but I doubt if the presentation would be much more arbitrary in this respect than most freshman courses. Indeed, some of the material might be said to be common knowledge today.

Almost every high-school graduate "knows" (I put quotation marks around the word) that air is primarily a mixture of oxygen gas and nitrogen gas; furthermore, when a candle or a match or a cigarette "burns," heat and light are being evolved by a chemical reaction involving oxygen. This is called "combustion." If we burn enough material in a closed space, the combustion stops because the oxygen is used up. What burns? Some but not all of the students will say that in the cases mentioned it is a group of carbon compounds, and some will add that the products of combustion are carbon dioxide, $CO_2$ and water, $H_2O$. Anyone who has an elementary knowledge of chemical symbols usually loves to share the information! Suppose you heat molten tin in air at a high temperature for a long time, and the bright metal becomes covered with a scum, obviously not a metal. What has happened? A combination with oxygen —an oxide is formed—the bright boys and girls answer. Correct. Suppose we heat this non-metallic substance, an oxide, with carbon. What would happen? The carbon would combine with the oxygen, giving an oxide of carbon and leaving the metal. This is what happens in making iron from iron ore, the very bright boy tells you.

All very simple and plain. And you can set students to work in high-school laboratories to prove it. Yet it is an historic fact that at the time of the American Revolution not one philosopher or experimentalist out of one hundred could have given you an inkling of this explanation which we now designate as "correct." Instead, they would have talked learnedly of "phlogiston," a name probably totally unfamiliar to all but the chemists who read this book. Nearly a hundred years after Newton, and still everyone was thoroughly bewildered by such a simple matter as combustion! This fact needs to be brought home to all who would understand science and who talk of the "scientific method."

The chemical revolution was practically contemporary with the American Revolution and, of course, just preceded the French Revolution. Lavoisier, the man who singlehanded but building on the work of others made the revolution, lost his head at the hands of the Revolutionary Tribune in 1794 (though he was by no means hostile to the basic aims of the great social and political upheaval). Whether or not he was betrayed by a scientific colleague (Fourcroy) who at least was an ardent supporter of the extreme party then in power, is an intriguing historical question; its study would be a by-product of this case history in which certain students would take great interest. Likewise, the fact that another prominent figure in the final controversy was Priestley, a Unitarian clergyman, who was made an honorary citizen by the French Assembly and then fled to America in the very year of Lavoisier's execution to escape a reactionary English mob, adds zest to the story. There is no lack of material to connect science with society in the late eighteenth century, though the connection I think is more dramatic than significant; at all events, for keeping up students' interest it can hardly be surpassed.

## THE CLASSIC EXPERIMENT ON THE ROLE OF
### OXYGEN IN COMBUSTION

The chemical revolution took place during the years 1772-78. By the later date Lavoisier had made clear to the scientific world the role of oxygen in combustion. His classic experiment, often described in elementary textbooks, was as follows: Mercury heated in common air produces a red material (an oxide we would say, a "calx" to the chemists of the eighteenth century). In a closed space about one fifth of the air disappears. The red material weighs more than the metal from which it was formed. Therefore, something has disappeared from the air and combined with the metal. The red material, the oxide or calx, is next strongly heated in an enclosed space with the sun's rays brought to a focus by a large lens or "burning glass," a gas is evolved and the metal regenerated. The new gas is the "something" which disappeared from the original air, for the amount is the same, and the calx has lost weight in the right amount.

The new gas (oxygen) mixed with the residue from the first experiment yields a mixture which is identical with common air. (Figures 2 and 3.)

The experiments are simple, the proof appears to be complete. (Lavoisier, of course, generalized far beyond the case of mercury.) But the new conceptual scheme was by no means accepted at once with great acclaim. Quite the contrary. Lavoisier had to drive home his points with telling arguments. Slowly

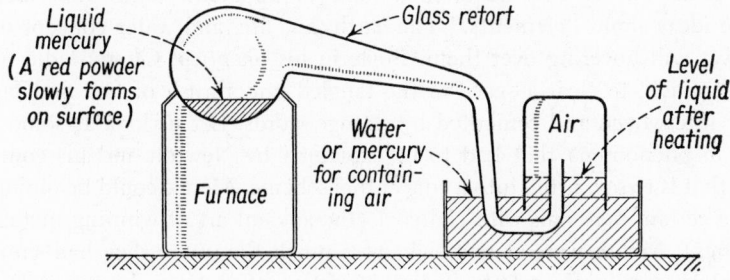

FIG. 2. *Mercury heated in air absorbs oxygen.*

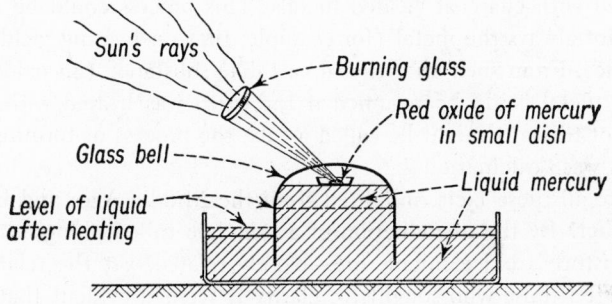

FIG. 3. *Red oxide of mercury heated very hot evolves oxygen. (The temperature in this experiment must be very much higher than in the formation of the oxide.)*

his French contemporaries were won over, but Priestley and Watt of the steam-engine fame and Cavendish and scores of others continued to cling to the phlogiston theory for a decade. Priestley's case is particularly interesting. This English experimenter had actually provided Lavoisier with an important clue when in 1774 he told him about his preparation of oxygen gas by heating red oxide of mercury. But Priestley died in 1804 without ever being converted to the new doctrine.

Why was there this reluctance to modify ideas in the light of beautifully clear experiments, and why were the men of the eighteenth century so long in getting on the right track? There were two reasons: first, one conceptual scheme—the phlogiston theory—had acquired an almost paralyzing hold on their minds; and second, elucidating the facts necessary to overthrow the theory involved experiments with gases which were then extremely difficult.

## THE SIGNIFICANCE OF THE PHLOGISTON THEORY

The phlogiston theory in its day was, we must first realize, a long step forward. In the sixteenth and seventeenth centuries those who were interested in making some sense out of what we now call chemistry were wandering in a bewildering forest. From the alchemists and the practical men, particularly the metal makers, they had acquired a mass of apparently unrelated facts and strange ideas about "elements." The earth, air, fire, and water concept of Aristotle was still hovering over them. Boyle in his *Skeptical Chymist* did a little, but not much, to clear a space in the tangled underbrush of fact and fancy so closely interwoven and cemented by strange words. Let us look at some of the common phenomena that had to be explained by Newton and his contemporaries, that is to say, fitted into a conceptual scheme. Metals could be obtained by heating certain materials with charcoal (the ancient art of winning metals from their ores). Metals were at first sight very much the same; they had similar superficial properties. Even today the classification of metal and nonmetal appeals at once to a layman. Other solids were called "earths" (oxides for us today) or else, like charcoal or sulfur, they were "combustible principles." Some earths when heated with charcoal yielded metals. This process could be reversed, for often but not always the metal (for example, tin) on heating yielded an earthlike substance. From such an artificial earthlike substance (an oxide in modern terms) the metal could be regained if the earth was heated with charcoal. A pure earth of this sort might be called a calx, the process of forming it by heating a metal was "calcination."

How were all these facts, inherited from the Middle Ages and before, to be fitted together? By the introduction of a principle called phlogiston, closely related to Aristotle's old element, fire—closely related, yet the relationship was never clear. To those who sought for clarity it seemed evident that there must be some common principle involved in the process of making various metals from their calces and vice versa. Therefore, let us call this something phlogiston, they in effect declared. When phlogiston was added to a calx you had a metal, when you removed it from a metal a calx was formed; phlogiston was in a sense a metalizing principle. Note there is a common-sense assumption more or less implied in this line of reasoning: except for gold, and occasionally a few other metals, calces *not* metals occur in nature. Therefore, these calces were the simpler materials, something must be added to them to make them metals. Since metals were so alike, the "something" was obviously the same in all cases. We shall call it phlogiston, said Becher, and his pupil Stahl in a series of books published in 1703-31.

Here was a key to unlock a maze, and it was immediately accepted. Here was a concept which provided a pattern into which a mass of otherwise unrelated phenomena could be fitted. Substances were rich or poor in phlogiston, this seemed easy to establish. What was phlogiston itself? It probably was never to be seen. Substances rich in phlogiston easily took fire and, indeed, fire was perhaps a manifestation of phlogiston, or worked with it at least. For some, fire was still an element. Charcoal was a phlogiston-rich material and on heating with a metallic calx gave up its phlogiston to the calx, making a metal. By itself charcoal burned, the phlogiston appearing as fire or combined with the air. Sulfur, using the word in its modern sense, was found free in nature; it burned when heated and yielded an acid, vitriolic acid (sulfuric acid in modern terms). Clearly, this sulfur was only vitriolic acid highly "phlogisticated"; the burning set the phlogiston free and yielded the acid.

We can write these changes in diagrammatic form to illustrate how the chemists of the eighteenth century thought:

Calx + phlogiston (from charcoal) ⟶ metal.
Metal heated in air ⟶ calx + phlogiston (to the air).
Charcoal burned yields phlogiston to the air accompanied by fire.
Phlogisticated vitriolic acid (sulfur to us) burns yielding phlogiston
    (to the air) + vitriolic acid (sulfuric acid).

There was one very simple flaw in all this argument and the interesting fact is that this flaw was known and talked about for fifty years before the phlogiston theory was even shaken, much less overthrown. This is a beautiful illustration of the principle in the Tactics and Strategy of Science referred to at the beginning of this section, namely, that a scientific discovery must fit the times. As early as 1630 (note the date—before Boyle was born) a Frenchman, Jean Rey, studied the calcination of tin and showed that the calx weighed more than the tin from which it was formed. More than that, he gave an explanation closely in accord with Lavoisier's ideas of 150 years later. For he said, "this increase in weight comes from the air, which in the vessel has been rendered denser, heavier, and in some measure adhesive . . . which air mixes with the calx . . . and becomes attached to its most minute particles. . . ." Boyle confirmed the increase in weight of metals in calcination in 1673 but added no support to Rey's shrewd guess (it was little more) as to the reason. In fact, if anything, he led subsequent investigators down the wrong path. At least in retrospect it seems that if he had followed up only a little more boldly his own experiments, the phlogiston theory might never have been proposed or, if proposed, never accepted seriously. Yet it is all too easy to imagine that even a still greater genius than Boyle could have discovered oxygen and revealed its role in combustion and calcination in the seventeenth century. Too much physics as well as chemistry lay under wraps which were only slowly removed by the labors of many men.

At all events, Boyle put forward the hypothesis that fire, the Aristotelian principle, had passed through the walls of the glass vessel used and combined with the metal, thereby giving it weight. This was, of course, not the same as the phlogiston theory formulated a generation later; in a sense it was the opposite because according to Boyle something was *added* to the metal in calcination, namely, fire. While in the phlogiston theory something, namely, phlogiston, was *removed*. But Boyle's writings did focus attention on the heat and flame (a characteristic of fire and calcination) rather than on the air which had figured in Rey's explanation.

### A SCIENTIFIC DISCOVERY MUST FIT THE TIMES

Rey's ideas about the air seem to have been lost in the subsequent 150 years, but not the facts of calcination. That a calx weighed more than the metal was well known throughout the eighteenth century, but this fact was *not* recognized as being fatal to the phlogiston theory. Here is an important point. Does it argue for the stupidity of the experimental philosophers of the day as a few writers once would have us think? Not at all; it merely demonstrates that in complex affairs of science, one is concerned with trying to account for a variety of facts and with welding them into a conceptual scheme; one fact is not by itself sufficient to wreck the scheme. In discussing Galileo's failure and Torricelli's successful interpretation of lift pumps, I referred to the principle that a conceptual scheme is never discarded merely because of a few stubborn facts with which it cannot be reconciled; a concept is either modified or replaced by a better concept, never abandoned with nothing left to take its place.

Not only was it known in 1770 that a calx weighed more than the metal from which it was formed (which means to us that something must have been taken up in its formation), but Boyle himself back in the 1660's showed that air was necessary for fire. John Mayow and Robert Hooke at about the same date had written about burning and the respiration of animals in terms of air being "deprived of its elastic force by the breathing of animals very much in the same way as by the burning of flame." Stephen Hales, fifty years later, spoke the same language. But these men were all ahead of their times. As we reread their papers we see in spite of strange words and ill-defined ideas they had demonstrated that air in which material had been burned or animals had respired would no longer sustain fire or life; furthermore, they showed that there was an actual diminution of the volume of the air in such cases. All of which seems to force the right explanation to our eyes; not so to the chemists of the eighteenth century.

Air which would no longer support combustion had merely become so rich in phlogiston it could take up no more, the "phlogistonists" declared. Indeed, when Priestley discovered how to prepare essentially pure nitrogen, it was quite natural for him to regard it as completely "phlogisticated air," because nitrogen will not support combustion. Likewise, when he discovered how to prepare essentially pure oxygen gas by heating red oxide of mercury, he called it "dephlogisticated air." He found this gas to be like common air, though a candle burned in it more brightly than even in common air. Upon the whole, said Priestley, it may safely be concluded, "that the purest air is that which contains the least phlogiston: that air is impure (by which I mean that it is unfit for respiration, and for the purpose of supporting flame) in proportion as it contains more of that principle." This letter was read to the Royal Society on

May 25, 1775. And in the same year in another letter he spoke of his newly discovered oxygen as "[an air] that is five or six times better than common air, for the purposes of respiration, inflammation and, I believe, every other use of common atmospherical air. As I think I have sufficiently proved that the fitness of air for respiration depends on its capacity to receive the *phlogiston* exhaled from the lungs this species of air may not improperly be called, *dephlogisti-- cated air.*"

### EXPERIMENTAL DIFFICULTIES WITH GASES

A chemist reading the papers of the phlogistonists clutches his head in despair; he seems to be transported to an Alice-through-the-looking-glass world! But if he is patient and interested he soon recognizes that much of the difficulty stemmed from the experimenters' inability to handle and characterize different gases. This fact illustrates once again the third point of the principles outlined in the last chapter, the difficulty of experimentation. Metals and calxes, inflammable substances like sulfur, charcoal, and phosphorus, the chemists of the eighteenth century could recognize and manipulate since they were solids. Even some liquids like vitriolic acid, water, and mercury were quite definite individuals. But two gases, neither of which would support fire, like nitrogen and carbon dioxide, were often hopelessly confused; or two which burned, like hydrogen and carbon monoxide. Nearly all gases look alike except for the few which are colored. They are compressible and subject to thermal expansion to about the same degree. Their densities, i.e., the weight of a unit volume, differ but that was something not easy to determine in those days. Indeed, in the eighteenth century the distinction between weight and density (i.e., weight per unit volume) even for solids and liquids was often confused. The chemical properties of each gas are characteristic and the way each gas is prepared is different; and it was these differences that finally led to a straightening out of some of the tangled skein.

To understand the difficulties of the chemists of 175 years ago, imagine yourself an elementary student in a laboratory given glass bottles of air, of oxygen, of nitrogen, and one containing air saturated with ether vapor, and asked to tell whether or not all the "airs" or gases in the bottles are identical. The air containing the ether vapor (actually still largely air) will be the only one at first recognized as distinct. A student does not know how to proceed to examine these gases except by looking at them, smelling them, or testing their solubility in water. And from Boyle's day to Priestley's the experimenters were largely in the same predicament. They spoke of different "airs," but hardly knew whether the differences were real or due to the presence of some impurity. Thus, Priestley, writing in 1777, said:

"Van Helmont and other chymists who succeeded him, were acquainted with the property of some *vapours* to suffocate, and extinguish flame, and of others to be ignited. . . . But they had no idea that the substances (if, indeed they knew that they were *substances*, and not merely *properties*, and *affections* of bodies which produced those effects) were capable of being separately exhibited in the form of a *permanently elastic vapour* . . . any more than the thing that constitutes *smell*. In fact they knew nothing at all of any air besides *common air*, and therefore they applied the term to no other substances whatever. . . ."

The history of the study of gases covers a hundred years from Boyle's day. A number of important improvements in techniques were made. They were brought to a focus by Priestley who in 1772 carried out extensive and very original experiments with "airs." He improved still further several techniques of handling these airs or gases which enormously simplified the experimental procedures. Before Priestley's work only three "different airs" were known. In a few years he had discovered eleven more, including oxygen. Here is another illustration of the importance of techniques, though here we meet with an evolutionary rather than a revolutionary change.

Though Priestley was the chief figure in extending the knowledge of gases, his stubborn refusal to accept the consequences of his own discoveries has already been mentioned. It is not necessary in this chapter to discuss either Priestley or Lavoisier as individuals, though the instructor using the case history of combustion would certainly wish to do so. Nor do I propose to digress by examining the priority problems involved in the work of these two men and the Swedish chemist, Scheele, who also discovered oxygen. Such matters fall within the province of the historian of science. For the purposes of the present exposition the important questions are: Why did it take the scientists of the eighteenth century so long to get on the right road? And why were there so many stubborn travelers on the wrong road after the right one had been discovered?

#### THE PHLOGISTON THEORY, A BLOCK TO A NEW CONCEPT

It is sometimes said that the experimenters before Lavoisier's day did not carry out quantitative experiments, that is, they did not use the balance. If they had, we are told, they would have discovered that combustion involves an increase in weight and would have rejected the phlogiston theory. This is nonsense. Rey, as I have already explained, long before the beginning of the phlogiston period showed that a calx weighed more than a metal. Quantitative experiments, though, of course, not very accurate ones, were repeatedly made. Everyone knew that a calx weighed more than the metal from which it was formed. No straightforward statement of the phlogiston theory could accommodate this fact. Yet the phlogiston theory was so useful that few if any in the mid-eighteenth century were looking to overthrow it or disprove it. Rather, they were interested in reconciling one inconvenient set of facts with what seemed from their point of view an otherwise admirable conceptual scheme. How they twisted and squirmed to accommodate the quantitative facts of calcination with the phlogiston theory makes an interesting chapter in the history of science. The eighteenth-century accounts are often confusing. Fortunately their many details need not concern the readers of this book, nor except in broad outline need they concern one teaching the principles of the Tactics and Strategy of Science with the aid of the eighteenth-century studies on combustion.

The principle which emerges is one already encountered, namely, that it takes a new conceptual scheme to cause the abandonment of an old one: when only a few facts appear to be irreconcilable with a well established conceptual scheme, the first attempt is *not* to discard the scheme but to find some way out of the difficulty and keep it. Likewise the proponents of new concepts are rarely shaken by a few alleged facts to the contrary. They seek at first to prove them wrong or to circumvent them. Thus Lavoisier persisted with his own new concept in spite of the fact that certain experiments seemed to be completely inexplicable in its terms. It was later found that the interpretation of the experiments was in error. Not so in the case of the calcination of metals: there could be no doubt in the mind of anyone by 1770 that the increase in weight during calcination was real. There was also no doubt that there should be a loss in weight according to the phlogiston theory. Or at best no change in weight if phlogiston were an imponderable substance like fire.

### ATTEMPTS TO RECONSTRUCT THE PHLOGISTON THEORY

One attempt to get out of the dilemma of calcination took refuge in a confusion between weight and density (calxes are less dense than metals, but the total weight in the calcination increased). This was soon put right by clear thinking. Another attempt involved assigning a negative weight to phlogiston. This illustrates how desperately men may strive to modify an old idea to make it accord with new experiments. But in this case the modification represented not a step forward but several steps to the rear! What was gained by accommodating the quantitative aspect of calcination was lost by following the consequences of negative weight to a logical conclusion. What manner of substance or principle could phlogiston be that when it was added to another material the total mass or weight diminished? The idea that phlogiston had negative weight strained the credulity, and for the most part this logical extension of the phlogiston theory (logical in one sense, highly illogical in another) was never widely accepted. But before we laugh too hard at the investigators of the eighteenth century, let us remember that before the nineteenth century heat was considered a corporeal substance and the whole concept of the atomic and molecular theory of matter lay over the distant horizon.

To some of the chemical experimenters, the dilemma presented by the quantitative facts of calcination seems to have been accepted as just one of those things which cannot be fitted in. And this attitude is much more common in the history of science than most historians would have you believe. Indeed, it is in a way a necessary attitude at certain stages of development of any concept. The keen-minded scientist, the real genius, is the man who keeps in the forefront of his thoughts these unsolved riddles. He then is ready to relate a new discovery or a new technique to the unsolved problems. He is the pioneer, the revolutionist. And it is this combination of strategy and tactics in the hands of a master which is well worthy of study if one would try to understand science through the historical approach.

## LAVOISIER'S CLUE

To recount the history of Lavoisier's development of his new theory, and the way in which the new discoveries of the time were fitted into his scheme would mean the recital of a long story. Such an account would be out of place in this volume, though a considerable portion of it would be involved in a thorough study of the case histories at hand. Let me take a few moments of the reader's time, however, to point out how Lavoisier first seems to have taken the right turn in the road. In a famous note of 1772, he wrote as follows:

"About eight days ago I discovered that sulphur in burning, far from losing weight, on the contrary gains it; . . . it is the same with phosphorus; this increase of weight arises from a prodigious quantity of air that is fixed during the combustion and combines with the vapours.

"This discovery, which I have established by experiments that I regard as decisive, has led me to think that what is observed in the combustion of sulphur and phosphorus may well take place in the case of all substances that gain in weight by combustion and calcination: and I am persuaded that the increase in weight of metallic calces is due to the same cause. . . ."

Here we seem to see the mental process at work to which I referred a few moments ago: the perception that a new fact properly interpreted enables one to explain an old dilemma, an outstanding unsolved problem. In a sense, in this note Lavoisier outlined the whole new chemistry, as he always later claimed. (The note was deposited sealed with the Secretary of the French Academy on November 1, 1772.) To be sure, at first Lavoisier mistook the gas evolved in the reduction of a calx with charcoal (carbon dioxide, the "fixed air" of that day) with the gas absorbed in calcination. The study we can now make of his notebooks as well as his later publications makes it plain that it was not until after Priestley's discovery of oxygen and Lavoisier's repetition of some of Priestley's experiments with the new gas that the nature of the gas absorbed in calcination became clear. It was only then that all the pieces of the puzzle fitted together, with the newly discovered oxygen occupying the central position in the picture. But at the outset Lavoisier recognized that something was absorbed from the air. Unconsciously he was retracing the steps Jean Rey had taken nearly 150 years earlier and which had never been followed up. Rey's almost forgotten book was called to Lavoisier's attention shortly after his first publications of his new theory.

An interesting question that will at once come to the mind of many is the following: why did the study of sulfur and phosphorus lead Lavoisier to the right type of explanation? Why after experiments with those substances did he set out full of confidence on a set of planned experiments along a new line?

This is one of those historical riddles which can never be answered, but concerning which it is not entirely profitless to speculate. I suggest that the key word in Lavoisier's note of November 1, 1772, is "prodigious"—"this increase of weight arises from a prodigious quantity of air that is fixed." If this is so, we have again another illustration of how experimental difficulties or the lack of them condition the evolution of new concepts. To determine whether air is absorbed or not during the calcination of a metal is not easy; the process takes a long time, a high temperature, and both the increase in weight and the amount of oxygen absorbed are small. But with phosphorus and sulfur the experiment was relatively easy to perform (the materials burn at once on ignition with a burning glass); furthermore, the effect observed is very large. The reason for this in terms of modern chemistry is that sulfur and phosphorus have low atomic weights of 32 and 31 (oxygen is 16), and in the combustion 1 atom of phosphorus combines with 5 of oxygen; 1 atom of sulfur with 3 of oxygen. The atomic weight of the metals is high, the number of atoms of oxygen combining with them, fewer. Thus 62 weights of phosphorus will yield $62 + (5 \times 16) = 142$ parts of combustion product; while in the case of tin, the atomic weight is 118 and only 2 atoms of oxygen are involved. Thus 118 weights of tin would yield only $118 + (2 \times 16) = 150$ weights of calx or an increase of only about 25 per cent. Note that with phosphorus the increase is more than double. The corresponding differences would be reflected in the volume of oxygen absorbed, and furthermore, since the calcination of tin was a long process at a high temperature in a furnace, no entirely satisfactory way of measuring the volume of air absorbed was at hand in 1770.

### QUANTITATIVE MEASUREMENTS AND ACCIDENTAL ERRORS

As a matter of fact, until Lavoisier was put on the track of the gas prepared by heating mercuric oxide by Priestley, he had a hard time proving that metallic calxes did gain in weight *because* of absorption of something from the air. The method he used was to repeat certain experiments of Boyle with a slight modification. Both the modification and the difficulties are of interest and point an obvious moral to the tale. Boyle had sealed tin in a glass vessel and heated the vessel a long time on a charcoal fire (which he says is a very dangerous operation as the glass may well explode). Boyle then removed the vessel from the fire and after cooling opened the glass, reweighed the vessel and noted the increase in weight. This was one of the many well-known experiments showing that the calx weighed more than the metal. (Boyle, the reader will recall, believed the increase to be due to the fire particles which passed through the glass). Now, said Lavoisier, where Boyle went wrong was in not weighing the vessel *before* opening it. For if his explanation were right and the fire had passed through the glass and combined with the tin, the increase would have occurred before the air was admitted. While if oxygen were involved, the increase in weight would occur *after* the air was admitted. The results obtained by Lavoisier on repeating this experiment were as expected, but were far from being as striking as those obtained with phosphorus for the reasons just explained. The increase was 10 parts in a total of 4,100 in one experiment and 3 parts in about the same amount in another! We now know that the difficulties of weighing a large glass vessel with a high degree of accuracy are great, due to film moisture and electrical charges. It is, therefore, not surprising that the glass retort, after heating, varied in weight from day to day almost as much as the total gain in weight in one of the two experiments.

These tough facts of experimentation are of great importance. To me, they indicate strongly that even if Boyle had weighed his vessel before and after admitting the air, the uncertainties of his figures would probably have been so great as to confuse him and subsequent investigators. *Important advances in science are based on quantitative measurements only if the measured quantity is large as compared with possible systematic and accidental errors.* The principle of significant figures which plays so large a part in later scientific history is foreshadowed in a crude way by this episode involving the combustion of phosphorus and the calcination of tin. Therefore, in considering the case history at hand the instructor would undoubtedly wish to enlarge at some length on the whole problem of the controlled variable and the role of quantitative measurements.

### LAVOISIER AND PRIESTLEY'S STUBBORN FACTS

For students who had some prior knowledge of chemistry, say a good high-school course, the study of the last days of the phlogiston theory might be rewarding. For the controversy between Lavoisier and Priestley not only illustrates with what tenacity an able man may cling to a hopeless position, but also the boldness with which the innovator pushes forward. Even if a few facts appear to be to the contrary, he still pushes his new ideas just as his conservative opponent stoutly maintains his own tenets in spite of contradictory evidence. In such tugs of war which are the commonest experience in science, though usually in highly restricted areas and with limited significance, the innovator is by no means always right. This point needs to be made perfectly clear. Several case histories to this end would be worth recounting. A few dramatic instances would be in order where some bold man put forward a new idea based on alleged facts which turned out to be erroneous or erroneously interpreted.

The record of Lavoisier was the opposite. For the facts he ignored were indeed not facts at all. Priestley's main points against Lavoisier's views were based on a mistaken identification of two different gases. This fact again emphasizes the difficulties of experimentation. Two gases, both inflammable, carbon monoxide and hydrogen, were at that period confused, even by the great experimenters with gases. Assuming their identity Priestley could ask Lavoisier to account for phenomena which were indeed inexplicable according to the new chemistry, but could be accommodated in the phlogiston theory, now being twisted more each day to conform to new discoveries. Not until long after Lavoisier's execution in 1794 was the relationship between the two gases straightened out. Therefore, Lavoisier was never able to respond to the most weighty of Priestley's arguments against his doctrine. He merely ignored the alleged facts, much as Priestley ignored the unexplained gain in weight or calcination. Each undoubtedly believed that some way would be found around the difficulty in question. Lavoisier's hopes, not Priestley's, proved well founded. So proceeds the course of science. Sometimes it turns out that difficulties with a concept or conceptual scheme are wisely ignored, sometimes unwisely. To suppose, with some who write about the "scientific method," that a scientific theory stands or falls on the issue of one experiment is to misunderstand science indeed.

A study of the overthrow of the phlogiston theory is thus seen to be more than a single case history; it is a related series of case histories. The student's knowledge of chemistry or willingness to take time to obtain this knowledge would be the limiting factor on the use of this material. Even without prior study of chemistry, I believe, a profitable excursion into this complicated bit of scientific history could be undertaken. From such an excursion would come a deeper appreciation of the two principles to which I earlier referred in this chapter. Having studied the phlogiston theory no one would fail to realize that old concepts may present barriers to the development of new ones; having traced the course of the history of experiments with gases and calcination, no one could fail to realize that scientific discoveries must fit the times if they are to be fruitful. In addition, other principles of the Tactics and Strategy of Science are constantly recurring throughout the somewhat lengthy story: the influence of new techniques, the difficulties of experimentation, the value of the controlled experiment, the evaluation of new concepts from experiment— all these are to be found illustrated more than once by those who have patience to study a strange and often neglected chapter in the history of science.

❦ ❦ ❦

*Abraham Flexner*

# The Usefulness of Useless Knowledge[1]

Is IT not a curious fact that in a world steeped in irrational hatreds which threaten civilization itself, men and women—old and young—detach themselves wholly or partly from the angry current of daily life to devote themselves to the cultivation of beauty, to the extension of knowledge, to the cure of disease, to the amelioration of suffering, just as though fanatics were not simultaneously engaged in spreading pain, ugliness, and suffering? The world has always been a sorry and confused sort of place—yet poets and artists and

1 "The Usefulness of Useless Knowledge," *Harper's Magazine*, CLXXIX (October, 1939), 544-550, with omissions. Reprinted by permission of the author.

scientists have ignored the factors that would, if attended to, paralyze them. From a practical point of view, intellectual and spiritual life is, on the surface, a useless form of activity, in which men indulge because they procure for themselves greater satisfactions than are otherwise obtainable. In this paper I shall concern myself with the question of the extent to which the pursuit of these useless satisfactions proves unexpectedly the source from which un-dreamed-of utility is derived.

We hear it said with tiresome iteration that ours is a materialistic age, the main concern of which should be the wider distribution of material goods and worldly opportunities. The justified outcry of those who through no fault of their own are deprived of opportunity and a fair share of worldly goods there-fore diverts an increasing number of students from the studies which their fathers pursued to the equally important and no less urgent study of social, economic, and governmental problems. I have no quarrel with this tendency. The world in which we live is the only world about which our senses can testify. Unless it is made a better world, a fairer world, millions will continue to go to their graves silent, saddened, and embittered. I have myself spent many years pleading that our schools should become more acutely aware of the world in which their pupils and students are destined to pass their lives. Now I sometimes wonder whether that current has not become too strong and whether there would be sufficient opportunity for a full life if the world were emptied of some of the useless things that give it spiritual significance; in other words, whether our conception of what is useful may not have become too narrow to be adequate to the roaming and capricious possibilities of the human spirit.

We may look at this question from two points of view: the scientific and the humanistic or spiritual. Let us take the scientific first. I recall a conversation which I had some years ago with Mr. George Eastman on the subject of use. Mr. Eastman, a wise and gentle farseeing man, gifted with taste in music and art, had been saying to me that he meant to devote his vast fortune to the promotion of education in useful subjects. I ventured to ask him whom he regarded as the most useful worker in science in the world. He replied instan-taneously: "Marconi." I surprised him by saying, "Whatever pleasure we derive from the radio or however wireless and the radio may have added to human life, Marconi's share was practically negligible."

I shall not forget his astonishment on this occasion. He asked me to explain. I replied to him somewhat as follows:

"Mr. Eastman, Marconi was inevitable. The real credit for everything that has been done in the field of wireless belongs, as far as such fundamental credit can be definitely assigned to anyone, to Professor Clerk Maxwell, who in 1865 carried out certain abstruse and remote calculations in the field of magnetism and electricity. Maxwell reproduced his abstract equations in a treatise published in 1873. At the next meeting of the British Association Pro-fessor H. J. S. Smith of Oxford declared that 'no mathematician can turn over the pages of these volumes without realizing that they contain a theory which

has already added largely to the methods and resources of pure mathematics.'
Other discoveries supplemented Maxwell's theoretical work during the next
fifteen years. Finally in 1887 and 1888 the scientific problem still remaining—
the detection and demonstration of the electromagnetic waves which are the
carriers of wireless signals—was solved by Heinrich Hertz, a worker in
Helmholtz's laboratory in Berlin. Neither Maxwell nor Hertz had any concern
about the utility of their work; no such thought ever entered their minds.
They had no practical objective. The inventor in the legal sense was of course
Marconi, but what did Marconi invent? Merely the last technical detail,
mainly the now obsolete receiving device called coherer, almost universally
discarded."

Hertz and Maxwell could invent nothing, but it was their useless theoretical
work which was seized upon by a clever technician and which has created
new means for communication, utility, and amusement by which men whose
merits are relatively slight have obtained fame and earned millions. Who were
the useful men? Not Marconi, but Clerk Maxwell and Heinrich Hertz. Hertz
and Maxwell were geniuses without thought of use. Marconi was a clever
inventor with no thought but use.

The mention of Hertz's name recalled to Mr. Eastman the Hertzian waves,
and I suggested that he might ask the physicists of the University of Rochester
precisely what Hertz and Maxwell had done; but one thing I said he could be
sure of, namely, that they had done their work without thought of use and that
throughout the whole history of science most of the really great discoveries
which had ultimately proved to be beneficial to mankind had been made by
men and women who were driven not by the desire to be useful but merely
the desire to satisfy their curiosity.

"Curiosity?" asked Mr. Eastman.

"Yes," I replied, "curiosity, which may or may not eventuate in something
useful, is probably the outstanding characteristic of modern thinking. It is not
new. It goes back to Galileo, Bacon, and to Sir Isaac Newton, and it must be
absolutely unhampered. Institutions of learning should be devoted to the cultivation of curiosity and the less they are deflected by considerations of immediacy of application, the more likely they are to contribute not only to
human welfare but to the equally important satisfaction of intellectual interest
which may indeed be said to have become the ruling passion of intellectual life
in modern times."

II

What is true of Heinrich Hertz working quietly and unnoticed in a corner
of Helmholtz's laboratory in the later years of the nineteenth century may be
said of scientist and mathematicians the world over for several centuries past.
We live in a world that would be helpless without electricity. Called upon to
mention a discovery of the most immediate and far-reaching practical use we
might well agree upon electricity. But who made the fundamental discoveries

out of which the entire electrical development of more than one hundred years has come?

The answer is interesting. Michael Faraday's father was a blacksmith; Michael himself was apprenticed to a bookbinder. In 1812, when he was already twenty-one years of age, a friend took him to the Royal Institution where he heard Sir Humphry Davy deliver four lectures on chemical subjects. He kept notes and sent a copy of them to Davy. The very next year, 1813, he became an assistant in Davy's laboratory, working on chemical problems. Two years later he accompanied Davy on a trip to the Continent. In 1825, when he was thirty-four years of age, he became Director of the Laboratory of the Royal Institution where he spent fifty-four years of his life.

Faraday's interest soon shifted from chemistry to electricity and magnetism, to which he devoted the rest of his active life. Important but puzzling work in this field had been previously accomplished by Oersted, Ampère, and Wollaston. Faraday cleared away the difficulties which they had left unsolved and by 1841 had succeeded in the task of induction of the electric current. Four years later a second and equally brilliant epoch in his career opened when he discovered the effect of magnetism on polarized light. His earlier discoveries have led to the infinite number of practical applications by means of which electricity has lightened the burdens and increased the opportunities of modern life. His later discoveries have thus far been less prolific of practical results. What difference did this make to Faraday? Not the least. At no period of his unmatched career was he interested in utility. He was absorbed in disentangling the riddles of the universe, at first chemical riddles, in later periods, physical riddles. As far as he cared, the question of utility was never raised. Any suspicion of utility would have restricted his restless curiosity. In the end, utility resulted, but it was never a criterion to which his ceaseless experimentation could be subjected.

In the atmosphere which envelops the world to-day it is perhaps timely to emphasize the fact that the part played by science in making war more destructive and more horrible was an unconscious and unintended by-product of scientific activity. Lord Rayleigh, president of the British Association for the Advancement of Science, in a recent address points out in detail how the folly of man, not the intention of the scientists, is responsible for the destructive use of the agents employed in modern warfare. The innocent study of the chemistry of carbon compounds, which has led to infinite beneficial results, showed that the action of nitric acid on substances like benzene, glycerine, cellulose, etc., resulted not only in the beneficent aniline dye industry but in the creation of nitro-glycerine, which has uses good and bad. Somewhat later Alfred Nobel, turning to the same subject, showed that by mixing nitroglycerine with other substances, solid explosives which could be safely handled could be produced—among others, dynamite. It is to dynamite that we owe our progress in mining, in the making of such railroad tunnels as those which now pierce the Alps and other mountain ranges; but of course dynamite has been abused by politicians and soldiers. Scientists are, however, no more to blame than they are to blame for an earthquake or a flood. The same thing can be said of poison gas. Pliny was killed by breathing sulphur dioxide in the eruption of Vesuvius almost two thousand years ago. Chlorine was not isolated by scientists for warlike purposes, and the same is true of mustard gas. These substances could be limited to beneficent use, but when the airplane was perfected, men whose hearts were poisoned and whose brains were addled perceived that the airplane, an innocent invention, the result of long disinterested and scientific effort, could be made an instrument of destruction, of which no one had ever dreamed and at which no one had ever deliberately aimed.

In the domain of higher mathematics almost innumerable instances can be cited. For example, the most abstruse mathematical work of the eighteenth and nineteenth centuries was the "Non-Euclidian Geometry." Its inventor, Gauss, though recognized by his contemporaries as a distinguished mathematician, did not dare to publish his work on "Non-Euclidian Geometry" for a quarter of a century. As a matter of fact, the theory of relativity itself with all its infinite practical bearings would have been utterly impossible without the work which Gauss did at Göttingen.

Again, what is known now as "group theory" was an abstract and inapplicable mathematical theory. It was developed by men who were curious and whose curiosity and puttering led them into strange paths; but "group theory" is today the basis of the quantum theory of spectroscopy, which is in daily use by people who have no idea as to how it came about. . . .

## III

I am pleading for the abolition of the word "use," and for the freeing of the human spirit. To be sure, we shall thus free some harmless cranks. To be sure, we shall thus waste some precious dollars. But what is infinitely more important is that we shall be striking the shackles off the human mind and setting it free for the adventures which in our own day have, on the one hand, taken Hale and Rutherford and Einstein and their peers millions upon millions of miles into the uttermost realms of space and, on the other, loosed the boundless energy imprisoned in the atom. What Rutherford and others like Bohr and Millikan have done out of sheer curiosity in the effort to understand the construction of the atom has released forces which may transform human life; but this ultimate and unforeseen and unpredictable practical result is not offered as a justification for Rutherford or Einstein or Millikan or Bohr or any of their peers. Let them alone. No educational administrator can possibly direct the channels in which these or other men shall work. The waste, I admit again, looks prodigious. It is not really so. All the waste that could be summed up in developing the science of bacteriology is as nothing compared to the advantages which have accrued from the discoveries of Pasteur, Koch, Ehrlich, Theobald Smith, and scores of others—advantages that could never have accrued if the idea of possible use had permeated their minds. These great artists —for such are scientists and bacteriologists—disseminated the spirit which prevailed in laboratories in which they were simply following the line of their own natural curiosity.

I am not criticising institutions like schools of engineering or law in which the usefulness motive necessarily predominates. Not infrequently the tables are turned, and practical difficulties encountered in industry or in laboratories stimulate theoretical inquiries which may or may not solve the problems by which they were suggested, but may also open up new vistas, useless at the moment, but pregnant with future achievements, practical and theoretical.

With the rapid accumulation of "useless" or theoretic knowledge a situation has been created in which it has become increasingly possible to attack practical problems in a scientific spirit. Not only inventors, but "pure" scientists have indulged in this sport. I have mentioned Marconi, an inventor, who, while a benefactor to the human race, as a matter of fact merely "picked other men's brains." Edison belongs to the same category. Pasteur was different. He was a great scientist; but he was not averse to attacking practical problems—such as the condition of French grapevines or the problems of beer-brewing—and not only solving the immediate difficulty, but also wresting from the practical problem some far-reaching theoretic conclusion, "useless" at the moment, but likely in some unforeseen manner to be "useful" later. Ehrlich, fundamentally speculative in his curiosity, turned fiercely upon the problem of syphilis and doggedly pursued it until a solution of immediate practical use—the discovery of salvarsan—was found. The discoveries of insulin by Banting for use in diabetes and of liver extract by Minot and Whipple for use in pernicious anemia belong in the same category; both were made by thoroughly scientific men, who realized that much "useless" knowledge had been piled up by men unconcerned with its practical bearings, but that the time was now ripe to raise practical questions in a scientific manner.

Thus it becomes obvious that one must be wary in attributing scientific discovery wholly to any one person. Almost every discovery has a long and precarious history. Some one finds a bit here, another a bit there. A third step succeeds later and thus onward till a genius pieces the bits together and makes the decisive contribution. Science, like the Mississippi, begins in a tiny rivulet in the distant forest. Gradually other streams swell its volume. And the roaring river that bursts the dikes is formed from countless sources.

I cannot deal with this aspect exhaustively, but I may in passing say this: over a period of one or two hundred years the contributions of professional schools to their respective activities will probably be found to lie, not so much in the training of men who may to-morrow become practical engineers or practical lawyers or practical doctors, but rather in the fact that even in the pursuit of strictly practical aims an enormous amount of apparently useless activity goes on. Out of this useless activity there come discoveries which may well prove of infinitely more importance to the human mind and to the human spirit than the accomplishment of the useful ends for which the schools were founded.

The considerations upon which I have touched emphasize—if emphasis were needed—the overwhelming importance of spiritual and intellectual freedom. I have spoken of experimental science; I have spoken of mathematics; but what I say is equally true of music and art and of every other expression of the untrammeled human spirit. The mere fact that they bring satisfaction to an individual soul bent upon its own purification and elevation is all the justification that they need. And in justifying these without any reference whatsoever, implied or actual, to usefulness we justify colleges, universities, and institutes of research. An institution which sets free successive generations of human souls is amply justified whether or not this graduate or that makes a so-called useful contribution to human knowledge. A poem, a symphony, a painting, a mathematical truth, a new scientific fact, all bear in themselves all the justification that universities, colleges, and institutes of research need or require. . . .

This is not a new idea. It was the idea which animated von Humboldt when, in the hour of Germany's conquest by Napoleon, he conceived and founded the University of Berlin. It is the idea which animated President Gilman in the founding of the Johns Hopkins University, after which every university in this country has sought in greater or less degree to remake itself. It is the idea to which every individual who values his immortal soul will be true whatever the personal consequences to himself.

❦ ❦ ❦

# The Sciences

*Arthur Stanley Eddington*

## The Evolution of the Physical World[1]

LOOKING back through the long past we picture the beginning of the world —a primeval chaos which time has fashioned into the universe that we know. Its vastness appalls the mind; space boundless though not infinite, according to the strange doctrine of science. The world was without form and almost void. But at the earliest stage we can contemplate the void is sparsely broken by tiny electric particles, the germs of the things that are to be; positive and negative they wander aimlessly in solitude, rarely coming near enough to seek or shun one another. They range everywhere so that all space is filled, and yet so empty that in comparison the most highly exhausted vacuum on earth is a jos-

[1] From Arthur Stanley Eddington, *Science and the Unseen World*, 1930, pp. 11-21. Copyright, 1930, by The Macmillan Company. By permission of The Macmillan Company, publishers.

tling throng. In the beginning was vastness, solitude and the deepest night. Darkness was upon the face of the deep, for as yet there was no light.

The years rolled by, million after million. Slight aggregations occurring casually in one place and another drew to themselves more and more particles. They warred for sovereignty, won and lost their spoil, until the matter was collected round centers of condensation leaving vast empty spaces from which it had ebbed away. Thus gravitation slowly parted the primeval chaos. These first divisions were not the stars but what we should call "island universes" each ultimately to be a system of some thousands of millions of stars. From our own island universe we can discern the other islands as spiral nebulae lying one beyond another as far as the telescope can fathom. The nearest of them is such that light takes 900,000 years to cross the gulf between us. They acquired rotation (we do not yet understand how) which bulged them into flattened form and made them wreathe themselves in spirals. Their forms, diverse, yet with underlying regularity, make a fascinating spectacle for telescopic study.

As it had divided the original chaos, so gravitation subdivided the island universes. First the star clusters, then the stars themselves were separated. And with the stars came light, born of the fiercer turmoil which ensued when the electrical particles were drawn from their solitude into dense throngs. A star is not just a lump of matter casually thrown together in the general confusion; it is of nicely graded size. There is relatively not much more diversity in the masses of new-born stars than in the masses of new-born babies. Aggregations rather greater than our Sun have a strong tendency to subdivide, but when the mass is reduced a little the danger quickly passes and the impulse to subdivision is satisfied. Here it would seem the work of creation might cease. Having carved chaos into stars, the first evolutionary impulse has reached its goal. For many billions of years the stars may continue to shed their light and heat through the world, feeding on their own matter which disappears bit by bit into aetherial waves.

Not infrequently a star, spinning too fast or strained by the radiant heat imprisoned within it, may divide into two nearly equal stars, which remain yoked together as a double star; apart from this no regular plan of further development is known. For what might be called the second day of creation we turn from the general rule to the exceptions. Amid so many myriads there will be a few which by some rare accident have a fate unlike the rest. In the vast expanse of the heavens the traffic is so thin that a star may reasonably count on travelling for the whole of its long life without serious risk of collision. The risk is negligible for any individual star, but ten thousand million stars in our own system and more in the systems beyond afford a wide playground for chance. If the risk is one in a hundred millions some unlucky victims are doomed to play the role of "one." This rare accident must have happened to our Sun—an accident to the Sun, but to us the cause of our being here. A star journeying through space casually overtook the Sun, not indeed colliding with it, but approaching so close as to raise a great tidal wave. By this disturbance jets of matter spurted out of the Sun; being carried round by their angular momentum they did not fall back again but condensed into small globes—the planets.

By this and similar events there appeared here and there in the universe something outside Nature's regular plan, namely a lump of matter small enough and dense enough to be cool. A temperature of ten million degrees or more prevails through the greater part of the interior of a star; it cannot be otherwise so long as matter remains heaped in immense masses. Thus the design of the first stage of evolution seems to have been that matter should ordinarily be endowed with intense heat. Cool matter appears as an afterthought. It is unlikely that the Sun is the only one of the starry host to possess a system of planets, but it is believed that such development is very rare. In these exceptional formations Nature has tried the experiment of finding what strange effects may ensue if matter is released from its usual temperature of millions of degrees and permitted to be cool.

Out of the electric charges dispersed in the primitive chaos ninety-two different kinds of matter—ninety-two chemical elements—have been built. This building is also a work of evolution, but little or nothing is known as to its history. In the matter which we handle daily we find the original bricks fitted together and cannot but infer that somewhere and somewhen a process of matter-building has occurred. At high temperature this diversity of matter remains as it were latent; little of consequence results from it. But in the cool experimental stations of the universe the differences assert themselves. At root the diversity of the ninety-two elements reflects the diversity of the integers from one to ninety-two; because the chemical characteristics of element No. 11 (sodium) arise from the fact that it has the power at low temperatures of gathering round it eleven negative electric particles; those of No. 12 (magnesium) from its power of gathering twelve particles; and so on.

It is tempting to linger over the development out of this fundamental beginning of the wonders studied in chemistry and physics, but we must hurry on. The provision of certain cool planetary globes was the second impulse of evolution, and it has exhausted itself in the formation of inorganic rocks and ores and other materials. We must look to a new exception or abnormality if anything further is to be achieved. We can scarcely call it an accident that among the integers there should happen to be the number 6; but I do not know how otherwise to express the fact that organic life would not have begun if Nature's arithmetic had overlooked the number 6. The general plan of ninety-two elements, each embodying in its structural pattern one of the first ninety-two numbers, contemplates a material world of considerable but limited diversity; but the element carbon, embodying the number 6, and because of the peculiarity of the number 6, rebels against limits. The carbon atoms love to string themselves in long chains such as those which give toughness to a soap-film. Whilst other atoms organise themselves in twos and threes or it may be in tens, carbon atoms organise themselves in hundreds and thousands. From this potentiality of carbon to form more and more elaborate structures, a third impulse of evolution arises.

I cannot profess to say whether anything more than this prolific structure-building power of carbon is involved in the beginning of life. The story of evolution here passes into the domain of the biological sciences for which I cannot speak, and I am not ready to take sides in the controversy between the Mechanists and the Vitalists. So far as the earth is concerned the history of development of living forms extending over nearly a thousand million years is recorded (though with many breaks) in fossil remains. Looking back over the geological record it would seem that Nature made nearly every possible mistake before she reached her greatest achievement Man—or perhaps some would say her worst mistake of all. At one time she put her trust in armaments and gigantic size. Frozen in the rock is the evidence of her failures to provide a form fitted to endure and dominate—failures which we are only too ready to imitate. At last she tried a being of no great size, almost defenceless, defective in at least one of the more important sense-organs; one gift she bestowed to save him from threatened extinction—a certain stirring, a restlessness, in the organ called the brain.

And so we come to Man.

❧ ❧ ❧

*William L. Laurence*

# A Primer of Atomic Energy[1]

THE material universe, the earth and everything in it, all things living and non-living, the sun and its planets, the stars and the constellations, the galaxies and the supergalaxies, the infinitely large and the infinitesimally small, manifests itself to our senses in two forms, matter and energy. We do not know, and probably never can know, how the material universe began, and whether, indeed, it ever had a beginning, but we do know that it is constantly changing and that it did not always exist in its present form. We also know that in whatever form the universe may have existed, matter and energy have always been inseparable, no energy being possible without matter, and no matter without energy, each being a form of the other.

While we do not know how and when matter and energy came into being, or whether they ever had a beginning in time as we perceive it, we do know that while the relative amounts of matter and energy are constantly changing, the total amount of both, in one form or the other, always remains the same. When a plant grows, energy from the sun, in the form of heat and light, is converted into matter, so that the total weight of the plant is greater than that of the ele-

[1] Reprinted from *The Hell Bomb* by William L. Laurence, by permission of Alfred A. Knopf, Inc. Copyright 1950 by William L. Laurence.

mentary material constituents, water and carbon-dioxide gas, out of which its substance is built up. When the substance of the plant is again broken up into its original constituents by burning, the residual ashes and gases weigh less than the total weight of the intact plant, the difference corresponding to the amount of matter that had been converted into energy, liberated once again in the form of heat and light.

All energy as we know it manifests itself through motion or change in the physical or chemical state of matter, or both, though these changes and motions may be so slow as to be imperceptible. As the ancient Greek philosopher Heraclitus perceived more than two thousand years ago, all things are in a constant state of flux, this flux being due to an everlasting conversion of matter into energy and energy into matter, everywhere over the vast stretches of the material universe, to its outermost and innermost limits, if any limits there be.

Each manifestation of energy involves either matter in motion or a change in its physical state, which we designate as physical energy; a change in the chemical constitution of matter, which we know as chemical energy; or a combination of the two. Physical energy can be converted into chemical energy and vice versa. For example, heat and light are forms of physical energy, each consisting of a definite band of waves of definite wave lengths in violent, regular, rhythmic oscillations. A mysterious mechanism in the plant, known as photosynthesis, uses the heat and light energy from the sun to create complex substances, such as sugars, starches, and cellulose, out of simpler substances, such as carbon dioxide and water, converting physical energy, heat and light into the chemical energy required to hold together the complex substances the plant produces. When we burn the cellulose in the form of wood or coal (coal is petrified wood), the chemical energy is once again converted into physical energy in the form of the original heat and light. As we have seen, the chemical energy stored in the plant manifested itself by an increase in the plant's weight as compared with that of its original constituents. Similarly, the release of the energy manifests itself through a loss in the total weight of the plant's substance.

It can thus be seen that neither matter nor energy can be created. All we can do is to manipulate certain types of matter in a way that liberates whatever energy had been in existence, in one form or another, since the beginning of time. All the energy that we had been using on earth until the advent of the atomic age had originally come from the sun. Coal, as already said, is a petrified plant that had stored up the energy of the sun in the form of chemical energy millions of years ago, before man made his appearance on the earth. Oil comes from organic matter that also had stored up light and heat from the sun in the form of chemical energy. Water power and wind power are also made possible by the sun's heat, since all water would freeze and no winds would blow were it not for the sun's heat energy keeping the waters flowing and the air moving, the latter by creating differences in the temperature of air masses.

There are two forms of energy that we take advantage of which are not due directly to the sun's radiations—gravitation and magnetism—but the only way we can utilize these is by employing energy derived from the sun's heat. In harnessing Niagara, or in the building of great dams, we utilize the fall of the water because of gravitation. But as I have already pointed out, without the sun's heat water could not flow. To produce electricity we begin with the chemical energy in coal or oil, which is first converted into heat energy, then to mechanical energy, and finally, through the agency of magnetism, into electrical energy.

The radiations of the sun, of the giant stars millions of times larger than the sun, come from an entirely different source, the greatest source of energy in the universe, known as atomic or, more correctly, nuclear energy. But even here the energy comes as the result of the transformation of matter. The difference between nuclear energy and chemical energy is twofold. In chemical energy, such as the burning of coal, the matter lost in the process comes from the outer shell of the atoms, and the amount of matter lost is so small that it cannot be weighed directly by any human scale or other device. In nuclear energy, on the other hand, the matter lost by being transformed into energy comes from the nucleus, the heavy inner core, of the atom, and the amount of matter lost is millions of times greater than in coal, great enough to be weighed.

An atom is the smallest unit of any of the elements of which the physical universe is constituted. Atoms are so small that if a drop of water were magnified to the size of the earth the atoms in the drop would be smaller than oranges.

The structure of atoms is like that of a minuscule solar system, with a heavy nucleus in the center as the sun, and much smaller bodies revolving around it as the planets. The nucleus is made up of two types of particles: protons, carrying a positive charge of electricity, and neutrons, electrically neutral. The planets revolving about the nucleus are electrons, units of negative electricity, which have a mass about one two-thousandth the mass of the proton or the neutron. The number of protons in the nucleus determines the chemical nature of the element, and also the number of planetary electrons, each proton being electrically balanced by an electron in the atom's outer shells. The total number of protons and neutrons in the nucleus is known as the mass number, which is very close to the atomic weight of the element but not quite equal. Protons and neutrons are known under the common name "nucleons."

There are two important facts to keep constantly in mind about protons and neutrons. The first is that the two are interchangeable. A proton, under certain conditions, loses its positive charge by emitting a positive electron (positron) and thus becomes a neutron. Similarly, a neutron, when agitated, emits a negative electron and becomes a proton. As we shall see, the latter process is taken advantage of in the transmutation of nonfissionable uranium into plutonium, and of thorium into fissionable uranium 233. The transmutation of all other elements, age-old dream of the alchemists, is made possible by the interchangeability of protons into neutrons, and vice versa.

The second all-important fact about protons and neutrons, basic to the understanding of atomic energy, is that each proton and neutron in the nuclei of the elements weighs less than it does in the free state, the loss of weight being equal to the energy binding the nucleons. This loss becomes progressively greater for the elements in the first half of the periodic table, reaching its maximum in the nucleus of silver, element 47. After that the loss gets progressively smaller. Hence, if we were to combine (fuse) two elements in the first half of the periodic table, the protons and the neutrons would lose weight if the newly formed nucleus is not heavier than that of silver, but would gain weight if the new nucleus thus formed is heavier than silver. The opposite is true with the elements in the second half of the periodic table, the protons and neutrons losing weight when a heavy element is split into two lighter ones, and gaining weight if two elements are fused into one.

Since each loss of mass manifests itself by the release of energy, it can be seen that to obtain energy from the atom's nucleus requires either the fusion of two elements in the first half of the periodic table or the fission of an element in the second half. From a practical point of view, however, fusion is possible only with two isotopes (twins) of hydrogen, at the beginning of the periodic table, while fission is possible only with twins of uranium, U-233 and U-235, and with plutonium, at the lower end of the table.

The diameter of the atom is 100,000 times greater than the diameter of the nucleus. This means that the atom is mostly empty space, the volume of the atom being 500,000 billion times the volume of the nucleus. It can thus be seen that most of the matter in the universe is concentrated in the nuclei of the atoms. The density of matter in the nucleus is such that a dime would weigh 600 million tons if its atoms were as tightly packed as are the protons and neutrons in the nucleus.

The atoms of the elements (of which there are ninety-two in nature, and six more man-made elements) have twins, triplets, quadruplets, etc., known as isotopes. The nuclei of these twins all contain the same number of protons and hence all have the same chemical properties. They differ, however, in the number of neutrons in their nuclei and hence have different atomic weights. For example, an ordinary hydrogen atom has a nucleus of one proton. The isotope of hydrogen, deuterium, has one proton plus one neutron in its nucleus. It is thus twice as heavy as ordinary hydrogen. The second hydrogen isotope, tritium, has one proton and two neutrons in its nucleus and hence an atomic mass of three. On the other hand, a nucleus containing two protons and one neutron is no longer hydrogen but helium, also of atomic mass three.

There are hundreds of isotopes, some occurring in nature, others produced artificially by shooting atomic bullets, such as neutrons, into the nuclei of the atoms of various elements. A natural isotope of uranium, the ninety-second and last of the natural elements, contains 92 protons and 143 neutrons in its nucleus, hence its name U-235, one of the two atomic-bomb elements. The most common isotope of uranium has 92 protons and 146 neutrons in its nucleus and hence is known as U-238. It is 140 times more plentiful than U-235, but cannot be used for the release of atomic energy.

Atomic, or rather nuclear, energy is the cosmic force that binds together the protons and the neutrons in the nucleus. It is a force millions of times greater than the electrical repulsion force existing in the nucleus because of the fact that the protons all have like charges. This force, known as the coulomb force, is tremendous, varying inversely as the square of the distance separating the positively charged particles. Professor Frederick Soddy, the noted English physicist, has figured out that two grams (less than the weight of a dime) of protons placed at the opposite poles of the earth would repel each other with a force of twenty-six tons. Yet the nuclear force is millions of times greater than the coulomb force. This force acts as the cosmic cement that holds the material universe together and is responsible for the great density of matter in the nucleus.

We as yet know very little about the basic nature of this force, but we can measure its magnitude by a famous mathematical equation originally presented by Dr. Einstein in his special theory of relativity in 1905. This formula, one of the great intellectual achievements of man, together with the discovery of the radioactive elements by Henri Becquerel and Pierre and Marie Curie, provided the original clues as well as the key to the discovery and the harnessing of nuclear energy.

Einstein's formula $E=mc^2$, revealed that matter and energy are two different manifestations of one and the same cosmic entity, instead of being two different entities, as had been generally believed. It led to the revolutionary concept that matter, instead of being immutable, was energy in a frozen state, while, conversely, energy was matter in a fluid state. The equation revealed that any one gram of matter was the equivalent in ergs (small units of energy) to the square of the velocity of light in centimeters per second—namely, 900 billion billion ergs. In more familiar terms, this means that one gram of matter represents 25,000,000 kilowatt-hours of energy in a frozen state. This equals the energy liberated in the burning of three billion grams (three thousands tons) of coal.

The liberation of energy in any form, chemical, electrical, or nuclear, involves the loss of an equivalent amount of mass, in accordance with the Einstein formula. When 3,000 metric tons of coal are burned to ashes, the residual ashes and the gaseous products weigh one gram less than 3,000 tons; that is, one three-billionth part of the original mass will have been converted into energy. The same is true with the liberation of nuclear energy by the splitting or fusing (as will be explained later) of the nuclei of certain elements. The difference is merely that of magnitude. In the liberation of chemical energy by the burning of coal, the energy comes from a very small loss of mass resulting from the rearrangement of electrons on the surface of the atoms. The nucleus of the coal atoms is not involved in any way, remaining exactly the same as before. The amount of mass lost by the surface electrons is one thirtieth of one millionth of one per cent.

On the other hand, nuclear energy involves vital changes in the atomic nucleus itself, with a consequent loss of as high as one tenth to nearly eight tenths of one per cent in the original mass of the nuclei. This means that from one to nearly eight grams per thousand grams are liberated in the form of energy, as compared with only one gram in three billion grams liberated in the burning of coal. In other words, the amount of nuclear energy liberated in the transmutation of atomic nuclei is from 3,000,000 to 24,000,000 times as great as the chemical energy released by the burning of an equal amount of coal. In terms of TNT the figure is seven times greater than for coal, as the energy from TNT, while liberated at an explosive rate, is about one seventh the total energy content for an equivalent amount of coal. This means that the nuclear energy from one kilogram of uranium 235, or plutonium, when released at an explosive rate, is equal to the explosion of twenty thousand tons of TNT.

Nuclear energy can be utilized by two diametrically opposed methods. One is fission—the splitting of the nuclei of the heaviest chemical elements into two uneven fragments consisting of nuclei of two lighter elements. The other is fusion—combining, or fusing, two nuclei of the lightest elements into one nucleus of a heavier element. In both methods the resulting elements are lighter than the original nuclei. The loss of mass in each case manifests itself in the release of enormous amounts of nuclear energy.

When two light atoms are combined to form a heavier atom, the weight of the heavier is less than the total weight of the two light atoms. If the heavier atom could again be split into the two lighter ones, the latter would resume their original weight. As explained before, however, this is true only with the light elements, such as hydrogen, deuterium, and tritium, in the first half of the periodic table of the elements. The opposite is true with the heavier elements of the second half of the periodic table. For example, if krypton and barium, elements 36 and 56, were to be combined to form uranium, element 92, the protons and the neutrons in the uranium nucleus would each weigh about 0.1 per cent more than they weighed in the krypton and barium nuclei. It can thus be seen that energy could be gained either through the loss of mass resulting from the fusion of two light elements, or from the similar loss of mass resulting from the fission of one heavy atom into two lighter ones.

In the fusion of two lighter atoms, the addition of one and one yields less than two, and yet half of two will be more than one. In the case of the heavy elements the addition of one and one yields more than two, yet half of two makes less than one. This is the seeming paradox of atomic energy.

Three elements are known to be fissionable. Only one of these is found in nature: the uranium isotope 235 (U-235). The other two are man-made.

One is plutonium, transmuted by means of neutrons from the nonfissionable U-238, by the addition of one neutron to the 146 present in the nucleus, which leads to the conversion of two of the 147 neutrons into protons, thus creating an element with a nucleus of 94 protons and 145 neutrons. The second man-made element (not yet in wide use, as far as is known) is uranium isotope 233 (92 protons and 141 neutrons), created out of the element thorium (90 protons, 142 neutrons) by the same method used in the production of plutonium.

When the nucleus of any one of these elements is fissioned, each proton and neutron in the two resulting fragments weighs one tenth of one per cent less than it weighed in the original nucleus. For example, if U-235 atoms totaling 1,000 grams in weight are split, the total weight of the fragments will be 999 grams. The one missing gram is liberated in the form of 25,000,000 kilowatt-hours of energy, equivalent in explosive terms to 20,000 tons of TNT. But the original number of protons and neutrons in the 1,000 grams does not change.

The fission process, the equivalent of the "burning" of nuclear fuels, is maintained by what is known as a chain reaction. The bullets used for splitting are neutrons, which, because they do not have an electric charge, can penetrate the heavily fortified electrical wall surrounding the positively charged nuclei. Just as a coal fire needs oxygen to keep it going, a nuclear fire needs the neutrons to maintain it.

Neutrons do not exist free in nature, all being tightly locked up within the nuclei of atoms. They are liberated, however, from the nuclei of the three fissionable elements by a self-multiplication process in the chain reaction. The process begins when a cosmic ray from outer space, or a stray neutron, strikes one nucleus and splits it. The first atom thus split releases an average of two neutrons, which split two more nuclei, which in turn liberate four more neutrons, and so on. The reaction is so fast that in a short time trillions of neutrons are thus liberated to split trillions of nuclei. As each nucleus is split, it loses mass, which is converted into great energy.

There are two types of chain reactions: controlled and uncontrolled. The controlled reaction is analogous to the burning of gasoline in an automobile engine. The atom-splitting bullets—the neutrons—are first slowed down from speeds of more than ten thousand miles per second to less than one mile per second by being made to pass through a moderator before they reach the atoms at which they are aimed. Neutron-"killers"—materials absorbing neutrons in great numbers—keep the neutrons liberated at any given time under complete control in a slow but steady nuclear fire.

The uncontrolled chain reaction is one in which there is no moderator—and no neutron-absorbers. It is analogous to the dropping of a match in a gasoline tank. In the uncontrolled chain reaction the fast neutrons, with nothing to slow them down or to devour them, build up by the trillion and quadrillion in a fraction of a millionth of a second. This leads to the splitting of a corresponding number of atoms, resulting in the release of unbelievable quantities of nuclear energy at a tremendously explosive rate. One kilogram of atoms split releases energy equivalent to that of 20,000,000 kilograms (20,000 metric tons) of TNT.

It is the uncontrolled reaction that is employed in the explosion of the atomic bomb. The controlled reaction is expected to be used in the production of vast quantities of industrial power. It is now being employed in the creation of radioactive isotopes, for use in medicine and as the most powerful research tool since the invention of the microscope for probing into the mysteries of nature, living and non-living.

In the controlled reaction the material used is natural uranium, which consists of a mixture of 99.3 per cent U-238 and 0.7 of the fissionable U-235. The neutrons from the U-235 are made to enter the nuclei of U-238 and convert them to the fissionable element plutonium, for use in atomic bombs. The large quantities of energy liberated by the split U-235 nuclei in the form of heat is at too low a temperature for efficient utilization as power, and is at present wasted. To be used for power, nuclear reactors capable of operating at high temperatures are now being designed.

In the atomic bomb only pure U-235, or plutonium, is used.

In both the controlled and the uncontrolled reactions a minimum amount of material, known as the "critical mass," must be used, as otherwise too many neutrons would escape and the nuclear fire would thus be extinguished, as would an ordinary fire for lack of oxygen. In the atomic bomb two masses, each less than a critical mass, which together equal or exceed it, are brought in contact at a predetermined instant. The uncontrolled reaction then comes automatically, since, in the absence of any control, the neutrons, which cannot escape to the outside, build up at an unbelievable rate.

Whereas the fission process for the release of nuclear energy entails making little ones out of big ones, the fusion process involves making big ones out of little ones. In both processes the products weigh less than the original materials, the loss of mass coming out in the form of energy. According to the generally accepted hypothesis, the fusion process is the one operating in the sun and the stars of the same family. The radiant energy given off by them, it is believed, is the result of the fusion of four hydrogen atoms into one atom of helium, two of the protons losing their positive charge, thus becoming neutrons. Since a helium atom weighs nearly eight tenths of one per cent less than the total weight of the four hydrogen atoms, the loss of mass is thus nearly eight times that produced by fission, with a corresponding eight-fold increase in the amount of energy liberated. This process, using light hydrogen, is not feasible on earth.

The nuclei of all atoms are thus vast storage depots of cosmic energy. We must think of them as cosmic safe-deposit vaults, in which the Creator of the universe, if you will, deposited at the time of creation most of the energy in the universe for safekeeping. The sun and the other giant stars that give light have, as it were, drawing accounts in this "First National Bank and Trust Company of the Universe," whereas we on this little planet of ours in the cosmic hinterland are much too poor to have such a bank account. So we have been forced all these years we have been on earth to subsist on small handouts from our close neighbor the sun, which squanders millions all over space, but can spare us only nickels, dimes, and quarters (depending on the seasons of the year) for a cup of coffee and a sandwich. We are thus in the true sense of the word cosmic beggars, living off the bounty of a distant relative.

The discovery of fission in 1939 meant that after a million years of exclusive dependence on the sun we had suddenly managed to open a modest drawing account of our own in this bank of the cosmos. We were enabled to do it by stumbling upon two special master keys to five of the cosmic vaults. One of these keys we call fission; the other, which allows us entry into a much richer chamber of the vault, we call fusion. We can get a lot of the stored-up cosmic treasure by using the key to the fission vaults alone, but, as with our terrestrial bank vaults, which generally require two keys before they can be opened, it is not possible to use the key to the fusion vault unless we first use the fission key.

Except for the payment of our heat and light bill, the sun gives us nothing directly in cash. Instead it deposits a very small pittance in the plants, which serve as its major terrestrial banks. The animals then rob the plants and we rob them both. When we eat the food we live by we thus actually eat sunshine.

The sun makes its deposits in the plant through an agent named chlorophyll, the stuff that makes the grass green. Chlorophyll has the uncanny ability to catch sunbeams and to hand them over to the plant. A chemical supergenius inside the plant changes the sunlight energy into chemical energy, just as a bank teller changes bills into silver. With this chemical energy at their disposal, a great number of devilishly clever chemists in the plants' chemical factory go to work building up many substances to serve as vaults in which to store up a large part of the energy, using only part of it for their own subsistence.

The building materials used by these chemists inside the plants consist mainly of carbon-dioxide gas from the atmosphere, and water from the soil, plus small amounts of minerals either supplied by the good earth or by fertilizers. Carbon dioxide, by the way, composed of one atom of carbon and two atoms of oxygen, is the stuff you exhale. In solid form it is what we know as dry ice, used in efforts to make rain. It is present in the atmosphere in large amounts.

Out of the carbon dioxide and water the chemists in the plants build cellulose, starch, sugar, fat, proteins, vitamins, and scores of other substances, all of which serve as vaults for the sun's rays caught by the chlorophyll. The biggest vaults of all, storing most of the energy, are the cellulose, sugars and starches, fats and proteins. There the stored energy remains until it is released by processes we call burning or digestion, both of which, as we shall see, are different terms for the same chemical reaction. When we burn wood, or the petrified ancient wood we know as coal, we burn largely the cellulose, the chief component of the solid part of plants. When we eat the plants, or the animals in whom the plant tissues are transformed into flesh by the solar energy stored within them, it is the sugars, starches, fats, and proteins that give us the energy we live by.

In the process of burning wood or coal the large cellulose vaults, composed of carbon, hydrogen, and oxygen, are broken up, thus allowing the original solar energy, stored up within them as chemical energy, to escape in the form of heat and light. This is the same heat and light deposited there by the sun many years before—in the case of coal, some two hundred million years back. The process of burning thus transforms the chemical energy in the plants back to its original form of light and radiant heat energy. The complex carbon and hydrogen units in the cellulose are broken up, each freed carbon atom uniting within two oxygen atoms in the air to form carbon dioxide again, while two hydrogen atoms unite with one of oxygen to form water. Thus we see that the cellulose vaults are broken up once more into the original building bricks out of which the chemists in the plants had fashioned them.

When we eat plant or animal food to get the energy to live by, exactly the same process takes place except at a lower temperature. The sunlight deposit vaults of sugar, starch, and fat, also composed, like cellulose, of carbon, hydrogen, and oxygen, are broken up by the digestive system into their component parts, thus allowing the original solar energy stored within them to get free in the form of chemical energy, which our body uses in its essential processes. Here, too, the end products are carbon dioxide, which we exhale, and water. About half the energy we thus obtain is used by us for the work we do. The other half is used by the body for building up the tissues burned up as part of the regular wear and tear of life.

We thus burn food for our internal energy as we burn cellulose for our external energy. The interesting thing here is that, in both types of burning, fission as well as fusion processes take place. The fission is the splitting of the cellulose, sugar, fats, starches, and proteins into carbon and hydrogen atoms. The fusion part is the union of the carbon and the hydrogen with oxygen to form carbon dioxide and water. The fusion part is just as necessary to release the stored-up solar energy in the wood or coal as is the fission part, for, as everyone knows, unless there is oxygen for the carbon to fuse with, no combustion (burning) can take place and hence no release of energy. The plant vaults would remain closed absolutely tight.

At this point two things become clear. We see, in the first place, that whenever we get any kind of energy in any form we do not in any way create any of it. All we do is merely draw on something that is already stored up; in the case of coal and wood by the sun, in the case of uranium and hydrogen by the same power that created the sun and all energy. We draw water from the spring, but we do not make the water. On the other hand, we cannot draw the water unless we first find the spring, and even then we cannot draw it unless we have a pitcher.

And we also see, in the second place, that fission and fusion are common everyday phenomena that occur any time you burn anything. Both are essential whenever energy is released, whether it is the chemical energy from coal or the atomic energy from the nuclei of uranium, deuterium, or tritium. When you light a cigarette you employ both fission and fusion or you don't smoke. The first fission and fusion take place in the lighting of the match, the cellulose in the match (whether it is wood or paper) being fissioned (that is, split into its component atoms of carbon and hydrogen). These atoms are then fusioned with the oxygen in the air. The same thing happens when the tobacco catches fire. In each case the fusion with the oxygen makes possible the fission of cellulose. When we burn U-235, or plutonium, we again get both fission and fusion, except that, instead of oxygen, the nuclei of these elements first fuse with a neutron before they are split apart. Thus we see that the process of burning U-235, or plutonium, requires not only fission but fusion as well, without which they could not burn. This is true also in hydrogen fusion. When you burn deuterium by fusing two deuterons (nuclei of deuterium) to form helium of atomic weight three, plus a neutron, one of the two deuterons is split in half in the process. Similarly, when you burn tritium by fusion two tritons (nuclei of tritium), one of the tritons splits into two neutrons and a proton, the one proton joining the other triton to form helium of atomic weight four.

Thus we see that fission and fusion are the cosmic firebrands that are always present whenever a fire is lighted, chemical or atomic, whether the fuel is wood, coal, or oil, or uranium, plutonium, deuterium, or tritium. Both, with some variations, are essential for opening the cosmic safe where the energy of the universe is kept in storage. The only reason you get much more energy in the fission and fusion of atomic nuclei is that so much more had been stored in them than in the cellulose vaults on this planet.

The same reason that limits our ability to obtain stored chemical energy to a few fuels also limits our ability to obtain atomic energy. Coal, oil, and wood are the only dividend-paying chemical-energy stocks. Similarly only five elements, uranium 233 and 235, plutonium, deuterium, and tritium are the only dividend-paying atomic-energy stocks, and of these only two (U-235 and deuterium) exist in nature. The other three are re-created from other elements by modern alchemical legerdemain. What is more, we know for a certainty that it will never be possible to obtain atomic energy from any other element, by either fission or fusion.

This should put to rest once and for all the notion of many, including some self-styled scientists, that the explosion of a hydrogen bomb would set the hydrogen in the waters, and the oxygen and the nitrogen in the air, on fire and thus blow up the earth. The energy in common hydrogen is locked up in one of those cosmic vaults which only the sun and the stars that shine can open and which no number of H-bombs could blow apart. Oxygen and nitrogen are locked even for the sun. As for the deuterium in the water, it cannot catch fire unless it is highly concentrated, condensed to its liquid form, and heated to a temperature of several hundred million degrees. Hence all this talk about blowing up the earth is pure moonshine.

But while we know that we have reached the limit of what can be achieved either by fission or by fusion, that by no means justifies the conclusion that we have reached the ultimate in discovery and that fission and fusion are the only possible methods for tapping the energy locked up in matter. We must remember that fifty years ago we did not even suspect that nuclear energy existed and that until 1939 no one, including Dr. Einstein, believed that it would ever become possible to use it on a practical scale. We simply stumbled upon the phenomenon of fission, which in its turn opened the way to fusion.

If science tells us anything at all, it tells us that nature is infinite and that the human mind, driven by insatiable curiosity and probing ever deeper into nature's mysteries, will inevitably find ever greater treasures, treasures that are at present beyond the utmost stretches of the imagination—as far beyond fission and fusion as these are beyond man's first discovery of how to make a fire by striking a spark with a laboriously made flint. The day may yet come, and past history makes it practically certain that it will come, when man will look upon the discovery of fission and fusion as we look today upon the crudest tools made by primitive man.

A great measure of man's progress has been the result of serendipity, the faculty of making discoveries, by chance or sagacity, of things not sought for. Many an adventure has led man to stumble upon something much better than he originally set out to find. Like Columbus, many an explorer into the realms of the unknown has set his sights on a shorter route to the spices of India only to stumble upon a new continent. Unlike Columbus, however, the explorers in the field of science, instead of being confined to this tiny little earth of ours, have the whole infinite universe as the domain of their adventures, and many a virgin continent, richer by far than any yet discovered, still awaits its Columbus.

Roentgen and Becquerel were exploring what they thought was an untrodden path in the forest and came upon a new road that led their successors to the very citadel of the material universe. Young Enrico Fermi was curious to find out what would happen if he fired a neutron into the nucleus of uranium, hoping only to create a heavier isotope of uranium, or at best a new element. His rather modest goal led five years later to the fission of uranium, and in another six years to the atomic bomb.

Yet, as we have seen, in both fission and fusion only a very small fraction of the mass of the protons and neutrons in the nuclei of the elements used is liberated in the form of energy, while 99.3 to 99.9 per cent of their substance remains in the form of matter. We know of no process in nature which converts 100 per cent of the matter in protons and neutrons into energy, but scientists are already talking about finding means for bringing about such a conversion. They are seeking clues for such a process in the mysterious cosmic rays that bombard the earth from outer space with energies billions of times greater than those released by fission or fusion, great enough to smash atoms of oxygen or nitrogen, or whatever other atoms they happen to hit in the upper atmosphere, into their component protons and neutrons. Luckily, their number is small and most of their energy is spent long before they reach sea level.

But we have already learned how to create secondary cosmic-ray particles of relatively low energies (350,000,000 electron-volts) with our giant cyclotrons. The creation of these particles, known as mesons which are believed to be the cosmic cement responsible for the nuclear forces, represents the actual conversion of energy into matter. This is the exact reverse of the process taking place in fission and fusion, in which, as we have seen, matter is converted into energy. And we are now about to complete multibillion-volt atom-smashers that will hurl atomic bullets of energies of from three to ten billion volts at the nuclei of atoms. With these gigantic machines, known as the cosmotron (at the Brookhaven National Laboratory of the Atomic Energy Commission) and the bevatron (at the University of California), we shall be able to smash nuclei into their individual component protons and neutrons and thus get a much more intimate glimpse of the forces that hold the nuclei together. What is more, instead of creating only mesons, particles with only 300 electron masses, we shall be able for the first time to convert energy into protons and neutrons, duplicating, as far as is known, an act of creation that has not taken place since the beginning of the universe. Man at last will be creating the very building blocks out of which the universe is made, as well as the cosmic cement that holds them together.

What new continents will our first glimpse into the mechanism of the very act of creation of matter out of energy reveal? What new secrets will be uncovered before the dazzled eyes and mind of man when he takes the nucleus of the atom completely apart at last? Not even Einstein could tell us. But, as Omar Khayyam divined, "a single Alif" may provide "the clue" that, could we but find it, leads "to the Treasure-House, and peradventure to the Master too." The fact is that we already have opened the door to the anteroom of the treasure-house, and we are about to unlock the door to one of its inner chambers. What shall we find there? No one as yet knows. But we do know that every door man has opened so far has led to riches beyond his wildest dreams, each new door bringing greater rewards than the one before. On the other hand, we also know that the treasure-house has many mansions, and that no matter how many chambers he may enter, he will always find new doors to unlock. For we have learned that the solution of any one secret always opens up a thousand new mysteries.

We have also learned, to our sorrow, that any new insight gained into nature's laws and forces can be used for great good and for equally great evil. The greater the insight, the greater the potentialities for good or evil. The new knowledge he is about to gain by his deeper insight into the heart of matter, and by his ability to create it out of energy, may offer man the means to make himself complete master of the world he lives in. It is equally true, alas, that he could use it to destroy that world even more thoroughly than with the hydrogen bomb.

As already stated, scientists are even now discussing the possibility of finding means for the complete annihilation of matter by the conversion of the entire mass of protons and neutrons into energy, instead of only o.1 to o.7 per cent. And while the total annihilation of protons and neutrons still seems highly speculative, we already know that such a process actually does take place in the realm of the electron. This is the phenomenon already achieved numerous times on a small scale in the laboratory, in which a positive electron (positron) and an electron with a negative charge completely destroy each other, their entire mass being converted into energy. Luckily, this is at present only a laboratory experiment, in which each positron must be individually produced, since there are hardly any positive electrons in our part of the universe. But suppose the new knowledge we are about to pry loose from the inner citadel of matter reveals to us a new process, at present not even suspected, that would release positrons in large numbers, just as the fission and fusion processes made possible for the first time the liberation of large quantities of neutrons. Such an eventuality, by no means beyond the realm of the possible, would open potentialities of horror alongside which those of the H-bomb, even the rigged one, would be puny. For any process that would release large numbers of positrons in the atmosphere, in a chain reaction similar to the one now liberating neutrons, may envelop the earth in one deadly flash of radioactive lightning that would instantly kill all sensate things. And although this is admittedly purely speculative, no one dare say that such a discovery will not be made, not when one remembers how remote and unlikely a process such as fission seemed to be just before it was made.

Though many of the great discoveries came about as the result of chance, they came because, as Pasteur said, "chance favors the prepared mind." Actually they came largely through the intellectual synthesis of what had originally appeared as unrelated phenomena or concepts. When Faraday discovered the principle of electromagnetic induction, he established for the first time that electricity and magnetism, looked upon since prehistoric times as two separate and distinct phenomena, were actually only two aspects of one basic natural force, which we know today as electromagnetism. This great intellectual synthesis led directly to the age of electricity and all its wonders. About thirty years later the great Scottish physicist James Clerk Maxwell demonstrated that electromagnetic action traveled through space in the form of transverse waves similar to those of light and having the same velocity. This revealed the existence in nature of electromagnetic waves, better known to us today as radio waves. About a quarter century later the great German-Jewish physicist Heinrich Hertz not only produced these electromagnetic waves but showed that they are propagated just as waves of light are, possessing all other properties of light, such as reflection, refraction, and polarization. This led directly to wire less telegraphy and telephony, radio and television, radiophotography and radar.

When Einstein, in his special theory of relativity of 1905, united matter and energy in one basic cosmic entity, the road was opened to the atomic age. Yet Einstein was never satisfied and has devoted more than forty-five years of his life to the search for a greater, all-embracing unity underlying the great diversity of natural phenomena. In his general theory of relativity of 1915 he formulated a concept that encompasses the universal law of gravitation in his earlier synthesis of space and time, of which matter and energy were an integral part. This synthesis, wrote Bertrand Russell in 1924, "is probably the greatest synthetic achievement of the human intellect up to the present time. It sums up the mathematical and physical labors of more than two thousand years. Pure geometry from Pythagoras to Riemann, the dynamics and astronomy of Galileo and Newton, the theory of electromagnetism as it resulted from the researches of Faraday, Maxwell, and their successors, all are absorbed, with the necessary modifications, in the theories of Einstein, Weyl, and Eddington.

"So comprehensive a synthesis," he continued, "might have represented a dead end, leading to no further progress for a long time. Fortunately, at this moment quantum theory [the theory applying to the forces within the atom] has appeared, with a new set of facts outside the scope of relativity physics [which applies to the forces governing the cosmos at large]. This has saved us, in the nick of time, from the danger of supposing that we know everything."

Yet Einstein, working away in majestic solitude, has been trying all these years to construct a vast intellectual edifice that would embrace all the laws of the cosmos known so far, including the quantum, in one fundamental concept, which he designates as a "unified field theory." Early in 1950 he published the results of his arduous labors since 1915. This he regards as the crowning achievement of his life's work, a unified theory that bridges the vast gulf that had existed between relativity and quantum, between the infinite universe of the stars and galaxies and the equally infinite universe within the nucleus of the atom. If he is right, and he has always been right before, his latest contribution will prove to be a greater synthetic achievement of the human intellect than ever before, embracing space and time, matter and energy, gravitation and electromagnetism, as well as the nuclear forces within the atom, in one all-encompassing concept. In due time this concept should lead to new revelations of nature's mysteries, and to triumphs even greater than those which followed as a direct consequence of all earlier intellectual syntheses.

If the synthesis of matter and energy led to the atomic age, what may we expect of the latest, all-inclusive synthesis? When Einstein was asked about it he replied: "Come back in twenty years!" which happens to coincide with the end of the hundred-year period recorded by the brothers Goncourt: God swinging a bunch of keys, and saying to humanity: "Closing time, gentlemen!"

The search for new intellectual syntheses goes on, and no doubt new relationships between the diverse phenomena of nature will be found, regardless of whether Einstein's latest theory stands or falls in the light of further discovery. Physicists, for example, are speculating about a fundamental relationship between time and the electronic charge, one of the most basic units of nature, and there are those who believe that this relationship will turn out to be much more fundamental than that between matter and energy. Should this be found to be true, then the discovery of the relationship between time and charge may lead to finding a way for starting a self-multiplying positron-electron chain reaction, just as the relationship between matter and energy led inevitably to the self-multiplying chain reaction with neutrons. If this comes about, then closing time will come much closer.

Yet the sound of the swinging keys need not necessarily mean closing time for man at the twilight of his day on this planet. It could also mean the opening of gates at a new dawn, to a new earth—and a new heaven.

❧ ❧ ❧

*Donald Culross Peattie*

# Chlorophyll: The Sun Trap[1]

WHAT we love, when on a summer day we step into the coolness of a wood, is that its boughs close up behind us. We are escaped, into another room of life. The wood does not live as we live, restless and running, panting after flesh, and even in sleep tossing with fears. It is aloof from thoughts and instincts; it responds, but only to the sun and wind, the rock and the stream— never, though you shout yourself hoarse, to propaganda, temptation, reproach, or promises. You cannot mount a rock and preach to a tree how it shall attain the kingdom of heaven. It is already closer to it, up there, than you will grow to be. And you cannot make it see the light, since in the tree's sense you are blind. You have nothing to bring it, for all the forest is self-sufficient; if you burn it, cut, hack through it with a blade, it angrily repairs the swathe with thorns and weeds and fierce suckers. Later there are good green leaves again, toiling, adjusting, breathing—forgetting you.

For this green living is the world's primal industry; yet it makes no roar. Waving its banners, it marches across the earth and the ages, without dust around its columns. I do not hold that all of that life is pretty; it is not, in purpose, sprung for us, and moves under no compulsion to please. If ever you fought with thistles, or tried to pull up a cattail's matted root-stocks, you will know how plants cling to their own lives and defy you. The pond-scums

[1] From *Flowering Earth* by Donald Culross Peattie, copyright 1939, G. P. Putnam's Sons.

SCIENCE

gather in the cistern, frothing and buoyed with their own gases; the storm waves fling at your feet upon the beach the limp sea-lettuce wrenched from its submarine hold—reminder that there too, where the light is filtered and refracted, there is life still to intercept and net and by it proliferate. Inland from the shore I look and see the coastal ranges clothed in chaparral—dense shrubbery and scrubbery, close-fisted, intricately branched, suffocating the rash rambler in the noon heat with its pungency. Beyond, on the deserts, under a fierce sky, between the harsh lunar ranges of unweathered rock, life still, somehow, fights its way through the year, with thorn and succulent cell and indomitable root.

Between such embattled life and the Forest of Arden, with its ancient beeches and enchanter's nightshade, there is no great biologic difference. Each lives by the cool and cleanly and most commendable virtue of being green. And though that is not biological language, it is the whole story in two words. So that we ought not speak of getting at the root of a matter, but of going back to the leaf of things. The orator who knows the way to the country's salvation and does not know that the breath of life he draws was blown into his nostrils by green leaves, had better spare his breath. And before anyone builds a new state upon the industrial proletariat, he will be wisely cautioned to discover that the source of all wealth is the peasantry of grass.

The reason for these assertions—which I do not make for metaphorical effect but maintain quite literally—is that the green leaf pigment, called chlorophyll, is the one link between the sun and life; it is the conduit of perpetual energy to our own frail organisms.

For inert and inorganic elements—water and carbon dioxide of the air, the same that we breathe out as a waste—chlorophyll can synthesize with the energy of sunlight. Every day, every hour of all the ages, as each continent and, equally important, each ocean rolls into sunlight, chlorophyll ceaselessly creates. Not figuratively, but literally, in the grand First Chapter Genesis style. One instant there are a gas and water, as lifeless as the core of earth or the chill of space; and the next they are become living tissue—mortal yet genitive, progenitive, resilient with all the dewy adaptability of flesh, ever changing in order to stabilize some unchanging ideal of form. Life, in short, synthesized, plant-synthesized, light-synthesized. Botanists say photosynthesized. So that the post-Biblical synthesis of life is already a fact. Only when man has done as much, may he call himself the equal of a weed.

Plant life sustains the living world; more precisely, chlorophyll does so, and where, in the vegetable kingdom, there is not chlorophyll or something closely like it, then that plant or cell is a parasite—no better, in vital economy, than a mere animal or man. Blood, bone and sinew, all flesh is grass. Grass to mutton, mutton to wool, wool to the coat on my back—it runs like one of these cumulative nursery rhymes, the wealth and diversity of our material life accumulating from the primal fact of chlorophyll's activity. The roof of my house, the snapping logs upon the hearth, the desk where I write, are my imports from the plant kingdom. But the whole of modern civilization is based upon a whirlwind spending of the plant wealth long ago and very slowly accumulated. For, fundamentally, and away back, coal and oil, gasoline and illuminating gas had green origins too. With the exception of a small amount of water power, a still smaller of wind and tidal mills, the vast machinery of our complex living is driven only by these stores of plant energy.

We, then, the animals, consume those stores in our restless living. Serenely the plants amass them. They turn light's active energy to food, which is potential energy stored for their own benefit. Only if the daisy is browsed by the cow, the maple leaf sucked of its juices by an insect, will that green leaf become of our kind. So we get the song of a bird at dawn, the speed in the hoofs of the fleeing deer, the noble thought in the philosopher's mind. So Plato's Republic was builded on leeks and cabbages.

Animal life lives always in the red; the favorable balance is written on the other side of life's page, and it is written in chlorophyll. All else obeys the thermodynamic law that energy forever runs down hill, is lost and degraded. In economic language, this is the law of diminishing returns, and it is obeyed by the cooling stars as by man and all the animals. They float down its Lethe stream. Only chlorophyll fights up against the current. It is the stuff in life that rebels at death, that has never surrendered to entropy, final icy stagnation. It is the mere cobweb on which we are all suspended over the abyss.

And what then is this substance which is not itself alive but is made by life and makes life, and is never found apart from life?

I remember the first time I ever held it, in the historic dimness of the old Agassiz laboratories, pure, in my hands. My teacher was an owl-eyed master, with a chuckling sense of humor, who had been trained in the greatest laboratory in Germany, and he believed in doing the great things first. So on the first day of his course he set us to extracting chlorophyll, and I remember that his eyes blinked amusement behind his glasses, because when he told us all to go and collect green leaves and most went all the way to the Yard for grass, I opened the window and stole from a vine upon the wall a handful of Harvard's sacred ivy.

We worked in pairs, and my fellow student was a great-grand-nephew or something of the sort, of Elias Fries, the founder of the study of fungi. Together we boiled the ivy leaves, then thrust them in alcohol. After a while it was the leaves which were colorless while the alcohol had become green. We had to dilute this extract with water, and then we added benzol, because this will take the chlorophyll away from the alcohol which, for its part, very conveniently retains the yellow pigments also found in leaves. This left us with a now yellowish alcohol and, floating on top of it, a thick green benzol; you could simply decant the latter carefully off into a test tube, and there you had chlorophyll extract, opaque, trembling, heavy, a little viscous and

oily, and smelling, but much too rankly, like a lawn-mower's blades after a
battle with rainy grass.

Then, in a darkened room where beams from a spectroscope escaped in
painful darts of light as from the cracks in an old-fashioned magic lantern, we
peered at our extracted chlorophyll through prisms. Just as in a crystal chande-
lier the sunlight is shattered to a rainbow, so in the spectroscope light is
spread out in colored bands—a long narrow ribbon, sorting the white light by
wave lengths into its elemental parts. And the widths, the presence or the
absence, of each cross-band on the ribbon, tell the tale of a chemical element
present in the spectrum, much as the bands on a soldier's insignia ribbon
show service in Asia, in the tropics, on the border, in what wars. When the
astronomer has fixed spectroscope instead of telescope upon a distant star, he
reads off the color bands as easily as one soldier reads another's, and will tell
you whether sodium or oxygen, helium or iron is present.

Just so our chlorophyll revealed its secrets. The violet and blue end of the
spectrum was almost completely blacked out. And that meant that chlorophyll
absorbed and used these high-frequency waves. So, too, the red and orange
were largely obliterated, over at the right hand side of our tell-tale bar. It
was the green that came through clearly. So we call plants green because they
use that color least. It is what they reject as fast as it smites the upper cells;
it is what they turn back, reflect, flash into our grateful retinas.

It was only routine in a young botanist's training to make an extraction and
spectrum analysis of chlorophyll. My student friends over in the chemistry
laboratories were more excited than I about it. They were working under
Conant, before he became president of Harvard and had to sneak into his old
laboratory at night with a key he still keeps. For chlorophyll was Conant's
own problem. His diagram of its structure, displayed to me by his students,
was closely worked over with symbols and signs, unfolded to something like
the dimensions of a blue print of Boulder Dam, and made clear—to anyone
who could understand it!—how the atoms are arranged and deployed and
linked in such a tremendous molecule as $MgN_4C_{55}H_{72}O_5$.

To Otto and Alfred and Mort every jot and joint in the vast Rube Goldberg machinery of that structural formula had meaning, and more than meaning—the geometrical beauty of the one right, inevitable position for every
atom. To me, a botanist's apprentice, a future naturalist, there was just one
fact to quicken the pulse. That fact is the close similarity between chlorophyll
and hemoglobin, the essence of our blood.

So that you may lay your hand upon the smooth flank of a beech and say,
"We be of one blood, brother, thou and I."

The one significant difference in the two structural formulas is this: that
the hub of every hemoglobin molecule is one atom of iron, while in chlorophyll it is one atom of magnesium.

Iron is strong and heavy, clamorous when struck, avid of oxygen and capable of corruption. It does not surprise us by its presence in our blood stream. Magnesium is a light, silvery, unresonant metal; its density is only one seventh that of iron, it has half of iron's molecular weight, and melts at half the temperature. It is rustless, ductile and pliant; it burns with a brilliant white light rich in actinic rays, and is widely distributed through the upper soil, but only, save at mineral springs, in dainty quantities. Yet the plant succeeds always in finding that mere trace that it needs, even when a chemist might fail to detect it.

How does the chlorophyll, green old alchemist that it is, transmute the dross of earth into living tissue? Its hand is swifter than the chemist's most sensitive analyses. In theory, the step from water and carbon dioxide to the formation of sugar (the first result readily discerned) must involve several syntheses; yet it goes on in a split hundredth of a second. One sunlight particle or photon strikes the chlorophyll, and instantaneously the terribly tenacious molecule of water, which we break down into its units of hydrogen and oxygen only with difficulty and expense, is torn apart; so too is the carbon dioxide molecule. Building blocks of the three elements, carbon, hydrogen and oxygen, are then whipped at lightning speed into carbonic acid; this is instantly changed over into formic acid—the same that smarts so in our nerve endings when an ant stings us. No sooner formed than formic acid becomes formaldehyde and hydrogen peroxide. This last is poisonous, but a ready enzyme in the plant probably splits it as fast as it is born into harmless water and oxygen, while the formaldehyde is knocked at top speed into a new pattern—and is grape sugar, glucose. And all before you can say Albert Einstein. Indeed, by the time you have said Theophrastus Bombastus Aureolus Paracelsus von Hohenheim, the sugar may have lost a modicum of water—and turned into starch, the first product of photosynthesis that could be detected by the methods of fifty years ago.

At this very instant, with the sun delivering to its child the earth, in the bludgeoning language of mathematics, $215 \times 10^{15}$ calories per second, photosynthesis is racing along wherever the leaf can reach the light. (All else goes to waste.) True, its efficiency is very low—averaging no better than one per cent, while our machines are delivering up to twenty-five per cent of the fuel they combust. But that which they burn—coal and gas, oils and wood—was made, once, by leaves in ancient geologic times. The store of such energy is strictly finite. Chlorophyll alone is hitched to what is, for earthly purposes, the infinite.

Light, in the latest theory, is not waves in a sea of ether, or a jet from a nozzle; it could be compared rather to machine gun fire, every photo-electric bullet of energy traveling in regular rhythm, at a speed that bridges the astronomical gap in eight minutes. As each bullet hits an electron of chlorophyll it sets it to vibrating, at its own rate, just as one tuning fork, when struck, will cause another to hum in the same pitch. A bullet strikes—and one electron is knocked galley west into a dervish dance like the madness of the atoms in the sun. The energy splits open chlorophyll molecules, recombines their atoms, and lies there, dormant, in foods.

The process seems miraculously adjusted. And yet, like most living processes it is not perfect. The reaction time of chlorophyll is not geared as high as the arrival of the light-bullets. Light comes too fast; plants, which are the very children of light, can get too much of it. Exposure to the sunlight on the Mojave desert is something that not a plant in my garden, no, nor even the wiry brush in the chaparral, could endure. Lids against the light plants do not have; but by torsions of the stalk some leaves may turn their blades edge-on to dazzling radiation, and present them again broadside in failing light. Within others the chlorophyll granules too, bun or pellet-shaped as they are, can roll for a side or frontal exposure toward the light. In others they can crowd to the top of a cell and catch faint rays, or sink or flee to the sides to escape a searing blast. . . .

When I began to write these pages, before breakfast, the little fig tree outside my window was rejoicing in the early morning light. It is a special familiar of my work, a young tree that has never yet borne fruit. It is but a little taller than I, has only two main branches and forty-three twigs, and the brave if not impressive sum of two hundred and sixteen leaves—I have touched every one with a counting finger. Though sparse, they are large, mitten-shaped, richly green with chlorophyll. I compute, by measuring the leaf and counting both sides, that my little tree has a leaf surface of about eighty-four square feet. This sun-trap was at work today long before I.

Those uplifted hand-like leaves caught the first sky light. It was poor for the fig's purpose, but plant work begins from a nocturnal zero. When I came to my desk the sun was full upon those leaves—and it is a wondrous thing how they are disposed so that they do not shade each other. By the blazing California noon, labor in the leaves must have faltered from very excess of light; all the still golden afternoon it went on; now as the sun sets behind a sea fog the little fig slackens peacefully at its task.

Yet in the course of a day it has made sugar for immediate burning and energy release, put by a store of starch for future use; with the addition of nitrogen and other salts brought up in water from the roots it has built proteins too—the very bricks and mortar of the living protoplasm, and the perdurable stuff of permanent tissue. The annual growth ring in the wood of stem and twigs has widened an infinitesimal but a real degree. The fig is one day nearer to its coming of age, to flowering and fruiting. Then, still leafing out each spring, still toiling in the sunlight that I shall not be here to see, it may go on a century and more, growing eccentric, solidifying whimsies, becoming a friend to generations. It will be "the old fig" then. And at last it may give up the very exertion of bearing. It will lean tough elbows in the garden walks, and gardeners yet unborn will scold it and put up with it. But still it will leaf out till it dies.

Dusk is here now. So I switch on the lamp beside my desk. The power-house burns its hoarded tons of coal a week, and gives us this instant and most marvelous current. But that light is not new. It was hurled out of the sun two hundred million years ago, and was captured by the leaves of the Carboniferous tree-fern forests, fell with the falling plant, was buried, fossilized, dug up and resurrected. It is the same light. And, in my little fig tree as in the ancient ferns, it is the same unchanging green stuff from age to age, passed without perceptible improvement from evolving plan to plant. What it is and does, so complex upon examination, lies about us tranquil and simple, with the simplicity of a miracle.

❧ ❧ ❧

*William Harvey*

# Of the Quantity of Blood Passing through the Heart[1]

THUS far I have spoken of the passage of the blood from the veins into the arteries, and of the manner in which it is transmitted and distributed by the action of the heart; points to which some, moved either by the authority of Galen or Columbus, or the reasonings of others, will give in their adhesion. But what remains to be said upon the quantity and source of the blood which thus passes, is of so novel and unheard-of character, that I not only fear injury to myself from the envy of a few, but I tremble lest I have mankind at large for my enemies, so much doth wont and custom, that become as another nature, and doctrine once sown and that hath struck deep root, and respect for antiquity influence all men: Still the die is cast, and my trust is in my love of truth, and the candour that inheres in cultivated minds. And sooth to say, when I surveyed my mass of evidence, whether derived from vivisections, and my various reflections on them, or from the ventricles of the heart and the vessels that enter into and issue from them, the symmetry and size of these conduits,—for nature doing nothing in vain, would never have given them so large a relative size without a purpose,—or from the arrangement and intimate structure of the valves in particular, and of the other parts of the heart in general, with many things besides, I frequently and seriously bethought me, and long revolved in my mind, what might be the quantity of blood which was transmitted, in how short a time its passage might be effected, and the like; and not finding it possible that this could be supplied by the juices of the ingested aliment without the veins on the one hand becoming drained, and the arteries on the other getting ruptured through the excessive

---

[1] From William Harvey, *On the Motion of the Heart and Blood in Animals,* Robert Willis trans., revised by Alexander Bowie in *Scientific Papers, Physiology, Medicine, Surgery, Geology* (New York: P. F. Collier & Son Corporation, 1910), p. 382. Reprinted by permission of the publishers.

charge of blood, unless the blood should somehow find its way from the arteries into the veins, and so return to the right side of the heart; I began to think whether there might not be a MOTION, AS IT WERE, IN A CIRCLE. Now this I afterwards found to be true; and I finally saw that the blood, forced by the action of the left ventricle into the arteries, was distributed to the body at large, and its several parts, in the same manner as it is sent through the lungs, impelled by the right ventricle into the pulmonary artery, and that it then passed through the veins and along the vena cava, and so round to the left ventricle in the manner already indicated. Which motion we may be allowed to call circular, in the same way as Aristotle says that the air and the rain emulate the circular motion of the superior bodies; for the moist earth, warmed by the sun, evaporates; the vapours drawn upwards are condensed, and descending in the form of rain, moisten the earth again; and by this arrangement are generations of living things produced; and in like manner too are tempests and meteors engendered by the circular motion, and by the approach and recession of the sun.

And so, in all likelihood, does it come to pass in the body, through the motion of the blood; the various parts are nourished, cherished, quickened by the warmer, more perfect, vaporous, spirituous, and, as I may say, alimentive blood; which, on the contrary, in contact with these parts becomes cooled, coagulated, and, so to speak, effete; whence it returns to its sovereign the heart, as if to its source, or to the inmost home of the body, there to recover its state of excellence or perfection. Here it resumes its due fluidity and receives an infusion of natural heat—powerful, fervid, a kind of treasury of life, and is impregnated with spirits, and it might be said with balsam; and thence it is again dispersed; and all this depends on the motion and action of the heart.

The heart, consequently, is the beginning of life; the sun of the microcosm, even as the sun in his turn might well be designated the heart of the world; for it is the heart by whose virtue and pulse the blood is moved, perfected, made apt to nourish, and is preserved from corruption and coagulation; it is the household divinity which, discharging its function, nourishes, cherishes, quickens the whole body, and is indeed the foundation of life, the source of all action. But of these things we shall speak more opportunely when we come to speculate upon the final cause of this motion of the heart.

Hence, since the veins are the conduits and vessels that transport the blood, they are of two kinds, the cava and the aorta; and this not by reason of there being two sides of the body, as Aristotle has it, but because of the difference of office; nor yet, as is commonly said, in consequence of any diversity of structure, for in many animals, as I have said, the vein does not differ from the artery in the thickness of its tunics, but solely in virtue of their several destinies and uses. A vein and an artery, both styled vein by the ancients, and that not undeservedly, as Galen has remarked, because the one, the artery to wit, is the vessel which carries the blood from the heart to the body at large, the other or vein of the present day bringing it back from the general system to the heart; the former is the conduit from, the latter the channel to, the heart; the latter contains the cruder, effete blood, rendered unfit for nutrition; the former transmits the digested, perfect, peculiarly nutritive fluid.

❦ ❦ ❦

*Claude Bernard*

# Carbon Monoxide Poisoning[1]

ABOUT 1846, I wished to make experiments on the cause of poisoning with carbon monoxide. I knew that this gas had been described as toxic, but I knew literally nothing about the mechanism of its poisoning; I therefore could not have a preconceived opinion. What, then, was to be done? I must bring to birth an idea by making a fact appear, i.e., make another experiment to see. In fact I poisoned a dog by making him breathe carbon monoxide and after death I at once opened his body. I looked at the state of the organs and fluids. What caught my attention at once was that its blood was scarlet in all the vessels, in the veins as well as the arteries, in the right heart as well as in the left. I repeated the experiment on rabbits, birds and frogs, and everywhere I found the same scarlet coloring of the blood. But I was diverted from continuing this investigation, and I kept this observation a long time unused except for quoting it in my course *a propos* of the coloring of blood.

In 1856, no one had carried the experimental question further, and in my course at the Collège de France on toxic and medicinal substances, I again took up the study of poisoning by carbon monoxide which I had begun in 1846. I found myself then in a confused situation, for at this time I already knew that poisoning with carbon monoxide makes the blood scarlet in the whole circulatory system. I had to make hypotheses, and establish a preconceived idea about my first observation, so as to go ahead. Now, reflecting on the fact of scarlet blood, I tried to interpret it by my earlier knowledge as to the cause of the color of blood. Whereupon all the following reflections presented themselves to my mind. The scarlet color, said I, is peculiar to arterial blood and connected with the presence of a large proportion of oxygen, while dark coloring belongs with absence of oxygen and presence of a larger proportion of carbonic acid; so the idea occurred to me that carbon monoxide, by keeping venous blood scarlet, might perhaps have prevented the oxygen from changing into carbonic acid in the capillaries. Yet it seemed hard to understand how that could be the cause of death. But still keeping on with my inner preconceived reasoning, I added: If that is true, blood taken from the

[1] From Claude Bernard, *An Introduction to the Study of Experimental Medicine*, translated by Henry Copley Greene (New York: The Macmillan Company, 1927), pp. 159-161. Reprinted by permission of the General Education Board.

veins of animals poisoned with carbon monoxide should be like arterial blood in containing oxygen; we must see if that is the fact.

Following this reasoning, based on interpretation of my observation, I tried an experiment to verify my hypothesis as to the persistence of oxygen in the venous blood. I passed a current of hydrogen through scarlet venous blood taken from an animal poisoned with carbon monoxide, but I could not liberate the oxygen as usual. I tried to do the same with arterial blood; I had no greater success. My preconceived idea was therefore false. But the impossibility of getting oxygen from the blood of a dog poisoned with carbon monoxide was a second observation which suggested a fresh hypothesis. What could have become of the oxygen in the blood? It had not changed with carbonic acid, because I had not set free large quantities of that gas in passing a current of hydrogen through the blood of the poisoned animals. Moreover, that hypothesis was contrary to the color of the blood. I exhausted myself in conjectures about how carbon monoxide could cause the oxygen to disappear from the blood; and as gases displace one another I naturally thought that the carbon monoxide might have displaced the oxygen and driven it out of the blood. To learn this, I decided to vary my experimentation by putting the blood in artificial conditions that would allow me to recover the displaced oxygen. So I studied the action of carbon monoxide on blood experimentally. For this purpose I took a certain amount of arterial blood from a healthy animal; I put this blood on the mercury in an inverted test tube containing carbon monoxide; I then shook the whole thing so as to poison the blood sheltered from contact with the outer air. Then, after an interval, I examined whether the air in the test tube in contact with the poisoned blood had been changed, and I noted that the air thus in contact with the blood had been remarkably enriched with oxygen, while the proportion of carbon monoxide was lessened. Repeated in the same conditions, these experiments taught me that what had occurred was an exchange, volume by volume, between the carbon monoxide and the oxygen of the blood. But the carbon monoxide, in displacing the oxygen that it had expelled from the blood, remained chemically combined in the blood and could no longer be displaced either by oxygen or by other gases. So that death came through death of the molecules of blood, or in other words by stopping their exercises of a physiological property essential to life.

This last example, which I have very briefly described, is complete; it shows from one end to the other, how we proceed with the experimental method and succeed in learning the immediate cause of phenomena. To begin with I knew literally nothing about the mechanism of the phenomenon of poisoning with carbon monoxide. I undertook an experiment to see, i.e., to observe. I made a preliminary observation of a special change in the coloring of blood. I interpreted this observation, and I made an hypothesis which proved false. But the experiment provided me with a second observation about which I reasoned anew, using it as a starting point for making a new hypothesis as to the mechanism, by which the oxygen in the blood was removed. By building up hypotheses, one by one, about the facts as I observed them, I finally succeeded in showing that carbon monoxide replaces oxygen in a molecule of blood, by combining with the substance of the molecule. Experimental analysis, here, has reached its goal. This is one of the cases, rare in physiology, which I am happy to be able to quote. Here the immediate cause of the phenomenon of poisoning is found and is translated into a theory which accounts for all the facts and at the same time includes all the observations and experiments. Formulated as follows, the theory posits the main facts from which all the rest are deduced: Carbon monoxide combines more intimately than oxygen with the hemoglobin in a molecule of blood. It has quite recently been proved that carbon monoxide forms a definite combination with hemoglobin. So that the molecule of blood, as if petrified by the stability of the combination, loses its vital properties. Hence everything is logically deduced: because of its property of more intimate combination, carbon monoxide drives out of the blood the oxygen essential to life; the molecules of blood become inert, and the animal dies, with symptoms of hemorrhage, from true paralysis of the molecules.

🌱 🌱 🌱

*Sigmund Freud*

# The Anatomy of the Mental Personality[1]

LADIES AND GENTLEMEN—I am sure you all recognise in your dealings, whether with persons or things, the importance of your starting-point. It was the same with psycho-analysis: the course of development through which it has passed, and the reception which it has met with have not been unaffected by the fact that what it began working upon was the symptom, a thing which is more foreign to the ego than anything else in the mind. The symptom has its origin in the repressed, it is as it were the representative of the repressed in relation to the ego; the repressed is a foreign territory to the ego, an internal foreign territory, just as reality is—you must excuse the unusual expression—an external foreign territory. From the symptom the path of psycho-analysis led to the unconscious, to the life of the instincts, to sexuality, and it was then that psycho-analysis was met by illuminating criticisms to the effect that man is not merely a sexual being but has nobler and higher feelings. It might have been added that, supported by the consciousness of those higher feelings, he often allowed himself the right to think nonsense and to overlook facts.

[1] From *New Introductory Lectures in Psycho-Analysis* by Sigmund Freud, by permission of W. W. Norton & Company, Inc. Copyright 1933 by Sigmund Freud. Translated by W. J. H. Sprott.

You know better than that. From the very beginning our view was that men fall ill owing to the conflict between the demands of their instincts and the internal resistance which is set up against them; not for a moment did we forget this resisting, rejecting and repressing factor, which we believed to be furnished with its own special forces, the ego-instincts, and which corresponds to the ego of popular psychology. The difficulty was that, since the progress of all scientific work is necessarily laborious, psycho-analysis could not study every part of the field at once or make a pronouncement on every problem in one breath. At last we had got so far that we could turn our attention from the repressed to the repressing forces, and we came face to face with the ego, which seemed to need so little explanation, with the certain expectation that there, too, we should find things for which we could not have been prepared; but it was not easy to find a first method of approach. That is what I am going to talk to you about to-day.

*THEME*

Before I start, I may tell you that I have a suspicion that my account of the psychology of the ego will affect you differently than the introduction into the psychological underworld that preceded it. Why that should be the case, I cannot say for certain. My original explanation was that you would feel that, whereas hitherto I have been telling you in the main about facts, however strange and odd they might appear, this time you would be listening chiefly to theories, that is to say, speculations. But that is not quite true; when I weighed the matter more carefully I was obliged to conclude that the part played by intellectual manipulation of the facts is not much greater in our ego-psychology than it was in the psychology of the neuroses. Other explanations turned out to be equally untenable, and I now think that the character of the material itself is responsible, and the fact that we are not accustomed to dealing with it. Anyhow I shall not be surprised if you are more hesitant and careful in your judgment than you have been hitherto.

The situation in which we find ourselves at the beginning of our investigation will itself suggest the path we have to follow. We wish to make the ego the object of our study, our own ego. But how can we do that? The ego is the subject *par excellence*, how can it become the object? There is no doubt, however, that it can. The ego can take itself as object, it can treat itself like any other object, observe itself, criticise itself, and do Heaven knows what besides with itself. In such a case one part of the ego stands over against the other. The ego can, then, be split; it splits when it performs many of its functions, at least for the time being. The parts can afterwards join up again. After all that is saying nothing new; perhaps it is only underlining more than usual something that every one knows already. But on the other hand we are familiar with the view that pathology, with its magnification and exaggeration, can make us aware of normal phenomena which we should otherwise have missed. Where pathology displays a breach or a cleft, under normal conditions there may well be a link. If we throw a crystal to the ground, it breaks, but it does not break haphazard; in accordance with the lines of cleavage it falls into fragments, whose limits were already determined by the structure of the crystal, although they were invisible. Psychotics are fissured and splintered structures such as these. We cannot deny them a measure of that awe with which madmen were regarded by the peoples of ancient times. They have turned away from external reality, but for that very reason they know more of internal psychic reality and can tell us much that would otherwise be inaccessible to us. One group of them suffer what we call delusions of observation. They complain to us that they suffer continually, and in their most intimate actions, from the observation of unknown powers or persons, and they have hallucinations in which they hear these persons announcing the results of their observations: "now he is going to say this, now he is dressing himself to go out," and so on. Such observation is not the same thing as persecution, but it is not far removed from it. It implies that these persons distrust the patient, and expect to catch him doing something that is forbidden and for which he will be punished. How would it be if these mad people were right, if we all of us had an observing function in our egos threatening us with punishment, which, in their case, had merely become sharply separated from the ego and had been mistakenly projected into external reality?

I do not know whether it will appeal to you in the same way as it appeals to me. Under the strong impression of this clinical picture, I formed the idea that the separating off of an observing function from the rest of the ego might be a normal feature of the ego's structure; this idea has never left me, and I was driven to investigate the further characteristics and relations of the function which had been separated off in this way. The next step is soon taken. The actual content of the delusion of observation makes it probable that the observation is only a first step towards conviction and punishment, so that we may guess that another activity of this function must be what we call conscience. There is hardly anything that we separate off from our ego so regularly as our conscience and so easily set over against it. I feel a temptation to do something which promises to bring me pleasure, but I refrain from doing it on the ground that "my conscience will not allow it." Or I allow myself to be persuaded by the greatness of the expectation of pleasure into doing something against which the voice of my conscience has protested, and after I have done it my conscience punishes me with painful reproaches, and makes me feel remorse for it. I might say simply that the function which I am beginning to distinguish within the ego is the conscience; but it is more prudent to keep that function as a separate entity and assume that conscience is one of its activities, and that the self-observation which is necessary as a preliminary to the judicial aspect of conscience is another. And since the process of recognizing a thing as a separate entity involves giving it a name of its own, I will henceforward call this function in the ego the "super-ego."

At this point I am quite prepared for you to ask scornfully whether our ego-psychology amounts to no more than taking everyday abstractions literally, magnifying them, and turning them from concepts into things—which would not be of much assistance. My answer to that is, that in ego-psychology it will be difficult to avoid what is already familiar, and that it is more a question of arriving at new ways of looking at things and new groupings of the facts than of making new discoveries. I will not ask you, therefore, to abandon your critical attitude but merely to await further developments. The facts of pathology give our efforts a background for which you will look in vain in popular psychology. I will proceed. No sooner have we got used to the idea of this super-ego, as something which enjoys a certain independence, pursues its own ends, and is independent of the ego as regards the energy at its disposal, than we are faced with a clinical picture which throws into strong relief the severity, and even cruelty, of this function, and the vicissitudes through which its relations with the ego may pass. I refer to the condition of melancholia, or more accurately the melancholic attack, of which you must have heard often enough, even if you are not psychiatrists. In this disease, about whose causes and mechanism we know far too little, the most remarkable characteristic is the way in which the super-ego—you may call it, but in a whisper, the conscience—treats the ego. The melancholiac during periods of health can, like any one else, be more or less severe towards himself; but when he has a melancholic attack, his super-ego becomes over-severe, abuses, humiliates, and ill-treats his unfortunate ego, threatens it with the severest punishments, reproaches it for long forgotten actions which were at the time regarded quite lightly, and behaves as though it had spent the whole interval in amassing complaints and was only waiting for its present increase in strength to bring them forward, and to condemn the ego on their account. The super-ego has the ego at its mercy and applies the most severe moral standards to it; indeed it represents the whole demands of morality, and we see all at once that our moral sense of guilt is the expression of the tension between the ego and the super-ego. It is a very remarkable experience to observe morality, which was ostensibly conferred on us by God and planted deep in our hearts, functioning as a periodical phenomenon. For after a certain number of months the whole moral fuss is at an end, the critical voice of the super-ego is silent, the ego is reinstated, and enjoys once more all the rights of man until the next attack. Indeed in many forms of the malady something exactly the reverse takes place during the intervals; the ego finds itself in an ecstatic state of exaltation, it triumphs, as though the super-ego had lost all its power or had become merged with the ego, and this liberated, maniac ego gives itself up in a really uninhibited fashion, to the satisfaction of all its desires. Happenings rich in unsolved riddles!

You will expect me to do more than give a mere example in support of my statement that we have learnt a great deal about the formation of the super-ego, that is of the origin of conscience. The philosopher Kant once declared that nothing proved to him the greatness of God more convincingly than the starry heavens and the moral conscience within us. The stars are unquestionably superb, but where conscience is concerned God has been guilty of an uneven and careless piece of work, for a great many men have only a limited share of it or scarcely enough to be worth mentioning. This does not mean, however, that we are overlooking the fragment of psychological truth which is contained in the assertion that conscience is of divine origin! but the assertion needs interpretation. Conscience is no doubt something within us, but it has not been there from the beginning. In this sense it is the opposite of sexuality, which is certainly present from the very beginning of life, and is not a thing that only comes in later. But small children are notoriously a-moral. They have no internal inhibitions against their pleasure-seeking impulses. The rôle, which the super-ego undertakes later in life, is at first played by an external power, by parental authority. The influence of the parents dominates the child by granting proofs of affection and by threats of punishment, which, to the child, mean loss of love, and which must also be feared on their own account. This objective anxiety is the forerunner of the later moral anxiety; so long as the former is dominant one need not speak of super-ego or of conscience. It is only later that the secondary situation arises, which we are far too ready to regard as the normal state of affairs; the external restrictions are introjected, so that the super-ego takes the place of the parental function, and thenceforward observes, guides and threatens the ego in just the same way as the parents acted to the child before.

The super-ego, which in this way has taken over the power, the aims and even the methods of the parental function, is, however, not merely the legatee of parental authority, it is actually the heir of its body. It proceeds directly from it, and we shall soon learn in what way this comes about. First, however, we must pause to consider a point in which they differ. The super-ego seems to have made a one-sided selection, and to have chosen only the harshness and severity of the parents, their preventive and punitive functions, while their loving care is not taken up and continued by it. If the parents have really ruled with a rod of iron, we can easily understand the child developing a severe super-ego, but, contrary to our expectations, experience shows that the super-ego may reflect the same relentless harshness even when the up-bringing has been gentle and kind, and avoided threats and punishment as far as possible. We shall return to this contradiction later, when we are dealing with the transmutation of instincts in the formation of the super-ego.

I cannot tell you as much as I could wish about the change from the parental function to the super-ego, partly because that process is so complicated that a description of it does not fit into the framework of a set of introductory lectures such as these, and partly because we ourselves do not feel that we have fully understood it. You will have to be satisfied, therefore, with the following indications. The basis of the process is what we call an identification, that is to say, that one ego becomes like another, one which results in the first ego behaving itself in certain respects in the same way as the second; it imitates it, and as it were takes it into itself. This identification

has been not inappropriately compared with the oral cannibalistic incorporation of another person. Identification is a very important kind of relationship
with another person, probably the most primitive, and is not to be confused
with object-choice. One can express the difference between them in this way:
when a boy identifies himself with his father, he wants to *be like* his father;
when he makes him the object of his choice, he wants to *have* him, to possess him; in the first case his ego is altered on the model of his father, in
the second case that is not necessary. Identification and object-choice are
broadly speaking independent of each other; but one can identify oneself
with a person, and alter one's ego accordingly, and take the same person as
one's sexual object. It is said that this influencing of the ego by the sexual
object takes place very often with women, and is characteristic of femininity.
With regard to what is by far the most instructive relation between identification and object-choice, I must have given you some information in my previous
lectures. It can be as easily observed in children as in adults, in normal as
in sick persons. If one has lost a love-object or has had to give it up, one
often compensates oneself by identifying oneself with it; one sets it up
again inside one's ego, so that in this case object-choice regresses, as it were,
to identification.

I am myself not at all satisfied with this account of identification, but it will
suffice if you will grant that the establishment of the super-ego can be described as a successful instance of identification with the parental function.
The fact which is decisively in favour of this point of view is that this new
creation of a superior function within the ego is extremely closely bound up
with the fate of the Oedipus complex, so that the super-ego appears as the
heir of that emotional tie, which is of such importance for childhood. When
the Oedipus complex passes away the child must give up the intense object-
cathexes which it has formed towards its parents, and to compensate for this
loss of object, its identifications with its parents, which have probably long
been present, become greatly intensified. Identifications of this kind, which
may be looked on as precipitates of abandoned object-cathexes, will recur often
enough in the later life of the child; but it is in keeping with the emotional
importance of this first instance of such a transformation that its product
should occupy a special position in the ego. Further investigation also reveals
that the super-ego does not attain to full strength and development if the
overcoming of the Oedipus complex has not been completely successful. During the course of its growth, the super-ego also takes over the influence of
those persons who have taken the place of the parents, that is to say of persons who have been concerned in the child's upbringing, and whom it has
regarded as ideal models. Normally the super-ego is constantly becoming more
and more remote from the original parents, becoming, as it were, more impersonal. Another thing that we must not forget is that the child values its
parents differently at different periods of its life. At the time at which the
Oedipus complex makes way for the super-ego, they seem to be splendid

figures, but later on they lose a good deal of their prestige. Identifications take place with these later editions of the parents as well, and regularly provide important contributions to the formation of character; but these only affect the ego, they have no influence on the super-ego, which has been determined by the earliest parental imagos.

I hope you will by now feel that in postulating the existence of a super-ego I have been describing a genuine structural entity, and have not been merely personifying an abstraction, such as conscience. We have now to mention another important activity which is to be ascribed to the super-ego. It is also the vehicle of the ego-ideal, by which the ego measures itself, towards which it strives, and whose demands for ever-increasing perfection it is always striving to fulfil. No doubt this ego-ideal is a precipitation of the old idea of the parents, an expression of the admiration which the child felt for the perfection which it at that time ascribed to them. I know you have heard a great deal about the sense of inferiority which is said to distinguish the neurotic subject. It crops up especially in the pages of works that have literary pretensions. A writer who brings in the expression "inferiority-complex" thinks he has satisfied all the demands of psycho-analysis and raised his work on to a higher psychological plane. As a matter of fact the phrase "inferiority-complex" is hardly ever used in psycho-analysis. It does not refer to anything which we regard as simple, let alone elementary. To trace it back to the perception in oneself of some organic disability or other, as the school of so-called Individual Psychologists like to do, seems to us a short-sighted error. The sense of inferiority has a strong erotic basis. The child feels itself inferior when it perceives that it is not loved, and so does the adult as well. The only organ that is really regarded as inferior is the stunted penis—the girl's clitoris. But the major part of the sense of inferiority springs from the relationship of the ego to its super-ego, and, like the sense of guilt, it is an expression of the tension between them. The sense of inferiority and the sense of guilt are exceedingly difficult to distinguish. Perhaps we should do better if we regarded the former as the erotic complement to the sense of moral inferiority. We have paid but little attention to such questions of conceptual differentiation in psycho-analysis.

Seeing that the inferiority-complex has become so popular, I shall venture to treat you to a short digression. A historical personage of our time, who is still living but who for the present has retired into the background, suffers from the mal-development of a limb caused by an injury at birth. A very well-known contemporary writer who has a predilection for writing the biographies of famous persons, has dealt with the life of the man to whom I am referring. Now if one is writing a biography, it is naturally very difficult to suppress the urge for psychological understanding. The author has therefore made an attempt to build up the whole development of his hero's character on the basis of a sense of inferiority, which was caused by his physical defect. While doing this he has overlooked a small but not unimportant fact.

It is usual for mothers to whom fate has given a sickly or otherwise defective child to try to compensate for this unfair handicap with an extra amount of love. In the case we are speaking of, the proud mother behaved quite differently; she withdrew her love from the child on account of his disability. When the child grew up into a man of great power, he proved beyond all doubt by his behaviour that he had never forgiven his mother. If you will bear in mind the importance of mother-love for the mental life of the child, you will be able to make the necessary corrections in the inferiority-theory of the biographer.

But let us get back to the super-ego. We have allocated to it the activities of self-observation, conscience, and the holding up of ideals. It follows from our account of its origin that it is based upon an overwhelmingly important biological fact no less than upon a momentous psychological fact, namely the lengthy dependence of the human child on its parents and the Oedipus complex; these two facts, moreover, are closely bound up with each other. For us the super-ego is the representative of all moral restrictions, the advocate of the impulse towards perfection, in short it is as much as we have been able to apprehend psychologically of what people call the "higher" things in human life. Since it itself can be traced back to the influence of parents, teachers, and so on, we shall learn more of its significance if we turn our attention to these sources. In general, parents and similar authorities follow the dictates of their own super-egos in the up-bringing of children. Whatever terms their ego may be on with their super-ego, in the education of the child they are severe and exacting. They have forgotten the difficulties of their own childhood, and are glad to be able to identify themselves fully at last with their own parents, who in their day subjected them to such severe restraints. The result is that the super-ego of the child is not really built up on the model of the parents, but on that of the parents' super-ego; it takes over the same content, it becomes the vehicle of tradition and of all the age-long values which have been handed down in this way from generation to generation. You may easily guess what great help is afforded by the recognition of the super-ego in understanding the social behaviour of man, in grasping the problem of delinquency, for example, and perhaps, too, in providing us with some practical hints upon education. It is probable that the so-called materialistic conceptions of history err in that they underestimate this factor. They brush it aside with the remark that the "ideologies" of mankind are nothing more than resultants of their economic situation at any given moment or superstructures built upon it. That is the truth, but very probably it is not the whole truth. Mankind never lives completely in the present; the ideologies of the super-ego perpetuate the past, the traditions of the race and the people, which yield but slowly to the influence of the present and to new developments, and, so long as they work through the super-ego, play an important part in man's life, quite independently of economic conditions.

In 1921 I tried to apply the distinction between the ego and the super-ego to the study of group psychology. I reached a formula, which ran like this: A psychological group is a collection of individuals, who have introduced the same person into their super-ego, and on the basis of this common factor have identified themselves with one another in their ego. This naturally only holds for groups who have a leader. If we could find more applications of this kind, the hypothesis of the super-ego would lose all its strangeness for us, and we should be entirely relieved of the embarrassment which we cannot help feeling when, used as we are to the atmosphere of the underworld, we make excursions into the more superficial and higher planes of the mental apparatus. Of course we do not for a moment think that the last word on ego-psychology has been spoken with the demarcation of the super-ego. It is rather the beginning of the subject, but in this case it is not only the first step that is difficult.

But now another task awaits us, as it were at the opposite end of the ego. This question is raised by an observation which is made during analytic work, an observation which is, indeed, an old one. As so often happens, it has taken a long time for its true value to be appreciated. As you are aware, the whole of psycho-analytic theory is in fact built up on the perception of the resistance exerted by the patient when we try to make him conscious of his unconscious. The objective indication of resistance is that his associations stop short or wander far away from the theme that is being discussed. He may also become subjectively aware of the resistance by experiencing painful feelings when he approaches the theme. But this last indication may be absent. In such a case we say to the patient that we conclude from his behaviour that he is in a state of resistance, and he replies that he knows nothing about it and is only aware of a difficulty in associating. Experience shows that we were right, but, if so, his resistance too must have been unconscious, just as unconscious as the repressed material which we were trying to bring to the surface. Long ago we should have asked from which part of the mind such an unconscious resistance could operate. The beginner in psycho-analysis will be ready at once with the answer that it must be the resistance of the unconscious. An ambiguous and useless answer! If it means that the resistance operates from the repressed, then we must say: "Certainly not!" To the repressed we must rather ascribe a strong upward-driving force, an impulsion to get through to consciousness. The resistance can only be a manifestation of the ego, which carried through the repression at one time or other and is now endeavouring to keep it up. And that too was our earlier view. Now that we have posited a special function within the ego to represent the demand for restriction and rejection, *i.e.* the super-ego, we can say that repression is the work of the super-ego,—either that it does its work on its own account or else that the ego does it in obedience to its orders. If now we are faced with the case where the patient under analysis is not conscious of his resistance, then it must be either that the super-ego and the ego can operate unconsciously in quite important situations, or, which would be far more significant, that parts of both ego and super-ego themselves are unconscious. In both cases we should have to take account of the disturbing view that the ego (including the super-ego) does not by any means completely coincide with the conscious, nor the repressed with the unconscious.

Ladies and Gentlemen—I feel I must have a little breathing space, which I expect you will welcome with relief, and before I go on I must make an apology. Here am I giving you a supplement to the introduction to psycho-analysis which I started fifteen years ago, and I am behaving as though you yourselves had been doing nothing but psycho-analysis all that time. I know it is a monstrous supposition, but I am helpless, I have no alternative. The reason is that it is exceedingly difficult to give an insight into psycho-analysis to any one who is not himself a psycho-analyst. I assure you that we do not like to give the effect of being members of a secret society carrying on a secret science. And yet we have been obliged to recognise and state as our considered opinion that no one has a right to say in psycho-analysis unless he has been through certain experiences which he can only have by being analysed himself. When I delivered my lectures to you fifteen years ago I tried to let you off certain speculative parts of our theory, but it is with those very parts that are connected the new discoveries which I am going to speak of to-day.

Now let me return to my theme. With regard to the two alternatives—that the ego and the super-ego may themselves be unconscious, or that they may merely give rise to unconscious effects—we have for good reasons decided in favour of the former. Certainly, large portions of the ego and super-ego can remain unconscious, are, in fact, normally unconscious. That means to say that the individual knows nothing of their contents and that it requires an expenditure of effort to make him conscious of them. It is true, then, that ego and conscious, repressed and unconscious do not coincide. We are forced fundamentally to revise our attitude towards the problem of conscious and unconscious. At first we might be inclined to think very much less of the importance of consciousness as a criterion, since it has proved so untrustworthy. But if we did so, we should be wrong. It is the same with life: it is not worth much, but it is all that we have. Without the light shed by the quality of consciousness we should be lost in the darkness of depth-psychology. Nevertheless we must try to orientate ourselves anew.

What is meant by "conscious," we need not discuss; it is beyond all doubt. The oldest and best meaning of the word "unconscious" is the descriptive one; we call "unconscious" any mental process the existence of which we are obliged to assume—because, for instance, we infer it in some way from its effects—but of which we are not directly aware. We have the same relation to that mental process as we have to a mental process in another person, except that it belongs to ourselves. If we want to be more accurate, we should modify the statement by saying that we call a process "unconscious" when we have to assume that it was active *at a certain time*, although *at that time* we knew nothing about it. This restriction reminds us that most conscious processes are conscious only for a short period; quite soon they become *latent*, though they can easily become conscious again. We could also say that they had become unconscious, if we were certain that they were still something mental when they were in the latent condition. So far we should have learnt nothing, and not even have earned the right to introduce the notion of the unconscious into psychology. But now we come across a new fact which we can already observe in the case of errors. We find that, in order to explain a slip of the tongue, for instance, we are obliged to assume that an intention to say some particular thing had formed itself in the mind of the person who made the slip. We can infer it with certainty from the occurrence of the speech-disturbance, but it was not able to obtain expression; it was, that is to say, unconscious. If we subsequently bring the intention to the speaker's notice, he may recognise it as a familiar one, in which case it was only temporarily unconscious, or he may repudiate it as foreign to him, in which case it was permanently unconscious. Such an observation as this justifies us in also regarding what we have called "latent" as something "unconscious." The consideration of these dynamic relations puts us in a position to distinguish two kinds of unconscious: one which is transformed into conscious material easily and under conditions which frequently arise, and another in the case of which such a transformation is difficult, can only come about with a considerable expenditure of energy, or may never occur at all. In order to avoid any ambiguity as to whether we are referring to the one or the other unconscious, whether we are using the word in the descriptive or dynamic sense, we make use of a legitimate and simple expedient. We call the unconscious which is only latent, and so can easily become conscious, the "preconscious," and keep the name "unconscious" for the other. We have now three terms, "conscious," "preconscious," and "unconscious," to serve our purposes in describing mental phenomena. Once again, from a purely descriptive point of view, the "preconscious" is also unconscious, but we do not give it that name, except when we are speaking loosely, or when we have to defend in general the existence of unconscious processes in mental life.

You will, I hope, grant that so far things are not so bad and that the scheme is a convenient one. That is all very well; unfortunately our psycho-analytic work has compelled us to use the word "unconscious" in yet another, third, sense; and this may very well have given rise to confusion. Psycho-analysis has impressed us very strongly with the new idea that large and important regions of the mind are normally removed from the knowledge of the ego, so that the processes which occur in them must be recognized as unconscious in the true dynamic sense of the term. We have consequently also attributed to the word "unconscious" a topographical or systematic meaning; we have talked of *systems* of the preconscious and of the unconscious, and of a conflict between the ego and the Ucs. system; so that the word "unconscious" has more and more been made to mean a mental province rather than a quality which mental things have. At this point, the discovery, inconvenient at first sight, that parts of the ego and super-ego, too, are unconscious in the dynamic sense, has a facilitating effect and enables us to remove a complication. We evidently have no right to call that region of the mind which is neither ego nor super-ego the Ucs. system, since the character of unconsciousness is not exclusive to it. Very well; we will no longer use the word "unconscious" in the sense of a system, and to what we have hitherto called by that name we will give a better one, which will not give rise to misunderstandings. Borrowing, at G. Groddeck's suggestion, a term used by Nietzsche, we will call it henceforward the "id." This impersonal pronoun seems particularly suited to express the essential character of this province of the mind—the character of being foreign to the ego. Super-ego, ego and id, then, are the three realms, regions or provinces into which we divide the mental apparatus of the individual; and it is their mutual relations with which we shall be concerned in what follows.

But before we go on I must make a short digression. I have no doubt that you are dissatisfied with the fact that the three qualities of the mind in respect to consciousness and the three regions of the mental apparatus do not fall together into three harmonious pairs, and that you feel that the clarity of our conclusions is consequently impaired. My own view is that we ought not to deplore this fact but that we should say to ourselves that we had no right to expect any such neat arrangement. Let me give you an analogy; analogies prove nothing, that is quite true, but they can make one feel more at home. Let us picture a country with a great variety of geographical configurations, hills, plains and chains of lakes, and with mixed nationalities living in it, Germans, Magyars and Slovaks, who, moreover, are engaged upon a number of different occupations. Now the distribution might be such that the Germans lived in the hills and kept cattle, the Magyars on the plains and grew corn and vines, while the Slovaks lived by the lakes and caught fish and plaited reeds. If this distribution were neat and exact it would no doubt give great satisfaction to a President Wilson; it would also be convenient for giving a geography lesson. It is probable, however, that you would find a less orderly state of affairs if you visited the region. Germans, Magyars and Slovaks would be living everywhere mixed up together, and there would be cornfields too in the hills, and cattle would be kept on the plains as well. One or two things would be as you expected, for one cannot catch fish on the mountains, and wine does not grow in water. The picture of the region which you had brought with you might on the whole fit the facts, but in details you would have to put up with departures from it.

You must not expect me to tell you much that is new about the id, except its name. It is the obscure inaccessible part of our personality; the little we know about it we have learnt from the study of dream-work and the formation of neurotic symptoms, and most of that is of a negative character, and can only be described as being all that the ego is not. We can come nearer to the id with images, and call it a chaos, a cauldron of seething excitement. We suppose that it is somewhere in direct contact with somatic processes, and takes over from them instinctual needs and gives them mental expression, but we cannot say in what substratum this contact is made. These instincts fill it with energy, but it has no organisation and no unified will, only an impulsion to obtain satisfaction for the instinctual needs, in accordance with the pleasure-principle. The laws of logic—above all, the law of contradiction—do not hold for processes in the id. Contradictory impulses exist side by side without neutralising each other or drawing apart; at most they combine in compromise formations under the over-powering economic pressure towards discharging their energy. There is nothing in the id which can be compared to negation, and we are astonished to find in it an exception to the philosophers' assertion that space and time are necessary forms of our mental acts. In the id there is nothing corresponding to the idea of time, no recognition of the passage of time, and (a thing which is very remarkable and awaits adequate attention in philosophic thought) no alteration of mental processes by the passage of time. Conative impulses which have never got beyond the id, and even impressions which have been pushed down into the id by repression, are virtually immortal and are preserved for whole decades as though they had only recently occurred. They can only be recognised as belonging to the past, deprived of their significance, and robbed of their charge of energy, after they have been made conscious by the work of analysis, and no small part of the therapeutic effect of analytic treatment rests upon this fact.

It is constantly being borne in upon me that we have made far too little use of our theory of the indubitable fact that the repressed remains unaltered by the passage of time. This seems to offer us the possibility of an approach to some really profound truths. But I myself have made no further progress here.

Naturally, the id knows no values, no good and evil, no morality. The economic, or, if you prefer, the quantitative factor, which is so closely bound up with the pleasure-principle, dominates all its processes. Instinctual cathexes seeking discharge,—that, in our view, is all that the id contains. It seems, indeed, as if the energy of these instinctual impulses is in a different condition from that in which it is found in the other regions of the mind. It must be far more fluid and more capable of being discharged, for otherwise we should not have those displacements and condensations, which are so characteristic of the id and which are so completely independent of the qualities of what is cathected. (In the ego we should call it an idea.) What would one not give to understand these things better? You observe, in any case, that we can attribute to the id other characteristics than that of being unconscious, and you are aware of the possibility that parts of the ego and super-ego are unconscious without possessing the same primitive and irrational quality. As regards a characterisation of the ego, in so far as it is to be distinguished from the id and the super-ego, we shall get on better if we turn our attention to the relation between it and the most superficial portion of the mental apparatus; which we call the Pcpt-cs (perceptual-conscious) system. This system is directed on to the external world, it mediates perceptions of it, and in it is generated, while it is functioning, the phenomenon of consciousness. It is the sense-organ of the whole apparatus, receptive, moreover, not only of excitations from without but also of such as proceed from the interior of the mind. One can hardly go wrong in regarding the ego as that part of the id which has been modified by its proximity to the external world and the influence that the latter has had on it, and which serves the purpose of receiving stimuli and protecting the organism from them, like the cortical layer with which a particle of living substance surrounds itself. This relation to the external world is decisive for the ego. The ego has taken over the task of representing the external world for the id, and so of saving it; for the id, blindly striving to gratify its instincts in complete disregard of the superior strength of outside forces, could not otherwise escape annihilation. In the fulfilment of this function, the ego has to observe the external world and preserve a true picture of it in the memory traces left by its perceptions, and, by means of the reality-test, it has to eliminate any element in this picture of the external world which is a contribution from internal sources of excitation. On behalf of the id, the ego controls the path of access to motility, but it interpolates between desire and action the procrastinating factor of thought, during which it makes use of the residues of experience stored up in memory. In this way it dethrones the pleasure-principle, which exerts undisputed sway over the processes in the id, and substitutes for it the reality-principle, which promises greater security and greater success.

The relation to time, too, which is so hard to describe, is communicated to the ego by the perceptual system; indeed it can hardly be doubted that the mode in which this system works is the source of the idea of time. What, however, especially marks the ego out in contradistinction to the id, is a tendency to synthesise its contents, to bring together and unify its mental processes which is entirely absent from the id. When we come to deal presently with the instincts in mental life, I hope we shall succeed in tracing this fundamental characteristic of the ego to its source. It is this alone that produces that high degree of organisation which the ego needs for its highest achievements. The ego advances from the function of perceiving instincts to that of controlling them, but the latter is only achieved through the mental representative of the instinct becoming subordinated to a larger organisation, and finding its place in a coherent unity. In popular language, we may say that the ego stands for reason and circumspection, while the id stands for the untamed passions.

So far we have allowed ourselves to dwell on the enumeration of the merits and capabilities of the ego; it is time now to look at the other side of the picture. The ego is after all only a part of the id, a part purposively modified by its proximity to the dangers of reality. From a dynamic point of view it is weak; it borrows its energy from the id, and we are not entirely ignorant of the methods—one might almost call them "tricks"—by means of which it draws further amounts of energy from the id. Such a method, for example, is the process of identification, whether the object is retained or given up. The object-cathexes proceed from the instinctual demands of the id. The first business of the ego is to take note of them. But by identifying itself with the object, it recommends itself to the id in the place of the object and seeks to attract the libido of the id on to itself. We have already seen that, in the course of a person's life, the ego takes into itself a large number of such precipitates of former object-cathexes. On the whole the ego has to carry out the intentions of the id; it fulfils its duty if it succeeds in creating the conditions under which these intentions can best be fulfilled. One might compare the relation of the ego to the id with that between a rider and his horse. The horse provides the locomotive energy, and the rider has the prerogative of determining the goal and of guiding the movements of his powerful mount towards it. But all too often in the relations between the ego and the id we find a picture of the less ideal situation in which the rider is obliged to guide his horse in the direction in which it itself wants to go.

The ego has separated itself off from one part of the id by means of repression-resistances. But the barrier of repression does not extend into the id; so that the repressed material merges into the rest of the id.

The proverb tells us that one cannot serve two masters at once. The poor ego has a still harder time of it; it has to serve three harsh masters, and has to do its best to reconcile the claims and demands of all three. These demands are always divergent and often seem quite incompatible; no wonder that the ego so frequently gives way under its task. The three tyrants are the external world, the super-ego and the id. When one watches the efforts of the ego to satisfy them all, or rather, to obey them all simultaneously, one cannot regret having personified the ego, and established it as a separate being. It feels itself hemmed in on three sides and threatened by three kinds of danger, towards which it reacts by developing anxiety when it is too hard pressed. Having originated in the experiences of the perceptual system, it is designed to represent the demands of the external world, but it also wishes to be a loyal servant of the id, to remain upon good terms with the id, to recommend itself to the id as an object, and to draw the id's libido on to itself. In its attempt to mediate between the id and reality, it is often forced to clothe the Ucs. commands of the id with its own Pcs. rationalisations, to gloss over the conflicts between the id and reality, and with diplomatic dishonesty to display a pretended regard for reality, even when the id persists in being stubborn and uncompromising. On the other hand, its every movement is watched by the severe super-ego, which holds up certain norms of behaviour, without regard to any difficulties coming from the id and the external world; and if these norms are not acted up to, it punishes the ego with the feelings of tension which manifest themselves as a sense of inferiority and guilt. In this way, goaded on by the id, hemmed in by the super-ego, and rebuffed by reality, the ego struggles to cope with its economic task of reducing the forces and influences which work in it and upon it to some kind of harmony; and we may well understand how it is that we so often cannot repress the cry: "Life is not easy." When the ego is forced to acknowledge its weakness, it breaks out into anxiety: reality anxiety in face of

the external world, normal anxiety in face of the super-ego, and neurotic anxiety in the face of the strength of the passions in the id.

I have represented the structural relations within the mental personality, as I
have explained them to you, in a simple diagram, which I here reproduce.

You will observe how the super-ego goes down into the id; as the heir to
the Oedipus complex it has, after all, intimate connections with the id. It lies
further from the perceptual system than the ego. The id only deals with the external world through the medium of the ego, at least in this diagram. It is certainly still too early to say how far the drawing is correct; in one respect I
know it is not. The space taken up by the unconscious id ought to be incomparably greater than that given to the ego or to the preconscious. You must, if you
please, correct that in your imagination.

And now, in concluding this certainly rather exhausting and perhaps not
very illuminating account, I must add a warning. When you think of this dividing up of the personality into ego, super-ego and id, you must not imagine
sharp dividing lines such as are artificially drawn in the field of political geography. We cannot do justice to the characteristics of the mind by means of

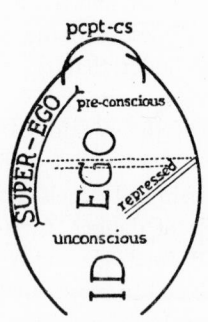

linear contours, such as occur in a drawing or in a
primitive painting, but we need rather the areas of
colour shading off into one another that are to be found
in modern pictures. After we have made our separations,
we must allow what we have separated to merge again.
Do not judge too harshly of a first attempt at picturing a
thing so elusive as the human mind. It is very probable
that the extent of these differentiations varies very greatly
from person to person; it is possible that their function
itself may vary, and that they may at times undergo a
process of involution. This seems to be particularly true
of the most insecure and, from the phylogenetic point of view, the most recent
of them, the differentiation between the ego and the super-ego. It is also incon-
testable that the same thing can come about as a result of mental disease. It
can easily be imagined, too, that certain practices of mystics may succeed in
upsetting the normal relations between the different regions of the mind, so
that, for example, the perceptual system becomes able to grasp relations in the
deeper layers of the ego and in the id which would otherwise be inaccessible to
it. Whether such a procedure can put one in possession of ultimate truths, from
which all good will flow, may be safely doubted. All the same, we must admit
that the therapeutic efforts of psycho-analysis have chosen much the same
method of approach. For their object is to strengthen the ego, to make it more
independent of the super-ego, to widen its field of vision, and so to extend its
organisation that it can take over new portions of the id. Where id was, there
shall ego be.

It is reclamation work, like the draining of the Zuyder Zee.

❧ ❧ ❧

# Technology

*Norbert Wiener*

## The First and the Second Industrial Revolution [1]

ONCE before in history, the machine has impinged upon human culture with an effect of the greatest moment. This previous impact is known as the Industrial Revolution, and it concerns the machine purely as an alternative to human muscle. In order to study the present crisis, which we shall term the second industrial revolution, it is perhaps wise to discuss the history of the earlier crisis as something of a model to which we may go back.

The first industrial revolution had its roots in the intellectual ferment of the eighteenth century, which found the scientific techniques of Newton and Huygens already well developed, but with applications which had yet scarcely transcended astronomy. It had, however, become manifest to all intelligent scientists that the new techniques were going to have a profound effect on the other sciences. The first field in which this came to pass was that of navigation and of clockmaking.

Navigation is an art which dates to ancient times, but it had one conspicuous weakness until the seventeen-thirties. The problem of determining latitude has always been an easy one even in the days of the Greeks. It is simply the problem of determining the angular height of the celestial pole. This may be done roughly by taking the pole star as the actual pole of the heavens and it may be done very precisely by further refinements which locate the center of the apparent circular path of the pole star. On the other hand, the problem of longitudes is always more difficult. Short of a geodetic survey, it can only be solved by a comparison of local time with some standard time such as that of Greenwich. In order to do this, we must either carry the Greenwich time with us on a chronometer or we must find some heavenly clock other than the sun to take the place of a chronometer.

Before either of these two methods had become available for the practical navigator, he was very considerably hampered in his techniques of navigation. He was accustomed to sail along the coast until he reached the latitude he wanted. Then he would strike out on an east or west course, along a parallel of latitude, until he made a landfall. Except by an approximate dead-reckoning, he could not tell how far he was along the course. It was therefore a matter of great importance to him that he should not come unawares onto a dangerous

[1] From *The Human Use of Human Beings* (New York: Houghton Mifflin Company, 1950), pp. 164-189. Reprinted by permission of the Houghton Mifflin Company.

coast. Having made his landfall, he again sailed along the coast until he came to his destination. It will be seen that under these circumstances every voyage was very much of an adventure. Nevertheless, this was the pattern of voyages for many centuries. It can be recognized in the course taken by Columbus, in that of the Silver Fleet, and that of the Acapulco galleons.

This slow and risky procedure was not satisfactory for the admiralties of the eighteenth century. In the first place, the overseas interests of England and France, unlike those of Spain, lay in high latitudes, where the advantage of a direct great-circle course over an east-and-west course is most conspicuous. In the second place, there was a great competition between the two northern powers for the supremacy of the seas, and the advantage of a better navigation was a serious one. It is not a surprise that both governments offered large rewards for an accurate technique of finding longitudes.

The history of these prize contests is complicated and not too edifying. More than one able man was deprived of his rightful triumph, and went bankrupt. In the end, these prizes were awarded in both countries for two very different achievements. One was the design of an accurate ship's chronometer —that is of a clock sufficiently well constructed and compensated to be able to keep the time within a few seconds over a voyage in which it was subject to the continual violent motion of the ship. The other was the construction of good mathematical tables of the motion of the moon, which enabled the navigator to use that body as the clock with which to check the apparent motion of the sun. These two methods have dominated all navigation until the recent development of radio and radar techniques.

Accordingly, the advance guard of the craftsmen of the industrial revolution consisted on the one hand of clockmakers, who used the new mathematics of Newton in the design of their pendulums and their balance wheels; and on the other hand, of optical-instrument makers, with their sextants and their telescopes. The two trades had very much in common. They both demanded the construction of accurate circles and accurate straight lines, and the graduation of these in degrees or in inches. Their tools were the lathe and the dividing engine. These machine tools for delicate work are the ancestors of our whole machine-tool industry of the present day.

It is an interesting reflection that every tool has a genealogy, and that it is descended from the tools by which it has itself been constructed. The clockmakers' lathes of the eighteenth century have led through a clear historical chain of intermediate tools to the great turret lathes of the present day. The series of intervening steps might conceivably have been foreshortened somewhat, but it has necessarily had a certain minimum length. In order to construct a great turret lathe, it is clearly impossible to depend on the unaided human hand for the pouring of the metal, for the placing of the castings on the instruments to machine them, and above all for the power needed in the task of machining them. These must be done through machines that have themselves been manufactured by other machines, and it is only through many stages of this that one reaches back to the original hand or foot lathes of the eighteenth century.

It is thus entirely natural that those who were to develop new inventions were either clockmakers or scientific-instrument makers themselves, or called on people of these crafts to help them. For instance, Watt was a scientific-instrument maker. To show how even a man like Watt had to bide his time before he could extend the precision of clockmaking techniques to larger undertakings, we must remember, as I have said earlier, that his standard of the fit of a piston in a cylinder was that it should be barely possible to insert and move a thin sixpence between them.

We must thus consider navigation and the instruments necessary for it as the locus of an industrial revolution before the main industrial revolution. The main industrial revolution begins with the steam engine. The first form of the steam engine was the crude and wasteful Newcomen engine, which was used for pumping mines. In the middle of the eighteenth century there were abortive attempts to use it for generating power, by making it pump water into elevated reservoirs, and employing the fall of this water to turn waterwheels. Such clumsy devices became obsolete with the introduction of the perfected engines of Watt, which were employed quite early in their history for factory purposes as well as for mine pumping. The end of the eighteenth century saw the steam engine thoroughly established in industry, and the promise of the steamboat on the rivers and of steam traction on land was not far away.

Let us notice that the first place where steam power came into practical use was in replacing one of the most brutal forms of human or animal labor: the pumping of water out of mines. At best, this had been done by draft animals or by crude machines turned by horses. At worst, as in the silver mines of New Spain, it was done by the labor of human slaves. It is a work that is never finished and which can never be interrupted without the possible closing-down of the mine forever. The use of the steam engine to replace this servitude must certainly be regarded as a great humanitarian step forward.

However, slaves do not only pump mines: they also drag loaded riverboats upstream. A second great triumph of the steam engine was the invention of the steamboat, and in particular of the river steamboat. The steam engine at sea was for many years but a supplement of questionable value to the sails carried by every seagoing steamboat; but it was steam transportation on the Mississippi which opened up the interior of the United States. Like the steamboat, the steam locomotive started where it seems now about to die, as a means of hauling heavy freight.

The next place where the Industrial Revolution made itself felt, perhaps a little later than in the field of the heavy labor of mine workers, and simultaneously with the revolution in transportation, was in the textile industry. This was already a sick industry. Even before the power spindle and the power looms, the condition of the spinners and the weavers left much to be desired. The bulk of production which they could perform fell far short of the demands of the day. It might thus appear to have been scarcely possible to conceive that the transition to the machine could have worsened their condition; but worsen it, it most certainly did.

The beginnings of textile-machine development go back of the steam engine. The stocking frame has existed in a form worked by hand ever since the time of Queen Elizabeth. Machine spinning first became necessary in order to furnish warps for hand looms. The complete mechanization of the textile industry, covering weaving as well as spinning, did not occur until the beginning of the nineteenth century. The first textile machines were for hand operation, although the use of horsepower and water power followed very quickly. Part of the impetus behind the development of the Watt engine, as contrasted with the Newcomen engine, was the desire to furnish power in the rotary form needed for textile purposes.

The textile mills furnished the model for almost the whole course of the mechanization of industry. On the social side, they began the transfer of the workers from the home to the factory and from the country to the city. There was an exploitation of the labor of children and women to an extent, and of a brutality, scarcely conceivable at the present time; that is, if we forget the South African diamond mines and ignore the new industrialization of China and India and the general terms of plantation labor in every country. A great deal of this was due to the fact that new techniques had produced new responsibilities, at a time at which no code had yet arisen to take care of these responsibilities. There was, however, a phase which was more technical than moral. This lay in the very nature of early steam power and its transmission. The steam engine was very uneconomical of fuel by modern standards, although this is not as important as it might seem, considering the fact that early engines had none of the more modern type with which to compete. However, among themselves they were much more economical to run on a large scale than on a small one. In contrast with the prime mover, the textile machine, whether it be loom or spindle, is a comparatively light machine, and uses little power. It was therefore economically necessary to assemble these machines in large factories, where many looms and spindles could be run from one steam engine.

At that time the only available means of transmission of power were mechanical. The first among these were the line of shafting, supplemented by the belt and the pulley. Even as late as the time of my own childhood, the typical picture of a factory was that of a great shed with long lines of shafts suspended from the rafters, and pulleys connected by belts to the individual machines. This sort of factory still exists; although in very many cases it has given way to the modern arrangement where the machines are driven individually by electric motors.

Indeed this second picture is the typical one at the present time. The trade of the millwright has taken on a totally new form. Here there is an important fact relevant to the whole history of invention. It was exactly these millwrights and other new craftsmen of the machine age who were to develop the inventions lying at the foundation of our patent system. Now, the mechanical connection of machines involves difficulties that are quite serious, but not easy to cover by any simple mathematical formulation. In the first place, long lines of shafting either have to be well aligned, or to employ ingenious modes of connection, such as universal joints or parallel couplings, which allow for a certain amount of freedom. In the second place, the long lines of bearings needed for such shafts are very high in their power consumption. In the individual machine, the rotating and reciprocating parts are subject to similar demands of rigidity, and to similar demands that the number of bearings must be reduced as far as possible for the sake of low power consumption and simple manufacture. These prescriptions are not easily filled on the basis of general formulas, and they offer an excellent opportunity for ingenuity and inventive skill of the old-fashioned artisan sort.

It is in view of this fact that the change-over in engineering between mechanical connections and electrical connections has had so great an effect. The electrical motor is a mode of distributing power which it is very convenient to construct in small sizes, so that the individual machine may have its own motor. The transmission losses in the wiring of a factory are relatively low, and the efficiency of the motor itself is relatively high. The connection of the motor with its wiring is not necessarily rigid, nor does it consist of many parts. There are still motives of traffic and convenience which may induce us to continue the custom of mounting the different machines of an industrial process in a single factory; but the need of connecting all the machines to a single source of power is no longer a serious reason for geographical proximity. In other words, we are now in a position to return to cottage industry, in places where it would otherwise be suitable.

Moreover, if it should be so desired, a single piece of machinery may contain several motors, each introducing power at the proper place. This relieves the designer of much of the need for the ingenuity in mechanical design which he would otherwise have been compelled to use. In an electrical design, the mere problem of the connection of the parts seldom involves much difficulty of a nature which does not lend itself to easy mathematical formulation and solution. This is an example of the way in which the art of invention is conditioned by the existing means.

In the third quarter of the last century, when the electric motor began to be employed in industry, it was at first supposed to be nothing more than an alternative device for carrying out existing industrial techniques. It was probably not foreseen that its final effect would be to give rise to a new concept of the factory.

That other great electrical invention, the vacuum tube, has had a similar history. Before the invention of the vacuum tube, it was a matter of a large number of separate tasks of design to develop the regulation of systems of great power. Indeed, most of the regulatory means employed did not involve a particularly low level of power. There were exceptions to this lack of development of methods of control, but they were in specific fields, such as the steering of ships.

As late as 1915, I crossed the ocean on one of the old ships of the American Line. It belonged to the transitional period when ships still carried sails and the masts on which to stretch them, as well as a pointed bow to carry a bowsprit. In a well-deck not far aft of the main superstructure, there was a formidable engine, consisting of four or five six-foot wheels with hand-spokes. These wheels were supposed to be the method of controlling the ship when its automatic steering engine had broken down. In a storm, it would have taken ten men or more, exerting their full strength, to keep that great ship on its course.

This was not the usual method of control of the ship, but an emergency replacement, or as sailors call it, a "jury steering wheel." For normal control, the ship carried, as had all other large ships for years, a steering engine which translated the relatively small forces of the quartermaster at the wheel into the movement of the massive rudder. Thus even on a purely mechanical basis, some progress had been made toward the solution of the problem of amplification of forces or torques. Nevertheless, at that time, this solution of the amplification problem did not range over extreme differences between the levels of input and of output, nor was it embodied in a convenient universal type of apparatus.

The most flexible universal apparatus for amplifying small energy-levels into high energy-levels is the vacuum tube, or electron valve. The history of this is interesting, though it is too complex for us to discuss here. It is however amusing to reflect that the invention of the electron valve goes back to the greatest scientific discovery of Edison, and perhaps the only one which he did not capitalize into an invention.

He observed that when an electrode was placed inside an electric lamp, and was taken as electrically positive with respect to the filament, then a current would flow, if the filament were heated, but not otherwise. Through a series of inventions by other people, this led to a more effective way than any known before of controlling a large current by a small voltage. This is the basis of the modern radio industry, but it is also an industrial tool which is spreading widely into new fields. It is thus no longer necessary to control a process at high energy-levels by a mechanism in which the important details of control are carried out at these levels. It is quite possible to form a certain pattern of behavior response at levels even much lower than those found in usual radio sets, and then to employ a series of amplifying tubes to control by this apparatus a machine as heavy as a steel-rolling mill. The work of discriminating and of forming the pattern of behavior for this is done under conditions under which the power losses are insignificant, and yet the final employment of this discriminatory process is at arbitrarily high levels of power.

It will be seen that this is an invention which alters the fundamental postulational conditions of industry, quite as vitally as the transmission and subdivision of power through the use of the small electric motor. The study of the pattern of behavior is transferred to a special part of the instrument in which power-economy is of very little importance. We have thus deprived of much of their importance the dodges and devices previously used to insure that a mechanical linkage should consist of the fewest possible elements, as well as the devices used to minimize friction and loss motion. The design of machines involving such parts has been transferred from the domain of the skilled shopworker to that of the research-laboratory man; and in this he has all the available tools of circuit theory to replace a mechanical ingenuity by the old sort. Invention in the old sense has been supplanted by the intelligent employment of the laws of nature. The step from the laws of nature to their employment has been reduced a hundred times.

I have previously said that when an invention is made, it is generally a considerable period before its full implications are understood. It was long before people became aware of the full impact of the airplane on international relations and on the conditions of human life. The effect of atomic energy on mankind and the future is yet to be assessed, although many stupid people of the present day assess it merely as a new weapon like all older weapons.

The situation with the vacuum tube was similar. In the beginning, it was regarded merely as an extra tool to supplement an already existing technique of telephone communication. The electrical engineers first mistook its real importance to such an extent that for years the vacuum tubes were relegated to a particular part of the communication network. This part was connected up with other parts consisting only of the traditional so-called inactive circuit elements —the resistance, the capacitances and the inductances. Only since the war have engineers felt free enough in their employment of vacuum tubes to insert them where necessary, with the same freedom with which they have previously inserted passive elements of these three kinds.

The vacuum tube was first used to replace previously existing components of long-distance telephone circuits and of the wireless telegraphy of the time. It was not long, however, until it had become clear that the radio-telephone had achieved the stature of the radio-telegraph, and that broadcasting was possible. Let not the fact that this great triumph of invention has been given over to the soap-opera and the hillbilly singer blind one to the excellent work which was done in developing it, and to the great civilizing possibilities which have been perverted into a national medicine-show.

Thus the vacuum tube received its début in the communications industry. The boundaries and extent of this industry were not fully understood for a long period. There were sporadic uses of the vacuum tube and of its sister invention, the photo-electric cell, for scanning the products of industry; as for example, for regulating the thickness of a web coming out of a paper machine, or for inspecting the color of a can of pineapples. These uses did not as yet form a reasoned new technique, nor were they associated in the engineering line with the task of communication.

All this changed in the war. One of the few things to be salvaged from the great conflict was the rapid development of invention, under the stimulus of necessity and the unlimited employment of money; and above all, the new blood called in to industrial research. At the beginning of the war, our greatest need was to keep England from being knocked out by an overwhelming air attack. Accordingly, the anti-aircraft cannon was one of the first objects of our scientific war effort, especially when combined with the airplane-detecting device of radar or ultra-high-frequency Hertzian waves. The technique of radar used the same modalities as the existing technique of radio besides inventing new ones of its own. It was thus natural to consider radar as a branch of communication theory. The speed of the airplane made it necessary to give the predicting machine itself communication functions which had previously been assigned to human beings. Thus the problem of anti-aircraft fire control made familiar the notion of a communication addressed to a machine rather than to a person.

During the pre-war period other uses were found for the vacuum tube coupled directly with the machine rather than with the human agent. The concept of the large-scale computing machine as developed by Vannevar Bush among others was originally a purely mechanical one. The integration was done by rolling disks engaging one another in a frictional manner; and the interchange of outputs and inputs between these disks was the task of a classical train of shafts and gears.

The mother idea of these first computing machines is much older than the work of Vannevar Bush. In certain respects it goes back to the work of Babbage early in the last century. Babbage had an idea of the computing machine which is surprisingly modern, but his mechanical means fell far behind his ambitions. The first difficulty he met, and with which he could not cope, was that a long train of gears requires a considerable energy to run it, so that its output of power and torque very soon becomes too small to actuate the remaining parts of the apparatus. Bush saw this difficulty and overcame it in a very ingenious way. Besides the electrical amplifiers depending on vacuum tubes and on similar devices, there are certain mechanical torque-amplifiers which are familiar to everyone acquainted with ships and the unloading of cargo. The stevedore raises the cargo-slings by taking a purchase of his load around the drum of a donkey-engine or cargo-hoist. In this way, the tension which he exerts mechanically is increased by a factor which grows extremely rapidly with the angle of contact between his rope and the rotating drum. Thus one man is able to control the lifting of a load of many tons.

This device is fundamentally a force- or torque-amplifier. By an ingenious bit of design, Bush inserted such mechanical amplifiers between the stages of his computing machine; and was thereby able to do effectively the sort of thing which Babbage had only dreamed of theoretically.

In one of the earlier models of the Bush Differential Analyzer, this sort of mechanical device performed all the principal amplification functions. The only use of electricity was to give power to the motors running the machine as a whole. This state of computing-mechanisms was intermediate and transitory. It very soon became clear that amplifiers of an electric nature, connected by wires rather than by shafts, were both less expensive and more flexible than mechanical amplifiers and mechanical connections. Accordingly, the later forms of Bush's machine made an adequate use of vacuum-tube devices. This has been continued in all their successors; whether they were what is called now analogy machines, which work primarily by the measurement of physical quantities, or digital machines, which work primarily by counting and the operations of arithmetic.

The development of these computing machines has been very rapid since the war. For a large range of computational work, they have shown themselves vastly more rapid and vastly more accurate than the human computer. Their speed has long since reached such a level that any intermediate human intervention in their work is out of the question. Thus they offer the same need to replace human capacities by machine capacities as those in the anti-aircraft computer. The parts of the machine must speak to one another through an appropriate language, without speaking to any person or listening to any person, except in the terminal and initial stages of the process. Here again we have an element which has contributed to the general acceptance of the extension to machines of the idea of communication.

In this conversation between the parts of a machine, it is often necessary to take cognizance of what the machine has already said. Here there enters the notion of feedback, which is older than its exemplification in the ship's steering engine, and is as old, in fact, as the governor which regulates the speed of Watts' steam engine. This governor is needed to keep the engine from running wild when its load is removed. If it starts to run wild, the balls of the governor fly upward from centrifugal action, and in their upward flight they move a lever which partly cuts off the admission of steam. Thus the tendency to speed up produces a partly compensatory tendency to slow down. This method of regulation received a thorough mathematical analysis at the hands of Clerk Maxwell in 1868.

Here feedback is used to regulate the velocity of a machine. In the ship's steering engine it regulates the position of the rudder. The man at the wheel operates a light transmission system, employing chains or hydraulic transmission, which moves a member in the room containing the steering engine. There is some sort of apparatus which notes the distance between this member and the tiller; and this distance controls the admission of steam to the ports of a steam steering-engine, or some similar electrical admission in the case of an electrical steering-engine. Whatever the particular connections may be, this change of admission is always in such a direction as to bring into coincidence the tiller and the member actuated from the wheel. Thus one man at the wheel can do with ease what a whole crew could only do with difficulty at the old man-power wheel.

We have so far given examples where the feedback process takes primarily a mechanical form. However, a series of operations of the same structure can be carried out through electrical and even vacuum-tube means. These means promise to be the future standard method of designing control apparatus.

Quite apart from the vacuum tube and the method of feedback, there has long been a tendency to render factories and machines automatic. Except for some special purpose, one would no longer think of producing screws by the use of the ordinary lathe, in which a mechanic must watch the progress of his cutter and regulate it by hand. The production of screws in quantity without serious human intervention is now the normal task of the ordinary screw machine. Although this does not make any special use of the process of feedback nor of the vacuum tube, it accomplishes a somewhat similar end. What the feedback and the vacuum tube have made possible is not the sporadic design of individual automatic mechanisms, but a general policy for the construction of automatic mechanisms of the most varied type. In this they have been reinforced by our new theoretical treatment of communication, which takes full cognizance of the possibilities of communication between machine and machine. It is this conjunction of circumstances which now renders possible the new automatic age.

The existing state of industrial techniques includes the whole of the results of the first industrial revolution, together with many inventions which we now see to be precursors of the second industrial revolution. What the precise boundary between these two revolutions may be, it is still too early to say. In its potential significance, the vacuum tube certainly belongs to an industrial revolution different from that of the age of power; and yet it is only at present that the true significance of the invention of the vacuum tube has been sufficiently realized to allow us to attribute the present age to a new and second industrial revolution.

Up to now we have been talking about the existing state of affairs. We have not covered more than a small part of the aspects of the previous industrial revolution. We have not mentioned the airplane, nor the bulldozer, together with the other mechanical tools of construction, nor the automobile, nor even one-tenth of those factors which have converted the form of modern life to something totally unlike the life of any other period. It is fair to say, however, that except for a considerable number of isolated examples, the industrial revolution up to the present has displaced man and the beast as a source of power, without making any great impression on other human functions. The best that a pick-and-shovel worker can do to make a living at the present time is to act as a sort of gleaner after the bulldozer. In all important respects, the

man who has nothing but his physical power to sell has nothing to sell which *THOUGHT*
it is worth anyone's money to buy.

Let us now go on to a picture of a more completely automatic age. Let us consider what for example the automobile factory of the future will be like; and in particular the assembly line, which is that one of the component parts of that sort of factory which employs the most labor. In the first place, the sequence of operations will be controlled by something like a modern high-speed computing machine. I have often said that the high-speed computing machine is primarily a logical machine, which confronts different propositions with one another and draws some of their consequences. It is possible to translate the whole of mathematics into the performance of a sequence of purely logical tasks. If this representation of mathematics is embodied in the machine, the machine will be a computing machine in the ordinary sense. Nevertheless, such a computing machine, besides ordinary mathematical tasks, will involve the logical task of channeling a series of orders concerning mathematical operations. Therefore, as present high-speed computing machines in fact do, it will contain at least one large assembly which is purely logical.

The instructions to such a machine, and here too I am speaking of present practice, are given by what we have called a taping. The orders given the machine may be fed into it by a taping which is completely predetermined. It is also possible that the actual contingencies met in the performance of the machine may be handed over as a basis of further regulation to a new control tape constructed by the machine itself, or to a modification of the old one.

It may be thought that the present great expense of computing machines bars them from use in industrial processes; and furthermore that the delicacy of the work needed in their construction and the variability of their functions precludes the use of the methods of mass production in constructing them. Neither of these charges is correct. In the first place, the enormous computing machines now used for the highest level of mathematical work cost something of the order of hundreds of thousands of dollars. Even this price would not be forbidding for the control machine of a really large factory, but it is not the relevant price. The present computing machines are developing so rapidly that practically every one constructed is a new model. In other words, a large part of these apparently exorbitant prices goes into new work of design, and into new parts, which are produced by a very high quality of labor under the most expensive circumstances. If one of these computing machines were therefore established in price and model, and put to use in quantities of tens or twenties, it is very doubtful whether its price would be in a higher range than that of tens of thousands of dollars. A similar machine of less capacity, not suited for the most difficult computational problems, but nevertheless quite adequate for factory control, would probably cost no more than a few thousand dollars in any sort of moderate-scale production.

Now let us consider the problem of mass production. If the only opportunity for mass production were the mass production of completed machines, it is quite clear that for a considerable period the best we could hope for would be a moderate-scale production. However, in each machine the parts are largely repetitive in very considerable numbers. This is true, whether we consider the memory apparatus, the logical apparatus, or the arithmetical subassembly. Thus production of a few dozen machines only, represents a potential mass production of the parts, and is accompanied with the same economic advantages.

It may still seem that the delicacy of the machines must mean that each job demands a special new model. This is also false. Given even a rough similarity in the type of mathematical and logical operations demanded of the mathematical and logical units of the machine, the over-all performance is regulated by the taping, or at any rate by the *original* taping. The taping of such a machine is a highly skilled intellectual task for a professional man of a very specialized type; but it is largely or entirely a once-for-all job, and need only be partly repeated when the machine is modified for a new industrial setup. Thus the cost of such a skilled technician will be distributed over a tremendous output, and will not really be a significant factor in the use of the machine.

The computing machine represents the center of the automatic factory, but it will never be the whole factory. On the one hand, it receives its detailed instructions from elements of the nature of sense organs. I am thinking of sense organs such as photo-electric cells, condensers for the reading of the thickness of a web of paper, thermometers, hydrogen-ion-concentration meters, and the general run of apparatus now built by instrument companies for the manual control of industrial processes. These instruments are already built to report electrically at remote stations. All they need to enable them to introduce their information into an automatic high-speed computor is a reading apparatus which will translate position or scale into a pattern of consecutive digits. Such apparatus already exists, and offers no great difficulty, either of principle or of constructional detail. The sense-organ problem is not new, and it is already effectively solved.

Besides these sense organs, the control system must contain effectors, or components which act on the outer world. Some of these are of a type already familiar, such as valve-turning motors, electric clutches, and the like. Some of them will have to be invented, to duplicate more nearly the functions of the human hand as supplemented by the human eye. It is altogether possible in the machining of automobile frames to leave on certain metal lugs, machined into smooth surfaces as points of reference. The tool, whether it be drill or riveter or whatever else we want, may be led to the rough neighborhood of these surfaces by a photo-electric mechanism, actuated for example by spots of paint. The final positioning may bring the tool up against the reference surfaces, so as to establish a firm contact, but not a destructively firm one. This is only one way of doing the job. Any competent engineer can think of a dozen more.

Of course, we assume that the instruments which act as sense organs to the system record not only the original state of the work, but also the result of the

functioning of all previous processes. Thus the machine may carry out feedback operations, either those of the simple type now so thoroughly understood,
or those involving more complicated processes of discrimination, regulated by
the central control as a logical or mathematical system. In other words, the all-
over system will correspond to the complete animal with sense organs, effectors
and proprioceptors, and not, as in the ultra-rapid computing machine, to an
isolated brain, dependent for its experiences and for its effectiveness on our
intervention.

The speed with which these new devices are likely to come into industrial
use will vary greatly with the different industries. Automatic devices, which
may not be precisely like those described here, but which perform roughly the
same functions, have already come into extensive use in continuous-process
industries like canneries, steel-rolling mills, and especially wire and tin-plate
factories. They are also familiar in paper factories, which likewise produce a
continuous output. Another place where they are indispensable is in that sort
of factory which is too dangerous for any considerable number of workers to
risk their lives in its control, and in which an emergency is likely to be so
serious and costly that its possibilities should have been considered in advance,
rather than left to the excited judgment of somebody on the spot. If a policy
can be thought out in advance, it can be committed to a taping which will
regulate the conduct to be followed in accordance with the readings of the
instrument. In other words, such factories should be under a régime rather like
that of the interlocking signals and switches of the railroad signal-tower. This
régime is already followed in oil-cracking factories, in many other chemical
works, and in the handling of the sort of dangerous materials found in the
exploitation of atomic energy.

We have already mentioned the assembly line as a place for applying the
same sorts of technique. In the assembly line, as in the chemical factory or the
continuous-process paper mill, it is necessary to exert a certain statistical control on the quality of the product. This control depends on a sampling process.
These sampling processes have now been developed by Wald and others into
a technique called *sequential analysis,* in which the sampling is no longer
taken in a lump, but is a continuous process going along with the production.
That which can be done then by a technique so standardized that it can be
put in the hands of a statistical computer who does not understand the logic
behind it, may also be executed by a computing machine. In other words,
except again at the highest levels, the machine takes care of the routine statistical controls, as well as of the production process.

In general, factories have an accounting procedure which is independent of
the production. As far as the data which occur in cost-accounting are concerned,
that part which comes from the machine or assembly line may be fed directly
into the computing machine. Other data may be fed in from time to time by
human operators, but the bulk of necessary clerical work will be cut to that
not of a completely routine nature. For example, girls will be needed to take

care of outside correspondence and the like. Even a large part of this may be received from the correspondents on punched cards, or transferred to punched cards by extremely low-grade labor. From this stage on, everything may go by machine. This mechanization also may apply to a not inappreciable part of the library and filing facilities of an industrial plant.

In other words, the machine plays no favorites as between overall labor and white collar labor. Thus the possible fields into which the new industrial revolution is likely to penetrate are very extensive; and include all labor performing judgments of a low level, in much the same way as the displaced labor of the earlier industrial revolution included every aspect of human power. There will, of course, be trades into which the new industrial revolution of judgment will not penetrate: either because the new control machines are not economical in industries on so small a scale as not to be able to carry the considerable capital costs involved, or because their work is so varied that a new taping will be necessary for almost every job. I cannot see automatic machinery of the judgment-replacing type coming into use in the corner grocery, or in the corner garage, although I can very well see it employed by the wholesale grocer and the automobile manufacturer. The farm laborer too, although he is beginning to be pressed by automatic machinery, is protected from the full pressure of it, because of the ground he has to cover, the variability of the crops he must till, and the special conditions of weather and the like that he must meet. Even here, the large-scale or plantation farmer is becoming increasingly dependent on cotton-picking and weed-burning machinery, as the wheat farmer has long been dependent on the McCormick reaper. Where such machines may be used, some use of machinery of judgment is not inconceivable.

The introduction of the new devices and the dates at which they are to be expected are, of course, largely economic matters, on which I am not an expert. Short of any violent political changes or another great war, I should give a rough estimate that it will take the new tools ten to twenty years to come into their own. A war would change all this overnight. If we should engage in a war with a major power like Russia, which would make serious demands on the infantry, and consequently on our man-power, we may be hard put to it to keep up our industrial production. Under these circumstances, the matter of replacing human production by other modes may well be a life-or-death matter to the nation. We are already as far along in the process of developing a unified system of automatic control machines as we were in the development of radar in 1939. Just as the emergency of the Battle of Britain made it necessary to attack the radar problem in a massive manner, and to hurry up the natural development of the field by what may have been decades, so too, the needs of labor replacement are likely to act on us in a similar way in the case of another war. The personnel of skilled radio amateurs, mathematicians, and physicists, who were so rapidly turned into competent electrical engineers for the purposes of radar design, is still available for the very similar task of automatic-machine design. There is a new and skilled generation coming up, which they have trained.

Under these circumstances, the period of about two years which it took for radar to get onto the battlefield with a high degree of effectiveness is scarcely likely to be exceeded by the period of evolution of the automatic factory. At the end of such a war, the "know-how" needed to construct such factories will be common. There will even be a considerable backlog of equipment manufactured for the government, which is likely to be on sale or available to the industrialists. Thus a new war will almost inevitably see the automatic age in full swing within less than five years.

I have spoken of the actuality and the imminence of this new possibility. What can we expect of its economic and social consequences? In the first place, we can expect an abrupt and final cessation of the demand for the type of factory labor performing purely repetitive tasks. In the long run, the deadly uninteresting nature of the repetitive task may make this a good thing, and the source of the leisure which is necessary for the full cultural development of man on all sides. It may also produce cultural results as trivial and wasteful as the greater part of those so far obtained from the radio and the movies.

Be that as it may, the intermediate period of the introduction of the new means, especially if it comes in the fulminating manner to be expected from a new war, will lead to an immediate transitional period of disastrous confusion. We have a good deal of experience as to how the industrialists regard a new industrial potential. Their whole propaganda is to the effect that it must not be considered as the business of the government but must be left open to whatever entrepreneurs wish to invest money in it. We also know that they have very few inhibitions when it comes to taking all the profit out of an industry that there is to be taken, and then letting the public pick up the pieces. This is the history of the lumber and mining industries, and is part of the traditional American philosophy of progress.

Under these circumstances, industry will be flooded with the new tools to the extent that they appear to yield immediate profits, irrespective of what long-time damage they can do. We shall see a process parallel to the way in which the use of atomic energy for bombs has been allowed to compromise the very necessary potentialities of the long-time use of atomic power to replace our oil and coal supplies, which are within centuries, if not decades, of utter exhaustion. Note well that atomic bombs do not compete with power companies.

Let us remember that the automatic machine, whatever we think of any feelings it may have or may not have, is the precise economic equivalent of slave labor. Any labor which competes with slave labor must accept the economic conditions of slave labor. It is perfectly clear that this will produce an unemployment situation, in comparison with which the present recession and even the depression of the thirties will seem a pleasant joke. This depression will ruin many industries—possibly even the industries which have taken advantage of the new potentialities. However, there is nothing in the industrial tradition which forbids an industrialist to make a sure and quick profit, and to get out before the crash touches him personally.

Thus the new industrial revolution is a two-edged sword. It may be used for the benefit of humanity, assuming that humanity survives long enough to enter a period in which such a benefit is possible. If, however, we proceed along the clear and obvious lines of our traditional behavior, and follow our traditional worship of progress and the fifth freedom—the freedom to exploit—it is practically certain that we shall have to face a decade or more of ruin and despair.

❦ ❦ ❦

## David M. Potter

# Democracy and Abundance[1]

ONE OF THE most widely current phrases of the second World War was the designation of the countries in arms against the axis as the "freedom-loving nations." It was a conveniently vague term for masking the diversity of the cobelligerents, and its essential irony was not at the time apparent, even when it was applied to the Soviet Union. But, apart from its value as an expedient, the phrase undoubtedly gained great vitality from a genuine belief among Americans that the peoples of the world fall into two categories: those who love freedom and those who do not. Implicitly, we understood, of course, that we were the most devoted of all and that, while other countries might prove fickle in their affection, we could pride ourselves upon a record of constant fidelity. It was as if all the world had been presented with a choice between a right principle of government and a wrong one, and we, more than any others, had been unequivocal in choosing the right.

It is not unnatural, of course, for Americans to take this view of their political institutions. Americans have always been especially prone to regard all things as resulting from the free choice of a free will. Probably no people have so little determinism in their philosophy, and as individuals we have regarded our economic status, our matrimonial happiness, and even our eternal salvation as things of our own making. Why should we not then regard our political felicity, likewise, as a virtue which is also virtue's reward?

If this way of explaining ourselves to ourselves had no other result than to nourish our self-esteem, it would hardly be worthy of any special attention, for excessive national pride is in no sense peculiar to the United States. But our conception of democracy as a simple matter of moral choice has caused us to hope falsely that other countries will embrace democracy as we understand it, and to misconstrue badly the reasons for their failure to do so. It has even led

[1] From *People of Plenty* (Chicago: The University of Chicago Press, 1954), chap. V. Copyright 1954 by the University of Chicago.

us to condemn, quite unjustly, the countries which fail to establish a democracy like our own, as if it were plain obstinacy or even outright iniquity which explains their behavior.[2]

By viewing democracy simply as a question of political morality, we have blinded ourselves to the fact that, in every country, the system of government is a by-product of the general conditions of life, including, of course, the economic conditions, and that democracy, like any other system, is appropriate for countries where these conditions are suited to it and inappropriate for others with unsuitable conditions, or at least that it is vastly more appropriate for some than for others. Viewed in these terms, there is a strong case for believing that democracy is clearly most appropriate for countries which enjoy an economic surplus and least appropriate for countries where there is an economic insufficiency. In short, economic abundance is conducive to political democracy.[3]

At first glance this proposition may seem abjectly deterministic and may seem to imply that our democracy, like our climate, is a mere matter of luck, involving no merit. But it does not necessarily mean that we enjoy democracy without achieving it; rather, it means that we have achieved it less by sheer ideological devotion to the democratic principle than by the creation of economic conditions in which democracy will grow. In doing this, we have, of course, enjoyed the advantage of unequaled natural resources, but, as I have already sought to show, abundant physical endowments do not automatically or invariably produce an economic surplus for the area which possesses them. For instance, New England, poorly endowed by nature, became, in the nineteenth century, one of the richest regions of the United States, while the Cotton South, richly endowed, committed itself to a slave-labor system, a one-crop system, and an economy restricted to producing raw materials, which, in the end, left it the poorest part of the nation.

These instances and many others indicate that man may, through cultural processes, use environment well or use it ill; he may make his political system one of the instruments for such use; he may apply democratic devices for the purpose of developing or distributing abundance, and then he may use abundance as a base for the broadening and consolidation of his democracy. Or, to put it another way, he may use an economic surplus for the purpose of furthering a democratic system which will, in turn, enable him to increase further his economic surplus.

But, though this view does not, in a deterministic sense, deny man credit for democratic accomplishments, it does argue that he should distinguish very care-

[2] "We have believed as a nation that other peoples had only to will our democratic institutions in order to repeat our own career" (Frederick Jackson Turner, *The Frontier in American History* [New York: Henry Holt & Co., 1920], p. 244).

[3] "Political democracy came to the United States as the result of economic democracy. . . . This nation came to be marked by political institutions of a democratic type because it had, still earlier, come to be characterized in its economic life by democratic arrangements and practices" (J. Franklin Jameson, *The American Revolution Considered as a Social Movement* [Princeton: Princeton University Press, 1926], p. 41).

fully the things for which credit is claimed. A nation may properly be proud that it has developed the economic means which enable it to afford a full-fledged democracy or that it has utilized democratic practices to create the economic base on which a democracy can be further broadened. But it cannot, with any validity, attribute its democracy to sheer moral and ideological virtue. Shaw stated the point forcibly in his Preface to *John Bull's Other Island*, when he said, "The virtues of the English soil are not less real because they consist of coal and iron, not of metaphysical sources of character. The virtues of Broadbent [the Englishman] are not less real because they are the virtues of the money that coal and iron have produced."

To understand why a democratic system depends upon an economic surplus, one has only to compare what a democracy offers to its citizens and what other regimes offer. All social systems, of course, seek to keep the bulk of their people contented, and all of them make promises of one kind or another in order to do this—some have promised a utopia in the indefinite future; others have offered, instead of real welfare, inexpensive distractions such as the bread and circuses of the Romans or the lotteries of modern Spain and Latin America; still others have attempted to provide real cradle-to-the-grave security. But however much or little a society, or a government acting for the society, may have to allot, it is axiomatic that it must not arouse expectations very much higher than it is able to satisfy. This means that it must not hold out the promise of opportunity unless there is a reasonable prospect of the opportunity's being fulfilled. It must not invite the individual to compete for prizes unless there are a substantial number of awards to be passed out.[4]

In all societies of economic insufficiency, which is the only kind that existed up to about two centuries ago, certain social conditions have been fixed and inevitable. The vast majority of the people were inescapably destined to heavy toil and bare subsistence, and the economic surplus in excess of such bare subsistence was not sufficient to give leisure and abundance to more than a tiny minority. In these circumstances, certainly the society could not afford either the economic or the emotional costs of conducting a great social steeplechase for the purpose of selecting a handful of winners to occupy the few enviable positions.[5] It was much sounder public policy to assign these positions by an arbitrary system of status and at the same time to assign to the great bulk of the people the burdens which most of them were destined to bear regardless of what regime was in power. Under a system of subordination transmitted by heredity, social competition, with its attendant loss of energy through friction,

[4] For extended, systematic consideration of the manner in which a society motivates its members to perform the roles necessary to the functioning of the social system see Talcott Parsons, *Essays in Sociological Theory* (Glencoe, Ill.: Free Press, 1949), and Robert K. Merton, *Social Theory and Social Structure* (Glencoe, Ill.: Free Press, 1949).

[5] "And yet, Burke might have countered, once the masses were fated by the laws of political economy to toil in misery, what else was the idea of equality but a cruel bait to goad mankind into self-destruction" (Karl Polanyi, *The Great Transformation* [New York: Rinehart & Co., 1944], p. 119).

was avoided; the status-bound individual often gained a sense of contentment with his lot and even of dignity within his narrow sphere, and all that he sacrificed for this psychological advantage was a statistically negligible chance for advancement. Moreover, in a relatively static and relatively simple society such as that of Tudor or Stuart England, the problems of government were not very intricate, and the only qualities required in the local ruling class were integrity and a willingness to accept responsibility. These qualities could usually be found and could readily be transmitted even in a squirearchy of low intellectual attainments, and therefore there was no need to recruit widely for leadership, as a society must do when it requires intelligence, specialized skill, and adaptability in its administration.

A country with inadequate wealth, therefore, could not safely promise its citizens more than security of status—at a low level in the social hierarchy and with a meager living. But this promise is, in its denial of equality, by definition, undemocratic. A democracy, by contrast, setting equality as its goal, must promise opportunity, for the goal of equality becomes a mockery unless there is some means of attaining it. But in promising opportunity, the democracy is constantly arousing expectations which it lacks the current means to fulfil and is betting on its ability to procure the necessary means by the very act of stimulating people to demand them and go after them. It is constantly educating large numbers of people without waiting to see whether jobs requiring education are available for all of them; it does this in the expectation that the supply will create a demand and that a society constantly rising in the level of its education will constantly generate new posts in which educated people are needed. Also, democracy is forever encouraging individuals to determine their own goals and set their own courses toward these goals, even though only a small proportion can attain complete success; the time and effort of many may be wasted in the pursuit, but the advantage to society of having the maximum number of people developing their maximum potentialities of intellect and personality is thought to justify the social cost.

All this is very well and works admirably if the country following these practices has the necessary physical resources and human resourcefulness to raise the standard of living, to create new occupational opportunities, and to find outlets for the abilities of an ever increasing class of trained men. But it must have this endowment to begin with, or it is certain to suffer intensely from the social waste that results from giving training which cannot be utilized and from the psychological damage that results when a competition has an excess of participants and a paucity of rewards. In short, to succeed as a democracy, a country must enjoy an economic surplus to begin with or must contrive to attain one.[6]

If this is true, it means that the principles of democracy are not universal

[6] John Taylor of Caroline said, "Wealth, like suffrage, must be considerably distributed to sustain a democratick republic; and hence, whatever draws a considerable proportion of either into a few hands will destroy it" (*An Inquiry into the Principles and Policy of the Government of the United States* [Fredericksburg, Va., 1814], pp. 274-75).

truths, ignored during centuries of intellectual darkness and brought to light at last in the age of the American Revolution, but rather that democracy is the foremost by far of the many advantages which our economic affluence has bought for us. To say this, of course, is also to say that, when we propose world-wide adoption of democracy, our problem is not merely to inspire a belief in it but to encourage conditions conducive to it. About a year ago an English visitor in America made a comparison between socialism and free-enterprise democracy, which illustrated extremely well, though quite unwittingly, the reliance of democracy upon these conditions.

The comparison was based on a contrast between the ways in which the two systems in question might deal with the departure of a passenger train. Under a thoroughgoing system of socialism, said the description, the seating of all passengers would be directed. Station attendants would supervise the seating of every ticket-holder. They would arbitrarily place together people who did not want to sit together or place individuals in seats with ventilation or sunlight which those individuals particularly disliked. At the scheduled hour of departure, they would delay the train in order to complete their arrangements. Cost of operations would be increased, passengers vexed, and timetables disrupted.

In a democracy of the American kind, said the comparison, those who particularly want good seats come early, while those who do not care come late, quite prepared to accept what is left. Individuals indulge their own preferences and aversions as to sunlight and in the choice of neighbors. They distribute themselves, automatically and to the maximum satisfaction of all concerned, throughout the train, and all this is accomplished without supervision, without expense, and without delay.

Like all analogies, this one probably has its pitfalls; but, without stopping to look for them, can we not observe one major unstated assumption in the description of the democratic train? It is the simple assumption that *there will be enough seats for everyone*; that the average passenger stands a reasonably good chance of finding one that will satisfy him. If the passenger train symbolizes the American economy, this assumption is valid, but for other countries it may or may not be valid, and certainly it is the sufficiency of seats, quite as much as the method of seat-selection, which makes the democratic system work.

Not only has the presence of more than enough seats, more than enough rewards for those who strive, made the maintenance of a democratic system possible in America; it has also given a characteristic tone to American equalitarianism as distinguished from the equalitarianism of the Old World. Essentially, the difference is that Europe has always conceived of redistribution of wealth as necessitating the expropriation of some and the corresponding aggrandizement of others; but America has conceived of it primarily in terms of giving to some without taking from others. Hence, Europe cannot think of altering the relationship between the various levels of society without assuming a class struggle; but America has altered and can alter these relationships without necessarily treating one class as the victim or even, in an ultimate sense, the antagonist of another. The European mind often assumes implicitly that the volume of wealth is fixed; that most of the potential wealth has already been converted into actual wealth; that this actual wealth is already in the hands of owners; and, therefore, that the only way for one person or group to secure more is to wrest it from some other person or group, leaving that person or group with less. The British Labour party, for instance, has, I believe, placed greater emphasis upon the heavy taxation of the wealthy and less upon the increase of productive capacity than an American labor party might have done. The American mind, by contrast, often assumes implicitly that the volume of wealth is dynamic, that much potential wealth still remains to be converted; and that diverse groups—for instance, capital and labor—can take more wealth out of the environment by working together than they can take out of one another by class warfare.

European radical thought is prone to demand that the man of property be stripped of his carriage and his fine clothes; but American radical thought is likely to insist, instead, that the ordinary man is entitled to mass-produced copies, indistinguishable from the originals. Few Americans feel entirely at ease with the slogan "Soak the rich," but the phrase "Deal me in" springs spontaneously and joyously to American lips.

This American confidence that our abundance will suffice for the attainment of all the goals of social justice is evident throughout the greater part of our national history. Even before the American Revolution, squatters who had entered into illegal occupation of land on the Pennsylvania frontier justified their action by declaring that "it was against the law of God and nature that so much land should be idle while so many Christians wanted it to labor on to raise bread." They did not contend, it is worth noticing, that it was wrong in general for man to want for bread. They probably had been taught to regard want as part of the order of nature; but, where so much land was available, then it was wrong for men to want. In other words, the availability of an economic surplus altered the standards of social justice.

It has been altering them ever since. It enabled Dr. Townsend to win a vast following for the belief that it was wrong for old people to receive less than thirty dollars every Thursday; it enabled Upton Sinclair to come within an ace of being elected governor of what is now the second state in the Union, on a platform that demanded an end of poverty in California. It was this same attitude of mind on which Huey P. Long capitalized in his "share-our-wealth" program—and capitalized to such good effect that he became for a while Franklin Roosevelt's most dangerous adversary. In his formal argument, Long employed a simple fallacy: he computed the value of America's wealth, developed and undeveloped, liquid and nonliquid, and then proceeded to treat the total sum as if it were in the form of cash available for distribution. Granted the validity of his calculation, the phrase "every man a king" did not seem excessive. But, despite this sophistry, Long was not relying primarily upon the arithmetical naïveté of the American people; he was relying upon their belief in the inexhaustible plenty of North America and in their own unrestrained right to enjoy this plenty without brain trust or dogma.

Long, Townsend, and Sinclair have provided striking though extreme examples of the American faith in plenty; but it is perhaps more revealing to consider a program which gained the support of a clear majority of all Americans —namely, the New Deal. For Franklin Roosevelt, too, was an apostle of abundance and, accordingly, of the view that the one-third who were unfortunate could be cared for without detriment to existing interests. Although hated in conservative circles as an expropriator and a fomenter of class antagonisms, Roosevelt in fact attempted to create a real balance between various class interests, such as those of labor and those of management; and this balance was predicated on an idea which was the very antithesis of the class struggle—the idea that no one need lose anything: debts were not scaled down, mortgages were not canceled, imminent bankruptcies which would have paved the way for nationalization were not permitted to occur. Even "the unscrupulous money-changers," as Roosevelt called them, were not driven from the temples of finance. They were simply required to suspend operations for a brief time. Landlords collected farm benefits; industrialists under the NRA secured indulgence for monopolistic practices that had been under fire from more conservative administrations for forty years; while little businesses were protected by Thurman Arnold and the TNEC. At the nadir of the Depression, when capitalism was fearfully vulnerable and almost unresisting to attack and when many doctrinaires would have said that the overthrow of capitalism was the prerequisite to reform, Roosevelt unhesitatingly assumed that the country could afford to pay capitalism's ransom and to buy reform, too. One of his most irritating and most successful qualities was his habit of assuming that benefits could be granted without costs being felt—an assumption rooted in his faith in the potentialities of the American economy.

Going beyond Roosevelt himself, it is interesting to consider the attitude of the American people as a whole toward the idea of class struggle. Antipathy to the concept is a well-known American trait, and it is frequently associated with or attributed to America's faith in the ideal of equality and America's reluctance to admit that social stratification exists. Certainly this commitment to the ideal of equality has a deep bearing; but is not our hostility to the class-struggle concept also linked with our reluctance to entertain the thought that American wealth has ceased to grow, that we can no longer raise the standard of living at one point without lowering it somewhere else?

Occasionally, one encounters the statement that Americans believe in leveling up rather than in leveling down. The truth of the assertion is more or less self-evident, but the basic meaning is less so. Clearly, if one is leveling a fixed number of items, say, personal incomes, the very process of leveling implies the reduction of the higher ones. But in order to raise the lower without reducing the higher, to level *up*, it is necessary to increase the total of all the incomes—

that is, to introduce new factors instead of solving the problem with the factors originally given. And it is by this stratagem of refusing to accept the factors given, of drawing on nature's surplus and on technology's tricks, that America has often dealt with her problems of social reform.

This, in turn, may explain another distinctive feature of the American record, and that is the relative lack of intellectualism in its reform or radical movements. For instance, by European standards the Populists of the late nineteenth century, and even more the Progressives of the early twentieth, would have seemed incredibly muddled, sentimental, and superficial in their thinking. European radicalism almost invariably has had a highly articulated rationale, a fully developed doctrinal system. European radicals have kept their ideological weapons sharpened to razor edge, so that they are ever ready to follow logic through the most complex maze or to split the hairs of heresy in disputes over minor points of doctrine. They do this, in part, I believe, because the social problems with which they deal are relatively fixed, and disciplined intelligence is the one means through which they can hope to attain a solution. But the social problems of America were not at all fixed, and their mutability has made logical solutions unnecessary.

Our practice, indeed, has been to overleap problems—to bypass them—rather than to solve them. For instance, in the 1880's and 1890's there seemed to be three major public problems—the problem of a shrinking bullion supply; the problem of the control of an entire industry by a small group of monopolists, like John D. Rockefeller and his associates in the oil industry; and the problem of regulation of the railroads, which enjoyed a natural monopoly of transportation. Reformers struggled with all three of these problems, and various political solutions were proposed: the adoption of a bimetallic currency to relieve the bullion stringency, the enactment of an anti-trust law to curb Mr. Rockefeller, and the adoption of an Interstate Commerce Act to protect the shipper vis-à-vis the railroads. But in each case technological change interposed to relieve the acuteness of the problem or even to make it obsolete: the discovery of new gold supplies in the Klondike and of new methods of recovering gold reversed the process of shrinkage in the bullion supply; the discovery of the vast new deposits of oil in Texas and elsewhere undermined the dominance of Rockefeller in the oil industry as no legislative prohibition was ever able to do; and the introduction of trucks moving over a network of national highways ended the natural monopoly of transportation by the railroads before Congress ceased the long quest for a legislative solution.

There is a widespread belief in the United States that the basic policy of our government underwent a sudden change about twenty years ago, with the advent of the New Deal. According to this belief, the American Republic had been a thoroughgoing laissez faire state during its first century and a half—a state where government scrupulously refrained from intervention in the economic sphere, and private enterprise alone shaped the country's economic progress. Then, it is supposed, an abrupt reversal of policy took place, and, turning our backs upon the principles that had guided us to our earlier economic triumphs, we embraced a paternalistic program of governmental regulation and control which started us on the road to the welfare state. This view is probably most widely prevalent in conservative circles, but among people who are left of center there is also a widespread belief that government in the nineteenth and early twentieth centuries held aloof from economic problems and that this negative attitude continued until the time of Franklin Roosevelt, who followed a trail blazed by the Progressives and asserted a more constructive function for public authority. In short, left and right are in dispute as to the merit of this change, but they are inclined to agree that a complete change took place.

Without denying that a major transformation occurred, we need to be aware of the strands of continuity, as well as of the shifts and new departures in our history. If we are to appreciate the links with the past, we must recognize that laissez faire was not the unique principle of policy in our eighteenth- and nineteenth-century development but that one of the key principles was certainly the constant endeavor of government to make the economic abundance of the nation accessible to the public. The tactics by which this was done changed as the form of abundance itself changed, but the basic purpose—to keep our population in contact with the sources of wealth—has remained steadily in the ascendant throughout our history.

In the early nineteenth century the major form in which abundance presented itself was the fertility of unsettled land. For a people of whom 90 per cent followed agricultural pursuits, access to abundance meant opportunity to settle the new lands. The government responded by a series of land laws, beginning with the Ordinance of 1785 and extending far past the Homestead Act of 1862, which made land progressively easier for settlers to attain, until at last they could acquire title to 160 acres absolutely free. Over the years, while this was happening, some eminently public spirited men like John Quincy Adams contended for a program that would have conserved the assets of the public domain by distributing it gradually and on a basis that would yield revenue to the Treasury; but all such proposals were defeated, and quick settlement was stimulated even by legislation which encouraged squatters to occupy the land before it had been opened to public entry. Widespread access to wealth was preferred over the public capitalization of a great economic asset.

Relatively early, however, it became clear that access to soil did not mean access to wealth unless it was accompanied by access to market. Fertile soil remained a mere potentiality when its products could not reach the consumer. The market was the source of wealth to which access was needed, and again government responded by providing the internal improvements which would give such access. Sometimes the federal government did this, as, for instance, by the construction of the Cumberland Pike; sometimes the state governments took the initiative, as New York did with the digging of the Erie Canal; and sometimes government did not execute the project itself but encouraged private interests to do so by offering such tangible inducements as direct financial support, use of the public credit, and use of the power of eminent domain. Even in so great a project as the building of the first transcontinental railroad, the government virtually furnished all the funds, and, though the ownership was private, a congressman from New York could truthfully point out that the government in fact had built the railroads.

Later still, the wealth to which access was needed appeared increasingly in forms that could not be handled by the individual acting as a solitary operator. Iron resources, coal resources, petroleum resources, water-power resources, and other physical assets promised to raise the standard of living; but the only means of access to their value was through large-scale concentration of capital and labor. Again, government responded by facilitating the means of access: it made easy the process of concentration by sanctioning the wide use of the practice of incorporation; it assured the new corporations, through judicial interpretation of the Fourteenth Amendment, that they would enjoy the fullest legal security and even advantage; by the tariffs of the Civil War and post-Civil War periods, it guaranteed the corporations control of the American market. In return they did what was expected of them: they converted potential wealth into usable wealth, wastefully, selfishly, and ruthlessly in many cases, but quickly— and results were the primary thing demanded of them.

By the third decade of the twentieth century, the form in which wealth appeared had again altered drastically. No longer did it consist in natural resources of soil or subsoil, requiring to be put into operation. Access to wealth was now dependent upon the continued movement of the production lines rather than upon the throwing open of untapped resources. In these circumstances, the operation of the business cycle, manifesting itself in the great Depression, seemed to block access to wealth as completely as the barriers of physical distance had blocked it a century earlier. In both cases, though the overt circumstances seemed wholly dissimilar, Americans found consolation in the same basic and comforting conviction—that abundance was there, and the problem was not to create it or to get along without it but simply to find how to get at it. And in both cases government responded with steps to provide access. If access depended upon the creation of purchasing power, government under the New Deal was ready to create it by spending, lending, priming the pump, and enacting minimum-wage laws; if it depended upon the capacity of workers to bargain collectively, government was ready to confer that capacity by law; if it depended upon securing industry against some of the hazards of competition, government offered a National Industrial Recovery Act to remove these hazards.

Writers on public questions often assume that in our early history we had a basic commitment to individualism and that we have recently abandoned this traditional principle just for the sake of security. But what we really were com-

mitted to was realizing on the potentialities of our unmatched assets and raising our standard of living. Because the standard of living involves comfort and
material things, a basic concern with it is commonly regarded as ignoble; yet, as
I have already suggested, it is only because we have attained a relatively high
standard of living that we can afford to own and operate a democratic system.
But, whether noble or not, our commitment to abundance was primary, and individualism was sanctioned as the very best means of fulfilling the possibilities of abundance. When it ceased to be the best means, we modified it with a
readiness alarming to people who had supposed that it was the individualism itself which was basic. We did this because a great many people had never regarded it, at bottom, as more than a means to an end. The politics of our democracy was a politics of abundance rather than a politics of individualism,[7] a politics of increasing our wealth quickly rather than of dividing it precisely, a
politics which smiled both on those who valued abundance as a means to safeguard freedom and on those who valued freedom as an aid in securing abundance.

In so far as Americans have succeeded in equating abundance and freedom, it
becomes something of an abstraction to question which is the means and which
is the end. The historical analyst may itch to discover which one is basic and
which derivative, but the purpose of Americans, generally, will be to make the
two coincide in such a way that, as factors, they cannot be isolated. In this sense
it may seem somewhat metaphysical to make heavy-handed distinctions between these two ingredients—freedom and abundance—which are to such a
great extent fused in American democratic thought.

But, though Americans have caused freedom and abundance to converge, the
two are not by nature prone to convergence, and for the world at large they
have not been closely linked. Consequently, when America, out of her abundance, preaches the gospel of democracy to countries which see no means of attaining abundance, the message does not carry the meaning which it is meant
to convey. No other part of American activity has been so consistently and so
completely a failure as our attempt to export democracy. At this point, the
duality between abundance and freedom in the American democratic formula
ceases to be abstract and becomes painfully concrete, for it is the lack of understanding of what we have to offer to the rest of the world that has vitiated
our efforts to fulfil a national mission which we undertook with real dedication
and for which we have made real sacrifices. But the discussion of this aspect of
the relation between democracy and abundance will involve a consideration of
the world relations of the American Republic, and this is so extensive a subject
that it must be left for another chapter.

---

[7] "Thomas Carlyle once said to an American: 'Ye may boast o' yer dimocracy, or any
ither 'cracy, or any kind o' poleetical roobish; but the reason why yer laboring folk are
so happy is thot ye have a vost deal o' land for a verra few people'" (Josiah Strong,
*Our Country* [1885], p. 153).

❦ ❦ ❦

# Challenges to Science
# and Technology

*I. I. Rabi*

## Scientist and Humanist[1]

1

FOR more than half a century, from the period of the Darwinian controversy till the end of the 1930's, science remained almost unchallenged as the source of enlightenment, understanding, and hope for a better, healthier, and safer world. The benefits brought by science were and are still visible everywhere one looks. Human ills are being overcome; food supplies are becoming more abundant; travel and communication are quick and easy; and the comforts of life, especially for the common man, are vastly increased. In the person of Albert Einstein science enjoyed a world-wide respect almost akin to reverence and hardly equaled since the time of Isaac Newton.

In the last decade or so we have begun to detect signs of significant change. The knowledge and techniques developed through science for the illumination of the mind and the elevation of the spirit, for the prolongation and the amelioration of life, have been used for the destruction of life and the degradation of the human spirit. Technological warfare, biological warfare, psychological warfare, brainwashing, all make use of science with frightening results.

I do not suggest that warfare and its attendant horror is a result of modern science. Ancient Greece, at the zenith of that remarkable civilization, in a land united by a common culture and a common religion, destroyed itself in a bitter and useless war more thoroughly than Europe has done in the present century even with the aid of electronics, aviation, and high explosives. What I mean is that our epoch in history, which has produced one of the greatest achievements of the human race, may be passing into a twilight that does not precede the dawn.

Science, the triumph of the intellect and the rational faculties, has resulted in the hydrogen bomb. The glib conclusion is that science and the intellect are therefore false guides. We must seek elsewhere, some people say, for hope and salvation; but, say the same people, while doing so we must keep ahead of the

[1] From the *Atlantic Monthly* (January, 1956), pp. 64-67. Copyright 1956 by The Atlantic Monthly Company, Boston 16, Massachusetts. Reprinted by permission of Professor I. I. Rabi, Higgins Professor of Physics, Columbia University.

Russians in technology and in the armaments race. Keep the fearsome fruits but reject the spirit of science. Such is the growing mood of some people at the present time. It is a mood of anti-intellectualism which can only hasten the destruction which these people fear. Anti-intellectualism has always been endemic in every society, perhaps in the heart of every human being. In times of stress this attitude is stimulated and people tend to become impatient and yield to prejudice and emotion just when coolness, subtlety, and reason are most needed.

We are told, and most of us believe, that we are living in a period of crisis unequaled in history. To be cheerful and proud of our accomplishment and optimistic of the future is almost akin to subversion. To be considered objective and realistic, one must view with alarm. Yet we are not living in a period of hard times and unemployment! We have, I cannot say enjoyed but, rather, bemoaned, a period of prosperity and world-wide influence for good unequaled in history. Nevertheless, despite all, we seem to be acquiring a complacency of despair. In this mood, unable to adjust to new values, we hark back to a past which now looks so bright in retrospect, and we raise the banner of "Back to the Humanities."

What is meant by the slogan "Back to the Humanities"? What are people really looking for? What knowledge, what guidance, what hope for salvation, what inspiration, or what relief from anxiety does a practical-minded people like ours expect from a knowledge of the humanities? They do not wish to re-establish the study of the Greek and Roman classics in their original tongues, or to re-create the Greek city-state in Metropolitan Boston.

I venture to suggest that what they mean is something quite different from what is meant by the humanities. The progress of civilization in the modern age, especially in our own century, has brought with it an immense increase of knowledge of every kind, from archaeology to zoology. More is known of the history of antiquity than was known to Herodotus. We have penetrated farther into the heavens and into the innermost secrets of the structure of matter than anyone could have dreamt of in previous generations. We have run through the satisfactions of representational art to the puzzling outlines of abstract art. The increase in physical comfort and in communication has brought with it a whole set of new problems. The great increase in population necessarily means further crowding and additional social and cultural adjustment. Under these circumstances, it is natural for people to look for guidance toward a balanced adjustment.

2

What people are really looking for is wisdom. To our great store of knowledge we need the added quality of wisdom.

Wisdom is inseparable from knowledge; it is knowledge plus a quality which is within the human being. Without it knowledge is dry, almost unfit for human consumption, and dangerous in application. The absence of wisdom is clearly noticeable; the learned fool and the educated bore have been with us since the beginnings of recorded history. Wisdom adds flavor, order, and measure to knowledge. Wisdom makes itself most manifest in the application of knowledge to human needs.

Every generation of mankind has to remake its culture, its values, and its goals. Changing circumstances make older habits and customs valueless or obsolete. New knowledge exposes the limitations and the contingent nature of older philosophies and of previously accepted guides to action. Wisdom does not come in formulas, proverbs, or wise saws, but out of the living actuality. The past is important for understanding the present, but it is not the present. It is in a real sense created in the present, and changes from the point of view of every generation.

When change is slow, the new is gradually assimilated, and only after a number of generations is it noticeable that the world is really different. In our century enormous changes in the circumstances of our lives and in our knowledge have occurred rapidly—in every decade. It is therefore not at all surprising that our intellectual, our social, and our political processes have failed to keep abreast of contemporary problems. It is not surprising that we become confused in the choice of our goals and the paths which we must take to reach them.

Clearly a study of the Greek and Roman classics in their original tongues or even in a good translation is a most rewarding venture in itself. This literature has never been surpassed in any age. And in reading this literature one is struck by how applicable the situations are to the present day. The fact that we can still be moved strongly by this literature is an illustration not merely of the constancy of structure of the human nervous system but also of the fact that great art and profound insights have a character which is independent of any age.

The humanities preserve and create values; even more they express the symbolic, poetic, and prophetic qualities of the human spirit. Without the humanities we would not be conscious of our history; we would lose many of our aspirations and the graces of expression that move men's hearts. Withal the humanities discern but a part of the life of man—true, a vital part but only a part.

It has often been claimed that the chief justification for the study of the humanities is that it teaches us values. In fact some people go even further and claim that the humanities, in which literature, parts of philosophy, and the history and appreciation of the fine arts are included, are the *only* sources of values other than the more spiritual values of religion.

This claim cannot pass without challenge. It cannot be said that it is absurd, but rather that it is a symptom of our failure in the present age to achieve a unity and balance of knowledge which is imbued with wisdom. It is a symptom of both ignorance and a certain anti-rational attitude which has been the curse of our century. It betrays a lack of self-confidence and faith in the greatness of the human spirit in contemporary man. It is the expression of a form of self-hatred which is rationally unjustifiable although deeply rooted.

Man is made of dust and to dust returneth; he lives in a universe of which he is also a part. He is free only in a symbolic sense; his nature is conditioned by the dust out of which he is made. To learn to understand himself he must learn to understand the universe in which he lives. There is more than enough in this enterprise to engage the boldest, the most imaginative, and the keenest minds and spirits of every generation. The universe is not given to us in the form of a map or guide. It is made by human minds and imaginations out of slight hints which come from acute observation and from the profound stratagems of experiments.

How can we hope to obtain wisdom, the wisdom which is meaningful in our own time? We certainly cannot attain it as long as the two great branches of human knowledge, the sciences and the humanities, remain separate and even warring disciplines.

Why is science, even more than the humanities, as a living component of our society so misunderstood? A glance at a current dictionary definition may give us a clue.

Science: "A branch of knowledge dealing with facts or truths systematically arranged and showing the operation of general law."

This definition brings to my mind a solitaire player or head bookkeeper for a mail-order concern. It is a partial truth which is also a caricature. It is out of harmony with the picture of Archimedes jumping out of his bath crying Eureka! or Galileo in misery and degradation during his trial and recantation, or Einstein creating the universe out of one or two deductions from observation and a profound aesthetic feeling for symmetry. Nor does this definition account for the violence of the opposition to scientific discovery which still exists in the same quarters in our own age.

It is often argued that physical science is inherently simple, whereas the study of man is inherently complicated. Yet a great deal is known of man's nature. Wise laws for government and personal conduct were known in remotest antiquity. The literature of antiquity shows a profound understanding of human natures and emotions. Not man but the external world was bewildering. The world of nature instead of seeming simple was infinitely complex and possessed of spirits and demons. Nature had to be worshiped and propitiated by offerings, ceremonies, and prayers. Fundamentally nature was unpredictable, antagonistic to human aspiration, full of significance and purpose, and generally evil. Knowledge of nature was suspect because of the power which it brought, a power which was somehow allied with evil. There were of course always men who had insights far beyond these seemingly naïve notions, but they did not prevail over what seemed to be the evidence of the senses and of practical experience.

It was therefore not until late in the history of mankind, not until a few seconds ago so to speak, that it was recognized that nature is understandable and that a knowledge of nature is good and can be used with benefit; that it does not involve witchcraft or a compact with the devil. What is more, any person of intelligence can understand the ideas involved and with sufficient skill learn the necessary techniques, intellectual and manual.

This idea which is now so commonplace represents an almost complete break with the past. To revere and trust the rational faculty of the mind—to allow no taboo to interfere in its operation, to have nothing immune from its examination—is a new value which has been introduced into the world. The progress of science has been the chief agent in demonstrating its importance and riveting it into the consciousness of mankind. This value does not yet have universal acceptance in this country or in any other country. But in spite of all obstacles it will become one of the most treasured possessions of all mankind because we can no longer live without it. We have gone too far along the direction which it implies ever to turn back without unimaginable disaster.

The last world war was started in an attempt to turn back to dark reaction against the rational faculty and to introduce a new demonology into the world. It failed as will every other such attempt. Once the mind is free it will be destroyed rather than be put back in chains.

### 3

To my mind the value content of science or literary scholarship lies not in the subject matter alone; it lies chiefly in the spirit and living tradition in which these disciplines are pursued. The spirit is almost always conditioned by the subject. Science and the humanities are not the same thing; the subject matter is different and the spirit and tradition are different. Our problem in our search for wisdom is to blend these two traditions in the minds of individual men and women.

Many colleges and universities are trying to do just this, but there is one serious defect in the method. We pour a little of this and a little of that into the student's mind in proportions which result from mediation between the departments and from the particular predilections of the deans and the president. We then hope that these ingredients will combine through some mysterious alchemy and the result will be a man educated, well-rounded, and wise. Most often, however, these ingredients remain well separated in the compartmentalized mind, or they may form an indigestible precipitate which is not only useless but positively harmful, until time the healer washes it all away.

Wisdom is by its nature an interdisciplinary quality and not the product of a collection of specialists. Although the colleges do indeed try to mold the student toward a certain ideal of the educated man of the twentieth century, it is too often a broad education administered by specialists. The approximate counterpart to this ideal of the educated man, embodied in a real living person, is a rare being on any college faculty. Indeed, in most colleges and universities the student is the only really active connecting link between the different departments. In a certain paradoxical sense the students are the only broadly educated body in the university community, at least in principle.

The affairs of this country—indeed of almost every country—whether in government, education, industry, or business, are controlled by people of broad experience. However, this broad experience rarely includes the field of science. How can our leaders make wise decisions now in the middle of the twentieth century without a deep understanding of scientific thought and feeling for scientific traditions? The answer is clear in the sad course that events have taken.

This anguished thought has impelled many scientists, often to their own personal peril, to concern themselves with matters which in the past were the exclusive domain of statesmen and military leaders. They have tried to advise, importune, and even cajole our leaders to include the scientific factor in our fateful policy decisions. They have been successful, but only in special instances.

I am not making a plea for the scientist statesman comparable to the philosopher king. The scientist rarely has this kind of ambition. The study of nature in its profundity, beauty, and subtlety is too attractive for him to wish to forsake his own creative and rewarding activity. The scientist away from his science is like an exile who longs for the sights and sounds of his native land. What the scientist really desires is for his science to be undertood, to become an integral part of our general culture, to be given proper weight in the cultural and practical affairs of the world.

The greatest difficulty which stands in the way of a meeting of the minds of the scientist and the non-scientist is the difficulty of communication, a difficulty which stems from some of the defects of education to which I have alluded. The mature scientist, if he has any taste in these directions, can listen with pleasure to the philosopher, the historian, the literary man, or even to the art critic. There is little difficulty from that side because the scientist has been educated in our general culture and lives in it on a day-to-day basis. He reads newspapers, magazines, books, listens to music, debates politics, and participates in the general activities of an educated citizen.

Unfortunately this channel of communication is often a one-way street. The non-scientist cannot listen to the scientist with pleasure and understanding. Despite its universal outlook and its unifying principle, its splendid tradition, science seems to be no longer communicable to the great majority of educated laymen. They simply do not possess the background of the science of today and the intellectual tool necessary for them to understand what effects science will have on them and on the world. Instead of understanding, they have only a naïve awe mixed with fear and scorn. To his colleagues in the university the scientist tends to seem more and more like a man from another planet, a creature scattering antibiotics with one hand and atomic bombs with the other.

The problems to which I have addressed myself are not particularly American. The same condition exists in England, France, and indeed in all other countries. From my observation we are perhaps better off than most. Our American colleges and universities, since they are fairly recent and are rapidly expanding, have not settled into complacency. They are quite ready to experiment to achieve desired ends. Our experimental methods have taught us how to impart the most diverse forms of knowledge. Although wisdom is more elusive, once the objective is clear that the ultimate end of education is knowledge imbedded in wisdom we shall find ways to move toward that ideal. The ideal of the well-rounded man is a meaningless ideal unless this sphericity means a fusion of knowledge to achieve balanced judgment and understanding, which are qualities of wisdom.

The problems are, of course, depressingly difficult. In the secondary schools—with their overcrowding, their teachers overworked and inadequately trained, the school boards, and, not least, the powerful clique of professional educators who form a society within our society—all that is unique and characteristic of science and mathematics is being crowded out of the curriculum and replaced by a fairy tale known as general science. The colleges and universities are in much better shape, although the great population increase is about to hit them with masses of inadequately prepared students. Most people would be quite content with a holding operation in which we could maintain the quality that is already possessed.

However, it seems to me that something could be done even now with the faculty members of the colleges and the universities. Wisdom can achieve a hybrid vigor by crossing the scientist and the humanist through a more extensive and intensive interaction within the faculty. Why should not the professor of physics be expected to refresh himself periodically by taking a course in aesthetics or comparative literature or in the Greek drama? Why shouldn't the professor of medieval philosophy or the professor of ancient history take a course in modern physics and become acquainted with the profound thoughts underlying relativity and quantum mechanics? It would let in some fresh air, or at least different air, to blow away some of the cobwebs which grow in the unventilated ivory towers.

Somewhere a beginning has to be made to achieve a more architectural quality in our culture, a quality of proportion and of organic unity, and it is reasonable to start with the members of the faculties of our institutions of higher learning. Here are all the strands of the tapestry which is to represent our culture, living in close proximity but separate, adding up to nothing more than the sum of the parts. The scientists must learn to teach science in the spirit of wisdom and in the light of the history of human thought and human effort, rather than as the geography of a universe uninhabited by mankind. Our colleagues in the non-scientific faculties must understand that if their teachings ignore the great scientific tradition and its accomplishments, their words, however eloquent and elegant, will lose meaning for this generation and be barren of fruit.

Only with a united effort of science and the humanities can we hope to succeed in discovering a community of thought which can lead us out of the darkness and the confusion which oppress all mankind.

❦ ❦ ❦

*Morris Bishop*

# The Reading Machine[1]

"I HAVE invented a reading machine," said Professor Entwhistle, a strident ener-
gumen whose violent enthusiasms are apt to infect his colleagues with nausea or
hot flashes before the eyes.

Every head in the smoking room of the Faculty Club bowed over a magazine, in an attitude of prayer. The prayer was unanswered, as usual.

"It is obvious," said Professor Entwhistle, "that the greatest waste of our
civilization is the time spent in reading. We have been able to speed up practically everything to fit the modern tempo—communication, transportation,
calculation. But today a man takes just as long to read a book as Dante did,
or—"

"Great Caesar!" said the Professor of Amphibology, shutting his magazine
with a spank.

"Or great Caesar," continued Professor Entwhistle. "So I have invented a machine. It operates by a simple arrangement of photoelectric cells, which scan a
line of type at lightning speed. The operation of the photoelectric cells is
synchronized with a mechanical device for turning the pages—rather ingenious.
I figure that my machine can read a book of three hundred pages in ten minutes."

⸎ "Can it read French?" said the Professor of Bio-Economics, without looking
up.

"It can read any language that is printed in Roman type. And by an alteration of the master pattern on which the photoelectric cells operate, it can be
fitted to read Russian, or Bulgarian, or any language printed in the Cyrillic
alphabet. In fact, it will do more. By simply throwing a switch, you can adapt
it to read Hebrew, or Arabic, or any language that is written from right to left
instead of from left to right."

"Chinese?" said the Professor of Amphibology, throwing himself into the
arena. The others still studied their magazines.

"Not Chinese, as yet," said Professor Entwhistle. "Though by inserting the
pages sidewise . . . Yes, I think it could be done."

"Yes, but when you say this contrivance reads, exactly what do you mean? It
seems to me—"

"The light waves registered by the photoelectric cells are first converted into
sound waves."

"So you can listen in to the reading of the text?"

"Not at all. The sound waves alter so fast that you hear nothing but a con-

[1] Reprinted by permission of the author. Copyright, 1947, The New Yorker Magazine, Inc. (Formerly The F-R. Publishing Corp.)

tinuous hum. If you hear them at all. You can't, in fact, because they are on a wave length inaudible to the human ear."

"Well, it seems to me—"

"Think of the efficiency of the thing!" Professor Entwhistle was really warming up. "Think of the time saved! You assign a student a bibliography of fifty books. He runs them through the machine comfortably in a weekend. And on Monday morning he turns in a certificate from the machine. Everything has been conscientiously read!"

"Yes, but the student won't remember what he has read!"

"He doesn't remember what he reads now."

"Well, you have me there," said the Professor of Amphibology. "I confess you have me there. But it seems to me we would have to pass the machine and fail the student."

"Not at all," said Professor Entwhistle. "An accountant today does not think of doing his work by multiplication and division. Often he is unable to multiply and divide. He confides his problem to a business machine and the machine does his work for him. All the accountant has to know is how to run the machine. That is efficiency."

"Still, it seems to me that what we want to do is to transfer the contents of the book to the student's mind."

"In the mechanized age? My dear fellow! What we want is to train the student to run machines. An airplane pilot doesn't need to know the history of aerodynamics. He needs to know how to run his machine. A lawyer doesn't want to know the development of theories of Roman law. He wants to win cases, if possible by getting the right answers to logical problems. That is largely a mechanical process. It might well be possible to construct a machine. It could begin by solving simple syllogisms, you know—drawing a conclusion from a major premise and a minor premise—"

"Here, let's not get distracted. This reading machine of yours, it must *do* something, it must make some kind of record. What happens after you get the sound waves?"

"That's the beauty of it," said Professor Entwhistle. "The sound waves are converted into light waves, of a different character from the original light waves, and these are communicated to an automatic typewriter, working at inconceivable speed. This transforms the light impulses into legible typescript, in folders of a hundred pages each. It tosses them out the way a combine tosses out sacked wheat. Thus, everything the machine reads is preserved entire, in durable form. The only thing that remains is to file it somewhere, and for this you would need only the services of a capable filing clerk."

"Or you could read it?" persisted the Professor of Amphibology.

"Why, yes, if you wanted to, you could read it," said Professor Entwhistle.

An indigestible silence hung over the Faculty Club.

"I see where the Athletic Association has bought a pitching machine," said the Assistant Professor of Business Psychology (Retail). "Damn thing throws any curve desired, with a maximum margin of error of three centimetres over the plate. What'll they be thinking of next?"

"A batting machine, obviously," said Professor Entwhistle.

❧ ❧ ❧

*Jacques Barzun*

# The Ivory Lab [1]

*I degrade Physics into an implement of culture, and this is
my deliberate design.*—JOHN TYNDALL, *Fragments of Science*

MOST of the excitement about "higher education" in the last three years has been about the teaching of history, languages, and "great books." But the most serious and pressing need in colleges today seems to me to be the teaching of science. It may appear paradoxical that I speak of a "need" which everyone believes to be adequately met, but paradox disappears when the point of view changes. From one point of view, science is taught in every American college; from another point of view, it is taught in none, or very few. Looked at in a certain light, science teaching today is the most efficient, up to date, and worldly-wise. In another light, it is backward, wasteful and "escapist." Let me explain these contrasts.

Fifty or sixty years ago, science was a new academic subject. People mistrusted its power to educate, and many of its proponents seemed as if they could never be educated themselves. The tradition of liberal studies had always included mathematics, because mathematics was supposed to train the mind; but the new physical sciences were first seen as manual arts, messy and expensive, and with no more "discipline" to them than a pair of elastic-sided boots. At the time of the fight for adding science to the curriculum, the defensive position was held by Greek and Latin, which unfortunately adopted a "scorched earth" policy. I mean that they allowed themselves to be invaded by the "scientific spirit" and in trying to compete with it reduced their field to a wasteland of verbal criticism, grammar, and philology. Literature was relegated to a second place and studying the classics came to mean research into the uses of *utor, fruor,* and *fungor.*

Naturally the classics were exterminated, for science could beat them at their own game. A young man trained in science could on graduation get any of a hundred desirable jobs in industry. A young "scientific" classicist could only hope to teach his own subject to a dwindling number of students. That is what invariably comes of trying to put belles-lettres into utilitarian envelopes. As

[1] From *Teacher in America* by Jacques Barzun. Copyright, 1944, 1945, by Jacques Barzun. Reprinted by permission of Little, Brown & Company and the Atlantic Monthly Press.

Dean Briggs of Harvard said when the Bachelor of Science degree was established: "It does not guarantee that the holder knows any science, but it does guarantee that he does *not* know any Latin." When the study of classical literature in translation was reintroduced for freshmen at Columbia College a few years ago, the undergraduate department of classics was surprised to find its enrollment in beginning Greek increased 150 per cent: they now had ten students.

But the bitter joke is not on the Classics alone. Having stepped into Greek's vacated place, Science now occupies its position, not with respect to size of enrollment, but with respect to educational attitude. It is now in power and it acts disdainful, holier-than-thou, and prudish. Someone once asked, "What is it that our men of science are guarding like a threatened virginity?" "Oh," was the answer, "they have a Vestal interest in their subject." Considered—somewhat unfairly—in the mass, science teachers may be said to contribute the greatest proportion of backward-looking, anti-intellectual, mechanic-minded members to the faculty. Characteristically, single departments of physical science have in certain institutions tried to set up separate schools, where only their one science would be taught for four years and rewarded with some kind of Bachelor's degree. The intention was to monopolize the student's time, cram him full of "practical" knowledge, and sell him to the highest bidder the moment he had clutched his diploma and redeemed his ten-dollar deposit for apparatus.

Doubtless there is a demand for such prefabricated industrial robots and I see no reason why such schools should not function in a manner useful to the commonwealth—off the campus. But departments that once clamored for admission to university status and have had it for fifty years are unwilling to give up all the *douceurs* of the association. They would still like to profit from the university connection, to color their degree with a faint tincture of liberal teaching—perhaps they would require a year of English and a year of history and economics—and to boast that their own subject, be it chemistry or geology, is also one of the "humanities." They want to eat their cake as many times over as a cow does her cud.

A crowd of evils springs from this ambiguous mood in the present college curriculum. There is an undignified scramble for the student's time, with broad hints on the part of the scientist that the rest of the program is folderol. Repressed antagonisms divide teachers of the humanities (vague, pointless, unpractical subjects—except economics) from teachers of the real stuff represented by science. Moreover, departments of physics and chemistry require mathematical preparation in strict amount and order of time, with the result that all scheduling revolves around their claims. Since most young Americans discover their vocational bent while undergraduates, the wish to qualify for a profession is a powerful lever to make everyone study science for one or two years under these barbaric conditions. The doctor, the engineer, the research man in any science must gobble up as many courses as he can; and the man uninterested in science must "fulfill the requirement." Both are often judged on their science record, in the belief that it unmistakably reveals "real brains" or the lack of them.

The worst of all this is that neither group of students learns much about science but goes to swell the ranks of the two great classes of modern men—the single-track expert and the scientific ignoramus. Could anything more plainly demonstrate the failure of science to become a subject fit for college teaching? What makes a subject fit for the higher curriculum is surely no novelty: it is that it shall enlighten all the corners of the mind and teach its own uses. The humble three R's begin in strict utility and end up in poetry, science, and the search for the Infinite. They can and should therefore be taught indefinitely. Men have known for three thousand years that other matters of knowledge naturally divide themselves into special and general, that both are needful, but that whereas the special *add* to one's powers, the general *enhance the quality* of all of them.

At a recent educational conference, the Dean of a Midwestern university complained humorously that he was always being asked to give credits for impossible subjects—subjects that, he said, deserved to be called *in-credible*. A transfer student, for example, wanted "points" for seven hours of saw filing. Undeniably saw filing is a necessary art, but its merits as a general enhancer of power and personality stop accruing so soon after study is begun that it is not properly a branch of academic learning. The same is true of still more complex matters like shorthand, typewriting, and dress designing. Farther on in the series, it becomes harder to draw the line: stamp collecting is subeducational but numismatics is a province of history.

Fortunately there is no doubt whatever about the place of the sciences: they *are* humanities and they belong in the college curriculum. Accordingly, they should be introduced into it *as humanities*, at the earliest possible moment. How? I have some tentative suggestions to make, but first I want to stress the danger of further delay and of the continuance of our present malpractice.

The worst danger is the creation of a large, powerful, and complacent class of college-trained uneducated men at the very heart of our industrial and political system. We may be too near to judge, but it strikes me that one of the conditions that made possible the present folly in Germany was the split among three groups: the technicians, the citizens, and the irresponsible rabble. This becomes persuasively plain if you consider the professional army caste as a group of unthinking technicians. The rabble together with the technicians can cow the citizenry; the technicians—wedded solely to their work-bench—will work for any group that hires; and the rabble, worshiping "science" to the exclusion of less tangible necessaries, are perfectly willing to sacrifice the citizen. They probably think that, if necessary, "science" could manufacture German citizens —out of wolfram.

Such principles will hardly give long life and happiness to a democracy. The only hope for a democratic state is to have more citizens than anything else. Hence technicians must not be allowed to hibernate between experiments, but must become conscious, responsible, politically and morally active men. Otherwise they will find not only that representative government has slipped out of their fingers, but that they have also lost their commanding position. They will be paid slaves in the service of some rabble, high or low. Meanwhile our present stock of citizens must not simply gape at the wonders of science, but must understand enough of its principles to criticize and value the results. As for the rabble, it must be transmuted as fast as it forms, by science and morals both.

All this clearly depends on teaching our easygoing, rather credulous college boys and girls what science is. If they leave college thinking, as they usually do, that science offers a full, accurate, and literal description of man and Nature; if they think scientific research by itself yields final answers to social problems; if they think scientists are the only honest, patient, and careful workers in the world; if they think that Copernicus, Galileo, Newton, Lavoisier, and Faraday were unimaginative plodders like their own instructors; if they think theories spring from facts and that scientific authority at any time is infallible; if they think that the ability to write down symbols and read manometers is fair grounds for superiority and pride, and if they think that science steadily and automatically makes for a better world—then they have wasted their time in the science lecture room; they live in an Ivory Laboratory more isolated than the poet's tower [2] and they are a plain menace to the society they belong to. They are a menace whether they believe all this by virtue of being engaged in scientific work themselves or of being disqualified from it by felt or fancied incapacity.

I return to what might perhaps be done preventively and constructively. To begin with, a change of direction must be imparted to the teaching of science. The fact must be recognized that most students still do not make science their profession.[3] Consequently, for future lay citizens the compulsory science requirement in force nearly everywhere must be justified by a course explicitly designed for them. Such a course must not play at making physicists or biologists, but must explain the principles of the physical sciences in a coherent manner. A "survey" of all the sciences is out of the question. It would be at once superficial and bewildering. But an intelligent introduction to principles can be given. The assumptions that connect and that differentiate the sciences of matter, of living beings, and of logical relation can be taught; the meaning and the grounds of great unifying theories can be explained, and significant demonstrations and experiments can be shown to and made by the students.

Out of such a course there would surely come a changed attitude on the part of teachers and indeed a change in teaching personnel. At present, side by side

[2] To judge by results, it would seem that the poet climbs to the top of his tower to look out on the world and write about it. Why cavil at the building material—at once durable and attractive and requiring no upkeep?

[3] Statistics for the Middle West, based on large freshman enrollments, show that 50 percent of those taking Chemistry 1, 60 percent of those taking Geology 1, 73 percent of those taking Physics 1, 75 percent of those taking Biology 1, and 82 percent of those taking Botany 1, never go further into the science.

with wise men and ripe teachers in the sciences, one finds many highly trained and absolutely uneducated practitioners. One also finds fanatics of the order that Dickens described in Professor Dingo, who, being caught defacing houses with his geological hammer, replied that "he knew of no building save the Temple of Science." Many university scientists openly scorn teaching and use their appointment to boil the pot of individual research. Now a life of research is a worthy one, but no amount of worthy motive justifies false pretenses and fraudulent impersonation—in this case the pretense of imparting knowledge and the impersonation of a teacher.

In the classroom, such men usually are neither civil, nor literate, nor even scientific, for their knowledge of science is purely from inside—a limitation equally bad but more misleading than the limitation of knowing it purely from outside. "What do they know of science who only science know?" They teach it as a set of rules, and speak of the profession as a "game." Drill in manual dexterity they entrust to laboratory assistants, who are only younger editions of themselves, and for whom a good notebook or speed in performing repetitious experiments is the passport to approval. There is seldom any consideration of the students as thinking minds, of the proper allocation of effort among the many interests legitimate at their time of life, nor of the philosophical implications which the words, the history, and the processes of the particular science disclose.

To offset this lamentable state of things, it must be said that two of the professions most concerned with scientific training—engineering and medicine —have lately amended their outlook and made overtures to the humanities. The medical schools have declared that cramming the student with science in college was a poor thing. He had better study other, less "practical," more formative subjects and postpone advanced chemistry and biology until medical school, where they will be taught him again in a fashion better tailored to his needs. This new policy is excellent, but it is not yet sufficiently enforced. The lesser medical schools—and some others—do not trust their own belief in the principle; they still appeal to "practical" views and judge applicants by A's in science.

Similarly, the Society for the Promotion of Engineering Education has passed splendid resolutions approving what they call the "social-humanistic stem"—by which they mean a few branches of non-engineering study; more accurately then, the "social-humanistic faggots." But here again, engineering thought is ahead of the engineer's emotions. When it comes to the test, the student or the program is pushed around to suit engineering subject matter.

If you add to this the important fact that many young Americans choose "engineering" in the belief that this means a career of research in pure science, you may form some notion of the present anarchical mess. The would-be engineer of seventeen finds that what he really wants to work at is pure research in electricity, that is, to be a physicist. He must therefore back water, change his

course, and take some new prerequisites. Meanwhile his upbringing as a man
and citizen goes by the board. He is caught between two grindstones, each indifferent to the effect of its motion, just as if the boy being put through this
mill were not a human being, a student of the university, and a future citizen
of the nation. Who is being "practical" now?

Some would probably still maintain that the professional schools in contact
with "the world" know best what is the practical view, and that the college is as
ever utopian. But there is one curious fact to be added. It is that the scientific
professional schools have a way of relaxing their jaws into a smile whenever the
market demand for their product decreases: it is a reflex action. They fall in
love with the humanities all over again and raise the amount they require for
admission, until outside pressure once again lowers the floodgates and the
frown succeeds the smile. This self-regulating action is a feat of engineering in
itself—or shall I say of doctoring the supply for public consumption?

The question is not whether this is the easy way to go about marketing
young men, but whether it is a responsible grown-up way of replenishing the
professional class of society. Granted that practice is the test of all schemes and
ideals, is this the most practical scheme that American ingenuity can devise? I
concede that in the present state of mind of the American public, desire for vocational training takes the lead over anything else. But are the directing members of the university world to follow other people's untutored impulses or to
guide and redirect them? We may well ask when we reflect that the first victims of the system are the children of the unthinking public and the public itself. For it is the oldest fallacy about schooling to suppose that it can train a
man for "practical" life. Inevitably, while the plan of study is being taught,
"practical life" has moved on. "They did it this way three months ago, now they
do it this way." No employer who knows anything about men will value a
beginner because he knows the ropes of a particular changeable routine. It
would be as sensible to require that newcomers know the floor plan of the
factory ahead of time.[4]

The corporations employing the largest numbers of engineers and scientific
research men are on this matter way ahead of the colleges. One such firm conducted a survey last year to find out where and how its first-rate executives had
been prepared. They came from the most unexpected places—including small
liberal arts colleges, the teaching profession, the stage, and the Baptist ministry. It was found that the engineering schools—particularly those sensible ones
that make no pretense at intellectual *cachet*—turned out a good average prod-

---

[4] The S.P.E.E. reports: "From its very nature, engineering education operates under
changing conditions which constantly challenge its processes and test its results . . ." so
as to adapt itself to changing needs." (*Draft of a Report*, etc. November 16, 1939, p. 1).
This is fine and good, but it holds true of every other professional subject and most academic ones. The old belief that only a few schools are in touch with the "real world"
is untrue, even if the newer belief should prove true that it is best for the world to have
the school conform to every change outside.

uct, but few leaders. The company's own institutes and night courses raised the chance of foremen and district managers—but only up to a point. The survey concluded that what it wanted as material to shape future executives was graduates of liberal arts colleges, trained in history and economics, in philosophy and in good English, and likewise possessed of *an intelligent interest in science and technology.* Gentlemen, the path lies open.

II

My friend Dean Finch, of the Columbia University School of Engineering, might not agree with all I have just said, but I think he would approve of one element in my suggestions which I casually threw in. I mean the utility of history in the teaching of science. He himself is an historian of technology and offers in Columbia College a most valuable course in the subject for the use of "lay" students. What is surprising is that similar courses, accompanied by others in the history of pure science, are not given—indeed required—on every American campus.

The very idea, it must be said, is shrouded in the smoke of battle. When I mention it, some of my scientific colleagues slap me on the back and say "more power to you." They may express doubts about persuading their fellows, or finding good instructors, but they want to see it tried. Moreover they do not feel robbed when in my own teaching of nineteenth-century history I discuss Dalton and Darwin, Liebig and Faraday, Mayer and Clerk Maxwell. Though scientists, these colleagues of mine can see that to complain of general ignorance about the role of science in modern history, and to prevent historians from mentioning it, is to love monopoly above riches.

Others take the view that science has no history because every new achievement supersedes previous ones. The history of science, they feel, is nothing but biographical chitchat about scientists. Or else they admit that it is useful to find out what the Middle Ages thought of natural science, but only in order to point the lesson of freedom from church authority and fight anew the old battle of science against religion.

This angry confusion about the history of science is dense but not impenetrable. Three things may be distinguished. First there is historical research into the beginnings of science—Greek or Arabic or Medieval. This goes on as advanced study and concerns undergraduates only in the form of broad tested conclusions. Then there is the biography of scientists, which is of immense educational importance—whatever laboratory men may say. Biography does not mean recounting Newton's imaginary embroilments with women or Lavoisier's perfectly real ones with public finance. It means finding out from the lives of great scientific creators what they worked at and how their minds functioned. How tiresome it is to hear nothing from our scientific departments but Sunday-school homilies on the gameness of Galileo, the patience of Pasteur, and the carefulness of Madame Curie. And how uninstructive! Any man who accomplishes anything in any field is as patient as he has to be, and even little boys know that glass being breakable, you have to be careful.[5]

What would be far more significant and novel, though true, would be to teach that Copernicus gambled on insufficient evidence; and Kepler was chiefly a horoscope-caster; that Faraday probably believed more wrong theories than any man alive—and turned them to good use in experiment; that Darwin, on his own admission, made awful blunders and admired the art of wriggling out of them; that T. H. Morgan's laboratory was rather messy; that Newton could not see how his own astronomy contradicted the Bible; that scientific men have suppressed and persecuted opponents of their theories, and that the best scientific truth can end in a rigid and mistaken orthodoxy—as happened after Newton and Darwin. The point is that science is made by man, in the light of interests, errors, and hopes, just like poetry, philosophy, and human history itself.

To say this is not to degrade science, as naïve persons might think; it is on the contrary to enhance its achievements by showing that they sprang not from patience on a monument but from genius toiling in the mud. I leave unexplained here all that accrues from studying how we came to use atoms or devise Absolute Zero or to state the Law of Conservation of Energy (including the reasons why energy is a better word than the earlier "force") or what steps led first to the abandonment and then to the later salvaging of Avogadro's hypothesis. A good scientist-historian would exhibit the assumptions and habits which affected scientific opinion at important turning points. He would unite science to other thought by discussing the nature of its evidence at various periods. And he would show the role of the pure imagination in all great scientific work. I know Bacon promised that science would level all the minds of its devotees to average size, and he is right insofar as drilling can make ordinary men into patient, careful laboratory workers. But science has not yet managed to get along without ideas, and these come only from men of special, powerful, and irreducible aptitudes. The chronological study of these men and ideas is the proper subject matter for an undergraduate course in the history of science.[6]

I know the common objection offered to all this—to an historical and a synoptic account of scientific principles in place of the "regular" science courses: it is that the substitutes would be merely talk about science and not

[5] The self-righteousness of the man of science is universal enough to sustain advertising appeals: "Like the scientist, NEWSWEEK . . . makes it its business to search out truth by continual research, relentless checking and re-checking of the facts." A grim grind!

[6] Some very useful works already exist which exemplify the historical and inductive method of teaching science; among others: Ostwald's *Schule der Chemie* (translated by E. C. Ramsay), Ida Freund's *The Study of Chemical Composition* and *The Experimental Basis of Chemistry*, Norman Campbell's *Physics: The Elements*, and H. T. Pledge's *Science Since 1500*.

science itself. Grant this for argument's sake. The objectors miss the point if they do not see that talk about science has a place in the curriculum and that such talk may be good or bad, quite all right or all quite wrong, exactly like talk about art. If science is one of the humanities it must be capable of being looked at and thought about apart from direct doing—at least until we require every concertgoer to write a symphony before being allowed to take his seat at Carnegie Hall. Besides, the synoptic course I have in view would include laboratory work, and it would rest with the scientists themselves whether the students mastered enough of the operative side of true science to keep them from irresponsible talk about it. If science teachers think that a year's drudgery in physics as now given prevents silly notions in those who take it in college, they are either inobservant or illogical.

Doubtless it is bad logic they suffer from—the usual weakness of scientists . . . and of the rest of mankind, who generally want to have things both ways. Take as an example a comment made on the relation of science and history in the excellent study of Lavoisier by J. A. Cochrane. The author complains that "although Lavoisier was at the time of his death and for at least fifteen years before it one of the most eminent men in France, the general historian does not think it worth while to make any mention of him. . . . Science has undoubtedly changed the face of the world, and yet practically the only credit given to it by the historian is the Industrial Revolution . . . and even then the facts are not always accurate."

This is very sound criticism, but the scientist at once reasserts his monopoly: "No doubt the historian, having no qualifications to discuss the progress of science, feels that he had best leave it severely alone, but he can scarcely claim to trace the evolution of the modern world if he omits one of the most important factors in that evolution." Which will the author have—treatment with inevitable errors or leaving the sacred objects "severely alone"? So long as we act like watchdogs over our little plots, it is obvious that we cannot have the comprehensive views that all profess to desire. Somebody has to take the first step—and suffer for his pains.

But it would be unfair if I gave the impression that the opposition to teaching the history of science to college students was universal or came only from certain scientists. At one great university near New York there was a thriving enterprise of this sort, popular with students and science departments alike. It was given by a young man, equally gifted in the humanities and in his chosen physical science—a budding *uomo universale*, whom fellow scientists were willing to aid, guide, and correct—if need be—on the remoter details of their science. After a few years this course built up a tradition, exerted an influence, reached a kind of perfection in the fulfillment of its aim.

With the war, changes came in staff and direction; the instructor left and the opposition rallied to abolish the course. It will scarcely be believed when I say that the prime mover in this *Putsch* was a philosopher. What inspired him, the Absolute only knows. The science course did not teach any philosophy contrary to his own; it only taught the historical fact that great men of science have employed varying philosophical assumptions to gain their ends. It taught, besides, that the several sciences do not look at the world all in the same way and that so far as science has a unified point of view, it is not exclusive of others —the ways, namely, of art, philosophy, religion, and common sense. Lastly, the course imparted a fair amount of matters of fact and showed how wrong was the man who said: "You don't have to teach the history of science to make a man understand that water is $H_2O$." It is precisely what you have to teach, unless you are willing to barter understanding for mere voodoo formulas.

What more could any philosophy department want? Their students were lucky enough to be taught to think. Is there any other use to make of the four years of college? The world being full of a number of things, it takes practice to think easily about the chief ones. Does philosophy pretend to monopolize cogitation because Descartes said, "Don't doubt I'm thinking!"

The fact is that philosophy has suffered emotionally, like Greek and Latin, from the triumph of science. Philosophy was a minor partner in the defeat of the classics, and that has left it laboring under the same sense of wrong, the same fancied need to be haughty—and even hoity-toity. In the '80s science said: "We bring you the answers. Philosophy will gradually be pushed out as we extend our certainty." Many philosophers agreed and looked for their retirement at the first outrush of some naked Archimedes shouting "Eureka." Other philosophers, courageously holding their ground, fought as critics of science's faulty logic or extreme arrogance, just as a few classicists kept saying, "Poison gas marks a great step forward but have you taken in the meaning of Thucydides's 'Peloponnesian War'?"

The time has now come for the three-cornered duel on the campus to cease. The classics, philosophy, and science are at once overlapping and complementary disciplines. No need even to adjust boundary differences. The students are well able to take care of seeming conflicts, and in truth profit from them, since opposition reinforces attention by heightening the drama of human thought. Science must be taught, and historically, too, or the people will perish. Philosophy likewise must have a voice in all courses throwing light on the history of ideas. It will save philosophy as a subject and save the students from caddishness and provincialism. But philosophy has other obvious collegiate duties. It must read its great masterpieces with the new generation, expound ethical and metaphysical theory, help teach logic, and do liaison work with historians, scientists, and theologians. Once in a while an original philosopher will arise, unsought, in the midst of his colleagues, and the world will know him to its own profit.

The classics, too, must enter the dance. They hold the key to the meaning of our long journey from the cave to—precisely—the laboratory.

❧ ❧ ❧

*Lewis Mumford*

# Looking Forward[1]

THE achievements of modern technology have been part of a culture whose central theme was the seizure and exploitation of power. But although the quest for power led to the ruthless exploitation of natural resources, the break-up of the natural balance of organisms, and the extermination of many valuable cultural traditions, it was not wholly a negative and destructive impulse. For up to the first World War this culture embraced people who lived in every part of the planet; and by means of an increasing interchange of trade, investments, and ideas, it brought over a billion people into a working partnership. In the field of politics there was a steady diffusion of power, through the spread of democratic and co-operative methods of control.

Unfortunately, technical improvements and economic facilities outran the moral capacities of the peoples who had fared best under this culture, and in particular of their governing classes. The very illusion of moral progress that was fostered by the prevailing optimistic philosophy of the nineteenth century tended to conceal the vast hiatus between technological and social achievements.

The underlying axiom of this power culture was that the increased use of non-human sources of energy, and the increase of wealth through the mechanization of the means of production, must automatically increase the possibilities of human well-being. This axiom, as Mr. Arnold Toynbee has amply shown in his *Study of History*, has no factual basis. Though there is a close relation between technics and every other aspect of human culture, material abundance often goes hand in hand with social decay.

As a corollary to this prime assumption about the desirability of material expansion went the notion that the increase of "power and wealth" had no limits, because human desires were boundless and insatiable. This corollary was as baseless as the axiom itself: it was merely an illusion which assumed as given the very fact that remained to be established, the notion that human satisfaction increased in proportion to the number of human desires and to society's capability of satisfying them. That vulgar notion has been responsible for a great deal of human misery. For the experience of the race has abundantly shown that moderation and restriction are essential to human well-being in every aspect of man's existence. This is true on the physiological level, since three dinners at a time are not three times as satisfactory as one; and it is true on the moral level, where the moderation and equilibration of desire have proved organically satisfactory, whereas its inordinate expression, or inordinate contraction, leads to conditions of social and personal maladjustment.

When Lord Acton said, "All power corrupts and absolute power corrupts absolutely," he was referring mainly to political power. But what he said likewise applies to power in all its manifestations. The more energy that man commands the more important it is that this energy should be at the service of his whole personality and his whole culture, and not merely at the command of some narrow ambition or some limited goal. Now the fact is that science and technology, for the last three hundred years, have been at the service of narrow, and often, one must add, quite primitive notions of human development and human well-being. They have given power to the military and political and financial despots: they have fed their egos and justified their ambitions; they have further brutalized the brutal and corrupted the corrupt. As a result they have made mankind the victim of the machine rather than its benign commander and controller. Although many high and humane achievements remain, the animus of this civilization has been a predatory one.

The familiar doctrines of technological materialism are without a sound sociological or psychological basis; and that by itself would be enough to condemn them from a human standpoint. But there is still another way in which their insufficiency may be demonstrated; and this is by reference to the facts of historic development. Technological materialism itself represents a passing phase of human history. The great age of expansion which it fostered is now coming to an end; the conditions that turned men's attention exclusively to the conquest and exploitation of the material environment have been subverted by the very success of Western man's enterprise and invention. We are now probably living through the last great crisis in this power civilization. This crisis will either ruin Western Society entirely—and with it the very advanced technics of science and invention—or it will permit this culture to establish itself on a much broader human basis. In the second instance, the process of materialization, by which one may characterize our culture during the last three centuries, will give way to a process of "etherealization" to use a term coined by Toynbee: quantitative interests will become secondary to qualitative interests; and the great advances that were once made in the physical sciences almost exclusively will now be paralleled by progress in the domain of sociology and personology—sciences which themselves will no longer be dominated by the categories and methods of the physical sciences.

This change within the domain of thought is the counterpart of a wider social process; as it is, no less, one of the means by which further social developments will be guided and applied. If we are to understand both its significance and its necessity, we must understand first of all how completely our technological achievements in the past have been conditioned by the historic movement of expansion: the land expansion of the conquistador and pioneer, the mechanical expansion of the inventor, the industrialist, and the financier, and finally, the population expansion which was the source of the vital energy of Europe during the nineteenth century.

The first thing to note about modern technics is that it is associated with the period of land expansion in the Western world, which began in the fifteenth century, when Europe had reached the limits of its own frontiers. This period of discovery was accompanied by a steady pushing back of the physical horizons; and it was marked by the quick spread of the European from his original habitat to the remotest shores of Asia, Africa, and America. Here was an attempt to break away from the bounded and walled horizons of the medi- eval city; an attempt to treat the whole world as the habitat of Western man and as the object of his curiosity as well as of his cupidity.

This world-wide immigration and colonization was itself the complex prod- uct of economic interests, seeking to widen the area of trade, of a missionary impulse to spread Christian doctrine, which grew up again with the new preaching orders, and of new technical instruments for commanding space and time. The compass, the three-masted sailing ship, the sailing chart, the accurate ship's chronometer—the latter not invented till the eighteenth century—made possible the era of exploration and colonization. It would be impossible to exaggerate the effect of the new spatial horizons upon men's minds. Samuel Morse's impulse to invent the electric telegraph dates from the moment when the lonely young American painter, in London, felt the gap between himself and his family, filled only by letters, to be an unbearably long one.

But the technical results of exploration and colonization were not one-sided ones. Though the Western European, by the nineteenth century, had dis- tributed his firearms and his friction matches, his iron hardware and his mis- sionary pocket-handkerchiefs all over the map, he rapidly acquired, from the primitive peoples he conquered by his "superior" civilization, a greater abundance of resources and technical methods, which could be utilized by his advancing industry, than had been diffused by slower processes during the pre- vious few milleniums. This account has never been accurately reckoned up, as far as I know: perhaps because its results would diminish Western man's self- satisfaction and conceit.

If, however, one goes no farther back than the fifteenth century and takes nothing more away than printing from movable types from Korea, cotton fab- rication from India, porcelain manufacture from China, rubber culture from the Amazons, and the new food crops that came from the Americas, the effect would be to bring the whole Western world to a literal standstill and to the verge of outright starvation. At all events, it is extremely doubtful whether anything that could be compared with modern technics could have resulted by the twentieth century out of Western man's unaided imagination. The mechan- ical conquest of the planet, by means of the sailing vessel, the steamship, the railroad, the cable, the telegraph, the radio—and above all, perhaps, by gun- powder—was a means by which the technological contributions of hitherto isolated cultures were enabled to influence the whole Western world. This happened at a moment when Western man's interests were becoming almost exclusively technological and materialistic; and it therefore had an overwhelm- ing effect.

Now, this period of land expansion has finally come to an end. What was true of the United States around 1890, as Frederick Jackson Turner pointed out, became true of the whole planet during the fifty years that followed: Siberia, Manchuria, and a few scattered outposts around the rest of the globe were the last regions to undergo the invasion and exploitation of modern man. The period of one-sided conquest now has come to its own natural terminus: the process of surface exploitation, of wholesale migration and colonization, with its careless wastage of capital resources and its greed for quick return belongs to the past.

We are now entering a period of settlement or rather of resettlement; and this involves the attempt to find a stable basis for living in the environments that have proved most favorable to human life. There are vast damages to be repaired: deforested areas to be restored to woodland, eroded soils to be built up, more organic patterns of living that are to be reinstated; and if science and technics are to benefit by the stimulus of other cultures, there must be a world-wide give-and-take, as between equals. Political skill must keep open the world-wide channels of intercourse and interco-operation, once established crudely at the point of a gun for the benefit of the Western exploiters.

But at this point it becomes obvious that the conditions for further technical advance, through the stimulus of other cultures and ways of life, rest not upon technicians and scientists, but upon political actions that lie far outside their immediate sphere of control. Once, the political instruments of cultural intercourse could be taken for granted: foreign scientists and explorers traveled freely in the remotest parts of the world, even without passports; unless they aroused purely local animosity they could come and go in safety and freedom. For the last twenty-five years the common vehicles of such intercourse have been one by one disappearing. The totalitarian states are even in times of peace closed regimes: the democratic states themselves have shared this vice in some degree, as compared with the open world which existed generally before 1914.

The danger should be plain. If each great state or empire becomes a rigid, self-contained unit, immune to outside influences and foreign ideas, the social basis for technological advance, which historically involves world-wide intercourse at all levels, will have disappeared. Doctrines of political and cultural isolationism—which are sometimes heretically preached even by men of science —are based upon historic ignorance as to the actual foundations of our present culture.

Now, world travel and intercourse rest ultimately on world trade. It is the passage of surpluses and specialties across frontiers that makes available the means of exchange that enables other people, besides the merchants involved, to travel freely and exchange their intellectual products. Where no such medium is available, the investigator who wishes to become familiar with foreign thought or technics must either imitate Alexander, and come with an army, or he must follow Plato's reputed example when he went to Egypt and covered his expenses by taking with him a cargo of oil which he sold to the Egyptians. Otherwise only beggars can be travelers. Already there are states in existence where Plato's method would be impossible, even if he were not denied a visa or stopped at the frontier because he was not a believer in "Aryan" anthropology or in "Marxian" genetics.

If the closed totalitarian states should remain in existence for as much as another generation, the international structure of scientific thought would probably collapse. For even before the present war passed into its active phase, the tactics of the Russian, German, and Italian governments had made the procedures of so-called International Congresses almost a farce, for they were either used as a vehicle for fascist propaganda or decimated of some of their most valued contributors by these totalitarian governments.

To mark the change that has taken place here one need only compare the treatment accorded to the Belgian historian, Henri Pirenne, during the World War with that accorded to representative scientists and scholars in the totalitarian states during the last ten years. When Pirenne was taken in custody by the German government, after the occupation of Belgium, that fact was quickly known to the rest of the world; and the expression of outrage was universal. Danish and Dutch scholars dared to denounce it, no less than Americans. As the result of a world-wide protest, headed by President Wilson and the Pope, he was taken out of a prison camp and sequestered in a quiet German village, with no other duty than that of reporting to the Mayor once a day. That was in war time. Outrages a thousand times worse have been committed by the totalitarian governments against world-respected scientists, sometimes without the news coming out, frequently without arousing a single organized protest, always without world opinion being able to effect the slightest improvement in their position.

The problems raised by the termination of the period of land expansion have not yet been widely grasped; for uncontrolled colonization, immigration, trade—all the methods whereby the exploited resources were put ultimately at the disposal of a world community—have now to be replaced by a rational world organization empowered to redistribute the resources and to widen the economic and political basis of international cooperation. The need of the new age is to create balanced regional communities, which will be capable of operating within a world-wide framework: no longer sealed behind the military frontiers of the bellicose state. *Every movement toward regional or self-sufficiency is a betrayal of the positive achievements of the age of conquest, unless it is accompanied by an equal movement toward planetary organization.* Similarly every attempt to resume the age of conquest, on the Nazi pattern, by re-introducing the principle of dominance and by restoring inequalities and slaveries, goes deeply against the grain of civilized effort. This last movement is not the wave of the future but the treacherous undertow of the past.

Extensive exploration and conquest must now yield to intensive cultivation and regional development; not for the purpose of achieving an illusory self-sufficiency but for the purpose of making the fullest contribution ultimately to the life of mankind.

One could trace a similar movement toward stabilization and balance within the domain of the machine itself, as a result of the purely mechanical and economic factors that are in operation. In *Technics and Civilization* (1934) I called attention to some of these factors. But here I prefer to dwell on another development; or rather, on two current changes that must have a bearing on the future of technics and science. The first is the increasing importance of the biological and social sciences. Before 1850 it would be hard to point to a single important invention that rested directly upon a knowledge of the structure and function of organisms; but during the last two generations some of the most critical advances have come about through the direct application of the biological sciences. The telephone grew out of an interest in the mechanism of human voice production, and the telephone receiver was modeled directly upon the structure of the human ear; experiments with heavier than air flying machines resulted directly from Pettigrew's and Marey's study of the locomotion of animals.

Meanwhile, the application of biological knowledge to the raising of food and to the planning of the human diet has effectively altered the whole problem of man's health and his survival: genetics and the new discoveries on the physiology of nutrition have done far more to assure mankind of an adequate food supply than all the gangplows and automatic reapers and binders that the nineteenth century boasted. We are now aware of many processes where chemical, biological, or social science will enable us to provide alternatives for the purely mechanical solutions that were chiefly available during the paleotechnical period. Most of these applications of biology are still in an early stage.

Let me give a simple illustration. By the use of costly apparatus and machinery it is possible to build a house without windows, in which the air shall be filtered, warmed or cooled, and circulated, and in which sun-lamps, applied at intervals, will make up for the need for natural sunlight: such a house will work almost as well in a crowded slum as anywhere else. Unfortunately, such an "advanced" technical form is compatible with hideous social disorder and economic waste—just as mechanical advances in war are, as in Germany, compatible with political barbarism. But with the full employment of other arts and sciences, such a house is actually a monstrosity. By utilizing current knowledge of meteorology, a house can be oriented and designed so that it utilizes to the full all available sunshine; by utilizing the political art of town-planning, the house can be assured permanent open spaces, pure air, freedom from noxious gases or effluvia without any provision of special machinery; by saving on the cost of mechanical equipment interior space and exterior gardens can be provided whose utilization and pleasure will help keep the occupants in health and psychological balance. In short, by employing all the knowledge at his command, the architect and planner of a modern community can reduce the expenditure on mechanical utilities, and create a far more effective human environment.

This simple example has a much wider bearing. The progress of the biological and social sciences will result in a shrinking of the province of the machine. Here, I believe, is a fact of deep significance: its implications have still to be grasped.

The coming utilization of social and political skills rests upon another condition, which held true even before the development of modern science; and that is, there is some relation between the degree of personal culture that prevails in a community and the quantity of physical goods it desires and commands. One can put this in a crude and comic form by saying that if all men were honest there would be no need for locksmiths and safes: if all men were co-operative there would be no need for handcuffs. In such simple relations it is easy to see that the achievement of a higher degree of moral culture would not result in a new form of machine: it would result in the elimination of a particular mechanical contraption.

What does this mean in the broader picture? It means that an effective transfer of interest to the realm of ethics and esthetics will result in a diminished demand for the machine and its products. If the use of speedy motor cars is the chief means of utilizing leisure, it is obvious that the output of motor cars, highroads, steel and concrete, and all the accessory supplies and services will increase: but if other means of utilizing leisure become popular, if more people paint and write and model and carpenter and garden, if more people study the stars or observe the behavior of children or become outdoor naturalists, there will be a lessened demand for swift agents of locomotion purely for the purposes of recreation. A transference of interest from the mechanical to the organic and human may be properly regarded either as a labor-saving device or as a brake upon production. At all events it introduces a new factor not embraced by the crude doctrine of "increasing wants." Such a change is one of the real possibilities that follows from a better scientific knowledge of the human personality.

Plainly, the process of etherealization has always been possible. There is plenty of historic evidence to show that it actually took place in Roman civilization, from the first century B.C. onwards, and that it contributed quite as much as the invasion of the barbarians to overthrow that society. Perhaps the chief problem of our society is to make allowance for these submerged and blockaded human impulses, left out of the mechanical world picture, without permitting them to undermine and disrupt our whole civilization through their uncontrolled eruption.

The facts, at all events, should be plain. Those who have put their faith in mechanical inventions and in the power theme have failed to see that only a modicum of our constant human needs is encompassed by the machine or included in the territory it conquers. We know pretty definitely that men do not live by machines alone, and that the power impulse, however deep and ineradicable, is not a self-sustaining or a self-sufficient one. This is not to deny the importance of the machine in its place; it is merely to acknowledge the fact that it is not a substitute for art and love and fellowship and beauty and contemplative understanding. Many vital human needs have been frustrated by our one-sided overemphasis on the quantitative and the mechanical: this is true both in thought and in social and personal development. Indeed, as Karl Mannheim has pointed out, the hiatus that now exists between those parts of our life that have been rationalized by the machine and those parts that lie outside its scope, constitutes one of the gravest problems of present-day society. There has been, he points out, an uneven development of the human faculties. A diversification and balance of interests will itself be one of the elements that will save science from its own vices: the vices of isolation, non-communicability.

Beyond what is needed to provide what Aristotle called the material basis of the good life, our absorption in the machine deprives us of leisure, of the means of cultivating the arts and sciences for our personal illumination and enjoyment, and of the possibility of taking active parts as citizens in the shaping and direction of our polity. The machine today often serves as a substitute for activities that should be translated directly into biological, social, and personal terms. Our power and leisure are, in fact, empty of significance unless our leisure is used to build up those elements in the human personality and in social relations which are thrust aside or perverted by the one-sided pursuit of power.

The lesson of balance, which comes both from physiology and ecology, is one that has wide applications throughout our culture; it carries with it a demand for co-ordination, for interrelationship, and for intercommunication between the various domains which were once considered free, independent, and sovereign. (Dr. Walter Cannon has very ably elaborated this theme.) Need I point out that there is a close relationship here between the underlying political and social motives of the opening age and the framework of thought in which all our new tasks must be achieved? In both domains power politics and belligerent national sovereignty have produced immediate gains at the expense of the life and integrity of the whole. The age of balance will be one of world-wide federation and interlinkage—in thought no less than in political action.

The real question today is not whether stabilization will take the place of expansion, and symbiosis will replace a more or less predatory economy. The process of stabilization cannot be avoided. The real question is whether this will take place, in disorderly fashion, by a relapse to a more primitive underworld culture, like that envisaged by the Nazis, or whether the change will take place rationally and purposefully: in a fashion that will conserve all of man's great achievements in science and technics during the last three centuries, and bring them to a far richer fruition. But the future of science and technics cannot, in the nature of things, be an automatic continuation of the processes, methods, and beliefs that served the period of expansion. The age of cultivation has new needs and makes new claims. To satisfy these needs every part of our culture must be revitalized and re-oriented; and success here will demand political skill no less than philosophic vision; for thought itself bears an organic relation to life.

## ❦ ❦ ❦ VI. Society

# Social Attitudes

*Clyde Kluckhohn*

## An Anthropologist Looks at the United States [1]

SUPPOSE that archaeologists five hundred years hence were to excavate the ruins of settlements of various sizes in Europe, in America, in Australia, and in other regions. They would properly conclude that American culture was a variant of a culture of world-wide occurrence, distinguished by elaboration of gadgets and especially by the extent to which these were available to all sorts and conditions of men. Careful studies of distribution and diffusion would indicate that the bases of this civilization had been developed in northern Africa, western Asia, and Europe. The shrewd archaeologist would, however, infer that twentieth-century American culture was no longer colonial. He would see that distinctive features in the physical environment of the United States had made themselves perceptible in the warp of the American cultural fabric and that large-scale cultural hybridization and native inventions were continuing to produce a new texture and new patterns in the weft.

Unfortunately, the social anthropologist of 1948 cannot develop this picture much farther and remain in the realm of demonstrated fact. The anthropological study of American communities was initiated in *Middletown* (1928) and *Middletown in Transition* (1937). Since then we have had a series of monographs on *Yankee City;* two books on *Southerntown; Plainville, U.S.A.;* brief studies of six different communities by the Department of Agriculture; Margaret Mead's popular book *And Keep Your Powder Dry;* and a score of scattered papers. Very recently Warner and Havighurst have published a study of class structure and education, *Who Shall be Educated?* Walter Goldschmidt has given us *As You Sow,* a report on California agricultural communities; and the publications on a Middle Western town, *Jonesville, U.S.A.,* have begun to appear. Yet contrast this total handful with the countless valuable volumes that have been published on the history, government, geography, and economy of the United States. Of this culture in the anthropological sense we know less than of Eskimo culture.

[1] From *Mirror for Man* (New York: McGraw-Hill Book Company, Inc., 1949), pp. 228-261. Copyright, 1949, McGraw-Hill Book Company, Inc.

In treating American culture one must resort to an analysis that goes only a shade beyond impressionism. There is the special danger, considering the small quantity of recent field work, of describing American culture more as it has been than as it is. Yet a sketch of characteristic thought patterns, values, and assumptions may help us a little to understand ourselves and thus to understand other peoples better. One can assemble points of agreement in the anthropological studies that have been made, in the testimony of astute European and Asiatic observers, in personal observations. This has been a business civilization—not a military, ecclesiastical, or scholarly one. The brevity of our national history has made for this dominance of the economic as well as for the stress upon the potential as opposed to the actual society. Lacking the inertia of a deeply rooted culture pattern and given the high standard of living, American customs have changed rapidly under the influence of automobiles, radio, and moving pictures. There are many culture traits which are too obvious to require a massing of evidence: love of physical comfort, a cult of bodily cleanliness, finance capitalism. Certain values, such as fair play and tolerance, are generally agreed to but represent modifications of our British heritage rather than anything distinctively American. Rather than cataloguing traits exhaustively, however, this chapter will treat selectively some related traits that appear best to bring out the underlying organization of the culture.

American culture has been called a culture of paradoxes. Nevertheless national advertising and a national moving-picture industry would be impossible were there not certain terms in which one can appeal to the vast majority of this capturable people. Though sectional, economic, and religious differences are highly significant in some respects, there are certain themes that transcend these variations. Some life goals, some basic attitudes tend to be shared by Americans of every region and of all social classes.

To start with the commonplace: even the most bitter critics of the United States have conceded us material generosity. In spite of the romanticism of "public-spirited disinterestedness" most Americans are outgoing and genuinely benevolent. Sometimes, to be sure, American humanitarianism is linked with the missionary spirit—the determination to help others by making the world over on the American model.

Perhaps no huge society has ever had such generalized patterns for laughter. In older civilizations it is commonly the case that jokes are fully understood and appreciated only by class or regional groups. It is true that it is some distance from the sophisticated humor of *The New Yorker* to the slapstick of popular radio programs. But the most widespread formulas reach all Americans. Some of the most characteristic of these are related to the cult of the average man. No one becomes so great that we cannot make fun of him. Humor is an important sanction in American culture. Probably the ridicule of Hitler did more than all the rational critiques of Nazi ideology to make the man in the street contemptuous of Nazism.

All European travelers are struck by American attitudes toward women.

They often note that "Americans spoil their women," or that "America is dominated by petticoats." The truth is more complicated. On the one hand, it is clear that a very large number of American women of privileged economic position are freed by labor-saving devices from much household drudgery—particularly after their few children have entered school. Their abundant leisure goes into women's clubs, community activities, "cultural" organizations, unhealthy devotion to their children, other mildly or seriously neurotic activities. It is also true that many American men are so wrapped up in pursuit of the success goal that they largely abdicate control over their children's upbringing to their wives. The responsibility of American women for moral and cultural questions is tremendous. On the other hand, it is too often forgotten that in 1940, 26 out of every 100 women of working age worked outside the home, that almost every girl who graduates from high school or college has had some job training. We interest women in careers but make it difficult for them to attain a full life in one. In a culture where "prestige" is everything we have felt it necessary to set aside Mother's Day as a symbolic atonement for the lack of recognition ordinarily given to domestic duties.

In Japan a year ago Japanese of many classes complained to me that it was difficult to understand American democracy because Americans seemed to lack an explicit ideology that they could communicate. The Japanese contrasted the Russians who could immediately give a coherent account of their system of beliefs. Various Americans have remarked that what the United States needed more than a good five-cent cigar was a good five-cent ideology. Such explicit ideology as we have derives largely from the political radicalism of the late eighteenth century. We repeat the old words, and some of the ideas are as alive now as then. But much of this doctrine is dated, and a new latent ideology inherent in our actual sentiments and habits is waiting for popular expression.

Particularly since the drastic disillusionment that followed the fine Wilsonian phrases of World War I, Americans have been shy at expressing their deepest convictions and have been verbally cynical about Fourth of July oratory. Yet devotion to the American Way has been none the less passionate. It is significant that aviators in this past war who were under narcotics in the course of psychotherapy would not only talk freely about personal emotional problems but were equally articulate on the ideological reasons for American participation in the war.

The pattern of the implicit American creed seems to embrace the following recurrent elements: faith in the rational, a need for moralistic rationalization, an optimistic conviction that rational effort counts, romantic individualism and the cult of the common man, high valuation of change—which is ordinarily taken to mean "progress," the conscious quest for pleasure.

Mysticism and supernaturalism have been very minor themes in American life. Our glorification of science and our faith in what can be accomplished through education are two striking aspects of our generalized conviction that secular, humanistic effort will improve the world in a series of changes, all or mainly for the better. We further tend to believe that morality and reason must coincide. Fatalism is generally repudiated, and even acceptance seems to be uncongenial—though given lip service in accord with Christian doctrine.

The dominant American political philosophy has been that the common man would think and act rationally. The same premises are apparent in typical attitudes toward parental responsibility. The individual, if "let alone" and not "corrupted by bad company" will be reasonable. If a child does not turn out well, the mother or both parents tend to blame themselves or to explain the failure by "bad blood"—as if action-guided-by-reason could of itself always produce well-adjusted children when the biological inheritance was adequate.

While many Americans are in some senses profoundly irreligious, they still typically find it necessary to provide moral justifications for their personal and national acts. No people moralizes as much as we do. The actual pursuit of power, prestige, and pleasure for their own sakes must be disguised (if public approval is to be obtained) as action for a moral purpose or as later justified by "good works." Conversely, a contemplative life tends to be considered "idleness."

The American mother offers her love to her child on the condition of his fulfilling certain performance standards. No conversational bromides are more characteristically American than "Let's get going"; "Do something"; "Something can be done about it." Although during the thirties there was widespread devaluation of present and future and though pessimism and apathy about the atomic bomb and other international problems are certainly strong currents in contemporary national thinking, the dominant American reaction is still—against the perspective of other cultures—that this is a world in which effort triumphs. A recent public opinion study showed that only 32 per cent of Americans were concerned about social security—for themselves.

Countless European observers have been impressed by "enthusiasm" as a typically American quality. During the war military analysts noted repeatedly that the British were better at holding a position but the Americans at taking one. As Margaret Mead has observed, the British cope with a problem; Americans start from scratch and build completely anew.

Americans are not merely optimistic believers that "work counts." Their creed insists that anyone, anywhere in the social structure, can and should "make the effort." Moreover, they like to think of the world as man-controlled. This view about the nature of life is thus intimately linked with that conception of the individual's place in society which may be called "romantic individualism."

In the English-speaking world there are two principal ideologies of individualism. The English variety (which may be tagged with the name of Cobden) is capitalistic in its basic outlook. American individualism has agrarian roots and may be associated with Jefferson. To this day Americans hate "being told what to do." They have always distrusted strong government. The social roles most frequently jibed at in comic strips are those that interfere with the freedom of others: the dog-catcher, the truant officer, the female social climber (Mrs. Jiggs) who forces her husband and family to give up their habitual satisfactions. "My rights" is one of the commonest phrases in the American language. This historically conditioned attitude toward authority is constantly reinforced by child-training patterns. The son must "go farther" than his father, and revolt against the father in adolescence is expected.

However, as de Tocqueville pointed out, Americans are characteristically more interested in equality than in liberty. "I'm as good as the next man," seems at first a contradiction of the American emphasis upon success and individual achievement within a competitive system. It is true that there are relatively few places at the top in a social pyramid—*at any one time*. But the American faith that "there is always another chance" has its basis in the historical facts of social mobility and the fluidity (at least in the past) of our economic structure. "If at first you don't succeed, try, try again." The American also feels that if he himself does not "get a break," he has a prospect for vicarious achievement through his children.

American individualism centers upon the dramatization of the individual. This is reflected in the tendency to personalize achievement, good or bad. Americans prefer to attack men rather than issues. Corporations are personified. Public power projects were advertised as much as a means of beating the Utility Devil as a way of getting better and cheaper service.

The less opportunity the greater the merit of success. "You can't keep a good man down." Conversely, failure is a confession of weakness, and status distinctions and even class lines are rationalized on such grounds as, "he got there by hard work," "it's his own fault that he didn't get on." Such attitudes—and the idealization of the "tough guy" and the "red-blooded American" and the fear of "being a sucker"—derive both from the Puritan ethic and from the American pioneer era. Aggressive activity and rapid mobility were effectual in the rapid development of a new country, and it made sense then that the rewards in money and status should be high.

The worship of success has gone farther than in any known culture, save possibly prewar Japan. This is reflected in countless staple phrases such as "bettering yourself," "getting ahead," and "how are you getting on?" The opposition to Roosevelt's proposal for a taxation program that would limit net income to $25,000, attests to the depth of feeling for slogans like "the sky's the limit." But the striving for money is not simply the pursuit of purposeless materialism. Money is primarily a symbol. The deeper competition is for power and prestige. "Aggressive" is, in American culture, a descriptive adjective of high praise when applied to an individual's personality or character. "You have to be aggressive to be a success." The obvious crudities of aggression are, as Lynd says, explained away by identifying them with the common good.

But there is a defensive note in this aggressiveness which is also symptomatic. Competitive aggressiveness against one's fellows is not just playing a part in a drama. The only way to be safe in American life is to be a success. Failure to "measure up" is felt as deep personal inadequacy. In a phrase, the American creed is equality of opportunity, not equality of man.

The cult of the average man might seem to imply disapproval of outstanding individuals of every sort. Certainly it is true that a great deal of hostility is directed upward. However, under the influence of the dramatic and success aspects of the "romantic individualism" orientation, the typical attitude toward leaders may best be described as one of mixed feelings. On the one hand, there is a tendency to snipe at superior individuals with a view to reducing them to the level of their fellows. On the other hand, their very success is a dramatic vindication of the American way of life and an invitation to identification and emulation.

The cult of the average man means conformity to the standards of the current majority. To de Tocqueville this was "enfeeblement of the individual." A more recent observer, Fromm, who also looked at the American scene from a European viewpoint, likewise finds this conformity repressive to self-expression. But he fails to see that the American is not a passive automaton submitting to cultural compulsives like European provincials. The American voluntarily and consciously seeks to be like others of his age and sex—without in any way becoming an anonymous atom in the social molecule. On the contrary, all the devices of the society are mobilized to glamorize the individual woman and to dramatize every achievement of men and women that is unusual—but still within the range of approved aspirations of the conforming majority. "Miss America" and "the typical American mother" are widely publicized each year, but an announced atheist (no matter of what brilliance and accomplishment) cannot be elected President.

American devotion to the underdog must be linked to this attitude. As Lynd points out, we worship bigness yet we idealize "the little man." "Griping" is a characteristic American trait, but the griping of American soldiers against the officer caste system is to be understood in terms of American egalitarian notions and especially of the cult of the average man. The fact that officers and enlisted men did not have equal access to various facilities for recreation and transportation enraged what were felt to be the most basic sentiments in the American code. To some extent this aspect of the cult of the average man doubtless represents a refuge for those who fail to "rise," a justification for envy of those who do.

Because of the cult of the average man, superficial intimacy is easy in America. People of every social class can talk on common topics in a way that is not so easy in Europe where life is based more on repetition of patterns of early family routines that are differentiated by class. However, American friendships tend to be casual and transitory.

Thanks to our expanding economy and to national folklore created by various historical accidents, the nineteenth-century faith in "progress" became intrenched in the United States as nowhere else. As Lovejoy and Boas have pointed out, America's golden age has been located mainly in the future

rather than in the past. To some extent, to be sure, the future has been brought
into the present by installment plan buying, the philosophy of "spend, don't
save," etc. But the basic underlying notions have been well made explicit by
Carl Becker.

> By locating perfection in the future and identifying it with the successive
> achievements of mankind, the doctrine of progress makes a virtue of novelty
> and disposes men to welcome change as in itself a sufficient validation of
> their activities.

Western Europeans and Americans tend to be fundamentally different in
their attitudes toward conforming. Americans believe in conforming only to
the standards of one's own age group and change-in-time is a strong value;
Europeans believe—or have believed—in conforming to a past society and
have found security in traditional behavior; yet conformity to contemporary
society is only incidental and not a value. There are, to be sure, wide disparities
in American hospitality to change. We take pride in material change but are,
on the whole, more hostile than contemporary Europeans to changes in our
institutions (say the Constitution or the free enterprise system). In some ways
the conformity of middle-class Englishmen, for instance, is more rigid than
that of Americans—but in other ways it is less so. American attitudes toward
change make generational conflicts more serious. These very generational conflicts, however, make certain types of social change possible. As Mead points
out, children can be more "successful" than their parents, hence "better."

Americans publicly state that having a good time is an important part of
life and admit to craving "something new and exciting." In terms of this
ideology we have created Hollywood, our Forest of Arden type of college life,
our National Parks, Monuments, and Forests. Leaders of our entertainment
industry are the best paid men and women in the United States. In 1947 the
American people spent nearly twenty billion dollars for alcoholic beverages,
theater and movie tickets, tobacco, cosmetics, and jewelry. We spend as much
for moving pictures as for churches, more for beauty shops than for social
service. However, because of the Puritan tradition of "work for work's sake,"
this devotion to recreation and material pleasure is often accompanied by a
sense of guilt—another instance of the bipolarity of many features of American culture. The pleasure principle attains its fullest development in American youth culture. Youth is the hero of the American Dream. Most especially,
the young girl ready for marriage is the cynosure of American society.

We have borrowed ideas and values from countless sources. If one takes single features, one can match almost every instance in a dozen or more cultures,
including the primitive. For example, during the last war many of our soldiers
carried magic amulets, such as a miniature wooden pig which was said to
have raised fogs, smoothed out a high sea, commuted an execution, or cured
assorted cases of illness. But if one looks at the total combination of premises
and attitudes one sees a pattern that has its own special flavor, even though

this description is too brief to take account of regional, class, ethnic group, and generational variations.

An anthropological snapshot of the American way of life cannot catch all the details, but, with other cultures in the background, it should highlight some meaningful interplay of light and shadow. And the attempt is needed. No amount of knowledge of Russian or Chinese culture will avail in the solution of our international problems unless we know ourselves also. If we can predict our own reactions to a probable next move in the Russian gambit and have some clues as to why we shall react in that manner, the gain to self-control and toward more rational action will be tremendous. Because of our tradition of assimilating immigrants and because of our overweening pride in our own culture it is particularly difficult to get Americans to understand other cultures.

Seen in the perspective of the range of human institutions, the following combination of outstanding features define the American scene: consciousness of diversity of biological and cultural origins; emphasis upon technology and upon wealth; the frontier spirit; relatively strong trust in science and education and relative indifference to religion; unusual personal insecurity; concern over the discrepancy between the theory and the practice of the culture.

"The melting pot" is one of the surest catchwords that has ever been applied to the United States. Probably much of the vitality of American life and the increased stature and other evidences of physical superiority for new generations of Americans must be attributed to the mingling of diverse cultural and biological strains as well as to dietary and environmental factors. The "Ballad for Americans" triumphantly proclaims our manifold origins. Newspapers during the war proudly referred to the fact that Eisenhower was a German name but he was an American, to the fact that another general was an Indian, to the variety of names in American platoons and in American graveyards overseas. The distinguished record of Japanese-Americans in the armed services was used to document the success of the American Way.

Heterogeneity has, in fact, become one of the organizing principles of American culture. Ripley's "Believe it or Not," "Quiz Kids" programs, "Information Please," and other formal and informal educational devices are evidence that Americans value disconnected pieces of information and feel that people must be prepared to live in a world in which generalizations are hard to apply.

If one looks at a culture as a system in which traits mainly received by borrowing are being patterned in response to situational factors and organic needs our American position at present bears a few compelling resemblances to that of Europe in perhaps the twelfth century. It was only then that a quasi-permanent integration had been attained in the European cultural melting pot. Pagan and Christian, Greco-Roman and Germanic culture elements had seethed in troubled opposition during the centuries of the movements of people. Our mass movements stopped only a generation ago with the closing of the frontier. During the tenth and eleventh centuries in Europe forests were cleared and swamps were drained; cities were built in large numbers in

Northern Europe, and there came to be some fixity in the distribution and density of population.

Because of the very fact that diversity is an explicit theme of American culture one must be careful not to overemphasize the threats of the admitted contradictions in our way of life. Those who look longingly back to the good old days of a fancied homogeneity in American values forget that the Tories almost equaled the Patriots in number, do not remember the details of the situation that demanded the Federalist papers, neglect the two radically opposed sets of values that led to the War between the States. Actually, we must agree with Frank Tannenbaum that the harmony best suited to a democratic society "is one which comes from many-sided inner tensions, strains, conflicts, and disagreements." Though the stability of a culture depends on how much the conflicts it engenders can be supplied adequate outlets, still the strength of the democratic process is that it not only tolerates but welcomes difference. Democracy is based not upon a single value but upon a subtle and intricate multiple of values. Its strength rests in the balance of social institutions.

Although the definition of an American as a person who is endlessly catching trains is a caricature, the phrase of G. Lowes Dickinson "contemptuous of ideas but amorous of devices" remains uncomfortably correct as a characterization of all save a tiny minority of Americans. And while we indignantly met the Fascist label of "plutocracy!" by pointing to our humanitarian organizations, our numerous foundations dedicated to the spending of untold millions for lofty aims, and the generosity of individual citizens, it remains true that not only are we the wealthiest nation in the world but that money comes closer with us than with any other people to being the universal standard of value.

This is why the level of intellectual ability is very much higher in the Harvard Law School than in the Harvard Graduate School of Arts and Sciences. The ablest undergraduates in Harvard College do not always receive the highest honors. The energies of many are often, realistically enough, consecrated to "making contacts" through "activities," through a sedulous campaign to acquire membership in a "final club." This is not necessarily because they are congenitally uninterested in ideas, but because they have been effectually conditioned by family pressure and by certain schools. They have considerable intuitive insight into the structure of our culture. They know that intellectual endeavor will lead them to little "recognition" and less salary. They know how vital is "success" to security in our society. Brilliant young men voluntarily condemn themselves to lives of cutthroat competition and narrow slavery.

Our economy is a prestige economy to a pathological extent. The wife must buy fur coats and drive an expensive automobile because she too is an item of conspicuous consumption. Even in the supposedly uncommercial halls of learning the awed whisper is heard, "Why, he is a $15,000-a-year professor." The numerical system of grading, an unmistakably American invention, is simply another projection of our conviction that all attainments can be expressed in figures.

Suppose that an intellectual Australian aborigine, who was also a trained anthropologist, were to write a monograph on our culture. He would unequivocally assert that machines and money are close to the heart of our system of symbolic logics. He would point out that the two are linked in a complex system of mutual interdependence. Technology is valued as the very basis of the capitalistic system. Possession of gadgets is esteemed as a mark of success to the extent that persons are judged not by the integrity of their characters or by the originality of their minds but by what they seem to be—so far as that can be measured by the salaries they earn or by the variety and expensiveness of the material goods which they display. "Success" is measured by two automobiles—not by two mistresses as in some cultures.

Could our aboriginal anthropologist introduce some time perspective into his study, he would note that this value system has shown some signs of alteration during the last two decades. However, against the background of all known cultures, American culture would still stand out for its quantitative and materialistic orientations.

Americans love bigness—so far as things and events are concerned. Their constant overstatement appears to others as boasting. Americans love to speak in numbers. They like to "get down to brass tacks" and "want the lowdown." Europeans are usually content to rate students according to categories corresponding to "high honors," "honors," "pass." Only Americans think that the relative standing of students in a course can be measured on a continuous scale from zero to 100. This emphasis on the quantitative must not be too easily taken as proof of a thoroughgoing materialism. But Americans do tend to get very excited about things as opposed to ideas, people, and aesthetic creations. "Virtuous materialism" has tended to be part of the American creed.

Status in the United States is determined more by the number and price of automobiles, air-conditioning units, and the like owned by a family than by the number of their servants or the learning and aesthetic skills of family members. In fact, Americans usually are scared out of being artists. There is reverence only for the man who *does things* in a big way." Most Americans do subscribe to the current Einstein legend, but *Time* has recently pointed out that many did not take this very seriously until they were told that Einstein's "theories" had made the atomic bomb possible. It is significant that Edison is a household name, whereas only the professors have heard of Willard Gibbs.

John Dewey says that American thinking is characterized by a "lust after absolutes." By this he does not, of course, mean a hankering for the "absolutes" of religion and philosophy. He refers to the tendency to think that, because simple questions can be posed, there exist simple answers, which classify ideas and individuals as all black or all white. For this reason "compromise" has an unfavorable connotation in American English. Worship of the external and quantitative leaves little patience for the infinite shadings and variations of direct experience. Doubtless the vastness of the American scene and the impermanence of social place create a need to generalize. Europeans are ordinarily more sensitive to the complexity of situations.

Our phrase "pioneer of industry" is not a haphazard combination of words. The patterns of the American Way were set during that period when the United States was on the skirmish line of civilization. The frontier has been a predominant influence in the shaping of American character and culture, in the molding of American political life and institutions; the frontier is the principal, the recurring theme in the American symphony. Whatever distinction we have as a people, whatever differentiates us from the other branches of Western European civilization we owe in large part to the presence of the frontier—its unappropriated wealth, its dangers and challenges.

Unfortunately, many of the responses which made for survival under those conditions are singularly unsuited to our present situation. To some considerable degree, frontier virtues are the intolerable vices of contemporary America. To extemporize and not to plan "paid off" then. Unhappily, we have tended to see these qualities as absolutes rather than from the perspective of cultural relativity. Aggressive and childish young Mickey Rooney was recently the hero of a population which ought to have grown up. A reactionary comic strip which portrays the triumphs Orphan Annie and Daddy Warbucks attain by stubborn clinging to pioneer attitudes and habits is still the inspirational reading of millions of Americans. Egoistic individualism remains long after the economic place for it has passed.

This same frontier spirit, however, affords the spiritual sources which can swiftly bring about potential reforms. If we Americans are restless, unanchored in our ideas as in our habitations, if also we may boast a certain freedom, a flexibility in our thinking and a vigor and independence in our action, it is in some degree traceable to the constant flux of American life, always westward, always away from old and permanent things. The American tempo has not become a sophisticated dignified one, measured in harmony with the persisting splendor of ancient palaces, and the symmetry of great parks carpeted with lawns such as only centuries of tending could produce. We have not evolved a splendid system of common law out of the crude folk code of the German forest by a millennium of patient and slow change. Our political institutions did not grow deep in the shadow which the *imperium Romanum,* the *pax Romana,* the *instituta Gaii* have always cast over the ideas of the men of Western Europe. We on this continent have not upreared under the goad of a common ecstasy and mighty aspiration a sky-striving shrine for Our Lady of Chartres, nor a great temple for the Three Kings of Cologne. We share, to be sure, in all the achievements of Western Europe because we have a common ancestry in blood and in ideas with the men of Western Europe, but we share more distantly, more and more differently. The common ecstasy of our great-grandfathers went toward the conquest of a vast and magnificent, a sometimes pitiless and terrible land; our grandfathers were born beside covered wagons in mountain passes, on the prairie, on the desert; the Vigilantes administered the laws in many of our early communities. If our whole economic development as a nation was conditioned by the fact that for more than a century there was always free land in the West for the man who had lost his job in the East, it is equally true that this terrible struggle for survival against the Indian and against the land itself begot in our forefathers not a slow, ordered, conventionalized response to a given stimulus but a quick tense reaction to fit each differing need: the temper of American life to this day.

Assembly-line factories and skyscrapers must, in part, be understood in terms of the frontier. Our so rapid development in invention and technique, our gigantic financial and industrial systems—in general, the fact that we adjusted so completely and quickly, albeit so inharmoniously, to the Technical Age is to be traced to the absence of an ancient order of society and the presence of the frontier where we had to adapt ourselves to vastness with decision, speed, and skill. In an old culture there is a belief in the established order, a rooted opposition to change, a constitutional imperviousness to new ideas which would involve radical alteration in the mode of life. The frontier liberated the American spirit. It developed generosity and radiant vitality, together with a restlessness which was both good and ill, but did certainly bring with it a resiliency of mind, fluidity of idea and of society, a willingness for bold experiment.

Mass education, like mass suffrage and mass production, is a leading trait of our code. During the last generation education has supplanted the frontier as a favorite means of social mobility, for we have continued to define success in terms of mobility rather than in terms of stability. Our educational system has recently been built upon a kind of watery intellectualism. We have too often naïvely assumed that, if people were "well informed" and taught to reason in accord with accepted canons of logic, their characters would take care of themselves, and they would automatically acquire the point of view requisite in the citizen of a great society. Meanwhile, the toughening influences of frontier conditions were becoming steadily more dilute. Children of the economically dominant classes were being brought up in relative luxury. Parents failed to condition their offspring to rigorous standards of conduct because they were themselves confused. Actually many educative functions formerly carried out by the family have been surrendered to the school. The existing educational system is hopelessly irresolute on many fronts. It vacillates between training girls to be housewives or career women; it is torn between conditioning children for the theoretically desirable cooperative objectives or to the existing competitive realities. In spite of the terrific demands made upon them, elementary and high-school teachers are underpaid and lack social status. Psychiatrists are agreed that the elimination of social disorganization, as well as of personal disorganization, can be furthered only by more consistent educational practices both in the home and in the school because automatic actions based on the habits of early life are the most stable.

The anthropologist must also characterize our culture as profoundly irreligious. More than half of our people still occasionally go through the forms, and there are rural and ethnic islands in our population where religion is still a vital force. But very few of our leaders are still religious in the sense that they are convinced that prayer or the observance of church codes will affect the course of human events. Public figures participate in public worship and contribute financially to a church for reasons of expediency or because they know that churches represent one of the few elements of stability and continuity in our society. But belief in God's judgments and punishments as a motive for behavior is limited to a decreasing minority. Feelings of *guilt* are common but the sense of *sin* is rare.

The legend of Jesus lives in men's hearts and the Christian ethic is far from dead. As Bridges reminds us: "They who understand not cannot forget, and they who keep not His commandments call Him Master and Lord." But, in the opinion of many acute observers, American Protestantism is vital today primarily as an agency of benign social work. Relatively few Protestants, except in a few sects and in some rural areas, manifest deep religious feeling. The Roman Church certainly retains vigor, and parts of the encyclicals of recent Popes are not the least impressive of utterances upon contemporary life. To more than a few intellectuals of recent years the Catholic Church has appeared as the one firm rock in a sea of chaos and decay. To others it seems that the authoritarian Church, for all the social wisdom she has shown, for all the subtlety of her doctors, has purchased peace of mind in their time for her communicants by identifying ephemeral cultural expedients with immutable human nature. A system of beliefs, profoundly felt, is unquestionably necessary to the survival of any society, but an increasing number of Americans debate the extent to which the dogmas of any organized Christian Church are compatible with contemporary secular knowledge.

Much of this debate reflects the shallowness of certain aspects of American culture. The alternative of science *or* religion is fictitious once it be granted that the functions of religion are primarily symbolic, expressive, and orientative. Every culture must define its ends as well as perfect its means. The logical and symbolic expressions of the ultimate values of a civilization cannot arise directly from scientific investigation, though it is fair to demand that they should not rest upon premises contrary to known fact or proven theory. A mechanistic, materialistic "science" hardly provides the orientations to the deeper problems of life that are essential for happy individuals and a healthy social order. Nor does a political philosophy such as "democracy." Men need tenets that do not outrage the brain but are meaningful to the viscera and the aesthetic sensibilities. They must be symbolized in rites that gratify the heart, please the ear and eye, fulfill the hunger for drama.

Observers agree on the poverty of American ceremonial life. American ceremonialism is too overwhelmingly that of Shriner conventions and labor rallies. If such national sentiments as we possess are to be maintained at a degree of intensity sufficient to preserve them, they must be given collective expression on suitable occasions. If the conduct of the individual is to be regulated in accord with the needs and purposes of the society, the society's sentiments must be periodically reinforced in the individual by gatherings in which all classes assert in symbolic form: "we are one people." [2]

Mass economic upheaval following upon unprecedented economic growth; lack of attention to the human problems of an industrial civilization; the impersonality of the social organization of cities; the melting pot, transitory geographical residence, social mobility, weakening of religious faith—all of these trends have contributed to make Americans feel unanchored, adrift upon a meaningless voyage. The American family system is in process of settling into a new type of organization and such a phase does not make for psychic ease. Why are Americans a nation of joiners? In part this is a defense mechanism against the excessive fluidity of our social structure. Weary of the tension of continual struggle for social place, people have tried to gain a degree of routinized and recognized fixity by allying themselves with others in voluntary associations.

The smooth working of all societies depends upon individuals not having to think about many of their acts. They can carry out their specialized functions better if much of their behavior is a more or less automatic reaction to a standardized situation in a socially appropriate fashion. A man meets a woman acquaintance on the street. He raises his hat. Such small acts bind a society together by making one's behavior intelligible to one's neighbors and give the participants a sense of security. Because one knows what to do and knows what the other person will do everything seems to be under control. Such patterns likewise release energy for the activities in which the individual is really interested. The trouble in our society is that the cluster of meanings upon which such an expective, repetitive way of behaving must depend is sadly disorganized. The cultural dislocation of emigrant groups, the rapid and disorderly expansion of cities, and many other factors have all contributed to the disorientation of individuals from a cohesive social matrix. Technicians have applied science to industry without either management, unions, or the state making more than feeble attempts at the indispensable compensatory adjustments in social structure.

A disproportionate technological development has given tempo to American life but denied it rhythm. It has provided the constant overstimulation necessary to throw many of us into a perpetual state of neurotic indecision. The disparity between our ingenuity in solving mechanical as opposed to human problems is a grave question. It would be infantile, of course, to say "away with the machine!" Obviously, it is not machines but our lack of scientific at-

---

[2] These statements may seem to imply an exaltation of nationalism or at least an acceptance of its inevitability for all time. Nothing of the sort is intended. I am primarily interested in calling attention to the empirical fact of the connection between means and ends. Also, I believe that certain American sentiments have a value to us and to the world—at least until the millennium of a world society arrives.

tention to the problems they raise which is evil. It is a legitimate hope that machines may free the majority of humans from drudgery and thus afford an escape from industrial feudalism. Further, as Mumford has urged, machines and the rapid transportation and distribution of goods which they make possible, create an international reciprocity and dependency such as to make the peace and order of nations more nearly a condition which *must* be attained rather than a pious desirability.

In rural areas and small towns, quick and direct response of neighbors can make for great personal security and for other values enriching to life. In cities, however, the economy is so finely organized and specialized that the dependency of one individual upon another, though actually more acute, is not felt in warm personal terms. People miss a network of relationships linking the job, the family, the church and other institutions. They feel the lack of personal appreciation of the products of their labors and of nonutilitarian creativity. Edward Sapir has well contrasted our psychological position with that of the primitive:

> So long as the individual retains a sense of control over the major goods of life, he is able to take his place in the cultural patrimony of his people. Now that the major goods of life have shifted so largely from the realm of immediate to that of remote ends, it becomes a cultural necessity for all who would not be looked upon as disinherited to share in the pursuit of these remoter ends. Nor harmony and depth of life . . . is possible when activity is well-nigh circumscribed by the sphere of immediate ends and when functioning within that sphere is so fragmentary as to have no inherent intelligibility or interest. Here lies the grimmest joke of our present American civilization. The vast majority of us, deprived of any but an insignificant and culturally abortive share in the satisfaction of the immediate wants of mankind, are further deprived of both opportunity and stimulation to share in the production of non-utilitarian values. Part of the time we are dray horses; the rest of the time we are listless consumers of goods which have received no least impress of our personality. In other words, our spiritual selves go hungry, for the most part, pretty much all of the time.

Most thoughtful Americans are concerned about the fact that the theory and the practice of our culture are hopelessly out of line. It is well established that while cultural content often changes rapidly, cultural forms often have extraordinary permanency. Thus it is only the *tradition* of economic independence which truly survives. For all our talk of free enterprise we have created the most vast and crushing monopolies in the world. Although the fable that every boy can become president has been repeatedly scoffed at in recent years, parents and children still act upon the ruling motivation that hard work, training, and aggressiveness can overcome almost all limitations. The result is, of course, countless disgruntled or bitter men and women, for as Veblen has shown, in a capitalistic economy the number of places at the top is disappointingly few. A cramping constriction will be felt by individuals so long as our ideal pattern is proclaimed as equality of opportunity for all. "Freedom" like-wise has become fertile of disillusioned cynicism because of increasing realiza-tion of the truth of Durkheim's words, "I can be free only to the extent that others are forbidden to profit from their physical, economic, or other superi-ority to the detriment of my liberty." And much of the exultation in our "high standard of living" is, as Norman Thomas contends, "ludicrously beside the point. What the workers have a right to demand of the machine age is not that it will give them more bath tubs than Henry VIII had for his troublesome domestic establishment; they have a right to ask that machinery will conquer poverty rather than increase insecurity."

A society may indeed be viewed as a structure of expectancies. Neuroses have been produced experimentally in laboratory animals by causing the rela-tion between stimulus and proper response to be irregular and haphazard. It follows that if the expectancies which are generated by the cultural ideology are notably unrealistic, mass frustration and mass neurosis are the inescapable con-sequences.

The diversity of ethnic origins in our forming nation provided strong psy-chological reinforcement of the doctrines of human equality which were the gospel of the Age of Enlightenment and of the Romantic Movement. Had not a belief in mystic equality become part of the official ideology of American culture and offered psychological security to non-Anglo-Saxons, these divergent groups might well have remained tight little islands of transplanted Europeans. But the contrast between this legal and political theory and the private the-ories and practices of too many American citizens (as symbolized in labels like "wops" and "greasers," in Jim Crow laws and lynchings) constitutes one of the severest strains undermining the equilibrium of the American social sys-tem. The Negroes and, to only a slightly lesser extent, the Spanish-speaking Americans constitute caste groups—that is, normal intermarriage does not oc-cur between them and the rest of the population. Segregation in housing and discriminatory practices in our armed services stand out as intolerable contra-dictions in the institutions of a free society.

In the last fifteen years anthropologists have presented evidence that, in con-trast to our official beliefs, a class structure has even now considerably crystal-lized in at least some parts of the United States. Lloyd Warner and his asso-ciates distinguish a six-class system: upper-upper, lower-upper, upper-middle, lower-middle, upper-lower, lower-lower. These groupings are not solely eco-nomic. In fact, members of the top class ordinarily have less money than those of the lower-upper group. Nor does stratification correspond entirely to occu-pational lines. Physicians, for example, are found in all of the first four classes. In Warner's sense a class consists of persons who visit in one another's home, belong to the same social clubs, exchange gifts, and show awareness of them-selves as a group set apart from others, and in a subordinate or superior posi-tion to others.

Whether the six-class system is generally valid or whether a larger or smaller subdivision better represents the facts in some communities is a factual question that cannot be answered until there have been more studies. The division of labor in a complex society makes some form of class stratification almost inevitable. It just so happens that in American culture recognition of the facts is repugnant to the American creed. Public-opinion polls indicate that 90 per cent of Americans insist that they are "middle class" despite wide variations in income level, occupation, and social habits. One study shows that 70 per cent of low-income groups claim middle-class social position. Warner, however, places 59 per cent of the people in one New England town in the two lower classes.

Under the influence of the depression and of Marxian theories discussion of class in the United States has increased greatly in the past twenty years. When class position is grudgingly recognized, it is often with anger—as something un-American and hence wrong. Some students of American class structure have failed to examine the significance of values—adhered to by almost all Americans—which operate to deny and tear down class divisions. Except possibly in limited areas of the eastern seaboard, the South, and the San Francisco area, the lines are still relatively fluid and everyone hopes to rise. The statement that American culture is dominantly a middle-class culture is something more than an acceptance of popular ideology which glosses over the sometimes ugly facts of differentiation. Hence "class," though a real phenomenon, does not have precisely the sense that it does in Europe. Certainly Americans are increasingly conscious of status, but the ranking of individuals and their immediate families is often still divorced from that of their close relatives. And the place of the whole body of kin in the smaller communities is frequently based primarily on length of residence there. Our society remains in important respects an open society.

Nevertheless the facts indicate that rapid rise through sheer ability and industry is much more difficult than it was a generation or two ago. Status is harder to achieve by one's own initiative and easier to acquire through family connections. In Washington during the war it was noted that considerable communication and power flowed through channels that were not only nonofficial but not those of political or other normal American interest groups. For the first time since the Age of Jackson an upper class appeared to be operating without much reference to regional or political lines. The class problem is also manifesting itself in the schools. Teachers, themselves usually of middle-class position, discriminate against lower-class children. The children sense that they are punished for following the cultural patterns of their parents. If effort and ability are not rewarded, the way to delinquency or stolid escapism is inviting. In short, class typing rather than individual typing has become one American mode of granting or denying recognition to other people.

Americans are at present seeing social change of a vastness difficult to comprehend. Concretely, social change has its origins in the strains and dissatisfactions felt by specific individuals. When personal insecurity is sufficiently intense and sufficiently widespread, new patterns are germinated in the few creative individuals, and there will be willingness to try them out on the part of larger numbers. Such is the present condition of American society. If a society be regarded as a system in equilibrium, it may be said that in the decade following 1918 the prewar equilibrium was precariously reattained. But the depression and World War II appear to have destroyed the old equilibrium beyond repair. At the moment Americans are in the tortures of attempting to reach a new and differently based equilibrium. The devastating appropriateness of the phrase, "the neurotic personality of our time," is both the condition and the result of this circumstance.

The basis of social life is the sensitivity of human beings to the behavior of other human beings. In a complex society the need for correct interpretation and response to the demands of others is especially great. But in American culture the first experiences of the growing child tend so to emphasize prestige (especially economic prestige) needs that the ego requirements of our adults are often too tremendous for them to follow any other pattern. As Horney says, "the striving for prestige as a means of overcoming fears and inner emptiness is certainly culturally prescribed." Such a device, however, like the intemperate devotion to the pleasure principle, is but a feeble palliative. The popular motto, "every man for himself," was less socially dangerous when firm and generally held beliefs in the afterworld provided some check upon rampant individualism.

The frontier code of sturdy individualism needs tempering and modification the more because it is seldom possible of attainment in the present situation. As Sirjamaki says, "The culture posits individualism as a basic social value but places overwhelming burdens upon its realization." In most aspects of social life American demands for conformity are too great. After the passing of the frontier, individualism was expressed mainly in the economic part of the culture. Today the United States is almost the only country in the world in which large numbers of people cling to laissez-faire principles in economics and government. In its extreme form this is utterly unrealistic, a fixation upon a vain phantasm of our past.

Some acceptance of planning and of stability as a value would decrease the envy and strife that go with incessant mobility. In a society where everybody is either going up or going down there is an excessive psychological necessity to cherish the familiar. This exaggerated stress upon conformity plus our business externalism has created what Fromm has recently termed "the personality of the market place" as the most frequent type in our culture. Given the pressures to conformity, personality fulfillment is denied to many, perhaps most, of our citizens.

America's claim to greatness thus far is not through its Whitmans and Melvilles, nor its Woods and Bentons, nor its Michelsons and Comptons. Still less does it consist in its having added to the contemplative or religious treasures of mankind. Emerson, Thoreau, James, and Dewey are distinguished thinkers, but that they are of the stature of many other ancient and modern philosophers is doubtful. Mary Baker Eddy, Joseph Smith, and other leaders of cultist or revivalistic sects represent all that is characteristically American in religion.

Americans have, however, been inventive in more than one sphere. Admirable and useful as are those material inventions which have made "the American standard of living" an international byword, American social inventions are the most distinctive contributions made by the United States to world culture. The cult of the average man is an even more characteristically American invention than the assembly line. Philosophers of many nations had dreamed of a state guided by a skillfully trained but small group of the good and wise. The United States, however, was the first country to dedicate itself to the conception of a society where the lot of the common man would be made easier, where the same opportunities would be available to all, where the lives of all men and women would be enriched and ennobled. This was something new under the sun.

We cannot rest upon the laurels of past achievement. E. H. Carr has bluntly stated the alternatives:

> The impact of the Soviet Union has fallen on a western world where much of the framework of individualism was already in decay, where faith in the self-sufficiency of individual reason had been sapped by the critique of relativism, where the democratic community was in urgent need of reinforcement against the forces of disintegration latent in individualism, and where the technical conditions of production on the one hand, and the social pressures of mass civilization on the other, were already imposing far-reaching measures of collective organization. . . . The fate of the western world will turn on its ability to meet the Soviet challenge by a successful search for new forms of social and economic action in which what is valid in individualist and democratic tradition can be applied to the problems of mass civilization.[3]

All advocates of government by an élite, from Plato to Hitler and Stalin, have ridiculed the competence of average citizens to form rational opinions upon complex issues. There is no doubt that many nineteenth-century utterances absurdly exalted rationality. Yet the best anthropological evidence, as Franz Boas pointed out, is that the judgment of the masses is sounder than the judgment of the classes on broad questions of policy where sentiments and values are concerned. This doctrine must not be perverted into a claim for the common man's expertness on technical or artistic matters. Nor does contemporary thought refer to the individual citizen's judgments. Rather, it refers to collective decisions arrived at in group interaction and dealing with "matters of common concern which depend upon estimates of probability." As Carl Friedrich continues:

> This concept of the common man salvages from the onslaught of the irrationalist revolt those elements in the older doctrine which are essential to democratic politics. It seeks a middle ground between the extreme rationalistic ideas of an earlier day and the denial of all rationality by those who

[3] From E. H. Carr, *The Soviet Impact on the Western World*. Copyright 1947 by The Macmillan Company and used with their permission and that of the author.

were disappointed over its limitations. . . . Enough common men, when confronted with a problem, can be made to see the facts in a given situation to provide a working majority for a reasonable solution, and such majorities will in turn provide enough continuing support for a democratic government to enforce such common judgments concerning matters of common concern.

What is the prospect for American culture? Let one anthropologist, though bearing in mind the principles of his science, speak unashamedly in terms of his own American sentiments. Given our biological and material wealth, given the adaptive genius which is the constructive heritage of our peculiarly American frontier spirit, it will be the fault not of angels but of ourselves if our problems are not in large part resolved. The decisive factor will be the extent to which individual Americans feel a personal responsibility. This, in turn, depends upon an intangible: their total philosophic attitude. James Truslow Adams in *The Epic of America* urges that the meaningful contribution which the United States has made to the totality of human culture is "the American Dream," "a vision of a society in which the lot of the common man will be made easier and his life enriched and ennobled." It was in the ideological field that America made its first and can still make its greatest contribution to the world. In the New World, peopled by robust men and women who had the courage to emigrate and many of whom were impelled by the active vision of a nobler society, Americans enlarged the meaning of freedom and gave it many new expressions.

It is this prospect for American culture which we must cherish and believe in. Nor is there anything in science which indicates that the dreams of man do not influence, nay sometimes determine, his behavior. While choice is most often a flattering illusion, while antecedent and existent hard-sense data usually shape our destinies, there are moments in the careers of nations, as well as in the careers of individuals, when opposing external forces are about equally balanced, and it is then that intangibles like "will" and "belief" throw the scales. Cultures are not altogether self-contained systems which inevitably follow out their own self-determined evolution. Sorokin and other prophets of doom fail to see that one of the factors which determines the next step in the evolution of a system is precisely the dominant attitudes of people. And these are not completely determined by the existent culture. John Dewey has shown us that in "judgments of practice" the hypothesis itself has a crucial influence upon the course of events: "to the extent that it is seized and acted upon, it weights events in its favor."

Even that erstwhile pessimist, Aldous Huxley, has seen that the discoveries of modern psychology have been perverted to bolster a false determinism. If responses can be conditioned, they can by the same token be deconditioned and reconditioned—though neither individuals nor peoples change suddenly and completely. We are now released from the dominantly external and material demands which frontier conditions made upon our society. Intelligent planning can ease the hostile tensions of national anarchy by providing both security and socialized freedom for the individual. Ideals of flourishing freshness that adapt to changed conditions and to what is sound and creative in the distinctive American Way are the only sure antidote for our social ills. Only those ideals will spread and be accepted which correspond to the culturally created emotional needs of the people. Scientific humanism is such an ideal. Rooted in the tradition of Americans to value scientific achievement highly, scientific humanism can actualize the American Dream. As our culture has come from all the world, so must we give back to all the world not that technological materialism which is science cheapened and debased but the scientific attitude woven into the stuff of people's daily lives. This is a vision of humility in the face of the complexity of things, of the joyous pursuit of ideas of which there is no exclusive possession. This is science not as the provider of the agencies of barbarism but science as revealing the order in experience, as heightening the sense of our precarious dependence one upon the other, as the surest and most powerful of internationalizing forces.

Scientific humanism should be the sturdy creed of the future. Despite uncritical worship of invention and technology, the masses are still, in Carlson's expression, "innocent of science, in the sense of the spirit and the method of science as part of their way of life. . . . Science in this sense has as yet hardly touched the common man or his leaders." An effective working majority of our citizens need no longer base their personal security upon expectation of future life or adult dependency upon the projected images of parent-persons. The scientific vision is the vision which Plato saw in the *Symposium,* a security system which is depersonalized but humanized rather than dehumanized. To try to make such a vision real, offers American men and women that common nobility of purpose which is the vitalizing energy of any significant culture. The venture demands a courage analogous to religious faith, a courage undismayed by the failure of any specific experiment, a courage ready to offer the renunciations of waiting long, a courage which recognizes that even negative knowledge means growth, a courage realizing that the general hypotheses underlying the venture will be proved only if diminished anxiety and greater gusto in day-to-day living transform the lives of us all.

❦ ❦ ❦

*Geoffrey Gorer*

# American Dating[1]

THE PRESENCE, the attention, the admiration of other people . . . becomes for Americans a necessary component to their self-esteem, demanded with a feeling of far greater psychological urgency than is usual in other countries.

This gives a special tone to the social relationships of Americans with their fellows (with the exception, on occasion, of marital and parental relationships): they are, in the first instance, devices by which a person's self-esteem is maintained and enhanced. They can be considered exploitative, but this exploitation is nearly always mutual: "I will assure you that you are a success if you will assure me that I am" might be the unspoken contract under which two people begin a mutual relationship. The most satisfying form of this assurance is not given by direct flattery or commendation (this by itself is suspect as a device to exploit the other) but by love, or at least the concentrated, exclusive attention which shows that one is worthy of interest and esteem.

It is only against this psychological background that what is probably the most singular feature of American social life can be understood: the "dating" which occupies so much of nearly every American's leisure time from before adolescence until betrothal, and which for many continues even after, if separation or satiety lessens the satisfactions to be derived from the betrothed, or if excessive individual anxiety demands more reassurance than betrothed or spouse or lover can give. "Dating" is idiosyncratic in many ways, but especially so in that it uses the language and gestures of courtship and love-making, without necessarily implying the reality of either. The overt differences of behavior which distinguish "dating" from courtship are so slight as to be barely perceptible; yet only in rare cases, and those involving unbalanced people, does confusion result—when both partners are American. "Dating" is a highly patterned activity or group of activities, comparable in some ways to a formal dance, in others to a very complicated competitive game; it is comparable to a dance in that the gestures employed do not have the significance they would have in other settings (witness the bows and curtsies of the minuet, the close embrace of the waltz and later ballroom dances); but it is more nearly comparable to such a competitive game as chess, in which the rules are known to, and observed by, both parties, but in which each move, after the opening gambit, is a response to the previous move of the other player. As in dances and games, the activity is felt to be enjoyable and rewarding for its own sake, and the more enjoyable the more nearly the partners or players are matched in skill and other necessary qualifications. The comparison with competitive games, such as chess, can be carried further; both partners must play with concentration and seriousness, using all their ingenuity, within the accepted rules, to be the victor; apart from the pleasure of the game, there is also the pleasant enhancement to one's self-esteem that winning the game provides. There is one aspect, however, in which the comparison of "dating" to chess breaks down; in a successful date there should not be a loser; both parties should feel their self-esteem, their assurance, enhanced.

As far as I know, no other society has been recorded which has developed a similar institutionalized type of behavior for its young people. A number of societies, of which the Samoans and the Trobrianders are well-known examples, allow for a period of sexual license and experiment before betrothal and

marriage; but these are, and are meant to be, years of sensual and sexual satisfaction, sought for their own sake. In American "dating" sensual and sexual
satisfactions may play a part (though this is by no means necessary) as counters in the game, but they are not the object of the exercise; the object of the
exercise is enhanced self-esteem, assurance that one is lovable, and therefore a
success.

A further complication arises from the fact that the words and gestures of
love are regularly employed in "dating" without either party taking them for
anything but counterfeit, moves in the game; and yet Americans believe very
deeply and passionately in love (a concept not shared by the Samoans, nor the
Trobrianders, nor many of the people of whom we have adequate studies). It
is difficult to find comparisons for thus using frivolously in one context words
and gestures which may be of the greatest importance in another. A very far-
fetched one could be derived from the game of chess. In a period of monar-
chical passions and court intrigue "Your queen is captured" or "Your king is
threatened" could have completely different significance according to the settings in which the phrases were used.

There is, finally, the complication that "dating," employing and being known
to employ the words and gestures of love-making, is admitted and abetted by
parents and teachers who, many of them, hold the puritan attitudes toward sex
and the pleasures of the body, even though these attitudes do not seem to be
held by most of the younger generation.

Because "dating" is so idiosyncratic to Americans (though the generality of
Americans do not suspect this, believing, like the rest of the world, that the behavior they are used to is "human nature") and because it employs the form—
but not the content—of love making, it has been the cause of innumerable and
serious misunderstandings whenever young Americans have come in contact
with foreigners of the opposite sex. An invitation to a "date"—a pleasant and
mutually profitable evening to enhance each other's self-esteem and demonstrate one's skill in the game—is almost always interpreted by a non-Ameri-
can as an attempt at seduction; if it is indignantly repudiated, both parties
are left angry and dissatisfied: if it is immediately acceded to, the American, at
least, feels defrauded, as if one had set out for a hunt and the fox had insisted
on sitting down in one's back yard.

In a "date" the opening move, at least overtly, should come from the boy, in
the form of an invitation to the girl to spend the evening in his company.
The basis of selection is somewhat different for the boy and for the girl. For
the girl the object is to have as many invitations as possible, so that she can
choose among them the partner who she thinks can give her the best time, or
who will be the most fun to compete with; for the boy the object is to have as
his partner the girl who is most admired and most sought after by his companions and fellow rivals. A girl who only got a single invitation to an important social event (say a commencement dance), even though it was from the
most desirable boy, the captain of the football team, would be doubtfully

pleased (this, of course, on condition that they are not courting); a boy whose invitation is accepted by the local "belle" in similar circumstances has already gained a major social triumph. Consequently, participation in the "dating" pattern is somewhat different for the two sexes: all boys can and should take part in it, the level to which they aspire being dependent on their qualifications; but only the most successful and popular girls in each set do so fully, the rest having to be content with a steady boy friend, or even the companionship of a fellow unfortunate.

Unless an American boy is very poor, very maladjusted, or for some reason almost totally excluded from social life, "dating" and earning money for "dates" will occupy the greater part of his leisure time from early adolescence until betrothal. The social pressure toward doing so is very great. Thus in a typical Midwestern college fraternity the senior members insisted that the juniors have at least three "dates" a week; and further that these "dates" should be with girls who did honor to the fraternity, and, barring betrothal, should not be too frequently with the same girl. Such open control and supervision is unusual, but few Americans would quarrel with the standard of behavior demanded.

The experience of girls is much less uniform, since they are dependent on the boys' invitations, and the boys will invite the most popular girls obtainable. As a consequence some girls will have almost all their time taken up by "dates," while others have at most an occasional one, and many others drop out of the competition altogether until betrothal. The picture is clearest in formal dances. The hostess attempts to have at least three men for every two girls, so that at any moment at least a third of the men are in the "stag line," whereas all the girls are dancing. A man from the stag line "cuts in on" a dancing couple by tapping the man on the shoulder and taking his place. By etiquette one cannot refuse to be cut in on, nor can one cut in on one's immediate successor; a third man must intervene before one can resume one's partner and conversation. A man should not abandon his partner until cut in on; and one of the greatest humiliations a girl can bear is not to be cut in on before her partner is satiated with her company. Such an unfortunate girl is not likely to be invited again, nor, if invited, to accept.

For many girls, consequently, the "dating" period is one of humiliation, of frustration, of failure. But though it is painful, it is not usually psychologically crippling. Such unsuccessful girls are often betrothed and married earlier and better than the "belles" who, many of them, find it difficult to give up such prebetrothal triumphs: and moreover a "belle" is rated by the amount of money spent on her, among other things, and the standard is too high for most young men to maintain regularly.

The "date" starts as an invitation from a young man to a girl for an evening's public entertainment, typically at his expense, though since the depression girls occasionally pay their share. The entertainment offered depends on the young man's means and aspirations, and the locality; but it is in a public place always, and nearly always includes eating food together, the food being anything from an ice-cream soda at the local drugstore to the most elaborate and expensive meal that the locality can provide. Besides the food, the most usual entertainment is dancing—the place of the dance ranging anywhere from the cheap roadside café with a jukebox to the most expensive cabaret or country club. The male (the "escort") should call for the girl in a car (unless he be particularly young or poor) and should take her back in the car. If the entertainment proposed is of a formal or expensive nature, the man should provide a corsage—flowers for the girl to wear on her dress or in her hair.

The corsage is the first sign of the man's estimate of his partner for the evening, partly through the expense of the flowers, and partly according to the extent to which they are particularly suited to the girl's appearance, personality, or costume. Every item of the subsequent entertainment gives further signs; the relative amount of money spent is important for the girl's self-esteem, and not in itself.

"Showing the girl a good time" is the essential background for a "date," but it is not its object, as far as the man is concerned; its object is to get the girl to prove that he is worthy of love, and therefore a success. In some cases superior efficiency in dancing will elicit the necessary signs of approval; but typically, and not unexpectedly, they are elicited by talk. Once again, the importance of words is paramount.

Since, on first "dates" the pair are normally comparative strangers to one another, a certain amount of autobiography is necessary in the hopes of establishing some common interest or experience, at the least to prove that one is worthy of the other's attention. These autobiographies, however, differ at most in emphasis, in tone of voice, from those which should accompany any American meeting between strangers. What distinguishes the "date" from other conversation is a mixture of persiflage, flattery, wit and love-making which was formerly called a "line" but which each generation dubs with a new name.

The "line" is an individual variation of a commonly accepted pattern which is considered to be representative of a facet of a man's personality. Most men are articulately self-conscious about their "lines" and can describe them with ease; they are constantly practiced and improved with ever differing partners. The object of the "line" is to entertain, amuse, and captivate the girl, but there is no deep emotional involvement; it is a game of skill.

The girl's skill consists of parrying the "line" without discouraging her partner or becoming emotionally involved herself. To the extent that she falls for the "line" she is a loser in this intricate game; but if she discourages her partner so much that he does not request a subsequent "date" in the near future she is equally a loser. To remain the winner, she must make the nicest discriminations between yielding and rigidity.

The man scores to the extent that he is able to get more favors from the girl than his rivals, real or supposed, would be able to do. The proving time is the return journey from the place of public entertainment to the girl's home. A good-night kiss is almost the minimum repayment for an evening's entertainment; but how much more depends on the enterprise of the man, the self-assurance of the woman, and the number of "dates" the pair have had together. This love-making is still emotionally uninvolved; it is still part of the game, though the gestures and intimacies and language are identical with true love-making; it is not, save most rarely, an attempt at seduction; and the satisfactions sought are not, in the first instance, sensual but self-regarding. The man should demonstrate his enterprise and prove that he is worthy to be loved by pressing for ever further favors; but the girl who yields too much, or too easily, may well be a disappointment, in exactly the same way as too easy a victory in tennis or chess may be a disappointment.

It is usual—but not essential—that intimacies should increase with each successive "date" with the same partner, up to the threshold of, but seldom including, actual intercourse. The contest continues in these later phases, though slightly less articulately; the victor is the one who makes the other lose self-control without losing it him (or her) self.

It must be repeated that the goal of "dating" is not in the first place sexual satisfaction. An "easy lay" is not a good "date," and conversely. Apart from professional or semiprofessional prostitutes, there are in most groups girls who create for themselves an illusion of popularity by promiscuity. Their telephone numbers may get bandied about, but they are not the girls who get the orchid corsages, or get taken to the ringside tables at the best restaurants. It would be a paradox, but not too great a one, to say that the converse was more nearly true: that the ideal date is one in which both partners are so popular, so skilled, and so self-assured that the result is a draw.

Although "dating" is a game for two players only, it is very often elaborated into a "double date" by two couples going to the same places together. Noteworthy in this is the fact that the deeper emotional bond is between the two friends of the same sex (usually, but by no means always, the men) who arranged the "double date." A still further elaboration is the "blind date," in which the couple have not met at all before the start of the evening's entertainment; this can occur through one partner of an arranged "date" asking the other to provide a companion for his (or her) friend, or through a visitor in a strange town calling up a girl whose number he has been given. . . .

"Dates" are public. The greater part of them, as has already been said, take place in public places; and even if there is not a witness for the final portion, as there is in "double dates," there is little expectation that what transpires will be secret. Though distorted by a certain amount of boasting, detailed accounts of past dates are among the most popular subjects of conversation with people of one's own sex and generation. As with the child recounting his triumphs in the play group or at school, it is a proper method of gaining other people's respect and admiration.

"Dating" is normally ended by betrothal, which is the almost inevitable sequel of a boy's concentration on one girl. "Dating" is by definition promiscuous; and America offers no pattern for prolonged concentration on a single partner for the young outside courtship and marriage—there is no analogue, for example, to the French student's *petite amie*. With the increase in emotional maturity, most young men feel the lack of content in the "dating" pattern as it is normally practiced; a few—the "wolves"—develop it into regular seductions; but for the majority it is succeeded by betrothal and marriage.

❦ ❦ ❦

*Philip Wylie*

# Common Women[1]

## *Mom[2] Is the End Product of She*

SHE is Cinderella . . . the shining-haired, the starry-eyed, the ruby-lipped virgo æternis, of which there is presumably one, and only one, or a one-and-only for each male, whose dream is fixed upon her deflowerment and subsequent perpetual possession. This act is a sacrament in all churches and a civil affair in our society. The collective aspects of marriage are thus largely compressed into the rituals and social perquisites of one day. Unless some element of mayhem or intention of divorce subsequently obtrudes, a sort of privacy engulfs the union and all further developments are deemed to be the business of each separate pair, including the transition of Cinderella into mom, which, if it occasions any shock, only adds to the huge, invisible burthen every man carries with him into eternity. It is the weight of this bundle which, incidentally, squeezes out of him the wish for death, his last positive biological resource.

Mom is an American creation. Her elaboration was necessary because she was launched as Cinderella. Past generations of men have accorded to their mothers, as a rule, only such honors as they earned by meritorious action in their individual daily lives. Filial *duty* was recognized by many sorts of civilizations and loyalty to it has been highly regarded among most peoples. But I cannot think, offhand, of any civilization except ours in which an entire division of living men has been used, during wartime, or at any time, to spell out the word "mom" on a drill field, or to perform any equivalent act.

The adoration of motherhood has even been made the basis of a religious cult, but the mother so worshipped achieved maternity without change in her

---

[1] From *Generation of Vipers*, copyright 1942, 1954, by Philip Wylie, and reprinted by permission of Rinehart & Company, Inc., New York.

[2] You are now about to read (or re-read) one of the most renowned (or notorious) passages in modern English Letters.

This chapter has put the word "momism" indelibly in our language; it has broken a path through sacred preserves into which all manner of amateur critics (along with the stateliest psychiatrists and the United States Armed Services) have since proceeded, virgin status—a distinction worthy of contemplation in itself—and she thus in no way resembled mom.

Hitherto, in fact, man has shown a considerable qui vive to the dangers which arise from momism and freely perceived that his "old wives" were often vixens, dragons, and Xanthippes. Classical literature makes a constant point of it. Shakespeare dwelt on it. Man has also kept before his mind an awareness that, even in the most lambent mother love, there is always a chance some extraneous current will blow up a change, and the thing will become a consuming furnace. The spectacle of the female devouring her young in the firm belief that it is for their own good is too old in man's legends to be overlooked by any but the most flimsily constructed society. . . .

Megaloid momworship has got completely out of hand. Our land, subjectively mapped, would have more silver cords and apron strings crisscrossing it than railroads and telephone wires. Mom is everywhere and everything and damned near everybody, and from her depends all the rest of the U.S. Disguised as good old mom, dear old mom, sweet old mom, your loving mom, and so on, she is the bride at every funeral and the corpse at every wedding. Men live for her and die for her, dote upon her and whisper her name as they pass away, and I believe she has now achieved, in the hierarchy of miscellaneous articles, a spot next to the Bible and the Flag, being reckoned part of both in a way. . . .

Mom is something new in the world of men. Hitherto, mom has been so busy raising a large family, keeping house, doing the chores, and fabricating everything in every home except the floor and the walls that she was rarely a problem to her family or to her equally busy friends, and never one to herself. Usually, until very recently, mom folded up and died of hard work somewhere in the middle of her life. Old ladies were scarce and those who managed to get old did so by making remarkable inner adjustments and by

---

pouring out articles, monographs, bulletins, research reports and shelves of books showing how right I was to speak as I did of a certain, prevalent sub-species of middle-class American woman; and the chapter has typed me apparently forever as a woman hater—indeed, as the all-out, all-time, high-scoring world champion misogynist.

It is this last I regret. The fact that legions of individuals, and finally the Army, followed me in condemnation of that special type of American mother I called "mom" merely affirms my work: the Oedipus complex had become a social fiat and a dominant neurosis in our land. It was past time somebody said so. As a way of life, it is shameful in grownups of both sexes; as a national cult, it is a catastrophe.

But, since I love women more than most men, I believe I love them more deeply and knowingly, and since I respect motherhood whenever and wherever it is worthy of respect, I find it somewhat distressing to be forever tagged as Woman's Nemesis. The fact is that only moms—or incipient moms—could imagine, after a close reading of this very chapter, that I had any other sensation for *real* women than love. Quite a few thousand ladies perceived that fact and so wrote to me. But millions, who thought they read otherwise—or who never read the text but took rumor of my diatribe as Gospel (in mom's fashion)—have given me a false name.

To such females, womanhood is more sacrosanct by a thousand times than the Virgin

virtue of a fabulous horniness of body, so that they lent to old age not only dignity but metal.

Nowadays, with nothing to do, and tens of thousands of men . . . to maintain her, every clattering prickamette in the republic survives for an incredible number of years, to stamp and jibber in the midst of man, a noisy neuter by natural default or a scientific gelding sustained by science, all tongue and teat and razzmatazz. The machine has deprived her of social usefulness; time has stripped away her biological possibilities and poured her hide full of liquid soap; and man has sealed his own soul beneath the clamorous cordillera by handing her the checkbook and going to work in the service of her caprices. . . .

Satan, we are told, finds work for idle hands to do. There is no mistaking the accuracy of this proverb. Millions of men have heaped up riches and made a conquest of idleness so as to discover what it is that Satan puts them up to. Not one has failed to find out. But never before has a great nation of brave and dreaming men absent-mindedly created a huge class of idle, middle-aged women. Satan himself has been taxed to dig up enterprises enough for them. But the field is so rich, so profligate, so perfectly to his taste, that his first effort, obviously, has been to make it self-enlarging and self-perpetuating. This he has done by whispering into the ears of girls that the only way they can cushion the shock destined to follow the rude disillusionment over the fact that they are not really Cinderella is to institute momworship. Since he had already infested both male and female with the love of worldly goods, a single step accomplished the entire triumph: he taught the gals to teach their men that dowry went the other way, that it was a weekly contribution, and that any male worthy of a Cinderella would have to work like a piston after getting one, so as to be worthy, also, of all the moms in the world. . . .

Mom got herself out of the nursery and the kitchen. She then got out of

---

Mary to popes—and motherhood, that degree raised to astronomic power. They have eaten the legend about themselves and believe it; they live it; they require fealty of us all.

From them, I received dozens of scurrilous, savage, illiterate, vulgar and obscene epistles, letters which but made my point that much clearer—to me. But I have had hundreds of *times* as many communications from moms who confessed, from the sons and daughters of moms who suddenly saw whence their sickly dependencies came, and from multitudes of the learned, the celebrated, the world's leaders, who said in effect: *Thanks.*

So, for individuals, the message has often been of value. But insofar as its effect on this great nation is concerned (about which possibility people sometimes enquire), my risky effort to sever the psychic umbilicus by which millions of moms hold millions of grown American men and women in diseased serfdom, *achieved nothing.*

Mom still commands. Mom's more than ever in charge. Hardly five Americans in a hundred know today that mom and her bogus authority have ever been questioned— by me, or by anybody else. The nation can no longer say it contains many great, free, dreaming men. We are deep in the predicted nightmare now and mom sits on its the house. She did not get out of the church, but, instead, got the stern stuff out of *it*, padded the guild room, and moved in more solidly than ever before. No longer either hesitant or reverent, because there was no cause for either attitude after her purge, she swung the church by the tail as she swung everything else. In a preliminary test of strength, she also got herself the vote and, although politics never interested her (unless she was exceptionally naïve, a hairy foghorn, or a size forty scorpion), the damage she forthwith did to society was so enormous and so rapid that even the best men lost track of things. Mom's first gracious presence at the ballot-box was roughly concomitant with the start toward a new all-time low in political scurviness, hoodlumism, gangsterism, labor strife, monopolistic thuggery, moral degeneration, civic corruption, smuggling, bribery, theft, murder, homosexuality, drunkenness, financial depression, chaos and war. Note that.

The degenerating era, however, marked new highs in the production of junk. Note that, also.

Mom, however, is a great little guy. Pulling pants onto her by these words, let us look at mom.

She is a middle-aged puffin with an eye like a hawk that has just seen a rabbit twitch far below. She is about twenty-five pounds overweight, with no sprint, but sharp heels and a hard backhand which she does not regard as a foul but a womanly defense. In a thousand of her there is not sex appeal enough to budge a hermit ten paces off a rock ledge. She none the less spends several hundred dollars a year on permanents and transformations, pomades, cleansers, rouges, lipsticks, and the like—and fools nobody except herself. If a man kisses her with any earnestness, it is time for mom to feel for her pocketbook, and this occasionally does happen.

---

decaying throne—who bore us, who will soon, most likely, wrap civilization in mom's final, tender garment: a shroud.

Today, as the news photos abundantly make plain, mom composes the majority of Senator McCarthy's shock troops—paying blind tribute to a blind authoritarianism like her own. Mom reaches out from her shrieking hordes, cries, "I touched him!" and faints away. The tragic Senator stalks smiling to the podium and leads the litany of panic, the rituals of logic perverted, the induced madness of those the gods have marked for destruction. "McCarthyism," the rule of unreason, is one with momism: a noble end aborted by sick-minded means, a righteous intent—in terrorism fouled and tyranny foundered.

Today, too, there is mom and her mass affaire with Liberace. . . .

Tomorrow, she will shriek around and dote upon some other Hero, as sick, or as fatuous.

Today, while decent men struggle for seats in government with the hope of saving our Republic, mom makes a condition of their election the legalizing of Bingo. What will she want tomorrow when the world needs saving even more urgently?

We must understand mom before we lose touch with understanding itself.

I showed her as she is—ridiculous, vain, vicious, a little mad. She is her own fault first of all and she is dangerous. But she is also everybody's fault. When we and our

She smokes thirty cigarettes a day, chews gum, and consumes tons of bon-bons and petit fours. The shortening in the latter, stripped from pigs, sheep and cattle, shortens mom. She plays bridge with the stupid voracity of a ham-merhead shark, which cannot see what it is trying to gobble but never stops snapping its jaws and roiling the waves with its tail. She drinks moderately, which is to say, two or three cocktails before dinner every night and a brandy and a couple of highballs afterward. She doesn't count the two cocktails she takes before lunch when she lunches out, which is every day she can. On Saturday nights, at the club or in the juke joint, she loses count of her drinks and is liable to get a little tiddly, which is to say, shot or blind. But it is her man who worries about where to acquire the money while she worries only about how to spend it, so he has the ulcers and colitis and she has the guts of a bear; she can get pretty stiff before she topples.

Her sports are all spectator sports.

She was graduated from high school or a "finishing" school or even a col-lege in her distant past and made up for the unhappiness of compulsory education by sloughing all that she learned so completely that she could not pass the final examinations of a fifth grader. She reads the fiction in three women's magazines each month and occasionally skims through an article, which usually angers her so that she gets other moms to skim through it, and then they have a session on the subject over a canister of spiked coffee in order to damn the magazine, the editors, the author, and the silly girls who run about these days. She reads two or three motion-picture fan magazines also, and goes to the movies about two nights a week. If a picture does not coincide precisely with her attitude of the moment, she converses through all of it and so whiles away the time. She does not appear to be lecherous toward the movie photographs as men do, but that is because she is a realist and a little shy on imagination. However, if she gets to Hollywood and encounters the flesh-and-blood article known as a male star, she and her sister moms will run forward in a mob, wearing a joint expression that must make God rue his invention of bisexuality, and tear the man's clothes from his body, yea, verily, down to his B.V.D.'s.

---

culture and our religions agreed to hold woman the inferior sex, cursed, unclean and sinful—we made her mom. And when we agreed upon the American Ideal Woman, the Dream Girl of National Adolescence, the Queen of Bedpan Week, the Pin-up, the Glamour Puss—we insulted woman and disenfranchised millions from love. We thus made mom. The hen-harpy is but the Cinderella chick come home to roost: the taloned, cackling residue of burnt-out puberty in a land that has no use for mature men or women.

Mom is a human calamity. She is also, like every calamity, a cause for sorrow, a re-proach, a warning siren and a terrible appeal for amends.

While she exists, she will exploit the little "sacredness" we have given motherhood as a cheap-holy compensation for our degradation of woman: she will remain irresponsi-ble and unreasoning—for what we have believed of her is reckless and untrue. She will act the tyrant—because she is a slave. God pity her—and us all!

Mom is organization-minded. Organizations, she has happily discovered, are intimidating to all men, not just to mere men. They frighten politicians to sniveling servility and they terrify pastors; they bother bank presidents and they pulverize school boards. Mom has many such organizations, the real purpose of which is to compel an abject compliance of her environs to her personal desires. With these associations and committees she has double parking ignored, for example. With them she drives out of the town and the state, if possible, all young harlots and all proprietors of places where "questionable" young women (though why they are called that—being of all women the least in question) could possibly foregather, not because she competes with such creatures but because she contrasts so unfavorably with them. With her clubs (a solid term!) she causes bus lines to run where they are convenient for her rather than for workers, plants flowers in sordid spots that would do better with sanitation, snaps independent men out of office and replaces them with clammy castrates, throws prodigious fairs and parties for charity and gives the proceeds, usually about eight dollars, to the janitor to buy the committee some beer for its headache on the morning after, and builds clubhouses for the entertainment of soldiers where she succeeds in persuading thousands of them that they are momsick and would rather talk to her than to take Betty into the shrubs. All this, of course, is considered social service, charity, care of the poor, civic reform, patriotism, and self-sacrifice. . . .

Knowing nothing about medicine, art, science, religion, law, sanitation, civics, hygiene, psychology, morals, history, geography, poetry, literature, or any other topic except the all-consuming one of momism, she seldom has any especial interest in *what*, exactly, she is doing as a member of any of these endless organizations, so long as it is *something*. . . .

In churches, the true purpose of organized momhood is to unseat bishops, snatch the frocks off prelates, change rectors just for variety, cross-jet community gossip, take the customary organizational kudos out of the pot each for each, bestow and receive titles, and short-circuit one another.

Mom also has patriotism. If a war comes, this may even turn into a genuine feeling and the departure of her son may be her means to grace in old age. Often, however, the going of her son is only an occasion for more show. She has, in that case, no deep respect for him. What he has permitted her to do to him has rendered him unworthy of consideration—and she has shown him none since puberty. She does not miss him—only his variety—but over that she can weep interminably. . . .

But, peace or war, the moms have another kind of patriotism that, in the department of the human spirit, is identical to commercialized vice, because it captures a good thing and doles it out for the coin of unctuous pride—at the expense of deceased ancestors rather than young female offspring. By becoming a Daughter of this historic war or that, a woman makes herself into a sort of madam who fills the coffers of her ego with the prestige that has accrued to the doings of others. A frantic emptiness of those coffers provides the impulse for the act. There are, of course, other means of filling them, but they are difficult, and mom never does anything that is difficult—either the moving of a piano or the breaking of a nasty habit. . . .

In the matter of her affiliation of herself with the Daughters of some war the Hitler analogue especially holds, because these sororities of the sword often constitute her Party—her shirtism. Ancestor worship, like all other forms of religion, contained an instinctual reason and developed rituals thought to be germane to the reason. People sedulously followed those rituals, which were basically intended to remind them that they, too, were going to be ancestors someday and would have to labor for personal merit in order to be worthy of veneration. But mom's reverence for her bold forbears lacks even a ritualistic significance, and so instructs her in nothing. She is peremptory about historical truth, mandates, custom, fact, and point. She brushes aside the ideals and concepts for which her forebears perished fighting, as if they were the crumbs of melba toast. Instead, she attributes to the noble dead her own immediate and selfish attitudes. She "knows full well what they would have thought and done," and in that whole-cloth trumpery she goes busting on her way.

Thus the long-vanished warriors who liberated this land from one George in order to make another its first president guide mom divinely as she barges along the badgering boulevard of her life, relaying fiats from the grave on birth control, rayon, vitamins, the power trust, and a hundred other items of which the dead had no knowledge. To some degree most people, these days, are guilty of this absurd procedure. There has been more nonsense printed lately detailing what Jefferson would say about matters he never dreamed of than a sensible man can endure. (I do not have any idea, for instance, and I am sure nobody has any idea, what Jefferson would think about the giddy bungle of interstate truck commerce; but people, columnists especially, will tell you.)

Mom, however, does not merely quote Thomas Jefferson on modern topics: she *is* Thomas Jefferson. This removes her twice from sanity. Mom wraps herself in the mantle of every canny man and coward who has drilled with a musket on this continent and reproduced a line that zigzagged down to mom. In that cloak, together with the other miters, rings, scepters, and power symbols which she has swiped, she has become the American pope.

People are feebly aware of this situation and it has been pointed out at one time or another that the phrase "Mother knows best" has practically worn out the staircase to private hell. Most decriers of matriarchy, however, are men of middle age, like me.

Young men whose natures are attuned to a female image with more feelings than mom possesses and different purposes from those of our synthetic archetype of Cinderella-the-go-getter bounce anxiously away from their first few brutal contacts with modern young women, frightened to find their shining hair is vulcanized, their agate eyes are embedded in cement, and their ruby lips case-hardened into pliers for the bending males like wire. These young men, fresh-startled by learning that She is a chrome-plated afreet, but not able to discern that the condition is mom's unconscious preparation of somebody's sister for a place in the gynecocracy—are, again, presented with a soft and shimmering resting place, the bosom of mom. . . .

"Her boy," having been "protected" by her love, and carefully, even shud-deringly, shielded from his logical development through his barbaric period, or childhood (so that he has either to become a barbarian as a man or else to spend most of his energy denying the barbarism that howls in his brain—an autonomous remnant of the youth he was forbidden), is cushioned against any major step in his progress toward maturity. Mom steals from the genera-tion of women behind her (which she has, as a still further defense, also sterilized of integrity and courage) that part of her boy's personality which should have become the love of a female contemporary. Mom transmutes it into sentimentality for herself. . . .

As men grow older, they tend to become more like women, and vice versa. Even physically, their characteristics swap; men's voices rise, their breasts grow, and their chins recede; women develop bass voices and mustaches. This is another complementary, or opposite, turn of nature. It is meant to reconcile sexuality and provide a fountainhead of wisdom uncompromised by it, in the persons of those individuals who are hardy enough and lucky enough to sur-vive to old age in a natural environment. But survival, as I have said, no longer depends on any sort of natural selection, excepting a great basic one which our brains are intended to deal with, and which, if allowed to go brainlessly on, will have to reduce our species to savagery in order to get back to a level on which instinct itself can rule effectively. . . .

I have explained how the moms turned Cinderellaism to their advantage and I have explained that women possess some eighty per cent of the nation's money (the crystal form of its energy) and I need only allude, I think, to the statistical reviews which show that the women are the spenders, wherefore the controlling consumers of nearly all we make with our machines. The steel puddler in Pittsburgh may not think of himself as a feminine tool, but he is really only getting a Chevrolet ready for mom to drive through a gar-den wall. I should round out this picture of America existing for mom with one or two more details, such as annual increase in the depth of padding in vehicles over the past thirty years due to the fact that a fat rump is more easily irritated than a lean one, and the final essential detail of mom's main subjective preoccupation, which is listening to the radio. The radio is mom's soul; a detail, indeed.

It is also a book in itself, and one I would prefer to have my reader write after he has learned a little of the art of catching overtones as a trained ear, such as mine, catches them. But there must be a note on it.

The radio has made sentimentality the twentieth century Plymouth Rock. As a discipline, I have forced myself to sit a whole morning listening to the soap operas, along with twenty million moms who were busy sweeping dust under carpets while planning to drown their progeny in honey or bash in their heads. This filthy and indecent abomination, this trash with which, until lately, only moron servant girls could dull their credulous minds in the tawdry privacy of their cubicles, is now the national saga. Team after team of feeble-minded Annies and Davids crawl from the loudspeaker into the front rooms of America. The characters are impossible, their adventures would make a saint spew, their morals are lower than those of ghouls, their habits are un-cleanly, their humor is the substance that starts whole races grinding bayonets, they have no manners, no sense, no goals, no worthy ambitions, no hope, no faith, no information, no values related to reality, and no estimate of truth. They merely sob and snicker—as they cheat each other. . . .

The radio is mom's final tool, for it stamps everybody who listens with the matriarchal brand—its superstitions, prejudices, devotional rules, taboos, musts, and all other qualifications needful to its maintenance. Just as Goebbels has revealed what can be done with such a mass-stamping of the public psyche in his nation, so our land is a living representation of the same fact worked out in matriarchal sentimentality, goo, slop, hidden cruelty, and the foreshadow of national death.

That alone is sinister enough, but the process is still more vicious, because it fills in every crack and cranny of mom's time and mind—and pop's also, since he has long ago yielded the dial-privilege to his female; so that a whole nation of people lives in eternal fugue and never has to deal for one second with itself or its own problems. Any interior sign of worry, wonder, speculation, anxiety, apprehension—or even a stirring of an enfeebled will to plan sanely—can be annihilated by an electrical click whereby the populace puts itself in the place, the untenable place—of somebody called Myrt—and never has even to try to *be* itself alone in the presence of this real world.

This is Nirvana at last. It is also entropy. For here the spirit of man, ab-sorbed, disoriented, confused, identified with ten thousand spurious personali-ties and motives, has utterly lost itself. By this means is man altogether lost. The radio, in very truth, sells soap. We could confine it to music, intelligent discourse, and news—all other uses being dangerous—but mom will not let us. Rather than study herself and her environment with the necessary honesty, she will fight for this poisoned syrup to the last. Rather than take up her democratic responsibility in this mighty and tottering republic, she will bring it crashing down simply to maintain to the final rumble of ruin her personal feudalism. Once, sentimentalism was piece work, or cost the price of a movie or a book; now it is mass produced and not merely free, but almost compul-sory.

I give you mom. I give you the destroying mother. I give you her justice—from which we have never removed the eye bandage. I give you the angel—and point to the sword in her hand. I give you death—the hundred million deaths that are muttered under Yggdrasill's ash. I give you Medusa and Stheno and Euryale. I give you the harpies and the witches, and the Fates.

I give you the woman in pants, and the new religion: she-popery. I give you Pandora. I give you Proserpine, the Queen of Hell. The five-and-ten-cent-store Lilith, the mother of Cain, the black widow who is poisonous and eats her mate, and I designate at the bottom of your program the grand finale of all the soap operas: the mother of America's Cinderella.

We must face the dynasty of the dames at once, deprive them of our pocket-books when they waste the substance in them, and take back our dreams which, without the perfidious materialism of mom, were shaping up a new and braver world. We must drive roads to Rio and to Moscow and stop spending all our strength in the manufacture of girdles: it is time that mom's sag became known to the desperate public; we must plunge into our psyches and find out there, each for each, scientifically, about immortality and miracles. To do such deeds, we will have to make the conquest of momism, which grew up from male default.

❦ ❦ ❦

*Thorstein Veblen*

# Pecuniary Canons of Taste [1]

THE caution has already been repeated more than once, that while the regulating norm of consumption is in large part the requirement of conspicuous waste, it must not be understood that the motive on which the consumer acts in any given case is this principle in its bald, unsophisticated form. Ordinarily his motive is a wish to conform to established usage, to avoid unfavourable notice and comment, to live up to the accepted canons of decency in the kind, amount, and grade of goods consumed, as well as in the decorous employment of his time and effort. In the common run of cases this sense of prescriptive usage is present in the motives of the consumer and exerts a direct constraining force, especially as regards consumption carried on under the eyes of observers. But a considerable element of prescriptive expensiveness is observable also in consumption that does not in any appreciable degree become known to outsiders—as, for instance, articles of underclothing, some articles of food, kitchen utensils, and other household apparatus designed for service rather than for evidence. In all such useful articles a close scrutiny will discover certain features which add to the cost and enhance the commercial value of the goods in question, but do not proportionately increase the service-ability of these articles for the material purposes which alone they ostensibly are designed to serve.

Under the selective surveillance of the law of conspicuous waste there

[1] From *The Theory of the Leisure Class* by Thorstein Veblen. Copyright 1899, 1912 by The Macmillan Company. Reprinted by permission of The Viking Press, Inc., New York.

grows up a code of accredited canons of consumption, the effect of which is to hold the consumer up to a standard of expensiveness and wastefulness in his consumption of goods and in his employment of time and effort. This growth of prescriptive usage has an immediate effect upon economic life, but it has also an indirect and remoter effect upon conduct in other respects as well. Habits of thought with respect to the expression of life in any given direction unavoidably affect the habitual view of what is good and right in life in other directions also. In the organic complex of habits of thought which make up the substance of an individual's conscious life the economic interest does not lie isolated and distinct from all other interests. Something, for instance, has already been said of its relation to the canons of reputability.

The principle of conspicuous waste guides the formation of habits of thought as to what is honest and reputable in life and in commodities. In so doing, this principle will traverse other norms of conduct which do not primarily have to do with the code of pecuniary honour, but which have, directly or incidentally, an economic significance of some magnitude. So the canon of honorific waste may, immediately or remotely, influence the sense of duty, the sense of beauty, the sense of utility, the sense of devotional or ritualistic fitness, and the scientific sense of truth.

It is scarcely necessary to go into a discussion here of the particular points at which, or the particular manner in which, the canon of honorific expenditure habitually traverses the canons of moral conduct. The matter is one which has received large attention and illustration at the hands of those whose office it is to watch and admonish with respect to any departures from the accepted code of morals. In modern communities, where the dominant economic and legal feature of the community's life is the institution of private property, one of the salient features of the code of morals is the sacredness of property. There needs no insistence or illustration to gain assent to the proposition that the habit of holding private property inviolate is traversed by the other habit of seeking wealth for the sake of the good repute to be gained through its conspicuous consumption. Most offences against property, especially offences of an appreciable magnitude, come under this head. It is also a matter of common notoriety and byword that in offences which result in a large accession of property to the offender he does not ordinarily incur the extreme penalty or the extreme obloquy with which his offence would be visited on the ground of the naïve moral code alone. The thief or swindler who has gained great wealth by his delinquency has a better chance than the small thief of escaping the rigorous penalty of the law; and some good repute accrues to him from his increased wealth and from his spending the irregularly acquired possessions in a seemly manner. A well-bred expenditure of his booty especially appeals with great effect to persons of a cultivated sense of the proprieties, and goes far to mitigate the sense of moral turpitude with which his dereliction is viewed by them. It may be noted also—and it is more immediately to the point—that we are all inclined to condone an offence against property in the case of a man whose motive is the worthy one of providing the means of a "decent" manner of life for his wife and children. If it is added that the wife has been "nurtured in the lap of luxury," that is accepted as an additional extenuating circumstance. That is to say, we are prone to condone such an offence where its aim is the honorific one of enabling the offender's wife to perform for him such an amount of vicarious consumption of time and substance as is demanded by the standard of pecuniary decency. In such a case the habit of approving the accustomed degree of conspicuous waste traverses the habit of deprecating violations of ownership, to the extent even of sometimes leaving the award of praise or blame uncertain. This is peculiarly true where the dereliction involves an appreciable predatory or piratical element.

This topic need scarcely be pursued farther here; but the remark may not be out of place that all that considerable body of morals that clusters about the concept of an inviolable ownership is itself a psychological precipitate of the traditional meritoriousness of wealth. And it should be added that this wealth which is held sacred is valued primarily for the sake of the good repute to be got through its conspicuous consumption. . . .

Obviously, the canon of conspicuous waste is accountable for a great portion of what may be called devout consumption; as, e.g., the consumption of sacred edifices, vestments, and other goods of the same class. Even in those modern cults to whose divinities is imputed a predilection for temples not built with hands, the sacred buildings and the other properties of the cult are constructed and decorated with some view to a reputable degree of wasteful expenditure. And it needs but little either of observation or introspection —and either will serve the turn—to assure us that the expensive splendour of the house of worship has an appreciable uplifting and mellowing effect upon the worshipper's frame of mind. It will serve to enforce the same fact if we reflect upon the sense of abject shamefulness with which any evidence of indigence or squalor about the sacred place affects all beholders. The accessories of any devout observance should be pecuniarily above reproach. This requirement is imperative, whatever latitude may be allowed with regard to these accessories in point of æsthetic or other serviceability.

It may also be in place to notice that in all communities, especially in neighbourhoods where the standard of pecuniary decency for dwellings is not high, the local sanctuary is more ornate, more conspicuously wasteful in its architecture and decoration, than the dwelling-houses of the congregation. This is true of nearly all denominations and cults, whether Christian or Pagan, but it is true in a peculiar degree of the older and maturer cults. At the same time the sanctuary commonly contributes little if anything to the physical comfort of the members. Indeed, the sacred structure not only serves the physical well-being of the members to but a slight extent, as compared with their humbler dwelling-houses; but it is felt by all men that a right and enlightened sense of the true, the beautiful, and the good demands that in all expenditure on the sanctuary anything that might serve the comfort of the worshipper should be conspicuously absent. If any element of comfort is admitted in the fittings of the sanctuary, it should at least be scrupulously screened and masked under an ostensible austerity. In the most reputable latter-day houses of worship, where no expense is spared, the principle of austerity is carried to the length of making the fittings of the place a means of mortifying the flesh, especially in appearance. There are few persons of delicate tastes in the matter of devout consumption to whom this austerely wasteful discomfort does not appeal as intrinsically right and good. Devout consumption is of the nature of vicarious consumption. This canon of devout austerity is based on the pecuniary reputability of conspicuously wasteful consumption, backed by the principle that vicarious consumption should conspicuously not conduce to the comfort of the vicarious consumer.

The sanctuary and its fittings have something of this austerity in all the cults in which the saint or divinity to whom the sanctuary pertains is not conceived to be present and make personal use of the property for the gratification of luxurious tastes imputed to him. The character of the sacred paraphernalia is somewhat different in this respect in those cults where the habits of life imputed to the divinity more nearly approach those of an earthly patriarchal potentate—where he is conceived to make use of these consumable goods in person. In the latter case the sanctuary and its fittings take on more of the fashion given to goods destined for the conspicuous consumption of a temporal master or owner. On the other hand, where the sacred apparatus is simply employed in the divinity's service, that is to say, where it is consumed vicariously on his account by his servants, there the sacred properties take the character suited to goods that are destined for vicarious consumption only. . . .

These canons of reputability have had a similar, but more far-reaching and more specifically determinable, effect upon the popular sense of beauty or serviceability in consumable goods. The requirements of pecuniary decency have, to a very appreciable extent, influenced the sense of beauty and of utility in articles of use or beauty. Articles are to an extent preferred for use on account of their being conspicuously wasteful; they are felt to be serviceable somewhat in proportion as they are wasteful and ill adapted to their ostensible use.

The utility of articles valued for their beauty depends closely upon the expensiveness of the articles. A homely illustration will bring out this dependence. A hand-wrought silver spoon, of a commercial value of some ten to twenty dollars, is not ordinarily more serviceable—in the first sense of the word—than a machine-made spoon of the same material. It may not even be more serviceable than a machine-made spoon of some "base" metal, such as aluminum, the value of which may be no more than some ten to twenty cents. The former of the two utensils is, in fact, commonly a less effective contrivance for its ostensible purpose than the latter. The objection is of course ready to hand that, in taking this view of the matter, one of the chief uses, if not the chief use, of the costlier spoon is ignored; the hand-wrought spoon gratifies our taste, our sense of the beautiful, while that made by machinery out of the base metal has no useful office beyond a brute efficiency. The facts are no doubt as the objection states them, but it will be evident on reflection that the objection is after all more plausible than conclusive. It appears (1) that while the different materials of which the two spoons are made each pos- sesses beauty and serviceability for the purpose for which it is used, the ma- terial of the hand-wrought spoon is some one hundred times more valuable than the baser metal, without very greatly excelling the latter in intrinsic beauty of grain or colour, and without being in any appreciable degree su- perior in point of mechanical serviceability; (2) if a close inspection should show that the supposed hand-wrought spoon were in reality only a very cleve: imitation of hand-wrought goods, but an imitation so cleverly wrought as to give the same impression of line and surface to any but a minute examination by a trained eye, the utility of the article, including the gratification which the user derives from its contemplation as an object of beauty, would imme- diately decline by some eighty or ninety per cent, or even more; (3) if the two spoons are, to a fairly close observer, so nearly identical in appearance that the lighter weight of the spurious article alone betrays it, this identity of form and colour will scarcely add to the value of the machine-made spoon, nor appreciably enhance the gratification of the user's "sense of beauty" in contemplating it, so long as the cheaper spoon is not a novelty, and so long as it can be procured at a nominal cost.

The case of the spoons is typical. The superior gratification derived from the use and contemplation of costly and supposedly beautiful products is, commonly, in great measure a gratification of our sense of costliness mas- querading under the name of beauty. Our higher appreciation of the superior article is an appreciation of its superior honorific character, much more fre- quently than it is an unsophisticated appreciation of its beauty. The require- ment of conspicuous wastefulness is not commonly present, consciously, in our canons of taste, but it is none the less present as a constraining norm selec- tively shaping and sustaining our sense of what is beautiful, and guiding our discrimination with respect to what may legitimately be approved as beautiful and what may not.

It is at this point, where the beautiful and the honorific meet and blend, that a discrimination between serviceability and wastefulness is most difficult in any concrete case. It frequently happens that an article which serves the honorific purpose of conspicuous waste is at the same time a beautiful object; and the same application of labour to which it owes its utility for the former purpose may, and often does, go to give beauty of form and colour to the article. The question is further complicated by the fact that many objects, as, for instance, the precious stones and metals and some other materials used for adornment and decoration, owe their utility as items of conspicuous waste to an antecedent utility as objects of beauty. Gold, for instance, has a high degree of sensuous beauty; very many if not most of the highly prized works of art are intrinsically beautiful, though often with material qualification; the like is true of some stuffs used for clothing, of some landscapes, and of many other things in less degree. Except for this intrinsic beauty which they possess, these objects would scarcely have been coveted as they are, or have become monopolised objects of pride to their possessors and users. But the utility of these things to the possessor is commonly due less to their intrinsic beauty than to the honour which their possession and consumption confers, or to the obloquy which it wards off.

Apart from their serviceability in other respects, these objects are beautiful and have a utility as such; they are valuable on this account if they can be appropriated or monopolised; they are, therefore, coveted as valuable possessions, and their exclusive enjoyment gratifies the possessor's sense of pecuniary superiority at the same time that their contemplation gratifies his sense of beauty. But their beauty, in the naïve sense of the word, is the occasion rather than the ground of their monopolisation or of their commercial value. "Great as is the sensuous beauty of gems, their rarity and price adds an expression of distinction to them, which they would never have if they were cheap." There is, indeed, in the common run of cases under this head, relatively little incentive to the exclusive possession and use of these beautiful things, except on the ground of their honorific character as items of conspicuous waste. Most objects of this general class, with the partial exception of articles of personal adornment, would serve all other purposes than the honorific one equally well, whether owned by the person viewing them or not; and even as regards personal ornaments it is to be added that their chief purpose is to lend éclat to the person of their wearer (or owner) by comparison with other persons who are compelled to do without. The æsthetic serviceability of objects of beauty is not greatly nor universally heightened by possession.

The generalisation for which the discussion so far affords ground is that any valuable object in order to appeal to our sense of beauty must conform to the requirements of beauty and of expensiveness both. But this is not all. Beyond this the canon of expensiveness also affects our tastes in such a way as to inextricably blend the marks of expensiveness, in our appreciation, with the beautiful features of the object, and to subsume the resultant effect under the head of an appreciation of beauty simply. The marks of expensiveness come to be accepted as beautiful features of the expensive articles. They are pleasing as being marks of honorific costliness, and the pleasure which they afford on this score blends with that afforded by the beautiful form and colour of the object; so that we often declare that an article of apparel, for instance, is "perfectly lovely," when pretty much all that an analysis of the æsthetic value of the article would leave ground for is the declaration that it is pecuniarily honorific.

This blending and confusion of the elements of expensiveness and of beauty is, perhaps, best exemplified in articles of dress and of household furniture. The code of reputability in matters of dress decides what shapes, colours, materials, and general effects in human apparel are for the time to be accepted as suitable; and departures from the code are offensive to our taste, supposedly as being departures from æsthetic truth. The approval with which we look upon fashionable attire is by no means to be accounted pure make-believe. We readily, and for the most part with utter sincerity, find those things pleasing that are in vogue. Shaggy dress-stuffs and pronounced colour effects, for instance, offend us at times when the vogue is goods of a high, glossy finish and neutral colours. A fancy bonnet of this year's model unquestionably appeals to our sensibilities to-day much more forcibly than an equally fancy bonnet of the model of last year; although when viewed in the perspective of a quarter of a century, it would, I apprehend, be a matter of the utmost difficulty to award the palm for intrinsic beauty to the one rather than to the other of these structures. So, again, it may be remarked that, considered simply in their physical juxtaposition with the human form, the high gloss of a gentleman's hat or of a patent-leather shoe has no more of intrinsic beauty than a similarly high gloss on a threadbare sleeve; and yet there is no question but that all well-bred people (in the Occidental civilised communities) instinctively and unaffectedly cleave to the one as a phenomenon of great beauty, and eschew the other as offensive to every sense to which it can appeal. It is extremely doubtful if any one could be induced to wear such a contrivance as the high hat of civilised society, except for some urgent reason based on other than æsthetic grounds.

By further habituation to an appreciative perception of the marks of expensiveness in goods, and by habitually identifying beauty with reputability, it comes about that a beautiful article which is not expensive is accounted not beautiful. In this way it has happened, for instance, that some beautiful flowers pass conventionally for offensive weeds; others that can be cultivated with relative ease are accepted and admired by the lower middle class, who can afford no more expensive luxuries of this kind; but these varieties are rejected as vulgar by those people who are better able to pay for expensive flowers and who are educated to a higher schedule of pecuniary beauty in the florist's products; while still other flowers, of no greater intrinsic beauty than these, are cultivated at great cost and call out much admiration from flower-lovers whose tastes have been matured under the critical guidance of a polite environment. . . .

It is not only with respect to consumable goods—including domestic animals—that the canons of taste have been coloured by the canons of pecuniary reputability. Something to the like effect is to be said for beauty in persons. In order to avoid whatever may be matter of controversy, no weight will be given in this connection to such popular predilection as there may be for the dignified (leisurely) bearing and portly presence that are by vulgar tradition associated with opulence in mature men. These traits are in some measure accepted as elements of personal beauty. But there are certain elements of feminine beauty, on the other hand, which come in under this head, and which are of so concrete and specific a character as to admit of itemised appreciation. It is more or less a rule that in communities which are at the stage of economic development at which women are valued by the upper class for their service, the ideal of female beauty is a robust, large-limbed woman. The ground of appreciation is the physique, while the conformation of the face is of secondary weight only. A well-known instance of this ideal of the early predatory culture is that of the maidens of the Homeric poems.

This ideal suffers a change in the succeeding development, when, in the conventional scheme, the office of the high-class wife comes to be a vicarious leisure simply. The ideal then includes the characteristics which are supposed to result from or to go with a life of leisure consistently enforced. The ideal accepted under these circumstances may be gathered from descriptions of beautiful women by poets and writers of the chivalric times. In the conventional scheme of those days ladies of high degree were conceived to be in perpetual tutelage, and to be scrupulously exempt from all useful work. The resulting chivalric or romantic ideal of beauty takes cognizance chiefly of the face, and dwells on its delicacy, and on the delicacy of the hands and feet, the slender figure, and especially the slender waist. In the pictured representations of the women of that time, and in modern romantic imitators of the chivalric thought and feeling, the waist is attenuated to a degree that implies extreme debility. The same ideal is still extant among a considerable portion of the population of modern industrial communities; but it is to be said that it has retained its hold most tenaciously in those modern communities which are least advanced in point of economic and civil development, and which show the most considerable survivals of status and of predatory institutions. That is to say, the chivalric ideal is best preserved in those existing communities which are substantially least modern. Survivals of this lackadaisical or romantic ideal occur freely in the tastes of the well-to-do classes of Continental countries.

In modern communities which have reached the higher levels of industrial development, the upper leisure class has accumulated so great a mass of wealth as to place its women above all imputation of vulgarly productive labour. Here the status of women as vicarious consumers is beginning to lose its place in the affections of the body of the people; and as a consequence the ideal of feminine beauty is beginning to change back again from the infirmly delicate, translucent, and hazardously slender, to a woman of the archaic type that does not disown her hands and feet, nor, indeed, the other gross material facts of her person. In the course of economic development the ideal of beauty among the peoples of the Western culture has shifted from the woman of physical presence to the lady, and it is beginning to shift back again to the woman; and all in obedience to the changing conditions of pecuniary emulation. The exigencies of emulation at one time required lusty slaves; at another time they required a conspicuous performance of vicarious

leisure and consequently an obvious disability; but the situation is now beginning to outgrow this last requirement, since, under the higher efficiency of
modern industry, leisure in women is possible so far down the scale of reputability that it will no longer serve as a definitive mark of the highest pecuniary grade.

Apart from this general control exercised by the norm of conspicuous waste
over the ideal of feminine beauty, there are one or two details which merit
specific mention as showing how it may exercise an extreme constraint in
detail over men's sense of beauty in women. It has already been noticed that
at the stages of economic evolution at which conspicuous leisure is much regarded as a means of good repute, the ideal requires delicate and diminutive
hands and feet and a slender waist. These features, together with the other
related faults of structure that commonly go with them, go to show that the
person so affected is incapable of useful effort and must therefore be supported
in idleness by her owner. She is useless and expensive, and she is consequently valuable as evidence of pecuniary strength. It results that at this cultural stage women take thought to alter their persons, so as to conform more
nearly to the requirements of the instructed taste of the time; and under the
guidance of the canon of pecuniary decency, the men find the resulting artificially induced pathological features attractive. So, for instance, the constricted
waist which has had so wide and persistent a vogue in the communities of
the Western culture, and so also the deformed foot of the Chinese. Both of
these are mutilations of unquestioned repulsiveness to the untrained sense. It
requires habituation to become reconciled to them. Yet there is no room to
question their attractiveness to men into whose scheme of life they fit as
honorific items sanctioned by the requirements of pecuniary reputability. They
are items of pecuniary and cultural beauty which have come to do duty as
elements of the ideal of womanliness. . . .

. . . Among objects of use the simple and unadorned article is æsthetically
the best. But since the pecuniary canon of reputability rejects the inexpensive
in articles appropriated to individual consumption, the satisfaction of our
craving for beautiful things must be sought by way of compromise. The canons
of beauty must be circumvented by some contrivance which will give evidence of a reputably wasteful expenditure, at the same time that it meets the
demands of our critical sense of the useful and the beautiful, or at least meets
the demand of some habit which has come to do duty in place of that sense.
Such an auxiliary sense of taste is the sense of novelty; and this latter is
helped out in its surrogateship by the curiosity with which men view ingenious
and puzzling contrivances. Hence it comes that most objects alleged to be
beautiful, and doing duty as such, show considerable ingenuity of design and
are calculated to puzzle the beholder—to bewilder him with irrelevant suggestions and hints of the improbable—at the same time that they give evidence
of an expenditure of labour in excess of what would give them their fullest
efficiency for their ostensible economic end. . . .

This process of selective adaptation of designs to the end of conspicuous waste, and the substitution of pecuniary beauty for æsthetic beauty, has been especially effective in the development of architecture. It would be extremely difficult to find a modern civilised residence or public building which can claim anything better than relative inoffensiveness in the eyes of any one who will dissociate the elements of beauty from those of honorific waste. The endless variety of fronts presented by the better class of tenements and apartment houses in our cities is an endless variety of architectural distress and of suggestions of expensive discomfort. Considered as objects of beauty, the dead walls of the sides and back of these structures, left untouched by the hands of the artist, are commonly the best feature of the building. . . .

The position here taken is enforced in a felicitous manner by the place assigned in the economy of consumption to machine products. The point of material difference between machine-made goods and the hand-wrought goods which serve the same purposes is, ordinarily, that the former serve their primary purpose more adequately. They are a more perfect product—show a more perfect adaptation of means to end. This does not save them from disesteem and depreciation, for they fall short under the test of honorific waste. Hand labour is a more wasteful method of production; hence the goods turned out by this method are more serviceable for the purpose of pecuniary reputability; hence the marks of hand labour come to be honorific, and the goods which exhibit these marks take rank as of higher grade than the corresponding machine product. Commonly, if not invariably, the honorific marks of hand labour are certain imperfections and irregularities in the lines of the hand-wrought article, showing where the workman has fallen short in the execution of the design. The ground of the superiority of hand-wrought goods, therefore, is a certain margin of crudeness. This margin must never be so wide as to show bungling workmanship, since that would be evidence of low cost, nor so narrow as to suggest the ideal precision attained only by the machine, for that would be evidence of low cost.

The appreciation of those evidences of honorific crudeness to which hand-wrought goods owe their superior worth and charm in the eyes of well-bred people is a matter of nice discrimination. It requires training and the formation of right habits of thought with respect to what may be called the physiognomy of goods. Machine-made goods of daily use are often admired and preferred precisely on account of their excessive perfection by the vulgar and the underbred who have not given due thought to the punctilios of elegant consumption. The ceremonial inferiority of machine products goes to show that the perfection of skill and workmanship embodied in any costly innovations in the finish of goods is not sufficient of itself to secure them acceptance and permanent favour. The innovation must have the support of the canon of conspicuous waste. Any feature in the physiognomy of goods, however pleasing in itself, and however well it may approve itself to the taste for effective work, will not be tolerated if it proves obnoxious to this norm of pecuniary reputability.

The ceremonial inferiority or uncleanness in consumable goods due to "commonness," or in other words to their slight cost of production, has been taken very seriously by many persons. This objection to machine products is often formulated as an objection to the commonness of such goods. What is common is within the (pecuniary) reach of many people. Its consumption is therefore not honorific, since it does not serve the purpose of a favourable invidious comparison with other consumers. Hence the consumption, or even the sight of such goods, is inseparable from an odious suggestion of the lower levels of human life, and one comes away from their contemplation with a pervading sense of meanness that is extremely distasteful and depressing to a person of sensibility. . . .

The position of machine products in the civilised scheme of consumption serves to point out the nature of the relation which subsists between the canon of conspicuous waste and the code of proprieties in consumption. Neither in matters of art and taste proper, nor as regards the current sense of the serviceability of goods, does this canon act as a principle of innovation or initiative. It does not go into the future as a creative principle which makes innovations and adds new items of consumption and new elements of cost. The principle in question is, in a certain sense, a negative rather than a positive law. It is a regulative rather than a creative principle. It very rarely initiates or originates any usage or custom directly. Its action is selective only. Conspicuous wastefulness does not directly afford ground for variation and growth, but conformity to its requirements is a condition to the survival of such innovations as may be made on other grounds. In whatever way usages and customs and methods of expenditure arise, they are all subject to the selective action of this norm of reputability; and the degree in which they conform to its requirements is a test of their fitness to survive in the competition with other similar usages and customs. Other things being equal, the more obviously wasteful usage or method stands the better chance of survival under this law. The law of conspicuous waste does not account for the origin of variations, but only for the persistence of such forms as are fit to survive under its dominance. It acts to conserve the fit, not to originate the acceptable. Its office is to prove all things and to hold fast that which is good for its purpose.

❧ ❧ ❧

*John Dos Passos*

# The Bitter Drink[1]

Veblen,
    a greyfaced shambling man lolling resentful at his desk with his cheek on his hand, in a low sarcastic mumble of intricate phrases subtly paying out

[1] From John Dos Passos, *U.S.A.* (Boston: Houghton Mifflin Company, 1936). Copyright by John Dos Passos, 1936, 1937.

the logical inescapable rope of matteroffact for a society to hang itself by,

dissecting out the century with a scalpel so keen, so comical, so exact that the professors and students ninetenths of the time didn't know it was there, and the magnates and the respected windbags and the applauded loudspeakers never knew it was there.

Veblen

asked too many questions, suffered from a constitutional inability to say yes.

Socrates asked questions, drank down the bitter drink one might when the first cock crowed,

but Veblen

drank it in little sips through a long life in the stuffiness of classrooms, the dust of libraries, the staleness of cheap flats such as a poor instructor can afford. He fought the boyg all right, pedantry, routine, timeservers at office desks, trustees, collegepresidents, the plump flunkies of the ruling businessmen, all the good jobs kept by yesmen, never enough money, every broadening hope thwarted. Veblen drank the bitter drink all right.

The Veblens were a family of freeholding farmers.

The freeholders of the narrow Norwegian valleys were a stubborn hardworking people, farmers, dairymen, fishermen, rooted in their fathers' stony fields, in their old timbered farmsteads with carved gables they took their names from, in the upland pastures where they grazed the stock in summer.

During the early nineteenth century the towns grew; Norway filled up with landless men, storekeepers, sheriffs, moneylenders, bailiffs, notaries in black with stiff collars and briefcases full of foreclosures under their arms. Industries were coming in. The townsmen were beginning to get profits out of the country and to finagle the farmers out of the freedom of their narrow farms.

The meanspirited submitted as tenants, daylaborers; but the strong men went out of the country

as their fathers had gone out of the country centuries before when Harald the Fairhaired and St. Olaf hacked to pieces the liberties of the northern men, who had been each man lord of his own creek, to make Christians and serfs of them,

only in the old days it was Iceland, Greenland, Vineland the northmen had sailed west to; now it was America.

Both Thorstein Veblen's father's people and his mother's people had lost their farmsteads and with them the names that denoted them free men.

Thomas Anderson for a while tried to make his living as a traveling carpenter and cabinetmaker, but in 1847 he and his wife, Kari Thorsteinsdatter, crossed in a whalingship from Bremen and went out to join friends in the Scandihoovian colonies round Milwaukee.

Next year his brother Haldor joined him.

They were hard workers; in another year they had saved up money to preempt a claim on 160 acres of uncleared land in Sheboygan County, Wisconsin; when they'd gotten that land part cleared they sold it and moved to an all-Norway colony in Manitowoc County, near Cato and a place named Valders after the valley they had all come from in the old country;

there in the house Thomas Anderson built with his own tools, the sixth of twelve children, Thorstein Veblen was born.

When Thorstein was eight years old, Thomas Anderson moved west again into the blacksoil prairies of Minnesota that the Sioux and the buffalo had only been driven off from a few years before. In the deed to the new farm Thomas Anderson took back the old farmstead name of Veblen.

He was a solid farmer, builder, a clever carpenter, the first man to import merino sheep and a mechanical reaper and binder; he was a man of standing in the group of Norway people farming the edge of the prairie, who kept their dialects, the manner of life of their narrow Norway valleys, their Lutheran pastors, their homemade clothes and cheese and bread, their suspicion and stubborn dislike of townsmen's ways.

The townspeople were Yankees mostly, smart to make two dollars grow where a dollar grew before, storekeepers, middlemen, speculators, moneylenders, with long heads for politics and mortgages; they despised the Scandihoovian dirtfarmers they lived off, whose daughters did their wives' kitchenwork.

The Norway people believed as their fathers had believed that there were only two callings for an honest man, farming or preaching.

Thorstein grew up a hulking lad with a reputation for laziness and wit. He hated the irk of everrepeated backbreaking chores round the farm. Reading he was happy. Carpentering he liked or running farmmachinery. The Lutheran pastors who came to the house noticed that his supple mind slid easily round the corners of their theology. It was hard to get farmwork out of him, he had a stinging tongue and was famous for the funny names he called people; his father decided to make a preacher out of him.

When he was seventeen he was sent for out of the field where he was working. His bag was already packed. The horses were hitched up. He was being sent to Carleton Academy in Northfield, to prepare for Carleton College.

As there were several young Veblens to be educated their father built them a house on a lot near the campus. Their food and clothes were sent to them from the farm. Cash money was something they never saw.

Thorstein spoke English with an accent. He had a constitutional inability to say yes. His mind was formed on the Norse sagas and on the matteroffact sense of his father's farming and the exact needs of carpenterwork and threshingmachines.

He could never take much interest in the theology, sociology, economics of Carleton College where they were busy trimming down the jagged dogmas of the old New England bibletaught traders to make stencils to hang on the walls of commissionmerchants' offices.

Veblen's collegeyears were the years when Darwin's assertions of growth and becoming were breaking the set molds of the Noah's Ark world,

when Ibsen's women were tearing down the portieres of the Victorian parlors,

and Marx's mighty machine was rigging the countinghouse's own logic to destroy the countinghouse.

When Veblen went home to the farm he talked about these things with his father, following him up and down at his plowing, starting an argument while they were waiting for a new load for the wheatthresher. Thomas Anderson had seen Norway and America; he had the squarebuilt mind of a carpenter and builder, and an understanding of tools and the treasured elaborated builtupseasonbyseason knowledge of a careful farmer,

a tough whetstone for the sharpening steel of young Thorstein's wits.

At Carleton College young Veblen was considered a brilliant unsound eccentric; nobody could understand why a boy of such attainments wouldn't settle down to the business of the day, which was to buttress property and profits with anything usable in the debris of Christian ethics and eighteenth-century economics that cluttered the minds of collegeprofessors, and to reinforce the sacred, already shaky edifice with the new strong girderwork of science Herbert Spencer was throwing up for the benefit of the bosses.

People complained they never knew whether Veblen was joking or serious.

In 1880 Thorstein Veblen started to try to make his living by teaching. A year in an academy at Madison, Wisconsin, wasn't much of a success. Next year he and his brother Andrew started graduate work at Johns Hopkins. Johns Hopkins didn't suit, but boarding in an old Baltimore house with some ruined gentlewomen gave him a disdaining glimpse of an etiquette motheaten now but handed down through the lavish leisure of the slaveowning planters' mansions straight from the merry England of the landlord cavaliers.

(The valley farmers had always been scornful of outlanders' ways.)

He was more at home at Yale where in Noah Porter he found a New England roundhead granite against which his Norway granite rang in clear dissent. He took his Ph.D. there. But there was still some question as to what department of the academic world he could best make a living in.

He read Kant and wrote prize essays. But he couldn't get a job. Try as he could he couldn't get his mouth round the essential yes.

He went back to Minnesota with a certain intolerant knowledge of the amenities of the higher learning. To his slight Norwegian accent he'd added the broad a.

At home he loafed about the farm and tinkered with inventions of new machinery and read and talked theology and philosophy with his father. In the Scandihoovian colonies the price of wheat and the belief in God and St.

Olaf were going down together. The farmers of the Northwest were starting their long losing fight against the parasite businessmen who were sucking them dry. There was a mortgage on the farm, interest on debts to pay, always fertilizer, new machines to buy to speed production to pump in a halfcentury the wealth out of the soil laid down in a million years of buffalograss. His brothers kept grumbling about this sardonic loafer who wouldn't earn his keep.

Back home he met again his college sweetheart, Ellen Rolfe, the niece of the president of Carleton College, a girl who had railroadmagnates and money in the family. People in Northfield were shocked when it came out that she was going to marry the drawling pernickety bookish badly dressed young Norwegian ne'erdowell.

Her family hatched a plan to get him a job as economist for the Santa Fe Railroad but at the wrong moment Ellen Rolfe's uncle lost control of the line. The young couple went to live at Stacyville where they did everything but earn a living. They read Latin and Greek and botanized in the woods and along the fences and in the roadside scrub. They boated on the river and Veblen started his translation of the *Laxdælasaga*. They read *Looking Backward* and articles by Henry George. They looked at their world from the outside.

In '91 Veblen got together some money to go to Cornell to do postgraduate work. He turned up there in the office of the head of the economics department wearing a coonskin cap and grey corduroy trousers and said in his low sarcastic drawl, "I am Thorstein Veblen,"

but it was not until several years later, after he was established at the new University of Chicago that had grown up next to the World's Fair, and had published *The Theory of the Leisure Class*, put on the map by Howells' famous review, that the world of the higher learning knew who Thorstein Veblen was.

Even in Chicago as the brilliant young economist he lived pioneerfashion (The valleyfarmers had always been scornful of outlanders' ways.) He kept his books in packingcases laid on their sides along the walls. His only extravagances were the Russian cigarettes he smoked and the red sash he sometimes sported. He was a man without smalltalk. When he lectured he put his cheek on his hand and mumbled out his long spiral sentences, reiterative like the eddas. His language was a mixture of mechanics' terms, scientific latinity, slang and Roget's Thesaurus. The other profs couldn't imagine why the girls fell for him so.

The girls fell for him so that Ellen Rolfe kept leaving him. He'd take summer trips abroad without his wife. There was a scandal about a girl on an ocean liner.

Tongues wagged so (Veblen was a man who never explained, who never could get his tongue around the essential yes; the valleyfarmers had always been scornful of the outlanders' ways, and their opinions) that his wife left him and went off to live alone on a timberclaim in Idaho and the president asked for his resignation.

Veblen went out to Idaho to get Ellen Rolfe to go with him to California when he succeeded in getting a job at a better salary at Leland Stanford, but in Palo Alto it was the same story as in Chicago. He suffered from woman trouble and the constitutional inability to say yes and an unnatural tendency to feel with the workingclass instead of with the profittakers. There were the same complaints that his courses were not constructive or attractive to big money bequests and didn't help his students to butter their bread, make Phi Beta Kappa, pick plums off the hierarchies of the academic grove. His wife left him for good. He wrote to a friend: "The president doesn't approve of my domestic arrangements; nor do I."

Talking about it he once said, "What is one to do if the woman moves in on you?"

He went back up to the shack in the Idaho woods.

Friends tried to get him an appointment to make studies in Crete, a chair at the University of Pekin, but always the boyg, routine, businessmen's flunkeys in all the university offices . . . for the questioner the bitter drink.

His friend Davenport got him an appointment at the University of Missouri. At Columbia he lived like a hermit in the basement of the Davenports' house, helped with the work round the place, carpentered himself a table and chairs. He was already a bitter elderly man with a grey face covered with a net of fine wrinkles, a vandyke beard and yellow teeth. Few students could follow his courses. The college authorities were often surprised and somewhat chagrined that when visitors came from Europe it was always Veblen they wanted to meet.

These were the years he did the most of his writing, trying out his ideas on his students, writing slowly at night in violet ink with a pen of his own designing. Whenever he published a book he had to put up a guarantee with the publishers. In *The Theory of Business Enterprise, The Instinct of Workmanship, The Vested Interests and the Common Man,*

he established a new diagram of a society dominated by monopoly capital, etched in irony

the sabotage of production by business,

the sabotage of life by blind need for money profits,

pointed out the alternatives: a warlike society strangled by the bureaucracies of the monopolies forced by the law of diminishing returns to grind down more and more the common man for profits.

or a new matteroffact commonsense society dominated by the needs of the men and women who did the work and the incredibly vast possibilities for peace and plenty offered by the progress of technology.

These were the years of Debs's speeches, growing laborunions, the I.W.W. talk about industrial democracy: these years Veblen still held to the hope that the workingclass would take over the machine of production before monopoly had pushed the western nations down into the dark again.

War cut across all that: under the cover of the bunting of Woodrow Wilson's phrases the monopolies cracked down. American democracy was crushed.

The war at least offered Veblen an opportunity to break out of the airless greenhouse of academic life. He was offered a job with the Food Administration, he sent the Navy Department a device for catching submarines by trailing lengths of stout bindingwire. (Meanwhile the government found his books somewhat confusing. The postoffice was forbidding the mails to *Imperial Germany and the Industrial Revolution* while propaganda agencies were sending it out to make people hate the Huns. Educators were denouncing *The Nature of Peace* while Washington experts were clipping phrases out of it to add to the Wilsonian smokescreen.)

For the Food Administration Thorstein Veblen wrote two reports: in one he advocated granting the demands of the I.W.W. as a wartime measure and conciliating the workingclass instead of beating up and jailing all the honest leaders; in the other he pointed out that the Food Administration was a businessman's racket and was not aiming for the most efficient organization of the country as a producing machine. He suggested that, in the interests of the efficient prosecution of the war, the government step into the place of the middleman and furnish necessities to the farmers direct in return for raw materials;

but cutting out business was not at all the Administration's idea of making the world safe for democracy,

so Veblen had to resign from the Food Administration.

He signed the protests against the trial of the hundred and one wobblies in Chicago.

After the armistice he went to New York. In spite of all the oppression of the war years, the air was freshening. In Russia the great storm of revolt had broken, seemed to be sweeping west, in the strong gusts from the new world in the east the warsodden multitudes began to see again. At Versailles allies and enemies, magnates, generals, flunkey politicians were slamming the shutters against the storm, against the new, against hope. It was suddenly clear for a second in the thundering glare what war was about, what peace was about.

In America, in Europe, the old men won. The bankers in their offices took a deep breath, the bediamonded old ladies of the leisure class went back to clipping their coupons in the refined quiet of their safedeposit vaults.

the last puffs of the ozone of revolt went stale

in the whisper of speakeasy arguments.


Veblen wrote for the *Dial*,
lectured at the New School for Social Research.

He still had a hope that the engineers, the technicians, the nonprofiteers whose hands were on the switchboard might take up the fight where the workingclass had failed. He helped form the Technical Alliance. His last hope was the British general strike.

Was there no group of men bold enough to take charge of the magnificent machine before the pigeyed speculators and the yesmen at office desks irrevocably ruined it

and with it the hopes of four hundred years?

No one went to Veblen's lectures at the New School. With every article he wrote in the *Dial* the circulation dropped.

Harding's normalcy, the new era was beginning;

even Veblen made a small killing on the stockmarket.

He was an old man and lonely.

His second wife had gone to a sanitarium suffering from delusions of persecution.

There seemed no place for a masterless man.

Veblen went back out to Palo Alto

to live in his shack in the tawny hills and observe from outside the last grabbing urges of the profit system taking on, as he put it, the systematized delusions of dementia praecox.

There he finished his translation of the *Laxdæelasaga*.

He was an old man. He was much alone. He let the woodrats take what they wanted from his larder. A skunk that hung round the shack was so tame he'd rub up against Veblen's leg like a cat.

He told a friend he'd sometimes hear in the stillness about him the voices of his boyhood talking Norwegian as clear as on the farm in Minnesota where he was raised. His friends found him harder than ever to talk to, harder than ever to interest in anything. He was running down. The last sips of the bitter drink.

He died on August 3, 1929.

Among his papers a penciled note was found:

*It is also my wish, in case of death, to be cremated if it can conveniently be done, as expeditiously and inexpensively as may be, without ritual or ceremony of any kind; that my ashes be thrown loose into the sea or into some sizeable stream running into the sea; that no tombstone, slab, epitaph, effigy, tablet, inscription or monument of any name or nature, be set up to my memory or name in any place or at any time; that no obituary, memorial, portrait or biography of me, nor any letters written to or by me be printed or published, or in any way reproduced, copied or circulated;*

but his memorial remains

riveted into the language:

the sharp clear prism of his mind.

❦ ❦ ❦

# H. L. Mencken

## Professor Veblen [1]

BACK in the year 1909, being engaged in a bombastic discussion with what was then known as an intellectual Socialist (like the rest of the *intelligentsia*, he succumbed to the first fife-corps of World War I, pulled down the red flag, damned Marx as a German spy, and began whooping for Woodrow Wilson and Otto Kahn), I was greatly belabored and incommoded by his long quotations from a certain Prof. Thorstein Veblen, then quite unknown to me. My antagonist manifestly attached a great deal of importance to these borrowed sagacities, for he often heaved them at me in lengths of a column or two, and urged me to read every word of them. I tried hard enough, but found it impossible going. The more I read them, in fact, the less I could make of them, an so in the end, growing impatient and impolite, I denounced this Prof. Veblen as a geyser of pish-posh, refused to waste any more time upon his incomprehensible syllogisms, and applied myself to the other Socialist witnesses in the case, seeking to set fire to their shirts.

That old debate, which took place by mail (for the Socialist lived in levantine luxury on his country estate and I was a wage-slave attached to a city newspaper), was afterward embalmed in a dull book, and got the mild notice of a day. The book, by name, *Men vs. the Man*,[2] is now as completely forgotten as Baxter's *Saint's Rest* or the Constitution of the United States. I myself am perhaps the only man who remembers it at all, and the only thing I can recall of my opponent's argument (beyond the fact that it not only failed to convert me to Marxism, but left me a bitter and incurable scoffer at democracy in all its forms) is his curious respect for the aforesaid Veblen, and his delight in the learned gentleman's long, tortuous and (to me, at least) intolerably flapdoodlish phrases.

There was, indeed, a time when I forgot even this—when my mind was empty of the professor's very name. That was, say, from 1909 or thereabout to the middle of 1917. During those years, having lost all my former interest in Socialism, even as a species of insanity, I ceased to read its literature, and thus lost track of its Great Thinkers. The periodicals that I then gave an eye to, setting aside newspapers, were chiefly the familiar American imitations of the English weeklies of opinion, and in these the dominant Great Thinker was, first, the late Dr. William James, and, after his decease in 1910, Dr. John Dewey. The reign of James, as the illuminated will recall, was long and glorious. For three or four years running he was mentioned in every one of

[1] From *A Mencken Chrestomathy* by H. L. Mencken, pp. 265-275. Copyright 1949 by Alfred A. Knopf, Inc. Reprinted from *Prejudices: First Series*, 1919, pp. 59-83. Copyright 1919 by Alfred A. Knopf, Inc. Reprinted by permission of Alfred A. Knopf, Inc.
[2] New York, 1910. The Socialist was Robert Rives La Monte.

those American *Spectators* and *Saturday Reviews* at least once a week, and often a dozen times. Among the less somber gazettes of the republic, to be sure, there were other heroes: Maeterlinck, Rabindranath Tagore, Judge Ben B. Lindsey, and so on, and still further down the literary and intellectual scale there were yet others: Hall Caine, Brieux and Jack Johnson among them, with paper-bag cookery and the twilight sleep to dispute their popularity. But on the majestic level of the pre-Villard *Nation*, among the white and lavender peaks of professorial ratiocination, there was scarcely a serious rival to James. Now and then, perhaps, Jane Addams had a month of vogue, and during one winter there was a rage for Bergson, but taking one day with another James held his own against the field. . . .

Then, of a sudden, Siss! Boom! Ah! Then, overnight, the upspringing of intellectual soviets, the headlong assault upon all the old axioms of pedagogical speculation, the nihilistic dethronement of Prof. Dewey—and rah, rah, rah for Prof. Dr. Thorstein Veblen! Veblen? Could it be—? Aye, it was! My old acquaintance! The *doctor obscurus* of my half-forgotten bout with the so-called intellectual Socialist! The Great Thinker redivivus! Here, indeed, he was again, and in a few months—almost it seemed a few days—he was all over the *Nation*, the *Dial*, the *New Republic* and the rest of them, his books and pamphlets began to pour from the presses, the newspapers reported his every wink and whisper, and everybody who was anybody began gabbling about him. The spectacle, I do not hesitate to say, somewhat disconcerted me and even distressed me. On the one hand, I was sorry to see so learned and interesting a man as Dr. Dewey sent back to the insufferable dungeons of Columbia, there to lecture in imperfect Yiddish to classes of Grand Street Platos. And on the other hand, I shrunk supinely from the appalling job, newly rearing itself before me, of rereading the whole canon of the singularly laborious and muggy, the incomparably tangled and unintelligible works of Prof. Veblen.

But if a sense of duty tortures a man, it also enables him to achieve prodigies, and so I managed to get through the whole infernal job. I read *The Theory of Business Enterprise* (1904), and then I read *The Instinct of Workmanship* (1914). A hiatus followed; I was racked by a severe neuralgia, with delusions of persecution. On recovering I tackled *Imperial Germany and the Industrial Revolution* (1915). Marasmus for a month, and then *The Nature of Peace and the Terms of Its Perpetuation* (1917). What ensued was never diagnosed; probably it was some low infection of the mesentery or spleen. When it passed off, leaving only an asthmatic cough, I read *The Higher Learning in America* (1918), and then went to Mt. Clemens to drink the Glauber's salts. Eureka! the business was done! It had strained me, but now it was over. Alas, a good part of the agony had been needless. What I found myself aware of, coming to the end, was that practically the whole system of Prof. Veblen was in his first book and his last—that is, in *The Theory of the Leisure Class*, and *The Higher Learning in America*.[3] I pass on the news to literary archeologists.

[3] He wrote four books between *The Higher Learning* and his death in 1929, but they were only reboilings of old bones, and attracted no notice.

Read these two, and you won't have to read the others. And if even two daunt you, then read the first. Once through it, though you will have missed many a pearl and many a pain, you will have an excellent grasp of the gifted metaphysician's ideas.

For those ideas, in the main, were quite simple, and often anything but revolutionary in essence. What was genuinely remarkable about them was not their novelty, or their complexity, nor even the fact that a professor should harbor them; it was the astoundingly grandiose and rococo manner of their statement, the almost unbelievable tediousness and flatulence of the gifted headmaster's prose, his unprecedented talent for saying nothing in an august and heroic manner. There are tales of an actress of the last generation, probably Sarah Bernhardt, who could put pathos and even terror into a recitation of the multiplication table. Something of the same talent, raised to a high power, was in this Prof. Veblen. If one tunneled under his great moraines and stalagmites of words, dug down into his vast kitchen-midden of discordant and raucous polysyllables, blew up the hard, thick shell of his almost theological manner, what one found in his discourse was chiefly a mass of platitudes—the self-evident made horrifying, the obvious in terms of the staggering.

Marx, I daresay had said a good deal of it long before him, and what Marx overlooked had been said over and over again by his heirs and assigns. But Marx, at this business, labored under a technical handicap; he wrote in German, a language he actually understood. Prof. Veblen submitted himself to no such disadvantage. Though born, I believe, in These States, and resident here all his life, he achieved the effect, perhaps without employing the means, of thinking in some unearthly foreign language—say Swahili, Sumerian or Old Bulgarian —and then painfully clawing his thoughts into a copious but uncertain and book-learned English. The result was a style that affected the higher cerebral centers like a constant roll of subway expresses. The second result was a sort of bewildered numbness of the senses, as before some fabulous and unearthly marvel. And the third result, if I make no mistake, was the celebrity of the professor as a Great Thinker. In brief, he stated his hollow nothings in such high, astounding terms that inevitably arrested and blistered the right-thinking mind. He made them mysterious. He made them shocking. He made them portentous. And so, flinging them at naïve and believing souls, he made them stick and burn.

Consider this specimen—the first paragraph of Chapter XIII of *The Theory of the Leisure Class:*

> In an increasing proportion as time goes on, the anthropomorphic cult, with its code of devout observances, suffers a progressive disintegration through the stress of economic exigencies and the decay of the system of status. As this disintegration proceeds, there come to be associated and blended with the devout attitude certain other motives and impulses that are not always of an anthropomorphic origin, nor traceable to the habit of personal subservience. Not all of these subsidiary impulses that blend with the bait of devoutness in the later devotional life are altogether congruous with

the devout attitude or with the anthropomorphic apprehension of sequence
of phenomena. Their origin being not the same, their action upon the
scheme of devout life is also not in the same direction. In many ways they
traverse the underlying norm of subservience or vicarious life to which the
code of devout observances and the ecclesiastical and sacerdotal institutions
are to be traced as their substantial basis. Through the presence of these
alien motives the social and industrial regime of status gradually disinte-
grates, and the canon of personal subservience loses the support derived
from an unbroken tradition. Extraneous habits and proclivities encroach upon
the field of action occupied by this canon, and it presently comes about that
the ecclesiastical and sacerdotal structures are partially converted to other
uses, in some measure alien to the purpose of the scheme of devout life as it
stood in the days of the most vigorous and characteristic development of the
priesthood.

Well, what have we here? What does this appalling salvo of rhetorical artillery signify? What was the sweating professor trying to say? Simply that in the
course of time the worship of God is commonly corrupted by other enterprises,
and that the church, ceasing to be a mere temple of adoration, becomes the
headquarters of these other enterprises. More simply still, that men sometimes
vary serving God by serving other men, which means, of course, serving themselves. This bald platitude, which must be obvious to any child who has ever
been to a church bazaar, was here tortured, worried and run through rollers
until it spread out to 241 words, of which fully 200 were unnecessary. The
next paragraph was even worse. In it the master undertook to explain in his
peculiar dialect the meaning of "that non-reverent sense of aesthetic congruity with the environment which is left as a residue of the latter-day act of
worship after elimination of its anthropomorphic content." Just what did he
mean by this "non-reverent sense of aesthetic congruity"? I studied the whole
paragraph for three days, halting only for prayer and sleep, and I came to certain conclusions. What I concluded was this: he was trying to say that many
people go to church, not because they are afraid of the devil but because they
enjoy the music, and like to look at the stained glass, the potted lilies and the
rev. pastor. To get this profound and highly original observation upon paper,
he wasted, not merely 241, but more than 300 words. To say what might have
been said on a postage stamp he took more than a page in his book.

And so it went, alas, alas, in all his other volumes—a cent's worth of information wrapped in a bale of polysyllables. In *The Higher Learning in
America* the thing perhaps reached its damndest and worst. It was as if the
practise of that incredibly obscure and malodorous style were a relentless disease, a sort of progressive intellectual diabetes, a leprosy of the horse sense.
Words were flung upon words until all recollection that there must be a meaning in them, a ground and excuse for them, were lost. One wandered in a laby-
rinth of nouns, adjectives, verbs, pronouns, adverbs, prepositions, conjunctions
and participles, most of them swollen and nearly all of them unable to walk. It

was, and is, impossible to imagine worse English, within the limits of intelligible grammar. It was clumsy, affected, opaque, bombastic, windy, empty. It was without grace or distinction and it was often without the most elementary order. The professor got himself enmeshed in his gnarled sentences like a bull trapped by barbed wire, and his efforts to extricate himself were quite as furious and quite as spectacular. He heaved, he leaped, he writhed; at times he seemed to be at the point of yelling for the police. It was a picture to bemuse the vulgar and to give the judicious grief.

Worse, there was nothing at the bottom of all this strident wind-music—the ideas it was designed to set forth were, in the overwhelming main, poor ideas, and often they were ideas that were almost idiotic. The concepts underlying, say, *The Theory of the Leisure Class* were simply Socialism and well water; the concepts underlying *The Higher Learning in America* were so childishly obvious that even the poor drudges who wrote editorials for newspapers often voiced them, and when, now and then, the professor tired of this emission of stale bosh and attempted flights of a more original character, he straightway came tumbling down into absurdity. What the reader then had to struggle with was not only intolerably bad writing, but also loose, flabby, cocksure and preposterous thinking. . . . Again I take refuge in an example. It is from Chapter IV of *The Theory of the Leisure Class*. The problem before the author here had to do with the social convention which, in pre-Prohibition 1899, frowned upon the consumption of alcohol by women—at least to the extent to which men might consume it decorously. Well, then, what was his explanation of this convention? Here, in brief, was his process of reasoning:

1. The leisure class, which is the predatory class of feudal times, reserves all luxuries for itself, and disapproves their use by members of the lower classes, for this use takes away their charm by taking away their exclusive possession.

2. Women are chattels in the possession of the leisure class, and hence subject to the rules made for inferiors. "The patriarchal tradition . . . says that the woman, being a chattel, should consume only what is necessary to her sustenance, except so far as her further consumption contributes to the comfort or the good repute of her master."

3. The consumption of alcohol contributes nothing to the comfort or good repute of the woman's master, but "detracts sensibly from the comfort or pleasure" of her master. Ergo, she is forbidden to drink.

This, I believe, was a fair specimen of the Veblenian ratiocination. Observe it well, for it was typical. That is to say, it started off with a gratuitous and highly dubious assumption, proceeded to an equally dubious deduction, and then ended with a platitude which begged the whole question. What sound reason was there for believing that exclusive possession was the hall-mark of luxury? There was none that I could see. It might be true of a few luxuries, but it was certainly not true of the most familiar ones. Did I enjoy a decent bath because I knew that John Smith could not afford one—or because I delighted in being clean? Did I admire Beethoven's Fifth Symphony because it was incomprehensible to Congressmen and Methodists—or because I genuinely loved music? Did I prefer kissing a pretty girl to kissing a charwoman because even a janitor may kiss a charwoman—or because the pretty girl looked better, smelled better and kissed better?

Confronted by such considerations, it seemed to me that there was little truth left in Prof. Veblen's theory of conspicuous consumption and conspicuous waste—that what remained of it, after it was practically applied a few times, was no more than a wraith of balderdash. What could have been plainer than his failure in the case of the human female? Starting off with a platitude, he ended in absurdity. No one could deny, I was willing to grant, that in a clearly limited sense, women occupied a place in the world—or, more accurately, aspired to a place in the world—that had some resemblance to that of a chattel. Marriage, the goal of their only honest and permanent hopes, invaded their individuality; a married woman (I was thinking, remember, of 1899) became the function of another individuality. Thus the appearance she presented to the world was often the mirror of her husband's egoism. A rich man hung his wife with expensive clothes and jewels for the same reason, among others, that he drove an expensive car: to notify everybody that he could afford it—in brief, to excite the envy of Marxians. But he also did it, let us hope, for another and far more powerful reason, to wit, that he delighted in her, that he loved her—and so wanted to make her gaudy and happy. This reason, to be sure, was rejected by the Marxians of the time, as it is rejected by those of ours, but nevertheless, it continued to appeal very forcibly, and so continues in our own day, to the majority of normal husbands in the nations of the West. The American husband, in particular, dresses his wife like a circus horse, not primarily because he wants to display his wealth upon her person, but because he is a soft and moony fellow and ever ready to yield to her desires, however preposterous. If any conception of her as a chattel were actively in him, even unconsciously, he would be a good deal less her slave. As it is, her vicarious practise of conspicuous waste commonly reaches such a development that her master himself is forced into renunciations—which brought Prof. Dr. Veblen's theory to self-destruction.

His final conclusion was as unsound as his premises. All it came to was a plain begging of the question. Why does a man forbid his wife to drink all the alcohol she can hold? Because, he said, it "detracts sensibly from his comfort or pleasure." In other words, it detracts from his comfort and pleasure because it detracts from his comfort and pleasure. Meanwhile, the real answer is so plain that even a professor should know it. A man forbids his wife to drink too much because, deep in his secret archives, he has records of the behavior of other women who drank too much, and is eager to safeguard his wife's connubial rectitude and his own dignity against what he knows to be certain invasion. In brief, it is a commonplace of observation, familiar to all males beyond the age of twenty-one, that once a woman is drunk the rest is a mere matter of time and place: the girl is already there. A husband, viewing this prospect, perhaps shrinks from having his chattel damaged. But let us be soft enough to think that he may also shrink from seeing humiliation and bitter regret inflicted upon one who is under his protection, and one whose dignity and happiness are precious to him, and one whom he regards with deep and (I surely hope) lasting affection. A man's grandfather is surely not his chattel, even by the terms of the Veblen theory, yet I am sure that no sane man would let the old gentleman go beyond a discreet cocktail or two if a bout of genuine bibbing were certain to be followed by the complete destruction of his dignity, his chastity and (if a Presbyterian) his immortal soul.

One more example of the Veblenian logic and I must pass on. On page 135 of *The Theory of the Leisure Class* he turned his garish and buzzing searchlight upon another problem of the domestic hearth, this time a double one. First, why do we have lawns around our country houses? Secondly, why don't we use cows to keep them clipped, instead of employing Italians, Croatians and blackamoors? The first question was answered by an appeal to ethnology: we delight in lawns because we are the descendants of "a pastoral people inhabiting a region with a humid climate"—because our dolicho-blond ancestors had flocks, and thus took a keen professional interest in grass. (The Marx motif! The economic interpretation of history in E flat.) But why don't we keep flocks? Why do we renounce cows and hire Jugo-Slavs? Because "to the average popular apprehension a herd of cattle so pointedly suggests thrift and usefulness that their presence . . . would be intolerably cheap." Plowing through a bad book from end to end, I could find nothing sillier than this. Here, indeed, the whole "Theory of conspicuous waste" was exposed for precisely what it was: one per cent platitude and ninety-nine per cent nonsense. Had the genial professor, pondering his great problems, ever taken a walk in the country? And had he, in the course of that walk, ever crossed a pasture inhabited by a cow (*Bos taurus*)? And had he, making that crossing, ever passed astern of the cow herself? And had he, thus passing astern, ever stepped carelessly, and—

❦ ❦ ❦

*David Riesman*

# Character and Society [1]

WHAT is the relation between social character and society? How is it that every society seems to get, more or less, the social character it "needs"? Erik H. Erikson writes, in a study of the social character of the Yurok Indians, that ". . . systems of child training . . . represent unconscious attempts at creating

[1] From *The Lonely Crowd* by David Riesman, Nathan Glazer, and Reuel Denney (New York: Doubleday & Co., 1955), pp. 19-48, with omissions. Copyright, 1950, 1953, by Yale University Press. Reprinted by permission of Yale University Press.

out of human raw material that configuration of attitudes which is (or once was) the optimum under the tribe's particular natural conditions and economic-historic necessities."[2]

From "economic-historic necessities" to "systems of child training" is a long jump. Much of the work of students of social character has been devoted to closing the gap and showing how the satisfaction of the largest "needs" of society is prepared, in some half-mysterious way, by its most intimate practices. Erich Fromm succinctly suggests the line along which this connection between society and character training may be sought: "In order that any society may function well, its members must acquire the kind of character which makes them *want* to act in the way they *have* to act as members of the society or of a special class within it. They have to *desire* what objectively is *necessary* for them to do. *Outer force* is replaced by *inner compulsion*, and by the particular kind of human energy which is channeled into character traits." [3]

Thus, the link between character and society—certainly not the only one, but one of the most significant, and the one I choose to emphasize in this discussion—is to be found in the way in which society ensures some degree of conformity from the individuals who make it up. In each society, such a mode of ensuring conformity is built into the child, and then either encouraged or frustrated in later adult experience. (No society, it would appear, is quite prescient enough to ensure that the mode of conformity it has inculcated will satisfy those subject to it in every stage of life.) I shall use the term "mode of conformity" interchangeably with the term "social character"—though certainly conformity is not all of social character: "mode of creativity" is as much a part of it. However, while societies and individuals may live well enough—if rather boringly—without creativity, it is not likely that they can live without some mode of conformity—even be it one of rebellion.

My concern . . . is with two revolutions and their relation to the "mode of conformity" or "social character" of Western man since the Middle Ages. The first of these revolutions has in the last four hundred years cut us off pretty decisively from the family- and clan-oriented traditional ways of life in which mankind has existed throughout most of history; this revolution includes the Renaissance, the Reformation, the Counter-Reformation, the Industrial Revolution, and the political revolutions of the seventeenth, eighteenth, and nineteenth centuries. This revolution is, of course, still in process, but in the most advanced countries of the world, and particularly in America, it is giving way to another sort of revolution—a whole range of social developments associated with a shift from an age of production to an age of consumption. . . . The second revolution, which is just beginning, has interested many contemporary

[2] "Observations on the Yurok: Childhood and World Image," *University of California Publications in American Archaeology and Ethnology,* XXXV (1943), iv.

[3] "Individual and Social Origins of Neurosis," *American Sociological Review,* IX (1944), 380; reprinted in *Personality in Nature, Society and Culture,* edited by Clyde Kluckhohn and Henry Murray (New York, Alfred A. Knopf, 1948).

observers, including social scientists, philosophers, and journalists. Both description and evaluation are still highly controversial; indeed, many are still preoccupied with the first set of revolutions and have not invented the categories for discussing the second set. In this book I try to sharpen the contrast between, on the one hand, conditions and character in those social strata that are today most seriously affected by the second revolution, and, on the other hand, conditions and character in analogous strata during the earlier revolution; in this perspective, what is briefly said about the traditional and feudal societies which were overturned by the first revolution is in the nature of backdrop for these later shifts.

One of the categories I make use of is taken from demography, the science that deals with birth rates and death rates, with the absolute and relative numbers of people in a society, and their distribution by age, sex, and other variables, for I tentatively seek to link certain social and characterological developments, as cause and effect, with certain population shifts in Western society since the Middle Ages.

It seems reasonably well established, despite the absence of reliable figures for earlier centuries, that during this period the curve of population growth in the Western countries has shown an S-shape of a particular type (as other countries are drawn more closely into the net of Western civilization, their populations also show a tendency to develop along the lines of this S-shape curve). The bottom horizontal line of the S represents a situation where the total population does not increase or does so very slowly, for the number of births equals roughly the number of deaths, and both are very high. In societies of this type, a high proportion of the population is young, life expectancy is low, and the turnover of generations is extremely rapid. Such societies are said to be in the phase of "high growth potential"; for should something happen to decrease the very high death rate (greater production of food, new sanitary measures, new knowledge of the causes of disease, and so on), a "population explosion" would result, and the population would increase very rapidly. This in effect is what happened in the West, starting with the seventeenth century. This spurt in population was most marked in Europe, and the countries settled by Europeans, in the nineteenth century. It is represented by the vertical bar of the S. Demographers call this the stage of "transitional growth," because the birth rate soon begins to follow the death rate in its decline. The rate of growth then slows down, and demographers begin to detect in the growing proportion of middle-aged and aged in the population the signs of a third stage, "incipient population decline." Societies in this stage are represented by the top horizontal bar of the S, again indicating, as in the first stage, that total population growth is small—but this time because births and deaths are low.

The S-curve is not a theory of population growth so much as an empirical description of what has happened in the West and in those parts of the world influenced by the West. After the S runs its course, what then? The developments of recent years in the United States and other Western countries do not seem to be susceptible to so simple and elegant a summing up. "Incipient population decline" has not become "population decline" itself, and the birth rate has shown an uncertain tendency to rise again, which most demographers think is temporary.[4]

It would be very surprising if variations in the basic conditions of reproduction, livelihood, and survival chances, that is, in the supply of and demand for human beings, with all it implies in change of the spacing of people, the size of markets, the role of children, the society's feeling of vitality or senescence, and many other intangibles, failed to influence character. My thesis is, in fact, that each of these three different phases on the population curve appears to be occupied by a society that enforces conformity and molds social character in a definably different way.

The society of high growth potential develops in its typical members a social character whose conformity is insured by their tendency to follow tradition: these I shall term *tradition-directed* people and the society in which they live *a society dependent on tradition-direction.*

The society of transitional population growth develops in its typical members a social character whose conformity is insured by their tendency to acquire early in life an internalized set of goals. These I shall term *inner-directed* people and the society in which they live *a society dependent on inner-direction.*

Finally, the society of incipient population decline develops in its typical members a social character whose conformity is insured by their tendency to be sensitized to the expectations and preferences of others. These I shall term *other-directed* people and the society in which they live one *dependent on other-direction.* . . .

### HIGH GROWTH POTENTIAL: TRADITION-DIRECTED TYPES

The phase of high growth potential characterizes more than half the world's population: India, Egypt, and China (which have already grown immensely in recent generations), most preliterate peoples in Central Africa, parts of Central and South America, in fact most areas of the world relatively untouched by industrialization. Here death rates are so high that if birth rates were not also high the populations would die out.

Regions where the population is in this stage may be either sparsely populated, as are the areas occupied by many primitive tribes and parts of Central and South America; or they may be densely populated, as are India, China, and Egypt. In either case, the society achieves a Malthusian bargain with the limited food supply by killing off, in one way or another, some of the potential

[4] The terminology used here is that of Frank W. Notestein. See his "Population— The Long View," in *Food for the World,* edited by Theodore W. Schultz (University of Chicago Press, 1945).

surplus of births over deaths—the enormous trap which, in Malthus' view, nature sets for man and which can be peaceably escaped only by prudent cultivation of the soil and prudent uncultivation of the species through the delay of marriage. Without the prevention of childbirth by means of marriage postponement or other contraceptive measures, the population must be limited by taking the life of living beings. And so societies have "invented" cannibalism, induced abortion, organized wars, made human sacrifice, and practiced infanticide (especially female) as means of avoiding periodic famine and epidemics.

Though this settling of accounts with the contradictory impulses of hunger and sex is accompanied often enough by upheaval and distress, these societies in the stage of high growth potential tend to be stable at least in the sense that their social practices, including the "crimes" that keep population down, are institutionalized and patterned. Generation after generation, people are born, are weeded out, and die to make room for others. The net rate of natural increase fluctuates within a broad range, though without showing any long-range tendency, as is true also of societies in the stage of incipient decline. But unlike the latter, the average life expectancy in the former is characteristically low: the population is heavily weighted on the side of the young, and generation replaces generation far more rapidly and less "efficiently" than in the societies of incipient population decline.

In viewing such a society we inevitably associate the relative stability of the man-land ratio, whether high or low, with the tenacity of custom and social structure. However, we must not equate stability of social structure over historical time with psychic stability in the life span of an individual: the latter may subjectively experience much violence and disorganization. In the last analysis, however, he learns to deal with life by adaptation, not by innovation. With certain exceptions conformity is largely given in the "self-evident" social situation. Of course nothing in human life is ever really self-evident; where it so appears it is because perceptions have been narrowed by cultural conditioning. As the precarious relation to the food supply is built into the going culture, it helps create a pattern of conventional conformity which is reflected in many, if not in all, societies in the stage of high growth potential. This is what I call tradition-direction.

## A Definition of Tradition-Direction

Since the type of social order we have been discussing is relatively unchanging, the conformity of the individual tends to be dictated to a very large degree by power relations among the various age and sex groups, the clans, castes, professions, and so forth—relations which have endured for centuries and are modified but slightly, if at all, by successive generations. The culture controls behavior minutely, and, while the rules are not so complicated that the young cannot learn them during the period of intensive socialization, careful and rigid etiquette governs the fundamentally influential sphere of kin relationships.

Moreover, the culture, in addition to its economic tasks, or as part of them, provides ritual, routine, and religion to occupy and to orient everyone. Little energy is directed toward finding new solutions of the age-old problems, let us say, of agricultural technique or "medicine," the problems to which people are acculturated.

It is not to be thought, however, that in these societies, where the activity of the individual member is determined by characterologically grounded obedience to traditions, the individual may not be highly prized and, in many instances, encouraged to develop his capabilities, his initiative, and even, within very narrow time limits, his aspirations. Indeed, the individual in some primitive societies is far more appreciated and respected than in some sectors of modern society. For the individual in a society dependent on tradition-direction has a well-defined functional relationship to other members of the group. If he is not killed off, he "belongs"—he is not "surplus," as the modern unemployed are surplus, nor is he expendable as the unskilled are expendable in modern society. But by very virtue of his "belonging," life goals that are *his* in terms of conscious choice appear to shape his destiny only to a very limited extent, just as only to a limited extent is there any concept of progress for the group.

In societies in which tradition-direction is the dominant mode of insuring conformity, relative stability is preserved in part by the infrequent but highly important process of fitting into institutionalized roles such deviants as there are. In such societies a person who might have become at a later historical stage an innovator or rebel, whose belonging, as such, is marginal and problematic, is drawn instead into roles like those of the shaman or sorcerer. That is, he is drawn into roles that make a socially acceptable contribution, while at the same time they provide the individual with a more or less approved niche. The medieval monastic orders may have served in a similar way to absorb many characterological mutations.

In some of these societies certain individuals are encouraged toward a degree of individuality from childhood, especially if they belong to families of high status. But, since the range of choice, even for high-status people, is minimal, the apparent social need for an individuated type of character is also minimal. It is probably accurate to say that character structure in these societies is very largely "adjusted," in the sense that for most people it appears to be in tune with social institutions. Even the few misfits "fit" to a degree; and only very rarely is one driven out of his social world.

This does not mean, of course, that the people are happy; the society to whose traditions they are adjusted may be a miserable one, ridden with anxiety, sadism, and disease. The point is rather that change, while never completely absent in human affairs, is slowed down as the movement of molecules is slowed down at low temperature; and the social character comes as close as it ever does to looking like the matrix of the social forms themselves.

In western history the Middle Ages can be considered a period in which the majority were tradition-directed. But the term tradition-directed refers to a common element, not only among the people of precapitalist Europe but also among such enormously different types of people as Hindus and Hopi Indians, Zulus and Chinese, North African Arabs and Balinese. . . .

### TRANSITIONAL GROWTH: INNER-DIRECTED TYPES

Except for the West, we know very little about the cumulation of small changes that can eventuate in a breakup of the tradition-directed type of society, leading it to realize its potential for high population growth. As for the West, however, much has been learned about the slow decay of feudalism and the subsequent rise of a type of society in which inner-direction is the dominant mode of insuring conformity.

Critical historians, pushing the Renaissance ever back into the Middle Ages, seem sometimes to deny that any decisive change occurred at all. On the whole, however, it seems that the greatest social and characterological shift of recent centuries did indeed come when men were driven out of the primary ties that bound them to the western medieval version of tradition-directed society. All later shifts, including the shift from inner-direction to other-direction, seem unimportant by comparison, although of course this latter shift is still under way and we cannot tell what it will look like when—if ever—it is complete.

A change in the relatively stable ratio of births to deaths, which characterizes the period of high growth potential, is both the cause and consequence of other profound social changes. In most of the cases known to us a decline takes place in mortality prior to a decline in fertility; hence there is some period in which the population expands rapidly. The drop in death rate occurs as the result of many interacting factors, among them sanitation, improved communications (which permit government to operate over a wider area and also permit easier transport of food to areas of shortage from areas of surplus), the decline, forced or otherwise, of infanticide, cannibalism, and other inbred kinds of violence. Because of improved methods of agriculture the land is able to support more people, and these in turn produce still more people.

Notestein's phrase, "transitional growth," is a mild way of putting it. The "transition" is likely to be violent, disrupting the stabilized paths of existence in societies in which tradition-direction has been the principal mode of insuring conformity. The imbalance of births and deaths puts pressure on the society's customary ways. A new slate of character structures is called for or finds its opportunity in coping with the rapid changes—and the need for still more changes—in the social organization.

## A Definition of Inner-Direction

In western history the society that emerged with the Renaissance and Reformation and that is only now vanishing serves to illustrate the type of society in which inner-direction is the principal mode of securing conformity. Such a society is characterized by increased personal mobility, by a rapid accumulation of capital (teamed with devastating technological shifts), and by an almost constant expansion: intensive expansion in the production of goods and people, and extensive expansion in exploration, colonization, and imperialism. The greater choices this society gives—and the greater initiatives it demands in order to cope with its novel problems—are handled by character types who can manage to live socially without strict and self-evident tradition-direction. These are the inner-directed types.

The concept of inner-direction is intended to cover a very wide range of types. Thus, while it is essential for the study of certain problems to differentiate between Protestant and Catholic countries and their character types, between the effects of the Reformation and the effects of the Renaissance, between the puritan ethic of the European north and west and the somewhat more hedonistic ethic of the European east and south, while all these are valid and, for certain purposes, important distinctions, the concentration of this study on the development of modes of conformity permits their neglect. It allows the grouping together of these otherwise distinct developments because they have one thing in common: *the source of direction for the individual is "inner" in the sense that it is implanted early in life by the elders and directed toward generalized but nonetheless inescapably destined goals.*

We can see what this means when we realize that, in societies in which tradition-direction is the dominant mode of insuring conformity, attention is focused on securing external *behavioral* conformity. While behavior is minutely prescribed, individuality of character need not be highly developed to meet prescriptions that are objectified in ritual and etiquette—though to be sure, a social character *capable* of such behavioral attention and obedience is requisite. By contrast, societies in which inner-direction becomes important, though they also are concerned with behavioral conformity, cannot be satisfied with behavorial conformity alone. Too many novel situations are presented, situations which a code cannot encompass in advance. Consequently the problem of personal choice, solved in the earlier period of high growth potential by channeling choice through rigid social organization, in the period of transitional growth is solved by channeling choice through a rigid though highly individualized character.

This rigidity is a complex matter. While any society dependent on inner-direction seems to present people with a wide choice of aims—such as money, possessions, power, knowledge, fame, goodness—these aims are ideologically interrelated, and the selection made by any one individual remains relatively unalterable throughout his life. Moreover, the means to those ends, though not fitted into as tight a social frame of reference as in the society dependent on tradition-direction, are nevertheless limited by the new voluntary associations—for instance, the Quakers, the Masons, the Mechanics' Associations—to which people tie themselves. Indeed, the term "tradition-direction" could be misleading if the reader were to conclude that the force of tradition has no weight for the inner-directed character. On the contrary, he is very considerably bound by traditions: they limit his ends and inhibit his choice of means. The point is rather that a splintering of tradition takes place, connected in part with the increasing division of labor and stratification of society. Even if the individual's choice of tradition is largely determined for him by his family, as it is in most cases, he cannot help becoming aware of the existence of competing traditions —hence of tradition as such. As a result he possesses a somewhat greater degree of flexibility in adapting himself to ever changing requirements and in return requires more from his environment.

As the control of the primary group is loosened—the group that both socializes the young and controls the adult in the earlier era—a new psychological mechanism appropriate to the more open society is "invented": it is what I like to describe as a psychological gyroscope.[5] This instrument, once it is set by the parents and other authorities, keeps the inner-directed person, as we shall see, "on course" even when tradition, as responded to by his character, no longer dictates his moves. The inner-directed person becomes capable of maintaining a delicate balance between the demands upon him of his life goal and the buffetings of his external environment.

This metaphor of the gyroscope, like any other, must not be taken literally. It would be a mistake to see the inner-directed man as incapable of learning from experience or as insensitive to public opinion in matters of external conformity. He can receive and utilize certain signals from outside, provided that they can be reconciled with the limited maneuverability that his gyroscope permits him. His pilot is not quite automatic.

Huizinga's The Waning of the Middle Ages gives a picture of the anguish and turmoil, the conflict of values, out of which the new forms slowly emerged. Already by the late Middle Ages people were forced to live under new conditions of awareness. As their self-consciousness and their individuality developed, they had to make themselves at home in the world in novel ways. They still have to.

### INCIPIENT DECLINE OF POPULATION: OTHER-DIRECTED TYPES

The problem facing the societies in the stage of transitional growth is that of reaching a point at which resources become plentiful enough or are utilized effectively enough to permit a rapid accumulation of capital. This rapid accumulation has to be achieved even while the social product is being drawn on at an accelerated rate to maintain the rising population and satisfy the consumer demands that go with the way of life that has already been adopted. For most countries, unless capital and techniques can be imported from other countries in still later phases of the population curve, every effort to increase national resources at a rapid rate must actually be at the expense of current standards of living. We have seen this occur in the U.S.S.R., now in the stage of

[5] Since writing the above I have discovered Gardner Murphy's use of the same metaphor in his volume Personality (New York, Harper, 1947).

transitional growth. For western Europe this transition was long-drawn-out and painful. For America, Canada, and Australia—at once beneficiaries of European techniques and native resources—the transition was rapid and relatively easy.

The tradition-directed person, as has been said, hardly thinks of himself as an individual. Still less does it occur to him that he might shape his own destiny in terms of personal, lifelong goals or that the destiny of his children might be separate from that of the family group. He is not sufficiently separated psychologically from himself (or, therefore, sufficiently close to himself), his family, or group to think in these terms. In the phase of transitional growth, however, people of inner-directed character do gain a feeling of control over their own lives and see their children also as individuals with careers to make. At the same time, with the shift out of agriculture and, later, with the end of child labor, children no longer become an unequivocal economic asset. And with the growth of habits of scientific thought, religious and magical views of human fertility—views that in an earlier phase of the population curve made sense for the culture if it was to reproduce itself—give way to "rational," individualistic attitudes. Indeed, just as the rapid accumulation of productive capital requires that people be imbued with the "Protestant ethic" (as Max Weber characterized one manifestation of what is here termed inner-direction), so also the decreased number of progeny requires a profound change in values—a change so deep that, in all probability, it has to be rooted in character structure.

As the birth rate begins to follow the death rate downward, societies move toward the epoch of incipient decline of population. Fewer and fewer people work on the land or in the extractive industries or even in manufacturing. Hours are short. People may have material abundance and leisure besides. They pay for these changes however—here, as always, the solution of old problems gives rise to new ones—by finding themselves in a centralized and bureaucratized society and a world shrunken and agitated by the contact—accelerated by industrialization—of races, nations, and cultures.

The hard enduringness and enterprise of the inner-directed types are somewhat less necessary under these new conditions. Increasingly, *other people* are the problem, not the material environment. And as people mix more widely and become more sensitive to each other, the surviving traditions from the stage of high growth potential—much disrupted, in any case, during the violent spurt of industrialization—become still further attenuated. Gyroscopic control is no longer sufficiently flexible, and a new psychological mechanism is called for.

Furthermore, the "scarcity psychology" of many inner-directed people, which was socially adaptive during the period of heavy capital accumulation that accompanied transitional growth of population, needs to give way to an "abundance psychology" capable of "wasteful" luxury consumption of leisure and of the surplus product. Unless people want to destroy the surplus product in war, which still does require heavy capital equipment, they must learn to enjoy and engage in those services that are expensive in terms of man power but not of capital—poetry and philosophy, for instance.[6] Indeed, in the period of incipient decline, nonproductive consumers, both the increasing number of old people and the diminishing number of as yet untrained young, form a high proportion of the population, and these need both the economic opportunity to be prodigal and the character structure to allow it.

Has this need for still another slate of character types actually been acknowledged to any degree? My observations lead me to believe that in America it has.

## A Definition of Other-Direction

The type of character I shall describe as other-directed seems to be emerging in very recent years in the upper middle class of our larger cities: more prominently in New York than in Boston, in Los Angeles than in Spokane, in Cincinnati than in Chillicothe. Yet in some respects this type is strikingly similar to *the* American, whom Tocqueville and other curious and astonished visitors from Europe, even before the Revolution, thought to be a new kind of man. Indeed, travelers' reports on America impress us with their unanimity. The American is said to be shallower, freer with his money, friendlier, more uncertain of himself and his values, more demanding of approval than the European. It all adds up to a pattern which, without stretching matters too far, resembles the kind of character that a number of social scientists have seen as developing in contemporary, highly industrialized, and bureaucratic America: Fromm's "marketer," Mills's "fixer," Arnold Green's "middle class male child." [7]

It is my impression that the middle-class American of today is decisively different from those Americans of Tocqueville's writings who nevertheless strike us as so contemporary, and much of this book will be devoted to discussing these differences. It is also my impression that the conditions I believe to be responsible for other-direction are affecting increasing numbers of people in the metropolitan centers of the advanced industrial countries. My analysis of the other-directed character is thus at once an analysis of the American and of contemporary man. Much of the time I find it hard or impossible to say where one ends and the other begins. Tentatively, I am inclined to think that the other-directed type does find itself most at home in America, due to certain unique elements in American society, such as its recruitment from Europe and its lack of any feudal past. As against this, I am also inclined to put more weight on capitalism, industrialism, and urbanization—these being international tendencies—than on any character-forming peculiarities of the American scene.

Bearing these qualifications in mind, it seems appropriate to treat contem-

---

[6] These examples are given by Allan G. B. Fisher, *The Clash of Progress and Security* (London, Macmillan, 1935).

[7] See Erich Fromm, *Man for Himself*; C. Wright Mills, "The Competitive Personality," *Partisan Review*, XIII (1946), 433; Arnold Green, "The Middle Class Male Child and Neurosis," *American Sociological Review*, XI (1946), 31. See also the work of Jurgen Ruesch, Martin B. Loeb, and co-workers on the "infantile personality."

porary metropolitan America as our illustration of a society—so far, perhaps, the only illustration—in which other-direction is the dominant mode of insuring conformity. It would be premature, however, to say that it is already the dominant mode in America as a whole. But since the other-directed types are to be found among the young, in the larger cities, and among the upper income groups, we may assume that, unless present trends are reversed, the hegemony of other-direction lies not far off.

If we wanted to cast our social character types into social class molds, we could say that inner-direction is the typical character of the "old" middle class— the banker, the tradesman, the small entrepreneur, the technically oriented engineer, etc.—while other-direction is becoming the typical character of the "new" middle class—the bureaucrat, the salaried employee in business, etc. Many of the economic factors associated with the recent growth of the "new" middle class are well known. They have been discussed by James Burnham, Colin Clark, Peter Drucker, and others. There is a decline in the numbers and in the proportion of the working population engaged in production and extraction—agriculture, heavy industry, heavy transport—and an increase in the numbers and the proportion engaged in white-collar work and the service trades. People who are literate, educated, and provided with the necessities of life by an ever more efficient machine industry and agriculture, turn increasingly to the "tertiary" economic realm. The service industries prosper among the people as a whole and no longer only in court circles.

Education, leisure, services, these go together with an increased consumption of words and images from the new mass media of communications. While societies in the phase of transitional growth begin the process of distributing words from urban centers, the flow becomes a torrent in the societies of incipient population decline. This process, while modulated by profound national and class differences, connected with differences in literacy and loquacity, takes place everywhere in the industrialized lands. Increasingly, relations with the outer world and with oneself are mediated by the flow of mass communication. For the other-directed types political events are likewise experienced through a screen of words by which the events are habitually atomized and personalized—or pseudo-personalized. For the inner-directed person who remains still extant in this period the tendency is rather to systematize and moralize this flow of words.

These developments lead, for large numbers of people, to changes in paths to success and to the requirement of more "socialized" behavior both for success and for marital and personal adaptation. Connected with such changes are changes in the family and in child-rearing practices. In the smaller families of urban life, and with the spread of "permissive" child care to ever wider strata of the population, there is a relaxation of older patterns of discipline. Under these newer patterns the peer-group (the group of one's associates of the same age and class) becomes much more important to the child, while the parents make him feel guilty not so much about violation of inner standards as about failure to be popular or otherwise to manage his relations with these other children. Moreover, the pressures of the school and the peer-group are reinforced and continued—in a manner whose inner paradoxes I shall discuss later—by the mass media: movies, radio, comics, and popular culture media generally. Under these conditions types of character emerge that we shall here term other-directed. . . . *What is common to all the other-directed people is that their contemporaries are the source of direction for the individual—either those known to him or those with whom he is indirectly acquainted, through friends and through the mass media. This source is of course "internalized" in the sense that dependence on it for guidance in life is implanted early. The goals toward which the other-directed person strives shift with that guidance: it is only the process of striving itself and the process of paying close attention to the signals from others that remain unaltered throughout life.* This mode of keeping in touch with others permits a close behavioral conformity, not through drill in behavior itself, as in the tradition-directed character, but rather through an exceptional sensitivity to the actions and wishes of others.

Of course, it matters very much who these "others" are: whether they are the individual's immediate circle or a "higher" circle or the anonymous voices of the mass media; whether the individual fears the hostility of chance acquaintances or only of those who "count." But his need for approval and direction from others—and contemporary others rather than ancestors—goes beyond the reasons that lead most people in any era to care very much what others think of them. While all people want and need to be liked by some of the people some of the time, it is only the modern other-directed types who make this their chief source of direction and chief area of sensitivity.[8]

It is perhaps the insatiable force of this psychological need for approval that differentiates people of the metropolitan, American upper middle class, whom we regard as other-directed, from very similar types that have appeared in capital cities and among other classes in previous historical periods, whether in imperial Canton, in eighteenth- and nineteenth-century Europe, or in ancient Athens, Alexandria, or Rome. In all these groups fashion not only ruled as a substitute for morals and customs, but it was a rapidly changing fashion that held sway. It could do so because, although the mass media were in their infancy, the group corresponding to the American upper middle class was comparably small and the elite structure was extremely reverberant. It can be argued, for example, that a copy of *The Spectator* covered its potential readership more thoroughly in the late eighteenth century than *The New Yorker* covers its readership today. In eighteenth- and nineteenth-century English, French, and Russian novels, we find portraits of the sort of people who operated in the upper reaches of bureaucracy and had to be prepared for rapid changes of signals.

[8] This picture of the other-directed person has been stimulated by, and developed from, Erich Fromm's discussion of the "marketing orientation" in *Man for Himself*, pp. 67-82. I have also drawn on my portrait of "The Cash Customer," *Common Sense*, XI (1942), 183.

Stepan Arkadyevitch Oblonsky in *Anna Karenina* is one of the more likeable and less opportunistic examples, especially striking because of the way Tolstoy contrasts him with Levin, a moralizing, inner-directed person. At any dinner party Stepan manifests exceptional social skills; his political skills as described in the following quotation are also highly social:

> Stepan Arkadyevitch took in and read a liberal newspaper, not an extreme one, but one advocating the views held by the majority. And in spite of the fact that science, art, and politics had no special interest for him, he firmly held those views on all subjects which were held by the majority and by his paper, and he only changed them when the majority changed them—or, more strictly speaking, he did not change them, but they imperceptively changed of themselves within him.
>
> Stepan Arkadyevitch had not chosen his political opinions or his views; these political opinions and views had come to him of themselves, just as he did not choose the shapes of his hats or coats, but simply took those that were being worn. And for him, living in a certain society—owing to the need, ordinarily developed at years of discretion, for some degree of mental activity—to have views was just as indispensable as to have a hat. If there was a reason for his preferring liberal to conservative views, which were held also by many of his circle, it arose not from his considering liberalism more rational, but from its being in closer accord with his manner of life. . . . And so liberalism had become a habit of Stepan Arkadyevitch's, and he liked his newspaper, as he did his cigar after dinner, for the slight fog it diffused in his brain.

Stepan, while his good-natured gregariousness makes him seem like a modern middle-class American, is not fully other-directed. This gregariousness alone, without a certain sensitivity to others as individuals and as a source of direction, is not the identifying trait. Just so, we must differentiate the nineteenth-century American—gregarious and subservient to public opinion though he was found to be by Tocqueville, Bryce, and others—from the other-directed American as he emerges today, an American who in his character is more capable of and more interested in maintaining responsive contact with others both at work and at play. This point needs to be emphasized, since the distinction is easily misunderstood. The inner-directed person, though he often sought and sometimes achieved a relative independence of public opinion and of what the neighbors thought of him, was in most cases very much concerned with his good repute and, at least in America, with "keeping up with the Joneses." These conformities, however, were primarily external, typified in such details as clothes, curtains, and bank credit. For, indeed, the conformities were to a standard, evidence of which was provided by the "best people" in one's milieu. In contrast with this pattern, the other-directed person, though he has his eye very much on the Joneses, aims to keep up with them not so much in external details as in the quality of his inner experience. That is, his great sensitivity keeps him in touch with others on many more levels than the externals of appearance and propriety. Nor does any ideal of independence or of reliance on God alone modify his desire to look to the others—and the "good guys" as well as the best people—for guidance in what experiences to seek and in how to interpret them.

## The Three Types Compared

One way to see the structural differences between the three types is to see the differences in the emotional sanction or control in each type.

The tradition-directed person feels the impact of his culture as a unit, but it is nevertheless mediated through the specific, small number of individuals with whom he is in daily contact. These expect of him not so much that he be a certain type of person but that he behave in the approved way. Consequently the sanction for behavior tends to be the fear of being *shamed*.

The inner-directed person has early incorporated a psychic gyroscope which is set going by his parents and can receive signals later on from other authorities who resemble his parents. He goes through life less independent than he seems, obeying this internal piloting. Getting off course, whether in response to inner impulses or to the fluctuating voices of contemporaries, may lead to the feeling of *guilt*.

Since the direction to be taken in life has been learned in the privacy of the home from a small number of guides and since principles, rather than details of behavior, are internalized, the inner-directed person is capable of great stability. Especially so when it turns out that his fellows have gyroscopes too, spinning at the same speed and set in the same direction. But many inner-directed individuals can remain stable even when the reinforcement of social approval is not available—as in the upright life of the stock Englishman isolated in the tropics.

Contrasted with such a type as this, the other-directed person learns to respond to signals from a far wider circle than is constituted by his parents. The family is no longer a closely knit unit to which he belongs but merely part of a wider social environment to which he early becomes attentive. In these respects the other-directed person resembles the tradition-directed person: both live in a group milieu and lack the inner-directed person's capacity to go it alone. The nature of this group milieu, however, differs radically in the two cases. The other-directed person is cosmopolitan. For him the border between the familiar and the strange—a border clearly marked in the societies depending on tradition-direction—has broken down. As the family continuously absorbs the strange and so reshapes itself, so the strange becomes familiar. While the inner-directed person could be "at home abroad" by virtue of his relative insensitivity to others, the other-directed person is, in a sense, at home everywhere and nowhere, capable of a rapid if sometimes superficial intimacy with and response to everyone.

The tradition-directed person takes his signals from others, but they come in a cultural monotone; he needs no complex receiving equipment to pick them up. The other-directed person must be able to receive signals from far and near; the sources are many, the changes rapid. What can be internalized, then, is not a code of behavior but the elaborate equipment needed to attend to such messages and occasionally to participate in their circulation. As against guilt-and-shame controls, though of course these survive, one prime psychological lever of the other-directed person is a diffuse *anxiety*. This control equipment, instead of being like a gyroscope, is like a radar.[9]

### The Case of Athens

Could other civilizations, such as the ancient Hebrew, Greek, and Roman, also be characterized at successive stages in their population-subsistence develment as tradition-directed, inner-directed, and other-directed? In all likelihood the tremendous growth of world population since about 1650—and consequently the S-curve of population growth—is unique in the history of mankind and the consequence of an altogether new (industrialized) type of technological, economic, and social organization. Nonetheless, the fact that every society has some form of organization and some "technology," be it the most unscientific ritual, constitutes proof of an effort, more or less successful, to bring down the death rate and improve the standard of living over that of mere animal existence. And an exploratory study of the Athenian empire suggests that there, too, a correlation between population growth and social character of the type we have described for the recent West may be discerned.[10]

What scant evidence we have of the long-term trend of population growth in the empire must be derived from the patient studies of present-day demographers and from the remarks of ancient Greek authors. The Homeric epics depict a volatile society in which the institution of private property had already disrupted the tradition-directed communal organization of tribe, phratry, and clan. Revolutionary improvements in cultivation of the soil, made possible by continued settlement in one place, increased the standard of living and, as a corollary, initiated a phase of population growth that was to continue for several centuries. Private ownership, the development of an exchange economy, and the patrilineal inheritance of property encouraged the concentration of wealth and produced economic and social inequality. A new, three-fold social stratification interpenetrated the traditional organization and not only loosened the hold of the clan upon its members but also encouraged the coalescence of individuals with like economic status from different tribes and phratries. The reform measures taken by Solon and others in succeeding generations also clearly imply that some individuals and families were far more successful than others in achieving the new economic goals of leisure and material wealth.

During the five hundred years after the founding of the Athenian state there seems to have existed an expanding "frontier" economy, based in part

[9] The "radar" metaphor was suggested by Karl Wittfogel.

[10] The following discussion draws on an unpublished monograph by Sheila Spaulding, "Prolegomena to the Study of Athenian Democracy" (Yale Law School Library, 1949).

upon the exploitation of internal resources, made possible by technological improvement and the institution of slavery, and in greater part upon the conquest of other peoples and the incorporation of their wealth into the domestic economy. One might well adduce as indications of inner-direction during this period the changing attitudes toward the family and the upbringing of children; the laws which enhanced the freedom of the individual, for example, the significant reforms which permitted the free alienation of property and the initiation of a criminal prosecution by a "third party"; the multiplication of opportunities for profitable employment in commerce, agriculture, and industry; the drift from country to city; the enthusiasm for exploration and conquest; and the increasing interest in philosophic speculation and science.

By the turn of the fifth century the Athenian empire had reached the zenith of its power; and the Greeks of this period were familiar with the idea of an expanding population. Both Plato and Aristotle advocated a stationary population. Two centuries later we find that the problem has radically shifted and the fear of overpopulation has been replaced by the fear of depopulation. Polybius, writing in the second century, declared that the population of Greece was dying out because of the practice of infanticide. This is undoubtedly an overstatement; infanticide was confined, as contraception tends to be today, largely to the upper and upper middle classes. Nevertheless, it indicates the trend toward artificial limitation of the size of the family and suggests that the population had reached the period not only of incipient but of actual decline. It is as an expanding population begins to reach its peak that we see the rise of social forms that seem to indicate the presence of the other-directed mode of conformity.

For example, the institution of ostracism, introduced as a means of preventing tyranny, became in the fifth century a formidable weapon of public opinion, wielded capriciously as a means of insuring conformity of taste and "cutting down to size" those statesmen, playwrights, and orators of markedly superior ability. In addition, the common people produced a numerous brood of informers "who were constantly accusing the better and most influential men in the State, with a view to subjecting them to the envy of the multitude." In *The Jealousy of the Gods and Criminal Law in Athens* Svend Ranulf has meticulously traced the incidence and development of the "disinterested tendency to inflict punishment" which, based upon a diffuse characterological anxiety, could perhaps be described as the ascendancy of an omnipotent "peer-group."

All this was accompanied by a decline in inner-directed dutifulness toward the political sphere. In spite of the deference shown by many authors to Athenian "democracy" of the fifth century, one is struck by the apathy of the voting population. What had earlier been a hard-won privilege of the lower classes—attendance at the ecclesia or popular assembly—became during the rule of the demos an obligation. Various punitive measures were introduced to insure a quorum; and when these failed, the "right to vote" became a paid service to the state.

Here in the history of the Athenian empire we have an area in which more detailed research and analysis might very profitably be undertaken; obviously, no more has been done in these remarks than to suggest certain problems that would be relevant for such research. Similarly, the problems of Rome during the reign of Augustus suggest the emergence and ascendancy of the other-directed character type as the population reached the phase of incipient decline. The importation of a new poetic language legitimating the importance of subtle states of personal feeling, in the Alexandrian-influenced work of such poets as Catullus, and probably Gallus, may evidence shifts toward other-direction in the dominant classes.

## Some Necessary Qualifications

The limitations of language lead me to speak as if I saw societies as always managing to produce the social organization and character types they need in order to survive. Such an assumption, raising the image of a separate body, "society," making certain demands on people and testing out various processes, would introduce an unwarranted teleology into social change. What seems to happen is that by sheer "accident" any of a number of ways of insuring characterological conformity may exist in a given society. Those which have been successful in preserving a coherent society are transmitted as unconsciously as they arose; but, since by their historical success they present themselves for study and investigation, it appears as if some teleological force, serving the interest of society, has introduced the successful—or fairly successful—mode of insuring conformity. Yet we must recognize that societies do disintegrate and die out despite what may appear to be successful methods of insuring character perpetuation. Correspondingly, we must not deny the probability that societies can tolerate, even without disintegration, much more disorganization and even ruin than many people recognize.

We must not overestimate the role of character in the social process. It is not a sufficient explanation, for instance, to say, as some students have said, that the German army held together because "the Germans" had an authoritarian character, since armies of very diverse character type do in fact hold together under given conditions of battle and supply. Nor will it do to assume, as American aptitude-testers sometimes do, that certain jobs can be successfully handled only by a narrowly limited range of character types: that we need "extrovert" or "oral" salesmen and administrators, and "introvert" or "anal" chemists and accountants. Actually, people of radically different types can adapt themselves to perform, adequately enough, a wide variety of complex tasks. Or, to put the same thing in another way, social institutions can harness a gamut of different motivations, springing from different character types, to perform very much the same kinds of socially demanded jobs. And yet, of course, this is not to say that character is merely a shadowy factor in history, like some Hegelian spirit. Character will affect the style and psychic costs of job performances that, in economic or political analysis, look almost identical.

Thus we are forced to take account of the possibility that people may be compelled to behave in one way although their character structure presses them to behave in the opposite way. Society may change more rapidly than character, or vice versa. Indeed, this disparity between socially required behavior and characterologically compatible behavior is one of the great levers of change. Fortunately we know of no society like the one glumly envisaged by Aldous Huxley in *Brave New World*, where the social character types have been completely content in their social roles and where consequently, barring accident, no social change exists.

Finally, it is necessary to point out that social character types are abstractions. They refer back to the living, concrete human being, and in order to arrive at them, as we saw at the beginning of this chapter, it is necessary first to abstract from the real individual his "personality," then to abstract from that his "character," finally to abstract from that the common element that forms "social character."

In fact, the discerning reader may already have realized that in the nature of the case there can be no such thing as a society or a person wholly dependent on tradition-direction, inner-direction, or other-direction: each of these modes of conformity is universal, and the question is always one of the degree to which an individual or a social group places reliance on one or another of the three available mechanisms. Thus, all human beings are inner-directed in the sense that, brought up as they are by people older than themselves, they have acquired and internalized some permanent orientations from them. And, conversely, all human beings are other-directed in the sense that they are oriented to the expectations of their peers and to the "field situation" (Kurt Lewin) or "definition of the situation" (W. I. Thomas) that these peers at any moment help to create.[11]

Since, furthermore, each of us possesses the capacity for each of the three modes of conformity, it is possible that an individual may change, in the course of his life, from greater dependence on one combination of modes to greater dependence on another (though radical shifts of this kind, even when circumstances encourage them, are unlikely). For, unless individuals are completely crazy—and, indeed, they are never *completely* crazy—they both organize the cues in their social environment and attend to those cues. Thus, if a predominantly other-directed individual were placed in an environment without peers,

[11] In this connection, it is revealing to compare the conceptions of the socialization process held by Freud and Harry Stack Sullivan. Freud saw the superego as the internalized source of moral life-directions, built in the image of the awesome parents, and transferred thereafter to parent-surrogates such as God, the Leader, Fate. Sullivan does not deny this happens but puts more emphasis on the role of the peer-group—the chum and group of chums who take such a decisive hand in the socialization of the American child. Sullivan's very insistence on the importance of interpersonal relations—which led him to believe, much more than Freud, in the adaptability of men and the possibilities of social peace and harmony—may itself be viewed as a symptom of the shift toward other-direction.

he might fall back on other patterns of direction. Similarly, it is clear that no individual, and assuredly no society, ever exists without a heavy reliance on tradition, much as this may appear to be overlaid by swings of fashion.

It is important to emphasize these overlappings of the several types in part because of the value judgments that readers are likely to attach to each type in isolation. Since most of us value independence we are likely to prefer the inner-directed type and overlook two things. First, the gyroscopic mechanism allows the inner-directed person to appear far more independent than he really is: he is no less a conformist to others than the other-directed person, but the voices to which he listens are more distant, of an older generation, their cues internalized in his childhood. Second, as just indicated, this type of conformity is only one, though the predominant, mechanism of the inner-directed type: the latter is not characteristically insensitive to what his peers think of him, and may even be opportunistic in the highest degree. Thus, he need not always react to other people as if they were merely stand-ins for his parents. Rather, the point is that he is somewhat less concerned than the other-directed person with continuously obtaining from contemporaries (or their stand-ins: the mass media) a flow of guidance, expectation, and approbation.

Let me repeat: the types of character and society dealt with in this book are *types:* they do not exist in reality, but are a construction, based on a selection of certain historical problems for investigation. By employing more types, or subtypes, one could take account of more facts (or mayhap, the same facts with less violence!), but my collaborators and I have preferred to work with a minimum of scaffolding; throughout, in seeking to describe by one interrelated set of characteristics both a society and its typical individuals, we have looked for features that connect the two and ignored those aspects of behavior—often striking—which did not seem relevant to our task.

❦ ❦ ❦

*Erich Fromm*

# The Illusion of Individuality[1]

BUT what about ourselves? Is our own democracy threatened only by Fascism beyond the Atlantic or by the "fifth column" in our own ranks? If that were the case, the situation would be serious but not critical. But although foreign and internal threats of Fascism must be taken seriously, there is no greater mistake and no graver danger than not to see that in our own society we are faced with the same phenomenon that is fertile soil for the rise of Fascism anywhere: the insignificance and powerlessness of the individual.

This statement challenges the conventional belief that by freeing the indi-

[1] From *Escape from Freedom*, copyright 1941 by Erich Fromm and reprinted by permission of Rinehart & Company, Inc., New York.

vidual from all external restraints modern democracy has achieved true individualism. We are proud that we are not subject to any external authority, that we are free to express our thoughts and feelings, and we take it for granted that this freedom almost automatically guarantees our individuality. *The right to express our thoughts,* however, *means something only if we are able to have thoughts of our own;* freedom from external authority is a lasting gain only if the inner psychological conditions are such that we are able to establish our own individuality. Have we achieved that aim, or are we at least approaching it? . . . In discussing the two aspects of freedom for modern man, we have pointed out the economic conditions that make for increasing isolation and powerlessness of the individual in our era; in discussing the psychological results we have shown that this powerlessness leads either to the kind of escape that we find in the authoritarian character, or else to a compulsive conforming in the process of which the isolated individual becomes an automaton, loses his self, and yet at the same time consciously conceives of himself as free and subject only to himself.

It is important to consider how our culture fosters this tendency to conform, even though there is space for only a few outstanding examples. The suppression of spontaneous feelings, and thereby of the development of genuine individuality, starts very early, as a matter of fact with the earliest training of a child. This is not say that training must inevitably lead to suppression of spontaneity if the real aim of education is to further the inner independence and individuality of the child, its growth and integrity. The restrictions which such a kind of education may have to impose upon the growing child are only transitory measures that really support the process of growth and expansion. In our culture, however, education too often results in the elimination of spontaneity and in the substitution of original psychic acts by superimposed feelings, thoughts, and wishes. (By original I do not mean, let me repeat, that an idea has not been thought before by someone else, but that it originates in the individual, that it is the result of his own activity and in this sense is *his* thought.) To choose one illustration somewhat arbitrarily, one of the earliest suppressions of *feelings* concerns hostility and dislike. To start with, most children have a certain measure of hostility and rebelliousness as a result of their conflicts with a surrounding world that tends to block their expansiveness and to which, as the weaker opponent, they usually have to yield. It is one of the essential aims of the educational process to eliminate this antagonistic reaction. The methods are different; they vary from threats and punishments, which frighten the child, to the subtler methods of bribery or "explanations," which confuse the child and make him give up his hostility. The child starts with giving up the expression of his feeling and eventually gives up the very feeling itself. Together with that, he is taught to suppress the awareness of hostility and insincerity in others; sometimes this is not entirely easy, since children have a capacity for noticing such negative qualities in others without being so easily deceived by words as adults usually are. They still dislike somebody "for no good reason"—

except the very good one that they feel the hostility, or insincerity, radiating from that person. This reaction is soon discouraged; it does not take long for the child to reach the "maturity" of the average adult and to lose the sense of discrimination between a decent person and a scoundrel, as long as the latter has not committed some flagrant act.

On the other hand, early in his education, the child is taught to have feelings that are not at all "his"; particularly is he taught to like people, to be uncritically friendly to them, and to smile. What education may not have accomplished is usually done by social pressure in later life. If you do not smile you are judged lacking in a "pleasing personality"—and you need to have a pleasing personality if you want to sell your services, whether as a waitress, a salesman, or a physician. Only those at the bottom of the social pyramid, who sell nothing but their physical labor, and those at the very top do not need to be particularly "pleasant." Friendliness, cheerfulness, and everything that a smile is supposed to express, become automatic responses which one turns on and off like an electric switch.[2]

To be sure, in many instances the person is aware of merely making a gesture; in most cases, however, he loses that awareness and thereby the ability to discriminate between the pseudo feeling and spontaneous friendliness.

It is not only hostility that is directly suppressed and friendliness that is killed by superimposing its counterfeit. A wide range of spontaneous emotions are suppressed and replaced by pseudo feelings. Freud has taken one such suppression and put it in the center of his whole system, namely the suppression of sex. Although I believe that the discouragement of sexual joy is not the only important suppression of spontaneous reactions but one of many, certainly its importance is not to be underrated. Its results are obvious in cases of sexual inhibitions and also in those where sex assumes a compulsive quality and is consumed like liquor or a drug, which has no particular taste but makes you forget yourself. Regardless of the one or the other effect, their suppression, because of the intensity of sexual desires, not only affects the sexual sphere but also weakens the person's courage for spontaneous expression in all other spheres.

In our society emotions in general are discouraged. While there can be no doubt that any creative thinking—as well as any other creative activity—is inseparably linked with emotion, it has become an ideal to think and to live without emotions. To be "emotional" has become synonymous with being unsound or unbalanced. By the acceptance of this standard the individual has be-

[2] As one telling illustration of the commercialization of friendliness I should like to cite *Fortune's* report on "The Howard Johnson Restaurants." (*Fortune*, September, 1940, p. 96.) Johnson employs a force of "shoppers" who go from restaurant to restaurant to watch for lapses. "Since everything is cooked on the premises according to standard recipes and measurements issued by the home office, the inspector knows how large a portion of steak he should receive and how the vegetable should taste. He also knows how long it should take for the dinner to be served and he knows the exact degree of friendliness that should be shown by the hostess and the waitress."

come greatly weakened; his thinking is impoverished and flattened. On the other hand, since emotions cannot be completely killed, they must have their existence totally apart from the intellectual side of the personality; the result is the cheap and insincere sentimentality with which movies and popular songs feed millions of emotion-starved customers.

There is one tabooed emotion that I want to mention in particular, because its suppression touches deeply on the roots of personality: the sense of tragedy. As we saw in an earlier chapter, the awareness of death and of the tragic aspect of life, whether dim or clear, is one of the basic characteristics of man. Each culture has its own way of coping with the problem of death. For those societies in which the process of individuation has progressed but little, the end of individual existence is less of a problem since the experience of individual existence itself is less developed. Death is not yet conceived as being basically different from life. Cultures in which we find a higher development of individuation have treated death according to their social and psychological structure. The Greeks put all emphasis on life and pictured death as nothing but a shadowy and dreary continuation of life. The Egyptians based their hopes on a belief in the indestructibility of the human body, at least of those whose power during life was indestructible. The Jews admitted the fact of death realistically and were able to reconcile themselves with the idea of the destruction of individual life by the vision of a state of happiness and justice ultimately to be reached by mankind in this world. Christianity has made death unreal and tried to comfort the unhappy individual by promises of a life after death. Our own era simply denies death and with it one fundamental aspect of life. Instead of allowing the awareness of death and suffering to become one of the strongest incentives for life, the basis for human solidarity, and an experience without which joy and enthusiasm lack intensity and depth, the individual is forced to repress it. But, as is always the case with repression, by being removed from sight the repressed elements do not cease to exist. Thus the fear of death lives an illegitimate existence among us. It remains alive in spite of the attempt to deny it, but being repressed it remains sterile. It is one source of the flatness of other experiences, of the restlessness pervading life, and it explains, I would venture to say, the exorbitant amount of money this nation pays for its funerals.

In the process of tabooing emotions modern psychiatry plays an ambiguous role. On the one hand its greatest representative, Freud, has broken through the fiction of the rational, purposeful character of the human mind and opened a path which allows a view into the abyss of human passions. On the other hand psychiatry, enriched by these very achievements of Freud, has made itself an instrument of the general trends in the manipulation of personality. Many psychiatrists, including psychoanalysts, have painted the picture of a "normal" personality which is never too sad, too angry, or too excited. They use words like "infantile" or "neurotic" to denounce traits or types of personalities that do not conform with the conventional pattern of a "normal" individual. This kind of influence is in a way more dangerous than the older and franker forms of name-calling. Then the individual knew at least that there was some person or some doctrine which criticized him and he could fight back. But who can fight back at "science"?

The same distortion happens to original *thinking* as happens to feelings and emotions. From the very start of education original thinking is discouraged and ready-made thoughts are put into people's heads. How this is done with young children is easy enough to see. They are filled with curiosity about the world, they want to grasp it physically as well as intellectually. They want to know the truth, since that is the safest way to orient themselves in a strange and powerful world. Instead, they are not taken seriously, and it does not matter whether this attitude takes the form of open disrespect or of the subtle condescension which is usual towards all who have no power (such as children, aged or sick people). Although this treatment by itself offers strong discouragement to independent thinking, there is a worse handicap: the insincerity— often unintentional—which is typical of the average adult's behavior toward a child. This insincerity consists partly in the fictitious picture of the world which the child is given. It is about as useful as instructions concerning life in the Arctic would be to someone who has asked how to prepare for an expedition to the Sahara Desert. Besides this general misrepresentation of the world there are the many specific lies that tend to conceal facts which, for various personal reasons, adults do not want children to know. From a bad temper, which is rationalized as justified dissatisfaction with the child's behavior, to concealment of the parents' sexual activities and their quarrels, the child is "not supposed to know" and his inquiries meet with hostile or polite discouragement.

The child thus prepared enters school and perhaps college. I want to mention briefly some of the educational methods used today which in effect further discourage original thinking. One is the emphasis on knowledge of facts, or I should rather say on information. The pathetic superstition prevails that by knowing more and more facts one arrives at knowledge of reality. Hundreds of scattered and unrelated facts are dumped into the heads of students; their time and energy are taken up by learning more and more facts so that there is little left for thinking. To be sure, thinking without a knowledge of facts remains empty and fictitious; but "information" alone can be just as much of an obstacle to thinking as the lack of it.

Another closely related way of discouraging original thinking is to regard all truth as relative.[3] Truth is made out to be a metaphysical concept, and if anyone speaks about wanting to discover the truth he is thought backward by the "progressive" thinkers of our age. Truth is declared to be an entirely subjective matter, almost a matter of taste. Scientific endeavor must be detached

[3] Cf. to this whole problem Robert S. Lynd's *Knowledge for What?* Princeton University Press, Princeton, 1939. For its philosophical aspects cf. M. Horkheimer's *Zum Rationalismusstreit in der Gegenwärtigen Philosophie*, Zeitschrift für Sozialforschung, Vol. 3, 1934, Alcan, Paris.

from subjective factors, and its aim is to look at the world without passion and interest. The scientist has to approach facts with sterilized hands as a surgeon approaches his patient. The result of this relativism, which often presents itself by the name of empiricism or positivism or which recommends itself by its concern for the correct usage of words, is that thinking loses its essential stimulus—the wishes and interests of the person who thinks; instead it becomes a machine to register "facts." Actually, just as thinking in general has developed out of the need for mastery of material life, so the quest for truth is rooted in the interests and needs of individuals and social groups. Without such interest the stimulus for seeking the truth would be lacking. There are always groups whose interest is furthered by truth, and their representatives have been the pioneers of human thought; there are other groups whose interests are furthered by concealing truth. Only in the latter case does interest prove harmful to the cause of truth. The problem, therefore, is not that there is *an* interest at stake, but *which kind* of interest is at stake. I might say that inasmuch as there is some longing for the truth in every human being, it is because every human being has some need for it.

This holds true in the first place with regard to a person's orientation in the outer world, and it holds especially true for the child. As a child, every human being passes through a state of powerlessness, and truth is one of the strongest weapons of those who have no power. But the truth is in the individual's interest not only with regard to his orientation in the outer world; his own strength depends to a great extent on his knowing the truth about himself. Illusions about oneself can become crutches useful to those who are not able to walk alone; but they increase a person's weakness. The individual's greatest strength is based on the maximum of integration of his personality, and that means also on the maximum of transparence to himself. "Know thyself" is one of the fundamental commands that aim at human strength and happiness.

In addition to the factors just mentioned there are others which actively tend to confuse whatever is left of the capacity for original thinking in the average adult. With regard to all basic questions of individual and social life, with regard to psychological, economic, political, and moral problems, a great sector of our culture has just one function—to befog the issues. One kind of smokescreen is the assertion that the problems are too complicated for the average individual to grasp. On the contrary it would seem that many of the basic issues of individual and social life are very simple, so simple, in fact. that everyone should be expected to understand them. To let them appear to be so enormously complicated that only a "specialist" can understand them, and he only in his own limited field, actually—and often intentionally—tends to discourage people from trusting their own capacity to think about those problems that really matter. The individual feels helplessly caught in a chaotic mass of data and with pathetic patience waits until the specialists have found out what to do and where to go.

The result of this kind of influence is a twofold one: one is a scepticism and cynicism towards everything which is said or printed, while the other is a childish belief in anything that a person is told with authority. This combination of cynicism and naïveté is very typical of the modern individual. Its essential result is to discourage him from doing his own thinking and deciding.

Another way of paralyzing the ability to think critically is the destruction of any kind of structuralized picture of the world. Facts lose the specific quality which they can have only as parts of a structuralized whole and retain merely an abstract, quantitative meaning; each fact is just *another* fact and all that matters is whether we know more or less. Radio, moving pictures, and newspapers have a devastating effect on this score. The announcement of the bombing of a city and the death of hundreds of people is shamelessly followed or interrupted by an advertisement for soap or wine. The same speaker with the same suggestive, ingratiating, and authoritative voice, which he has just used to impress you with the seriousness of the political situation, impresses now upon his audience the merits of the particular brand of soap which pays for the news broadcast. Newsreels let pictures of torpedoed ships be followed by those of a fashion show. Newspapers tell us the trite thoughts or breakfast habits of a debutante with the same space and seriousness they use for reporting events of scientific or artistic importance. Because of all this we cease to be genuinely related to what we hear. We cease to be excited, our emotions and our critical judgment become hampered, and eventually our attitude to what is going on in the world assumes a quality of flatness and indifference. In the name of "freedom" life loses all structure; it is composed of many little pieces, each separate from the other and lacking any sense as a whole. The individual is left alone with these pieces like a child with a puzzle; the difference, however, is that the child knows what a house is and therefore can recognize the parts of the house in the little pieces he is playing with, whereas the adult does not see the meaning of the "whole," the pieces of which come into his hands. He is bewildered and afraid and just goes on gazing at his little meaningless pieces.

What has been said about the lack of "originality" in feeling and thinking holds true also of the act of *willing*. To recognize this is particularly difficult; modern man seems, if anything, to have too many wishes and his only problem seems to be that, although he knows what he wants, he cannot have it. All our energy is spent for the purpose of getting what we want, and most people never question the premise of this activity: that they know their true wants. They do not stop to think whether the aims they are pursuing are something they themselves want. In school they want to have good marks, as adults they want to be more and more successful, to make more money, to have more prestige, to buy a better car, to go places, and so on. Yet when they do stop to think in the midst of all this frantic activity, this question may come to their minds: "If I do get this new job, if I get this better car, if I can take this trip —what then? What is the use of it all? Is it really I who wants all this? Am I not running after some goal which is supposed to make me happy and which eludes me as soon as I have reached it?" These questions, when they arise, are frightening, for they question the very basis on which man's whole activity is built, his knowledge of what he wants. People tend, therefore, to get rid as soon as possible of these disturbing thoughts. They feel that they have been bothered by these questions because they were tired or depressed—and they go on in the pursuit of the aims which they believe are their own.

Yet all this bespeaks a dim realization of the truth—the truth that modern man lives under the illusion that he knows what he wants, while he actually wants what he is *supposed* to want. In order to accept this it is necessary to realize that to know what one really wants is not comparatively easy, as most people think, but one of the most difficult problems any human being has to solve. It is a task we frantically try to avoid by accepting ready-made goals as though they were our own. Modern man is ready to take great risks when he tries to achieve the aims which are supposed to be "his"; but he is deeply afraid of taking the risk and the responsibility of giving himself his own aims. Intense activity is often mistaken for evidence of self-determined action, although we know that it may well be no more spontaneous than the behavior of an actor or a person hypnotized. When the general plot of the play is handed out, each actor can act vigorously the role he is assigned and even make up his lines and certain details of the action by himself. Yet he is only playing a role that has been handed over to him.

The particular difficulty in recognizing to what extent our wishes—and our thoughts and feelings as well—are not really our own but put into us from the outside, is closely linked up with the problem of authority and freedom. In the course of modern history the authority of the Church has been replaced by that of the State, that of the State by that of conscience, and in our era, the latter has been replaced by the anonymous authority of common sense and public opinion as instruments of conformity. Because we have freed ourselves of the older overt forms of authority, we do not see that we have become the prey of a new kind of authority. We have become automatons who live under the illusion of being self-willing individuals. This illusion helps the individual to remain unaware of his insecurity, but this is all the help such an illusion can give. Basically the self of the individual is weakened, so that he feels powerless and extremely insecure. He lives in a world to which he has lost genuine relatedness and in which everybody and everything has become instrumentalized, where he has become a part of the machine that his hands have built. He thinks, feels, and wills what he believes he is supposed to think, feel, and will; in this very process he loses his self upon which all genuine security of a free individual must be built.

The loss of the self has increased the necessity to conform, for it results in a profound doubt of one's own identity. If I am nothing but what I believe I am supposed to be—who am "I"? We have seen how the doubt about one's own self started with the breakdown of the medieval order in which the individual had had an unquestionable place in a fixed order. The identity of the individual has been a major problem of modern philosophy since Descartes. Today we take for granted that we are we. Yet the doubt about ourselves still exists, or has ever grown. In his plays Pirandello has given expression to this feeling of modern man. He starts with the question: Who am I? What proof have I for my own identity other than the continuation of my physical self? His answer is not like Descartes'—the affirmation of the individual self—but its denial: I have no identity, there is no self excepting the one which is the reflex of what others expect me to be: I am "as you desire me."

This loss of identity then makes it still more imperative to conform; it means that one can be sure of oneself only if one lives up to the expectations of others. If we do not live up to this picture we not only risk disapproval and increased isolation, but we risk losing the identity of our personality, which means jeopardizing sanity.

By conforming with the expectations of others, by not being different, these doubts about one's own identity are silenced and a certain security is gained. However, the price paid is high. Giving up spontaneity and individuality results in a thwarting of life. Psychologically the automaton, while being alive biologically, is dead emotionally and mentally. While he goes through the motions of living, his life runs through his hands like sand. Behind a front of satisfaction and optimism modern man is deeply unhappy; as a matter of fact, he is on the verge of desperation. He desperately clings to the notion of individuality; he wants to be "different," and he has no greater recommendation of anything than that "it is different." We are informed of the individual name of the railroad clerk we buy our ticket from; handbags, playing cards, and portable radios are "personalized," by having the initials of the owner put on them. All this indicates the hunger for "difference" and yet these are almost the last vestiges of individuality that are left. Modern man is starved for life. But since, being an automaton, he cannot experience life in the sense of spontaneous activity he takes as surrogate any kind of excitement and thrill: the thrill of drinking, of sports, of vicariously living the excitements of fictitious persons on the screen.

What then is the meaning of freedom for modern man?

He has become free from the external bonds that would prevent him from doing and thinking as he sees fit. He would be free to act according to his own will, if he knew what he wanted, thought, and felt. But he does not know. He conforms to anonymous authorities and adopts a self which is not his. The more he does this, the more powerless he feels, the more is he forced to conform. In spite of a veneer of optimism and initiative, modern man is overcome by a profound feeling of powerlessness which makes him gaze toward approaching catastrophes as though he were paralyzed.

Looked at superficially, people appear to function well enough in economic and social life; yet it would be dangerous to overlook the deep-seated unhappiness behind that comforting veneer. If life loses its meaning because it is not lived, man becomes desperate. People do not die quietly from physical starvation; they do not die quietly from psychic starvation either. If we look only at the economic needs as far as the "normal" person is concerned, if we do not see the unconscious suffering of the average automatized person, then we fail to see the danger that threatens our culture from its human basis: the readiness to accept any ideology and any leader, if only he promises excitement and offers a political structure and symbols which allegedly give meaning and order to an individual's life. The despair of the human automaton is fertile soil for the political purposes of Fascism.

❦ ❦ ❦

*Adam Smith*

# Of the Wages of Labour[1]

THE produce of labour constitutes the natural recompense or wages of labour.

In that original state of things, which precedes both the appropriation of land and the accumulation of stock, the whole produce of labour belongs to the labourer. He has neither landlord nor master to share with him.

Had this state continued, the wages of labour would have augmented with all those improvements in its productive powers to which the division of labour gives occasion. All things would gradually have become cheaper. They would have been produced by a smaller quantity of labour; and as the commodities produced by equal quantities of labour would naturally in this state of things be exchanged for one another, they would have been purchased likewise with the produce of a smaller quantity. . . .

But this original state of things, in which the labourer enjoyed the whole produce of his own labour, could not last beyond the first introduction of the appropriation of land and the accumulation of stock. It was at an end, therefore, long before the most considerable improvements were made in the productive powers of labour, and it would be to no purpose to trace further what might have been its effects upon the recompense or wages of labour.

· As soon as land becomes private property, the landlord demands a share of almost all the produce which the labourer can either raise, or collect from it. His rent makes the first deduction from the produce of the labour which is employed upon land.

It seldom happens that the person who tills the ground has wherewithal to maintain himself till he reaps the harvest. His maintenance is generally advanced to him from the stock of a master, the farmer who employs him, and who would have no interest to employ him, unless he was to share in the produce of his labour, or unless his stock was to be replaced to him with a profit. This profit makes a second deduction from the produce of the labour which is employed upon land.

[1] *The Wealth of Nations* (New York: E. P. Dutton & Co., Inc., 1937, Everyman's Library), pp. 57-67, 69-72, with omissions. First printed in 1776.

The produce of almost all other labour is liable to the like deduction of profit. In all arts and manufactures the greater part of the workmen stand in need of a master to advance them the materials of their work, and their wages and maintenance till it be completed. He shares in the produce of their labour, or in the value which it adds to the materials upon which it is bestowed; and in this share consists his profit. . . .

What are the common wages of labour, depends everywhere upon the contract usually made between those two parties, whose interests are by no means the same. The workmen desire to get as much, the masters to give as little as possible. The former are disposed to combine in order to raise, the latter in order to lower the wages of labour.

It is not, however, difficult to foresee which of the two parties must, upon all ordinary occasions, have the advantage in the dispute, and force the other into a compliance with their terms. The masters, being fewer in number, can combine much more easily; and the law, besides, authorises, or at least does not prohibit their combinations, while it prohibits those of the workmen. We have no acts of parliament against combining to lower the price of work; but many against combining to raise it. In all such disputes the masters can hold out much longer. A landlord, a farmer, a master manufacturer, a merchant, though they did not employ a single workman, could generally live a year or two upon the stocks which they have already acquired. Many workmen could not subsist a week, few could subsist a month, and scarce any a year without employment. In the long-run the workman may be as necessary to his master as his master is to him; but the necessity is not so immediate.

We rarely hear, it has been said, of the combinations of masters, though frequently of those of workmen. But whoever imagines, upon this account, that masters rarely combine, is as ignorant of the world as of the subject. Masters are always and everywhere in a sort of tacit, but constant and uniform combination, not to raise the wages of labour above their actual rate. . . . Masters, too, sometimes enter into particular combinations to sink the wages of labour even below this rate. These are always conducted with the utmost silence and secrecy, till the moment of execution, and when the workmen yield, as they sometimes do, without resistance, though severely felt by them, they are never heard of by other people. Such combinations, however, are frequently resisted by a contrary defensive combination of the workmen; who sometimes too, without any provocation of this kind, combine of their own accord to raise the price of their labour. Their usual pretences are, sometimes the high price of provisions; sometimes the great profit which their masters make by their work. But whether their combinations be offensive or defensive, they are always abundantly heard of. In order to bring the point to a speedy decision, they have always recourse to the loudest clamour, and sometimes to the most shocking violence and outrage. They are desperate, and act with the folly and extravagance of desperate men, who must either starve, or frighten their masters into an immediate compliance with their demands. The masters upon these occasions are just as clamorous upon the other side, and never cease to call aloud for the assistance of the civil magistrate, and the rigorous execution of those laws which have been enacted with so much severity against the combinations of servants, labourers, and journeymen. The workmen, accordingly, very seldom derive any advantage from the violence of those tumultuous combinations, which, partly from the interposition of the civil magistrate, partly from the superior steadiness of the masters, partly from the necessity which the greater part of the workmen are under of submitting for the sake of present subsistence, generally end in nothing, but the punishment or ruin of the ringleaders.

But though in disputes with their workmen, masters must generally have the advantage, there is, however, a certain rate below which it seems impossible to reduce, for any considerable time, the ordinary wages even of the lowest species of labour.

A man must always live by his work, and his wages must at least be sufficient to maintain him. They must even upon most occasions be somewhat more; otherwise it would be impossible for him to bring up a family, and the race of such workmen could not last beyond the first generation. . . .

There are certain circumstances, however, which sometimes give the labourers an advantage, and enable them to raise their wages considerably above this rate; evidently the lowest which is consistent with common humanity.

When in any country the demand for those who live by wages, labourers, journeymen, servants of every kind, is continually increasing; when every year furnishes employment for a greater number than had been employed the year before, the workmen have no occasion to combine in order to raise their wages. The scarcity of hands occasions a competition among masters, who bid against one another, in order to get workmen, and thus voluntarily break through the natural combination of masters not to raise wages.

The demand for those who live by wages, it is evident, cannot increase but in proportion to the increase of the funds which are destined for the payment of wages. These funds are of two kinds; first, the revenue which is over and above what is necessary for the maintenance; and, secondly, the stock which is over and above what is necessary for the employment of their masters. . . .

It is not the actual greatness of national wealth, but its continual increase, which occasions a rise in the wages of labour. It is not, accordingly, in the richest countries, but in the most thriving, or in those which are growing rich the fastest, that the wages of labour are highest. England is certainly, in the present times, a much richer country than any part of North America. The wages of labour, however, are much higher in North America than in any part of England. . . . The price of provisions is everywhere in North America much lower than in England. A dearth has never been known there. In the worst seasons they have always had a sufficiency for themselves, though less for exportation. If the money price of labour, therefore, be higher than it is anywhere in the mother country, its real price, the real command of the necessaries and conveniencies of life which it conveys to the labourer must be higher in a still greater proportion.

But though North America is not yet so rich as England, it is much more thriving, and advancing with much greater rapidity to the further acquisition of riches. The most decisive mark of the prosperity of any country is the increase of the number of its inhabitants. In Great Britain, and most other European countries, they are not supposed to double in less than five hundred years. In the British colonies in North America, it has been found that they double in twenty or five-and-twenty years. Nor in the present times is this increase principally owing to the continual importation of new inhabitants, but to the great multiplication of the species. . . . The value of children is the greatest of all encouragements to marriage. We cannot, therefore, wonder that the people in North America should generally marry very young. Notwithstanding the great increase occasioned by such early marriages, there is a continual complaint of the scarcity of hands in North America. The demand for labourers, the funds destined for maintaining them, increase, it seems, still faster than they can find labourers to employ.

Though the wealth of a country should be very great, yet if it has been long stationary, we must not expect to find the wages of labour very high in it. The funds destined for the payment of wages, the revenue and stock of its inhabitants, may be of the greatest extent; but if they have continued for several centuries of the same, or very nearly of the same extent, the number of labourers employed every year could easily supply, and even more than supply, the number wanted the following year. There could seldom be any scarcity of hands, nor could the masters be obliged to bid against one another in order to get them. The hands, on the contrary, would, in this case, naturally multiply beyond their employment. There would be a constant scarcity of employment, and the labourers would be obliged to bid against one another in order to get it. If in such a country the wages of labour had ever been more than sufficient to maintain the labourer, and to enable him to bring up a family, the competition of the labourers and the interest of the masters would soon reduce them to this lowest rate which is consistent with common humanity. China has been long one of the richest, that is, one of the most fertile, best cultivated, most industrious, and most populous countries in the world. It seems, however, to have been long stationary. Marco Polo, who visited it more than five hundred years ago, describes its cultivation, industry, and populousness, almost in the same terms in which they are described by travellers in the present times. It had perhaps, even long before his time, acquired that full complement of riches which the nature of its laws and institutions permits it to acquire. The accounts of all travellers, inconsistent in many other respects, agree in the low wages of labour, and in the difficulty which a labourer finds in bringing up a family in China. . . . .

China, however, though it may perhaps stand still, does not seem to go backwards. Its towns are nowhere deserted by their inhabitants. The lands which had once been cultivated are nowhere neglected. The same or very nearly the same annual labour must therefore continue to be performed, and the funds destined for maintaining it must not, consequently, be sensibly diminished. The lowest class of labourers, therefore, notwithstanding their scanty subsistence, must some way or another make shift to continue their race so far as to keep up their usual numbers.

But it would be otherwise in a country where the funds destined for the maintenance of labour were sensibly decaying. Every year the demand for servants and labourers would, in all the different classes of employments, be less than it had been the year before. Many who had been bred in the superior classes, not being able to find employment in their own business, would be glad to seek it in the lowest. The lowest class being not only over-stocked with its own workmen, but with the overflowings of all the other classes, the competition for employment would be so great in it, as to reduce the wages of labour to the most miserable and scanty subsistence of the labourer. Many would not be able to find employment even upon these hard terms, but would either starve, or be driven to seek a subsistence either by begging, or by the perpetration perhaps of the greatest enormities. Want, famine, and mortality would immediately prevail in that class, and from thence extend themselves to all the superior classes, till the number of inhabitants in the country was reduced to what could easily be maintained by the revenue and stock which remained in it, and which had escaped either the tyranny or calamity which had destroyed the rest. . . .

The liberal reward of labour, therefore, as it is the necessary effect, so it is the natural symptom of increasing national wealth. The scanty maintenance of the labouring poor, on the other hand, is the natural symptom that things are at a stand, and their starving condition that they are going fast backwards. . . .

The real recompense of labour, the real quantity of the necessaries and conveniencies of life which it can procure to the labourer, has, during the course of the present century, increased perhaps in a still greater proportion than its money price. Not only grain has become somewhat cheaper, but many other things from which the industrious poor derive an agreeable and whole-some variety of food have become a great deal cheaper. . . . The common complaint that luxury extends itself even to the lowest ranks of the people, and that the labouring poor will not now be contented with the same food, clothing, and lodging which satisfied them in former times, may convince us that it is not the money price of labour only, but its real recompense, which has augmented.

Is this improvement in the circumstances of the lower ranks of the people to be regarded as an advantage or as an inconvenience to the society? The answer seems at first sight abundantly plain. Servants, labourers, and workmen of different kinds, make up the far greater part of every great political society. But what improves the circumstances of the greater part can never be regarded as an inconveniency to the whole. No society can surely be flourishing and happy, of which the far greater part of the members are poor and miserable. It is but equity, besides, that they who feed, clothe, and lodge the whole body of the people, should have such a share of the produce of their own labour as to be themselves tolerably well fed, clothed, and lodged. . . .

❦ ❦ ❦

*John Maynard Keynes*

# Gold-Mining[1]

WHEN involuntary unemployment exists, the marginal disutility of labour is necessarily less than the utility of the marginal product. Indeed it may be much less. For a man who has been long unemployed some measure of labour, instead of involving disutility, may have a positive utility. If this is accepted, the above reasoning shows how "wasteful" loan expenditure may nevertheless enrich the community on balance. Pyramid-building, earthquakes, even wars may serve to increase wealth, if the education of our statesmen on the principles of the classical economics stands in the way of anything better.

It is curious how common sense, wriggling for an escape from absurd conclusions, has been apt to reach a preference for *wholly* "wasteful" forms of loan expenditure rather than for *partly* wasteful forms, which, because they are not wholly wasteful, tend to be judged on strict "business" principles. For example, unemployment relief financed by loans is more readily accepted than the financing of improvements at a charge below the current rate of interest; whilst the form of digging holes in the ground known as gold-mining, which not only adds nothing whatever to the real wealth of the world but involves the disutility of labour, is the most acceptable of all solutions.

If the Treasury were to fill old bottles with banknotes, bury them at suitable depths in disused coal-mines which are then filled up to the surface with town rubbish, and leave it to private enterprise on well-tried principles of *laissez-faire* to dig the notes up again (the right to do so being obtained, of course, by tendering for leases of the note-bearing territory), there need be no more unemployment and, with the help of the repercussions, the real income of the community, and its capital wealth also, would probably become a good deal greater than it actually is. It would, indeed, be more sensible to build houses and the like; but if there are political and practical difficulties in the way of this, the above would be better than nothing.

[1] From *The General Theory of Employment, Interest, and Money* by John Maynard Keynes. Reprinted by permission of Harcourt, Brace and Company, Inc.

The analogy between this expedient and the gold-mines of the real world is complete. At periods when gold is available at suitable depths experience shows that the real wealth of the world increases rapidly; and when but little of it is so available, our wealth suffers stagnation or decline. Thus gold-mines are of the greatest value and importance to civilisation. Just as wars have been the only form of large-scale loan expenditure which statesmen have thought justifiable, so gold-mining is the only pretext for digging holes in the ground which has recommended itself to bankers as sound finance; and each of these activities has played its part in progress—failing something better. To mention a detail, the tendency in slumps for the price of gold to rise in terms of labour and materials aids eventual recovery, because it increases the depth at which gold-digging pays and lowers the minimum grade of ore which is payable.

In addition to the probable effect of increased supplies of gold on the rate of interest, gold-mining is for two reasons a highly practical form of investment, if we are precluded from increasing employment by means which at the same time increase our stock of useful wealth. In the first place, owing to the gambling attractions which it offers it is carried on without too close a regard to the ruling rate of interest. In the second place the result, namely, the increased stock of gold, does not, as in other cases, have the effect of diminishing its marginal utility. Since the value of a house depends on its utility, every house which is built serves to diminish the prospective rents obtainable from further house-building and therefore lessens the attraction of further similar investment unless the rate of interest is falling *pari passu*. But the fruits of gold-mining do not suffer from this disadvantage, and a check can only come through a rise of the wage-unit in terms of gold, which is not likely to occur unless and until employment is substantially better. Moreover, there is no subsequent reverse effect on account of provision for user and supplementary costs, as in the case of less durable forms of wealth.

Ancient Egypt was doubly fortunate, and doubtless owed to this its fabled wealth, in that it possessed *two* activities, namely, pyramid-building as well as the search for the precious metals, the fruits of which, since they could not serve the needs of man by being consumed, did not stale with abundance. The Middle Ages built cathedrals and sang dirges. Two pyramids, two masses for the dead, are twice as good as one; but not so two railways from London to York. Thus we are so sensible, have schooled ourselves to so close a semblance of prudent financiers, taking careful thought before we add to the "financial" burdens of posterity by building them houses to live in, that we have no such easy escape from the sufferings of unemployment. We have to accept them as an inevitable result of applying to the conduct of the State the maxims which are best calculated to "enrich" an individual by enabling him to pile up claims to enjoyment which he does not intend to exercise at any definite time.

🌺 🌺 🌺

*Henry David Thoreau*

# On the Duty of Civil Disobedience[1]

I HEARTILY accept the motto,—"That government is best which governs least";
and I should like to see it acted up to more rapidly and systematically. Carried
out, it finally amounts to this, which also I believe,—"That government is best
which governs not at all"; and when men are prepared for it, that will be the
kind of government which they will have. Government is at best but an expedient; but most governments are usually, and all governments are sometimes,
inexpedient. The objections which have been brought against a standing army,
and they are many and weighty, and deserve to prevail, may also at last be
brought against a standing government. The standing army is only an arm of
the standing government. The government itself, which is only the mode which
the people have chosen to execute their will, is equally liable to be abused and
perverted before the people can act through it. Witness the present Mexican
war, the work of comparatively a few individuals using the standing government as their tool; for, in the outset, the people would not have consented to
this measure.

This American government,—what is it but a tradition, though a recent one,
endeavoring to transmit itself unimpaired to posterity, but each instant losing
some of its integrity? It has not the vitality and force of a single living man;
for a single man can bend it to his will. It is a sort of wooden gun to the people
themselves. But it is not the less necessary for this; for the people must have
some complicated machinery or other, and hear its din, to satisfy that idea of
government which they have. Governments show us how successfully men
can be imposed on, even impose on themselves, for their own advantage. It is
excellent, we must all allow. Yet this government never of itself furthered any
enterprise, but by the alacrity with which it got out of its way. *It* does not keep
the country free. *It* does not settle the West. *It* does not educate. The character
inherent in the American people has done all that has been accomplished; and
it would have done somewhat more, if the government had not sometimes
got in its way. For government is an expedient by which men would fain
succeed in letting one another alone; and, as has been said, when it is most
expedient, the governed are most let alone by it. Trade and commerce, if they
were not made of India-rubber, would never manage to bounce over the
obstacles which legislators are continually putting in their way; and, if one
were to judge these men wholly by the effects of their actions and not partly
by their intentions, they would deserve to be classed and punished with those
mischievous persons who put obstructions on the railroads.

[1] From Norman Holmes Pearson, ed., *Walden* and *On the Duty of Civil Disobedience* (New York: Rinehart & Co. Inc., 1948), pp. 281-304, with omissions. "Rinehart
Editions." First printed in 1849.

But, to speak practically and as a citizen, unlike those who call themselves no-government men, I ask for, not at once no government, but *at once* a better government. Let every man make known what kind of government would command his respect, and that will be one step toward obtaining it.

After all, the practical reason why, when the power is once in the hands of the people, a majority are permitted, and for a long period continue, to rule is not because they are most likely to be in the right, nor because this seems fairest to the minority, but because they are physically the strongest. But a government in which the majority rule in all cases cannot be based on justice, even as far as men understand it. Can there not be a government in which majorities do not virtually decide right and wrong, but conscience?—in which majorities decide only those questions to which the rule of expediency is applicable? Must the citizen ever for a moment, or in the least degree, resign his conscience to the legislator? Why has every man a conscience, then? I think that we should be men first, and subjects afterward. It is not desirable to cultivate a respect for the law, so much as for the right. The only obligation which I have a right to assume is to do at any time what I think right. It is truly enough said, that a corporation has no conscience; but a corporation of conscientious men is a corporation *with* a conscience. Law never made men a whit more just; and, by means of their respect for it, even the well-disposed are daily made the agents of injustice. A common and natural result of an undue respect for law is, that you may see a file of soldiers, colonel, captain, corporal, privates, powder-monkeys, and all, marching in admirable order over hill and dale to the wars, against their wills, ay, against their common sense and consciences, which makes it very steep marching indeed, and produces a palpitation of the heart. They have no doubt that it is a damnable business in which they are concerned; they are all peaceably inclined. Now, what are they? Men at all? or small movable forts and magazines, at the service of some unscrupulous man in power? Visit the Navy-Yard, and behold a marine, such a man as an American government can make, or such as it can make a man with its black arts,—a mere shadow and reminiscence of humanity, a man laid out alive and standing, and already, as one may say, buried under arms with funeral accompaniments, though it may be,—

> Not a drum was heard, not a funeral note,
>     As his corpse to the rampart we hurried;
> Not a soldier discharged his farewell shot
>     O'er the grave where our hero we buried.

The mass of men serve the state thus, not as men mainly, but as machines, with their bodies. They are the standing army, and the militia, jailors, constables, posse comitatus, etc. In most cases there is no free exercise whatever of the judgment or of the moral sense; but they put themselves on a level with wood and earth and stones; and wooden men can perhaps be manufactured that will serve the purpose as well. Such command no more respect than men of straw or a lump of dirt. They have the same sort of worth only as horses and dogs. Yet such as these even are commonly esteemed good citizens. Others—as most legislators, politicians, lawyers, ministers, and office-holders—serve the state chiefly with their heads; and, as they rarely make any moral distinctions, they are as likely to serve the Devil, without *intending* it, as God. A very few, as heroes, patriots, martyrs, reformers in the great sense, and *men*, serve the state with their consciences also, and so necessarily resist it for the most part; and they are commonly treated as enemies by it. A wise man will only be useful as a man, and will not submit to be "clay," and "stop a hole to keep the wind away," but leave that office to his dust at least:—

> I am too high-born to be propertied,
> To be a secondary at control,
> Or useful serving-man and instrument
> To any sovereign state throughout the world.

He who gives himself entirely to his fellow-men appears to them useless and selfish; but he who gives himself partially to them is pronounced a benefactor and philanthropist.

How does it become a man to behave toward this American government to-day? I answer, that he cannot without disgrace be associated with it. I cannot for an instant recognize that political organization as *my* government which is the *slave's* government also.

All men recognize the right of revolution; that is, the right to refuse allegiance to, and to resist, the government, when its tyranny or its inefficiency are great and unendurable. But almost all say that such is not the case now. But such was the case, they think, in the Revolution of '75. If one were to tell me that this was a bad government because it taxed certain foreign commodities brought to its ports, it is most probable that I should not make an ado about it, for I can do without them. All machines have their friction; and possibly this does enough good to counterbalance the evil. At any rate, it is a great evil to make a stir about it. But when the friction comes to have its machine, and oppression and robbery are organized, I say, let us not have such a machine any longer. In other words, when a sixth of the population of a nation which has undertaken to be the refuge of liberty are slaves, and a whole country is unjustly overrun and conquered by a foreign army, and subjected to military law, I think that it is not too soon for honest men to rebel and revolutionize. What makes this duty the more urgent is the fact that the country so overrun is not our own, but ours is the invading army. . . .

> A drab of state, a cloth-o'-silver slut,
> To have her train borne up, and her soul trail in the dirt.

Practically speaking, the opponents to a reform in Massachusetts are not a hundred thousand politicians at the South, but a hundred thousand merchants and farmers here, who are more interested in commerce and agriculture than they are in humanity, and are not prepared to do justice to the slave and to

Mexico, *cost what it may*. I quarrel not with far-off foes, but with those who, near at home, coöperate with, and do the bidding of, those far away, and without whom the latter would be harmless. We are accustomed to say, that the mass of men are unprepared; but improvement is slow, because the few are not materially wiser or better than the many. It is not so important that many should be as good as you, as that there be some absolute goodness somewhere; for that will leaven the whole lump. There are thousands who are *in opinion* opposed to slavery and to the war, who yet in effect do nothing to put an end to them; who, esteeming themselves children of Washington and Franklin, sit down with their hands in their pockets, and say that they know not what to do, and do nothing; who even postpone the question of freedom to the question of free-trade, and quietly read the prices-current along with the latest advices from Mexico, after dinner, and, it may be, fall asleep over them both. What is the price-current of an honest man and patriot to-day? They hesitate, and they regret, and sometimes they petition; but they do nothing in earnest and with effect. They will wait, well disposed, for others to remedy the evil, that they may no longer have it to regret. At most, they give only a cheap vote, and a feeble countenance and God-speed, to the right, as it goes by them. There are nine hundred and ninety-nine patrons of virtue to one virtuous man. But it is easier to deal with the real possessor of a thing than with the temporary guardian of it.

All voting is a sort of gaming, like checkers or backgammon, with a slight moral tinge to it, a playing with right and wrong, with moral questions; and betting naturally accompanies it. The character of the voters is not staked. I cast my vote, perchance, as I think right; but I am not vitally concerned that that right should prevail. I am willing to leave it to the majority. Its obligation, therefore, never exceeds that of expediency. Even voting *for the right* is *doing* nothing for it. It is only expressing to men feebly your desire that it should prevail. A wise man will not leave the right to the mercy of chance, nor wish it to prevail through the power of the majority. There is but little virtue in the action of masses of men. When the majority shall at length vote for the abolition of slavery, it will be because they are indifferent to slavery, or because there is but little slavery left to be abolished by their vote. *They* will then be the only slaves. Only *his* vote can hasten the abolition of slavery who asserts his own freedom by his vote.

I hear of a convention to be held at Baltimore, or elsewhere, for the selection of a candidate for the Presidency, made up chiefly of editors, and men who are politicians by profession; but I think, what is it to any independent, intelligent, and respectable man what decision they may come to? Shall we not have the advantage of his wisdom and honesty, nevertheless? Can we not count upon some independent votes? Are there not many individuals in the country who do not attend conventions? But no: I find that the respectable man, so called, has immediately drifted from his position, and despairs of his country, when his country has more reason to despair of him. He forthwith adopts one of the candidates thus selected as the only *available* one, thus proving that he is himself *available* for any purposes of the demagogue. His vote is of no more worth than that of any unprincipled foreigner or hireling native, who may have been bought. O for a man who is a *man*, and, as my neighbor says, has a bone in his back which you cannot pass your hand through! Our statistics are at fault: the population has been returned too large. How many *men* are there to a square thousand miles in this country? Hardly one. Does not America offer any inducement for men to settle here? The American has dwindled into an Odd Fellow,—one who may be known by the development of his organ of gregariousness, and a manifest lack of intellect and cheerful self-reliance; whose first and chief concern, on coming into the world, is to see that the Almshouses are in good repair; and, before yet he has lawfully donned the virile garb, to collect a fund for the support of the widows and orphans that may be; who, in short, ventures to live only by the aid of the Mutual Insurance company, which has promised to bury him decently.

It is not a man's duty, as a matter of course, to devote himself to the eradication of any, even the most enormous wrong; he may still properly have other concerns to engage him; but it is his duty, at least, to wash his hands of it, and, if he gives it no thought longer, not to give it practically his support. If I devote myself to other pursuits and contemplations, I must first see, at least, that I do not pursue them sitting upon another man's shoulders. I must get off him first, that he may pursue his contemplations too. See what gross inconsistency is tolerated. I have heard some of my townsmen say, "I should like to have them order me out to help put down an insurrection of the slaves, or to march to Mexico;—see if I would go"; and yet these very men have each, directly by their allegiance, and so indirectly, at least, by their money, furnished a substitute. The soldier is applauded who refuses to serve in an unjust war by those who do not refuse to sustain the unjust government which makes the war; is applauded by those whose own act and authority he disregards and sets at naught; as if the state were penitent to that degree that it hired one to scourge it while it sinned, but not to that degree that it left off sinning for a moment. Thus, under the name of Order and Civil Government, we are all made at last to pay homage to and support our own meanness. After the first blush of sin comes its indifference; and from immoral it becomes, as it were, *un*moral, and not quite unnecessary to that life which we have made.

The broadest and most prevalent error requires the most disinterested virtue to sustain it. The slight reproach to which the virtue of patriotism is commonly liable, the noble are most likely to incur. Those who, while they disapprove of the character and measures of a government, yield to it their allegiance and support are undoubtedly its most conscientious supporters, and so frequently the most serious obstacles to reform. Some are petitioning the state to dissolve the Union, to disregard the requisitions of the President. Why do they not dissolve it themselves—the union between themselves and the state,—and refuse to pay their quota into its treasury? Do not they stand in the same relation to the state that the state does to the Union? And have not the same reasons prevented the state from resisting the Union which have prevented them from resisting the state?

How can a man be satisfied to entertain an opinion merely, and enjoy *it*? Is there any enjoyment in it, if his opinion is that he is aggrieved? If you are cheated out of a single dollar by your neighbor, you do not rest satisfied with knowing that you are cheated, or with saying that you are cheated, or even with petitioning him to pay you your due; but you take effectual steps at once to obtain the full amount, and see that you are never cheated again. Action from principle, the perception and the performance of right, changes things and relations; it is essentially revolutionary, and does not consist wholly with anything which was. It not only divides states and churches, it divides families; ay, it divides the *individual*, separating the diabolical in him from the divine.

Unjust laws exist: shall we be content to obey them, or shall we endeavor to amend them, and obey them until we have succeeded, or shall we transgress them at once? Men generally, under such a government as this, think that they ought to wait until they have persuaded the majority to alter them. They think that, if they should resist, the remedy would be worse than the evil. But it is the fault of the government itself that the remedy *is* worse than the evil. *It* makes it worse. Why is it not more apt to anticipate and provide for reform? Why does it not cherish its wise minority? Why does it cry and resist before it is hurt? Why does it not encourage its citizens to be on the alert to point out its faults, and *do* better than it would have them? Why does it always crucify Christ, and excommunicate Copernicus and Luther, and pronounce Washington and Franklin rebels?

One would think, that a deliberate and practical denial of its authority was the only offense never contemplated by government; else, why has it not assigned its definite, its suitable and proportionate penalty? If a man who has no property refuses but once to earn nine shillings for the state, he is put in prison for a period unlimited by any law that I know, and determined only by the discretion of those who placed him there; but if he should steal ninety times nine shillings from the state, he is soon permitted to go at large again.

If the injustice is part of the necessary friction of the machine of government, let it go, let it go: perchance it will wear smooth,—certainly the machine will wear out. If the injustice has a spring, or a pulley, or a rope, or a crank, exclusively for itself, then perhaps you may consider whether the remedy will not be worse than the evil; but if it is of such a nature that it requires you to be the agent of injustice to another, then, I say, break the law. Let your life be a counter friction to stop the machine. What I have to do is to see, at any rate, that I do not lend myself to the wrong which I condemn.

As for adopting the ways which the state has provided for remedying the evil, I know not of such ways. They take too much time, and a man's life will be gone. I have other affairs to attend to. I came into this world, not chiefly to make this a good place to live in, but to live in it, be it good or bad.

A man has not everything to do, but something; and because he cannot do *everything*, it is not necessary that he should do *something* wrong. It is not my business to be petitioning the Governor or the Legislature any more than it is theirs to petition me; and if they should not hear my petition, what should I do then? But in this case the state has provided no way: its very Constitution is the evil. This may seem to be harsh and stubborn and unconciliatory; but it is to treat with the utmost kindness and consideration the only spirit that can appreciate or deserves it. So is all change for the better, like birth and death, which convulse the body.

I do not hesitate to say, that those who call themselves Abolitionists should at once effectually withdraw their support, both in person and property, from the government of Massachusetts and not wait till they constitute a majority of one, before they suffer the right to prevail through them. I think that it is enough if they have God on their side, without waiting for that other one. Moreover, any man more right than his neighbors constitutes a majority of one already.

I meet this American government, or its representative, the state government, directly, and face to face, once a year—no more—in the person of its tax-gatherer; this is the only mode in which a man situated as I am necessarily meets it; and it then says distinctly, Recognize me; and the simplest, most effectual, and, in the present posture of affairs, the indispensablest mode of treating with it on this head, of expressing your little satisfaction with and love for it, is to deny it then. My civil neighbor, the tax-gatherer, is the very man I have to deal with,—for it is, after all, with men and not with parchment that I quarrel,—and he has voluntarily chosen to be an agent of the government. How shall he ever know well what he is and does as an officer of the government, or as a man, until he is obliged to consider whether he shall treat me, his neighbor, for whom he has respect, as a neighbor and well-disposed man, or as a maniac and disturber of the peace, and see if he can get over this obstruction to his neighborliness without a ruder and more impetuous thought or speech corresponding with his action. I know this well, that if one thousand, if one hundred, if ten men whom I could name,—if ten *honest* men only,—ay, if *one* HONEST man, in this State of Massachusetts, *ceasing to hold slaves*, were actually to withdraw from this copartnership, and be locked up in the county jail therefor, it would be the abolition of slavery in America. For it matters not how small the beginning may seem to be: what is once well done is done forever. But we love better to talk about it: that we say is our mission. Reform keeps many scores of newspapers in its service, but not one man. If my esteemed neighbor, the State's ambassador, who will devote his days to the settlement of the question of human rights in the Council Chamber, instead of being threatened with the prisons of Carolina, were to sit down the prisoner of Massachusetts, that State which is so anxious to foist the sin of slavery upon her sister,—though at present she can discover only an act of inhospitality to be the ground of a quarrel with her,—the Legislature would not wholly waive the subject the following winter.

Under a government which imprisons any unjustly, the true place for a just man is also a prison. The proper place to-day, the only place which Massachusetts has provided for her freer and less desponding spirits, is in her prisons, to be put out and locked out of the State by her own act, as they have already put themselves out by their principles. It is there that the fugitive slave, and the Mexican prisoner on parole, and the Indian come to plead the wrongs of his race should find them; on that separate, but more free and honorable ground, where the State places those who are not *with* her, but *against* her,—the only house in a slave State in which a free man can abide with honor. If any think that their influence would be lost there, and their voices no longer afflict the ear of the State, that they would not be as an enemy within its walls, they do not know by how much truth is stronger than error, nor how much more eloquently and effectively he can combat injustice who has experienced a little in his own person. Cast your whole vote, not a strip of paper merely, but your whole influence. A minority is powerless while it conforms to the majority; it is not even a minority then; but it is irresistible when it clogs by its whole weight. If the alternative is to keep all just men in prison, or give up war and slavery, the State will not hesitate which to choose. If a thousand men were not to pay their tax-bills this year, that would not be a violent and bloody measure, as it would be to pay them, and enable the State to commit violence and shed innocent blood. This is, in fact, the definition of a peaceable revolution, if any such is possible. If the tax-gatherer, or any other public officer, asks me, as one has done, "But what shall I do?" my answer is, "If you really wish to do anything, resign your office." When the subject has refused allegiance, and the officer has resigned his office, then the revolution is accomplished. But even suppose blood should flow. Is there not a sort of blood shed when the conscience is wounded? Through this wound a man's real manhood and immortality flow out, and he bleeds to an everlasting death. I see this blood flowing now.

I have contemplated the imprisonment of the offender, rather than the seizure of his goods,—though both will serve the same purpose,—because they who assert the purest right, and consequently are most dangerous to a corrupt State, commonly have not spent much time in accumulating property. To such the State renders comparatively small service, and a slight tax is wont to appear exorbitant, particularly if they are obliged to earn it by special labor with their hands. If there were one who lived wholly without the use of money, the State itself would hesitate to demand it of him. But the rich man —not to make any invidious comparison—is always sold to the institution which makes him rich. Absolutely speaking, the more money, the less virtue; for money comes between a man and his objects, and obtains them for him; and it was certainly no great virtue to obtain it. It puts to rest many questions which he would otherwise be taxed to answer; while the only new question which it puts is the hard but superfluous one, how to spend it. Thus his moral ground is taken from under his feet. The opportunities of living are diminished in proportion as what are called the "means" are increased. The best thing a man can do for his culture when he is rich is to endeavor to carry out those schemes which he entertained when he was poor. Christ answered the Herodians according to their condition. "Show me the tribute-money," said he;—and one took a penny out of his pocket;—if you use money which has the image of Cæsar on it and which he has made current and valuable, that is, *if you are men of the State,* and gladly enjoy the advantages of Cæsar's government, then pay him back some of his own when he demands it. "Render therefore to Cæsar that which is Cæsar's, and to God those things which are God's,"—leaving them no wiser than before as to which was which; for they did not wish to know. . . .

I have paid no poll-tax for six years. I was put into a jail once on this account, for one night; and, as I stood considering the walls of solid stone, two or three feet thick, the door of wood and iron, a foot thick, and the iron grating which strained the light, I could not help being struck with the foolishness of that institution which treated me as if I were mere flesh and blood and bones, to be locked up. I wondered that it should have concluded at length that this was the best use it could put me to, and had never thought to avail itself of my services in some way. I saw that, if there was a wall of stone between me and my townsmen, there was a still more difficult one to climb or break through before they could get to be as free as I was. I did not for a moment feel confined, and the walls seemed a great waste of stone and mortar. I felt as if I alone of all my townsmen had paid my tax. They plainly did not know how to treat me, but behaved like persons who are underbred. In every threat and in every compliment there was a blunder; for they thought that my chief desire was to stand the other side of that stone wall. I could not but smile to see how industriously they locked the door on my meditations, which followed them out again without let or hindrance, and *they* were really all that was dangerous. As they could not reach me, they had resolved to punish my body; just as boys, if they cannot come at some person against whom they have a spite, will abuse his dog. I saw that the State was half-witted, that it was timid as a lone woman with her silver spoons, and that it did not know its friends from its foes, and I lost all my remaining respect for it, and pitied it.

Thus the State never intentionally confronts a man's sense, intellectual or moral, but only his body, his senses. It is not armed with superior wit or honesty, but with superior physical strength. I was not born to be forced. I will breathe after my own fashion. Let us see who is the strongest. What force has a multitude? They only can force me who obey a higher law than I. They force me to become like themselves. I do not hear of *men* being *forced* to live this way or that by masses of men. What sort of life were that to live? When I meet a government which says to me, "Your money or your life," why should I be in haste to give it my money? It may be in a great strait, and not know what to do: I cannot help that. It must help itself; do as I do. It is not worth the while to snivel about it. I am not responsible for the successful working of the machinery of society. I am not the son of the engineer. I perceive that, when an acorn and a chestnut fall side by side, the one does not remain inert to make way for the other, but both obey their own laws, and spring and grow and flourish as best they can, till one, perchance, over-shadows and destroys the other. If a plant cannot live according to its nature, it dies; and so a man. . . .

When I came out of prison,—for some one interfered, and paid that tax,—I did not perceive that great changes had taken place on the common, such as he observed who went in a youth and emerged a tottering and gray-headed man; and yet a change had to my eyes come over the scene,—the town, and State, and country,—greater than any that mere time could effect. I saw yet more distinctly the State in which I lived. I saw to what extent the people among whom I lived could be trusted as good neighbors and friends; that their friendship was for summer weather only; that they did not greatly propose to do right; that they were a distinct race from me by their prejudices and superstitions, as the Chinamen and Malays are; that in their sacrifices to humanity they ran no risks, not even to their property; that after all they were not so noble but they treated the thief as he had treated them, and hoped, by a certain outward observance and a few prayers, and by walking in a particular straight though useless path from time to time, to save their souls. This may be to judge my neighbors harshly; for I believe that many of them are not aware that they have such an institution as the jail in their village.

It was formerly the custom in our village, when a poor debtor came out of jail, for his acquaintances to salute him, looking through their fingers, which were crossed to represent the grating of a jail window. "How do ye do?" My neighbors did not thus salute me, but first looked at me, and then at one another, as if I had returned from a long journey. I was put into jail as I was going to the shoemaker's to get a shoe which was mended. When I was let out the next morning, I proceeded to finish my errand, and, having put on my mended shoe, joined a huckleberry party, who were impatient to put themselves under my conduct; and in half an hour,—for the horse was soon tackled, —was in the midst of a huckleberry field, on one of our highest hills, two miles off, and then the State was nowhere to be seen. . . .

I have never declined paying the highway tax, because I am as desirous of being a good neighbor as I am of being a bad subject; and as for supporting schools, I am doing my part to educate my fellow-countrymen now. It is for no particular item in the tax-bill that I refuse to pay it. I simply wish to refuse allegiance to the State, to withdraw and stand aloof from it effectually. I do not care to trace the course of my dollar, if I could, till it buys a man or a musket to shoot with,—the dollar is innocent,—but I am concerned to trace the effects of my allegiance. In fact, I quietly declare war with the State, after my fashion, though I will still make what use and get what advantage of her I can, as is usual in such cases.

If others pay the tax which is demanded of me, from a sympathy with the State, they do but what they have already done in their own case, or rather they abet injustice to a greater extent than the State requires. If they pay the tax from a mistaken interest in the individual taxed, to save his property, or prevent his going to jail, it is because they have not considered wisely how far they let their private feelings interfere with the public good.

This, then, is my position at present. But one cannot be too much on his guard in such a case, lest his action be biased by obstinacy or an undue regard for the opinions of men. Let him see that he does only what belongs to himself and to the hour.

I think sometimes, Why, this people mean well, they are only ignorant; they would do better if they knew how: why give your neighbors this pain to treat you as they are not inclined to? But I think again, This is no reason why I should do as they do, or permit others to suffer much greater pain of a different kind. Again, I sometimes say to myself, When many millions of men, without heat, without ill will, without personal feeling of any kind, demand of you a few shillings only, without the possibility, such is their constitution, of retracting or altering their present demand, and without the possibility, on your side, of appeal to any other millions, why expose yourself to this overwhelming brute force? You do not resist cold and hunger, the winds and the waves, thus obstinately; you quietly submit to a thousand similar necessities. You do not put your head into the fire. But just in proportion as I regard this as not wholly a brute force, but partly a human force, and consider that I have relations to those millions as to so many millions of men, and not of mere brute or inanimate things, I see that appeal is possible, first and instantaneously, from them to the Maker of them, and, secondly, from them to themselves. But if I put my head deliberately into the fire, there is no appeal to fire or to the Maker of fire, and I have only myself to blame. If I could convince myself that I have any right to be satisfied with men as they are, and to treat them accordingly, and not according, in some respects, to my requisitions and expectations of what they and I ought to be, then, like a good Mussulman and fatalist, I should endeavor to be satisfied with things as they are, and say it is the will of God. And, above all, there is this difference between resisting this and a purely brute or natural force, that I can resist this with some effect; but I cannot expect, like Orpheus, to change the nature of the rocks and trees and beasts.

I do not wish to quarrel with any man or nation. I do not wish to split hairs, to make fine distinctions, or set myself up as better than my neighbors. I seek rather, I may say, even an excuse for conforming to the laws of the land. I am but too ready to conform to them. Indeed, I have reason to suspect myself on this head; and each year, as the tax-gatherer comes round, I find myself disposed to review the acts and position of the general and State governments, and the spirit of the people, to discover a pretext for conformity.

> We must affect our country as our parents,
> And if at any time we alienate

> Our love or industry from doing it honor,
> We must respect effects and teach the soul
> Matter of conscience and religion,
> And not desire of rule or benefit.

I believe that the State will soon be able to take all my work of this sort out of my hands, and then I shall be no better a patriot than my fellow-countrymen. Seen from a lower point of view, the Constitution, with all its faults, is very good; the law and the courts are very respectable; even this State and this American government are, in many respects, very admirable, and rare things, to be thankful for, such as a great many have described them; but seen from a point of view a little higher, they are what I have described them; seen from a higher still, and the highest, who shall say what they are, or that they are worth looking at or thinking of at all?

However, the government does not concern me much, and I shall bestow the fewest possible thoughts on it. It is not many moments that I live under a government, even in this world. If a man is thought-free, fancy-free, imagination-free, that which *is not* never for a long time appearing *to be* to him, unwise rulers or reformers cannot fatally interrupt him.

I know that most men think differently from myself; but those whose lives are by profession devoted to the study of these or kindred subjects content me as little as any. Statesmen and legislators, standing so completely within the institution, never distinctly and nakedly behold it. They speak of moving society, but have no resting-place without it. They may be men of a certain experience and discrimination, and have no doubt invented ingenious and even useful systems, for which we sincerely thank them; but all their wit and usefulness lie within certain not very wide limits. They are wont to forget that the world is not governed by policy and expediency. Webster never goes behind government, and so cannot speak with authority about it. His words are wisdom to those legislators who contemplate no essential reform in the existing government; but for thinkers, and those who legislate for all time, he never once glances at the subject. I know of those whose serene and wise speculations on this theme would soon reveal the limits of his mind's range and hospitality. Yet, compared with the cheap professions of most reformers, and the still cheaper wisdom and eloquence of politicians in general, his are almost the only sensible and valuable words, and we thank Heaven for him. Comparatively, he is always strong, original, and, above all, practical. Still, his quality is not wisdom, but prudence. The lawyer's truth is not Truth, but consistency or a consistent expediency. Truth is always in harmony with herself, and is not concerned chiefly to reveal the justice that may consist with wrong-doing. He well deserves to be called, as he has been called, the Defender of the Constitution. There are really no blows to be given by him but defensive ones. He is not a leader, but a follower. His leaders are the men of '87. "I have never made an effort," he says, "and never propose to make an effort; I have never countenanced an effort, and never mean to countenance an effort, to disturb the arrangement as origi-

nally made, by which the various States came into the Union." Still thinking of
the sanction which the Constitution gives to slavery, he says, "Because it was
a part of the original compact,—let it stand." Notwithstanding his special
acuteness and ability, he is unable to take a fact out of its merely political relations, and behold it as it lies absolutely to be disposed of by the intellect,—
what, for instance, it behooves a man to do here in America to-day with regard
to slavery,—but ventures, or is driven, to make some such desperate answer as
the following while professing to speak absolutely, and as a private man,—
from which what new and singular code of social duties might be inferred?
"The manner," says he, "in which the governments of those States where
slavery exists are to regulate it is for their own consideration, under their responsibility to their constituents, to the general laws of propriety, humanity, and
justice, and to God. Associations formed elsewhere, springing from a feeling of
humanity, or other cause, have nothing whatever to do with it. They have never
received any encouragement from me, and they never will."

They who know of no purer sources of truth, who have traced up its stream
no higher, stand, and wisely stand, by the Bible and the Constitution, and drink
at it there with reverence and humility; but they who behold where it comes
trickling into this lake or that pool, gird up their loins once more, and continue
their pilgrimage toward its fountainhead.

No man with a genius for legislation has appeared in America. They are
rare in the history of the world. There are orators, politicians, and eloquent
men, by the thousand; but the speaker has not yet opened his mouth to speak
who is capable of settling the much-vexed questions of the day. We love eloquence for its own sake, and not for any truth which it may utter, or any
heroism it may inspire. Our legislators have not yet learned the comparative
value of free-trade and of freedom, of union, and of rectitude, to a nation.
They have no genius or talent for comparatively humble questions of taxation
and finance, commerce and manufactures and agriculture. If we were left solely
to the wordy wit of legislators in Congress for our guidance, uncorrected by
the seasonable experience and the effectual complaints of the people, America
would not long retain her rank among the nations. For eighteen hundred years,
though perchance I have no right to say it, the New Testament has been written; yet where is the legislator who has wisdom and practical talent enough to
avail himself of the light which it sheds on the science of legislation?

The authority of government, even such as I am willing to submit to,—for I
will cheerfully obey those who know and can do better than I, and in many
things even those who neither know nor can do so well,—is still an impure
one: to be strictly just, it must have the sanction and consent of the governed.
It can have no pure right over my person and property but what I concede to
it. The progress from an absolute to a limited monarchy, from a limited monarchy to a democracy, is a progress toward a true respect for the individual.
Even the Chinese philosopher was wise enough to regard the individual as the
basis of the empire. Is a democracy, such as we know it, the last improvement

possible in government? Is it not possible to take a step further towards recognizing and organizing the rights of man? There will never be a really free and enlightened State until the State comes to recognize the individual as a higher and independent power, from which all its own power and authority are derived, and treats him accordingly. I please myself with imagining a State at last which can afford to be just to all men, and to treat the individual with respect as a neighbor; which even would not think it inconsistent with its own repose if a few were to live aloof from it, not meddling with it, nor embraced by it, who fulfilled all the duties of neighbors and fellow-men. A State which bore this kind of fruit, and suffered it to drop off as fast as it ripened, would prepare the way for a still more perfect and glorious State, which also I have imagined, but not yet anywhere seen.

❧ ❧ ❧

*E. B. White*

# Walden—1954[1]

IN HIS journal for July 10-12, 1841, Thoreau wrote: "A slight sound at evening lifts me up by the ears, and makes life seem inexpressibly serene and grand. It may be in Uranus, or it may be in the shutter." The book into which he later managed to pack both Uranus and the shutter was published in 1854, and now, a hundred years having gone by, *Walden*, its serenity and grandeur unimpaired, still lifts us up by the ears, still translates for us that language we are in danger of forgetting, "which all things and events speak without metaphor, which alone is copious and standard."

*Walden* is an oddity in American letters. It may very well be the oddest of our distinguished oddities. For many it is a great deal too odd, and for many it is a particular bore. I have not found it to be a well-liked book among my acquaintances, although usually spoken of with respect, and one literary critic for whom I have the highest regard can find no reason why anyone gives *Walden* a second thought. To admire the book is, in fact, something of an embarrassment, for the mass of men have an indistinct notion that its author was a sort of Nature Boy.

I think it is of some advantage to encounter the book at a period in one's life when the normal anxieties and enthusiasms and rebellions of youth closely resemble those of Thoreau in that spring of 1845 when he borrowed an axe, went out to the woods, and began to whack down some trees for timber. Received at such a juncture, the book is like an invitation to life's dance, assuring the troubled recipient that no matter what befalls him in the way of success or failure he will always be welcome at the party—that the music is played for

[1] From *The Yale Review*, XLIV, No. 1 (Autumn, 1954). Copyright, 1954, by Yale University Press. Reprinted by permission.

him, too, if he will but listen and move his feet. In effect, that is what the book is—an invitation, unengraved; and it stirs one as a young girl is stirred by her first big party bid. Many think it a sermon; many set it down as an attempt to rearrange society; some think it an exercise in nature-loving; some find it a rather irritating collection of inspirational puffballs by an eccentric show-off. I think it none of these. It still seems to me the best youth's companion yet written by an American, for it carries a solemn warning against the loss of one's valuables, it advances a good argument for traveling light and trying new adventures, it rings with the power of positive adoration, it contains religious feeling without religious images, and it steadfastly refuses to record bad news. Even its pantheistic note is so pure as to be noncorrupting—pure as the flute-note blown across the pond on those faraway summer nights. If our colleges and universities were alert, they would present a cheap pocket edition of the book to every senior upon graduating, along with his sheepskin, or instead of it. Even if some senior were to take it literally and start felling trees, there could be worse mishaps: the axe is older than the Dictaphone and it is just as well for a young man to see what kind of chips he leaves before listening to the sound of his own voice. And even if some were to get no farther than the table of contents, they would learn how to name eighteen chapters by the use of only thirty-nine words and would see how sweet are the uses of brevity.

If Thoreau had merely left us an account of a man's life in the woods, or if he had simply retreated to the woods and there recorded his complaints about society, or even if he had contrived to include both records in one essay, *Walden* would probably not have lived a hundred years. As things turned out, Thoreau, very likely without knowing quite what he was up to, took man's relation to nature and man's dilemma in society and man's capacity for elevating his spirit and he beat all these matters together, in a wild free interval of self-justification and delight, and produced an original omelette from which people can draw nourishment in a hungry day. *Walden* is one of the first of the vitamin-enriched American dishes. If it were a little less good than it is, or even a little less queer, it would be an abominable book. Even as it is, it will continue to baffle and annoy the literal mind and all those who are unable to stomach its caprices and imbibe its theme. Certainly the plodding economist will continue to have rough going if he hopes to emerge from the book with a clear system of economic thought. Thoreau's assault on the Concord society of the mid-nineteenth century has the quality of a modern Western: he rides into the subject at top speed, shooting in all directions. Many of his shots ricochet and nick him on the rebound, and throughout the melee there is a horrendous cloud of inconsistencies and contradictions, and when the shooting dies down and the air clears, one is impressed chiefly by the courage of the rider and by how splendid it was that somebody should have ridden in there and raised all that ruckus.

When he went to the pond, Thoreau struck an attitude and did so deliberately, but his posturing was not to draw the attention of others to him but rather to draw his own attention more closely to himself. "I learned this at least by my experiment: that if one advances confidently in the direction of his dreams, and endeavors to live the life which he has imagined, he will meet with a success unexpected in common hours." The sentence has the power to resuscitate the youth drowning in his sea of doubt. I recall my exhilaration upon reading it, many years ago, in a time of hesitation and despair. It restored me to health. And now in 1954 when I salute Henry Thoreau on the hundredth birthday of his book, I am merely paying off an old score—or an installment on it.

In his journal for May 3-4, 1838—Boston to Portland—he wrote: "Midnight —head over the boat's side—between sleeping and waking—with glimpses of one or more lights in the vicinity of Cape Ann. Bright moonlight—the effect heightened by seasickness." The entry illuminates the man, as the moon the sea on that night in May. In Thoreau the natural scene was heightened, not depressed, by a disturbance of the stomach, and nausea met its match at last. There was a steadiness in at least one passenger if there was none in the boat. Such steadiness (which in some would be called intoxication) is at the heart of *Walden*—confidence, faith, the discipline of looking always at what is to be seen, undeviating gratitude for the life-everlasting that he found growing in his front yard. "There is nowhere recorded a simple and irrepressible satisfaction with the gift of life, any memorable praise of God." He worked to correct that deficiency. *Walden* is his acknowledgment of the gift of life. It is the testament of a man in a high state of indignation because (it seemed to him) so few ears heard the uninterrupted poem of creation, the morning wind that forever blows. If the man sometimes wrote as though all his readers were male, unmarried, and well-connected, it is because he gave his testimony during the callow years, and, for that matter, never really grew up. To reject the book because of the immaturity of the author and the bugs in the logic is to throw away a bottle of good wine because it contains bits of the cork.

Thoreau said he required of every writer, first and last, a simple and sincere account of his own life. Having delivered himself of this chesty dictum, he proceeded to ignore it. In his books and even in his enormous journal, he withheld or disguised most of the facts from which an understanding of his life could be drawn. *Walden*, subtitled "Life in the Woods," is not a simple and sincere account of a man's life, either in or out of the woods; it is an account of a man's journey into the mind, a toot on the trumpet to alert the neighbors. Thoreau was well aware that no one can alert his neighbors who is not wide awake himself, and he went to the woods (among other reasons) to make sure that he would stay awake during his broadcast. What actually took place during the years 1845-47 is largely unrecorded, and the reader is excluded from the private life of the author, who supplies almost no gossip about himself, a great deal about his neighbors and about the universe.

As for me, I cannot in this short ramble give a simple and sincere account of my own life, but I think Thoreau might find it instructive to know that this memorial essay is being written in a house that, through no intent on my part, is the same size and shape as his own domicile on the pond—about ten by fifteen, tight, plainly finished, and at a little distance from my Concord. The house in which I sit this morning was built to accommodate a boat, not a man, but by long experience I have learned that in most respects it shelters me better than the larger dwelling where my bed is, and which, by design, is a manhouse not a boathouse. Here in the boathouse I am a wilder and, it would appear, a healthier man, by a safe margin. I have a chair, a bench, a table, and I can walk into the water if I tire of the land. My house fronts a cove. Two fishermen have just arrived to spot fish from the air—an osprey and a man in a small yellow plane who works for the fish company. The man, I have noticed, is less well equipped than the hawk, who can dive directly on his fish and carry it away, without telephoning. A mouse and a squirrel share the house with me. The building is, in fact, a multiple dwelling, a semidetached affair. It is because I am semidetached while here that I find it possible to transact this private business with the fewest obstacles.

There is also a woodchuck here, living forty feet away under the wharf. When the wind is right, he can smell my house; and when the wind is contrary, I can smell his. We both use the wharf for sunning, taking turns, each adjusting his schedule to the other's convenience. Thoreau once ate a woodchuck. I think he felt he owed it to his readers, and that it was little enough, considering the indignities they were suffering at his hands and the dressing-down they were taking. (Parts of *Walden* are pure scold.) Or perhaps he ate the woodchuck because he believed every man should acquire strict business habits, and the woodchuck was destroying his market beans. I do not know. Thoreau had a strong experimental streak in him. It is probably no harder to eat a woodchuck than to construct a sentence that lasts a hundred years. At any rate, Thoreau is the only writer I know who prepared himself for his great ordeal by eating a woodchuck; also the only one who got a hangover from drinking too much water. (He was drunk the whole time, though he seldom touched wine or coffee or tea.)

Here in this compact house where I would spend one day as deliberately as Nature if I were not being pressed by *The Yale Review*, and with a woodchuck (as yet uneaten) for neighbor, I can feel the companionship of the occupant of the pondside cabin in Walden woods, a mile from the village, near the Fitchburg right of way. Even my immediate business is no barrier between us: Thoreau occasionally batted out a magazine piece, but was always suspicious of any sort of purposeful work that cut into his time. A man, he said, should take care not to be thrown off the track by every nutshell and mosquito's wing that falls on the rails.

There has been much guessing as to why he went to the pond. To set it down to escapism is, of course, to misconstrue what happened. Henry went forth to battle when he took to the woods, and *Walden* is the report of a man torn by two powerful and opposing drives—the desire to enjoy the world (and not be derailed by a mosquito wing) and the urge to set the world straight. One cannot join these two successfully, but sometimes, in rare cases, something good or even great results from the attempt of the tormented spirit to reconcile them. Henry went forth to battle, and if he set the stage himself, if he fought on his own terms and with his own weapons, it was because it was his nature to do things differently from most men, and to act in a cocky fashion. If the pond and the woods seemed a more plausible site for a house than an intown location, it was because a cowbell made for him a sweeter sound than a churchbell. *Walden,* the book, makes the sound of a cowbell, more than a churchbell, and proves the point, although both sounds are in it, and both remarkably clear and sweet. He simply preferred his churchbell at a little distance.

I think one reason he went to the woods was a perfectly simple and commonplace one—and apparently he thought so, too. "At a certain season of our life," he wrote, "we are accustomed to consider every spot as the possible site of a house." There spoke the young man, a few years out of college, who had not yet broken away from home. He hadn't married, and he had found no job that measured up to his rigid standards of employment, and like any young man, or young animal, he felt uneasy and on the defensive until he had fixed himself a den. Most young men, of course, casting about for a site, are content merely to draw apart from their kinfolks. Thoreau, convinced that the greater part of what his neighbors called good was bad, withdrew from a great deal more than family: he pulled out of everything for a while, to serve everybody right for being so stuffy, and to try his own prejudices on the dog.

The house-hunting sentence above, which starts the Chapter called "Where I Lived, and What I Lived For," is followed by another passage that is worth quoting here because it so beautifully illustrates the offbeat prose that Thoreau was master of, a prose at once strictly disciplined and wildly abandoned. "I have surveyed the country on every side within a dozen miles of where I live," continued this delirious young man. "In imagination I have bought all the farms in succession, for all were to be bought, and I knew their price. I walked over each farmer's premises, tasted his wild apples, discoursed on husbandry with him, took his farm at his price, at any price, mortgaging it to him in my mind; even put a higher price on it—took everything but a deed of it—took his word for his deed, for I dearly love to talk—cultivated it, and him too to some extent, I trust, and withdrew when I had enjoyed it long enough, leaving him to carry it on." A copydesk man could get a double hernia trying to clean up that sentence for the management, but the sentence needs no fixing, for it perfectly captures the meaning of the writer and the quality of the ramble.

"Wherever I sat, there I might live, and the landscape radiated from me accordingly." Thoreau, the home-seeker, sitting on his hummock with the entire State of Massachusetts radiating from him, is to me the most humorous of the New England figures, and *Walden* the most humorous of the books, though its humor is almost continuously subsurface and there is nothing funny any-where, except a few weak jokes and bad puns that rise to the surface like the perch in the pond that rose to the sound of the maestro's flute. Thoreau tended to write in sentences, a feat not every writer is capable of, and *Walden* is, rhetorically speaking, a collection of certified sentences, some of them, it would now appear, as indestructible as they are errant. The book is distilled from the vast journals, and this accounts for its intensity: he picked out bright particles that pleased his eye, whirled them in the kaleidoscope of his content, and produced the pattern that has endured—the color, the form, the light.

On this its hundredth birthday, Thoreau's *Walden* is pertinent and timely. In our uneasy season, when all men unconsciously seek a retreat from a world that has got almost completely out of hand, his house in the Concord woods is a haven. In our culture of gadgetry and the multiplicity of convenience, his cry "Simplicity, simplicity, simplicity!" has the insistence of a fire alarm. In the brooding atmosphere of war and the gathering radioactive storm, the innocence and serenity of his summer afternoons are enough to burst the remembering heart, and one gazes back upon that pleasing interlude—its confidence, its pur-ity, its deliberateness—with awe and wonder, as one would look upon the face of a child asleep.

"This small lake was of most value as a neighbor in the intervals of a gentle rain-storm in August, when, both air and water being perfectly still, but the sky overcast, midafternoon had all the serenity of evening, and the wood-thrush sang around, and was heard from shore to shore." Now, in the perpetual over-cast in which our days are spent, we hear with extra perception and deep gratitude that song, tying century to century.

I sometimes amuse myself by bringing Henry Thoreau back to life and show-ing him the sights. I escort him into a phone booth and let him dial Weather. "This is a delicious evening," the girl's voice says, "when the whole body is one sense, and imbibes delight through every pore." I show him the spot in the Pacific where an island used to be, before some magician made it vanish. "We know not where we are," I murmur. "The light which puts out our eyes is darkness to us. Only that day dawns to which we are awake." I thumb through the latest copy of "Vogue" with him. "Of two patterns which differ only by a few threads more or less of a particular color," I read, "the one will be sold readily, the other lie on the shelf, though it frequently happens that, after the lapse of a season, the latter becomes the most fashionable." Together we go outboarding on the Assabet, looking for what we've lost—a hound, a bay horse, a turtledove. I show him a distracted farmer who is trying to repair a hay baler before the thunder shower breaks. "This farmer," I remark, "is en-deavoring to solve the problem of a livelihood by a formula more complicated than the problem itself. To get his shoe strings he speculates in herds of cattle."

I take the celebrated author to Twenty-One for lunch, so the waiters may study his shoes. The proprietor welcomes us. "The gross feeder," remarks the proprietor, sweeping the room with his arm, "is a man in the larva stage." After lunch we visit a classroom in one of those schools conducted by big corporations to teach their superannuated executives how to retire from business without serious injury to their health. (The shock to men's systems these days when relieved of the exacting routine of amassing wealth is very great and must be cushioned.) "It is not necessary," says the teacher to his pupils, "that a man should earn his living by the sweat of his brow, unless he sweats easier than I do. We are determined to be starved before we are hungry."

I turn on the radio and let Thoreau hear Winchell beat the red hand around the clock. "Time is but the stream I go a-fishing in," shouts Mr. Winchell, rattling his telegraph key. "Hardly a man takes a half hour's nap after dinner, but when he wakes he holds up his head and asks, 'What's the news?' If we read of one man robbed, or murdered, or killed by accident, or one house burned, or one vessel wrecked, or one steamboat blown up, or one cow run over on the Western Railroad, or one mad dog killed, or one lot of grasshoppers in the winter—we need never read of another. One is enough."

I doubt that Thoreau would be thrown off balance by the fantastic sights and sounds of the twentieth century. "The Concord nights," he once wrote, "are stranger than the Arabian nights." A four-engined air liner would merely serve to confirm his early views on travel. Everywhere he would observe, in new shapes and sizes, the old predicaments and follies of men—the desperation, the impediments, the meanness—along with the visible capacity for elevation of the mind and soul. "This curious world which we inhabit is more wonderful than it is convenient; more beautiful than it is useful; it is more to be admired and enjoyed than used." He would see that today ten thousand engineers are busy making sure that the world shall be convenient if they bust doing it, and others are determined to increase its usefulness even though its beauty is lost somewhere along the way.

At any rate, I'd like to stroll about the countryside in Thoreau's company for a day, observing the modern scene, inspecting today's snowstorm, pointing out the sights, and offering belated apologies for my sins. Thoreau is unique among writers in that those who admire him find him uncomfortable to live with—a regular hairshirt of a man. A little band of dedicated Thoreauvians would be a sorry sight indeed: fellows who hate compromise and have compromised, fellows who love wildness and have lived tamely, and at their side, censuring them and chiding them, the ghostly figure of this upright man, who long ago gave corroboration to impulses they perceived were right and issued warnings against the things they instinctively knew to be their enemies. I should hate to be called a Thoreauvian, yet I wince every time I walk into the barn I'm pushing before me, seventy-five feet by forty, and the author of *Walden* has served as my conscience through the long stretches of my trivial days.

Hairshirt or no, he is a better companion than most, and I would not swap him for a soberer or more reasonable friend even if I could. I can reread his famous invitation with undiminished excitement. The sad thing is that not more acceptances have been received, that so many decline for one reason or another, pleading some previous engagement or ill health. But the invitation stands. It will beckon as long as this remarkable book stays in print—which will be as long as there are August afternoons in the intervals of a gentle rainstorm, as long as there are ears to catch the faint sounds of the orchestra. I find it agreeable to sit here this morning, in a house of correct proportions, and hear across a century of time his flute, his frogs, and his seductive summons to the wildest revels of them all.

❧ ❧ ❧

*Plato*

# The Apology of Socrates[1]

## SOCRATES' DEFENCE

WHAT effect my accusers had upon you, Men of Athens, I know not. As for me, they well-nigh made me forget who I was, so telling were their speeches! And yet, so to say, not one atom of truth did they utter. But that which astonished me most among all their fabrications was this, that they said you must be on your guard, and not be deceived by me, as I was a masterly speaker. That they should not be ashamed when they were promptly going to be caught by me in a lie, through the fact, since I shall show myself to be no orator at all, therein methought they reached the very height of their effrontery; unless perchance what they call masterly speaker means the one who tells the truth. If that is what they are saying, then I will admit I am an orator, though not of the sort they describe.

Well then, as I say, these men have uttered nothing, or next to nothing, that is true. From me, however, you shall hear the simple truth. But, by Heaven! fellow citizens, it will not be in language like theirs, decked out with epithets and phrases, nor beautifully ordered; rather you shall hear such utterances as come to me, in any words that offer, for of the justice of what I say I am convinced, and from me you need none of you expect aught else. No, Gentlemen! it would hardly befit a man of my age to come into your presence moulding phrases like a youngster. And nevertheless, my fellow citizens, and above all, I do request and beg of you this thing: if you should hear me pleading my cause with the same expressions I habitually have used in speaking, whether at the market by the counters, where many of you have heard me, or elsewhere, do not for that reason marvel and make a disturbance. The facts stand thus. At the age of seventy years I now for the first time have come up before a tribunal,

[1] *Plato on the Trial and Death of Socrates*, Lane Cooper trans. (Ithaca: Cornell University Press, 1941), pp. 49-77. Reprinted by permission of the publishers.

and so I am an absolute stranger to the language of this place. Let it be as if I really were a foreigner here, since then you surely would excuse me if I used the accent and manner of speech in which I was reared. And so I now make this request of you, a matter of justice as it seems to me, that you let me use my way of speaking; it may be better, it may be worse, but the only thing you have to consider is this, and this is what you have to put your mind on, whether that which I say is right or not. That is the merit of a judge; the merit of a speaker is to tell the truth.

To begin with, fellow citizens, it is right for me to answer the earliest charges falsely brought against me, and my first accusers, and then I must answer the charges and accusers that come later.

Many, in fact, were they who formerly brought charges against me, yes many years ago, and spoke not a word of truth. And them I fear more than I do the group of Anytus, dangerous as these are too. No, Gentlemen, those others are more dangerous, for they have prejudiced the major part of you since your childhood, convincing you of an utterly false charge against me; to wit, 'There is a person, Socrates by name, a "wise man," who speculates about the heavens above, and also searches into everything below the earth, and in argument can make the worse case win.' [2] Those persons who have spread this charge abroad, they, fellow citizens, are my dangerous accusers; for people who listen to them think that men who make the said investigations do not believe in any gods. Add that these accusers are many in number, have brought their charges for a long time now, and, moreover, made them to you when you most readily believed things, when some of you were children or striplings; sheer accusation of an absent person without anybody to defend him. And what is most baffling of all, it is impossible to identify and name them, unless perchance in the case of a certain comic poet. For the rest, for all who through jealousy and malice misled you, and those who, once they were misled, got others to believe the same—with all these it is impossible to deal. There is no means of bringing one of them here to court, or putting a single one to cross-examination. No, in making my defense I am simply forced to fight, as it were, with shadows, and to question with nobody to make reply. Accordingly, I ask you to assume with me that, as I say, my accusers fall into these two classes, one group who are accusing me at present, the other those who of old accused me as aforesaid; and understand that it is these I must reply to first, for it is they whom you heard bringing charges earlier, and far more than this group who now come after.

Well then, fellow citizens, I must now make my defence, and must try to clear away in this brief time that calumny which you have entertained so long. I would that this might come to pass, if so it should be better for both you and me, and if it profits me to plead. But I think the task to be a hard one, and what its nature is I am by no means unaware. Still, let the outcome be as it pleases God; the law must be obeyed, and the defence be made.

Let us, then, go back and look at the original accusation from which the

[2] The proverbial translation is: 'To make the worse appear the better reason.'

slander arose, the slander that gave Meletus his ground for this indictment he has lodged against me. Let us see. Precisely what did the slanderers say when they slandered? We must read their complaint as if it were a legal accusation: 'Socrates is wicked; overdoes inquiry into what occurs below the earth and in the heavens; in arguing makes the worse case win; and teaches others to do the same as he.' Such is in substance the accusation—what you actually saw in the comedy [the *Clouds*] of Aristophanes, where a man called 'Socrates' is swung about, declaring that he treads the air, and sputtering a deal of other nonsense on matters of which I have not one bit of knowledge either great or small. And I do not say so in disparagement of any science such as that, if any one is learned in such matters; I should not wish to be attacked by Meletus upon so grave a charge. But actually, fellow citizens, to me these matters are of absolutely no concern. I call the greater part of you yourselves to witness, and beg all who ever heard me in discussion to tell one another and declare it; many of you are in a position to do this. Declare to one another, therefore, whether any of you ever heard me dealing with such matters either briefly or at length. In that way you will see what all the rest amounts to of what the generality of people say concerning me.

No, there is nothing in it whatsoever. And if you have heard anybody say that I profess to give instruction, and get money in that way, neither is that true; although to my mind it is very fine indeed if any one is able to instruct his fellows, as are Gorgias of Leontini, and Prodicus of Ceos, and Hippias of Elis. Each one of them is able, Gentlemen, to go to city after city and attract young men; youths who might without expense consort with any one they chose among their own fellow citizens, these they persuade to give up that fellowship, to consort with them, to pay them money, and to be grateful to them besides. And indeed there is another man of learning here, from Paros, who, I learned, was staying in the City, for I happened to be calling on a man, Callias son of Hipponicus, who has paid more money to the Sophists than have all the others put together. And so I questioned him, he having, in fact, two sons:

'Callias,' said I, 'if your two sons had been colts or calves, we should have no trouble in finding some one to look after them, who for pay would make them fine and good according to the standard of their kind. We should pick some trainer of horses, say, or farmer. But now that they are human beings, whom have you in mind to put in charge of them? Who is there with a knowledge of their proper quality, the excellence of a human being and a citizen? I fancy you have given thought to this since you have sons. Is there any one,' said I, 'or not?'

'Yes, certainly,' said he.

'Who?' said I. 'Whence comes he? What does he charge for teaching?'

'Socrates,' he said, 'it is Evenus; comes from Paros; charge, five minae.' So I thought Evenus was a lucky man if he really had this art, and would teach it at so reasonable a rate. For myself, I should be very proud and self-conceited if I knew all that. But the truth is, fellow citizens, I have no such knowledge.

Then perhaps some one of you may be inclined to ask: 'But, Socrates, what *is* the matter with you? What is the origin of these charges that are made against you? Unless you acted very differently from everybody else, surely no such story and repute would have arisen—if you did not do something other than most people do. Tell us what it is, in order to keep us from rushing to our own conclusion about you.'

That, I take it, would be fairly spoken; and I shall try to show you what it is that has given me this name and ill repute. Pray listen. Some of you, perhaps, will take me to be joking, but be assured that I shall tell you the simple truth. The fact is, fellow citizens, that I have got this name through my possession of a certain wisdom. What sort of wisdom is it? A wisdom, doubtless, that appertains to man. With respect to this, perhaps, I actually am wise; whereas those others whom I just now mentioned may possibly be wise with a wisdom more than human, or else I do not know what to say of it; as for me, I certainly do not possess it, and whoever says I do is lying, and seeks to injure me.

And, fellow citizens, do not interrupt me even if I say what seems extravagant, for the statement I shall make is not my own; instead, I shall refer you to a witness whose word can be accepted. Your witness to my wisdom, if I have any, and to its nature, is the god at Delphi. You certainly knew Chaerephon. He was a friend of mine from our youth, and a friend of your popular party as well; he shared in your late exile, and accompanied you on your return. Now you know the temper of Chaerephon, how impulsive he was in everything he undertook. Well so it was when once he went to Delphi, and made bold to ask the oracle this question—and, Gentlemen, please do not make an uproar over what I say; he asked if there was any one more wise than I. Then the Pythian oracle made response that there was no one who was wiser. To this response his brother here will bear you witness, since Chaerephon himself is dead.

Now bear in mind the reason why I tell you this. It is because I am going on to show you whence this calumny of me has sprung; for when I heard about the oracle, I communed within myself: 'What can the god be saying, and what does the riddle mean? Well I know in my own heart that I am without wisdom great or small. What is it that he means, then, in declaring me to be most wise? It cannot be that he is lying; it is not in his nature.' For a long time I continued at a loss as to his meaning, then finally decided, much against my will, to seek it in the following way.

I went to one of those who pass for wise men, feeling sure that there if anywhere I could refute the answer, and explain to the oracle: 'Here is a man that is wiser than I, but you said I was the wisest.' The man I went to see was one of our statesmen; his name I need not mention. Him I thoroughly examined, and from him, as I studied him and conversed with him, I gathered, fellow citizens, this impression. This man appeared to me to seem to be wise to others, and above all to himself, but not to be so. And then I tried to show him that he thought that he was wise, but was not. The result was that I gained his enmity and the enmity as well of many of those who were present. So, as I went away, I reasoned with myself: 'At all events I am wiser than this man is. It is quite possible that neither one of us knows anything fine and good. But this man fancies that he knows when he does not, while I, whereas I do not know, just so I do not fancy that I know. In this small item, then, at least, I seem to be wiser than he, in that I do not fancy that I know what I do not.' Thereafter I went to another man, one of those who passed for wiser than the first, and I got the same impression. Whereupon I gained his enmity as well as that of many more.

Thereafter I went from one man to another, perceiving, with grief and apprehension, that I was getting hated, but it seemed imperative to put the service of the god above all else. In my search for the meaning of the oracle I must go to all who were supposed to have some knowledge. And, fellow citizens, by the Dog, since I have to tell you the truth, here is pretty much what I encountered. The persons with the greatest reputation seemed to me to be the ones who were well-nigh the most deficient, as I made my search in keeping with the god's intent; whereas others of inferior reputation I found to be men superior in regard to their possession of the truth. I needs must tell you all about my wandering course, a veritable round of toils heroic, which I underwent to prove that the oracle was not to be refuted.

After the statesmen, I went to the poets, tragic, dithyrambic, and the rest. There, I thought, my ignorance would be self-evident in comparison with them. So I took those poems of theirs which seemed to me to have been most carefully wrought by them, and asked the authors what they meant, in order that I might at the same time learn from them. Well, Gentlemen, I am ashamed to tell you the truth; and yet it must be done. The fact is, pretty nearly everybody, so to say, who was present could have spoken better than the authors did about the poems they themselves had written. So here again in a short time I learned this about the poets too, that not by wisdom do they make what they compose, but by a gift of nature and an inspiration similar to that of the diviners and the oracles. These also utter many beautiful things, but understand not one of them. And such, I saw, was the experience of the poets. At the same time I perceived that their poetic gift led them to fancy that in all else, too, they were the wisest of mankind, when they were not. So I went away from them as well, believing that I had the same advantage over them as over the statesmen.

To make an end, I went, then, to the artisans. Conscious that I did not, so to say, know anything myself, I was certain I should find that they knew many things and fine. Nor in that was I deceived; they did indeed know things which I did not, and in that they were wiser than I. But, fellow citizens, these excellent workmen seemed to me to have the same defect as the poets. Because they were successful in the practice of their art, each thought himself most wise about all other things of the highest import, and this mistake of theirs beclouded all that wisdom. So I asked myself the question, for the oracle, whether I preferred to be just what I was, neither wise as they were wise nor ignorant as they were ignorant, or to be both wise and ignorant like them. And my response to myself and the oracle was that it paid me to be as I was.

Such, fellow citizens, was the quest which brought me so much enmity, hatreds so utterly harsh and hard to bear, whence sprang so many calumnies, and this name that is given me of being 'wise'; for every time I caught another person in his ignorance, those present fancied that I knew what he did not. But, Gentlemen, in all likelihood it really is the god who is wise, and by that oracle he meant to say that human wisdom is of little worth, or none. And it appears that when he picked out 'Socrates,' he used my name to take me for an example; it was as if he said: 'O race of men, he is the wisest among you, who, like Socrates, knows that in truth his knowledge is worth nothing.' So even now I still go about in my search, and, in keeping with the god's intent, question anybody, citizen or stranger, whom I fancy to be wise. And when it seems to me that he is not, in defence of the god I show that he is not. And this activity has left me without leisure either to take any real part in civic affairs or to care for my own. Instead, I live in infinite poverty through my service to the god.

In addition, the young men who of their own accord are my companions, of the class who have most leisure, sons of the very rich—they listen with joy to the men who are examined; they often imitate me, and in turn attempt to test out others. And thereupon, I take it, they find a great abundance of men who imagine they have some knowledge, and yet know little or nothing. And then these men whom they examine get angry, not at them, but at me, and say there is one Socrates, a perfect blackguard, who corrupts the young. Yet when anybody asks them how he does it, and by teaching what, they have nothing to tell, nor do they know. But in order not to seem quite at a loss, they make the usual attacks that are leveled at philosophers, namely, about 'things occurring in the heavens and below the earth,' 'not believing in the gods,' and 'making the worse case win.' What they do not care to utter, I imagine, is the truth: that they have been shown up in their pretense to knowledge when they actually knew nothing. Accordingly, since they are proud, passionate, and numerous, and organized and effective in speaking about me, they have long since filled your ears with their violent calumnies.

From among them have come Meletus, Anytus, and Lycon to attack me; Meletus aggrieved on behalf of the poets, Anytus on behalf of the artists and the politicians, Lycon on behalf of the rhetoricians. Consequently, as I said at the beginning, I shall be surprised if I succeed, within so short a time, in ridding you of all this swollen mass of calumny.

There, fellow citizens, you have the truth. I hide nothing from you, either great or small, nor do I dissimulate. And yet I know that even by this I stir up hatred, which itself proves that I tell the truth, and that it is precisely this that constitutes the charge against me, and is the cause of it. And whether now or later you investigate the matter, you will find it to be so.

Therewith let me close my defence to you on the charges made against me by my first accusers. As for Meletus, that honest man and good friend of the

City, as he styles himself, to him and my more recent foes I will now endeavor to reply.

Here again, since the present charges vary from the former, let us take the actual text of the complaint. It runs, in effect, as follows: 'Socrates,' it declares, 'offends against the law since he corrupts the young, does not believe in the gods the State believes in, and believes in novel deities [spirits, *daimonia*] instead.' Such is the accusation. Let us examine it point by point.

First, it holds that I offend by corrupting the young. But I, fellow citizens, I hold that Meletus offends in that he makes a jest of a serious matter, when he lightly brings men to trial on questions in which he pretends to be deeply interested and concerned, whereas he never took the slightest interest in any of them. That this is so, I will try to prove to you.

Your attention, Meletus! Answer! Do you not attach the utmost importance to the moral improvement of our youth?

[MELETUS.] I do indeed.

Well then, tell the assembly here, who makes the young men better? You obviously know, for it is your special concern. You have discovered, so you state, who it is that corrupts them: I, whom you bring hither and accuse. Come now, tell who the person is who makes them better, and name him to these judges.

See, Meletus, you are silent. Have you nothing to say? Doesn't that seem shameful to you, and proof enough of my assertion that you have had no interest in the matter? But come, friend, say who makes them better?

[MELETUS.] The laws.

No, my good fellow, that is not what I ask. I mean, what man? for, obviously, first of all he will have to know this very thing, the laws.

[MELETUS.] These judges, Socrates.

What say you, Meletus? These judges here are competent to instruct the young, and make them better?

[MELETUS.] Most certainly.

All are able? Or some are, and some are not?

[MELETUS.] All of them!

By Hera, that is welcome news! We have an ample store of men who benefit their kind! What next? What about the audience here, do these too make them better?

[MELETUS.] Yes, they too.

What about the Council?

[MELETUS.] Yes, the Council also.

But, Meletus, what about the men in the Assembly, the members of it, do they corrupt the young, or do they one and all make young men better?

[MELETUS.] Yes, they do it too.

So it seems that every one in Athens except me makes them fine and good, and I alone corrupt them. Is that your meaning?

[MELETUS.] Precisely that.

You detect me in a most unlucky situation. Answer me, though. Does the same thing seem to you to hold for horses too? Do you think all other men make horses better, and only one man ruins them? Or is it just the opposite of this, that some one man, or a very few, the horsemen, can improve them, whereas most people, if they have to deal with horses, and to make use of them, will spoil them? Is that not so, Meletus, both with horses and all other animals? It surely is, whether Anytus and you deny it or admit it. And what wonderful luck it would be for the young people if there were only one who did them harm, and all others did them good! But no, Meletus, you give ample proof that you never cared at all about the young; and your indifference is clearly shown—that you had no interest whatever in the things for which you bring me into court.

Now, Meletus, another question. In the name of Zeus, tell us whether it is better to live with honest citizens or with bad ones. Answer, friend; I ask you nothing difficult. Don't the wicked always do some evil to their neighbors, and the good some good?

[MELETUS.] Certainly.

Well, is there anybody who would rather be harmed than helped by those he lives with? Answer, my friend; the law requires you to do so. Does anybody like to be injured?

[MELETUS.] Certainly not.

Come now. When you bring me into court for corrupting the younger generation and making them worse, do you charge that I do so purposely or without design?

[MELETUS.] Purposely, say I.

What's that, Meletus? Are you at your age so much wiser than I am at mine? And thus, while you know that the wicked always do some injury to their nearest neighbors, and the good some good, I, you think, am come to such a state of ignorance as not to know that if I make some one I live with bad, I run the risk of getting injured by him? So according to you I do myself all this harm on purpose! That, Meletus, you will not get me to believe, nor, I fancy, anybody else in all the world. No, either I do not corrupt them, or if I do corrupt them, it is not by design. So either way you lie. If I ruin them unwittingly, the case is that of an involuntary error which does not legally bring me before this court; the proper thing would be to take me privately, and to instruct and warn me; for obviously when I learn better I shall stop doing what I do unwittingly. But you avoided joining me in order to instruct me; you chose not to do it. You bring me to this court where it is legal to try those who stand in need of punishment, not of learning.

There, fellow citizens, you have evidence enough of what I said, that Meletus has not taken the slightest interest in these matters.

Yet tell us, Meletus: in what way do you say I corrupt the younger men? Or is it not clear from the text of your complaint that you mean I teach them not to believe in the gods the State believes in, but in other new divinities? Isn't that the way you mean I corrupt them by my teaching?

[MELETUS.] Yes, that is just what I assert.

In that case, Meletus, in the name of those very gods we are discussing, explain your meaning still more clearly to these gentlemen here and me, for there is a point I am unable to make out. If you mean that I teach them to believe in the existence of certain gods, then I myself believe that there are gods, and so I am not out and out an atheist, and do not break the law in that respect. Or do you mean that they are not the gods the State believes in, but other gods instead, and is this the point of your complaint, that they are different? Or do you say that I myself do not believe in any gods at all, and that I teach this disbelief to others?

[MELETUS.] Yes, that is what I maintain, that you do not believe in any gods at all.

You amaze me, Meletus. How can you say so? Do you mean that I do not, like other men, regard the sun and moon as gods?

[MELETUS.] By Heaven, Gentlemen of the Jury, he does not; he holds that the sun is a stone, and the moon an earth.

You must think you are accusing Anaxagoras, my dear Meletus. Have you such a poor opinion of these men here, and do you think them so illiterate as not to know that the works of Anaxagoras of Clazomenae are full of these ideas? And so you think that the young men learn these things from me, when on occasion they could buy the books for a drachma at most in the orchestra, and then laugh at Socrates if he pretended that these theories were his—apart from the fact that they are so bizarre! But, by Heaven, is that the way you think of me, that I don't believe in any god whatever?

[MELETUS.] No, by Heaven, not a single one.

Now that, Meletus, is incredible, and something that I take it you do not believe yourself. In my opinion, fellow citizens, this man is an utterly over-weening and unbridled person, who has brought this accusation simply out of insolence, intemperance, and youthful rashness. It looks as if he had made up a riddle with which to try me out: 'See whether Socrates, the wise man, will know that I am jesting and self-contradictory, or whether I shall fool him and all the rest who listen'; for to me he clearly contradicts himself in the complaint. where in effect he says: 'Socrates offends by not believing in gods, but by believing in gods.' And that is simply joking.

Examine with me, Gentlemen, my way of showing that he says this. And, Meletus, you answer us. But, Gentlemen, remember the request I made at the outset, and do not interrupt if I pursue the argument in my customary fashion.

Is there any living man, Meletus, who believes that there are human things, but does not believe that there are human beings? Let him answer, Gentlemen, and not make noisy protests beside the point. Does any one believe in horse-manship, and not in horses? Or does any one believe there is an art of piping, but that there are no pipers? No, honorable sir, there isn't any one who does it. If you do not choose to answer, I will speak for you and these others here as well. But give the answer to this. Is there anybody who believes in the doings of spirits [*daimonia*], but thinks there are no spirits [*daimones*]?

THE APOLOGY OF SOCRATES

[MELETUS.] No.

How you oblige me by the grudging answer these gentlemen force you to make! Well then, you admit, I believe and teach that there are doings of spirits, whether recent or of old. At all events I do believe in them according to your statement; you have even sworn to this in your complaint. But if I believe in them, then quite necessarily, I suppose, I must believe in spirits. Isn't it so? It must be. I put you down as in agreement since you make no reply.

Now, must we not consider spirits as either gods or the offspring of gods? Say yes or no.

[MELETUS.] Yes, certainly.

If, then, I think that there are spirits, as you assert, and if the spirits are in some way gods, am I not right in saying that you talk in riddles and are jesting? First you say that I do not believe in gods, and next that I do believe in them inasmuch as I believe in spirits. Or again: if the spirits [daimones] are illegitimate children of the gods, whether by nymphs or other mothers as report will have it, who on earth will ever think that there are children of the gods, but that there are no gods? It would be as queer as to think that mules were the offspring of horses and asses, but that horses and asses did not exist. No, Meletus, there is no way out of it; either you formulated this complaint in order to try us out, or else you could find no real crime with which to charge me. That you could get a living person with the least intelligence to admit that a given man believed in the doings of spirits but not of gods, and that the same man, again, believed in neither spirits, gods, nor heroes, is quite beyond the bounds of possibility.

No, fellow citizens, that I am guiltless with respect to Meletus' indictment seems to me to call for no long defence; rather, let this argument suffice. But what I have said before, that much antagonism has arisen against me in the minds of many, rest assured that it is true. And this it is that will undo me, if I am undone, not Meletus nor Anytus, but the slander of the many, and their malice. Many another man, and good ones, has it undone, and, methinks, it will yet undo. There is no danger that the thing may stop with me.

Perhaps some one will say: 'Well, Socrates, aren't you ashamed that you pursued a course from which you now are in danger of death?' To that it would be right for me to reply: 'Good sir, it is not well said if you think that a man of any worth at all ought to calculate his chances of living or dying, and not rather look to this alone, when he acts, to see if what he does is right or wrong, and if his are the deeds of a good man or a bad. By your account, the demigods who fell at Troy would be sorry fellows, all of them, and notably the son of Thetis, who so despised all danger in comparison with any disgrace awaiting him, and with what result? When his mother saw him eager to slay Hector, she, the goddess, addressed him, as I recall, approximately thus: "My child, if you avenge the death of your comrade Patroclus by slaying Hector, then you yourself will die. For you the lot of death," she said, "comes straightway after Hector's." But he, on hearing that, made light of death and danger, fearing far more to live a coward and not avenge his loved ones. "Straightway let me die," said he, "once I give the villain his reward, and not continue here, a laughing-stock, beside the hollow ships, a burden to the earth." Do you think that he took heed of death or danger?

That, fellow citizens, is the way things really stand. If any one is stationed where he thinks it is best for him to be, or where his commander has put him, there, as it seems to me, it is his duty to remain, no matter what the risk, heedless of death or any other peril in comparison with disgrace.

It would have been dreadful conduct, fellow citizens, had I acted otherwise. When the leaders you had chosen to command me assigned a post to me at Potidaea, at Amphipolis, and at Delium, in the face of death itself I was as steadfast as any one could be in holding the position where they placed me; and when the god, as I believed and understood, assigned to me as my duty that I should live the life of a philosopher, and examine myself and others, it would have been dreadful had I through fear of death, or of anything else whatever, deserted my post. Dreadful indeed would it be, and verily any one would then be justified in bringing me to trial for not believing in gods, when I had disobeyed the oracle, feared death, and thought that I was wise when I was not.

For, Gentlemen, to be afraid of death is nothing else than thinking that one is wise when one is not, since it means fancying that one knows what one does not. Nobody knows, in fact, what death is, nor whether to man it is not perchance the greatest of all blessings; yet people fear it as if they surely knew it to be the worst of evils. And what is this but the shameful ignorance of supposing that we know what we do not? It is there and in that perhaps that I differ, Gentlemen, from the majority of mankind; and if I might call myself more wise than another, it would be in this, that as I do not know enough about what goes on in Hades, so too I do not think that I know. But doing wrong, and disobeying the person who is better than myself, be it god or man, that I know is base and wicked. Therefore never for the sake of evils which I know to be such will I fear or flee from what for all I know may be a good.

Accordingly, suppose you were now to acquit me, and went against Anytus; he who says that either I ought not to have been summoned hither to begin with, or, once I appeared I must inevitably be put to death; for he tells you that, if I am freed, your sons, who already put in practice what Socrates teaches, will all be utterly ruined. Suppose with reference to that you were to say to me: 'Socrates, at present we shall not give Anytus our assent, but will acquit you, yet upon one condition, namely, that hereafter you shall not pass your time in this investigation nor pursue philosophy; if you are caught doing it again, you die.' Well, as I said, if you were ready to let me go upon these conditions, my reply to you would be:

'Fellow citizens, I respect and love you, but I must obey the god rather than you, and so long as I draw breath, and can pursue philosophy, I will not cease from it nor from exhorting you, and ever pointing out the way to any one of you I meet, saying to him as I have been wont: "Good friend, you are a citizen of Athens, the greatest of all cities and the most renowned for power and learning, and yet you feel no shame at giving your mind to money so that you may get as much as possible, and to your reputation and to honor; but for insight, for the truth, for your soul and how it shall be at its best, you do not care nor trouble." '

And if any one of you disputes it, and says that he does care, I shall not forthwith dismiss him and go away, but will question him, and sift him, and put him to the test; and if he seems to me to have no fund of virtue, while professing to have it, I shall reproach him with attaching little value to what has most importance, and taking paltry things for what is larger. So will I do with young and old, whatever he be that I meet with, foreigner or native, yet rather with you citizens since you are nearer to me by kin; for this, you may rest assured, is what the god demands of me. And I think that there never came to you a greater good in the City than the service I render the god.

All I do is to go about persuading you, both young and old, not to think first of your bodies or your property, nor to be so mightily concerned about them as about your souls, how the spirit shall be at its best; it is my task to tell you that virtue does not spring from wealth, but that wealth and every other good that comes to men in private life or in public proceed from virtue. If it is by saying this that I corrupt the young, then this must be injurious; but any one who holds that I say anything save this says nothing. On that head, fellow citizens, I may assure you that whether you trust Anytus or not, and whether you acquit me or do not acquit me, I shall not alter my course, no matter if I have to die a hundred times.

Now, fellow citizens, do not interrupt, but continue granting my request of you not to cry out at what I may say, but to listen; I do believe that you will profit if you listen. I am, in fact, about to tell you certain other things at which you might possibly protest. Yet please do not. No; for you may rest assured that if you condemn me to death, I being such a person as I say, you will do yourselves more harm than you do me. As for me, Meletus will no more hurt me than will Anytus. It does not lie in his power, for in my belief the eternal order does not permit a better man to be harmed by a worse. Oh yes! quite possibly he might kill or banish me, or rob me of my civic rights; and doubtless this man and the next will think that these are major evils. I do not think them such; no, I think it a far greater evil for a man to do what this man now is doing, namely trying to get a man condemned to death unjustly.

So, fellow citizens, at present I am far from making my defence upon my own account, as one might think; I make it for your sake, in order that you may not, by condemning me, do wrong about the gift of the god to you; for if you have me put to death, you will not easily find another of the sort, fastened upon the City by the god, for all the world (if I may use a rather ludicrous comparison) like a gadfly on a great and noble horse that is somewhat sluggish on account of his size and needs the fly to wake him up. So, it seems to me, the god has fastened me like that upon the City, to rouse, exhort, and rebuke each one of you, everywhere besetting you, and never once ceasing all day long. Another one like that, Gentlemen, you will not come by so easily; but if you listen to me, you will take good care of me. You may, however, quite possibly be annoyed, like people awakened from their slumbers, and, striking out at me, may listen readily to Anytus and condemn me to death. Then you would finish out the rest of your life in sleep, unless the god were in mercy to send you some one else to take my place. That it is the deity by whom I, such as I am, have been given to the City you may see from this: it is not like human nature for me to neglect all my own concerns, to put up with a neglected household all these years, and to attend to your affair, ever going to you individually in private, like a father or an elder brother, urging you to care for your moral welfare. And if I got any profit from it all, if these exhortations brought me any pay, there would seem to be some reason in my conduct. As it is, you see for yourselves that my accusers, who, unashamed, have brought so many other charges against me, have yet not had the effrontery to present a witness to allege that I ever took any sort of fee or sought one. Why not? Because, methinks, the witness I present to show that I speak the truth is quite enough—my poverty.

Possibly it may look odd that I should busily go about in private with my counsels, but in public dare not approach the mass of you with counsel for the City. The reason for that is something you have often heard me speak of in many a place; it is that there comes to me a thing divine and spiritual, what Meletus has mockingly referred to in his indictment. From childhood on, this sign has come to me; it is a voice, which, when it comes, always deters me from what I am about to do, but never urges me to act. It is this that fights against my entering political affairs; and the opposition strikes me as being altogether good; for, fellow citizens, you may rest assured that if I, long ago, had tried to take up politics, I should long ago have perished, and been of no service whatever either to you or to myself. And do not be aggrieved at me for telling the truth: there is not a man on earth that is safe if he nobly puts himself in opposition to you or to any other crowd, and strives to stop all sorts of wrong and lawlessness in the State. But if any one is really going to battle for the right, and to be safe for some short time in doing it, he must perforce remain a private citizen; he must not appear in public life.

Of that I will furnish you with telling evidence, not arguments, but what you value, facts. Listen to what happened in my case, and you will see that I am not a man to yield to any one unjustly for fear of death, not even if by my not yielding I were at once to perish. The tale I shall tell you is of the legal sort and uninspiring, but is true.

I never held any public office, fellow citizens, but one: I was a member of the Council. And it happened that our tribe, Antiochis, had the executive function [prytany] at the time you wished to sentence in a body the ten commanders who failed to pick up the survivors of the naval action [at Arginusae]. The procedure was illegal, as after a while you all admitted. But at the time I was the only one of the prytanes who stood out against your doing an illegal act and voted against you; and although the orators were ready to indict me and arrest me, while you urged them on and made an uproar, I thought that I ought to risk all danger on the side of law and justice rather than side with you in an unjust decree for fear of imprisonment or death.

This took place while Athens still was a democracy. But again, when the oligarchy was established, the Thirty had me and four others summoned to the Rotunda, and ordered us to go get Leon of Salamis, and bring him thence to have him put to death; they gave such orders frequently to many other persons in order to involve as many as they could in their crimes. But there again I showed, by deeds, and not by words, that death, if I may speak quite baldly, meant nothing at all to me, while not to do an unjust or an impious act, this meant everything; for that power, however huge its sway, did not terrify me into doing what was wrong. No, when we came out of the Rotunda, the other four went off to Salamis and brought back Leon, and as for me I went to my home. And for that I might well have paid with my life, had the government not promptly fallen. Of these facts many persons will bear witness to you.

Well then, do you think I could have survived through all these years if I had taken part in state affairs, and, acting properly as a good citizen, had fought for justice, making this perforce of paramount importance? Far from it, fellow citizens; nor could any other living man have done it. As for me, all my life long, if ever I did anything in an official way, I showed myself to be that sort of person, and in private just the same; never once did I yield to anyone in any point against the right, not even to one of those whom my slanderers declare to be my pupils.

But I never have been anybody's teacher. If any one cares to listen to me as I speak and carry on my special function, be he young or old, I never have begrudged it. I am not one who will engage in discussion if he gets money, and if not refuses. No, rich and poor alike I am prepared to question, and whoever will may listen to what I say when I make reply. And for my part, if any of them turns out well or ill, I cannot rightly be held responsible when I never offered to give any one instruction, nor gave it. If any one asserts that he ever learned or heard a thing from me other than what all the others heard as well, rest assured that he who says so does not tell the truth.

Well then, why do certain persons like to spend so much of their time with me? I told you, fellow citizens, what the reason is. The truth of the matter is just what I said: they like to hear the sifting out of those who think that they are wise, but are not. The thing, in fact, is not unpleasant. But for me, as I aver, it is a task enjoined upon me by the deity, through oracles, through dreams, and in every single way that ever a divine injunction was laid upon a man to do a thing. These statements, fellow citizens, are true and are easily proved. Suppose I am at present ruining some of the young people, and already have perverted others; then necessarily, no doubt, a number of them, when they grew older, would have seen that on occasion, when they were young, I gave them evil advice, and would now appear in court to accuse and punish me. Or, if they themselves were unwilling to do it, then some of their relations, fathers, brothers, or others of their kin—if it were true that members of the family had received some injury from me—would now remember it, and have me punished. Certainly there are many of them present whom I see: first Crito here, a man of my own generation and my deme, father of yon Critobulus; next, Lysanias of Sphettus, father of yon Aeschines; add Antiphon here of Kephisia, father of Epigenes. Among others, men whose brothers have attended at the pastime, Nicostratus son of Theozotides and brother of Theodotus—as for Theodotus, he is dead, and therefore could not plead for me against him; so also Paralus here whose father is Demodocus and whose brother is Theages, Adeimantus son of Ariston whose brother is Plato here, and Aiantodorus, whose brother is yon Apollodorus. And many others I could name to you, of whom Meletus surely ought to have offered somebody as witness in his accusation. If he forgot it then, let him present it now—I yield the point—and let him say if he has any evidence of the sort. But, Gentlemen, you will find the case to be the very opposite of that; will find them all prepared to help me, the ruiner, the man who has done injury to their kin, as Meletus and Anytus aver. The ruined themselves, of course, might have some reason for coming to my aid. But those who are not ruined, men already mature, the relatives of these, what other reason could they have for coming to my aid except the straight and just one, that they know that Meletus is lying, and that I am telling the truth?

There you have it, Gentlemen. That is pretty much what I might have to say in my defence, that with possibly some additions to the like effect. Perhaps, however, one or another of you will be angry when he recalls his own experience, in some trial he was engaged in of less gravity than this; if he besought and with many tears implored the judges, and, in order to arouse the greatest pity, brought in his children along with others of his kin and many friends; while, as for me, I shall do nothing of the sort, although I am in danger, as I might suppose, to the last degree of peril. Perhaps, then, as he thinks of this, he will bear himself with the less remorse towards me, and, irritated by these very things, will cast his vote in anger. Now if any of you feels so, though for my part I do not impute it—but if anybody feels that way, then it seems to me the proper thing for me to say to him would be: 'Good friend, I too have friends and relatives; in fact, my case is just as Homer says. "I did not spring from either oak or rock," but from mankind, and so I have a family and sons; three sons, my fellow citizens, one a youth, and the other two are little boys.' Nevertheless not one of them will I bring hither imploring you to let me off. And why shall I do nothing of all that? Not, fellow citizens, out of hardihood, nor in disdain of you. And whether I fear death or not is another question; but for my own honor, and yours, and the honor of the entire City, it does not seem proper for me at my age, and with the name I have, to do any of these things. The opinion may be true, or may be false; at all events the view is held that Socrates is somehow different from the mass of men. Well, if those of you who are regarded as distinguished in point of wisdom, or of courage, or of any other quality, behaved like that, it would be shameful. And yet, often enough, I have seen persons of such sort, persons of some reputation, behaving in extraordinary fashion when they were to hear the verdict, as if they thought they must be going to suffer something terrible if they had to die—as if they thought that they would be immortal in case you did not condemn them. To my mind, they brought shame upon the City; anybody from another city would infer that the Athenians who were eminent for their virtue, those whom their fellows selected as their rulers and for other places of distinction, were in no way better than women. These things, fellow citizens, it behoves us not to do if we have any reputation whatsoever; and if we do them, you should not allow it. No; you should make this very thing quite clear, that you will far more readily give your vote against the person who drags in these tearful dramas, and makes the City ridiculous, than against the man who argues quietly.

But apart from the question of propriety, Gentlemen, it does not seem right to me to beg the judge for mercy, or, by doing it, to get away, when one ought rather to enlighten and convince him. He does not take his seat for this, the judge, to render justice as a favor, but to decide on what is just. Indeed he took an oath that he would not favor people according to his notion of them, but that he would give judgment in accordance with the laws. And so we should not get you into the habit of perjuring yourselves, nor should you get into it; neither of us should commit impiety. So do not ask me, fellow citizens, to treat you in a way which I take to be dishonorable, wrong, and impious; above all, by Zeus! when I am under accusation of impiety by this Meletus here present; for obviously, if I swayed you and by begging forced you to act against your oath, I would be teaching you not to believe that there are gods, and by my defence would simply accuse myself of not believing in them. But that be far from me! I do believe in them, my fellow citizens, as none of my accusers does; and to you I commend myself, and to the Deity, to judge concerning me what shall be best at once for me and for you.

### AFTER THE VOTE AGAINST HIM

If I am not distressed, my fellow citizens, at what has happened in that you voted to convict me, there are many reasons for it, and in particular that the outcome was to me not unexpected. What is to me far more surprising is the actual division of the votes. I thought for my part that the vote would go not by this small majority, but by a large one. As it is, apparently, if only thirty votes had gone the other way, I should have been acquitted. Accordingly, so far as Meletus is concerned, it seems to me I do now stand acquitted, and not only that, but it must be clear to every one that if Anytus and Lycon had not come hither to accuse me, he would have had to pay one thousand drachmas as a fine for not obtaining a fifth part of the votes.

Meanwhile the man proposes for me the penalty of death. So be it. What penalty, fellow citizens, am I to offer you instead? Evidently what I ought to get? What is it, then? What do I deserve to get or pay? I who, when I had learned a thing, did not lead my life in peace, but neglecting what the many care for—wealth, household matters, military leadership and civic and the other high positions, coalitions, factions that arise in the State—thought myself in fact too good a man to enter into these affairs with safety. I did not enter there where if I came I was not to be of any use either to you or to myself, but going to you one by one in private, I did you, I aver, the greatest service possible. There I went trying to persuade each one of you not to care first for his own possessions before caring for himself and how he might be at his best and wisest, nor to set the affairs of the City above the City itself, and to give attention to all other things in just that way. Being a man of that description, what ought I to get? Something good, my fellow citizens, if the award must truly square with the desert; and the good ought further to be something that fits my case. What, then, befits a poor man, a benefactor, who needs leisure for the office of exhorting you? Nothing is so proper as the maintenance of such a man in the Prytaneum, a reward far more befitting him than for any one of you who may have won a victory at Olympia with a horse or a pair of them or four. He makes you think that you are happy; I cause you to be so. He, moreover, has no need of maintenance; I stand in need of it. And so if I must get what I de-serve, there is my proposal: maintenance in the Prytaneum.

Perhaps when I say that to you, you will think that I am talking with the same bravado as about the tears and supplications. It is not, fellow citizens, as you think; no, it is more like this. I am persuaded that I never willingly wronged any man, but I have not persuaded you, since we have had small time to reach an understanding; whereas if the law with you were what it is with others, if a case involving the penalty of death could not be settled in a day, but took a number, I believe I would have won you over. As matters stand, it is not easy in a limited time to refute a mass of slanders.

Persuaded that I do no wrong to any one, I am far from ready to do injustice to myself, and will not say of myself that I merit some evil, and should allot myself that sort of penalty. In fear of what? For fear that otherwise I shall suffer the thing which Meletus proposes, that of which I say I know not whether it is good or evil? Instead of that ought I to choose one of the things that I know for certain to be ills, and penalize myself with that? Imprisonment? Why should I live in prison, a slave to a recurrent board of governors, the Eleven? Or say a fine, and to be jailed until I pay it? But that would be no different for me from what I just now mentioned, since I have no money to pay with. Well, suppose I offered to go into exile. Perhaps you would accept that. But truly, fellow citizens, the love of life must have a powerful hold on me, and make me heedless, if I cannot reason thus: You who are my fellow citizens could not endure my doings and discussions; no, they were too much for you, and so irritating that now you seek to be rid of them. Well, will others bear them easily? Far from it, fellow citizens. And what a fine existence that would be, for a man of my age to go away and live a wanderer and a waif driven from city to city; for well I know that wherever I went the young would listen to me just as they do here. And if I drove them off, they would get the older men's permission, and themselves expel me. And if I did not, their fathers and relations would expel me on the sons' account.

Well, perhaps some one will say: 'Why can't you go away from us, and then keep quiet, Socrates, and live in peace?' But that is the thing that is hardest of all to make some of you see. If I say that this means disobedience to the god, and for that very reason I cannot keep still, you will not believe me, but will think I speak in irony. If, on the other hand, I say it is perhaps the greatest good that can befall a man, daily to argue about virtue, and to discuss the other subjects about which you have heard me debating and examining myself as well as others, if I add that for mankind the unexamined life is not worth living, still less will you believe me when I tell you that. These matters stand, however, Gentlemen, precisely as I say, only it is not easy to convince you. And meanwhile, for my part, I am not in the habit of thinking that I merit ill at all. If I had wealth, I would suggest a sum that I was in a position to pay, for in that case I should do myself no harm. But now the fact is that I haven't, unless you chose to set a fine for me at a rate that I could pay. Perhaps I could pay you a silver mina; so that is what I offer.

But Plato here, my fellow citizens, and Crito, Critobulus, and Apollodorus, bid me offer thirty minæ upon their security. Well then, I offer that; these men will be adequate security to you for the amount.

### AFTER HE IS CONDEMNED TO DEATH

For no great thrift in time, my fellow citizens, you will have from those who wish to vilify the City the name and blame of having put to death the wise man, Socrates; for they will call me wise, even if I am not, they who would defame you. If only you had waited for a little while, the thing would have occurred for you in the course of nature; for you can see my age, that I am far along in life, and near to death. I say this, not to all of you, but only to those who voted for my death. And to them I have also to say this as well. It may be, Gentlemen, that you think I lost my cause for lack of arguments of the sort with which I might have won you over, if I had thought that I ought to say and do all things in order to escape the verdict. Far from it. I lost for a lack, but not of arguments; it was for lack of impudence and daring, and for not being ready to say to you the sort of thing it would have given you most pleasure to hear—me weeping and wailing, and doing and saying any and every sort of thing that I hold to be unworthy of me, but you are accustomed to hear from the rest. No, I did not then believe that, to avoid a danger, I ought to do anything unseemly in a freeman, nor do I now regret my manner of defence. No, far rather would I choose this manner of defence, and die, than follow that, and live. Whether in a court of justice or in war neither I nor any other man should seek by using every means conceivable to escape from death; for in battle you very often see that if you throw away your weapons and beg those who are pursuing you for mercy, you may get out of dying. Indeed, in every sort of danger there are various ways of winning through, if one is ready to do and say anything whatever. No, Gentlemen, that is not the hard thing, to escape from death; ah no, far harder is it to escape from sin, for sin is swifter than death. And so I, being old and slow, am overtaken by the slower enemy; while my accusers, who are strong and swift, have been caught by the swifter, namely wickedness. And so I now depart, by you condemned to pay the penalty of death; and they, by the truth convicted of a base injustice. And as I abide the payment, so do they. Who knows? Perhaps it had to be so, and I think that things are as they ought to be.

Touching the future, I desire to make for you who voted to condemn me, a prediction; for I am at the point where men foresee the future best—when they are soon to die. Let me tell you then, you men who have condemned me, that after I am gone there will straightway come upon you a chastisement far heavier, by Zeus, than the death you have set for me. You have now done this in the belief that you have freed yourselves from giving any reckoning for your life; but I tell you the result will be the very opposite for you. There will be more inquisitors to sift you, men whom I now hold in check without your knowing it. And they will be more critical as they are younger, and will annoy you more; for if you think that by putting men to death you will prevent the slur from being cast at you that you do not live aright, you are in error. This way of getting freedom is neither very sure nor fine; no, the finest and readiest way is this, not to interfere with other people, but to render oneself as good a man as possible. There is the prophecy I make for you who voted to condemn me. And of them I take my leave.

With those of you who voted to acquit me I should be glad to talk about this thing that has occurred, while the magistrates are busy and it is not time for me to go to the place where I must die. So, Gentlemen, please wait with me as long as that. There is nothing to keep us from talking to each other as long as it is allowed. To you as to friends I wish to explain the real meaning of what has just happened to me.

Justices, for when I call you that I am naming you aright, the thing that has come to me is wonderful.

My customary warning, by the spirit, in previous times has always, up to now, come to me very often to oppose me, even when a matter was quite unimportant, if ever I was going to do something amiss. But to-day, as you yourselves have witnessed, that thing has happened to me which anybody might suppose, and which is considered, to be the uttermost of evils. Yet neither did the sign from god oppose me when I left my house this morning, nor at the point when I ascended here to the tribunal, nor in my speech at anything I was about to say; though often when I have been talking elsewhere it has stopped me in the middle of a speech. But to-day, with reference to the whole procedure, not once did it oppose me in a thing I did or said. What, then, do I take to be the cause of this? No doubt this thing that has happened to me is good, and it cannot be that our supposition is correct when any of us think that death is a misfortune. For me, the proof of this is telling: it cannot be but that the customary sign would have opposed me, if I had not been about to do a thing that was good.

Let us view in another way how ample are the grounds for our hope that death is good. To be dead is one of two things. Either it is a sort of non-existence, and the dead man has no feeling about anything whatever, or else, as people say, the soul experiences a shift and a migration from here into another place. Now if there is no feeling, if death is like a sleep in which one does not even dream, what a wonderful gain it would be! I believe if a man were to take that night in which he slept so deeply that he did not have a single dream, and compared it with the other nights and days of his life; if he had to say, upon reflection, how many days and nights, all told, in his life, he has passed better and more sweetly than that night; I believe that every one, not merely any private citizen, but the Great King himself, would find them easy to count up in comparison with all the others. So if death is a sleep like that, I say it is a gain; for thus all time appears to be no more than a single night. If, on the other hand, death is like a journey from here to another place, and if what they say is true, that everybody who has died is there, then, Justices, what greater good than this could there be? If, on arriving in Hades, one could be freed from those who here pretend that they are Justices, and there find those who by report deal real justice, Minos, Rhadamanthus, Aæcus, and Triptolemus, and all the rest of the demigods who were just in their lives here, what a small thing would that journey seem! Or, again, to be with Orpheus and Musæus, with Hesiod and Homer, what price would not any of you pay for that? I would gladly die repeatedly, if all that is true. To me it would be a wonderful way to pass my time, there where I could meet with Palamedes and with Ajax son of Telamon, and any one else among the ancients who died through an unjust decision. To compare my lot with theirs, methinks, would not be so unpleasant; and most important of all would be to go on sifting people there, as here, and finding out who is wise, and who thinks he is so, but is not. What would not anybody give to examine, Justices, the leader of that mighty expedition against Troy, or else Odysseus, or Sisyphus, or a myriad of others one might mention, men and women too? There to talk with them, consort with them, examine them, would be a happiness beyond compare! Surely there, I take it, they do not put a man to death for doing that; for, happy in all else, people are happier there than here in that henceforth they are immortal, at all events if what is said is true.

But, Justices, you also it behoves to have good hope with reference to death, and this one thing you must bear in mind as true, that, living or dead, to a good man there can come no evil, nor are his affairs a matter of indifference to the gods. Nor has my destiny now come about by chance; rather, it is clear to me that it was better for me now to die and to be released from my troubles. That is why the sign did not at any point deter me, and why

I am not very bitter at those who voted to condemn me, or at my accusers. It is true they did not have this notion in condemning and accusing me; no, they thought to injure me, and therein they merit blame.

One thing, however, I do beg of them. When my sons grow up, then, Gentlemen, I ask you to punish them, you hurting them the same as I hurt you, if they seem to you to care for money, or aught else, more than they care for virtue. And if they pretend to be somewhat when they are nothing, do you upbraid them as I upbraided you, for not regarding as important what they ought to think so, and for thinking they have worth when they do not. If you do that, I shall have received just treatment from you, and my sons as well.

And now the time has come for our departure, I to die, and you to live. Which of us goes to meet the better lot is hidden from all unless it be known to God.

❧ ❧ ❧

*Jonathan Swift*

# A Modest Proposal[1]

### For Preventing the Children of Poor People From Being A Burthen to Their Parents or Country, and for Making Them Beneficial to the Public.

It is a melancholy object to those who walk through this great town, or travel in the country, when they see the streets, the roads, and cabin-doors crowded with beggars of the female sex, followed by three, four, or six children, *all in rags*, and importuning every passenger for an alms. These mothers, instead of being able to work for their honest livelihood, are forced to employ all their time in strolling, to beg sustenance for their helpless infants, who, as they grow up, either turn thieves for want of work, or leave their dear Native Country to fight for the Pretender in Spain, or sell themselves to the Barbadoes.

I think it is agreed by all parties that this prodigious number of children, in the arms, or on the backs, or at the heels of their mothers, and frequently of their fathers, is in the present deplorable state of the kingdom a very great additional grievance; and therefore whoever could find out a fair, cheap, and easy method of making these children sound useful members of the commonwealth would deserve so well of the public as to have his statue set up for a preserver of the nation.

But my intention is very far from being confined to provide only for the children of professed beggars; it is of a much greater extent, and shall take in the whole number of infants at a certain age who are born of parents

[1] First published in 1729.

in effect as little able to support them as those who demand our charity in the streets.

As to my own part, having turned my thoughts, for many years, upon this important subject, and maturely weighed the several schemes of other projectors, I have always found them grossly mistaken in their computation. It is true a child, just dropped from its dam, may be supported by her milk for a solar year with little other nourishment, at most not above the value of two shillings, which the mother may certainly get, or the value in scraps, by her lawful occupation of begging, and it is exactly at one year old that I propose to provide for them, in such a manner as, instead of being a charge upon their parents, or the parish, or wanting food and raiment for the rest of their lives, they shall, on the contrary, contribute to the feeding and partly to the clothing of many thousands.

There is likewise another great advantage in my scheme, that it will prevent those voluntary abortions, and that horrid practice of women murdering their bastard children, alas, too frequent among us, sacrificing the poor innocent babes, I doubt, more to avoid the expense than the shame, which would move tears and pity in the most savage and inhuman breast.

The number of souls in this kingdom being usually reckoned one million and a half, of these I calculate there may be about two hundred thousand couple whose wives are breeders, from which number I subtract thirty thousand couple who are able to maintain their own children, although I apprehend there cannot be so many under the present distresses of the kingdom, but this being granted, there will remain an hundred and seventy thousand breeders. I again subtract fifty thousand for those women who miscarry, or whose children die by accident or disease within the year. There only remain an hundred and twenty thousand children of poor parents annually born: The question therefore is, how this number shall be reared, and provided for, which, as I have already said, under the present situation of affairs, is utterly impossible by all the methods hitherto proposed, for we can neither employ them in handicraft, or agriculture; we neither build houses (I mean in the country), nor cultivate land: they can very seldom pick up a livelihood by stealing till they arrive at six years old, except where they are of towardly parts, although, I confess they learn the rudiments much earlier, during which time they can however be properly looked upon only as *probationers*, as I have been informed by a principal gentleman in the County of Cavan, who protested to me that he never knew above one or two instances under the age of six, even in a part of the kingdom so renowned for the quickest proficiency in that art.

I am assured by our merchants that a boy or a girl, before twelve years old, is no saleable commodity, and even when they come to this age, they will not yield above three pounds, or three pounds and half-a-crown at most on the Exchange, which cannot turn to account either to the parents or the kingdom, the charge of nutriment and rags having been at least four times that value.

I shall now therefore humbly propose my own thoughts, which I hope will not be liable to the least objection.

I have been assured by a very knowing American of my acquaintance in London, that a young healthy child well nursed is at a year old a most delicious, nourishing, and wholesome food, whether stewed, roasted, baked, or boiled, and I make no doubt that it will equally serve in a fricassee, or a ragout.

I do therefore humbly offer it to public consideration, that of the hundred and twenty thousand children already computed, twenty thousand may be reserved for breed, whereof only one fourth part to be males, which is more than we allow to sheep, black-cattle, or swine, and my reason is that these children are seldom the fruits of marriage, a circumstance not much regarded by our savages, therefore one male will be sufficient to serve four females. That the remaining hundred thousand may at a year old be offered in sale to the persons of quality, and fortune, through the kingdom, always advising the mother to let them suck plentifully in the last month, so as to render them plump, and fat for a good table. A child will make two dishes at an entertainment for friends, and when the family dines alone, the fore or hind quarter will make a reasonable dish, and seasoned with a little pepper or salt will be very good boiled on the fourth day, especially in winter.

I have reckoned upon a medium, that a child just born will weigh 12 pounds, and in a solar year if tolerably nursed increaseth to 28 pounds.

I grant this food will be somewhat dear, and therefore very proper for landlords, who, as they have already devoured most of the parents, seem to have the best title to the children.

Infants' flesh will be in season throughout the year, but more plentiful in March, and a little before and after, for we are told by a grave author, an eminent French physician, that fish being a prolific diet, there are more children born in Roman Catholic countries about nine months after Lent than at any other season; therefore reckoning a year after Lent, the markets will be more glutted than usual, because the number of Popish infants is at least three to one in this kingdom, and therefore it will have one other collateral advantage by lessening the number of Papists among us.

I have already computed the charge of nursing a beggar's child (in which list I reckon all cottagers, labourers, and four-fifths of the farmers) to be about two shillings *per annum*, rags included, and I believe no gentleman would repine to give ten shillings for the carcass of a good fat child, which, as I have said, will make four dishes of excellent nutritive meat, when he hath only some particular friend or his own family to dine with him. Thus the Squire will learn to be a good landlord, and grow popular among his tenants, the mother will have eight shillings net profit, and be fit for work till she produces another child.

Those who are more thrifty (as I must confess the times require) may flay the carcass; the skin of which, artificially dressed, will make admirable gloves for ladies, and summer boots for fine gentlemen.

As to our City of Dublin, shambles may be appointed for this purpose, in the most convenient parts of it, and butchers we may be assured will not be wanting, although I rather recommend buying the children alive, and dressing them hot from the knife, as we do roasting pigs.

A very worthy person, a true lover of this country, and whose virtues I highly esteem, was lately pleased, in discoursing on this matter, to offer a refinement upon my scheme. He said that many gentlemen of this kingdom, having of late destroyed their deer, he conceived that the want of venison might be well supplied by the bodies of young lads and maidens, not exceeding fourteen years of age, nor under twelve, so great a number of both sexes in every country being now ready to starve, for want of work and service: and these to be disposed of by their parents if alive, or otherwise by their nearest relations. But with due deference to so excellent a friend, and so deserving a patriot, I cannot be altogether in his sentiments; for as to the males, my American acquaintance assured me from frequent experience that their flesh was generally tough and lean, like that of our schoolboys, by continual exercise, and their taste disagreeable, and to fatten them would not answer the charge. Then as to the females, it would, I think with humble submission, be a loss to the public, because they soon would become breeders themselves: And besides, it is not improbable that some scrupulous people might be apt to censure such a practice (although indeed very unjustly) as a little bordering upon cruelty, which, I confess, hath always been with me the strongest objection against any project, however so well intended.

But in order to justify my friend, he confessed that this expedient was put into his head by the famous Psalmanazar, a native of the island Formosa, who came from thence to London, above twenty years ago, and in conversation told my friend that in his country when any young person happened to be put to death, the executioner sold the carcass to persons of quality, as a prime dainty, and that, in his time, the body of a plump girl of fifteen, who was crucified for an attempt to poison the emperor, was sold to his Imperial Majesty's Prime Minister of State, and other great Mandarins of the Court, in joints from the gibbet, at four hundred crowns. Neither indeed can I deny that if the same use were made of several plump young girls in this town, who, without one single groat to their fortunes, cannot stir abroad without a chair, and appear at the playhouse, and assemblies in foreign fineries, which they never will pay for, the kingdom would not be the worse.

Some persons of a desponding spirit are in great concern about that vast number of poor people, who are aged, diseased, or maimed, and I have been desired to employ my thoughts what course may be taken to ease the nation of so grievous an encumbrance. But I am not in the least pain upon that matter, because it is very well known that they are every day dying, and rotting, by cold, and famine, and filth, and vermin, as fast as can be reasonably expected. And as to the younger labourers they are now in almost as hopeful a condition. They cannot get work, and consequently pine away for want of nourishment, to a degree, that if at any time they are accidentally hired to common labour, they have not strength to perform it; and thus the country and themselves are happily delivered from the evils to come.

I have too long digressed, and therefore shall return to my subject. I think the advantages by the proposal which I have made are obvious and many, as well as of the highest importance.

For first, as I have already observed, it would greatly lessen the number of Papists, with whom we are yearly over-run, being the principal breeders of the nation, as well as our most dangerous enemies, and who stay at home on purpose with a design to deliver the kingdom to the Pretender, hoping to take their advantage by the absence of so many good Protestants, who have chosen rather to leave their country than stay at home, and pay tithes against their conscience to an Episcopal curate.

Secondly, The poorer tenants will have something valuable of their own, which by law be made liable to distress, and help to pay their landlord's rent, their corn and cattle being already seized, and *money a thing unknown*.

Thirdly, Whereas the maintenance of an hundred thousand children, from two years old, and upwards, cannot be computed at less than ten shillings a piece *per annum*, the nation's stock will be thereby increased fifty thousand pounds *per annum*, besides the profit of a new dish, introduced to the tables of all gentlemen of fortune in the kingdom, who have any refinement in taste, and the money will circulate among ourselves, the goods being entirely of our own growth and manufacture.

Fourthly, The constant breeders, besides the gain of eight shillings sterling *per annum*, by the sale of their children, will be rid of the charge of maintaining them after the first year.

Fifthly, This food would likewise bring great custom to taverns, where the vintners will certainly be so prudent as to procure the best receipts for dressing it to perfection, and consequently have their houses frequented by all the fine gentlemen, who justly value themselves upon their knowledge in good eating; and a skilful cook, who understands how to oblige his guests, will contrive to make it as expensive as they please.

Sixthly, This would be a great inducement to marriage, which all wise nations have either encouraged by rewards, or enforced by laws and penalties. It would increase the care and tenderness of mothers toward their children, when they were sure of a settlement for life, to the poor babes, provided in some sort by the public to their annual profit instead of expense. We should see an honest emulation among the married women, which of them could bring the fattest child to the market, men would become as fond of their wives, during the time of their pregnancy, as they are now of their mares in foal, their cows in calf, or sows when they are ready to farrow, nor offer to beat or kick them (as it is too frequent a practice) for fear of a miscarriage.

Many other advantages might be enumerated: For instance, the addition of some thousand carcasses in our exportation of barrelled beef; the propagation of swine's flesh, and improvement in the art of making good bacon, so much wanted among us by the great destruction of pigs, too frequent at our tables, which are no way comparable in taste or magnificence to a well-grown, fat yearling child, which roasted whole will make a considerable figure at a Lord Mayor's feast, or any other public entertainment. But this and many others I omit, being studious of brevity.

Supposing that one thousand families in this city would be constant customers for infants' flesh, besides others who might have it at merry-meetings, particularly weddings and christenings, I compute that Dublin would take off annually about twenty thousand carcasses, and the rest of the kingdom (where probably they will be sold somewhat cheaper) the remaining eighty thousand.

I can think of no one objection that will possibly be raised against this proposal, unless it should be urged that the number of people will be thereby much lessened in the kingdom. This I freely own, and was indeed one principal design in offering it to the world. I desire the reader will observe, that I calculate my remedy for this one individual *Kingdom of Ireland, and for no other that ever was, is, or, I think, ever can be upon earth*. Therefore let no man talk to me of other expedients: *Of taxing our absentees at five shillings a pound: Of using neither clothes, nor household furniture, except what is of our own growth and manufacture: Of utterly rejecting the materials and instruments that promote foreign luxury: Of curing the expensiveness of pride, vanity, idleness, and gaming in our women: Of introducing a vein of parsimony, prudence, and temperance: Of learning to love our Country, wherein we differ even from* LAPLANDERS, *and the inhabitants of* TOPI-NAMBOO: *Of quitting our animosities and factions, nor act any longer like the Jews, who were murdering one another at the very moment their city was taken: Of being a little cautious not to sell our country and consciences for nothing: Of teaching landlords to have at least one degree of mercy toward their tenants. Lastly, of putting a spirit of honesty, industry, and skill into our shopkeepers, who, if a resolution could now be taken to buy only our native goods, would immediately unite to cheat and exact upon us in the price, the measure, and the goodness, nor could ever yet be brought to make one fair proposal of just dealing, though often and earnestly invited to it.*

Therefore I repeat, let no man talk to me of these and the like expedients, till he hath at least some glimpse of hope that there will ever be some hearty and sincere attempt to put them in practice.

But as to myself, having been wearied out for many years with offering vain, idle, visionary thoughts, and at length utterly despairing of success, I fortunately fell upon this proposal, which as it is wholly new, so it hath something solid and real, of no expense and little trouble, full in our own power, and whereby we can incur no danger in *disobliging* ENGLAND. For this kind of commodity will not bear exportation, the flesh being of too tender a consistence to admit a long continuance in salt, *although perhaps I could name a country which would be glad to eat up our whole nation without it.*

After all I am not so violently bent upon my own opinion as to reject any offer, proposed by wise men, which shall be found equally innocent, cheap, easy, and effectual. But before something of that kind shall be advanced in contradiction to my scheme, and offering a better, I desire the author, or authors, will be pleased maturely to consider two points. First, as things now stand, how they will be able to find food and raiment for an hundred thousand useless mouths and backs. And secondly, there being a round million of creatures in human figure, throughout this kingdom, whose whole subsistence put into a common stock would leave them in debt two millions of pounds sterling; adding those, who are beggars by profession, to the bulk of farmers, cottagers, and labourers with their wives and children, who are beggars in effect. I desire those politicians, who dislike my overture, and may perhaps be so bold to attempt an answer, that they will first ask the parents of these mortals whether they would not at this day think it a great happiness to have been sold for food at a year old, in the manner I prescribe, and thereby have avoided such a perpetual scene of misfortunes as they have since gone through, by the oppression of landlords, the impossibility of paying rent without money or trade, the want of common sustenance, with neither house nor clothes to cover them from the inclemencies of the weather, and the most inevitable prospect of entailing the like, or greater miseries upon their breed for ever.

I profess in the sincerity of my heart that I have not the least personal interest in endeavouring to promote this necessary work, having no other motive than the *public good of my country, by advancing our trade, providing for infants, relieving the poor, and giving some pleasure to the rich.* I have no children by which I can propose to get a single penny; the youngest being nine years old, and my wife past child-bearing.

❀ ❀ ❀

*Thomas Jefferson*

# Declaration of Independence

*The unanimous declaration of the thirteen United
States of America, in Congress, July 4, 1776*

WHEN, in the course of human events, it becomes necessary for one people to dissolve the political bands which have connected them with another, and to assume among the powers of the earth the separate and equal station to which the laws of nature and of nature's God entitle them, a decent respect to the opinions of mankind requires that they should declare the causes which impel them to the separation.

We hold these truths to be self-evident: That all men are created equal; that they are endowed by their Creator with certain inalienable rights; that among these are life, liberty, and the pursuit of happiness. That, to secure these rights, governments are instituted among men, deriving their just powers from the consent of the governed; that, whenever any form of government becomes destructive of these ends, it is the right of the people to alter or to abolish it, and to institute a new government, laying its foundation on such principles, and organizing its powers in such form, as to them shall seem most likely to effect their safety and happiness. Prudence, indeed, will dictate that governments long established should not be changed for light and transient causes; and accordingly all experience hath shown that mankind are more disposed to suffer, while evils are sufferable, than to right themselves by abolishing the forms to which they are accustomed. But when a long train of abuses and usurpations, pursuing invariably the same object, evinces a design to reduce them under absolute despotism, it is their right, it is their duty, to throw off such government and to provide new guards for their future security. Such has been the patient suffering of these colonies, and such is now the necessity which constrains them to alter their former systems of government. The history of the present king of Great Britain is a history of repeated injuries and usurpations, all having in direct object the establishment of an absolute tyranny over these states. To prove this, let facts be submitted to a candid world.

He has refused his assent to laws the most wholesome and necessary for the public good.

He has forbidden his governors to pass laws of immediate and pressing importance, unless suspended in their operation till his assent should be obtained, and, when so suspended, he has utterly neglected to attend to them.

He has refused to pass other laws for the accommodation of large districts of people, unless those people would relinquish the right of representation in the legislature—a right inestimable to them and formidable to tyrants only.

He has called together legislative bodies, at places unusual, uncomfortable, and distant from the repository of their public records, for the sole purpose of fatiguing them into compliance with his measures.

He has dissolved representative houses repeatedly for opposing with manly firmness his invasions on the rights of the people.

He has refused for a long time after such dissolutions to cause others to be elected; whereby the legislative powers, incapable of annihilation, have returned to the people at large for their exercise: the state remaining, in the meantime, exposed to all the dangers of invasion from without and convulsions within.

He has endeavored to prevent the population of these states; for that purpose obstructing the laws for naturalization of foreigners; refusing to pass others to encourage their migration hither, and raising the conditions of new appropriations of lands.

He has obstructed the administration of justice by refusing his assent to laws for establishing his judiciary powers.

He has made judges dependent on his will alone for the tenure of their offices and the amount and payment of their salaries.

He has erected a multitude of new offices and sent hither swarms of officers to harass our people and eat out their substance.

He has kept among us, in times of peace, standing armies without the consent of our legislatures.

He has affected to render the military independent of and superior to the civil power.

He has combined with others to subject us to a jurisdiction foreign to our constitutions and unacknowledged by our laws, giving his assent to their acts of pretended legislation:

For quartering large bodies of armed troops among us;

For protecting them by a mock trial from punishment for any murders which they should commit on the inhabitants of these states;

For cutting off our trade with all parts of the world;

For imposing taxes on us without our consent;

For depriving us in many cases of the benefits of trial by jury;

For transporting us beyond seas to be tried for pretended offenses;

For abolishing the free system of English laws in a neighboring province, establishing therein an arbitrary government, and enlarging its boundaries so as to render it at once an example and fit instrument for introducing the same absolute rule into these colonies;

For taking away our charters, abolishing our most valuable laws, and altering fundamentally the forms of our governments;

For suspending our own legislatures and declaring themselves invested with power to legislate for us in all cases whatsoever.

He has abdicated government here by declaring us out of his protection and waging war against us.

He has plundered our seas, ravaged our coasts, burnt our towns and destroyed the lives of our people.

He is at this time transporting large armies of foreign mercenaries to complete the work of death, desolation, and tyranny already begun, with circumstances of cruelty and perfidy scarcely parallelled in the most barbarous ages and totally unworthy the head of a civilized nation.

He has constrained our fellow citizens taken captive upon the high seas to bear arms against their country, to become the executioners of their friends and brethren, or to fall themselves by their hands.

He has excited domestic insurrection amongst us, and has endeavored to bring on the inhabitants of our frontiers the merciless Indian savages, whose known rule of warfare is an undistinguished destruction of all ages, sexes, and conditions.

In every stage of these oppressions we have petitioned for redress, in the most humble terms; our repeated petitions have been answered only by repeated injury. A prince whose character is thus marked by every act which may define a tyrant is unfit to be the ruler of a free people.

Nor have we been wanting in attention to our British brethren. We have warned them, from time to time, of attempts by their legislature to extend an unwarrantable jurisdiction over us. We have reminded them of the circumstances of our emigration and settlement here. We have appealed to their native justice and magnanimity; and we have conjured them by the ties of our common kindred, to disavow these usurpations, which would inevitably interrupt our connections and correspondence. They, too, have been deaf to the voice of justice and consanguinity. We must, therefore, acquiesce in the necessity which denounces our separation, and hold them, as we hold the rest of mankind, enemies in war; in peace, friends.

We, therefore, the representatives of the United States of America, in general congress assembled, appealing to the Supreme Judge of the World for the rectitude of our intentions, do, in the name and by the authority of the good people of these colonies, solemnly publish and declare that these united colonies are, and of right ought to be, free and independent states; that they are absolved from all allegiance to the British crown, and that all political connection between them and the state of Great Britain is, and ought to be, totally dissolved; and that as free and independent states they have full power to levy war, conclude peace, contract alliances, establish commerce, and to do all other acts and things which independent states may of right do. And for the support of this declaration, with a firm reliance on the protection of Divine Providence, we mutually pledge to each other our lives, our fortunes, and our sacred honor.

❧ ❧ ❧

*Thomas Paine*

# The American Crisis, I

THESE are the times that try men's souls: The summer soldier and the sunshine patriot will, in this crisis, shrink from the service of his country; but he that stands it NOW, deserves the love and thanks of man and woman. Tyranny, like hell, is not easily conquered; yet we have this consolation with us, that the harder the conflict, the more glorious the triumph. What we obtain too cheap, we esteem too lightly:—'Tis dearness only that gives everything its value. Heaven knows how to put a proper price upon its goods; and it would be strange indeed if so celestial an article as FREEDOM should not be highly rated. Britain, with an army to enforce her tyranny, has declared that she has a right (*not only to* TAX) but "to BIND us in ALL CASES WHATSOEVER"; and if being *bound in that manner* is not slavery, then is there not such a thing as slavery upon earth. Even the expression is impious; for so unlimited a power can belong only to GOD.

Whether the independence of the continent was declared too soon, or delayed too long, I will not now enter into as an argument; my own simple opinion is, that had it been eight months earlier, it would have been much better. We did not make a proper use of last winter; neither could we, while we were in a dependent state. However, the fault, if it were one, was all our own; we have none to blame but ourselves. But no great deal is lost yet. All that Howe has been doing for this month past is rather a ravage than a conquest, which the spirit of the Jersies a year ago would have quickly repulsed, and which time and a little resolution will soon recover.

I have as little superstition in me as any man living; but my secret opinion has ever been, and still is, that God Almighty will not give up a people to military destruction, or leave them unsupportedly to perish, who have so earnestly and so repeatedly sought to avoid the calamities of war, by every decent method which wisdom could invent. Neither have I so much of the infidel in me as to suppose that he has relinquished the government of the world, and given us up to the care of devils; and as I do not, I cannot see on what grounds the king of Britain can look up to Heaven for help against us; a common murderer, a highwayman, or a house-breaker, has as good a pretense as he.

'Tis surprising to see how rapidly a panic will sometimes run through a country. All nations and ages have been subject to them: Britain has trembled like an ague at the report of a French fleet of flat-bottomed boats; and in the fourteenth century the whole English army, after ravaging the kingdom of France, was driven back like men petrified with fear; and this brave exploit was performed by a few broken forces collected and headed by a woman, Joan of Arc. Would that heaven might inspire some Jersey maid to spirit up her countrymen, and save her fair fellow sufferers from ravage and ravishment! Yet panics, in some cases, have their uses; they produce as much good as hurt. Their duration is always short; the mind soon grows through them, and acquires a firmer habit than before. But their peculiar advantage is, that they are the touchstones of sincerity and hypocrisy, and bring things and men to light, which might otherwise have lain forever undiscovered. In fact, they have the same effect on secret traitors which an imaginary apparition would have upon a private murderer. They sift out the hidden thoughts of man, and hold them up in public to the world. Many a disguised tory has lately shown his head, that shall penitentially solemnize with curses the day on which Howe arrived upon the Delaware.

As I was with the troops at Fort Lee, and marched with them to the edge of Pennsylvania, I am well acquainted with many circumstances which those who live at a distance know but little or nothing of. Our situation there was exceedingly cramped, the place being a narrow neck of land between the North River and Hackensack. Our force was inconsiderable, being not one-fourth so great as Howe could bring against us. We had no army at hand to have relieved the garrison, had we shut ourselves up and stood on our defence. Our ammunition, light artillery, and the best part of our stores, had been removed, on the apprehension that Howe would endeavor to penetrate the Jerseys, in which case Fort Lee could be of no use to us; for it must occur to every thinking man, whether in the army or not, that these kind of field forts are only for temporary purposes, and last in use no longer than the enemy directs his force against the particular object which such forts are raised to defend. Such was our situation and condition at Fort Lee on the morning of the 20th of November, when an officer arrived with information that the enemy with 200 boats had landed about seven miles above. Major General Green, who commanded the garrison, immediately ordered them under arms, and sent express to General Washington at the town of Hackensack, distant by the way of the ferry, six miles. Our first object was to secure the bridge over the Hackensack, which laid up the river between the enemy and us, about six miles from us, three from them. General Washington arrived in about three-quarters of an hour, and marched at the head of the troops towards the bridge, which place I expected we should have a brush for; however, they did not choose to dispute it with us, and the greatest part of our troops went over the bridge, the rest over the ferry except some which passed at a mill on a small creek between the bridge and the ferry, and made their way through some marshy grounds up to the town of Hackensack, and there passed the river. We brought off as much baggage as the wagons could contain, the rest was lost. The simple object was to bring off the garrison, and march them on till they could be strengthened by the Jersey or Pennsylvania militia, so as to be enabled to make a stand. We staid four days at Newark, collected our outposts with some of the Jersey militia, and marched out twice to meet the enemy on being informed that they were advancing, though our numbers were greatly inferior to theirs. Howe, in my opinion, committed a great error in generalship in not throwing a body of forces off from Staten Island through Amboy, by which means he might have seized all our stores at Brunswick and intercepted our march into Pennsylvania; but if we believe the power of hell to be limited, we must likewise believe that their agents are under some providential control.

I shall not now attempt to give all the particulars of our retreat to the Delaware; suffice it for the present to say that both officers and men, though greatly harassed and fatigued, frequently without rest, covering, or provision, the inevitable consequences of a long retreat, bore it with a manly and martial spirit. All their wishes centered in one; which was, that the country would turn out and help them to drive the enemy back. Voltaire has remarked that King William never appeared to full advantage but in difficulties and in action; the same remark may be made on General Washington, for the character fits him. There is a natural firmness in some minds which cannot be unlocked by trifles, but which, when unlocked, discovers a cabinet of fortitude; and I reckon it among those kinds of public blessings, which we do not immediately see, that GOD hath blessed him with uninterrupted health, and given him a mind that can even flourish upon care.

I shall conclude this paper with some miscellaneous remarks on the state of our affairs; and shall begin with asking the following question, Why is it that the enemy have left the New England provinces, and made these middle ones the seat of war. The answer is easy: New England is not infested with tories, and we are. I have been tender in raising the cry against these men, and used numberless arguments to show them their danger, but it will not do to sacrifice a world either to their folly or their baseness. The period is now arrived in which either they or we must change our sentiments, or one or both must fall. And what is a tory? Good GOD! What is he? I should not be afraid to go with a hundred whigs against a thousand tories, were they to attempt to get into arms. Every tory is a coward; for servile, slavish self-interested fear is the foundation of toryism; and a man under such influence, though he may be cruel, never can be brave.

But, before the line of irrecoverable separation be drawn between us, let us reason the matter together: Your conduct is an invitation to the enemy, yet not one in a thousand of you has heart enough to join him. Howe is as much deceived by you as the American cause is injured by you. He expects you will all take up arms and flock to his standard with muskets on your shoulders. Your opinions are of no use to him unless you support him personally, for 'tis soldiers, and not tories, that he wants.

I once felt all that kind of anger, which a man ought to feel, against the mean principles that are held by the tories: A noted one, who kept a tavern at Amboy, was standing at his door, with as pretty a child in his hand, about eight or nine years old, as I ever saw, and after speaking his mind as freely as he thought was prudent, finished with this unfatherly expression, "Well! Give me peace in my day." Not a man lives on the continent but fully believes that a separation must some time or other finally take place, and a generous parent should have said, "If there must be trouble, let it be in my day, that my child may have peace"; and this single reflection, well applied, is sufficient to awaken every man to duty. Not a place upon earth might be so happy as America. Her situation is remote from all the wrangling world, and she has nothing to do but to trade with them. A man can distinguish himself between temper and principle, and I am as confident as I am that GOD governs the world, that America will never be happy till she gets clear of foreign dominion. Wars, without ceasing, will break out till that period arrives, and the continent must in the end be conqueror; for though the flame of liberty may sometimes cease to shine, the coal can never expire.

America did not, nor does not want force; but she wanted a proper application of that force. Wisdom is not the purchase of a day, and it is no wonder that we should err at the first setting off. From an excess of tenderness, we were unwilling to raise an army, and trusted our cause to the temporary defence of a well-meaning militia. A summer's experience has now taught us better; yet with those troops, while they were collected, we were able to set bounds to the progress of the enemy, and thank God! they are again assembling. I always considered militia as the best troops in the world for a sudden exertion, but they will not do for a long campaign. Howe, it is probable, will make an attempt on this city; should he fail on this side of the Delaware, he is ruined. If he succeeds, our cause is not ruined. He stakes all on his side against a part on ours; admitting he succeeds, the consequences will be, that armies from both ends of the continent will march to assist their suffering friends in the middle states; for he cannot go everywhere, it is impossible. I consider Howe as the greatest enemy the Tories have; he is bringing a war into their country, which, had it not been for him and partly for themselves, they had been clear of. Should he now be expelled, I wish with all the devotion of a Christian, that the names of Whig and Tory may never more be mentioned; but should the Tories give him encouragement to come, or assistance if he come, I as sincerely wish that our next year's arms may expel them from the continent, and the Congress appropriate their possessions to the relief of those who have suffered in well-doing. A single successful battle next year will settle the whole. America could carry on a two years' war by the confiscation of the property of disaffected persons, and be made happy by their expulsion. Say not that this is revenge; call it rather the soft resentment of a suffering people, who, having no object in view but the GOOD of ALL, have staked their OWN ALL upon a seemingly doubtful event. Yet it is folly to argue against determined hardness; eloquence may strike the ear, and the language of sorrow draw forth the tear of compassion, but nothing can reach the heart that is steeled with prejudice.

Quitting this class of men, I turn with the warm ardor of a friend to those who have nobly stood, and are yet determined to stand the matter out: I call not upon a few, but upon all: not on THIS state or THAT state, but on EVERY state: up and help us; lay your shoulders to the wheel; better have too much force than too little, when so great an object is at stake. Let it be told to the future world, that in the depth of winter, when nothing but hope and virtue could survive, that the city and the country, alarmed at one common danger, came forth to meet and to repulse it. Say not that thousands are gone, turn out your tens of thousands; throw not the burden of the day upon Providence, but *"shew your faith by your works,"* that God may bless you. It matters not where you live, or what rank of life you hold, the evil or the blessing will reach you all. The far and the near, the home counties and the back, the rich and the poor, will suffer or rejoice alike. The heart that feels not now is dead; the blood of his children will curse his cowardice who shrinks back at a time when a little might have saved the whole and made *them* happy. I love the man that can smile in trouble, that can gather strength from distress and grow brave by reflection. 'Tis the business of little minds to shrink; but he whose heart is firm, and whose conscience approves his conduct, will pursue his principles unto death. My own line of reasoning is to myself as straight and clear as a ray of light. Not all the treasures of the world, so far as I believe, could have induced me to support an offensive war, for I think it murder; but if a thief breaks into my house, burns and destroys my property, and kills or threatens to kill me or those that are in it, and to *"bind me in all cases whatsoever"* to his absolute will, am I to suffer it? What signifies it to me whether he who does it is a king or a common man; my countryman or not my countryman; whether it be done by an individual villain, or an army of them? If we reason to the root of things we shall find no difference; neither can any just cause be assigned why we should punish in the one case and pardon in the other. Let them call me rebel and welcome, I feel no concern from it; but I should suffer the misery of devils, were I to make a whore of my soul by swearing allegiance to one whose character is that of a sottish, stupid, stubborn, worthless, brutish man. I conceive likewise a horrid idea in receiving mercy from a being, who at the last day shall be shrieking to the rocks and mountains to cover him, and fleeing with terror from the orphan, the widow, and the slain of America.

There are cases which cannot be overdone by language, and this is one. There are persons, too, who see not the full extent of the evil which threatens them; they solace themselves with hopes that the enemy, if he succeed, will be merciful. It is the madness of folly, to expect mercy from those who have refused to do justice; and even mercy, where conquest is the object, is only a trick of war. The cunning of the fox is as murderous as the violence of the wolf, and we ought to guard equally against both. Howe's first object is, partly by threats and partly by promises, to terrify or seduce the people to deliver up their arms and receive mercy. The ministry recommended the same plan to Gage, and this is what the tories call making their peace, *"a peace which passeth all understanding,"* indeed! A peace which would be the immediate forerunner of a worse ruin than any we have yet thought of. Ye men of Pennsylvania, do reason upon these things! Were the back counties to give up their arms, they would fall an easy prey to the Indians, who are all armed: this perhaps is what some tories would not be sorry for. Were the home counties to deliver up their arms, they would be exposed to the resentment of the back counties, who would then have it in their power to chastise their defection at pleasure. And were any one state to give up its arms, THAT state must be garrisoned by all Howe's army of Britons and Hessians to preserve it from the anger of the rest. Mutual fear is the principal link in the chain of mutual love, and woe be to that state that breaks the compact. Howe is mercifully inviting you to barbarous destruction, and men must be either rogues or fools that will not see it. I dwell not upon the vapors of imagination; I bring reason to your ears, and, in language as plain as ABC, hold up truth to your eyes.

I thank GOD that I fear not. I see no real cause for fear. I know our situation well, and can see the way out of it. While our army was collected, Howe dared not risk a battle; and it is no credit to him that he decamped from the White Plains, and waited a mean opportunity to ravage the defenceless Jerseys; but it is great credit to us, that with a handful of men, we sustained an orderly retreat for near an hundred miles, brought off our ammunition, all our field pieces, the greatest part of our stores, and had four rivers to pass. None can say that our retreat was precipitate; for we were near three weeks in performing it, that the country might have time to come in. Twice we marched back to meet the enemy, and remained out till dark. The sign of fear was not seen in our camp, and had not some of the cowardly and disaffected inhabitants spread false alarms through the country, the Jersies had never been ravaged. Once more we are again collected and collecting; our new army at both ends of the continent is recruiting fast, and we shall be able to open the next campaign with sixty thousand men, well armed and clothed. This is our situation, and who will may know it. By perseverance and fortitude we have the prospect of a glorious issue; by cowardice and submission, the sad choice of a variety of evils: a ravaged country—a depopulated city—habitations without safety, and slavery without hope—our homes turned into barracks and bawdy-houses for Hessians—and a future race to provide for, whose fathers we shall doubt of. Look on this picture and weep over it! and if there yet remains one thoughtless wretch who believes it not, let him suffer it unlamented.

❦ ❦ ❦

# The Bill of Rights[1]

### ARTICLE I

CONGRESS shall make no law respecting an establishment of religion, or prohibiting the free exercise thereof; or abridging the freedom of speech, or of the press; or the right of the people peaceably to assemble, and to petition the government for a redress of grievances.

### ARTICLE II

A well regulated militia, being necessary to the security of a free State, the right of the people to keep and bear arms, shall not be infringed.

### ARTICLE III

No soldier shall, in time of peace be quartered in any house, without the consent of the owner, nor in time of war, but in a manner to be prescribed by law.

### ARTICLE IV

The right of the people to be secure in their persons, houses, papers, and effects, against unreasonable searches and seizures, shall not be violated, and

[1] Passed by Congress, September 25, 1789; ratified by three-fourths of the States, December 15, 1791.

no warrants shall issue, but upon probable cause, supported by oath or affirmation, and particularly describing the place to be searched, and the persons or things to be seized.

## ARTICLE V

No person shall be held to answer for a capital, or otherwise infamous crime, unless on a presentment or indictment of a grand jury, except in cases arising in the land or naval forces, or in the militia, when in actual service in time of war or public danger; nor shall any person be subject for the same offense to be twice put in jeopardy of life or limb; nor shall be compelled in any criminal case to be a witness against himself, nor be deprived of life, liberty, or property, without due process of law; nor shall private property be taken for public use without just compensation.

## ARTICLE VI

In all criminal prosecutions, the accused shall enjoy the right to a speedy and public trial, by an impartial jury of the State and district wherein the crime shall have been committed, which district shall have been previously ascertained by law, and to be informed of the nature and cause of the accusation; to be confronted with the witnesses against him; to have compulsory process for obtaining witnesses in his favor, and to have the assistance of counsel for his defense.

## ARTICLE VII

In suits at common law, where the value in controversy shall exceed twenty dollars, the right of trial by jury shall be preserved, and no fact tried by a jury shall be otherwise reexamined in any court of the United States, than according to the rules of the common law.

## ARTICLE VIII

Excessive bail shall not be required, nor excessive fines imposed, nor cruel and unusual punishments inflicted.

## ARTICLE IX

The enumeration in the Constitution of certain rights shall not be construed to deny or disparage others retained by the people.

## ARTICLE X

The powers not delegated to the United States by the Constitution, nor prohibited by it to the States, are reserved to the States respectively, or to the people.

❦ ❦ ❦

*Learned Hand*

# A Plea for the Freedom of Dissent[1]

WHAT do we mean by "principles of civil liberties and human rights"? We cannot go far in that inquiry until we have achieved some notion of what we mean by Liberty; and that has always proved a hard concept to define. The natural, though naïve, opinion is that it means no more than that each individual shall be allowed to pursue his own desires without let or hindrance; and that, although it is true that this is practically impossible, still it does remain the goal, approach to which measures our success. Why, then, is not a beehive or an anthill a perfect example of a free society? Surely you have been a curious and amused watcher beside one of these.

In and out of their crowded pueblo the denizens pass in great number, each bent upon his own urgent mission, quite oblivious of all the rest except as he must bend his path to avoid them. It is a scene of strenuous, purposeful endeavor in which each appears to be, and no doubt in fact is, accomplishing his own purpose; and yet he is at the same time accomplishing the purpose of the group as a whole. As I have gazed at it, the sentence from the Collect of the Episcopal prayerbook has come to me: "Whose service is perfect freedom."

Why is it, then, that we so positively rebel against the hive and the hill as a specimen of a free society? Why is it that such prototypes of totalitarianisms arouse our deepest hostility? Unhappily it is not because they cannot be realized, or at least because they cannot be approached, for a substantial period. Who can be sure that such appalling forecasts as Aldous Huxley's *Brave New World* or Orwell's *1984* are not prophetic? Indeed, there have often been near approaches to such an order.

Germany at the end of 1940 was probably not far removed from one, and who of us knows that there are not countless persons today living within the boundaries of Russia and perhaps of China who are not willing partners, accepting as their personal aspirations the official definitions of the good, the true and the beautiful? Indeed, there have been, and still are, in our own United States large and powerful groups who, if we are to judge their purposes by their conduct, see treason in all dissidence and would welcome an era in which all of us should think, feel and live in consonance with duly prescribed patterns.

Human nature is malleable, especially if you can indoctrinate the disciple with indefectible principles before anyone else reaches him. (I fancy that the Janissaries were as fervent Mohammedans as the authentic Turks.) Indeed, we hear from those who are entitled to an opinion that at times the abject con-

1 From *The New York Times Magazine* (February 6, 1955), p. 11 ff. Copyright, 1955, by *The New York Times*. Reprinted by permission.

fessions made in Russia by victims who know that they are already marked for slaughter are not wrung from them by torture or threats against their families. Rather, they come from partisans, so obsessed with the faith that when they are told that the occasion calls for scapegoats and that they have been selected, recognize and assent to the propriety of the demand and cooperate in its satisfaction. It is as though, when the right time comes, the drones agreed to their extinction in the interest of the hive.

Nor need we be surprised that men so often embrace almost any doctrines, if they are proclaimed with a voice of absolute assurance. In a universe that we do not understand, but with which we must in one way or another somehow manage to deal, and aware of the conflicting desires that clamorously beset us, between which we must choose and which we must therefore manage to weigh, we turn in our bewilderment to those who tell us that they have found a path out of the thickets and possess the scales by which to appraise our needs.

Over and over again such prophets succeed in converting us to unquestioning acceptance; there is scarcely a monstrous belief that has not had its day and its passionate adherents, so eager are we for safe footholds in our dubious course. How certain is any one of us that he, too, might not be content to follow any fantastic creed, if he was satisfied that nothing would ever wake him from the dream? And, indeed, if there were nothing to wake him, how should he distinguish its articles from the authentic dictates of verity?

Remember, too, that it is by no means clear that we are happier in the faith we do profess than we should be under the spell of an orthodoxy that was sage against all heresy. Cruel and savage as orthodoxies have always proved to be, the faithful seem able to convince themselves that the heretics, as they continue to crop up, get nothing worse than their due, and to rest with an easy conscience.

In any event, my thesis is that the best answer to such systems is not so much in their immoral quality—immoral though they be—as in the fact that they are inherently unstable because they are at war with our only trustworthy way of living in accord with the facts. For I submit that it is only by trial and error, by insistent scrutiny and by readiness to re-examine presently accredited conclusions that we have risen, so far as in fact we have risen, from our brutish ancestors, and I believe that in our loyalty to these habits lies our only chance, not merely of progress, but even of survival.

They were not indeed a part of our aboriginal endowment: Man, as he emerged, was not prodigally equipped to master the infinite diversity of his environment. Obviously, enough of us did manage to get through; but it has been a statistical survival, for the individual's native powers of adjustment are by no means enough for his personal safety any more than are those of other creatures. The precipitate of our experience is far from absolute verity, and our exasperated resentment at all dissent is a sure index of our doubts. Take, for instance, our constant recourse to the word, "subversive," as a touchstone of impermissible deviation from accepted canons.

All discussion, all debate, all dissidence tends to question and in consequence to upset existing convictions: that is precisely its purpose and its justification. He is, indeed, a "subversive" who disputes those precepts that I most treasure and seeks to persuade me to substitute his own. He may have no shadow of desire to resort to anything but persuasion; he may be of those to whom any forcible sanction of conformity is anathema; yet it remains true that he is trying to bring about my apostasy, and I hate him just in proportion as I fear his success.

Contrast this protective resentment with the assumption that lies at the base of our whole system that the best chance for truth to emerge is a fair field for all ideas. Nothing, I submit, more completely betrays our latent disloyalty to this premise to all that we pretend to believe than the increasingly common resort to this and other question-begging words. Their imprecision comforts us by enabling us to suppress arguments that disturb our complacency and yet to continue to congratulate ourselves on keeping the faith as we have received it from the Founding Fathers.

Heretics have been hateful from the beginning of recorded time; they have been ostracized, exiled, tortured, maimed and butchered; but it has generally proved impossible to smother them, and when it has not, the society that has succeeded has always declined. Façades of authority, however imposing, do not survive after it has appeared that they rest upon the sands of human conjecture and compromise.

And so, if I am to say what are "the principles of civil liberties and human rights," I answer that they lie in habits, customs—conventions, if you will—that tolerate dissent and can live without irrefragable certainties; that are ready to overhaul existing assumptions; that recognize that we never see save through a glass, darkly, and that at long last we shall succeed only so far as we continue to undertake "the intolerable labor of thought"—that most distasteful of all our activities.

If such a habit and such a temper pervade a society, it will not need institutions to protect its "civil liberties and human rights"; so far as they do not, I venture to doubt how far anything else can protect them: whether it be Bills of Rights, or courts that must in the name of interpretation read their meaning into them.

This may seem to you a bleak and cheerless conclusion, too alien to our nature to be practical. "We must live from day to day"—you will say—"to live is to act, and to act is to choose and decide. How can we carry on at all without some principles, some patterns to meet the conflicts in which each day involves us?" Indeed, we cannot, nor am I suggesting that we should try; but I *am* suggesting that it makes a vital difference—*the* vital difference—whether we deem our principles and our patterns to be eternal verities, rather than the best postulates so far attainable.

Was it not Holmes who said: "The highest courage is to stake everything on a premise that you know tomorrow's evidence may disprove"? "Ah"—you will reply—"there's the rub. That may be the highest courage, but how many have it? You are hopelessly wrong if you assume the general prevalence of such a virtue; ordinary men must be given more than conjectures if they are to face grave dangers."

But do you really believe that? Do you not see about you every day and everywhere the precise opposite? Not alone on the battlefield but in the forest, the desert and the plain; in the mountains, at sea, on the playing field, even in the laboratory and the factory—yes (do not laugh), at the card table and the racetrack—men are forever putting it "upon the touch to win or lose it all." Without some smack of uncertainty and danger, to most of us the world would be a tepid, pallid show.

Surely, like me, you have all felt something of this when you have looked on those pathetic attempts to depict in paint or stone the delights of Paradise. I own that the torments of hell never fail to horrify me; not even the glee of the demons in charge is an adequate relief, though the artist has generally been successful in giving a veracious impression of the gusto with which they discharge their duties.

But when I turn to the Congregation of the Blessed, I cannot avoid a sense of anticlimax; strive as I may, the social atmosphere seems a bit forced; and I recall those very irreverent verses of Lowes Dickinson:

> Burning at first no doubt would be worse,
> But time the impression would soften,
> While those who are bored with praising the Lord,
> Would be more bored with praising him often.

By some happy fortuity man is a projector, a designer, a builder, a craftsman; it is among his most dependable joys to impose upon the flux that passes before him some mark of himself, aware though he always must be of the odds against him. His reward is not so much in the work as in its making; not so much in the prize as in the race. We may win when we lose, if we have done what we can; for by so doing we have made real at least some part of that finished product in whose fabrication we are most concerned—ourselves.

And if at the end some friendly critic shall pass by and say, "My friend, how good a job do you really think you have made of it all?" we can answer, "I know as well as you that it is not of high quality, but I did put into it whatever I had, and that was the game I started out to play."

It is still in the lap of the gods whether a society can succeed, based on "civil liberties and human rights," conceived as I have tried to describe them; but of one thing at least we may be sure: the alternatives that have so far appeared have been immeasurably worse, and so, whatever the outcome, I submit to you that we must press along. Borrowing from Epictetus, let us say to ourselves: "Since we are men we will play the part of a Man," and how can I better end than by recalling to you the concluding passage of "Prometheus Unbound"?

> To suffer woes which Hope thinks infinite;
> To forgive wrongs darker than death or night;

To defy Power, which seems omnipotent
To love, and bear; to hope till Hope creates
From its own wreck the thing it contemplates;
Neither to change, nor falter, nor repent;
This, like thy glory, Titan, is to be
Good, great and joyous, beautiful and free;
This is alone Life, Joy, Empire and Victory.

❧ ❧ ❧

# Problems of the Social Sciences

*Frederick Jackson Turner*

## The Significance of the Frontier
## in American History [1]

IN A RECENT bulletin of the Superintendent of the Census for 1890 appear these significant words: "Up to and including 1880 the country had a frontier of settlement, but at present the unsettled area has been so broken into by isolated bodies of settlement that there can hardly be said to be a frontier line. In the discussion of its extent, its westward movement, etc., it can not, therefore, any longer have a place in the census reports." This brief official statement marks the closing of a great historic movement. Up to our own day American history has been in a large degree the history of the colonization of the Great West. The existence of an area of free land, its continuous recession, and the advance of American settlement westward, explain American development.

Behind institutions, behind constitutional forms and modifications, lie the vital forces that call these organs into life and shape them to meet changing conditions. The peculiarity of American institutions is the fact that they have have been compelled to adapt themselves to the changes of an expanding people—to the changes involved in crossing a continent, in winning a wilderness, and in developing at each area of this progress out of the primitive economic and political conditions of the frontier into the complexity of city life. Said Calhoun in 1817, "We are great, and rapidly—I was about to say fearfully—growing!" So saying, he touched the distinguishing feature of American life. All peoples show development; the germ theory of politics has been sufficiently emphasized. In the case of most nations, however, the development has occurred in a limited area; and if the nation has expanded, it has met other growing peoples whom it has conquered. But in the case of the United States

---

[1] From *The Frontier in American History* (with omissions) by Frederick Jackson Turner. Copyright, 1920, by Frederick J. Turner. Copyright, 1948, by Caroline M. S. Turner. By permission of Henry Holt and Company, Inc.

we have a different phenomenon. Limiting our attention to the Atlantic coast, we have the familiar phenomenon of the evolution of institutions in a limited area, such as the rise of representative government; the differentiation of simple colonial governments into complex organs; the progress from primitive industrial society, without division of labor, up to manufacturing civilization. But we have in addition to this a recurrence of the process of evolution in each western area reached in the process of expansion. Thus American development has exhibited not merely advance along a single line, but a return to primitive conditions on a continually advancing frontier line, and a new development for that area. American social development has been continually beginning over again on the frontier. This perennial rebirth, this fluidity of American life, this expansion westward with its new opportunities, its continuous touch with the simplicity of primitive society, furnish the forces dominating American character. The true point of view in the history of this nation is not the Atlantic coast, it is the Great West. Even the slavery struggle, which is made so exclusive an object of attention by writers like Professor von Holst, occupies its important place in American history because of its relation to westward expansion.

In this advance, the frontier is the outer edge of the wave—the meeting point between savagery and civilization. Much has been written about the frontier from the point of view of border warfare and the chase, but as a field for the serious study of the economist and the historian it has been neglected.

The American frontier is sharply distinguished from the European frontier —a fortified boundary line running through dense populations. The most significant thing about the American frontier is, that it lies at the hither edge of free land. In the census reports it is treated as the margin of that settlement which has a density of two or more to the square mile. The term is an elastic one, and for our purposes does not need sharp definition. We shall consider the whole frontier belt, including the Indian country and the outer margin of the "settled area" of the census reports. This paper will make no attempt to treat the subject exhaustively; its aim is simply to call attention to the frontier as a fertile field for investigation, and to suggest some of the problems which arise in connection with it.

In the settlement of America we have to observe how European life entered the continent, and how America modified and developed that life and reacted on Europe. Our early history is the study of European germs developing in an American environment. Too exclusive attention has been paid by institutional students to the Germanic origins, too little to the American factors. The frontier is the line of most rapid and effective Americanization. The wilderness masters the colonist. It finds him a European in dress, industries, tools, modes of travel, and thought. It takes him from the railroad car and puts him in the birch canoe. It strips off the garments of civilization and arrays him in the hunting shirt and the moccasin. It puts him in the log cabin of the Cherokee and Iroquois and runs an Indian palisade around him. Before long he has gone to planting Indian corn and plowing with a sharp stick; he shouts the war cry and takes the scalp in orthodox Indian fashion. In short, at the frontier the environment is at first too strong for the man. He must accept the conditions which it furnishes, or perish, and so he fits himself into the Indian clearings and follows the Indian trails. Little by little he transforms the wilderness, but the outcome is not the old Europe, not simply the development of Germanic germs, any more than the first phenomenon was a case of reversion to the Germanic mark. The fact is, that here is a new product that is American. At first, the frontier was the Atlantic coast. It was the frontier of Europe in a very real sense. Moving westward, the frontier became more and more American. As successive terminal moraines result from successive glaciations, so each frontier leaves its traces behind it, and when it becomes a settled area the region still partakes of the frontier characteristics. Thus the advance of the frontier has meant a steady movement away from the influence of Europe, a steady growth of independence on American lines. And to study this advance, the men who grew up under these conditions, and the political, economic, and social results of it, is to study the really American part of our history. . . .

The Atlantic frontier was compounded of fisherman, fur-trader, miner, cattle-raiser, and farmer. Excepting the fisherman, each type of industry was on the march toward the West, impelled by an irresistible attraction. Each passed in successive waves across the continent. Stand at Cumberland Gap and watch the procession of civilization, marching single file—the buffalo following the trail to the salt springs, the Indian, the fur-trader and hunter, the cattle-raiser, the pioneer farmer—and the frontier has passed by. Stand at South Pass in the Rockies a century later and see the same procession with wider intervals between. The unequal rate of advance compels us to distinguish the frontier into the trader's frontier, the rancher's frontier, or the miner's frontier, and the farmer's frontier. When the mines and the cow pens were still near the fall line the traders' pack trains were tinkling across the Alleghenies, and the French on the Great Lakes were fortifying their posts, alarmed by the British trader's birch canoe. When the trappers scaled the Rockies, the farmer was still near the mouth of the Missouri.

Why was it that the Indian trader passed so rapidly across the continent? What effects followed from the trader's frontier? The trade was coeval with American discovery. The Norsemen, Vespucius, Verrazani, Hudson, John Smith, all trafficked for furs. The Plymouth pilgrims settled in Indian corn-fields, and their first return cargo was of beaver and lumber. The records of the various New England colonies show how steadily exploration was carried into the wilderness by this trade. What is true for New England is, as would be expected, even plainer for the rest of the colonies. All along the coast from Maine to Georgia the Indian trade opened up the river courses. Steadily the trader passed westward, utilizing the older lines of French trade. The Ohio, the Great Lakes, the Mississippi, the Missouri, and the Platte, the lines of western advance, were ascended by traders. They found the passes in the Rocky Mountains and guided Lewis and Clark, Frémont, and Bidwell. The explanation of the rapidity of this advance is connected with the effects of the trader on the

Indian. The trading post left the unarmed tribes at the mercy of those that had
purchased fire-arms—a truth which the Iroquois Indians wrote in blood, and so
the remote and unvisited tribes gave eager welcome to the trader. "The savages," wrote La Salle, "take better care of us French than of their own children; from us only can they get guns and goods." This accounts for the trader's
power and the rapidity of his advance. Thus the disintegrating forces of civilization entered the wilderness. Every river valley and Indian trail became a fissure
in Indian society, and so that society became honeycombed. Long before the
pioneer farmer appeared on the scene, primitive Indian life had passed away.
The farmers met Indians armed with guns. The trading frontier, while steadily
undermining Indian power by making the tribes ultimately dependent on the
whites, yet, through its sale of guns, gave to the Indian increased power of resistance to the farming frontier. French colonization was dominated by its
trading frontier; English colonization by its farming frontier. There was an antagonism between the two frontiers as between the two nations. Said Duquesne
to the Iroquois, "Are you ignorant of the difference between the king of England and the king of France? Go see the forts that our king has established
and you will see that you can still hunt under their very walls. They have been
placed for your advantage in places which you frequent. The English, on the
contrary, are no sooner in possession of a place than the game is driven away.
The forest falls before them as they advance, and the soil is laid bare so that
you can scarce find the wherewithal to erect a shelter for the night."

And yet, in spite of this opposition of the interests of the trader and the
farmer, the Indian trade pioneered the way for civilization. The buffalo trail became the Indian trail, and this became the trader's "trace"; the trails widened
into roads, and the roads into turnpikes, and these in turn were transformed
into railroads. The same origin can be shown for the railroads of the South,
the Far West, and the Dominion of Canada. The trading posts reached by
these trails were on the sites of Indian villages which had been placed in positions suggested by nature; and these trading posts, situated so as to command
the water systems of the country, have grown into such cities as Albany, Pittsburgh, Detroit, Chicago, St. Louis, Council Bluffs, and Kansas City. Thus civilization in America has followed the arteries made by geology, pouring an ever
richer tide through them, until at last the slender paths of aboriginal intercourse have been broadened and interwoven into the complex mazes of modern commercial lines; the wilderness has been interpenetrated by lines of
civilization growing ever more numerous. It is like the steady growth of a
complex nervous system for the originally simple, inert continent. If one
would understand why we are to-day one nation, rather than a collection of
isolated states, he must study this economic and social consolidation of the
country. . . .

The exploitation of the beasts took hunter and trader to the west, the exploitation of the grasses took the rancher west, and the exploitation of the
virgin soil of the river valleys and prairies attracted the farmer. Good soils

have been the most continuous attraction to the farmer's frontier. The land hunger of the Virginians drew them down the rivers into Carolina, in early colonial days; the search for soils took the Massachusetts men to Pennsylvania and to New York. As the eastern lands were taken up migration flowed across them to the west. Daniel Boone, the great backwoodsman, who combined the occupations of hunter, trader, cattle-raiser, farmer, and surveyor—learning, probably from the traders, of the fertility of the lands of the upper Yadkin, where the traders were wont to rest as they took their way to the Indians, left his Pennsylvania home with his father, and passed down the Great Valley road to that stream. Learning from a trader of the game and rich pastures of Kentucky, he pioneered the way for the farmers to that region. Thence he passed to the frontier of Missouri, where his settlement was long a landmark on the frontier. Here again he helped to open the way for civilization, finding salt licks, and trails, and land. His son was among the earliest trappers in the passes of the Rocky Mountains, and his party are said to have been the first to camp on the present site of Denver. His grandson, Col. A. J. Boone, of Colorado, was a power among the Indians of the Rocky Mountains, and was appointed an agent by the government. Kit Carson's mother was a Boone. Thus this family epitomizes the backwoodsman's advance across the continent. . . .

Omitting those of the pioneer farmers who move from the love of adventure, the advance of the more steady farmer is easy to understand. Obviously the immigrant was attracted by the cheap lands of the frontier, and even the native farmer felt their influence strongly. Year by year the farmers who lived on soil whose returns were diminished by unrotated crops were offered the virgin soil of the frontier at nominal prices. Their growing families demanded more lands, and these were dear. The competition of the unexhausted, cheap, and easily tilled prairie lands compelled the farmer either to go west and continue the exhaustion of the soil on a new frontier, or to adopt intensive culture. Thus the census of 1890 shows, in the Northwest, many counties in which there is an absolute or a relative decrease of population. These States have been sending farmers to advance the frontier on the plains, and have themselves begun to turn to intensive farming and to manufacture. A decade before this, Ohio had shown the same transition stage. Thus the demand for land and the love of wilderness freedom drew the frontier ever onward.

Having now roughly outlined the various kinds of frontiers, and their modes of advance, chiefly from the point of view of the frontier itself, we may next inquire what were the influences on the East and on the New World. . . .

First, we note that the frontier promoted the formation of a composite nationality for the American people. The coast was preponderantly English, but the later tides of continental immigration flowed across to the free lands. This was the case from the early colonial days. The Scotch-Irish and the Palatine Germans, or "Pennsylvania Dutch," furnished the dominant element in the stock of the colonial frontier. With these peoples were also the freed indented servants, or redemptioners, who at the expiration of their time of service passed to the frontier. . . . Very generally these redemptions were of non-English stock. In the crucible of the frontier the immigrants were Americanized, liberated, and fused into a mixed race, English in neither nationality nor characteristics. The process has gone on from the early days to our own. . . .

In another way the advance of the frontier decreased our dependence on England. The coast, particularly of the South, lacked diversified industries, and was dependent on England for the bulk of its supplies. In the South there was even a dependence on the Northern colonies for articles of food. . . . Before long the frontier created a demand for merchants. As it retreated from the coast it became less and less possible for England to bring her supplies directly to the consumer's wharfs, and carry away staple crops, and staple crops began to give way to diversified agriculture for a time. The effect of this phase of the frontier action upon the northern section is perceived when we realize how the advance of the frontier aroused seaboard cities like Boston, New York, and Baltimore, to engage in rivalry for what Washington called "the extensive and valuable trade of a rising empire."

The legislation which most developed the powers of the national government, and played the largest part in its activity, was conditioned on the frontier. Writers have discussed the subjects of tariff, land, and internal improvement, as subsidiary to the slavery question. . . . This is a wrong perspective. The pioneer needed the goods of the coast, and so the grand series of internal improvement and railroad legislation began, with potent nationalizing effects. Over internal improvements occurred great debates, in which grave constitutional questions were discussed. Sectional groupings appear in the votes, profoundly significant for the historian. Loose construction increased as the nation marched westward. But the West was not content with bringing the farm to the factory. Under the lead of Clay—"Harry of the West"—protective tariffs were passed, with the cry of bringing the factory to the farm. The disposition of the public lands was a third important subject of national legislation influenced by the frontier.

The public domain has been a force of profound importance in the nationalization and development of the government. The effects of the struggle of the landed and the landless States, and of the Ordinance of 1787, need no discussion. Administratively the frontier called out some of the highest and most vitalizing activities of the general government. The purchase of Louisiana was perhaps the constitutional turning point in the history of the Republic, inasmuch as it afforded both a new area for national legislation and the occasion of the downfall of the policy of strict construction. But the purchase of Louisiana was called out by frontier needs and demands. As frontier States accrued to the Union the national power grew. In a speech on the dedication of the Calhoun monument Mr. Lamar explained: "In 1789 the States were the creators of the Federal Government; in 1861 the Federal Government was the creator of a large majority of the States."

When we consider the public domain from the point of view of the sale and disposal of the public lands we are again brought face to face with the frontier. The policy of the United States in dealing with its lands is in sharp contrast with the European system of scientific administration. Efforts to make his domain a source of revenue, and to withhold it from emigrants in order that settlement might be compact, were in vain. The jealousy and the fears of the East were powerless in the face of the demands of the frontiersmen. John Quincy Adams was obliged to confess: "My own system of administration, which was to make the national domain the inexhaustible fund for progressive and unceasing internal improvement, has failed." The reason is obvious; a system of administration was not what the West demanded; it wanted land. Adams states the situation as follows: "The slaveholders of the South have bought the cooperation of the western country by the bribe of the western lands, abandoning to the new Western States their own proportion of the public property and aiding them in the design of grasping all the lands into their own hands." . . .

It is safe to say that the legislation with regard to land, tariff, and internal improvements—the American system of the nationalizing Whig party—was conditioned on frontier ideas and needs. But it was not merely in legislative action that the frontier worked against the sectionalism of the coast. The economic and social characteristics of the frontier worked against sectionalism. The men of the frontier had closer resemblances to the Middle region than to either of the other sections. Pennsylvania had been the seed-plot of frontier emigration, and, although she passed on her settlers along the Great Valley into the west of Virginia and the Carolinas, yet the industrial society of these Southern frontiersmen was always more like that of the Middle region than like that of the tide-water portion of the South, which later came to spread its industrial type throughout the South.

The Middle region, entered by New York harbor, was an open door to all Europe. The tide-water part of the South represented typical Englishmen, modified by a warm climate and servile labor, and living in baronial fashion on great plantations; New England stood for a special English movement— Puritanism. The middle region was less English than the other sections. It had a wide mixture of nationalities, a varied society, the mixed town and county system of local government, a varied economic life, many religious sects. In short, it was a region mediating between New England and the South, and the East and the West. It represented that composite nationality which the contemporary United States exhibits, that juxtaposition of non-English groups, occupying a valley or a little settlement, and presenting reflections of the map of Europe in their variety. It was democratic and nonsectional, if not national; "easy, tolerant, and contented"; rooted strongly in material prosperity. It was typical of the modern United States. . . .

It was this nationalizing tendency of the West that transformed the democracy of Jefferson into the national republicanism of Monroe and the democracy of Andrew Jackson. The West of the War of 1812, the West of Clay, and Benton and Harrison, and Andrew Jackson, shut off by the Middle States and the mountains from the coast sections, had a solidarity of its own with national tendencies. On the tide of the Father of Waters, North and South met and mingled into a nation. Interstate migration went steadily on—a process of cross-fertilization of ideas and institutions. The fierce struggle of the sections over slavery on the western frontier does not diminish the truth of this statement; it proves the truth of it. Slavery was a sectional trait that would not down, but in the West it could not remain sectional. It was the greatest of frontiersmen who declared: "I believe this Government can not endure permanently half slave and half free. It will become all of one thing or all of the other." Nothing works for nationalism like intercourse with the nation. Mobility of population is death to localism, and the western frontier worked irresistibly in unsettling population. The effect reached back from the frontier and affected profoundly the Atlantic coast and even the Old World.

But the most important effect of the frontier has been in the promotion of democracy here and in Europe. As has been indicated, the frontier is productive of individualism. Complex society is precipitated by the wilderness into a kind of primitive organization based on the family. The tendency is anti-social. It produces antipathy to control, and particularly to any direct control. The tax-gatherer is viewed as a representative of oppression. Prof. Osgood, in an able article, has pointed out that the frontier conditions prevalent in the colonies are important factors in the explanation of the American Revolution, where individual liberty was sometimes confused with absence of all effective government. The same conditions aid in explaining the difficulty of instituting a strong government in the period of the confederacy. The frontier individualism has from the beginning promoted democracy.

The frontier States that came into the Union in the first quarter of a century of its existence came in with democratic suffrage provisions, and had reactive effects of the highest importance upon the older States whose peoples were being attracted there. An extension of the franchise became essential. It was *western* New York that forced an extension of suffrage in the constitutional convention of that State in 1821; and it was *western* Virginia that compelled the tide-water region to put a more liberal suffrage provision in the constitution framed in 1830, and to give to the frontier region a more nearly proportionate representation with the tide-water aristocracy. The rise of democracy as an effective force in the nation came in with western preponderance under Jackson and William Henry Harrison, and it meant the triumph of the frontier —with all of its good and with all of its evil elements. . . .

So long as free land exists, the opportunity for a competency exists, and economic power secures political power. But the democracy born of free land, strong in selfishness and individualism, intolerant of administrative experience and education, and pressing individual liberty beyond its proper bounds, has its dangers as well as its benefits. Individualism in America has allowed a laxity in regard to governmental affairs which has rendered possible the spoils system and all the manifest evils that follow from the lack of a highly developed civic spirit. . . .

From the conditions of frontier life came intellectual traits of profound importance. The works of travelers along each frontier from colonial days onward describe certain common traits, and these traits have, while softening down, still persisted as survivals in the place of their origin, even when a higher social organization succeeded. The result is that to the frontier the American intellect owes its striking characteristics. That coarseness and strength combined with acuteness and inquisitiveness; that practical, inventive turn of mind, quick to find expedients; that masterful grasp of material things, lacking in the artistic but powerful to effect great ends; that restless, nervous energy; that dominant individualism, working for good and for evil, and withal that buoyancy and exuberance which comes with freedom—these are traits of the frontier, or traits called out elsewhere because of the existence of the frontier. Since the days when the fleet of Columbus sailed into the waters of the New World, America has been another name for opportunity, and the people of the United States have taken their tone from the incessant expansion which has not only been open but has even been forced upon them. He would be a rash prophet who should assert that the expansive character of American life has now entirely ceased. Movement has been its dominant fact, and unless this training has no effect upon a people, the American energy will continually demand a wider field for its exercise. But never again will such gifts of free land offer themselves. For a moment, at the frontier, the bonds of custom are broken and unrestraint is triumphant. There is not *tabula rasa*. The stubborn American environment is there with its imperious summons to accept its conditions; the inherited ways of doing things are also there; and yet, in spite of environment, and in spite of custom, each frontier did indeed furnish a new field of opportunity, a gate of escape from the bondage of the past; and freshness, and confidence, and scorn of older society, impatience of its restraints and its ideas, and indifference to its lessons, have accompanied the frontier. What the Mediterranean sea was to the Greeks, breaking the bond of custom, offering new experiences, calling out new institutions and activities, that, and more, the ever retreating frontier has been to the United States directly, and to the nations of Europe more remotely. And now, four centuries from the discovery of America, at the end of a hundred years of life under the Constitution, the frontier has gone, and with its going has closed the first period of American history.

❧ ❧ ❧

*Arnold J. Toynbee*

# Does History Repeat Itself? [1]

DOES history repeat itself? In our Western world in the eighteenth and nineteenth centuries, this question used to be debated as an academic exercise. The spell of well-being which our civilization was enjoying at the time had daz-

---

[1] From *Civilization on Trial* (New York: Oxford University Press, 1948), pp. 29-41. Copyright, 1948, Oxford University Press, Inc.

zled our grandfathers into the quaint pharisaical notion that they were "not as other men are"; they had come to believe that our Western society was exempt from the possibility of falling into those mistakes and mishaps that have been the ruin of certain other civilizations whose history, from beginning to end, is an open book. To us, in our generation, the old question has rather suddenly taken on a new and very practical significance. We have awakened to the truth (how, one wonders, could we ever have been blind to it?) that Western man and his works are no more invulnerable than the now extinct civilizations of the Aztecs and the Incas, the Sumerians and the Hittites. So today, with some anxiety, we are searching the scriptures of the past to find out whether they contain a lesson that we can decipher. Does history give us any information about our own prospects? And, if it does, what is the burden of it? Does it spell out for us an inexorable doom, which we can merely await with folded hands—resigning ourselves, as best we may, to a fate that we cannot avert or even modify by our own efforts? Or does it inform us, not of certainties, but of probabilities, or bare possibilities, in our own future? The practical difference is vast, for, on this second alternative, so far from being stunned into passivity, we should be roused to action. On this second alternative, the lesson of history would not be like an astrologer's horoscope; it would be like a navigator's chart, which affords the seafarer who has the intelligence to use it a much greater hope of avoiding shipwreck than when he was sailing blind, because it gives him the means, if he has the skill and courage to use them, of steering a course between charted rocks and reefs.

It will be seen that our question needs defining before we plunge into an attempt to answer it. When we ask ourselves "Does history repeat itself?" do we mean no more than "Does history turn out to have repeated itself, on occasions, in the past?" Or are we asking whether history is governed by inviolable laws which have not only taken effect in every past case to which they have applied but are also bound to take effect in every similar situation that may arise in the future? On this second interpretation, the word "does" would mean "must"; on the other interpretation it would mean "may." On this issue, the writer of the present article may as well put his cards on the table at once. He is not a determinist in his reading of the riddle of human life. He believes that where there is life there is hope, and that, with God's help, man is master of his own destiny, at least to some extent in some respects.

But as soon as we have taken our stand on this issue between freedom and necessity that is raised by the ambiguous word "does," we find ourselves called upon to define what we mean by the word "history." If we have to limit the field of history to events that are wholly within the control of human wills, then, to be sure, for a non-determinist no difficulty would arise. But do such events ever actually occur in real life? In our personal experience, when we are making a decision, do we not always find ourselves only partly free and partly bound by past events and present facts in our own life and in our social and physical environment? Is not history itself, in the last analysis, a vision of the whole universe on the move in the four-dimensional framework of spacetime? And, in this all-embracing panorama, are there not many events that the most staunch believer in the freedom of the human will would admit, as readily as the most thoroughgoing determinist, to be inexorably recurrent and precisely predictable?

Some events of this undisputedly recurrent predictable order may have little apparent bearing upon human affairs—as, for example, the repetitions of history in nebulae outside the system of the Milky Way. There are, however, some very obvious cyclic movements in physical nature that do affect human affairs in the most intimate fashion—as, for example, the recurrent predictable alternations of day and night and of the seasons of the year. The day-and-night cycle governs all human work; it dictates the schedules of the transportation systems of our cities, sets the times of their rush hours, and weighs on the minds of the commuters whom it shuttles to and fro, twice in every twenty-four hours, between "dormitory" and "workshop." The cycle of the seasons governs human life itself by governing our food supply.

It is true that man, by taking thought, can win a measure of freedom from these physical cycles that is beyond the reach of birds and beasts. Though the individual cannot break the tyranny of the day-and-night cycle by leading a waking life for twenty-four hours in the day, like the legendary Egyptian Pharaoh Mycerinus, human society can achieve Mycerinus' mythical feat collectively by a planned co-operation and a division of labour. Industrial plants can be operated for twenty-four hours in the day by successive shifts of workers, and the labours of workers who work by day can be prepared for and be followed up by the labours of other workers who rest by day and work by night. The tyranny of the seasons, again, has been broken by a Western society that has expanded from the northern temperate zone into the tropics and the southern temperate zone and has devised a technique of refrigeration. Nevertheless, these triumphs of man's mind and will over the tyranny of the two physical cycles of the day and the year are comparatively small gains for human freedom, remarkable though these triumphs are. On the whole, these recurrent predictable events in physical nature remain masters of human life—even at the present level of Western man's technology—and they show their mastery by subduing human affairs, as far as their empire over them extends, to their own recurrent predictable pattern.

But are there, perhaps, human acts, in other fields of action, that are not—or at any rate not so completely—under physical nature's control? Let us examine this question in a familiar concrete case. When, in the last days of April 1865, the horses that, in the first days of that month, had been the cavalry and artillery horses of the Army of Northern Virginia, were being driven behind the plough by the men who, at the beginning of that April, had been General Lee's cavalrymen and artillerymen, those men and horses were once again performing an annually recurrent agricultural operation which they themselves had performed a number of times before in their lives and which predecessors of theirs, in the Old World before Europeans discovered the New World, and in other societies before our Western society's birth, had been performing, year by year, for some five or six thousand years past. The invention of ploughing is coeval with the species of society that we call civilizations, and pre-plough methods of agriculture—likewise governed by the year cycle—were already in use for perhaps an equal length of time before that, during the neolithic dawn by which the sunrise of civilization was heralded. In the spring of 1865, agriculture in the ex-Confederate States of North America was governed by the seasons very rigidly. A few weeks' delay, and the season would have been too late—with the disastrous consequence that the food-producing capacities of those horses and men would have been lost to the community for a whole year longer.

Thus, in the last days of April 1865, the horses and men of the former Army of Northern Virginia were performing a historical act—the spring ploughing—which had repeated itself, by that date, some five or six thousand times at least, and was still repeating itself in 1947. (In that year the writer of this article witnessed the spring ploughing in Kentucky, and noted the farmers' anxiety when, in the middle of that April, their work was interrupted by heavy rainfall.)

But what about the history that General Lee's horses and men were making, not at the end of April, but at the beginning? Is the kind of history that is represented by the last act of the Civil War a kind that repeats itself—as ploughing and commuting repeat themselves owing to their close and obvious dependence on recurrent predictable cycles in physical nature? Are we not confronted here with a kind of human action that is more or less independent of physical cycles and is capable of overriding them? Suppose that General Lee had not found himself constrained to capitulate till June 1865? Or suppose that, General Lee having capitulated when he did, General Grant had not been moved to make his celebrated concession of allowing the Confederate soldiers who had just laid down their arms to take their horses back with them to their farms, notwithstanding the contrary provision in the terms of surrender that had just been agreed upon. Would not either of these hypothetical man-made variations on the actual course of historical events have prevented history from repeating itself in the Southern States in the spring ploughing of 1865?

The province of history that we are considering now is one that used to be treated as the whole field of history before the provinces of economic and social history were opened up. In this old-fashioned field of battles and policies, captains and kings, does history turn out to have repeated itself as it does in fields of human activity that are manifestly governed by cycles in the movement of physical nature? Was the Civil War, for instance, a unique event, or do we find other historical events that display sufficient similarity and affinity to it to warrant us in treating it and them as so many representatives of a class of events in which history has repeated itself at least to some extent? The present writer inclines to this latter view

The crisis represented in American history by the Civil War was, surely, repeated in a significant sense in the contemporary crisis in German history that is represented by the Bismarckian wars of 1864-71. In both cases an imperfect political union had threatened to dissolve altogether. In both cases, the issue between the dissolution of the union and its effective establishment was decided by war. In both cases, the partisans of effective union won, and, in both, one of the causes of their victory was their technological and industrial superiority over their opponents. In both, finally, the victory of the cause of union was followed by a great industrial expansion which turned both the post-bellum United States and the Second German Reich into formidable industrial competitors of Great Britain. And here we have hit upon another repetition of history; for, throughout the century ending about 1870, the industrial revolution in Great Britain might have appeared to be a unique historical event, whereas, since 1870, it has come to appear, in its true light, as simply the earliest instance of an economic transformation which was eventually to occur likewise in a number of other Western countries and in some non-Western countries too. Moreover, if we shift our attention from the economic common feature of industrialization to the political common feature of federal union, we shall see the history of the United States and Germany at this point repeating itself once again in the history of a third country—in this case not Great Britain but Canada, whose constituent provinces entered into their present federation in 1867, two years after the *de facto* re-establishment of the unity of the United States in 1865 and four years before the foundation of the Second German Reich in 1871.

In the formation, in the modern Western world, of a number of federal unions, and in the industrialization of these and other countries, we see history repeating itself in the sense of producing a number of more or less contemporary examples of the same human achievement. The contemporaneity of the different instances is, however, no more than approximate. The industrial revolution occurred as an apparently unique event in Great Britain at least two generations before its occurrence in America, and Germany proved it to be a repetitive phenomenon. The insecurely welded pre-Civil-War United States had existed for "four score and seven years," and the ramshackle post-Napoleonic German Confederation for half a century, before the crucial events of the eighteen-sixties proved that federal union was a repetitive pattern which was to recur not only in Canada but in Australia, South Africa, and Brazil. Contemporaneity is not an essential condition for the repetition of history on the political and cultural plane of human affairs. The historical events that repeat themselves may be strictly contemporary or they may overlap in time or they may be entirely non-contemporaneous with one another.

The picture remains the same when we turn to the consideration of the greatest human institutions and experiences that are known to us: the civilizations in their births and growths, their breakdowns, declines, and falls; the higher religions in their foundation and evolution. Measured by our subjective personal measuring rod of the average span of the memory of a single human being who lives to a normal old age, the time interval that divides our present generation from the date of the emergence of the Sumerian civilization in the fourth millennium B.C. or from the date of the beginning of the Christian era itself seems, no doubt, a very long one. Yet it is infinitesimally small on the objective time scale that has recently been given to us by the discoveries of our geologists and astronomers. Our modern Western physical science tells us that the human race has been in existence on this planet for at least 600,000 and perhaps a million years, life for at least 500 million and perhaps 800 million years, and the planet itself for possibly 2000 million years. On this time scale the last five or six thousand years that have seen the births of civilizations, and the last three or four thousand years that have seen the births of higher religions are periods of such infinitesimal brevity that it would be impossible to show them, drawn to scale, on any chart of the whole history of this planet up to date. On this true time scale, these events of "ancient history" are virtually contemporary with our own lifetime, however remote they may appear to be when viewed through the magnifying lens of the individual human midget's subjective mental vision.

The conclusion seems to be that human history does turn out, on occasions, to have repeated itself up to date in a significant sense even in spheres of human activity in which the human will is at its nearest to being master of the situation and is least under the domination of cycles in physical nature. Must we go on to conclude that, after all, the determinists are right and that what looks like free will is an illusion? In the present writer's opinion, the correct conclusion is just the opposite. As he sees it, this tendency towards repetition, which thus asserts itself in human affairs, is an instance of one of the well-known devices of the creative faculty. The works of creation are apt to occur in bunches: a bunch of representatives of a species, a bunch of species of a genus. And the value of such repetitions is, after all, not difficult to discern. Creation could hardly make any headway at all if each new form of creature were not represented by numerous eggs distributed among numerous baskets. How else could a creator, human or divine, provide himself with sufficient materials for bold and fruitful experiment and with effective means of retrieving inevitable failures? If human history repeats itself, it does so in accordance with the general rhythm of the universe; but the significance of this pattern of repetition lies in the scope that it gives for the work of creation to go forward. In this light, the repetitive element in history reveals itself as an instrument for freedom of creative action, and not as an indication that God and man are the slaves of fate.

What is the bearing of these conclusions about history in general on the particular question of the prospects of our Western civilization? As we observed at the beginning of this paper, the Western world has become rather suddenly very anxious about its own future, and our anxiety is a natural reaction to the formidableness of the situation in which we now find ourselves. Our present situation is formidable indeed. A survey of the historical landscape in the light of our existing knowledge shows that, up to date, history has repeated itself about twenty times in producing human societies of the species to which our Western society belongs, and it also shows that, with the possible exception of our own, all these representatives of the species of society called civilizations are already dead or moribund. Moreover, when we study the histories of these dead and moribund civilizations in detail, and compare them with one another, we find indications of what looks like a recurring pattern in the process of their breakdowns, declines, and falls. We are naturally asking ourselves today whether this particular chapter of history is bound to repeat itself in our case. Is that pattern of decline and fall in store for us in our turn, as a doom for which no civilization can hope to escape? In the writer's opinion, the answer to this question is emphatically in the negative. The effort to create a new manifestation of life—be it a new species of mollusc or a new species of human society—seldom or never succeeds at the first attempt. Creation is not so easy an enterprise as that. It wins its ultimate successes through a process of trial and error; and accordingly the failure of previous experiments, so far from dooming subsequent experiments to fail in their turn in the same way, actually offers them their oportunity of achieving success through the wisdom that can be gained from suffering. Of course a series of previous failures does not guarantee success to the next comer, any more than it condemns him to be a failure in his turn. There is nothing to prevent our Western civilization from following historical precedent, if it chooses, by committing social suicide. But we are not doomed to make history repeat itself; it is open to us, through our own efforts, to give history, in our case, some new and unprecedented turn. As human beings, we are endowed with this freedom of choice, and we cannot shuffle off our responsibility upon the shoulders of God or nature. We must shoulder it ourselves. It is up to us.

What shall we do to be saved? In politics, establish a constitutional co-operative system of world government. In economics, find working compromises (varying according to the practical requirements of different places and times) between free enterprise and socialism. In the life of the spirit, put the secular super-structure back onto religious foundations. Efforts are being made in our Western world today to find our way towards each of these goals. If we had arrived at all three of them, we might fairly feel that we had won our present battle for our civilization's survival. But these are, all of them, ambitious undertakings, and it will call for the hardest work and the highest courage to make any progress at all towards carrying any one of them through to achievement.

Of the three tasks, the religious one is, of course, in the long run by far the most important, but the other two are the more urgent, because, if we were to fail in these in the short run, we might lose forever our opportunity of achieving a spiritual rebirth which cannot just be whistled for at our convenience, but will only come, if it comes at all, at the unhurrying pace at which the deepest tides of spiritual creation flow.

The political task is the most urgent of all. The immediate problem here is a negative one. Faced, as we are, with the prospect that—given our present interdependence and present weapons—the world is now on the eve of being unified politically by one means or another, we have to stave off the disastrous dénouement of unification by force of arms: the familiar method of the forcible imposition of a *Pax Romana* which is probably the line of least resistance for the resolution of the formidable political forces in whose grip our own world finds itself today. Can the United States and the other Western countries manage to co-operate with the Soviet Union through the United Nations? If the United Nations organization could grow into an effective system of world government, that would be much the best solution of our political crux. But we have to reckon with the possibility of this enterprise's failing, and to be ready, should it fail, with an alternative to fall back upon. Could the United Nations split, *de facto*, into two groups without a breach of the peace? And, supposing that the whole face of the planet could be partitioned peacefully into an American and a Russian sphere, could two worlds on one planet live side by side on a footing of "non-violent non-co-operation" for long enough to give a chance for a gradual mitigation of the present differences in their social and ideological climates? The answer to this question would depend on whether, on these terms, we could buy the time needed to carry out our economic task of finding a middle way between free enterprise and socialism.

These riddles may be hard to read, but they do tell us plainly what we most need to know. They tell us that our future largely depends upon ourselves. We are not just at the mercy of an inexorable fate.

❦ ❦ ❦

*E. M. Forster*

# Toward a Definition of Tolerance[1]

CAN you define tolerance? I can't, any more than I could define love or faith, or fate, or any other abstraction. My mind slips about, tries a definition, finds it won't quite work, drops it, tries another, and so on. And people whose minds are better than my own seem to be in the same plight here. They propound definitions, they defend them stoutly and philosophically, but sooner or later the definition crumbles under the onslaught of some other philosopher, and the world is left where it was. Well, not quite where it was. Despite the failure, two valuable things have occurred. Firstly, the human mind has been exercising itself, and, my goodness, how desirable that is! It has been trying to discover something, and it has become stronger and more agile in conse-

---

[1] From *The New York Times Magazine* (February 22, 1953), p. 13. Copyright, 1953, by The New York Times. Reprinted by permission of the author.

quence, even though nothing has been discovered. And, secondly, the abstract subjects on which it has exercised itself have gained in prestige. Tolerance is important, no one can deny that, and if it is talked about so that people dispute what it is, or isn't, its importance should be maintained or increased.

Let me therefore set up an Aunt Sally.

Aunt Sallys are not as common in my country as they were, and for all I know they may have never crossed the Atlantic. Certainly I cannot imagine one on the Mayflower. So I had better define, and definition in this case is not so difficult. Aunt Sally is, or was, an elderly doll who was set up on a fairground to be shied at. She was tied to a stick or attached to a hinge. Three shies for a penny at Aunt Sally! Perhaps there was a prize if one hit her; perhaps the pleasure of bashing her face in was in itself sufficient reward. I forget. But she has become a symbol for the tentative definition. Knock her over if you can.

Let me therefore define tolerance as tolerating other people even when they don't tolerate you.

It is an austere definition. No politician would accept it. But if tolerance is to play any practical part in the modern world, if any headway is to be made against fanaticism, if there is to be any easing of the tensions between class and class, race and race, country and country, then tolerance must be more than a pious wish, more than a woolly assertion of goodwill. It must have courage, and it must be prepared to take risks.

At this point someone shies a ball at my Aunt Sally. It hits her. She staggers.

Someone has in effect said: "The modern world is indeed dangerous, and that is exactly why one can't take risks in it. It is so dangerous that tolerance is a luxury, which we can only indulge with those who reciprocate it. I don't like the color of so-and-so's face—it's green and I dislike green faces—still I'll put up with his face if he'll put up with mine. Mine is, of course, blue, the proper color for faces, and if he complains of it, if he threatens it, then my only remedy is to drop a bomb on him before he drops one on me. Tolerance is all very well, but there is such a thing as self-preservation."

Aunt Sally staggers but she does not fall. From her vantage post she can see that the modern world is not only dangerous: it is crowded, it is small and it has been contracted by science. A few hundred years ago she might not have said, "Tolerate other people even when they don't tolerate you." She might have said, "Fight it out, little blue face and little green face, if you want to. There is plenty of room for your quarrel; your muskets don't carry far and even if both of you are killed, civilization will survive." Today she is not so sure. One explosion may destroy us all. Tolerance assumes a new importance in a crowded world. The duty of running a risk has increased.

The heavenly counterpart of tolerance is love. Between the two a great gulf is set. Love is positive; tolerance negative. Love involves passion; tolerance is humdrum and dull. Love may explain the universe; tolerance, through common sense and good temper, tries to avert further disaster from the earth. Yet despite the gulf between, these two abstractions have problems in common. Love, too, has been asked to take risks: "Love your enemies, do good to them that hate you" is a text that has needed a good deal of explanation on the part of theologians. And love, in a pregnant line of W. H. Auden's, has been assigned the role which I have here claimed for tolerance: "We must love one another or die," the line runs. In another poem he tells us that we must love our crooked neighbor with our crooked heart; and how else shall we tolerate him?

Tolerance is not only needed to avoid disaster. It is also needed in peace conditions, if a community is to remain healthy and creative. An intolerant community, exacting the "right point of view" is condemned to monotony, even if the right point view is a good one. Its citizens would lack curiosity. They would tend to be all alike for the sake of avoiding friction. They would educate their children the same way, eat the same food at the same time, laugh at the same jokes, succumb to the same advertisements, go to the same places in the same planes, and they would denounce as subversive any one who criticized them. Money—and money alone—would distinguish one human being in that community from another and the spiritual tyranny of the income-bracket would triumph.

I would certainly sooner live in a montonous community than in a world of universal war, but I would sooner be dead than live in either of them. My heart is in the world of today, with its varieties and contrasts, its blue and green faces, and my hope is that, through courageous tolerance, the world of today may be preserved. Risks must be taken. It's difficult. Aunt Sally trembles on her perch as the well-directed missiles hit her. But what's your alternative?

❧ ❧ ❧

*Bertrand Russell*

# Co-existence or No Existence: The Choice Is Ours [1]

THE RECENT changes in the technique of war have produced a situation which is wholly unprecedented. War has existed ever since there were organized states, that is to say for some six thousand years. This ancient institution is now about to end. There are two ways in which the end may come about: the first is the extinction of the human race; the second is an agreement not to fight. I do not know which of these will be chosen.

Neither the general public nor the majority of powerful statesmen have as yet realized that war with modern weapons cannot serve the purposes of any government in the world. It is of the first importance that this should be realized by those who control policy both in the East and in the West. It is generally conceded by those who are in a position to speak with authority that

[1] From *The Nation*, CLXXX, No. 25 (June 18, 1955). Copyright 1955 by *The Nation*. Reprinted by permission of the author, of Public Interest, Inc., and of *The Nation*.

no complete defense against an H-bomb attack is possible. We must, I think, consider it the most likely hypothesis that if a great war broke out tomorrow each side would be successful in attack and unsuccessful in defense. This means that in the first days of such a war all the great centers of population on each side would be obliterated. Those who survived this first disaster would perish slowly or quickly as a result of the fall-out from radioactive cloud. Destruction of life from this cause would not be confined to the belligerent countries. The winds would gradually spread death throughout the world. This, at least, is what is to be feared. It cannot be said that the worst outcome is certain, but it is sufficiently probable to deter any sane man from incurring the risk.

Apart from the totality of destruction, there is another new element in the situation. In old days if you had a military advantage over your enemy, you might hope to win in time. But now, if each side has enough H-bombs to wipe out the other, there is no longer any advantage in having twice as many as your adversary.

Both in the United States and in Great Britain there has been much talk of civil defense. Russian military journals contain talk of the same kind. All such plans, I am convinced, show either ignorance or hypocrisy in those who advocate them. Deep shelters would enable a portion of the population to survive the first explosion, but sooner or later these people would have to emerge from their shelters into a radioactive world.

Although the H-bomb is the center of public attention at the moment, it is only one of the possibilities of destruction which science has put in the hands of irresponsible politicians. Chemical and bacteriological warfare are studied by all powerful states and may have consequences at least as horrifying as those of the H-bomb. There is no visible end to the methods of inflicting death that may be invented. Even if a portion of the human race were to survive a great war now, it cannot be doubted that the next war, if scientific technique survives, would complete what its predecessor had left unfinished.

There is therefore no escape from the choice that lies before us: Shall we renounce war, or shall we bring our species to an end?

### ESCAPE FROM REALITY

If men realized that these are the only alternatives, no one can doubt that they would choose peace. But there are various ways in which people escape the realization of unpleasant facts. I have seen statements by Russians and Chinese that a thermonuclear war would of course destroy the rotten capitalistic civilization of the West but would not vitally injure the sturdy Communist nations of the East. I have also seen statements by American authorities claiming that the West would be victorious. Both seemed to me, if genuinely believed, to be mere fantasies of wish-fulfilment and, if not genuinely believed, to be part of the silly game of bluff which great nations have been allowing themselves. I hope that this is beginning to be understood. Recently there have been hopeful signs that neither side is willing to push issues to the point of war. And with every month that passes there is a better chance that statesmen both in the East and in the West will become aware of some of the important facts by which their policy ought to be guided.

Another widespread delusion is that perhaps in a great war H-bombs would not be employed. People point to the fact that gas was not employed in the Second World War. They forget that gas had not proved a decisive weapon even in the First World War and that in the meantime gas-masks had been provided which were a complete protection. Any analogy is therefore entirely misleading.

It is thought by many that the first step forward should be an international agreement not to use H-bombs in the event of war, and this is generally coupled with the suggestion that both sides should destroy their existing stock of these weapons. This suggestion has certain merits but also certain drawbacks. Its chief merit is that if the destruction of existing stocks were honestly carried out, the danger of a sudden attack in the style of Pearl Harbor would be lessened. Against this we must set the fact that no system of inspection can now make sure that bombs are not being manufactured. This is a new fact. At the time of the Baruch proposal it was still possible for an inspectorate to gain control of the raw materials, but this is so no longer. Each side would therefore suspect that the other side was manufacturing bombs surreptitiously, and this might make relations worse than if no agreement had been concluded. What is even more important is that, if war did break out, neither side would consider itself bound by the agreement, and after a certain number of months H-bomb warfare would be in full swing. Only by not making war can the danger be avoided. We must therefore turn our thoughts away from war to the methods by which peace can be made secure.

The transition from the cold war to a condition of secure peace cannot be made in a day. But it can be made, and it must be made. It will have to be made by stages. The first stage will consist in persuading all powerful governments of the world that their aims, whatever they may be, cannot be achieved by war. In this first stage, scientists—not only nuclear physicists but also physiologists, geneticists, and bacteriologists—have a very important part to play. Their discoveries have created the dangers, and it is their obvious duty to arouse the public and the governments to a sense of the risks they are running. They may, in performing this duty, be compelled to take action of which their governments disapprove, but loyalty to mankind should be for them the paramount consideration. I am convinced that it is within their power to persuade the governments both of the East and of the West to look to negotiation rather than war for a solution of their problems.

The next stage must be to create temporary machinery to negotiate settlements of all the questions at present causing conflict between East and West. It will be necessary to refer such questions to a body of negotiators in which East and West have equal representation and the balance of power is in the hands of the neutrals. I do not venture to suggest what solution should be reached on any of the vexed questions of the present. I think that a body constituted as I have suggested would avoid gross unfairness to either side, and subject to this condition almost any settlement would be preferable to a continuation of the present state of tension. A very important part of any settlement should of course be a drastic reduction of armaments. It is hardly to be supposed that the very delicate negotiations which will be required can be conducted successfully in the atmosphere of strained hostility that has existed during recent years. Each side will have to abandon perpetual abuse of the other and learn to practice that degree of toleration which after centuries of warfare was at last achieved between Christians and Moslems and between Catholics and Protestants. We cannot now wait for the slow operation of reason through the discouragements of long indecisive wars. We must learn in advance a manner of thinking and feeling which in the past has been learned slowly and through bitter experience. I will not pretend that this is easy. But if men can be made to realize the dreadful alternative I do not think it will prove impossible.

### THE THIRD STEP

If the immediate problems that now divide East and West were settled in some such way, we could reach the third stage of progress toward secure peace. The international problems of our day are not the last that will ever arise. There will be new problems, perhaps dividing the world quite differently from the way in which it is now divided between Communist and anti-Communist blocs. So long as there is not an established international authority capable of enforcing peace, the risk of war will remain, and with every advance in science the risk will become more terrible. The international anarchy resulting from a multitude of states with unrestricted sovereignty must be brought to an end. The international authority which is to end it will have to be federal and endowed with only such powers as are necessary for preserving the peace of the world. The most important of these powers, and also the most difficult to secure, will be an obvious preponderance of armed forces over those of any national state or alliance of states. The anarchic liberty at present enjoyed by sovereign states is dear to most people and will not be surrendered easily, but it will have to be surrendered if the human species is to survive. The process required is a continuation of that which occurred in the fifteenth and sixteenth centuries. Before that time powerful barons in their castles could defy national governments, and there was the same sort of anarchy within a nation as now exists between nations. Gunpowder and artillery put an end to internal anarchy in France, Spain, and England. The hydrogen bomb has the same part to play in ending international anarchy. The loss of liberty, though it may be distasteful, is precisely of the same kind as that which private individuals suffer by being forbidden to commit murder, for after all it is the right to murder which hitherto sovereign states will be asked to surrender.

## LEGITIMATE HOPES

I have been speaking of dangers and how to avoid them, but there is another thing which it is just as important to emphasize, for while fears are at present unavoidable, hopes are equally legitimate. If we take the measures needed to end our fears, we shall thereby create a world capable of such well-being as has never been known and scarcely even imagined. Throughout the long ages since civilization began, the bulk of mankind have lived lives of misery and toil and bondage. All the long burden of misery that has darkened the slow progress of mankind has now become unnecessary. If we can learn to tolerate each other and to live in amity, poverty can be abolished everywhere more completely than it is now abolished in the most fortunate nations. Fear can be so much diminished that a new buoyancy and a new joy will brighten the daily lives of all. The work of science, which while war survives is largely evil, will become wholly beneficent. Nothing stands in the way but the darkness of atavistic evil passions. New technical possibilities of well-being exist, but the wisdom to make use of them has hitherto been lacking. Shall we collectively continue to turn our back upon the things that each one of us individually desires? We can make a world of light, or we can banish life from our planet. One or other we must do, and do soon. A great duty rests upon those who realize these alternatives, for it is they who must persuade mankind to make the better choice.

# ❧ ❧ ❧ VII. *Philosophy and Religion*

# The Good Life

*Aristotle*

## Virtue[1]

BUT it may be asked what we mean by saying that people must become just by doing what is just and temperate by doing what is temperate. For if they do what is just and temperate, they are *ipso facto* proved, it will be said, to be just and temperate in the same way as, if they practise grammar and music, they are proved to be grammarians and musicians.

But is not the answer that the case of the arts is not the same? For a person may do something that is grammatical either by chance or at the suggestion of somebody else; hence he will not be a grammarian unless he not only does what is grammatical but does it in a grammatical manner, i.e. in virtue of the grammatical knowledge which he possesses.

There is another point too of difference between the arts and the virtues. The productions of art have their excellence in themselves. It is enough therefore that, when they are produced, they should be of a certain character. But actions in accordance with virtue are not e.g. justly or temperately performed because they are in themselves just or temperate. It is necessary that the agent at the time of performing them should satisfy certain conditions, i.e. in the first place that he should know what he is doing, secondly that he should deliberately choose to do it and to do it for its own sake, and thirdly that he should do it as an instance of a settled and immutable moral state. If it be a question whether a person possesses any art, these conditions, except indeed the condition of knowledge, are not taken into account; but if it be a question of possessing the virtues, the mere knowledge is of little or no avail, and it is the other conditions, which are the results of frequently performing just and temperate actions, that are not of slight but of absolute importance. Accordingly deeds are said to be just and temperate, when they are such as a just or temperate person would do, and a just and temperate person is not merely one who does these deeds but one who does them in the spirit of the just and the temperate.

[1] From *The Nichomachean Ethics of Aristotle*, translated by J. E. C. Weldon (London: Macmillan & Co., Ltd., 1920), Book II, with omissions. Reprinted by permission of Macmillan & Co., Ltd.

It may fairly be said then that a just man becomes just by doing what is just and a temperate man becomes temperate by doing what is temperate, and if a man did not so act, he would not have so much as a chance of becoming good. But most people, instead of doing such actions, take refuge in theorizing; they imagine that they are philosophers and that philosophy will make them virtuous; in fact they behave like people who listen attentively to their doctors but never do anything that their doctors tell them. But it is as improbable that a healthy state of the soul will be produced by this kind of philosophizing as that a healthy state of the body will be produced by this kind of medical treatment.

We have next to consider the nature of virtue.

Now, as the qualities of the soul are three, viz. emotions, faculties and moral states, it follows that virtue must be one of the three. By the emotions I mean desire, anger, fear, courage, envy, joy, love, hatred, regret, emulation, pity, in a word whatever is attended by pleasure or pain. I call those faculties in respect of which we are said to be capable of experiencing these emotions, e.g. capable of getting angry or being pained or feeling pity. And I call those moral states in respect of which we are well or ill disposed towards the emotions, ill-disposed e.g. towards the passion of anger, if our anger be too violent or too feeble, and well-disposed, if it be duly moderated, and similarly towards the other emotions.

Now neither the virtues nor the vices are emotions; for we are not called good or evil in respect of our emotions but in respect of our virtues or vices. Again, we are not praised or blamed in respect of our emotions; a person is not praised for being afraid or being angry, nor blamed for being angry in an absolute sense, but only for being angry in a certain way; but we are praised or blamed in respect of our virtues or vices. Again, whereas we are angry or afraid without deliberate purpose, the virtues are in some sense deliberate purposes, or do not exist in the absence of deliberate purpose. It may be added that while we are said to be moved in respect of our emotions, in respect of our virtues or vices we are not said to be moved but to have a certain disposition.

These reasons also prove that the virtues are not faculties. For we are not called either good or bad, nor are we praised or blamed, as having an abstract capacity for emotion. Also while Nature gives us our faculties, it is not Nature that makes us good or bad, but this is a point which we have already discussed. If then the virtues are neither emotions nor faculties, it remains that they must be moral states.

The nature of virtue has been now generically described. But it is not enough to state merely that virtue is a moral state, we must also describe the character of that moral state.

It must be laid down then that every virtue or excellence has the effect of producing a good condition of that of which it is a virtue or excellence, and of enabling it to perform its function well. Thus the excellence of the eye makes the eye good and its function good, as it is by the excellence of the eye that we see well. Similarly, the excellence of the horse makes a horse excellent and good at racing, at carrying its rider and at facing the enemy.

If then this is universally true, the virtue or excellence of man will be such a moral state as makes a man good and able to perform his proper function well. We have already explained how this will be the case, but another way of making it clear will be to study the nature or character of this virtue.

Now in everything, whether it be continuous or discrete,[2] it is possible to take a greater, a smaller, or an equal amount, and this either absolutely or in relation to ourselves, the equal being a mean between excess and deficiency. By the mean in respect of the thing itself, or the absolute mean, I understand that which is equally distinct from both extremes; and this is one and the same thing for everybody. By the mean considered relatively to ourselves I understand that which is neither too much nor too little; but this is not one thing, nor is it the same for everybody. Thus if 10 be too much and 2 too little we take 6 as a mean in respect of the thing itself; for 6 is as much greater than 2 as it is less than 10, and this is a mean in arithmetical proportion. But the mean considered relatively to ourselves must not be ascertained in this way. It does not follow that if 10 pounds *of meat* be too much and 2 be too little for a man to eat, a trainer will order him 6 pounds, as this may itself be too much or too little for the person who is to take it; it will be too little e.g. for Milo,[3] but too much for a beginner in gymnastics. It will be the same with running and wrestling; *the right amount will vary with the individual.* This being so, everybody who understands his business avoids alike excess and deficiency; he seeks and chooses the mean, not the absolute mean, but the mean considered relatively to ourselves.

Every science then performs its function well, if it regards the mean and refers the works which it produces to the mean. This is the reason why it is usually said of successful works that it is impossible to take anything from them or to add anything to them, which implies that excess or deficiency is fatal to excellence but that the mean state ensures it. Good artists too, as we say, have an eye to the mean in their works. But virtue, like Nature herself, is more accurate and better than any art; virtue therefore will aim at the mean; —I speak of moral virtue, as it is moral virtue which is concerned with emotions and actions, and it is these which admit of excess and deficiency and the mean. Thus it is possible to go too far, or not to go far enough, in respect of fear, courage, desire, anger, pity, and pleasure and pain generally, and the excess and the deficiency are alike wrong; but to experience these emotions at the right times and on the right occasions and towards the right persons and for the right causes and in the right manner is the mean or the supreme good, which is characteristic of virtue. Similarly there may be excess, deficiency, or the mean, in regard to actions. But virtue is concerned with emotions and

[2] In Aristotelian language, as Mr. Peters says, a straight line is a "continuous quantity" but a rouleau of sovereigns a "discrete quantity."

[3] The famous Crotoniate wrestler.

actions, and here excess is an error and deficiency a fault, whereas the mean is successful and laudable, and success and merit are both characteristics of virtue.

It appears then that virtue is a mean state, so far at least as it aims at the mean.

Again, there are many different ways of going wrong; for evil is in its nature infinite, to use the Pythagorean[4] figure, but good is finite. But there is only one possible way of going right. Accordingly the former is easy and the latter difficult; it is easy to miss the mark but difficult to hit it. This again is a reason why excess and deficiency are characteristics of vice and the mean state a characteristic of virtue.

> For good is simple, evil manifold.[5]

Virtue then is a state of deliberate moral purpose consisting in a mean that is relative to ourselves, the mean being determined by reason, or as a prudent man would determine it.

It is a mean state *firstly as lying* between two vices, the vice of excess on the one hand, and the vice of deficiency on the other, and secondly because, whereas the vices either fall short of or go beyond what is proper in the emotions and actions, virtue not only discovers but embraces the mean.

Accordingly, virtue, if regarded in its essence or theoretical conception, is a mean state, but, if regarded from the point of view of the highest good, or of excellence, it is an extreme.

But it is not every action or every emotion that admits of a mean state. There are some whose very name implies wickedness, as e.g. malice, shamelessness, and envy, among emotions, or adultery, theft, and murder, among actions. All these, and others like them, are censured as being intrinsically wicked, not merely the excesses or deficiencies of them. It is never possible then to be right in respect of them; they are always sinful. Right or wrong in such actions as adultery does not depend on our committing them with the right person, at the right time or in the right manner; on the contrary it is sinful to do anything of the kind at all. It would be equally wrong then to suppose that there can be a mean state or an excess or deficiency in unjust, cowardly or licentious conduct; for, if it were so, there would be a mean state of an excess or of a deficiency, an excess of an excess and a deficiency of a deficiency. But as in temperance and courage there can be no excess or deficiency because the mean is, in a sense, an extreme, so too in these cases there cannot be a mean or an excess or deficiency, but, however the acts may be done, they are wrong. For it is a general rule that an excess or deficiency does not admit of a mean state, nor a mean state of an excess or deficiency.

But it is not enough to  lay down this as a general rule; it is necessary to

---

[4] The Pythagoreans, starting from the mystical significance of number, took the opposite principles of "the finite" (τὸ πέρασ or τὸ πεπερασμένον) and "the infinite" (τὸ απειρον ) to represent good and evil.

[5] A line—perhaps Pythagorean—of unknown authorship.

apply it to particular cases, as in reasonings upon actions, general statements, although they are broader, are less exact than particular statements. For all action refers to particulars, and it is essential that our theories should harmonize with the particular cases to which they apply.

We must take particular virtues then from the catalogue[6] of *virtues*.

In regard to feelings of fear and confidence, courage is a mean state. On the side of excess, he whose fearlessness is excessive has no name, as often happens, but he whose confidence is excessive is foolhardy, while he whose timidity is excessive and whose confidence is deficient is a coward.

In respect of pleasures and pains, although not indeed of all pleasures and pains, and to a less extent in respect of pains than of pleasures, the mean state is temperance, the excess is licentiousness. We never find people who are deficient in regard to pleasures; accordingly such people again have not received a name, but we may call them insensible.

As regards the giving and taking of money, the mean state is liberality, the excess and deficiency are prodigality and illiberality. Here the excess and deficiency take opposite forms; for while the prodigal man is excessive in spending and deficient in taking, the illiberal man is excessive in taking and deficient in spending.

(For the present we are giving only a rough and summary account *of the virtues*, and that is sufficient for our purpose; we will hereafter determine their character more exactly.)

In respect of money there are other dispositions as well. There is the mean state which is magnificence; for the magnificent man, as having to do with large sums of money, differs from the liberal man who has to do only with small sums; and the excess *corresponding to it* is bad taste or vulgarity, the deficiency is meanness. These are different from the excess and deficiency of liberality; what the difference is will be explained hereafter.

In respect of honour and dishonour the mean state is highmindedness, the excess is what is called vanity, the deficiency littlemindedness. Corresponding to liberality, which, as we said, differs from magnificence as having to do *not with great but* with small sums of money, there is a moral state which has to do with petty honour and is related to highmindedness which has to do with great honour; for it is possible to aspire to honour in the right way, or in a way which is excessive or insufficient, and if a person's aspirations are excessive, he is called ambitious, if they are deficient, he is called unambitious, while if they are between the two, he has no name.

Anger, like other emotions, has its excess, its deficiency, and its mean state. It may be said that they have no names, but as we call one who observes the mean gentle, we will call the mean state gentleness. Among the extremes, if a person errs on the side of excess, he may be called passionate and his vice

---

[6] It would seem that a catalogue of virtues ( διαγραφή or ὑπογραφή ) must have been recognized in the Aristotelian school. Cp. *Eud. Eth.* ii, ch. 3.

passionateness, if on that of deficiency, he may be called impassive and his deficiency impassivity.

There are also three other mean states with a certain resemblance to each
other, and yet with a difference. For while they are all concerned with intercourse in speech and action, they are different in that one of them is concerned with truth in such intercourse, and the others with pleasantness, one
with pleasantness in amusement and the other with pleasantness in the various
circumstances of life. We must therefore discuss these states in order to make
it clear that in all cases it is the mean state which is an object of praise, and
the extremes are neither right nor laudable but censurable. It is true that these
mean and extreme states are generally nameless, but we must do our best here
as elsewhere to give them a name, so that our argument may be clear and
easy to follow.

In the matter of truth then, he who observes the mean may be called truthful, and the mean state truthfulness. Pretence, if it takes the form of exaggeration, is boastfulness, and one who is guilty of pretence is a boaster; but if it
takes the form of depreciation it is irony, and he who is guilty of it is ironical.

There are also mean states in the emotions and in the expression of the
emotions. For although modesty is not a virtue, yet a modest person is praised
as if he were virtuous; for here too one person is said to observe the mean and
another to exceed it, as e.g. the bashful man who is never anything but modest,
whereas a person who has insufficient modesty or no modesty at all is called
shameless, and one who observes the mean modest.

Righteous indignation, again, is a mean state between envy and malice. They
are all concerned with the pain and pleasure which we feel at the fortunes
of our neighbours. A person who is righteously indignant is pained at the
prosperity of the undeserving; but the envious person goes further and is
pained at anybody's prosperity, and the malicious person is so far from being
pained that he actually rejoices *at misfortunes*. . . .

There are then three dispositions, two being vices, viz. one the vice of excess and the other that of deficiency, and one virtue, which is the mean state
between them; and they are all in a sense mutually opposed. For the extremes
are opposed both to the mean and to each other, and the mean is opposed to
the extremes. For as the equal if compared with the less is greater but if compared with the greater is less, so the mean states, whether in the emotions or
actions, if compared with the deficiencies, are excessive, but if compared with
the excesses are deficient. Thus the courageous man appears foolhardy as compared with the coward, but cowardly as compared with the foolhardy. Similarly, the temperate man appears licentious as compared with the insensible
but insensible as compared with the licentious, and the liberal man appears
prodigal as compared with the illiberal, but illiberal as compared with the
prodigal. The result is that the extremes mutually repel and reject the mean;
the coward calls the courageous man foolhardy, but the foolhardy man calls him
cowardly, and so on in the other cases.

But while there is this mutual opposition between the extremes and the mean, there is greater opposition between the two extremes than between either extreme and the mean; for they are further removed from each other than from the mean, as the great from the small and the small from the great than both from the equal. Again, while some extremes exhibit more or less similarity to the mean, as foolhardiness to courage and prodigality to liberality, there is the greatest possible dissimilarity between the extremes. But things which are fur-thest removed from each other are defined to be opposites; hence the further things are removed, the greater is the opposition between them.

It is in some cases the deficiency and in others the excess which is the more opposed to the mean. Thus it is not foolhardiness the excess, but cowardice the deficiency which is the more opposed to courage, nor is it insensibility the deficiency, but licentiousness the excess which is the more opposed to temper-ance. There are two reasons why this should be so. One lies in the nature of the thing itself; for as one of the two extremes is the nearer and more similar to the mean, it is not this extreme, but its opposite, that we chiefly set against the mean. For instance, as it appears that foolhardiness is more similar and nearer to courage than cowardice, it is cowardice that we chiefly set against courage; for things which are further removed from the mean seem to be more opposite to it. This being one reason which lies in the nature of the thing itself, there is a second which lies in our own nature. It is the things to which we ourselves are naturally more inclined that appear more opposed to the mean. Thus we are ourselves naturally more inclined to pleasures *than to their opposites*, and are more prone therefore to licentiousness than to decorum. Accordingly we speak of those things, in which we are more likely to run to great lengths, as being more opposed to the mean. Hence it follows that licentiousness which is an excess is more opposed to temperance than insensi-bility.

It has now been sufficiently shown that moral virtue is a mean state, and in what sense it is a mean state; it is a mean state as lying between two vices, a vice of excess on the one side and a vice of deficiency on the other, and as aiming at the mean in the emotions and actions.

# The Sermon on the Mount[1]

AND seeing the multitudes, he went up into a mountain; and when he was set, his disciples came unto him: and he opened his mouth, and taught them, say-ing, Blessed are the poor in spirit: for theirs is the kingdom of heaven.

[1] From *The Gospel According to Saint Matthew* (King James Version of *The Bible*), Chapters 5, 6, 7.

Blessed are they that mourn: for they shall be comforted. Blessed are the meek: for they shall inherit the earth. Blessed are they which do hunger and thirst after righteousness: for they shall be filled. Blessed are the merciful: for they shall obtain mercy. Blessed are the pure in heart: for they shall see God. Blessed are the peacemakers: for they shall be called the children of God. Blessed are they which are persecuted for righteousness' sake: for theirs is the kingdom of heaven. Blessed are ye, when men shall revile you, and persecute you, and shall say all manner of evil against you falsely, for my sake. Rejoice, and be exceeding glad: for great is your reward in heaven: for so persecuted they the prophets which were before you.

Ye are the salt of the earth: but if the salt have lost his savour, wherewith shall it be salted? it is thenceforth good for nothing, but to be cast out, and to be trodden under foot of men. Ye are the light of the world. A city that is set on an hill cannot be hid. Neither do men light a candle, and put it under a bushel, but on a candlestick; and it giveth light unto all that are in the house. Let your light so shine before men, that they may see your good works, and glorify your Father which is in heaven. Think not that I am come to destroy the law, or the prophets; I am not come to destroy, but to fulfil. For verily I say unto you, Till heaven and earth pass, one jot or one tittle shall in no wise pass from the law, till all be fulfilled. Whosoever therefore shall break one of these least commandments, and shall teach men so, he shall be called the least in the kingdom of heaven: but whosoever shall do and teach them, the same shall be called great in the kingdom of heaven. For I say unto you, That except your righteousness shall exceed the righteousness of the scribes and Pharisees, ye shall in no case enter into the kingdom of heaven.

Ye have heard that it was said by them of old time, Thou shalt not kill; and whosoever shall kill shall be in danger of the judgment: but I say unto you, That whosoever is angry with his brother without a cause shall be in danger of the judgment: and whosoever shall say to his brother, Raca, shall be in danger of the council: but whosoever shall say, Thou fool, shall be in danger of hell fire. Therefore if thou bring thy gift to the altar, and there rememberest that thy brother hath ought against thee; leave there thy gift before the altar, and go thy way; first be reconciled to thy brother, and then come and offer thy gift. Agree with thine adversary quickly, whiles thou art in the way with him; lest at any time the adversary deliver thee to the judge, and the judge deliver thee to the officer, and thou be cast into prison. Verily I say unto thee, Thou shalt by no means come out thence, till thou hast paid the uttermost farthing.

Ye have heard that it was said by them of old time, Thou shalt not commit adultery; but I say unto you, That whosoever looketh on a woman to lust after her hath committed adultery with her already in his heart. And if thy right eye offend thee, pluck it out, and cast it from thee: for it is profitable for thee that one of thy members should perish, and not that thy whole body should be cast into hell. And if thy right hand offend thee, cut it off, and cast it from thee:

for it is profitable for thee that one of thy members should perish, and not that thy whole body should be cast into hell. It hath been said, Whosoever shall put away his wife, let him give her a writing of divorcement: but I say unto you, That whosoever shall put away his wife, saving for the cause of fornication, causeth her to commit adultery: and whosoever shall marry her that is divorced committeth adultery.

Again, ye have heard that it hath been said by them of old time, Thou shalt not forswear thyself, but shalt perform to the Lord thine oaths: but I say unto you, Swear not at all; neither by heaven; for it is God's throne: nor by the earth; for it is his footstool: neither by Jerusalem; for it is the city of the great King. Neither shalt thou swear by thy head, because thou canst not make one hair white or black. But let your communication be, Yea, yea; Nay, nay: for whatsoever is more than these cometh of evil.

Ye have heard that it hath been said, An eye for an eye, and a tooth for a tooth: but I say unto you, That ye resist not evil: but whosoever shall smite thee on thy right cheek, turn to him the other also. And if any man will sue thee at the law, and take away thy coat, let him have thy cloke also. And who-soever shall compel thee to go a mile, go with him twain. Give to him that asketh thee, and from him that would borrow of thee turn not thou away.

Ye have heard that it hath been said, Thou shalt love thy neighbor, and hate thine enemy. But I say unto you, Love your enemies, bless them that curse you, do good to them that hate you, and pray for them which despitefully use you, and persecute you; that ye may be the children of your Father which is in heaven; for he maketh his sun to rise on the evil and on the good, and sendeth rain on the just and on the unjust. For if ye love them which love you, what reward have ye? do not even the publicans the same? And if ye salute your brethren only, what do ye more than others? do not even the publicans so? Be ye therefore perfect, even as your Father which is in heaven is perfect.

Take heed that ye do not your alms before men, to be seen of them: other-wise ye have no reward of your Father which is in heaven. Therefore when thou doest thine alms, do not sound a trumpet before thee, as the hypocrites do in the synagogues and in the streets, that they may have glory of men. Verily I say unto you, They have their reward. But when thou doest alms, let not thy left hand know what thy right hand doeth: that thine alms may be in secret: and thy Father which seeth in secret himself shall reward thee openly. And when thou prayest, thou shalt not be as the hypocrites are: for they love to pray standing in the synagogues and in the corners of the streets, that they may be seen of men. Verily I say unto you, They have their reward. But thou, when thou prayest, enter into thy closet, and when thou hast shut thy door, pray to thy Father, which is in secret; and thy Father which seeth in secret shall reward thee openly. But when ye pray, use not vain repetitions, as the heathen do: for they think that they shall be heard for their much speaking. Be not ye therefore like unto them: for your Father knoweth what things ye have need of, before ye ask him. After this manner therefore pray ye: Our Father which art in heaven, Hallowed be thy name. Thy kingdom come. Thy will be done in earth, as it is in heaven. Give us this day our daily bread. And forgive us our debts, as we forgive our debtors. And lead us not into temptation, but deliver us from evil: for thine is the kingdom, and the power, and the glory, for ever. Amen. For if ye forgive men their trespasses, your heavenly Father will also forgive you: but if ye forgive not men their trespasses, neither will your Father forgive your trespasses.

Moreover when ye fast, be not, as the hypocrites, of a sad countenance: for they disfigure their faces, that they may appear unto men to fast. Verily I say unto you, They have their reward. But thou, when thou fastest, anoint thine head, and wash thy face; that thou appear not unto men to fast, but unto thy Father which is in secret; and thy Father, which seeth in secret, shall reward thee openly.

Lay up not for yourselves treasures upon earth, where moth and rust doth corrupt, and where thieves break through and steal: but lay up for yourselves treasures in heaven, where neither moth nor rust doth corrupt, and where thieves do not break through nor steal: for where your treasure is, there will your heart be also. The light of the body is the eye: if therefore thine eye be single, thy whole body shall be full of light. But if thine eye be evil, thy whole body shall be full of darkness. If therefore the light that is in thee be darkness, how great is that darkness! No man can serve two masters: for either he will hate the one, and love the other; or else he will hold to the one, and despise the other. Ye cannot serve God and mammon. Therefore I say unto you, Take no thought for your life, what ye shall eat, or what ye shall drink; nor yet for your body, what ye shall put on. Is not the life more than meat, and the body than raiment? Behold the fowls of the air: for they sow not, neither do they reap, nor gather into barns; yet your heavenly Father feedeth them. Are not ye much better than they? Which of you by taking thought can add one cubit unto his stature? And why take ye thought for raiment? Consider the lilies of the field, how they grow; they toil not, neither do they spin: and yet I say unto you, That even Solomon in all his glory was not arrayed like one of these. Wherefore, if God so clothe the grass of the field, which to day is, and to morrow is cast into the oven, shall he not much more clothe you, O ye of little faith? Therefore take no thought, saying, What shall we eat? or, What shall we drink? or, Wherewithal shall we be clothed? (For after all these things do the Gentiles seek:) for your heavenly Father knoweth that ye have need of all these things. But seek ye first the kingdom of God, and his righteousness; and all these things shall be added unto you. Take therefore no thought for the morrow: for the morrow shall take thought for the things of itself. Sufficient unto the day is the evil thereof.

Judge not, that ye be not judged. For with what judgment ye judge, ye shall be judged: and with what measure ye mete, it shall be measured to you again.

And why beholdest thou the mote that is in thy brother's eye, but considerest not the beam that is in thine own eye? Or how wilt thou say to thy brother, Let me pull out the mote out of thine eye; and, behold, a beam is in thine own eye? Thou hypocrite, first cast out the beam out of thine own eye; and then shalt thou see clearly to cast out the mote out of thy brother's eye.

Give not that which is holy unto the dogs, neither cast ye your pearls before swine, lest they trample them under their feet, and turn again and rend you. Ask, and it shall be given you; seek and ye shall find; knock, and it shall be opened unto you: for every one that asketh receiveth; and he that seeketh findeth; and to him that knocketh it shall be opened. Or what man is there of you, whom if his son ask bread, will he give him a stone? Or if he ask a fish, will he give him a serpent? If ye then, being evil, know how to give good gifts unto your children, how much more shall your Father which is in heaven give good things to them that ask him? Therefore all things whatsoever ye would that men should do to you, do ye even so to them: for this is the law and the prophets.

Enter ye in at the strait gate: for wide is the gate, and broad is the way, that leadeth to destruction, and many there be which go in thereat: because strait is the gate, and narrow is the way, which leadeth unto life, and few there be that find it. Beware of false prophets, which come to you in sheep's clothing, but inwardly they are ravening wolves. Ye shall know them by their fruits. Do men gather grapes of thorns, or figs of thistles? Even so every good tree bringeth forth good fruit; but a corrupt tree bringeth forth evil fruit. A good tree cannot bring forth evil fruit, neither can a corrupt tree bring forth good fruit. Every tree that bringeth not forth good fruit is hewn down, and cast into the fire. Wherefore by their fruits ye shall know them. Not every one that saith unto me, Lord, Lord, shall enter into the kingdom of heaven; but he that doeth the will of my Father which is in heaven. Many will say to me in that day, Lord, Lord, have we not prophesied in thy name? And in thy name have cast out devils? and in thy name done many wonderful works? And then will I profess unto them, I never knew you: depart from me, ye that work iniquity. Therefore whosoever heareth these sayings of mine, and doeth them, I will liken him unto a wise man, which built his house upon a rock: and the rain descended, and the floods came, and the winds blew, and beat upon that house; and it fell not: for it was founded upon a rock. And every one that heareth these sayings of mine, and doeth them not, shall be likened unto a foolish man, which built his house upon the sand: and the rain descended, and the floods came, and the winds blew, and beat upon that house; and it fell: and great was the fall of it. And it came to pass, when Jesus had ended these sayings, the people were astonished at his doctrine: For he taught them as one having authority, and not as the scribes.

❦ ❦ ❦

*Søren Kierkegaard*

# A Panegyric upon Abraham[1]

## PRELUDE

ONCE upon a time there was a man who as a child had heard the beautiful story[2] about how God tempted Abraham, and how he endured temptation, kept the faith, and a second time received again a son contrary to expectation. When the child became older he read the same story with even greater admiration, for life had separated what was united in the pious simplicity of the child. The older he became, the more frequently his mind reverted to that story, his enthusiasm became greater and greater, and yet he was less and less able to understand the story. At last in his interest for that he forgot everything else; his soul had only one wish, to see Abraham, one longing, to have been witness to that event. His desire was not to behold the beautiful countries of the Orient, or the earthly glory of the Promised Land, or that godfearing couple whose old age God had blessed, or the venerable figure of the aged patriarch, or the vigorous young manhood of Isaac whom God had bestowed upon Abraham— he saw no reason why the same thing might not have taken place on a barren heath in Denmark. His yearning was to accompany them on the three days' journey when Abraham rode with sorrow before him and with Isaac by his side. His only wish was to be present at the time when Abraham lifted up his eyes and saw Mount Moriah afar off, at the time when he left the asses behind and went alone with Isaac up unto the mountain; for what his mind was intent upon was not the ingenious web of imagination but the shudder of thought.

That man was not a thinker, he felt no need of getting beyond faith; he deemed it the most glorious thing to be remembered as the father of it, an enviable lot to possess it, even though no one else were to know it.

That man was not a learned exegete, he didn't know Hebrew, if he had known Hebrew, he perhaps would easily have understood the story and Abraham.

### I

And God tempted Abraham and said unto him, Take Isaac, thine only son, whom thou lovest, and get thee into the land of Moriah, and offer him there for a burnt offering upon the mountain which I will show thee.

[1] From *Fear and Trembling* and *The Sickness unto Death* by S. Kierkegaard, translated by Walter Lowrie (New York: Doubleday and Co., 1955), pp. 26-37. Copyright, 1941, 1954, by Princeton University Press. Reprinted by permission.
[2] Genesis, Chapter 22.

It was early in the morning, Abraham arose betimes, he had the asses saddled, left his tent, and Isaac with him, but Sarah looked out of the window after them until they had passed down the valley and she could see them no more.[3] They rode in silence for three days. On the morning of the fourth day Abraham said never a word, but he lifted up his eyes and saw Mount Moriah afar off. He left the young men behind and went on alone with Isaac beside him up to the mountain. But Abraham said to himself, "I will not conceal from Isaac whither this course leads him." He stood still, he laid his hand upon the head of Isaac in benediction, and Isaac bowed to receive the blessing. And Abraham's face was fatherliness, his look was mild, his speech encouraging. But Isaac was unable to understand him, his soul could not be exalted; he embraced Abraham's knees, he fell at his feet imploringly, he begged for his young life, for the fair hope of his future, he called to mind the joy in Abraham's house, he called to mind the sorrow and loneliness. Then Abraham lifted up the boy, he walked with him by his side, and his talk was full of comfort and exhortation. But Isaac could not understand him. He climbed Mount Moriah, but Isaac understood him not. Then for an instant he turned away from him, and when Isaac again saw Abraham's face it was changed, his glance was wild, his form was horror. He seized Isaac by the throat, threw him to the ground, and said, "Stupid boy, dost thou then suppose that I am thy father? I am an idolater. Dost thou suppose that this is God's bidding? No, it is my desire." Then Isaac trembled and cried out in his terror, "O God in heaven, have compassion upon me. God of Abraham, have compassion upon me. If I have no father upon earth, be Thou my father!" But Abraham in a low voice said to himself, "O Lord in heaven, I thank Thee. After all it is better for him to believe that I am a monster, rather than that he should lose faith in Thee."

When the child must be weaned, the mother blackens her breast, it would indeed be a shame that the breast should look delicious when the child must not have it. So the child believes that the breast has changed, but the mother is the same, her glance is as loving and tender as ever. Happy the person who had no need of more dreadful expedients for weaning the child!

## II

It was early in the morning, Abraham arose betimes, he embraced Sarah, the bride of his old age, and Sarah kissed Isaac, who had taken away her reproach, who was her pride, her hope for all time. So they rode on in silence along the way, and Abraham's glance was fixed upon the ground until the fourth day when he lifted up his eyes and saw afar off Mount Moriah, but his glance turned again to the ground. Silently he laid the wood in order, he bound Isaac, in silence he drew the knife—then he saw the ram which God had prepared Then he offered that and returned home. . . . From that time on Abraham became old, he could not forget that God had required this of him. Isaac throve as before, but Abraham's eyes were darkened, and he knew joy no more.

[3] Judith 10:11.

When the child has grown big and must be weaned, the mother virginally hides her breast, so the child has no more a mother. Happy the child which did not in another way lose its mother.

### III

It was early in the morning, Abraham arose betimes, he kissed Sarah, the young mother, and Sarah kissed Isaac, her delight, her joy at all times. And Abraham rode pensively along the way, he thought of Hagar and of the son whom he drove out into the wilderness, he climbed Mount Moriah, he drew the knife.

It was a quiet evening when Abraham rode out alone, and he rode to Mount Moriah; he threw himself upon his face, he prayed God to forgive him his sin, that he had been willing to offer Isaac, that the father had forgotten his duty toward the son. Often he rode his lonely way, but he found no rest. He could not comprehend that it was a sin to be willing to offer to God the best thing he possessed, that for which he would many times have given his life; and if it was a sin, if he had not loved Isaac as he did, then he could not understand that it might be forgiven. For what sin could be more dreadful?

When the child must be weaned, the mother too is not without sorrow at the thought that she and the child are separated more and more, that the child which first lay under her heart and later reposed upon her breast will be so near to her no more. So they mourn together for the brief period of mourning. Happy the person who has kept the child as near and needed not to sorrow any more!

### IV

It was early in the morning, everything was prepared for the journey in Abraham's house. He bade Sarah farewell, and Eleazar, the faithful servant, followed him along the way, until he turned back. They rode together in harmony, Abraham and Isaac, until they came to Mount Moriah. But Abraham prepared everything for the sacrifice, calmly and quietly; but when he turned and drew the knife, Isaac saw that his left hand was clenched in despair, that a tremor passed through his body—but Abraham drew the knife.

Then they returned again home, and Sarah hastened to meet them, but Isaac had lost his faith. No word of this had ever been spoken in the world, and Isaac never talked to anyone about what he had seen, and Abraham did not suspect that anyone had seen it.

When the child must be weaned, the mother has stronger food in readiness, lest the child should perish. Happy the person who has stronger food in readiness!

Thus and in many like ways that man of whom we are speaking thought concerning this event. Every time he returned home after wandering to Mount

Moriah, he sank down with weariness, he folded his hands and said, "No one is so great as Abraham! Who is capable of understanding him?"

## A PANEGYRIC UPON ABRAHAM

If there were no eternal consciousness in a man, if at the foundation of all there lay only a wildly seething power which writhing with obscure passions produced everything that is great and everything that is insignificant, if a bottomless void never satiated lay hidden beneath all—what then would life be but despair? If such were the case, if there were no sacred bond which united mankind, if one generation arose after another like the leafage in the forest, if the one generation replaced the other like the song of birds in the forest, if the human race passed through the world as the ship goes through the sea, like the wind through the desert, a thoughtless and fruitless activity, if an eternal oblivion were always lurking hungrily for its prey and there was no power strong enough to wrest it from its maw—how empty then and comfortless life would be! But therefore it is not thus, but as God created man and woman, so too He fashioned the hero and the poet or orator. The poet cannot do what that other does, he can only admire, love and rejoice in the hero. Yet he too is happy, and not less so, for the hero is as it were his better nature, with which he is in love, rejoicing in the fact that this after all is not himself, that his love can be admiration. He is the genius of recollection, can do nothing except call to mind what has been done, do nothing but admire what has been done; he contributes nothing of his own, but is jealous of the intrusted treasure. He follows the option of his heart, but when he has found what he sought, he wanders before every man's door with his song and with his oration, that all may admire the hero as he does, be proud of the hero as he is. This is his achievement, his humble work, this is his faithful service in the house of the hero. If he thus remains true to his love, he strives day and night against the cunning of oblivion which would trick him out of his hero, then he has completed his work, then he is gathered to the hero, who has loved him just as faithfully, for the poet is as it were the hero's better nature, powerless it may be as a memory is, but also transfigured as a memory is. Hence no one shall be forgotten who was great, and though time tarries long, though a cloud [4] of misunderstanding takes the hero away, his lover comes nevertheless, and the longer the time that has passed, the more faithfully will he cling to him.

No, not one shall be forgotten who was great in the world. But each was great in his own way, and each in proportion to the greatness of that which he *loved*. For he who loved himself became great by himself, and he who loved other men became great by his selfless devotion, but he who loved God became greater than all. Everyone shall be remembered, but each became great in proportion to his *expectation*. One became great by expecting the possible, another by expecting the eternal, but he who expected the impossible became

[4] Alluding to various passages in Homer (e.g. *Iliad* III, 381) where a divinity saves a hero by enveloping him in a cloud and carrying him away.

greater than all. Everyone shall be remembered, but each was great in proportion to the greatness of that with which he *strove*. For he who strove with the
world became great by overcoming the world, and he who strove with himself
became great by overcoming himself, but he who strove with God became
greater than all. So there was strife in the world, man against man, one against
a thousand, but he who strove with God was greater than all. So there was
strife upon earth: there was one who overcame all by his power, and there
was one who overcame God by his impotence. There was one who relied upon
himself and gained all, there was one who secure in his strength sacrificed all,
but he who believed God was greater than all. There was one who was great
by reason of his power, and one who was great by reason of his wisdom, and
one who was great by reason of his hope, and one who was great by reason
of his love; but Abraham was greater than all, great by reason of his power
whose strength is impotence, great by reason of his wisdom whose secret is
foolishness, great by reason of his hope whose form is madness, great by reason
of the love which is hatred of oneself.

By faith Abraham went out from the land of his fathers and became a so-
journer in the land of promise. He left one thing behind, took one thing with
him: he left his earthly understanding behind and took faith with him—otherwise he would not have wandered forth but would have thought this unreasonable. By faith he was a stranger in the land of promise, and there was nothing
to recall what was dear to him, but by its novelty everything tempted his soul
to melancholy yearning—and yet he was God's elect, in whom the Lord was
well pleased! Yea, if he had been disowned, cast off from God's grace, he could
have comprehended it better; but now it was like a mockery of him and of
his faith. There was in the world one too who lived in banishment [5] from the
fatherland he loved. He is not forgotten, nor his Lamentations when he sorrow-
fully sought and found what he had lost. There is no song of Lamentations by
Abraham. It is human to lament, human to weep with them that weep, but it is
greater to believe, more blessed to contemplate the believer.

By faith Abraham received the promise that in his seed all races of the world
would be blessed. Time passed, the possibility was there, Abraham believed;
time passed, it became unreasonable, Abraham believed. There was in the
world one who had an expectation, time passed, the evening drew nigh, he was
not paltry enough to have forgotten his expectation, therefore he too shall not
be forgotten. Then he sorrowed, and sorrow did not deceive him as life had
done, it did for him all it could, in the sweetness of sorrow he possessed his
delusive expectation. It is human to sorrow, human to sorrow with them that
sorrow, but it is greater to believe, more blessed to contemplate the believer.
There is no song of Lamentations by Abraham. He did not mournfully count
the days while time passed, he did not look at Sarah with a suspicious glance,
wondering whether she were growing old, he did not arrest the course of the
sun, that Sarah might not grow old, and his expectation with her. He did not

[5] It is evident from the sequel that Jeremiah is meant.

sing lullingly before Sarah his mournful lay. Abraham became old, Sarah became a laughing-stock in the land, and yet he was God's elect and inheritor of the promise that in his seed all the races of the world would be blessed. So were it not better if he had not been God's elect? What is it to be God's elect? It is to be denied in youth the wishes of youth, so as with great pains to get them fulfilled in old age. But Abraham believed and held fast the expectation. If Abraham had wavered, he would have given it up. If he had said to God, "Then perhaps it is not after all Thy will that it should come to pass, so I will give up the wish. It was my only wish, it was my bliss. My soul is sincere, I hide no secret malice because Thou didst deny it to me"—he would not have been forgotten, he would have saved many by his example, yet he would not be the father of faith. For it is great to give up one's wish, but it is greater to hold it fast after having given it up, it is great to grasp the eternal, but it is greater to hold fast to the temporal after having given it up.

Then came the fulness of time. If Abraham had not believed, Sarah surely would have been dead of sorrow, and Abraham, dulled by grief, would not have understood the fulfilment but would have smiled at it as at a dream of youth. But Abraham believed, therefore he was young; for he who always hopes for the best becomes old, and he who is always prepared for the worst grows old early, but he who believes preserves an eternal youth. Praise therefore to that story! For Sarah, though stricken in years, was young enough to desire the pleasure of motherhood, and Abraham, though gray-haired, was young enough to wish to be a father. In an outward respect the marvel consists in the fact that it came to pass according to their expectation, in a deeper sense the miracle of faith consists in the fact that Abraham and Sarah were young enough to wish, and that faith had preserved their wish and therewith their youth. He accepted the fulfilment of the promise, he accepted it by faith, and it came to pass according to the promise and according to his faith—for Moses smote the rock with his rod, but he did not believe.

Then there was joy in Abraham's house, when Sarah became a bride on the day of their golden wedding.

But it was not to remain thus. Still once more Abraham was to be tried. He had fought with that cunning power which invents everything, with that alert enemy which never slumbers, with that old man who outlives all things—he had fought with Time and preserved his faith. Now all the terror of the strife was concentrated in one instant. "And God tempted Abraham and said unto him, Take Isaac, thine only son, whom thou lovest, and get thee into the land of Moriah, and offer him there for a burnt offering upon the mountain which I will show thee."

So all was lost—more dreadfully than if it had never come to pass! So the Lord was only making sport of Abraham! He made miraculously the preposterous actual, and now in turn He would annihilate it. It was indeed foolishness, but Abraham did not laugh at it like Sarah when the promise was announced. All was lost! Seventy years of faithful expectation, the brief joy at the fulfilment of faith. Who then is he that plucks away the old man's staff, who is it that requires that he himself shall break it? Who is he that would make a man's gray hairs comfortless, who is it that requires that he himself shall do it? Is there no compassion for the venerable oldling, none for the innocent child? And yet Abraham was God's elect, and it was the Lord who imposed the trial. All would now be lost. The glorious memory to be preserved by the human race, the promise in Abraham's seed—this was only a whim, a fleeting thought which the Lord had had, which Abraham should now obliterate. That glorious treasure which was just as old as faith in Abraham's heart, many, many years older than Isaac, the fruit of Abraham's life, sanctified by prayers, matured in conflict—the blessing upon Abraham's lips, this fruit was now to be plucked prematurely and remain without significance. For what significance had it when Isaac was to be sacrificed? That sad and yet blissful hour when Abraham was to take leave of all that was dear to him, when yet once more he was to lift up his head, when his countenance would shine like that of the Lord, when he would concentrate his whole soul in a blessing which was potent to make Isaac blessed all his days—this time would not come! For he would indeed take leave of Isaac, but in such a way that he himself would remain behind; death would separate them, but in such a way that Isaac remained its prey. The old man would not be joyful in death as he laid his hands in blessing upon Isaac, but he would be weary of life as he laid violent hands upon Isaac. And it was God who tried him. Yea, woe, woe unto the messenger who had come before Abraham with such tidings! Who would have ventured to be the emissary of this sorrow? But it was God who tried Abraham.

Yet Abraham believed, and believed for this life. Yea, if his faith had been only for a future life, he surely would have cast everything away in order to hasten out of this world to which he did not belong. But Abraham's faith was not of this sort, if there be such a faith; for really this is not faith but the furthest possibility of faith which has a presentiment of its object at the extremest limit of the horizon, yet is separated from it by a yawning abyss within which despair carries on its game. But Abraham believed precisely for this life, that he was to grow old in the land, honored by the people, blessed in his generation, remembered forever in Isaac, his dearest thing in life, whom he embraced with a love for which it would be a poor expression to say that he loyally fulfilled the father's duty of loving the son, as indeed is evinced in the words of the summons, "the son whom thou lovest." Jacob had twelve sons, and one of them he loved; Abraham had only one, the son whom he loved.

Yet Abraham believed and did not doubt, he believed the preposterous. If Abraham had doubted—then he would have done something else, something glorious; for how could Abraham do anything but what is great and glorious! He would have marched up to Mount Moriah, he would have cleft the firewood, lit the pyre, drawn the knife—he would have cried out to God, "Despise not this sacrifice, it is not the best thing I possess, that I know well, for what is an old man in comparison with the child of promise; but it is the best I am able to give Thee. Let Isaac never come to know this, that he may console himself with his youth." He would have plunged the knife into his own breast. He would have been admired in the world, and his name would not have been forgotten; but it is one thing to be admired, and another to be the guiding star which saves the anguished.

But Abraham believed. He did not pray for himself, with the hope of moving the Lord—it was only when the righteous punishment was decreed upon Sodom and Gomorrha that Abraham came forward with his prayers.

We read in those holy books: "And God tempted Abraham, and said unt him, Abraham, Abraham, where art thou? And he said, Here am I." Thou t whom my speech is addressed, was such the case with thee? When afar off thou didst see the heavy dispensation of providence approaching thee, didst thou not say to the mountains, Fall on me, and to the hills, Cover me? Or if thou wast stronger, did not thy foot move slowly along the way, longing as it were for the old path? When a call was issued to thee, didst thou answer, or didst thou not answer perhaps in a low voice, whisperingly? Not so Abraham: joyfully, buoyantly, confidently, with a loud voice, he answered, "Here am I." We read further: "And Abraham rose early in the morning"—as though it were to a festival, so he hastened, and early in the morning he had come to the place spoken of, to Mount Moriah. He said nothing to Sarah, nothing to Eleazar. Indeed who could understand him? Had not the temptation by its very nature exacted of him an oath of silence? He cleft the wood, he bound Isaac, he lit the pyre, he drew the knife. My hearer, there was many a father who believed that with his son he lost everything that was dearest to him in the world, that he was deprived of every hope for the future, but yet there was none that was the child of promise in the sense that Isaac was for Abraham. There was many a father who lost his child; but then it was God, it was the unalterable, the unsearchable will of the Almighty, it was His hand took the child. Not so with Abraham. For him was reserved a harder trial, and Isaac's fate was laid along with the knife in Abraham's hand. And there he stood, the old man, with his only hope! But he did not doubt, he did not look anxiously to the right or to the left, he did not challenge heaven with his prayers. He knew that it was God the Almighty who was trying him, he knew that it was the hardest sacrifice that could be required of him; but he knew also that no sacrifice was too hard when God required it—and he drew the knife.

Who gave strength to Abraham's arm? Who held his right hand up so that it did not fall limp at his side? He who gazes at this becomes paralyzed. Who gave strength to Abraham's soul, so that his eyes did not grow dim, so that he saw neither Isaac nor the ram? He who gazes at this becomes blind.—And yet rare enough perhaps is the man who becomes paralyzed and blind, still more rare one who worthily recounts what happened. We all know it—it was only a trial.

If Abraham when he stood upon Mount Moriah had doubted, if he had gazed about him irresolutely, if before he drew the knife he had by chance discovered the ram, if God had permitted him to offer it instead of Isaac—then he would have betaken himself home, everything would have been the same, he has Sarah, he retained Isaac, and yet how changed! For his retreat would have been a flight, his salvation an accident, his reward dishonor, his future perhaps perdition. Then he would have borne witness neither to his faith nor to God's grace, but would have testified only how dreadful it is to march out to Mount Moriah. Then Abraham would not have been forgotten, nor would Mount Moriah, this mountain would then be mentioned, not like Ararat where the Ark landed, but would be spoken of as a consternation, because it was here that Abraham doubted.

Venerable Father Abraham! In marching home from Mount Moriah thou hadst no need of a panegyric which might console thee for thy loss; for thou didst gain all and didst retain Isaac. Was it not so? Never again did the Lord take him from thee, but thou didst sit at table joyfully with him in thy tent, as thou dost in the beyond to all eternity. Venerable Father Abraham! Thousands of years have run their course since those days, but thou hast need of no tardy lover to snatch the memorial of thee from the power of oblivion, for every language calls thee to remembrance—and yet thou dost reward thy lover more gloriously than does any other; hereafter thou dost make him blessed in thy bosom; here thou dost enthral his eyes and his heart by the marvel of thy deed. Venerable Father Abraham! Second Father of the human race! Thou who first wast sensible of and didst first bear witness to that prodigious passion which disdains the dreadful conflict with the rage of the elements and with the powers of creation in order to strive with God; thou who first didst know that highest passion, the holy, pure and humble expression of the divine madness[6] which the pagans admired—forgive him who would speak in praise of thee, if he does not do it fittingly. He spoke humbly, as if it were the desire of his own heart, he spoke briefly, as it becomes him to do, but he will never forget that thou hadst need of a hundred years to obtain a son of old age against expectation, that thou didst have to draw the knife before retaining Isaac; he will never forget that in a hundred and thirty years thou didst not get further than to faith.

❦ ❦ ❦

*Marcus Aurelius*

# The Stoic Code[1]

BEGIN the morning by saying to thyself, I shall meet with the busybody, the ungrateful, arrogant, deceitful, envious, unsocial. All these things happen to them by reason of their ignorance of what is good and evil. But I who have seen the nature of the good that it is beautiful, and of the bad that it is ugly,

[6] Cf. Plato's *Phaedrus*, 22 and 37.

[1] From *The Thoughts of the Emperor Marcus Aurelius*, translated by George Long (Boston: Little, Brown & Company, 1897), Book II.

and the nature of him who does wrong, that it is akin to me, not [only] of the same blood or seed, but that it participates in [the same] intelligence and [the same] portion of the divinity, I can neither be injured by any of them, for no one can fix on me what is ugly, nor can I be angry with my kinsman, nor hate him. For we are made for co-operation, like feet, like hands, like eyelids, like the rows of the upper and lower teeth. To act against one another, then, is contrary to nature; and it is action against one another to be vexed and to turn away.

2. Whatever this is that I am, it is a little flesh and breath, and the ruling part. Throw away thy books; no longer distract thyself: it is not allowed; but as if thou wast now dying, despise the flesh; it is blood and bones and a network, a contexture of nerves, veins, and arteries. See the breath also, what kind of a thing it is; air, and not always the same, but every moment sent out and again sucked in. The third, then, is the ruling part; consider thus: Thou art an old man; no longer let this be a slave, no longer be pulled by the strings like a puppet to unsocial movements, no longer be either dissatisfied with thy present lot, or shrink from the future.

3. All that is from the gods is full of providence. That which is from fortune is not separated from nature or without an interweaving and involution with the things which are ordered by providence. From thence all things flow; and there is besides necessity, and that which is for the advantage of the whole universe, of which thou art a part. But that is good for every part of nature which the nature of the whole brings, and what serves to maintain this nature. Now the universe is preserved, as by the changes of the elements so by the changes of things compounded of the elements. Let these principles be enough for thee; let them always be fixed opinions. But cast away the thirst after books, that thou mayest not die murmuring, but cheerfully, truly, and from thy heart thankful to the gods.

4. Remember how long thou hast been putting off these things, and how often thou hast received opportunity from the gods, and yet dost not use it. Thou must now at last perceive of what universe thou art a part, and of what administrator of the universe thy existence is an efflux, and that a limit of time is fixed for thee, which if thou dost not use for clearing away the clouds from thy mind, it will go and thou wilt go, and it will never return.

5. Every moment think steadily as a Roman and a man to do what thou hast in hand with perfect and simple dignity, and feeling of affection, and freedom, and justice, and to give thyself relief from all other thoughts. And thou wilt give thyself relief if thou doest every act of thy life as if it were the last, laying aside all carelessness and passionate aversion from the commands of reason, and all hypocrisy, and self-love, and discontent with the portion which has been given to thee. Thou seest how few the things are, the which if a man lays hold of, he is able to live a life which flows in quiet, and is like the existence of the gods; for the gods on their part will require nothing more from him who observes these things.

6. Do wrong to thyself, do wrong to thyself, my soul; but thou wilt no longer have the opportunity of honoring thyself. Every man's life is sufficient. But thine is nearly finished, though thy soul reverences not itself, but places thy felicity in the souls of others.

7. Do the things external which fall upon thee distract thee? Give thyself time to learn something new and good, and cease to be whirled around. But then thou must also avoid being carried about the other way; for those too are triflers who have wearied themselves in life by their activity, and yet have no object to which to direct every movement, and, in a word, all their thoughts.

8. Through not observing what is in the mind of another a man has seldom been seen to be unhappy; but those who do not observe the movements of their own minds must of necessity be unhappy.

9. This thou must always bear in mind, what is the nature of the whole, and what is my nature, and how this is related to that, and what kind of a part it is of what kind of a whole, and that there is no one who hinders thee from always doing and saying the things which are according to the nature of which thou art a part.

10. Theophrastus, in his comparison of bad acts—such a comparison as one would make in accordance with the common notions of mankind—says, like a true philosopher, that the offences which are committed through desire are more blamable than those which are committed through anger. For he who is excited by anger seems to turn away from reason with a certain pain and unconscious contraction; but he who offends through desire, being overpowered by pleasure, seems to be in a manner more intemperate and more womanish in his offences. Rightly, then, and in a way worthy of philosophy, he said that the offence which is committed with pleasure is more blamable than that which is committed with pain; and on the whole the one is more like a person who has been first wronged and through pain is compelled to be angry; but the other is moved by his own impulse to do wrong, being carried towards doing something by desire.

11. Since it is possible that thou mayest depart from life this very moment, regulate every act and thought accordingly. But to go away from among men, if there are gods, is not a thing to be afraid of, for the gods will not involve thee in evil; but if indeed they do not exist, or if they have no concern about human affairs, what is it to me to live in a universe devoid of gods or devoid of providence? But in truth they do exist, and they do care for human things, and they have put all the means in man's power to enable him not to fall into real evils. And as to the rest, if there was anything evil, they would have provided for this also, that it should be altogether in a man's power not to fall into it. Now that which does not make a man worse, how can it make a man's life worse? But neither through ignorance, nor having the knowledge but not the power to guard against or correct these things, is it possible that the nature of the universe has overlooked them; nor is it possible that it has made so great a mistake, either through want of power or want of skill, that good

and evil should happen indiscriminately to the good and the bad. But death certainly, and life, honor and dishonor, pain and pleasure,—all these things equally happen to good men and bad, being things which make us neither better nor worse. Therefore they are neither good nor evil.

12. How quickly all things disappear,—in the universe the bodies themselves, but in time the remembrance of them. What is the nature of all sensible things, and particularly those which attract with the bait of pleasure or terrify by pain, or are noised abroad by vapory fame; how worthless, and contemptible, and sordid, and perishable, and dead they are,—all this it is the part of the intellectual faculty to observe. To observe too who these are whose opinions and voices give reputation; what death is, and the fact that, if a man looks at it in itself, and by the abstractive power of reflection resolves into their parts all the things which present themselves to the imagination in it, he will then consider it to be nothing else than an operation of nature; and if any one is afraid of an operation of nature, he is a child. This, however, is not only an operation of nature, but it is also a thing which conduces to the purposes of nature. To observe too how man comes near to the Deity, and by what part of him, and when this part of man is so disposed.

13. Nothing is more wretched than a man who traverses everything in a round, and pries into the things beneath the earth, as the poet says, and seeks by conjecture what is in the minds of his neighbors, without perceiving that it is sufficient to attend to the daemon within him, and to reverence it sincerely. And reverence of the daemon consists in keeping it pure from passion and thoughtlessness, and dissatisfaction with what comes from gods and men. For the things from the gods merit veneration for their excellence; and the things from men should be dear to us by reason of kinship; and sometimes even, in a manner, they move our pity by reason of men's ignorance of good and bad; this defect being not less than that which deprives us of the power of distinguishing things that are white and black.

14. Though thou shouldest be going to live three thousand years, and as many times ten thousand years, still remember that no man loses any other life than this which he now lives, nor lives any other than this which he now loses. The longest and shortest are thus brought to the same. For the present is the same to all, though that which perishes is not the same; and so that which is lost appears to be a mere moment. For a man cannot lose either the past or the future: for what a man has not, how can any one take this from him? These two things then thou must bear in mind; the one, that all things from eternity are of like forms and come round in a circle, and that it makes no difference whether a man shall see the same things during a hundred years, or two hundred, or an infinite time; and the second, that the longest liver and he who will die soonest lose just the same. For the present is the only thing of which a man can be deprived, if it is true that this is the only thing which he has, and that a man cannot lose a thing if he has it not.

15. Remember that all is opinion. For what was said by the Cynic Moni-

mus is manifest: and manifest too is the use of what was said, if a man receives what may be got out of it as far as it is true.

16. The soul of man does violence to itself, first of all, when it becomes an
abscess, and, as it were, a tumor on the universe, so far as it can. For to be vexed
at anything which happens is a separation of ourselves from nature, in some
part of which the natures of all other things are contained. In the next place,
the soul does violence to itself when it turns away from any man, or even
moves towards him with the intention of injuring, such as are the souls of those
who are angry. In the third place, the soul does violence to itself when it is
overpowered by pleasure or by pain. Fourthly, when it plays a part, and does
or says anything insincerely and untruly. Fifthly, when it allows any act of its
own and any movement to be without an aim, and does anything thoughtlessly
and without considering what it is, it being right that even the smallest things
be done with reference to an end; and the end of rational animals is to follow
the reason and the law of the most ancient city and polity.

17. Of human life the time is a point, and the substance is in a flux, and
the perception dull, and the composition of the whole body subject to putre-
faction, and the soul a whirl, and fortune hard to divine, and fame a thing
devoid of judgment. And, to say all in a word, everything which belongs to
the body is a stream, and what belongs to the soul is a dream and vapor, and
life is a warfare and a stranger's sojourn, and after-fame is oblivion. What then
is that which is able to conduct a man? One thing, and only one, philosophy.
But this consists in keeping the daemon within a man free from violence and
unharmed, superior to pains and pleasures, doing nothing without a purpose,
nor yet falsely and with hypocrisy, not feeling the need of another man's doing
or not doing anything; and besides, accepting all that happens, and all that is
allotted, as coming from thence, wherever it is, from whence he himself came;
and, finally, waiting for death with a cheerful mind, as being nothing else than
a dissolution of the elements of which every living being is compounded. But
if there is no harm to the elements themselves in each continually changing
into another, why should a man have any apprehension about the change and
dissolution of all the elements? For it is according to nature, and nothing is
evil which is according to nature.

❧ ❧ ❧

*Michel Eyquem de Montaigne*

# The Enjoyment of Living [1]

I AM NOT excessively fond of salads or fruit, with the exception of melons.
My father hated every kind of sauce; I like them all. Eating too much makes
me uncomfortable; but in respect of its properties I am not yet very certain

[1] From *The Essays of Montaigne*, translated by E. J. Trechmann (London: Oxford
University Press, 1927), II, 584-601. Reprinted by permission of the publishers.

that any kind of food disagrees with me. Nor have I noticed that I am affected by full or new moons, by autumn or spring.

We are subject to fickle and inexplicable changes. For example, radishes, which I first found to agree with me, afterwards disagreed, and now they agree again. In several things I have found my stomach and palate to vary in the same way: I have changed more than once from white wine to claret, and back again from claret to white wine.

I have a dainty tooth for fish, and the meatless days are my meat-days; my fasts are my feasts. Besides, I believe that it is, as some people say, more easily digested than meat. As it goes against my conscience to eat meat on fish-days, so my taste rebels against mixing meat and fish; the difference seems to me too wide.

From my youth up I have occasionally skipped a meal; either to sharpen my appetite for the next day (for, as Epicurus used to fast and make lean meals in order to accustom his greed to dispense with plenty, I do so, on the contrary, in order to train my greed to take better advantage of plenty and to enjoy it more cheerfully); or I used to fast to keep my strength for the performance of some mental or bodily action; for both my body and mind are made cruelly sluggish by repletion. (And especially do I hate the foolish idea of coupling so healthy and active a goddess with that little pot-bellied, belching god, all swelled up with the fumes of his liquor.) Or again, to cure my ailing digestion; or for want of congenial company; for with that same Epicurus I say that we should not so much look to what we eat as to whom we eat with. And I applaud Chilo, who would not promise to accept Periander's invitation to a feast until he was informed who were the other guests.

To me no dressing is so acceptable, and no sauce so appetising, as that derived from good company.

I think it is more wholesome to eat more at leisure, and less, and to eat oftener. But I would give hunger and appetite their due; I should take no pleasure in dragging through three or four wretched repasts a day, restricted by doctors' orders. Who will assure me that I can recover at supper-time the good appetite I had this morning? Let us old men especially take the first opportunity that comes our way. Let us leave the making of dietaries to doctors and almanac-makers.

The best fruit of my health is sensual pleasure; let us seize the first that is present and known. I avoid consistency in these laws of fasting. He who wishes to benefit by a habit, let him avoid continuing it. We become hardened, our powers are dulled by it; six months after your stomach will be so inured to it, that all the advantage you have gained will be to have lost the freedom of doing otherwise except to your prejudice.

I do not cover my legs and thighs more in winter than in summer: simple silk hose. For the relief of my colds I gave way to the habit of keeping my head warmer, and my belly on account of the colic. But in a few days my ailments became accustomed to them and scorned my ordinary precautions: from a cap I advanced to a kerchief, and from a bonnet to a lined hat. The wadding of my doublet is now only ornamental. All that would be of no avail unless I added a hare's skin or a vulture's plumage, with a skull-cap for the head. Continue this gradual progress and you will go a long way. I shall take care not to do so, and would gladly go back to where I began, if I dared.

"Have you developed a new ailment? Is the remedy no longer of any avail? You have grown accustomed to it? Then try another." In this way they ruin their health who allow themselves to be fettered by enforced rules, and superstitiously adhere to them; they need more and more, and after that more again. There is no end.

To suit our occupations, and for pleasure, it is much more convenient to lose one's dinner, as the ancients did, and defer making good cheer till the time of retirement and rest, instead of cutting up the day: that is what I used to do. For health's sake, on the other hand, I have since found by experience that it is better to dine, and that I digest better when awake.

I am not very subject to thirst, whether I am well or ill; in the latter case I very often have a dry mouth, but without thirst, and as a rule I only drink from the desire which comes with eating, and when the meal is well advanced. I drink pretty well for a man of ordinary build; in summer, and with an appetizing repast, I not only exceed the limits of Augustus, who drank only three times and no oftener, but, in order not to violate Democritus' rule, which forbade stopping at four as an unlucky number, I slide on, if need be, to the fifth: about three half-pints. For little glasses are my favourites, and I like to drain them, a thing which others avoid as unbecoming.

As a rule I dilute my wine with half, sometimes a third part of water. And when at home, following an old custom which my father's doctor recommended to him and himself followed, the wine I need is mixed in the buttery, two or three hours before it is served.

It is said that Cranaus, King of the Athenians, first introduced the custom of mixing wine with water; whether beneficially or not has been a matter for debate. I think it more seemly and more wholesome for children not to take wine before they are sixteen or eighteen years of age.

The best mode of life is that which is most usual and common; I think all singularity should be avoided. And I should hate to see a German putting water into his wine as I should to see a Frenchman drinking his pure. General use lays down the law in such things.

I fear a confined atmosphere, and have a mortal dread of smoke (the first repairs I set about in my house were those of the chimneys and the privies which are commonly defective in old buildings, and not to be tolerated); and among the discomforts of war I include the thick clouds of dust in which we are buried in the hot weather for a whole day's march.

My breathing is free and easy, and my colds generally pass off without a cough, and without injury to the lungs.

The rigour of summer is more hostile to me than that of winter; for, besides the discomfort caused by the heat, which is less easily to be remedied than that of cold, and the force of the sunbeams that strike upon my head, my eyes are afflicted by any dazzling light. I cannot even now sit down to dinner opposite a brightly burning fire.

To counteract the whiteness of the paper, when I used to read more than I do now, I laid a piece of glass upon my book, and felt great relief from it. To this moment I am ignorant of the use of spectacles, and can see as far as I ever did, and as any other person. As the day declines my eyes certainly begin to feel a little dim and weak when reading, an exercise that has always tried them, but especially at night-time.

That is a step backwards, but very hardly perceptible. I shall be retiring another step, from the second to the third, from the third to the fourth, so softly that I must needs become really blind before I feel the age and decay of my sight. So cunningly do the Fates unwind our life's thread!

And so I doubt whether my hearing is hesitating on its way to hardness, and you will see that, before I have half lost it, I shall still blame the voices of those who are speaking to me. We must, indeed, put great pressure on the soul to make it feel how it ebbs away.

My step is quick and firm; and I know not which of the two, my mind or my body, I have had most difficulty in arresting at the same point. The preacher who can hold my attention during a whole sermon is very much my friend. On solemn occasions, when the faces of all are so rigid, and when I have seen ladies keep even their eyes so steady, I could never succeed in keeping some part or other of me from ever wandering; though I may be seated, I am anything but settled.

As the house-slave of Chrysippus the philosopher said of her master that he was only drunk in his legs (for he had the habit of moving them about, in whatever position he was in; and she said it when the others were excited by wine and he felt no effects from it), it might have been said of me too that from my childhood I had madness in my feet, or quicksilver, so restless and fidgety are they, wherever I place them.

It is unmannerly, besides being prejudicial to health and even to one's pleasure, to eat greedily as I do. I often bite my tongue in my haste, and sometimes my fingers. Diogenes, meeting a boy who was eating in that way, gave his tutor a box on the ear. There were people at Rome who taught others to masticate, as well as to walk,[2] gracefully. This habit leaves me no time for talking, which gives so agreeable a relish to the dinner-table, provided that the conversation be in keeping, agreeable, and brief.

There is jealousy and envy between our pleasures; they clash and counteract one another. Alcibiades, a man who understood the art of entertainment, banished even music from his tables, lest it should disturb the pleasure of conversation, for the reason that Plato ascribes to him, "that it is the custom of vulgar men to call singers and instrumentalists to their feasts, for want of

[2] A *mascher comme à marcher*. Montaigne cannot keep away from his *jeux de mots*.

good conversation and agreeable entertainment, with which intelligent men know how to regale each other."

Varro makes the following requirements for a banquet:

"A company of persons of handsome presence and pleasing conversation, who must be neither dumb nor loquacious; cleanliness and daintiness in the food and in the chamber; and fine weather." It needs no little skill to provide good entertainment, and it is attended with no little pleasure. Neither great generals nor great philosophers have disdained the knowledge and practice of good eating. My imagination has given three repasts to my memory's keeping, which chanced to be particularly pleasant to me, at different times of my greater prime. For each of the guests brings the principal charm with him, according to the good temper of body and mind in which he happens to be at the time. My present condition excludes me from those pleasures.

I who am but of the earth earthy, dislike that inhuman sapience which would have us despise and hate the care of the body. I think it equally wrong to be out of love with natural pleasures and to be too much in love with them.

Xerxes was a coxcomb who, lapped in all human delights, offered a prize to the man who should invent others; but not much less of a coxcomb is a man who cuts himself off from those that Nature has invented for him. We must neither pursue nor flee them; we must accept them. I accept them a little more generously and graciously, and allow myself more readily to follow the bent of Nature.

We have no need to exaggerate their emptiness; it makes itself sufficiently felt and manifest, thanks to our morbid, kill-joy mind, which disgusts us with them as well as with itself. It treats both itself and all that it takes in, now well, now ill, according to its insatiable, erratic and versatile nature.

> Unless the vessel you would use be sweet,
> 'Twill sour whatever you may pour therein. (HORACE.)

I who boast of embracing so eagerly and particularly all amenities of life, find in them, when I look at them thus closely, little more than wind. But what would you have? We are all wind throughout. And the wind too, more wisely than we, loves to bluster and shift about, and is content with its own functions, with no desire for stability and solidity, which are none of its properties.

The unmixed pleasures of the imagination, as well as its unmixed pains, are, as some say, greater than all others, as hinted at by Critolaus and his scales.[3] It is not to be wondered at, since she composes them at her own sweet will, and cuts them out of the whole cloth. Of this I see every day notable and perhaps desirable examples. But I, who am of a mixed and coarse grain,

---

[3] "Supposing all the goods of the mind to be put into one scale, and the goods of the body into the other, Critolaus thought the goods of the mind would outweigh the others so far, that they would require the whole earth and sea to equalize the balance."— Cicero, *Tusc. Quaes.*, v. 17.

cannot so fully bite at this single and so simple object presented by the imagination, but that I let myself go, in all my grossness, after the present pleasures prescribed by human and universal laws, intellectually perceptible and perceptibly intellectual.

The Cyronaic philosophers hold that, like bodily pains, so also bodily pleasures are the more powerful, as being both twofold[4] and more rational.

There are some who with savage stupidity, as Aristotle says, express disgust of pleasures; I know some who do so from ambition. Why do they not also forswear breathing? Why do they not live on their own breath, and refuse the light, because it shines gratis, and costs them neither invention nor strength? Let them try to find sustenance in Mars or Pallas or Mercury, and see what happens, instead of Venus, Ceres, and Bacchus. Are not those the sort of people who will try to square the circle when perched on their wives?

I hate to be told that my spirit should be in the clouds whilst my body is at table. I would have the spirit not nailed down to it, nor sprawling upon it, but attending to it; it should sit at it, and not lie upon it.

Aristippus stood up for the body alone, as if we had no soul; Zeno embraced only the soul, as if we had no body. Both of them mistakenly. They say that Pythagoras followed a philosophy that was all contemplation, Socrates one that was all conduct and action; Plato found the adjustment of it between the two. But they say that to make up a tale. And the true adjustment is found in Socrates, and Plato is much more Socratic than Pythagorean; and it becomes him better.

When I dance, I dance; when I sleep, I sleep. Aye, and when I take a solitary stroll in a beautiful garden, if some part of the time my thoughts dwell on outside events, for some other part I recall them to my walk, to the garden, to the sweetness of the solitude and to myself.

Nature has, with motherly care, observed this rule, that the actions she has laid upon us for our need should give us pleasure; and she invites us to them, not only through our reason but also through our desire. It is wrong to infringe her rules.

When I see both Caesar and Alexander, in the thick of their great labours, so fully enjoying natural, and therefore necessary and reasonable pleasures, I do not call it a relaxing of their minds; I call it a stiffening of their minds to subordinate, by strength of spirit, their strenuous occupations and heavy thoughts to the usages of everyday life. Wise they would have been if they could have believed that the latter was their ordinary, the former their extraordinary vocation.

What fools we are! "He has spent his life in idleness," we say; "I have done nothing to-day." What, have you not lived? That is not only the fundamental but the most honourable of your occupations. "If I had been given an opportunity to manage great affairs, I might have shown what I can do." Have you been able to meditate and manage your own life? Then you have performed

4 i.e., both physical and mental.

the greatest work of all. In order to show herself and get to work, Nature has no need of a great destiny; she will show herself equally in all ranks, both behind a curtain and without one.

It is our duty to compose our character, not to compose books, and to win, not battles and provinces, but order and tranquillity for our conduct of life.

Our great and glorious masterpiece is to live to the purpose; all other things, ruling, laying up treasures, building, are at the most but appendicles and adminicles.

I delight in contemplating an army-general, at the foot of a breach he is about to attack, devoting himself entirely and free from cares to his dinner and to his table-talk among his friends. And Brutus, with heaven and earth conspiring against him and Roman liberty, stealing an hour or two from his nightly rounds, to read and epitomize Polybius in all security. It is the part of a little soul, buried under the weight of business, not to be able to get clean away from it, to lay it aside and take it up again:

> Now ye brave hearts that have weathered
>     Many a sorer strait with me,
> Chase your cares with wine—to-morrow
>     We shall plough the mighty sea! (HORACE.)

Whether it be in jest or in earnest that the wine of the Divines[5] and the Sorbonne has become proverbial, like their banquets, I think it reasonable that they should dine more agreeably and cheerfully for having been usefully and seriously employed in the morning teaching their classes. The consciousness of having made good use of the other hours is the right savory sauce for the table.

Thus did the Sages live. And that inimitable straining after virtue which excites our admiration in both of the Catos, that austere turn of mind that is carried to obtrusiveness, has thus tamely and complacently submitted to the laws of human nature, and of Venus and Bacchus; in accordance with the teachings of their school, which require the perfect sage to be as skilled and experienced in the enjoyment of natural pleasures, as in any other of life's duties. A *wise palate should go with a wise judgement* (Cicero).

The power to relax and assume easy manners is highly honourable, I think, and the most becoming trait in a strong and generous soul. Epaminondas never imagined it to be derogatory to the honour of his glorious victories and the perfect purity of his morals to mingle with the dance of the boys in his town, and to sing, play an instrument, and give his whole mind to these recreations.

And among the many admirable actions of Scipio, the grandfather,[6] a man

---

[5] *Vin Théologal*: notable good and strong wine; or the best wine, of what kind soever.—Cotgrave.

[6] The original reading of the 1588 edition was "of the younger Scipio (when all is considered, the first of the Romans)." Montaigne seems to have forgotten that it was the younger Scipio who was contemporary with Laelius and Terence.

worthy to be reputed of celestial origin, there is none that shows him in such
a charming light as to see him strolling along the beach with Laelius, playing
the fool like a careless boy, picking up and selecting shells and playing ducks
and drakes; and in bad weather amusing and tickling himself with reproducing
in written comedies the commonest and most vulgar actions of the people;[7]
and, with his thoughts taken up with that wonderful expedition against
Hannibal and Africa, visiting the schools in Sicily and attending lectures in
Philosophy, thus arming the teeth of the blind envy of his enemies at Rome.

And there is nothing more remarkable in the life of Socrates than that he
found time in his old age to learn to dance and play on instruments, and
thought it was time well spent.

This same man was once seen standing for a whole day and night in a
trance, in the presence of the whole Greek army, his mind caught and
carried away by some deep thought. He first, among so many valiant men of
the army, ran to the help of Alcibiades, when the latter was overwhelmed by
the enemy, covered him with his body and by main force of arms extricated
him from the throng. And he first, among all the Athenians, who, like him,
were incensed by so shameful a sight, came forward to rescue Theramenes,
who was being led to his death by the satellites of the Thirty Tyrants. And,
although he was joined by only two other men, all told, only at the instance
of Theramenes himself did he desist from this bold undertaking. Although he
was run after by a fair lady with whom he was in love, he was known, in
spite of pressing need, to observe strict chastity. At the battle of Delium he
was seen to pick up and save Xenophon, who had been thrown by his horse. He
was always seen to march to war and tread the ice barefoot, to wear the same
gown winter and summer, to surpass all his comrades in enduring hardships,
and to eat no more at a banquet than at his ordinary. He was seen for twenty-
seven years to endure, with unchanged countenance, hunger, poverty, the
perverseness of his children, his wife's clawings, and in the end, calumny,
tyranny, imprisonment, fetters, and poison.

But if ever he was challenged to a drinking-bout, he accepted as a matter
of civility, and of all the army he was the man who came off best. And he
never disdained to play at knuckle-bones with the boys or to ride with them
on a hobby-horse, and he did it all gracefully; for all actions, says Philosophy,
are equally becoming and honourable in a sage. We have material enough, and
we should never weary of presenting the picture of this great man as a pattern
and ideal of perfection in all things.

There are very few examples of a pure and perfect life, and our education
is all wrong when every day we are shown such crazy and defective models,

[7] Montaigne was quite convinced that Scipio and Laelius wrote the comedies of
Terence; see Book I, ch. 4. The 1588 edition had this passage, afterwards deleted. "I
am exceedingly vexed that the lives of those two great men, Epaminondas and the
younger Scipio, by common consent of the world, the one the first of the Greeks, the
other the first of the Romans, the finest pair of lives that Plutarch wrote, should
have been among the first to be lost."

scarce to be commended for any quality, which rather pull us backward; corrupters rather than correctors.

People generally go wrong: it is much easier to go along the side-path, where the boundary serves as a check and guide, than by the broad and open middle way to be guided by art rather than by Nature; but also much less noble and less commendable.

Greatness of soul consists not so much in soaring high and in pressing forward, as in knowing how to adapt and limit oneself. It regards as great all that is sufficient, and shows its distinction in choosing the mean things rather than the eminent.

There is nothing so noble and so right as to play the man well and fitly, nor anything so difficult to learn as how to live this life well and according to Nature; and the most inhuman of our diseases is to despise our being.

❦ ❦ ❦

# Religion

*Bertrand Russell*

## A Free Man's Worship [1]

To DR. FAUSTUS in his study Mephistopheles told the history of the Creation, saying:

"The endless praises of the choirs of angels had begun to grow wearisome; for, after all, did he not deserve their praise? Had he not given them endless joy? Would it not be more amusing to obtain undeserved praise, to be worshipped by beings whom he tortured? He smiled inwardly, and resolved that the great drama should be performed.

"For countless ages the hot nebula whirled aimlessly through space. At length it began to take shape, the central mass threw off planets, the planets cooled, boiling seas and burning mountains heaved and tossed, from black masses of cloud hot sheets of rain deluged the barely solid crust. And now the first germ of life grew in the depths of the ocean, and developed rapidly in the fructifying warmth into vast forest trees, huge ferns springing from the damp mould, sea monsters breeding, fighting, devouring, and passing away. And from the monsters, as the play unfolded itself, Man was born, with the power of thought, the knowledge of good and evil, and the cruel thirst for worship. And Man saw that all is passing in this mad, monstrous world, that all is struggling to snatch, at any cost, a few brief moments of life before Death's inexorable decree. And Man said: 'There is a hidden purpose, could we but

[1] Reprinted from *Mysticism and Logic*, pp. 46-57, by Bertrand Russell, by permission of W. W. Norton & Company, Inc. Copyright 1929 by the publishers.

fathom it, and the purpose is good; for we must reverence something, and in the visible world there is nothing worthy of reverence.' And Man stood aside from the struggle, resolving that God intended harmony to come out of chaos by human efforts. And when he followed the instincts which God had transmitted to him from his ancestry of beasts of prey, he called it Sin, and asked God to forgive him. But he doubted whether he could be justly forgiven, until he invented a divine Plan by which God's wrath was to have been appeased. And seeing the present was bad, he made it yet worse, that thereby the future might be better. And he gave God thanks for the strength that enabled him to forgo even the joys that were possible. And God smiled; and when he saw that Man had become perfect in renunciation and worship, he sent another sun through the sky, which crashed into Man's sun; and all returned again to nebula.

" 'Yes,' he murmured, 'it was a good play; I will have it performed again.' "

Such, in outline, but even more purposeless, more void of meaning is the world which Science presents for our belief. Amid such a world, if anywhere, our ideals henceforward must find a home. That Man is the product of causes which had no prevision of the end they were achieving; that his origin, his growth, his hopes and fears, his loves and his beliefs, are but the outcome of accidental collocations of atoms; that no fire, no heroism, no intensity of thought and feeling, can preserve an individual life beyond the grave; that all the labours of the ages, all the devotion, all the inspiration, all the noonday brightness of human genius, are destined to extinction in the vast death of the solar system, and that the whole temple of Man's achievement must inevitably be buried beneath the débris of a universe in ruins—all these things, if not quite beyond dispute, are yet so nearly certain, that no philosophy which rejects them can hope to stand. Only within the scaffolding of these truths, only on the firm foundation of unyielding despair, can the soul's habitation henceforth be safely built.

How, in such an alien and inhuman world, can so powerless a creature as Man preserve his aspirations untarnished? A strange mystery it is that Nature, omnipotent but blind, in the revolutions of her secular hurryings through the abysses of space, has brought forth at last a child, subject still to her power, but gifted with sight, with knowledge of good and evil, with the capacity of judging all the works of his unthinking Mother. In spite of Death, the mark and seal of the parental control, Man is yet free, during his brief years, to examine, to criticise, to know, and in imagination to create. To him alone, in the world with which he is acquainted, this freedom belongs; and in this lies his superiority to the resistless forces that control his outward life.

The savage, like ourselves, feels the oppression of his impotence before the powers of Nature; but having in himself nothing that he respects more than Power, he is willing to prostrate himself before his gods, without inquiring whether they are worthy of his worship. Pathetic and very terrible is the long history of cruelty and torture, of degradation and human sacrifices endured in the hope of placating the jealous gods: surely, the trembling believer thinks, when what is most precious has been freely given, their lust for blood must be appeased, and more will not be required. The religion of Moloch—as such creeds may be generically called—is in essence the cringing submission of the slave, who dare not, even in his heart, allow the thought that his master deserves no adulation. Since the independence of ideals is not yet acknowledged, Power may be freely worshipped, and receive an unlimited respect, despite its wanton infliction of pain.

But gradually, as morality grows bolder, the claim of the ideal world begins to be felt; and worship, if it is not to cease, must be given to gods of another kind than those created by the savage. Some, though they feel the demands of the ideal, will still consciously reject them, still urging that naked Power is worthy of worship. Such is the attitude inculcated in God's answer to Job out of the whirlwind: the divine power and knowledge are paraded, but of the divine goodness there is no hint. Such also is the attitude of those who, in our own day, base their morality upon the struggle for survival, maintaining that the survivors are necessarily the fittest. But others, not content with an answer so repugnant to the moral sense, will adopt the position which we have become accustomed to regard as specially religious, maintaining that, in some hidden manner, the world of fact is really harmonious with the world of ideals. Thus Man creates God, all-powerful and all-good, the mystic unity of what is and what should be.

But the world of fact, after all, is not good; and, in submitting our judgment to it, there is an element of slavishness from which our thoughts must be purged. For in all things it is well to exalt the dignity of Man, by freeing him as far as possible from the tyranny of non-human Power. When we have realised that Power is largely bad, that Man, with his knowledge of good and evil, is but a helpless atom in a world which has no such knowledge, the choice is again presented to us: Shall we worship Force, or shall we worship Goodness? Shall our God exist and be evil, or shall he be recognised as the creation of our own conscience?

The answer to this question is very momentous, and affects profoundly our whole morality. The worship of Force, to which Carlyle and Nietzsche and the creed of Militarism have accustomed us, is the result of failure to maintain our own ideals against a hostile universe: it is itself a prostrate submission to evil, a sacrifice of our best to Moloch. If strength indeed is to be respected, let us respect rather the strength of those who refuse that false "recognition of facts" which fails to recognise that facts are often bad. Let us admit that, in the world we know, there are many things that would be better otherwise, and that the ideals to which we do and must adhere are not realised in the realm of matter. Let us preserve our respect for truth, for beauty, for the ideal of perfection which life does not permit us to attain, though none of these things meet with the approval of the unconscious universe. If Power is bad, as it seems to be, let us reject it from our hearts. In this lies Man's true freedom:

in determination to worship only the God created by our own love of the good, to respect only the heaven which inspires the insight of our best moments. In action, in desire, we must submit perpetually to the tyranny of outside forces; but in thought, in aspiration, we are free, free from our fellowmen, free from the petty planet on which our bodies impotently crawl, free even, while we live, from the tyranny of death. Let us learn, then, that energy of faith which enables us to live constantly in the vision of the good; and let us descend in action, into the world of fact, with that vision always before us.

When first the opposition of fact and ideal grows fully visible, a spirit of fiery revolt, of fierce hatred of the gods, seems necessary to the assertion of freedom. To defy with Promethean constancy a hostile universe, to keep its evil always in view, always actively hated, to refuse no pain that the malice of Power can invent, appears to be the duty of all who will not bow before the inevitable. But indignation is still a bondage, for it compels our thoughts to be occupied with an evil world; and in the fierceness of desire from which rebellion springs there is a kind of self-assertion which it is necessary for the wise to overcome. Indignation is a submission of our thoughts, but not of our desires; the Stoic freedom in which wisdom consists is found in the submission of our desires, but not of our thoughts. From the submission of our desires springs the virtue of resignation; from the freedom of our thoughts springs the whole world of art and philosophy, and the vision of beauty by which, at last, we half reconquer the reluctant world. But the vision of beauty is possible only to unfettered contemplation, to thoughts not weighted by the load of eager wishes; and thus Freedom comes only to those who no longer ask of life that it shall yield them any of those personal goods that are subject to the mutations of Time.

Although the necessity of renunciation is evidence of the existence of evil, yet Christianity, in preaching it, has shown a wisdom exceeding that of the Promethean philosophy of rebellion. It must be admitted that, of the things we desire, some, though they prove impossible, are yet real goods; others, however, as ardently longed for, do not form part of a fully purified ideal. The belief that what must be renounced is bad, though sometimes false, is far less often false than untamed passion supposes; and the creed of religion, by providing a reason for proving that it is never false, has been the means of purifying our hopes by the discovery of many austere truths.

But there is in resignation a further good element: even real goods, when they are unattainable, ought not to be fretfully desired. To every man comes, sooner or later, the great renunciation. For the young, there is nothing unattainable; a good thing desired with the whole force of a passionate will, and yet impossible, is to them not credible. Yet, by death, by illness, by poverty, or by the voice of duty, we must learn, each one of us, that the world was not made for us, and that, however beautiful may be the things we crave, Fate may nevertheless forbid them. It is the part of courage, when misfortune comes, to bear without repining the ruin of our hopes, to turn away our thoughts from vain regrets. This degree of submission to Power is not only just and right; it is the very gate of wisdom.

But passive renunciation is not the whole of wisdom; for not by renunciation alone can we build a temple for the worship of our own ideals. Haunting foreshadowings of the temple appear in the realm of imagination, in music, in architecture, in the untroubled kingdom of reason, and in the golden sunset magic of lyrics, where beauty shines and glows, remote from the touch of sorrow, remote from the fear of change, remote from the failures and disenchantments of the world of fact. In the contemplation of these things the vision of heaven will shape itself in our hearts, giving at once a touchstone to judge the world about us, and an inspiration by which to fashion to our needs whatever is not incapable of serving as a stone in the sacred temple.

Except for those rare spirits that are born without sin, there is a cavern of darkness to be traversed before that temple can be entered. The gate of the cavern is despair, and its floor is paved with the gravestones of abandoned hopes. There Self must die; there the eagerness, the greed of untamed desire must be slain, for only so can the soul be freed from the empire of Fate. But out of the cavern the Gate of Renunciation leads again to the daylight of wisdom, by whose radiance a new insight, a new joy, a new tenderness, shine forth to gladden the pilgrim's heart.

When, without the bitterness of impotent rebellion, we have learnt both to resign ourselves to the outward rule of Fate and to recognise that the non-human world is unworthy of our worship, it becomes possible at last so to transform and refashion the unconscious universe, so to transmute it in the crucible of the imagination, that a new image of shining gold replaces the old idol of clay. In all the multiform facts of the world—in the visual shapes of trees and mountains and clouds, in the events of the life of Man, even in the very omnipotence of Death—the insight of creative idealism can find the reflection of a beauty which its own thoughts first made. In this way mind asserts its subtle mastery over the thoughtless forces of Nature. The more evil the material with which it deals, the more thwarting to untrained desire, the greater is its achievement in inducing the reluctant rock to yield up its hidden treasures, the prouder its victory in compelling the opposing forces to swell the pageant of its triumph. Of all the arts, Tragedy is the proudest, the most triumphant; for it builds its shining citadel in the very centre of the enemy's country, on the very summit of his highest mountain; from its impregnable watch-towers, his camps and arsenals, his columns and forts, are all revealed; within its walls the free life continues, while the legions of Death and Pain and Despair, and all the servile captains of tyrant Fate, afford the burghers of that dauntless city new spectacles of beauty. Happy those sacred ramparts, thrice happy the dwellers on that all-seeing eminence. Honour to those brave warriors who, through countless ages of warfare, have preserved for us the priceless heritage of liberty, and have kept undefiled by sacrilegious invaders the home of the unsubdued.

But the beauty of Tragedy does but make visible a quality which, in more or less obvious shapes, is present always and everywhere in life. In the spectacle of Death, in the endurance of intolerable pain, and in the irrevocableness of a vanished past, there is a sacredness, an overpowering awe, a feeling of the vastness, the depth, the inexhaustible mystery of existence, in which, as by some strange marriage of pain, the sufferer is bound to the world by bonds of sorrow. In these moments of insight, we lose all eagerness of temporary desire, all struggling and striving for petty ends, all care for the little trivial things, that, to a superficial view, make up the common life of day by day; we see, surrounding the narrow raft illumined by the flickering light of human comradeship, the dark ocean on whose rolling waves we toss for a brief hour; from the great night without, a chill blast breaks in upon our refuge; all the loneliness of humanity amid hostile forces is concentrated upon the individual soul, which must struggle alone, with what of courage it can command, against the whole weight of a universe that cares nothing for its hopes and fears. Victory, in this struggle with the powers of darkness, is the true baptism into the glorious company of heroes, the true initiation into the overmastering beauty of human existence. From that awful encounter of the soul with the outer world, renunciation, wisdom, and charity are born; and with their birth a new life begins. To take into the inmost shrine of the soul the irresistible forces whose puppets we seem to be—Death and change, the irrevocableness of the past, and the powerlessness of Man before the blind hurry of the universe from vanity to vanity—to feel these things and know them is to conquer them.

This is the reason why the Past has such magical power. The beauty of its motionless and silent pictures is like the enchanted purity of late autumn, when the leaves, though one breath would make them fall, still glow against the sky in golden glory. The Past does not change or strive; like Duncan, after life's fitful fever it sleeps well; what was eager and grasping, what was petty and transitory, has faded away, the things that were beautiful and eternal shine out of it like stars in the night. Its beauty, to a soul not worthy of it, is unendurable; but to a soul which has conquered Fate it is the key of religion.

The life of Man, viewed outwardly, is but a small thing in comparison with the forces of Nature. The slave is doomed to worship Time and Fate and Death, because they are greater than anything he finds in himself, and because all his thoughts are of things which they devour. But, great as they are, to think of them greatly, to feel their passionless splendour, is greater still. And such thought makes us free men; we no longer bow before the inevitable in Oriental subjection, but we absorb it, and make it a part of ourselves. To abandon the struggle for private happiness, to expel all eagerness of temporary desire, to burn with passion for eternal things—this is emancipation, and this is the free man's worship. And this liberation is effected by a contemplation of Fate; for Fate itself is subdued by the mind which leaves nothing to be purged by the purifying fire of Time.

United with his fellow-men by the strongest of all ties, the tie of a common doom, the free man finds that a new vision is with him always, shedding over every daily task the light of love. The life of Man is a long march through the night, surrounded by invisible foes, tortured by weariness and pain, towards a goal that few can hope to reach, and where none may tarry long. One by one, as they march, our comrades vanish from our sight, seized by the silent orders of omnipotent Death. Very brief is the time in which we can help them, in which their happiness or misery is decided. Be it ours to shed sunshine on their path, to lighten their sorrows by the balm of sympathy, to give them the pure joy of a never-tiring affection, to strengthen failing courage, to instil faith in hours of despair. Let us not weigh in grudging scales their merits and demerits, but let us think only of their need—of the sorrows, the difficulties, perhaps the blindnesses, that make the misery of their lives; let us remember that they are fellow-sufferers in the same darkness, actors in the same tragedy with ourselves. And so, when their day is over, when their good and their evil have become eternal by the immortality of the past, be it ours to feel that, where they suffered, where they failed, no deed of ours was the cause; but wherever a spark of the divine fire kindled in their hearts, we were ready with encouragement, with sympathy, with brave words in which high courage glowed.

Brief and powerless is Man's life; on him and all his race the slow, sure doom falls pitiless and dark. Blind to good and evil, reckless of destruction, omnipotent matter rolls on its relentless way; for Man, condemned to-day to lose his dearest, to-morrow himself to pass through the gate of darkness, it remains only to cherish, ere yet the blow falls, the lofty thoughts that ennoble his little day; disdaining the coward terrors of the slave of Fate, to worship at the shrine that his own hands have built; undismayed by the empire of chance, to preserve a mind free from the wanton tyranny that rules his outward life; proudly defiant of the irresistible forces that tolerate, for a moment, his knowledge and his condemnation, to sustain alone, a weary but unyielding Atlas, the world that his own ideals have fashioned despite the trampling march of unconscious Power.

❦ ❦ ❦

# The Providence of God[1]

LORD, thou hast been our dwelling place in all generations.

Before the mountains were brought forth, or ever thou hadst formed the earth and the world, even from everlasting to everlasting, thou art God.

Thou turnest man to destruction; and sayest, Return, ye children of men.

For a thousand years in thy sight are but as yesterday when it is past, and as a watch in the night.

[1] From *The Book of Psalms* (King James Version of *The Bible*), 90, 91.

Thou carriest them away as with a flood; they are as a sleep: in the morning they are like grass which groweth up.

In the morning it flourisheth, and groweth up; in the evening it is cut down, and withereth.

For we are consumed by thine anger, and by thy wrath are we troubled.

Thou hast set our iniquities before thee, our secret sins in the light of thy countenance.

For all our days are passed away in thy wrath: we spend our years as a tale that is told.

The days of our years are threescore years and ten; and if by any reason of strength they be fourscore years, yet is their strength labour and sorrow; for it is soon cut off, and we fly away.

Who knoweth the power of thine anger? even according to thy fear, so is thy wrath.

So teach us to number our days, that we may apply our hearts unto wisdom.

Return, O LORD, how long? and let it repent thee concerning thy servants.

O satisfy us early with thy mercy; that we may rejoice and be glad all our days.

Make us glad according to the days wherein thou hast afflicted us, and the years wherein we have seen evil.

Let thy work appear unto thy servants, and thy glory unto their children.

And let the beauty of the LORD our GOD be upon us: and establish thou the work of our hands upon us; yea, the work of our hands establish thou it.

He that dwelleth in the secret place of the most High shall abide under the shadow of the Almighty.

I will say of the LORD, He is my refuge and my fortress: my God; in him will I trust.

Surely he shall deliver thee from the snare of the fowler, and from the noisome pestilence.

He shall cover thee with his feathers and under his wings shalt thou trust: his truth shall be thy shield and buckler.

Thou shalt not be afraid for the terror by night; nor for the arrow that flieth by day;

Nor for the pestilence that walketh in darkness; nor for the destruction that wasteth at noonday.

A thousand shall fall at thy side, and ten thousand at thy right hand; but it shall not come nigh thee.

Only with thine eyes shalt thou behold and see the reward of the wicked.

Because thou hast made the LORD, which is my refuge, even the most High, thy habitation;

There shall no evil befall thee, neither shall any plague come nigh thy dwelling.

For he shall give his angels charge over thee, to keep thee in all thy ways.

They shall bear thee up in their hands, lest thou dash thy foot against a stone.

Thou shalt tread upon the lion and adder: the young lion and the dragon shalt thou trample under feet.

Because he hath set his love upon me, therefore will I deliver him: I will set him on high, because he hath known my name.

He shall call upon me, and I will answer him: I will be with him in trouble; I will deliver him, and honour him.

With long life will I satisfy him, and shew him my salvation.

❧ ❧ ❧

## John Donne

# Meditation XVII[1]

### Nunc lento sonitu dicunt, morieris[2]

PERCHANCE he for whom this bell tolls may be so ill as that he knows not it tolls for him; and perchance I may think myself so much better than I am as that they who are about me and see my state may have caused it to toll for me, and I know not that. The church is catholic, universal, so are all her actions; all that she does belongs to all. When she baptizes a child, that action concerns me; for that child is thereby connected to that body which is my head too and ingrafted into that body whereof I am a member. And when she buries a man, that action concerns me. All mankind is of one author, and is one volume; when one man dies, one chapter is not torn out of the book, but translated into a better language; and every chapter must be so translated. God employs several translators; some pieces are translated by age, some by sickness, some by war, some by justice; but God's hand is in every translation, and his hand shall bind up all our scattered leaves again for that library where every book shall lie open to one another. As therefore the bell that rings to a sermon calls not upon the preacher only but upon the congregation to come, so this bell calls us all; but how much more me who am brought so near the door by this sickness! There was a contention as far as a suit—in which piety and dignity, religion and estimation, were mingled—which of the religious orders should ring to prayers first in the morning; and it was determined that they should ring first that rose earliest. If we understand aright the dignity of this bell that tolls for our evening prayer, we would be glad to make it ours by rising early, in that application, that it might be ours as well as his, whose indeed it is. The bell doth toll for him that thinks it doth; and though it intermit again, yet from that minute that that occasion wrought upon him he is united to God. Who casts not up his eye to the sun when it rises? but who

[1] From *Devotions upon Emergent Occasions* by John Donne (London, 1624).
[2] Now this bell tolling softly says, you must die.

takes off his eye from a comet when that breaks out? Who bends not his ear
to any bell which upon any occasion rings? but who can remove it from that
bell which is passing a piece of himself out of this world? No man is an
island entire of itself; every man is a piece of the continent, a part of the main.
If a clod be washed away by the sea, Europe is the less, as well as if a prom-
ontory were, as well as if a manor of thy friend's or of thine own were.
Any man's death diminishes me, because I am involved in mankind, and
therefore never send to know for whom the bell tolls; it tolls for thee. Neither
can we call this a begging of misery or a borrowing of misery, as though we
were not miserable enough of ourselves but must fetch in more from the next
house, in taking upon us the misery of our neighbors. Truly it were an
excusable covetousness if we did, for affliction is a treasure, and scarce any man
hath enough of it. No man hath affliction enough that is not matured and
ripened by it and made fit for God by that affliction. If a man carry treasure
in bullion or in a wedge of gold and have none coined into current money,
his treasure will not defray him as he travels. Tribulation is treasure in the
nature of it, but it is not current money in the use of it, except we get nearer
and nearer our home, heaven, by it. Another man may be sick too, and sick
to death, and this affliction may lie in his bowels as gold in a mine and be of
no use to him; but this bell that tells me of his affliction digs out and applies
that gold to me, if by this consideration of another's danger I take mine own
into contemplation and so secure myself by making my recourse to my God,
who is our only security.

❧ ❧ ❧

*John Woolman*

# In His Will Is Our Peace [1]

TWENTY-SIXTH of eighth month [1772].—Being now at George Crosfield's, in
the county of Westmoreland, I feel a concern to commit to writing the following uncommon circumstance.

In a time of sickness, a little more than two years and a half ago, I was
brought so near the gates of death that I forgot my name. Being then desirous
to know who I was, I saw a mass of matter of a dull gloomy color between the
south and the east, and was informed that this mass was human beings in as
great misery as they could be, and live, and that I was mixed with them, and
that henceforth I might not consider myself as a distinct or separate being. In
this state I remained several hours. I then heard a soft melodious voice, more
pure and harmonious than any I had heard with my ears before; I believed
it was the voice of an angel who spake to the other angels; the words were,
"John Woolman is dead." I soon remembered that I was once John Woolman,

[1] From the *Journal* of John Woolman. First printed in 1774.

and being assured that I was alive in the body, I greatly wondered what that heavenly voice could mean. I believed beyond doubting that it was the voice of an holy angel, but as yet it was a mystery to me.

I was then carried in spirit to the mines where poor oppressed people were digging rich treasures for those called Christians, and heard them blaspheme the name of Christ, at which I was grieved, for his name to me was precious. I was then informed that these heathens were told that those who oppressed them were the followers of Christ, and they said among themselves, "If Christ directed them to use us in this sort, then Christ is a cruel tyrant."

All this time the song of the angel remained a mystery; and in the morning, my dear wife and some others coming to my bedside, I asked them if they knew who I was, and they telling me I was John Woolman, thought I was lightheaded, for I told them not what the angel said, nor was I disposed to talk much to any one, but was very desirous to get so deep that I might understand this mystery.

My tongue was often so dry that I could not speak till I had moved it about and gathered some moisture, and as I lay still for a time I at length felt a Divine power prepare my mouth that I could speak, and I then said, "I am crucified with Christ, nevertheless I live; yet not I, but Christ liveth in me. And the life which I now live in the flesh I live by the faith of the Son of God, who loved me and gave himself for me." Then the mystery was opened and I perceived there was joy in heaven over a sinner who had repented, and that the language "John Woolman is dead," meant no more than the death of my own will. . . .

After this sickness I spake not in public meetings for worship for nearly one year, but my mind was very often in company with the oppressed slaves as I sat in meetings; and though under his dispensation I was shut up from speaking, yet the spring of the gospel ministry was many times livingly opened in me, and the Divine gift operated by abundance of weeping, in feeling the oppression of this people. It being so long since I passed through this dispensation, and the matter remaining fresh and lively in my mind, I believe it safest for me to commit it to writing.

❧ ❧ ❧

*Alfred North Whitehead*

# Religion and Science[1]

THE difficulty in approaching the question of the relations between Religion and Science is, that its elucidation requires that we have in our minds some clear idea of what we mean by either of the terms, "religion" and "science." Also I wish to speak in the most general way possible, and to keep in the back-

[1] From *Science and the Modern World*. Copyright, 1925, by The Macmillan Company, and reprinted by permission of The Macmillan Company.

ground any comparison of particular creeds, scientific or religious. We have got to understand the type of connection which exists between the two spheres, and then to draw some definite conclusions respecting the existing situation which at present confronts the world.

The *conflict* between religion and science is what naturally occurs to our minds when we think of this subject. It seems as though, during the last half-century, the results of science and the beliefs of religion had come into a position of frank disagreement, from which there can be no escape, except by abandoning either the clear teaching of science, or the clear teaching of religion. This conclusion has been urged by controversialists on either side. Not by all controversialists, of course, but by those trenchant intellects which every controversy calls out into the open.

The distress of sensitive minds, and the zeal for truth, and the sense of the importance of the issues, must command our sincerest sympathy. When we consider what religion is for mankind, and what science is, it is no exaggeration to say that the future course of history depends upon the decision of this generation as to the relations between them. We have here the two strongest general forces (apart from the mere impulse of the various senses) which influence men, and they seem to be set one against the other—the force of our religious intuitions, and the force of our impulse to accurate observation and logical deduction.

A great English statesman once advised his countrymen to use large-scale maps, as a preservative against alarms, panics, and general misunderstanding of the true relations between nations. In the same way in dealing with the clash between permanent elements of human nature, it is well to map our history on a large scale, and to disengage ourselves from our immediate absorption in the present conflicts. When we do this, we immediately discover two great facts. In the first place, there has always been a conflict between religion and science; and in the second place, both religion and science have always been in a state of continual development. In the early days of Christianity, there was a general belief among Christians that the world was coming to an end in the lifetime of people then living. We can make only indirect inferences as to how far this belief was authoritatively proclaimed; but it is certain that it was widely held, and that it formed an impressive part of the popular religious doctrine. The belief proved itself to be mistaken, and Christian doctrine adjusted itself to the change. Again in the early Church individual theologians very confidently deduced from the Bible opinions concerning the nature of the physical universe. In the year A.D. 535, a monk named Cosmas wrote a book which he entitled, *Christian Topography*. He was a travelled man who had visited India and Ethiopia; and finally he lived in a monastery at Alexandria, which was then a great centre of culture. In this book, basing himself upon the direct meaning of Biblical texts as construed by him in a literal fashion, he denied the existence of the antipodes, and asserted that the world is a flat parallelogram whose length is double its breadth.

In the seventeenth century the doctrine of the motion of the earth was con-

demned by a Catholic tribunal. A hundred years ago the extension of time demanded by geological science distressed religious people, Protestant and Catholic. And today the doctrine of evolution is an equal stumbling-block. These are
only a few instances illustrating a general fact.

But all our ideas will be in a wrong perspective if we think that this recurring perplexity was confined to contradictions between religion and science;
and that in these controversies religion was always wrong, and that science was
always right. The true facts of the case are very much more complex, and refuse
to be summarized in these simple terms.

Theology itself exhibits exactly the same character of gradual development,
arising from an aspect of conflict between its own proper ideas. This fact is a
commonplace to theologians, but is often obscured in the stress of controversy.
I do not wish to overstate my case; so I will confine myself to Roman Catholic
writers. In the seventeenth century a learned Jesuit, Father Petavius, showed
that the theologians of the first three centuries of Christianity made use of
phrases and statements which since the fifth century would be condemned as
heretical. Also Cardinal Newman devoted a treatise to the discussion of the development of doctrine. He wrote it before he became a great Roman Catholic
ecclesiastic; but throughout his life, it was never retracted and continually re-
issued.

Science is even more changeable than theology. No man of science could
subscribe without qualification to Galileo's beliefs, or to Newton's beliefs, or
to all his own scientific beliefs of ten years ago.

In both regions of thought, additions, distinctions, and modifications have
been introduced. So that now, even when the same assertion is made today as
was made a thousand, or fifteen hundred years ago, it is made subject to limitations or expansions of meaning, which were not contemplated at the earlier
epoch. We are told by logicians that a proposition must be either true or false,
and that there is no middle term. But in practice, we may know that a proposition expresses an important truth, but that it is subject to limitations and
qualifications which at present remain undiscovered. It is a general feature of
our knowledge, that we are insistently aware of important truths; and yet that
the only formulations of these truths which we are able to make presuppose a
general standpoint of conceptions which may have to be modified. I will give
you two illustrations, both from science: Galileo said that the earth moves and
that the sun is fixed; the Inquisition said that the earth is fixed and the sun
moves; and Newtonian astronomers, adopting an absolute theory of space, said
that both the sun and the earth move. But now we say that any one of
these three statements is equally true, provided that you have fixed your sense
of "rest" and "motion" in the way required by the statement adopted. At the
date of Galileo's controversy with the Inquisition, Galileo's way of stating the
facts was, beyond question, the fruitful procedure for the sake of scientific research. But in itself it was not more true than the formulation of the Inquisition. But at that time the modern concepts of relative motion were in nobody's

mind; so that the statements were made in ignorance of the qualifications required for their more perfect truth. Yet this question of the motions of the earth and the sun expresses a real fact in the universe; and all sides had got hold of important truths concerning it. But with the knowledge of those times, the truths appeared to be inconsistent.

Again I will give you another example taken from the state of modern physical science. Since the time of Newton and Huyghens in the seventeenth century there have been two thories as to the physical nature of light. Newton's theory was that a beam of light consists of a stream of very minute particles, or corpuscles, and that we have the sensation of light when these corpuscles strike the retinas of our eyes. Huyghens' theory was that light consists of very minute waves of trembling in an all-pervading ether, and that these waves are travelling along a beam of light. The two theories are contradictory. In the eighteenth century Newton's theory was believed, in the nineteenth century Huyghens' theory was believed. Today there is one large group of phenomena which can be explained only on the wave theory, and another large group which can be explained only on the corpuscular theory. Scientists have to leave it at that, and wait for the future, in the hope of attaining some wider vision which reconciles both.

We should apply these same principles to the questions in which there is a variance between science and religion. We would believe nothing in either sphere of thought which does not appear to us to be certified by solid reasons based upon the critical research either of ourselves or of competent authorities. But granting that we have honestly taken this precaution, a clash between the two on points of detail where they overlap should not lead us hastily to abandon doctrines for which we have solid evidence. It may be that we are more interested in one set of doctrines than in the other. But, if we have any sense of perspective and of the history of thought, we shall wait and refrain from mutual anathemas.

We should wait: but we should not wait passively, or in despair. The clash is a sign that there are wider truths and finer perspectives within which a reconciliation of a deeper religion and a more subtle science will be found.

In one sense, therefore, the conflict between science and religion is a slight matter which has been unduly emphasized. A mere logical contradiction cannot in itself point to more than the necessity of some readjustments, possibly of a very minor character on both sides. Remember the widely different aspects of events which are dealt with in science and in religion respectively. Science is concerned with the general conditions which are observed to regulate physical phenomena; whereas religion is wholly wrapped up in the contemplation of moral and aesthetic values. On the one side there is the law of gravitation, and on the other the contemplation of the beauty of holiness. What one side sees, the other misses; and vice versa.

Consider, for example, the lives of John Wesley and of Saint Francis of Assisi. For physical science you have in these lives merely ordinary examples

of the operation of the principles of physiological chemistry, and of the dynamics of nervous reactions: for religion you have lives of the most profound
significance in the history of the world. Can you be surprised that, in the absence of a perfect and complete phrasing of the principles of science and
of the principles of religion which apply to these specific cases, the accounts
of these lives from these divergent standpoints should involve discrepancies?
It would be a miracle if it were not so.

It would, however, be missing the point to think that we need not trouble
ourselves about the conflict between science and religion. In an intellectual age
there can be no active interest which puts aside all hope of a vision of the
harmony of truth. To acquiesce in discrepancy is destructive of candour, and
of moral cleanliness. It belongs to the self-respect of intellect to pursue every
tangle of thought to its final unravelment. If you check that impulse, you will
get no religion and no science from an awakened thoughtfulness. The important question is, In what spirit are we going to face the issue? There we come
to something absolutely vital.

A clash of doctrines is not a disaster—it is an opportunity. I will explain my
meaning by some illustrations from science. The weight of an atom of nitrogen was well known. Also it was an established scientific doctrine that the
average weight of such atoms in any considerable mass will be always the same.
Two experimenters, the late Lord Rayleigh and the late Sir William Ramsay,
found that if they obtained nitrogen by two different methods, each equally
effective for that purpose, they always observed a persistent slight difference between the average weights of the atoms in the two cases. Now I ask you, would
it have been rational of these men to have despaired because of this conflict
between chemical theory and scientific observation? Suppose that for some reason the chemical doctrine had been highly prized throughout some district as
the foundation of its social order:—would it have been wise, would it have
been candid, would it have been moral, to forbid the disclosure of the fact that
the experiments produced discordant results? Or, on the other hand, should Sir
William Ramsay and Lord Rayleigh have proclaimed that chemical theory was
now a detected delusion? We see at once that either of these ways would have
been a method of facing the issue in an entirely wrong spirit. What Rayleigh
and Ramsay did was this: They at once perceived that they had hit upon a line
of investigation which would disclose some subtlety of chemical theory that had
hitherto eluded observation. The discrepancy was not a disaster: it was an opportunity to increase the sweep of chemical knowledge. You all know the end
of the story: finally argon was discovered, a new chemical element which had
lurked undetected, mixed with the nitrogen. But the story has a sequel which
forms my second illustration. This discovery drew attention to the importance of
observing accurately minute differences in chemical substances as obtained by
different methods. Further researches of the most careful accuracy were under
taken. Finally another physicist, F. W. Aston, working in the Cavendish Labora
tory at Cambridge in England, discovered that even the same element might

assume two or more distinct forms, termed *isotopes,* and that the law of the constancy of average atomic weight holds for each of these forms, but as between the different isotopes differs slightly. The research has effected a great stride in the power of chemical theory, far transcending in importance the discovery of argon from which it originated. The moral of these stories lies on the surface, and I will leave to you their application to the case of religion and science.

In formal logic, a contradiction is the signal of a defeat: but in the evolution of real knowledge it marks the first step in progress towards a victory. This is one great reason for the utmost toleration of variety of opinion. Once and forever, this duty of toleration has been summed up in the words, "Let both grow together until the harvest." The failure of Christians to act up to this precept, of the highest authority, is one of the curiosities of religious history. But we have not yet exhausted the discussion of the moral temper required for the pursuit of truth. There are short cuts leading merely to an illusory success. It is easy enough to find a theory, logically harmonious and with important applications in the region of fact, provided that you are content to disregard half your evidence. Every age produces people with clear logical intellects, and with the most praiseworthy grasp of the importance of some sphere of human experience, who have elaborated, or inherited, a scheme of thought which exactly fits those experiences which claim their interest. Such people are apt resolutely to ignore, or to explain away, all evidence which confuses their scheme with contradictory instances. What they cannot fit in is for them nonsense. An unflinching determination to take the whole evidence into account is the only method of preservation against the fluctuating extremes of fashionable opinion. This advice seems so easy, and is in fact so difficult to follow.

One reason for this difficulty is that we cannot think first and act afterwards. From the moment of birth we are immersed in action, and can only fitfully guide it by taking thought. We have, therefore, in various spheres of experience to adopt those ideas which seem to work within those spheres. It is absolutely necessary to trust to ideas which are generally adequate, even though we know that there are subtleties and distinctions beyond our ken. Also apart from the necessities of action, we cannot even keep before our minds the whole evidence except under the guise of doctrines which are incompletely harmonized. We cannot think in terms of an indefinite multiplicity of detail; our evidence can acquire its proper importance only if it comes before us marshalled by general ideas. These ideas we inherit—they form the tradition of our civilization. Such traditional ideas are never static. They are either fading into meaningless formulae, or are gaining power by the new lights thrown by a more delicate apprehension. They are transformed by the urge of critical reason, by the vivid evidence of emotional experience, and by the cold certainties of scientific perception. One fact is certain, you cannot keep them still. No generation can merely reproduce its ancestors. You may preserve the life in a flux of form, or preserve the form amid an ebb of life. But you cannot permanently enclose the same life in the same mold.

The present state of religion among the European races illustrates the statements which I have been making. The phenomena are mixed. There have been reactions and revivals. But on the whole, during many generations, there has been a gradual decay of religious influence in European civilization. Each revival touches a lower peak than its predecessor, and each period of slackness a lower depth. The average curve marks a steady fall in religious tone. In some countries the interest in religion is higher than in others. But in those countries where the interest is relatively high, it still falls as the generations pass. Religion is tending to degenerate into a decent formula wherewith to embellish a comfortable life. A great historical movement on this scale results from the convergence of many causes. I wish to suggest two of them which lie within the scope of this chapter for consideration.

In the first place for over two centuries religion has been on the defensive, and on a weak defensive. The period has been one of unprecedented intellectual progress. In this way a series of novel situations have been produced for thought. Each such occasion has found the religious thinkers unprepared. Something, which has been proclaimed to be vital, has finally, after struggle, distress, and anathema, been modified and otherwise interpreted. The next generation of religious apologists then congratulates the religious world on the deeper insight which has been gained. The result of the continued repetition of this undignified retreat, during many generations, has at last almost entirely destroyed the intellectual authority of religious thinkers. Consider this contrast: when Darwin or Einstein proclaim theories which modify our ideas, it is a triumph for science. We do not go about saying that there is another defeat for science, because its old ideas have been abandoned. We know that another step of scientific insight has been gained.

Religion will not regain its old power until it can face change in the same spirit as does science. Its principles may be eternal, but the expression of those principles requires continual development. This evolution of religion is in the main a disengagement of its own proper ideas from the adventitious notions which have crept into it by reason of the expression of its own ideas in terms of the imaginative picture of the world entertained in previous ages. Such a release of religion from the bonds of imperfect science is all to the good. It stresses its own genuine message. The great point to be kept in mind is that normally an advance in science will show that statements of various religious beliefs require some sort of modification. It may be that they have to be expanded or explained, or indeed entirely restated. If the religion is a sound expression of truth, this modification will only exhibit more adequately the exact point which is of importance. This process is a gain. In so far, therefore, as any religion has any contact with physical facts, it is to be expected that the point of view of those facts must be continually modified as scientific knowledge advances. In this way, the exact relevance of these facts for religious thought will grow more and more clear. The progress of science must result in the unceasing codification of religious thought, to the great advantage of religion.

The religious controversies of the sixteenth and seventeenth centuries put theologians into a most unfortunate state of mind. They were always attacking and defending. They pictured themselves as the garrison of a fort surrounded by hostile forces. All such pictures express half-truths. That is why they are so popular. But they are dangerous. This particular picture fostered a pugnacious party spirit which really expresses an ultimate lack of faith. They dared not modify, because they shirked the task of disengaging their spiritual message from the associations of a particular imagery.

Let me explain myself by an example. In the early medieval times, Heaven was in the sky, and Hell was underground; volcanoes were the jaws of Hell. I do not assert that these beliefs entered into the official formulations: but they did enter into the popular understanding of the general doctrines of Heaven and Hell. These notions were what everyone thought to be implied by the doctrine of the future state. They entered into the explanations of the influential exponents of Christian belief. For example, they occur in the *Dialogues* of Pope Gregory, the Great, a man whose high official position is surpassed only by the magnitude of his services to humanity. I am not saying what we ought to believe about the future state. But whatever be the right doctrine, in this instance the clash between religion and science, which has relegated the earth to the position of a second-rate planet attached to a second-rate sun, has been greatly to the benefit of the spirituality of religion by dispersing these medieval fancies.

Another way of looking at this question of the evolution of religious thought is to note that any verbal form of statement which has been before the world for some time discloses ambiguities; and that often such ambiguities strike at the very heart of the meaning. The effective sense in which a doctrine has been held in the past cannot be determined by the mere logical analysis of verbal statements, made in ignorance of the logical trap. You have to take into account the whole reaction of human nature to the scheme of thought. This reaction is of a mixed character, including elements of emotion derived from our lower natures. It is here that the impersonal criticism of science and of philosophy comes to the aid of religious evolution. Example after example can be given of this motive force in development. For example, the logical difficulties inherent in the doctrine of the moral cleansing of human nature by the power of religion rent Christianity in the days of Pelagius and Augustine—that is to say, at the beginning of the fifth century. Echoes of that controversy still linger in theology.

So far, my point has been this: that religion is the expression of one type of fundamental experiences of mankind: that religious thought develops into an increasing accuracy of expression, disengaged from adventitious imagery: that the interaction between religion and science is one great factor in promoting this development.

I now come to my second reason for the modern fading of interest in religion. This involves the ultimate question which I stated in my opening sentences. We have to know what we mean by religion. The churches, in their presentation of their answers to this query, have put forward aspects of religion which are expressed in terms either suited to the emotional reactions of bygone times or directed to excite modern emotional interests of nonreligious character. What I mean under the first heading is that religious appeal is directed partly to excite that instinctive fear of the wrath of a tyrant which was inbred in the unhappy populations of the arbitrary empires of the ancient world, and in particular to excite that fear of an all-powerful arbitrary tyrant behind the unknown forces of nature. This appeal to the ready instinct of brute fear is losing its force. It lacks any directness of response, because modern science and modern conditions of life have taught us to meet occasions of apprehension by a critical analysis of their causes and conditions. Religion is the reaction of human nature to its search for God. The presentation of God under the aspect of power awakens every modern instinct of critical reaction. This is fatal; for religion collapses unless its main positions command immediacy of assent. In this respect the old phraseology is at variance with the psychology of modern civilizations. This change in psychology is largely due to science, and is one of the chief ways in which the advance of science has weakened the hold of the old religious forms of expression. The non-religious motive which has entered into modern religious thought is the desire for a comfortable organization of modern society. Religion has been presented as valuable for the ordering of life. Its claims have been rested upon its function as a sanction to right conduct. Also the purpose of right conduct quickly degenerates into the formation of pleasing social relations. We have here a subtle degradation of religious ideas, following upon their gradual purification under the influence of keener ethical intuitions. Conduct is a by-product of religion—an inevitable by-product, but not the main point. Every great religious teacher has revolted against the presentation of religions as a mere sanction of rules of conduct. Saint Paul denounced the Law, and Puritan divines spoke of the filthy rags of righteousness. The insistence upon rules of conduct marks the ebb of religious fervor. Above and beyond all things, the religious life is not a research after comfort. I must now state, in all diffidence, what I conceive to be the essential character of the religious spirit.

Religion is the vision of something which stands beyond, behind, and within, the passing flux of immediate things; something which is real, and yet waiting to be realized; something which is a remote possibility, and yet the greatest of present facts; something that gives meaning to all that passes, and yet eludes apprehension; something whose possession is the final good, and yet is beyond all reach; something which is the ultimate ideal, and the hopeless quest.

The immediate reaction of human nature to the religious vision is worship. Religion has emerged into human experience mixed with the crudest fancies of barbaric imagination. Gradually, slowly, steadily the vision recurs in history under nobler form and with clearer expression. It is the one element in human experience which persistently shows an upward trend. It fades and then recurs. But when it renews its force, it recurs with an added richness and purity of content. The fact of the religious vision, and its history of persistent expansion, is our one ground for optimism. Apart from it, human life is a flash of occasional enjoyments lighting up a mass of pain and misery, a bagatelle of transient experience.

The vision claims nothing but worship; and worship is a surrender to the claim of assimilation, urged with the motive force of mutual love. The vision never overrules. It is always there, and it has the power of love presenting the one purpose whose fulfilment is eternal harmony. Such order as we find in nature is never force—it presents itself as the one harmonious adjustment of complex detail. Evil is the brute motive force of fragmentary purpose, disregarding the eternal vision. Evil is overruling, retarding, hurting. The power of God is the worship He inspires. That religion is strong which in its ritual and its modes of thought evokes an apprehension of the commanding vision. The worship of God is not a rule of safety—it is an adventure of the spirit, a flight after the unattainable. The death of religion comes with the repression of the high hope of adventure.

*Reinhold Niebuhr*

# Christis vs. Socrates[1]

THE discussion in a group of enlightened moderns centered on comparison of the outstanding moral exemplars in world history. Inevitably, as in college days of bygone years, Socrates and Christ were presented as outstanding exemplars of virtue. That was not surprising. In purely moral terms there was little to choose between the "martyrdom" of the two: Socrates drinking the cup of hemlock and Jesus on the Cross. (It is significant that a martyr's death is regarded as the supreme act of goodness in an age which implicitly defines the end of life as "the pursuit of happiness." But perhaps this observation is beside the point.) The point of the discussion was that the champions of Socrates were quite convinced that Christ would have a far better chance with our generation if Christians did not insist on confusing the issue by making absurd claims for His divinity. These claims, it was felt, were unfair and prejudiced His example.

This debate illustrates the profound misunderstanding between a so-called "secular" and idealistic culture and the character of the Christian faith. The idea that Christians are unenlightened people who insist on incredible divinities in human life is very widespread. It obscures the real debate between a "Socratic" and a Christian view of man and the mystery of existence. And this second debate is centered on different issues from the relative merits of Jesus and Socrates as moral exemplars.

We may define as "Socratic" any view which shares Socrates's conviction that

[1] From *The Saturday Review*, XXXVII, No. 51 (Dec. 18, 1954). Copyright 1954 by Saturday Review Associates, Inc. Reprinted by permission of the author and of Saturday Review Associates, Inc.

men "would do the good if they only knew it." This conviction makes virtue
the consequence of reason and naturally assumes that the only prerequisite of
good conduct is the right formula and exemplar of good conduct. In contrast to
this Socratic view, which has been accepted by most moderns since the Renaissance, and which seemed to have triumphed completely over Christianity in the
eighteenth and nineteenth centuries, we can put the simple Pauline confession:
"The good that I would do I do not do and the evil that I would not, that I do."
According to the Christian interpretation every man is at variance with himself
and ultimately with God because there is a "law in his members which wars
against the law that is in his mind." The acceptance of the highest ideals of
conduct is no guarantee against the force of self-regard, expressed either individually or collectively. Much evil is undoubtedly done in sheer stupidity, but
the basic human problem is the constant expression of the self's pride, will-to-
power, and avarice. Bertrand Russell defines the basic human inclination as the
desire for "power and glory." That is probably as good a definition of sin as
any.

But what has this analysis of the human situation—which any thoughtful observer must recognize as being more illuminating about man, particularly man
in the contemporary setting, than all the Socratic interpretations which try to
derive virtue from intelligence—what has this to do with the worship of Christ
as a revelation of God?

In answering that question we must recognize that interpretations of the self
and of the ultimate mystery of existence are closely related. The conception of
the self's freedom to defy the laws of its own existence is part and parcel of
the Christian conception of the self's radical freedom, particularly its freedom
over its own mind. In short, the self has a mystery which cannot be equated
with its reason. The self uses its reason but it is not reason. The self has the
freedom to transcend nature and reason to survey all the world's coherences and
rational intelligibilities and to inquire after the source and end of the meaning
of its existence. This freedom either proves the existentialists right in their insistence that the self has no law but its freedom; or it points to the validity of
the Biblical faith that there is a deeper and higher source of meaning than the
coherences discovered by science and philosophy. The Biblical faith, in short,
does not equate God with cosmic reason any more than it equates the self with
its own reason. It declares that the mystery of the divine is related to the
mystery of creation, and that creation is not identical with the causal sequences
which science can chart. The worship of God is thus in the first instance the
worship of "God, the Almighty maker of heaven and earth," the mysterious
power transcending the causal sequences and coherences of the world. It must
be noted that only on the presupposition of such a God does the self have
"headroom" for the unique freedom which gives it a vantage point above natural and rational coherences. This divine source and end of all things is a mystery beyond every rational intelligibility, though it is the capstone of every system of meaning.

Perhaps the reader will impatiently insist that faith in a mysterious creator-God and the knowledge of the radical character of human freedom still leave us far from any knowledge of faith in Christ as the revelation of God. In an effort to draw nearer it may be relevant to observe that the modern "Socratic" culture has not stated the questions for which such a faith is the answer, even if it acknowledged the reality and the "dignity" of human selfhood. It did not do so because it prided itself on the "dignity" of man but never came to terms with the "misery" of man. Briefly, that "misery" is man's inclination to use his freedom not as the instrument of virtue, but as a tool of self-glorification, and consequently as an instrument of social strife and injustice. There has been a strain of uneasy conscience in human life, to which the Babylonian penitential Psalms and the Pyramid texts of Egypt first gave eloquent expression. It expressed itself before and outside of the Biblical faith. It has only been in this post-Christian era of Western civilization that men have tried to obscure the guilt, in which all men are involved, and to pretend that the problem of being "good" could be solved if only men had the proper moral exemplars. Ironically enough, it is this age which has involved us in the collective guilt of possible atomic warfare and has initiated even the "pure" scientists into the problem of guilt, as they found themselves unwittingly becoming the weapon-manufacturers of an atomic age.

Through all ages men have wondered about the divine mystery which hovered over the strange drama of human history and was obviously more than the mystery of creation. They felt that the meaning in the mystery obviously spelled judgment upon evil, but they wondered how mercy and forgiveness were related to the judgment.

It was to these questions that the revelation in Christ offered the definitive answer. The Church was founded on the faith that this revelation was final and definitive. The drama of Christ's life was seen by faith to be more than a drama in history, and therefore Jesus was more than a revered historical martyr. This drama furnished the clue to the ultimate mystery. Through it faith was able to discern that the power of God and the love of God are one; and that the love of God contains both the severity of his justice and the kindness of his mercy to those who contritely acknowledge their sins and cease to pretend that men are virtuous and possess a "dignity" which is not contaminated by the false and idolatrous use they make of their freedom. The Christian doctrine of the "Atonement" asserts that judgment and forgiveness are contradictory, yet two facets of the same divine love. Those who recognize this clue to the mystery will stop pretending they are more righteous than they are; and will, with broken spirit and contrite heart, be enabled to live charitably with their neighbors.

Humility is the basis of charity. This age, which has extolled "humanism" so much, is singularly lacking in the spirit of charity. It is filled with the fury of self-righteousness expressed by the warring political, national, and rationalistic and pious groups. A few intellectuals, having discerned the mystery of selfhood

above the level of nature, have found Christian faith incredible and have preferred the mystical way defined by—among others—Aldous Huxley in "The
Perennial Philosophy." These intellectuals seem not to have noticed that this
alternative does indeed assert a divine, but also a total mystery. It suggests an
"eternity" which may purify, but which also annuls, history with all its strange
dramas, its joys and its sorrows, its responsibilities, victories, and defeats. It also
annuls the meaning of the existence of this strange creature—the human individual.

To assert that the Jesus of history is the Christ, and that "God was in Christ
reconciling the world unto Himself," is an affirmation of faith which insists
that the variance between man and God cannot be finally overcome by the virtue of man. All human virtue remains ambiguous to the end. It can be overcome only by a "suffering" God who takes the sins of the world upon Himself.

Of course, this faith will seem quite incredible to modern men partly because they have suppressed the internal problems of the human soul for which
it is the answer, and partly because they find it difficult to believe that a character and drama in history are lifted into the ultimate dimension as a clue to
the very meaning and mystery of existence. They are accustomed to find the
ultimate either in some eternal pattern within the flux of the temporal or (in
more modern terms) to find the very flux to be the ultimate (Bergson).

Nevertheless, it is not only the modern mind which finds the affirmation that
a crucified Saviour is the "very image of God" scandalous. St. Paul gloried in
the fact that this faith was a scandal but nevertheless that it was, once accepted, the source of "wisdom and power." In other words, it is incredible in
prospect but the source of wisdom in retrospect. It furnishes the clue through
which we can make sense out of the seeming nonsense of the historical drama
and the drama of our own existence.

When the problems of man are deeply felt men will come to such a faith in
any age, no matter how sophisticated it may think itself. Thus, Pascal lived in
an age dominated by Cartesian rationalism. He was himself a very great mathematician and scientist. He could not, of course, find peace in the knowledge of
"the God of the philosophers," which means the God revealed in the rational or
natural structure of things but having no word of judgment and mercy for
proud and tortured human souls. We have no Pascal in our own day to match
our numerous Cartesian rationalists. But Pascal's experience is undoubtedly
analogous to the experience of many who have found their way back to faith in
the "God and Father of our Lord Jesus Christ" even under the derision of their
peers, who worried about the growing "irrationalism" and piety of a culture
which had so recently celebrated its emancipation from every religious belief.

The figure of Christ in Christian faith is not that of a theophany—a miraculous appearance of the divine in history. Even those traditions which insist upon
the Virgin Birth as a part of the accreditation of His divinity fully understand
that He was "true man." He walked on earth, subject to the necessities of human
life, and did not escape either death or the tragedy of martyrdom. But it is not

in the first instance as moral exemplar that He is the key figure in Christian faith, though He is defined in the tradition as the "second Adam," who restores the lost innocence of man and defines the *summum bonum* of human life. In brief, that is the sacrificial love which His life incarnated. But when modern Christians sought to interpret Him merely as man, as moral example, in trying to adjust themselves to the prejudices of the age, they succeeded only in reducing the Christian faith to the general moral sentimentality of the age or even in aggravating that sentimentality. This was true because this view of Christ rested upon a false estimate of human nature. According to that view love was a simple possibility of human existence. The power and persistence of self-regard were obscured. An ancillary consequence was that Christian thought became as irrelevant to every political problem as did every other form of modern utopianism.

There is thus a vast difference in seeing in Jesus an exemplar of the nobility of vicarious suffering, from regarding the whole drama of His life as "the light that shineth in darkness" as a revelation of the mystery of God's justice and mercy as it comes to terms with the perpetual rebellion of human ambitions against the divine will. To regard Him as this key which resolves mystery into meaning is to look at the whole drama of human existence without either obscuring the tragic factors in man's persistent egotism or in seeking vain methods of eliminating that egotism by mystical techniques of self-annulment or dangerous political strategies of suppressing self-interest, the most consistent form of which has generated the horrible tyranny of Communism. These alternative techniques are defined in Koestler's "The Yogi and the Commissar."

The Christian answer to the problem is that there are indeterminate possibilities of escaping from the prison-house of self and establishing creative relations with our fellows, both by the shattering of the self-concerned self through divine judgment and by the operations of "common grace," which is to say, the erosion of egotism through our affections and responsibilities. But there is no final possibility of an ultimate redemption of the self from itself. In the end God must take the sins of human history upon Himself and heal the breach between man and God. Wherever that is recognized it is possible for sinful men to lead charitable lives because the fury of their self-righteousness has been overcome and they know themselves to be "forgiven sinners." The New Testament is full of admonitions which are well summarized in the Pauline advice "Be ye kindly affectioned one with another, forgiving each other as God also in Christ has forgiven you."

It is this sense of humility and contrition which must restore the lost charity and humaneness of an age which is submerged in all the inhumanities of self-righteous men who suppose that they can establish a more genuine "humanity" with enlightenment and moral idealism. Men do not forgive each other because they are compelled by duty to do so. This kind of charity is beyond the power of the sense of obligation. It is possible only to those who are of "broken spirit and contrite heart." In short, the principles by which modern men have sought to do justice to the drama of human existence have been inadequate to contain either the heights or the depths of the drama or the complexities of the endless variations of love and self-love in human history. The "humanitarian" principles have been drawn from either nature or reason. But man in his freedom is not contained in either nature or mind. He is able to elaborate an historical drama in which he discerns more or less rational "causes and effects," but the ultimate dimension and motif of the world transcend every system of rational intelligibility. Life ends in mystery. The issue between Christianity, with its assertion of a "revelation" which has pierced the mystery and given it meaning, and classical mysticism is whether the final mystery annuls all historical meanings or whether meaning can feed on mystery on the one hand even as it must be supported by rational intelligibility on the other hand.

A final word must be said about the way Christians enter into this debate on Christ and modern culture. They are certainly justified to call attention to ironic distortions which have overwhelmed the idealism, the humanism, and the utopianism of modern culture and have given new relevance to the Christian interpretation of life. But every lesson thus learned can be obscured if Christians fail to understand that piety as well as "idealism" can be made the servant of human self-esteem, that religion has been as fruitful of fanaticism as of charity in the past and present; that modern culture began with a justified protest against religiously inspired fanaticism; and that the religious life is frequently conventional, bigoted, narrow, and graceless. An adequate view of life from the standpoint of the Christian revelation must be able to appreciate all the virtues which may develop through cultural enlightenment and to know that religion may be the engine of cruelty.

If this is not done Christ ceases to be the mediator of the divine judgment and mercy upon all men and becomes the dubious ally of the pious "righteous" against the "secular humanists." It is certainly revealing about human nature that pious men are as rarely truly charitable as rationalists are "reasonable." This is so because both use their supposed devotion to God or the "truth" as an instrument of the self. True Christians will understand this better than the pure rationalists. But they are not true Christians if they imagine that their understanding of the mysteries of sin is a badge of virtue.

Thus, one writes apologetically of the Christian faith. A humanist and idealist generation is prepared to entertain the "moral ideals" of Jesus if only the Christians will abate their claims of His divinity. But involved in those claims is the whole Biblical view of the character of the human drama and of the self-contradiction in which all men are involved. It has become fashionable among some Christians to assert that the Christian ethic, which even secular humanists cherish, is not possible without "faith in God." We accuse the Communists of being "atheists," and imply that faith in God will somehow guarantee virtue. But these defenses of the faith miss the point. The question is whether the self has encountered at the ultimate reaches of consciousness the

God both just and merciful, and whether the self has no illusions about itself on the one hand and no despair about the inner contradictions of the soul. The question in short is whether it has encountered the "God who is revealed in Christ." From that encounter come the "truth and grace" which make it possible to enjoy the beauty of life and to be unafraid of its terrors; to assume responsibilities in the complex tasks of achieving community and justice amidst the claims and counter-claims of men without either seeking the perfect and impossible solution or of being unconscious of the dangers of trying.

One word must be said about the explicit faith which must be summoned for the venture of accepting Christ as the revelation of the mystery of the divine, particularly the mystery of the divine justice and mercy. Every world view, philosophy, or religion rests upon an act of faith. But most faith is implicit rather than explicit. The commitment of faith is obscured by the belief that the view is arrived at not by faith, but by a rational analysis of the coherences of the world. The liberal idea of historical progress and the Marxist idea of an historical dialectic are both faiths; and both faiths have some evidence to support them. But they both depend upon a commitment which selects the evidence by which they are supposedly supported. Whether the faith is implicit or explicit it must ultimately be validated by the evidence, but the commitment tends to select the evidence.

The Christian commitment is more explicit than any of its secular alternatives because it deals with discontinuities rather than continuities, with the human person and with the person of God in their respective freedoms. Personality is imbedded in an order, but it rises in freedom above its organism. The relation between personalities must be by faith and love rather than by reason because persons are discrete, unique, and discontinuous; they cannot be comprehended in a rational form. In terms of Biblical faith the encounter between man and God is analogous to the encounter between persons. Personality, or any other human quality, is ascribed to God with due regard to the inadequacy of analogy. But analogy is necessary to emphasize a freedom in both God and man, above the organism of man and above the order of the world. In this encounter the fact that man has made a false use of his freedom to center life upon and in himself is discovered. Therefore, the encounter is one which produces an uneasy conscience in man. He discerns the divine judgment. The revelation in Christ assures man that there is not only judgment but mercy; that the two are facets of the same holiness and love, though justice and forgiveness stand in provisional contradiction to each other. If the judgment is accepted the forgiveness becomes a reality in a "new" life.

This is the revelation in Christ upon which the Christian church is founded and which is the capstone of a Christian view of life. The relative merits of Jesus and Socrates as exemplars of goodness have little relevance to this assurance. It must of course be accepted by faith. That is to say, there is no rational analysis of the structure of the world which compels anyone to accept the truth about himself and his relation to God. Such acceptance comes not primarily through the mind but through the whole personality. Faith requires repentance and repentance produces faith. In that sense the Christian faith is "existential." The "existing" individual ceases to be an observer of the world and comes to terms with his own situation ultimately. This observation might persuade us to say a qualifying word about Socrates. He is supposed to be the fountain and source of all rational identifications of virtue and reason. But after all it was Socrates who said "Know thyself." By that much the view of Socrates and Christ share a common "existentialism."

It is of course not easy to follow Socrates's advice within a Socratic framework. The problem of self-knowledge is essentially unsolved despite the glories of the psychological sciences. It is unsolved because the human self is a creature, and moreover a rational creature; but also one which possesses this curious yearning for the ultimate. Either the self engages in the abortive enterprise of regarding itself as ultimate (existentialism) or of losing itself, and annulling its contingent existence, in the ultimate (mysticism); or in finding itself in a dialogic relation with the divine. The revelation of Christ has meaning only in the context of such a dialogic relationship. The Christian faith stands or falls by the affirmation that true self-knowledge, in which the self becomes aware of both its dignity and its sinful self-assertion, is the fruit of such a dialogue. The Revelation in Christ is the definitive exposition of the character of the dialogue.

❦ ❦ ❦

*Martin Buber*

# God and the Spirit of Man[1]

THIS book discusses the relations between religion and philosophy in the history of the spirit, and deals with the part that philosophy has played in its late period in making God and all absoluteness appear unreal.

If philosophy is here set in contrast to religion, what is meant by religion is not the massive fulness of statements, concepts, and activities that one customarily describes by this name and that men sometimes long for more than for God. Religion is essentially the act of holding fast to God. And that does not mean holding fast to an image that one has made of God, nor even holding fast to the faith in God that one has conceived. It means holding fast to the existing God. The earth would not hold fast to its conception of the sun (if it had one), nor to its connection with it, but to the sun itself.

In contrast to religion so understood, philosophy is here regarded as the

---

[1] From *Eclipse of God: Studies in the Relation Between Philosophy and Religion* (New York: Harper and Brothers, 1952), Chapter VIII. Copyright, 1952, by Harper and Brothers. Reprinted by permission. "God and the Spirit of Man" is the substance of a lecture delivered by Buber at a number of American universities in 1951.

process, reaching from the time when reflection first became independent to its more contemporary crisis, the last stage of which is the intellectual letting go of God.

This process begins with man's no longer contenting himself, as did the pre-philosophical man, with picturing the living God, to whom one formerly only called—with a call of despair or rapture which occasionally became his first name—as a Something, a thing among things, a being among beings, an It.

The beginning of philosophizing means that this Something changes from an object of imagination, wishes, and feelings to one that is conceptually comprehensible, to an object of thought. It does not matter whether this object of thought is called "Speech" (*Logos*), because in all and each one hears it speak, answer, and directly address one; or "the Unlimited" (*Apeiron*), because it has already leapt over every limit that one may try to set for it; or simply "Being," or whatever. If the living quality of the conception of God refuses to enter into this conceptual image, it is tolerated alongside of it, usually in an unprecise form, as in the end identical with it or at least essentially dependent on it. Or it is depreciated as an unsatisfactory surrogate, helpful to men incapable of thought.

In the progress of its philosophizing, the human spirit is ever more inclined to fuse characteristically this conception, of the Absolute as an object of an adequate thought, with itself, the human spirit. In the course of this process, the idea which was at first noetically contemplated finally becomes the potentiality of the spirit itself that thinks it, and it attains on the way of the spirit its actuality. The subject, which appeared to be attached to being in order to perform for it the service of contemplation, asserts that it itself produced and produces being. Until, finally, all that is over against us, everything that accosts us and takes possession of us, all partnership of existence, is dissolved in free-floating subjectivity.

The next step already takes us to the stage familiar to us, the stage that understands itself as the final one and plays with its finality: the human spirit, which adjudges to itself mastery over its work, annihilates conceptually the absoluteness of the absolute. It may yet imagine that it, the spirit, still remains there as bearer of all things and coiner of all values; in truth, it has also destroyed its own absoluteness along with absoluteness in general. The spirit can now no longer exist as an independent essence. There now exists only a product of human individuals called spirit, a product which they contain and secrete like mucus and urine.

In this stage, there first takes place the conceptual letting go of God because only now philosophy cuts off its own hands, the hands with which it was able to grasp and hold him.

But an analogous process takes place on the other side, in the development of religion itself (in the usual broad sense of the word).

From the earliest times, the reality of the relation of faith, man's standing before the face of God, world-happening as dialogue, has been threatened by the impulse to control the power yonder. Instead of understanding events as calls which make demands on one, one wishes oneself to demand without having to hearken. "I have," says man, "power over the powers I conjure." And that continues, with sundry modifications, wherever one celebrates rites without being turned to the Thou and without really meaning its Presence.

The other pseudo-religious counterpart of the relation of faith, not so elementally active as conjuration but acting with the mature power of the intellect, is unveiling. Here one takes the position of raising the veil of the manifest, which divides the revealed from the hidden, and leading forth the divine mysteries. "I am," says man, "acquainted with the unknown, and I make it known." The supposedly divine It that the magician manipulates as the technician his dynamo, the gnostic lays bare—the whole divine apparatus. His heirs are not "theosophies" and their neighbors alone; in many theologies also, unveiling gestures are to be discovered behind the interpreting ones.

We find this replacement of I-Thou by an I-It in manifold forms in that new philosophy of religion which seeks to "save" religion. In it, the "I" of this relation steps ever more into the foreground as "subject" of "religious feeling," as profiter from a pragmatist decision to believe, and the like.

Much more important than all this, however, is an event penetrating to the innermost depth of the religious life, an event which may be described as the subjectivizing of the act of faith itself. Its essence can be grasped most clearly through the example of prayer.

We call prayer in the pregnant sense of the term that speech of man to God which, whatever else is asked, ultimately asks for the manifestation of the divine Presence, for this Presence becoming dialogically perceivable. The single presupposition of a genuine state of prayer is thus the readiness of the whole man for this Presence, simple-turned-towardness, unreserved spontaneity. This spontaneity, ascending from the roots, succeeds time and again in overcoming all that disturbs and diverts. But in this our stage of subjectivized reflection not only the concentration of the one who prays, but also his spontaneity, is assailed. The assailant is consciousness, the overconsciousness of this man here that he is praying, that he is *praying*, that *he* is praying. And the assailant appears to be invincible. The subjective knowledge of the one turning-toward about his turning-toward, this holding back of an I which does not enter into the action with the rest of the person, an I to which the action is an object —all this de-possesses the moment, takes away its spontaneity. The specifically modern man who has not yet let go of God knows what that means: he who is not present perceives no Presence.

One must understand this correctly: this is not a question of a special case of the known sickness of modern man, who must attend his own actions as spectator. It is the confession of the Absolute into which he brings his unfaithfulness to the Absolute, and it is the relation between the Absolute and him upon which this unfaithfulness works, in the midst of the statement of trust. And now he too who is seemingly holding fast to God becomes aware of the eclipsed Transcendence.

What is it that we mean when we speak of an eclipse of God which is even now taking place? Through this metaphor we make the tremendous assumption that we can glance up to God with our "mind's eye," or rather being's eye, as with our bodily eye to the sun, and that something can step between our existence and his as between the earth and the sun. That this glance of the being exists, wholly unillusory, yielding no images yet first making possible all images, no other court in the world attests than that of faith. It is not to be proved; it is only to be experienced; man has experienced it. And that other, that which steps in between, one also experiences, today. I have spoken of it since I have recognized it, and as exactly as my perception has allowed me.

The double nature of man, as the being that is both brought forth from "below" and sent from "above," results in the duality of his basic characteristics. These cannot be understood through the categories of the individual man existing-for-himself, but only through the categories of his existing as man-with-man. As a being who is sent, man exists over against the existing being before which he is placed. As a being who is brought forth, he finds himself beside all existing beings in the world, beside which he is set. The first of these categories has its living reality in the relation I-Thou, the second has its reality in the relation I-It. The second always brings us only to the aspects of an existing being, not to that being itself. Even the most intimate contact with another remains covered over by an aspect if the other has not become Thou for me. Only the first relation, that which establishes essential immediacy between me and an existing being, brings me precisely thereby not to an aspect of it, but to that being itself. To be sure, it brings me only to the existential meeting with it; it does not somehow put me in a position to view it objectively in its being. As soon as an objective viewing is established, we are given only an aspect and ever again only an aspect. But it is also only the relation I-Thou in which we can meet God at all, because of him, in absolute contrast to all other existing beings, no objective aspect can be attained. Even a vision yields no objective viewing, and he who strains to hold fast an after-image after the cessation of the full I-Thou relation has already lost the vision.

It is not the case, however, that the I in both relations, I-Thou and I-It, is the same. Rather where and when the beings around one are seen and treated as objects of observation, reflection, use, perhaps also of solicitude or help, there and then another I is spoken, another I manifested, another I exists than where and when one stands with the whole of one's being over against another being and steps into an essential relation with him. Everyone who knows both in himself—and that is the life of man, that one comes to know both in himself and ever again both—knows whereof I speak. Both together build up human existence; it is only a question of which of the two is at any particular time the architect and which is his assistant. Rather, it is a question of whether the I-Thou relation remains the architect, for it is self-evident that it cannot be employed as assistant. If it does not command, then it is already disappearing.

In our age, the I-It relation, gigantically swollen, has usurped, practically uncontested, the mastery and the rule. The I of this relation, an I that possesses all, makes all, succeeds with all, this I that is unable to say Thou, unable to meet a being essentially, is the lord of the hour. This selfhood that has become omnipotent, with all the It around it, can naturally acknowledge neither God nor any genuine absolute which manifests itself to men as of non-human origin. It steps in between and shuts off from us the light of heaven.

Such is the nature of this hour. But what of the next? It is a modern superstition that the character of an age acts as fate for the next. One lets it prescribe what is possible to do and hence what is permitted. One surely cannot swim against the stream, one says. But perhaps one can swim with a new stream whose source is still hidden? In another image, the I-Thou relation has gone into the catacombs—who can say with how much greater power it will step forth! Who can say when the I-It relation will be directed anew to its assisting place and activity!

The most important events in the history of that embodied possibility called man are the occasionally occurring beginnings of new epochs, determined by forces previously invisible or unregarded. Each age is, of course, a continuation of the preceding one, but a continuation can be confirmation and it can be refutation.

Something is taking place in the depths that as yet needs no name. Tomorrow even it may happen that it will be beckoned to from the heights, across the heads of the earthly archons. The eclipse of the light of God is no extinction; even tomorrow that which has stepped in between may give way.

❧ ❧ ❧

*Jacques Maritain*

## Confession of Faith [1]

As a child I was brought up in "Liberal Protestantism." Later on I became acquainted with the different phases of secularistic thought. The scientist and phenomenist philosophy of my teachers at the Sorbonne at last made me despair of reason. At one time I thought I might be able to find complete certitude in the sciences, and Felix Le Dantec thought that my fiancée and I would become followers of his biological materialism. The best thing I owe to my studies at that time is that they let me meet, in the School of Sciences, the woman who since then has always, happily for me, been at my side in a perfect and blessed communion. Bergson was the first to answer our deep desire for metaphysical truth—he liberated in us the sense of the absolute.

Before being captured by St. Thomas Aquinas, I underwent some great in-

[1] From *The Social and Political Philosophy of Jacques Maritain*, edited by Joseph W. Evans and Leo R. Ward, copyright 1955 by Charles Scribner's Sons and reprinted with their permission.

fluences, those of Charles Péguy, Bergson, and Leon Bloy. A year after we met Bloy, my wife and I were baptized Catholics, and we chose him as our god-father.

It was after my conversion to Catholicism that I came to know St. Thomas. I had voyaged passionately among all the doctrines of modern philosophers and had found in them nothing but deception and grandiose uncertainty. What I now experienced was like an illumination of reason. My vocation as philosopher became perfectly clear to me. *Woe to me if I do not thomisticize*, I wrote in one of my first books. And through thirty years of work and battles I have kept to this same path, with the feeling of sympathizing all the more profoundly with the researches, the discoveries and the agonies of modern thought, the more I tried to penetrate them with the light which comes to us from a wisdom worked out through the centuries, a wisdom resistant to the fluctuations of time.

In order to advance in this path we are obliged constantly to bring together singularly distant extremes, for no solution of our problems is found ready-made in the heritage of the ancients. We are also obliged to make a difficult sifting of the pure substance of truths which many a modern rejects in his loathing of the trashy opinions of the past, from all the dross, the prejudices, the out-of-date images and arbitrary constructions which many a traditionalist confuses with what is really worthy of being venerated by intelligence.

I have spoken of the different experiences through which I passed, because they gave me the occasion to try personally the state of mind of the idealist freethinker, of the inexperienced convert, and of the Christian who becomes aware, in proportion as his faith takes root, of the purifications to which that faith must be subjected. I was also able to obtain some experimental idea of what the anti-religious camp and the straddlers' camp are worth. Neither of them is worth very much. And the worst disgrace of the second camp is that it runs the risk of compromising along with itself the innocent and persecuted Church, the Mystical Body of Christ, whose essential life, *sine macula sine ruga*, is in the Truth and in the saints, and which travels towards its fulness through the weaknesses of its own and the ferocity of the world. In my view, God educates us through our deceptions and mistakes, in order to make us understand at last that we ought to believe only in Him and not in men—which readily brings one to marvel at all the good which is in men despite everything and at all the good they do in spite of themselves.

I have decidedly come to the conclusion that in practice there are only two ways to know the depths of things, or, if one wishes, two "wisdoms," each of them a kind of folly, though in opposite manners. One is the way of sinners, who in order to drain things to the dregs embrace the nothingness of which all things are made and thereby have a full experience of this world, in the evil of the world more than in its good. The other way is the way of the saints, who adhere to subsisting Goodness, maker of all things, and receive in love a full experience of God and of creation, and who stand surety for all the world

by their suffering and compassion. Well, it is normal to hope that the disciples
of vain wisdom, if they are not hardened by pride and if they are loyal to their
own experience, will finally be saved "through fire" by the lovers of true wisdom. And if they should live to be converted, they will perhaps be harsher than
others in censuring any of their brothers still in darkness, so that, after having
long tasted the delights of the world, they will taste for a moment the delights
of their virtues and will continue vain till the last day, till they enter eternity.

This is not the place to give an exposition of theses in speculative philosophy. I will only say that I consider Thomistic philosophy to be a living and
present philosophy, with all the greater power to make conquests in new fields
of discovery just because its principles are so firm and so organically bound together. Confronted with the succession of scientific hypotheses, some minds are
surprised that anyone could find inspiration today in metaphysical principles
acknowledged by Aristotle and Thomas Aquinas and rooted in the oldest intellectual heritage of the race. My reply is that the telephone and the radio do not
prevent man from still having two arms, two legs and two lungs, or from falling in love and seeking happiness as did his faraway ancestors. Besides, truth
recognizes no chronological criteria, and the art of the philosopher is not to be
confused with the art of the great dressmakers.

On a deeper level, we must explain that progress in the sciences of phenomena, where the "problem" aspect is so characteristic, takes place chiefly by
*substitution* of one theory for another which saved less well the known facts
and phenomena; but in metaphysics and philosophy, where the "mystery" aspect
is predominant, progress takes place chiefly by *deeper penetration*. Besides, the
different philosophical systems, however ill founded they may be, constitute in
some way, in their totality, a virtual and fluent philosophy, overlapping contrary formulations and unfriendly doctrines and carried along by the elements
of truth they all contain. If, therefore, there exists among men a doctrinal organism entirely supported by true principles, it will incorporate—more or less
tardily, due to the laziness of its defenders—it will progressively realize within
itself this virtual philosophy, and this will thereby, and in a proportionate degree, take on form and organic arrangement. Such is my idea of progress in
philosophy.

If I say next that the metaphysics which I hold to be founded on truth may
be described as a critical realism and as a philosophy of intelligence and of being, or still more precisely as a philosophy of the *act of existing* regarded as
the act and perfection of all perfections, these formulas, of course, will be of
interest only to specialists. A brief reflection on the historical significance of
modern philosophy will no doubt be more appropriate.

In the Middle Ages, philosophy was in fact ordinarily treated as an instrument in the service of theology. Culturally, it was not in the state required by
its nature. The coming of a philosophical or lay wisdom which had completed
its own formation for itself and according to its own finalities was therefore a

response to an historical necessity. But unfortunately this work was brought about under the aegis of division and of a sectarian rationalism; Descartes *separated* philosophy from any higher wisdom, from anything in man which comes from above man. I am convinced that what the world and civilization have lacked in the intellectual order for three centuries has been a philosophy which would develop its autonomous exigencies in a Christian climate, a wisdom of reason not closed but open to the wisdom of grace. Today reason must battle an irrational deification of elemental and instinctive forces that threatens to ruin all civilization. In this struggle, reason's task is one of integration; understanding that intelligence is not the enemy of mystery, but lives on it, reason must come to terms with the irrational world of affectivity and instinct, as well as with the world of the will, of freedom and of love, and the suprarational world of grace and of divine life.

The dynamic harmony of the degrees of knowledge will at the same time become manifest. From this point of view, the problem proper to the age we are entering will be, it seems, to reconcile *science* and *wisdom*. The sciences themselves seem to invite intelligence to this work. We see them stripping themselves of the remains of materialistic and mechanistic metaphysics which for a time hid their true features. They call for a philosophy of nature, and the wonderful progress in contemporary physics restores to the scientist the sense of the mystery stammered by the atom and by the universe. A critique of knowledge formed in a genuinely realist and metaphysical spirit has a chance henceforth to be heard when it affirms the existence of structures of knowledge specifically and hierarchically distinct—distinct, but not separated—and shows that they correspond to original types of explanation which cannot be substituted one for another.

The Greeks recognized the great truth that contemplation is in itself superior to action. But they at once transformed this truth into a great error: they believed that the human race exists for a few intellectuals. As they saw it, there was a category of specialists, the philosophers, who lived a superhuman life, and the properly human life, namely, civil or political life, existed to serve them. To serve civil or political life, in turn, there was the subhuman life of labor, which in final analysis was the life of the slave. The lofty truth of the superiority of the contemplative life was thus bound to a contempt for labor and to the evil of slavery.

Christianity transfigured all this. It taught men that love is of more value than intelligence. It transformed the notion of contemplation, which henceforth does not stop in the intellect, but only in the love of God, the contemplated object. It restored to action its human significance as a service to our neighbor, and rehabilitated work by disclosing in it a value of natural redemption, as it were, and even a natural prefiguration of the communications of charity. It called to the contemplation of the saints and to perfection, not a few specialists or privileged persons, but all men, who are all bound proportionately by the law of work. Man is at once "homo faber" and "homo sapiens," and he is "homo faber" before truly and actually being "homo sapiens" and in order to become the latter. In this way Christianity saved, but by transforming and delivering from the error which tainted it, the Greek idea of the superiority of the contemplative life.

The saints' contemplation completes and consummates a natural aspiration to contemplation consubstantial to man, of which the sages of India and Greece especially give testimony. It is through love that the knowledge of divine things becomes experimental and fruitful. And precisely because this knowledge is the work of love in act, it also passes into action by virtue of the very generosity and abundance of love, which is gift of self. Then action proceeds from the superabundance of contemplation, and that is why, far from suppressing action or being opposed to it, contemplation vivifies it. It is in this sense, which relates to the essential generosity of the contemplation of love, that we must recognize with Bergson, in the superabundance and excess of the giving of self shown by the Christian mystics, the sign of their success in reaching the heroic summit of human life.

The pursuit of the highest contemplation and the pursuit of the highest freedom are two aspects of the same pursuit. In the order of spiritual life, man aspires to a perfect and absolute freedom, and therefore to a superhuman condition; sages of all times give evidence of this. The function of law is a function of protection and education of freedom, the function of a pedagogue. At the conclusion of this tutelage the perfect spiritual man is freed from every servitude, even, St. Paul says, from the servitude of the law, because he does spontaneously what is of the law and is simply one spirit and one love with the Creator.

To my way of thinking, the pursuit of freedom is also at the base of the social and political problem. But in the order of temporal life, it is not a divine freedom which is the object of our desires, but rather a freedom proportionate to the human condition and to the natural possibilities of our earthly existence. It is important not to deceive ourselves on the nature of the good thus pursued. It is not simply the preservation of each one's *freedom of choice*, nor the social community's *freedom of power*. The good in question is the *freedom of expansion* of human persons making up a people and participating in its good. Political society has as an end to develop conditions of life in common which, while assuring first of all the good and peace of the whole, will positively aid each person in the progressive conquest of this freedom of expansion, a freedom which consists above all in the flowering of moral and rational life.

Thus justice and friendship are the very foundations of society's life; and it is to truly human goods that society ought to subordinate all material goods, technical progress and the implements of power which also make up part of society's common good.

I believe that historical conditions and the yet backward state of human development make it difficult for social life fully to reach its end, and that in regard to the possibilities and demands which the Gospel brings to us in the socio-temporal order, we are still in a prehistoric age. As we see today in the psychoses of the masses which adore Stalin or Hitler, or dream of exterminating certain groups that they judge to be diabolical, in particular the Jews, doubtless because they are the people of God, human collectivities bear such a burden of willingly diseased animality that it will still require many centuries for the life of personality to be able truly to take on among the masses the fulness to which it aspires. But it still remains that the end towards which social life of itself tends is to procure the common good of the multitude in such a way that the concrete person, not merely in a privileged class but in the entire mass, may truly reach that measure of independence which belongs to civilized life and which is assured alike by the economic guarantees of work and property, by political rights, civic virtues and the cultivation of the mind.

These ideas are tied up with wider views which seem to me most properly designated by the expression *integral humanism,* and which involve a whole philosophy of modern history. Such a humanism, considering man in the integral wholeness of his natural and supernatural being and setting no a priori limits to the descent of the divine into man, may also be called a humanism of the Incarnation.

In the socio-temporal order it does not ask men to sacrifice themselves to the imperialism of race, of class or of nation. It asks them to sacrifice themselves to a better life for their brothers and to the concrete good of the community of human persons. That is why it cannot be less than an heroic humanism.

It has often been remarked that "bourgeois" liberalism, which tries to base everything on the individual taken as a little god and on his good pleasure, on an absolute freedom of ownership, of business and the pleasures of life, ends up fatally in statism. The rule of numbers produces the omnipotence of the State, of a ruminant or plutocratic State. Communism may be regarded as a reaction against this individualism. It claims to be orientated towards the absolute emancipation of man, who would thus become the god of history, but in reality this emancipation, supposing it were accomplished, would then be that of collective man, not that of the human person. Society as economic community would enslave the whole life of the person, because the essential work of civil society would be made to consist in economic functions, instead of subordinating this work to the freedom of expansion of persons: what the Communists propose as the emancipation of collective man would be the enslavement of human persons.

What of the anti-communist and anti-individualistic reactions of a totalitarian or dictatorial type? It is not in the name of the social community and the freedom of collective man, it is in the name of the sovereign dignity of the State, a state of the carnivorous type, or in the name of the spirit of a people, in the name of race or of blood, that they would annex man in his entirety to a social whole where the person of the ruler is the only one, properly speaking, to enjoy the privileges of personality. This is why totalitarian states, needing for themselves the total devotion of the person and having no sense of or respect for the person, inevitably seek a principle of human exaltation in myths of external grandeur and in the never-ending struggle for power and prestige. By its nature this tends to war and the self-destruction of the civilized community. If there are people in the Church—and they are fewer and fewer—who count on dictatorships of this kind to promote the religion of Christ and Christian civilization, they forget that the totalitarian phenomenon is an aberrant religious phenomenon in which an earthly mysticism devours every other mysticism whatever it may be, and will tolerate none besides itself.

Confronted with "bourgeois" liberalism, communism and totalitarian statism, what we need, I do not cease to say, is a new solution, one that is at the same time personalist and communal, one that sees human society as an organization of freedoms. We are thus brought to a conception of democracy, the community of free men, very different from that of Jean-Jacques Rousseau. We may call it *pluralist*, because it requires that the body politic guarantee the organic freedoms of the different spiritual families and different social bodies assembled within it, beginning with the basic natural community, the society of the family. The drama of modern democracies is that, under the appearance of an error—the deification of a fictitious individual entirely closed up in himself—they have without knowing it pursued a good thing: the expansion of the real person open to higher realities and to the common service of justice and friendship.

Personalist democracy holds that each is called, by virtue of the common dignity of human nature, to participate actively in political life, and that those who hold authority—which is a vital function in society and a real right to direct people—should be freely designated by the people. This is why personalist democracy sees in universal suffrage the first practical token by which a democratic society becomes aware of itself and which it may not in any case renounce. It has no better or more meaningful motto than the republican motto, understood as indicating, not an established condition in which man has only to be installed, but an end to be reached, a difficult and lofty goal to which man must tend by force of courage, justice and virtue. For freedom must be conquered, by the progressive elimination of the several forms of servitude, and it is not enough to proclaim equality of the fundamental rights of human persons, whatever one's race, one's religion, one's condition. This equality ought to pass in a real way into custom and into social structures and ought to yield fruit in a larger and larger participation by all in the common good of civilization. Finally, fraternity in the body politic requires that the loftiest and most generous of virtues, the love to which the Gospel has called our ungrateful species, pass into the very order of political life. A personalist democracy is not really conceivable without the super-elevations which nature and temporal civilizations receive, each in its own order, from the energies of the Christian leaven.

I am convinced that the coming of such a democracy, which presupposes that class antagonism has been overcome, demands that, by a genuine renewal of life and of justice, we truly go beyond "capitalism" and beyond socialism, each of which is vitiated by a materialistic conception of life. Nothing is more opposed to personalist democracy than fascist totalitarianism—whether social-nationalist or national-socialist; for it goes beyond "capitalism" only through the paroxysm of the evils it begets.

Let me remark that Christians are confronted today, in the socio-temporal order, with problems quite similar to those their sixteenth- and seventeenth-century ancestors encountered in the area of the philosophy of nature. At that time modern physics and astronomy, then in their beginnings, were simply one with philosophies set against tradition. The defenders of tradition did not know how to make the necessary distinctions. They took sides against what was to become modern science, at the same time that they took sides against the philosophical errors which at the start were parasitic on science. It took three centuries to get rid of this misunderstanding, if indeed the world is yet rid of it. It would be a sad story if we should be guilty today, in the field of practical and social philosophy, of like errors.

In the words of Pope Pius XI, the great scandal of the nineteenth century was the divorce of the working classes from the Church of Christ. In the temporal order, the moral secession of the working masses from the political community was a comparable tragedy. The awakening in the working masses of what the socialist vocabulary calls "class consciousness" appears to us as a great gain, so far as we see in it man's becoming aware of an offended and humiliated human dignity and of a vocation. But it has been chained to an historic calamity, because this awakening has been spoiled by the gospel of despair and of social warfare which is at the bottom of the Marxist idea of class struggle and the dictatorship of the proletariat. And it was precisely into this *secessionist* conception, whose protagonist was Marx and whose demand is that proletarians of all countries should recognize no other common good than that of their class, that the blindness of the possessing classes in the nineteenth century precipitated the working masses.

Whoever has pondered on these fundamental facts and on the history of the labor movement understands that the central problem of our times is the temporal and spiritual problem of the *reintegration of the masses*. In my view, it is only an artificial and illusory solution of this problem when the attempt is made, as in the case of German National Socialism, to manufacture happy slaves through violence linked with material ameliorations good in themselves but achieved in a spirit of domination, and with a psychotechnic solicitude vowed to satisfy and to benumb appetites. The fact is that one manufactures only unhappy slaves, robots of non-being.

However difficult, slow and painful it may be, the reintegration of the proletariat within the national community, not to exercise a class dictatorship in it, but to collaborate body and soul in the work of the community, will take place really, which means humanly, only by a recasting of social structures worked out in the spirit of justice. I am not naive enough to believe that this reintegration can be accomplished without knocks and sacrifices, on the one hand as regards the well-being of the privileged sons of fortune and on the other as regards the theories and the destructive instincts of fanatical revolutionaries. But I am persuaded that it requires above all else the free cooperation of the workers' leaders (elites) and of the masses who follow them, and this cooperation must go along with a better general understanding of historical realities and with an awareness, not wiped out but heightened, of the human being's dignity as worker and citizen. In like manner the return of the masses to Christianity will be brought about only through love, I mean love stronger than death, the fire of the Gospel.

We shall never give up hope of a new Christendom, a new temporal order of Christian inspiration. Now the means should correspond to the end, and already are the end itself as in the state of movement and preparation. If this is so, it is clear that in order to prepare a Christian social order we must use Christian means, that is to say true means, just means, and these are means animated, even when they are of necessity harsh, by a genuine spirit of love. In two books published in 1930 and 1933[2] I have insisted at length on these axiomatic truths. Nothing is more serious or scandalous than to see, as we have for some years seen in certain countries, iniquitous and barbarous means used by men in the name of Christian order and Christian civilization. It is a truth embedded in the very nature of things that Christendom will be renewed through Christian means or it will be completely eclipsed.

The present state of nations obliges us to declare that never has the spirit been so profoundly humiliated in the world. And yet pessimism in the end always dupes itself. It disregards the great law which may be called the law of the double movement involving the energy of history. While the wear and tear of time naturally dissipates and degrades the things of this world and the "energy of history," and this means the mass of human activity on which the movement of history depends, the creative forces which are characteristic of spirit and freedom and are a witness to them, forces which ordinarily find their point of application in the effort of the few—who are thereby bound to sacrifice—improve more and more the quality of this energy. This is exactly the work of the sons of God in history, it is the work of Christians if they do not belie their name.

People do not understand this work at all if they imagine that it aims at installing the world in a state from which all evil and all injustice would have disappeared. If this were the aim, it would be quite easy, considering the results, stupidly to condemn the Christian as utopian. The work the Christian has to do is to keep up and to increase in the world the internal tension and

[2] *Religion et culture; Du regime temporel et de la liberté.* (*Religion and Culture; Freedom in the Modern World.*)

movement of slow and painful deliverance, a tension and movement due to the invisible powers of truth and justice, of goodness and love, acting on the mass which is opposed to them. This work cannot be in vain, it assuredly bears its fruit.

Woe to the world should Christians turn their back on it, should they fail to do their work, which is to heighten here on earth the charge and tension of the spiritual; should they listen to blind leaders of the blind who seek the means to order and to good in things which of themselves lead to dissolution and death. We have no illusions about the misery of human nature and the malice of this world. But neither have we any illusions about the blindness and malfeasance of pseudo-realists who cultivate and exalt evil in order to fight evil, and who take the Gospel as a decorative myth which cannot be regarded seriously without wrecking the machinery of the world. They themselves, meantime, take it upon themselves to ruin, to distract, and to torment this unhappy world.

The ferment of the pharisees, against which Christ put us on our guard, is a permanent temptation for the religious conscience. Undoubtedly, this ferment will not be altogether driven out of the world till the end of history. Meantime, in the social as well as in the spiritual order, we must never let up the fight against it. However great may be the mass of evil which a mass of pharisaism means to oppose, the latter is always as great an evil, because the good it sets against that evil is a good which does not give life but kills, as does the letter without the spirit: it is a good which leaves God without resources in man.

One of the gravest lessons afforded us by the experience of life is that, in fact, in the practical conduct of most people, all those things which in themselves are good and very good—science, technical progress, culture, etc., and even the knowledge of moral laws, and religious faith itself, faith in the living God (which of itself demands the love of charity)—all these things, *without love and good will*, serve to make men all the more evil and the more unhappy. So far as religious faith is concerned, this was demonstrated in the Spanish civil war by the inhuman feelings that surged up in the "crusaders" as well as in the "reds," but were confirmed in the former in the sanctuary of the soul. What happens is that, without love and charity, man turns the best in him into an evil that is yet greater.

When one has understood this, he no longer puts his hope on earth in anything less than that good will of which the Gospel speaks—it speaks of good will, not of good velleity; he puts his hope in these obscure energies of a little real goodness which persists in making life germinate and regerminate in the secret depths of things. There is nothing more destitute, nothing more hidden, nothing nearer to the weakness of the infant. And there is no wisdom more fundamental or more effective than that simple and tenacious confidence, not in the means of violence, deceit and malice, which certainly are capable of crushing men and of triumphing, but which a grain of sand is nevertheless enough to cause to be smashed one against the other—but simple and tenacious

confidence in the resources of personal courage to give oneself, and of good
will set to do as one ought the tasks of every day. Through this disinterested
spirit flows the power of nature and the Author of nature.

❧ ❧ ❧

*William Ernest Hocking*

# Living Religions and a World Faith [1]

IF ONE were still able to travel by train from the New Harbor of Dubrovnik
to Serajevo, climbing noisily (and smokily) up the mountain slopes bordering
the fine estuary of the Ombla, he would be aware of a swift change of cultural
as well as of physical climate. The Dalmatian coast bears everywhere the
Roman and Venetian mark in architecture and religion; there are a few Greek
Orthodox Churches and numerous Jewish synagogues. But as one reaches
Mostar he sees minarets as well as steeples and domes. And at Serajevo it is
evident that the religion of Mohammed is a lively factor in the community.
Christianity, Judaism, Islam—three religions of Asiatic origin, dominate the
Balkan peninsula. At Spalato, Mestrovic's gigantic statue of Bishop Gregory set
up in the ruins of the palace of Diocletian symbolizes the almost complete
submersion of the religious influence of classical antiquity, both Roman and
Greek, under these faiths from the East.

Except in point of proportion the story of the Balkans is repeated everywhere in Europe and America: whatever forms of religion are alive among us
we owe to Asia. We are less conscious of the presence of Islam than of Judaism
and Christianity, hardly at all aware of Hinduism. Many do not realize that
there are (or were) active Moslem missions in England (as at Woking in
Surrey), Germany, and France; and that besides the monumental mosque in
Paris built to signalize the fact that France was a great Moslem power, there
are active mosques in Brooklyn and Chicago; nor that Bahai is an offshoot of
Islam, as the Vedanta movement with a dozen American centers is an offshoot
of Hinduism.

There are no religions indigenous to Europe and America which compare
with these religions from Asia either in their present vitality or in their influence on our civilization. This fact has sometimes been taken as a reproach
against the religious originality of the Western world. Sometimes it has been
taken as an argument that religion itself is a peculiar Oriental export, not
really suited to our mentality, which we should do well to lay aside quietly,
with all due gratitude for its historic services.

To comment on the latter point first, it is not at all certain that these historic services have been finished. What they amount to, in sum, is supplying

[1] From William Ernest Hocking in *The Asian Legacy*, ed. by Arthur E. Christy
(New York: The John Day Company, 1942), pp. 193-214.

the fecundity and the backbone for all that we call "Western civilization." This has been chiefly the work of Christianity. The Christian version of Roman-Stoic law, eked out by canon law, and administered by officers of the church, tided Europe over its darker hours of disorder, and laid the foundation for all civil law in Europe. The common law of England and America is an offspring of Anglo-Saxon conscience under the guidance of the church. The whole conception of the rights of man is directly traceable to Christian conceptions of human nature, and with that, all we call individualism, liberalism, democracy in the modern sense. The art of Europe, including architecture, music, painting, sculpture, was shaped by the medieval church; likewise its literature and philosophy. And as for its science, which we are inclined to think of as the result of a revolt against religious authority, and especially as one point which sets us off from everything Oriental—the whole development of scientific method in the seventeenth century, with its spirit of revolt—not against religion nor Christianity but against the authority of Aristotle and the Bible in matters of logic and science, is demonstrably an application of Christian ethics to the study of Nature, and was carried on by men who regarded themselves as more religious than those who criticized them. No historian can explain why and how what we call the modern era arose in Europe and America and nowhere else, who does not recognize the religion of Europe and America as one of the parents of that era.

And though we owe so much to Christianity, it is not at all clear that we yet know what it means. It still seems strange to us—otherworldly, remote, extravagant, impractical—in short "Oriental." Probably the Orient does in fact understand it better than we do. This means that we claim too much when we say we have taken our religion from the East: it has not yet been completely taken. We still have to learn religion from Asia, both in terms of the living religions which are there, and in terms of Asiatic versions of Christianity. Certainly, the learning business has to go in both directions, but our own culture will lack catholicity, poise, and security until we know what we have to do with religion in an age which is rightly committed to the humanistic spirit and the technology which is the gift of science.

As to the other matter—that we ought to be ashamed to take our religion from Asia—there are two things to be said. First, that religion is always original or nothing: nobody can use the religion of anybody else but himself. Whatever he accepts by way of suggestion or teaching from outside has to become his own conviction before it can do him any good. And as he appropriates it, he remolds it and produces his own version, even when he accepts it most humbly as the authoritative word of God. Second, the Western world is not behind in religious fecundity. Every ethnic region of Europe has produced its religious forms, still discernible in the undercurrents of folklore. There have been magnificent pantheons among them, from the urbane Olympians of Greece to the stormy Aesir, denizens of Asgard (from two of whom, Odin and Thor, we derive the words Wednesday and Thursday—our weekday names remaining obstinately pagan). And with these there have come splendid poetic literatures, mythologies, theologies, and parable-wisdoms. There have not been lacking efforts to resuscitate some of these buried cities of the spirit or to recover for use some of their ideas. Lutoslawski, for example, labored over the doctrine of transmigration as found in the Polish epics in order to show that it was an improvement on either the Hindu doctrine, associated with Karma, or Plato's picture of rebirth. But these European religions remain local reminiscences, held in the subconscious mold of peasant usages or absorbed into the framework of the dominant faith. Why, then, have the great Asiatic religions taken their place? The fact, I believe, is neither accidental nor humiliating: it is an inevitable consequence of the nature of religion and its history. I shall try to make this evident.

I

Religion is man's practical dealing with the enduring auspices of his destiny, his communion with what is eternal and total in his world, conceived as a source of direction to right living. By definition, religion reached toward what is universally true, that which concerns all men alike, no matter of what place, color, sex, race, or nation. Its nature is, therefore, to unite men in the consciousness of a common lot and obligation. Wherever it arises, and however it expresses itself, its whole meaning is to find that one reality and that one law which are valid for all mankind. At the same time, every religion, having its local origins, dealing with the less tangible sides of the world, having to use symbols, metaphors, and appeals rather than market-literalities, is steeped in localism. Belonging as it does to the working balance of a culture, it grows with the given culture, and the early religions naturally observe the limits drawn by language and political control. It is this paradoxical union of the local and the universal by which we have to understand the strange facts of religious history and dominance.

The strain between the local and the universal is relieved by the fact that the worshiper is usually unaware of the local quality of his religion. The Arab does not think of his religion as Arabian; it is his way of dealing with Allah, who, in his view, is the God of all men: so far from being felt as local, it is his way of escaping from localism. But he has something specific to do about his faith; he must make his prayers, and in doing so, orient his prayer-rug toward Mecca. He may well be wholly unconscious that in tethering his religion to a particular point in space, he has thereby separated himself from— let us say, a Japanese for whom a certain brass plate in a temple near Nara marks the spot where Amaterasu Omikami began the creation of the world. It is not the Arab but the outsider who finds that this Arab's religion has an "Oriental" flavor, or if he the outsider is a connoisseur, an Arab flavor, racy with the grandeur and masculinity of the imagination of the great peninsula.

And let us notice, too, that whatever the strain may be between the local and the universal, it does not amount to a contradiction. No religion is more local than Hinduism: it is steeped in the atmosphere of the land whose name it insists on keeping: it is a vast tree with a thousand branches and a thousand roots, almost oppressive to the European-American taste by the exuberance of its imagery and the fruitiness of its sense of life. Yet it is just Hinduism which distills itself into the most ethereal of all essences: its Brahman, the absolute being, is devoid of all describable attributes, has no temples, is not worshiped, stands one might say for a sort of dark North Pole in the night sky of the mind. It is as if Hinduism, as it strove to give an exact account of its faith, derived from its soil enough energy to reject every trace of the soil, every trace of the earth itself and of human life, everything that could serve as an identifying mark, and in the guise of Vedanta spread everywhere like a religious ether, pervasive and nonresistant.

This case of Hinduism suggests what happens to a religion as it becomes thoughtful. It becomes aware that its *truth* has no national boundaries, and on that ground, it begins to travel.

It is likely to be handicapped in this undertaking by the fact that a religion does not consist of truth alone; if it did, the problem of a world faith might be much easier. A religion is always a truth (embodied in a creed), a ritual, and a code. The moral code is likely, in early stages, to embody much of the common law of the community and therefore to be so characteristic as not to be applicable to other groups: the Hindu sacred law (*The Book of Manu*) could not be practiced in China. And as for the ritual, these symbolic observances belong so much to the special histories and feelings of the groups in which they arise that they are with difficulty so much as understood by others. Primitive peoples hide their rituals, not because they are ashamed of them, but because they do not wish to expose what is so closely bound up with their own feelings to an unsympathetic eye: early ritual is inherently private to its group—which is one reason of course for the exceptional curiosity it awakens in anthropologists and others. It is for this reason that a great Hindu like Gandhi, whose creed is in many respects coincident with Christianity, has no inclination to identify himself with Christianity. When he says that God has set his lot in India and that he must remain Hindu, he means not that his beliefs are different but that his religion is inseparable from the code, the ritual, and the sacred literature of his people (including their development and reform), and cannot lightly migrate with the universal scope of their thought. The name Rama is to him the most friendly and homely name of God.

Now Gandhi is certainly right about the localism of the whole concrete working of a religion: it has to have roots in the place it lives in. But if this were the last word, we Americans neither ought to be nor could be using Asiatic religions. God knows what religion we would have—possibly Druidism, if we have a Celtic rill in our veins! For a migratory people, localism presents difficulties, and certainly cannot be the determining factor. But there is a state at which *religion itself becomes migratory*; and this stage was reached in India itself For Buddhism is an Indian product, and Buddhism is inherently a traveling religion. By its own view of its teachings it was incapable of staying at home; and its wandering saved its life, for after a time it died out in India, and lived only in its newer homes—Burma, Ceylon, Siam, Afghanistan, Tibet, China, Japan. Christianity likewise almost abandoned Palestine, spreading to the north and west. Islam, the third among the great traveling religions, has still its central hearth in Arabia and Palestine, but its great mass of adherents lie across southern Asia and northern Africa. What is the peculiar point of view of the traveling religions?

In my judgment it is a matter of religious maturity. It is a phase which was bound to come with full religious self-consciousness, favored by a long history of civilization. (We may leave Islam aside for the moment, since Mohammed was largely influenced by Judaism and Christianity as he met them in Arabia, the other "religions of the Book," as he called them.) The simple reason why we are all using Asiatic religions is that Asia, having a longer consecutive religious history, and producing the men of genius who were able to read the meaning of this history, reached this stage first. What they did was so well conceived that there is no more reason for rejecting it—in the interest of a specious originality—than there would be for rejecting the alphabet or the multiplication table as "Oriental" because these too were first elaborated in Asia. Every part of the world has its indigenous religion; but only in Asia did the local cult have time to come to full flower and send its seeds, detached from the mother plant, to the four winds.

The local religions of Europe have not traveled, because they were not ready to travel when the era of traveling was on. The Germanic and Scandinavian cults had not been ripened by that wide political experience which plays its part in tempering and saddening the human spirit. Not only were they unchastened and unremorseful with respect to their own inherent powers of right living, they had not encountered that experience of political disillusionment which could make a mental distinction between "the world" and "the spirit," or between "the realm of appearance" and "the realm of true being." In brief, the problem of evil, as an accompaniment of high political civilization, could not so much as be formulated by these European cults: they were exuberant, thoughtless, and aggressive; like the Wends of whom Carlyle wrote, their peoples had to be "damped down into Christianity." And if something was extinguished in them—as no doubt it was—they endured the chastening because there was opened to them, at the same moment, a whole new dimension of moral experience which they were able to recognize—not as Asiatic—but as their own. The West-bound religion of Asia engulfed them only because it showed them their own destiny in the concrete. Those who wish to decry Christianity in Europe call it an "Oriental religion." Those in Asia who wish to decry the Christianity which Europe and America have at times tried to bring back to it have sometimes called it a "Western religion." Very likely it is both, in various details; since a much-traveled religion, like a much-traveled man, will bear traces of all the regions in which he has been at home. But in its original out-push it was neither; it intended to be simply "the way" for men everywhere; its founder never heard the word "Christian"; he considered himself a Jew, calling for a reform or a reconception of the Jewish faith such as would shake off its local restrictions. Five hundred years earlier a young Indian, Siddhartha, whom we now call "The Buddha" or "The Enlightened One," had undertaken a similar liberation of the local religion of his people. He offered his "way" (under the name of the Noble or Aryan Eightfold Path) not to Indians but to mankind. He never heard the word Buddhism. These religions traveled because they had to: having reached self-consciousness about what a religion has to do, a local boundary became a self-contradiction.

They did not as a rule spread automatically, as science has done, throughout human history, but by propaganda. Of each it is said that the founder "sent forth" disciples to preach the message—a new function in the life of religion. The words attributed to Buddha are these:

> Go, ye Bhikkus, for the weal of many, for the enlightenment of gods and of men; go not two together; let your abode be the shade of trees, your food what is given you . . .

Whether words like these were actually uttered is less important than the fact that they expressed what the original groups of believers thought of their duties and acted on. These religions had reached the traveling-point, as water reaches the boiling-point. I suggest that we now test this theory by examining some of the significant circumstances attending the origins of the great traveling faiths.

## II

First note the circumstances that these religions (again excepting Islam) arose within a limited period of world history—let us say between the eighth century B.C. and our era. The eighth century we may take as the period of the great Hebrew prophets, who, considering Jehovah as god of the whole earth, laid the foundations for present-day Judaism. About this time, India's forests were yielding an esoteric wisdom, Aranyakas and Upanishads, drawing from the robust polytheism of the Vedas a strict and abstract monism, the basis of the Vedanta. Here, in the sixth and fifth centuries B.C. Buddha appeared (562-482 perhaps). And almost precisely contemporary with him, Confucius in China (550-478); while Lao Tze, founder of Taoism, whose date is uncertain, may have been an older contemporary of both. About the same time, various so-called mystery religions in the Near East and in Greece, symptomatic of the religious unrest of the era, developed traveling propensities. Socrates and Plato (fourth and third centuries B.C.) were not unrelated to the religious concerns of the time. In Palestine, the hill country of Judaea and Galilee offered retreats for reflective spirits, aside from the main travel routes yet not far from them; its rabbis were called philosophers by the Greeks. Alexander paid it little heed, though his teacher, Aristotle, was said to have conversed with one of these wise men from the hills. But when Rome absorbed the small land the stage was set whereby a local disturbance, started by a dreamer from Galilee, could become a world movement.

The greater traveling religions are all products of religious revolt or reform; all of them shake off as unessential some of the local characters of the traditional religion of their several regions; all of them emphasize the universal aspect of religion. All of them make religion an individual matter, and an inward matter, more concerned with motives than with visible conduct. As revolts, they had to be the work of outstanding personalities. And partly on this account they have all come to be identified by the names or titles of their founders; they are "founded" religions, in contrast to the great local background of religious tradition whose authorship (generally speaking) is as little known as the authorship of the several languages. To identify a religion as "the religion of the Buddha" or "the religion of the Christ" or "the religion of the Prophet" does indeed introduce a new localism, a note of partisanship which promises much future trouble in the way of the world faith; but it does, at least, set the religion in question free from the older localism of habitat or race or people.

Was this striking set of similarities among the traveling religions a coincidence, or was there something like a world situation to which these several movements were responses? One suspects that the latter is the case, because no matter how great the genius of a prophet, he can start no historic movement unless the minds of men are asking the questions to which he offers the answers.

Perhaps the world situation was this—that men began to be aware that there *is* a "world." It was a period in which contact, commerce, and conquest within the area of Asia, Egypt, and Greece were destroying cultural isolation without destroying cultures. The "world" began to be thought of as a cultural pluralism, in which it was no longer possible for each one, having grown strong in solitude, to think of itself as the hearth of mankind, the rest being in peripheral twilight as "barbarian" or "gentile." What was taking place was the Copernican revolution of the cultural universe; the center could no longer be securely located at home! When Rome came, it merely finished what had been going on: to all but Rome itself, the political disasters implied by the Roman conquests toppled the easy mental supremacies of all local deities. Local religion had begun to be under suspicion.

More than this: individual men were forced to realize that they could not find complete human satisfaction any longer in their careers as citizens of their own communities. Standing, in the social world, was full of accident and injustice; the problem of happiness or of "salvation" could not be solved within the human social or political order. Religion, which had hitherto gone along with group life, inspiring its codes and sanctioning its loyalties, begins to pull apart from politics and address itself to the individual soul. The other world becomes important, and immortality a desired prospect, if there is any way to secure it. The career of the soul becomes the dominant theme of the religious "way."

This disaffection from the actual world and its natural ambitions does not need to go to the extent of despair, or what Gilbert Murray calls "loss of nerve," in order to present religion with its primary problem, that of the meaning of life. The distinction between the present world and another world is itself a source of profound unhappiness. How can a man wean away his desires and interests from the world in which he must act? He does not do so unless he is compelled to, not merely by circumstances, but by his thinking which convinces him that the separation *has to be made*, alike whether he is personally fortunate or unfortunate: the world of human experience is simply not capable of satisfying the demands of the human soul. Things at their best are finite and man is infinite; this is the root of the "problem of evil" which religion now faces in its full scope.

The great traveling religions are, accordingly, religions of "salvation." Each gives its own analysis of the human dilemma; each offers its own recipe for cure; each gives its teaching as to what men ought to hope for, here and hereafter. These answers are diverse, and this constitutes a part of the problem of the world faith of the future. We shall speak of these differences. For the moment we have been concerned simply to see why religion, arriving at a certain maturity in Asia, naturally came to Europe and America from that source.

At the same time, we can understand why certain other religious movements of the same period did not have the same tendency to universal spread. The Confucian world view had its religious elements; but Confucius was a reformer in this field only in the sense that, leaning against the superstition of his time, he selected and simplified its working elements, and confronted the rest with a prudent pragmatism. For him the working element of religion was a belief in Heaven (Tien) as an appointer of human destiny; every man had his task, and was bound to qualify himself to fulfil it. For the ordinary conduct of life, Confucius' genius was that of clarifying usage, with great loyalty to tradition, and much sensitiveness of conscience. He has given us one of the great religious sayings of all time: "He who offends the gods has no one to whom he can pray"—the self-created moral solitude of the man who holds himself able to defy duty. There was sufficient universality in the Confucian outlook to permit its spread to Korea and Japan; but China was, in the period we have described, still somewhat apart from the main current of Asiatic thought. Confucius reminds us in many ways of Socrates, in his concern for definitions of ethical ideas, and his indisposition to speculate. But through Socrates and Plato, the career of Greek religious thought took a directly opposite turn, emptying itself almost wholly into philosophy. Now philosophy, like mathematics, is universal by its nature, and neither requires nor can use the methods of preaching and propaganda. Socrates remained the inspiration of various schools of classical thought, especially of the Stoics; but he founded no community, and his thought entered namelessly into the body of Platonism, and thus of Western theology.

Judaism toward the beginning of our era was led into the way of spreading by propaganda. Its own dispersed situation, partly compelled and partly chosen, favored this type of activity. But the impulse subsided in favor of another method of advance. The true religion must indeed become the religion of all men; but this may occur either by transmission or by a gathering in. For Judaism the sense of the community on a family pattern was so strong as to decide the issue for the second type. Judaism was not to be given broadcast to the world, but the world was to be absorbed, so far as it could become worthy, within the Jewish community. The appropriate ceremony of acceptance, involving circumcision, resembled a ceremony of adoption. Judaism may thus be included among the traveling religions; but its mode of travel being corporate, its spread is at present limited to the multiplication of the community under its Law.

### III

I said that the answers given by the great religions to the problem of man's suffering and moral misery in the best of civilizations were diverse. It will be sufficient to illustrate this point if we contrast the answers given by Buddhism and Christianity.

To Buddha, the outstanding defect of human life is suffering, to Christ it is moral aimlessness. Buddhism accordingly undertakes to save men from suffering; Christianity to save them from "lostness." Buddha finds the escape from suffering in cutting the root of desire. His "Noble Fourfold Truth" runs in substance as follows:

Life in all its aspects is suffering;

The cause of suffering is the root of all desire, which is the craving for individual existence and that separateness from others implied by individual life.

The cure of suffering must therefore be the extirpation of that root, the overcoming of the craving to be, as a separate entity.

The way to achieve this cure (the Noble Eightfold Path) is neither asceticism nor indulgence, but a middle path, in which a union of activity with periods of meditation works steadily to the disenchantment which is Enlightenment and Nirvana—eternal peace, a goal which may be attained while one yet lives.

Christ finds the cure for moral lostness in nothing short of a rebirth, in which the struggling affections of secular human nature are unified in a dominant affection, a love of God and neighbor which brings desire and ambition to heel without killing them off. For both Christ and Buddha, the important thing about any human being is not what he does but what he cares about; both have long anticipated the psychiatry of today by showing that "integration" or peace can only come about by a rulership of natural desire under a single principle which puts first things first. But Buddha could not say "Seek ye first the Kingdom of God and his righteousness," for to Buddha there was no God in the usual sense—there was only the inexorable law of Karma (which carried over an uncured desire into another spell of existence and hence of more suffering) and the equally infallible law, his own discovery, of the escape from Karma, and therefore from further "existence." By the terms of his problem, the hope held out to men might indeed be called an eternal life, but not an eternal "existence," rather an eternity of unseparateness, the overcoming of individuality, Nirvana, the end of striving. For Christ the hope held out to men was also eternal life, but in a positive sense of personal continuance and effect; it took the vague form of an invitation to membership in a "Kingdom of God," an inner cure of the affections and an outer cure of human history, a long work like the slow leavening of an inert lump—at any rate, something to do.

It is easy to draw up handsome oppositions between these two teachings, and say that Buddha's goal is negative, Christ's is positive; Buddha's attitude toward life is pessimistic, Christ's optimistic; Buddha solaces the bewildered individual by getting him to resign all individual claim on life-satisfaction, Christ by making him individually precious in the sight of God, and a cooperator in a divine work. But these differences do not stand in stark contrast as the two systems are more fully understood; since the life of Buddha and his disciples, like that of Jesus, was one of active endeavor for the good of men. And the later history of Buddhism qualified many of the tenets of the early preaching. It is to be noticed, further, that Buddha and Christ were not asking precisely the same question, and hence their answers cannot be directly compared. Christ was not concerned for the cure of suffering; he tried to get men to face the certainty of "tribulation" with joy. Buddha was not concerned with the category of sin; he was rather a psychologist who inquired how man might train himself out of his earth-bound impulsiveness through a sort of sublimation. Hence many of the observations of each might be accepted by the other, within their diverse frame. The valid comparison of Buddhism and Christianity, though there have been many attempts, has yet to be worked out. Especially must it be remembered that Buddhism, in the forms it assumed in China and Japan, taught that every man participates in the "Buddha nature," and that his chief task is to realize that devotion to his kind, that superiority to selfishness, that power which comes from inner control, which were characteristic of the great sage. In this respect, Buddhism has dignified the conception of the human individual for Asia, as Christianity has done in the West.

But when all is said, the world views are surely not identical. The one is personal, the other impersonal; the one lives in a universe whose reality is moral will, the other in a universe whose reality is moral law; the one is aggressive, the other pacific—except, we must add, in Japan, where Buddhism long ago, in two of its sects, acquired a militant flavor. The ultimate world faith, therefore, will have to be one in which these differences must be resolved.

We have, then, a group of religions each of which accepts the responsibility of spreading its way of life to all men. Arising in widely separated centers and moving in different directions, they have in some measure divided the world among themselves, no one of them being effectively universal. The problem of a world faith will raise the practical question of the relations of these religions to one another, and to the local religions which they meet in the course of their expansion.

Nowhere is there a religious vacuum into which the migrant can move. Buddhism encounters Confucianism and Taoism in China, Confucianism and Shinto in Japan. But it came rather as a supplement than as a contestant. Confucianism had no dogmas regarding the other world and the career of the soul after death which it cared to oppose to the new doctrine, rich with metaphysical analysis and imaginative tapestry, supported by vast tomes of esoteric wisdom, and bringing to the human scene a new sense of divine compassion and of moral appeal to the Buddha nature in each one. Buddhism in China released a great wealth of artistic genius, giving it new themes in architecture, painting, sculpture. But chiefly it dignified human life by making it, in its inner struggle with suffering and desire, the central theme of the meaning of the cosmic process. A Chinese could thus be a good Confucianist and a good Buddhist at the same time. There was of course a silent competition on the plane of subsistence; for an organization must have an economic basis: what is given to Taoist priests cannot be given to Buddhist monks. But on the religious plane, there was room for all.

Christianity has been as a rule more belligerent toward the local religions. Professing to supply all the religious needs of mankind, it has called for singleness of allegiance. Buddhism in China presented the paradox of a religion with no God and at the same time with many divine figures, Buddhas, Bodhisattvas, and saints. A multiform system can flexibly add to its number or find cross-identities, whereas a monotheism such as Christianity or Islam must set itself against the whole apparatus of polytheistic worship, especially the images of the gods. The march of Christianity has therefore been a demand for Either-Or decisions; the temples and idols of the "heathen" have had to fall. But here also the conflict has not extended to the ground-level of the local structure. The tenacity of folk-custom and festival has led to many local amalgamations, and the sagacity especially of the Catholic missionaries has seen possibilities of conserving rather than destroying many a local observance within the body of the new faith. Hence the Christianities of the German forests, the Druid countries, the Mexican mountains, the old Spanish Southwest, are markedly different in temper: they are variations on a common theme.

In principle, since religion must be both local and universal, there should always be the possibility of uniting the mature, self-conscious superstructure of the traveling religion with elements of code and rite which belong to local feeling and history. But the problem is in each case a special one, since codes and rites are not separable from creeds; and the union, whatever it may be, must be natural and coherent, not an eclectic patchwork.

But the major problem of world faith arises when the great traveling religions encounter one another.

It belongs to the accidents of history that Buddhism and Christianity are themselves the result of a slow selection among various movements of similar nature—Buddhism and Jainism rising together in India; Christianity, Orphism, Mithraism, and other cults finding themselves together in the Empire. But these survivors, spreading in opposite directions, did not encounter one another, so far as we know, for several centuries; and then understood so little of one another that a romanticized Buddha, under the name of Josaphat, an Indian prince who in the tale was converted by the monk Barlaam, was innocently canonized by the Christian Church, both Byzantine and Roman (though later dropped by the Roman church)! In point of fact, their teachings are very unlike, and Buddha (who died about 480 B.C.) had he met the monk Barlaam, would have been from the monk's point of view sadly in need of conversion, and vice versa.

It belongs also to the accidents of history that Buddhism in its eastward progress encountered no other traveling faith. Its extension was pacific. Pandit Das Gupta's statement, at the opening of the new Buddhist temple at Sarnath, to the effect that Buddhism had never used force, nor inspired the use of force in its behalf, is well justified. He drew a damaging contrast between this history and that of Christianity. The early expansion of Islam brought it into Christian territory, in the Near East—Damascus, Jerusalem, Constantinople, the Balkans, Egypt, North Africa, Spain. Islam had its own methods of tolerating the presence of Christians in its precincts, as witness the division of the great church of Saint John at Damascus into two parts, the Christians using one half, while the other was used as a mosque! But the issue of ownership of the "sphere of influence" between these two religions was determined by the sword; and the political element in the establishment of Christianity in Europe and the Near East is one of the least creditable chapters of religious history. It has to be remembered, however, that from the fourth century onward Christianity had become identified with the maintenance of public law in Europe, tiding over a period in which secular authority was in confusion, and that it had created a "Christian" Europe largely through its power over the sources of legislation and teaching. Likewise for Islam, though to an even higher degree, the religion was at the same time a code of law and a government. For neither religion, during the centuries of Islamic growth, was it possible to separate church and state. With this consolidation of authority, a given territory had to be either Moslem or Christian; and the matter could not be settled by either prayer or philosophy.

We have now reached a point in the evolution of both politics and religion at which a degree of mutual independence is seen to be necessary to the health of both. Religion must influence law, if it is of any value at all. And government must have its religious presuppositions. But when they are united as organizations, religion is corrupted by patronage, the "extension of the faith"

becomes an undercover pretext for the extension of empire, politics loses the
correction of an independent moral judgment, and the relations between
nations lose the tempering influence of a religion which is beyond every state,
because it is effectively universal. We have not yet realized this ideal of mu-
tuality and detachment between church and state; but we are sufficiently
advanced toward it, so that the relations between the great faiths will henceforth be determined more by persuasion, on the ground of intrinsic merit, than
by the political complexion of the world—assuming that the world of tomorrow will allow the free intercourse of faiths, and the free play of thought in
regard to them.

Meanwhile, we have three or four promising aspirants for the position of
world religion. It is hardly correct to call them competitors, for the impulse to
spread is not a matter either of self-interest or of pride—though these motives
creep into every man-staffed large-scale enterprise—but of duty in the meeting
of human need. And since it is the consumer and not the promoter who, in the
end, determines whether the need is met, whatever rivalry there is should be of
the most frank and generous character, like the rivalry of physicians in the
cure of disease. The presence of these many aspirants is itself an anomaly; if
the plurality were acquiesced in, that would be equivalent to saying that there
is no world religion at all, and is to be none such, but only a group of differing
faiths having no way to settle their differences, since each appeals not to
reason nor to experience but to the undebatable and uncompromisable finalities
of revelation.

On the other hand, the magnitude of the field of dominance of each of the
great religions is so great that we must accord to each of them a large measure
of success in satisfying the religious craving of men; no other factor could
have maintained them over so long a period. We cannot, then, be dealing with
three falsehoods and one verity—one revealed and necessary way, and three
works of the devil—with the fateful problem in hand of recognizing the true
light; what we have is a variety of versions of truth, struggling through media
of human expression, vagary, conceit, superstition—with the problem in hand
of recognizing and releasing the essence of the matter, and with the large
probability that each of the group will have its own unique contribution to
that essence.

IV

There are now two questions before us. What are the elements of agreement
among these several aspirants? What are the outstanding differences, and
what processes are at work to resolve them?

A certain amount of agreement seems implied in the common circumstances
of origin of the traveling faiths. All religion accepts the reality of an invisible
order of being which in some way both commands and satisfies the root-aware-
ness of life. It implies belief in the extra-natural, which usually takes shape
as a belief in divine personal beings. All the mature religions recognize in the

human individual a "soul," that is to say, a phase of the self deeper than the current phase of conversation and the day's work, reflecting on and guiding the current excursions in view of the total picture of destiny: the soul is the self in its dealings with the whole, and therefore with the extra-natural world as well as the natural. All the traveling religions see and teach that the soul is in peril, life being an opportunity which may be missed. They teach that the obvious world attracts and blinds the vision so that spiritual things become obscure, and life runs to frustration. They all offer cure, and guidance to what we may call the cosmic success. All of them propose a code of life, which is in part a condition of the cure; and all of them, whatever their other precepts, include in the code a requirement of good will toward the fellow man, and a degree of detachment from the pressures of physical desire and greed and social ambition.

To the extent of this agreement, we may say that a world faith already exists. This does not imply that all the world assents to the items in which all the religions agree. The advance of science and of positivistic logic has carried with it a wide swath of negation of the first assertion of all religion, the invisible order as a moral order. To this wholly secular and this-worldly temper, all religion is "Oriental" in the sense that it assigns reality to something not "verifiable" by physical observation. This secularism now pervades the Orient, and in order to burn off that religious excess we call superstition proposes to burn off religion itself; it aims to reclaim for pressing mundane business the energy drafted off into the fruitless catalepsies of the mystic. If there is soundness in religion it will accept the ordeal, learn its lessons, and hold to what it perceives, seeing that science itself is an extra-natural structure of the soul, responding partially to a demand of the cosmos for truth. The truth about tangible things is not itself a tangible thing; nor is the truth about perishable things itself perishable. To Gandhi, Truth and God are interchangeable terms, and the scientist has but to become more fully self-conscious to see that he also is a worshiper. We need not therefore make secularism an exception to our statement that a world faith already exists.

All the great religions further agree that the soul has a career not limited to the physical life of man; they have their pictures of continuance or of supplementation. The notion of immortality, once vivid and near, burns dim today; but the concern it stands for, as a part of the problem of the meaning of life, is even more insistent as our noble social orders reveal their insecurity. They agree also on another matter, and one which becomes the kernel of disagreement: all give a unique religious position to their founders. The names of Buddha, Jesus Christ, Mohammed, become the party-signs of religious cleavage, and present the most refractory obstacles to mutual understanding. They incorporate in themselves the contemporary problem of world faith in its sharpest form. To many minds, this represents the crowning perversity of the ecclesiastical nostrumizing of religion, and provokes a disposition to reach a common faith, as Professor Dewey does, by discarding once for all the entire specialized apparatus of the religious organizations. My belief is, however, that there is a reason for the apparent perversity, and that we shall move ahead toward religious understanding far faster if we inquire why it is that the great faiths all take this turn.

We may profitably remember that there have been repeated attempts in history to bring men together on the basis of what they already agree upon, discarding their points of difference, as though differences were less important than agreements, only to discover once more that likenesses are abstractions, and are never enough by themselves to constitute a living organism. Why, then, do the traveling religions give a special divine status to their founders?

## v

We may approach the answer to our question by asking another. Why do men make holidays of the anniversaries of the advent of an idea? If an idea is true and valuable, it has no mark of time and place about it: it belongs by its nature to all minds who can apprehend it. The announcers of important ideas may not wish to be remembered in connection with the ideas—and most of them have not been—yet science itself strangely rebels against the impersonality of its product, attaches Napier's name to a set of logarithms, Newton's to certain laws of motion, and a motley array of personal roots to the names of various species of plants and animals. This impulse signalizes the fact that however timeless an idea may be, it is only "realized" when it is born in a time-occupied mind. And in proportion to the scope of the idea will men make holidays of such dates of birth. The "Noble Fourfold Truth" would on this score always be Buddha's doctrine. The "Ideas" of Plato have ceased to be merely platonic beings, since they are forever Platonic. Time makes a time-festival of its capture of the eternal. That is the beginning.

Buddh Gaya, the reputed scene of Buddha's Enlightenment, has long been a holy place for Buddhist visitors. As late as 1931 a temple was opened at Sarnath, near Benares, at the site of the ancient Deer Park where the story places the scene of Buddha's First Sermon. Buddha himself taught the doctrine of non-permanence, non-God-substance, non-soul-substance, and the timeless peace of Nirvana as his own portion; contrary to the spirit of his own thought, he has become an object of personal devotion, in the course of the time-changes which his doctrine has suffered. The Buddha-principle is hardly separable from the Buddha-image. The Buddhist initiate professes, "I take refuge in the Buddha." In much the same way, with careful avoidance of any deification of Mohammed, Islam makes its confession of faith: "There is no God but Allah, and Mohammed is his Prophet." This is not intended to be mere grateful reminiscence; it could not on that ground alone enter into the creed.

We come nearer to the secret when we recall that the founders were not merely seers and thinkers but teachers, planting their ideas in living minds as the best way, perhaps the only way, of securing their continuance. They were concerned to make their ideas forces in history, and to this end their concern was "Have they understood? Will they transmit?" Intentionally or not, they begot communities, bound together by the destiny of the faith in a world of opposition. It was not irrelevant that the founders, as reformers—and in the religious sphere which is the most bitterly conservative of all spheres because the landmarks are so few—had to be fighters as well as dreamers. Such communities, which as Royce has well said, will be communities of memory and of hope, have also to be communities of struggle, burdened with the trust of the teaching: the nerving memory of the original founder-fighter was needed as the living spirit of the effort. He would be thought of as present with them; the career of his idea in history would be the continuance of his cosmic career. The full profession of the Buddhist monk is, "I take refuge in the Buddha; I take refuge in the Dharma (the Law); I take refuge in the Samgha (the brotherhood)." By a similar process to that by which corporations in modern law become legal persons, these communities took on quasi-personal life, promoted by but also promoting the lives of their members. In them, something of the divine nature of truth had not alone entered time, but had taken on an historic career. It belonged to the nature of the divine to act in this way in history; and this nature is identical in quality with the nature of the founder, freed by death from bodily limitations. To take refuge in him is equivalent to taking refuge in God-in-history. We now see why the founder's name, with various shadings of the superhuman attribute, enters into the creedal statements of the several faiths. It is because, consciously or not, they all agree on a farther point, that God must have a human and temporal aspect, and that the human scene is ennobled by his working presence there.

Neither Buddha nor Mohammed would have accepted the phrase I used above, "God in history." Not Buddha, for to him there was no Brahman, but only the divine law, saving men from suffering and the misery of endless rebirth. Not Mohammed, for to him the divine majesty is unreachable, ungraspable, unembodied in any finite form: Allah rules all things, inscrutably, but he "neither begets nor is begotten," and with that denial Islam feels a permanent gulf set between itself and the Christian doctrine of the Son of God. But the chief agency in working toward a world faith is to see beyond language to meanings, by the aid of a sympathetic interpretation, aided by psychology. In the sense I have mentioned, it is the idea of incarnation which has given each of the founders his salient place in the creed. It is this idea which Tagore's "Religion of Man" is calling for and which many a movement which regards itself as atheistic is unknowingly using.

As these implicit meanings become slowly emergent into the general consciousness of men, the abstract world faith already present becomes by so much more concrete, and the obstacles of creedal difference melt away, because the truth namelessly persuades. But it is important that differences should be worked through, not abandoned; for men must differ according to their insights in order that their union when it comes may hold *all* their truth.

❦ ❦ ❦

# The Nature of Reality

*Plato*

## The Allegory of the Cave[1]

NEXT, said I, here is a parable to illustrate the degrees in which our nature may be enlightened or unenlightened. Imagine the condition of men living in a sort of cavernous chamber underground, with an entrance open to the light and a long passage all down the cave.[2] Here they have been from childhood, chained by the leg and also by the neck, so that they cannot move and can see only what is in front of them, because the chains will not let them turn their heads. At some distance higher up is the light of a fire burning behind them; and between the prisoners and the fire is a track[3] with a parapet built along it, like the screen at a puppet-show, which hides the performers while they show their puppets over the top.

I see, said he.

Now behind this parapet imagine persons carrying along various artificial objects, including figures of men and animals in wood or stone or other materials, which project above the parapet. Naturally, some of these persons will be talking, others silent.[4]

It is a strange picture, he said, and a strange sort of prisoners.

Like ourselves, I replied; for in the first place prisoners so confined would have seen nothing of themselves or of one another, except the shadows thrown by the fire-light on the wall of the Cave facing them, would they?

Not if all their lives they had been prevented from moving their heads.

---

[1] From *The Republic*, translated by Francis MacDonald Cornford (Oxford: The Clarendon Press, 1941), pp. 227-231. Reprinted by permission of The Clarendon Press.

[2] The *length* of the "way in" (*eisodos*) to the chamber where the prisoners sit is an essential feature, explaining why no daylight reaches them.

[3] The track crosses the passage into the cave at right angles, and is *above* the parapet built along it.

[4] A modern Plato would compare his Cave to an underground cinema, where the audience watch the play of shadows thrown by the film passing before a light at their backs. The film itself is only an image of "real" things and events in the world outside the cinema. For the film Plato has to substitute the clumsier apparatus of a procession of artificial objects carried on their heads by persons who are merely part of the machinery, providing for the movement of the objects and the sounds whose echo the prisoners hear. The parapet prevents these persons' shadows from being cast on the wall of the Cave.

And they would have seen as little of the objects carried past.

Of course.

Now, if they could talk to one another, would they not suppose that their words referred only to those passing shadows which they saw? [5]

Necessarily.

And suppose their prison had an echo from the wall facing them? When one of the people crossing behind them spoke, they could only suppose that the sound came from the shadow passing before their eyes.

No doubt.

In every way, then, such prisoners would recognize as reality nothing but the shadows of those artificial objects.[6]

Inevitably.

Now consider what would happen if their release from the chains and the healing of their unwisdom should come about in this way. Suppose one of them set free and forced suddenly to stand up, turn his head, and walk with eyes lifted to the light; all these movements would be painful, and he would be too dazzled to make out the objects whose shadows he had been used to see. What do you think he would say, if someone told him that what he had formerly seen was meaningless illusion, but now, being somewhat nearer to reality and turned towards more real objects, he was getting a truer view? Suppose further that he were shown the various objects being carried by and were made to say, in reply to questions, what each of them was. Would he not be perplexed and believe the objects now shown him to be not so real as what he formerly saw?

Yes, not nearly so real.

And if he were forced to look at the fire-light itself, would not his eyes ache, so that he would try to escape and turn back to the things which he could see distinctly, convinced that they really were clearer than these other objects now being shown to him?

Yes.

And suppose someone were to drag him away forcibly up the steep and rugged ascent and not let him go until he had hauled him out into the sunlight, would he not suffer pain and vexation at such treatment, and, when he had come out into the light, find his eyes so full of its radiance that he could not see a single one of the things that he was now told were real?

Certainly he would not see them all at once.

He would need, then, to grow accustomed before he could see things in that upper world. At first it would be easiest to make out shadows, and then the images of men and things reflected in water, and later on the things themselves. After that, it would be easier to watch the heavenly bodies and the sky

[5] Adam's text and interpretation. The prisoners, having seen nothing but shadows, cannot think their words refer to the objects carried past behind their backs. For them shadows (images) are the only realities.

[6] The state of mind call *eikasia* in the previous chapter.

itself by night, looking at the light of the moon and stars rather than the Sun and the Sun's light in the day-time.

Yes, surely.

Last of all, he would be able to look at the Sun and contemplate its nature, not as it appears when reflected in water or any alien medium, but as it is in itself in its own domain.

No doubt.

And now he would begin to draw the conclusion that it is the Sun that produces the seasons and the course of the year and controls everything in the visible world, and moreover is in a way the cause of all that he and his companions used to see.

Clearly he would come at last to that conclusion.

Then if he called to mind his fellow prisoners and what passed for wisdom in his former dwelling-place, he would surely think himself happy in the change and be sorry for them. They may have had a practice of honouring and commending one another, with prizes for the man who had the keenest eye for the passing shadows and the best memory for the order in which they followed or accompanied one another, so that he could make a good guess as to which was going to come next.[7] Would our released prisoner be likely to covet those prizes or to envy the men exalted to honour and power in the Cave? Would he not feel like Homer's Achilles, that he would far sooner "be on earth as a hired servant in the house of a landless man"[8] or endure anything rather than go back to his old beliefs and live in the old way?

Yes, he would prefer any fate to such a life.

Now imagine what would happen if he went down again to take his former seat in the Cave. Coming suddenly out of the sunlight, his eyes would be filled with darkness. He might be required once more to deliver his opinion on those shadows, in competition with the prisoners who had never been released, while his eyesight was still dim and unsteady; and it might take some time to become used to the darkness. They would laugh at him and say that he had gone up only to come back with his sight ruined; it was worth no one's while even to attempt the ascent. If they could lay hands on the man who was trying to set them free and lead them up, they would kill him.[9]

Yes, they would.

Every feature in this parable, my dear Glaucon, is meant to fit our earlier analysis. The prison dwelling corresponds to the region revealed to us through the sense of sight, and the fire-light within it to the power of the Sun. The

[7] The empirical politician, with no philosophic insight, but only a "knack of remembering what usually happens" (*Gorg.* 501 A). He has *eikasia* = conjecture as to what is likely (*eikos*).

[8] This verse, being spoken by the ghost of Achilles, suggests that the Cave is comparable with Hades.

[9] An allusion to the fate of Socrates.

ascent to see the things in the upper world you may take as standing for the upward journey of the soul into the region of the intelligible; then you will be in possession of what I surmise, since that is what you wish to be told. Heaven knows whether it is true; but this, at any rate, is how it appears to me. In the world of knowledge, the last thing to be perceived and only with great difficulty is the essential Form of Goodness. Once it is perceived, the conclusion must follow that, for all things, this is the cause of whatever is right and good; in the visible world it gives birth to light and to the lord of light, while it is itself sovereign in the intelligible world and the parent of intelligence and truth. Without having had a vision of this Form no one can act with wisdom, either in his own life or in matters of state.

❧ ❧ ❧

*René Descartes*

# A Discourse on Method[1]

I was then in Germany, attracted thither by the wars in that country, which have not yet been brought to a termination; and as I was returning to the army from the coronation of the emperor, the setting in of winter arrested me in a locality where, as I found no society to interest me, and was besides fortunately undisturbed by any cares or passions, I remained the whole day in seclusion, with full opportunity to occupy my attention with my own thoughts. Of these one of the very first that occurred to me was, that there is seldom so much perfection in works composed of many separate parts, upon which different hands had been employed, as in those completed by a single master. Thus it is observable that the buildings which a single architect has planned and executed, are generally more elegant and commodious than those which several have attempted to improve, by making old walls serve for purposes for which they were not originally built. Thus also, those ancient cities which, from being at first only villages, have become, in course of time, large towns, are usually but ill laid out compared with the regularly constructed towns which a professional architect has freely planned on an open plain; so that although the several buildings of the former may often equal or surpass in beauty those of the latter, yet when one observes their indiscriminate juxtaposition, there a large one and here a small, and the consequent crookedness and irregularity of the streets, one is disposed to allege that chance rather than any human will guided by reason must have led to such an arrangement. And if we consider that nevertheless there have been at all times certain officers whose duty it was to see that private buildings contributed to public ornament, the difficulty of

[1] From *A Discourse on Method* (1637), by René Descartes, in *The Method, Meditations, and Philosophy of Descartes*, translated by John Veitch (New York: Tudor Publishing Co., n.d.), pp. 155-172, omitting Ch. 3.

reaching high perfection with but the materials of others to operate on, will be readily acknowledged. In the same way I fancied that those nations which, starting from a semibarbarous state and advancing to civilization by slow degrees, have had their laws successively determined, and, as it were, forced upon them simply by experience of the hurtfulness of particular crimes and disputes, would by this process come to be possessed of less perfect institutions than those which, from the commencement of their association as communities, have followed the appointment of some wise legislator. It is thus quite certain that the constitution of the true religion, the ordinances of which are derived from God, must be incomparably superior to that of every other. And, to speak of human affairs, I believe that the past pre-eminence of Sparta was due not to the goodness of each of its laws in particular, for many of these were very strange, and even opposed to good morals, but to the circumstance that, originated by a single individual, they all tended to a single end. In the same way I thought that the sciences contained in books (such of them at least as are made up of probable reasonings, without demonstrations), composed as they are of the opinions of many different individuals massed together, are farther removed from truth than the simple inferences which a man of good sense using his natural and unprejudiced judgment draws respecting the matters of his experience. And because we have all to pass through a state of infancy to manhood, and have been of necessity, for a length of time, governed by our desires and preceptors (whose dictates were frequently conflicting, while neither perhaps always counselled us for the best), I farther concluded that it is almost impossible that our judgments can be so correct or solid as they would have been, had our reason been mature from the moment of our birth, and had we always been guided by it alone.

It is true, however, that it is not customary to pull down all the houses of a town with the single design of rebuilding them differently, and thereby rendering the streets more handsome; but it often happens that a private individual takes down his own with the view of erecting it anew, and that people are even sometimes constrained to this when their houses are in danger of falling from age, or when the foundations are insecure. With this before me by way of example, I was persuaded that it would indeed be preposterous for a private individual to think of reforming a state by fundamentally changing it throughout, and overturning it in order to set it up amended; and the same I thought was true of any similar project for reforming the body of the sciences, or the order of teaching them established in the schools: but as for the opinions which up to that time I had embraced, I thought that I could not do better than resolve at once to sweep them wholly away, that I might afterwards be in a position to admit either others more correct, or even perhaps the same when they had undergone the scrutiny of reason. I firmly believed that in this way I should much better succeed in the conduct of my life, than if I built only upon old foundations, and leaned upon principles which, in my youth, I had taken upon trust. For although I recognized various difficulties in this undertaking, these were not, however, without remedy, nor once to be compared with such as attend the slightest reformation in public affairs. Large bodies, if once overthrown, are with great difficulty set up again, or even kept erect when once seriously shaken, and the fall of such is always disastrous. Then if there are any imperfections in the constitutions of states (and that many such exist the diversity of constitutions is alone sufficient to assure us), custom has without doubt materially smoothed their inconveniences, and has even managed to steer altogether clear of, or insensibly corrected a number which sagacity could not have provided against with equal effect; and, in fine, the defects are almost more tolerable than the change necessary for their removal; in the same manner that highways which wind among mountains, by being much frequented, become gradually so smooth and commodious, that it is much better to follow them than to seek a straighter path by climbing over the tops of rocks and descending to the bottoms of precipices.

Hence it is that I cannot in any degree approve of those restless and busy meddlers who, called neither by birth nor fortune to take part in the management of public affairs, are yet always projecting reforms; and if I thought that this tract contained aught which might justify the suspicion that I was a victim of such folly, I would by no means permit its publication. I have never contemplated anything higher than the reformation of my own opinions, and basing them on a foundation wholly my own. And although my own satisfaction with my work has led me to present here a draft of it, I do not by any means therefore recommend to everyone else to make a similar attempt. Those whom God has endowed with a larger measure of genius will entertain, perhaps, designs still more exalted; but for the many I am much afraid lest even the present undertaking be more than they can safely venture to imitate. The single design to strip one's self of all past beliefs is one that ought not to be taken by every one. The majority of men is composed of two classes, for neither of which would this be at all a befitting resolution: in the first place, of those who with more than a due confidence in their own powers, are precipitate in their judgments and want the patience requisite for orderly and circumspect thinking; whence it happens, that if men of this class once take the liberty to doubt of their accustomed opinions, and quit the beaten highway, they will never be able to thread the byway that would lead them by a shorter course, and will lose themselves and continue to wander for life; in the second place, of those who, possessed of sufficient sense or modesty to determine that there are others who excel them in the power of discriminating between truth and error, and by whom they may be instructed, ought rather to content themselves with the opinions of such than trust for more correct to their own reason.

For my own part, I should doubtless have belonged to the latter class, had I received instruction from but one master, or had I never known the diversities of opinion that from time immemorial have prevailed among men of the greatest learning. But I had become aware, even so early as during my college life, that no opinion, however absurd and incredible, can be imagined, which has not been maintained by some one of the philosophers; and afterwards in the course of my travels I remarked that all those whose opinions are decidedly repugnant to ours are not on that account barbarians and savages, but on the contrary that many of these nations make an equally good, if not a better, use of their reason than we do. I took into account also the very different character which a person brought up from infancy in France or Germany exhibits, from that which, with the same mind originally, this individual would have possessed had he lived always among the Chinese or with savages, and the circumstance that in dress itself the fashion which pleased us ten years ago, and which may again, perhaps, be received into favour before ten years have gone, appears to us at this moment extravagant and ridiculous. I was thus led to infer that the ground of our opinions is far more custom and example than any certain knowledge. And, finally, although such be the ground of our opinions, I remarked that a plurality of suffrages is no guarantee of truth where it is at all of difficult discovery, as in such cases it is much more likely that it will be found by one than by many. I could, however, select from the crowd no one whose opinions seemed worthy of preference, and thus I found myself constrained, as it were, to use my own reason in the conduct of my life.

But like one walking alone and in the dark, I resolved to proceed so slowly and with such circumspection, that if I did not advance far, I would at least guard against falling. I did not even choose to dismiss summarily any of the opinions that had crept in my belief without having been introduced by reason, but first of all took sufficient time carefully to satisfy myself of the general nature of the task I was setting myself, and ascertain the true method by which to arrive at the knowledge of whatever lay within the compass of my powers.

Among the branches of philosophy, I had, at an earlier period, given some attention to logic, and among those of the mathematics to geometrical analysis and algebra,—three arts or sciences which ought, as I conceived, to contribute something to my design. But, on examination, I found that, as for logic, its syllogisms and the majority of its other precepts are of avail rather in the communication of what we already know, or even as the art of Tully, in speaking without judgment of things of which we are ignorant, than in the investigation of the unknown; and although this science contains indeed a number of correct and very excellent precepts, there are, nevertheless, so many others, and these either injurious or superfluous, mingled with the former, that it is almost quite as difficult to effect a severance of the true from the false as it is to extract a Diana or a Minerva from a rough block of marble. Then as to the analysis of the ancients and the algebra of the moderns, besides that they embrace only matters highly abstract, and, to appearance, of no use, the former is so exclusively restricted to the consideration of figures, that it can exercise the understanding only on condition of greatly fatiguing the imagination; and, in the latter, there is so complete a subjection to certain rules and formulas, that there results an art full of confusion and obscurity calculated to embarrass, instead of a science fitted to cultivate the mind. By these considerations I was induced to seek some other method which would comprise the advantages of the three and be exempt from their defects. And as a multitude of laws often only hampers justice, so that a state is best governed when, with few laws, these are rigidly administered; in like manner, instead of the great number of precepts of which logic is composed, I believed that the four following would prove perfectly sufficient for me, provided I took the firm and unwavering resolution never in a single instance to fail to observe them.

The first was never to accept anything for true which I did not clearly know to be such; that is to say, carefully to avoid precipitancy and prejudice, and to comprise nothing more in my judgment than was presented to my mind so clearly and distinctly as to exclude all ground of doubt.

The second, to divide each of the difficulties under examination into as many parts as possible, and as might be necessary for its adequate solution.

The third, to conduct my thoughts in such order that, by commencing with objects the simplest and easiest to know, I might ascend by little and little, and, as it were, step by step, to the knowledge of the more complex; assigning in thought a certain order even to those objects which in their own nature do not stand in a relation of antecedence and sequence.

And the last, in every case to make enumerations so complete, and reviews so general, that I might be assured that nothing was omitted.

The long chains of simple and easy reasonings by means of which geometers are accustomed to reach the conclusions of their most difficult demonstrations, had led me to imagine that all things, to the knowledge of which man is competent, are mutually connected in the same way, and that there is nothing so far removed from us as to be beyond our reach, or so hidden that we cannot discover it, provided only we abstain from accepting the false for the true, and always preserve in our thoughts the order necessary for the deduction of one truth from another. And I had little difficulty in determining the objects with which it was necessary to commence, for I was already persuaded that it must be with the simplest and easiest to know, and, considering that of all those who have hitherto sought truth in the sciences, the mathematicians alone have been able to find any demonstrations, that is, any certain and evident reasons, I did not doubt but that such must have been the rule of their investigations. I resolved to commence, therefore, with the examination of the simplest objects, not anticipating, however, from this any other advantage than that to be found in accustoming my mind to the love and nourishment of truth, and to a distaste for all such reasonings as were unsound. But I had no intention on that account of attempting to master all the particular sciences commonly denominated mathematics: but observing that, however different their objects, they all agree in considering only the various relations or proportions subsisting among those objects, I thought it best for my purpose to consider these proportions in the most general form possible, without referring them to any objects in particular, except such as would most facilitate the knowledge of them, and without by any means restricting them to these, that afterwards I might thus be the better able to apply them to every other class of objects to which they are legitimately applicable. Perceiving further, that in order to understand these relations I should sometimes have to consider them one by one, and sometimes only to bear them in mind, or embrace them in the aggregate, I thought that, in order the better to consider them individually, I should view them as subsisting between straight lines, than which I could find no objects more simple, or capable of being more distinctly represented to my imagination and senses; and on the other hand, that in order to retain them in the memory, or embrace an aggregate of many, I should express them by certain characters the briefest possible. In this way I believed that I could borrow all that was best both in geometrical analysis and in algebra, and correct all the defects of the one by help of the other.

And in point of fact, the accurate observance of these few precepts gave me, I take the liberty of saying, such ease in unravelling all the questions embraced in these two sciences, that in the two or three months I devoted to their examination, not only did I reach solutions of questions I had formerly deemed exceedingly difficult, but even as regards questions of the solution of which I continued ignorant, I was enabled, as it appeared to me, to determine the means whereby, and the extent to which, a solution was possible; results attributable to the circumstance that I commenced with the simplest and most general truths, and that thus each truth discovered was a rule available in the discovery of subsequent ones. Nor in this perhaps shall I appear too vain, if it be considered that, as the truth on any particular points is one, whoever apprehends the truth, knows all that on that point can be known. The child, for example, who has been instructed in the elements of arithmetic, and has made a particular addition, according to rule, may be assured that he has found, with respect to the sum of the numbers before him, all that in this instance is within the reach of human genius. Now, in conclusion, the method which teaches adherence to the true order, and an exact enumeration of all the conditions of the thing sought includes all that gives certitude to the rules of arithmetic.

But the chief ground of my satisfaction with this method, was the assurance I had of thereby exercising my reason in all matters, if not with absolute perfection, at least with the greatest attainable by me: besides, I was conscious that by its use my mind was becoming gradually habituated to clearer and more distinct conceptions of its objects; and I hoped also, from not having restricted this method to any particular matter, to apply it to the difficulties of the other sciences, with not less success than to those of algebra. I should not, however, on this account have ventured at once on the examination of all the difficulties of the sciences which presented themselves to me, for this would have been contrary to the order prescribed in the method, but observing that the knowledge of such is dependent on principles borrowed from philosophy, in which I found nothing certain, I thought it necessary first of all to endeavour to establish its principles. And because I observed, besides, that an inquiry of this kind was of all others of the greatest moment, and one in which precipitancy and anticipation in judgment were most to be dreaded, I thought that I ought not to approach it till I had reached a more mature age (being at that time but twenty-three), and had first of all employed much of my time in preparation for the work, as well by eradicating from my mind all the erroneous opinions I had up to that moment accepted, as by amassing variety of experience to afford materials for my reasonings, and by continually exercising myself in my chosen method with a view to increased skill in its application. . . .

I am in doubt as to the propriety of making my first meditations, in the place above mentioned, matter of discourse; for these are so metaphysical, and so uncommon, as not, perhaps, to be acceptable to every one. And yet, that it may be determined whether the foundations that I have laid are sufficiently secure, I find myself in a measure constrained to advert to them. I had long before remarked that, in relation to practice, it is sometimes necessary to adopt, as if above doubt, opinions which we discern to be highly uncertain, as has been already said; but as I then desired to give my attention solely to the search after truth, I thought that a procedure exactly the opposite was called for, and that I ought to reject as absolutely false all opinions in regard to which I could suppose the least ground for doubt, in order to ascertain whether after that there remained aught in my belief that was wholly indubitable. Accordingly, seeing that our senses sometimes deceived us, I was willing to suppose that there existed nothing really such as they presented to us; and because some men err in reasoning, and fall into paralogisms, even on the simplest matters of geometry, I, convinced that I was as open to error as any other, rejected as false all the reasonings I had hitherto taken for demonstrations; and finally, when I considered that the very same thoughts (presentations) which we experience when awake may also be experienced when we are asleep, while there is at that time not one of them true, I supposed that all the objects (presentations) that had ever entered into my mind when awake, had in them no more truth than the illusions of my dreams. But immediately upon this I observed that, whilst I thus wished to think that all was false, it was absolutely necessary that I, who thus thought, should be somewhat; and as I observed that this truth, I THINK, HENCE I AM, was so certain and of such evidence, that no ground of doubt, however extravagant, could be alleged by the sceptics capable of shaking it, I concluded that I might, without scruple, accept it as the first principle of the philosophy of which I was in search.

In the next place, I attentively examined what I was, and as I observed that I could suppose that I had no body, and that there was no world nor any place in which I might be; but that I could not therefore suppose that I was not; and that, on the contrary, from the very circumstance that I thought to doubt of the truth of other things, it most clearly and certainly followed that I was; while, on the other hand, if I had only ceased to think, although all the other objects which I had ever imagined had been in reality existent, I would have had no reason to believe that I existed; I thence concluded that I was a substance whose whole essence or nature consists only in thinking, and which, that it may exist, has need of no place, nor is dependent on any material thing; so that "I," that is to say, the mind by which I am what I am, is wholly distinct from the body, and is even more easily known than the latter, and is such, that although the latter were not, it would still continue to be all that it is.

After this I inquired in general into what is essential to the truth and certainty of a proposition; for since I had discovered one which I knew to be true, I thought that I must likewise be able to discover the ground of this certitude. And as I observed that in the words *I think, hence I am,* there is nothing at all which gives me assurance of their truth beyond this, that I see very clearly that in order to think it is necessary to exist, I concluded that I might take, as a general rule, the principle, that all the things which we very clearly and distinctly conceive are true, only observing, however, that there is some difficulty in rightly determining the objects which we distinctly conceive.

❧ ❧ ❧

## John Locke

# An Essay Concerning Human Understanding[1]

1. Every man being conscious to himself that he thinks; and that which his mind is applied about whilst thinking being the *ideas* that are there, it is past doubt that men have in their minds several ideas,—such as are those expressed by the words *whiteness, hardness, sweetness, thinking, motion, man, elephant, army, drunkenness,* and others: it is in the first place then to be inquired, *How he comes by them?*

I know it is a received doctrine, that men have native ideas, and original characters, stamped upon their minds in their very first being. This opinion I have at large examined already; and, I suppose what I have said in the foregoing Book will be much more easily admitted, when I had shown whence the understanding may get all the ideas it has; and by what ways and degrees they may come into the mind;—for which I shall appeal to every one's own observation and experience.

2. Let us then suppose the mind to be, as we say, white paper, void of all characters, without any ideas:—How comes it to be furnished? Whence comes it by that vast store which the busy and boundless fancy of man has painted on it with an almost endless variety? Whence has it all the *materials* of reason and knowledge? To this I answer, in one word, from EXPERIENCE. In that all our knowledge is founded; and from that it ultimately derives itself. Our observation employed either about external sensible objects, or about the internal

[1] *An Essay Concerning Human Understanding* (1690), ed., Alexander Campbell Fraser (Oxford: The Clarendon Press, 1894), Book II, Ch. I.

operations of our minds perceived and reflected on by ourselves, is that which supplies our understandings with all the *materials* of thinking. These two are the fountains of knowledge, from whence all the ideas we have, or can naturally have, do spring.

3. First, our Senses, conversant about particular sensible objects, do convey into the mind several distinct perceptions of things, according to those various ways wherein those objects do affect them. And thus we come by those *ideas* we have of *yellow, white, heat, cold, soft, hard, bitter, sweet,* and all those which we call sensible qualities; which when I say the senses convey into the mind, I mean, they from external objects convey into the mind what produces there those perceptions. This great source of most of the ideas we have, depending wholly upon our senses, and derived by them to the understanding, I call SENSATION.

4. Secondly, the other fountain from which experience furnisheth the understanding with ideas is,—the perception of the operations of our own mind within us, as it is employed about the ideas it has got;—which operations, when the soul comes to reflect on and consider, do furnish the understanding with another set of ideas, which could not be had from things without. And such are *perception, thinking, doubting, believing, reasoning, knowing, willing,* and all the different actings of our own minds;—which we being conscious of, and observing in ourselves, do from these receive into our understandings as distinct ideas as we do from bodies affecting our senses. This source of ideas every man has wholly in himself; and though it be not sense, as having nothing to do with external objects, yet it is very like it, and might properly enough be called *internal sense.* But as I call the other Sensation, so I call this REFLECTION, the ideas it affords being such only as the mind gets by reflecting on its own operations within itself. By reflection then, in the following part of this discourse, I would be understood to mean, that notice which the mind takes of its own operations, and the manner of them, by reason whereof there come to be ideas of these operations in the understanding. These two, I say, viz. external material things, as the objects of SENSATION, and the operations of our own minds within, as the objects of REFLECTION, are to me the only originals from whence all our ideas take their beginnings. The term *operations* here I use in a large sense, as comprehending not barely the actions of the mind about its ideas, but some sort of passions arising sometimes from them, such as is the satisfaction or uneasiness arising from any thought.

5. The understanding seems to me not to have the least glimmering of any ideas which it doth not receive from one of these two. *External objects* furnish the mind with the ideas of sensible qualities, which are all those different perceptions they produce in us; and *the mind* furnishes the understanding with ideas of its own operations.

These, when we have taken a full survey of them, and their several modes, [combinations, and relations,] we shall find to contain all our whole stock of ideas; and that we have nothing in our minds which did not come in one of these two ways. Let any one examine his own thoughts, and thoroughly search into his understanding; and then let him tell me, whether all the original ideas he has there, are any other than of the objects of his senses, or of the operations of his mind, considered as objects of his reflection. And how great a mass of knowledge soever he imagines to be lodged there, he will, upon taking a strict view, see that he has not any idea in his mind but what one of these two have imprinted;—though perhaps, with infinite variety compounded and enlarged by the understanding, as we shall see hereafter.

6. He that attentively considers the state of a child, at his first coming into the world, will have little reason to think him stored with plenty of ideas, that are to be the matter of his future knowledge. It is *by degrees* he comes to be furnished with them. And though the ideas of obvious and familiar qualities imprint themselves before the memory begins to keep a register of time and order, yet it is often so late before some unusual qualities come in the way, that there are few men that cannot recollect the beginning of their acquaintance with them. And if it were worth while, no doubt a child might be so ordered as to have but a very few, even of the ordinary ideas, till he were grown up to a man. But all that are born into the world, being surrounded with bodies that perpetually and diversely affect them, variety of ideas, whether care be taken of it or not, are imprinted on the minds of children. Light and colours are busy at hand everywhere, when the eye is but open; sounds and some tangible qualities fail not to solicit their proper senses, and force an entrance to the mind; —but yet, I think, it will be granted easily, that if a child were kept in a place where he never saw any other but black and white till he were a man, he would have no more ideas of scarlet or green, than he that from his childhood never tasted an oyster, or a pine-apple, has of those particular relishes.

7. Men then come to be furnished with fewer or more simple ideas from without, according as the objects they converse with afford greater or less variety; and from the operations of their minds within, according as they more or less reflect on them. For, though he that contemplates the operations of his mind, cannot but have plain and clear ideas of them; yet, unless he turn his thoughts that way, and considers them *attentively,* he will no more have clear and distinct ideas of all the operations of his mind, and all that may be observed therein, than he will have all the particular ideas of any landscape, or of the parts and motions of a clock, who will not turn his eyes to it, and with attention heed all the parts of it. The picture, or clock may be so placed, that they may come in his way every day; but yet he will have but a confused idea of all the parts they are made up of, till he applies himself with attention, to consider them each in particular.

8. And hence we see the reason why it is pretty late before most children get ideas of the operations of their own minds; and some have not any very clear or perfect ideas of the greatest part of them all their lives. Because, though they pass there continually, yet, like floating visions, they make not deep impressions enough to leave in their mind clear, distinct, lasting ideas, till the un-

derstanding turns inward upon itself, reflects on its own operations, and makes them the objects of its own contemplation. Children, when they come first into it, are surrounded with a world of new things, which, by a constant solicitation of their senses, draw the mind constantly to them; forward to take notice of new, and apt to be delighted with the variety of changing objects. Thus the first years are usually employed and diverted in looking abroad. Men's business in them is to acquaint themselves with what is to be found without; and so growing up in a constant attention to outward sensations, seldom make any considerable reflection on what passes within them, till they come to be of riper years; and some scarce ever at all.

❧ ❧ ❧

*William James*

# What Pragmatism Is[1]

SOME years ago, being with a camping party in the mountains, I returned from a solitary ramble to find every one engaged in a ferocious metaphysical dispute. The *corpus* of the dispute was a squirrel—a live squirrel supposed to be clinging to one side of a tree-trunk; while over against the tree's opposite side a human being was imagined to stand. This human witness tries to get sight of the squirrel by moving rapidly round the tree, but no matter how fast he goes, the squirrel moves as fast in the opposite direction, and always keeps the tree between himself and the man, so that never a glimpse of him is caught. The resultant metaphysical problem now is this: *Does the man go round the squirrel or not?* He goes round the tree, sure enough, and the squirrel is on the tree; but does he go round the squirrel? In the unlimited leisure of the wilderness, discussion had been worn threadbare. Every one had taken sides and was obstinate; and the numbers on both sides were even. Each side, when I appeared, therefore appealed to me to make it a majority. Mindful of the scholastic adage that whenever you meet a contradiction you must make a distinction, I immediately sought and found one, as follows: "Which party is right," I said, "depends on what you *practically mean* by 'going round' the squirrel. If you mean passing from the north of him to the east, then to the south, then to the west, and then to the north of him again, obviously the man does go round him, for he occupies these successive positions. But if on the contrary you mean being first in front of him, then on the right of him, then behind him, then on his left, and finally in front again, it is quite obvious that the man fails to go round him, for by compensating movements the squirrel makes, he keeps his belly turned towards the man all the time, and his back turned away. Make the

[1] From William James, *Pragmatism* (New York: Longmans, Green & Company, Inc., 1907, 1928), pp. 43-55. Reprinted by permission of Paul R. Reynolds & Son, 599 Fifth Avenue, New York 17, N.Y.

distinction, and there is no occasion for any further dispute. You are both right and both wrong, according as you conceive the verb 'to go round' in one practical fashion or the other."

Although one or two of the hotter disputants called my speech a shuffling evasion, saying they wanted no quibbling or scholastic hair-splitting, but meant just plain honest English "round," the majority seemed to think that the distinction had assuaged the dispute.

I tell this trivial anecdote because it is a peculiarly simple example of what I wish now to speak of as *the pragmatic method*. The pragmatic method is primarily a method of settling metaphysical disputes that otherwise might be interminable. Is the world one or many?—fated or free?—material or spiritual? —here are notions either of which may or may not hold good of the world; and disputes over such notions are unending. The pragmatic method in such cases is to try to interpret each notion by tracing its respective practical consequences. What difference would it practically make to any one if this notion rather than that notion were true? If no practical difference whatever can be traced, then the alternatives mean practically the same thing, and all dispute is idle. Whenever a dispute is serious, we ought to be able to show some practical difference that must follow from one side or the other's being right.

A glance at the history of the idea will show you still better what pragmatism means. The term is derived from the same Greek word πράγμα, meaning action, from which our words "practice" and "practical" come. It was first introduced into philosophy by Mr. Charles Peirce in 1878. In an article entitled "How to Make Our Ideas Clear," in the *Popular Science Monthly* for January of that year, Mr. Peirce, after pointing out that our beliefs are really rules for action, said that, to develop a thought's meaning, we need only determine what conduct it is fitted to produce: that conduct is for us its sole significance. And the tangible fact at the root of all our thought-distinctions, however subtle, is that there is no one of them so fine as to consist in anything but a possible difference of practice. To attain perfect clearness in our thoughts of an object, then, we need only consider what conceivable effects of a practical kind the object may involve—what sensations we are to expect from it, and what reactions we must prepare. Our conception of these effects whether immediate or remote, is then for us the whole of our conception of the object, so far as that conception has positive significance at all.

This is the principle of Peirce, the principle of pragmatism. It lay entirely unnoticed by any one for twenty years, until I, in an address before Professor Howison's philosophical union at the University of California, brought it forward again and made a special application of it to religion. By that date (1898) the times seemed ripe for its reception. The word "pragmatism" spread, and at present it fairly spots the pages of the philosophic journals. On all hands we find the "pragmatic movement" spoken of, sometimes with respect, sometimes with contumely, seldom with clear understanding. It is evident that the term applies itself conveniently to a number of tendencies that hitherto have lacked a collective name, and that it has "come to stay."

To take in the importance of Peirce's principle, one must get accustomed to applying it to concrete cases. I found a few years ago that Ostwald, the illustrious Leipzig chemist, had been making perfectly distinct use of the principle of pragmatism in his lectures on the philosophy of science, though he had not called it by that name.

"All realities influence our practice," he wrote me, "and that influence is their meaning for us. I am accustomed to put questions to my classes in this way: In what respects would the world be different if this alternative or that were true? If I can find nothing that would become different, then the alternative has no sense."

That is, the rival views mean practically the same thing, and meaning, other than practical, there is for us none. Ostwald in a published lecture gives this example of what he means. Chemists have long wrangled over the inner constitution of certain bodies called "tautomerous." Their properties seemed equally consistent with the notion that an instable hydrogen atom oscillates inside of them, or that they are instable mixtures of two bodies. Controversy raged, but never was decided. "It would never have begun," says Ostwald, "if the combatants had asked themselves what particular experimental fact could have been made different by one or the other view being correct. For it would then have appeared that no difference of fact could possibly ensue; and the quarrel was as unreal as if, theorising in primitive times about the raising of dough by yeast, one party should have invoked a 'brownie,' while another insisted on an 'elf' as the true cause of the phenomenon."

It is astonishing to see how many philosophical disputes collapse into insignificance the moment you subject them to this simple test of tracing a concrete consequence. There can *be* no difference anywhere that doesn't *make* a difference elsewhere—no difference in abstract truth that doesn't express itself in a difference in concrete fact and in conduct consequent upon that fact, imposed on somebody, somehow, somewhere, and somewhen. The whole function of philosophy ought to be to find out what definite difference it will make to you and me, at definite instants of our life, if this world-formula or that world-formula be the true one.

There is absolutely nothing new in the pragmatic method. Socrates was an adept at it. Aristotle used it methodically. Locke, Berkeley, and Hume made momentous contributions to truth by its means. Shadworth Hodgson keeps insisting that realities are only what they are "known as." But these forerunners of pragmatism used it in fragments: they were a prelude only. Not until in our time has it generalized itself, become conscious of a universal mission, pretended to a conquering destiny. I believe in that destiny, and I hope I may end by inspiring you with my belief.

Pragmatism represents a perfectly familiar attitude in philosophy, the empiricist attitude, but it represents it, as it seems to me, both in a more radical and in a less objectionable form than it has ever yet assumed. A pragmatist turns his back resolutely and once for all upon a lot of inveterate habits dear to professional philosophers. He turns away from abstraction and insufficiency, from verbal solutions, from bad *a priori* reasons, from fixed principles, closed systems, and pretended absolutes and origins. He turns towards concreteness and adequacy, towards facts, towards action and towards power. That means the empiricist temper regnant and the rationalist temper sincerely given up. It means the open air and possibilities of nature, as against dogma, artificiality, and the pretence of finality in truth.

At the same time it does not stand for any special results. It is a method only. But the general triumph of that method would mean an enormous change in what I called in my last lecture the "temperament" of philosophy. Teachers of the ultra-rationalistic type would be frozen out, much as the courtier type is frozen out in republics, as the ultra-montane type of priest is frozen out in protestant lands. Science and metaphysics would come much nearer together, would in fact work absolutely hand in hand.

Metaphysics has usually followed a very primitive kind of quest. You know how men have always hankered after unlawful magic, and you know what a great part in magic *words* have always played. If you have his name, or the formula of incantation that binds him, you can control the spirit, genie, afrite, or whatever the power may be. Solomon knew the names of all the spirits, and having their names, he held them subject to his will. So the universe has always appeared to the natural mind as a kind of enigma, of which the key must be sought in the shape of some illuminating or power-bringing word or name. That word names the universe's *principle*, and to possess it is after a fashion to possess the universe itself. "God," "Matter," "Reason," "the Absolute," "Energy," are so many solving names. You can rest when you have them. You are at the end of your metaphysical quest.

But if you follow the pragmatic method you cannot look on any such word as closing your quest. You must bring out of each word its practical cash-value, set it at work within the stream of your experience. It appears less as a solution, then, than as a programme for more work, and more particularly as an indication of the ways in which existing realities may be *changed*.

*Theories thus become instruments, not answers to enigmas, in which we can rest.* We don't lie back upon them, we move forward, and, on occasion, make nature over again by their aid. Pragmatism unstiffens all our theories, limbers them up and sets each one at work. Being nothing essentially new, it harmonizes with many ancient philosophic tendencies. It agrees with nominalism, for instance, in always appealing to particulars; with utilitarianism in emphasizing practical aspects; with positivism in its disdain for verbal solutions, useless questions, and metaphysical abstractions.

All these, you see, are *anti-intellectualist* tendencies. Against rationalism as a pretension and a method pragmatism is fully armed and militant. But, at the outset, at least, it stands for no particular results. It has no dogmas, and no doctrines save its method. As the young Italian pragmatist Papini has well said, it lies in the midst of our theories like a corridor in a hotel. Innumerable chambers open out of it. In one you may find a man writing an atheistic volume; in the next some one on his knees praying for faith and strength; in a third a chemist investigating a body's properties; in a fourth a system of idealistic metaphysics is being excogitated; in a fifth the impossibility of metaphysics is being shown. But they all own the corridor, and all must pass through it if they want a practicable way of getting into or out of their respective rooms.

No particular results then, so far, but only an attitude of orientation, is what the pragmatic method means. *The attitude of looking away from first things, principles, "categories," supposed necessities; and of looking towards last things, fruits, consequences, facts.*

So much for the pragmatic method! You may say that I have been praising it rather than explaining it to you, but I shall presently explain it abundantly enough by showing how it works on some familiar problems. Meanwhile the word pragmatism has come to be used in a still wider sense, as meaning also a certain *theory of truth.* I mean to give a whole lecture to the statement of that theory, after first paving the way, so I can be very brief now. But brevity is hard to follow, so I ask for your redoubled attention for a quarter of an hour. If much remains obscure, I hope to make it clearer in the later lectures.

One of the most successfully cultivated branches of philosophy in our time is what is called inductive logic, the study of the conditions under which our sciences have evolved. Writers on this subject have begun to show a singular unanimity as to what the laws of nature and elements of fact mean when formulated by mathematicians, physicists, and chemists. When the first mathematical, logical, and natural uniformities, the first *laws*, were discovered, men were so carried away by the clearness, beauty, and simplification that resulted that they believed themselves to have deciphered authentically the eternal thoughts of the Almighty. His mind also thundered and reverberated in syllogisms. He also thought in conic sections, squares, and roots and ratios, and geometrized like Euclid. He made Kepler's laws for the planets to follow; he made velocity increase proportionally to the time in falling bodies; he made the law of the sines for light to obey when refracted; he established the classes, orders, families, and genera of plants and animals, and fixed the distances between them. He thought the archetypes of all things, and devised their variations; and when we rediscover any one of these his wondrous institutions, we seize his mind in its very literal intention.

But as the sciences have developed farther, the notion has gained ground that most, perhaps all, of our laws are only approximations. The laws themselves, moreover, have grown so numerous that there is no counting them; and so many rival formulations are proposed in all the branches of science that investigators have become accustomed to the notion that no theory is absolutely a transcript of reality, but that any one of them may from some point of view be useful. Their great use is to summarize old facts and to lead to new ones. They are only a man-made language, a conceptual shorthand, as some one calls them, in which we write our reports of nature; and languages, as is well known, tolerate much choice of expression and many dialects.

Thus human arbitrariness has driven divine necessity from scientific logic. If I mention the names of Sigwart, Mach, Ostwald, Pearson, Milhaud, Poincaré, Duhem, Heymans, those of you who are students will easily identify the tendency I speak of, and will think of additional names.

Riding now on the front of this wave of scientific logic, Messrs. Schiller and Dewey appear with their pragmatistic account of what truth everywhere signifies. Everywhere, these teachers say, "truth" in our ideas and beliefs means the same thing that it means in science. It means, they say, nothing but this, *that ideas (which themselves are but parts of our experience) become true just in so far as they help us to get into satisfactory relation with other parts of our experience*, to summarize them and get about among them by conceptual shortcuts instead of following the interminable succession of particular phenomena. Any idea upon which we can ride, so to speak; any idea that will carry us prosperously from any one part of our experience to any other part, linking things satisfactorily, working securely, simplifying, saving labour—is true for just so much, true in so far forth, true *instrumentally*. This is the "instrumental" view of truth taught so successfully at Chicago, the view that truth in our ideas means their power to "work," promulgated so brilliantly at Oxford.

Messrs. Dewey, Schiller, and their allies, in reaching this general conception of all truth, have only followed the example of geologists, biologists, and philologists. In the establishment of these other sciences, the successful stroke was always to take some simple process actually observable in operation—as denudation by weather, say, or variation from parental type, or change of dialect by incorporation of new words and pronunciations—and then to generalize it, making it apply to all times, and produce great results by summating its effects through the ages.

The observable process which Schiller and Dewey particularly singled out for generalization is the familiar one by which any individual settles into *new opinions*. The process here is always the same. The individual has a stock of old opinions already, but he meets a new experience that puts them to a strain. Somebody contradicts them; or in a reflective moment he discovers that they contradict each other; or he hears of facts with which they are incompatible; or desires arise in him which they cease to satisfy. The result is an inward trouble to which his mind till then had been a stranger, and from which he seeks to escape by modifying his previous mass of opinions. He saves as much of it as he can, for in this matter of belief we are all extreme conservatives. So he tries to change first this opinion, and then that (for they resist change very variously), until at last some new idea comes up which he can graft upon the ancient stock with a minimum of disturbance of the latter, some idea that mediates between the stock and the new experience and runs them into one another most felicitously and expediently.

This new idea is then adopted as the true one. It preserved the older stock of truths with a minimum of modification, stretching them just enough to make them admit the novelty, but conceiving that in ways as familiar as the case leaves possible. An *outrée* explanation, violating all our preconceptions, would never pass for a true account of a novelty. We should scratch round industriously till we found something less eccentric. The most violent revolutions in an individual's beliefs leave most of his old order standing. Time and space, cause and effect, nature and history, and one's own biography remain untouched. New truth is always a go-between, a smoother-over of transitions. It marries old opinion to new fact so as ever to show a minimum of jolt, a maximum of continuity. We hold a theory true just in proportion to its success in solving this "problem of maxima and minima." But success in solving this problem is eminently a matter of approximation. We say this theory solves it on the whole more satisfactorily than that theory; but that means more satisfactorily to ourselves, and individuals will emphasize their points of satisfaction differently. To a certain degree, therefore, everything here is plastic.

❧ ❧ ❧

# Can Philosophy Save Civilization?

*Étienne Gilson*

## The Breakdown of Modern Philosophy[1]

WHEN Oswald Spengler first published *The Decline of the West*, many readers of his now famous book felt at variance with more than one of its conclusions; yet few among them would have thought of questioning the fact that the West was actually declining. Most of them had already known it for a long time. Not in the least because of the World War; on the contrary, the war had been a time of enthusiasm and complete self-dedication to a sacred cause, when old fears and solicitous misgivings as to the future of Western culture had been forgotten. I know that it is now fashionable to laugh at that sacred cause; yet there are still a few people who remember how they were then trying to redeem war by giving it a meaning and who remember what that meaning was. A certain idea of man and a corresponding ideal of social life were not to be allowed to perish. Yet it now seems clear that even at that time Western culture was steadily following its process of dissolution, and we know it from within, by a sort of immediate and personal experience. For we are the bearers of that culture; it cannot be dying, and dying in us, without our being aware of it.

In its broadest sense, what we call Western culture is essentially the culture

[1] From *The Unity of Philosophical Experience* by Étienne Gilson, copyright 1937 by Charles Scribner's Sons, and reprinted with their permission.

of Greece, inherited from the Greeks by the Romans, transfused by the fathers
of the church with the religious teachings of Christianity, and progressively
enlarged by countless numbers of artists, writers, scientists, and philosophers
from the beginning of the Middle Ages up to the first third of the nineteenth
century. It would be a waste of time to look for a turning point in its history
—in the continuous stream of historical events every point is a turning point
—but it can safely be assumed that the French Revolution marks the time when
the more clear-sighted among the representatives of Western culture began to
feel that there was something wrong with it. They offered various diagnoses,
and they began to suggest remedies. For the reasons we have noted, Comte
failed to provide Europe with a living dogma; his new scientific religion was
stillborn, and he died, a self-appointed pope, with a very small number of disciples. On the whole, his Reformation was a failure, but Comte had at least seen
clearly that the European crisis was essentially a crisis of Western culture: Can
a social order, begotten by a common faith in the value of certain principles,
keep on living when all faith in these principles is lost?

The meaning of that question will be illustrated best by a summary description of what may be called, for brevity's sake, the Western creed. Its most
fundamental feature is a firm belief in the eminent dignity of man. The Greeks
of classical times never wavered in their conviction that of all the things that
can be found in nature, man is by far the highest, and that of all the things
important for man to know, by far the most important is man. When Socrates,
after unsuccessful attempts to deal with physical problems, made up his mind
to dedicate himself to the exclusive study of man, he was making a momentous
decision. "Know thyself" is not only the key to Greek culture but to the classical culture of the Western world as well. What the Greeks left to their successors was a vast body of knowledge, mainly related to man's nature and his
various needs: logic, which is the science of how to think; several different
philosophies, all of them culminating in ethics and politics, which are the sciences of how to live; remarkable specimens of history and political eloquence,
related to the life of the city. As to what we today call positive science, the
greatest achievements of the Greek genius were along the lines of mathematics,
a knowledge which man draws from his own mind without submitting to the
degrading tyranny of material facts, and medicine, whose proper object is to insure the well-being of the human body. And they stopped there, checked by an
obscure feeling that the rest was not worth having, at least not at the price
which the human mind would have to pay for it; its freedom from matter, its
internal liberty.

Of the heirs to Greek culture it can truly be said that while they enlarged
and deepened their heritage, they always respected its nature and never thought
of displacing its center of gravity. When the Romans added the lofty structure
of Roman law to it, man and the betterment of human life still remained their
essential interest. As to Christianity, though it be true that God was its ultimate
goal and its center of reference, the fact remains that it conceived man, created

by God in His own image and likeness, as the most perfect of all earthly beings, with no higher duty than to achieve his own salvation. And why is man an image of God? Because, says St. Augustine, he has a mind. All the Greek philosophers would have gladly subscribed to that statement.

Hence the second fundamental feature of Western culture, which is a definite conviction that reason is the specific difference of man. Man is best described as a rational animal; deprive man of reason, and what is left is not man, but animal. This looks like a very commonplace statement; yet Western culture is dying wherever it has been forgotten, for the rational nature of man is the only conceivable foundation for a rational system of ethics. Morality is essentially normality; for a rational being to act and to behave either without reason or contrary to its dictates is to act and behave, not exactly as a beast, but as a beastly man, which is worse. For it is proper that a beast should act as a beast —that is, according to its own nature—but it is totally unfitting for a man to act as a beast, because that means the complete oblivion of his own nature, and hence his final destruction.

It is hardly possible to realize the continuity that prevails throughout the whole history of Western culture unless one keeps in mind the important part played by the church in the work of its transmission. The Greek and the Latin fathers of the church had so carefully preserved the classical notion of man that when St. Thomas Aquinas, in the thirteenth century, undertook to build up a complete exposition of the Christian truth, he did not scruple to borrow for his technical equipment from the pagan Aristotle, whose logic, physics, biology, ethics, and metaphysics were then transformed by his mediaeval disciple into as many elements of a Christian synthesis.

The Reformation of the sixteenth century was to wreck that stately edifice, whose two component elements then fell apart, Christianity on the one side and Greek culture on the other. Yet not only Catholic humanists such as Erasmus but even Protestants such as Melanchthon immediately set about rebuilding it. Luther himself, despite his fierce attacks upon pagan culture, was fond of Ovid, and he always remained partial to Cicero. The humanists who, more or less consciously, swerved from Christianity to paganism were either going back to what seemed to them the pure doctrine of Aristotle or testing the truth value of the doctrines left by the Stoics and Epicureans. Throughout the Renaissance and until the middle of the nineteenth century, the classical tradition remained the common ground on which both pagans and Christians could still meet and carry on fruitful intellectual intercourse. Even the most brilliant scientific discoveries were made by men who, like Descartes, Pascal, Fermat, Leibniz, and Newton, had learned little more at school than classical Latin, a philosophy which more or less resembled that of St. Thomas or Aristotle, and the elements of mathematics. So long as, and in so far as, science itself kept faith with its own nature, it remained the healthy exercise of reason, reason seeking to know, because knowing is its natural function. Even the most stupendous progress made by the physical and biological sciences entailed no disruption in the continuity of

Western culture. While man remained in control of nature, culture could still survive. It was lost from the very moment nature began to control man.

Such a development was by no means inevitable, but the progressive growth of natural science had made it more and more probable. The growing interest taken by men in the practical results of science was in itself both natural and legitimate, but it helped them to forget that science is knowledge, and practical results but its by-products. Moreover, the constant accumulation of hitherto unknown facts and of their recently formulated laws was destroying the old balance between the human and the physical sciences, to the advantage of the latter. This, however, was not the main point. It lay rather in the fact that before their unexpected success in finding conclusive explanations of the material world, men had begun either to despise all disciplines in which such demonstrations could not be found or to rebuild those disciplines after the pattern of the physical sciences. As a consequence, metaphysics and ethics had to be ignored or, at least, replaced by new positive sciences; in either case, they would be eliminated.

A very dangerous move indeed, which accounts for the perilous position in which Western culture has now found itself. The European burned his old ships before making sure that the new ones would float. Moreover, the first article of the scientific creed is the acceptance of nature such as it is. Far from making up for the loss of philosophy, the discovery of the scientific substitutes for it leaves man alone with nature such as it is and obliges him to surrender to natural necessity. Philosophy is the only rational knowledge by which both science and nature can be judged. By reducing philosophy to pure science, man has not only abdicated his right to judge nature and to rule it, but he has also turned himself into a particular aspect of nature, subjected, like all the rest, to the necessary law which regulates its development. A world where accomplished facts are unto themselves their own justification is ripe for the most reckless social adventures. Its dictators can wantonly play havoc with human institutions and human lives, for dictatorships are facts, and they also are unto themselves their own justification.

❦ ❦ ❦

*Lewis Mumford*

# The Basis of Renewal[1]

## THE EXTERNAL CRISIS

HENRY ADAMS was right: the last thirty years have been witnessing the active disintegration of Western civilization. In a disintegrating society, decay is its form of life; and all the dynamic forces that are available have worked either to

[1] From *The Condition of Man* by Lewis Mumford, copyright, 1944, by Lewis Mumford, pp. 391-423, with omissions. Reprinted by permission of Harcourt, Brace and Company, Inc. With minor changes of the text made by the author.

corrupt the human fiber or to multiply the agents of physical destruction. If we go further along the same route we shall fare worse. On our courage in facing this fact and on our promptness in meeting it, all plans for the renewal of personality and community depend. "Bombs educate vigorously," Adams observed, "and even wireless telegraphy or airships might require the reconstruction of society."

Has the destruction yet gone far enough to promote a genuine renewal—or has it already gone so far that it will prevent it? No one can yet answer this question. But only the ability to put the question to ourselves will provide an effectual answer in life and action.

The makers of the New World idolum confidently expected that the older part of the human heritage would disappear: science and technics seemed thoroughly able not merely to reconstruct man's institutions and his personality, but to displace any older forms of art, thought, or practice. If anything, the utilitarians would have been surprised at the persistence of institutions that were manifestly at odds with the utilitarian way of life. But they forgot that the moral and intellectual traditions of Judaea, Greece, and Rome were essential to the development of the New World ideology itself: so that, with the ebbing away of this older tide of culture, the insufficiency of their own creed as a guide to life would become plain. A science that disclaimed all interest in human values, except the satisfaction of curiosity and the increase of manipulative skill, cannot be useful even in its own limited sphere when the general dissolution of values leads to a contempt for science and a deliberate perversion of its results.

Modern civilization has been arrested in mid-flight: its technical advances in saving labor, perfecting automatism, mechanizing the daily processes of life, multiplying the arts of destruction, and dehumanizing the personality, have been responsible for this arrest. The rise of the machine and the fall of man are two parts of the same process: never before have machines been so perfect, and never before have men sunk so low, for the sub-human conduct that the Nazis have exhibited in the torture and extermination of their victims drops below any level of merely animal brutality. That degradation is shared by those who passively condone this sub-human conduct, by belittling its horror and denying its terrible significance.

This catastrophe and this debasement have no parallels in earlier history; for now, for the first time, the entire world is involved. All consolations that are based on past recoveries are meaningless. What happened to Greece, Rome, China, or India has no parallel in the world today: when those civilizations collapsed, they were surrounded by neighbors that had reached nearly equal levels of culture, whereas if Western civilization should continue its downward course it will spread ruin to every part of the planet; and its going will consume the very forces and ideas within its own tradition that might have given a start to its successor.

The present crisis has long been visible. Jacob Burckhardt observed its early stages in the middle of the nineteenth century: in the series of brilliant essays, now published in English under the title, Force and Freedom, he not merely diagnosed the malady but accurately predicted its outward manifestations. In a letter written to Henry Osborn Taylor in 1905, Henry Adams remarked: "At the present rate of progression since 1600, it will not need another century or half century to tip thought upside down. Law, in that case, would disappear as theory or *a priori* principle and give place to force. Morality would become police. Explosives would reach cosmic violence. Disintegration would overcome integration." Henry Adams did not live to observe fascism: he anticipated it. He knew that the detonators of violence and destruction were present in every part of the social structure of Western society.

Like the die-hards of fourth century Rome, most of our contemporaries are still unaware of the dimensions of the present catastrophe. They were so completely self-hypnotized by pride in man's control over nature that they overlooked all the palpable evidence of the fact that this control did not extend to his own self and his own very life: they were unprepared to believe that a fiendish barbarism could arise in the midst of an advanced scientific country like Germany; and they were unable to analyze in their own reactions to this the characteristic symptoms of decay: a moral inertia, a flight from reality, an unwillingness to face danger or hardship on behalf of an ideal cause. The democratic peoples, inheritors of a universal culture that had actually spread throughout the globe, were willing to barter all their advances for the sake of "peace." When they finally found that the choice was not in their hands, they made ready to fight—but skeptically, reluctantly, stupidly, as men answer an alarm clock when still thick with sleep. This feeble response to the challenge of barbarism was as much a sign of disintegration as the barbarism itself.

The war itself has shocked people into facing the grimmest of realities; but it is not in itself sufficient to promote an understanding of the forces that have promoted this world catastrophe. In its later phases, the war has caused people to accept unthinkable sacrifices: but they have yet to accept the hardest sacrifice of all, and that is, to give up their illusions about this civilization. Modern man is the victim of the very instruments he values most. Every gain in power, every mastery of natural forces, every scientific addition to knowledge, has proved potentially dangerous because it has not been accompanied by equal gains in self-understanding and self-discipline. We have sought to achieve perfection by eliminating the human element. Believing that power and knowledge were by nature beneficent or that man himself was inherently good when freed from external obligations to goodness, we have conjured up a genius capable of destroying our civilization. The disproportionate development of the sciences themselves only hastens this malign end.

The physical victory over the barbarian in war is no answer to the problem that the barbarian's existence has conjured up: it merely clears the way for an answer. Even if valor and skill in war give the democratic peoples a temporary military ascendancy, that in itself will not be sufficient either to secure a lasting peace or to raise up this battered civilization. For the disease that threatens us is an organic one: it is no localized infection that can be lanced, cleaned, bandaged; on the contrary, it requires a reorientation of our whole life, a change in occupation, a change in regimen, a change in personal relationships, not least, a change in attitude and conscious direction: fundamentally, a change in religion, our total sense of the world and life and time. If we seek salvation more cheaply, we shall not be ready to undertake the heroic feats and sacrifices, the spiritual and practical efforts that will be necessary to create a life-sustaining community and a life-directed personality. To make use of our vitalities and energies—and potentially these were never greater—we must reassert once more the primacy of the person.

The obstacle to renewal does not merely lie in the fact that in so many parts of society the agents of destruction have gained the upper hand, and the organization of destruction has been forced upon us by the barbarian's attempt at world enslavement. Worse than that: organization has become in itself destructive of human values: everywhere the machine holds the center and the personality has been pushed to the periphery: a process which remains sinister even when the intention is benign—as it undoubtedly is, for example, in our over-organized institutions for teaching the young or for healing disease. The only way to renew the forces of life is to begin once again with the repressed and displaced elements: to dismantle a large part of the physical structure, to loosen up the automatisms of habit, to challenge even successful forms of routine, to give time, thought, attention, to all those changes which do not, in their first stages, require the collaboration and support of existing institutions. Our society is now at the stage where conversion—an inner change and redirection—must precede every outer change or transformation.

Here is the benign moment of disintegration: the moment when the old life is sufficiently shattered and broken to make a new life conceivable. When this moment of germination comes, the individual's experience of renewal, or at least his radical readiness for renewal, widens into a collective act. Such a change took place in classic civilization during the fourth century: it occurred again on a similar scale throughout the Western world in the eighteenth century: in both cases responses to disintegration. That inner change, under the pressure of a powerful experience, universally shared, is the prelude to every significant outer change. If rational demonstration cannot bring such a change about, it can nevertheless hasten it and clarify its goals once the personality has made itself ready and the conditions favoring it have come into being.

## THE INERTIA OF "PROGRESS"

The Chinese symbol for crisis is composed of two elements: one signifies danger and the other opportunity. If the dangers that the world faces today are greater than the majority yet fully realize, the opportunities are equally great. But these opportunities are of a different order than those of the past. Talk of goods and benefits to be shared among mankind after the war too often has been in the familiar utilitarian terms, and those who have been most confident of technical progress show themselves pitifully incapable of understanding either current dangers or future promises. Such people are the bemused victims of the very values they question least.

In anticipation of the post-war tasks, perhaps the most important thing to remember is that our mission is not the simple one of re-building demolished houses and ruined cities, converting war industries to peacetime manufactures, repairing the broken bodies of the wounded or the broken souls of those who have borne witness to more violence, terror, and misery than the human spirit can endure. All these tasks are essential; but they are only first aid. If the material shell of our society alone needed repair, if only the more obvious human wreckage needed to be restored to the human estate, our designs might follow familiar patterns. But the fact is our task is a far heavier one. In every department of our culture, we must lay the foundations for a new set of purposes, a new drama, a radically different mode of life. The "New World" of the fifteenth century is now the *Old* World: our dawning new world must take in far larger tracts of both the earth and the human personality. The bulk of our institutions no longer corresponds to the needs and possibilities of human life; and this is true, not merely of traditional structures, but of many that boast their unqualified modernity: some of the last, indeed, are already the seediest, the most completely disserviceable, in terms of valid human purposes.

In short, the crisis we are now in the midst of does not admit of a return to our original condition, in the fashion that a crisis in pneumonia, once passed, enables the patient to recover his original health. The fact is that before the war there was spiritually little health in us. Our elaborate mechanical organization of life had resulted in an increasingly purposeless society, in which some of the parts were neatly articulated and ordered, while the whole made little sense in terms of life-satisfactions and life-fulfillments. In its very mechanical elaboration, our civilization had become emptier, because it had not originally been shaped in conformity to the basic needs of human life. Only after the human voice had been transmitted around the world with the speed of light did it become plain that the words so widely disseminated might still be the same words one could hear from the village gossip or the village idiot or the village clown or the village hoodlum.

Man himself did not mirror the perfection of his instruments. Behind this empty technical fabric was an emptier ideology: one which multiplied quantities and forgot qualities: one which centered on the means of life and forgot its consummations.

Western man has exhausted the dream of mechanical power which so long dominated his imagination. If he is to preserve the instruments he has so cunningly created, if he is to continue to refine and perfect the whole apparatus of life, he can no longer let himself remain spellbound in that dream: he must attach himself to more humane purposes than those he has given to the machine. We can no longer live, with the illusions of success, in a world given over to devitalized mechanisms, desocialized organisms, and depersonalized societies: a world that had lost its sense of the ultimate dignity of the person

THE BASIS OF RENEWAL

almost as completely as the Roman Empire did at the height of its military greatness and technical facility. All that the Nazis have done has been to bring to a more rapid climax a process that was more slowly, more insidiously, undermining our whole civilization.

But another symptomatic weakness should by now be equally plain: even those who cling to the old drama of expansion and conquest, of mechanical organization and material exploitation, no longer wholly believe in the plot. Georges Sorel observed this fact early in the twentieth century: he compared the new capitalists disparagingly with the American robber barons of the mid-nineteenth century, and he was afraid that the revolutionary élan would disappear in a society whose business men and industrialists had lost their original ruthlessness if not their original greed. The signs of this inner exhaustion multiplied steadily during the last thirty years; one of the most critical of them is the widespread unwillingness to play the game if the player happens to be losing. When people are really interested in a life-theme, they cling to it even under the most adverse conditions; indeed, the pressure of difficulty only intensifies their interest. When the Christian theme was in the making, persecutions welded the faithful together and finally resulted in a unified Church. When the interests of capitalism were dominant, adventurous enterprisers accepted losses and bankruptcies without wincing and began all over again; the Christian did not cease to believe in his religion because it brought personal grief, nor the capitalist in capitalism because it might result in personal ruin.

Now, we have seen just the opposite of these qualities in our time. Capitalists accepted the closing down of the world market for the same reason that democratic peoples accepted without even a timid counter-movement the cancerous spread of fascism. And why? For the sake of peace: for the reason that a counter-movement implied risk and sacrifice; and risk and sacrifice were not accepted, since the faith that would have made them self-justifying had evaporated.

Had the old plot become too complicated to follow? Had the old rewards proved disappointing? Had new motives appeared which cast into disrepute the accepted themes of the old drama? In varying ways all these things had indeed happened; but the main fact to be noted is that the old game no longer thrilled the players: until the war actually was forced upon the anti-fascist powers, neither nationalism nor capitalism had the pride, the self-confidence, the initiative to summon together energies that were still visible as late as 1914. In the course of fighting the war, nationalism and capitalism have both received a powerful stimulant: the nationalist shows a truculent egoism toward allies in victory that might have staved off the war altogether had it been originally present in the face of fascist bluff and bullying; while capitalism, like an old man who has miraculously begotten a baby, actually fancies it has recovered the potencies of youth. Both responses, however, are automatic ones: mere by-products of the war. Examine the motives that are still dominant and they turn out to end up in dreams of escape, escape via the golf-links, the motor highway, the night club, the helicopter, a life of expensive automatism and automatic expense: the tag ends of baroque luxury and baroque futility in a setting of slick machines.

Unlike the rapacious industrialists of the nineteenth century, the leaders today no longer treat the industrial system as an end in itself. Western man demands a special price for further mechanization: bread and shows, physical security, and semi-mental distractions. He must be bribed and coaxed to perform acts his forefathers performed gladly, wholeheartedly, with an almost religious conviction. This applies to both owners and workers, leaders and led. The very economies the machine makes possible bring with them a train of dissipations.

In general, one may say that in the present crisis nothing was real enough to fight for at the beginning because nothing was significant enough to live for at the end.

If technics is the sole key to success, the American cartels that connived with the Nazis to suppress patents essential to democracy's preparation for war might write off their treason to the account of profit. If technics alone constitutes man's desirable future, then the Nazis, who have applied cold technics to the state-controlled copulation of future mothers or to the bestial murder of Jews, were indeed the "wave of the future." But what a future! The danger to human society today does not come solely from the active barbarians: it comes even more perhaps from those who have in their hearts assented to the barbarian's purposes. This lapse was part of a decay of faith in the primacy of the person that people of the most widely assorted convictions succumbed to: the very Churches that had originally sprung from this faith were among its most sinister betrayers.

Unfortunately, the war itself has reawakened a confidence in the future on the basis of a simple restoration of the motives and methods of the past—that very past which has terminated in the present catastrophe. Above all, the capitalist dog has returned to his old vomit. The investor, the organizer, the industrial worker, even the farmer, have once again had a glimpse of that hitherto unattainable heaven which the innocent regard as a practical equivalent of the good life: the heaven of full productivity based on unlimited demand and leading to the hope of unlimited profits. That heaven, it is true, will remain real only until the day of reckoning comes: the day when each country adds up the costs and starts to balance the books. Indeed, no better evidence exists of the mental disorder that is rife in present-day society than the capitalist's confidence in his ability to resume this game on his own terms—when *on his own terms,* that is, on the terms of redeeming the existing debt at par value, and paying to boot the interest charges he has already lost.

Mazzini long ago remarked when he was promoting the national independence of Italy that people were much more willing to sacrifice their lives to the good cause than their pennies. When the time comes to shift from war production to peace production, we shall find that the utopia of full production is a capitalist mirage, as long as the old capitalist super-ego remains in control. Capitalism by nature and principle subordinates public need to private profit. On capitalist terms, there is no satisfactory "moral equivalent of war." That was the illusion of the new capitalism: an illusion that should have been buried forever by the calamitous depression that started in 1929.

But there is far more impressive evidence of the vanity of all these great expectations than I have yet shown. The fact is that most of the current plans for remolding our civilization ignore the vast secular change that has crept up on Western Civilization during the past century, almost unawares. That change is nothing less than the end of the Era of Expansion, and the collapse of the major premises, metaphysical, moral, social, economic, on which it was based.

### THE END OF EXPANSION

The world crisis that has existed for the lifetime of a whole generation indicates that a radical shift in the direction of social movement has taken place: this shift began during the last quarter of the nineteenth century and now, directly and indirectly, has affected almost every institution. The crisis has two aspects: an external and an internal one. Here I shall deal mainly with the causes of the external crisis. The external change may be summed up in a brief sentence: an age of expansion is giving place to an age of equilibrium. The achievement of this equilibrium is the task of the next few centuries.

So far this change has been a blind and blundering one. Not merely have the underlying causes themselves been ignored, but the interests and attitudes that were formed by the tradition of expansion have kept every community from meeting by rational means the new conditions of life that open up. Those that have accepted the premises of stabilization have attached the movement itself to regressive purposes and have cut it off from its creative mission. Those who have resisted stabilization have striven to perpetuate a past that is beyond recall: a past that would not be worth recalling even if that were possible. Both the tempo and the direction of our life are about to undergo a profound change: this will prove a change for the better provided we can throw off the fatal temptation to worship our dead selves and perpetuate our past mistakes.

The present period is a painful transition between two eras. The first I have traced in some detail since the fourteenth century: it is associated with the rise of capitalism, militarism, scientism, and mechanization: likewise with the counter-movements of protestantism, romanticism, and democracy. All of these institutions made positive contributions to human culture: even militarism. The total effect of the era of expansion, however, was to increase man's power over nature, and in particular Western man's power over the more amiable or more feebly armed peoples that inhabited the rest of the planet; but the civilization that resulted has been rent by internal conflicts and contradictions which have nullified many of its real triumphs.

The outlines of the period of humanization that approaches are not so easy to describe: many of the characters have still to be invented and their lines have still to be written: at best, some of their costumes and a few odd parcels of scenery indicate what the play is to be about. But by way of broad contrast one may characterize the approaching period as one of dynamic equilibrium, such an equilibrium as the human body maintains at every stage in its growth. The theme for the new period will be neither arms and the man nor machines and the man: its theme will be the resurgence of life, the displacement of the mechanical by the organic, and the re-establishment of the person as the ultimate term of all human effort. Cultivation, humanization, co-operation, symbiosis: these are the watchwords of the new world-enveloping culture.

Many of the miscarriages of the present period are due to the fact that our statesmen, our industrial leaders, our administrators are still trying to apply the ideology of the age of expansion to a social organization that has an entirely different set of requirements: an organization in which the careful timing and spacing of activities, in which the proper diversification of opportunities and the balancing and interlocking of functions must take the place of those spectacular one-sided advances, colossal but incoherent, which were characteristic of the period of expansion. Every department of life will record this change: it will affect the task of education and the procedures of science no less than the organization of industrial enterprises, the planning of cities, the development of regions, the interchange of world resources.

The facts of the present stabilization are familiar to students of history and sociology; but the interpretation of these facts has proved tardy. Yet strangely enough, our present state was accurately forecast by at least one early observer, John Stuart Mill: witness what has become, by force of events, a great chapter in the second volume of his Principles of Political Economy. That chapter is devoted to a theoretical discussion of what Mill misleadingly called the "stationary state." By this he meant an economic order in which the area for new capital investments had dwindled by a natural process of self-limitation, in which, through birth control, the population had become stable, and in which the rates of profit and interest tended, as a result of this twofold curb, to fall toward zero.

This is the chapter that most people know by only a single sentence, one in which Mill doubted whether labor-saving machinery had yet lightened the day's burdens of a single worker. But it was here he made a far more significant observation: namely, that a state of dynamic equilibrium, though it might be dreaded by the profiteer, was precisely the condition required for translating mechanical improvements into social welfare. In restating Mill's observations as history I only accentuate their merit as prophecy.

The era of Western expansion had three overlapping and interacting phases: land expansion, population expansion, and industrial expansion. All three phases have usually been treated as if they were constant phenomena in any healthy society; whereas they were extremely unusual and highly localized changes that had a definite beginning and an inevitable terminus. In our time the whole process has come to an end, or very nearly approaches an end. Other peoples who a hundred years ago existed on a primitive level have fast become masters of Western machines and weapons, producers in their own right. Such people will no longer consent to being treated as packbearers and servants: they properly claim their place as partners, and they reinforce their claim with the Christian doctrine of the infinite worth of the individual, and the democratic doctrine of the freedom and equality of all men as men. We cannot disown either doctrine without betraying our own precious heritage. World trade, world production, world intercourse must now be based upon equivalent advantages for all the regions concerned: it must now be a two-way process: consciously and deliberately so. Meanwhile, equally radical changes are under way in the other departments where expansion has prevailed. I propose to examine these changes and to point out their consequences. . . .

## THE INTERNAL CRISIS

The internal crisis in our civilization has been visible for a much longer time than the external crisis; for it grew out of the inadequacy of the New World idolum and the failure of utilitarian man to fulfill the ends of life.

The materialist creed by which a large part of humanity has sought to live during the last few centuries confused the needs of survival with the needs of fulfillment; whereas man's life requires both. For survival, the physiological needs are uppermost; and the most imperative, obviously, are the needs for air and water: then food and shelter against extremes of temperature, and so by degrees one passes to those social needs for communication and co-operation, that never wholly limit themselves to life-preservation in the narrow sense. Within the life-span of a generation, the needs for sexual intercourse and parental care are as imperative as those for air and water.

In terms of life-fulfillment, however, this ascending scale of needs, from bare physical life to social stimulus and personal growth, must be reversed. The most important needs from the standpoint of life-fulfillment are those that foster spiritual activity and promote spiritual growth: the needs for order, continuity, meaning, value, purpose and design—needs out of which language and poesy and music and science and art and religion have grown. The deepest, the most organic, of these higher needs is that for love: all the stronger because it is rooted in survival. Neither group of needs is in a watertight compartment: lovers must eat and even greedy eaters have been known to share their food with the starving. Nevertheless there are conflict and tension between these two sets of needs, as there are between the primitive institutions of the tribe, seeking self-preservation, and the order of an open society, prepared to share its highest values with all other men.

Lured by his elemental needs, man tends to rest content with their satisfaction: instead of using them as the basis of the good life, he often seeks, by merely elaborating and refining them, to use them as a substitute for the good life. Here is one of the chief causes of social fixation and personal arrest. The more complicated and costly the physical and social apparatus for ensuring man's survival, the more likely will it smother the purposes for which it humanly exists. The threat was never stronger than it is today; for the very exquisiteness of our mechanical apparatus, in every department of life, tends to put the non-human process above the human end.

But no matter how primitive the community, and no matter how terrible the pressure of war, pestilence, or natural disaster, there must always be a sufficient margin of time and energy to carry forward the processes that make life-fulfill-ment possible. No matter how harassed a mother may be, she must give her child the gift of language as well as food. When life-fulfillment is put first, an intensification of activity takes place in all the subordinate needs, for they then have a meaning and a purpose that they do not possess in themselves: they do not merely sustain life but raise it to a higher level.

The emergence of man from his purely animal state consists in the constant increase of the ratio of higher needs to lower needs, and in the fuller contri-bution of his vitalities and energies to the molding of more richly endowed and more fully expressive personalities. Up to now, the fullest kind of human growth has been possible only to small groups of men: a privileged class, or at best, a city; and the fact that men as a body have not participated fully in man's own highest activities has always undermined and disordered the very growth that even the most fortunate achieved. Only now has mankind itself arrived at the point of inheriting man's whole estate. There lies the meaning and the promise of the democratic ideal.

The great gains that were made in technics during the last few centuries were largely offset by a philosophy that either denied the validity of man's higher needs or that sought to foster only that limited set of interests which enlarged the power of science and gave scope to a power personality. At a moment when a vast surplus was available for the goods of leisure and culture, the very ideals of leisure and culture were cast into disrepute—except when they could be turned to profit. Here lies the core of the inner crisis that has afflicted our civilization for at least two centuries. In the heyday of expan-sionism, the middle of the nineteenth century, scarcely a single humane voice could be found to defend either the means or the ideals of a power civiliza-tion. The wisdom of the race revolted against the inhuman fruits of its knowl-edge: Blake, Ruskin, Morris, Arnold, Emerson, Whitman, Thoreau, Melville, Dickens, Howells, Hugo, Zola, Mazzini, Tolstoy, Dostoyevsky, Ibsen—almost all the representative minds of Europe and America—denounced the human results of the whole process of mechanization and physical conquest. As with one voice, they protested against the inhuman sacrifices and brutalizations, the tawdry materialisms, the crass neglect of the human personality.

In the course of the last generation, the wisdom of this protest has become plain. As a result, many of the plans and projects that seemed like mere escapist dreams in the nineteenth century have become conditions for renewal; indeed only those who are aware of the importance of man's higher needs will be capable even of providing intelligently for bare food and shelter. This is one of those periods when only the dreamers are practical men. By the same token, the so-called practical men have become makers and perpetuators of nightmares: for it is their attempt to crawl back into the crumbled wreckage of the immediate past that has condemned our society to frustration, to sterility, to savage barbarism.

The inner crisis in our civilization must be resolved before the outer crisis can be effectively met. Our first duty is to revamp our ideas and values and to reorganize the human personality around its highest and most central needs. If we ask ourselves as we face the future, not how to keep our old institutions and organizations running in their accustomed grooves, but how to keep life itself running, with or without the aid of these institutions, our problem immediately clarifies itself. There is no wealth, as Ruskin said, but life; and there is no consummation of life except in the perpetual growth and renewal of the human person: machines, organizations, institutions, wealth, power, culture, cities, landscapes, industries, are all secondary instruments in that process. Whatever nourishes the personality, humanizes it, refines it, deepens it, intensifies its aptitude and broadens its field of action is good: whatever limits it or thwarts it, whatever sends it back into tribal patterns and lessens its capacity for human co-operation and communion must be counted as bad. Nothing that man has created is outside his capacity to change, to remold, to supplant, or to destroy: his machines are no more sacred or substantial than the dreams in which they originated.

In the end, all our contrivances have but one object: the continued growth of human personalities and the cultivation of the best life possible. What sort of personality must we now seek to foster and nourish? What kind of common life? What traits and disciplines are needed in an age of stabilization, co-operation, and balance? What is the order of value in our life needs: do we put babies above motor cars, art above plumbing, the well-being of the worker above the mechanical efficiency or cheapness of his product? If so, we must create a different ego-ideal from that which was the norm in a capitalistic and mechanical civilization: our mode of education and our plan of life must be directed to more humane ends than those that have hitherto governed us.

### THE NEED FOR HUMAN BALANCE

As our culture developed during the last five centuries, its center lay more and more outside the human personality: hence a fragment of the personality displaced the whole. In attempting to restore balance in the community and in the personality, we need not be troubled by references to the undoubted existence of individual differences or to the fact, as true in society as in the individual organism, that all equilibrium is necessarily unstable and is constantly upset by the continued act of growth. The first condition makes the effort to achieve a fuller and more balanced development necessary: the second makes it an ideal goal—one always to be aimed at but never, in the nature of things, fully achieved.

Differences in temperament, capacity, aptitude, and interest, differences that have their origin in diversities of biological inheritance, characterize all men, as they characterize the same men at successive moments in life: Who would doubt it? Who would change it? These differences are the inexhaustible source of the richness of human experience. But no man is an island: every age has a common ideal of personality which represents the goals of living toward which the whole community is more or less set. To the extent that an individual shares in this personality, he is fit for his daily tasks and can co-operate freely with his fellows and make the fullest use of his culture. The more representative the common type, the more it meets the claims of its historic moment, the fewer repressions must be exercised over those whose inner tendency is to depart from it.

If the era of stabilization is to be one devoted to the intensive but balanced cultivation of our natural and social resources, balance and intensity are equally, I believe, the key to the sort of personality that is needed to work effectively within this culture and to create the necessary changes in our disrupted institutions. The age of mechanical specialization produced a quite different ideal: that of the one-sided specialist, the piece worker, the operative conditioned by repetition and reward, as Dr. E. L. Thorndike puts it: the end product of a long period of mechanization in which one by one the higher attributes of the personality have disappeared or have been reduced to mere whims and hobbies. The fatal results of this process were pointed out by Comte a full century ago. "If we have been accustomed to deplore the spectacle, among the artisan class, of a workman occupied during his whole life in nothing but making knife handles or pinheads, we may find something quite as lamentable in the intellectual class, in the exclusive employment of the human brain in resolving equations or classifying insects. The moral effect is, unhappily, analogous in the two cases. It occasions a miserable indifference about the general course of human affairs as long as there are equations to resolve or pins to manufacture."

One of Comte's most able successors in sociology, Dr. Karl Mannheim, has carried this observation even further: he notes the growing irrationality of the personality engaged in production in proportion to the technical refinement and "rationalization" of the process. The dismembered man, whether as engineer or workman, as organizer or salesman, needs less directive insight and intelligence once he is geared to the whole machine than the carpenter or the weaver needed in his workshop. The behaviorist man, with his slot-machine mind, responding mechanically to external stimuli, passive until acted upon, incapable of taking the initiative or choosing his destination, is the typical by-product of current society: fascist minds are thus more common than the conscious philosophy of fascism. Indeed our whole civilization has put a premium upon this primitive kind of automatism and compulsion: the very humanity that quickens the life-like machine leaves the person depleted and empty.

Dr. Mannheim has well pointed out that the chief element in our inner crisis today is the disproportionate development of human faculties: "individuals as well as historical and social groups may, under certain circumstances, suffer from the danger of disintegration because their capacities fail to develop equally and harmoniously." This observation has been reinforced by an experienced psychiatrist and a profound reader of the modern soul, Dr. C. G. Jung, who has sought to combat this unfortunate lopsidedness and disparity by counseling his patients to cultivate their weaker sides. None of our dominant institutions today correct this lack of balance: on the contrary, they encourage it in the name of efficiency, an efficiency which fosters a single function at the expense of the whole life that finally supports it. Only by making the personality itself central, and by drawing forth its repressed or thwarted capacities, can this mischief be cured: balance and autonomy go together.

The ideal of balance itself is an ancient one: common to philosophers as far apart in time and culture as Confucius, Aristotle, and Spencer: the Confucian ideal of the superior man, the Greek ideal of the Golden Mean, and the renascence ideal of the gentleman all embodied this conception. Behind the notion of balance is the ethical principle laid down by Herbert Spencer: "Strange as the conclusion looks, it is nevertheless a conclusion to be drawn, that the performance of every function is, in general, a moral obligation. It is usually thought that morality requires us only to restrain such vital activities as in our present state are often pushed to excess, or such as conflict with average welfare, special or general; but it also requires us to carry on these vital activities up to their normal limits."

Spencer's doctrine of organic balance was handicapped by the same weakness that crippled Marx's socialism, a defective incarnation: his formulation remained a tissue of abstractions. But it is important to realize how well the deliverances of this nonconformist and individualist expressed the mature beliefs of Marx himself. These indications are significant because the period of formulation almost always anticipates by at least half a century or more the stages of incarnation and fulfillment: so that, if we are to achieve a balanced economy and a balanced community and a balanced personality, it will be with the aid of ideas that have long been in existence: ripened sufficiently to be ready now for assimilation. Hence it is important to realize that Marx, in a brief passage in *Capital*, anticipated the present arguments. He said: "In a socialist society, the 'fragmentary man' would be replaced by the 'completely developed individual,' one for whom different social functions are but alternative forms of activity. Men would fish, hunt, or engage in literary criticism without becoming professional fishermen, hunters, or critics."

In every department of life, man's activity is limited by his capacities for assimilation; and the greater the resources man can potentially use the more disciplined and many-sided must be his response. The difficulty our culture faces was well diagnosed by Shelley: "The accumulations of the materials of external life exceed the quantity of power of assimilating them to the internal laws of human nature." When these accumulations heap up as recklessly as they have in our time and when the internal laws and the internal capacities of human nature are disregarded, the result is to turn each potential gain *against* man: he functions as a distracted atom in a growing chaos, made poor by his wealth, made empty by his fullness, reduced to monotony by his very opportunities for variety, the victim of changes that have in themselves become fixations: all beyond his power to assimilate or control.

Civilizations do not die of old age: they die of the complications of old age. Observing this process long ago, Burckhardt predicted the coming of the "terrible simplifiers": people who would reject all the goods modern man had acquired in order to restore the capacity to act. Those terrible simplifiers have appeared. They are the barbarians who renounce every part of our culture that makes a claim upon man's higher needs: avowed barbarians like the Nazis and more insidious barbarians who, by advertising, propaganda, and education, would turn every part of our life into the mean handiwork of coachman, cook, and groom, of beauty shop, assembly-line, and roadhouse. We cannot save our culture from these barbarians, external or internal, by clinging to the habits that make us a prey to their corrupt vitality. To recover life and health again we must, like the Christian confronting the classic world, find a benign method of simplification. We must find a method that will assert the primacy of the person and that will re-endow the person with all its attributes, all its heritage, all its potentialities. But unlike the Christian, we must undertake this transformation before the barbarian has finally wrecked our civilization: only thus shall we be able to carry forward the many life-promoting activities that man has created since the breakup of the medieval synthesis.

The task for our age is to decentralize power in all its manifestations. To this end, we must build up balanced personalities: personalities that will be capable of drawing upon our immense stores of energy, knowledge, and wealth without being demoralized by them. On this point, Plato's words in *The Laws* cannot be improved: "If anyone gives too great power to anything, too large a sail to a vessel, too much food to the body, too much authority to the mind, and does not observe the mean, everything is overthrown, and in the wantonness of excess runs in the one case to disorders, and in the other to injustice, which is the child of excess."

If we are to control machines and organizations, then, we must make men; and our first task is that of self-examination, self-education, self-control. Those who fail at this point will be incapable of contributing to the political, economic, and social transformations that are now so long overdue.

### THE ORGANIC PERSON

The ideal personality for the opening age is a balanced personality: not the specialist but the whole man. Such a personality must be in dynamic interaction with every part of his environment and every part of his heritage. He must be capable of treating economic experiences and esthetic experiences, parental experiences and vocational experiences, as the related parts of a single whole, namely, life itself. His education, his discipline, his daily routine must tend toward this wholeness. To achieve this, he must be ready to spurn the easy successes that come, in a dying culture, through self-mutilation.

Such a dynamic balance is not easily achieved: its consummations are precious and its stability is precarious: it demands a vigilance and an athletic readiness for new shifts and stresses that more specialized vocations do not habitually achieve. For balance is not a matter of allotting definite amounts of time and energy to each segment of life that requires attention: even our mechanical partition of functions does that. It means that the whole personality must be constantly at play, at least at ready call, at every moment of its existence and that no one part of life should be segregated from another part, incapable of influencing it or being influenced by it.

But qualitative balance is as important as quantitative balance: many kinds of experience have the role in life that vitamins have in the diet: quantitatively minute elements may be as important for spiritual health as the vitamins and minerals are for bodily health. Most of man's higher activities are in the latter category. No healthy person can look at pictures all day any more than he can make love all day. But for even the humblest person, a day spent without the sight or sound of beauty, the contemplation of mystery, or the search for truth and perfection is a poverty-stricken day; and a succession of such days is fatal to human life. That is why even the most superstitious forms of religion, which have at least kept alive some wraith of beauty or perfection, still contain for the mass of mankind something valuable that a bare scientific positivism has allowed to be lost both in thought and practice.

The importance of balance to both the community and the personality will come out more clearly, perhaps, if we call to mind the patent dangers that will attend stabilization: dangers that are already plainly visible in the bureaucratism and time-serving that have begun to infect every department of life: not alone government but business; and not alone business but education. Those who lack the creative capacity to establish a dynamic balance are already caught by its counterfeit and its negation: Alexandrianism or Byzantinism.

Organizations that have been stabilized for any length of time—the army is an excellent example—become embedded in routine and hostile to change: they are unable to meet fresh challenges, and their very "adjustment" becomes a profound cause of maladjustment. Scientific progress does not alter this fact, for scientific advances themselves tend to follow inflexible institutional forms, and they often seek perfection within a more and more obsolete frame of reference. Stability and security, pursued for their own sake, will result in a caste division of labor and in the denial of any changes that would upset an increasingly sessile routine: forms, precedents, stereotypes would supplant human needs, and the very attributes of life, its capacity for readjustment, for insurgence, for renewal, would be forfeited by these ill-conceived efforts to guard life more effectively.

These regressive forms of stabilization have already taken shape: they have been seized upon by Nazi philosophers and leaders as the basis for enforcing permanent caste divisions. But the danger is not confined to the conscious fascists: many of those who talk loudest about rugged individualism prove themselves in their daily practice the upholders of a Byzantine rigidity and hollowness. The standard examination papers that have appeared in so many departments of American education under the guise of progressive method would, in a short generation, paralyze the acquisition and extension of fresh knowledge: this symbolizes a much wider menace to life and thought.

Precisely because stabilization brings with it these dangers, we must introduce into our conception of the type of personality needed the ability to touch life at many points, to travel light, and to keep every part of experience in a state of constant interplay and interaction: so that fresh challenges will appear at unexpected points, in unforeseeable circumstances. For the age of balance we need a new race of pioneers, of deliberate amateurs, in order to offset the tendency to harden practice into smooth molds and to sacrifice the growing personality to the machine. Such stereotyping of activity as will free the organism for its higher functions—like those human automatisms that put a large part of the burden of behavior on the vertebral column and the cerebellum—must not halt on its way to this destination.

In this respect the varied war experiences that people in many countries have undergone, as soldiers, air raid wardens, fire fighters, nurses, and so forth, must be regarded as essential contributions to the task of peacetime co-operation: typical of a new kind of citizenship and a more vivid routine of life. But we cannot afford to promote a war every generation to break up social fixations: that is burning down the house to roast the pig. We must erect these social and personal counterpoises to rigidity and fixity as the basic requirements for a maturing personality.

The custom of our time is to think no change worth even discussing unless it can be at once organized into a visible movement: the mass enlistment of thousands, preferably millions, of men and women. The very appearance of millions of men in black shirts and brown shirts gave fascism publicity that made its rancid ideas seem important. Many of the actual movements that claim allegiance today are little better than devices of publicity: decorative devices that change nothing and move nothing. Such, even, would be a revolutionary movement, unless those who took part in it remodeled the instruments with which they work: first of all themselves.

Only in one place can an immediate renewal begin: that is, within the person; and a remolding of the self is an inescapable preliminary to the great changes that must be made throughout every community, in every part of the world. Each one, within his or her own field of action—the home, the neighborhood, the city, the region, the school, the church, the factory, the mine, the office, the union—must carry into his immediate day's work a changed attitude toward all his functions and obligations. His collective work cannot rise to a higher level than his personal scale of values. Once a change is effected in the person, every group will record and respond to it.

Today our best plans miscarry because they are in the hands of people who have undergone no inner growth. Most of these people have shrunk from facing the world crisis and they have no notion of the manner in which they themselves have helped to bring it about. Into every new situation they carry only a fossilized self. Their hidden prejudices, their glib hopes, their archaic desires and automatisms—usually couched in the language of assertive modernity—recall those of the Greeks in the fourth century B.C. or those of the Romans in the fourth century A.D. They are in a power dive and their controls have frozen. By closing their eyes they think they can avoid a crash.

Those who look for swift wholesale changes to take place in our institutions under-rate the difficulties we now face: the inroads of barbarism and automatism, those twin betrayers of freedom, have been too deep. In their impatience, in their despair, such people secretly long to cast the burden of their own regeneration upon a savior: a president, a pope, a dictator—vulgar counterparts of a divinity debased or a corruption deified. But such a leader is only the mass of humanity writ small: the incarnation of our resentments, hates, sadisms, or of our cowardices, confusions, and complacencies. There is no salvation through such naked self-worship: God must work within us. Each man and woman must first silently assume his own burden.

We need not wait for bombs and bullets actually to strike us before we strip our lives of superfluities: we need not wait for events to bend our wills to unison. Wherever we are, the worst has already happened and we must meet it. We must simplify our daily routine without waiting for ration cards; we must take on public responsibilities without waiting for conscription; we must work for the unity and effective brotherhood of man without letting further wars prove that the current pursuit of power, profit and all manner of material aggrandizement is treason to humanity: treason and national suicide. Year by year, we must persevere in all these acts, even though the restrictions are lifted and the urgencies of war have slackened. Unless we now rebuild our selves all our external triumphs will crumble.

There is no easy formula for this renewal. It is not enough for us to do all that is possible: we must do that which seems impossible. Our first need is not for organization but for orientation: a change in direction and attitude. We must bring to every activity and every plan a new criterion of judgment: we must ask how far it seeks to further the processes of life-fulfillment and how much respect it pays to the needs of the whole personality.

More immediately we must demand: What is the purpose of each new political and economic measure? Does it seek the old goal of expansion or the new one of equilibrium? Does it work for conquest or co-operation? And what is the nature of this or that industrial or social achievement—does it produce material goods alone or does it also produce human goods and good men? Do our individual life-plans make for a universal society, in which art and science, truth and beauty, religion and sanctity, enrich mankind? Do our public life-plans make for the fulfillment and renewal of the human person, so that they will bear fruit in a life abundant: ever more significant, ever more valuable, ever more deeply experienced and more widely shared?

If we keep this standard constantly in mind, we shall have both a measure for what must be rejected and a goal for what must be achieved. In time, we shall create the institutions and the habits of life, the rituals, the laws, the arts, the morals that are essential to the development of the whole personality, and the balanced community: the possibilities of progress will become real again once we lose our blind faith in the external improvements of the machine alone. But the first step is a personal one: a change in direction of interest *towards* the person. Without that change, no great betterment will take place in the social order. Once that change begins, everything is possible.

# Biographical Notes

HOLLIS ALPERT (1916–) has been a movie critic for *The Saturday Review of Literature* since 1950. Author of several short stories, he was formerly on the editorial staff of *The New Yorker* magazine.

ARISTOTLE (384–322 B.C.), versatile Greek philosopher, was a student of Plato. He was appointed by Philip of Macedon to tutor his son, Alexander the Great. Later he returned to Athens where he lectured to many disciples and wrote his numerous works on poetry, logic, natural science, politics, rhetoric, philosophy, and metaphysics. His influence, particularly great during the Middle Ages, continues to this day.

MATTHEW ARNOLD (1822–1888), critic of the strains in contemporary culture, in his poems voiced the doubts of an age "wandering between two worlds, one dead, the other powerless to be born"—the world of religious faith and the world of doubt engendered by science.

FRANCIS BACON (1561–1626), scientist, philosopher, and man of letters, became Lord Chancellor of England. His works, which have influenced the development of human thought and progress, include *The Advancement of Learning* (1605), *Instauratio Magna,* and *Novum Organum* (1627).

JACQUES BARZUN (1907–) was born in Paris and received his early education at a Paris *lycée*. Now a United States citizen, he has taught history at Columbia since 1937, from which he received his Ph.D. in 1932. Among his many books are *Teacher in America* (1945), *Berlioz and the Romantic Century* (1950), and *God's Country and Mine* (1954).

CLAUDE BERNARD (1813–1878), French physiologist and opponent of "vitalism," carried out experimental investigation on nerves and chemical research. He discovered the function of the vasomotor nerves. His theory of the "interior environment" has been of major importance. Two of his books are *An Introduction to Experimental Medicine* (1865) and *General Physiology* (1872).

MORRIS GILBERT BISHOP (1893–), scholar and teacher of Romance Languages at Cornell University, is also known as a satirist and humorist. He has published biographical and critical works on Cabeza de Vaca, Pascal, and Ronsard, and a number of volumes of humorous poems and sketches.

ROLLO WALTER BROWN (1880–), author and teacher, was born in Ohio. He has taught English at Carleton College and Harvard, lectured, contributed to magazines, and written a number of books, among which are *Next Door to a Poet*, *The Writer's Art*, and *Harvard Yard in the Golden Age*.

MARTIN BUBER (1878–), Jewish theologian and philosopher, is a native of Vienna. He has done much to interpret Judaism to contemporary America. The present selection is substantially a lecture which he delivered in 1951 at a number of American universities. Among his books are *I and Thou* (1923), *Israel and the World* (1948), and *Good and Evil* (1952).

INGRAM BYWATER (1841–1914) was an English Hellenist and translator of Aristotle.

JAMES BRYANT CONANT (1893–), American scientist and former president of Harvard University, is Ambassador to the Federal Republic of West Germany. He is the author of *The Chemistry of Organic Compounds* (1933) and *Education and Liberty* (1953).

ROBERT GORHAM DAVIS (1908–), a graduate of Harvard, is professor of English and chairman of the department at Smith College. The author of many critical essays and reviews, he has also published short stories.

RENÉ DESCARTES (1596–1650), was the French philosopher whose system did much to sweep aside the subtleties of medieval thinkers and thus to influence greatly the formation of the modern mind. A mathematician as well as a philosopher, Descartes aimed at the ideal of mathematical certitude in metaphysical problems. His principal works are *Discours de la Methode*, *Meditationes de Prima Philosophia*, and *Principia Philosophiae*.

JOHN DONNE (1573–1631), the famous Dean of St. Paul's and metaphysical poet, was born a Roman Catholic. After his conversion to the Anglican Church he took holy orders at the suggestion of King James I, who was pleased to grant him several preferments in the Church, culminating in the Deanship of St. Paul's. Though Donne in early youth was worldly, and wrote some of the most passionate love poetry in English literature, he now became fervent in the spirit and zealous for the Lord. His sermons, many of them preached before Charles I, are among the most eloquent in all English pulpit oratory. His *Devotions*, occasioned by a grave illness, were written in 1623. Donne is considered one of the greatest of English prose writers by many critics.

JOHN DOS PASSOS (1896–), novelist and essayist, became first known for his novel *Three Soldiers* in 1921. Many other novels have appeared, among them *The Big Money* (1936) and *The Grand Design* (1949).

SIR ARTHUR STANLEY EDDINGTON (1882–1944), English physicist and astronomer, made distinguished contributions to astrophysics and the theory of relativity with such books as *Space, Time and Gravitation* (1920), *The Internal Constitution of the Stars* (1926), and *The Expanding Universe* (1933).

IRWIN EDMAN (1896–1954) received both his B.A. and Ph.D. at Columbia and taught there in the Department of Philosophy. A posthumous collection of his essays is entitled *The Uses of Philosophy* (1955).

WILLIAM FAULKNER (1897–), one of the foremost living American novelists, has published some twenty books of fiction, notably *The Sound and the Fury* (1931), *Light in August* (1932) and *A Fable* (1954). In 1950 he was awarded the Nobel Prize for literature.

ABRAHAM FLEXNER (1866–), American educator and physician, was director of the Institute for Advanced Studies at Princeton from 1930 to 1939 and is now director emeritus. He has been associated with the General Education Board and has written many books on medical education and higher education in the United States and Europe.

E. M. FORSTER (1879–), British novelist, is author of the celebrated *A Passage to India* (1924). He was educated at Cambridge, where he is now an Honorary Fellow of King's College. He is also author of *A Room with a View* (1908) and *Howard's End* (1910), as well as two books of short stories, *The Eternal Moment* (1928), and *The Celestial Omnibus* (1911).

SIGMUND FREUD (1856–1939), Viennese neurologist and psychologist and the founder of psychoanalysis, has exerted a profound influence upon modern art, literature, and philosophy as well as on psychology and medicine. He is best known for such writings as *The Interpretation of Dreams* (1913) and *A General Introduction to Psychoanalysis* (1920).

ERICH FROMM (1900–) was born in Frankfurt, Germany. Trained in psychoanalysis in Munich and at the Psychoanalytic Institute in Berlin, he has devoted his time since 1925 partly to work as a consultant psychologist, and partly to theoretical work especially in the field of the application of psychoanalytic theory to problems of culture and society. In 1934 he settled permanently in America and is now an American citizen. His latest books are *Escape from Freedom* (1941), *Man for Himself* (1947), *The Forgotten Language* (1951), and *The Sane Society* (1955).

ÉTIENNE GILSON (1884–), French philosopher and historian, was educated at the Sorbonne, where he has been professor of medieval philosophy. Since 1929 he has been director of the Institute of Medieval Studies at Toronto. A popular lecturer in English as well as French, he has frequently lectured in England and at universities in the United States. He is considered one of the most distinguished medievalists in the world. A devout Roman Catholic in religion, in philosophy he is a follower of St. Thomas Aquinas. Some of his books are *The Philosophy of St. Thomas Aquinas*, *The Unity of Philosophical Experience*, and *Christianity and Philosophy*.

GEOFFREY GORER (1905–), British anthropologist, was born in London and educated at Cambridge. As a result of travels in Africa and the Dutch East Indies he became interested in anthropology, which he later studied with Margaret Mead and Ruth Benedict at Columbia. He lives in Sussex on a farm. He is the author of *The American People* (1948) and *Exploring English Character* (1953).

LEARNED HAND (1872–) was born at Albany and educated at Harvard and the Harvard Law School. Now retired, he was Judge of the United States Circuit

Court, Second Circuit, from 1924 to 1951. The probity and wisdom of his decisions have made other lawyers, as well as the public, revere him as the dean of the American bar.

WILLIAM HARVEY (1578–1657), English physiologist and physician to Charles I, was educated at Cambridge and Padua. A series of experiments, now regarded as classic, led to his discovery and description of the circulation of the blood. *On the Motion of the Heart and Blood in Animals* was published under a Latin title in 1628.

S. I. HAYAKAWA (1906–) is a leader in the general semantics movement and editor of *Etc.* His *Language in Action* (1941) was distributed by the Book of the Month Club; more recently he has written *Language, Meaning, and Maturity* (1954).

GEOFFREY T. HELLMAN (1907–), a graduate of Yale, has been associated with *The New Yorker* since 1929, except for brief intervals with *Fortune* and *Life* and for governmental and military service during World War II.

ROBERT HERRIDGE (1917–), a graduate of Northwestern University, is a television producer, writer, and director. He has adapted Melville, Mark Twain, and Shakespeare to this medium, and his credits further include such programs as "Camera Three," "Westinghouse Summer Theatre," and "Studio One." Author of numerous articles and reviews, he has published in *Poetry, The Atlantic Monthly,* and the *Yale Review.*

GILBERT HIGHET (1906–), born in Scotland and a graduate of Glasgow and Oxford, came to the United States in 1937. A professor of Latin at Columbia, he is widely known for his radio and television talks. Among his books are *The Classical Tradition* (1949) and *Juvenal the Satirist* (1954).

HILAIRE HILER (1898–) is an artist and psychologist. *Why Expressionism?* (1946) is one of several books by him on painting.

WILLIAM ERNEST HOCKING (1873–), professor of philosophy emeritus at Harvard, was educated at Harvard and at German universities. Alford Professor of Philosophy at Harvard until his retirement in 1943, he has also taught at the University of California and Yale University. He has lectured at the Universities at Glasgow, Oxford, and Cambridge. Some of his books are *The Meaning of God in Human Experience, Man and the State, Recent Trends in American Philosophy, What Man Can Make of Man,* and *Contemporary Science and the Idea of God.*

ALFRED EDWARD HOUSMAN (1859–1936), distinguished English poet and classical scholar, was educated at Oxford, where he failed to receive honors and took a pass degree. In 1892 he became professor of Latin at University College, London, and in 1911, professor of Latin at Cambridge. His "Introductory Lecture" was delivered upon the occasion of his becoming professor of Latin at University College. He edited Manilius, Juvenal, and Lucan. He ranks among the greatest classical scholars England has produced. But he is more highly esteemed by most readers for his three slender volumes of poems: A *Shropshire Lad* (1896), *Last Poems* (1922), and *More Poems* (1936).

ROBERT MAYNARD HUTCHINS (1899–), formerly president of the University of Chicago and now director of the Fund for the Republic, was educated at Oberlin and Yale. A controversial figure in American education, he has published many articles and books.

THOMAS JEFFERSON (1743–1826) composed his own epitaph: "Here was buried Thomas Jefferson, Author of the Declaration of Independence, of the Statute of Virginia for Religious Freedom, and Father of the University of Virginia."

E. J. KAHN, JR. (1916–) graduated from Harvard in 1937, and in the same year began his career of writer and reporter in New York City. He served with the U.S. Army from 1941 to 1945. Among his books are *The Army Life* (1942) and *Who, Me?* (1949).

JOHN MAYNARD KEYNES (1883–1946), was an English economist and Director of the Bank of England, and is perhaps best known for his volumes *The Economic Consequences of the Peace* (1919) and *A Treatise on Money* (2 vols., 1930). His economic theory has been influential in both Great Britain and the United States.

SÖREN KIERKEGAARD (1813–1855), Danish theologian and philosopher, has profoundly influenced twentieth-century existentialists. Some of his works are *Either/Or, Stages on Life's Way, Fear and Trembling,* from which "A Panegyric upon Abraham" was selected, and *The Sickness unto Death.* Kierkegaard is now rather generally regarded as the greatest theologian of the last century.

CLYDE KLUCKHOHN (1905–), Professor of Anthropology at Harvard and Director of Harvard's Russian Research Center, first became interested in anthropology when he began to study the Navajos and other peoples of the Southwest. He has traveled and studied in Europe, was chief of the Policy Division in the Far East of the O. W. I. He is the author of such books as *To the Foot of the Rainbow* (1927), *Personality in Nature, Society and Culture* (1948), and *How the Soviet System Works* (1955).

ARTHUR KOESTLER (1905–), born in Hungary, has been a correspondent and a soldier in the French and British armies. Two of his books are the novel *Darkness at Noon* (1941) and the commentary on politics, *The Track of the Dinosaur* (1955).

SUSANNE LANGER (1895–), a graduate of Radcliffe (A.B., A.M., Ph.D.), is professor of philosophy at Connecticut College. Her best known works are *Philosophy in a New Key* (1942) and its sequel *Feeling and Form* (1953).

WILLIAM L. LAURENCE (1888–) is science-news reporter for the New York *Times* and has won the Pulitzer prize twice. He is especially skilled in understanding and interpreting to the everyday reader the complexities of modern science, and was the only civilian to go along on the mission to bomb Nagasaki in World War II. He is the author of *The Hell-Bomb* (1951).

DONALD J. LLOYD (1910–) is a graduate of Wayne University (A.B., M.A.) and Yale (Ph.D.). Now associate professor of English at Wayne, he has written, with Harry R. Warfel, *American English in Its Cultural Setting* (1956).

JOHN LOCKE (1632–1704) was an English philosopher whose writings turned from the subtleties of Aristotle and the Schoolmen and helped point the modern world toward experimental science. Locke has been called the father of English empiricism, and his influence on the development of psychology, philosophy, education, and political science has been tremendous. His principal philosophical work is *An Essay Concerning Human Understanding*. His two *Treatises of Government* denied the divine right of kings and justified the Revolution of 1688, thus indirectly providing justification for the American Revolution. He was probably the most influential English thinker of the seventeenth century, and his influence is still felt in Western democracies.

MARCUS AURELIUS ANTONINUS (121–180), Roman emperor and philosopher, was one of the greatest Stoics. His *Meditations*, written in Greek, consist of twelve books of sage advice on conduct and living. Learned and gentle, he nevertheless opposed Christianity, even to the extent of persecuting Christians.

JACQUES MARITAIN (1882–), Catholic philosopher, was born in Paris and educated at the University of Paris and at Rome. In 1906, he was converted to Roman Catholicism, and since then he has been widely regarded as one of the most influential Catholic spokesmen in the world. For many years he has specialized in the scholastic philosophy of St. Thomas Aquinas, upon which he has lectured at many of the great universities of the world. From 1948–1953 he was professor of philosophy at Princeton, and since 1953 he has been professor emeritus. Author of many books, some of his most important are *The Person and the Common Good* (1947), *Existence and the Existent* (1948), *Man and the State* (1950), *The Range of Reason* (1952), *Creative Intuition in Art and Poetry* (1953), *Approaches to God* (1954).

FRANK JEWETT MATHER, JR. (1868–1953), was a professor of art and archaeology at Princeton University. His specialty was Italian painting.

H. L. MENCKEN (1880–1956), critic, editor, and philologist, edited *The American Mercury* from 1924 until 1933, and long was associated with the Baltimore *Evening Sun*. His six series of *Prejudices* (1919–1927) exemplify his work as a critic, and *The American Language* (1918, with later revisions) is his philological masterpiece.

ARTHUR MILLER (1915–) graduated from Michigan in 1938. Most famous of his plays is *Death of a Salesman* (1949); others are *All My Sons* (1947) and *The Crucible* (1953). In the summer of 1956 he married the motion picture actress Marilyn Monroe.

MICHEL EYQUEM DE MONTAIGNE (1533–1592) was a French courtier and essayist. His *Essais*, important both for their matter and for their style, have exercised a considerable influence on the development of the essay in English literature.

GEOFFREY MOORE (1920–), a graduate of Cambridge, has taught at six colleges and universities in the United States. Long active in BBC radio and television, he was appointed lecturer in American literature at the University of Manchester in 1955.

THEODORE MORRISON (1901–), director of English A at Harvard, is the author of several volumes of poetry and frequent critical papers. His books include *The Portable Chaucer* (1949) and a novel *The Stones of the House* (1953).

LEWIS MUMFORD (1895–) has written a number of books on American civilization. Though his most distinguished work has concerned architecture (as in *Sticks and Stones*, 1924), he has also made notable contributions in literary and cultural history (as in *The Golden Day*, 1926, and *The Brown Decades*, 1931) and in philosophical analysis (as in *Values for Survival*, 1946, *The Conduct of Life*, 1951, *The Human Prospect*, 1955, and *Transformations of Man*, 1956).

REINHOLD NIEBUHR (1892–), influential American theologian, studied at Elmhurst College (Illinois) and the Yale Divinity School. After graduation, he was ordained to the ministry of the Evangelical Synod of North America in 1915. Since 1930 he has taught theology at Union Theological Seminary in New York. His most important works are *Moral Man and Immoral Society* (1932), *Beyond Tragedy* (1937), *The Nature and Destiny of Man* (1941–43), *Discerning the Signs of the Times* (1946) and *Faith and History* (1949). He is one of contemporary Protestantism's most profound spokesmen.

GEORGE ORWELL is the pseudonym of Eric Blair (1904–1950), British essayist and novelist. Among his best known books are *Animal Farm* (1945) and *1984* (1949).

THOMAS PAINE (1737–1809), American political philosopher, encouraged the American Revolution by publishing *Common Sense*, which called for an immediate declaration of independence (January 10, 1776), and *The Crisis*, twelve issues of which appeared during the course of the war. He is also the author of *The Rights of Man* and *The Age of Reason*.

FREDERIC E. PAMP, JR. (1916–), a graduate of Harvard (A.B., A.M., Ph.D.), is division manager of the American Management Association.

DONALD CULROSS PEATTIE (1898–) worked in the Department of Agriculture from 1922 to 1925. Since then, writing in the tradition of Agassiz and Thoreau, he has published many books on the natural scene in America, including *Audubon's America* (1940).

S. J. PERELMAN (1904–) has written constantly since his graduation from Brown University in 1925. He is best known for his regular contributions to *The New Yorker* and his collected essays, such as *Listen to the Mocking Bird* (1949) and *The Ill-Tempered Clavicord* (1953).

PLATO (428–347 B.C.), the Greek philosopher, was a pupil and admirer of Socrates. Most of his adult life was spent in teaching at Athens, his native city, and in the composition of his *Dialogues*, all of which are extant. The *Dialogue* are based on the teachings of Socrates, who figures largely in them as the conductor of the discussions.

DAVID M. POTTER (1910–), Coe professor of American history at Yale University, has written many historical studies, the latest of which is *People of Plenty* (1954).

I. I. RABI (1898–), professor of physics in Columbia University, was awarded the Nobel Prize in 1944 for his work in nuclear physics. He is Chairman of the Advisory Committee of the U.S. Atomic Energy Commission.

DAVID RIESMAN (1909–) is a graduate of Harvard College and Harvard Law School. After legal practice and teaching, he became a member of the social science department at the University of Chicago in 1946. Two of his books are *The Lonely Crowd* (1950) and *Individualism Reconsidered and Other Essays* (1954).

JAMES HARVEY ROBINSON (1863–1936), a native of Illinois, held degrees from Harvard and the University of Freiburg. For many years he was professor of history at Columbia, but resigned in 1917 as a protest against what he considered a suppression of academic freedom in the University. As a historian, his work has done much to change the emphasis of historical writing from wars, territorial changes, and treaties to the development of ideas and beliefs. He is the author of *The Mind in the Making, Introduction to the History of Western Europe,* and many other books.

LEONARD Q. ROSS is the pseudonym of Leo Calvin Rosten (1908–), who, after beginning an academic career as English teacher and student in the social sciences, has been largely associated with motion-picture projects (since 1937). From this latter part of his career has come *Hollywood: the Movie Colony—the Movie Makers* (1941). More recently he has edited *The Religions of America* (1955).

BERTRAND RUSSELL (1872–), philosopher and mathematician, was educated at Cambridge. He has taught mathematics and philosophy at Cambridge, Harvard, the University of Chicago, and the University of California at Los Angeles. He is co-author with Alfred North Whitehead of *Principia Mathematica* (1910–1913). Among his other books are *Introduction to Mathematical Philosophy* (1919), *The Analysis of Matter, Philosophical Essays, Marriage and Morals, Education and the Social Order.* He has recently published *Nightmares of Eminent Persons* (1954) and *Human Society in Ethics and Politics* (1955). His views on marriage and pacificism have at times involved him in controversies. Though he is an English nobleman, he refuses to use his title.

ROGER SESSIONS (1896–) is a composer and music teacher who is generally recognized to be a leading contemporary American practitioner of both arts. His *Symphony No. 1,* first performed by the Boston Symphony in 1927, has been followed by other symphonies, sonatas, concertos, and chorales, which have been performed by leading ensembles around the world. He teaches at Princeton University. *Harmonic Practice* (1951) is his second book.

NATHANIEL SOUTHGATE SHALER (1841–1906), a Kentuckian by birth, was a distinguished American geologist. During most of his life he was identified with Harvard, and it was there that he studied with the great Louis Agassiz. He was graduated from Lawrence School of Science, Harvard, in 1862. After serving two years as an artillery officer in the Union Army, he taught at Harvard successively zoology, geology, and paleontology, becoming professor of geology in 1888, a position he held until his death. He was director of the Kentucky Geologic Survey, and later geologist in charge of the Atlantic division of the U. S. Geological Survey. He wrote *A First Book in Geology, Aspects of the Earth, The Interpretation of Nature,* and *Man and Death.*

GEORGE BERNARD SHAW (1856–1950), born in Dublin, joined the Fabian Society in London and wrote music, drama, and art criticism before turning to the stage. He was a socialist, satirist, and meliorist. His wit and stagecraft and his belief in a "Life Force" are evident in such different plays as *Candida* (1898), *Androcles and the Lion* (1912), and *St. Joan* (1924).

ADAM SMITH (1723–1790) published his *Inquiry into the Nature and Causes of the Wealth of Nations* in 1776. The book revolutionized the economic theories of the day, and has remained a classic statement of the doctrine of "laissez faire."

FRANK SULLIVAN (1892–), a graduate of Cornell, is the author of humorous sketches collected under such titles as *A Pearl in Every Oyster* (1938), *A Rock in Every Snowball* (1946), and *The Night the Old Nostalgia Burned Down* (1953).

JONATHAN SWIFT (1667–1745), greatest English prose satirist, was born in Dublin and educated at Trinity College. In addition to his masterpiece, *Travels into Several Remote Nations of the World,* commonly known as *Gulliver's Travels,* he is also the author of *A Tale of a Tub,* a brilliant satire on the divisions of the Christian church, *The Battle of the Books, A Modest Proposal,* a masterpiece of irony, and *The Journal to Stella,* as well as a number of poems, most of which are humorous.

HENRY DAVID THOREAU (1817–1862) called himself "a mystic, a transcendental philosopher, and a natural philosopher to boot." His dominant individualism is evident in his most famous book, *Walden* (1854). It also appears, but tempered by a belief in acting collectively "according to the spirit of our institutions," in the three John Brown speeches (1859–1860) and *Life without Principle* (1863) as well as in the essay printed here.

JAMES THURBER (1894–), one of the best contemporary humorists and cartoonists, was educated at Ohio State University. After working on several newspapers, he joined the staff of *The New Yorker,* where he was for a time managing editor. Later he wrote the "Talk of the Town" for the same magazine. He is now a free-lance writer, but still remains a frequent contributor to *The New Yorker.* He has written *My Life and Hard Times, Let Your Mind Alone, The Male Animal, Fables for Our Times, My World—and Welcome to It!* and others.

CHAUNCEY B. TINKER (1876–) is the Sterling Professor of English Literature emeritus at Yale and keeper of rare books at the library.

ARNOLD JOSEPH TOYNBEE (1889–) is Director of Studies in the Royal Institute of International Affairs. An English historian, he has covered much of the history of East and West in a series of studies, and in 1954 completed his monumental ten-volume *A Study of History*. He is also the author of *Civilization on Trial* (1948) and *An Historian's Approach to Religion* (1956).

LIONEL TRILLING (1905–) is the author of a novel, *The Middle of the Journey*, (1947) and of short stories that have been frequently anthologized. Critical volumes by him include *E. M. Forster* (1943), *The Liberal Imagination* (1950), and *The Opposing Self* (1955). He teaches English at Columbia University.

FREDERICK JACKSON TURNER (1861–1932) taught history at the University of Wisconsin and at Harvard University. His carefully documented account of the frontiers of the discoverer and explorer, the missionary, soldier, trapper, and farmer constituted a new synthesis and a new point of view in American history.

BARRY ULANOV (1918–) is a graduate of Columbia University and has written biographies of Duke Ellington and Bing Crosby. He edits *Metronome* and *Your Music* and teaches English at Barnard College.

THORSTEIN VEBLEN (1857–1929), American teacher and economist, became a leading figure in the "institutional school" of economic theory and was in part responsible for the trend toward social control in the decade 1930–1940. *The Instinct of Workmanship* (1914) and *The Engineers and the Price System* (1921) are important books by him.

GRAHAM WALLAS (1858–1932) was a British political scientist who taught at the London School of Economics and at the University of London. He wrote *Human Nature in Politics* and a number of other works.

ROBERT PENN WARREN (1905–), professor of English at Yale, is a poet, critic, and novelist, and a founder of *The Southern Review*. Two of his best known books are *Understanding Poetry* (1938, with Cleanth Brooks) and the novel *World Enough and Time* (1950).

PHILIP WHEELWRIGHT (1901–), a graduate of Princeton (A.B., Ph.D.), has been professor of philosophy at the University of California at Riverside since 1954. Besides *The Burning Fountain*, he has written *A Critical Introduction to Ethics* (revised edition, 1949) and *The Way of Philosophy* (1954).

E. B. WHITE (1899–), essayist, lives at North Brooklyn, Maine. Born at Mt. Vernon, New York, he was educated at Cornell. He began his career as a reporter. Formerly a contributor to *Harper's*, he has been for a number of years a contributing editor of *The New Yorker*. In addition to his frequent contributions to magazines, he has written many books: *Is Sex Necessary?* (in collaboration with James Thurber), *One Man's Meat* (1944), *Stuart Little* (1945), *Charlotte's Web* (1952), *The Second Tree from the Corner* (1953). In 1941 he edited *A Subtreasury of American Humor*.

ALFRED NORTH WHITEHEAD (1861–1947) was an English philosopher and mathematician. One of the most influential thinkers of the twentieth century, Whitehead taught at Trinity College, Cambridge, the University of London, and at Harvard. Among his books are *Principia Mathematica*, which he wrote with Bertrand Russell in 1910, *The Principles of Natural Knowledge, Science and the Modern World, Adventures of Ideas*, and *Nature and Life*.

WILLIAM H. WHYTE, JR. (1917–) graduated from Princeton in 1939. A staff writer and editor of *Fortune* since 1946, he has written two books based on a series of articles in that magazine: *Is Anybody Listening?* (1952) and *Why Do People Buy?* (1954).

NORBERT WIENER (1894–), after receiving his Ph.D. from Harvard, studied at Cornell, Columbia, Cambridge, Göttingen, and Copenhagen. His achievements in mathematics have brought him international recognition. During World War II he devised a method of solving problems of fire control and developed improvements in radar and controlled missiles. He teaches and conducts research in cybernetics at M.I.T.

EDMUND WILSON (1895–), a graduate of Princeton, is a leading literary critic. The author of fiction, drama, and poetry, his books of criticism are his most significant achievement. Among them are *Axel's Castle* (1931), *The Triple Thinkers* (1938), and *Classics and Commercials* (1952).

JOHN WOOLMAN (1720–1772), Quaker preacher and author, was born in New Jersey, where he was apprenticed to a tailor. He traveled widely throughout the Colonies, visiting meetings of the Friends and denouncing slavery. His most famous work is his *Journal*, which gives an account of these activities. It has been frequently reprinted and is much praised for its style. Charles Lamb once suggested that aspiring writers "get Woolman's writings by heart."

FRANK LLOYD WRIGHT (1869–) began his illustrious career in 1893 at Chicago. *An Autobiography—Frank Lloyd Wright* (1932, rev. 1943) tells the long story of his struggle in establishing modern architecture.

PHILIP WYLIE (1902–), editor, columnist, and author of the popular "Crunch and Des" fishing stories, is also a satirist and moralist. His virulent criticisms of many aspects of American civilization appear in *Generation of Vipers* (1942), *Night unto Night* (1944), *An Essay on Morals* (1947), and *Tomorrow!* (1954).

# Index